MW00637649

The fourth volume of *The New Cambridge Medieval History* covers the eleventh and twelfth centuries, which comprised perhaps the most dynamic period in the European middle ages.

This is a history of Europe, but the continent is interpreted widely to include the Near East and North Africa as well. The volume is divided into two Parts of which this, the second, deals with the course of events, ecclesiastical and secular, and major developments in an age marked by the transformation of the position of the papacy in a process fuelled by a radical reformation of the church, the decline of the western and eastern empires, the rise of western kingdoms and Italian elites, and the development of governmental structures, the beginnings of the recovery of Spain from the Moors and the establishment of western settlements in the eastern Mediterranean region in the wake of the crusades.

The New Cambridge Medieval History

EDITORIAL BOARD

David Abulafia   Rosamond McKitterick
Martin Brett   Edward Powell
Simon Keynes   Jonathan Shepard
Peter Linehan   Peter Spufford

Volume IV *c.* 1024–*c.* 1198

Part II

THE NEW
CAMBRIDGE
MEDIEVAL HISTORY

Volume IV c. 1024–c. 1198
Part II

EDITED BY

DAVID LUSCOMBE

Professor of Medieval History,
University of Sheffield

AND

JONATHAN RILEY-SMITH

Dixie Professor of Ecclesiastical History,
University of Cambridge

 CAMBRIDGE
UNIVERSITY PRESS

CAMBRIDGE
UNIVERSITY PRESS

University Printing House, Cambridge CB2 8BS, United Kingdom

Cambridge University Press is part of the University of Cambridge.

It furthers the University's mission by disseminating knowledge in the pursuit of education, learning and research at the highest international levels of excellence.

www.cambridge.org
Information on this title: www.cambridge.org/9781107460638

© Cambridge University Press 2004

This publication is in copyright. Subject to statutory exception and to the provisions of relevant collective licensing agreements, no reproduction of any part may take place without the written permission of Cambridge University Press.

First published 2004
Reprinted 2006
First paperback edition 2015

A catalogue record for this publication is available from the British Library

ISBN 978-0-521-41411-1 Hardback
ISBN 978-1-107-46063-8 Paperback

Cambridge University Press has no responsibility for the persistence or accuracy of URLs for external or third-party internet websites referred to in this publication, and does not guarantee that any content on such websites is, or will remain, accurate or appropriate.

CONTENTS

MAPS

GENEALOGICAL TABLES

LISTS OF RULERS

Christian rulers

Muslim rulers (with dates of accession)

CONTRIBUTORS

MICHAEL ANGOLD: Professor of Byzantine History, University of Edinburgh

BENJAMIN ARNOLD: Professor of Medieval History, University of Reading

JOHN W. BALDWIN: Charles Homer Haskins Professor of History Emeritus, The Johns Hopkins University, Baltimore, Maryland, and Corresponding Fellow of the British Academy

GEOFFREY BARROW: Sir William Fraser Professor Emeritus of Scottish History and Palaeography, University of Edinburgh, and Fellow of the British Academy

SIMON BARTON: Professor of Spanish, University of Exeter

NORA BEREND: Lecturer in History and Fellow of St Catharine's College, University of Cambridge

UTA-RENATE BLUMENTHAL: Professor in The Catholic University of America, Washington DC

CONSTANCE BRITTAIN BOUCHARD: Distinguished Professor of History, University of Akron, Ohio

MICHAEL BRETT: Professor in the History of North Africa, School of Oriental and African Studies, University of London

MICHEL BUR: Emeritus Professor, University of Nancy II

MARJORIE CHIBNALL: Fellow of Clare Hall, Cambridge, and Fellow of the British Academy

MARTIN DIMNIK: Professor in the Pontifical Institute of Mediaeval Studies, Toronto

STEPHEN HUMPHREYS: King Abdul Aziz Ibn Saud Professor of Islamic Studies, University of California, Santa Barbara

†THOMAS K. KEEFE: Professor, Appalachian State University, Boone, North Carolina

PETER LINEHAN: Fellow of St John's College, Cambridge, and Fellow of the British Academy

G. A. LOUD: Reader in Medieval History, University of Leeds

DAVID LUSCOMBE: Professor of Medieval History, University of Sheffield, and Fellow of the British Academy

PAUL MAGDALINO: Professor of Byzantine History, University of St Andrews, and Fellow of the British Academy

HANS EBERHARD MAYER: Emeritus Professor, University of Kiel

JONATHAN RILEY-SMITH: Dixie Professor of Ecclesiastical History and Fellow of Emmanuel College, University of Cambridge

I. S. ROBINSON: Professor of Medieval History, Trinity College, Dublin

PETER SAWYER: Emeritus Professor of Medieval History, University of Leeds

†GIOVANNI TABACCO: Associate Professor of Church History, University of Turin, and Corresponding Fellow of the British Academy

HANNA VOLLRATH: Professor in the Ruhr-Universität, Bochum

JERZY WYROZUMSKI: Professor in the Jagiellonian University, Cracow

PREFACE

To all the contributors to both parts of this volume the editors extend their warmest thanks for their co-operation, patience and considerable efforts. No collaborative venture is free of collective risk, and volume IV of *The New Cambridge Medieval History* – the largest volume in the series – has been no exception: more than ten years have passed in its compilation.

In Part 1, of those scholars originally planning to contribute, five were unable to deliver. We are exceptionally grateful to the distinguished historians who stepped forward and wrote chapters for us in their place.

In Part 2 the fluctuations and the obstacles which we encountered were more problematic. Of those scholars originally planning to contribute three died before beginning to write, and five others were unable to deliver. We are similarly and exceptionally grateful to the distinguished historians who also stepped forward and wrote chapters for us in their place and at short notice. We have also to express our regrets at the more recent deaths of Giovanni Tabacco and of Tom Keefe who wrote his contribution while terminally ill.

D.E.L.

J.R.-S.

ACKNOWLEDGEMENTS

We have many debts to acknowledge with gratitude in the course of the preparation of this volume. Expertise has been generously provided by copy-editors, translators, secretaries, cartographers, illustrationists, typesetters and others. Our copy-editors – Frances Brown and Linda Randall – have given invaluable help as have our indexer – Auriol Griffith-Jones – and our team of translators which has included Jean Birrell, Monika Coghlan, Caroline Stone and Martin Thom among others. Pat Holland in the University of Sheffield has given unstinting secretarial assistance. To William Davies of Cambridge University Press we express our very special gratitude for support at every stage. The editors have reason too to thank each other for a most fruitful and agreeable partnership. But our greatest thanks by far go to all who have written in this volume.

D.E.L.
J.R.-S.

ABBREVIATIONS

AHP	*Archivum Historiae Pontificiae*
AHR	*American Historical Review*
Annales ESC	*Annales: Economies, Sociétés, Civilisations*
ANS	*Anglo-Norman Studies*
BEC	*Bibliothèque de l'Ecole des Chartes*
BF	*Byzantische Forschungen*
BHL	*Bibliotheca Hagiographica Latina*
BIHR	*Bulletin of the Institute of Historical Research*
BISI	*Bullettino dell'Istituto Storico Italiano per il Medio Evo e Archivio Muratoriano*
BMGS	*Byzantine and Modern Greek Studies*
BS	*Byzantinoslavica*
BSOAS	*Bulletin of the School of Oriental and African Studies*
BZ	*Byzantinische Zeitschrift*
CCCM	Corpus Christianorum, Continuatio Mediaevalis
CCM	*Cahiers de Civilisation Médiévale*
COD	*Conciliorum oecumenicorum decreta*, ed. J. Alberigo, J. A. Dossetti *et al.*, 3rd edn, Bologna (1973)
DA	*Deutsches Archiv für Erforschung des Mittelalters*
DOP	*Dumbarton Oaks Papers*
EEBΣ	*Epeteris Etaireias Vizantinon Spoudon*
EEMCA	*Estudios de Edad Media de la Corona de Aragón*
EHR	*English Historical Review*
FmaSt	*Frühmittelalterliche Studien*
FSI	Fonti per la Storia d'Italia, ed. Istituto Storico Italiano, 118 vols. so far, Rome (1887–)
HZ	*Historische Zeitschrift*
JEH	*Journal of Ecclesiastical History*

JL	*Regesta pontificum Romanorum ab condita ecclesia ad annum post Christum natum MCXCVIII*, ed. P. Jaffé, 2nd edn, rev. ed. S. Loewenfeld, F. Kaltenbrunner and P. Ewald, 2 vols., Leipzig (1885–8)
JMH	*Journal of Medieval History*
JöB	*Jahrbuch des österreichischen Byzantinistik*
JRAS	*Journal of the Royal Asiatic Society*
MA	*Le Moyen Age*
Mansi	*Sacrorum conciliorum nova et amplissima collectio*, ed. G. D. Mansi, 55 vols., Venice and Florence (1759–98)
MGH	*Monumenta Germaniae Historica*, ed. G. H. Pertz *et al.*, Hanover, Weimar, Stuttgart and Cologne (1826–)
Constitutiones	*Constitutiones et acta publica imperatorum et regum*, 11 vols. so far (1893–)
Diplomata	*Diplomata regum et imperatorum Germaniae*, 19 vols. so far (1879–)
Epistolae	*Die Briefe des deutschen Kaiserzeit*, 8 vols. so far (1949–)
Epp. sel.	*Epistolae selectae*, 5 vols. so far (1916–)
Libelli	*Libelli de lite imperatorum et pontificum saeculis XI. et XII. conscripti*, 3 vols. (1891–7)
S	*Scriptores*, 38 vols. so far (1826–)
Schriften	*Schriften der Monumenta Germaniae Historica*, 51 vols. so far (1938–)
SRG	*Scriptores rerum Germanicarum in usum scholarum separatim editi*, 75 vols. so far (1871–)
SRG NS	*Scriptores rerum Germanicarum. Nova series*, 18 vols. so far (1922–)
MIÖG	*Mitteilungen des Instituts für österreichische Geschichtsforschung*
NA	*Neues Archiv*
NCMH	*The New Cambridge Medieval History*
OCP	*Orientalia Christiana Periodica*
PaP	*Past and Present*
PBA	*Proceedings of the British Academy*
PL	*Patrologiae cursus completus, Series Latina*, comp. J. P. Migne, 221 vols., Paris (1844–64)
QFIAB	*Quellen und Forschungen aus italienischen Archiven und Bibliotheken*
RBén	*Revue Bénédictine*
REB	*Revue des Etudes Byzantines*
RES-EE	*Revue des Etudes Sud-est Européennes*

RHC Occ.	*Recueil des historiens des croisades. Historiens occidentaux,* ed. Académie des Inscriptions et Belles-Lettres, 5 vols., Paris (1844–95)
RHE	*Revue d'Histoire Ecclésiastique*
RHGF	*Recueil des historiens des Gaules et de la France,* ed. M. Bouquet and M.-J.-J. Brial, 24 vols., Paris (1738–1904)
RIS NS	*Rerum Italicarum Scriptores,* 2nd edn, ed. G. Carducii *et. al.*, 34 vols. so far, Città di Castello and Bologna (1900–)
RS	Rerum Britannicarum Medii Aevi Scriptores, publ. under the direction of the Master of the Rolls, 99 vols., London (1858–96)
SG	*Studi Gregoriani*
TM	*Travaux et Mémoires*
TRHS	*Transactions of the Royal Historical Society*
VV	*Vizantiniskij Vermmenik*
ZDPV	*Zeitschrift des Deutschen Palästina-Vereins*
ZRG	*Zeitschrift für Rechtsgeschichte*
ZRVI	*Zbornik Radova Vizantinoloshkog Instituta*
ZSSRG	*Zeitschrift der Savigny-Stiftung für Rechtsgeschichte*
KA	*Kanonistische Abteilung*

CHAPTER I

INTRODUCTION

Jonathan Riley-Smith and David Luscombe

THE recovery in July 1099 of the city of Jerusalem by crusaders after four and a half centuries of Muslim rule was the strongest indication yet of a shift in the balance of power from the eastern Mediterranean region to the west. The Balkans and the Levant were in no state to take advantage of beneficial economic forces which were just as much at work in them as in western Europe. The Byzantine empire had been gravely damaged by the occupation of most of Asia Minor by nomadic Turks, although, in a situation reminiscent of the barbarian incursions of the third century, rebellious 'Roman' generals had to a large extent brought this on themselves by inviting the Turks in as mercenaries. The empire had no more than a shadow of a presence in central Greece and the Balkans and it suffered from the fact that it had never had great trading or industrial sectors which could have helped to compensate for its territorial losses: Constantinople had been at best a great consumer city. Profitable commercial centres needed to be on trade routes rather than at the end of them and when he encouraged Venetian and Pisan merchants to come to Constantinople the emperor Alexios I may have been trying to create the vital extra overseas leg that an international market of this kind would need.

Syria and Palestine had been devastated in the wars between the Shi'ite Fatimids in Cairo and the Sunni Seljuq Turks ruling on behalf of the 'Abbasid caliphate in Baghdad. The Muslim Near East had fallen into even deeper disarray just before the arrival of the First Crusade. In 1092 the greatest figure in Seljuq history, the vizier Nizam al-Mulk, the power behind the sultans for over thirty years, was murdered. A month later the sultan, Malikshah, died in suspicious circumstances, as did his wife, his grandson and other powerful figures. The 'Abbasid caliph, al-Muqtadi, himself expired in 1094. The Seljuq sultanate disintegrated into localities in which pretenders and members of the family fought each other for power. In 1094 the Fatimid caliph, al-Mustansir, who had ruled in Cairo for fifty-eight years and had fiercely resisted the Seljuqs,

I

also died; so did his vizier, Badr al-Jamali. The First Crusade swept, therefore, into a region in which there was a vacuum of power.

Western Europe may not have been a cosy place in which to live, but conditions there were infinitely better. With no significant outside threat the developments in education and administration described in the first part of this volume could proceed apace. The engine for change was provided by the Latin church, the only institution with a truly transcontinental role. Its transformation into an advanced governmental machine was partly a consequence of initiatives taken by the centre in a climate of opinion, secular as well as religious, which was in its favour. They proved to be astonishingly ambitious, although they did not at first comprise a detailed programme, since none of the main actors had a clear idea where they were going. These men wanted simply to restore the whole church to what they believed had been its pristine purity and were determined to use the central organs of ecclesiastical government to bring this about. Over the course of the next three centuries, in one of the most revolutionary periods in the history of the church, the papacy, insisting on its independent authoritative voice and reinforcing this with institutional controls, was able to loosen the framework of pre-existing doctrinal authority, provided above all by the decisions of the first seven (or eight) general councils. It would be going too far to assert that it was now free-wheeling – indeed it always assured anyone who would listen of its devotion to precedent, previous councils and scripture – but its pre-eminence and the respect with which its voice was generally heard meant that it could oversee doctrinal adaptation and development. Between 1123 and 1312 it summoned no less than seven new general councils while the judgements streaming from the papal curia meant that the standard codification of canon law, Gratian's *Decretum*, had to be regularly updated with supplementary works. Authority for Latins, therefore, came to be not static, but continually developing, and Catholic doctrine came to be characterized by a succession of pronouncements on faith and morals, each claiming, of course, to be only expressing what had been in the mind of the church from the start.

Ambition alone would not have been enough, of course, to transform the role of the popes from a relatively passive to a consistently proactive one. It cannot be said often enough that advances in government depend as much on the governed as the governors. Few rulers have proved themselves to be so foolish as to establish elaborate machinery with nothing to do; central offices have emerged in response to the creation of business. In the middle ages this was on the whole generated from below as subjects sought arbitration or judgement, but nobody would seek a judicial decision from a court impractically distant from his or her home or from one whose procedures were perceived to be uncertain. The church already had an apparatus of public courts, each within a reasonable distance of every baptized Christian. These were the courts of the bishops, which is one of the reasons why control over the episcopate became such an issue in the eleventh century. The papacy's encouragement of the scholarship needed if the law – canon law – applicable everywhere by these courts was to be clarified and systematized created the conditions for ordinary Christians to seek judgement in them.

The process of change began with the arrival in Rome after the election of Pope Leo IX in 1049 of a group of radical reformers, under the influence of a movement which had been growing in monastic circles for half a century. The papacy, powered by an intense moral seriousness, placed itself in the forefront of change for almost the only time in its history, risking its own prestige in the process. Its radicalism was of a historical kind, based in its eyes on precedent and past authority, and it seems to have been barely conscious of the consequences of some of its initiatives, but no one can question the energy and intransigence with which it pursued its goals: it challenged the Byzantine empire and the patriarchate of Constantinople; it tried to establish free papal elections; it revived ancient half-forgotten legislation on clerical celibacy, episcopal schools and legations; it claimed lordship over important regions of western Europe; it developed the unprecedented notion of penitential warfare and invented crusading; and it set out to submit all episcopal hierarchies, including those in the eastern patriarchates, to the see of Peter. In a remarkably short time the sacramental and penitential theology of the Latin church was transformed, much of it in ways that directly affected ordinary Christians such as the geographical location of purgatory and the establishment of universal rules for canonization and for the verification of relics.

The way that the reformers' trains of thought could lead them in directions far from that originally intended is illustrated by the election decree of 1059. This established that thenceforward papal elections were to be free. The cardinal bishops should first confer about the candidate and then summon the cardinal clergy. The remaining Roman clergy and people should assent to the choice. The king of Germany, the heir to the empire, was to have 'due honour'. In effect the papacy was renouncing its traditional protector, in the name of the freedom, to which it was so committed, of the church from lay patronage. The reformers were inclined to ignore the many benefits that customary lay patronage had brought – not least the reform of their own institution by the emperor – but it would be wrong to suppose that they rejected protection in principle. On the contrary, they ardently desired it, since they knew that the church could not fulfil its functions efficiently without a strong secular arm assuring the order and security which was needed. That was why the election decree was ambiguously worded, why the policy enunciated in it was not consistently applied and why even two centuries later there remained an ambivalence in the relationship between church and state. But while to the eleventh-century reformers the prime justification of rulership and the chief duty given it by God was the protection of the church, a protector should know his place and should never try to interfere or control. They were convinced that lay patronage had got out of hand, to the point at which it was, in their eyes, wrong in itself.

Their boldness can only be appreciated in the context of the uneasy relationship between Rome and its own bishops which had been a constant in papal history. The city was now barely recognizable as a former imperial capital. Fields and marshes took up much of the space within the ancient walls. Scattered among them were the tower-houses of the Roman nobles, whom the popes feared most of all, because it was in the nature of things that these men would try to dominate their local bishopric. Everyone knew, or thought they knew, that periods of papal degradation had coincided with those times when the nobles had had the upper hand. That is why the popes had sought assistance from Byzantine, Carolingian, Ottonian and Salian emperors. By renouncing imperial protection, which is what the reformers in Rome were effectively doing, they were exposing the papacy to real danger. A century and a half later Pope Innocent III, who was himself a member of a Roman noble family, thought he had found a solution in the exploitation of the papal patrimony – so that as a powerful prince himself the pope could dominate the local magnates – but in the interim popes were often exiled from their see and forced to look for defenders who had the advantage, in their eyes, of being too weak to threaten them: south Italian Normans, *fideles beati Petri* and so on. Nothing demonstrates the force of the papacy's commitment to its reform programme so much as its option for insecurity, but the extent of its achievement can be measured by comparing what was at the disposal of Innocent III around 1200 with the shadowy rights of his predecessors two centuries before.

The energy of the reformers can easily be demonstrated by taking a half-hour's drive through the countryside of western Europe today and counting the sites where a church was built in the central middle ages. The resources committed to the construction of major stone edifices in almost every village – if that is what a miserable collection of huts could be called – almost passes comprehension. There had been no building programme on this scale since the Roman empire, but to a society which appreciated display it demonstrated the standing of the church and its influence. This was coming to be felt everywhere, even in warfare, that most political of all activities, which was not only sacralized in the crusades, but also ritualized at every level. In the heartlands of Latin Europe, where the concern was, often against the odds, for a more efficient government, the church provided at the same time a model and a hindrance in that its insistence on the management of its own affairs limited the influence that kings and magnates could have over an important institution on which they had relied in their administration. A theme of the period is the forms of resistance rulers employed, from waging war in late eleventh-century Italy to fomenting schism or demanding a redrawing of the boundaries between secular and ecclesiastical jurisdiction in the twelfth century.

Wherever in western Europe an apparatus of courts was still recognizably under a ruler's control and was staffed by officials answerable in some degree to him centralization was possible. In England the Normans took care not to dismantle the system they found there, although, as elsewhere, it coexisted with local jurisdictions and with courts Christian. King Henry II's introduction of the possessory assizes is an example of the importance of having accessible courts and easily understandable procedures working in tandem; the result, in the aftermath of a period of disorder, was a stream of cases flowing into royal courts and a consequent growth in royal authority. Historians of medieval England take pride in what they consider to be a precociously advanced system of government with a wealth of records, but England was not unique. The Norman kingdom of Sicily, divided between the island, which following its conquest in the eleventh century was firmly in the hands of its ruler, and the mainland, where a number of individual principalities had grown up, was an example of experimentation in government every bit as impressive as that in England. In both cases, however, rulership worked well because the country concerned was relatively small geographically.

Size was always an important factor. The western empire, which in the year 1000 had looked somewhat similar to England in governmental terms, had begun to disintegrate by 1100. In Germany this was to lead to the rise of the principalities and in northern Italy to the communes. The empire suffered from a succession of civil wars, but it is arguable that it was simply too big to be effectively administered as a whole once the expectations of its subjects had grown beyond a certain level. It is noticeable that none of its constituent parts challenged the theory of its existence; all of them found a way of managing their own affairs within a framework which they nevertheless succeeded in emasculating. France, another country too large for effective centralized control, had already fragmented and in the early eleventh century this led to intolerable levels of internal disorder. The situation had improved by 1100, but for almost a century thereafter parts of the kingdom suffered intermittently from internal warfare, often because the princes were trying to reduce their own territories to order. The steps taken around 1200 by King Philip II to raise his profile by advancing royal authority into lordships which had already been reconsolidated were, however, made harder than they need have been, because one magnate, the king of England, had accumulated far more land than was healthy for the kingdom as a whole.

Centralization is not everything and where an apparatus of jurisdiction had fragmented or decayed it was not possible to rebuild it, which is why the empire under Frederick Barbarossa and the crown of France under a succession of Capetian kings had to make use of other means to enlarge the scope of royal authority. In both Germany and France the rulers exploited feudal relationships, since these at least provided them with services of various kinds and a legal framework for loyalty and obedience, but over time the consequences were to be completely different, because in Germany the fragmentation came to be reinforced, whereas in France the crown was eventually going to triumph. Before 1200 these processes were only in their early stages and, without agreeing entirely with the communitarian theories which have been argued recently, it is certainly the case that feudal lordship was not yet the force it was to be by the end of the thirteenth century.

Indeed if there was one issue that was at the forefront of the minds of landowners in the late eleventh and twelfth centuries it was not lordship and the possession of tenancies, which are characteristic of feudal holdings, but family. Blood relationships, which endured, of course, as a major political factor into modern times, provided western Europe with another kind of internal unity. The most significant difference between them and association by lordship was that whereas lordship tended to operate in the localities they were cosmopolitan, as families searched further afield for suitable spouses, partly in response to the very strict rules of consanguinity which the church was trying to impose. Rotrou of Perche, the count of Mortagne on the frontiers of Normandy around 1100, for example, was related to the kings of Aragón through his aunt and to the viscount of Turenne in Limousin through the marriage of his sister. At about the same time the daughters of Count William Tête Hardi of Burgundy were married to the duke of Burgundy and the counts of Flanders, Savoy and Bar-le-Duc. And one of William's sons was married to the heiress of Castile. International bonds of kinship straggled, like Cistercian filiations, from Britain and Scandinavia to the Levant, binding westerners together culturally.

Dynastic relationships had strong effects on the periphery. Recent research on the settlers in Syria and Palestine has shown how closely they were in touch with their relations in the west. The families thrown into prominence there were often not of the highest rank. The Montlhérys, the first clan to exploit the crusading movement, must have been predisposed in some way to respond to the earliest calls to crusade since so many members took part. Two Montlhérys were among the first settlers in the Levant, and one of them was independently related to the greatest figures there and was talented enough to be rewarded by them with lordship. He in turn patronized other relations, including new arrivals. Members of the family were, therefore, well placed when they were provided with an opportunity to seize the crown in 1118. And the characteristic way that the instinct for cooperation and mutual assistance would bring a whole kindred-group, or a substantial part of it, into line behind an initiative is demonstrated by the attempts by relations, in the west as well as in the east, to respond to needs of their colonial cousins through visits to Palestine, through the use of whatever influence they had at home or through settlement themselves. The path taken by the Montlhérys was to be followed a few decades later by the Lusignans and in the thirteenth century by the Briennes. Crusading was so dependent on the reactions of committed European kin-groups that it could be manipulated by them relatively easily.

Western government was marked everywhere by experimentation and innovation. This was particularly the case in the new settlements in which characteristic features of frontier administration, marcher lordships, gave their holders freedom to experiment. In Spain and in the Levant western conquerors were faced by the absorption of large numbers of indigenous of other religions and evolved measures to cope with them, most being variations on existing Muslim *dhimmi* regulations for subject peoples. But a feature before 1200 was that on many frontiers the papacy had much less influence than in the heartlands, in spite of the facts that the Levantine colonies had been created out of the papal crusading movement, Spain was a region on which it had concentrated much of its effort in the eleventh century and the king of Sicily was a papal vassal. The nature of the conquest, the accession of rulers who had not been in the forefront of reform and the poor quality of the clergy who had accompanied the First Crusade were responsible for a patriarchate of Jerusalem which comprised possibly the most backward and unreformed collection of provinces in Latin Christendom. In Spain and Sicily the church fell into the pockets of the kings. The reason for its relative weakness seems to have been that it had not yet evolved instruments to cope with the imposition of Latin Christianity in regions which had not known it. So on the frontiers, at a time when it was trumpeting its freedom from lay influence, it was still as dependent on secular power as it had been in the days of Charlemagne and the Ottonian emperors.

CHAPTER 2

THE PAPACY, 1024–1122

Uta-Renate Blumenthal

INTRODUCTION

General

The author of a chapter on the history of the papacy from 1024 to 1122 confronts the unusual task of giving in a few pages an account of both the *Adelspapsttum* and of the popes of the Gregorian reform period. No greater contrast could be imagined, one might think. After the clean-sweep of Sutri and Rome in 1046, when ecclesiastical councils under the guidance of Emperor Henry III cleared the way for the first of the northern newcomers, Pope Clement II (1046–7), a fundamentally altered papacy is supposed to have arisen from the ashes of a papacy dominated by the corrupt local Roman nobility. And, indeed, profound changes occurred in the second half of the eleventh century, although with regard less to the papacy itself as an institution than to its relationship with the churches of the empire (Germany, Italy and, at times, Burgundy), the Normans of Italy, the principalities and kingdom of France and the Byzantine patriarchate. Because of the Conquest and the special relationship between the papacy and the English kings from William I to Henry I, England stood somewhat apart in this reordering, as did Spain on account of the *Reconquista*.[1] It involved the successful realization of the papal primacy. This was not limited to the secular realm, but also deeply affected relationships within the church. The history of these changes can be found in an earlier chapter as well as in many handbooks and will only be sketched very briefly here.[2] The present chapter will emphasize the administrative underpinning that allowed a strengthened papacy to emerge at the end of the twelfth century under Innocent III (1198–1216) as the single most influential political and spiritual institution of Latin Christendom. It will cover the initial stages of this development, since they

[1] Cowdrey (1972) and (1989); Fornasari (1989); Garcia y Garcia (1989); Erdmann (1935).
[2] *NCMH*, IV, Part I, ch. 9.

unfolded precisely in the period from *c.* 1012 to 1123 and form a continuous theme.

The tenth-century background

The popes of the tenth and early eleventh centuries never renounced the proud papal traditions represented in the more recent past by Nicholas I (858–67) and John VIII (872–82). But because the ties between the pope and the Frankish rulers, which had helped to shift the focus of the papacy from Byzantium to northern Europe in the eighth century, had weakened considerably during the break-up of the Carolingian empire and the effectiveness of the popes had declined, the papacy of the tenth century came to depend increasingly on local Roman and Italian factions. Near-anarchy north and south of the Alps greatly constricted the papal vision as well as the papal sphere of action. Not even the revival of the western imperial tradition by the Ottonian rulers in 962 could break the vicious cycle which threatened to make the papacy permanently a merely local force. The affair of Pope Formosus (891–6) shows vividly that it was even an advantage for the church, when with Sergius III (904–11) one of the several rival factions in Rome gained the definite ascendancy over the others. Formosus had been bishop before his election, and canon law forbade the translation of bishops to other sees, since they were considered married to their churches of ordination. The opponents of Formosus, therefore, possessed an excellent weapon. At the infamous synod of 896/7, Pope Stephen VII had the decaying corpse of Formosus dressed in papal regalia, deprived him of his rank and finally had the mutilated corpse cast into the Tiber. For almost two decades afterwards it was hotly debated whether or not Formosus had been pope legally and whether or not, therefore, his ordinations had been and remained valid. Writings supporting Formosus are vivid illustrations of the confusion and violence reigning in Rome at the time, and incidentally provided some of the most potent arguments in the eleventh-century quarrel over the validity of simoniacal ordination between Peter Damian and Humbert of Silva Candida.

The success of Sergius III, since 897 the anti-Formosan candidate for the papacy, was primarily due to the support of his cause by Theophylact. Theophylact and his direct heirs dominated Rome until 963, when the Crescentians and eventually the Tusculans succeeded to his role. Under the *princeps* Alberic II (932–955), grandson of Theophylact, Rome enjoyed the greatest degree of security and tranquillity in the entire century. Alberic completely dominated the papacy, but his rule also brought monastic reforms to Rome. They were inspired and personally guided by Abbot Odo of Cluny. Alberic's son, Octavian, not only continued to rule temporal Rome, but also became pope under the name of John XII (955–64). Not until 1012 was Crescentian control over the papacy to be broken. The Tusculan party succeeded in replacing the Roman branch of the Crescentians in May of that year, when within a week both Pope Sergius IV (1009–12) and the patrician John had died. Gregory, elevated to the papacy by the Crescentian party, was defeated and replaced by the Tusculan Theophylact as Benedict VIII.

The Tusculan popes

Benedict VIII (1012–24)

In contrast to the Crescentians, who had largely relied on the entrenchment of their own dynasty and their supporters in the duchy of Rome as secular magnates and landowners – often at the expense of the temporal property of the Roman church – the Tusculans used their secular power and successes to shore up the standing of the papacy among the Roman nobility. The position of patrician, so important to Crescentian rule, remained vacant. Benedict VIII, in particular, fought successfully to restore to the Roman church some of the properties that had been alienated through long-term emphyteusis to lay magnates. At the same time the pontiff also lent his support to monasteries such as Farfa south of Rome in reclaiming alienated property. The synod of Pavia of 1022, celebrated jointly by Benedict and Emperor Henry II, betrays the same spirit, although an element of moral reform of the clergy was also present and should not be underestimated.[3] Successful restitutions of rights and property to the apostolic see were none the less negligible, if the abject poverty of the papacy in the mid-eleventh century provides an acceptable measure. In the long run, therefore, other aspects of Benedict's reign were better suited to shore up and preserve traditional papal rights as they had evolved in the Carolingian period. Benedict's cooperation with the emperor and his need for a military alliance brought about a visit to Henry II at Bamberg in 1020. On this occasion the pope received an imperial privilege which repeated with a few additions the *Ottonianum*, which had confirmed the papal lands granted in earlier Frankish donations. The document, known as the *Henricianum*, played a subsidiary but nevertheless important role in conjunction with the Donation of Constantine in documenting papal sovereignty and the geographical extent of the papal states for centuries to come.

The cooperation between pope and emperor also shaped other aspects of papal policy far beyond the reigns of the Tusculan popes themselves. Among them are administrative changes with regard to the chancery, as well as the seemingly innocuous introduction of the *filioque* clause. A synod gathered

---

[3] *MGH Constitutiones*, I, no. 34, pp. 70–7; cf. Capitani (1966), Pavia 1046. The fight for the restitution of ecclesiastical property might itself constitute reform, cf. Garcia y Garcia (1989), p. 246.

in Rome on the occasion of Henry's imperial coronation in 1014 agreed to follow in future the Frankish custom of including the Nicene creed among the prayers of the mass on Sundays and holidays. The venerable creed was now to contain the *filioque* whose Frankish origin was quickly forgotten. It was accepted as so typically Roman that Byzantine objections to the *filioque* became a fundamental issue in the break between Rome and Constantinople in 1054.

More important still was the fact that since the time of Charlemagne it had become customary for new archdioceses to be established only through the papacy. The pontiff would determine the geographical extent of an ecclesiastical province as well as the seat of the new archbishop. An archbishop, furthermore, could only assume his duties after he had obtained the pallium, once it had been consecrated by the pope over the tomb of St Peter in Rome. Eventually, in the late eleventh century, the conferring of the pallium made the archbishop seem more like the pope's deputy with a delegated share in the universal primacy. It is true, of course, that rulers who were powerful enough to establish new archbishoprics like Otto I (Magdeburg 963) or Henry II (Bamberg 1020) also were strong enough to influence the papacy, but formally at least papal control determined the shape of the church in the particular kingdoms. When political circumstances permitted, the papacy could translate such control into real terms, or try to do so. Gregory IV (827–44), for example, intervened in the revolt of 830 against Louis the Pious on the side of Lothar I and his bishops. The pope was unsuccessful on this occasion, because most of the Frankish episcopate supported Louis, but in the course of the negotiations Gregory IV had reinterpreted instructions of Pope Leo I (440–61), stating that the pope alone possessed the fullness of power (*plenitudo potestatis*) whereas the bishops were entrusted only with partial responsibility (*pars sollicitudinis*). By the end of the eleventh century this declaration was frequently used to justify papal supremacy. By then it encountered little opposition among the episcopate which thus abandoned the old collegial understanding of the church at least in practice. With an attribution to Pope Vigilius, the text found its place in the Pseudo-Isidorian Decretals, thus becoming part of this sophisticated corpus of Frankish forgeries from the mid-ninth century, which also included the Donation of Constantine.[4]

Monastic privileges

In addition to the use of legates, who continued to represent the papacy on solemn occasions, especially councils, throughout the *seculum obscurum*, the influence of the papacy and veneration for St Peter is also evident in the growing

---

[4] *Decretales Pseudo-Isidorianae*; Fuhrmann (197–4).

appeals to Rome for papal protection or even exemption of monasteries and, eventually, bishoprics. Papal protection, well into the eleventh century usually side by side with royal or imperial protection, meant that a particular abbey was protected by St Peter; an attack on such an abbey was at the same time an attack on St Peter. Frequently such a privilege included the right to the free election of the abbot or abbess. Expanded protection brought with it the exemption of an abbey from episcopal supervision at least in part. The extent of the exemption varied and was never absolute. The history of the Burgundian abbey of Cluny, founded by the duke of Aquitaine in 909, is an example of the various stages of protection/exemption. The foundation charter immediately provided for full independence from secular authority, free abbatial elections and papal protection (*tuitio* and *defensio*). The monastery was given to St Peter and St Paul. Every five years Cluny was to pay a census of ten *solidi* in recognition of this protection. The right of free abbatial elections, interpreted as the right to the designation of a worthy successor, contributed at first far more to Cluny's development than did papal protection. The abbots were thus able to prevent any decline in reforming zeal or the strictness of life and morals. It was only the later protection of Cluny by kings and popes that eventually led to Cluny's exemption from diocesan authority through the papacy. The final step in a complex process was the privilege of 1024 bestowed by Pope John XIX on Cluny to terminate all the bitter disputes and struggles between the abbey and the bishops of Mâcon, who had lost large portions of diocesan income because of Cluny's partial exemption.[5] Given the fame and influence of Cluny it is easy to understand how the abbey's links to St Peter strengthened not only the monastery but also the prestige and influence of St Peter's earthly successor, the pope. In general it must be said, however, that the two successors of Benedict VIII, John XIX (1024–32) and Benedict IX (1032–44; 1045–6; 1047–8), were less successful than their predecessor. The regnal years of Benedict IX's pontificate with their frequent interruptions are a tell-tale sign. His pontificate was interrupted by first a resignation, secondly a deposition and thirdly a defeat.[6]

Legacy

Nevertheless, veneration for the successor of St Peter was kept alive in many ways: by the many pilgrims; probably hardly less so by the export of Italian relics; the papal right to the imperial coronation; and the first instances of the canonization of saints through popes. Up to the end of the tenth century, the cult of a saint had evolved spontaneously and locally, but in 993 John XV

[5] Cowdrey (1970).
[6] Kempf (1969), pp. 247–57; Herrmann (1973); Schimmelpfennig (1984), ch. 5, pp. 122ff.

became the first pope to proclaim a saint officially at the request of the German ruler. The cult of Bishop Ulrich of Augsburg prescribed for the universal church by John, of five Polish martyrs by John XVIII and of the Armenian hermit Symeon by Benedict VIII were the first steps in a process that was to lead under Pope Innocent III to the exclusive papal prerogative of canonization. The role of the imperial coronation in the history of the papacy has been evaluated in an earlier chapter.[7] Here a reminder suffices that no king who hoped to be emperor, or needed the title to maintain his sovereignty, could afford to forget his dependence on papal support.

Whatever the strengths and weaknesses of an individual who occupied the throne of St Peter, therefore, the papacy as an institution was well prepared for the universal role it was to assume under the popes of the reform period. The foundations on which they could build were laid firmly, not least in the canonical collections of the time. In practical terms the successes of a great pontiff like Nicholas I were ephemeral,[8] but they were invaluable in legal and theoretical terms. The increasing separation between the eastern and the western halves of the church in intellectual and political terms brought a decisive turn in the development of the Roman primacy. Without the patriarchate of Constantinople as a constant, practical reminder of the division of the patriarchal authority among five sees, the Roman patriarchal role was readily superseded by that of the universal primacy which had been attributed to the bishop of Rome as successor of St Peter for centuries in the Latin west. In 1054 two legates of Leo IX, the cardinals Frederick of Lorraine and Humbert of Silva Candida, excommunicated the patriarch of Constantinople, Michael Keroularios, as well as Emperor Constantine IX, an important step towards the permanent schism between the Greek Orthodox and Roman Catholic churches but also towards the universal papal primacy.

The papacy during the reform period

Simony and nicolaitism

From the days of the synods of Sutri and Rome in 1046 to the Lateran council of 1123, where the compromise regarding royal investitures of bishops and abbots concluded at Worms between Henry V and legates of Pope Calixtus II was reluctantly ratified, the papacy developed into an international institution of the first rank. The aim in 1046 had simply been the reform of the church in Rome. Conditions there had become urgent concerns of ecclesiastical reformers, among them monks, regular canons, bishops, princes, nobles and the laity in general. The twin evils corrupting the church and blemishing the

7 *NCMH*, iv, Part i, ch. 9.   8 *NCMH*, ii, ch. 21, pp. 563–86.

image of the pure bride of Christ were simony and nicolaitism, that is clerical marriage. Simony took its name from Simon Magus (Acts 8:18–24) and was understood as the buying or selling of spiritual goods and offices as defined by Gregory the Great. Gregory distinguished three forms of simony: the *munus a manu* (money or gift), *munus ab obsequio* (services, favours) and *munus a lingua* (intercession) and reinforced the older notion that whoever sinned against the Holy Spirit by committing simony was a heretic. By the eleventh century, when the concept of the proprietary church had penetrated the church, simony appeared in numerous guises, especially that of different types of fees, for instance those required by monasteries for admissions. Investiture, a ceremony for the handing over of the symbols of office (crosier and ring for a bishop), was often also seen as linked to simony. Simony, therefore, was a complex problem and extremely difficult to pursue. The fight for celibacy among the clergy was much more clear-cut, but it also required much persistence on the part of the papacy, which had taken over the leadership of church reform since the days of Leo IX. On both issues much headway was made, as described in an earlier chapter,[9] although neither sin could be extirpated entirely. Simony and nicolaitism had troubled the church for centuries and continued to do so in future, albeit less blatantly. But it is clear that the pertinent ecclesiastical legislation laid down standards that were now accepted throughout Latin Christendom as a measure of commitment to the clerical life, giving rise to the criticism of the clergy among the laity which is so pronounced a factor in the later middle ages. Nevertheless, historians who emphasize ecclesiastical reforms as the chief characteristics of the papacy of the eleventh century are hard pressed to explain differences between this and other periods of reformation and renewal in the church. It is increasingly recognized that the crucial difference is the interpretation of the old concept of the papal primacy by the reformers. The two issues, primacy and reform, interacted, but constitute separate strands none the less.

The papal primacy

Even in the tenth century, when the popes were not particularly respected, nobody ever doubted the primacy of Rome, notwithstanding the quarrel over the archbishopric of Rheims which came to a head at the synod of Chelles. But Yves Congar put it well when he pointed out that on the whole in the pre-reform period the primacy of Rome was seen as an office or ministry distinguished by wisdom and moral authority within a church that was led by bishops and regulated through councils.[10] Since the mid-eleventh century a forceful emphasis on canonical traditions, as handed down in the Pseudo-Isidorian Decretals and

[9] *NCMH*, IV, Part I, ch. 9.   [10] Congar (1961), p. 196; Klinkenberg (1955).

especially the *Decretum* of Burchard of Worms (d. 1025),[11] gradually enriched the concept of primacy until the Petrine texts (Matthew 16:18–19; Luke 22:32; John 21:15–17) were related *exclusively* to the Roman church and thus turned into a dogmatic truth.[12] Obedience to the pope became an aspect of faith; disobedience now was idolatry and therefore heresy. Disobedience is the fundamental reason given for the excommunication of Henry IV by Gregory VII[13] and that of Henry V by Urban II and by Paschal II in 1102.[14] The occasion was the Lateran council of that year. It also introduced as a new requirement a written profession of obedience to the pontiff from the participants of the council and from those being granted the pallium.[15]

The roots of this eleventh-century transformation of the concept of papal primacy were many; they can be found throughout the Latin church. Northern polemics apparently stressed the old rule that the pope could not be judged by anyone, especially not a layman like Emperor Henry III, who moreover had no rights with regard to the election of any cleric. The views of the Italian reformer Peter Damian had developed long before Leo IX and his Lotharingian/Burgundian companions brought reforms to Rome. Like many of his contemporaries throughout Latin Christendom, Damian literally regarded the authentic decrees of the fathers as *sacri canones*, as the sacred pronouncements of popes, councils and church fathers inspired by the Holy Spirit. Canons were equated with the divine law, and Peter Damian like others was convinced that it was impossible for the laws of God to contradict each other. Harmonization of seemingly contradictory passages was one of his main concerns. Of these there were many, since for Damian all councils, even if not papal or legatine, and all papal decretals – because the pope is the successor of St Peter – represented legal sources of universal validity. There was one exception. Damian declared that a canon was no longer valid when it contradicted authentic papal decretals ('si decretis Romanorum pontificum non concordat'). This straightforward principle served Damian as the touchstone for the authenticity of any canon, whatever its origin.[16] Differing from Cardinals Atto and Humbert of Silva Candida, Damian thus did not presuppose positive papal confirmation of a canon. Instead, he was in agreement with the *Decretum* of Burchard of Worms, a canonical collection he frequently used. Reasoning from the principle of concordance just mentioned, Damian came to declare anyone a heretic who did not agree with the Roman church ('haereticus esse

---

[11] Fuhrmann (1972–4), II, pp. 442–85.   [12] Congar (1961).
[13] Gregory VII, *Register* III, 10a: 'Et quia sicut christianus contempsit oboedire . . . meaque monita . . . spernendo . . . vinculo eum anathematis vice tua alligo'; *ibid.*, VII, 14a: 'Heinricus . . . non timens periculum inoboedientie, quod est scelus idolatrie . . . excommunicationem incurrit.'
[14] Blumenthal (1978), p. 21.   [15] *Ibid.*, pp. 21 ff; Gottlob (1936), pp. 8–10 and 49ff.
[16] Ryan (1956), pp. 137ff.

constat, qui Romanae ecclesiae non concordat'). Slightly altered, this sentence is frequently attributed to Ambrose of Milan and is found in a very similar form in the *dictatus papae* of Gregory VII.[17] Many though not all of the reformers (Cardinal Deusdedit is one exception) implicitly and even explicitly equated the Apostle Peter, the pope and the Roman church. Thus obedience owed to the pontiff became absolute.

This conviction, displayed so prominently in the *dictatus papae* of Gregory VII but shared equally by his immediate predecessors and successors, carried over into the secular sphere, as we would say today. It was expressed strikingly in the day-to-day activities of the papacy. The crusades, envisioned under papal leadership by Gregory VII and initiated by Urban II at the council of Clermont in 1095; the deposition of the French king and of the emperors Henry IV and Henry V; the policies towards Byzantium and last but not least towards the Normans in southern Italy: everywhere to some extent at least the principle of the papal primacy is at play, albeit indirectly. The Latin church, by now understood as the universal church, was directly under the control of the pope. The pontiff possessed the *plenitudo potestatis* and could not be judged or deposed. By the second half of the twelfth century at the latest the right to issue new legislation had become his alone; papal decretals became the most significant influence on the jurisprudence arising particularly at the universities in southern France and Italy. The popes alone could issue dispensations, make monasteries and collegiate churches exempt, create new dioceses or divide or relocate old bishoprics. The relative autonomy of the archbishops in particular was considerably weakened. The most important aids in the execution of papal policies were the new organization of the papal bureaucracy, the rise of the college of cardinals and the systematic use of legates.

In addition to stressing the papal primacy within the church, Gregory VII and his successors also inverted the customary relationship between the monarchies and the papacy. The Gelasian concept of the priestly and the secular power side by side within the one church whose head was Christ had been typical for the Carolingian world of the ninth century. This image dominated thought well into the later eleventh century. Gregory's deposition of Henry IV and his claims to soverignty in Italy, Spain, the Mediterranean islands, Scandinavia, Poland, Bohemia, Hungary and last but not least England created conditions not at all unlike those envisioned in the forged Donation of Constantine.[18] By the early twelfth century the papacy was well on the way towards what has been described as the papal monarchy.

---

[17] Gregory VII, *Register* II, 55a, c. 26: 'Quod catholicus non habeatur, qui non concordat Romane ecclesie.'

[18] Robinson (1990), pp. 17–27.

THE PAPAL ADMINISTRATION

From the Lateran palace to the curia

The Lateran palace, for much of the period under consideration the papal residence, also served as administrative centre of the Roman church as well as of her temporal properties: the duchy of Rome and the patrimonies (landed estates) of the see of St Peter. Known simply as the *episcopium* in the time of Gregory the Great, the Lateran soon thereafter also was called *patriarchium Lateranense* in analogy to the eastern patriarchates. Finally, by the tenth century, *sacrum palatium Lateranense* became the standard expression, a designation that had appeared in the Donation of Constantine, most likely an eighth-century Roman forgery. Best known among early papal officials are the seven deacons of Rome, an influential oligarchy from whose ranks many of the early popes, including Gregory I, were elected. By the mid-tenth century, however, the leading officials were the 'judges', a term then meaning dignitary rather than judge. The title might be replaced by 'duke', 'consul romanorum', prince and even 'sentatrix' in the case of the Roman lay magnates, who as *iudices de militia* were closely associated with the papacy.[19] This is also true for the prefect whose ancient office was specifically linked with criminal and civic jurisdiction in the city of Rome. It was still significant under the popes of the reform period, gaining yet new lustre during the twelfth-century communal movement.[20] The office of *vestararius* should perhaps be thought of at times as even more influential.[21] Side by side and intermingled with the lay 'judges' were the *iudices de clero*, the chief papal administrators. They, too, were members of the Roman nobility and usually married, for despite their misleading name they were only in minor orders. The group included the *primicerius* of the defensors and the *primicerius* and *secundicerius* of the notaries (organized like other groups into *scholae*), the *arcarius* and *sacellarius* responsible since the seventh century for finances, and the *nomenculator* in charge of alms; in the ninth century the *protoscrinarius* was also numbered among the 'judges'. The offices of these seven 'judges' are described in two documents, known as the older and younger (1002–49, before 1032?) list of judges, respectively.[22] Whether the younger list reflects the influence of the imperial *sacrum palatium* at Pavia or not, it is certainly one of the traces

[19] *Regesta pontificum Romanorum: Italia pontificia*, I, p. 185, no. 1. Jordan (1947), p. 112. Fundamental are the lists for various officials in Halphen (1907). For the rarely used expression *iudices de militia* see *ibid.*, p. 37 n. 1. For members of the family of Theophylact addressed as 'senatrix' see Toubert (1973), p. 1027 n. 3, in addition to Kehr.

[20] One example is the abduction of Gregory VII in 1075 by Cencius Stephani (Bonizo of Sutri, 'Liber ad amicum', pp. 606, 610–11) and another the revolt of 1116/17 against Paschal II (*Liber pontificalis*, II, pp. 302, 303). See Partner (1972), pp. 152ff.

[21] Jordan (1947), pp. 116–18.

[22] Schramm (1929), pp. 199–218; Elze (1952), pp. 29–33, arguing persuasively for *c.* 962 as a possibility.

left by the attempts of the Tusculan popes to strengthen the papacy. Another
is evidence which seems to imply that members of the Roman clergy were now
more closely associated with the pope as palace clergy, including by 1018 acolytes
and subdeacons (JL 4024) and by 1049 at the latest deacons (JL 4067 and JL
4163).[23] The link between the popes and cardinal priests and cardinal bishops,
still predominantly liturgical, was reemphasized, for the later tenth- and early
eleventh-century papal ceremonial in the Lateran palace as well as papal processions and station liturgies in the city of Rome were further elaborated, as
witnessed by the younger list of judges.[24] Pope John XIX not only requested the
bishop of Silva Candida to restore the liturgy at St Peter's basilica in 1026 (JL
4076), but also invited Guido of Arezzo to come to Rome in order to reform
church music.[25] Benedict VIII as well as John XIX, moreover, paid particular
attention to the suburbicarian sees, like Porto, Silva Candida and Tivoli.[26]

The chancery

Tentative reform efforts – and perhaps it is only to us that they appear so
tentative – extended beyond the papal ceremonial and the cardinal-bishoprics,
however. By the later tenth century practical reforms must have been urgent,
if the deterioration in the Roman curial script of the few extant original documents is any guide. The studies of Rabikauskas support the suggestions of Elze
that many of the papal scribes, whether designated as notaries or *scriniarii*, were
identical with Roman urban notaries, the *tabelliones*. This can only mean that
the papal writing office had become so insignificant that it no longer needed
permanent officials of its own.[27] The renewal of the imperial dignity in 962
and new links with the imperial Ottonian/Saxon court influenced this later
tenth- and early eleventh-century reorganization of the Lateran bureaucracy.
The office of chancellor is the most important example. Under John XVIII
(1004–9) the *cancellarius sacri palatii Lateranensis* became a constant designation for the papal chancellor who functioned next to the *bibliothecarius* as a
second official in charge of correspondence and privileges.[28] By 1023, when

[23] Elze (1952), pp. 40–6.
[24] Elze (1952), pp. 50ff, with references to the Ordo of Benedict. The liturgical roles of the judges recall
their former eminence but also indicate that they no longer practise their official functions. From
the late tenth century they had been replaced by the *bibliothecarius* (Jordan (1947), p. 116). See also
Blaauw (1987).
[25] Elze (1952), p. 53 n. 140.
[26] *Regesta pontificum Romanorum: Italia pontificia*, III, nos. p. 20, 10 and 11 for Porto; pp. 25–7, nos. 2–5
for Silva Candida; p. 77, no. 9 for Tivoli. In this context Toubert (1973), p. 1036, refers to Tusculan
activity 'pre-reformateur'.
[27] *Protoscrinarius* is explained in the younger list of judges as follows: 'Quintus est protus qui praeest
scriniariis, quos nos tabelliones vocamus' (Rabikauskas (1958), pp. 69–71). See *ibid.*, p. 68 n. 12 for
examples of the identity of papal scribe and urban notary.
[28] See Rabikauskas (1958), pp. 95ff, and especially Santifaller, (1940), pp. 113ff.

Pope Benedict VIII named Archbishop Pilgrim of Cologne *bibliothecarius*, the chancellor evidently had assumed the functions of the librarian entirely.[29] Both offices were combined in 1037 by Pope Benedict IX in the person of Peter of Silva Candida (JL 4110).[30] Peter continued to hold these offices to his death in 1050, notwithstanding the extraordinary and fateful changes touching the papacy upon the intervention of Emperor Henry III at the synods of Sutri and Rome in 1046. Benedict IX had granted the offices to the bishops of Silva Candida in perpetuity, but only Humbert, one of the ecclesiastics who had accompanied Pope Leo IX to Rome, and his successor Mainard could secure the office of librarian/chancellor in the years 1057–63, when they were cardinal bishops of Silva Candida.[31] In general, it was preferred to entrust the office of chancellor to a lower-ranking cleric who would be able to devote himself exclusively to his secretarial duties. From 1063 the acolyte Peter occupied the position until 1084, when he deserted the cause of Pope Gregory VII and went over to Antipope Clement III. Famous is the long tenure of the chancellor John of Gaeta who took over in 1088 and remained until 1118, when he was elected pope as Gelasius II. John of Gaeta had been a monk at Monte Cassino where he had studied under the rhetorician Alberic. It was he who introduced the *cursus* into papal documents, used a new period for the calculation of the indiction and a new date for the beginning of the year.[32]

However, despite the continuity of leadership in the papal chancery, located in the Lateran palace, the church reform of the eleventh century meant numerous changes in its personnel and, most visibly, in its products, primarily papal letters and privileges, although the chancery also maintained official registers. The antique custom of keeping official registers was revived at the latest under Pope Alexander II (1061–73), although from this period only the original manuscript of the register of Gregory VII (1073–85) has survived in the Archivio Segreto of the Vatican.[33] The papal archives seem to have been kept in part at the Lateran palace and in part at a tower near the arch of Constantine.[34] Only Roman scribes were trained in the traditional curial script, but they rarely

---

[29] Bresslau (1912), pp. 219ff.

[30] Herrmann (1973), p. 24, inappropriately describes the new office as a *Superministerium*. See Elze (1952) and Rabikauskas (1958).

[31] Huels (1977), pp. 131–4 for Humbert, and pp. 134–6 for Mainard. Mainard was replaced by the acolyte Peter in January 1063 when he became abbot of the abbey of Pomposa.

[32] Santifaller (1940), pp. 183–9 for the acolyte Peter, and pp. 208–14 for John of Gaeta; Sydow (1954/5), p. 50.

[33] Bresslau (1912), pp. 101–24; Caspar (1913), pp. 214–26; Lohrmann (1968); Schmidt (1977), pp. 220–35; Blumenthal (1986), pp. 1–18, and (1988b), p. 135 n. 2.

[34] Schieffer (1971), pp. 169–84; for the *Archivo sacri palatii Lateranensis* see Deusdedit, *Kanonessammlung*, III. 278 and III. 279; Kurze (1990), p. 35 n. 48; Ehrle (1910), p. 448. The influential thesis of Kehr (1901) that *scrinium* and chancery were two different institutions with different personnel has been convincingly rejected by Elze (1952) as noted by Toubert (1973), p. 1043 n. 2.

accompanied pontiffs like Leo IX or Victor II on their extended travels. The
popes, therefore, had to rely on local assistants or members of their entourage,
who usually were obliged to substitute Carolingian minuscule for the curial
script. Moreover, it was necessary to use parchment instead of papyrus, which
was becoming rare at this time and could not be obtained north of the Alps.
The replacement of the curial script, however, was certainly not intentional,
for under Stephen IX and his successors to Pope Calixtus II (1119–24) it reappeared and was used side by side with the minuscule until it disappeared for
good after 1123.

Of greater interest are textual and formulaic changes in the privileges, which
were introduced most likely through papal initiatives. Some of them clearly
reflect imperial usages. Certain historians suggest a linkage with the lively
interest in the Donation of Constantine displayed by the popes since Leo IX,
but the evidence is too ambiguous to be certain.[35] Leo IX and his advisers,
including Humbert of Silva Candida, introduced the rota into the eschatocol,
the last lines of a privilege following upon the body of the text. The rota, a
double circle surrounding a cross and with an inscription specific to each pope,
replaced a simple cross. One other notable change is the transformation of the
old *Bene valete* of the popes into a monogram.[36] The gradual, overall evolution
of the chancery brought with it, intentionally or not, a differentiation and
separation from local Roman institutions. Thus it fits in well with the evolution
of the papacy from a locally dominated institution to an international one. The
chancellor, dating back to the early eleventh century at least, thus finds his place
with ease in the papal curia developing since the pontificate of Urban II (1088–
99), like the *camera* and the *capella papalis* in analogy to the courts of the
European monarchies.[37]

The financial administration and the lands of St Peter

Particularly significant for the history of the papacy was the creation of the
camera under Pope Urban II. Apart from the cardinal bishops, many members
of the Roman clergy (the old 'iudici de clero') had deserted the cause of Gregory
VII in 1084 and transferred their allegiance to the antipope Clement III and
Emperor Henry IV. Both the chancellor and the *archidiaconus* had been among

---

[35] This is often assumed, but such assumptions are contradicted by the fact that the German imperial
chancery influenced the papal chancery certainly from the pontificate of John XIII (965–72) and
into the reign of Pope Stephen IX. By the end of the eleventh century, by contrast, the influence
was flowing in the opposite direction. See Bresslau (1918), especially pp. 27–37.

[36] Santifaller (1973), pp. 29–38. Frenz (1986), pp. 15–22, provides an excellent recent description for
the evolution of letters, simple and solemn privileges in this period and includes a bibliography. For
details on development under Leo IX, see Dahlhaus (1989).

[37] Jordan (1947), pp. 114ff and n. 15, and Jordan (1973), pp. 32–43.

them. Urban, therefore, could begin with a clean slate and transfer the *camera*, the financial institution which had proven its value at the Burgundian abbey of Cluny, to Rome without being hamstrung by ancient traditions there or consideration of the claims of the old bureaucracy. Indeed, other monasteries north of the Alps also used a *camera* to keep their financial affairs in order,[38] but it can hardly be doubted that Urban, formerly prior at Cluny, was influenced by the very institution which he had come to know and appreciate as a monk, especially since his first treasurer, the *camerarius* Peter, was also a monk from Cluny. Moreover, Cluny itself directly assisted the papacy with financial trans-actions in the late eleventh and early twelfth centuries, so much so that the *Historia Compostellana* referred to Cluny as *camera et asseda* of the pope at the time of Calixtus II.[39] Peter continued as treasurer under Paschal II (1099–1118). Calixtus II, the former Archbishop Guy of Vienne, once again installed a monk from Cluny, Stephen of Besançon, as *camerarius*. Only after his pontificate did the financial ties between the papacy and Cluny begin to weaken.

Records for the activities of the *camera* in the beginning of its history are very scanty. The financial situation of the papacy in this period was very precarious, as the many papal appeals for assistance to English, French and German ec-clesiastics demonstrate. Ordinarily, the chief expenses of the pontiffs were the *presbyteria*, gifts to the Romans due on many different ceremonial occasions, and the maintenance and embellishment of the churches and monasteries of Rome, including the Lateran palace and St Peter's basilica. The clergy of Rome, particularly if they were foreigners or members of the bureaucracy, also depended to some extent on the papacy for financial support. The reform papacy, however, was in addition not only involved in a struggle, armed or otherwise, with the Roman noble opposition but was also trying to reconquer the papal states, having to fend off the Normans in the process. Expenses cer-tainly rose, therefore. The papal income was originally derived primarily from the 'lands of St Peter', the huge estates, villages and towns of the patrimony found throughout the western half of the former Roman empire, but especially in southern Italy and Africa. Once, at the end of the sixth century, this income readily sufficed to provide for the entire city of Rome. By the eleventh century, when the *camera* was created, matters had changed dramatically. Again and again the popes had tried to prevent the appropriation of church lands by the great Roman families, but to no avail. The nobles took advantage of long-term leases, customarily granted for the term of three lives, which they exacted from popes, bishops or abbots in return for a small recognition fee, the *pensio* or *census*. At the synod of 877 at Ravenna Pope John VIII jointly with Emperor Charles the Bald (840–77) very tellingly prohibited not only alienations by

---

[38] Sydow (1954/5), p. 43 n. 161.   [39] *Ibid.*, p. 57 n. 249.

the papacy but also *requests* for the alienation of the patrimony or of any of the fiscal rights of the Roman church. Such income was to go directly to the Lateran palace, nor were any monasteries, manors or estates to be given out as benefices. Both of these conciliar canons contained significant exceptions: familiars of the popes and persons to whom such grants were owed for their special service to holy Roman church.[40] The arenga of the privilege of Otto III (983–1002) of 1001 granting Pope Sylvester II (999–1003) eight counties in the Pentapolis, severely criticized the territorial policies of the papacy: 'we are witness to the fact that the Roman church is the mother of all churches, but the carelessness and ignorance of the popes has long obscured the monuments of her greatness. For not only did they sell and alienate ... things outside the City, but also ... what they held in this our royal City.' The arenga eventually lists the Donation of Constantine as one of the fabrications of the papacy under the name of the great Constantine in order to make up for losses by appropriating what belonged to the emperor.[41] In the rest of Italy similar conditions prevailed; Otto III decreed in 998 that leases were to be valid only during the lifetime of the lessor, since the ecclesiastical institutions should not be made to suffer through alienations based on greed and personal ties.[42] Such and similar leases together with outright grants transformed, for instance, the Sabina north of Rome into a Crescentian power base.[43] Improvements were very slow to come, the great Donation of Emperor Henry II to the Roman church of 1020 notwithstanding.[44] Two privileges of Nicholas II (1059–61) for Rocca Antica and Montasola, established collective communities under the protection of the pope in return for a yearly census, provisions (*fodrum*), and subjection to papal jurisdiction. The inhabitants of Rocca Antica were also obliged to rebuild the fort (*castellum*).[45] Documents from the reign of Paschal II, which were excerpted in the *camera* around the middle of the twelfth century from his register, and eventually made their way into the *Liber Censuum*, show similar features in grants in the patrimony.[46] With the aid of the Normans Paschal

---

[40] Mansi 17, pp. 335ff, cc. 15 and 17; Jordan (1932), p. 31.

[41] Otto III, *Die Urkunden*, no. 389, pp. 818–20, at p. 820: 'Romanam ecclesiam matrem omnium ecclesiarum esse testamur, sed incuria et inscientia pontificum longe sue claritatis titulos obfuscasse. Nam non solum quae extra urbem esse videbantur, vendiderunt et ... alienaverunt, sed ... si quid in hac nostra urbe regia habuerunt ... omnibus iudicante pecunia in commune dederunt ... Hec sunt enim commenta ab illis ipsis inventa ... et sub titulo magni Constantini longi mendacii tempora finxit.'

[42] Jordan (1932), p. 37.

[43] Toubert (1973), pp. 1029ff, esp. n. 3. Specifically for the Sabina see Vehse (1929–30).

[44] Herrmann (1973), p. 34 n. 75.

[45] *Regesta pontificum Romanorum: Italia pontificia*, II, p. 72, no. 1 for Rocca Antica; Vehse (1929–30), pp. 172–5, appendices 1 and 2 for Montasola.

[46] *Liber censuum*, I, p. 407, no. 132, and *ibid.*, 2, p. 95 = x. 54; *Regesta pontificum Romanorum: Italia pontificia* II, p. 109, no 1; Jordan (1932), pp. 49ff.

had conquered the *castellum* Ninfa south of Rome in the diocese of Velletri around 1108. Its inhabitants had to swear fealty to St Peter and the Lord Pope Paschal as well as to his rightful successors; they had to render military service, owed suit at the papal court, and aid (*servitutem*). What is new is the reliance on feudal ties with what has been described as collective seigneuries as a means to maintain papal sovereignty.

The slender evidence for Nicholas and his successors shows how slowly papal authority expanded again. The pontiffs apparently governed the patrimony directly from the Lateran without the old rectors as intermediaries. The evidence for the evolution of the *camera* is so fragmentary that definite conclusions are hard to reach, but perhaps it can be said that the early twelfth century showed clearly a turning away from the old models for the government of papal states which still dominated under Alexander II and Gregory VII (1073–85). When Count Raymond William of Urgel had granted St Peter two forts (*castelli*) in the time of Alexander II, taking them back for himself and for his heirs in return for an annual census payment (*pensio*), the census was to be collected by Abbot Frotard of St-Pons-de-Thomières, who is described as *actionarius*, the old title of the collectors of rents and other payments in the Patrimony.[47] At the time of Paschal II the old titles have almost entirely disappeared, and new ones linked to the chamber are bewildering in their variety, from a *serviens domni Petri camerarii* to *dapifer* (steward), *familiaris* and *thesaurarius*.[48] The variations are a typical sign of evolution and growth and just what one would expect. Under Adrian IV (1154–9) the *camerarius* Boso was exclusively responsible for the Patrimony of St Peter. By then the papal treasury had evolved into a much better defined institution, despite ups and downs such as papal schism and the Roman revolt of the 1140s. But even then its activities left much to be desired, at least in the eyes of Cencius Savelli, treasurer and later pope as Honorius III. He compiled the *Liber Censuum*, as he explained in the preface, to make sure that the financial rights of the papacy throughout western Christendom would be adequately recorded and preserved forever. Besides income from counties, principalities and kingdoms that were under the protection and/or lordship of St Peter as fiefs, or from customary gifts such as Peter's Pence from England, the *Liber Censuum* noted the names of numerous monasteries and churches which owed an annual census. For the late twelfth century it has been calculated that the income from secular sources amounted to four times as much as the income from protected or exempt churches.[49] The collection of these fees was one of the primary duties of the treasury, the other being the administration of the Patrimony. No wonder, then, that its agents were intensely disliked as far back

---

[47] Deusdedit, *Kanonessammlung*, III. 271.   [48] Sydow (1954/5), p. 56.
[49] Robinson (1990), pp. 281–3; Pfaff (1953), p. 114.

as the late eleventh century. The first satire on papal greed and Roman avarice, the *Tractatus Garsiae Tholetani canonici de Albino et Rufino*, was composed during the pontificate of Urban II.[50]

Legates

From a very early period the popes were more than just bishops of Rome. Their position of leadership in the rest of Christendom, with regard to jurisdiction going back to the council of Sardica (343) which allowed deposed bishops and other clergy to appeal to the Roman see,[51] brought with it the frequent use of emissaries or legates as papal representatives, for instance at ecumenical councils. They were also used for political negotiations as in the case of the Lombard or Frankish kings. The sources usually describe them as *missi* or *missi apostolicae sedis*, but also as *legati*. The last term is the usual one used in the register of Gregory VII. During the reform period missions of legates intensified greatly. For the Iberian peninsula, for example, practically all of the papal business was entrusted to emissaries who enjoyed papal confidence. With the important exception of Archbishop Diego Gelmirez of Santiago de Compostela, all of them came either from Rome or from southern France, not excluding Archbishop Bernard of Toledo, the former abbot of St Victor of Marseilles. The local councils held by these legates in 'Spain' were essential to the reform and constitute the primary measure for papal influence in peninsula affairs.[52]

By the time of Gregory VII, who was a legate to France and Germany himself on several occasions before his election to the papacy, what might be called a regular system of representatives and legates to enforce papal decrees and claims functioned relatively smoothly. In an interesting letter of April 1075 to King Sven of Denmark Gregory contrasted the conditions of the early church with the present. The pope explained that it had been the custom among his predecessors to teach all nations through legates, to correct all kings and princes and to invite all to eternal life, for, Gregory wrote, the law of the earth used to be in the hands of the popes rather than of the emperors. Now, however, the kings and magnates (*presides*) of the land had become so contemptuous of the ecclesiastical laws that hardly any legates were being sent out, because they achieved no results; papal words were now only directed in prayer to the Lord of kings and the God of punishment. But because he, Gregory, knew the

[50] *MGH Libelli*, II, pp. 423–35; Robinson (1990), pp. 244–91.
[51] Hess (1958), pp. 121ff for canons 4 and 7; see pp. 126ff for the appeals of presbyters or deacons.
[52] Garcia y Garcia (1989), pp. 251–3.

king from the time of his archdiaconate and was aware of his reverence for the mother of all churches, he was none the less sending this letter through legates (*nuntios*), expecting a royal reply and Danish *nuntios* in return.[53] Gregory must have tried to flatter the Danish king, for legates were his favoured way of communication and often highly esteemed collaborators. Several months earlier the pope had confirmed in a letter the interdict which his legate, Bishop Gerald of Ostia, had pronounced upon Bishop Isembert of Poitiers.[54] Other legates adjudicated ecclesiastical cases, including disputed elections.[55] They might supervise new elections,[56] hold councils in the name of the pope[57] and excommunicate kings.[58] One of the clauses of the *dictatus papae* (c. 4) stipulates that papal legates, even if of inferior rank, would preside over bishops at councils and could depose them, clearly transferring papal prerogatives to the legate.[59] A letter of accreditation for the legates Gepizo and Maurus of January 1075 further details the authority Gregory vested in his representatives who were sent, Gregory explained, because it was impossible for him to be personally present as would be necessary if the church were to be reformed;[60] the same letter requested in addition to obedience and moral support the maintenance of the legates. This right to hospitality, later known as *procuratio*, was also included in the new oath of obedience demanded of archbishops and gave rise to complaints almost immediately. Bishop Ivo of Chartres implied in a letter to Paschal II that the pontiff even used legations as a pretext to provide for his clergy.[61] In 1179 the Third Lateran Council saw itself obliged to declare that the entourage of a visiting cardinal was not to exceed twenty-five persons at most.[62] Gregory VII himself, however, strictly supervised the legates through detailed instructions and, if necessary, by means of additional legates, making sure they returned in timely fashion to give account of their doings.[63] There never was any question about their subordination to the pope. On at least three occasions Gregory VII quashed major legatine decisions.

In addition to these legates, some dispatched from Rome, others dignitaries from the regions concerned, Gregory VII also used permanent papal representatives, the so-called standing legates. Hugh of Lyons, Girard of Angoulême,

[53] Gregory VII, *Register*, II, 76.   [54] *Ibid.*, II, 23.

[55] *Ibid.*, II, 25, IV, 17, IV, 26, in very comprehensive terms: 'Quapropter misimus ad vos hunc dilectum filium nostrum Gregorium et diaconum sancte Romane ecclesie, quatenus una vobiscum de ecclesiasticis causis et christiane religionis sacrosanctis institutionibus, que necessaria sunt, Deo adiuvante pertractans nostra vice, que corrigenda sunt, corrigat, que statuenda, constituat et ecclesiastice libertatis atque iustitie diu et in multis neglectas rationes et studia ad formam canonice et apostolice discipline reducere ... efficaciter valeat confirmare.' Gregory is sent 'de sinu nostro' conveying the same meaning as the later *a latere*.

[56] *Ibid.*, V, 19.   [57] *Ibid.*, II, 28.   [58] *Ibid.*, IV, 23.   [59] *Ibid.*, II, 55a, c. 4.   [60] *Ibid.*, II, 40.

[61] Hinschius (1869), p. 511 n. 1; Ivo of Chartres, 'Epistolae', *PL* 162, ep. 109.

[62] C. 4 = *COD*, pp. 213ff.   [63] Gregory VII, *Register*, I, 6.

Amatus of Oléron, Altmann of Passau and Gebhard of Constance held such an office under Gregory VII and his successors in France, northern Spain and the empire. An exceptional case was Sicily. Under Urban II Roger of Sicily and his heir obtained a privilege permitting them to control the access and activities of papal legates, even to exercise legatine powers in accordance with the instructions of papal vicars sent from Rome.[64] Papal control over the church was immensely strengthened by all of these steps. The pope in fact was able to act as the universal ordinary of the church.[65] A similar intention to centralize the control of the church probably lies behind measures to restore, as Gregory and Urban believed, the ancient primatial-patriarchal dignity as described by Pseudo-Isidore. In 1079 Gregory granted the rank of primate to Archbishop Gebuin of Lyons, the *prima sedes* of the ancient province *Lugdunensis* I. The archbishops of Rouen, Tours and Sens were subjected to him.[66] Under Urban II the archbishops of Narbonne, Bourges and Toledo were confirmed in this supposedly ancient dignity and under Calixtus II the archbishop of Vienne. If the new, quasi-patriarchal rank in the ecclesiastical hierarchy had been better defined in the canonical source, it could have aided centralization under the pope even further, especially in connection with the office of legate, as witnessed by the career of Hugh of Lyons, Gebuin's successor.

Councils

In the eleventh century, next to the systematic use of different types of legates, papal councils or synods were probably the most important instrument for the centralized governing of Latin Christendon.[67] It even has been argued that under Pope Leo IX crucial innovations created 'an assembly attended by bishops from outside the Roman ecclesiastical province and from outside the imperial territories, an assembly under the sole presidency of the pope, the decrees of which were regarded as binding on the whole of Latin Christendom'.[68] But is it correct to speak of innovations rather than transformation of the customary papal synods in the course of the reform? It is difficult to speak of radical departures when there is so much continuity. Leo certainly never intended to innovate, either at the synod of Mainz which he celebrated in October 1049 jointly with Emperor Henry III or at the synod of Rheims, held

---

[64] The clearest formulation of the Sicilian privilege is that of Paschal II, JL 6562.

[65] Ryan (1966).

[66] The sees were the capitals of the old provinces *Lugdunensis* II, III and IV.

[67] Contemporary sources use *concilium* and *synodus* as synonyms, a practice followed here; Somerville (1989), p. 34 n. 2. Schmale (1976) and Robinson (1990) try to differentiate between these and similar terms.

[68] Robinson (1990), p. 22.

a fortnight earlier, from 3 to 5 October, in conjunction with the dedication of the new basilica at the abbey of St-Rémi. In a later letter (JL 4185) to all French Christians, bishops and laymen alike (*fratribus et filiis catholicis per universum regnum Francorum*), the pontiff declared that the canons from Rheims, which he had ordered to be phrased as canons and which he had confirmed at his other councils, should be kept in the same manner as those of the ancient ecumenical councils to which they were appended.[69] The near-contemporary *Vita Leonis* tells us that Leo had insisted all along that the 'catholic law' should be observed. At his very first council (Rome, April 1049) the pontiff confirmed aloud the statutes of the first four ecumenical councils and the decrees of all his predecessors.[70] This declaration is reminiscent of the *Liber diurnus* formula for the profession of faith at a papal consecration,[71] and Leo had just been consecrated in February, but the profession also recalls age-old procedures at ecclesiastical councils. One very visible focus at many a working session was a canonical collection, solemnly displayed in the midst of the assembly. This was also the procedure at Rheims as the 'Historia dedicationis' confirms.[72] Nobody has ever argued that the pope could celebrate councils only in Rome or only in the empire.[73] The apparent innovation at the council of Rheims was due to force of circumstance: the French king and his advisers were unwilling to have French clergy subjected to the kind of papal reform legislation which already had created havoc in April 1049 at Rome[74] and refused to collaborate. Leo decided to proceed on his own, thus revealing the increased self-confidence of the foreign successors of the Tusculan popes as well as their urgent concern for the reform of clerical morals.

A comparison of the thematically connected synods of Pavia of August 1022, held jointly by Pope Benedict VIII and Emperor Henry II, and of Leo's three councils of 1049 reflects continuity of papal synodal traditions as well as change. The overriding concern at both was simony and married clergy, accompanied at Pavia by a theme familiar from the tenth century – lamentations over the poverty of the once richly endowed church – and at Rheims

---

[69] *PL* 143, cols. 616 ff; '[at Rheims] plurima ad utilitatem Christianae religionis necessaria ... statuendo confirmavimus: quae omni capitulis digesta inter canones haberi praecepimus, et ... in omnibus synodis quas habuimus, idipsum confirmare curavimus'.

[70] For the *Vita Leonis* see *BHL* no. 481. A critical edition is under preparation under the aegis of the *MGH*; Krause (1976).

[71] *Liber diurnus*, no. LXXXIII, pp. 90–3; Santifaller (1976), pp. 81ff and pp. 226ff; Blumenthal (1988), p. 246 and n. 22. The *Liber diurnus* formula refers to seven ecumenical councils.

[72] 'Historia dedicationis', p. 721: 'lectis sententiis super hac re olim promulgatis ab orthodoxis patribus, declaratum est quod solus Romanae sedis pontifex universalis ecclesia primas esset et apostolicus'; p. 723: 'quod in canonibus de sacrorum ordinum venditoribus sit decretum, iussit tantum modo recitari ...; lectae sunt sententiae super huiuscemodi re promulgatae ab orthodoxis patribus'.

[73] Schmale (1976), p. 97.   [74] Hauck (1958), pp. 600–3.

by demands for canonical elections. At Pavia the pope declared the decrees of the synod universally valid and confirmed them forever as applying to all of the earth.[75] Henry II, a ruler anointed and crowned by the pope, also confirmed and approved the decisions as a loyal son, declaring them immutable public law (*publica iura*).[76] Several canons in both the papal and the royal version concerned *iudices* and *tabelliones*.[77] At least in theory, therefore, the imperial confirmation should have had a practical effect. But neither papal nor imperial confirmation seem to have been effective, as Leo's legislation of 1049 goes to show. The lack of approval by the French king Henry I at Rheims, therefore, cannot have distressed Leo to any notable extent, especially given the division of the secular sovereignty between king and princes in France. The princes were not powerful enough to maintain their customary rights over and against the reformed papacy and King Henry could decide upon neutrality quite readily, since only theoretical rights were threatened.[78] Pope Leo IX, as we have seen, did not hesitate to order the addition of his synodal decrees to the canons of the old ecumenical councils in terms recalling thematically the announcement of Benedict VIII at Pavia.[79] He had arrived at Rheims fresh from the council of Mainz which he had celebrated jointly with Emperor Henry III. As in Italy and at Mainz, so at Rheims he obliged bishops who were accused of simony or nicolaitism to clear themselves by oath. Throughout his reign (1049–54), he travelled from synod to synod, consecrated churches and altars and protected abbeys and monasteries through papal privileges. The response was overwhelming. Abbot John of Fécamp praised Leo IX in the most extravagant terms, singling out for special mention the synods held north of the Alps:

For who has not wondered and erupted into jubilant applause seeing the care of this pastor, unheard of in our times? He who was not content to advise the one people of his own see of the city of Rome, or only to irrigate the Italian soil with heavenly words, but who in addition perambulated and nourished the transalpine churches with synodal examination, and who... quickly emended and corrected... through ecclesiastical censure and rule. *Ave, Pater papa mirabilis....*[80]

The general enthusiasm for reform measures promulgated by the popes begining with Leo IX on occasions such as synods is one of the distinguishing characteristics of the papal councils of the second half of the eleventh century.

---

[75] *MGH Constitutiones*, I, no. 34, pp. 70–7, at p. 75: 'Et ut firmum posthac quod sancimus permaneat et in fines orbis terrae conservandum perveniat, totius huius summa sentenciae hac nostri forma decreti, fratribus et coepiscopis nostris subscribentibus, confirmabitur.'

[76] *Ibid.*, p. 76: 'Omnia quidem, quae pro ecclesiae necessaria reparatione synodaliter instituit et reformavit paternitas tua, ut filius laudo, confirmo et approbo.'

[77] *Ibid.*, cc. 4, 6 and 7.   [78] Kempf (1969), pp. 194–7; Becker (1955).

[79] See n. 75 above.   [80] *PL* 143, cols. 797–800, at col. 797.

The other is the vastly expanded exercise of papal jurisdiction over clergy and laity, including kings and emperors,[81] at both papal and legatine synods. Leo's successors Urban II, Paschal II and Calixtus II still held synods in France – particularly famous is Urban's council of Clermont in 1095 which initiated the First Crusade[82] – but more usual were Italian, especially Roman, councils when the popes were in control of the Eternal City. Synods were held frequently. Attendance became obligatory for archbishops, bishops and abbots from throughout Latin Christendom. They were invited by the popes or might be cited to appear before them. Failure to come to Rome, or to attend legatine councils closer to home, automatically brought with it excommunication, even if the individual concerned had grown grey in devoted service to the Roman church.[83] Some of the entries in the official register for the synods of Gregory VII look like mere lists of excommunicated and/or suspended members of the nobility, including Philip I of France and Henry IV of Germany, and of ecclesiastics, usually because they had failed to attend as requested.[84] Pastoral concerns were perhaps always present, but were rarely thought worth recording, it seems; after all, the care of souls was the primary duty of every priest and especially of the pope.[85] What needed to be recorded was the relationship between the pope and individual clerics and laymen if it was in any way unusual.[86]

Often the expansion of the sphere of papal and legatine jurisdiction was the result of appeals to Rome. Appeals from imperial Germany usually were complaints by a lower ranking member of the hierarchy against a superior, as for example in the case of the canons of Bamberg against their Bishop Hermann because of his monastic policy; or of the monks of Reichenau against an abbot whom they were refusing to accept. Papal synodal judgement for much of the period tended to favour the appellants, provoking fury and indignation among the episcopate everywhere, but especially in Germany. The Declaration of Worms of January 1076, withdrawing obedience from Gregory VII, claimed that parishioners had been given to understand that only the pope himself or his legate could condemn or pardon individuals who had approached the pope;[87] as far as he could, the bishops wrote, Gregory had deprived them of all power which was known to have been granted to the bishops divinely through

---

[81] *NCMH*, IV, Part I, ch. 9.   [82] Somerville (1990), nos. VII and VIII.

[83] Blumenthal (1978), pp. 99ff for the council of Troyes (1107).

[84] Gregory VII, *Register*, II, 52a, III, 10a, and VIII, 20a, are telling examples.

[85] For Urban II see Somerville (1990), no. V; for Gregory VII, *Register*, V, 14a, and VII, 14a. The synodal records in Gregory's register are clearly incomplete: Somerville (1989), p. 35.

[86] The *Liber pontificalis* customarily recorded papal ordinations at the end of the *vita* of each pope. Gregory VII, *Register*, I, 85a (year-end summary or *Jahresschlussbericht*), likewise recorded the names of archbishops and bishops who had been consecrated by the pope, but then went on to record also the other side of the coin; specifically, the excommunication of Robert Guiscard and his followers.

[87] Henry IV, *Die Briefe*, p. 67, lines 4–8; Schieffer (1972), p. 46 n. 138.

the Holy Spirit.[88] This is exaggerated, but not by much. The popes of the reform period vigorously acted upon their claim to jurisdiction of the *causae maiores*. The relevant Pseudo-Isidorian material, the related conciliar canons of Nicaea and Sardica as well as the decretals of Innocent I, Leo I and Nicholas I can be found in all of the eleventh- and early twelfth-century canonical collections, ending up in the *Decretum* of Gratian of *c.* 1140 (c.2 q.6 c.3ff).[89]

The difference in this respect between the early and the late eleventh century cannot be over-emphasized, although the much-maligned Roman popes of the later tenth and early eleventh centuries in theory had always held firmly to certain basic principles, such as the papal right to bestow the pallium on metropolitans, the pope's competence in the trials or disputes of bishops, and last but not least the pope's jurisdiction over all the faithful. Disputes over the archbishopric of Rheims had pitted French bishops and abbots against the papacy at the synod held in the monastery of St Basle at Verzy in 991, and even more pointedly at the meeting held at Chelles, probably in 994. Pope John XV (985–96) refused to yield at the time, but the Carolingian Arnulf who had been deposed by the French was returned to the see of Rheims only by default, and, ironically, by a dispensation granted by Pope Sylvester II (999–1003). Sylvester, before his election Gerbert of Aurillac, had been Arnulf's opponent as Capetian-supported archbishop of Rheims.[90] Benedict VIII, the first pope from the house of Tusculum, ably maintained papal jurisdictional supremacy both with regard to the English clergy, supported by King Cnut, and with regard to Archbishop Aribo of Mainz. In 1017, on a pilgrimage to Rome, Archbishop Lyfing of Canterbury requested the archiepiscopal pallium from Benedict in accordance with a respective papal demand, but not without a strong protest. The English clergy claimed as customary right the consecration of their metropolitans and asserted that the pallium had always been sent by Rome. Their ire had been caused last but not least by the papal demand for fees in return for the pallium. They castigated the practice as heretical simony.[91] The opposition of Aribo of Mainz to Benedict is more complex. Countess Irmingard of Hammerstein had appealed to Benedict in 1023, after a synod held at Mainz had dissolved her marriage to Otto of Hammerstein because of consanguinity. In response to the appeal, the synod of Seligenstadt issued a decree in 1023 that no penitent was allowed to seek absolution in Rome or to appeal there before he had obtained his own bishop's permission and

---

[88] Henry IV, *Die Briefe*, p. 66, lines 19ff: 'Sublate enim quantum in te fuit, omni potestate ab episcopis, que eis divinitus per gratiam sancti spiritus ... collata esse dinoscitur.'

[89] Maleczek (1981), p. 60 n. 135; Gregory VII, *Register*, II, 55a, c. 21: 'Quod maiores cause cuiuscunque ecclesie ad eam [ecclesia romana] referri debean'; Robinson (1988), pp. 272ff; Winroth (2000).

[90] Kempf (1969), p. 299, highlighted the important principles involved.

[91] Hermann (1973), pp. 109–17; Barlow (1963), p. 299.

had performed the penance imposed. The quarrel between pope and synodal assembly in the care of Aribo of Mainz was ended by Benedict's death in 1024, when pressure by King Conrad II induced Aribo to abandon the proceedings against Irmingard. All of these cases show that the papacy certainly intended to maintain its rights, and, moreover, was successful when occasion demanded. But this is just the point – when occasion demanded – and there was not much demand for papal intervention, nor did the popes chose to intervene on their own. The church reform in the mid-eleventh century ushered in a radical change in this respect.

In keeping with tradition, the *causae maiores* which came before the popes of the reform period were often adjudicated in papal synods, or by a papal legate at a more local council. Not least for this reason, papal synods became the chief forum for papally led ecclesiastical reform; the large number of attendees, in addition to papal letters and papal legates – often specially sent out to repromulgate decrees from papal councils at local synods – soon came to ensure a relatively wide dissemination of canons and judicial decisions made at such councils. Eventually, it became customary for synods to entrust committees of papal advisers with the preparation of documents or cases that were to be submitted for approval either to the entire council or to the pope. At the Lateran council of March 1112, when the investiture concession granted under duress by Pope Paschal II to Henry V was revoked, Paschal confessed that the privilege for the emperor was invalid[92] and ordered that it should be corrected by the advice and judgement of the assembled brethren. In response, the synod formed a committee of cardinals and bishops who presented a corresponding resolution on the following day. It was unanimously accepted by the council and is preserved with the inscription *actio concilii contra heresim de investitura*.[93] It is sometimes assumed that such committees were the forerunner of the thirteenth-century consistory which eventually was composed of cardinals and came to replace the councils. However, this is not the case, for as late as the reign of Pope Innocent III the term consistory described solemn, publicly held judicial proceedings.[94]

The fragmentary nature of the information preserved in often unedited manuscripts of the period has often been stressed, as well as the resulting uncertainty about conciliar proceedings in the early twelfth century. Robinson's description of some of the better known synods illustrates the point clearly.[95]

---

[92] *Liber pontificalis*, II, p. 370, lines 7–20, with the reference *pravefactum* for the document which hence is called *pravilegium* in the revocation.

[93] *MGH Constitutiones*, I, p. 571 with recension 1.

[94] Maleczek (1984), pp. 299–302, proving with a wealth of evidence the distinction between the advisory meeting of the cardinals (*Ratsversammlung*) and the *consistorium*.

[95] Robinson (1990), pp. 121–35; Somerville (1990), nos. v and vii; Schmale (1976).

Surviving records, however, irrespective of the ever changing relationship between individual popes and the assembled fathers, leave no room for doubt
that papal councils now held the central position in the life of the Latin church;
that numerous archbishops, bishops, abbots and prominent laymen attended
the regularly held synods from throughout Europe; that although the lower
clergy is rarely mentioned by name, their presence is pointed out. Moreover,
late eleventh- and twelfth-century councils were purely papal affairs. After the
death of Henry III in 1056 no pope ever again jointly presided with an emperor. Popes promulgated canons and judicial decisions, known as the acta of
the councils, at the conclusion of councils without reference to secular authority. Papal synods had become general or universal councils. By the sixteenth
century, some of them, beginning with the First Lateran Council of 1123, were
regarded and counted as ecumenical councils in the western church.[96] A canonical principle, based on the early ninth-century Pseudo-Isidorian Decretals and
formulated in the *Decretum* of Bishop Burchard of Worms (d. 1025), had shown
its effectiveness in forming mental attitudes as well as papal practice during
the reform: 'The apostolic see has been entrusted with the right to convoke
synods by special empowerment; we do not read anywhere that a general synod
is legal which has not been assembled or supported by its authority.'[97] In 1117
Paschal II wrote to Count Roger of Sicily, confirming but also limiting the
privilege Roger's father, Robert Guiscard, had been granted by Pope Urban II.
In his letter Paschal specifically excluded the count from the right to convoke
synods, his legatine powers notwithstanding. Only the pope had the right to
convene councils, and only he could decide to do so through his special legate
in the case of Sicily. How could it be otherwise, Paschal asked rhetorically.[98]

THE COLLEGE OF CARDINALS

In 1148, the cardinals accompanying Pope Eugenius III to the synod of Rheims
complained bitterly about Bernard of Clairvaux who had deprived them of
their prerogatives. They were able to force Eugenius's hand. He rescinded
the decisions of Bernard and his friends with regard to Gilbert of Poitiers,
postponing the discussion for a future occasion.[99] By that time the college of
cardinals had accumulated most of the powers that pertain to it to this very
day, such as the papal elections. The cardinals indeed had become the 'spiritual
senators of the universal church' as Peter Damian (+1072), himself cardinal

---

[96] Fuhrmann (1961), pp. 677–89.
[97] Burchard of Worms, 'Decretorum libri xx', 1, 42 (*PL* 140, col. 561): 'Synodorum . . . congregandarum
auctoritas apostolicae sedi privata commissa est potestas. Nec ullam synodum generalem ratam esse
legimus, quae eius non fuerit auctoritate congregata vel fulta'; Fuhrmann (1961), pp. 683ff.
[98] JL 6562.   [99] Robinson (1990), p. 109.

bishop of Ostia since late 1057, had called them.[100] Advisory functions in the church government, subscriptions under privileges as well as acta, participation in the judicial supremacy of the papacy and the papal election gradually had become their inalienable prerogatives from the reign of Leo IX onwards.[101] The term cardinal is much older, but underwent a pronounced change in meaning under the popes of the reform period: its liturgical significance was gradually superseded by its political connotations. Klewitz recognized the reforms of Leo IX as the 'birth' of the college of cardinals.[102]

In the early twelfth century the college of cardinals included three ranks: bishops, priests and deacons. The title with the most ancient history is that of cardinal bishop. From the fourth century on bishops from certain dioceses in the vicinity of Rome, the suburbicarian sees, appear in the entourage of the pope. By then the bishop of Ostia already had the prerogative of consecrating the newly elected pope, assisted by the bishops of Porto and Albano. The constant number of seven cardinal bishoprics emerges first in the eighth century, but for practical reasons, impoverishment and depopulation, as well as political reasons the names of the seven suburbicarian sees kept changing until, by the mid-twelfth century, the number seven ceased to matter.[103] Ordinarily included were the bishoprics of (Velletri-) Ostia, Albano, Porto, Palestrina, (Silva Candida-) Tivoli, (Gabii-Labicum-) Tusculum and Sabina. According to the *Vita* of Pope Stephen III (768–72) in the *Liber pontificalis*, this pontiff associated the 'cardinal' bishops with the liturgy at the Lateran basilica, functions still clearly delineated in the *Descriptio ecclesiae Lateranensis* from *c.* 1100.[104] 'However, the seven bishops who are the vicars of the lord pope and who celebrate masses there at the altar of the Saviour, shall divide oblations with the clerics of the church [the Lateran basilica], and when the week has been completed they shall return to their sees.'[105] The term 'cardinal', therefore, described a cleric who celebrated the liturgy on a regular basis at a church other than his church of ordination. According to Leo IX, however, the term pointed to the close association of the cardinals with the Roman church, the *cardo* (hinge) and *caput* (head) of the entire church.[106] At that time this etymology was erroneous, for cardinals were to be found in non-Roman churches as well.

Under Leo IX and his successors these liturgical functions of the Roman cardinals quickly receded into the background. Instead, they became increasingly active in papal government and were to be found among the foremost

---

[100] *Contra philargyriam* = Peter Damian, *Die Briefe*, part 3, pp. 64–83, at p. 80, line 18; Kuttner (1945), p. 174 n. 100.

[101] Maleczek (1981). See also n. 113.   [102] Klewitz (1936); Huels (1977).   [103] *Ibid.*, p. 4.

[104] *Ibid.*, pp. 38–44.   [105] Valentini and Zucchetti (1946), III, pp. 360ff.

[106] See n. 115.

collaborators of the popes. When the election decree of 1059 was issued under
Pope Nicholas II in 1059, the leadership role of the cardinal bishops was already
prominent.[107] The responsibility for the reform of the church rested upon their
shoulders. Leo himself apparently nominated only Humbert of Moyenmoutier
as cardinal bishop of Silva Candida in 1050; Bonizo's references to Azelin of
Sutri, who had come from Compiègne, are unclear. Victor II (1055–7) was the
next pope who could fill a vacant suburbicarian see. He selected an Italian
monk, Boniface, for the see of Albano. Peter Damian, also Italian, was named
to the cardinal bishopric of Ostia by Pope Stephen IX (1057–8) at the urging
of Hildebrand, the later Gregory VII. When Stephen died in 1058 at Florence,
the Roman opposition took advantage of the absence of curia and elected
cardinal bishop John of Velletri as successor. John chose the name Benedict
X, reviving the Tusculan tradition, not a surprising move given that his most
prominent noble supporters were Count Gregory II of Tusculum, Count Gerard of Galeria and the sons of Crescentius of Monticelli. However, only one
other cardinal bishop, Rainerius of Palestrina, also abbot of the monastery of
SS. Cosmas and Damian (S. Cosimato) in Trastevere, supported John, thus
defying the express wishes of Stephen IX. With the defeat of this opposition
clustered around Benedict X by about 1060, all of the cardinal bishops could
be considered supporters of the reform. The victory was an astonishing success for the papacy, when it is remembered that the lands surrounding the
sees of Albano, Palestrina, Velletri, Sutri and Tusculum were in the hands of
the feudal nobility. The hold on the papacy by magnates propertied in and
around Rome had been broken. The election decree of 1059 took advantage of
the situation. The decree which was solemnly promulgated stipulated in part
that the cardinal bishops were to debate papal elections in the first instance;
subsequently the other cardinals should be admitted to their deliberations and
finally, once the election had been determined, the remaining Roman clergy
and the laity were to give their consent.[108] The rights of the Romans were
strictly limited, the decree explains, because they usually voted on the basis of
blood relationship or in return for payments; in other words, they committed
simony, an unforgivable crime in the eyes of the reformers.

By the early twelfth century the cardinal bishops had to share their responsibilities with cardinal priests as well as cardinal deacons.[109] The complex history
of the deacons has been elucidated by Huels in the context of the schisms of the

---

[107] Jasper (1986).   [108] *Ibid.*, pp. 101–4.
[109] Klewitz (1936), p. 20 n. 1, with the pertinent text of the *Descriptio*: 'Quando papa S. Petri vicarius
in dominicis vel in praecipuis sollempnitatibus missam celebrat in altare s. Salvatoris Lateranensis
ecclesiae . . . praedicti VII episcopi debent assistere cum XXVIII cardinalibus totidem ecclesiis infra
muros urbis Romae praesidentibus . . . Debent etiam ibi praesens esse archidiaconus Romae cum
VI diaconibus palatinis . . . et alii XII diacones regionarii.'

Investiture Controversy.[110] As for the cardinal priests, a privilege of Pope John VIII that granted corporate jurisdiction over the clergy and laity of Rome to the cardinal priests is probably not authentic.[111] The *Descriptio*, however, speaks in glowing terms of the privileges of both the cardinal priests and the bishops. They supposedly had the right to judge all bishops of the entire Roman empire – the ancient Roman empire is surely meant – at all the councils or synods which they attended.[112] Since at least the fourth century, the presbyters or priests of Rome were associated with specific title churches, churches originally taking their name from private houses which had served as places of worship for Christians before their place was taken by public buildings such as basilicas. For the early fifth century twenty-five title churches are known. Klewitz deduced from the evidence a system of 5 × 5, associating title priests of groups of five churches each with weekly liturgical functions at the five patriarchal basilicas of medieval Rome: S. Paolo fuori le mura, S. Lorenzo f.l.m., S. Maria Maggiore, St Peter and the Lateran basilica. This hypothetically reconstructed system must have changed when Pope Stephen III entrusted the cardinal bishops with liturgies at the Lateran, reviving ancient traditions. The *Descriptio* of *c.* 1100 reflects an arrangement which linked seven cardinal priests with each of the four remaining major basilicas, reserving the services at the Lateran to the cardinal bishops.[113] The names of twenty-eight title churches are given in the document, but only four of them are represented by signatures under the election decree of 1059. One additional piece of information is a grant of Pope Alexander II. It reserved to the cardinal priests rights of a quasi-episcopal jurisdiction in their titles.[114]

The primary attention of the reform papacy was focused on the cardinal bishops. Pope Leo IX took up the Pseudo-Isidorian definition of *cardo*, hinge, as pointed out earlier. In this view the apostolic see becomes the head and hinge of the universal church; writing to the patriarch of Constantinople Leo declared in 1054 that 'like the immovable hinge which sends the door forth and back, thus Peter and his successors have the sovereign judgment over the entire Church . . . Therefore his clerics are named cardinals, for they belong more closely to the hinge by which everything else is moved.'[115] These, his clerics, were the cardinal bishops. Given the traditional role of the cardinal priests and deacons of Rome, it is not surprising that these groups protested vehemently against the singling out of the neighbouring bishops. The cardinal presbyter

---

[110] Huels (1977), pp. 14ff, 255–72.   [111] Kuttner (1945), pp. 173 and 193–7.

[112] *Ibid.*, p. 177, points out that this privilege is shared by bishops and priests. And the passage is always understood in this sense. The Latin, however, is ambiguous. See Klewitz (1936), p. 20.

[113] Klewitz (1936), pp. 56–60 and *ibid.*, p. 16 for the *Descriptio* text; Huels (1977), pp. 8–14.

[114] JL 4736; *Regesta pontificum Romanorum: Italia pontificia*, I, p. 7, no 9; Kuttner (1945), p. 176 n. 105.

[115] Kuttner (1945), p. 176, whose translation I quote.

of S. Pietro in Vincoli, Deusdedit, emerged as one of their chief spokesmen, although he remained a staunch supporter of the reform popes throughout his life. Among long forgotten documents which Deusdedit brought back into circulation by including them in his canonical collection (1087) and his *Libellus adversus simoniacos*, completed shortly before his death in either 1098 or 1099, was a decree from the Roman synod of 769. The 769 canon stipulated that only a cardinal priest or deacon could be elected to the Holy See, and, furthermore, that priests, ecclesiastical magnates and the entire clergy of the Roman church were to carry out the election.[116] Both points were flatly contradicted by the election decree of 1059. And not by accident. Deusdedit's preface, dedicating his canonical collection to Pope Victor III in 1087, railed against the 1059 provisions, stating that they violated every single one of the decrees of God and of the holy fathers.[117] In keeping with his view of the role of the Roman cardinal priests and deacons is Deusdedit's interpretation of Isidore's definition of *cardo* which he expressed in the second book of his collection (II. 160). According to Deusdedit's text the cardinals themselves are responsible for leading the people of God to eternal salvation. They are the kings who rule the people; they are the hinges which move the door – and heaven revolves around them.[118]

Not much might have come of these apparently extreme claims despite Deusdedit's prominent position in the circle of the reformers, had it not been for the Wibertine schism. When in 1084 the Romans finally opened their gates to Henry IV and the pope-elect Wibert of Ravenna (Clement III), they were influenced in no small part by the action of the Roman clergy, especially cardinal priests and deacons, who had deserted the cause of Gregory VII. With one exception, the cardinal bishops had remained loyal to the pope. The hostile schismatic cardinal Beno blamed Gregory for separating the bishops from the consortium of the Roman cardinals, 'because their hand had been forced by Gregory'.[119] The loyalty of most of the recently appointed bishops can be readily explained, however, by their prominent place in the papal government. The absence of such a role and the attendant loss of dignity for the churches of Roman priests and deacons equally well explains a good deal of the antagonism of the latter. Klewitz noted that during the pontificate of Urban II seventeen

[116] Deusdedit, *Kanonessammlung*, II. 261 and II. 262 (p. 268). Interesting is the differentiation of *laici* and *proceres ecclesie* in II. 262.
[117] *Ibid.*, *Prologus*, pp. 4ff, lines 30ff. Victor III had signed the 1059 decree as cardinal priest of S. Cecilia and was clearly meant by Deusdedit's *quidam*.
[118] *Ibid.*, II. 160 (p. 268): 'Sicut a basibus...basilei idest reges dicuntur, quia populum regunt: ita et cardinales deriuatiue dicuntur a cardinibus ianue, qui tam regunt et mouent, quod plebem dei...moueant. Item cardinales mundi duo sunt in septemtrione et meridie et ideo dicuntur cardines, quia in ipsis uoluitur celum.' See Kuttner (1945), pp. 176ff. for additional texts from the collection extolling the lower ranks of the cardinals.
[119] The list of the names is found in the contemporary *Gesta Romanae Ecclesiae contra Hildebrandum* = *MGH Libelli*, II, pp. 369–422, here p. 369, lines 19ff; Zafarana (1966).

cardinal presbyters supported the antipope Clement as well as about half of the cardinal deacons at any one time.[120] The relationship between 'orthodox' pontiffs and the Roman cardinals remained extremely fluid, however, especially after the popes had allied themselves with the 'new' Pierleoni and Frangipani families and thus garnered magnate support.[121] Because of Beno's pronounced hostility to Gregory, too little weight is sometimes given to his accusation that Gregory had dismissed the cardinals from his counsel and had not consulted them when he suddenly excommunicated Henry IV without calling a synod and without the subscription of the cardinals.[122] Wibert–Clement turned this situation to his favour, giving cardinal presbyters and deacons a prominent place in his administration – and among the signatories to his privileges. Gregory's legitimate successors, Urban II and Paschal II, had to follow suit. The support of the cardinal presbyters was vital for any pope who wished to maintain himself in Rome. The result was an undivided college of cardinals which successfully asserted and maintained its increasing share in the papal government.

[120] Klewitz (1936), pp. 70–6. [121] Huels (1977), pp. 255–72. [122] *Liber pontificalis*, II, p. 370.

CHAPTER 3

THE WESTERN EMPIRE UNDER THE SALIANS

Hanna Vollrath

THE BEGINNING OF THE SALIAN CENTURY

Just as his predecessor Otto III in 1002, Henry II died without issue in 1024. Although this may look like a repetition of events, there were marked differences: Otto III had not been married, and being still very young, marriage with the prospect of an heir must have seemed probable. He died, however, of malaria in Italy at the age of twenty-one. Henry II, on the other hand, had been married for almost thirty years when he died at the age of about fifty. The probability that his death would leave the realm without an obvious successor must have presented itself to the magnates for quite some time. Yet the detailed account of the election procedure written by the royal chaplain Wipo some twenty years after the event gives the impression that it was only after Henry's death on 13 July 1024 that the magnates, who had been summoned to Kamba on the Rhine for the election of a new king by Archbishop Aribo of Mainz, began to give the question any thought: according to Wipo, first several candidates were named, then their number gradually reduced to two men both by the name of Conrad – one called 'the Younger', the other 'the Elder' – the sons of two brothers; finally 'Conrad the Elder' was elected king. Like the other lay nobles of his time he was an 'idiota', illiterate. This was anything but a compliment from the Italian monk who called him that. But as it did not prevent the German electors from regarding him as the most suitable candidate, it shows that literacy was held in rather less esteem in the German lands than south of the Alps.[1] Wipo fails to mention, however, that Conrad was the great-grandson of Otto the Great's daughter Liutgard by Otto's first English wife Eadgyth (Edith) and thereby the closest of kin to the deceased king. As it was only more than a century later that genealogies of noble families came to be written down, the electors of 1024 had none at hand. But were they really

---

[1] For an overview of lay and of ecclesiastical literacy with emphasis on the German kings and nobles see Wendehorst (1996).

unaware of the fact that by electing Conrad the Elder they adhered closely to the royal kin? If, however, they were guided by considerations of blood relationship, how can this be reconciled with Wipo's stipulation that after King Henry's death people began to look far and wide for a suitable successor? Was it really a 'free' election with free deliberation? Did the electors of 1024 act in the belief that they were giving their support to the foremost member of the established royal family or did they think they were deciding on a new royal house? To the present day historians cannot agree how to answer these questions.

Whatever the electors of 1024 thought they were doing, modern historiography, anyway, sees Conrad as the first king of a new royal family, which like all the other noble kin-groups still lacked family name and came to be called the Salians (Salier) only in the twelfth century. Conrad and his chancery were aware of the fact that there had been a king named Conrad a little more than a century earlier (911–19). So the first Salian king called himself Conrad II.

The Salians reigned for a century, every one of the Salian kings securing the succession of a son during his own lifetime: Conrad II (1024–39) was succeeded by his only son Henry III (1039–56), who after a premature death at the age of thirty-nine was followed by his son Henry IV (1056–1105/6), a child of five at the time of his accession to the throne. Henry IV ended his stormy career by being deposed by his son Henry V (1105–25). The latter turned out to be the last of the Salians, as he and his English wife Matilda, the notorious 'Empress Maud' after her return to England, had no children.

The Salian century can been seen as falling more or less into two parts: whereas Conrad II and Henry III reigned according to established customs, Henry IV was faced with problems that left him and most of his contemporaries without orientation. For Henry IV the revolutionary momentum of the 'Gregorian Reform' coincided and combined forces with the Saxon rebellion, bringing about a 'crisis of medieval Germany'[2] that jeopardized the very survival of his kingship and the coherence of his German kingdom, a crisis that continued well into the reign of Henry V.

An election at the beginning of the eleventh century – be it that of a king, pope, bishop or abbot – did not follow a formal procedure. There was no defined body of electors, no counting of votes. A candidate for whatever office could only succeed if he was accepted as lord and thereby won the support of those who were to be his followers, and he would only gain this acceptance if he was believed to be the 'right' person for the office, the one pre-chosen by custom and divine will. This fundamentalist approach began to be challenged during the Salian period when disputed elections and civil war made people give election procedures more thought than before. Conrad's elevation to the

---

[2] Leyser (1983) repr. (1994).

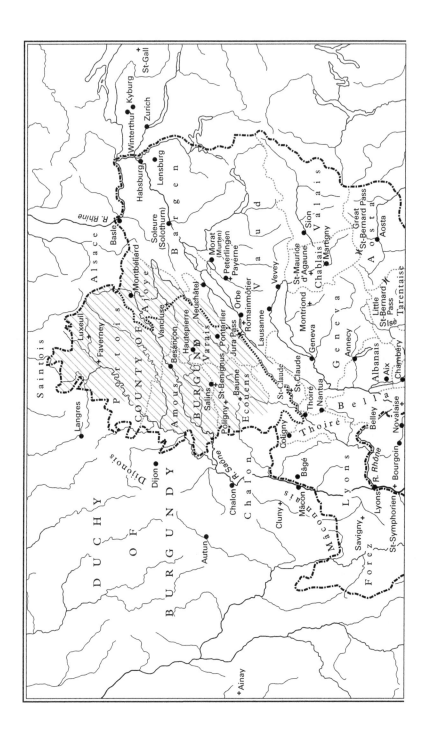

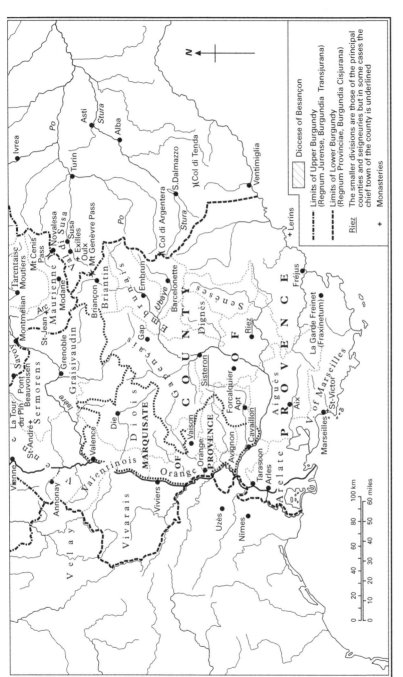

Map 1a The western empire: Burgundy and Provence in the eleventh century

Map 1b The western empire: Germany and the north-eastern

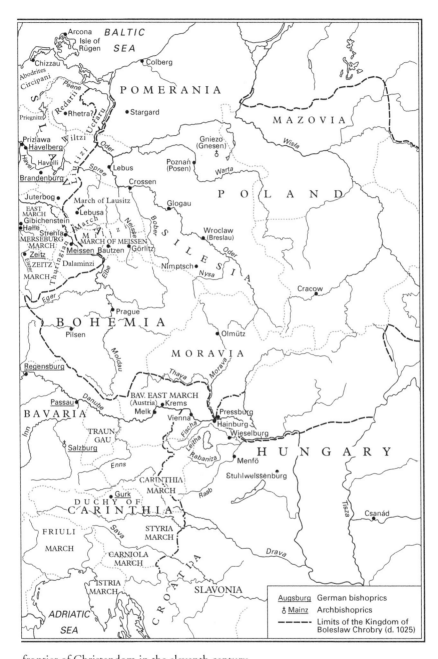

frontier of Christendom in the eleventh century

throne can almost be seen as a turning-point in this development in that it
established that the leading men of the realm united in collective action were
to be those with whom the election of the new king should lie.[3] The homage
rendered to Conrad by the nobles at Kamba did not dispense him, however,
from seeking the support of those who had not been present there, above all the
support of the Saxons, who seemed to have been altogether absent. If feeling
of identify transcended blood relations and local or regional affiliations at all,
it still rested very much with one of the tribes of which the German kingdom
consisted. The new king was of Frankish extraction, his family's landed wealth
lay in the Rhineland around Worms and Speyer. By his election the Saxons
lost the kingship that had hitherto been vested in an Ottonian (a Saxon) king
and they seem to have had misgivings about the 'foreign' king. They were
only willing to do homage to him on the condition that he guaranteed their
'particularly cruel Saxon law' (as the historian Wipo put it), which Conrad did
when he met them in the Saxon town of Minden on his first circuit of his realm.

Conrad's German kingdom was still very 'archaic' – economically as well as
socially and intellectually. The land was thinly populated with long stretches
of woods and uncultivated swamps or heaths separating the settlements. This
made communication and travel difficult. The king with his entourage depended just as much upon the navigable rivers and a few ancient routes for his
horse-saddle reign as did the traders, who traversed northern Europe with their
merchandise. As yet trade and manufacture were still a very minor economic
factor in the German lands as compared to agriculture, and towns as places
with a diversified economy were virtually non-existent. The vast majority of
the people lived and worked in dependence upon an ecclesiastical or secular
lord. The inhabitants of the ancient Roman towns that had survived in a much
reduced state as bishoprics along the Rhine and Danube rivers were just as dependent upon their lords, the bishops or archbishops, as were the people living
in hamlets around the manors. Literacy and learning were confined to the big
monasteries and to some teachers, who gathered a few students on their own
initiative or on that of their bishops.

All was quite different in Conrad's second kingdom, Italy, the crown of which
he demanded on the ground of a traditional union between the two realms.
The 'regnum Italiae' was more or less conterminous with the Lombard north of
the pensinsula. Although there, too, self-government had collapsed, the urban
character of the settlements persisted to a much larger degree than in Conrad's
northern kingdom. The inhabitants were considered free by birth. The nobles
continued to reside in the towns. Thus, the inhabitants of the Lombard towns
were in a far better position to refute the dominion by their bishops or other

---

[3] Keller (1983); Fried (1994), pp. 731–6.

lords. At the very beginning of his reign Conrad II was confronted with an incident that stood witness to a growing sense of independence in the towns: the inhabitants of Pavia had destroyed the imperial palace in the city immediately after Henry II's death. Conrad might not have been aware of the fact that the inhabitants of other Lombard towns such as Cremona, Brescia, Parma and Lodi had already been challenging the government of their respective episcopal lords for quite some time, organizing themselves into communes and also destroying their lords' town palaces just as the people of Pavia had done. Conrad denounced this act of violence as illegal and demanded the reconstruction of the palace, which, however, never took place.

The trade revolution with its renaissance of urban prosperity and urban self-assurance was already well under way in Italy when Conrad went there to win the imperial crown in 1027 at the hands of the pope as custom demanded. One may doubt whether his feudal views permitted him to interpret the economic and social situation in the Italian towns as precursor of a general development that was to transform the whole of western Europe in the decades to come.

Conrad's reign was guided by tradition and he stuck to the ways paved by his predecessors. On the one hand this led to the acquisition of the kingdom of Burgundy; on the other hand it brought him the accusation of having been a simoniac.

Rudolf II king of Burgundy had bound himself by several treaties to leave his crown to Henry II, who was his relative as well as his liege lord. When Rudolf died in September 1032 Conrad claimed the Burgundian crown as successor of Henry II in the office of king, whereas Rudolph's nephew Count Odo of Blois as well as Conrad's step-son Duke Ernst of Swabia claimed Burgundy as the closest of kin and heirs to the deceased. In the feud that ensued Conrad prevailed and succeeded in being crowned king of Burgundy in February 1033. Although the Burgundian feudal lords prevented his Burgundian kingship from amounting to more than an honour, a *dignitas*, Burgundy was nevertheless henceforth considered as part of the *imperium*, the lands of the *imperator*.

In Conrad's views, formed by Ottonian tradition, *regnum* and *sacerdotium* were bound to each other by their mutual responsibility for the order of the world ordained by divine will. As the Lord's anointed he considered himself responsible for the Christian faith and the Christian churches of his realms, making pious donations and intervening in their affairs when he deemed necessary. In response to his pious efforts he expected the support of the bishops and abbots, both spiritually and materially. It seems, however, that in this he did not quite act in ways the clerics and monks of his kingdom expected from a king anointed.[4] He probably had no qualms about bullying the newly installed

[4] Hoffmann (1993).

bishop of Basle in 1025 into paying him a considerable amount of money; he would have considered it part of the *servitium regis*, which the churches had been accustomed to render from time immemorial. Some twenty years later this was considered to be not only inappropriate but a sin. When Wipo finished his *Gesta Cuonradi* shortly after 1046 during the reign of Conrad's son and successor Henry III he reports that simoniac heresy suddenly appeared when King Conrad and his queen accepted an immense amount of money from the cleric Udalrich upon the latter's instalment on the episcopal throne of Basle. Conrad, Wipo was eager to continue, later repented of this sin vowing never to accept money again for an abbey or a bishopric and, so Wipo added, he more or less kept this promise.

Wipo's judgement mirrors the state of the debate in the late 1040s when simony and nicolaitism had come to be used as synonyms for an utterly depraved state of the church. Historians have tried for a long time to answer the question why these two themes came to the fore around the middle of the eleventh century. Why did 'church reform' become so much more important a topic, and why did it become equated with the demand to fight simony and nicolaitism? For a long time historians followed the contemporary sources in their verdict that morally and spiritually the church was indeed in a damnable state and that the cry for reform of the church meant that people had become aware of the growing abuse. A closer look at the early medieval parishes reveals, however, that clerical marriage, that is nicolaitism, must have been a matter of some importance; that, in fact, the position of priest more often than not was handed down from father to son, a situation that must even be considered beneficial to church life, as there was no regular training for the priesthood, and a son, who had been watching his father fulfil the sacerdotal rites, must have been in a much better position to act as priest than someone who had not had this experience from his early boyhood.

As far as the 'Reichskirche' (imperial church) was concerned, nobody would have denied that according to the holy canons the conferment of a bishopric included an election by the clergy and the people. But in the early middle ages *clerus et populus* were not conceived of as a defined electoral body that arrived at independent decisions according to established rules. Rather clergy and people 'voted' by accepting their new spiritual lord as any lay band of followers would have to accept their lord. This acceptance was regulated by custom and the notion of propriety. With lay people hereditary rights played the most decisive part. No hereditary succession was valid, however, without a solemn rite of conferment through the hands of the lord. It was the lord's investiture that transformed entitlement into legitimate succession. Both were so much bound together in unseparable unity that there were no rules as to how to proceed if customary titles of heredity clashed with a lord's right to invest. We tend to think of these two factors as two separable and hence separate titles.

People of the earlier middle ages did not. They thought of men as acting in unison to achieve what everybody considered to be the right thing. Lack of unity called for compromise (in which the conflicting parties agreed to have finally found the solution according to what was right) or – probably more often – for violence in a feud.

Episcopal appointments were handled along these lines. As direct hereditary succession was, however, precluded by the obligation of celibacy there was a wider scope of action for those who were responsible for the appointment, namely clergy, people and king. Although the venerated canons knew nothing of royal investiture, it was unquestionably accepted as part of the world of personal dependencies and obligations. It was the king's lordly power and position in his relation to local dignitaries that decided on how strong his influence would be.[5]

Also the churches high and low formed part of a society the economic and social basis of which was feudal lordship with dependent villains bound together in the manorial system. A bishop 'received' a church with all its revenues from his lord the king through investiture, as did a priest who was invested with a parish church by the lord of the manor and thereby 'received' the landed property of 'his' church. By conferring the church the respective lords gave them an income just as they did with their secular vassals. For their gifts they demanded a gift in return – the prayers of the clergy, to be sure, but material gifts as well: the lord king could expect to be housed and entertained with his retinue; the bishops and abbots owed him mounted knights for his expeditions and some other services, which could also be commuted into a money donation. Nobody had equated these donations with simony forbidden by the holy canons. The donations formed part of the gift-exchange economy of the early middle ages and as such it made sense and must have seemed quite normal to everybody.

In view of these long-established customs a growing number of scholars tend to attribute the demand for church reform with the fight against simony and nicolaitism to a change of perception.[6] Practices that up until then only a very few people had objected to came to be looked at as abuses. The church must be reformed by abolishing simony and nicolaitism. The sacraments, the faithful began to fear, could only work for the salvation of souls if they had been administered by priests, whose hands were 'pure', i.e. unpolluted by money and fleshly contacts.

---

[5] Traditional German historiography attributes the most decisive influence in all the German bishoprics and royal monasteries to the king's will, who is seen as delegating men from his royal chapel (*Hofkapelle*) in order to weld the single churches into an 'imperial church system' serving king and kingdom. This view was successfully challenged by Reuter (1982). For an assessment of the lively debate that ensued see Fried (1991), pp. 165ff, and (1994), especially pp. 666ff.

[6] Leyser, English version (1994).

In Conrad's days, so it seems, these views were still confined to some strict religious circles in northern Italy, where clauses forbidding simony began to turn up in monastic foundation charters shortly after the turn of the century. Reports on the persecution of heretics also indicate that religious consciousness was beginning to change. Church councils had been denouncing a variety of religious practices and beliefs as heretical in the late Roman period. In the early middle ages, however, heresy was no topic. When Burchard of Worms compiled his *Decretum* in about 1025 which for more than a century came to be one of the most often copied canon law collections in the western church, he had nothing to say about heretics. At just about the same time the Milanese historian Landulf reports his archbishop Aribert as having discovered a group of 'heretics' living in the castle of the countess of Monteforte near Turin. On interrogation by the archbishop they confessed to an extremely ascetic life with continuous prayers, vigils, declining not only personal property, sexual intercourse and everything fleshly, but also the sacraments and the authority of the Roman pontiff. The archbishop took them prisoners to Milan where he could not prevent the leading citizens from burning those to death who refused to confess the 'Catholic faith'.

This is one of the earliest medieval instances where people were put to death through the hands of fellow-Christians because of divergent religious practices. The report given by Landulf discloses some of the features that were to become elements of a religious mass movement all over western Europe by the end of the century: voluntary poverty with individual and sometimes eccentric if not blasphemous devotional practices combined with a repudiation of the sacraments administered by the anointed agents of the church. To live the apostles' lives as true followers of Christ was to ensure salvation and make sacramental mediation superfluous. As yet there were only a few isolated incidents in Italy and France. King Conrad and his German countrymen will not have taken notice of them. Their devotion was traditional, manifesting itself in almsgiving and in pious gifts to monasteries and churches, where the *memoriae* for the dead were being held and prayers for the well-being of the living said. Burial in or by a church near the holy relics was to promote salvation. Conrad chose the episcopal church of Speyer to be his own family's resting-place and started the reconstruction of what was to be one of the most impressive Romanesque cathedrals in Germany.

HENRY III (1039–1056)

In his more passionate approach to all matters religious Conrad's son Henry struck contemporaries as a man of exceptional seriousness and piety. Upon his designation as king by his father in 1026 the nine-year-old boy had been handed over to the bishop of Augsburg for education. His piety might well have been reinforced when he married the equally fervent Agnes of Poitou and Aquitaine in 1043. Medieval historians tend to put down as personal vices and virtues what to our modern understanding indicates a change of values reflecting long-term developments. To them Henry III was a pious ruler because he fought simony and his father Conrad II was rather less so because he did not.

There can be no doubt, however, that Henry III was very much aware of the spiritual demands inherent in his own as well as in any other ecclesiastical office. For episcopal investitures he preferred royal chaplains from his own foundations at Kaiserswerth (on the lower Rhine near Duisburg) and at Goslar (in the Harz mountains). He preached peace from the pulpit in the churches of Constance and Trier, as became a Christian king; he appeared as a penitent before his host after having won the battle of Menfö against the Hungarians. For his son Henry born in 1050 he fervently requested Hugh abbot of Cluny as godfather and finally succeeded.[7] All this was nothing really new, but rather a more intense way of dealing with traditional practices. As for the really new concern about simony and nicolaitism it seems that Henry III became aware of it only in 1046 when he arrived in northern Italy on his way to Rome for imperial coronation. The French historian Radulf Glaber reports Henry delivering a sermon against simony, when sitting together in a synod with the Italian bishops at Pavia, in which he denounced as prevalent practice that clerical offices (and their stipends) were being bought and sold like merchandise. A little later he met Pope Gregory VI. The king's and the pope's names in the fraternity book of the church of San Savino at Piacenza[8] stand witness to the fact that Henry was quite unaware of the accusations levelled against Gregory, namely of his having committed the very crime of simony Henry had just denounced. It was part of a confused situation in the Roman church in that there were several popes at the same time. Benedict IX, from the Roman noble family of the Tusculans, had been sitting on the papal throne since 1032; in 1045 he was confronted with Sylvester III from the rival Crescentians, and whom that part of the Roman clergy and people hostile to his own family had elected pope. As a way out of this stalemate situation Benedict was brought to resign in favour of Gregory VI, his own godfather and a man of unquestioned piety. However, Benedict demanded – and received – a payment as compensation for the loss of revenues his abdication entailed.

Although religiously minded persons like the pious hermit Peter Damian welcomed the solution, others found Gregory VI guilty of simony. Here as in the decades to come simony was a rather vague concept, which nobody took care to define properly. Any kind of economic transaction perpetrated

---

[7] Lynch (1985) and (1986); Angenendt (1984), pp. 97ff.   [8] Schmid (1983).

in any kind of connection with an ecclesiastical office might upon scrutiny reveal its simoniacal character. As some such connection could almost always be detected if somebody had an interest in finding it, later some episcopal chapters which had a grudge against their bishops on quite different grounds succeeded in getting rid of them by accusing them of simony.[9]

From ancient canons it was learnt that simony was heresy – *simoniaca heresis* – and as such a horrifying crime. As the Lord's anointed and emperor to be Henry felt it his responsibility to free the Roman church of this heresy. He convened synods at Sutri and Rome and had all three popes deposed, installing the German bishop Suitger of Bamberg as Pope Clement II on the papal throne. A few days later upon his imperial coronation he was given the title *patricius Romanorum* which was to secure this influence in further papal elections. Clement was the first of several imperial popes. The most important of them was Leo IX (1048–54), a man of noble Alsatian extraction and like Henry III imbued with the fervour to reform the church by cutting down the weeds of bad customs that had overgrown its primeval purity. Unlike his Roman-born predecessors with their entrenchment in local Roman affairs, Leo saw the papal office as meaning the leadership of the church and therefore as being called upon to promote the ideas of reform wherever necessary in Christendom. After a long period during which the numerous local churches were more or less held together by their allegiance to their mutual lord, the king, Leo reactivated the notion of the one and indivisible holy church, the members of which looked to the Roman pontiff as their head. Neither Henry nor Leo seem to have feared any problem from this dual allegiance. On his deathbed Henry resigned his six-year-old only son Henry IV into the hands of Pope Victor II, a German, too, who was present when Henry died prematurely in 1056 at the age of thirty-nine.

HENRY IV (1056–1105/6)

Some twenty years after Henry III's death, Pope Gregory VII formally abjured this dual allegiance of the bishops towards king and pope when he declared all investitures performed by laymen including the kings to be illegal. This was directed at all laymen including all kings in western Christendom. In Germany, however, it had greater effects than elsewhere because it coincided with a rebellion of most of the nobles in the eastern part of the duchy of Saxony, who succeeded in forming alliances with magnates from other parts of the realm as well as with Henry's adversary on the papal throne, plunging Germany into a civil war that was to last with varying intensity for more than forty years.

[9] Schieffer (1972); Vollrath (1993).

In retrospect a number of incidents from the mid 1050s on appear as precursors of the decisive clash in the 1070s making it appear almost inevitable. And yet Henry IV and his followers evidently failed to grasp the revolutionary impetus behind the group of people at Rome who acted in the name of church reform. Among them there was general agreement that church reform should mean first and foremost the abolition of simony and nicolaitism and that the reformed church should be modelled after the unpolluted *ecclesia primitiva*. Nobody, however, seems to have had a clear notion of what that should mean, except that the primeval church had been of ideal purity, where Christians and their communities had been virtuous instead of vicious. There was no agreed plan, no defined concept of how this ideal former status of the church could be won back. Reformers like Pope Leo IX and Peter Damian, who had been made cardinal bishop of Ostia by the same pope, envisaged an *ecclesia*, in which the king as the Lord's anointed cooperated with pope and bishops for the benefit of all Christians. Others like Humbert, cardinal bishop of Silva Candida, who had accompanied Leo from Lorraine to Rome, argued that basically simony had its roots in lay predominance in the church. Therefore the fight against simony should start with cutting down that dominance. In his treatise *Adversus simoni- acos libri tres*, written in 1057/8, he sees the world in a preposterous order in that the secular power comes first in an episcopal election, pushing the consent of the people and the clergy and the judgement of the metropolitan to an inferior place, whereas the holy canons decreed that it should be the other way around. This was a reference to a well-known sentence by Pope Leo I which said that no one should be counted among the bishops who had not been elected by the clergy, demanded by the people and consecrated by his fellow-provincials with the judgement of the metropolitan, a passage that was being quoted over and over again to define what a canonical election should be like. Neither Leo nor, in fact, Humbert specified, however, who precisely should do what, when and where in the election of a bishop. Humbert particularly found fault with lay investiture because no lay person, not even a king, should be allowed to confer an ecclesiastical office. Although this was to become the essence of papal policy after 1078 Humbert's treatise of 1057/8 was not a platform which 'the' reformers adopted for successive implementation. Even Humbert's rather radical views did not amount to a clear concept of what the 'reformed' church should be like. As far as our source material allows us to judge, a general, if unspecific, climate of unrest and discontent with the state of the church prevailed in the middle of the century which made people clamour for reform. Up to 1056, until the death of Henry III, they did this with the support of the emperor. After that date they had to do without it. The German king and emperor-to-be was a child of six. There was no institutionalized regency. The child Henry was anointed and crowned and therefore considered to be the reigning king;

but, being still a minor, he was in need of a guardian, a position which fell as
a matter of course to his mother Agnes. She had a difficult task to fulfil: like
all other German kings before him her husband had been faced with recur-
rent rebellions by disaffected nobles. As yet royal government knew of only a
few means to secure allegiances: above all to honour its noble retainers with
lavish 'gifts' and thereby to secure their fidelity as a 'gift' in return. Landed
property as well as prestigious offices given as fiefs lent themselves to this. But
as custom allowed sons of loyal vassals to expect their fathers' fiefs upon the
latter's death, fiefs were not readily at a king's disposal. Agnes was lucky in
that the ducal lines of Carinthia, Bavaria and Swabia had died out during her
husband's reign and Henry III had not filled the posts. In giving Swabia and
the administration of Burgundy to Rudolf of Rheinfelden in 1057, and in 1061
Bavaria to the Saxon noble Otto of Northeim and Carinthia to the Swabian
Berthold of Zähringen, she could allow herself to believe that she had won the
allegiance of three exceptionally formidable men with particularly important
family backgrounds. Moreover Rudolf, who might have been connected with
the Ottonian family through cognatic ties,[10] was given Agnes's four year-old
daughter Matilda for a bride, and when Matilda died before her marriage, he
took Adelaide of Turin for his wife, sister to Henry IV's bride Bertha. Modern historians tend to citicize Agnes for 'squandering' royal resources, first by
handing out the free dukedoms which her husband had so wisely reserved
for the crown's own use, and secondly for having chosen the wrong persons,
as all three dukes played a prominent part in the rebellions which shook her
son's kingship in the 1070s. It must be remembered, however, that a king who
was a minor was in need of support even more than an adult king and that it
was more difficult to get. Agnes followed tradition when she used the vacant
dukedoms to this end. As far as the nobles chosen by her were concerned none
of the three had so far engaged in anti-Salian activities.

   Given the nature of the German kings' various dignities and obligations
Agnes's first preoccupation had to be the German lands, as they formed the
basis for all other far-ranging activities. It looks as if she herself and her counsellors did not have a very clear notion of what was going on in Rome. This
is far less surprising than it might seem. The developments certainly lacked
the moral unambiguity our partisan source material implies and the logical
consistency that we who know the eventual outcome tend to discern in them.
As elsewhere the election of the Roman pontiff traditionally rested with the
clergy and the people of the episcopal city. In Rome as in many other places
local rivalries and conflicts extended to the episcopal dignity. Henry III had
succeeded in pushing his German candidates, thereby quenching local rivalries

---

[10] Jackman (1990).

for a while but without, of course, being able to eliminate them altogether. When in 1059 the party of the cardinal bishops saw a member of the old Roman aristocratic kindred elected as Pope Benedict X, they pitted Pope Nicholas II as the candidate of 'church reform' against him. A synod was held immediately afterwards that passed a papal election decree to legitimize Nicholas's election. It accorded the most decisive weight to the votes of the cardinal bishops which it deduced from ancient canons. It did not mean to challenge the traditional role of the German kings as protectors of the Roman church. If it was rather vague about the latter's legal status in papal elections it was because kings did not figure in the ancient canons that dated from pre-medieval times. In 1059 it was not the German king whom the cardinals feared as a rival in the leadership of the Roman church, but the local noble factions which were reclaiming their traditional influence. It can be doubted that the decree was perceived of as a norm for all future papal elections. But it certainly mirrored the leading role the *collegium* of cardinal bishops envisaged for itself in the Roman church. Anyone who ignored this would have to reckon with their resistance.[11]

When after the death of Nicholas II in 1061 a delegation of Roman nobles sent the patrician's insignia to young Henry asking him to give them a pope, Agnes acting for her son nominated Bishop Cadalus of Parma. In doing this she indeed ignored the cardinals. The reason for this might lie in a disagreement over some German bishops, which was disturbing the relations between the papal curia and the German royal court at the time of Nicholas's death. Agnes was probably not aware of the election decree of 1059, and certainly had only a limited knowledge of the intricacies of the Roman situation. Nevertheless, the German court found itself supporting 'the Romans' against the cardinal bishops who elected Bishop Anselm of Lucca to be Pope Alexander II and had him enthroned with the help of the Norman troops of Richard of Capua.

Eventually Agnes's move turned out to be a grave mistake. In spite of her personal piety she had manoeuvred her son into a position which made the German court appear as an opponent to church reform as personified in the cardinal bishops. Her failure merits particular attention as it reveals a problem that was to recur with her son and which touches upon the basics of early medieval society, namely long-distance policy-making. A history of early medieval communication remains yet to be written. It mainly rested on face-to-face contacts, in which verbal exchanges were supplemented by gestures and rituals, forming together a specific language.[12] Long-distance contacts seem to have been upheld mainly by messengers and sometimes by letters. But as far as

---

[11] As the Papal Election Decree of 1059 eventually became the basis of all further legal provisions for the election of the pope, it has received extensive scholarly treatment. For a new edition and a summary of the discussions see Jasper (1986).

[12] Schmitt (1990); Koziol (1992); Althoff (1993).

we know long-distance communication lacked systematic organization and as such was sporadic, haphazard and knew of no systematically employed means to ensure dependably balanced information.

In addition to the Roman disaster, leading ecclesiastics and lay nobles felt that she was listening rather too much to the counsel of Bishop Henry of Augsburg and ignoring theirs. Spreading discontent made Anno, the archbishop of Cologne and one of the leading magnates of the realm, end Agnes's de facto regency by having young Henry abducted in 1062 from Kaiserswerth, a royal palace then situated on an island in the Rhine river, some fifty miles north of Cologne. Although Henry tried to get away by jumping into the river, the twelve-year-old boy was caught and handed over to Anno. In the person of the king kingship was in Anno's hands. He used it to demonstrate his support for Alexander II and eventually end the papal schism in securing the obedience of the German episcopate for Alexander.

Anno's regency did not last long. In 1065 Henry reached the age of fifteen and thereby adulthood. He started to reign in his own right. Just as that of the other kings of his time his royal position rested on feudal obligations: the leading nobles of his realm owed him counsel and support (*consilium et auxilium*). They rendered their counsel by coming to his itinerant court and by sitting with him in council until consent was reached. A king who failed to reach consent with the most of his leading men had no means of enforcing their rendering the support they owed him. On the other hand the royal court was a kind of social nucleus of the kingdom, the place where fiefs and honours were won and where prestige and dignity were assessed and demonstrated in the ranking of peers. For the king as well as for the nobility it was a constant balancing of mutual dependencies. If nobles fell into enmity with each other the king's endeavour to appease let him appear only too easily as partisan of one side in the eyes of the man who felt himself discriminated against. If a king diverged from what his nobles considered to be established custom and therefore their right he had to reckon with their resistance. Controversial feudal heritages in which the king favoured the claim of one side by exercising his right to invest might only too easily bring him the enmity of the other as well as that of its kin and sworn friends. This was even more likely if a king tried to push his own claims against that of one or several powerful men. In that case he could easily face a rebellion of the nobility of a whole region intent on fighting him as a tyrant.

One such region was the eastern part of the duchy of Saxony in the eleventh century. The violence of the Saxon war after 1073 and the ample coverage it gets in the contemporary sources led historians for a long time to ignore the fact there were already disturbances during the reign of Henry III and during Henry IV's minority. Unfortunately but quite typically for the time the historians lent their pens as weapons in the feud and therefore did not feel obliged to give a balanced account with background information as to the causes underlying the violence. They stand witness to the fact that every side described the other as utterly base and depraved and ruthlessly breaking the law. Therefore historians have not been able to agree on the causes underlying the tensions that developed into civil war in the beginning of the 1070s. Was Henry claiming royal possessions his widowed mother had been too weak to secure? Was he demanding Ottonian property as a royal successor challenging the titles based on kinship? Was he trying to take back into direct royal administration lands that had been leased out for several lives, thereby denying that customs of usufruct traditionally merged into lasting rights? Whatever the causes were it is evident that they made Henry adopt administrative measures that were considered novel and therefore illegal by his opponents: he fortified castles built on Saxon hills and manned them with Swabian *ministeriales*, retainers of mostly unfree condition who had been able to rise socially through military service. Both their Swabian and their servile extraction made them abominable to Saxon nobles, who saw themselves oppressed by ignoble foreigners.

At just about the same time a conflict with the papacy was building up over the archbishopric of Milan. In Milan as in other Lombard cities the citizens had come to speak with a voice of their own against their lord, the archbishop, who was invested by the German king in his capacity as king of Italy. Important factions of the population of Milan rallied behind noble leaders in accusing Archbishop Guido and his adherents of endangering their salvation by tolerating simoniac and nicolaitistic priests. Whereas the name *placitum Dei* (judgement of God) adopted by the disaffected citizens suggests purely religious motives, the name *Pataria* (trash) given to them by their enemies and then used by themselves seems to indicate concomitant social reasons in the ancient city, where the ancient social system was being upset by the growth of a money economy as part of the trade revolution of the high middle ages.

Archbishop Guido, who was faced with continuous criticism and saw the priests he felt his duty to protect being physically assaulted, decided to resign his position in 1070. He and his followers chose a canon by the name of Godfrey to succeed him and sent him over the Alps to Henry for investiture. The *Pataria* maintained that a canonical election by the clergy and the people had not taken place. The dissent that had been disrupting the city of Milan for some time precluded consent of clergy and people in the archiepiscopal election and practically forced the king to support the candidate of one faction by bestowing royal investiture. Henry IV nevertheless made a grave mistake by investing Godfrey far away from the site of turmoil and then sending him back demanding his acceptance. Like his mother the king got involved in long-distance policy-making with probably no clear picture of the situation.

He exercised the right of investiture which by custom he knew to be his. Even well-meaning Milanese contemporary historians, however, who did not dispute this royal prerogative, criticized his way of ignoring public opinion in the town by supporting the archbishop from afar, who was resigning precisely because he lacked support. The *Pataria* answered by setting up a churchman called Atto as a candidate of their own and by turning to Pope Alexander II asking support for their candidate. Alexander II approved Atto and maintained that in a disputed election the candidate who got the support to St Peter was to be considered canonically elected. As yet the pope did not contest royal investiture as such, but demanded that Henry revoke it in this particular case as it had been given to the wrong person. This was an altogether novel assertion in medieval ecclesiastical elections, one which mirrored the new role the Roman pontiffs had come to assert for themselves as leaders of the universal church. With that the local conflict had developed into one between king and papacy. Again it made the Salian court appear to be opposing church reform.

The conflict had been dragging on when Gregory VII was made pope in 1073. He had virtually dedicated himself to church reform. But whereas he was just as hazy as his predecessors about what that actually should mean, he had a visionary knowledge of the role of the pope and the Roman church in it: he knew the Roman church to be established by Jesus Christ himself, as testified by his words that Peter was to be the rock upon which he would build his church (Matthew 16: 18). Hence he saw St Peter himself as speaking through every canonically elected pope and hence he himself as St Peter's mouthpiece was right by divine ordination. Many of the twenty-seven sentences which Gregory inserted into his register in 1075 and headed *Dictatus papae* (the pope's own dictation) are just logical deductions from this tenet: that the Roman church never erred and according to scripture never will err (22); that every canonically elected Roman pontiff is through St Peter's merits undoubtedly holy (23); that only those who agree with the Roman church are orthodox in faith (26). From this it followed that everybody was subject to the pope's judgements: that nobody could quash any of his judgements whereas he could quash the judgements of all others (18); that he was allowed to depose emperors (12).[13] The *Dictatus papae* did not elicit vehement protests, simply because for the time being it remained unknown. But Pope Gregory acted according to it and consequently met with violent resistance: from the German bishops who saw their God-given episcopal dignity impaired by this dangerous man, and from Henry IV, from whom he peremptorily demanded obedience in the Milanese case. The most uncompromising papal letter happened to reach the

---

[13] Gregory VII, *Register*. That the *Dictatus papae* was but rarely referred to in canon law collections was shown by Gilchrist (1973, 1980).

king at the end of the year 1075, just when he was celebrating an important victory over the Saxon rebels. He felt strong enough to refute all papal claims to superiority, the more so as he saw himself in agreement with the greater part of his bishops. The royal council that he convened at Worms in January 1076 denounced Gregory's presumptuous behaviour, abjured all obedience to the pope and declared his election and hence his papacy illegal. It carefully avoided an outright deposition, thereby acknowledging the conviction that a pope stands above the judgement of men. A second letter to the Romans shows, however, that the pronouncement was meant to amount to just that: it asked the Romans to chase the false pope away, claiming that he had been a false pope all along because his election had been illegal. German kings and emperors were known to have had popes deposed before. But they all had been on the spot when doing this, whereas Henry again tried to impose his will from afar. Again he failed. Gregory chose the papal Lenten council as the scene for his reply. In a prayer to St Peter he declared Henry IV excommunicate and released everybody from the fealty he had sworn him. The effect of this is echoed in the words of Bonizo of Sutri, who saw the earth quake when the papal verdict was heard. The excommunication of a king was without precedent, indeed. The Lord's anointed, the king and emperor-to-be whose predecessors had been known to be the special defenders of the *Romana ecclesia*, had been ousted from the church by the bishop of Rome.

Like Henry the pope had acted from afar. With the German bishops who had rallied behind their king just a little time before, it was a question of loyalty that had never presented itself before: did their ecclesiastical order and their forming part of the hierarchy of the universal church add up to a greater commitment than their fealty to their lord king and the web of feudal bonds in their native kingdom? As lords demanding the obedience due to a superior the popes had but rarely and with varying success intervened in German ecclesiastical affairs and only when one of several quarrelling parties had thought it expedient to bring them in. Never before, however, had loyalty to the king been pitted against loyalty to the pope; never before had the ecclesiastical princes of the realm been asked to choose between pope and king.

By summer it became clear that for many of them allegiance to St Peter outweighed that to their liege lord. From the royal Easter council at Utrecht, to the one convened at Pentecost in Worms and the assembly in June in Mainz, the number of participants kept dwindling. Leading churchmen like the archbishops of Mainz and Trier, Bishop Hermann of Metz and Bishop Adalbero of Würzburg expressly sought and received reconciliation with Gregory VII. This rather unexpected course of events must be attributed to a growing sense of corporate clerical identity which had been developing with the commitment to church reform and to the reformed papacy since the 1040s and which made it unbearable for many conscientious ecclesiastics to be cut off altogether from the Roman church. Likewise the opposition of the lay princes and their ecclesiastical allies in Saxony as well as in the duchies of Swabia, Bavaria and Carinthia began to reassert itself as early as Easter. Often enmity due to a lay feud merged with religious motivations springing from adherence to church reform and its most uncompromising protagonist, Gregory VII. In other cases, however, religious issues seem to have played little or no part: Margrave Ekbert of Meissen started his stormy career when still a young boy. He was foremost in organizing the Saxon opposition against the king, his relative. But as he was a formidable figure in eastern Saxony the king could not help receiving him back into his allegiance several times when he sought reconciliation. No religious motives are known for his insurrections. It appears that even some of the leading Saxon ecclesiastics such as the Archbishops Werner (1063–78) and Hartwig of Magdeburg (1079–1102) fought Henry on particularist Saxon grounds rather than on religious ones.[14] It is impossible to tell just when and why Rudolf of Rheinfelden, duke of Swabia, became a champion of the anti-Salian cause. As mentioned above, the beginning of his ducal career had been associated with a marriage contract with the Salians. He might even have been a long-distant blood relative of that family. On the other hand he had evinced a pronounced concern for church reform. The reform monastery of Hirsau in the Black Forest, which was developing into a Gregorian bulwark once the disagreement between Gregory VII and Henry IV had led to open feud, enjoyed his generous support. He had not taken part in the royal court at Worms in January and together with his ducal colleagues from Bavaria and Carinthia was active in organizing the opposition to the king almost immediately after Gregory's Lenten verdict became known. From then on he was known to be one of those who was putting forward the idea of electing a new king should Henry refuse or fail to have the papal ban lifted before the year's end. By October 1076 Henry could not avoid admitting that all the opponents in his realm had agreed on this line of action. In order to save his kingship he made a move his enemies apparently had not foreseen, as they had already fixed a date for the election of a new king: he set out to cross the Alps in winter to seek reconciliation with the pope. He encountered Gregory who was already in Tuscany on his way to Germany, and he made it known to the surprised pope that he had not come to fight him but to do penance.

Penance and reconciliation were not spontaneous pious acts but the ritual-ized stagings of contrition, humiliation and purification. In a case as conspic-uous as the one under consideration the order of events was agreed upon by negotiation: Henry, who had his god-father Hugh, the abbot of Cluny, and

[14] Claude (1972); Fenske (1977).

Countess Matilda of Tuscany to act as intermediaries on his behalf, consented to appear on three consecutive days in a penitent's garb before the walls of the fortified castle of Canossa, Gregory's temporary residence. His imploring for the pope's forgiveness was to be answered on the third day, 25 January, when the pope would lift the repentent sinner from the floor, where he would be lying flat on his face. A joint meal was to conclude the ceremony.

The date reveals the meaning that the scene was intended to convey. In the church calendar 25 January is the feast of the *conversio Pauli*, the conversion of the apostle Paul. Just as *the scales fell from Saul's eyes* when he was changed into the believer Paul after having lain three days in blindness before Damascus, so the king would be changed from a persecutor of the faithful into a Christian, whose eyes had finally been opened to the truth.

In German historical writing as in political discourse 'Canossa' came to be considered as a shameful abasement of the German sovereign before papist presumption. The assessment of the event in its medieval context has been coloured by this supposition until very recently, when scholars began to give more attention to medieval mentality.[15] Historians have come to realize that contemporaries seem to have been far more disturbed by the papal ban than by Henry's act of penance. Although some of the particulars were unusual, penance and reconciliation had after all a fixed place in medieval religious life. Although this takes the sting of national humiliation away, the deciphering of the symbolic message makes it even more obvious to what degree Henry had had to succumb to Gregory's view: disobedience to the pope made a man appear as though blind to God's truth and was equivalent to being a persecutor of the faithful. In the ninth and tenth centuries the kings were seen as the anointed heads of their several churches, the lords of their bishops, with their sceptres given by God himself. Now Gregory had been successful with his view that the bishops with their flocks constituted the church as a single body with the pope as its head. Kings, though exalted in the world, were part of the flock; they needed guidance and owed obedience to him.

Although Henry could hope that he had saved his crown by doing penance before the pope at Canossa, he seems to have been quite aware of the fact that he had indeed acknowledged the pope's view of the right order of the world. He is reported to have sat at the meal with a grim mien, not touching the food and working the wooden table with his fingernails. Joint meals, too, were a meaningful ritual in medieval social relationships. They were an indispensable part of sworn friendship alliances (*amicitiae*), the essence of which they meant to embody: friendship, mutual help, absence of ill-will and feud. The sharing

---

[15] For the changing perception of Canossa as revealed in writings from the eleventh century onward see Zimmermann (1975).

of food at a joint meal demonstrated that enmity was absent and that peace and amity reigned. It is impossible to tell whether Henry had really broken the rules of accepted behaviour in not touching the food or whether the historian Rangerius, who wrote some twenty years after the event, handed down an early legend connected with it. The meaning Rangerius wanted to convey with the details is quite obvious, however. As far as the king was concerned, the feud had ended, but peace was only superficially restored, as ill-will and distrust remained.[16]

It was neither the pope's intention nor was it, in fact, in his interest that open strife recommenced only two months after Canossa. Although Gregory was satisfied with Henry's penance and could very well be, a small yet determined group of German princes went ahead with the election of a new king anyway. On 15 March 1077 they elected Rudolf of Rheinfelden as their king. Some of them had fought Henry before: the archbishop of Magdeburg and the bishop of Halberstadt had been prominent anti-Salians in the Saxon wars, as had been the Saxon noble Otto of Northeim, whom Henry IV had deposed as duke of Bavaria in 1070. And yet the election of a king of their own was more than a rekindling of the old enmities. Never before in the history of the medieval German kingdom had an anti-king been elected. As yet undisputed custom saw the son of a king as his natural successor. Did not the fact that God had blessed a king with an heir show that God himself wanted kingship to continue in his line?[17] The princes who in the past had invariably elected the son, or, where biology precluded this, the closest of kin to the deceased king had not interviewed different candidates before doing this. An election meant that they accepted the right person as their royal lord, the one determined by custom and the established God-given order of things. This mental background made formal rules for an election superfluous. Neither was there an agreed number of electors. A king's royal position rested on the support he was able to gain from the important princes of his realm, those with illustrious names and formidable family backgrounds, who could if need be muster blood relations, sworn friends and large retinues of men bound to them by all kinds of obligations. Up to the year 1077 many a German king had seen nobles turn away from him and had seen them form alliances against him when they felt their king had wronged them. But never before had a group of feudal lords subtracted its allegiance for good by transferring it to another royal lord. This was new, indeed, as was the stipulation that Rudolf of Rheinfelden had only been elected as an individual and that a succession of his son should not be taken for granted. Was this

[16] For medieval meals as meaningful rituals see Althoff (1987).
[17] Charlemagne argued along this line to justify his plan for a partition of his realm among his three sons in 806 'Divisio regnorum', ed. *MGH Capitularia regum Francorum*, 1, no. 45, pp. 126–30. His reasoning is indicative of the mental background of medieval elections.

a precursor of the 'free' elections that were to become normal in Germany after the extinction of the Staufen in the mid-thirteenth century?[18] Did the rebellious nobles want to limit the breach of custom to Henry IV with the intention of returning to the established royal line once this particular enemy of theirs was dead? Whatever the long-term intentions might have been, the immediate result was civil war which went on even after Rudolf's death in battle in 1080. The effects differed over time and by region. Where people were more or less unanimous in the support of one of the two kings the region was simply closed to the other and his party. This was the case in eastern Saxony, which supported Rudolf, and in Bavaria, which stayed loyal to Henry. But in many parts of Germany the situation was more complicated. As a direct reaction to the breach of fealty Henry had Rudolf of Rheinfelden convicted in a court of peers and then declared the duchy of Swabia forfeit. In 1079 he installed Frederick of Büren as duke in Rudolf's stead and corroborated the alliance by giving him his daughter Agnes for a bride. Frederick's decendants were to call themselves Staufer (Staufen) after their fortified castle Stauf on the mountain Hohenstaufen near Waiblingen. As Henry's candidate Frederick was the natural enemy of the Rheinfelden and their allies, particularly the noble family clans of the Welfs and Zähringen, who had elected Rudolf's son Berthold for their ducal lord. Both dukes tried to conquer the duchy and attacks on the rival's supporters and their dependants and acts of violence were endemic, just as they were in some of the bigger towns in the Rhine valley. In Mainz the burghers supported Henry, whereas their town lord, the archbishop, sided with Rudolf. When he had him anointed and crowned in his episcopal church the burghers rioted and expelled both the rival king and their own lord, just as the burghers of Worms and Cologne had done during the Saxon wars. It seems as if the rising social classes of the town burghers generally tended more to support the traditional royal line than did elements of the nobility.

As the archbishops and bishops were traditionally installed by the king after having been elected by the clergy and the people, factions in the bishoprics would easily lead to schisms, as in Augsburg, where Wigolt sought installation as bishop from King Rudolf, disputing the right of the royal chaplain Siegfried, whom King Henry had invested. As Wigolt, who was supported by the Bavarian Welf party, and Siegfried with his Heinrician backing resorted to feuding to win the bishopric of Augsburg, its men and goods suffered devastations for many years. In some cases the torn kingship only provided a new means of continuing old feuds, as in the region of Lake Constance, where old animosities between

---

[18] Because of the later developments which distinguished German kingship from that in countries like England and France that adopted primogeniture, historians have called the election of 1077 a turning-point in the history of Germany, giving it much attention. The turning-point hypothesis was elaborated by Schlesinger (1973), repr. (1987). For a more recent discussion see Keller (1983).

the bishopric of Constance and the neighbouring monasteries of Reichenau and St Gall were continued under the pretext of fighting the supporters of the enemy king. But notwithstanding divergent local conditions the support for King Henry steadily grew.

Meanwhile Gregory was advancing his vision of an unpolluted church by generally banning lay investiture. In May 1077 he let his legate in France know that should an archbishop consecrate an elect who had received his church through the hands of a lay person, he risked his own office. The legate duly proclaimed this at two French synods, but it is unlikely that the ban became known in the German lands at that time.[19] In November 1078, however, Gregory took advantage of the Lateran council to make his views known:

Since we know that contrary to the statutes of the holy fathers investitures by lay persons are being performed in many places and that multifarious disturbances arise therefrom in the church, harming the Christian religion, we decree that no cleric is to receive the investiture of a bishopric, an abbey or a church through the hands of an emperor, a king or any other lay person, be it man or woman. If, however, he should attempt to do this, let him be informed that by apostolic authority this investiture is invalid and he himself is excommunicated until due satisfaction is done.[20]

This ban, in fact, upset the feudal system based on personal ties and mutual personal obligations, of which the ecclesiastics were a part. By investing a bishop in a solemn rite with ring and staff the king made it known that the church was his to give because it belonged to his realm, that its incumbent owed him fealty and all kinds of services in return for the protection the king owed his churches, and in return for the many donations and privileges kings had been accustomed to give for centuries. A king, after all, raised no taxes to help him run the country. He had to rely on the obligations his lay and ecclesiastical magnates owed him and these were established by the solemn rites of fealty and investiture. Ecclesiastical investitures were the equivalent to the feudal bonds that had to be renewed whenever lord or vassal died. Pope Gregory thought along quite different lines. He was not concerned with the functioning of kingdoms but with religious truths: the hands of the priests who touched Christ's flesh and blood in the eucharist must not come into contact with the blood-stained hands of a layman. In his eyes it was a *mala consuetudo* (a bad custom) that the church of God was integrated into the feudal world. For him *libertas ecclesiae* (liberty of the church) meant freedom from all secular ties and obligations.

[19] Until recently the first general papal bans on lay investiture were dated 1075 or even as early as 1059 and scholars have argued that it was precisely this ban that made Henry IV and his bishops denounce their obedience to the pope at Worms in January 1076. Rudolf Schieffer (1981), who dates it 1077/8, thoroughly discusses the dating question with its political implications.

[20] Gregory VII, *Register*, VI, 5b, c. 3.

Although Gregory's ban was a clear rejection of the basic structure of feudal society, it had only a limited influence on the wars that were going on in Germany.[21] The parties in the conflict did not define themselves as fighting for or against lay investiture. Even Pope Gregory himself did not take this line. In the Augsburg case mentioned above King Rudolf might indeed have performed what Gregorians would consider a model royal installation, abstaining from the traditional rite of investiture, whereas King Henry certainly went on investing bishops and abbots in the customary way. And yet Gregory refused to confirm the ban that one of his legates in Germany had pronounced against Henry in the autumn of 1077, just as he hesitated to acknowledge Rudolf as the legitimate German king. It was not the question of lay investiture but that of obedience which again aggravated the situation in 1080. Seeing the number of his followers grow, Henry demanded from the pope the excommunication of the rival king, announcing the election of a new pope should Gregory refuse. At this Gregory renewed the ban against Henry[22] and acknowledged Rudolf as the legitimate king. He was so confident that God himself would punish Henry's insurrection against St Peter's vicar that he predicted the king's death before 1 August, the feast of St Peter's chains.

Henry reconvened his episcopal supporters, who again broke off their relations with the pope. But this time the Salian party went further than at Worms in 1076. Henry went south with a large retinue and had a synod meet in the south Tyrolean town of Brixen in June 1080 and elect Bishop Wibert of Ravenna pope. Wibert, who adopted the papal name Clement III, was anything but an opponent to church reform in the sense of improving the religious attitudes and practices of clergy and people. He appears to have shown great interest in the stricter monastic foundations in his diocese.[23] But as his papal activities show, he expected church reform in cooperation with his anointed royal lord, as had the reformers in the 1040s and 1050s. Times, however, had changed since then. Many people had come to equate church reform with obedience to the *Romana ecclesia*, which made those who refused that obedience enemies of reform. Feudal ways of thinking had reduced a very complex problem to a matter of personal ties.

The rival king's death in battle in October 1080 greatly reinforced Henry's position. The fact that Rudolf died of the loss of his right hand gave his death the significance of an ordeal, as it was with this hand that he had once sworn fealty to his royal lord. And it belied Gregory's prophesy of Henry's imminent death. In spite of the election of Hermann of Salm as another anti-king Henry

---

[21] This is the somewhat surprising result of the study by Stefan Beulertz (1991).

[22] Bonizo of Sutri gives this explanation for the course of events. For a recent discussion of its credibility see Vogel (1983).

[23] Heidrich (1984).

felt secure enough to leave Germany for Rome for his imperial coronation. He and his wife Bertha received it on Easter 1084 at the hands of Pope Clement III. Gregory, who had had to leave the city, died in exile the following year. As far as their personal dispute was concerned, Henry had definitely triumphed over his adversary.

The success in Italy had strengthened Henry's party in Germany by winning him new followers. But although many had changed sides, others remained adamant in their resistance. The most obvious among them were the bishops who had declared themselves obedient to Gregory at the beginning of the open strife between king and pope in 1076 and who, after having taken part in the election of Rudolf, had been ousted from their episcopal towns by their parishioners with Salian leanings. The archbishops of Mainz and Salzburg and the bishops of Würzburg, Passau, Worms and Metz had all been living in exile for several years or been reduced to controlling parts of their dioceses when an Easter synod convened at Mainz in 1085 in the presence of Pope Clement III declared them deposed and others elected in their stead. The same synod deposed the fiercest of Henry's ecclesiastical enemies in Saxony, the archbishop of Magdeburg and the bishops of Halberstadt, Meissen and Merseburg. Altogether there were fifteen dioceses for which new bishops were named at Mainz. The investitutres were performed by the king in the customary way. The effects of these nominations differed. In the diocese from which Gregorians had been exiled they ended vacancies. In Saxony the situation was different, as there the hostile bishops were well established in their dioceses. The bishops Henry had elected in their stead needed and received the king's armed support in trying to take possession of their dioceses, but often their situation remained precarious. For those who considered Clement and his German followers to be schismatics in the first place all these depositions were, of course, illegal, and the subsequent elections were only legitimizing usurpers. So war went on and dioceses where both sides were strong enough to fight for what everyone considered his right continued to suffer devastations.

Political developments in the eleventh century were very much a matter of persons and personal allegiances, a fact that can be illustrated by the course of events in the 1090s. The anti-king Hermann, who had never been a significant rival to Henry, died in 1088 and in April of that year Bishop Burchard II of Halberstadt, who had been the fiercest of all of Henry's Saxon ecclesiastical enemies, was murdered; in 1090 his most pronounced lay adversary, the margrave of Meissen, suffered the same fate.[24] There were others who must have stayed alive and remained hostile. But altogether Henry's German enemies definitely

[24] For a categorizing assessment of the numerous acts of violence in the Salian period, which for the first time in German history included the murdering of bishops, see Reuter (1992).

seemed to have been on the decline by the end of the 1080s and even with regard to the papacy it looked as if the emperor had prevailed.

Although Clement III had failed to win recognition outside the German ruler's sphere of influence, Henry IV could very well believe that by the mid-1080s he had subjected the party of cardinals as well. With the death of the exiled Gregory VII in Salerno it looked as if it had received the decisive blow. It took the cardinal bishops a whole year to have the very reluctant abbot of Montecassino elected pope. He never took residence in war-torn Rome and died in September 1087. In March 1088, however, they elected Odo cardinal bishop of Ostia to become their pope. He called himself Urban II and proved to be a formidable adversary as an intellectual as well as a crafty politician. He was French born and trained and he was also well versed in German affairs as he had been trying to weld the Gregorian party together as papal legate in Germany in 1085. He had not been very successful at that because the ban he had hurled at defectors had not made them abjure King Henry's cause. But he had helped to install Gebhard, a member of the Zähringen noble clan, as bishop of Constance, and he became a bulwark of the Gregorian cause.

The first of his schemes to isolate Henry was a marriage he helped to arrange in 1089 between the unwavering Gregorian Matilda, countess of Tuscany, then forty-three years old and Welf V, aged seventeen. When King Henry went to Italy in 1090 to execute a verdict for high treason against the countess he found himself trapped near Verona, because cooperation between the Tuscan and Welf followers hindered him from moving north again until 1096, when Welf had grown tired of his aging wife and returned into his fealty. In 1093 the pope won Henry's son Conrad, the young king, over to his side and in 1095 he let Henry's second wife Adelaide-Praxedis use the papal synod at Piacenza as a forum for accusing her husband of the grossest sexual aberrations.

It is hard to tell whether these schemes had much effect, except perhaps in helping to establish Henry's bad personal reputation in historiography up to the present day. After all, Adelaide's accusations corroborated that of the enemy historians of the Saxon wars who had also pilloried his sexual excesses. It must nevertheless be doubted that these imputations are to be understood literally, because according to Isidore, the seventh-century bishop of Seville, whose *Etymologies* were used as an encyclopaedia in the middle ages, licentiousness and the cruel oppression of peoples defined a tyrant,[25] who by that very definition was no longer entitled to the fealty due to a king. By letting Henry appear as

[25] Isidore of Seville, *Etymologiarum sive originum libri viginti*, Lib. IX, III, 20: 'in usum accidit tyrannos vocari pessimos atque inprobos reges luxuriosae dominationis cupiditatem et crudelissimam dominationem in populis exercentes'.

a sexual monster his enemies imputed the characteristics of a tyrant to Henry, which, of course, legitimized their defection.[26]

It was not these schemes that made Pope Urban II famous, but rather the fact that he reestablished the reform papacy's leadership over the Latin church. Above all, he is remembered as the pope who initiated the First Crusade. When Byzantine envoys addressed the pope in 1095 with a demand for help against the infidels at their borders, they probably hoped for trained mercenaries, which the pope, however, misunderstood deliberately or not as a general appeal to western Christendom. In the sermon which he preached at the council of Clermont in November 1095 the pope called all Christians rich or poor to arms to free the holy sites from the domination of the infidels, promising remission of sins to all who answered the call. Further propagation of the plan of an armed pilgrimage to the Holy Land was to lie with the bishops.[27] The original text of the sermon has not come down to us. The summaries that we have differ one from another. Although the pope might not have intended anything dramatically new it can nevertheless be assumed that it was the pope himself who summed up all non-Christians as enemies of the Christian name, thereby introducing a dichotomy into people's perception which allowed them to draw disastrous conclusions.[28] It made non-Christians, who apparently had lived more or less undisturbedly in early medieval Christian society, objects of persecution, especially since travelling preachers spontaneously took to preaching the crusade. In France as well as in Germany Jewish communities fell victim to rabid bands. It has been estimated that altogether about 5,000 Jews were slain.[29] In none of the medieval kingdoms had the Jews been integrated into the networks of dependence and protection provided by blood relationships and feudal or other personal bonds. Instead their legal status was that of being under the 'protection' of the respective king, as was the status of widows and orphans. When appealed to by the heads of some of the Jewish communities King Henry obligingly issued charters of protection, which was about all he could do. In reality the fate of the German Jews depended on the protection that the bishops as lords of the towns were able – or willing – to give. Whereas the bishop of Speyer succeeded in saving virtually the whole Jewish community by receiving its members into his fortified town house, the Jews of Worms and Mainz suffered enormous losses. Other than these gruesome side-effects the call to the First Crusade seems more or less to have by-passed the German lands at first. It was predominantly a French, Flemish and English affair. Few German bishops were present at the

[26] For the problem of deciphering the symbolic language and of establishing Henry's personality in our sense of the word, see Tellenbach (1988); Vollrath (1992).
[27] See Riley-Smith (1986).   [28] Rousset (1983).
[29] Mertens (1981); Chazan (1987) draws primarily on the Jewish sources in trying to establish the situation of the Jewish communities as a part of medieval society before and after the First Crusade.

council of Clermont, and the German king was trapped in Lombardy at the time when crusade preaching and preparation began. Moreover, he was still bound to Clement III; Pope Urban was his enemy, who almost immediately after his enthronement had renewed the papal ban against him.

From its beginning, church reform with its questioning of established customs and traditions had prompted theoretical reflections on the nature of secular and ecclesiastical rule and the right order of the world. In the course of the intellectual debate Bishop Ivo of Chartres had transformed the rather blurred notions about the different sides of a bishop's position into a definition of functions by distinguishing the *spiritualia* from the *temporalia*. *Temporalia* stood for temporal rights of rule and property, whereas the *spiritualia* summed up the religious functions. By the end of the century it had become widely accepted that the traditional symbols for ecclesiastical investitures, namely ring and staff, stood for the spiritual rights and obligations of the episcopal office and should be employed by ecclesiastics only in religious rites. This opened the question of how the incumbent was to receive the landed wealth with its dependants and the judicial and other privileges connected with his office. Before he could act as the lord of all this he had to be made the lord of it. The theoretical dividing up of a bishop's position into its several functions led to the idea that several separate acts were necessary for the making of a bishop. Gregory VII had banned investitures meaning investitures by ring and staff. Urban aggravated the situation by extending the papal ban to feudal commendations.[30] It was his answer to the fact that the king and other feudal lords in France had begun to sacrifice investitures in favour of feudal rites in analogy to the rites by which a lord bestowed lay fiefs thought to have returned into his possession upon the death of each holder. This, the pope argued, could not be, as it would sever the churches from their possessions, which through analogy would – at least theoretically – acquire the legal status of leased lands and rights. On the other hand the lords insisted on some sort of rite, as the structure of kingdoms was not yet maintained institutionally but through personal bonds of dependence and allegiance.

This turned out to be a theoretical deadlock. It was Ivo of Chartres who with all the weight of his authority showed a way out: after having received an oath of fealty the lords would give the temporal possessions of a bishopric by way of a simple *concessio*, which the pope would abstain from punishing. It was meant as a momentary expedient. But whereas in France it simply became normal to proceed along these lines, a formal treaty was concluded between the English king and Archbishop Anselm of Canterbury in 1107 to the same effect.

---

[30] Minninger (1978); Southern (1990), pp. 280ff.

In Germany the controversy dragged on. Although Henry IV abstained from having a new antipope elected after Clement III's death in 1100, the relationship between the king and the then reigning pope Paschal II had been far too much disturbed to allow for an easy reconciliation. Moreover the divided allegiances in the German episcopate and its lay followers stood in the way of a non-formal agreement. For many Henry IV had been the enemy incarnate for so long that they would welcome whatever promised to stimulate the old animosities. It is therefore hard to tell whether the disturbed relationship with the papacy served as a mere pretext or whether it really won important magnates over to the side of the king's son Henry V when he started a rebellion against his father late in 1104. In any case the pope was willing to oblige by freeing Henry V from his promise never to break the oath of fealty to his father. Again Henry IV was confronted with enemies who fought him for very different reasons, and again he was ready to take up the fight. He was out collecting allies in the lower Rhineland when he suddenly died at Liège in August 1106 at the age of fifty-six. The bishop of Liège, who had remained on the old king's side, had him interred in his cathedral church, whence his son had him exhumed. The man banned by the church was allotted a grave in a yet unconsecrated chapel at Speyer cathedral, the Salians' imperial place of burial. But people were far from unanimous on this verdict on the old king: they flocked to his coffin on its way up the Rhine valley, touching and venerating it as if it was that of a martyr and saint. It was only when Henry V himself ran into trouble with the papacy in 1111 that he had his father demonstratively translated into the royal tomb in Speyer cathedral. His remains have been lying there to the present day.

HENRY V (1105/6–1125)

It seemed as though the death of the old king had indeed paved the way for peace. In August 1106 the Saxon duke Magnus died leaving no male heir who would have stood for an undisputed succession. But surprisingly Henry V found no resistance when he appointed Lothar of Supplinburg as duke, although both of Magnus's daughters were married to ambitious men who later claimed the duchy. The new king was equally successful in other contentious parts of his realm such as the duchy of Lorraine. Men who had fought Henry IV on ecclesiastical grounds somewhat surprisingly accepted investiture in the traditional way from Henry V. They had apparently failed to grasp the complicated judicial and religious issues inherent in investitures and had reduced the problem to the moral question of good king versus bad king, king versus tyrant. They therefore had no apprehension about being invested by the king who had been approved by the pope. In 1110 Henry was able to win the hand of Matilda, daughter to the English king Henry I, who after her husband's death in 1025 and her subsequent return to her native land was to become the notorious 'Empress Maud' of English history. This prestigious connection not only strengthened his position, but also brought him a rich dowry and made him even consider a claim to the English throne after the death of the English king's only legitimate son in the 'tragedy of the white ship.'[31]

As far as the contest over investitures was concerned, Henry V opened negotiations almost immediately after his father's death. As king of Italy and emperor-to-be and as the son and successor of the pope's personal enemy, Henry V had to come to terms with Pope Paschal II himself. Moreover, only an agreement with the pope would bring the war-torn German churches back to unity. Delegations met at Guastalla in Lombardy (October 1106), at Châlons-sur-Marne in the French kingdom (1107) and in Rome (1109). In all of these meetings it became apparent that a formal treaty between pope and emperor-to-be would have to be based on a treatment of the whole question. Although both sides showed the good-will needed to end the controversy they failed to reach agreement.

It was the *regalia*, the rights of the kingdom, which Henry saw in danger and which he felt his duty to defend. But whereas both sides agreed that these did not encompass the *spiritualia*, they were not able to reach an agreement of how the *regalia* were related to the *temporalia*.[32] Henry seems to have understood his position as that of a lord of proprietary churches: everything *his* churches possessed was in the end his, which he, as custom demanded, put at the disposal of *his* bishops. For the king the *temporalia* of the imperial churches were equivalent to *regalia*. The pope, on the other hand, seems to have distinguished provenance and function; in his view the material goods of the churches had been acquired through pious gifts by innumerable donors including the kings; they had been given to the churches inalienably and could therefore not be made the objects of a royal transference. From these the pope distinguished rights and revenues which the king possessed as royal prerogatives in his capacity as governmental head of the kingdom, together with judicial rights, taxes, and the rights to mint coins, to hold markets and to raise fortified castles. These he considered to be just as unalienably part of the reigning powers of kings. Where ecclesiastical and lay princes held them, they did so through concession by the king. The pope was more or less willing to concede that these could be the objects of a secular investiture in connection with a bishop's assumption of office, whereas others in the papal curia felt that this was going too far.

Descriptions of the negotiations at Châlons have been handed down to us in vivid scenes by a famous contemporary, the abbot Suger of St Denis, the French king's most influential adviser. He depicts the German delegation as a band

[31] Leyser (1991).   [32] Fried (1973).

of ruffians, ready to resort to brutal force and not leaders in the intellectual debate. However, his report was written after the turn events took when Henry went to Italy in IIII to receive his imperial crown. Although it probably does not convey a true picture of what happened at Châlons, it nevertheless shows to what an extent the German king had altogether alienated himself through his subsequent acts from what was thought acceptable.

It is hard to believe that Henry himself could have thought that any of his moves would restore peace. At first he concluded a secret treaty with the pope in the Roman church Santa Maria in Turri which he must have known would be utterly unacceptable to German ecclesiastical princes. He promised the pope to abstain from investitures on the condition that the bishops would abandon the *regalia*, which, he now conceded, not did encompass pious donations. When the treaty was made known at the imperial coronation ceremony in the Lateran church, the German princes, ecclesiastical and lay, rose in tumult, as they saw the order of the kingdom upset. Theoretically it was a clean freak and not devoid of logic. It is hard to see, however, how it could possibly have worked. When the king saw his plan frustrated through the violent opposition of his magnates, he resorted to another rash expedient. He claimed investiture with ring and staff as his royal prerogative. When the pope refused to concede this, Henry took him prisoner, extorting from him the privilege of Ponte Mammolo, which granted him just that as an ancient custom of the empire.

In view of the compromises people had come to accept as sensible means of doing justice to both sides in France and in England the German king's claims were untimely, even though he was eager to clarify that he meant his investiture only to transfer the *temporalia*. This explanation did not make his move any more acceptable, of course. The Lateran synod of III2 revoked the papal privilege denouncing it as a 'pravilege' and had the emperor excommunicated.

With the return of the open feud between pope and emperor, the old alliances from the time of his father seemed to repeat themselves. Saxon discontent over how Henry V handled the inheritance of Count Ulrich II of Weimar-Orlamünde, who had died without issue in III2, initiated an alliance of malcontents within and without Saxony, with Duke Lothar as its head. After the king had lost two battles in III4 and III5, the rebels received reinforcements from Archbishop Adalbert of Mainz, who, as a member of the mighty house of the counts of Saarbrücken, had seen his family's territorial interests thwarted by the king. His animosity had secular grounds. But as head of the largest and most renowned archbishopric in the German kingdom he almost inevitably assumed the position of spokesman for the ecclesiastical opposition.

Despite the papal ban, the fiercest moral accusations and the election of yet another anti pope, negotiations over the question of investitures never broke down entirely. When violence escalated into civil war again it was the magnates who in 1121 peremptorily demanded a reconciliation between pope and emperior. Papal legates came to Germany to negotiate a treaty which materialized as the 'Concordate of Worms'. Each side drew up a list of promises, which were given the form of a papal and a royal privilege and then were exchanged on 23 September 1122 on the *Lobwiese* just outside the Worms town gate. Henry's central promise was his renunciation of all investitures with ring and staff. In view of the many futile discussions on *temporalia* and *regalia* over the past fifteen years the central sentence of the papal *promissio* reads like an ingenious escape. The pope allowed the elect to receive the *regalia* at the hands of the emperor through the symbol of a sceptre and conceded the fulfilment of the obligations resulting from it. A year later the Lateran Council approved the treaty and declared the Investiture Contest to have come to an end with it.

It is not only this declaration which seems to assign this concordat a decisive role in the course of political events. It is therefore surprising to realize that many German episcopal churches remained virtually ignorant of it. Only few of them had a text of the treaty. It was never referred to in particular cases and when later writers mentioned it they betrayed only a limited knowledge of it.[33] Apparently customs which had come to be observed anyway had finally been cast into writing. Essentially it was a proclamation of peace between the pope and the emperor. Given the implications that the contest had had for the factions and for the civil wars that for decades had disrupted many parts of the German kingdom it is hard to see what kind of a difference the writing down of accepted customs could possibly have made. There can be no doubt, however, that the practice as such, namely the investiture of the archbishops, bishops and the abbots of royal monasteries with the *regalia* through a sceptre, a symbol of rulership, guaranteed that they all were considered to be princes of the realm (*Reichsfürsten*). It put them on the same level as the dukes and ensured that they were to wield vice-regal power in their territories.[34]

The year 1123 saw another confrontation between the emperor and the Saxon Duke Lothar over the appointment of a margrave in which the duke prevailed. It is impossible to predict whether the peace treaty with the papacy would eventually have helped Henry to reassert his royal authority in his German kingdom because he died childless in May 1125. The magnates whom Archbishop Adalbert called to Mainz for the royal election chose Lothar, the duke of Saxony, Henry's most formidable foe, to succeed him.

[33] Schieffer (1986), esp. pp. 62ff.   [34] Heinemeyer (1986).

NORTHERN AND CENTRAL ITALY IN THE ELEVENTH CENTURY

Giovanni Tabacco

THE RULING POWER IN ITALY: THE HOUSE OF FRANCONIA FROM CONRAD II TO HENRY III

The kingdom of Italy, extending from the Alps to its unsettled borders with the papal states, suffered its most serious crisis during the transition from the imperial house of the Saxons to that of the Salians in 1024, when the capital itself, Pavia, rose, destroyed the royal palace and scattered the officials in charge of the central administration. At that point the throne was vacant and the great lords of Italy divided over the problem of the succession. The subordination of the Italian to the German crown was not yet a peacefully accepted fact and some of the major powers sought their own candidate in France. But the bishops of northern Italy, remembering the disagreements over inheritance which had arisen between the church and the laity and the resulting violence, chose a different way. Under the guidance of the archbishop of Milan, Aribert of Antimiano and the bishop of Vercelli, Leo, they offered the crown to the king who had just been elected in Germany, Conrad II of the house of Franconia.

In 1026, Conrad came down into Italy through the Brenner pass with a considerable army and was welcomed at Milan by Aribert. He besieged Pavia and set about reducing the nobles reluctant to recognize him. In 1027, he created Boniface of Canossa, already powerful through his estates, castles and titles of count in various regions of the Po valley, marquess in Tuscany. He had himself crowned emperor in Rome by Pope John XIX, of the family of the counts of Tusculum. From him he also obtained recognition of the ecclesiastical jurisdiction over the Lagoon of Venice claimed by the patriarch of Aquileia, Poppo of Carinthia, to the detriment of the patriarchate of Grado and Venetian autonomy. Throughout his time in Italy, he confirmed landed estates and distributed them on a large scale, as well as privileges, temporal jurisdictions and patronage to monasteries, bishoprics and canonical chapters

Map 2 Italy

from the Alps, in particular from the eastern side, as far as the monastery of
Farfa in Sabina and that of Casauria in Abruzzo. In this way, there came to be
developed the type of organization which the kings of Germany had granted
the kingdom of Italy since the time of Otto. It was a form of organization based
not on the workings of a rationally distributed hierarchy of public officials, but
rather on the binding of royal power, through an exchange of protection and

loyalty, to institutions and nobles, in particular princes of the church, rooted in the area through their lands and with authority derived either from their religious responsibilities or their dynastic power.

After spending a number of years in Germany, Conrad II was elected king of Burgundy in 1033 by various of the great men of that kingdom, among them the powerful count Humbert, head of the house of Savoy and possessor of estates and rights in several counties, from the Val d'Aosta to the frontier with the kingdom of Italy. In 1034 an Italian army led by the archbishop of Milan, Aribert, and Boniface, marquess of Tuscany, took part in the military operations necessary to ensure Conrad's effective domination over his new kingdom. When at the end of 1036, however, Conrad came down into Italy for the second time, the increase in the influence of the church and the temporal power of the archbishop of Milan were such that the emperor was forced to listen to the complaints of the lords and cities of Lombardy about his encroachments and, faced with his contemptuous behaviour, he had him imprisoned. Aribert fled and took refuge in Milan, where he was protected by the people. Conrad besieged the city, but in vain. Vain too was his wish to remove Aribert from office and appoint as his successor a court chaplain, Ambrose, a member of the higher clergy of Milan.

During the fruitless siege of Milan, on 28 May 1037, the emperor promulgated his famous edict on the rights of vassals. In a situation which had become dangerous for the prestige of the ruling power in Italy, this was a fundamental legislative move and one which attempted to restore the king-emperor to his place at the heart of the natural development of institutions within the region. The Milanese problem was not in fact only a problem of the competition between the city and its metropolitan church and the other Lombard centres of major economic, ecclesiastical and political importance, but also one of the great military power of the archbishop, who was at the summit of a complex and elaborately stratified network of client vassals. There were strong tensions within this network: with the archbishop at the top, among the various strata and with the non-military population of the city. The tensions suffered by Milan served in their turn as models for the internal dissension of all the major military centres of the ecclesiastical and lay nobility in Lombardy. The edict of Conrad was indeed officially presented as the solution of these problems, by establishing, at least theoretically, an ordered hierarchy of vassals possessing fiefs, following a unified concept of the military organization of the kingdom.

The disagreements between individual vassals and their immediate superiors in the fluid hierarchy of personal dependencies in fact hinged on the precarious estate-based nature of the fiefs granted in exchange for service as a vassal. Conrad II, faced with the contradictions among the practices which had arisen on this account, referred back to a comprehensive hierarchy of vassals who had been remunerated by fiscal lands or lands of fiscal origin or ecclesiastical lands. He confirmed each vassal in the possession of the fiefs he was enjoying, declaring that such grants to beneficiaries were irrevocable and thus hereditary, as long as the vassal or his heir in the male line faithfully continued to perform his required service, with horses and arms, for his feudal superior, the originator of the grant. In this way, the solidity of the reciprocal bond between lord and vassal was clarified by the fief appearing at one and the same time in the estate of each party, the bond itself being based on military service, which the edict interpreted as an integral part of the vassalic hierarchy of the royal army. In order to give a greater appearance of reality to an all-embracing and hierarchic military structure, culminating in the person of the king, the edict officially ignored the existence of fiefs which had neither a fiscal origin – and hence were not directly or indirectly related to the ruling power – nor were part of the ecclesiastical estates, held under a special royal protection. The kingdom, which we have already seen was not functioning according to a rational system of public ordinances but as a heterogeneous collection of patron and client relationships, now began to reassume its unity, by observing the patronage system with the help of a legal fiction.

This does not mean that the royal and imperial authority in Italy was completely inefficacious. It frequently influenced both the choice of bishops, a choice which formally belonged to the local clergy, and that of the abbots in the case of monasteries belonging to the crown. It can in fact be said that the sovereign, in so far as he succeeded in governing, above all made use of the symbolism of vassalage in his relationships with those powerful lords – for the most part ecclesiastics or those whom family tradition invested with the dignities of marquess or count – who, by swearing loyalty to the ruler in person, legitimized punitive action which might come to be taken as a result of the most obvious infractions of the oath. The promotion of Boniface of Canossa to the marquessate of Tuscany should likewise be borne in mind. This shows the possibility of royal intervention in the line of succession of certain non-ecclesiastical regional powers; in other words when the power of the marquess or count was not firmly established in dynastic form, as in the case with the Tuscan march. The crown's intervention could also take the form of an agreement with the power of a great family, using marriages favoured by or acceptable to the sovereign. This was the case with Adelaide of Turin, in 1034 daughter and heir of the Marquess Olderico Manfredi and the wife of three spouses in succession, each of whom was recognized in his turn – under Conrad II and then Henry III – as holder of the title to the Turin march, a large area of the kingdom. Similarly, Conrad II favoured the marriage of his faithful Marquess Boniface of Tuscany with

Beatrice of Lorraine, who grew up in the imperial court and was the relative of a descendant of the marquess of Obertenghi, Alberto Azzo II d'Este, and of the powerful German family of the Welfs. To these more or less occasional incursions of the ruling house into the workings of powerful churches and great noble dynasties should be added the appointment – although these too were only occasional – of royal messengers who represented their sovereign in presiding over legal assemblies in one area or another of the kingdom.

As regards the edict on fiefs, it had a certain general effect: not of course in the sense of giving rise to a homogeneous and strictly ordered hierarchy of vassals, but in that it came to form an element in the uncertain play of feudal–vassal customs and helped the evolution, which had already begun, towards greater guarantees for the vassals endowed with fiefs. It did not, on the other hand, have any perceptible repercussions on the relationship of Conrad II with the Milanese neighbourhood, which continued to resist the siege. A plot hatched by certain of the bishops of the Po valley against the emperor was also discovered and there was an attempt on the part of Aribert to ally himself with the count of Champagne, who had invaded the western provinces of Germany. Conrad II, in his turn, visited central Italy in 1038 and obtained from Pope Benedict IX, the nephew and successor of John XIX, the excommunication of Aribert and the recognition of Ambrose, the imperial candidate to the see of Milan, but with no real success. Agreements having, therefore, been reached with the pope, Conrad proceeded south to the defence of Monte Cassino, to which he appointed as abbot a German monk, faithful to his cause, assigning him the prince of Salerno as protector. After other kingly acts in Campania, the emperor turned north along the Adriatic coast and continued to distribute privileges to both nobles and institutions. Putting off the subjection of Milan to another occasion, he went back up the valley of the Adige and recrossed the Alps. The Italian lords who had remained faithful to the emperor then took up the siege of Milan again, but in 1039 they were surprised by news of his death, which reached them from Germany.

When one considers the extent of Conrad II's activities in Europe, from Lorraine and Burgundy to the Slavic world and from the North Sea to southern Italy, it cannot be said that the kingdom of Italy was left on the fringes of his interests. But the attraction which the most various and far-flung parts of the unstable imperial complex gradually came to exercise over him prevented a lasting pacification of the kingdom of Italy. It also considerably increased the difficulties of a political strategy essentially based on the interplay of alliances among groups rooted in the various regions of Italy. The kingdom had no territorially based administration. The collecting of the right to fodder, the contribution in kind owed to the emperor during his stays in Italy for the maintenance of the court and the army, was to some extent problematical, because it always depended on the degree of loyalty which the nobles vouchsafed to the person of the emperor. This loyalty was constant in the relationships between Conrad II and Boniface of Canossa, who was the ruler's greatest support in Italy. It was changeable, however, in other cases, beginning with that of Aribert whose rebellion was at the same time a clear demonstration of the powerlessness of Conrad when faced with the most determined forces in Italy and those richest in material resources and prestige. His government of the kingdom was not, generally considered, lacking in success, as is indicated by the peaceful succession in Italy of his son Henry III as ruler.

The succession had in fact already been prepared during the reign of Conrad II and by an election and coronation in Germany. This fact serves to show that the close links between the German and Italian crowns had by this time been accepted. There would certainly have been political reasons to oppose the young king in Italy, when one considers the unresolved problem of Milan; but in this regard he behaved prudently, giving up the struggle against Aribert and accepting the oaths of loyalty which the prelate brought him in Germany. At the same time, he lavished on churches and monasteries confirmations and privileges which had been requested from Italy. He took a particular interest, in these first years of his reign, in the imperial monastery of Farfa in Sabina, to which, acting on his own judgement, he gave as abbot a monk who had been a learned teacher of his own, and he took care to appoint two German canons as patriarch of Aquileia and archbishop of Ravenna. In 1043, he sent the chancellor Adalgar to Lombardy, where he presided over judicial assemblies and took action in various cities with the general aim of pacification. After the death of Aribert in 1045, the king refused the candidates for the succession put forward by the higher clergy of Milan and appointed as archbishop a prelate coming from the area around Milan – Guido da Velate – clearly with the intention of exercising closer control over the great men of the city, who were divided among themselves and insecure in their loyalty. In the spring of 1046, at an assembly of great men called at Aachen, he deposed the archbishop of Ravenna, Widgero, whom he had himself appointed two years earlier. Serious accusations of incompetence and corruption had been raised against him in Italy, under the influence of the incipient movement for ecclesiastical reform and particularly by the great rhetorician and monk, Peter Damian of Ravenna. Meanwhile, the king prepared for his first journey to Italy.

At the end of the summer, he crossed the Alps at the Brenner with a large suite of vassals and in October he was at Pavia presiding over a great ecclesiastical synod of a reforming character. In December, at the synods of Sutri and Rome, he put an end to the papal crisis which had begun two years earlier with the rising of Rome against Benedict IX, the last Tusculan pope. Three popes who claimed rights to the papal throne were deposed and the king appointed the bishop of Bamberg supreme pontiff, under the name Clement II. The king was crowned emperor by him and was invested by the Romans with the title of patrician, thus accentuating his function as protector of Rome, with the right to participate in every papal election, casting the first vote. By means of a strict control of the papacy and the three powerful metropolitan sees of northern Italy – Milan, Aquileia and Ravenna – Henry III ensured the submission of the whole episcopate throughout the kingdom of Italy in the territories formally lying within the political control of the Roman church. During the first months of 1047, he also concerned himself with the affairs of the great abbeys of Farfa, Monte Cassino and San Vincenzo al Volturno and with the political order of the Campania, into which the Normans were beginning to penetrate. The concept of an imperial kingdom in Italy, extending from the Alps throughout the whole peninsula, was thus reinforced.

The death of Clement II in the autumn of 1047, when the emperor had already been back in Germany for several months, caused the Tusculan party at Rome, which had at first found favour even with Boniface of Tuscany, to revive. But Henry III designated as pope the bishop of Bressanone, who took the name of Damasus II, and ordered Boniface to escort him to Rome. The new pope also died some weeks later and again the emperor opposed the Tusculan party with his own candidate, his cousin, the bishop of Toul, who became Leo IX. He proceeded with great firmness against the Tusculan party without, however, succeeding in dislodging them from their castles in Lazio. The pontificate of Leo IX represented, from a politico-ecclesiastical point of view, the definitive meeting point between Henry III's imperial plans and the reform movement on a European scale, which now found its centre in Rome in the person of Leo IX and some of his eminent collaborators of various national origins. This convergence served to stress the system which had by now become traditional in the Romano-German empire: the political supremacy of the crown, based on the episcopate and the religious communities; it also served, however, to aggravate the problem of the relationship of the ruling house with the great secular aristocracy. The seriousness of the situation became obvious especially on the far side of the Alps, but signs of trouble also began to appear in Italy.

Already, the fidelity of the powerful Marquess Boniface had faltered in 1048 when faced with the problem of the papal succession. Boniface died in 1052, but his widow, Beatrice of Lorraine, took over his rich estates and pre-eminent political position both north and south of the Apennines and some time later chose as her new husband the most dangerous adversary whom Henry III had in Germany: Godfrey the Bearded, made powerful by his estates and clients and already the duke of Upper Lorraine, although formally stripped of his dukedom by the emperor for rebelliousness. The union of two regional forces, which both in Germany and Italy were in conflict with the imperial supremacy, came at the same time as the military misfortunes of Leo IX in southern Italy against the Normans and made the whole problem of the kingdom of Italy a matter of urgency for Henry III. He was in fact already observing conditions in Italy with some attention, as two pieces of legislation, one criminal, one civil, promulgated in 1052 at Zurich in an assembly of the great men of the kingdom of Italy, indicate. This was an important sign of legislative renovation, even if still only sporadic, after the edict on fiefs of Conrad II. In 1054 he again summoned the great men of Italy to an assembly at Zurich at which the members of the Lombard episcopate appeared in force and he made provision for a successor to the late Leo IX, appointing a German bishop, his expert and faithful court counsellor, who was consecrated at Rome in the spring of 1055 with the name of Victor II. Meanwhile, the emperor had come down into Italy, as usual by way of the Brenner, with a following of bishops and vassals.

During Henry III's stay of several months in Italy his acts favouring churches and lively small towns such as Mantua and Ferrara take on a particular importance. They lay in the geographical region bounded by the Po and the Arno, where the influence of the Canossa family was at its strongest. It was one way of answering the legacy left by Boniface and vindicated by Beatrice and Godfrey through direct relations with the local powers. At the same time, the emperor delegated control of the duchy of Spoleto and all of the coastal areas from the Adriatic to central Italy to Victor II. The papal authority over these regions had not previously been recognized, although Victor had personally been made the representative of the empire within them. This served to extend imperial authority over the territories which marked the transition from the kingdom of Italy with its Carolingian tradition, to southern Italy, as far as Monte Cassino, as it faced the dynamic power of the Normans.

Henry the III was once again in Germany in 1056, where a reconciliation was effected with Godfrey the Bearded and Beatrice. In October he died prematurely. He left a difficult legacy in Italy. How would the Canossas act? And what would be the fate of the imperial union with the Roman church once the faithful German pope died – as he did the following year? How were the local powers now at full expansion to be incorporated? And how were the fortunes of the Normans to be checked or overthrown?

THE REGIONAL FORCES IN THE KINGDOM OF ITALY (FIRST HALF
OF THE ELEVENTH CENTURY)

The progressive incorporation of temporal jurisdiction and military power into
the ecclesiastical estates from the end of the Carolingian period and throughout
that of the imperial dynasty of Saxony, and at the same time the dynastic
orientation of such power pertaining to marquesses and counts as had remained
in lay hands, had so radically altered the public order as to make it impossible
to compare regional power structures – in the Italy of Conrad II and Henry
III – with the district divisions of Carolingian origin. The activity of the royal
messengers occurred as circumstances dictated, outside permanent territorial
plans and was limited to supplementing the normal exercise of power by the
great ones of the kingdom: churches and dynasties, rooted economically in
their landed estates and militarily in their fortresses which were increasing in
number.

Among the ecclesiastical bodies, there now emerged those holders of
metropolitan authority in whom very diverse elements of power converged:
disciplinary authority over the bishops of the suffragan dioceses, control of
the monasteries within the province of the archbishopric, authority over the
communities inhabiting the scattered estates of the metropolitan church, civil
and military government – whether by royal grant or customary law – of the
metropolis and its surrounding countryside, and the increasing presence of
armed supporters and castles. The archbishop of Milan, whose ecclesiastical
province extended from the western Alps to the Ligurian coast until it met
with the ecclesiastical province of Aquileia on Lake Garda, radiated political
and territorial influence from Milan throughout much of Lombardy, following
in the tracks of the economic expansion of the city. In spite of the absence of
a territory unified from the legal point of view and in temporal terms, the
political weight of Archbishop Aribert was such that at the crucial moment of
his struggle with Conrad II he was publicly able to mobilize the inhabitants
of his diocese of Milan, calling them all, without distinction, from peasants to
knights, to arms against the emperor.

The patriarch of Aquileia, whose ecclesiastical province included the Veneto,
Friuli, Istria and the eastern Alps, had the greater part of his remarkable estates, his exemptions and his castles concentrated in Friuli, but he was closely
bound to the authority of the emperor who appointed faithful members of
the German clergy to the patriarchate. The ecclesiastical province of Ravenna
and the archbishop held numerous countships in Romagna, within the old
exarchate, with imperial recognition, but in competition with the church of
Rome. Above all, he was supported by enormous landed estates, frequently in
alliance with the numerous aristocracy of Ravenna, composed of landowners

and perpetual leaseholders. At Ravenna, too, the metropolitan was appointed by the German ruler and chosen from among the German prelates.

Within the ecclesiastical province of Aquileia, which was fully independent of the patriarchate in temporal terms, but coordinated with it in its exemptions and subjected to the German influences operating on this ecclesiastical body, the marquess of Verona exercised the prime public authority over counties corresponding to the present-day Veneto and the county of Friuli – in other words over a territorial complex essential as a passage between the kingdoms of Germany and Italy and for the control of the hinterland of the Lagoon of Venice. The marquesses of Verona were at the same time, through personal links which went back to the time of Otto, dukes of Carinthia, and belonged to the high German aristocracy. The union of the Italian marquisate with the German duchy was the most visible expression – thanks to the special imperial attentions paid to these regions – of the connection between the two kingdoms in which they were respectively located. The military interest felt by the empire in their operations preserved in these two regions, albeit in a colourless way, the legal form of the great public districts based on land which had completely disappeared in Lombardy.

The march of Turin also preserved the original form of a great public district, which extended in a wide band along the south-western Alps from the valleys of Susa and the Canavese as far as the Ligurian Sea. Entrusted since the middle of the tenth century to the Arduinici family, the march of Turin had become an hereditary landed principality, where the power of the marquess in almost all the counties which made up the march was supported by the rich allodial estates of the family and a series of monastic foundations and endowments. The firmness of the Arduinici's roots in the region is shown by the fact that even when the male line died out in 1034, the Countess Adelaide, daughter of Marquess Olderico Manfredi, was able to maintain control of the whole area by obtaining for her successive husbands – as we have seen above – investiture with the title of marquess by the empire. The last of these was the count of Maurienne, Odo, the son and successor of that same Humbert, the founder of the house of Savoy, who had helped Conrad II to conquer the Burgundian kingdom. Maurienne, in the valley of the Arc, a tributary of the Rhône, was one of the counties belonging to Odo in Burgundy and adjacent to the lands of the Arduinici in the Susa valley, with which it communicated via the Montcenis pass.

The marriage of Odo and Adelaide, therefore, implied the union, on the two sides of the Alps, of the two dynastic powers which controlled the passage between the kingdom of Burgundy and that of Italy. This ran along the so-called 'Via Francigera', travelled by merchants, pilgrims and military detachments coming from western Europe and heading for Rome. It is easily understandable, therefore, that imperial interest in this region remained very much alive, as has been shown analagously in the case of the convergence of the duchy of Carinthia and the march of Verona. This was all the more the case since in the kingdom of Burgundy Count Odo also held the valley of Aosta. Through this ran the road which, crossing the Great St Bernard, kept the three kingdoms of Italy, Burgundy and Germany, which constituted the Romano-German empire, in touch. Proof of this persistent interest is the betrothal agreed by Henry III at the end of 1055 between his own son Henry IV, still a small child, but already elected king of Germany, and Bertha, the daughter of Odo of Maurienne and Adelaide of Turin.

Among the regional complexes of lands which had a certain unity in the kingdom of Italy, the richest and most influential was undoubtedly that brought together at the time of Conrad II by Boniface of Canossa. It became hostile in the reign of Henry III, thanks to the activities of the widow of Marquess Boniface and her new consort, Godfrey the Bearded. Here too, as was the case with the Arduinici in the march of Turin, the house of Canossa was so deeply rooted that even the disappearance of the direct male line was not enough for the vast estates to break up. The military and territorial roots, seen in terms of farms, castles, client-vassals and noble churches, were most vigorous north of the Apennines, starting in geographical terms with the counties of Brescia and Mantua and then following the line of the Po and so to Emilia and Romagna, where the Canossas had the titles to other counties and had made the city of Mantua a fulcrum of their power. The other fulcrum of the Canossas' government was in the Tuscan march at Lucca, where, after their acquisition of the march, they tried to create a juridical centre with a wide sphere of action. The character of the Canossas' domain in so far as it concerned regions which little by little came to border on each other, from the Brescia region to the papal states, still maintained that of a large heterogeneous area. It did not have any restraining tradition to unify its various members, as was the case with the march of the Arduinici, admittedly in a substantially smaller geographical area. This was the result of very different political origins; the effort of constant expansion had always been characteristic of the Canossas. The Canossas were also, undoubtedly, much inclined to create a vigorous land-based principality but they found in their very policy, dynamic and wide-ranging as it was, a good number of obstacles to be overcome in achieving their goal.

Meanwhile, other great families with a military tradition, which had obtained the title of marquess as a result of a royal decision, from the mid-tenth century on – in other words at the same time as the Arduinici – had had fortunes very different from theirs. There were the Aleramici of southern Piedmont and the Obertenghi of eastern Liguria and of Tortona and Milan. The marches or groups of counties to which they bore titles had broken up at the turn of the tenth and eleventh centuries. Faced with the Salian dynasty, the two great families now appeared to have divided into numerous smaller units, each of which had preserved the title of marquess and were scattered widely through the kingdom, with considerable differences in terms of estates and military capacity. They constituted a large number of autonomous powers, often with estates which not only did not abut upon each other, but were scattered in themselves; they were also, for the most part, rural or mountainous, around the northern Apennines and its valleys. One branch of the Obertenghi even ended up in eastern Italy, between the Veneto and Romagna, and to it belonged that same Alberto Azzo d'Este who married into the German family of the Welfs at the request of Conrad II. In these cases, the title of marquess meant no more than fidelity to a family tradition and the desire to preserve a rank which made it easier to exercise power locally, wherever their castles and armed clients might happen to be.

These seigneuries known as marquessates thus came to intertwine and become confused with innumerable counties or even offices without any public title. Henceforth, these, together with the ecclesiastical seigneuries, were to constitute the true political fabric of the kingdom. This was the case both with those which were within the areas of the regional powers and those which found themselves without, directly faced by imperial authority. In the kingdom of Italy, as elsewhere in the west, this untidy coexistence of permanently evolving local nobility, largely installed on allodial estates, gave rise to a juxtaposition and superimposition, whereby the relationships of power often found juridical support in the institution of feudal ties, or in particular forms of protection inherent in the functioning of the religious bodies.

ROYAL POWER AND REGIONAL POWERS IN ITALY FROM HENRY IV TO HENRY V

In 1056 Henry III, on his deathbed, entrusted his son Henry, a child of six, to Pope Victor II, who was present with him in Germany. Victor assured the succession of the child Henry IV to the kingdom of Germany and that of the widowed empress, Agnes of Poitou and Aquitaine, to the regency. On returning to Italy, he continued to be on good terms with Godfrey the Bearded and his brother Frederick, who became abbot of Monte Cassino. On the death of Victor in the summer of 1057, Frederick succeeded to the papal throne under the name of Stephen IX. Here was another German pope, therefore, but not one appointed by the imperial court. On the contrary, he came from the reform movement of the Roman clergy and was chosen from that very house of Lorraine which, in the person of Godfrey, had in previous years been a grave threat to Henry III, both in Germany and in Italy. The new pope recognized his brother's position as representative of the empire in the duchy of Spoleto and in those Adriatic territories where Henry III had appointed Victor II his vicar.

Stephen IX died in 1058 and the Roman aristocracy, which was hostile to the reform movement, caused the election of Benedict X. Even his choice of name seemed to connect him to the tradition of the Tusculan popes, but the reformers managed to oppose him and caused the bishop of Florence to prevail. He became Nicholas II and arrived at Rome escorted by Godfrey the Bearded. Reversing the previous political stance of the papacy, Nicholas placed his trust in the Normans of southern Italy. In this way, the political alignment which took shape around the reforming papacy put the German imperial court out of play as protector of the church of Rome. After the death of Nicholas II in 1061 this led to the papal schism, which witnessed a broad new confrontation between the anti-reform Roman aristocracy and the imperial court. The latter supported Cadalus, bishop of Parma, who was elected pope under the name of Honorius II in an Italo-German synod convened at Basle. Against him was the pope chosen by the reformers at Rome: Anselm, bishop of Lucca, of Lombard origin, who became Alexander II.

During the schism, Godfrey the Bearded remained neutral, but his wife Beatrice tried to prevent the forces which were bringing Cadalus to Rome from crossing the Apennines. Meanwhile, in Germany, the imperial court, where the influence of the archbishop of Cologne, Anno, was paramount, inclined towards recognition of Alexander II. Godfrey then came to an agreement with Anno and himself adopted the cause of Alexander, with the result that in 1063 he escorted him to Rome. In 1065, the arrival in Italy of Henry IV was awaited, that he might receive the imperial crown from Pope Alexander at Rome. But nothing came of this, either then or in the years that followed. During the minority of Henry IV and his persistent absence from Italy, the metropolitan churches of Aquileia and Ravenna remained linked to the imperial court, but at Milan, at least until 1067, the desperate struggle between the upper clergy and the Paterines continued without any German intervention: indeed, the only outside interference was papal. The abbey of Monte Cassino had been the pivot of understanding between the empire and the papacy as regards the problem of the south. Now, from 1057, and for many decades more, it became, under Abbot Desiderius, a very different type of fulcrum in the alliance between the reforming papacy and the Normans. When in the years 1066–7 there was a moment of crisis in the relationship between Alexander II and the Norman prince Richard of Capua, it was not the slow-moving imperial power, but the swift personal initiative of Godfrey the Bearded that drove back the Normans from Roman territory. Godfrey's wife Beatrice was also present at these events, as was Matilda, the daughter of Boniface of Canossa and Beatrice. This is all the more worthy of note in that Godfrey's intervention was interpreted in Germany as a slight to the authority of the very young king.

Godfrey's power had been both recognized and augmented by Henry IV in 1065 through the grant of the duchy of Lower Lorraine, which should not be confused with the duchy of Upper Lorraine of which he had been stripped in the days of Henry III. It served to strengthen Godfrey in Germany, but it also resulted in a consolidation of the prevailing position of the Canossas in Italy, as can indeed be seen in the part played by the Italian and German forces which accompanied the duke against Richard of Capua. This was all the more dangerous for imperial authority in that the function of protecting Rome had become a defence of ecclesiastical reform, which had taken on a European dimension and was leading to an incipient centralization of papal power in the ecclesiastical government of western Christendom. The importance of Godfrey's help can be seen in 1068, when in consonance with the fluctuations in attitude of King Henry and Anno of Cologne, he too began to pay new attention to the excommunicated bishop of Parma, Cadalus, thus provoking the indignant surprise of Peter Damian, who wrote exhorting him to maintain himself worthy of the high responsibility which he bore as first, after the king, of all of the princes of the Romano-German empire. In Italy the predominance of the house of Canossa–Lorraine was further consolidated by the carefully planned marriage arranged between Godfrey the Hunchback and Matilda of Canossa, the daughter and heir of the late Marquess Boniface and Beatrice. The union of the duchy of Lower Lorraine and the Tuscan march, with all the other jurisdictions and immense estates belonging to the two houses, thus lasted beyond the death of Godfrey the Bearded, which occurred at the end of 1069.

The union did not, however, last much longer, on account of the disagreements which arose between the second Godfrey and his wife Matilda. Politically, a separation was determined between the German might of Godfrey, allied to the king, and the Italian power of Matilda and Beatrice, allied to the reforming papacy. This was seen particularly clearly after the death of Alexander II in 1073 and the accession to the papal throne of the brave and spirited Archdeacon Hildebrand, who took the name of Gregory VII and whose election involved no German intervention. The heterogeneous complex under the sway of the house of Canossa remained intact from eastern Lombardy to the Tuscan march, but was entrusted to two women who, formally, were empowered to inherit lands and castles, but not the functions of marquess, except through marriage with the young duke and marquess Godfrey. The difference between the legal situation at a high official level and the real position of this far-flung regional domination, which was essentially the convergence of numerous local powers, the inheritance of Boniface of Canossa, made imperial intervention possible, with destabilizing consequences. This aggravated processes which had been operating for decades within the whole structure, as a result of the energy of the urban centres and the client-vassals. After the death of Beatrice in Tuscany in 1076 and, tragically, Godfrey in the north of Germany, Matilda, in Italy, found herself alone at the apex of a power structure menaced by internal movements and the hostility of the king.

Meanwhile, during the last years of the pontificate of Alexander II, the king had become involved in the struggle which had flared up in Milan over the replacement of Archbishop Guido, who had been solemnly chosen by him and then condemned by Pope Alexander and had not been able to maintain his position in the city. The most powerful metropolitan in northern Italy thus seemed about to escape permanently from the control of the German court, just as had occurred with the Roman papacy. But the increasing rigour of the reform movement and its concentration at Rome, as a result of the action of Gregory VII – in contrast to much of the episcopate – offered the king new opportunities for intervention, both in the see of Milan and, after the clamorous rupture with Rome, in the papacy itself.

When at the beginning of 1077, the king visited Italy for the first time, Matilda of Canossa played a leading part in the fragile reconciliation between the pope and the king. Nevertheless, the profound humiliation, both at the personal and at the political-institutional level, which Henry IV endured in 1076 on account of the upsetting of the traditional balance between the supreme imperial power and the authority of the church of Rome – and which had been obvious to all at Canossa – remained. This resulted in such general confusion and such violent clashes between the supporters of Pope Gregory and those of the antipope Clement III, archbishop of Ravenna, and between those of the king and of the anti-king who had arisen in Germany, that Matilda, faced by the double schism which had developed in the church and in the kingdom, involving most of the bishoprics, soon found herself dangerously involved. The internal rifts which troubled all her many lands were aggravated by privileges granted by the king to cities aspiring to independence and upset all plans to consolidate her various political holdings into a working unit. It was this which induced her in 1080 to ensure her own political survival by formally making over all her own allodial estates to the church of Rome, reserving, however, the personal right to dispose of them freely, albeit under the aegis of the papacy. This did not, however, prevent Henry IV in the following year, on the occasion of his second incursion into Italy, from putting Matilda beyond the pale of the empire and declaring all her rights and possessions, both allodial and feudal, abolished. The sentence was in almost no case effectively carried out, but it served to legitimize all the attacks made against her power.

The varying fortunes of war, which had spread throughout the whole of the kingdom of Italy and the lands formally belonging to the papacy, brought the king to Rome on more than one occasion. It was there at last, in 1084, that the antipope Clement crowned him emperor. But Rome was threatened by the Normans, supporters of Gregory VII, and the emperor abandoned the city and returned shortly afterwards to Germany. He remained at a distance for three unbroken years. After the brutal Norman occupation of Rome, the pope took refuge at Monte Cassino and died at Salerno in 1085, still under the protection of the Normans. The Roman cardinals chose as his successor Desiderius, abbot of Monte Cassino, who became Victor III. He was the candidate suggested by one of the Norman princes and accepted by Matilda of Canossa.

Notwithstanding the serious disturbances within her dominions and although she felt the need for a general policy of reconciliation, Matilda remained – over and above her personal intentions and those of her vassals – the centre of the opposition to Henry IV. This became clear when Victor III's successor, Urban II (1088–99), persuaded her to take a new husband: the eighteen-year-old Welf V, the son of Welf IV, duke of Bavaria. Thus two powerful sources of hostility to the emperor in Germany and Italy were realigned. It was a connection associated with and attuned to that between the Welfs and the Este, which Conrad II had in his time sought to promote as part of his imperial plans and which now persisted to the prejudice of the empire. Duke Welf IV was the son of the Obertenghi marquess Alberto Azzo II d'Este, who was still alive in 1090 when Henry IV once again entered Italy. This political constellation had been functioning for years as a military power and in 1093 it could also reckon on the rebellion of King Conrad against his father, the emperor. Conrad had already, some years earlier in Germany, been raised by his father to the royal title and was now crowned king by the archbishop of Milan, against the background of an alliance of Milan and other cities with Matilda and Welf V. In fact, in 1095 Matilda found herself once again alone at the height of her power in Italy, owing to the breakdown of her unnatural marriage with the young Welf, who returned to Germany and, with his father Welf IV, began to veer towards the supporters of Henry IV. In this same year, at the urgent request of Matilda and Urban II, a very different political marriage was contracted by King Conrad with the daughter of Roger, the powerful Norman count of Sicily. It served to confirm the increasing isolation of the emperor within the whole Italian framework, especially when viewed in the context of the vast success of Pope Urban's ecclesiastical actions throughout Europe.

Henry IV was forced to take action in the Veneto and then in 1097 crossed back to the further side of the Alps. He had spent seven years of hard and taxing personal effort in Italy and in the end they had been barren of results. Conrad in his turn became an unwilling instrument of Matilda, while his father in Germany declared his deposition as king and raised another son in his place: Henry V. This Henry, after the premature death of Conrad in Italy, also ended by rebelling against his father, who died two years later in 1106. For years, the greater part of the kingdom of Italy was aligned with Urban II's successor, Paschal II (1099–1118), supported by the Countess Matilda. She confirmed the new pontiff in the gift of all her allodial estates made to Gregory VII some twenty years earlier.

The fortress of Canossa in the Emilian Apennines held sway over lands which radiated out in all directions and virtually everywhere, given its inter-regional scope, acquired the characteristics of countship and marquisate. The tendency to adopt symbols appropriate to the mentality of a principality imitating a kingdom was made clear both in the activities of the chancellery and in the poem by the monk Donizo celebrating Matilda and the house of Canossa. This symbolism was in keeping with the influential presence of famous jurists in the countess's suite. As a princedom, however, it was weak, for it was increasingly split internally by local forces, in spite of the gradual settling of the ecclesiastical disputes. It can quite accurately be pointed out that although the great ecclesiastical struggle caused problems within the domains, it also gave Matilda a position of the greatest prominence in the Italian theatre of action and caused her to seek out powerful allies. This serves to explain her two marriages, although both ended badly, and explains the rather different expedient which she adopted in 1099, when she chose an enterprising and militarily vigorous gentleman as her adopted son. This was Guido Guerra I, rich in estates in the Tuscan and Romagnan Apennines. But in the end it was the need for a reconciliation between Matilda and the king which prevailed.

In 1111, after Henry V's journey to Italy and the imperial coronation that Paschal II was constrained to perform, the emperor and Matilda finally met. The countess, presumably with the intention of avoiding the breaking up of the Canossa lands, declared Henry personally to be the heir to all her allodial possessions and enormous mass of lands and castles, particularly in the regions of Italy adjacent to the Po. Henry occupied these for the most part on his second journey to Italy, after the death of the countess in 1115. This legacy could only be reconciled with Matilda's previous bequests to the church of Rome in so far as the countess had, in these donations, reserved the right to dispose of the estates which she placed under papal protection as she chose. This created a delicate legal situation from which arose the interminable controversy that was destined to poison relations between the empire and the papacy in Italy at both a territorial and a political level. As regards the jurisdiction over the marquisate that the countess exercised, this was a matter for Henry as emperor and he entrusted the Tuscan march to people from Germany, who proved completely incapable of pacifying the region.

Thus, against Matilda's hopes, there crumbled away the concentration of lands and power representing a large part of the kingdom of Italy, which for almost a century the family of Canossa had controlled, in harmony or dishar-mony with the empire. Meanwhile, in 1091, the march of Turin had also broken up on the death of the Countess Adelaide, who had always maintained an equi-librium in the very thick of the fight between the empire and the papacy. The march of Turin did not dissolve, as did the dominions of the Canossas, through the dying out of the dynastic line, but because of the numerous claimants to the succession and the prevalence of the dynasty's transalpine interests over those of the branches present in Italy. The most profound reason, however, for the dissolution of these two dynastic powers – Canossa and Turin – lay in the development of local forces. This was also true of the march of Verona which, although still formally united to the duchy of Carinthia, provides evidence of its last signs of jurisdictional activity in 1123, towards the end of the reign of Henry V. The patriarchs of Aquileia, on the other hand, consolidated their own lands in a relatively coherent manner. These were originally landed estates, which took on the quality of a princely domain in 1077, through Henry IV's gift of the countship of Friuli to the patriarch in perpetuity. The estate of the bishop of Trento also assumed the form of territorial principality through the county of Trento, which was assigned to the bishop as early as 1027 in a charter issued by Conrad II. These two ecclesiastical principalities of Trento and Aquileia, of fundamental importance for communications between Germany and Italy, remained under imperial control. The metropolitan see of Ravenna, however, was involved in the schism of the antipope Clement III and thus escaped the domination of the empire during the last years of Henry V. By submitting to the reforming papacy, it lost that strength of political independence which had made it a pivot of power on a regional basis. The same had already happened to the metropolitan see of Milan.

The more or less general disintegration of regional coordination among the metropolitan churches and the dynasties of marquesses in the kingdom of Italy gave room for the military undertakings of Henry V, which were made easier by the occupation of the lands of the Countess Matilda and had been caused by new disagreements with the reforming popes. When, finally, in 1122 agreement was reached with Pope Calixtus II in the Concordat of Worms, the radical change which had occurred in Italy to the prejudice of the empire became clear. The presence of the king or of his representative at episcopal and abbatial elections had been laid down for Germany, but not for Italy, and this meant that south of the Alps it was impossible for the empire to control with any degree of efficiency the functioning of the centres of power, the bishoprics and great abbeys, which had for a long time been the main stable points of reference for the royal authority. Futhermore, when Henry V died in 1125, a controversy arose over the bequest of the estates of the Countess Matilda, the acquisition of which had been the greatest political triumph achieved by the emperor in Italy.

THE WIDESPREAD DISINTEGRATION OF THE KINGDOM OF ITALY
AND THE DEVELOPMENT OF THE CITIES AND THE PAPAL DOMAIN

The progressive decline of royal power in Italy under the Salian dynasty and the accompanying crisis of the regional authorities, whether operating in alliance with or in opposition to the kingdom, brought into evidence numerous local forces. These had for some time been building, on a small scale, but often very efficiently, potential political frameworks for the social development of the kingdom. The process occurred at the same time though in different forms in both rural and urban contexts, but it was clearly linked to the increase in population and production and to the greater mobility of men and the wider dispersal of new institutional models.

Throughout the countryside of northern and central Italy, small territories were being formed, as was occurring more or less everywhere in the post-Carolingian west. These territories were often fairly coherent from a topographical point of view and were protected by the military force of a landed owner, which might be an episcopal church, a community of canons, a monastery or a family with a military tradition. The territory rarely coincided with the farm lands of the lord, even when its fulcrum was the administrative centre of the estate. This was because it included a complex of lands which might well belong to different proprietors and were unified only by the protection offered by the lord to all the residents of the area by means of armed force. As a rule, the heart of each of these local dominions was a fortress or castle and the strength of an ecclesiastical body or a noble family was commensurate with the number of castles they held and their strategic positions. This was true for all those who held power, from those who had only a single local estate to the metropolitan churches and ecclesiastical princedoms and the families bearing the titles of count or marquess. The most notable case was that of the Canossas, whose power was rooted not so much in their public offices given by the king, but in the number of fortresses they possessed and the innumerable local armed clients at their disposal. The title of count or marquess was, however, an important instrument coordinating the numerous noble estates of a great dynasty.

This widespread process of the accumulation of local power had its roots in the crisis of public order of the tenth century, but becomes much clearer in Italy during the eleventh in the reports of the local ruling and legal powers, as the activity of the notaries gradually increased, creating documents for the transmission of lands and titles. The terminology used for the estate of a noble to distinguish the rights inherent in any landed property from those judicial and coercive rights of a potentially public nature shows that the legal world realized that responsibilities which really belonged to the royal appanage were now being incorporated into the powers of the local nobility and were helping these lords to become aware of it. The consequent fragmentation of political power created the possibility of communication between the lords and the rural people who were their dependants in terms of land, as the agreements drawn up locally from the mid-eleventh century show. These were the roots of the rural communes which subsequently came to be organized in the twelfth century.

The political fragmentation had, however, both complications and correctives in the web of relationships which proliferated among all the centres of power. There were, first of all, the connections at all levels between the churches and the lay nobility, who might be their founders or patrons, or else their vassals. Especially vast were the donations and protection granted to the monastic churches by Adelaide of Turin and Matilda of Canossa. To these should be added the associations, not only religious, but also involving protection and temporal dependence, among the churches themselves, both greater and lesser. The control exercised by the metropolitan churches over those to which they held title should be particularly considered. Again, feudal relationships among lay nobles persisted and increased. This might either be because the holders of fortresses, the representatives of the nobles who were the true owners of the fiefs, were in the process of becoming lords themselves, bound to the owner by the claims of vassalage, or, alternatively, because certain allodial lords took on the bonds of vassalage from other lords through acquiring lands as fiefs. There were also relationships among equals within a group of vassals, all depending on the same feudal lord. The most famous case is that of the many vassals of Matilda, who maintained a certain unity even after the death of the countess, electing a leader although not thereby disavowing their fealty as vassals to Henry V as heir to the estates of the house of Canossa.

The demographic and economic growth in both the countryside and the cities was remarkable in the kingdom of Italy, as opposed to the lands on the other side of the Alps, and this too had its political implications. In most cases, from the tenth century on, the urban centres showed their inclination to self-government, in collaboration or the reverse with the temporal government of the bishop; and their awareness of their own strength was much clearer than in the countryside. Under the Salian dynasty, thanks to the development of commerce and the means of production, the growing attention paid to the landed proprietors of the surrounding area and the client vassals of the bishop and other powerful men served to stress, especially in the Po valley, the importance of this military class, an aristocracy which was also urban. This led to alternating alliances and disagreements with the other groups within the urban population, which served at the same time to feed ecclesiastical, commercial and military competition among the various cities. The disagreements were complicated by the spread of a number of religious movements, Patarine in flavour, and also by the conflicts between the reforming papacy and the empire, with resulting ecclesiastical schisms in the episcopal cities. This became obvious from the late eleventh to the early twelfth centuries through the appearance in the main cities of a suitable organ for political administration: the 'consulate'. This was an office of variable duration, although it subsequently tended to become annual: it was formed by a limited group of eminent citizens, chosen from among the notables outstanding for their economic position or their military standing.

The most powerful communes, through their economic and military strength and the breadth of their fields of action, were Milan, heir to the political authority of the archbishop in Lombardy, and the maritime republics of Genoa and Pisa. In Milan, the dominant military class was formed from the military clients of the archbishop and was in its turn distinct within the socially supreme group of the 'capitanei' and within that immediately below, the vavasours. At Genoa and Pisa, the dominant class was a mixture of shipowners and great landowners. They were generally speaking active in the hinterland, in the tradition of the minor aristocracy, and also to a large extent at sea. They undertook military operations against the Muslims settled in the large islands of the Tyrrhenian Sea, in North Africa and in the Iberian peninsula. The events in the Lagoon of Venice held a position all their own, for the region had always remained apart from the kingdom of Italy and from the developments, both aristocratic and urban, typical of western Europe. This was because of the Venetians' highly individual political traditions of Byzantine origin and also because of their close relationship, both commercial and diplomatic, with the Byzantine world as well as with the Germano-Latin one. During the eleventh century, the city of Venice, as a result of the coordination of the island communities which gravitated around the Rialto, continued to rule itself politically under a duke, who held the position for life, helped by an aristocracy which was daring at sea and so strengthened its predominance in the Adriatic.

The political disintegration which has been observed in the kingdom of Italy can also be seen in the regions where the rights of the empire intersected with the more or less theoretical ones of the church of Rome, of Romagna and Marche, across the territories of Perugia and as far as Lazio. But the ecclesiastical expansion of the reforming papacy was reflected also at a level of regional politics, above all in Lazio. Here, steps were taken to eliminate or reduce the power of the aristocratic centres most dangerous to the independent action of the papacy; among the numerous noble and allodial fortresses, those belonging to the church of Rome increased and multiplied. Meanwhile, a central financial administration and a chancery were organized and use was made of the college of cardinals, with the help of the new bureaucracy in order to ensure likewise the temporal dominion of Lazio. While local ascendancy, whether on an ecclesiastical or dynastic basis, was in decline in the heart of the kingdom of Italy, along its southern edges a form of regional rule was being organized, hinging on the church of Rome, which was destined to play an active role in the political history of Italy, together with the city communes of the north and the Norman might in the south.

SOUTHERN ITALY IN THE
ELEVENTH CENTURY

G. A. Loud

IN the year 1000 southern Italy was divided into three distinct zones. Apulia and Calabria were ruled by the Byzantine empire, the island of Sicily by the Arabs (as it had been since the conquest of the ninth century) and the central mountains and the Campania were divided between three Lombard principalities, those of Capua (from a few miles north of Naples to the Monti Ausoni and the upper valley of the River Liri, the border with the papal states), Salerno in the south (from the Amalfitan peninsula down to the Gulf of Policastro) and Benevento (in the inland mountain district, from Avellino northwards to the Adriatic). In addition, to the north of the principality of Benevento, in the Abruzzi (roughly from the River Trigno northwards), lay a series of independent counties, partly Lombard, partly Frankish in origin, but this region was in almost every aspect, geographic, economic and social, separate from the south proper. On the west coast there were three small duchies, Gaeta, Naples and Amalfi, which had throughout the earlier middle ages retained a determined, if at times precarious, independence from their larger neighbours, the principalities of Capua and Salerno. Both Naples and Amalfi still acknowledged some dependence on the Byzantine empire, largely as a means of protection against the aggressive instincts of the Lombard princes.

Fragmented as the political divisions of southern Italy were, the cultural and religious divide was more complex still, for it did not coincide with the political boundaries. In the Byzantine dominions the population of northern and central Apulia was almost entirely Lombard, by this stage speaking a Latin-Romance dialect, and observing Latin religious rites. Southern Apulia and Lucania were more mixed, although the Greek part of the population was probably in the majority, and had been strengthened in Lucania by emigration from further south during the course of the tenth century. Calabria was mainly, and in the south entirely, Greek, but with still some Lombards in the area north of the Sila Grande which had in the ninth century been part of the principality of Salerno. On the island of Sicily, although conversion and emigration had taken their toll, a substantial Greek Christian population remained, concentrated in the north-east of the island between Mount Etna and Messina.[1] Hence in both the Byzantine and the Muslim zones there were potentially disaffected sections of the population whose loyalties, particularly their religious affiliations, were suspect.

The Byzantine government in Italy was under considerable threat *c.* 1000, both from internal disaffection and from sporadic, but from the 990s increasingly serious, raids from Arab Sicily, which affected both Calabria and southern Apulia. In the summer of 1003 Bari, the capital of Byzantine Italy, was besieged for four months, and only relieved by the arrival of a fleet from Venice. In 1009, quite possibly sparked off by the impact of a very harsh winter immediately before, revolt broke out in the coastal cities of Apulia, and for some months, and possibly longer, Bari and Trani were in the hands of the rebels. Reinforcements had to be despatched from Constantinople to quell the uprising, whose leader, a Lombard from Bari called Melus, fled to the Lombard principalities of the west. The threat had been made more serious by a simultaneous Muslim attack on northern Calabria, in which Cosenza had been sacked.[2]

Byzantine rule was becoming unpopular in Apulia, not least because of the fiscal burden exacted by a centralized and efficient administration, and the 1009 revolt, and a second and almost equally serious one in 1017–18, were put down only with difficulty. Nevertheless it would be wrong to see Byzantium as necessarily weak. If anything its power grew stronger in the early eleventh century, certainly by comparison with the other zones where authority was tending to disintegrate. In Sicily the emirs of the Kalbid dynasty were still more or less in control, but the deposition of the amir Ja'far in 1019 after a revolt in Palermo was a sign that all was not well, and indeed from the 1030s onwards the internal cohesion of the island was to collapse almost completely, which had the beneficial effect of freeing the Christian mainland from the threat of piratical raids. In the Lombard principalities central authority was already growing progressively weaker, particularly in Benevento, and although for a brief period between 1008 and 1014 the two principalities of Benevento and Capua were re-united, as they had been for most of the tenth century, this had no practical effect.[3] Already, in the 960s and 970s, the Byzantines had been able to consolidate their hold over Lucania, and in the closing years of the

---

[1] The extent of this emigration and of the shift of the Greek population northwards in Calabria has been much debated. See Ménager (1958/9); Guillou (1963) and (1965); Loud (1988), pp. 215–18, and (2000), pp. 54–8, for a summary.

[2] Hoffmann (1969), pp. 112–14, would prefer to date Melus's rebellion to 1011 on the basis of the *Annales Barenses* (*MGH S*, v, p. 53), but most authorities prefer 1009.

[3] Capua and Benevento were ruled by two branches of the same family. Pandulf IV of Capua (1014–49) and Landulf V of Benevento were in fact brothers. Given this relationship, the practice of associating sons with their fathers' rule during the latter's lifetime, and the use of a very limited stock of personal

tenth century they had extended their rule into the area between the southern Apennines and the Gargano peninsula, northwards as far as the River Fortore, at the expense of the prince of Benevento to whose authority this region had earlier at least nominally been subject. The Byzantine catepan (governor) from 1018, Basil Boiannes, was to devote considerable attention to strengthening the empire's hold in this area.

Southern Italy was thus politically and culturally fragmented, and something of a power vacuum. If Byzantium was, despite all local difficulties, the strongest force in the south of the peninsula, the ability of the Byzantine government to intervene there was dependent on having resources to spare from its heavy commitments in other parts of its far-flung empire. In the first years of the eleventh century the emperor Basil II was grappling to enforce his authority in the Balkans and to incorporate the Bulgarian kingdom into the empire. Only when this was successfully accomplished could troops and money be spared on any scale for southern Italy. Similarly, while the German empire claimed overlordship over the whole of Italy – including the south, and in particular over the Lombard principalities – in practice imperial intervention was sporadic and ineffective. Only when Otto I had worked in alliance with Pandulf I of Capua in the 960s and 970s had the German emperor had much influence, and Otto II's disastrous defeat by the Arabs in Calabria in 982 was not a precedent designed to encourage German involvement in the south. Nor indeed was Otto III's foray to Capua and Benevento in 999; while less catastrophic, it had been equally barren in result.[4] Distance, and the pressure of other and more vital interests, inevitably prevented the western empire from taking more than an occasional interest in southern Italy.

Despite the political fragmentation of the region, contemporary chroniclers believed it to be prosperous: 'the land which brings forth milk and honey, and so many good things'.[5] Clearly this ecstatic opinion cannot have applied to every part of it. Much of inland southern Italy is very mountainous, with communication largely confined to narrow river valleys. The Abruzzi and Lucania in particular were heavily forested. Several coastal districts were marshy and malarial, most unsuitable therefore for settlement, while other areas such as the limestone Murge in inland Apulia and the eastern coast of Calabria are arid and infertile. Calabria, with the Sila mountains in the north and the Aspromonte

---

names, the numbering of the princes (itself anachronistic) poses pitfalls for the unwary, and in consequence not all historians agree on such numbers. The numbers used here for the Lombard princes are those most commonly found.

[4] Benevento had recently resisted an imperial siege, and his nominee as prince of Capua was expelled a year later, Loud (2000), p. 27.

[5] 'la terre qui mene lat et miel et tant belles coses', Amatus of Monte Cassino, *Storia de' Normanni* [henceforth Amatus], lib. 1 c. 19, p. 24.

in the south, can never have supported a very large population. But there were other areas, the Terra di Lavoro around Capua and Naples, the Tavoliere of northern Apulia, the slopes of Mount Etna in eastern Sicily, which were (and are) notable for their rich soil and fertility. Grain from Apulia, Campania and Sicily, wine from almost everywhere under 800 metres in height, fruit (much of it exotic to northern eyes like figs, almonds and water melons) from the Campania and northern and eastern Sicily, olive production which was growing in the eleventh century, especially in central Apulia, and the surprisingly extensive cultivation of mulberries and silkworms in Calabria, again expanding very rapidly in the eleventh century, all contributed to this picture of prosperity. Letters from Jewish merchants in Cairo suggest that Calabria was second only to Muslim Spain as a source for silk in the eleventh-century Mediterranean. And not only parts of Calabria and Lucania but other seemingly unpromising areas like the Cilento in the south of the principality of Salerno, another steeply mountainous region, were being opened up for settlement at this time. The cities of the west coast, above all Amalfi, played a significant role in Mediterranean trade, which had developed despite the Christian/Muslim division. From there corn, timber, even wine, were exported to North Africa and Egypt, while luxury items were imported from the Byzantine empire. Salerno, according to a contemporary, 'furnished all that one could desire by land and sea' and Amalfi was 'a wealthy and populous city, none richer in silver, gold and garments from innumerable places'.[6]

When therefore *c.* 1000 men from northern Europe whom the contemporary sources call 'Normans' began to arrive in the south of Italy, at first as pilgrims and then in the hope of employment and profit, the region was both temptingly prosperous and also unstable enough, particularly in the area of Lombard rule in the west and centre, to provide ample opportunities for soldiers of fortune. By the 1030s the mercenaries were sufficiently numerous to be themselves a factor undermining the stability of the south, and from the early 1040s onwards the erstwhile mercenaries began to become masters, until by the end of the century they controlled the whole of mainland southern Italy and had conquered the island of Sicily from the Arabs. But, because the Normans secured mastery of southern Italy, it would be misleading to see that process as inevitable. It was only gradually that they transformed their role from employees to conquerors. Their takeover was slow and piecemeal, a process of infiltration as much as invasion. Furthermore, while the newcomers took over the existing provinces and principalities, provided new rulers and introduced new institutions like

---

[6] 'Et quodcunque velis terrave marive ministrat . . . Urbs haec dives opum, populoque referta videtur', William of Apulia, *La Geste de Robert Guiscard* [henceforth W. Apulia], lib. III lines 475–9, p. 190. See generally Citarella (1968); Guillou (1974); and von Falkenhausen (1975).

the fief, they were not that numerous and never constituted a complete and homogeneous ruling class, either in lay society or the church. Native traditions remained strong, especially in the towns, and there was never such a polarity between the Norman governing class and indigenous subjects as there was in Anglo-Norman England.

The view that the Norman takeover was inexorable is largely derived from the contemporary chronicles celebrating the conquest. The three most important chronicle sources of the time, all written towards the end of the century, presented the viewpoint of the conquerors, and all concluded that the victory of the Normans was divinely ordained. To quote William of Apulia's verse biography of Robert Guiscard (duke of Apulia 1059–85), which was written c. 1095–9, 'it was pleasing to the All-Powerful King who controls seasons and kingdoms that the Apulian littoral which had for a long time been held by the Greeks should no longer be inhabited by them, and that the Norman race, distinguished by its fierce knighthood, should enter it, expel the Greeks and rule over Italy'.[7] Similar sentiments were expressed in the 'History of the Normans' by Amatus of Monte Cassino, written c. 1080. Some twenty years later a Norman monk of Catania, Geoffrey Malaterra, writing the 'Deeds of Count Roger of Sicily', took as his theme a slightly different but still closely related concept, the moral qualities of the Normans as against the deficiencies of the natives, whether Lombard or Greek, which had therefore made the conquest inevitable and divinely sanctioned.[8] Yet all these viewpoints were *partis pris*, and were written in the consciousness that the conquest had happened, was by then irreversible and, because it had taken place, must therefore have been in accordance with God's will. But that does not mean that we should necessarily allow medieval teleology to distort rational historical explanation, and the use of documentary sources must inevitably modify the cut-and-dried picture of contemporary historians. Nor should we assume that every action of the invaders was from the first directed towards conquest. William of Apulia might, for example, suggest that the Normans deliberately fostered discord among the Lombards to prevent any one party gaining a decisive advantage, which indeed they may have done.[9] But we cannot assume that the idea of conquest was therefore present from the first; such a tactic may have been intended to

[7] 'Postquam complacuit regi mutare potenti, Tempora cum regnis, ut Graecis Apulia tellus iam possessa diu non amplius incoleretur, Gens Normannorum feritate insignis equestri intrat, et expulsis Latio dominatur Achivis', W. Apulia, I lines 1–5, p. 98.

[8] Amatus, dedication, p. 3. Geoffrey Malaterra, *De rebus gestis Roger Rogerii Calabriae et Siciliae comitis* [henceforth Malaterra]. On the Lombards, 'gens invidissima', 'genus semper perfidissimum', *ibid.*, lib. I cc. 6, 13, pp. 10–14; on the Greeks, 'gens deliciis et voluptatibus, potius quam belli studiis ex more dedita', lib. III c. 13, p. 64. On Malaterra, Capitani (1977), especially pp. 6–11, 30–3; Wolf (1995), pp. 143–71.

[9] W. Apulia, I lines 156–64, pp. 106–8.

continue the need for their own employment rather than a Machiavellian ploy to undermine their hosts.

The conquest of southern Italy thus fell into three distinct stages. First, up to the early 1040s the Normans acted as mercenaries, selling their swords to almost every power in the south, except for the Arabs, 'fighting for the purpose of gain' in Malaterra's succinct phrase.[10] From 1042 onwards they acted in their own right, extending their operations from the Lombard zone into Apulia, and in the 1040s and 1050s employment turned into conquest. The capture of Capua in 1058 and the investiture of the Norman leaders Robert Guiscard and Richard of Aversa by the pope in 1059 as, respectively, duke of Apulia and prince of Capua effectively closed this phase, even though not all of southern Italy was yet in Norman hands. The papal investiture was a sign that the Normans were there to stay, and it recognized that *by then* their takeover was inevitable. The third phase was one of consolidation on the mainland, mopping up the last bastions of Byzantine rule in Apulia and Calabria, combined with a new enterprise, the conquest of the island of Sicily. This last operation, begun in 1061, lasted a full generation, not being completed until the capture of the last Muslim fortresses in the south-east of the island in 1091. While this was still going on the Norman ruler of Apulia, Robert Guiscard, began to play a significant role on the European stage. From 1080 he was the main supporter and ally of the Gregorian reform papacy in its dispute with the German emperor Henry IV, and in addition he launched a full-scale assault on the mainland provinces of the Byzantine empire.

THE CONQUEST: THE MERCENARY PHASE

The first significant involvement in southern Italy of those whom the contemporary sources call the Normans came in the second Apulian revolt led by Melus in 1017. According to the 'Deeds of Robert Guiscard' of William of Apulia (written, it must be remembered, seventy years later) it was preceded by a seemingly chance meeting between the rebel leader and a group of Norman pilgrims at the shrine of St Michael on Monte Gargano.[11] Whether William's poem was recounting fact or legend, and whether such involvement was purely chance or if it occurred with the connivance of one or more of the Lombard princes or of Pope Benedict VIII, has been endlessly debated. Two points are however clear. This was *not* the very first contact of the Normans with southern Italy, and their role in the rebellion was essentially auxiliary, as mercenaries strengthening, probably in no great numbers, an indigenous rising.

---

[10] 'Causa militari aliquid lucrandi', Malaterra, 1.6, p. 10.   [11] W. Apulia, 1 lines 11–27, pp. 98–100.

The tradition preserved by the *History* of Amatus of Monte Cassino was that a group of Normans first arrived in southern Italy, as pilgrims returning from Jerusalem, at Salerno 'before 1000', and helped to repel an Arab attack on the city. Once again attempts have been made to dismiss this episode as legend, or to re-date it to shortly before the Apulian rebellion of 1017. But there is good reason to suggest that there was a Muslim attack on Salerno around the turn of the century, and it would be quite explicable if Norman mercenaries were employed in small numbers in the south from that time onwards.[12] Several different sources suggest that political exiles from Normandy were among them. The question of numbers is also a difficult one. Amatus said that there were forty pilgrims in the group aiding Salerno. His account of the 1017–18 revolt contradicts itself, saying first that some 250 Normans were involved and then that 3,000 were, of whom only 500 survived.[13] One might tend towards the smaller figure, but whatever the case it seems clear that there were not very many Normans present, and that casualties were heavy. After initial successes in northern Apulia, the rebels were crushingly defeated in October 1018 by a substantially reinforced Byzantine army led by the new catepan Basil Boiannes. Melus fled, ultimately to seek the aid of the German emperor Henry II, and the surviving Normans either went to the Lombard principalities or, soon afterwards, enlisted in the pay of the victor.

During the decade when Basil Boiannes was catepan (1018–28), Byzantine prestige and power in Italy was at its height. The successful conclusion of the war with Bulgaria released resources for Italy in a way that had not been possible for many years, and Boiannes consolidated his hold on northern Apulia by the construction of a series of fortified settlements on hill sites along the fringe of the Apulian plain at Troia, Dragonara, Fiorentina and Civitate, each of which was established as a garrison and a bishopric.[14] Furthermore the Lombard princes were now much more amenable to Byzantine influence than hitherto (though it may be that Guaimar III of Salerno had always been well disposed to the eastern empire).[15] Pandulf IV of Capua had not been, however, and had supported and aided Melus's rebellion. But after its failure he not only formally acknowledged Byzantine overlordship, but accepted a substantial bribe to permit Byzantine troops to enter his principality and arrest Melus's brother-in-law, Dattus, who was taken back to Bari and there executed.

---

[12] Amatus, 1.17–18, pp. 21–3, and cf. *Chronica monasterii Casinensis* [henceforth *Chron. Cas.*], lib. II c. 37, p. 236. The discussion by Hoffmann (1969) is fundamental and supersedes earlier ones such as Joranson (1948). Damage done by an earlier Muslim attack is referred to in a charter of November 1005, *Codex diplomaticus Cavensis*, pp. 40–2 no. 898 (there misdated to 1035). See now Loud (2000), pp. 60–6.

[13] Amatus, 1.22–3, pp. 30–1.   [14] See Borsari (1966–7); von Falkenhausen (1967), pp. 55–7.

[15] Hoffmann (1969), pp. 123–4. The Catepan Basil Mesardonites had been at Salerno in October 1011, von Falkenhausen (1967), pp. 175–6.

It was this strengthening of the Byzantine position, combined with the pleas of the exiled Melus and Pope Benedict VIII, which led Henry II of Germany to intervene in southern Italy in 1022. His motive was to vindicate the imperial overlordship which had been recognized, at least in the Lombard principalities, in the later tenth century. The pope wished to have his authority recognized over the Latin churches of Apulia, as opposed to that of the patriarch of Constantinople, an issue which had already inflamed relations between the two from the 960s onwards, and which the general breakdown in relations between Rome and Constantinople after 1009 (over the western use of the *filioque* clause in the creed) can only have made worse. However, just as in 999 with Otto III's intervention, that of Henry II had a purely short-term effect. Pandulf IV of Capua was deposed and replaced as prince by his cousin the count of Teano, but Salerno successfully resisted a half-hearted siege by imperial forces and an attempted invasion of Apulia was defeated by the equally successful defiance of the new border fortress of Troia, manned by Norman mercenaries now in the catepan's employment. With his army wilting in the heat of the south Italian summer the emperor withdrew. His nominee as prince of Capua lasted longer than Otto III's, but within four years had been driven out by Pandulf IV, whom Henry's successor, Conrad II, had released from his German prison.

After 1022 Byzantine authority in Apulia and Calabria remained unchallenged for almost twenty years. During this period the internal unity of Islamic Sicily collapsed, and indeed an expedition to reconquer the island, already planned but never executed in the 1020s, was set in motion in 1038, to be frustrated by quarrels among its leaders and the recall of the commander-in-chief George Maniakes. Meanwhile Pandulf IV sought to restore his authority in the principality of Capua and the Lombard princes fought each other. The details of these internecine wars may be passed over very briefly, but two aspects should be considered significant. One was the attempts, first by Pandulf IV and then by Guaimar IV of Salerno (1027–52), to achieve overall predominance in Lombard south Italy. To quote William of Apulia, 'a great desire for rule stirred up the conflicts of these princes. Each wished to be the more powerful, and strove to seize the rightful property of the other.'[16] Pandulf succeeded first in recovering Capua in 1026, and then in seizing Naples in the late 1020s, although he only retained control of that city for some three years. In 1036 he unsuccessfully besieged Benevento, held by his nephew Pandulf III, and soon afterwards he secured Gaeta. However, in 1038 a further imperial intervention, by Conrad II, led Pandulf to flee to Constantinople, and Conrad installed

---

[16] 'Illis principibus dominandi magna libido bella ministrabat. Vult quisque potentior esse, Alter et alterius molitur iura subire', W. Apulia, 1 lines 148–50, p. 106.

Guaimar IV as prince of Capua. A few months later, in March or April 1039, the prince of Salerno took over Amalfi. He also installed his brother as ruler of Sorrento, formerly subject to Naples.[17] It seems probable that both Pandulf and Guaimar were aiming quite deliberately to become masters of, or at least the dominant power in, the whole of the once-unified duchy of Benevento, as well as to realize long-standing ambitions to take over the small, but rich, coastal duchies. The model for such pre-eminence was the career of Pandulf Ironhead of Capua, who, with the support of Otto II, had for a time unified all the Lombard principalities in the late 970s. What in practice such control meant is another matter. Princely authority in Capua had long been confined to little more than the immediate vicinity of Capua itself, and, significantly, in the end the duchy of Gaeta escaped from princely rule and, after being held briefly by Rainulf, the Norman count of Aversa, was eventually taken over in 1045 by Count Atenulf of Aquino, whose lordship was not only much closer to Gaeta than was Capua, but was also effectively independent of princely rule. Prince Pandulf's oppression of the monastery of Monte Cassino in the 1030s, denounced at length both by Amatus and by the later abbey chronicle of Leo of Ostia, might be better interpreted not merely as the product of the prince's innate malice (as the chroniclers suggest), but as part of his attempts to restore his authority in the north of his principality, an area physically separated from the Capuan plain by the Roccamonfina barrier. In the event this policy rebounded disastrously, for (at least according to the Cassinese tradition) it was the monks' complaints which brought about, or contributed to, the imperial intervention of 1038.[18]

The second aspect was the military support of Norman mercenaries, who played an increasingly important role in the conflicts in the Lombard zone in the 1020s and 1030s. A crucial step was taken when, on recovering Naples c. 1029/30, Duke Sergius IV installed a group of Normans at Aversa to defend the border of his duchy. This was the first landed base the Normans possessed in Italy, and their leader at Aversa, Rainulf, was in 1038, at Guaimar of Salerno's request, invested as count of the city by Conrad II, thus securing imperial legitimization of this territorial acquisition. But Aversa was by no means the only focus of activity for Norman mercenaries. Pandulf IV used Norman troops to seize Monte Cassino's lands in the 1030s, and Guaimar sent 300 Normans to assist the Byzantines in their expedition to Sicily in 1038.[19] One cannot help suspecting that now, at least for the present unchallenged as the dominant figure in the Lombard principalities, he used this opportunity to remove those who were surplus to his requirements or potential troublemakers.

---

[17] For Pandulf's attack on Benevento, 'Annales Beneventani', p. 154; Amatus, I.40, p. 53. For Guaimar as prince of Capua, Amatus, II.6, pp. 63–4, and as duke of Amalfi, Schwarz (1978), pp. 49, 247.
[18] *Chron. Cas.*, II.63, p. 288.   [19] Amatus, II.8, pp. 66–7.

By 1040 therefore the Norman immigrants had developed a considerable reputation as 'swords for hire' and were growing more numerous. Amatus wrote, somewhat over-enthusiastically, that after the acquisition of Aversa 'the lordship of the Normans grew daily, and the most valiant knights increased in number every day'.[20] But, Aversa apart, they still had no landed base in southern Italy. It was in the early 1040s that the situation was to change dramatically and that the foundations for the conquest and settlement of the south were to be established. The catalyst for this was a new revolt in Byzantine Apulia in 1041–2. Yet even here, to begin with, the Normans were once again only auxiliaries. A dissident Byzantine officer called Arduin, himself clearly little more than a mercenary, who originally came from Milan in northern Italy, seized the border town of Melfi with the help of a group of Normans and the collaboration of the local inhabitants. From there, within a very short space of time, his troops seized the neighbouring towns of Venosa and Lavello, and in the next few months inflicted a series of heavy defeats on the Byzantine forces of the province. But, even before Arduin's *coup de main*, Apulia had already been in turmoil, with local revolts in 1040 at Bari and at the key inland fortress of Ascoli, insurrections almost certainly sparked off by the demands of Byzantine tax collectors and recruiting officers for the Sicilian expedition of 1038. And when in May 1041, after a second successive defeat, the then catepan abandoned inland Apulia and retired with what was left of his forces to Bari, the insurgents chose as their leader not a Norman but Atenulf, the brother of the then prince of Benevento.

After a further victory near Montepeloso in September 1041 most of the coastal towns joined the rebels. Describing this William of Apulia's language is significant. Bari, Monopoli, Giovenazzo and other towns 'abandoned their alliance with the Greeks and made a pact with the Franks'.[21] This was clearly not a matter of conquest but of these Lombard-inhabited towns joining the insurrection. Furthermore, the Normans were by no means united, particularly when Atenulf of Benevento proved unsatisfactory as leader. Those Normans who had come from Aversa still recognized the authority of Guaimar of Salerno; others who had been mercenaries in Apulia before the uprising looked, along with the Lombard rebels, to Argyros, the son of the leader of the 1009 and 1017 revolts, Melus. It was not until the autumn of 1042 that the Normans united around a leader of their own, and acted independently of the rebellious townsmen of Apulia. By this stage a counter-attack by the new catepan, George Maniakes, re-appointed by the new emperor, Constantine IX, had recovered

---

[20] 'Li honor de li Normant cressoit chascun jor, et li chevalier fortissime multiplioient chascun jor', Amatus, 1.43, pp. 54–5.

[21] 'Foedere spreto Graecorum, pactum cum Francigenis iniere', W. Apulia, 1 lines 400–1, p. 120. Cf. Amatus, 11.25, p. 88, on the Normans' efforts to gain local recruits for their army. The discussion of Chalandon (1907), 1, pp. 95–105, remains very useful for this period.

most of southern Apulia, and Argyros (who may have been suspicious of Norman motives) had defected to the Greeks.

THE CONQUEST OF THE MAINLAND

The election of William of Hauteville as count of Apulia in September 1042 marks a watershed in the history of the Norman takeover in southern Italy. Up to this point the newcomers had been working for others; from now on they were working for themselves. In addition, despite the Byzantine counter-attack, which came to an abrupt halt when Maniakes abandoned Italy to make a challenge for the imperial throne, they were left in control of most of inland Apulia. However, despite William's election as overall leader the Normans of Apulia were still not united, but were rather a loose confederation of different interest groups and leaders, the twelve *nobiliores* to whom William of Apulia referred and of whom Amatus gave a list.[22] And they still acknowledged the overall lordship of Guaimar of Salerno. But the picture was beginning to change. Up to this point Aversa, as the only possession of the Normans, had been the focus of their activity and Count Rainulf the dominant figure. But the real gains were now to be made in Apulia, and it is symptomatic that in the early 1040s Rainulf was unable to consolidate his hold on Gaeta, although the city was for a time in his hands.[23] The Apulian dominions increased at a spectacular rate, and although Rainulf and the Aversan Normans were given the option of involvement there – the planned share-out of 1043 assigned the Gargano peninsula to him – he and his successors confined their attention to the west of the peninsula.

Throughout the 1040s both Apulian and Aversan Normans continued to work in partnership with Guaimar, who from January 1043 onwards claimed the title of 'duke of Apulia and Calabria', and in that same year joined Count William in an unsuccessful attack on Bari. The *History* of Amatus, which furnishes most detail about this relationship, continues to use the language of vassalage and dependence – thus Count Rainulf of Aversa 'persevered in loyalty to the prince', after his death his Norman vassals 'came to the prince of Salerno and asked for a successor to their dead lord', Drogo of Hauteville's succession to his brother William received the prince's consent, and Drogo later 'hurried to avenge the injury done to his lord'.[24] None the less, Amatus makes clear that the

---

[22] W. Apulia, 1 lines 232–4, p. 110; Amatus, II.31, pp. 95–6.

[23] Rainulf's rule was acknowledged in two charters of January 1042, *Codex diplomaticus Caietanus*, I, pp. 335–7 nos. 169–70; cf. Amatus, II.32, p. 97. Atenulf of Aquino dated his rule as duke of Gaeta from 1044.

[24] 'Et cestui conte Raynolfe persevera en loïalte a lo Prince', Amatus, II.7, p. 65. 'Li fidel Nomant . . . vindrent a lo Prince de Salerne et requistrent subcessor de lor seignor qui estoit mort', *ibid.*,

relationship was increasingly one of partnership rather than deference. After the death of Rainulf's nephew Asclettin Guaimar was unsuccessful in his attempt to impose a new count from a different family on the Normans of Aversa, and it was Drogo who forced him to accept the choice of the Aversan Normans, 'not a request but a command'.[25] That the relationship continued was because it was one of mutual advantage, sealed by gifts and family alliance (Drogo was married to Guaimar's daughter). 'Guaimar exalted himself in the company of the Normans, and the Normans grew great in the gifts of their prince.'[26] When Guaimar and Drogo were both murdered within a year of each other, in 1051–2, William of Apulia could still describe them jointly as 'the leaders of the Normans'.[27] But by then the circumstances were beginning to change. In 1047 the Emperor Henry III had intervened in southern Italy, depriving Guaimar of the principality of Capua, which he had returned to the former prince, Pandulf, and investing not only the count of Aversa (as his father had done in 1038), but also Drogo as count of Apulia. From the emperor's point of view at least they were no longer dependent on Guaimar, and the latter abandoned his self-proclaimed ducal title. Furthermore, while Amatus's *History* still wrote of Drogo as Guaimar's 'loyal count', and Richard (yet another of Rainulf's nephews) who became count of Aversa in 1050 did fealty to Guaimar, the author made clear that without the Normans the Lombard princes could do nothing. After Guaimar's death the chroniclers ceased to use language with vassalic implications, and the 'presents' given by Guaimar to the Normans became 'tribute'.

Meanwhile, the activities of the Normans extended into new areas and the lands under their control increased. In 1044 a foray was made into Calabria, by 1047 a Norman count was ruling at Lesina on the Adriatic,[28] to the north of the Gargano peninsula, and in 1048 Drogo invaded Lucania and northern Calabria, threatening Cosenza and establishing garrisons in the Val di Crati. He posted his half-brother Robert in command of one of these, and from this base the latter's raids penetrated deep into the surrounding region. At the same time smaller towns on or near the Apulian coast, like Andria and Barletta, fell into Norman hands. Within the principality of Capua the Normans posed a

---

II.32, p. 97. 'Et a lui succedi son frere, liquel se clamoit Drogo; . . . et estoit approve de Guaymere', *ibid.*, II.35, p. 101. 'Et Drogo se festina de deffendre la injure de son seignor', *ibid.*, II.37, p. 104. The arguments of Clementi (1982–3) that there was no vassalic relationship here seem misconceived. For a more balanced treatment, Tramontana (1970), pp. 125–88. The work of Amatus needs to be treated with care since it only survives in a much later French translation of the original Latin.

[25] 'Mes non fut proïre, ains fu comandent', Amatus, II.39, p. 106.

[26] 'Guaymere se glorifia en la compaignie de li Normant, et li Normant se magnificoient en li don de lor Prince', Amatus, III.2, p. 117.

[27] W. Apulia, II lines 75–6, p. 136. D' Alessandro (1978), pp. 107–16, has a useful discussion here.

[28] *Le colonie Cassinesi in capitanata*, I: *Lesina*, pp. 71–2, no. 23.

most serious threat to the lands of Monte Cassino, leading the German abbot Richer (appointed by Conrad II in 1038) to gather the local population together in fortified *castella*, and in 1052 Count Richard of Aversa besieged Capua itself, albeit unsuccessfully.

By the early 1050s, therefore, the threat of a Norman conquest of all, or most, of southern Italy was growing increasingly clear, and the area was becoming more and more destabilized. Furthermore, the methods the Normans employed were often brutal in the extreme, and the burning of crops and cutting down of vines and olive trees did little to endear them to the native inhabitants. The freebooting of Robert Guiscard in northern Calabria in the late 1040s, however heroic the terms used by the admiring chroniclers to dignify it, was precisely the sort of behaviour calculated to inflame the local population. The murder of Drogo and several other Norman leaders in the summer of 1051 was their reaction to this mayhem. Two other factors led to the formation of a general anti-Norman coalition. Pope Leo IX, the first great pope of the reform movement, from the early days of his pontificate devoted considerable attention to southern Italy. His primary concern was the eradication of simony and the administrative reorganization of the church in the south, but the scale of Norman depredations was brought very forcibly to his attention, especially when in the spring of 1051 the citizens of Benevento, who had some months earlier expelled their prince, asked the pope to become ruler of their city. Secondly, the Lombard Argyros was appointed in 1051 as governor of what was left of Byzantine Apulia. His viewpoint was, and had always been, that of the urban patriciate of Bari and the other Apulian cities. His defection to the Byzantine side in 1042 marked the recognition that the Normans were more of a threat to the interests of his class than was Byzantine rule. As catepan he was prepared to cooperate with the pope against the Normans. The assassination of Guaimar IV of Salerno in June 1052, though not directly connected with this anti-Norman coalition but rather caused by rivalries within the princely family, removed the Normans' only local ally.

The army that Leo IX raised and led into Apulia in 1053 thus represented the first and as it turned out the only serious and concerted effort to reduce the newcomers to a state of subordination or even to drive them out of southern Italy altogether. What was intended is far from clear, because on 18 June 1053 the papal army was annihilated at Civitate in northern Apulia by the combined forces of the Apulian and Aversan Normans under the command of Drogo of Hauteville's brother and successor, Humphrey. The chroniclers naturally ascribe the victory to the superior courage and military expertise of the Normans, but one might also point to the failure of the Byzantine forces to link up with the papal army, and to the very small contingent of German troops which was all the help that Henry III sent to aid his papal ally. The victory at Civitate effectively ensured the Norman conquest of the south. Thereafter the progress of the invaders on the mainland was not seriously challenged, and the pace of conquest quickened appreciably.

In 1054–5 the Normans penetrated deep into southern Apulia, capturing Conversano (south of Bari) in 1054 and then pressing on into the heel of Italy, where next year the important port of Otranto was captured. Soon afterwards deep inroads began into the principality of Salerno, whose new prince, Gisulf II, had very rapidly fallen out with both Richard of Aversa and Humphrey of Apulia. From 1057 too Robert Guiscard, who in that year succeeded his brother Humphrey as leader of the Apulian Normans, embarked in earnest on the conquest of Calabria, penetrating right down to Reggio. Despite some setbacks, problems in Apulia which needed his attention and disputes with his younger brother Roger about the division of the conquests, the operation was completed in no more than three years, and by 1060, when Reggio surrendered, the whole province was in Norman hands. Meanwhile Richard of Aversa attacked Capua in the spring of 1058 and secured the city's surrender on terms after a short siege. He was recognized as the new prince, and in the next four years enforced his rule over the whole of the old Lombard principality. The culmination of this process was the recognition of the two chief Norman leaders, Robert Guiscard and Richard of Capua, by Pope Nicholas II at the synod of Melfi in August 1059. Both swore fealty to the pope and his successors in return for the pope (borrowing a symbol hitherto the prerogative of the emperor) investing them with their lands by banner. Guiscard was granted the title of duke of Apulia, Calabria and Sicily.[29]

Why the Norman leaders should have been willing to become papal vassals is clear; this recognized their status as territorial rulers and legitimized their conquests. The motives for such a drastic reversal of previous papal policy were more complex. In part it was, perhaps, a recognition of the inevitable, that the Normans were there to stay and therefore that the interests of the church required an accommodation with them. But the 1059 investiture also reflected the situation of the reform papacy in Rome. A year earlier, on the death of Stephen IX there had been a double election, in which the Roman nobility had chosen their own candidate for the papal throne against Nicholas II, the choice of the circle of ecclesiastical reformers who had gathered in Rome

---

[29] Some historians have doubted whether Richard of Capua was at Melfi since his presence there was not mentioned in the account of the synod by W. Apulia, II lines 387–404, pp. 152–4, and only Robert's oath was preserved by the *Liber censuum*, I, p. 422 (English translation, Loud (2000), pp. 188–9). However, not only does *Chron. Cas.*, III.15, p. 377, imply that Richard was present, but this is expressly recorded by a contemporary charter, Loud (1981b), pp. 119–20 no. 3. It is, however, possible that Richard had already sworn fealty to the papacy in 1058. The view that Drogo had earlier been made duke of Apulia, e.g. Chalandon (1907), I, p. 114, is based on a forgery, Deér (1972), p. 48.

since the days of Leo IX. Nicholas had only prevailed in the ensuing struggle by securing the military support of the new Norman prince of Capua, and papal recognition was the price paid for that help and to ensure such assistance in the future, which the Norman princes swore to give. Furthermore, the desire to reform and restructure the church in southern Italy, already apparent under Leo IX, and to recover the disciplinary rights of the papacy over churches which the Byzantines had kept subject to the patriarch of Constantinople, both required the assistance of the *de facto* ruling authorities. The combination of these motives was made clear at the synod of Melfi. Not only did the pope invest the Norman leaders with their lands and titles; he condemned clerical marriage, and deposed several bishops guilty of simony. These activities were to be continued by his successor Alexander II, who also deposed Archbishop John of Trani, the chief ecclesiastical supporter in Apulia of the Byzantine patriarch.[30] In short, the pope's interests now coincided with those of the new Norman rulers.

THE CONSOLIDATION OF THE MAINLAND AND THE CONQUEST OF SICILY

After 1059 these Norman rulers cemented their authority on the mainland. At the time of the synod of Melfi Bari and several of the most important towns of southern Apulia were still in Byzantine hands, and Guiscard's immediate problem was to complete the conquest of Calabria, and to mop up these pockets of resistance. Although the conquest of Calabria was accomplished within a few months, in the event it took some twelve years to complete the conquest of the last bastions of Byzantine rule in Apulia. However, this was due more to internal divisions among the Normans, by no means all of whom were disposed to accept Robert's status as their overlord, than to any great determination on the part of Byzantium, which at this time was facing a growing threat from the Turks to its eastern frontier in Asia Minor. Thus when Guiscard returned to Apulia after the surrender of Reggio in 1060, there was already disaffection in the ranks of his vassals, and in his absence some of his personal lands had been plundered.[31] In the early 1060s Robert was preoccupied with renewed problems in Calabria and with the early stages of the invasion of Sicily. So while in 1063/4 both Taranto and Matera were captured from the Byzantines, this was the work of other Normans, seemingly acting independently. Finally, in the autumn of 1067 Guiscard faced a serious rebellion, financed and encouraged by the Byzantines, in which most of the more important lords of Apulia were

---

[30] Peter Damian, *Die Briefe*, no. 97, pp. 77–8. For John, Gay (1904), pp. 495, 506.

[31] Amatus, IV.32, p. 206; Malaterra, II.2, p. 30.

involved, including his own nephews Geoffrey of Conversano and Abelard.[32] It was only after the last embers of this revolt had been suppressed in the summer of 1068 that Robert could begin the siege of Bari, the one remaining bastion of Byzantine rule. With Bari being supplied and reinforced from the sea that siege took almost three years to bring to a successful conclusion, and then it was division among its Lombard inhabitants which led to the city's surrender.

Richard of Capua similarly took some years to complete the takeover of his principality. The original surrender of Capua in 1058 had left its citizens in control of the town's defences, and a second siege was required in 1062 before he was fully master of his new capital. A major rebellion in the north of the principality in 1063 involved most of the Lombard nobles of the area, as well as Richard's own son-in-law William of Montreuil, and took some two years to quell. Richard's chief ally was the great monastery of Monte Cassino, whose abbot, Desiderius, had thrown in his lot with the Normans even before the capture of Capua in 1058, seeing in the prospect of an effective central authority the best safeguard for the extensive territorial interests of his house. Monte Cassino was the chief profiteer from the 1063–5 rebellion, for Richard granted the abbey a series of *castella* and lands confiscated from the Lombard rebels, greatly extending the bounds of its franchise in the north of the principality, the 'Lands of St Benedict'.[33]

By this time the conquest of Sicily was already underway. In 1059 Nicholas II had invested Guiscard with future title to Sicily, and from 1061 onwards his forces secured a foothold in the north-east of the island. Messina was quickly captured, but thereafter, despite the help of the local Greek population and divisions among the Muslims, progress was slow. Only in the very early stages, and for a brief period in 1064 when an unsuccessful attack was made on Palermo, was Guiscard himself and his main field army involved – his difficulties on the mainland saw to that – and he was forced to leave operations on the island to his brother Roger, with only a small number of troops. At the beginning of 1062 the latter had only 300 men, and in 1063 at Cerami he defeated a major Muslim force sent over from North Africa with, according to Malaterra, only 136 knights.[34] That the Norman invasion was not driven out altogether was due partly to the difficult terrain of north-east Sicily, which enabled the Normans to fortify and hold on to what they had already gained, partly to superior Norman armour and tactics, which gained a second major victory at Misilmeri in 1068, but probably mainly to the divisions within the Muslim ranks. Count Roger little by little extended his rule along the north

[32] For the dating, revising older accounts, Jahn (1989), pp. 101–5.
[33] Loud (1981a), pp. 120–2, nos. 5, 12–14. Notice also a grant to a loyal Lombard count, *ibid.*, no. 8.
[34] Malaterra, II.29, 33, pp. 39, 42–3.

coast until by 1068 his outposts were close to Palermo. But it was not until the surrender of Bari in April 1071 that enough forces were available to launch a fresh attack on this city, this time with effective naval aid which seems to have been lacking in the unsuccessful 1064 attempt. Palermo surrendered in January 1072.

The conquest of the rest of the island still took almost twenty years. Throughout the 1070s Robert Guiscard was fully involved in suppressing renewed revolt on the mainland and continuing his attempts to absorb all that remained of the principalities of Benevento and Salerno, and by the early 1080s his attention and military forces were concentrated on the invasion of the Byzantine empire. After 1072 he never returned to Sicily. Twice, in 1074/5 and 1081, Count Roger was hurriedly summoned to the mainland to help suppress revolt there, and on both occasions there were serious reverses in Sicily during his absence. But despite this, and the small number of troops involved, the western end of the island was secured with the capture of Trapani in 1077 and the Mount Etna region (with the exception of Castrogiovanni) by the fall of Taormina two years later. Problems on the mainland and internal dissension in their own ranks prevented much further progress for some years, but a renewed offensive largely extinguished further resistance in the mid-1080s. Syracuse was captured in October 1086, Agrigento in July 1087, Castrogiovanni (modern Enna) finally surrendered a short time later, Butera in the summer of 1089 and Noto, the last town in Muslim hands, in February 1091.

On the mainland the capture of Bari had completed the conquest of the former Byzantine provinces. But Robert Guiscard's rule was never entirely secure. He returned from Sicily in the autumn of 1072 to suppress a further revolt, involving the Norman lords of the most of the Apulian coastal towns, including several of his own relatives, and supported by Gisulf of Salerno and Richard of Capua. The most persistent of the rebels were his nephews Abelard and Herman, the sons of his elder brother Humphrey, who had never forgotten that Robert had usurped what they felt to be their rightful position at the head of the Normans of Apulia.[35] Though the Apulian rebellion was fairly rapidly suppressed, Abelard held out in his Calabrian stronghold of S. Severino until probably 1075, and a little over a year later was in revolt again, defying the duke for nearly two years from his base at S. Agata di Puglia. Only a few months after he had finally surrendered there was another, and much more widespread, insurrection in Apulia, sparked off by Robert's demand for a financial 'aid' from his vassals on the occasion of one of his daughters' marriage.[36] This involved not only Herman, the count of Canne, but two of Guiscard's other nephews, the counts of Conversano and Montescaglioso, and in addition the counts

[35] W. Apulia, III lines 517–18, p. 192.   [36] *Ibid.*, lines 498–501, p. 190.

of Monte S. Angelo, Andria and Giovenazzo. For a brief period Robert lost control even of Bari, although when he appeared in person in northern Apulia the revolt very quickly collapsed. In 1081, while Guiscard was fighting the Byzantines on the other side of the Adriatic, there was a final rebellion, once again led by Abelard and Herman, which forced the duke to return to Italy early in 1082 and took nearly a year to suppress. By this stage he seems to have been losing patience, and while generally merciful even to the ringleaders of previous rebellions he now resorted to more drastic measures, including the total destruction of Canne.[37]

These continued difficulties all primarily involved Normans, and only to a very limited extent the Lombard inhabitants of Apulia. Despite these problems, and also despite their own mutual rivalry, the 1070s saw both Richard of Capua and Robert Guiscard attempting to complete their dominions by absorbing what was left of the other petty states of the west and centre of the region. Here they were only partly successful. Amalfi acknowledged Robert's rule in October 1073, not least to secure protection from the hostility of Gisulf of Salerno. Salerno itself was conquered after a six-month siege in 1076, and in defiance of unavailing papal censures. But Richard of Capua was unable to capture Naples, despite naval help from Robert, nor was the latter able to capture Benevento after the death of its last prince, who had been prudent enough to submit his city to papal overlordship some years earlier, in 1077. The distractions in Apulia hindered these efforts at the complete consolidation of Norman rule, and Naples and Benevento remained bastions of independence, albeit isolated ones, in Norman south Italy. In this very limited sense the Norman conquest of southern Italy was incomplete, and the continued revolts against Guiscard show how far the conquerors themselves were and remained disunited.

THE NORMANS AND THE PAPACY

The investitures of 1059 provided the formal, theoretical basis for the rule of the dukes of Apulia and the princes of Capua. However, both Robert Guiscard and Richard of Capua were already ruling, or were in the course of taking over, their respective principalities before 1059, and their rule in practice depended on their control over and recognition by their vassals and subjects. Malaterra, for example, recorded that when Robert returned to Apulia from Calabria in the autumn of 1060 he had to restore his authority there and 'the Apulian leaders accepted his ducal rule once again'.[38] Papal recognition added moral weight to his rule and that of the prince of Capua, but that rule was not dependent on it;

---

[37] *Ibid.*, IV lines 528–9, p. 232.
[38] 'Apuliensesque principes, de novo ducatu accepto, sibi congaudentes', Malaterra, II.2, p. 30.

nor did papal investiture prevent rebellion, as that faced by Richard of Capua in 1063–5 and by Guiscard for much of his career: in 1067–8, 1072–3, again in the late 1070s, when he lay under excommunication, and in 1081–3 when he was the papacy's most important ally. It became established that the Norman rulers should swear fealty to, and be formally reinvested with their lands and titles by, each new pope – and that each new duke or prince should do this. But their status as papal vassals was not the basis for their rule. The princes of Capua also took over the princely style and the inauguration rituals of their Lombard predecessors, the *collaudatio*, formal crown-wearings and, perhaps (the evidence here is scanty and difficult), anointing by the archbishop of Capua to validate their rule. Soon after his capture of Capua in 1058 Prince Richard visited Monte Cassino and 'he was received in procession as a king'.[39] This occurred *before* he had received formal investiture from the pope.

The relationship between the Norman rulers and the papacy could at times be very tense. Robert Guiscard was excommunicated by Gregory VII in 1073 and only absolved in 1080. Richard I of Capua was excommunicated in 1076, to be absolved only when he lay dying in 1078, and his son Jordan was laid under excommunication in 1079–80 and 1082–3. It has been argued that such difficulties stemmed from two opposing concepts of the vassalic relationship between the south Italian Normans and the papacy: the Normans considering that their rule was held on a hereditary and essentially unconditional basis, and the popes by contrast believing that these grants of investiture were conditional and could be withdrawn, and need not necessarily be granted to the successor of a dead ruler.[40] However, such a view is fundamentally mistaken. Certainly the Norman rulers regarded their rule as hereditary and in no way the product of papal investiture. The popes may well have attached greater importance to the recognition of their overlordship, but there is no evidence that they considered such grants other than hereditary. The Norman rulers might delay their fealty to new popes (or new rulers to the existing pope) and the receipt of investiture for some years. That Guiscard did not formally become Gregory VII's vassal until 1080, seven years after he had become pope, is explicable because of their quarrel and Robert's excommunication in 1073. But he may not have received investiture from Gregory's predecessor, Alexander II, until 1067, when the latter had been pope for some six years,[41] and his grandson Duke William of Apulia did not receive investiture from Paschal II until three years after his own accession in 1111. This strongly suggests that the function of the formal ceremony renewing the investiture was declarative, not constitutive,

---

[39] 'Il fu rechut o procession come roy', Amatus, IV.13, p. 191. See more generally the important discussion by Hoffmann (1978), especially pp. 142–52, and on the princely *scriptorium* and style Loud (1981b), pp. 106–7.

[40] Deér (1972), *passim*.   [41] Houben (1989), p. 127; Loud (2000), pp. 196, 208.

and was viewed as such by both sides. Furthermore, although Robert Guiscard lay under excommunication for seven years there was never any hint that Gregory wished to depose him or to declare him suspended from office, as he did to the German Emperor Henry IV. In 1073–4 Gregory proposed to lead a military expedition to southern Italy but its aim, he stated, was to restore peace and order to southern Italy. That achieved, the expedition would go on to fight the Turks who were threatening the Byzantine empire.[42] In the event the expedition collapsed, but Gregory continued to look for a reconciliation with Robert, not to depose him. Nor did he ever support the Apulian nobles rebelling against Guiscard.

The 'feudal' relationship between the Norman rulers and the pope was in fact an alliance, given visible expression by the vassalic link and the formal ceremonies of investiture, but not, it must be noted, homage which the Norman rulers did not perform before 1120. The problems which that alliance went through were caused, not by differing concepts of that vassalic link, but by more practical and political reasons. No contemporary source states exactly why Gregory VII excommunicated Duke Robert in 1073 after a proposed meeting at Benevento had ended in confusion with the two never actually coming face-to-face. But it seems very probable that this was caused by the continued territorial incursions of the Normans. Men subject to Robert, and particularly his nephew, Count Robert of Loritello, were penetrating into lands claimed by the papacy in the Abruzzi; while the duke himself was threatening both Benevento, which in August 1073 was formally handed over by its prince to papal rule, and the remains of the principality of Salerno, whose prince, Gisulf II, had become closely allied with the papacy. In subsequent years Gregory condemned these incursions several times.[43] The excommunication of Richard of Capua in 1076 came when the prince abandoned his loyalty to Gregory, attacked the duchy of Naples and aided Guiscard in his seizure of Salerno from Prince Gisulf. Jordan was excommunicated for attacks on ecclesiastical property in 1079, and for becoming the vassal of the excommunicate (and in papal eyes deposed) emperor, Henry IV, in 1082. But in all these cases what the pope wanted was for the Norman rulers to abandon their evil ways and observe the oaths they had sworn to him and his predecessors. He never intended to attempt to deprive them of their lands, even though these were technically papal fiefs. And after 1090, when the authority of both the duke of Apulia and the prince of Capua suffered serious setbacks, Urban II did his best to assist and strengthen their power.

If therefore we should treat the alleged importance of the vassalic relationship with caution, we should also be careful not to attribute overtly political

---

[42] Gregory VII, *Register*, I, 25, 46.
[43] *Ibid.*, II, 52a, IV, 7, V, 14a, VII, 14a. For Benevento, Vehse (1930–1), especially pp. 99–107.

motives to the popes. They did not, for example, seek deliberately to 'divide and rule', to play off the principality of Capua against the duchy of Apulia,[44] or what was left of the Lombard principalities against the Normans. They wanted peace and harmony in southern Italy, and this for three reasons. First, there was their natural repugnance to bloodshed among Christians. Secondly, with the reform party's hold on Rome still far from secure, and relations with the empire deteriorating until they broke down irretrievably in 1080, they needed the political and military support of the Normans. Capuan troops installed Nicholas II in Rome in 1059 and Alexander II there in 1061, and Duke Robert was to rescue Gregory VII from the imperialists in 1084. Thirdly, only through good relations with the Norman rulers, and particularly the duke of Apulia, could the popes push forward the reform and reorganization of the south Italian church which was so clearly needed, and on which Leo IX and Nicholas II had made only a start. The rivalry between Rome and Constantinople over the previous century had left in Apulia and Calabria a maelstrom of contending ecclesiastical claims, rival metropolitans and sometimes chapters, autocephalous archbishoprics and ill-organized church provinces. The effort to bring order to this confusion was to continue until the early years of the twelfth century.[45] Furthermore, Duke Robert and his brother Roger were restoring Christian rule to Sicily, an enterprise which the papacy had sanctioned and approved. Robert's reconciliation with the church in June 1080 at the synod of Ceprano can only have been a matter of profound relief to the pope.

Yet even after this the essentially pragmatic nature of the relationship remained clear. Despite the pope's desire for him to remain in Italy and protect Rome against the imperialists, Duke Robert preferred to launch an invasion of the Byzantine empire in 1081, to attempt to profit from what seemed to be the terminal decline of that once-great power. When he returned to Italy he lingered for more than a year suppressing rebellion in Apulia before marching to aid Pope Gregory in 1084. The military aid of the south Italian Normans was the aspect of the vassalic relationship which was most important to the pope, not any theoretical rights over their territories; but how weak his position as overlord had become was very apparent by the 1080s. After Gregory's death his successor was Abbot Desiderius of Monte Cassino (Victor III), the ally and collaborator of the Normans, who was elected at Capua under the aegis of their leaders, and whose return to Rome for his consecration was made possible by Norman troops. By the 1080s the papacy needed the Normans more than they needed it.

---

[44] Cowdrey (1983), pp. 121–36, emphasizes this aspect too much, in what is otherwise a most valuable book.

[45] See Kamp (1977); Fonseca (1977); Houben (1989), pp. 121–35.

THE SOCIETY OF NORMAN ITALY

By the death of Robert Guiscard in 1085 the conquest was effectively completed, apart from 'mopping-up operations' in south-east Sicily. By that stage too emigration from northern France to southern Italy had largely ceased. How had that influx changed south Italian society?

First of all one needs to examine the validity of the label 'Norman', which has, up to this point, been used for the sake of convenience. Were the newcomers to southern Italy actually Normans? After all to an Italian 'Norman' or 'northman' might mean anyone from north of the Alps. As William of Apulia wrote, 'they are called Normans, that is men of the north (wind)'.[46] Is it significant that William's verse used the words *Normanni, Galli* and *Francigeni* interchangeably to describe the newcomers?

In fact it is not. The literary nature of William's work meant that the demands of scansion were more important than terminological accuracy, and anyway the Normans *were* French-speaking. By contrast both Amatus and Malaterra began their histories by discussing very specifically the duchy of Normandy as the source of the invaders. From documentary sources it has been calculated that between two-thirds and three-quarters of the clearly non-indigenous persons from southern Italy whose names are known from the eleventh and early twelfth centuries were actually from the duchy of Normandy. Either these persons had family names which can be traced back to somewhere in the duchy, or they described themselves specifically as 'Norman' (as opposed to Bretons, Flemings etc. who also appear in charters), or their names had a Scandinavian element which can only be linked with the Scandinavian area of France, that is Normandy.[47] Of course, this means that there was also a substantial minority who came to Italy from other parts of France, a few from northern Italy and even Germany. For example, the lords of S. Agata di Puglia from the 1080s, whom Guiscard installed there instead of his errant nephew Abelard, and who became hereditary ducal constables, were Bretons.[48] Count Roger of Sicily's marriage to Adelaide of Savona in the late 1080s (his third wife) led to the establishment of a veritable colony of north Italians in eastern Sicily under the aegis of her brother Count Henry of Paterno, who was, after the ruler, probably the most significant lay landowner in Sicily in the early twelfth century. But the majority of the incomers were genuinely Normans. Furthermore, most of the really important mainland landowners were Normans, many of whom in Apulia were relatives of the duke and in Capua of the prince. In the east of the principality the counts of Caiazzo (who had displaced several former Lombard counts) were

---

[46] 'Normanni dicuntur, id est homines boreales', W. Apulia, 1 line 10, p. 98.
[47] Ménager (1975a). For wider aspects of this same problem, Loud (1981b).
[48] Ménager (1975b), pp. 375–6, for references.

descended from a brother of Richard I, while the counts of Carinola in the centre of the principality stemmed from his youngest son. In Sicily the lands of Henry of Paterno were bordered by those of the lordship of Syracuse, held first by Roger I's bastard son Jordan and then by his nephew Tancred, and the lordship (or perhaps county) of Ragusa, held by another of his sons, Godfrey.[49] Where important landowners were not Normans they might well not be other Frenchmen, but indigenous survivors from the pre-Norman regime. In the north of the principality of Capua the lands of Monte Cassino were bordered by those of the Lombard counts of Aquino, who continued to hold their property, if not their comital title, through to the thirteenth century.[50] In the borderlands between the principality of Capua and the Abruzzi the dominant family continued to be, as it had been in the tenth century, a dynasty of counts of mixed Lombard–Frankish descent called the Burrells. In the Stilo region of Calabria Greek landowners retained their property and importance. While parts of the principality of Salerno fell into the hands of Norman families such as the counts of the Principate, descended from Duke Robert's younger brother William, and the lords of S. Severino (whose forebear Turgisius proudly described himself as *Normannus ex normannis*), several cadet branches of the old princely family survived the fall of Gisulf II and retained their lands into the twelfth century. Intermarriage was here a potent factor, above all that of Sichelgaita, daughter of Guaimar IV, with Guiscard himself in 1058, but this was only the most notable among several other examples.[51]

The most salient feature of the Norman takeover of southern Italy was the relatively small numbers of the invaders, never more than a few thousand at the most. Furthermore, although many of the Apulian lordships were based on towns, these were generally not among the most important. The major urban centres of the south Italian mainland, notably Bari, Benevento, Salerno, Amalfi, Naples and Capua, remained the more or less exclusive preserves of the existing population. Apart from perhaps in coastal Apulia, Norman and French landowners tended to reside on their properties outside the towns, not just because of any possible aversion to or unfamiliarity with urban life, but also because most of the important towns of southern Italy fell into Norman hands relatively late, and in the case of Benevento and Naples not at all. Aversa, a predominantly Norman town, was very much the exception, and that of course had been in the hands of the newcomers since 1030 and was effectively a new foundation (there may have been a village on the site already, but certainly

---

[49] Tramontana (1977), pp. 216–21, and *passim* for landownership in Sicily under Roger I. See also Loud (2000), pp. 173–9.

[50] The most illustrious of its later members was St Thomas Aquinas.

[51] See here Loud (1987), especially pp. 159–63, and (1996), pp. 329–32, and for the issue of continuity in general, and for most of what follows here, von Falkenhausen (1977).

no fortified town). Thus the impact of the Normans on the countryside was stronger than on the towns. In some areas at least the rural population may have suffered, and not just through the short-term impact of warfare, though we should not underestimate the effect of the (largely man-made) Calabrian famine of 1058, graphically described by Malaterra.[52] But, before the Normans, Calabria had been a society of primarily free peasant cultivators. After the conquest the long lists of serfs donated to local monasteries by the new rulers are very striking, as are the *jarida* (surveys of the servile population) detailing the mainly Muslim peasants on Sicilian lordships. The condition of the rural population may well have worsened over much of southern Italy, but here too one must make qualifications. Southern Italy was a rentier, not a demesne-based, economy and serfdom was far more a matter of customary dues than labour services. In those areas most advanced economically, such as the principality of Capua and eastern Sicily, servile obligations as such were relatively rare (at any rate in Sicily on Christian settlers, since the count wished to attract them). Obligations would more frequently be tenurial (that is attached to the holding as a species of rent) than personal.[53]

Furthermore, the rudimentary infrastructure of the new governments needed indigenous participation, not least because of the survival of a tradition of lay literacy among Lombards, Greeks and Arabs which the Normans did not possess. In Apulia many of the officials of the Norman counts remained Lombards, Lombard officials were prominent in the entourage of the princes of Capua, and one, and probably the most important, of Duke Robert's ecclesiastical advisers, Archbishop Ursus of Bari, was a Lombard. The church was only partially taken over. In the principality of Capua French bishops were installed in the southern sees, near Capua itself, but those in the north of the principality were largely filled from the ranks of the monks of Monte Cassino, a monastery whose recruitment remained almost exclusively Lombard. If any part of the church was dominated by 'Normans' it was the newly founded abbeys and bishoprics of Sicily, although in fact the first bishop of Syracuse came from Provence and that of Agrigento from Burgundy. But whereas Roger I set up six Latin bishoprics in the island, and a seventh on Malta, as well as four Latin abbeys, he also founded or endowed some seventeen Greek ones; a ratio which reflected the demographic structure of the island, the Christian population of which remained primarily Greek until well into the twelfth century.[54]

---

[52] Malaterra, 1.27, pp. 21–2.

[53] Cf. *ibid.*, IV.16, pp. 95–6, describing Roger I's attempts to encourage captives from Malta to stay in Sicily by promising them freedom from servile exactions. See generally D'Alessandro (1987), especially pp. 310–12.

[54] White (1938), especially pp. 38–46; Scaduto (1947), chapter 3, especially pp. 69–70. For the first bishops, Malaterra, IV.7, p. 89.

The ecclesiastical patronage of the new rulers, and the very considerable redistribution of property to churches which they carried out, also reflected the limitations of the 'Norman' conquest. Those abbeys founded by the conquerors profited, as Venosa and St Euphemia did from the patronage of Robert Guiscard, and Mileto from Roger I. This was particularly apparent on the island of Sicily where the monasteries of Lipari and Catania (the latter the seat of a bishopric) were very generously endowed. But other churches which profited just as much if not more from the conquerors were not Norman foundations. Above all Monte Cassino benefited from Desiderius's collaboration with the conquerors, not only through his partnership with the princes of Capua, but also by greatly extending its properties in Apulia. The patronage of Robert Guiscard in his last years and of his son Roger Borsa played a significant part in this, as did the pressure on laymen under the influence of the reform papacy to surrender their proprietary churches. In the period 1038–1105 Monte Cassino was given at least 150 such churches, profiting both from the Norman conquerors and often from Lombards who hoped that under the abbey's protection they might safeguard at least some of their property from the invader.[55] But Monte Cassino always remained a Lombard monastery. Very few of its monks and none of its abbots were Normans. The same was true of the Holy Trinity, Cava, which became the most important monastic house of the principality of Salerno, and the chief recipient of the pious generosity of Dukes Roger Borsa and William, as well as a considerable landowner in Apulia. In the latter area its benefactors were almost entirely Norman, but the abbey itself remained one in which the Lombard element predominated.[56] So too did St Sophia, Benevento, which attracted considerable benefactions from the Norman nobility of Molise, but which was itself in a city which was never subject to Norman rule.

It has been argued that in Calabria there was a deliberate attempt if not to 'Normanize' at least to Latinize the area, by discrimination against the Greek church and the conversion of Greek sees to Latin ones, and indeed that policy resulted in the emigration of Calabrian Greeks back to Sicily.[57] However, such conclusions have been disputed, and if there was a Latinization of Calabria it was a very slow process, although several sees in northern and central Calabria were converted to the Latin rite in the last years of the eleventh century. But the churches (and the population) of southern Calabria remained Greek for a long time to come, and there is little evidence for religious tension. There were still Greek clergy in northern Calabrian dioceses with Latin bishops in the early twelfth century, Norman barons patronized Greek monasteries, and Greek and Latin prelates cooperated on important liturgical and legal occasions. If

---

[55] Dormeier (1979), p. 56.   [56] See Loud (1987).   [57] Ménager (1958/9), *passim*.

Greek religious observance went into decline it was far more a product of the acculturation of the Greek population by the Latins over a couple of centuries than of direct oppression.[58]

If relations were at times still tense between the newcomers and the local population, and above all with some of the Lombards, at the end of the century, the reason was not the conquest as such, but rather the problems of government and the breakdown of order in the years after the death of Robert Guiscard in 1085 and Jordan I of Capua in 1090. Roger Borsa faced a determined challenge from his elder half-brother Bohemond, whose mother Robert had repudiated before his marriage to Sichelgaita of Salerno; and he was unable to prevent him from carving out his own independent principality in southern Apulia, based on the city of Taranto. But in addition several other powerful Apulian nobles, who had always been restive under Duke Robert, threw off the shackles of ducal rule, ceased to mention the duke's regnal years in the dating clauses of their charters and set about aggrandizing their power bases. Pope Urban II's proclamation of the Truce of God at the councils of Melfi in 1089 and Troia in 1093 was the direct consequence of this breakdown of central authority in Apulia. The townsmen of Capua twice expelled the prince during the 1090s, and were only eventually reduced to heel in 1098 by a full-scale siege conducted by the prince, the duke of Apulia and Count Roger of Sicily. Whereas up to the 1090s Lombard officials were prominent at the princely court, his charters issued from Aversa in that decade reveal an exclusively French, and indeed almost exclusively Norman, entourage. After 1090 too the Normans were expelled for a time from Gaeta and the prince largely lost control of the northern part of his principality. But by contrast in the principality of Salerno Roger Borsa's rule remained stable, not least because his descent via his mother from the old princely family gave him legitimacy in the eyes of the Lombard population. While Duke Roger did not entirely abandon Apulia, nor those parts of Calabria which his father had retained in his own hands (rather than handing over to his brother Roger), his activities concentrated more and more on Salerno and the west coast. Southern Calabria and Sicily remained firmly in the hands of Count Roger, and not even the fact that his death in 1101 was followed by a long minority disturbed the equilibrium of his dominions.

If therefore the Norman conquest had brought stability to those areas which were inhabited almost exclusively by Greeks and Muslims it was very far from having done so in much of southern Italy, which in 1100 was as much if not more fragmented than it had been a century earlier. It was to be a long and bloody process before the entire region was united under the rule of Roger of Sicily's son.

---

[58] Guillou (1963); Loud (1988).

CHAPTER 5

THE KINGDOM OF THE FRANKS
TO 1108

Constance Brittain Bouchard

THE eleventh century in France was a period in which both political and social structures were transformed. Much of the heritage of the tenth century continued, from the assumption that Benedictine monasticism was the purest form of the religious life to the very political units over which the territorial princes of the eleventh century ruled. Yet old institutions were modified within a new cultural matrix and entirely new institutions were formed. While the changes were not sudden enough – or even synchronous enough – to speak of the eleventh century as a 'rupture' in French history, the Carolingian heritage was modified during the eleventh century until it was virtually unrecognizable.

In politics, although the form of governmental institutions remained initially unchanged, the Carolingian assumption that the king was at the top, surrounded by his great *fideles* and bishops, was no longer automatic, regardless of how much reality it might or might not once have had. The narrowness of the eleventh-century kings' political domain, which had already shrunk under the last French Carolingian kings and continued to shrink under the first Capetians, points to a profound transformation of authority.

But the political weakness of the eleventh-century kings should not be seen purely as a negative feature. Rather than saying that the collapse of royal power made necessary new political and social structures, it would be better to say that *all* aspects of society underwent significant transformations, and that the role of the king was one of these aspects. The eleventh-century kings did not simply lose power that the twelfth-century kings regained. The eleventh-century kings, who actually had an advantage over the tenth-century Carolingians in that they were never seriously challenged for the throne, lived in a period in which there were far-reaching attempts to organize, create hierarchies and understand the moral and social structures of the universe. These new forms of organization involved many more people than had taken part in Carolingian politics. The French kings had to find a place for themselves in a new political and social order, and in doing so laid the foundations for the power of their successors a century later.

Between the death of Robert II in 1031 and the accession of Louis VI in 1108, the kings of France had little obvious impact beyond their somewhat migratory court itself. Henry I (1031–60) and Philip I (1060–1108) were recognized as kings and overlords to the French dukes and counts who in many cases wielded appreciably greater temporaral power. They were asked to confirm monastic possessions and intermittently attempted, with greater or lesser success, to make one of their favourites a bishop, though only in a relatively narrow area. They did keep the loyalty of the French episcopate, even when it was greatly strained by Philip's marital problems. But these kings have been most frequently examined by modern scholarship not for their policies but for their often tumultuous marriages, and the conclusion of all studies on the extent of their leadership and authority has been how highly limited these were.

One must, however, avoid being too dismissive of Kings Henry and Philip. They certainly kept alive and viable both the monarchy and the Capetian dynasty which Hugh Capet and Robert II had established in the late tenth and early eleventh centuries. They thus made possible the great advances in royal power and royal governmental institutions in the twelfth century. Kings need not, after all, always be at the head of all political, social or institutional developments. And the modern historian must be careful not to let the absence of a contemporary biographer – such as both Robert II and Louis VI had – make one discount the kings in between who did not have one. The nickname of 'The Battler' which the *Miracula Sancti Benedicti* gave Henry does not make up for the lack of a biography, and of course Suger lauded Louis VI in part by drawing sharp comparisons with Philip. But one is still left with the overall impression that eleventh-century France was a very exciting place, everywhere except for the royal court.

For while these two men held the French throne, French society and culture changed rapidly. The various transformations of the eleventh century had different causes and took place at different rates, yet most of them can be seen as related to various attempts to become more organized in everything from theology to politics, with a pronounced move toward greater hierarchy. The eleventh century could only be a period of such broad changes because it was a period of economic growth. Although France's commercial economy grew less precociously than Italy's, during the eleventh century the market economy began to spread, and forests were cut and swamps drained as both rural population and the extent of agricultural land began to increase.

The system of fief-holding (the only reasonable meaning of the term 'feu- dalism' in medieval France) was essentially created entirely anew during the

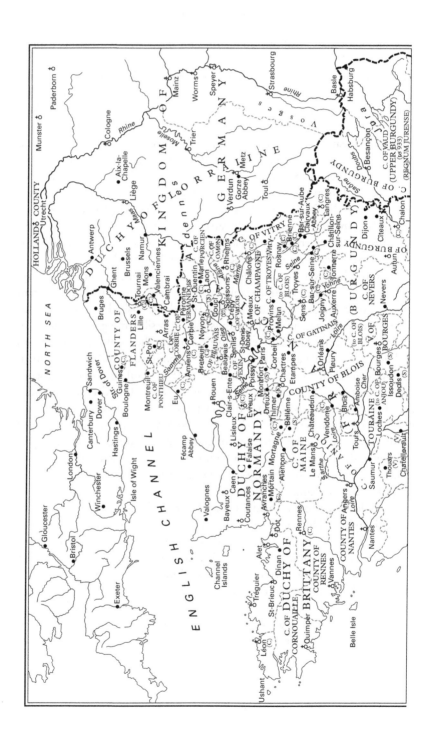

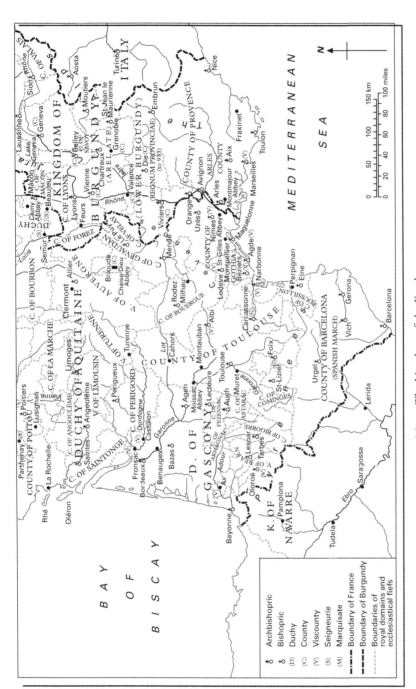

Map 3 The kingdom of the Franks

reigns of Henry and Philip. Yet it is a sign of their social and political separation from many of the events of their kingdom that the French kings, unlike their contemporaries in England, did not become properly involved in fief-holding until the twelfth century. Castles, which had first made their appearance at the very end of the tenth century, spread rapidly across eleventh-century France, and with castles the newly generated and newly important social groups of castellans and knights.

Rapid expansion and development of the religious life took place under these kings – though essentially without their involvement – as many of the old French monasteries, ruined or abandoned for centuries, were refounded and rebuilt. Cluny acquired an affiliated group of priories, canons regular first made their appearance, hermits appeared in some numbers in the French forests and the new monastery of Cîteaux was founded. The Gregorian reform and the Investiture Controversy profoundly changed both elections to bishoprics and the morals of the men who held high ecclesiastical office, and indeed restructured the Christian church so that the lines of authority within it all led eventually to the pope. But the kings of France played no leadership role in the Controversy either, only providing haven to the popes when they were driven out of Rome and acceding to compromises after they had been worked out by others.

Intellectually, the later eleventh century was a period of the development of the first of the French cathedral schools of national (or even international) reputation, which would later influence the rise of the universities. Theological debates of great intensity were carried on in these schools, as certain beliefs were declared to be heretical, and convicted heretics were put to death for the first time in centuries. The rather desultory attempts of the Carolingian era to create systematic compilations of canon law took on a new vitality.

In short, the foundations of most of the aspects of high medieval culture in France, which came to fruition in the twelfth century, were laid firmly during the more fluid era of the eleventh century, during the long reigns of Henry and Philip.

HENRY I

Henry I (1031–60) was not supposed to be king. His older brother Hugh had in 1017 been consecrated king, along with their father, Robert II. Only after Hugh's untimely death in 1025, caused by a fall from a horse according to the *Miracula Sancti Benedicti*, was Henry put forward as Robert's designated successor. Even this choice was problematic. According to Radulf Glaber, the formidable Queen Constance preferred her third son, Robert, as royal heir. But Henry was finally designated king in 1027, and his younger brother Robert was given the duchy of Burgundy, originally intended for Henry. Constance and Robert's final son, Odo, received no territory from his parents, and in later years he frequently fomented rebellions against the king.

After King Robert II died in 1031, on 20 July, the queen began a brief war against her sons, for reasons that are not clear, but after this Henry settled down to some thirty years of relative obscurity as king. He married at least one German princess named Matilda, and may indeed have married two, for the *Vita* of Emperor Conrad dates the death of his daughter Matilda, *desponsata* to Henry, to 1034, while the *Miracula Sancti Benedicti* states that Queen Matilda died in 1044, when a child was taken from her by Caesarean section.[1] But neither Matilda bore Henry living sons. Finally, in 1051, after twenty years as king, Henry married Anna, daughter of Jaroslav I, archduke of Kiev. The French kings had been having difficulties for three generations in finding brides of suitably elevated status to whom they were not already related, and a Russian princess (contemporary chronicles called Jaroslav a king), of the first generation to be raised as Christians, was a welcome if novel solution.[2]

By Anna, Henry had three sons, named Philip, Robert and Hugh. Philip was born in 1052, within a year of his parents' marriage. The name Philip, given to the royal heir and very common among later Capetians, probably entered the lineage via Anna's Russian connections; Anna's grandmother had been of a Macedonian dynasty that claimed descent from Philip of Macedon. Of the younger two sons of Henry I, Robert died young, and Hugh (d. 1102) became count of Vermandois by marriage with Adela, daughter of Heribert IV of Vermandois. King Henry died on 4 August 1060.

PHILIP I

Philip I (1060–1108), who was described in almost uniformly negative terms by his contemporaries, is best known to modern scholarship for his marital problems. He had been associated with his father on the French throne at Pentecost of 1059, consecrated by the archbishop of Rheims, before an assembly of French bishops and secular lords. Since he was no more than eight when his father died in the following year, the kingdom was governed for several years by his uncle Baldwin V of Flanders, who had married a sister of Henry I. Baldwin had been Henry's choice, an interesting one considering that Henry's brother Robert, duke of Burgundy, might have been a more obvious selection. Baldwin exercised effective control over his nephew and the kingdom until his own death in 1067; the queen-mother, Anna, who also assisted in the regency

---

[1] Wipo, 'Vita Chuonradi', p. 32; *Miracula sancti Benedicti* VII.3; Vajay (1971), pp. 241–56.
[2] Bouchard (1981b), p. 277.

at first, played little part in royal affairs after 1062, when she married Ralph of Crépy and Vermandois.

Probably in 1072, Philip married Bertha, daughter of the late count of Holland, Florent I, and stepdaughter of Robert of Frisia, count of Flanders. Philip and Robert of Frisia had agreed to a peace treaty very shortly before. For some years Philip and Bertha were troubled by their failure to have a son. The birth of the future Louis VI in 1081 was striking enough for a miracle story to grow up around the event, in which the saintly abbot of Soissons told the queen that she was pregnant and that it would be appropriate to give her son the (Carolingian) name of Louis.[3]

As well as Louis, Philip and Bertha had a daughter named Constance and apparently a second son, Henry, who died young. After the birth of his children, Philip grew tired of his wife. She was 'too fat' for him according to one contemporary account, although he himself became too heavy to ride a horse late in life. In 1092, announcing he was divorcing Bertha, Philip took up with Bertrada of Montfort, wife of Count Fulk Réchin (Fulk IV) of Anjou, which naturally earned him that count's hatred. In spite of strong opposition, Philip and Bertrada seem to have remained together for the rest of their lives, and were even reconciled to Count Fulk in 1106. Philip and Bertrada had three children, named Philip, Cecilia, and Florus. These children remained illegitimate and outside the line of inheritance. Louis appears with the title *rex designatus* in the year 1100.

Philip's second marriage provoked very strong reactions and one of the most prolonged and public attempts to force the developing idea of the Christian marriage bond on unwilling parties. The difficulty was that the organized church did not present a united front against the pair. The French episcopate would not desert their king, and even the pope, locked in a struggle with the emperor, seems to have sought to compromise. Philip initially hoped in 1092 that Ivo of Chartres would bless his marriage. Although Ivo refused to do so, since Philip was still married to Bertha, Philip was able to have his second marriage celebrated by several French bishops, probably including the archbishop of Rheims, to whom the pope wrote a strong letter of reproach. The king imprisoned Ivo in 1093 in retribution for his opposition.

In 1094, after Queen Bertha's death, which should have left Philip (although not Bertrada) free to marry again, two councils were held to consider the royal marriage. Philip may have hoped for a favourable decision from the council convoked by the archbishop of Rheims, but more important was the council held by the papal legate, which ended up excommunicating the king. Negotiations followed for a year, after which the pope himself excommunicated

---

[3] Hariulf, 'Vita S. Arnulfi episcopi Suessionensis'.

Philip in 1095 at Clermont, at the complaint of Count Fulk. Philip thus played no part in the First Crusade, which was preached at Clermont – though he was so prematurely old and fat at this point that an active role would have been unlikely anyway.

In 1096, Philip agreed to separate from Bertrada and was reconciled to the pope. When, in fact, he refused to keep his promise, France was put under interdict in 1097. Further negotiations and councils followed for seven years, until a final compromise was reached in 1104. Again, Philip agreed to separate from Bertrada, and again he failed to carry out his promise, but after this the pope seems to have turned a blind eye to their relationship.

After these events, Philip retired from active life, leaving Louis VI effective French king well before he succeeded in fact. When he died, on 29/30 July 1108, Philip asked to be buried at Fleury (St-Benoît-sur-Loire), rather than at St-Denis with most preceding French kings. According to Suger and Orderic Vitalis, he felt he was unworthy to be buried among his more illustrious predecessors.

ROYAL GOVERNMENT

Henry's and Philip's reigns, like those of Hugh Capet and Robert II before them, were in many ways an institutional continuation of the royal rule of the Carolingians, but were marked by institutional evolution as well as continuity. Like the Carolingians, the Capetians were consecrated at Rheims with holy oil. Indeed, the first Capetians were described by their chancelleries in even more grandiloquent terms than their predecessors, and the kings exercised a thaumaturgical healing power which seems to have been unknown among the Carolingians. Able to heal the 'king's evil' (scrofula), Robert II and his son and grandson enjoyed a spiritual authority beyond that of the Carolingians – and indeed beyond that of their descendants in the twelfth century.

The royal household

Like the Carolingians, the eleventh-century Capetians ruled through royal officers who were in many respects indistinguishable from their household officers. The royal entourage travelled fairly constantly, both because the court could use revenues and food more easily if they came to where it was raised and because the king needed to be personally present to exercise many of his functions, from justice to the confirmation of privileges. One of the most important members of the royal court, almost always with the king in the eleventh century, was the queen; as already noted, the queen was often a source of controversy, and she frequently signed royal charters.

The royal household officers became increasingly vital members of court during the eleventh century, and their counsel and signatures were sought by the king rather than those of his great *fideles*. The most important of the royal household officers was the seneschal (*dapifer*), the institutional heir of the mayor of the palace of Merovingian and Carolingian times. He was the master of the king's household, in some ways an actual viceroy. The constable (*comes stabuli*), in charge of the royal army, and the butler (*buticularius*), who supervised the income and wine from royal estates, were subject to the seneschal. During the eleventh century the chamberlain (*camerarius*), in charge of the royal treasury, often signed royal charters, though this officer never gained the power of the royal chamberlain in England. These four officers were all in origin domestic officials, and the offices were held by laymen. The other important royal office, that of the chancellor (*cancellarius*), who was in charge both of the royal archives (including the king's seal) and the royal chapel, was held under the early Capetians by high ecclesiastics.

Capetian royal charters initially took the same form as the public charters of their predecessors, but during the course of the eleventh century they increasingly took the appearance of 'private' charters, especially in their long list of witnesses. Carolingian royal charters had been signed only by the king and his chancellor, but by the time Henry I took office the royal entourage frequently signed as well. The list of witnesses, which had long been common in private charters, also became the rule in royal charters, as castellans and lesser lords, as well as the counts and bishops who constituted the king's *fideles*, affixed their names. Indeed, bishops declined in frequency among the witnesses to royal charters in the late eleventh century, leaving secular lords the most common signatories. In addition, these secular lords were increasingly from the Ile-de-France region, suggesting that local men rather than the great princes of the kingdom were most influential on a daily basis at the royal court.[4]

Royal power

The kings exercised their most direct power in an area between the territories of the great French princes, a gap between the counties and duchies of Normandy, Aquitaine, Flanders, Vermandois, Troyes, Burgundy and Chartres–Blois–Tours. In addition, the Capetians had acquired, in becoming kings of France, a handful of *villae* once part of the Carolingian domain, most situated in the valleys of the Oise and the Aisne. Yet even within this area there were counties and castellanies headed by independently minded castellans. Indeed, during the eleventh century the count of Anjou and duke of Normandy had

---

[4] Lemarignier (1965), pp. 42–59, 107–28.

much more thorough control over their regions than did the king of France over his, although the rise of independent castellans also marked other parts of the kingdom, including the counties of Mâcon and Poitou.

The domain over which the eleventh-century Capetians ruled directly was smaller than the territory which their Carolingian predecessors had ruled. The kings' authority in the royal domain was a rather inconsistent mixture of judicial, administrative and fiscal rights. The king received some income from such regalian rights as market taxes and tolls and minting in this region; similar rights were exercised by the great French dukes and counts in their own principalities. In the eleventh century, the heart of the royal political domain was the Ile-de-France, the area surrounding Paris and Orleans, the former duchy of Hugh Capet. Paris had been the centre of Robertian/Capetian power since at least the end of the ninth century, when Odo was elected king of France in 888 after fighting back the Vikings from Paris in the celebrated siege of 885/6.

Even smaller than the kings' political domain was the domain from which they derived the majority of their income. This economic domain, in the eleventh century as later in the middle ages, was not a coherent geographic unit, but rather was constituted of those lands within the kingdom which were administered directly by the king and his agents. The king received rents and dues from a much smaller agglomeration of territories than those over which he exercised rights.[5] Those territories – or those people – which owed their revenues directly to him constituted the principal base for the upkeep of the royal court.

In practice, the kings exercised their rights over both their political and their economic domains through some of the same people. They administered justice and collected revenues through their provosts (*praepositi*), an office which had been created by the end of the tenth century, although there are few details on it until the second half of the eleventh century. These were primarily domanial agents, concerned with economic revenues, although they did have under them such officers as the *vicarius* of a town and the *maior* of a rural village. A *prévôté* may have a name suggesting a fixed geographic unit, but the provosts did not hold any more complete or coherent authority in a particular area than the king himself.

Henry seems to have been quite satisfied with a small royal domain, smaller in fact than that of some of his territorial princes. He did not even travel or write to a number of nearby territories where Robert II had frequently been, most notably Burgundy, where his younger brother was duke. Royal authority was primarily exercised north of the Loire. There is, however, some indication that Philip tightened and systematized administrative control over the royal

---

[5] Newman (1937), pp. x–xii, 1–5.

domain. In the last twenty years or so of his reign his provosts regularly received
royal instructions. These provosts also acted as witnesses to some royal charters.
They and the household officials were by the late eleventh century drawn from
powerful castellan families of the region, rather than being the petty aristocrats
who had served earlier. This may suggest that the king, even if not yet the
undisputed leader of the region as Louis VI later set out to be, was able to
command respect and service among an upper social stratum.

There were few significant additions to the royal domain in the eleventh
century, and these were for the most part balanced by losses of other territory.
Robert II acquired Burgundy after the death of his uncle Henry in 1002, but it
took him close to fifteen years to do so, and in 1031 it was separated from the
crown and became an independent duchy until the middle of the fourteenth
century. Henry I took over the county of Sens in 1055, when Count Raynard
II died, although the city continued to be ruled by its viscounts, but the king
also gave the county of Corbie to the count of Flanders when his sister Adela
married the latter.

Philip I was a little more successful in increasing the size of the royal domain.
He acquired the Gâtinais in 1069 from the count of Anjou, as a bribe or reward
for staying out of the count's conflicts with his brother; took Corbie back from
the count of Flanders around 1071, perhaps as a reward for attempting to help
the young count hold off his usurping uncle; and took over the Vexin when
Count Simon of Vermandois and the Vexin, step-son of King Philip's mother
Anna, retired to the cloister in 1077. Finally, Philip bought Bourges from the
viscount sometime around 1100, when the latter was leaving for Jerusalem and
needed to raise money.

Bishops and monasteries

At least in the kings' own minds, an important part of their rights was the right
to help choose new bishops. Indeed, modern scholars attempting to define the
extent of the royal domain (or at least royal political authority) in the eleventh
century – something the kings never explicitly did themselves – have based
their conclusions in part on the cities in which the kings received revenues as an
exercise of regalian rights during vacancies, played a role in episcopal elections
and invested new bishops. It is clear that the kings treated as 'royal' an array
of bishoprics spread out over a far larger area than that of their economic
domain. Some of the sees to which the eleventh-century kings attempted
to name bishops were located within the great territorial principalities. The
Carolingians had routinely nominated bishops and received diocesan revenues
during vacancies, and the German emperors continued to do so, but Henry
and Philip exercised such rights in only some twenty or twenty-five sees: the

exact number is disputed, and indeed it seems rather pointless to try to come up with an exact count, as circumstances varied both from see to see and over the course of the century.

Henry I never became involved in the reform of the church which Leo IX began at the council of Rheims in 1049. He continued to nominate bishops, and indeed was accused by Cardinal Humbert in 1058 of simony, of buying and selling ecclesiastical offices. While Philip was king, this initial wave of 'Gregorian' reform (as it is commonly called by modern scholars) took on a new twist, as Gregory VII became embroiled with the German heir to the empire over the specific issue of the election and investiture of new bishops and the broader issue of whether the king or the pope wielded the ultimate authority in a Christian empire. Philip, however, continued to push for his favorites for episcopal office and indeed removed bishops he found unsuitable. For example, he deposed Archbishop Ralph of Tours in 1082.

The kings relied on the bishops of certain sees, especially those of Rheims, Laon, Châlons and Beauvais, as supporters of royal power. Indeed, the archbishop of Rheims, as well as traditionally crowning French kings, had been the normal candidate for the royal chancellor under the Carolingians. Although the eleventh-century Capetians never had quite so close or exclusive a relationship to the bishops of any one see – the Capetians/Robertians before Hugh Capet who had become king had been crowned by the archbishops of Sens – they continued to treat certain bishops as key to their realm.

The kings were not consistent, as they might ignore a city in which they had previously approved of the new bishop, or attempt to put their candidate into a see which had previously been influenced more by a local duke or count than the king. And, by late in Philip I's reign, the issue had become complicated by the debates of the Investiture Controversy, in which the reformers simultaneously sought to keep laymen out of episcopal elections and arranged for a specific role for the king to play in holding and releasing the temporal possessions attached to a bishopric. Yet the Investiture Controversy never became the burning political issue in France that it was in the empire. Part of the reason is doubtless the limited number of sees in which the French kings had invested bishops during the eleventh century. Popes forced to flee from Rome in the eleventh century inevitably came to France, and the greatest of the reforming councils, starting with the council of Rheims in 1049, were held within the French kingdom.

Philip's clashes with the papacy over his relations with the French bishops are overshadowed by those caused by his marital problems. In 1107, the pope, Philip and his heir Louis VI all declared at a council at Troyes a mutually acceptable agreement over royal investiture, fifteen years before the pope and the emperor were able to compromise. Although the exact details of this agreement are not known, they seem based on a distinction, initially arrived at by Ivo of Chartres, between the spiritualities, symbolized by ring and staff, which were forbidden to the king, and the temporalities, the lands and revenues of a bishopric, which the king might confer.

If the definition of a 'royal' bishopric is problematic, the definition of a 'royal' monastery is even more so.[6] The kings granted confirmations of possessions and rights of immunity to a number of monasteries, but these can certainly not all be said to be 'royal' houses. The purpose of a grant of immunity, declaring that a monastery was subject to no layman but the king, was not to subject the monks to the crown so much as to establish its independence. The king's reform of a monastic house similarly increased its independence of any layman, including himself. But there were some houses in which the eleventh-century kings acted as the monks' protector, their *advocatus*, and also exercised rights of justice (rather than having the local bishop judge their cases), generally also playing a major role in the election of new abbots. These houses included St-Benoît-sur-Loire, St-Denis and St-Aignan of Orleans, as well as St-Martin-des-Champs, the latter founded by Henry I as a house of canons and reformed by Philip I as a Cluniac priory in 1079.

During the course of the eleventh century, the French kings gradually changed from men who were virtually treated as priests themselves, or at least as an important mediator between their subjects and God, to laymen who could not be sanctified persons in the same way that priests were. The royal anointing ceremony of the late tenth century was very close to the ceremony of anointing a bishop. That the kings could heal scrofula emphasized their sacral nature. Yet by the first half of the twelfth century the sacral nature of kingship had been devalued in favour of the pope's spiritual authority, a change which was influential in France even though the arguments were almost all fought out in relation to the empire.

THE PRINCIPALITIES IN ELEVENTH-CENTURY FRANCE

The king and the princes

The eleventh-century French kings were scarcely more politically powerful than many of their counts and dukes. The great duchies and counties had been Carolingian administrative units before they became quasi-independent principalities in the tenth and eleventh centuries. Some of these princes were virtual kings within their own territories. However, they recognized the suzerainty of the kings and treated them at least intermittently with respect. Not until late

---

[6] *Ibid.*, pp. 69–85.

in the eleventh century did counts start drawing up family genealogies showing their glorious descent, often from the Carolingians, to assert their own
independence; and by the twelfth century the kings were actively engaged in
reducing any such independence. In most of the principalities, the eleventh-
century counts and dukes played an active role in the choice of new bishops,
who might either be from their own families or from the group of their clients.

The eleventh-century Capetians could count on the fidelity of only a handful
of the territorial princes, and not even on all of them consistently. The princes
of the far south-west of the kingdom were especially far from royal authority.
This restricted authority over the princes, and the retreat of French royal power
towards the north, was already becoming evident in the tenth century, under
the last of the French Carolingians.

Such political success as Henry and Philip enjoyed was achieved by playing
different sides off against each other. As the powerful princes who held territory
adjacent to royal territory, especially the counts of Anjou and the counts of
Blois, jostled for position and authority, the kings were able to gain advantages
by supporting one side or the other; and often by switching allegiance at key
points. Henry had had to ask for help at the beginning of his reign from the
duke of Normandy against his mother; the dukes of Normandy had already
assisted King Robert in his Burgundian wars two decades earlier. After settling
his war with his mother, Henry spent the next decade or so preoccupied with
the counts of Blois and Troyes, first Odo II and then Odo's sons. Initially, he
supported the count of Anjou, also an enemy of the house of Blois, though by
late in his reign Henry turned against first the count of Anjou and then the
duke of Normandy.

Philip, who grew up under the tutelage of the count of Flanders, intervened
in 1070/1 in the war over the succession to the county and strove to reduce the
power of the dukes of Normandy, allied both politically and by marriage to
Flanders. Since the duke of Normandy was also king of England after 1066, and
thus during Philip's entire adulthood, the French king considered these dukes
his chief rivals. Beginning a policy which was continued by his successors in the
twelfth century, Philip exploited every division within the English royal family
by supporting rebellions against the king, in his case especially the revolts of
Robert Curthose against first his father, William the Conqueror, and then his
brother, William Rufus.

In surveying the secular princes of the eleventh-century French kingdom,
several themes emerge. The French dukes and counts faced the same challenge
as did the kings in keeping their viscounts and castellans from acting independently. In some principalities, the counts' authority was eroded, but in others
dukes and counts were more successful than were Kings Henry and Philip
in continuing to control their territories. The dukes and counts also worried

about their inheritance and whether to leave everything to one son or to divide it among several sons; both methods were tried. Most commonly – although it was far from the rule – the oldest son would inherit the patrimony that his own father had inherited, while the second (or all younger) son(s) might receive what their father had acquired during his lifetime.

All the different families of dukes and counts were related to each other – and to the kings – by blood or marriage by the end of the eleventh century. Shifting political alliances mark the eleventh century, so that one can never say that two principalities were natural allies; but it is evident that the kings were always a potential enemy, for almost all the families of princes fought against the king at one time or another. But one can still see a remarkable stability among the French duchies and counties during the eleventh century. All of them were important principalities at the end as at the beginning of the century, and, with few exceptions, they were ruled by members of the same families. Indeed, their political histories are inextricably bound to the tangled histories of these families and their marital allegiances.

Burgundy

By far the most complex example is the duchy of Burgundy. Burgundy had a special connection to the French kings in the tenth century, and in the eleventh century its dukes were Capetians. King Robert II took Burgundy from Count Otto-William and his supporters at the beginning of the century and designated his second son as the new duke. The dukes of Burgundy after 1031 were first the brother and then the cousins of the kings, but they did not necessarily act in concert with the royal court. Duke Robert I (1031–75), the brother of King Henry I, and the two grandsons who succeeded him, Hugh I (1075–8) and Odo I (1078–1102), who succeeded after his older brother retired to Cluny, were primarily involved in trying – not always successfully – to establish control over the duchy. The experience of the French kings, in having *fideles* within their kingdom nearly as strong as they were, was duplicated on a smaller scale by that of the dukes of Burgundy. There were also monasteries like Cluny, which claimed complete immunity from any secular overlord, and even one county, that of Langres, held by the bishop of Langres independently of the duke.

But by the final decades of the eleventh century, the dukes of Burgundy had become involved in a major external concern, the *Reconquista* in Spain. Duke Robert's daughter Constance married King Alfonso VI of Castile; and his grandson Henry (brother of Dukes Hugh and Odo) became prince of Portugal by marriage. Once the 'crusading' emphasis shifted from Spain to the Holy Land, the dukes shifted their attention there too; Odo I died on a crusade to Jerusalem.

The chief competitors for the dukes within Burgundy came from the counts of Burgundy and Mâcon, the descendants of Count Otto-William (981–1026). Besides the dukes and the counts, the other two principal lineages were those of the counts of Nevers and of the counts of Chalon. Count Otto-William was son of Adalbert, last king of Italy (d. *c.* 965), and of Gerberge of Chalon; he was adopted by Duke Henry of Burgundy, Hugh Capet's brother, after Henry married Gerberge.

When Duke Henry died in 1002, Otto-William seems originally to have hoped to succeed to the duchy. He was assisted especially by his uncle, Count Hugh I of Chalon, who was also bishop of Auxerre (999–1039). Close to fifteen years of war between Otto-William and King Robert II ended with Otto-William settling for the county of Mâcon, which he had acquired around 981, and for the title of count of Burgundy. This latter title came during the course of the eleventh century to represent the counts' authority over much of the old kingdom of trans-Saône Burgundy. This kingdom was essentially ignored by its titular kings, the German emperors, after the death of Rudolf III, the last Burgundian king, in 1032.

Otto-William married his children to other powerful lords of Burgundy and France. His son Raynald, who took the title of count of Burgundy, married Adelaide of Normandy; their marriage probably took place at the end of the Burgundian wars, for the dukes of Normandy had been major allies of the king against Otto-William and his allies. Otto-William's three daughters married respectively Count Landric of Nevers, Count William II of Provence and Duke William V of Aquitaine.

It should be noted that although the Nivernais was separated from Burgundy during the time of the Valois dukes in the late middle ages, in the eleventh century it was very much part of the duchy of Burgundy. Count Landric, who seems to have become count of Nevers through his marriage with Count Otto-William's daughter, was one of that count's most important allies against the king after 1002, even though he had earlier played an active part in Robert II's attempts to stay married to Bertha, from whom the French bishops had insisted he must separate. Landric's reconciliation with the king when the Burgundian wars finally ended was marked by the engagement of his son and heir to Robert II's daughter. Landric's descendants, the counts of Nevers and Auxerre, also acquired the county of Tonnerre in the second half of the century when Landric's grandson married the heiress of Tonnerre.

After Otto-William died, the county of Mâcon was held by the descendants of his eldest son, Guy, who had predeceased his father. Guy was succeeded by his son Otto and then his grandson Geoffrey. The separate line of counts of Mâcon ended in 1078, when Guy's great-grandson, Guy II, retired to Cluny along with the duke of Burgundy. In the meanwhile the county of Burgundy went to Otto-William's son Raynald (d. *c.* 1057) and Raynald's son, William 'Tête-Hardi'. The latter inherited Mâcon from his cousin and left it to his eldest son, Raynald II (d. *c.* 1095), while his second son, Stephen I (d. 1102), inherited the county of Burgundy.

Normandy

The dukes of Normandy were among the most vigorous and powerful princes to challenge the authority of the French kings during the eleventh century, and their principality, in contrast to Burgundy, was one of the most cohesive. Originally a Viking settlement, recognized by Charles the Simple in 911, the duchy of Normandy had become thoroughly French in language and culture by the beginning of the eleventh century. But the Normans did not become Franks; their institutions and community organization developed out of their Norse heritage. Their method of tying their dependants to them was highly effective; the dukes of Normandy wielded far more direct power in their duchy than did the eleventh-century kings in the Ile-de-France.

Duke Richard II, who ruled Normandy in the early part of the eleventh century (996–1026), was a supporter of the Capetians; he helped King Robert II take the duchy of Burgundy from Otto-William and his allies. At the end of the Burgundian wars, he married his daughter Adelaide to Otto-William's son, Count Raynald of Burgundy. Richard's son and successor, Duke Richard III, ruled for a very brief period (1026–7). He married Adela, the daughter of King Robert II who later married Baldwin V of Flanders. Richard III was succeeded when he died in 1027 not by his son but by his brother Robert, often known as Robert the Devil. Robert had already challenged Richard's authority over him earlier. This competition between close kin was to be repeated in the family of the dukes of Normandy, and later the kings of England. The duchy was treated as indivisible, with only one son inheriting. Although other sons were often given land or income of their own, the new dukes generally set out to deprive their kin of their holdings; Robert was one of the very few brothers who had not been ousted violently.[7] When Robert the Devil died on pilgrimage to the Holy Land in 1037, his entire inheritance went to his bastard son William.

William was still a minor when he inherited, and a rash of private castles and wars threatened the authority of the dukes. Not until 1047, when William crushed the chief of the insurgents with the aid of King Henry I, was he able to enjoy the same power as his father. Also probably in 1047, William introduced the Peace of God into Normandy, making a movement which had had its origins in episcopal councils fifty years earlier (see below) part of ducal rule.

[7] Searle (1988), pp. 143–8.

In the following years, he fought against Geoffrey Martel of Anjou, first while allied with King Henry I and then against both Henry and Geoffrey. These wars did not end until both Henry and Geoffrey died in 1060. William allied himself to the count of Flanders in 1050/1 by marrying Count Baldwin V's daughter Matilda, even though they were related within the forbidden degrees.

During the 1060s, William rapidly expanded Norman ducal power, but his greatest expansion of authority was his 1066 conquest of England. After William became king, he continued to be duke of Normandy, and as most of the Norman lords who took over Anglo-Saxon estates also held on to their Norman possessions, rule and authority were exercised in cross-channel lordship. When William died in 1087, he divided his inheritance, leaving the duchy of Normandy to his eldest son, Robert Curthose, and England to his second son, William Rufus.

Blois

Another powerful family which challenged the authority of the kings of France was that of the counts of Blois, Troyes and Chartres, the family which called themselves counts of Champagne by the twelfth century. They were the descendants of Count Odo I, count of Tours, Blois and Chartres (d. 996), who had married Bertha, sister of King Rudolf III of Burgundy. After Odo I's death Bertha married King Robert II of France, even though they were eventually forced to separate on grounds of consanguinity. The king was highly supportive of the son of Odo I and Bertha, Odo II, and indeed royal support for the count of Blois was highly useful to him in his conflicts with the count of Anjou. But the break-up of the marriage of Robert and Bertha and the king's remarriage to a granddaughter of the count of Anjou (Constance) can be seen in part as a restructuring of the alliances between the kings and the counts of Blois and of Anjou. Odo II tried unsuccessfully to claim Burgundy for himself after Rudolf III's death in 1032. He acquired the regions near Rheims and Provins around 1004 on his brother's death, even though the archbishop of Rheims continued to insist on his own independence, and inherited the county of Troyes from his second cousin Stephen, after the latter died in 1021 (his hereditary claim was backed up by war).

Once Odo II added the Champagne territories located east of Paris (Rheims, Provins and Troyes), which had been in the tenth century the heart of Vermandois power, to his counties to the south-west of Paris (Tours, Blois and Chartres), his possessions essentially surrounded the French royal domain. Although he willingly referred to the king as his lord, and both he and his successors appeared more frequently at the royal court than did the other great French princes, he also was careful to assert that his counties were his by hereditary right, not by the king's grant. He plotted against both King Robert II and King Henry I, although his ambitions, which led to wars over the Touraine, Lorraine and the kingdom of Burgundy, may have been too wide to succeed. His wars against Henry in the early 1030s finally came to an end when Henry made an alliance with the emperor Conrad II, Odo's chief rival for the Burgundian throne.

Upon Odo's death in 1037, his sons divided his inheritance. His western counties, centred on Blois, went to Theobold I (d. 1089), and the eastern (Champagne) counties, centred on Troyes, went to Stephen (d. 1045/8) and then to Stephen's son Odo III. Theobold lost Tours to the count of Anjou in 1044. The brothers Theobold and Stephen plotted unsuccessfully against the king, in a conspiracy led by Henry's younger brother Odo. When Odo III of Champagne moved to England after the Norman Conquest, Theobold took his counties as well. He was in an excellent position to challenge the king and called himself 'count palatine', a title that had fallen out of use since Carolingian times. But on his death in 1089, Philip I was able to insist successfully that Blois and Champagne be divided between Theobold's sons, Stephen (or Stephen-Henry) and Odo IV.

Flanders

Flanders had been a strong and independent county on the fringes of the French kingdom since Carolingian times, and in the eleventh century the region was an important commercial centre, noted both for its wool trade and for cloth weaving. Counts Baldwin IV (988–1037) and Baldwin V (1037–67) began to expand their territory from the kingdom of France into the empire. Baldwin V was a close ally of the French throne. He married Adela, sister of King Henry I; and he acted as regent for his young nephew Philip I from Henry's death in 1060 to his own in 1067.

Baldwin V had two sons, Baldwin VI (1067–70), his heir for Flanders, and Robert, usually called Robert of Frisia, who married the widowed countess of Holland. But Baldwin VI ruled for a very short time and after his death Robert (1070–92) seized Flanders from Baldwin's son Arnulf. Although Philip intervened on behalf of Arnulf, the latter was killed in 1071, and Philip soon made peace with Robert. Shortly thereafter, Philip married Robert's stepdaughter, Bertha of Holland, and for the rest of the eleventh century the counts of Flanders were staunch allies of the kings. Robert was one of the most successful of the French territorial princes in quelling dissent within his county. He and Gertrude, Queen Bertha's mother, bore Robert II of Flanders (1092–1116), the succeeding count. Robert II, one of the richest of the French princes of his time, was also among the most powerful lords to go on the First Crusade.

Anjou

The county of Anjou was one of the strongest principalities in eleventh-century France and its redoubtable ruling family was one of the kings' perpetual challenges. Count Fulk Nerra (987–1040) spent much of his long rule consolidating his power. His niece Constance was King Robert II's final wife, and this marriage has been seen as representing a triumph of the Angevins. Fulk was the first of the French princes to build and use castles effectively. He managed to claim a fair amount of independence from the kings and expanded his territory substantially. He was almost constantly at war, went on pilgrimage several times and made the counts of Anjou a formidable ally or enemy to have.

His son, Geoffrey Martel (1040–60), who had fought against his own father, as count made war variously on the kings of France, the dukes of Normandy, the dukes of Aquitaine and the counts of Blois, from whom he took Tours in 1044. He exercised what might be considered royal, rather than merely princely, rights within his territory, claiming that his court was the court for all free men under him, that all free men had to fight in his armies and that he himself had the right to reform bad legal customs. He married Agnes, widow of William V of Aquitaine and daughter of Otto-William of Burgundy. But he had no children, and his heirs were the children of his sister Ermengard. She had married the count of Château-Landon (the Gâtinais) and later struck up a relationship with Duke Robert of Burgundy. Robert and Ermengard had one daughter, Hildegard, who married William VIII of Aquitaine.

When Geoffrey Martel died in 1060, the county of Anjou was disputed between his nephews, Geoffrey Barbu and Fulk Réchin. The latter eventually won, by 1068, due to an alliance with both the king and the pope, and ruled Anjou until his death in 1109. He brought back under firm comital control those Angevin castellans who had tried to take advantage of the wars between the brothers to establish independent lordships. It was Fulk Réchin's wife Bertrada whom King Philip I left his own wife to marry in 1092, earning him that count's hatred.

Aquitaine

The duchy of Aquitaine, in the central and western part of the French kingdom, was for long the most independent of the great principalities. From the middle of the tenth century on, the title of duke of Aquitaine had been taken by the counts of Poitou. Duke William V 'the Great' (993–1030) inherited a broad territory, and he exercised at least some influence over the more southerly counties of Languedoc. His rule, however, was only unquestioned within Poitou itself, and his reign was marked by struggles with the neighbouring counts, especially the count of Anjou. He was a strong supporter of the churches of his region, and was one of the first princes to support the Peace of God movement; he also went on pilgrimage repeatedly.

He married several times; his last wife was Agnes, daughter of Otto-William of Burgundy. When the first two of William's sons succeeded him (as William VI and William VII) without producing heirs of their own, the castellans of Aquitaine were able to assert their independence, and Geoffrey Martel of Anjou built up Angevin authority on the borders of Aquitaine. The last of William V's sons, Gui-Geoffrey-William, or William VIII (1058–86) (he was originally named Gui, became Geoffrey when his mother married Geoffrey Martel and William when he became duke of Aquitaine), managed to regain ground, including control in 1063 of Gascony, to the south of Aquitaine. He was at the head of the *fideles* at the coronation of King Philip, but his contact with the king was at best infrequent.

William VIII married Hildegard, daughter of Duke Robert of Burgundy, making consanguineous the marriage between Eleanor of Aquitaine and Louis VII three generations later.[8] His son William IX (1086–1126), a noted troubadour poet, was kept busy both on the borders of Aquitaine, with quarrels with Anjou, Angoulême and Gascony, and in the broader world: he went on crusade and campaigned in Spain.

Brittany

In spite of being located in northern France, bordered by Normandy and Anjou, Brittany stood apart from French politics and society both culturally and linguistically. The dukes acted essentially as kings within their own territory; Radulf Glaber even reports that Conan I celebrated his consolidation of power over the duchy by putting a diadem on his head, 'in the manner of kings.'[9] In spite of this symbolic authority, the Breton dukes of this period scrambled, without always great success, to hold their own against neighbouring princes and against the increasingly independent castellans.

During the tenth century the duchy of Brittany had been disputed between the counts of Rennes and the counts of Nantes; by the late tenth century, Conan I (d. 992) had secured the victory (at least temporarily) for the counts of Rennes. He married Ermengard, sister of Fulk Nerra of Anjou. His son Geoffrey (992–1008) allied himself, both politically and through marriage, to the dukes of neighbouring Normandy: he married Hadwidis, sister of Duke Richard II of Normandy, while having that duke marry his own sister. Geoffrey initiated a number of monastic reforms in Brittany during his short reign. His

---

[8] *Chronique de Saint Maixent*, c. 1067.   [9] Radulf Glaber, *Historia* II.iii.4, 'more regio'.

young son, Alain III, who succeeded him (1008–40), was able to suppress two revolts by the Breton lords and kept very firm control of the episcopate. By his wife Bertha, daughter of Odo II of Blois, Alain had Conan II (1040–66), whose reign again began with a minority. Even after taking ducal power himself, Conan was faced by uprisings against him, several led by his uncle, who had acted as regent while he was still a boy. The counts of Nantes and Anjou and the duke of Normandy also joined the ongoing conflict. It is an indication of the independence of many of the great Breton lords that a number fought with William of Normandy at Hastings. Even though Conan was relatively successful in maintaining his position in Brittany, his death in late 1066, without a son to succeed, meant a change in the Breton dynasty.

Conan's sister Hadwidis had married Hoël, count of Nantes. In 1066, he became duke of Brittany. Under Hoël and his son, Alain IV (1084–1115), the dukes of Brittany were frequently at war with the dukes of Normandy and their own vassals. It was during this period that the Breton bishops, who had earlier been closely allied with the dukes, became much more subject to outside influence as the Gregorian reform penetrated the duchy.

Toulouse

The county of Toulouse, like the duchy of Aquitaine, was one of the most independent of the French principalities. Oriented towards the Mediterranean, the counts essentially ignored northern politics. The city of Toulouse grew rapidly into an important urban centre in the eleventh century and the counts kept firm control over both the bishops and the viscounts of the city. The old system of Roman law, written agreements between laymen and the public court system, stayed alive here when they were long gone in the north, even while castles multiplied and new lands were cleared.

At the beginning of the eleventh century, William, nicknamed 'Taillefer' (d. 1037), was count of Toulouse and Gothia. He married Emma, niece of Count William I of Provence. The two sons of William Taillefer, Pons and Raymond, split their family lands and titles, by separating the counties of Toulouse and Gothia. Pons's sons, William IV (d. 1093) and Raymond IV (d. 1105), did the same on that count's death in 1061. But Pons's younger son, Raymond IV, called 'of St-Gilles' from the time when he became marquis of Provence (and subjected the monastery of St-Gilles to Cluny), reunited Toulouse and Gothia as well as adding Provence to his inheritance. Raymond IV's remarkable political success was short-lived, however; when he went on crusade in 1096, the duke of Aquitaine, who had married Raymond's niece Philippa, took the opportunity to attack Toulouse. Raymond ended up establishing a principality in Tripoli which continued to distract his heirs from southern France.

Provence

Provence had been the heart of an independent kingdom in the late ninth and early tenth centuries, but by the late tenth century it had become no more than a county, centred on the city of Arles. Until the death of the last king of Burgundy in 1032, it was under his authority but not part of his kingdom. Although it lay in the empire rather than, strictly speaking, in the French kingdom, culturally and politically it was French in the eleventh century.

William I was count of Arles and marquis of Provence at the end of the tenth century (d. 993). He married Adelaide-Blanche, the aunt of Fulk Nerra of Anjou. Adelaide-Blanche had earlier been married to the Carolingian Louis V. The son and heir of William and Adelaide, William II (993–1019), married Gerberge, daughter of Count Otto-William of Burgundy. As well as William II, William I had Constance, who became queen of France by marrying Robert II.

William II was succeded in turn by his three sons, William, Bertran (also known as Fulk-Bertran) and Jouffre. For much of the eleventh century, comital rights were exercised by all three of these sons and their sons. But after these three had died, as had Bertran's son William Bertran (d. 1065) and Jouffre's son Bertran II (d. 1090), only women were left as heirs. The county of Provence went to their cousin, Raymond IV of Toulouse (1065–1105), descended from a niece of William I of Provence, who became marquis of Provence and took the title 'St-Gilles'.

OTHER ELEVENTH-CENTURY DEVELOPMENTS

The eleventh century in France was in many ways a turning-point, when fundamental changes took place in social and economic structures, power structures and in the religious and intellectual life. The changes did not take place all at the same time or at the same speed, and even within the area one might loosely call France – or at least northern France – there were enormous regional differences. But there can be no question that France (however defined) was vastly different in the year 1100 than it had been in the year 1000.

This change has sometimes been characterized as the development of 'feudal' society, or, if one is talking specifically about the kings, the development of 'feudal monarchy'. Any such use of the term 'feudal' is highly problematic in itself, and, if it is defined at all sensibly, refers neither to society in a broad sense nor to the eleventh-century French kings.

If one feels compelled to give a sweeping name to the new social and governmental forms, one possibility is to refer to 'Capetian' society; after all, the terms 'Merovingian' and 'Carolingian' are already widely used to refer to everything from artistic styles to judicial systems in, respectively, the fifth to the ninth and the ninth and tenth centuries. Another possibility would be to borrow the architectural term 'Romanesque' and refer to the birth of 'Romanesque' society, which would have the advantage over 'Capetian' in referring specifically to the eleventh and twelfth centuries.

Economic developments

However one defines the new society and structures that emerged in eleventh-century France it is clear that significant changes were taking place. It was the period in which the economic foundations were laid which made the rapid urban and commercial growth of the twelfth century possible. At base was an overall improvement in the climate, the end of the 'mini ice-age' which had marked the early middle ages. The climate was already improving by the tenth century, but only in the eleventh century did the slightly longer growing season and the slightly drier climate, which made possible the cultivation of the rich, heavy soils of northern France's river valleys, begin to be widely noted. Several parts of France suffered through disastrous harvests in the first decades of the century, when many people starved and rumours of cannibalism were rampant, but after the 1030s major, widespread famine disappeared from France until the beginning of the fourteenth century.

New lands began to be cultivated as forests were cleared, slowly at first, although the tempo accelerated in the late eleventh and early twelfth centuries. The gradual and sporadic spread of heavy ploughs and of horses instead of oxen made possible cultivation of damper lands and more rapid ploughing. Although the eleventh century's agricultural expansion is outshone by that of the twelfth century, it is quite clear that more people were growing more food successfully in France by the end of the eleventh century than 100 years earlier.

While French peasants of the eleventh century increased the size of the arable and made some improvements in agricultural technique, they also in many cases broke free from the servitude which had characterized their ancestors. The terms *servus* and *ancilla*, male and female serf, common since late antiquity, essentially disappeared in northern France by the first decades of the twelfth century. Free peasants were by no means the social equal of their lords; indeed, the development of the distinction between 'those who fight' and 'those who work' put a sharp barrier between lords and peasants. But the normal twelfth-century term for a dependent peasant, *homo*, was the same term used for a vassal, even a vassal of noble birth.

Accompanying the agricultural expansion were the foundations of urban and commercial growth. In urbanization, France, or at least northern France, seems to have been close to a century behind Italy, where growth of the cities is evident from the very beginning of the eleventh century. But commercial exchange multiplied during the eleventh century, as the markets and tolls which had never died out during Carolingian times became more active. The number of coins in circulation (especially small coins) increased markedly, an indication that broad commercial exchange had reached to the lowest economic levels. New bridges were built to accommodate the increased traffic in goods.

The economic growth of eleventh-century France is reflected in the expansionism of the second half of the century. Already in the first half of the eleventh century, Normans had begun going to fight in southern Italy, where they laid the foundations of what eventually became the kingdom of Sicily. In the 1070s, political and marriage alliances were formed between the kings of Spain and French nobles, especially those of Burgundy, who played a major role in the *Reconquista*. The First Crusade, launched in 1095, was dominated by French soldiers.

Castles and castellans

Many of the changes in the upper levels of society can be related to the development and spread of castles. Fortifications of course had a long history, going back to the Bronze Age, and a number of French cities had had substantial walls since the early middle ages. The term *castrum* had been in at least intermittent use for a fortified place for some time. But castles were a new phenomenon at the end of the tenth century. They were built not to defend a large population behind their walls, for longer or shorter periods of time, and not as a defence against Viking or Muslim invasions, long over by the time when castles began to appear in any numbers, but rather to serve as the permanent home for a powerful lord and his household. Castles thus combined the functions of a fortress with those of a palace, which had earlier been a larger, more open hall. Castles are also an example of both the eleventh century's rapid changes and the continuities from an earlier period. The stone keeps which proliferated during the century were built initially by men whose principalities – and usually whose ancestors – had been in place since Carolingian times.

Castles spread rapidly across France, on major routes, along rivers, at political frontiers. Some were built at the command of princes, others by powerful allodists, at their own initiative, on their own lands. The political weakness of the French kings meant that there was no question here, as there was in post-Conquest England, of having castles royally licensed. Individual counts or dukes, however, might strictly control the building and manning of castles within their territories. The counts of Anjou, who at the beginning of the century were some of the most assiduous castle builders, sought to maintain the loyalty of the men they put into their castles.

The castellans were undoubted members of the aristocracy from the time when they first appeared. And yet in many cases they seem to have been 'new men', whose ancestors had not had political authority. Their appearance swelled the ranks of the nobility, and, once they became established, they quickly created ties of marriage between themselves and the counts and viscounts – with much more venerable ancestries – who had in many cases put them into their castles in the first place.

The castellans soon began to organize their families and personal identities as well as their political and military power around their castles. By the final decades of the eleventh century, it was fairly common for a noble to be referred to in the charters as being 'of' somewhere – for example to be called 'Milo of Noyers' – whereas for over 500 years nobles had usually been known only by a single name. As the *cognomen* (second name), most commonly taken from the name of the castle, became more common, there was a sharp reduction in the number of Christian names in circulation, and cousins might end up sharing only a few names, taking preferentially the names of their most glorious ancestors. Inheritance as well as naming patterns was organized around the castellany. Castles very quickly became hereditary, and castellans usually decided to leave their castles only to the eldest son.

The power that a castle gave a lord allowed the castellans to begin to exercise 'banal' rights (from the Latin *bannum*, meaning the area subject to a person or institution's authority). These rights constituted the economic, military and judicial authority that the castellan exercised over everyone who lived within the region of his castellany. Castles thus became instruments of territorial rule. Banal rights seem in origin to have been a combination of public and private rights. Judicial and military functions, which were once levied in the name of the king but now devolved from kings and their counts and viscounts to the new castellans, were combined with many of the economic obligations to which tenants and serfs had always been subject.

What was different here was that these banal rights were enforced on all local inhabitants, whether they were personally dependent on that particular lord or not. They quickly were transformed from being a form of delegated authority to become part of the banal lord's patrimonial possessions. It is an indication of how much these rights had lost their public character that banal rights were frequently called *consuetudines*, customary rights, based on collective memory rather than royal authority; and, interestingly, by the middle of the eleventh century French kings were starting to use the term *consuetudines* for their own exercise of power.

The most important of these banal rights was that to the taille, essentially a fee payable on demand to the lord; it might now be termed protection money. Banal rights also included monopolies on mills and ovens, tolls on roads and bridges, the right to demand hospitality and especially the administration of justice. Thus, at the time many serfs were escaping from servitude, many peasants whose ancestors had been free allodists began to owe dues to the local lords for the first time. The lords with banal rights were able to consolidate their economic position during the eleventh and twelfth centuries, at a time when rising monetary expenses (for everything from new castles to crusades to gifts to the church) cut into the wealth of many aristocrats.

Simultaneous with the spread of castles was the spread of a new social group, the knights (*milites*). The term *miles* had originally meant a Roman footsoldier, but from the end of the tenth century onward its significance was changed, and it meant specifically someone who served and fought for a lord or castellan, generally on horseback. The idea of service was integral to the concept of knighthood when it first appeared, but the kind of service that knights owed their lords was very different from the service of peasant tenants. The knight of the eleventh century, sometimes referred to as *caballarius* instead of *miles*, served in the castles and followed his lord in warfare, to regional councils and on excursions to cities and monasteries. The knights, professionals in warfare as those of noble blood had not necessarily been before, were not originally identical with the nobles, although the two groups did eventually fuse in the twelfth and thirteenth centuries.[10]

At the same time as knights began to be common in France, there began to be a new perception of how society was structured. Earlier, the most prevalent distinction between laymen had been between free and servile, with free peasants and free nobles thus lumped into a single category. But in the eleventh century it became increasingly common to divide society not by status but by function. The classic statement of this division was made by Adalbero of Laon in the early eleventh century, when he distinguished between those who fight, those who pray and those who work.[11] Adalbero's formulation did not immediately replace earlier descriptions of society. Even ecclesiastics who agreed with a separation within secular society between workers and warriors did not generally treat members of the secular clergy and the regular clergy as part of the same order. But increasingly nobles and their knights, the fighters (including many dependent knights who would have been considered servile in the tenth century), were distinguished by their warlike activities from the rest of society.

The Peace of God

Contemporary with the spread of castles and knights was the development of the Peace of God movement. This movement marks a shift in underlying ideas (at least among the bishops who led it), from the acceptance of war as

---

[10] Flori (1988), pp. 260–4.   [11] Adalbero, *Poème*, lines 295–6.

the normal occupation of men to the equation of God's will with peace.[12] The disintegration of Carolingian public justice – however effective it might or might not once have been – in the face of groups of powerful men provoked an alternative method of preserving order within society. As a new social group of professional warriors grew, and as the multiplication of castles provided loci for warfare, the bishops of first southern and then northern France reacted by holding Peace of God councils. The southern bishops were often assisted by the local counts. The sworn oaths that had been used in southern France for some time to reinforce the protection of persons and goods dependent on the church, and to maintain the right of sanctuary in the churches, became an instrument for establishing – or attempting to establish – general order and justice within society.[13]

In these councils the bishops brought out relics to use spiritual persuasion to make nobles and knights swear oaths to limit violence to, and exactions from, the unarmed and clerics. The councils first appeared in the 980s and multiplied during the eleventh century. By the 1030s and 1040s, the French bishops felt that they had made enough headway in persuading the powerful not to attack the helpless to allow them to expand their efforts by preaching the Truce of God, an attempt to make knights and nobles agree not even to kill each other on certain days of the week. The Truce started with establishing Sunday as a day of peace and spread out to cover several other days and certain seasons of the year (especially Advent and Lent). The peace movement was revived at the end of the eleventh century with the result that virtually every ecclesiastical council in France, even those led by the pope (such as the 1095 council of Clermont, which launched the First Crusade), proclaimed the Peace of God.

These peace councils were probably not notably successful in reducing the overall level of violence in society – after all, mercenary soldiers first appeared in France in the second half of the century, at the same time the peace movement was at its height[14] – although they doubtless made some nobles think about what they were doing and occasionally moderate their behaviour. But there are several conclusions that can be drawn from the fact that the bishops held these councils.

First, it is striking that the Capetian kings of France were not considered even worth consulting in these efforts to reduce violence toward the helpless. The bishops called their councils in a royal power vacuum. The Carolingian kings – and even kings from other families during the ninth and tenth centuries – had been war leaders, and those who had not been effective war leaders had been considered incompetent kings. Now, even though the eleventh-century Capetians did not immediately take up this role, it was assumed that effective

[12] Duby (1973), pp. 450–1.   [13] Magnou-Nortier (1974), p. 304.   [14] Duby (1973), p. 462.

leaders would be peace-makers. Some dukes realized this well before the kings; the dukes of Normandy and Aquitaine took the lead in calling peace councils in their duchies.

Secondly, although the councils uniformly decried the violence of their age, and although the endemic fighting of the period is well documented, one still comes away with the impression that the eleventh century was less violent than the tenth. It would not have been even worth trying to make nobles and knights agree to give up random attacks on the helpless if there had been no chance that they would comply. Even the building of castles suggests at least respites in fighting; one cannot, after all, fortify an important hilltop or river crossing while it is being actively besieged.

Fief-holding

This is one of the chief examples of the ways in which the eleventh century reformulated the structures and even the legal terms inherited from an earlier period. Because fief-holding used Latin words which had been in use in the Carolingian period, with different meanings, such as *fidelis*, *vassus* and *beneficium*, scholars used to assume that the feudal relationships which become evident in eleventh-century records had also existed a century or two earlier. But a number of close regional studies have revealed the novelty of this institution.

In the fief-holding system, which was carried out exclusively between nobles or between nobles and knights, that is between members of the upper echelons of society, one man swore an oath of fidelity to another in return for a lifetime right to a piece of property, the fief (*feudum*). The man who received the fief, the vassal, did not owe specific dues or rents, only faithful support and military service as needed. He did not assume ownership of the fief, which continued to belong to the lord, but he had possession and use of it. The vassal's right to the fief was conditional, in that it was predicated on continued support of his lord, even though the lord was expected to allow his vassal to keep his fief for life barring loss of that support; in this respect a fief was quite different from the *beneficia* which the Carolingians had granted for longer or shorter terms.

Fulbert of Chartres described the correct relationship of a vassal to his lord around 1020 in a letter which is the earliest to give a full description of feudal relationships (*forma fidelitatis*), emphasizing especially the negative obligations of the vassal.[15] He should not cause his lord any harm, Fulbert said, or betray either his secrets or his castles. He should not detract from the lord's judicial rights, cause him any loss of possessions or do anything which would make it harder, or even impossible, for the lord to do what would be of value to him.

---

[15] Fulbert of Chartres, *Letters* 51, pp. 90–2.

Fulbert added that these negative obligations were not enough, however, for the vassal to be entitled to a fief. He was also supposed to aid his lord, both physically and with good counsel, and his lord should in return be faithful and helpful to him.

When fief-holding first appeared in France, it was extremely *ad hoc* and extremely limited. It certainly had antecedents in earlier centuries, in the oaths of fidelity which counts and dukes had sworn to the Carolingian kings, or for that matter in the groups of lords and clients which characterized both Roman and early Germanic society. But eleventh-century fief-holding was as often a relationship between equals as between superiors and clients, and it necessarily involved the grant of a fief, whereas *fideles* in the Carolingian period were *fideles* whether or not the king had granted them anything – or whether or not he took it back. Another important distinction, one which can be seen most clearly in southern France but which is also applicable in the north, is that Carolingian *fideles* received grants of public land and income in their position as officials, whereas eleventh-century feudal lords granted their own personal allodial land to their vassals.

The mutual obligations which Fulbert mentioned created a sense of equality between lord and vassal. Fief-holding was used to cement alliances as well as to bind knights and petty aristocrats to the more powerful. By the late twelfth century, the system was one of the most powerful tools that the territorial princes had to forge links between themselves and the castellans below them. But in the eleventh century – and, indeed, for much of the twelfth – fiefs were in the minority among aristocratic holdings, as they held most of their land outright, as allods.

Monastic reform

At the same time as castles, knights and fiefs began to spread, French monasticism experienced rapid expansion. Radulf Glaber, describing Burgundy, dates the beginning of a major period of ecclesiastical rebuilding to around 1030, when he said France became covered with a 'white mantle of churches'.[16] In fact, even in Burgundy, eleventh-century monastic expansion had long tenth-century roots, but there is no doubt that the eleventh century was a great period for rebuilding, refounding and reforming French monasteries, so that by the beginning of the twelfth century there were very few ruined churches left which had at any time in their histories sheltered monks. Not all were monasteries in the twelfth century; many, especially in the cities, were refounded instead as houses of secular or regular canons. But by the time of Molesme's foundation

---

[16] Radulf Glaber, *Historia* III.iv.13, 'passim candidam ecclesiarum vestem indueret'.

in 1075 and Cîteaux's in 1098, two houses which were to be enormously influential in twelfth-century monasticism, most new monasteries were indeed
new foundations, rather than reformations of Merovingian or Carolingian
houses.

The monastic revival of the eleventh century contained several different
and not necessarily related aspects. Houses which needed to be reformed were
reformed; houses of an already exemplary life were rebuilt or expanded; and a
number of monasteries sought to free themselves from episcopal control. Privileges from the ninth or early tenth centuries, putting houses directly under the
papacy, were revived and used as defences against the local bishops. Although
some monasteries, like Cluny, were able to exempt themselves fairly thoroughly
from their diocesan bishops during the eleventh century, the abrupt emergence
of the papacy into the active life of the French church in the later part of the
century led, somewhat ironically, to the reestablishment of episcopal authority,
as the popes sought a hierarchical structure in which the bishops certainly had
an important role to play, even if it was as mediators between the papacy and
local churches and monasteries.

Although reform of existing monasteries, whether because they had been
physically ruined or because the monks no longer seemed to be following a life
of appropriate rigour, was as old as monasticism itself, and had been carried out
repeatedly in France since Merovingian times, the wave of reform which began
in the final quarter or so of the tenth century was unprecedented in intensity.
It is doubtless related to the same (even if slight) reduction in the overall level
of violence which made the Peace of God movement even thinkable.

The usual late tenth- and eleventh-century pattern was for a monastery of
undoubted regularity and sanctity of life to be given responsibility for reforming
a ruined or dissolute house, sometimes by taking over its direction, sometimes
by sending one of its own monks to be abbot there, generally with a group
of companions. In different parts of France, different monasteries were sought
out as sources of monastic reform. In Burgundy, Cluny was so treated in the
late tenth and eleventh centuries, even though in the first part of the tenth
century its influence had been felt more in the Auvergne and even in Italy than
in Burgundy. In Lorraine, Gorze played a similar role, as did Marmoutier in
western France, Montmajour in Provence, Moissac in the county of Toulouse
(subjected to Cluny in the second half of the eleventh century) and Chaise-
Dieu in the Auvergne.

These reforms tended to be quite *ad hoc* in the eleventh century, with
nothing like the orderly establishment of daughter-houses, permanently bound
into an institutionalized relationship, which characterized the Cistercian order
in the twelfth century. Reforms were in almost all cases initiated not by the
monastery which ended up carrying out these reforms but by a local bishop or

powerful layman; indeed, in many cases the abbot might be highly reluctant to use his resources and monks to reestablish another monastery. It is striking that eleventh-century reforms and foundations were rarely carried out at the initiative of the kings, who were not even asked to confirm those outside the royal domain, as the Carolingians had routinely been. Interestingly, both Henry and Philip paid more attention to houses of canons than to monasteries; the latter, it has been suggested, presented more of a threat to a monarchy whose authority was already weakened.[17]

In some cases, the reformed monastery might become a priory of the re-forming monastery, having the abbot of the reforming house serve as its abbot, an arrangement which might last indefinitely or only as long as the original abbot lived. Fécamp in Normandy was reformed by the abbot of St-Bénigne of Dijon, but, after thirty years of being under the abbot of St-Bénigne, it received its own abbot at the request of the duke of Normandy. In other cases the newly reformed house would have its own abbot from the beginning, one of the monks sent out to reestablish a house's religious life.

By whatever method monastic reform was carried out, it was highly effective. By the final decades of the eleventh century, there were few religious houses capable of supporting a large group of religious men or women which did not indeed do so. Even small churches frequently had a small chapter of canons attached. Many of these were secular canons, but beginning in the 1060s regular or 'Augustinian' canons began to appear in France. These became established especially in urban churches, although also in some rural churches and even castle chapels, where they combined care for the souls of their secular neighbors with a communal way of life. About the same time as these canons appeared in urban churches, hermits began to appear scattered through the French countryside. By the end of the eleventh century, some of these hermitages became the nodes of new monastic foundations; Cîteaux, for example, was founded on the site of a *hermemum*.

During the course of the eleventh century, monasteries, which had once relied on kings or at least territorial princes to give them grants of immunity, increasingly turned to the pope. This process was well under way even before the Gregorian reform, when it was accelerated. Cluny, for example, received no charters from the French kings during the reigns of Henry and Philip. The perceived independence of the monks from royal authority was distressing to royal supporters. Adalbero of Laon's description of the 'three orders' of society was not a simple observation but part of a polemic, an argument that 'those who pray' were beginning to interfere in the activities more rightly belonging to 'those who fight'.

---

[17] Lemarignier (1965), pp. 93–107.

The eleventh century was a major period for gifts from powerful laymen to monks. Fairly frequent were gifts of parish churches, given to the monks by the secular nobles who had previously held them; one of the ways that monasteries became more important in the eleventh century was in controlling more parish churches. It was fairly common for monks to receive large tracts of land, even entire *villae*, from the most powerful of their benefactors: interestingly, often the same men who at other periods in their lives might attempt to appropriate monastic property for themselves. Although it would be extremely difficult to compare eleventh-century donations overall to those of the twelfth century, since there were many new foundations in the twelfth century, and since the knights who had rarely made gifts of their own in the eleventh century began to do so in the twelfth, it is clear that the very large gift, often from the layman who had either initiated the reform of a particular house himself or whose ancestors had done so, was more characteristic of the period before rather than after 1100. At some houses, indeed, the great bulge in gifts came even earlier; Cluny received enough sizable gifts from its neighbours in the 980s to reduce their resources for eleventh-century gifts.

Scholarship

While both monks and the laymen who made them gifts sought to forward the regular monastic life with new intensity in the eleventh century, a number of episcopal schools attracted teachers and attracted to their doors people interested in intellectual studies even if not in joining the particular church. Even some houses of secular canons opened schools; Bernard of Clairvaux had studied with the canons of Châtillon-sur-Seine while still a layman. At many of these schools, theological questions which had not been broadly debated in the west since the patristic period were examined anew.

Canonists like Ivo of Chartres went through the great mass of papal pronouncements, conciliar decisions and real or forged canonical collections from the first millennium of Christianity and attempted to establish what the church's position actually was on a number of issues involving both theology and canon law. Schools like the school of Chartres attracted both masters and students interested in the study of theology, and interest in such issues was high enough that, by the final years of the eleventh century, itinerant theologians attracted large audiences. Heresy reappeared in the west during this period, not that it had been gone in a strict sense, but that no one had had time, energy or knowledge to dispute orthodoxy versus heresy for some centuries. With the reappearance of heresy came the reappearance of burning heretics, although the practice, unknown in France since the end of the Roman empire, was still very sporadic in the eleventh century.

Accompanying the developments in scholarship within the church were, as the example of Bernard of Clairvaux suggests, the beginnings of a revival of lay literacy. At least in northern France, lay literacy seems to have died out in the tenth century, and it did not become at all common again until the thirteenth, but there is no question that the number of charters issued on behalf of laymen increased markedly in the eleventh. The majority of the surviving documents are monastic, and therefore one cannot separate this documentary increase from the increase in gifts to monks, but it is clear that the written word was taking on a new significance.

Related to – although one could not say directly caused by – the resurgence in monasticism and interest in church law and doctrine was the so-called Gregorian reform of the episcopate. In France this led fairly rapidly to a series of bishops who, unlike many (though certainly not all) of their predecessors were dedicated to the church above their own families, were chaste, and had acceded to office by election rather than by purchase. One of the most striking results of the dramatic lessening of the role of the kings and great princes in choosing bishops was the change in the social origins of the men who became bishop in almost all the French sees. Once they had been men who had served the powerful, perhaps as their chaplains, or had even been the brothers and cousins of princes. When the cathedral chapters took over the choice of new bishops, they tended to choose one of their own rather than the dependants or relatives of the most powerful secular lords of the area. Starting in the last quarter of the eleventh century, new bishops, while certainly aristocratic, no longer tended to be from the highest ranks of the nobility, and they were also much more frequently local in origin.[18]

The eleventh century, then, was a period of major and rapid evolution in all aspects of French society. It has been relatively neglected in the past, due in part to the blandness of the kings who reigned during this period, and in part to the greater scholarly attention to the twelfth century. But the eleventh was a key transitional century, when the economic, cultural and political institutions inherited from the Carolingian period were transformed.

[18] Bouchard (1987), pp. 67–76.

CHAPTER 6

SPAIN IN THE ELEVENTH CENTURY

Simon Barton

THE death of Muhammad ibn Abi 'Amir – better known to history by his hon-orific al-Mansur or Almanzor ('the Victorious') – at Medinaceli on 11 August 1002 was doubtless greeted with grim satisfaction, not to say considerable relief, by the inhabitants of the realms of Christian Spain. For a quarter of a century al-Mansur had firmly held the reins of power in al-Andalus (Muslim Spain), eliminating his political rivals within the state bureaucracy in Córdoba and rel-egating the ruling Umayyad caliph, Hisham II (976–1009), to little more than a ceremonial role. Commanding fear and respect in roughly equal measure, al-Mansur's authority as *hajib*, or chief minister to the caliph, and as *de facto* ruler of al-Andalus appears to have gone largely unchallenged. The sheer size and strength of the armies that he had under his command ensured that Cordoban control over the provinces of al-Andalus was never seriously called into ques-tion; just as they also enabled him to win considerable personal prestige, as well as impressive quantities of booty, by virtue of the devastating twice-yearly razzias that he led far and wide into Christian territory, from Barcelona in the north-east to Santiago de Compostela in the far north-west. By the beginning of the eleventh century al-Andalus was not simply the dominant political force in the Iberian peninsula, but it was probably the most powerful state in the en-tire western Mediterranean region, its boundaries stretching from North Africa to the Duero. Under al-Mansur's rule, a writer later observed, 'Islam enjoyed a glory which al-Andalus had never witnessed before, while the Christians suffered their greatest humiliation.'[1] For all that, the impression of strength was to prove illusory. Within only a decade of al-Mansur's death, unitary political authority in al-Andalus collapsed and in 1031 the western Umayyad caliphate passed into history, never to be resurrected. Although, towards the end of the century, Muslim Spain was to achieve short-lived unity under the Berber Almoravids, the balance of power in the peninsula had already shifted

---

[1] 'Abd Allah, *The Tibyan*, p. 43.

decisively away from al-Andalus. Spanish Islam had begun what was to prove a long and humiliating retreat in the face of the increasingly self-confident and expansionist states of the Christian north.

Al-Mansur's son and successor, 'Abd al-Malik al-Muzaffar, was regarded by some as a libertine and a wine-bibber, but the policies he pursued were very much a continuation of those that had been implemented by his illustrious father.[2] The new *hajib* in Córdoba took steps to tighten his grip on power at home, eliminating those whom he perceived to be potential rivals to his position, and ensuring that the caliph remained far removed from the affairs of state. He also strove to maintain the pressure against his enemies abroad, leading raiding expeditions deep into Catalonia, Castile, León and Navarre, with varying degrees of success. In 1004 he was even asked to arbitrate in a dispute over the regency of the throne of León. But respite was at hand for the beleaguered inhabitants of the Christian north. The untimely death of al-Muzaffar from a heart attack in October 1008 was to plunge al-Andalus into political crisis and reveal the fundamental structural weaknesses of the political and military edifice which al-Mansur had so painstakingly constructed. For one thing, although al-Mansur and his son had claimed to be acting in the name of Hisham II, the effective isolation of the young caliph from government and the emergence of the *hajib* as the true power behind the throne had served only to diminish the already fast-fading prestige of the caliphal office and to undermine the established basis of authority in al-Andalus. Though the caliph's name still appeared on the coins that were minted and he continued to be mentioned at Friday prayers, by 1008 the Umayyad ruler had long since become a political irrelevance.[3] Secondly, the rapid expansion of the state army had not simply proved an intolerable strain on the public purse, but the recruitment of large numbers of Berbers into its ranks had introduced into al-Andalus a foreign and volatile element which owed its loyalty to its paymasters in Cordoba rather than to the institution of the Umayyad caliphate *per se*. When, subsequently, that institution came under threat, few among the military would think it worthwhile taking up arms to ensure its survival.

In the short term, for so long as the ruling 'Amirids were willing to pay lip-service to the pretence of caliphal authority and were able to command the support of the armed forces, their political supremacy seemed assured. But the decision by al-Muzaffar's vainglorious brother 'Abd al-Rahman (known as Shanjul) to have himself appointed heir to the caliphal throne late in 1008 was to have fateful consequences both for the 'Amirid dynasty his father had founded and for centralized government in al-Andalus as a whole. Faced with

---

[2] Ibn 'Idhari, *La caída del Califato de Córdopa*, p. 11.
[3] Ibn al-Kardabus, *Historia de al-Andalus*, p. 84; Wasserstein (1985), pp. 40–1, n. 47.

the prospect of imminent political extinction, members of the Umayyad family launched a daring *coup d'état* in February 1009 in the course of which they managed to oust the hapless Hisham II, install another member of their dynasty, Muhammad al-Mahdi, as caliph in his stead, and then assassinate the hated *hajib* Shanjul. To cap it all, the sumptuous palace which al-Mansur had built for his family to the east of Córdoba at Madinat al-Zahira ('the glittering city') was razed to the ground by the insurgents. Yet, if the Umayyad conspirators fondly imagined that by their rebellion they might turn back the clock and restore to the caliphate the power and prestige which it had enjoyed in the days of 'Abd al-Rahman III (912–61) they were to be sorely disappointed. For far from shoring up Umayyad unitary authority, the events of 1008/9 simply encouraged other would-be rulers to throw their hats into the ring and to make their own bids for power. The state army, which hitherto had enabled central government in Córdoba to retain control over the provinces, fragmented into any number of competing warbands, and with it the unity of Muslim Spain was broken.

In the course of the intense struggle for power that unfolded between the death of al-Muzaffar in 1008 and the final extinction of the caliphate in 1031, the authority of the centre evaporated and al-Andalus dissolved into a number of independent principalities known to historians as taifa kingdoms (in Arabic the word *ta'ifa* means 'party' or 'faction'). Contemporary Arabic writers referred to this period of strife as the *fitna*, meaning discord, rebellion or punishment.[4] According to the version of events provided in his memoirs by 'Abd Allah al-Ziri, taifa king of Granada between 1073 and 1090, after the fall of the 'Amirid dynasty 'every military commander rose up in his own town and entrenched himself behind the walls of his own fortress, having first secured his own position, created his own army, and amassed his own resources. These persons vied with one another for worldly power, and each sought to subdue the other.'[5] Most of the successor-states that emerged immediately after 1008 were based on administrative units (*kuwar*) – a city and its dependent territory – that had already existed during the period of 'Amirid rule. Likewise, many of the men who successfully established themselves as taifa rulers had already exercised positions of power under the previous regime. Zawi ibn Ziri, for example, who took over the province of Elvira at the foot of the Sierra Nevada in about 1013 and later transferred his seat of government to what was to become the city of Granada, was but one among several Berber generals who successfully set themselves up as independent rulers after the demise of unitary authority. In other areas, notably in Almería, Denia and Valencia, those who took control were not military men but prominent civil administrators, some

---

[4] Scales (1994), pp. 2–5.   [5] 'Abd Allah, *The Tibyan*, p. 45.

of whom were *saqaliba*, or slaves of European origin, who had previously exercised their functions under the 'Amirids. A handful of other taifa rulers belonged to Andalusi families of long-standing wealth and influence: like the Tujibids who seized control of Saragossa in 1010 and the Hudids who later displaced them in 1039, the Dhu al-Nunids who occupied Toledo in 1018; or the 'Abbadids who successfully assumed power in Seville in 1023.[6] What all of these ambitious men had in common was a keen awareness of the opportunities for self-advancement that the demise of the centre presented. Although the vast majority owed their former positions of power to the 'Amirid dictatorship, they seemed no keener to fight for the survival of that regime than they were to ensure the survival of the caliphate. And the stark truth was that the former centre, Cordoba itself, racked by bloody infighting after the coup of 1009, was simply in no position to reassert control. Although there were those who still considered that the Umayyad caliphal institution was worth resuscitating, however feeble and discredited it had become, a feverish atmosphere of plot and counterplot ensured that no one was able to hold on to power for long. By the time the last of the caliphs, Hisham III (1027–31), was deposed in 1031, Córdoba had been reduced to the status of a taifa statelet like any other, its former pretensions to authority over the whole of al-Andalus but a rapidly fading memory.

During the period of greatest political turmoil, between about 1010 and 1040, there were as many as three dozen of these taifa states. They varied considerably in size, population and resources, from tiny though prosperous coastal enclaves, such as Almería, Cartagena and Málaga, whose wealth depended in large part upon long-distance maritime trade, to vast border regions like Badajoz, Toledo and Saragossa. By the middle of the eleventh century, however, the political map of Muslim Spain had simplified somewhat. Given the great disparities in wealth and military strength between the various taifas, it was only a matter of time before some of the lesser statelets fell victim to the predatory ambitions of their more powerful neighbours. Most predatory of all was the 'Abbadid kingdom of Seville, which in the course of the 1040s and 1050s succeeded in bringing as many as a dozen lesser taifas – Algeciras, Huelva and Ronda, to name but three – under its rule. In 1070 Córdoba itself was annexed by the 'Abbadids. Seville may have been the most powerful and renowned of the taifa kingdoms, so much so that it could plausibly lay claim to be the true heir to the caliphal tradition, but its pretensions to hegemony over the whole of al-Andalus were to be fiercely resisted. The taifas of Toledo and Saragossa, and to

---

[6] On the collapse of the caliphate, see Wasserstein (1985), pp. 55–81; Scales (1994). There are good studies of the taifa successor-states in Wasserstein (1985), Viguera Molíns (1992) and (1994). For a regional focus, see for example Dunlop (1942), Huici Miranda (1969–70), Terrón Albarrán (1971), Turk (1978) and Tapia Garrido (1978).

a slightly lesser extent those of Badajoz, Granada and Valencia, were important political entities in their own right. Heirs to the wealth of the caliphate and economically buoyant, the major taifa kingdoms each had the wherewithal to sustain both a capital city and a royal court of considerable splendour. Their rulers sought to demonstrate their magnificence to the world by undertaking prestigious building projects, such as the luxurious Aljafería palace which was erected in Saragossa by its ruler al-Muqtadir (1046–82), and by exercising artistic patronage on a lavish scale. It was in this extravagant though refined milieu that poets, philosophers and scientists of renown were able to thrive. Some of the taifa kings, notably al-Muzaffar of Badajoz (1045–68), and al-Mu'tadid (1042–69) and al-Mu'tamid of Seville (1069–91), were accomplished poets and scholars in their own right.[7]

But for all their prodigious wealth, their splendid palaces and mosques, and their centres of cultural excellence, the taifa kingdoms were vulnerable. Their very number and size meant that the majority lacked the political and military clout to make territorial expansion a practical proposition. For most of the taifa kings, rather, personal survival was the order of the day. The political activity of these rulers was set against a constantly shifting background of petty dynastic rivalries, local diplomatic manoeuvring and small-scale military conflict. As the political horizons of its rulers became increasingly limited, so 'Muslim Spain shrank in upon itself.'[8] Diplomatic relations with overseas powers gradually began to dry up; and offensive military campaigns against the Christian north, which had been such a feature of external politics under the 'Amirids, became few and far between. Instead, the feuding taifa kings looked increasingly towards the Christian states of the north to provide them with the military muscle they desperately needed in their regular territorial squabbles with their neighbours. It was to be only a matter of time before the Christians would seek to turn this state of affairs to their own advantage.

In the immediate aftermath of the death of al-Muzaffar in the autumn of 1008, however, the rulers of the Christian realms of the peninsula could scarcely have foreseen the political upheaval that within a very short time would lead to the disintegration of unitary rule in Muslim Spain, let alone the opportunities for spectacular self-enrichment and wholesale territorial expansion that would subsequently present themselves. Moreover, with the notable exception of the contingents of Castilian and Catalan troops who became embroiled in the post-'Amirid power struggle in Córdoba in 1009–10, there appears to have been little attempt by the Christian sovereigns to gain any immediate advantage from the collapse of the caliphate.[9] Besides, most of them had problems

---

[7] Viguera Molíns (1994), pp. 497–647.   [8] Wasserstein (1985), p. 135.
[9] Scales (1994), pp. 182–204.

enough of their own to contend with. The plain fact of the matter was that the Christians had long since become accustomed to playing second-fiddle to the potentates of al-Andalus. For most of the tenth century the caliph 'Abd al-Rahman III and his successor al-Hakam II (961–76) had held the military and political ascendancy over the Christian states, to the extent that several rulers had become their clients. In the latter quarter of the century the devastating raids that the *hajib* al-Mansur had regularly visited upon the Christian north had not simply reinforced the dominance of Cordoba, but had left deep physical and psychological wounds on the demoralized Christians that would not immediately heal.

Nowhere was this more the case than in the kingdom of León, the largest and most powerful of the Christian realms.[10] Descended from the Asturian principality which had emerged in the wake of the Muslim conquest of 711–18, by the early eleventh century the kingdom had come to embrace not only the mountainous regions of the Asturias and Galicia, but also the vast open plains of the northern half of the Spanish *meseta* that stretched as far south as the River Duero. The colonization of the *meseta* and the fortification of the southern frontier along the Duero had long since been one of the principal preoccupations of the Leonese monarchs and would continue to be so for some time to come. Another was to keep the armies of the caliphate at bay and to take the fight to them whenever the opportunity arose. But the latter was easier said than done. During the second half of the tenth century there had been precious few moments of military success to crow about. The period had been more notable for internal political conflict, exemplified by the struggle for the throne between Sancho I the Fat (956–66) and Ordoño IV the Bad (958–9) in 958–9, and between Ramiro III (966–85) and Vermudo II (982–99) in 982–5, than for any noteworthy feats of Leonese arms.[11] With their political survival seemingly in the balance, an increasingly powerful and independent-minded aristocracy to contain, and Muslim attacks mounting in their frequency, range and ferocity by the day, ambitious raids into Umayyad-controlled territory had simply no longer been an option for an increasingly beleaguered Leonese monarchy. The decision by Vermudo II to offer an annual tribute to al-Mansur in return for a garrison of Muslim troops with which to bolster his position at home spoke volumes for the prostration of the Leonese crown. Moreover, when in 987 Vermudo had later tried to free himself from Cordoban dominance, al-Mansur had swiftly responded by sacking Coimbra, León and Zamora. To rub salt into the wound, in 997 the *hajib*'s forces had

---

[10] For the history of the various Christian realms, see in particular the works of Valdeavellano (1968), Lacarra (1975), Ubieto Arteta (1981) and Salrach (1987). In English, there are useful single-volume surveys by O'Callaghan (1975), Lomax (1978), Bisson (1986) and Reilly (1992).

[11] *Historia Silense*, pp. 169–77.

plundered the holy city of Santiago de Compostela and carried off the doors and bells of its church to adorn the great mosque in Córdoba.[12]

Although the perennial Muslim threat to León quickly evaporated after the demise of al-Muzaffar in 1008, Vermudo's son and successor, Alfonso V (999–1028), had more than enough on his plate to cope with as it was: he had to face up to repeated challenges to his authority by rebellious elements within the local aristocracy; repel the Viking marauders whose raids regularly devastated the Galician coastline; and attend to the reconstruction and repopulation of his battered kingdom. It was not until 1028 that Alfonso considered himself to be in a strong enough position to be able to profit from the political turmoil in al-Andalus, but he then met an untimely end while engaged in the siege of the Portuguese town of Viseu.[13] The accession to the throne of his nine-year-old son, Vermudo III (1028–37), ushered in a period of renewed political instability.

The sovereigns of León had traditionally considered themselves to be the legitimate successors to the unitary Visigothic kingdom which had perished at the hands of the Muslim invaders in 711. Back in the ninth century, propagandists at the Asturian royal court in Oviedo had already begun to nurture the neo-Gothic ideal and had enthusiastically proclaimed the rights of the Asturian monarchs to rule over all Spain. What is more, it had confidently been predicted that the expulsion of the infidel from the peninsula was just around the corner.[14] But political infighting within León meant that these lofty claims had become increasingly hard to sustain as the tenth century wore on, although there were still those, like Bishop Sampiro of Astorga (fl. 992 × 1042), who struggled manfully to keep the flickering flame of reconquest alive.[15] Beyond the rhetoric, however, political realities on the ground were considerably more complex. By the early eleventh century Christian Spain was made up of a patchwork of competing principalities. East of León, for example, lay the county of Castile, once part of the domains of the Leonese kings, which had successfully established itself as an independent principality under the able leadership of Count Fernán González (930–70) and that of his successors García Fernández (970–95) and Sancho Garcés (995–1017). While the Leonese monarchy struggled to keep a grip on power, the Castilian counts displayed an increasingly self-confident and expansionary mood; none more so than Count Sancho Garcés who, although thwarted in his attempt to hold the reins of power during the minority of Alfonso V, profited from the political unrest in León by extending his lordship westwards over the territories that lay between the Cea and Pisuerga Rivers. Even more daring was his brief involvement on the side of the Berber insurgents

---

[12] On the campaigns of al-Mansur, see Lévi-Provençal (1944), I, pp. 432–47; Ruiz Asencio (1968); Seco de Lucena Paredes (1970); Molina (1981).

[13] Fernández del Pozo (1984), pp. 31–162.   [14] *Crónicas asturianas*, p. 188.

[15] Fernández-Armesto (1992), pp. 133–7.

who seized power in Cordoba in 1009, as a consequence of which the count was able to recover a number of fortresses along the Duero valley, including Gormaz, San Esteban, Clunia and Osma, which had previously been lost to al-Mansur.[16]

Beyond Castile lay the Basque country and the diminutive kingdom of Pamplona, or Navarre. Although its early history is obscure in the extreme, a recognizably independent realm based upon the old Roman town of Pamplona had emerged from first Muslim and then Frankish lordship by the second quarter of the ninth century.[17] Under the rule of Sancho Garcés I (905–25) of the newly installed Jiménez dynasty, the kingdom had undertaken a comparatively modest expansion of its frontiers into the fertile region of the Rioja. It was in the opening decades of the eleventh century, however, that the Navarrese kingdom was to experience the most spectacular, if ultimately short-lived, extension of its boundaries. Sancho Garcés III (1004–35), known to posterity as 'the Great', combined ruthless opportunism and not inconsiderable diplomatic skill, backed up by military force, to bring an impressive array of Christian-held territories under his rule.[18] To the east, he annexed the central Pyrenean counties of Sobrarbe and Ribagorza, whilst to the north he extended his lordship over the Basque coastal regions of Guipúzcoa and Vizcaya and for a very brief period towards the end of his reign even claimed authority over Gascony.[19] To the west, meanwhile, Sancho skilfully used marriage alliances to extend his interests yet further: thus, he himself wed Mayor Sánchez, the daughter of Count Sancho Garcés of Castile; he married off his sister Urraca to Alfonso V of León in 1023; and when his youthful brother-in-law Count García Sánchez of Castile (1017–29) was murdered in 1029, thereby frustrating a proposed Leonese–Castilian alliance, Sancho installed his own son Fernando as count and then betrothed the latter to Sancha, the sister of Vermudo III of León, in 1032. He followed up this diplomatic coup by establishing a protectorate over the kingdom of León. Towards the end of his reign, by which time he claimed to exercise hegemony over a vast area stretching from Zamora to Gascony by way of Barcelona, Sancho was proudly styling himself emperor (*imperator*) and king of the Spains (*rex Hispaniarum*).[20] However, his much-vaunted empire was dismembered almost as soon as it came into being. Navarrese claims to authority over León and Gascony evaporated within months of Sancho's death

[16] Scales (1994), pp. 188–200.   [17] Lacarra (1975), pp. 21–33; Collins (1990), pp. 104ff.

[18] Pérez de Urbel (1950).

[19] *Cartulario de San Juan de la Peña*, I, nos. 58–9; *Documentación medieval de Leire*, no. 23; cf. Bull (1993), pp. 90–2.

[20] 'Regnante rex Sancio Gartianis in Aragone et in Castella et in Legione, de Zamora usque in Barcinona, et cunta Guasconia imperante': *Cartulario de San Juan de la Peña*, I, no. 59. As *imperator* and *rex Hispaniarum*, see Menéndez Pidal (1956), I, p. 109, II, pp. 671–2; *Cartulario de San Millán de la Cogolla*, no. 193.

in 1035 and the remaining territories were partitioned among his sons, in accordance with the late king's wishes: García, the eldest, receiving Navarre, Fernando Castile, Ramiro Aragón and Gonzalo Sobrarbe and Ribagorza.

The origins of the tiny Pyrenean county of Aragón, like those of its neighbour the kingdom of Navarre, are shrouded in obscurity. The territory emerges as a historically recognizable entity in the early ninth century, by which time it had successfully resisted attempts by both Muslims and Franks to impose their respective authority. Under Count Galindo Aznar (c. 844–67), however, Aragón came under the orbit of the monarchs of Navarre and that influence would persist until the county was elevated to the status of a kingdom in its own right on the death of Sancho Garcés III in 1035. Under its first monarch, Ramiro I (1035–63), the fledgling kingdom soon began to flex its muscles and to expand its boundaries further. In 1045 Ramiro took advantage of the murder of his half-brother Gonzalo to extend his lordship over the territories of Sobrarbe and Ribagorza. However, subsequent efforts to push westwards into Navarre and southwards into the territory of the taifa kingdom of Saragossa met with only very limited success. Under Ramiro I, it has been said, Aragón 'did little more than survive behind its mountain ramparts'.[21] To make matters worse, when Ramiro finally broke out of his mountain fastness and captured Graus in the foothills of the Pyrenees in 1063, he was promptly defeated and killed in battle by al-Muqtadir of Saragossa and his Castilian allies. It was left to Sancho Ramírez I (1063–94) to continue the aggressive policy of expansion that his father had initiated; but the decisive military breakthrough which was to allow the Aragonese to move down on to the plain of Huesca was not to materialize until two further decades of military frustration had elapsed.

At the far eastern end of the Pyrenees, in the region known today as Catalonia, lay a cluster of small, independent Christian principalities. Their origins are to be found in the Frankish protectorate – the so-called Spanish March – that had been established in the region in the early ninth century.[22] With the disintegration of the Carolingian empire in the latter half of that century, however, the newly established Catalan counties had been left increasingly to their own devices until Frankish control had ceased altogether. The power vacuum had been filled by a number of local magnates who set themselves up as independent rulers, the most powerful of whom was Count Wifred 'the Hairy' of Barcelona (870–97). Even so, the political link with the Frankish empire was not finally broken until the Carolingian dynasty expired in the late tenth century, and the frontiers of the marcher territory that had been established by the Franks remained relatively stable, notwithstanding the devastating attacks on

[21] Reilly (1992), p. 106. On the early history of Aragón, see Ubieto Arteta (1981), pp. 9–76.
[22] Salrach (1987), pp. 117–81; Collins (1995), pp. 250ff.

the region by al-Mansur and al-Muzaffar. Following the death of the latter in 1008, Count Ramón Borrell I of Barcelona (992–1017) and his brother Count Armengol I of Urgel (992–1010) became caught up in the wild disorder that afflicted al-Andalus when in 1010 they led an army south to help the would-be caliph Muhammad al-Mahdi recover Córdoba from Berber control. However, what came to be known as 'the year of the Catalans' was not to be the prelude to a prolonged period of campaigning against the Muslim south.[23] Although there were further Catalan raids into al-Andalus in 1018 and 1024, there appears to have been little systematic attempt at territorial conquest and the frontier with Muslim Spain scarcely altered. Instead, Catalan–Muslim relations in the first half of the eleventh century were characterized by increasingly close political and economic ties. Partly as a direct consequence of the stagnation of the frontier, the history of Barcelona in the first half of the eleventh century was marked by internal strife on a grand scale, as Count Berenguer Ramón I (1017–35) showed himself unable to maintain his authority over his increasingly rebellious Catalan magnates. During the second quarter of the century there was a progressive breakdown in public order, as comital power was attacked head-on by the great nobles, private armies abounded and 'adulterine' fortresses proliferated in the hands of a 'new aristocracy' of petty castellans. The task of restoring order fell to Count Ramón Berenguer I (1035–76), who was gradually able to regain control by skilfully exploiting the divisions between his opponents, by using the large sums of money he received in tribute from his taifa clients to buy off those who resisted him and to regain control of their castles, and by binding his subordinates to him with ties of personal fidelity.[24]

A decade before Ramón Berenguer I of Barcelona began to impose his 'new political order' in the Catalan territories under his authority, renewed political turmoil had begun to brew on the other side of the peninsula.[25] The death of Sancho Garcés III of Navarre in 1035 seems to have been greeted by Vermudo III of León as an opportunity settle old scores. In 1037, he led an army across the River Cea with a view to recovering the territory that had been acquired by Fernando of Castile on the occasion of his marriage to Vermudo's sister in 1032. But the daring strategy backfired. Vermudo was defeated and killed by Fernando at the battle of Tamarón in September 1037, whereupon the latter moved rapidly to establish his own right to the Leonese throne by virtue of his wife Sancha.

The consecration of Fernando and Sancha on the throne of León in June 1038, in the presence of most of the secular and ecclesiastical magnates of the realm, marked the formal birth of a new kingdom of León-Castile which in

---

[23] Scales (1994), pp. 191–5.
[24] Bonnassie (1975–6), II, pp. 539–680; Salrach (1987), pp. 312ff.   [25] Bisson (1986), p. 25.

the succeeding decades would come to dominate the Christian north. In the short term, however, the new monarch's priority was not to indulge in further ambitious empire-building, but to consolidate his authority over his newly established realms. However, such is the poverty of the sources for Fernando I's reign – a few dozen charters and some lacklustre chronicle narrative is almost all we have to go on – that we know very little indeed about the early years of his rule. Nevertheless, if the witness-lists that were attached to his diplomas are anything to go by, the new king seems to have been able to win over most of the nobility of León and Castile to his side.[26] In Galicia, however, the death of Vermudo III and the arrival of the new Navarro-Castilian dynasty seems to have been greeted with considerably less enthusiasm. It is a striking feature of Fernando's reign that he visited Galicia so rarely and that he made so very few donations to the churches and monasteries of the region. The rebellion that was orchestrated by the Countess Odrocia, her daughter Elvira and her grandson Count Nuño Rodríguez in the region of Monterroso may merely have been part of a wider show of disaffection against Fernando's authority. It is probably no mere coincidence that several of the oldest aristocratic families of the region disappear from the record at this time.[27] The likelihood is that the old Galician aristocracy decided to stand up to Fernando I and that it paid the price as a result.

Fernando I's other pressing concern during the first half of his reign was the stability of his frontier with Navarre. Although García Sánchez V (1035–54) had sent troops to assist Fernando in his struggle with Vermudo III of León in 1037 and had received the northern part of the former county of Castile as the price for his support, the two brothers had later quarrelled. Mutual hostility eventually gave rise to outright warfare. On 1 September 1054 Fernando defeated and killed García in battle at Atapuerca near Burgos, as a result of which he was able to annex the territory of the Bureba on the west bank of the upper Ebro and reduce the new Navarrese king, Sancho Garcés IV (1054–76), to vassalage.

With any potential Navarrese threat neutralized, Fernando was at long last in a position to capitalize upon the political and military weakness of the taifa kingdoms of al-Andalus. His best-publicized territorial conquests came at the expense of the taifa of Badajoz. In November 1057 Fernando's forces captured the town of Lamego and with it the upper reaches of the Duero valley. Viseu fell in 1058 and in 1064 Coimbra followed suit, with the result that the basin of the River Mondego also came under Leonese control. These conquests were matched by important gains at the other end of the Duero, where in 1060 Fernando stormed a number of fortresses belonging to al-Muqtadir of

---

[26] *Colección diplomática de Fernando I*, nos. 8–13.   [27] *Ibid.*, no. 59; Fletcher (1984), p. 31.

Saragossa. On top of these successes, Fernando kept up the pressure on the taifa kings by dispatching regular raiding expeditions far and wide into Muslim territory, from Seville in the south-west to Valencia in the south-east.

Territorial conquests were all very well and good, but the rewards in land, plunder and slaves, not to mention the prestige that accrued to the victor, might easily be offset by the elevated costs of campaigning. Thus, the occupation of Coimbra by Fernando I in 1064 was achieved only after a punishing and no doubt costly six-month-long siege.[28] It was hardly surprising, therefore, that for a monarch with his eye on the profit margin the exaction of tribute was often the preferred course of action. The Christian rulers of eastern Spain, and in particular Count Ramón Berenguer I of Barcelona, who set the trend in or around 1045, were the first to demand tribute or *parias*, as such payments were known, from the enfeebled taifa kings of al-Andalus in return for military 'protection'.[29] Fernando I of León-Castile does not seem to have levied *parias* in any systematic way until the final years of his reign; but he soon made up for lost time. By the time of his death in 1065 Fernando was receiving regular payments of *parias* from the taifas of Badajoz, Toledo and Saragossa, and occasional ones from the rulers of Seville and Valencia too. Substantial sums of money were involved. If the payment of 5,000 gold dinars that Fernando I was reportedly promised by al-Muzaffar of Badajoz was in any way typical, then it is likely that by the time of his death the Leonese-Castilian king was in receipt of an annual income well in excess of 25,000 gold pieces.[30] In addition to hard currency, tribute might also take the form of jewellery, textiles and other luxury goods, while in 1063 Fernando I even recovered the mortal remains of St Isidore from his client al-Mu'tadid of Seville.[31]

Although no details have survived of the arrangements which regulated the agreements between Fernando I and his client states, we can get a good idea of the mechanics of the *paria* system from the treaties that were drawn up between al-Muqtadir of Saragossa and Sancho Garcés IV of Navarre in 1069 and 1073.[32] The latter agreement stipulated, among other things, that al-Muqtadir was to pay the Navarrese king the sum of 12,000 gold pieces a year, or their equivalent in silver. In return, Sancho undertook to persuade the king of Aragón, by force if necessary, to withraw from the territory around Huesca, from where he had been harrying the kingdom of Saragossa. The two rulers further agreed

[28] Rodrigo Jiménez de Rada, *Historia de rebus Hispanie*, pp. 189–90.
[29] Lacarra (1981a), pp. 52ff. Cf. Grassotti (1964), pp. 45–64.
[30] Ibn 'Idhari, *La caída del Califato de Córdoba*, p. 198. Fernando's son and successor, Alfonso VI, may have realized an annual income of as much as 70,000 gold dinars from his Muslim tributaries: Reilly (1992), p. 58.
[31] *Historia Silense*, pp. 198–204; *Colección diplomática de Fernando I*, no. 66; Viñayo González (1961).
[32] Lacarra (1981b).

to provide military assistance to one another whether against Christians or against Muslims.

The gigantic sums that were paid over in *parias* by the taifa kings brought unheard of wealth to the previously impoverished Christian rulers. The lion's share of the money was probably designated towards the military budget. The influx of Moorish gold and silver enabled the kings and counts of the north to put ever bigger and better equipped armies into the field, to engage in castle-building on an unprecedented scale, to build or acquire ships and even, in one notable case, to engage the services of an expert in siege techniques from abroad. Thus, between 1062 and 1072 Ramón Berenguer I of Barcelona is reckoned to have lavished at least 10,000 ounces of gold on the purchase of castles alone.[33] Large amounts of cash also found their way into the hands of the warrior nobles upon whose considerable military expertise their rulers relied so heavily. Few could match the achievements of the Catalan nobleman Arnal Mir de Tost, who amassed a vast fortune for himself in money, land, castles and luxury goods during the course of his long and highly successful military career.[34] Religious institutions, such as the cathedral churches of Jaca, Pamplona and Urgel, and the monastic houses of Nájera and San Juan de la Peña, were the other great beneficiaries of *parias*. In 1048, Count Armengol III of Urgel (1038–65) undertook to deliver to his local see one tenth of his future income from Muslim tributes.[35] The new wealth was also diverted to churches beyond the Pyrenees, notably to the Burgundian abbey of Cluny, which was promised an annual donative of 1,000 gold pieces by Fernando I of León-Castile in or around 1063, and twice that amount by his son Alfonso VI in 1077.[36]

Although tribute-gathering and territorial aggrandizement were far from being the exclusive preserve of the Leonese-Castilian monarchy, by the time of his death on 29 December 1065 Fernando I's victories on the battlefield, his by no means inconsiderable conquests and his success in reducing several of the wealthiest of the taifa kingdoms to tributary status had confirmed him as by far the most powerful monarch on the peninsular political stage.

We seek only our lands which you conquered from us in times past at the beginning of your history. Now you have dwelled in them for the time allotted to you and we have become victorious over you as a result of your own wickedness. So go to your own side of the Straits and leave our lands to us, for no good will come to you from dwelling here with us after today. For we shall not hold back from you until God decides between us,

Fernando I is alleged to have declared to an embassy from Toledo. Or so Ibn 'Idhari, writing in the early fourteenth century, would have us believe.[37]

---

[33] Lacarra (1981a), pp. 61–4; Bonnassie (1975–6), II, pp. 670–4; Sobrequés i Vidal (1985), pp. 62–3.
[34] Bonnassie (1975–6), II, pp. 789–97.   [35] Lacarra (1981a), p. 65 n. 76.
[36] Bishko (1980), pp. 23ff.   [37] Wasserstein (1985), p. 250.

Whether by this time Fernando I had truly committed himself to a deliberate policy of reconquest is very much a moot point. Certainly, the dynastic arrangements which the ailing king made in December 1063, just two years before his death, do not suggest that, like the ninth-century kings of the Asturias, he considered the restoration of a unitary Christian state embracing the length and breadth of the peninsula to be either a viable or a pressing objective. For, like his father Sancho Garcés III before him, Fernando chose to partition his realms amongst his sons. To the eldest, Sancho II (1065–72), he granted the kingdom of Castile as far west as the River Pisuerga, together with the *parias* owed by the taifa of Saragossa. To Alfonso VI went the territories of León and the Asturias and the *parias* of Toledo. And to his youngest son, García I (1065–73), he granted Galicia and the Portuguese territories as far south as Coimbra, as well as the tributes payable by the taifa of Badajoz.[38]

The death of Fernando I's widow Sancha, on 7 November 1067, appears to have been greeted by the king's sons as an opportunity to undo their late father's dynastic arrangements and to redraw the political map of north-west Spain. In 1068 forces loyal to Sancho II of Castile and Alfonso VI of León clashed inconclusively at Llantadilla on the River Pisuerga. In the spring of 1071 Alfonso also took up arms against his sibling García, who was forced to seek refuge in Coimbra. Alfonso may have proposed to Sancho some form of power-sharing arrangement in Galicia, but mutual suspicion between the brothers soon gave rise to further territorial squabbles. In January 1072 Alfonso was defeated and captured by Sancho in battle at Golpejera near Carrión. Shortly afterwards, Sancho in turn overthrew García and brought the Galician and Portuguese territories under his sole rule.

On the face of things, Sancho II's aggressive strategy had proved a brilliant *tour de force*. Not only had he reunited the kingdom which his father had dismembered, but his brothers had been forced into exile, Alfonso to the taifa court of al-Mam'un of Toledo (1043–75) and García to that of al-Mu'tamid of Seville. The pacification of the newly conquered realms proved rather more difficult to achieve, however. Despite his crushing feats of arms, the newly crowned monarch of León and Castile faced opposition to his rule both among the ecclesiastical hierarchy and among the landed aristocracy of León. He also had to contend with the hostility of his sister Urraca who, according to one account, sought to rally supporters of Alfonso to her side from her headquarters at Zamora on the north bank of the Duero.[39] Sancho moved swiftly to neutralize this threat to his authority by besieging Zamora, but on 7 October 1072 he

---

[38] *Historia Silense*, pp. 204–5; Pelayo of Oviedo, *Crónica*, pp. 75–6; 'Chronicon Compostellanum', p. 609.
[39] 'Chronicon Compostellanum', pp. 609–10.

was murdered outside the walls of the city. His rule as king of Castile, León and Galicia had lasted barely nine months.

Whether the Zamora uprising and the subsequent murder of Sancho II were directly instigated by Alfonso VI with a view to recovering his lost inheritance we cannot say for sure. Although Alfonso himself was quick to claim that his recovery of the throne of León had been achieved without bloodshed, later accounts of Sancho's murder were in no doubt that foul play had been involved.[40] In any case, Alfonso evidently had much to gain from his brother's demise. While Sancho's corpse was being conveyed back to Castile for burial at the monastery of Oña, Alfonso headed swiftly north to León to reclaim his throne. In December he may have been in Burgos, where he made a generous grant to the monks of the nearby abbey of Cardeña, seeking to win over the Castilian episcopate and aristocracy to his side.[41] Later literary accounts were to make great play of the grave misgivings which some Castilan nobles supposedly harboured about the role Alfonso VI had played in the death of Sancho II. The Leonese monarch was allegedly forced to swear an oath in Burgos denying any complicity in his brother's death before the Castilian nobility would accept him as their king.[42] But whether or not this episode has any historical basis in fact, Alfonso was presumably successful in his attempt to seek Castilian support, for there is no record of any challenge being mounted against his authority after 1072. With Castile pacified, Alfonso was able to turn his attention to Galicia. In February 1073 he captured his brother García, recently returned from exile, and had him imprisoned in the castle of Luna to the north of León, where he was to remain until his death on 22 March 1090.

The death of Sancho II of Castile and the incarceration of García I of Galicia enabled Alfonso VI to gather into his own hands all of the territories which Fernando I had divided up among his sons. With no other obvious claimants to the throne on the horizon, the lay and ecclesiastical magnates of Castile and Galicia may simply have accepted the ruthless unravelling of Fernando I's dynastic arrangements as a *fait accompli*. In any case, the expansionist policies which Alfonso VI pursued soon after his restoration to the throne in the winter of 1072 do not suggest a man uncertain of his position at home, but rather a monarch bent on restoring León-Castile to the dominant position

---

[40] In his charter issued on 17 November 1072 the king declared: 'Ego quidem Adefonsus rex...sensi uindictam Dei omnipotentis presenti tempore factus extorris a potestate regni mei et postea restituit me Deus in id ipsum quod amiseram, sine sanguine hostium, sine depredatione regionis, et subito, quum non extimabatur, accepi terram sine inquietudine, sine alicuius contradictione et sedi in sede genitoris mei Dei donante clementia': *Colección documental...de León*, no. 1182. Cf. Menéndez Pidal (1956), II, pp. 178ff.

[41] *Becerro Gótico de Cardeña*, no. lxxxvi.

[42] Lucas of Túy, 'Chronicon Mundi', p. 100; cf. Menéndez Pidal (1956), I, pp. 193–9, II, pp. 709–11.

it had enjoyed under his father Fernando I only a few years before. One of Alfonso's immediate priorities after his restoration was to secure recognition of his suzerainty by his cousin Sancho Garcés IV of Navarre. However, on 4 June 1076 Sancho was murdered, pushed over a cliff at Peñalén by his brother Ramiro and sister Ermesinda, or so it was alleged. Before any of Sancho's kinsmen could establish themselves on the throne, Navarre's neighbours resolved to make their own bids for power. To the east Sancho Ramírez I of Aragon promptly seized Pamplona, while to the west Alfonso VI led an army into the Rioja. Under the terms of the treaty that was subsequently agreed between the two monarchs, Alfonso was to receive both the Rioja and the Basque provinces of Alava, Vizcaya and part of Guipúzcoa. Sancho Ramírez was to hold the territory of Pamplona as far west as Estella, in return for which he undertook to pay homage to the Leonese-Castilian monarch. Barely forty years after the death of the self-styled 'king of the Spains', Sancho Garcés III, the partition of Navarre in 1076 signified the disappearance of that kingdom as an independent political power for the next fifty-eight years. By the time it was resuscitated in 1134 not only was Navarre to find its power much reduced, but the loss of the Rioja meant that any further expansion into Muslim territory was effectively barred.

The occupation of the Rioja confirmed Alfonso VI's hegemonic position over the other Christian powers of the peninsula. It may have been no accident that within a year of his Navarrese conquests the Leonese-Castilian monarch bombastically began to style himself emperor of all Spain (*imperator totius Hispaniae*).[43] Alfonso VI's other chief preoccupation during the early years of his reign was with the taifa kingdoms of al-Andalus. The fratricidal strife which had unfolded in León-Castile between 1067 and 1072 had encouraged the taifa kings to cease paying the great sums in *parias* which they had been obliged to render in the days of Fernando I. Alfonso VI now moved swiftly to remedy this state of affairs. As early as 1074 al-Muqtadir of Saragossa, whose treaty with Sancho Garcés IV of Navarre we referred to earlier, was probably prevailed upon to resume payment of *parias* which had lapsed after the death of Sancho II. Al-Ma'mun of Toledo, who had offered political asylum to Alfonso after the latter was banished by Sancho II in 1072, probably followed suit shortly afterwards. Furthermore, in the summer of 1074 Alfonso led an army against the taifa kingdom of 'Abd Allah of Granada, backed by forces loyal to his ally al-Ma'mun. Skilfully exploiting the divisions between 'Abd Allah and his Muslim opponents, Alfonso soon brought the Granadan king to the negotiating table. 'Abd Allah's own candid account of the bargaining which ensued, preserved in the pages of the memoirs which the taifa king composed whilst in exile in Morocco in the 1090s, claims that Alfonso's

---

[43] Reilly (1988), p. 104; cf. Menéndez Pidal (1956), II, pp. 725–31.

strategy was clear-cut:

> He...came with the intention of taking money from both sides and crushing their heads against one another. It was not his hope to seize the country for himself, for he had pondered the matter and said to himself: 'I am not of their faith, and all the inhabitants hate me. On what basis should I aspire to take it? By submission? No, that's impossible. By combat? No, my men will perish, my money will disappear and my losses will be greater than any benefit I could hope to derive should the city fall into my hands. Even if it does fall to me, it cannot be held without the cooperation of its inhabitants – but then, they are not to be trusted. Nor is it possible to massacre the inhabitants and settle some of my co-religionists in it. The best plan, indeed the only plan, is to threaten one with the other and to take their money all the time until their cities are impoverished and weakened. When they are weakened, they will surrender and become mine of their own accord.' [44]

This should not be dismissed as mere fanciful speculation on 'Abd Allah's part, for he claimed to have been told of Alfonso's thinking by the Leonese monarch's right-hand man Count Sisnando Davídez of Portugal. Besides, other Arab sources present a substantially similar analysis.[45] In any case, after prolonged negotiations between the two rulers, backed by veiled threats on Alfonso's part, an agreement was reached. The treaty stipulated that neither monarch should attack the other and that 'Abd Allah should pay Alfonso the enormous sum of 30,000 gold *mithqals* immediately and an additional 10,000 *mithqals* per annum thereafter.

As 'Abd Allah's illuminating exposition of Alfonso VI's policy towards the taifas suggests, the conquest of al-Andalus was not an immediate priority for the Leonese king. Indeed, given the vast sums of money that were paid to him annually in *parias*, not to mention all the other precious objects which customarily accompanied the tribute-payments, the incentives to do so could not have been great. As one historian has put it, 'the condition upon which the system of *parias* depended was the continued existence and economic vitality of the tribute-payers. It would have been foolish to kill the goose that laid the golden eggs.'[46] And yet, within only a few years of the Granadan expedition, that was exactly what Alfonso VI resolved to do.

The root cause of this sudden shift in Alfonso's policy towards the taifa rulers of al-Andalus was the changing political situation in the kingdom of Toledo. Under the leadership of al-Ma'mun, Alfonso VI's friend and ally of long standing, Toledo had enjoyed a notable period of prosperity and expansion. Valencia had been annexed in 1065 and Córdoba ten years after that. The death of al-Ma'mun in 1075, however, gave rise to a period of intense political

[44] 'Abd Allah, *The Tibyan*, pp. 89–90.
[45] See, for example, Ibn al-Kardabus, *Historia de al-Andalus*, p. 102.   [46] Fletcher (1987), p. 35.

instability in the kingdom. His grandson and successor, al-Qadir, proved ill-suited to the demands of government. Valencia and Córdoba soon slipped from his grasp and, worse still, in 1079 fierce political infighting within Toledo itself forced al-Qadir to withdraw from the city to his family power-base at Cuenca. His enemies in Toledo invited the ruler of neighbouring Badajoz, 'Umar al-Mutawakkil (1067–94), to assume the throne. But accomplished poet and celebrated gourmand though he was, al-Mutawakkil was no warrior. With the forces of Alfonso VI, who had conquered Coria, bearing down on him, the king of Badajoz quickly recognized that his own position in Toledo was untenable and withdrew, allowing al-Qadir to resume control. As the price for Alfonso's support, al-Qadir not only had to deliver yet larger sums of money in *parias*, but he was persuaded to cede a number of fortresses in the northern reaches of his kingdom to Leonese control. But al-Qadir's position remained highly precarious. The humiliating installation of Christian garrisons on Toledan soil, the imposition of further heavy taxes on his already long-suffering subjects, not to mention his savage persecution of his political opponents in Toledo all added to his unpopularity. In the end, however, the final, decisive blow that toppled al-Qadir from power was delivered not by his enemies within, or even by one of his taifa rivals, but by his ally and supposed 'protector' Alfonso VI.

It may have been the renewed outbreak of civil war in Toledo in 1082, together with the realization that al-Qadir's days as a reliable ally were seriously numbered, that ultimately persuaded Alfonso VI to make his own bid for power. According to one account, it was al-Qadir himself who offered to surrender Toledo and its territories to Alfonso if the latter would help him to capture Valencia.[47] In the autumn of 1084 Alfonso's army laid siege to Toledo. Requests for military assistance were hastily dispatched by the citizens to the other taifa rulers, but their appeals fell on deaf ears. Terms of surrender were finally agreed on 6 May 1085. Alfonso could afford to be generous: the citizens of Toledo were guaranteed the security of their persons and property and were to be free to practise their own religion. Those who chose to leave the city could do so without let or hindrance. On 25 May Alfonso VI entered Toledo in triumph. For the Leonese king it was to prove the crowning-point of his long military career. Toledo was a relatively wealthy city. The territory of the former taifa kingdom encompassed a vast area that stretched from the Sierra de Guadarrama in the north to the Sierra Morena in the south, and from the Tagus valley around Talavera in the west to Guadalajara in the east. Overnight the kingdom of León-Castile had expanded by as much as a third to occupy an area more than twice the size of England. Yet, if the spoils of war were prodigious,

47 Ibn al-Kardabus, *Historia de al-Andalus*, pp. 104–5. On the background to the fall of Toledo, see Lévi-Provençal (1931); Miranda Calvo (1980); Reilly (1988), pp. 161ff.

the psychological consequences of conquest were possibly even greater still. It was not simply that Toledo was the first major Muslim city to have fallen into Christian hands since the peninsula had been overrun in the eighth century and that, at a time when the frontiers of Christendom were under attack from Islam elsewhere, Alfonso could plausibly claim to be the defender of the faith. More important still, Toledo was the ancient capital of the Visigoths. For a monarch like Alfonso VI, who claimed to rule as 'emperor of all the Spains', the conquest of the city was an act that was imbued with immense symbolic significance.

Viewed from a wider European perspective, the 'great leap forward' of León-Castile from the Duero to the Tagus after the fall of Toledo was symptomatic of the spectacular expansion of Latin Christendom into the European periphery during the high middle ages. Everywhere, from Spain to the Baltic to the eastern Mediterranean, the pattern of expansion was broadly the same: military conquest, followed by a less dramatic, but by no means less remarkable, movement of migration and colonization. But in north-western Spain the process of settlement had got under way long before the delivery of Toledo into the hands of Alfonso VI. Indeed, ever since the Asturian kingdom had spilled over on to the Leonese plain in the early ninth century, the territorial expansion of the realm had been accompanied by a slow, piecemeal movement of colonization, as small groups of settlers had advanced down the numerous river valleys that cross the northern *meseta* until they had reached the banks of the Duero between the years 850 and 900.[48] In the early tenth century, driven in part by the search for new pasture lands, settlers from the Leonese and Castilian heartlands had gradually begun to occupy territories south of the Duero. But the timid process of colonization had been rudely interrupted by the devastating series of raids that had been visited upon the region by al-Mansur's armies between 977 and 986.[49] The Duero had then remained the frontier between Christian and Muslim for decades, until the military push led first by Fernando I and then by Alfonso VI, which culminated in the conquest of Toledo, brought with it a vast swathe of largely unpopulated territory, known as the Extremaduras, which had to be systematically colonized, governed and defended.

Sepúlveda, strategically situated between the River Duero to the north-west and the Somosierra pass across the Guadarrama mountains to the south-east, was one of the earliest settlements to be established in the Trans-Duero. Although the destruction of the town by al-Mansur in 984 had brought an abrupt halt to the colonizing movement that had been in progress since the early tenth century, the dramatic shift in Christian–Muslim relations in the wake of the collapse of the caliphate of Córdoba encouraged the process of

---

[48] Sánchez-Albornoz (1966); cf. García de Cortázar (1985).   [49] Villar García (1986), pp. 59–71.

repoblación to begin anew. On 17 November 1076, Alfonso VI granted a *fuero*, or charter of liberties, to Sepúlveda in which he confirmed the rights and obligations of those who had already taken up residence in the territory and sought to encourage new colonists from the north to settle at the frontier outpost.[50] A number of generous and eye-catching incentives, ranging from tax breaks for all to immunity from prosecution for murderers on the run, were offered to those who were willing to take up residence. For Sepúlveda was no ordinary town; just as those who colonized it were no ordinary settlers. From the very outset, rather, Sepúlveda was conceived of as a military settlement whose citizens, categorized simply as *caballeros* (horsemen) or *peones* (footsoldiers), were expected to defend the frontier against attack and take the fight to the enemy whenever the need should arise. The militarization of municipal life in Sepúlveda was soon mirrored at other settlements in the Trans-Duero. By the early twelfth century an entire defensive frontier system stretching from Salamanca to Soria had been established, a string of strategically situated fortress towns designed both to bear the brunt of Muslim attacks and to act as a springboard for future campaigns of conquest. Although, in the event, the defensive capabilities of walled cities such as Avila, Salamanca and Segovia were never to be seriously put to the test, the militia forces they put into the field were to play an increasingly vital role in the Leonese-Castilian fighting machine. It was to be thanks in large part to their military expertise that the frontier with Islam did not buckle.[51]

Elsewhere in the Christian north the migratory movement towards the southern frontier was being pursued with equal vigour. Indeed, decades before Alfonso VI issued his invitation to the criminals and ne'er-do-wells of Castile to make a new life for themselves in Sepúlveda, significant numbers of emigrants had already begun to leave their home villages in the Aragonese and Catalan uplands in order to seek out new opportunities on the frontier with al-Andalus.[52] However, the expansionism of Christian Spain in the eleventh century was exemplified not only by the step-by-step conquest and colonization of Muslim-held territories, but by the equally dynamic process of 'internal expansion' that occurred well behind the front line. In northern Spain, as in most areas of the west after 950, a combination of factors, including rapid population growth, climatic change, technological innovation and extensive land clearance, contributed to a steady increase in agricultural output. As the rural economy flourished, so the demand for land grew. The net result was a dramatic upturn in the property market, as wealthy aristocratic families

---

[50] Sáez (1953), pp. 45–51.
[51] Barrios García (1983–4), I, pp. 128–71; Villar García (1986), pp. 91–103; González Jiménez (1989), pp. 52–9. On the municipal militias, see Powers (1988).
[52] Nelson (1984); Bonnassie (1975–6), I, pp. 436–40; Salrach (1987), pp. 256–62.

and ecclesiastical institutions eagerly sought to extend their landholdings at the expense of independent peasant proprietors. Witness, for example, the 67 property transactions that are known to have been conducted by the Leonese magnate Count Froila Muñoz between 1007 and 1045; or the 119 estates that were acquired by the monks of San Pedro de Cardeña near Burgos between 999 and 1090.[53] And it was the same story at the other end of the peninsula, in Catalonia, where in the hinterland around Barcelona a surge in land clearance was accompanied by a marked increase in agricultural production from the 980s onwards.[54]

The steady rise in human population and agricultural output after the millennium encouraged urban centres to grow. Although none of the modest settlements that passed for towns in the Christian north in the eleventh century could possibly have competed in terms of population and wealth with the flourishing commercial centres of al-Andalus, most of them experienced some significant growth in this period. In Catalonia, for example, increased profits from agricultural surpluses, coupled with an influx of precious metals through *parias*, acted as a stimulus to commercial activity and transformed the city of Barcelona into an important centre of regional exchange.[55] In other areas of the north, however, where the boom in the agrarian economy does not seem to have been quite so pronounced as in the Catalan territories, by far the most important spur to urban development was the pilgrimage to Santiago de Compostela.[56] Pilgrims from beyond the Pyrenees had been making the arduous journey to the shrine of St James in Galicia from at least the middle of the tenth century. However, the flow of pilgrim traffic to the tomb of the apostle grew in intensity as the eleventh century progressed, to reach a climax in the first half of the twelfth. Four principal pilgrim-routes ran from starting-points in France and converged in the western Pyrenees at Puente la Reina, from where the so-called *camino francés*, or French road, wound its way westwards across northern Spain via Logroño, Burgos, Carrión, Sahagún, León and Astorga before entering Galicia itself.[57]

---

[53] On the emergence of the great landholders, see Carlé (1973), pp. 23–92; Sánchez-Albornoz (1978), pp. 19–57; Pastor (1980), pp. 56–73; Carzolio de Rossi (1981); Martínez Sopena (1985), pp. 215ff. For the property conveyances of Froila Muñoz, see *Catálogo de documentos… de Santa Maria de Otero de las Dueñas*, nos. 154–7, 161–2, 165, 167; *Colección diplomática de Santa María de Otero de las Dueñas*, nos. 58, 61, 82–3, 89–91, 93–4, 101–6, 109–13, 116, 118, 122–3, 126–30, 135–6, 138–40, 142, 145–6, 148, 150, 154, 157–61, 163, 166, 91a, 96a, 107a–b, 122a, 124a–b, 125a, 137a, 145a, 156a, 158a, 165a, 166a. Cf. Prieto Prieto (1975). On the acquisitions of the monks of Cardeña, see Moreta Velayos (1971), pp. 125–6.

[54] Bonnassie (1964) and (1975–6), I, pp. 435ff; Ruiz Doménec (1977).

[55] Bonnassie (1975–6), I, pp. 488–96; Ruiz Doménec (1977).

[56] Valdeavellano (1969), pp. 103–76; Gautier Dalché (1989), pp. 67–85.

[57] Vázquez de Parga, Lacarra and Uría Ríu (1948–9); Fletcher (1984), pp. 78–101.

The pilgrim-road left a lasting impression on the communities through which it passed. Kings, clerics and laymen competed to enhance the facilities available to the passing pilgrims, mending roads, building bridges and churches, and erecting hostels and hospitals for those in need, such as the one that Bishop Pelayo of León founded opposite his cathedral on 13 December 1084.[58] The arrival of so many foreign, though mostly French, pilgrims left a profound cultural imprint too. It was reflected in the French forms of writing, which by the end of the century had begun to displace the traditional Visigothic hand employed in many parts of the peninsula hitherto; in the innovative sculptural forms which came into vogue in places as far apart as Jaca in the Pyrenees and Sahagún in the Tierra de Campos; and in the buildings designed in the popular Romanesque style which sprang up in such numbers along the pilgrim-route at this time, such as the exquisite church of San Martín de Frómista near Carrión.[59]

The pilgrimage to Santiago de Compostela helped to put Spain on the map and opened the peninsula up to foreign influences as never before. But piety was not the only force that drew outsiders to set foot on Spanish soil. It was probably rumours of the immense wealth flowing north in *parias* from the taifa kingdoms of al-Andalus that prompted some warrior-aristocrats from beyond the Pyrenees to view the Spanish front line as the ideal place in which to feather their nests. At any rate, it now seems plain that it was the prospect of plunder, not the promise of spiritual rewards, that was uppermost in the minds of the force of French knights who helped an army of Catalan and Aragonese troops to besiege and conquer the Saragossan fortress town of Barbastro in 1064.[60] Marriage alliances with peninsular dynasties were also influential in encouraging French nobles to travel to Spain. Thus, among the leaders of the French military force that campaigned inconclusively around Tudela in 1087, Duke Odo of Burgundy was the nephew of Alfonso VI's second wife Constance, and Raymond of St-Gilles, whose mother Almodis had married Count Ramón Berenguer I of Barcelona, was the uncle of Philippa, the wife of Sancho Ramírez of Aragon.[61]

News of the profits that were to be made in the peninsula also encouraged colonies of foreign merchants and artisans to set up shop along the *camino francés* in order to cater for the needs of the faithful who passed through in droves. The Aragonese city of Jaca, situated at the foot of the Somport pass across the central Pyrenees, provides an illuminating case in point. During the course of the eleventh century the ever-increasing flow of pilgrims into Spain

---

[58] Vázquez de Parga, Lacarra and Uría Ríu (1948–9), I, pp. 281ff; the collected articles in Santiago-Otero (1992); *Colección documental... de León*, no. 1236.

[59] Fletcher (1978), pp. 115–16; Moralejo (1985); Whitehill (1941).

[60] Ferreiro (1983); Bull (1993), pp. 72–81. [61] Bull (1993), pp. 86–9.

transformed Jaca from a comparatively insignificant fortified settlement into an important staging-post on the route to Compostela and a major conduit for commercial traffic between France and the peninsular realms.[62] Significant numbers of settlers, or *burgenses* as they were labelled, had already begun to be drawn to the burgeoning mercantile centre by the time Sancho Ramírez awarded a charter of privileges to Jaca in 1077.[63] What is more, the volume of merchandise that passed through the town annually – a good deal of it apparently carried by self-declared pilgrims – came to be such that the Aragonese king was prompted to slap tariffs on the incoming goods.[64] A similar process of urban development can be glimpsed at other points on the *camino francés*. At Estella, south-west of Pamplona, for example, where French settlers arrived in such numbers that they were also granted a special *fuero* of privileges by Sancho Ramírez in 1090; and at the bustling mercantile *burgo* that was established by Alfonso VI alongside the monastery of Sahagún, south-east of León, some time prior to 1085 and which reportedly attracted traders and craftsmen from all parts of Europe and of all manner of professions, including smiths, carpenters, tailors, furriers and shoemakers.[65] At Santiago de Compostela itself, meanwhile, commercial life had flourished to such an extent by 1095 that the local lord, Raymond of Burgundy, found it necessary to issue a decree protecting the rights of the merchants who made their way to the Holy City to sell their wares.[66]

Pilgrims, warriors and merchants were not the only foreigners to make their presence felt on Spanish soil. Churchmen, too, began to cross the Pyrenees in ever-increasing numbers as the century wore on. There were French monks like Adelelm of the abbey of La Chaise-Dieu in the Auvergne, who travelled to Spain in about 1081 at the invitation of Alfonso VI's second wife, Constance of Burgundy, and who was later to rule over the religious community and hospital of San Juan in Burgos, which was affiliated to La Chaise-Dieu in 1091; Peter of Andouque of the house of Ste-Foy-de-Conques, who was appointed to the see of Pamplona in 1082; and Frotard, abbot of St-Pons-de-Thomières, and Richard, abbot of St-Victor de Marseille, whose monasteries built up an important network of subordinate foundations among the religious houses of Catalonia in the closing quarter of the century.[67] Particularly prominent on

---

[62] Lacarra (1951).   [63] *Cartas de población del Reino de Aragón*, no. 2.
[64] Vázquez de Parga, Lacarra and Uría Ríu (1948–9), III, no. 76.
[65] On Estella, see Défourneaux (1949), pp. 247–8; Valdeavellano (1969), pp. 140–3. On Sahagún, see Herrero de la Fuente (1988), no. 823; *Crónicas anónimas de Sahagún*, pp. 19–24; Gautier Dalché (1989), pp. 70–3. In a wider context, see Ruiz de la Peña Solar (1993).
[66] López Ferreiro (1898–1911), III, Ap., no. VII; *Historia Compostellana*, pp. 51–2.
[67] On Adelelm see Vázquez de Parga, Lacarra and Uría Ríu (1948–9), II, pp. 184–5; *Documentación . . . de San Juan de Burgos*, no. 1. On Peter of Andouque, bishop of Pamplona, see Müssigbrod (1994). On Frotard and Richard, see Linage Conde (1973), II, pp. 872, 885, 908, 912–13, 979–81.

the Iberian scene, however, was the Burgundian abbey of Cluny.[68] It was in or around 1025 that Sancho Garcés III of Navarre asked Abbot Odilo of Cluny for help in introducing reformed Benedictine customs into the monasteries of his kingdom. The abbot responded by dispatching a party of monks to Spain, under the leadership of a certain Paternus, who took up residence at the Aragonese monastery of San Juan de la Peña, from where they may have extended Cluniac customs to other religious houses in Sancho's domains. In return, the Navarrese king made a number of munificent gifts to Cluny which secured him a place as a lay member of the community and the promise of the intercessionary prayer of the monks thereafter.

Notwithstanding the close confraternal ties which Sancho Garcés III had established with the Burgundian monastery, Cluniac influence in Spain spread only very slowly. The abbey did not build up a dense network of daughter-houses in the peninsula, as it was doing in other areas of the west, nor is there any evidence of an influx of Cluniac monks to Spanish monasteries. What is more, after the death of Sancho Garcés III, his sons García, Ramiro and Gonzalo appear to have demonstrated a studied indifference to the abbey their father had held in such high esteem.[69] In the kingdom of León-Castile, by contrast, Cluniac influence eventually came to be especially strongly felt. It was some time in the 1050s that Fernando I was prompted to revive the bond of friendship that his father had earlier forged with Cluny. Moreover, towards the end of his reign, probably in 1063, by which time the royal coffers were full to overflowing with Moorish tribute, Fernando secured for himself a permanent place in the liturgical commemorations of the monks when he undertook to make an annual payment of 1,000 gold pieces to Cluny.[70] His son Alfonso VI was even more generous. Between 1073 and 1077 the newly restored monarch of León-Castile granted four monasteries to the Cluniacs, including the royal abbey of Sahagún, and in 1077 he doubled the annual Cluniac *census* to 2,000 gold pieces. Alfonso had good reason to hold Cluny in particular esteem. After all, it had been thanks to the good offices of Abbot Hugh of Cluny that Sancho II of Castile had been persuaded to release him from prison in Burgos in 1072. And the abbot may also have been instrumental in arranging the marriage of his niece Constance to Alfonso in 1079. The marriage served to strengthen the Leonese–Cluniac connection yet further. Increasing numbers of Cluniac churchmen entered the kingdom during the last quarter of the century and many came to achieve high office in the Leonese-Castilian church hierarchy. None did better for themselves than Bernard of Sédirac, who was appointed

[68] On the Cluniacs in Spain, see in particular Bishko (1961), (1965) and (1980); Cowdrey (1970), pp. 214–47; Linage Conde (1973), II, pp. 861–997; Segl (1974).
[69] Bishko (1980), pp. 5–8.   [70] *Ibid.*, pp. 23ff.

abbot of Sahagún in 1080, archbishop of Toledo in 1086 and primate of the whole Spanish church in 1088, a position which he held until his death in 1124.[71]

Until the middle of the eleventh century, contacts between the Spanish Christian realms and the popes had been sporadic to say the least. Although the Catalan counties had successfully kept open a channel of communication with the papacy, the rest of Christian Spain appears to have remained relatively isolated from the mainstream of European religious practice and thought.[72] However, with the development of the ecclesiastical reform movement in the second half of the century, this state of affairs was to change. The reform movement encouraged the papacy to broaden its horizons as never before and it was thus that the Holy See came to take a far closer interest in Iberian affairs. Under Alexander II and Gregory VII increasingly determined efforts were made to override local ecclesiastical customs and to bind the Spanish church more closely to the Holy See. Evidence of this new-found interest in Spanish affairs is provided by the three legatine missions that were carried out at the behest of Alexander II by Cardinal Hugh Candidus between 1065 and 1072.[73]

Taking up where his predecessor Alexander II had left off, and displaying a cavalier disregard for either peninsular political realities or local sensibilities, Pope Gregory VII launched a blistering diplomatic offensive designed to advance his authority over what he inaccurately termed the 'kingdom of Spain'. In a letter of 30 April 1073, in which he underlined his support for a projected military expedition to Spain under Count Ebles of Roucy, Gregory boldly asserted papal lordship over the peninsula and reminded those who were to take part in the forthcoming campaign that any lands they conquered from the Muslims were to be held as papal fiefs.[74] In this respect Gregory was doubtless encouraged by the example of Sancho Ramírez of Aragon, who in 1068 had been persuaded by Alexander II to become a *fidelis beati Petri*, or papal vassal, and had duly placed his kingdom under the suzerainty of Rome.[75] As things turned out, Count Ebles's expedition appears to have been something of a damp squib, but this did not stop Pope Gregory stepping up the diplomatic pressure on the Spanish kingdoms. In a further letter, dated 28 June 1077, he audaciously informed the Spanish monarchs and their nobles that the kingdom of Spain had been given by 'ancient constitutions' – by which he presumably was referring to the Donation of Constantine – to Blessed Peter and the holy Roman church in right and ownership and that as a consequence the rulers of

---

[71] Rivera Recio (1966), ch. 3; cf. Défourneaux (1949), pp. 32ff.
[72] Linage Conde (1973), II, pp. 866–87; Bonnassie (1975–6), I, pp. 326–32; cf. Kehr (1946), pp. 77–89; Fletcher (1994), pp. 461–4.
[73] Säbekow (1931), pp. 13–17.   [74] *La documentación pontificia hasta Inocencio III*, no. 6.
[75] Kehr (1945).

the Spanish realms were bound to owe obedience to Rome.[76] However, with the exception of the Catalan Bernat of Besalú, who placed his county under papal lordship in 1077, Gregory VII's wildly ambitious diplomatic campaign in the peninsula received notably short shrift.[77] It is probably no mere coincidence that it was in 1077, the very same year that Gregory had issued his forthright letter to the Spanish kings, that Alfonso VI chose to underline his own claim to peninsular hegemony by adopting the style *imperator totius Hispaniae* in the products of his chancery.[78] Gregory appears to have got the message, for the matter of papal suzerainty was never raised again.

The question of liturgical reform was not to be side-stepped so easily. The so-called Mozarabic liturgy had been developed in Spain during the Visigothic period. Its customs varied from standard Roman practice in innumerable ways, from the prayers that were recited to the colour of the vestments worn by its priests. In the second half of the eleventh century, however, papal concern to enforce liturgical standardization throughout the Latin west brought the Spanish kingdoms (with the exception of Catalonia which had long since accepted the Roman rite) under increasing pressure to step into line. What had once struck foreign observers as merely an oddity was now portrayed as an affront. Alexander II expressed his concerns on the matter in the letter he sent to Abbot Aquilino of San Juan de la Peña in 1071 and reform of what the pope labelled 'confused rites' was one of the chief objectives of Hugh Candidus's legatine mission of that same year.[79] The pressure began to bear fruit. With the pope's encouragement, Sancho Ramírez of Aragon gradually replaced the Visigothic rite in the bishoprics and monasteries of his kingdom between 1071 and 1092.[80] In neighbouring León-Castile, Alfonso VI was also willing enough to obey the papal directive on the matter, but his attempts to impose the Roman liturgy provoked a long and bruising dispute.[81] Some of the Spanish bishops who had attended the Lenten synod in Rome in 1074 and who had agreed to implement the reform may subsequently have had second thoughts on the matter. In a letter Alfonso VI sent to Abbot Hugh of Cluny in 1077 he confessed that his kingdom was completely desolated by the change.[82] According to later accounts, Alfonso resorted to increasingly

---

[76] 'Preterea notum vobis fieri volumus, quod nobis quidem facere non est liberum, vobis autem non solum ad futuram sed etiam ad presentem gloriam valde necessarium, videlicet, regnum Hyspanie ex antiquis constitutionibus beato Petro et sancte Romane ecclesie in ius et proprietatem esse traditum': *La documentación pontificia hasta Inocencio III*, no. 13.

[77] Menéndez Pidal (1956), I, p. 234. [78] See above, n. 43.

[79] *La documentación pontificia hasta Inocencio III*, no. 4. [80] Ubieto Arteta (1948), pp. 308–24.

[81] For what follows, see Cowdrey (1970), pp. 228–39; Hitchcock (1973); O'Callaghan (1985), pp. 105–13; Reilly (1988), pp. 97ff. Cf. Menéndez Pidal (1956), I, pp. 237–51, for whom the controversy over the liturgy represented nothing less than a full-blooded 'crisis de nacionalismo'.

[82] *Recueil des chartes de l'abbaye de Cluny*, IV, pp. 551–3.

desperate means, including a judicial duel and a bizarre trial by fire, in the course of which the king had copies of each liturgy burned on a bonfire only to see the Mozarabic rite leap undamaged from the flames, as he endeavoured to resolve the dispute once and for all.[83] Alfonso enlisted the help of Abbot Hugh of Cluny and Queen Constance turned to the monk Adelelm, in an attempt to pour oil on troubled waters; but another Cluniac, the monk Robert, who had been installed as abbot of Sahagún, seems to have come out in support of the Mozarabic liturgy. The dispute dragged on. Papal legates came and went and a lively correspondence between the chief players ensued. Finally, in May 1080, the papal trouble-shooter Cardinal Richard of St-Victor de Marseille celebrated a council at Burgos during the course of which the Mozarabic liturgy was formally abandoned and the Roman rite introduced. Gregory VII had won a signal victory. The integration of the northern Spanish kingdoms into the wider community of western Christendom was to continue apace.

The fall of Toledo in 1085 marked a watershed in Christian–Muslim political relations in the peninsula. The conquest of that city and the annexation of the vast territory it controlled not only gave rise to a spectacular expansion of the Leonese-Castilian kingdom, but it also represented a decisive and, as events would prove, permanent shift in the balance of power in favour of the Christian north. 'Abd Allah of Granada was later to recall that the conquest of Toledo 'sent a great tremor through al-Andalus and filled the inhabitants with fear and despair of continuing to live there'.[84] The poet Ibn al-'Assal painted an even more graphic picture:

> O people of al-Andalus, spur on your mounts; it is nothing but a blunder to
>   stay on here.
> A robe (normally) unravels from its edges, but I see the robe of the
>   peninsula unravelled from the centre.
> We are caught up with an enemy who will not leave us alone: How can one
>   live in a basket together with snakes?[85]

Similarly apocalyptic fears had been expressed at the time of the fall of Barbastro to a force composed of French, Catalan and Aragonese troops in 1064. 'We are standing on the edge of a cliff, looking down on disaster', Ibn Hayyan had despairingly observed at the time.[86] But Barbastro had been recaptured by al-Muqtadir of Saragossa the following year and the mood of despair had quickly subsided. Now, twenty-one years later, a renewed bout of hysteria swept through the Muslim community.

[83] *Crónica Najerense*, p. 116.   [84] 'Abd Allah, *The Tibyan*, p. 113.
[85] *Christians and Moors in Spain*, III: *Arabic Sources*, pp. 90–1.
[86] Scales (1994), p. 210; cf. Marín (1992).

This widespread sense of mounting alarm would have been reinforced by subsequent events in Toledo itself, where Alfonso VI's conciliatory policy towards the Muslim inhabitants quickly seems to have been abandoned. At some point in 1086 the city governor Count Sisnando Davídez, who had previously served in the household of al-Mu'tadid of Seville and who was presumably well attuned to the sensibilities of the Muslim community, was removed from office.[87] At roughly the same time, allegedly at the behest of Queen Constance and her fellow-Frenchman Archbishop Bernard of Toledo, and apparently in clear breach of the surrender terms of the previous year, the principal mosque of the city was taken over and converted into a Christian cathedral.[88] In the meantime, an increasingly belligerent Alfonso VI had begun to tighten the screw yet further on the remaining taifa tributaries. In the spring of 1086 he fulfilled his side of the bargain that he had made with al-Qadir shortly before the surrender of Toledo by sending an army under Alvar Fáñez to install his former client as ruler of Valencia. He is reported to have called upon al-Mu'tamid of Seville to surrender his kingdom; and he dispatched a raiding expedition into the territory of Abd 'Allah of Granada. It may also have been at this time that one of his lieutenants, García Jiménez, captured the fortress of Aledo south-west of Murcia. The siege of Saragossa, which was begun by Alfonso VI in the early summer of 1086, may have been undertaken in order to persuade its new ruler, al-Musta'in (1085–1110), to resume the payment of *parias* which had lapsed the previous year, rather than with a view to outright conquest. But coming so soon after the fall of Toledo, Alfonso's actions were hardly designed to allay the growing apprehension among the other taifa kings that their own positions as independent rulers were in jeopardy. With their backs to the wall, the taifa kings sent a desperate appeal across the Straits of Gibraltar to the court of the Almoravid amir, Yusuf ibn Tashufin, at Marrakesh, requesting military assistance to enable them to push back what appeared to them to be an inexorable Christian advance.

The Almoravid movement is said to have had its origins in the *ribat*, or fortified post, that was established in the basin of the River Senegal by a Malikite scholar and missionary named Ibn Yasin some time after 1039.[89] Ibn Yasin's followers, who came to be known as the al-Murabitun, from which the Spanish form Almoravid derives, aspired to live a life of religious purity and were committed to extending the frontiers of Islam by *jihad*, or holy war.

---

[87] García Gómez and Menéndez Pidal (1947).

[88] Rodrigo Jiménez de Rada, *Historia de rebvs Hispanie*, pp. 205–7; cf. García Gómez and Menéndez Pidal (1947), pp. 32–3, 38–41.

[89] On the origins and development of the Almoravid movement, see in particular Bosch Vilá (1956); Lagardère (1989a). For a useful review of recent scholarship, see Hrbek and Devisse (1988); Molina López (1990), pp. liii–lxxix.

With its compelling brand of austerity and revivalist vigour, the Almoravid movement enjoyed a rapid growth in popularity. By the time of Ibn Yasin's death in 1059, the Almoravids had extended their authority over the Sanhaja Berber tribes of the western Sahara and over several of the other Berber peoples of southern Morocco. Leadership of the movement then fell to one of Ibn Yasin's disciples, the Sanhaja chief Abu Bakr ibn'Umar. While Abu Bakr set about reinforcing his position in the south, his cousin Yusuf ibn Tashufin advanced north across the Atlas mountains, established his headquarters at Marrakesh in 1070 and rapidly overran the plain of Morocco, conquering Fez, Tlemcen and Tangier in quick succession. On Abu Bakr's death in 1087, Yusuf assumed supreme leadership of the entire Almoravid movement.

No sooner had Yusuf gained a foothold on the southern Mediterranean shore, than he had begun to receive requests for military aid from the taifa rulers of al-Andalus. In 1079, shortly after the fall of Coria, al-Mutawakkil of Badajoz dispatched a letter imploring the Almoravid amir to intervene on his behalf. And in 1083 a plea in similar vein was sent by al-Mu'tamid of Seville, still smarting from the devastation of his kingdom by a raiding party led by Alfonso VI. But it was the fall of Toledo in 1085 that finally decided Yusuf to act. From the outset, however, there appears to have been little love lost between the austere Almoravid amir and the taifa rulers. To the latter, Yusuf was simply an uncouth barbarian, and a religious zealot to boot. In Yusuf's opinion, the effete taifa kings had betrayed the Islamic faith by leading a licentious lifestyle, by kowtowing to the Christians and by imposing non-Qur'anic taxes on their subjects with which to pay their Christian 'protectors'. The taifa sovereigns evidently had deep misgivings about seeking Berber intervention, but desperate times called for desperate measures. Given the dire straits in which they found themselves in the winter of 1085–6, the taifa kings could scarcely afford to be choosy about their allies. Al-Mu'tamid of Seville's celebrated remark that he 'would rather be a camel-driver in Morocco than a swineherd in Castile' pithily summed up the prevailing mood.[90]

In June 1086 Yusuf crossed the Straits at the head of a large Berber army. He established his base at Algeciras and then moved inland, first to Seville and then north to Badajoz. Alfonso VI was forced to raise the siege of Saragossa and hurried southwards to meet the threat. On 23 October 1086 the two armies clashed at Sagrajas, a little to the north of Badajoz. The Christian army was routed and Alfonso barely escaped with his life.[91] But the Almoravid amir chose not to reap any immediate territorial advantage from his military success and withdrew to Morocco shortly afterwards. However, renewed appeals for help from the taifa kings prompted Yusuf to return to Spain in 1089, when he

---

[90] Pérès (1953), p. 11.   [91] Huici Miranda (1956), pp. 19–82; Lagardère (1989b).

vainly tried to reduce Aledo, and again the following year, when he mounted an unsuccessful attack upon Toledo. By this time, however, the already strained relations between the amir and the taifa monarchs had broken down altogether. Dismayed by the lukewarm support he had received from the taifas hitherto and by the continual bickering that prevented them from presenting any sort of united front against the Christian north, and suspecting – correctly as it turned out – that at least some of them had secretly reopened negotiations with Alfonso VI, Yusuf resolved to make himself the master of al-Andalus. He was helped in this regard by the fact that the Muslim populace appears to have regarded the Almoravids as liberators. The spectacular victory at Sagrajas, which offered hope that decades of humiliation and suffering at Christian hands might at last be at an end, as well as the prospect of sizeable tax cuts, helped to endear Yusuf to the population at large. As one chronicler later put it, the Almoravid amir was widely regarded both 'as a good omen and a blessing'.[92] With the encouragement of the *fuqaha'* and the *qudat*, the theologians and judges who were responsible for upholding the tenets of Islamic law and who had long since become disenchanted by the conduct of the taifa kings, it was not long before citizens were virtually queuing up to denounce their rulers before the amir.

As for the taifa rulers themselves, they appeared virtually powerless to oppose Yusuf. 'Abd Allah of Granada was the first to fall, stripped of his wealth and office and exiled to Morocco in September 1090. In 1091 it was the turn of al-Muʻtamid of Seville and some of the lesser taifas. And in early 1094 al-Mutawakkil was deposed and murdered, as a result of which the Almoravids overran the cities of central Portugal – Lisbon, Santarém and Sintra – which the desperate king of Badajoz had ceded to Alfonso VI the previous year as the price of a new military alliance. By 1094 all of the taifa rulers of western al-Andalus had been toppled and their territories absorbed into the Almoravid empire. In the meantime, Yusuf's lieutenants had been busily mopping up resistance in south-eastern Spain, as Murcia, Aledo, Denia, Játiva and Alcira all fell in quick succession. At Valencia, however, the Almoravid juggernaut was stopped rudely in its tracks. There, resistance came not in the shape of some plucky taifa monarch determined to defend his dynasty and kingdom to the last, but in the unlikely form of a Castilian warrior-adventurer named Rodrigo Díaz de Vivar.

Rodrigo Díaz (*c.* 1043–99), better known to posterity as El Cid, has traditionally been portrayed as one of the great heroes of Spanish history. The inspiration of the greatest work of medieval Spanish epic poetry, the *Poema de mio Cid*, as well as a host of other literary works, El Cid was portrayed after

---

[92] *Christians and Moors in Spain*, III: *Arabic Sources*, p. 99.

his lifetime as a pious crusading warrior whose overriding concern had been to liberate the peninsula from Muslim domination.[93] If we disentangle the man from the legend and the patriotic rhetoric, however, a rather different picture emerges. Rodrigo Díaz was a Castilian nobleman who rose to prominence in the household of Sancho II. In 1081, after he had led an unauthorized raid into the taifa of Toledo, he was exiled by Alfonso VI. Having unsuccessfully sought asylum in Catalonia, he eventually took up employment as a mercenary captain in the service of al-Muqtadir of Saragossa and then in that of his son al-Mu'tamin (1082–5). By all accounts a soldier of some genius, Rodrigo's exploits on the field of battle, against Muslim and Christian foes alike, rapidly won him great wealth and fame, as well as the epithet *Campidoctor* (whence the Spanish *Campeador*). In 1082 he defeated and captured Count Berenguer Ramón II of Barcelona (1076–97) in battle at Almenar near Lérida, prompting a monk of Ripoll, who was a supporter of Berenguer Ramón's erstwhile sibling rival, Ramón Berenguer II (1076–82), to pen the celebratory *Carmen Campi Doctoris* in Rodrigo's honour.[94] Two years after that, Rodrigo routed an army led by Sancho Ramírez of Aragon. In 1086, shortly after the Sagrajas debacle, he was reconciled to Alfonso VI and returned to Castile, but three years later, apparently because of his failure to help raise the Almoravid siege of Aledo, he was cast into exile once more. Between 1089 and 1094 El Cid operated as a freelance soldier of fortune in eastern Spain. By dint of his military expertise and his success in attracting sufficient troops to his service, he was able to exact prodigious sums in *parias* from a number of the lesser taifas in the region. In June 1094 he conquered Valencia and beat off the Almoravid army that was dispatched by Yusuf to deal with him. His position secure, Rodrigo Díaz ruled the principality of Valencia until his death on 10 July 1099.

The long and chequered career of Rodrigo Díaz was undeniably a remarkable one. Later literary works, notably the *Poema de mio Cid*, keen to present a suitable role model to which the warrior nobility of thirteenth-century Castile might aspire, took pains to emphasize the fact that El Cid's conquests had been carried out on behalf of his lord, Alfonso VI, and that he held them as his loyal vassal.[95] Earlier, and more reliable, evidence strongly suggests that between 1094 and 1099 Rodrigo remained very much his own man.[96] The

---

[93] *Poema de mio Cid*; Menéndez Pidal (1956), II, pp. 593–622. For a timely reappraisal of the Cid's career, see Fletcher (1989).

[94] Wright (1979).

[95] *Poema de Mio Cid*, lines 815–18, 875–80, 895, 1271–4, 1334–9, 1809–14; cf. West (1977), pp. 204–6; Fletcher (1989), pp. 193–6; Pattison (1996), pp. 108–10.

[96] Fletcher (1989), pp. 179–85.

likelihood is that the rulers of Christian Spain looked down on Rodrigo Díaz as little more than a troublesome parvenu with ideas and ambitions well above his station. Nevertheless, El Cid's deeds on the battlefield demonstrated that the Almoravids were far from invincible and gave fresh hope to the Christian north at a time when its own defensive lines were beginning to show dangerous signs of fracturing altogether. His stubborn resistance not only prevented the Almoravids from advancing up through the Levante towards Barcelona, but also provided a useful distraction at a time when Muslim military efforts were being geared towards the reconquest of Toledo. In the long run, however, Rodrigo Díaz's rule as prince of Valencia amounted to little more than a curious parenthesis in the overall dynamic of events. Once Rodrigo was dead, the principality he had carved out for himself dissolved almost as quickly as it had come into being. His widow Jimena did what she could to hold Valencia, but renewed Almoravid attacks in 1102 forced her to evacuate the city and return to Castile. By that stage, only Saragossa of the former taifa kingdoms maintained a fragile independence and that was to be ruthlessly extinguished by Yusuf's son, 'Ali ibn Yusuf, in 1110.

The appearance of Rodrigo Díaz on the already crowded political stage of eastern Spain in 1081 was to be viewed with increasing alarm by the leading Christian powers of the region in the years that followed. Under Ramiro I and his successor Sancho Ramírez I, the principal strategic objective of the Aragonese had long since been the southwards expansion of their kingdom into the upper reaches of the taifa of Saragossa. Thanks to the support of his Christian allies in Castile and Navarre, al-Muqtadir of Saragossa had been able to keep the Aragonese at bay, but the balance of power at the eastern end of the peninsula had been dramatically altered by the murder of Sancho Garcés IV of Navarre in 1076. The subsequent annexation of the territory of Pamplona firmly established Aragon as the foremost Christian power in the region and emboldened Sancho Ramírez to take the military initiative against Saragossa once more. He was further encouraged in this respect by Alfonso VI's increasing preoccupation with events on his own southern frontier after 1080, by the division of the taifa of Saragossa between al-Mu'tamin and his brother Mundhir in 1081, and not least by the departure of Rodrigo Díaz from the Saragossan court in 1086. As a result of Sancho's efforts a string of important Saragossan border fortresses fell into Aragonese hands during the 1080s, including Graus in 1083, Montearagón in 1088 and Monzón in 1089. Although the Aragonese king was to meet an untimely end whilst engaged in the siege of the city of Huesca in July 1094, his son and successor Pedro I (1094–1104) soon took up where his father had left off. Huesca finally fell to the Aragonese and their French allies in November 1096, Barbastro was reconquered in 1100 and the following year the city of Saragossa itself was the object of an unsuccessful attack.[97]

For most of the eleventh century, indeed ever since Ramón Borrell had travelled to Cordoba in 1010 to become embroiled in the power-struggle for the caliphate, the principal aim of the counts of Barcelona had been to turn the political fragmentation of al-Andalus to their own financial advantage. Count Ramón Berenguer I, in particular, who was the very first among the rulers of Christian Iberia to levy *parias* on a regular basis, received vast quantities of precious metals in tribute from the neighbouring taifas of Lérida, Tortosa and Saragossa. It was thanks in large part to this steady flow of Muslim gold and silver northwards that the count was able to consolidate his authority over the unruly barons of his realms in the 1040s and 1050s, while the cash surplus also helped him to extend his rule over a number of territories in southern France, including the counties of Carcassonne and Razès which he acquired by a series of purchase agreements carried out between 1067 and 1070.[98] Later, some time between 1076 and 1078, Ramón Berenguer I's twin sons and joint heirs, Ramón Berenguer II and Berenguer Ramón II, in league with their ally and kinsman Count Armengol IV of Urgel (1065–92), drew up ambitious plans to establish a vast protectorate which would have embraced not only their tributaries of long-standing, but the taifas of Valencia, Denia, Murcia and Granada too.[99] However, their efforts to put those plans into practice were to be resoundingly unsuccessful. In 1082 Ramón Berenguer II was murdered and all-out civil war in Barcelona was only averted by the agreement of 1086 which allowed the suspected fratricide, Berenguer Ramón, to continue to rule until his nephew, who was later to be known as Ramón Berenguer III (1097–1131), came of age. To make matters worse, the presence of Rodrigo Díaz in the region not only frustrated Berenguer Ramón's designs on the kingdom of Valencia, culminating in his humiliating defeat at Tévar in 1090, but it encouraged Lérida, Tortosa and Denia to place themselves under the protection of the powerful Castilian war-lord. Even after El Cid had disappeared from the scene in 1099, the steady advance of Almoravid armies into eastern Spain between 1102 and 1110 ensured that for Catalonia, just as for the other Christian powers of the peninsula, the golden age of *parias* was truly at an end.[100]

In the years that followed their victory at Sagrajas in 1086 Almoravid strategic thinking was dominated by the desire to recover Toledo. By the end of the eleventh century, all the territories that had belonged to the former taifa kingdom as far north as the Tagus had been overrun by Yusuf's armies. But

---

[97] Ubieto Arteta (1981), pp. 77–138. On the reigns of Sancho Ramírez and Pedro I respectively, see Buesa Conde (1996) and Ubieto Arteta (1951), pp. 53–126.

[98] Bonnassie (1975–6), II, pp. 860–3.   [99] *Ibid.*, II, pp. 865–7.   [100] Bensch (1995), pp. 98ff.

the embattled city of Toledo itself managed to hold out – despite the fact that it was to be subjected to siege on numerous occasions after 1090 – and was to remain the principal base for Leonese-Castilian military operations on the southern frontier for over a century to come. For his part, Alfonso VI did what he could to the stem the Almoravid tide, though with notable lack of success. In 1091 the army he sent to help raise the Almoravid siege of Seville was routed at Almodóvar del Río; and in 1092, in alliance with Aragon, Barcelona and the Italian maritime city-states of Genoa and Pisa, he unsuccessfully invested Valencia.

Diplomatic initiatives were only marginally more successful. In the immediate aftermath of his humiliating reverse at Sagrajas, Alfonso VI had issued an urgent appeal for military aid to his neighbours beyond the Pyrenees. The call had been answered by a large French expeditionary force led by, among others, Duke Odo of Burgundy, Hugh VI of Lusignan and, probably, Count Raymond IV of Toulouse, all of whom had family ties in the peninsula. The army crossed into Spain in the winter of 1087 and besieged Tudela in the Ebro valley before returning home having accomplished little.[101] Yet the French expedition was not to prove entirely fruitless. Perhaps encouraged by the French show of force, Alfonso VI, who had married Duke Odo's aunt Constance in 1079, was keen to strengthen diplomatic ties with the Burgundian ducal house yet further. It was therefore agreed that Constance's cousin, Count Raymond of comital Burgundy, should marry Alfonso's eldest daughter Urraca. Some time afterwards Raymond's cousin Henry of ducal Burgundy was betrothed to one of Alfonso's illegitimate daughters, Teresa; another daughter, Elvira, was married off to Count Raymond of Toulouse in or before 1094. These marriage alliances were doubtless a source of great pride and prestige for the Leonese-Castilian royal house, but in power-political terms they did not really amount to very much. So far as we can tell, Raymond and Henry were not accompanied to Spain by a military entourage of any size; nor is there any evidence that the Burgundian connection subsequently led to further contingents of French troops crossing the Pyrenees to lend Alfonso VI a hand in his struggle for ascendancy with the Almoravids.

Nevertheless, Raymond and Henry did well for themselves at the Leonese-Castilian court. In 1087, at about the same time he was betrothed to the Infanta Urraca, Raymond was granted authority over the province of Galicia, where a rebellion led by Count Rodrigo Ovéquiz had been put down only shortly before, and over the Portuguese marcher territories, although these were later to be transferred to Henry in 1096. According to a Compostelan source, Raymond may even have been designated heir apparent to the throne of León-Castile.[102]

[101] Bull (1993), pp. 83–6.   [102] 'Chronicon Compostellanum', p. 611.

Whether or not this was truly the case, the fact that Alfonso VI's only close male relative, his brother García, had died in prison in 1090 and that the king had hitherto failed to produce a legitimate male heir meant that Raymond may well have harboured expectations that the throne would eventually be his. However, these hopes were turned on their head in 1093 when the king's mistress Zaida, the former daughter-in-law of al-Muʿtamid of Seville, gave birth to a son, Sancho. Fearing, with good reason, that his aspirations to rule León-Castile were now in jeopardy, Raymond decided to act. Some time between 1095 and 1107 – the precise date has been the subject of considerable though inconclusive scholarly debate – Raymond and Henry, with the connivance of Abbot Hugh of Cluny and his envoy Dalmatius Geret, drew up a secret treaty.[103] Under the terms of the so-called 'Succession Pact', the cousins resolved that on the death of Alfonso VI Henry would assist Raymond to succeed to the throne of León-Castile and that they would partition the kingdom between them. Henry was to hold Toledo as Raymond's vassal, or else, if that were impossible – a strong intimation that nobody was very confident that the city could hold out against Almoravid attack for that long – the province of Galicia; Raymond would get the rest. Furthermore, the cousins agreed that one third of the treasury of Toledo was to pass to Henry. The name of the Infante Sancho is conspicuous by its absence. However, the death of Raymond in September 1107 rendered the treaty redundant. Besides, in 1106 Alfonso VI had already further strengthened Sancho's claims to the throne by marrying the boy's mother Zaida, thereby legitimizing the heir apparent.

The final years of Alfonso VI's reign were to be dominated by the succession question and the military struggle with the Almoravids. Although the king had good reason to be encouraged by the capture of Santarém on the Tagus in 1095, and by the fall of Huesca to Pedro I of Aragon the following year, the vulnerability of his position was forcefully underlined in 1097 when Yusuf inflicted another humiliating defeat on him, this time at Consuegra near Toledo, and followed it up by routing an army led by Alfonso's right-hand man Alvar Fáñez near Cuenca. In 1100 Toledo was besieged once more and in 1102 Alfonso had to supervise the evacuation of Valencia. To add to the king's problems, he was desperately short of manpower, to the point at which in 1100 and in 1101 Pope Paschal II had to send letters warning would-be Spanish crusaders to the Holy Land not to abandon the peninsula.[104] What is more, with *parias* now a thing of the past, the king was seriously strapped for cash.[105] Nevertheless, Alfonso

---

[103] *Documentos medievais Portugueses*, I, pt 1, pp. 1–2, and pt 2, pp. 547–53. On the background to the 'Pact of Succession', see David (1948); Bishko (1971); Fletcher (1984), pp. 121–5; Reilly (1988), pp. 247–54.

[104] *Historia Compostellana*, pp. 24–6, 77–8.   [105] Sánchez-Albornoz (1965), pp. 483–519.

was still prepared to take the fight to the enemy. Taking advantage of the fact that the Almoravid amir was now severely incapacitated by ill health, he captured the fortress town of Medinaceli in 1104 and led further raiding parties into Muslim territory in 1104 and 1106. When Yusuf finally died in September 1106, to be succeeded by his son 'Ali ibn Yusuf, the Almoravid military machine cranked up a gear again, and in May 1108 an army led by 'Ali's brother Tamim headed north to Toledo once more. Before it reached its objective, however, it was intercepted by Leonese forces at Uclés some 100 kilometres to the east. In the ensuing battle the Christian army was annihilated. Seven counts reportedly perished in the battle, as well as Alfonso's son and heir Sancho.[106]

Despite the spectacular Almoravid victory on the field of Uclés the Tagus frontier was not overrun. Toledo did not fall. However, the political consequences of the defeat were devastating. The untimely death of the Infante Sancho meant that the thorny question of the royal succession had to be settled all over again. To make matters worse, a decision was required speedily, for Alfonso VI himself was stricken with illness and bedridden. But the options open to the ailing monarch were severely limited to say the least. Altough Raymond was no longer on the scene, he had left a widow, Urraca, and their three-year-old son, the future Alfonso VII (1126–57). For their part, Count Henry and Countess Teresa of Portugal were to be blessed with a child, also called Alfonso (Atonso), in 1109. In the end, Alfonso VI formally proclaimed his daugter Urraca as his successor and announced her betrothal to the king of Aragon, Alfonso I 'the Battler' (1104–34). Though the precise terms of the Aragonese marriage are not altogether clear, on paper at least the project had much to be said for it. For one thing, it held out the prospect of a joint military alliance between the two most powerful Spanish Christian kingdoms which just might have been able to turn back the increasingly perilous Almoravid advance. For another, it avoided leaving León-Castile under the sole rule of a woman, something which many contemporaries – not least Alfonso VI himself – may well have found difficult to countenance. True, Alfonso I and Urraca were related by common descent from Sancho Garcés III of Navarre, but given the desperate position in which the kingdom found itself, Alfonso VI doubtless anticipated – incorrectly as it turned out – that the church authorities would be willing to turn a blind eye to this minor matter. Indeed, when Alfonso VI finally passed away in Toledo, the scene of his greatest triumph, on 1 July 1109, by which time the frontiers of his *imperium* stretced from the Atlantic seaboard in

---

[106] *Crónica Najerense*, p. 118. Cf. Lucas of Túy, 'Chronicon Mundi', pp. 101–2; Rodrigo Jiménez de Rada, *Historia de rebvs Hispanie*, pp. 216–17. On the background to the Uclés campaign, see Huici (1956), pp. 103–34; Slaughter (1974–9); Reilly (1988), pp. 348–55.

the west to the Ebro in the east and from the Cantabrian littoral as far south as the Tagus, he may well have thought that he had done enough to safeguard his achievements. The reality was to prove very different. Far from reinforcing the kingdom, the immediate result of the Aragonese marriage was to be a renewed succession crisis and an eight-year civil war that was to tear the Leonese empire apart.

CHAPTER 7

ENGLAND AND NORMANDY,
1042–1137

Marjorie Chibnall

THE century after Edward the Confessor returned from exile in Normandy to be crowned king of England in 1042 might be called the century of the Norman Conquest, which led to the formation of a short-lived Anglo-Norman realm. Already foreshadowed by personal dynastic ties, it became a visible reality when William the Conqueror, having restored the ducal authority and the military power of the duchy, united Normandy with the kingdom of England in 1066. Under his sons William Rufus and Henry some further conquest and consolidation continued, accompanied by a measure of social and administrative cross-fertilization; though closer union continued to seem a possibility it had not been achieved by the time King Stephen lost his grip on the duchy. Union of a different kind was restored only for a time in the wider complex known as the Angevin empire.

Edward the Confessor, the son of King Æthelred II and Emma of Normandy, returned to a kingdom that had recently undergone a major territorial upheaval as a result of the Scandinavian conquest. Most of the older nobility had been replaced either by Scandinavian followers of the Danish rulers or by newly enriched members of obscure Saxon families; pre-eminent among the new earls were Earl Godwine and his sons. The earls at this time were in the position of provincial governors, with particular responsibilities for defence. Initially their power and wealth posed no immediate threat to the king; the monarchy was strong, the underlying structure of local communities stable and the kingdom wealthy. Variations in local law and custom, particularly noticeable in the eastern counties of the Danelaw where Danish settlement had left its mark, did not destroy the unity achieved by the West-Saxon kings and reinforced under Cnut.

The needs of defence during the period of Danish wars and Danish rule had stimulated the development of both royal taxation and military organization. Even in the tenth century King Edgar had been able to collect general taxes or gelds assessed territorially. The demand for both cash and service increased

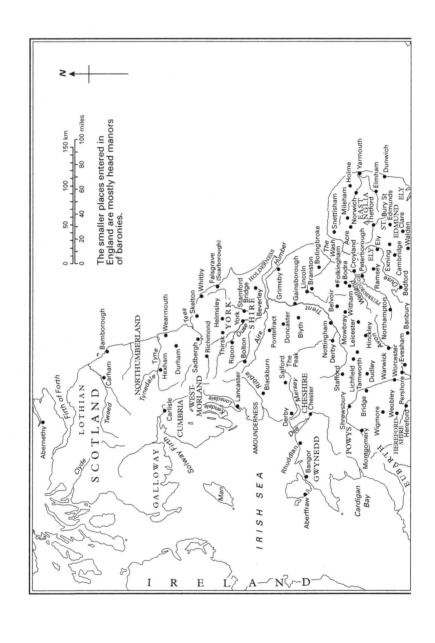

The smaller places entered in England are mostly head manors of baronies.

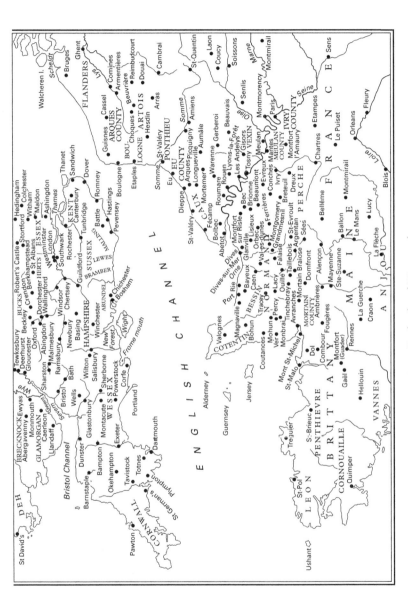

Map 4 England and Normandy

spectacularly with the Danish invasions. The amount levied in danegeld, said by the Anglo-Saxon chroniclers to have amounted to £36,000 in 1012 and £80,000 in 1017, may have been exaggerated; but the value of coin issued in one of the periodical recoinages could have raised such sums in an emergency. There is no reason to doubt that King Æthelred had been able to raise £4,000 annually as heregeld or army tax, and this was levied regularly until 1051. Some military obligations were discharged in person, others in cash or kind; the paid element was important. Royal and comital retainers were maintained in the household and paid some wages; and in times of emergency temporary mercenaries were hired; up to 1051 a regular fleet was maintained at a cost estimated at £3,000 to £4,000 a year. All this would have been impossible without an administration sufficiently sophisticated to exploit the wealth of the country.

During the eleventh century shire reeves or sheriffs increased in importance as the king's principal officers in the shire. Appointed by the king, they were directly responsible to him, not to the earl, for the administration of finance as well as for presiding in the shire court. They collected the dues from the royal estates as well as the general gelds, and played their part in assessing the liability of the district. In this they were assisted both by the reeves in the smaller administrative divisions of hundred and wapentake and by the lords of the large estates, who had their own reeves and servants. Village reeves shared in the responsibility for collecting geld, and some tenants owed riding services that may have included carrying the king's writs, by which he conveyed his instructions to the sheriffs and other local officers. Townsmen too played their part in collecting some local revenues.[1] All this business led to an increase in the number of written documents and probably too in the central rolls recording geld liability. The number of clerks in the writing office must have increased, though the formal organization of a true chancery still lay some way in the future.

The peace and stability of the kingdom depended on the king's good relations with his thegns and greater magnates. At first there were no serious tensions, and the handful of Normans or Bretons who accompanied or followed King Edward and settled on the Welsh border and in East Anglia contributed to the defence of the frontiers. The one serious threat came from the growing power of the family of Godwine, earl of Wessex. Godwine's daughter Edith became King Edward's wife, and his sons Harold, Swein, Tostig, Gyrth and Leofwine acquired earldoms in the course of the reign. King Edward's one attempt to expel them in 1050–1 ended in failure; thereafter he accepted the need to work with them. Swein and Tostig lost their earldoms through their own errors and misgovernment; but the power of Harold, particularly after he inherited his

[1] Campbell (1987).

father's earldom, increased. He and his brothers had their own military house-holds and formed alliances with important churchmen like Wulfstan, bishop of Worcester. By 1066 the family's estates had been considerably augmented by grants from the king, made partly to enable them to carry out their military duties and to defend the shires where their responsibilities lay. They included, however, lands which had previously been used for endowing royal officials, which now became family lands; and the total wealth of the Godwine family far exceeded that of the king. The evidence supports the charge recently made against King Edward, that if he approved of the aggrandizement of the family he was foolish, and if he acquiesced he cannot have been in full control of the kingdom.[2] In spite of the wealth and military organization of England, it was becoming dangerously unstable when Edward died childless, leaving the succession an open question. Earl Harold, though not of the royal blood, was a strong contender because of his power, presence at the king's deathbed and possible designation by Edward. There were also two serious contenders on grounds of distant kinship: Harald Hardrada, king of Norway, and William duke of Normandy, who also professed to have been promised the crown in 1051.

Normandy under Duke William was in the process of becoming the most powerful principality in the French kingdom. By 1047 the troubles of the duke's minority were over, and a victory over rebels at Val-ès-Dunes left him in a commanding position, strong enough to meet any new rebellion. The 1050s were a time of consolidation, when the frontiers of the duchy were strengthened, the authority of the king of France though acknowledged in principle was virtually excluded and a slow military expansion was begun. This prepared the way for the external conquests and triumphs of the 1060s. The dukes profited from inheriting both some of the public powers of the former Carolingian counts of Rouen and the military authority exercised by the leaders of the Scandinavian warbands who had settled in the tenth century. At first the duke may have been a Frankish count to some of his subjects, a Viking jarl to others; by the mid-eleventh century the fusion was complete. Lucien Musset calculated that the ducal *coutumes* showed a proportion of four Frankish royal customs to two Nordic elements.[3] Among the duke's public powers were the right to levy general taxes, to control the coinage and to demand that castles could be taken over by ducal castellans. The Scandinavia contribution to the machinery of government included some of the roots of the Norman public peace and probably also the procedure for mobilizing the fleet.

Besides this, Duke William began in the early 1050s to work closely with reforming churchmen and to cultivate good relations with the pope. He led the way in founding Benedictine monasteries and used all his traditional rights and

---

[2] Fleming (1991), p. 102.   [3] Musset (1970), pp. 112–14.

his powers of enforcing the public peace to assume a general guardianship over monasteries founded by his vassals. While keeping the control of episcopal and abbatial elections in his own hands, he was careful to avoid selling benefices. His removal of his uncle Mauger from the archbishopric of Rouen may have been due as much to doubts of Mauger's loyalty as to the worldly life that had been tolerated for some fifteen years, but William was careful to depose him in a church council and to replace him with a man of exemplary character. At St-Evroult similarly he drove out Robert of Grandmesnil, whose family had been involved in rebellion, and replaced him with an abbot as acceptable to reformers as to himself. He presided over church councils that promulgated decrees against simony and clerical marriage, and laid the foundations for the good relations with reforming popes that were to last for the greater part of his reign after the conquest of England.

After an unsuccessful rebellion by William, count of Arques, and his forfeiture in 1053, the great Norman families worked closely with the duke and throve as he prospered, in this age of 'predatory kinship'.[4] The new Norman counts who emerged from the 1020s onwards were kinsmen and vassals of the duke; many were connected with the families of Duke Richard I's widow, the Duchess Gunnor, or his half-brother, Count Rodulf. Their comtés were usually situated near the frontiers, for defence and attack; the earliest counts appeared at Ivry, Eu and Mortain. Their titles, at first personal, had all become territorialized by 1066, with the possible exception of Brionne, where Count Gilbert was never called 'count of Brionne'. They were an aristocracy of power, who held castles and founded monasteries, but did not exercise any public functions by virtue of their office. Predatory and outward looking, they sometimes acquired lands beyond the Norman frontiers, which involved them in fealty to the kings of France. Non-comital lords too, like Roger of Beaumont who married a daughter of Waleran, count of Meulan, or Roger of Montgomery, who married Mabel of Bellême, combined estates in Normandy and other French provinces. Some were acquiring estates across the Channel. In 1002 Duke Richard II's daughter Emma had married King Æthelred, so giving Duke William his claim to the English throne through kinship; Edward the Confessor's accession in 1042 attracted a scattering of Normans to settle in England. Pre-conquest penetration was building up there as well as in the provinces of Brittany, Maine and Perche. Initially this extended Norman influence, but dual allegiance was in time to strain the loyalty of the cross-frontier magnates.

Public duties fell mostly on the *vicomtes*, who were the true representatives of the duke in his traditional capacity as count of Rouen. These men were responsible for the administration of justice and collection of revenues, for

---

[4] Searle (1988).

military levies and the defence of castles; they performed many of the duties that in England would have fallen to the sheriff. In some important respects, however, they were different. Normandy, in spite of Viking influence, had no popular assemblies like the Scandinavian *things* or the English county and hundred courts. The *vicomtes* were directly responsible to the duke; there were no local assemblies over which they might preside, and they were not in any way deputies of the counts. Such structural differences were bound to influence later changes. Some *vicomtal* families held office for two or more generations and became wealthy and influential. Roger I of Montgomery, *vicomte* of the Hiémois, was succeeded by his son Roger II. Hugh I of Montfort-sur-Risle too was succeeded by his son. The Crispin family were establishing themselves in the Norman Vexin and the Goz family at Avranches. Ralph, *vicomte* of Bayeux, and Nigel of the Cotentin were likewise securing *vicomtés* for their heirs. For some of these men, who were rising to be important magnates, their wealth and power was to serve as a springboard to greater dignities in England.

When Duke William began to look towards England, Normandy, partly through the temporary weakness of the counts of Anjou and the French king, had become the most powerful province in northern France. He had taken advantage of a disputed succession in Maine to invade the county, arrange for the betrothal of his son Robert to the young heiress of Maine and secure the recognition of Robert as count even though his bride died before the marriage could take place. In the east Guy, count of Ponthieu, was compelled to swear fealty and promise military support; and relations with Count Baldwin of Flanders had been good after William's marriage to Baldwin's daughter Matilda. In 1064 he campaigned in Brittany during the minority of Count Conan II in support of Rivallon of Combour, and asserted his authority there. These wars brought out his remarkable skill as a military commander and attracted knights from neighbouring provinces to serve in his household troops, both to gain experience and to win booty. The obligations of his own vassals included military service, which as yet was normally of unspecified quantity and duration; quite probably the only men who contracted to supply an exact quota of knights were the holders of money fiefs. Abbeys which later provided knights may have owed them from former church lands which had become secularized and then restored to the church with knights settled on them. Good service brought ample rewards for the laity: lands, castellanships and *vicomtés*, or the hand of an heiress in marriage. In the mid-eleventh century war has been described as 'the national industry of the Normans'.

Edward the Confessor's childlessness and his gratitude to the Norman kins-men who had given him a refuge and recognized his rights during his exile may have encouraged William to hope from an early date to be designated as Edward's heir. His serious bid for the crown began, however, only after

Edward's death in January 1066, when Harold Godwineson was crowned king. William consulted his vassals and gained their support for his enterprise. The months of preparation show that he did not underestimate the task ahead; all his resources and experience were directed towards it. His own vassals provided men and ships; an early, incomplete ship-list contains some figures which look convincing.[5] The contributions from leading vassals and allies ranged from 120 and 100 ships provided by his half-brothers, Robert of Mortain and Odo bishop of Bayeux respectively, and 80 from William count of Evreux, through 60 each from Hugh of Avranches, Roger of Beaumont, Robert of Eu, Roger of Montgomery and William fitz Osbern, down to a single ship from Remigius of Fécamp Abbey. The core army of Normans was strongly supported by allies and knights from nearby provinces and even further afield. Eustace of Boulogne brought a substantial force from his county, and there were Bretons, Flemings, Poitevins and some men from Maine, Aquitaine and Anjou and possibly southern Italy. The 1066 conquest of England has been described, not without reason, as 'Duke William's Breton, Lotharingian, Flemish, Picard, Artesian, Cenomanian, Angevin, general-French and Norman Conquest.'[6] During the two or three months in the summer of 1066, when the army was first assembling at Dives-sur-Mer and then, after a move to St-Valéry, waiting to launch the invasion, there was ample time for a rigorous training to weld the individual units into a single effective striking force. Their success in the long and hard-fought battle at Hastings shows that William made good use of his time.

Whether or not he had prior information about an attempted invasion of King Harold Hardrada, supported by Tostig, in the north of England, he waited until Harold Godwineson had been forced to leave the south coast unprotected and hurry to Yorkshire to repel the invader. If, as Norman writers anxious to detect the will of God liked to claim, William was delayed by unfavourable winds which only changed in response to prayer, the fact that a change came at the first moment when a good commander would have chosen to embark is a remarkable coincidence. Harold, hurrying south after a successful battle at Stamford Bridge, had with him only the hard core of his army and local levies. Formidable as even this force was, it could not stand up to the combined assaults of William's well-rehearsed cavalry charges supported by archers. Harold was killed in the battle of Hastings. The destruction of the English army and the Norman victory was, however, only the beginning of the first stage of conquest. Even after William's acceptance by the English magnates who had survived the battle, and his coronation at Westminster by Archbishop Ældred of York, he had to face serious rebellions in the west and north of England for some four years. In spite of his claim to legitimate succession, and his attempt to retain existing

---

[5] Van Houts (1988).   [6] Ritchie (1954), p. 157.

English institutions as far as possible, his army was in many ways an army of occupation. This was to determine the military structure of his new realm.

In the twenty years after the Conquest a major redistribution of lands took place. Abbots and bishops were allowed to retain the bulk of their former church lands after making submission; but by the end of the reign Normans and their allies had been granted all but about 5 per cent of the land previously held by English secular magnates. The change, however, took place by stages. William had at his immediate disposal the royal demesne and the confiscated lands of the Godwine family, as well as the lands of the thegns who had fallen at Hastings. He was prepared to retain three of the former earls – Edwin, Morcar and Waltheof the son of Siward – and to preserve as much as possible of the administrative structure of the kingdom. When he left on a visit to Normandy he had to entrust others with military and political leadership in the earldoms formerly held by Harold and his brothers Gyrth and Leofwine. William fitz Osbern was given authority in Hampshire and Herefordshire and the title of earl. William's half-brother, Odo of Bayeux, appointed earl of Kent, was active in several shires; and Ralf the Staller, a Breton lord of Gael who had settled in East Anglia in King Edward's reign, apparently replaced Gyrth as earl of East Anglia. These were still earldoms of the traditional type; not until after the rebellion of Edwin and Morcar in 1068 had led to their forfeiture did the king establish earls analogous to the Norman counts in frontier areas with limited territorial authority. Roger of Montgomery became earl of Shrewsbury, probably from 1068, and Hugh of Avranches, earl of Chester from about 1070.[7]

By this time William's attitude to the kingdom had changed. Harold Godwineson was no longer called 'king'; and William, who dated his acts from the day of his coronation at Westminster, regarded himself as the immediate successor of King Edward after a nine months' usurpation. Further confiscations of the lands of rebels followed; and Normans or their allies replaced the last of the greatest English magnates. The king continued to exercise jurisdiction through the existing local courts, to collect traditional gelds and to employ established English moneyers to mint the coins of the realm. The invaders built on English foundations and appropriated English traditions, but the men themselves were 'Normans', speaking their own French language and observing different customs. The society that resulted was neither English nor Norman, and new forms of government and military organization were devised to meet new needs. Twelfth-century chroniclers, like Gaimar and Wace, who took over the English past as their own history and celebrated it in their vernacular French poems, were expressing in a different medium what had happened in society.

---

[7] Lewis (1991).

During the great distributions of property land was allocated to the new lords principally in two ways; by *antecessor* or by block grant in a particular county or group of counties. *Antecessores* were those who had been legally in possession on the day that King Edward died; the method of allocating the lands of a named *antecessor* was particularly common in the early years of the reign. The new lords sometimes held the lands of a Saxon *antecessor* only in one or two counties; Geoffrey of Mandeville, for example, was granted the lands of Ansgar the Staller in Essex but not in Hertfordshire or Buckinghamshire. Moreover, this was not the most common method of distribution; only about 10 per cent of the land can be positively accounted for in this way.[8] The king needed to have compact territorial blocks focused on castles for defence of the sea-coast and the frontiers. The Sussex lordships of Hastings, Pevensey, Lewes, Arundel and Bramber were established at an early date, and other compact lordships were created in Hampshire and the Welsh marches as well as along the moving northern frontier. These were built up by the second method: allocation in the shire court of the lands not already legally held by churches or early enfeoffed lay lords. A high proportion of later grants to lesser lords may have been made in roughly the same way. Some of the transfers were authenticated by royal writ; many depended on the witness of the court where they were made. Details of distribution might be settled in the local courts of hundred or wapentake.

Since some of the *antecessores* had held lands, particularly church lands, by lease for a limited number of lives, or had unlawfully occupied them, litigation was inevitable. A series of land pleas began within a decade of the Conquest; one of the greatest, held on Penenden Heath, concerned the lands of the church of Canterbury, and there was prolonged litigation over the lands of Ely. Twenty years of flux and change produced many changes both in landholding and in lordship. In estates with scattered sokes the shape of the pre-Conquest estate had a better chance of being preserved than in those where lordship extended only over men, not land. Some Saxon and other undertenants, anxious for protection, commended themselves to new Norman lords and formed a personal and legal connection that was not necessarily tenurial also. Such changes added further complexities to forms of landholding that were already confused by regional variations and the diversity of settlement customs. In the process of transfer many old estates were broken up and the consequent disruption of agrarian life was probably more important than the devastation caused by invading armies in reducing the value of lands as recorded in Domesday Book. Whereas estates transferred intact to new lords fell by only about 13 per cent

---

[8] The statistics in this section are taken from Fleming (1991), who provides the most full and detailed analysis of the relevant Domesday statistics at present available, and from Hollister (1987).

of their pre-Conquest values, those that were reconstituted from the lands of more than one landholder fell by an average 22 per cent.

With the regranting of land went some clarification of the terms of service.[9] In all probability quotas of military service were allocated to some leading ecclesiastical tenants-in-chief when their lands were confirmed or when a new prelate was appointed. The size of the monastic quotas seems to have been determined in part at least by military needs. Peterborough and Glastonbury, with quotas of sixty knights, and Ely and Bury St Edmunds, with quotas of forty, were all in regions vulnerable to invasion and attack and some distance from the centres of lay power. Abingdon, with a quota of thirty, controlled a vital ford on the north/south route to the midlands. The general obligations of lay lords to provide military support were more gradually expressed in precise quotas. Most had been defined by the end of the reign, though major changes in lordship through forfeiture or escheat were to take place up to and sometimes beyond the turn of the century. Sub-infeudation, with the establishment of knights' fees, was left to the individual lords, lay and ecclesiastical. Within a few decades it was to be of greater fiscal than military significance. Both the wealth of the estates granted and the size of the quotas imposed may have been related to the size of the military followings that the great magnates had brought with them and were obliged to support. In Normandy too the Conquest acted as a catalyst. With so many knights absent in England, the duke needed to be sure of adequate support from the great vassals who remained behind to keep the peace and defend the frontiers. If, as seems likely, most formal quotas were allocated in Normandy at about the same time as in England, this would account for the rough correlation that has been noted between the size of quotas in the Norman returns of 1172 and the wealth of the greatest magnates as suggested by the 1066 ship-list.

Many of the changes in landholding and resources resulting from two decades of conquest and settlement in England were summed up in the *Inquisitio geldi* (surviving for five shires only) and in Domesday Book. In 1085 King William needed to summon all available resources to meet the threat of invasion by King Cnut of Denmark, who was supported by Count Robert the Frisian of Flanders. Permanent household troops were always an important element in the armed forces, and the danger forced him to recruit an unusually large body of additional hired mercenaries. The duchy of Normandy too demanded his attention, and he was ready to settle a long-running border dispute in the Vexin by going on the offensive against the king of France. Financial needs were met by the exaction of heavy gelds. King Edward had dropped the heregeld in 1051; but by the early 1070s, if not before, William the Conqueror

---

[9] Holt (1984).

was collecting gelds and they became an important element in his revenue. The laments of the chroniclers show that exceptionally heavy gelds were levied in the last years of the reign. The *Inquisitio geldi* was most probably carried out in 1086, at almost the same time as the much more extensive Domesday survey. There were, however, needs other than financial that prompted the great survey. A series of land pleas, resulting from both lawful changes in tenure and unlawful appropriations dating even from before the Conquest, constantly demanded the attention of the king and his deputies. Disputes involved far more than the great ecclesiastical estates of Canterbury and Ely; the hundreds of *clamores* revealed by the Domesday inquest show that many small tenants were demanding redress. Norman sheriffs were among the predators; some lands had been occupied for non-payment of geld, and it seems likely that even before 1066 payment of geld had been taken to give some kind of title to land in dispute.[10] Norman landholders had an interest in securing official recognition of their rights by sworn testimony or royal writ. The machinery for the survey already existed in the courts of shire and hundred in which estate reeves participated alongside representatives of the vills. But without the co-operation of the magnates it could never have been carried through, as it was, within six months of being set in motion at King William's Christmas court in 1085. Only the exceptional circumstances of the Conquest made a survey on such a scale possible; no comparable inquest could have been attempted in Normandy, even if it had seemed desirable there.

The survey was made in seven, or more probably eight, circuits. Evidence was collected in the courts of shire and hundred with the assistance of local estate reeves and stewards, many of whom were already accustomed to accounting to their lords, and was checked by the sworn testimony of local juries before being submitted to the commissioners in each circuit. It covered the whole of England except Durham and the north and the great cities of London and Winchester. In the East Anglian circuit the tenures were so complicated that the returns had not been digested into their final form when returns from other circuits were complete, and they contained many details of stock omitted in the final version for the other circuits. It is beginning to be generally recognized that, though the writing up of Domesday Book continued into the next reign, the returns were completed by June 1086. They were available at the Salisbury court where 'all the land-holding men who were of any account' swore oaths of fealty and did homage to King William.[11] If the Salisbury oaths were indeed connected with the Domesday survey, it would be a sign that homage, initially a binding but general obligation between lord and man, was already being more specifically done in return for some definite grant of lands or rights. So it

---

[10] Hyams (1987).   [11] Holt (1987a).

is not unreasonable to describe the survey as 'the title-deed of all the Norman conquerors of England'.[12] Besides this, it provided the king, county by county, with the information which his officers, in particular the sheriffs, could use in administering the royal demesne and the lands of vassals and churches which came into the king's hands through vacancy, escheat or forfeiture. It shows too the mixture of fiscal and judicial elements that was to characterize royal government throughout the twelfth century.

The evidence collected, which included statements of landholders in the time of King Edward, when lands were first granted, and in 1066, brings out forcibly the changes in landed power brought about by the Conquest. Most striking is the different ratio between the extent of the royal demesne and that of the greatest tenants-in-chief. Of the lands held by the king and the wealthiest magnates before the Conquest, Edward the Confessor had held only 34 per cent, compared with 43 per cent in the hands of the Godwine family (even after Tostig's fall) and 23 per cent held by the families of Leofric and Siward. After the Conquest the proportions were reversed: King William had 64 per cent and the leading magnates together barely half that amount. Moreover, the wealth of William's greatest vassals was more modest than that of the powerful Saxon earls, and their lands were geographically slightly less scattered. The Godwines had land in thirty counties, whereas the estates of Hugh of Avranches were spread over twenty, and those of the king's half-brothers, Odo of Bayeux and Robert of Mortain together, over twenty-one.

A rough calculation of the wealth of William's vassals holding lands valued at over £750 a year shows Odo of Bayeux (£3,000), Robert of Mortain (£2,100), Roger of Montgomery (£2,100), William of Warenne (£1,165), Alan of Brittany, lord of Richmond (£1,100) at the top of the list, followed by Hugh of Avranches, earl of Chester (£820), Richard of Clare, Geoffrey bishop of Coutances and Geoffrey of Mandeville (each £780), and Eustace II of Boulogne (£770). Most of these men were ducal kinsmen and all had served him well. The church retained properties amounting to a little over 25 per cent of the landed wealth of the kingdom. The bishops of Bayeux and Coutances held their English lands as secular fees and performed the duties of lay barons in return; they were among the men most frequently appointed on judicial commissions. Odo of Bayeux, however, came under suspicion of disloyalty and was arrested and imprisoned in 1083; it was possible that his sympathies were with the king's rebel son, Robert Curthose. Released on the death of the Conqueror, he rebelled openly at the beginning of the next reign and suffered exile and forfeiture. Not one of the great magnates was strong enough to challenge the king as the Godwines had done; events were to prove that the king's resources, carefully used, were enough

[12] Davis (1987b), p. 28.

to bring down any rebellion in England or Normandy, even one backed by external powers, for the next half-century at least. William's great achievement has been described as giving such stability to Norman rule in England and the union of Normandy and England that his successors should want both to continue.[13]

The succession was, however, a serious problem facing all the Norman kings. When William died in September 1087 the danger of dividing the inheritance became apparent. Normandy was a part of the kingdom of France, even though the exact nature of the French king's lordship is uncertain and may have been differently interpreted by king and duke. William had probably sworn fealty first to King Henry, and then in 1060 to the young king Philip. Possibly homage was performed in the marches, but references to homage come from twelfth-century sources and may be anachronistic. Before he left for England in 1066 he made his magnates swear fealty to his eldest son Robert; the fealty was repeated later and Robert was recognized by King Philip in both Normandy and Maine. When he quarrelled with his father and even fought against him with help from King Philip he may have done homage to the French king. Although the association of father and son in the duchy of Normandy was little more than nominal in William's lifetime, it was a commitment from which the king could not escape on his deathbed. His wish may have been to keep the whole realm united, but he was not prepared to see Robert as king of England. He made it clear to Archbishop Lanfranc that he wished his second son, William Rufus, to be crowned; Lanfranc concurred without question, and so the realm was for the time being divided.

It would not be right to see the division between William Rufus and Robert as an application of the Norman custom of parage, whereby the eldest son often took the patrimony and the second son the acquisitions. Even if general inheritance customs had crystallized in 1087 – and in fact they remained flexible – they would not have been applicable either to the kingdom or to the duchy, and the previous history of both tended to ever greater union. Once the early English kingdoms were united the rulers obtained undivided authority over the whole realm; and the Norman dukes had never divided the duchy. Even the nominal association of the duke's son with his father did not amount to delegation, far less to division of authority; it was rather a guarantee of succession. Circumstances rather than calculated planning left Robert as duke of Normandy and William Rufus as king of England, while Henry, the third son, received only cash, though he claimed to have a right to his mother's lands. William Rufus and Robert at first agreed to make the other his heir if either died without issue. Later William's actions between 1096 and 1100 when he

[13] Bates (1989b), p. 185.

was ruling Normandy during his brother's absence on crusade, Henry's ruthless planning and effective action after William's death and Robert's vain struggle to recover England show that each one of the three brothers aimed to reunite the realm in his own hand. Both William and Henry, who showed something of their father's ability in ruling, enjoyed a fair measure of success; whereas Robert, who for all his military prowess as a crusader proved unable to hold the loyalty of his vassals except by giving away vital resources, failed to preserve even what he had.

Norman expansion continued during the reign of William Rufus. He carried on the enterprises begun by his father, helped by a continuing influx of new immigrants, many of whom were younger sons. The northern frontier was pushed forward into Cumbria. William I, on his one expedition against Malcolm Canmore king of Scots, had secured at Abernethy an oath of allegiance that may have been equivalent to homage in the marches. In 1092 Rufus led a great army northward, established a castle at Carlisle, planted settlers there and gave the lordship to Ralph of Briquessart. King Malcolm reluctantly agreed to attend his court at Gloucester in 1094, but remained a potential threat to the northern frontier. It was his murder shortly afterwards, the struggle for succession in Scotland and the friendly relations established with Malcolm's younger sons and daughters who were brought up in England that reduced tension on the frontier about the turn of the century. In northern and central Wales the Norman advance remained in the hands of the great marcher earls, Hugh of Chester and Roger of Shrewsbury, and was halted for a time after their deaths. In the south, where William fitz Osbert had begun to fortify the march, the treason and forfeiture of his son in 1075 brought the king more directly into the advance along the shore of the Bristol Channel. A surge of Norman settlers into this region followed; they established castles, monasteries and small boroughs. After the death in 1093 of Rhys ap Tewdwr there was no focus of Welsh power, and Rufus planted new Norman and Breton families at Abergavenny, Caerleon and Glamorgan. Welsh risings during the reign checked the Normans; but at least Rufus maintained his father's position.

He met with greater success on the Norman frontiers once Robert Curthose had left for Jerusalem. The skills of Robert of Bellême, the eldest son of Roger of Montgomery, as a military engineer helped him to strengthen the frontier defences with new castles. Gisors was a bastion against the unruly lords of the Vexin; though Rufus failed to advance on this frontier he left it better defended. In the south he successfully reasserted Norman claims to hold Maine directly under the count of Anjou, placed a garrison in Le Mans which held out until his death and successfully influenced an episcopal election there. Along the whole southern frontier the lords, some of whom held lands also of the king of France, gave the main weight of their support to whichever of the two kings had most to offer them. William Rufus successfully retained the loyalty of the count of Meulun; the family of Montfort l'Amaury was more divided, and at one time the brothers Simon and Amaury fought on opposite sides. In spite of divided allegiances Rufus was sufficiently secure in that region to be believed to be planning a major enterprise in Aquitaine when he was killed, in what was most probably a hunting accident, in the New Forest on 2 August 1100.

His overall success, in spite of a serious revolt led by Robert of Mowbray in 1095 and ruthlessly put down, depended both on military leadership and on the skilful use of resources inherited from his father. He kept a tight control over the royal castles; whereas Curthose, as long as he governed Normandy, allowed his vassals to turn out the royal garrisons and treat castles as part of the family patrimony. Curthose even abandoned Brionne, in the very heart of the duchy, to Roger of Beaumont, who had previously held it as castellan. Rufus did not squander his inheritance; and as long as there was a supply of new lands in Wales and in the north to settle, in addition to confiscated estates to be redistributed and the hope of profitable marriages, vassals knew that their interest lay in keeping the king's love. The forces they brought with them to war were not necessarily limited to their agreed quotas, and while so many had interests in Normandy there was no resistance to serving without question on either side of the Channel. In any case the king's very numerous household troops bore the brunt of the sustained campaigns in Normandy and Maine. There were complaints of extortion, especially from churchmen, and of the ravaging of the king's large and unruly household as it travelled in his company. Nevertheless, he remained popular with his knights and his younger vassals in particular, even though Anselm, his archbishop of Canterbury, went into exile to seek advice and help at the papal court and the church chroniclers reviled him. To them his sudden, unshriven, death was a judgement of God.

When Rufus died Robert Curthose was on his way home from Jerusalem, bringing with him Sibyl of Conversano as his wife and a dowry substantial enough to pay off his debts. Before he reached Normandy his younger brother Henry, by swift action, had had himself accepted as king of England and been crowned at Westminster. Robert's attempt to invade England in 1101 failed. Within six years Henry had forced him out of Normandy also and taken him prisoner at Tinchebray, so uniting the two parts of the Anglo-Norman realm. Robert's imprisonment lasted until his death in 1134; his claims remained alive in his young son William Clito.

Henry's aim during his long reign was consolidation rather than expansion, and he went further than his predecessors in tightening the bonds between England and Normandy. Like his father, he turned conquest into legitimate rule. His marriage to Matilda, daughter of Malcolm Canmore and Edgar Atheling's sister Margaret, united his line with that of King Alfred as well as helping to secure the northern frontier. In 1102 he faced the only major rebellion of his reign in England, from Robert of Bellême, who had brought together the immense Montgomery–Bellême inheritance on both sides of the Channel and favoured the cause of Curthose. Robert, defeated, forfeited all his English lands and was exiled with his younger brothers Arnulf and Roger. Ten years later Henry was able to confiscate his continental honours also, and imprison him for life. It was the only case of total dispossession of a whole great family in Henry's reign, and his relentless pursuit of the Bellême family continued until the end of his life.

Normandy was less secure. Henry's later wars, apart from two Welsh expeditions, were all fought on the Norman side of the Channel. Some vassals, particularly those on the Vexin frontier, supported the claims of Curthose, which were revived by William Clito as soon as he was old enough to bear arms. They were helped by King Louis VI and by the count of Anjou, who had inherited the rights of the counts of Maine and come into direct conflict with Norman interests there. In the struggle with Anjou Henry was powerfully assisted by the son of his sister Adela, Theobald count of Blois; family loyalties were reinforced by the traditional rivalry of Blois and Anjou. In 1113 Count Fulk V of Anjou finally made peace and agreed to the betrothal of his young daughter Matilda to Henry's only legitimate son, William Adelin. Maine was to be her dowry, and Henry now set about securing the whole inheritance for his son. In 1115 the Norman barons swore fealty and did homage to the twelve-year-old boy; a year later the English magnates likewise did homage at Salisbury. It was the first time the succession had been secured by homage as well as fealty. In 1119 the forces of King Louis VI were decisively defeated by Henry's knights at Brémule, and a year later Louis finally agreed to accept Henry's right to Normandy and received the homage of William Adelin. By establishing a right to Normandy without himself doing homage to anyone, Henry demonstrated the practical unity of the Anglo-Norman realm. Orderic Vitalis, writing in the later years of Henry's reign, saw his rule there as royal, and was prepared to regard disrespect for his person as a form of lèse-majesté. No one, however, suggested that Normandy was a province of England, and this language may have amounted to no more than a mark of personal distinction. Henry himself began after 1120 to use the title of duke of Normandy, which he had refrained from using when he first dispossessed his brother. The suzerainty of the kings of France may have been little more than a tradition, but it had the potential of becoming a reality; 'ignored, resisted or denied, but never forgotten', it 'introduced an important qualification into the notion of a progressive unification of the Norman lands and lordships'.[14]

---

[14] Le Patourel (1976), pp. 219–21.

Henry's actions in Normandy show that his concern was with legitimizing his position and strengthening his frontiers, not with expansion. More than fifteen castles on the frontiers of Brittany, Maine, Perche, the Vexin Français, the Beauvaisis and Eu-Ponthieu were either built of refortified. Royal rights were rigorously enforced in private castles; for example, during the hostilities with France in 1119 royal household troops were stationed in the archbishop of Rouen's castle at Andely. Henry's natural daughters were married to frontier lords: to Conan III duke of Brittany, Rotrou count of Perche, Eustace of Breteuil, William Gouet of Montmirail, Matthew of Montmorency, Roscelin of Beaumont-le-Vicomte and, at the other end of his dominions, to Alexander king of Scots and Fergus earl of Galloway. His only legitimate daughter, Matilda, was destined for a more illustrious marriage to the emperor Henry V, who gave support on the eastern frontiers of France and helped to ensure trading links with the wealthy cities of the Rhineland. His natural sons and his Blois nephews either earned preferment and the hand of an heiress by serving in his household troops, or were provided with church benefices. Robert of Caen, the eldest, was given the honour of Gloucester with the hand of Robert fitz Hamo's daughter and heir. His nephew, Stephen of Blois, received the county of Mortain and the hand of Matilda, heiress of Boulogne as well as lands in England; and Stephen's younger brother Henry of Blois was made abbot of Glastonbury and bishop of Winchester.

Henry aimed too at preserving the bonds between England and Normandy by promoting the interests of his magnates on both sides of the Channel. From the time that Normans secured rich estates in England they had an interest in avoiding the complication of dual allegiance. Orderic Vitalis put into words their wish to serve under one lord because of the honours they held in England and Normandy. The ties might become loosened with each new generation; in the course of time one branch of some families, like the Clares and the Tosnys, became rooted in England, while another remained in the Norman patrimony. Henry partially countered this by strengthening other cross-Channel lordships. The elder Beaumont twin, Robert, who inherited the honour of Leicester and was made an earl, was also given the hand of the heiress of Breteuil in marriage. Robert of Briquessart retained his Norman lands after inheriting the honour of Chester. Although some lords, like the younger Beaumont twin, Waleran, count of Meulan, might be distracted by conflicting obligations as vassals of the king of France, the cross-Channel interests of powerful English magnates were later to work to the advantage of the empress Matilda in her hard struggle for the crown against her cousin Stephen.

The succession question was reopened in an acute form when William Adelin was drowned in the wreck of the *White Ship* within a few months of doing homage to Louis VI. Henry's immediate object was to exclude William

Clito, who had the support of some Norman barons and of King Louis, and was precariously established as count of Flanders in 1127. Henry pursued him relentlessly; he persuaded the pope to annul Clito's marriage to a daughter of the count of Anjou, and during the Flemish war of succession encouraged the supporters of his rival Thierry of Alsace. The danger passed with Clito's death in battle in 1128. By that time Henry, whose second marriage to Adeliza of Louvain had proved sterile, had a candidate of his own blood for the succession. His daughter Matilda, widowed in 1125, was brought home from Germany; three years later, just before the death of William Clito, she was married to Geoffrey, the eldest son of the count of Anjou. Immediately after her return Henry had insisted that his vassals should accept her as his heir in England and Normandy and swear fealty to her. He never asked for homage; but the oaths were renewed in 1131 after her marriage, and the rights of any children of the marriage to succeed to the whole inheritance were secured in principle. Henry made clear his intention that the inheritance he had spent his life in consolidating should remain intact. Important practical details, however, were left vague. The position of Matilda's husband Geoffrey, who had been accepted by the baronage only with reluctance, was never clearly defined; he was not mentioned in the oaths. Matilda, as a woman, could not at that date have done homage, though she could have received it. Henry had himself avoided doing homage for Normandy and may have hoped that the French king would allow the same freedom to his daughter until she had a son old enough to do homage on her behalf. This may not have been enough to satisfy Geoffrey, who may even have hoped for a position of joint rule in England comparable to that enjoyed by his father Fulk, who married as his second wife Melisende, the heiress of Jerusalem.

When King Henry died at Lyons-la-Foret on 1 December 1135, after a very short illness, relations with Geoffrey and Matilda had become strained because of a dispute over border fortresses and the rights of William Talvas, the son of Robert of Bellême, to succeed to some of his father's Norman inheritance. Henry's nephew Stephen of Blois, who was in Boulogne at the time, moved quickly to seize the throne regardless of the oaths he had taken to Matilda. He too had no thought of dividing the inheritance, and in this he was backed by the great magnates, who recognized him as duke as soon as they heard of his coronation. Following King Henry's example, he himself avoided doing homage to the king of France but allowed his son Eustace to do homage in 1137. Unlike Henry, because his claims were even more dubious and involved the violation of an oath, he immediately sent to Pope Innocent II and secured papal confirmation of his coronation. Since 1066 churchmen had been able to insist on coronation as an essential element in the making of a king. Regnal years were dated from the day of coronation, and the first three Norman kings had all learnt the value of it in securing the loyal support of their prelates. Stephen's lawful coronation was to prove the strongest guarantee that he might hope to wear the crown for his lifetime. Normandy, however, proved to be his Achilles heel; the disputed border fortresses, including Argentan, had formed part of Matilda's dowry, and she immediately occupied them, keeping open a gateway into Normandy from Anjou. While the lords of the frontier pursued their private border wars, Stephen paid his one visit to Normandy in 1137, and succeeded only in making a temporary truce without establishing any lasting order. This failure might be said to mark the end of the old Anglo-Norman realm, which had reached its apogee under Henry I.

It was always dependent on the personal ability of the monarch, who united the disparate parts of his realm in his person and in his court and household. By constant movement around his domains he and the vassals and household officers who followed him became familiar with different customs and administrative practices. There was considerable cross-fertilization, though the difference in the underlying structures of England and Normandy ensured that developments would never be identical. As long as King Henry lived his court was 'at the centre of a network of power and influence spreading out into the localities'.[15] The men who had his ear enjoyed the benefit of his patronage, whether they were great magnate counsellors like Robert of Meulan, royal chaplains who continued to serve him after being promoted to bishoprics or commanders of his knights who acted when required as castellans and sometimes sheriffs. This group, changing in composition but always immensely influential, preserved the unity of the realm to the end of the reign.

The process of detaching financial and judicial institutions from the undifferentiated household-court and of establishing them in kingdom or duchy had barely begun, and terms such as chancery or treasury must be applied, if at all, with caution. In spite of the rapid increase in the use of written instruments there were not two separate writing offices for England and Normandy. A group of royal clerks travelled with the king and served his chapel. Before the Conquest both the Norman dukes and the English kings had had chapels of this kind; in both the chief clerk was occasionally given the title of 'chancellor'. Dudo of St-Quentin, drafting charters for Duke Richard II, had sometimes assumed this title, as had Regenbald the 'chancellor', who was taken over by William I from King Edward's household, though it would be premature to speak of a distinct chancery. Whatever may be argued about the existence of a seal in either England or Normandy before 1066, the instrument of the writ was becoming more widely used as a means of sending instructions to the officers and suitors in the English shire courts. The Conquest led to a speeding

---

[15] Green (1986), pp. 36–7.

up of developments in England and the increased use of the same instruments in Normandy. The sealed writ became an essential element in the royal government. Numbers of scribes increased, though some charters, particularly in Normandy, were written by the beneficiaries and taken to the king for authentication. There was, however, only one seal and one keeper of the seal and, once a rudimentary chancery began to emerge towards the end of Henry's reign, one chancellor. Other household officials – the chamberlains, constables and marshals – might be more localized. Nevertheless, some officers were mobile; for example Robert Mauduit served in the treasuries of both countries and Robert de la Haye, constable of Lincoln Castle, served at another time as a baron of the exchequer in Normandy.

All three of the first Norman kings necessarily divided their time between England and Normandy and were obliged to leave kinsfolk or trusted magnates to act as vice-regents in their place during their absence. William I often left his wife Matilda as his representative in Normandy. In England he relied at first on William fitz Osbern and then on Odo of Bayeux until Odo's disgrace. Archbishop Lanfranc had an important role in transmitting the king's orders, and both Robert of Mortain and Geoffrey bishop of Coutances were frequently commissioned to act in important pleas. When William Rufus governed Normandy during his brother's absence on crusade he employed an official of a new type in England: Ranulf Flambard, who had emerged as one of the ablest of the clerks in the royal household at the end of the Conqueror's reign. Ranulf never had quite the status of the later justiciar, but his duties were both judicial and fiscal. Henry was absent for long periods in Normandy; though the central curia remained the nucleus of all important business the practical difficulties arising from his movements and the steady increase in administrative business made it necessary to begin to detach more tightly organized departments of government from the household-court on both sides of the Channel. Until 1118 Henry's queen Matilda was the official regent in England during his absences, but Roger bishop of Salisbury gradually took over more of the vice-regal duties, and after her death emerged as second after the king. A small group of men, including Robert Bloet bishop of Lincoln, Richard Belmeis bishop of London, Adam of Port and Ralph Basset, were frequently associated with him, acting both as justices in pleas that did not follow the king and presiding over financial business. In Normandy John bishop of Lisieux performed similar functions during Henry's years in England.

Finance was crucial, and the need to meet recurring threats of invasion or rebellion, particularly in Normandy, determined many of Henry's decisions. He had to provide at all times for the knights serving in his household troops or as garrisons in his castles on the Norman frontiers and wherever feudal obligations were insufficient to meet the needs of defence. The periods of greatest danger were from the time he secured Normandy in 1106 to 1113, and in the 1120s when William Clito, supported by Louis VI, posed a real threat to the succession; and these saw the most vigorous financial reforms. It was necessary to control the unruly retinues of knights and household servants, whose ravagings had made the journeys of the court during the reign of Rufus a terror to the neighbourhood. By 1108 Henry had introduced greater discipline both by ruthlessly punishing abuses and by planning his perambulations in advance so that orderly arrangements for provisioning could be made. The evidence of the 1130 Pipe Roll shows how the sheriffs planned ahead to provide wine, wheat and clothing and much more besides for the needs of the itinerant household. His first great reform of the moneyers came in 1108; there was an even more radical overhaul in 1125, when he reduced the number of mints and finally abandoned the regular cycles of recoinage inherited from Anglo-Saxon England.[16] As more and more of both the produce from the royal demesne and the feudal obligations of vassals were converted into financial payments the need for tight control of the collection of cash and efficient auditing of receipts became necessary.

A momentous innovation took place in England in the first ten years of the twelfth century; by 1110 a central receipt and audit was held at the same place and in the same curial session. Still an event, not an institution, it was known as the Exchequer from the checked cloth of the abacus on which calculations were made as the sheriffs and other officers brought in their cash receipts and the tallies for sums already disbursed. The court met regularly twice a year, initially at Winchester; its composition varied from time to time, and the magnates active in each session, called barons of the Exchequer, handled judicial no less than financial business. Roger of Salisbury presided without ever being called treasurer – a title later given to his nephew Nigel. For convenience money continued to be stored in repositories in several places, including the Tower of London and Westminster as well as Winchester in England, and Caen and Falaise in Normandy. The treasure needed for day-to-day expenses was carried with the king, in the charge of a household chamberlain. Before the end of the reign, possibly only in the last few years, a central receipt and audit had begun to be held in Normandy at Caen, at a separate Exchequer presided over by John bishop of Lisieux.[17] There was close contact between the financial agents on both sides of the Channel; and though some chamberlains were active only on one side, information and experience were exchanged. The position of the treasurer, as described in the *Constitutio Domus Regis* at the end of Henry's reign, was still anomalous; half in the household and half out of it, he possibly supervised all the chamberlains and had overall responsibility for all the treasuries, English and Norman. There were similarities in organization at the

---

[16] Blackburn (1991).   [17] Green (1989), pp. 115–23.

level of the household; but, because the position of the English sheriffs differed from that of the *vicomtes* who were responsible for farming and collecting the Norman revenues and there was no Norman equivalent of the county court, differences were bound to persist. The first surviving English record of the central audit, the Pipe Roll of 1129–30 antedates anything available for Normandy; later Norman Exchequer Rolls (from 1172) show common influences offset by variations in local practice.

In judicial matters also, even though a single *curia regis*, moving with the king, might handle cases from any part of the realm wherever it happened to be, the development of institutions of government tended to 'perpetuate and intensify the different traditions and customs of the two countries'.[18] So the application of law through different local courts made in the long run for a good deal of variation below the baronial level, while the upper ranks of feudal society were tending towards greater uniformity all over the realm. At that level, intermarriage, attendance at the royal court, service in the royal household and widespread travel both on the king's business and to oversee their own far-flung estates, produced assimilation of the Normans, Bretons, Flemings, Poitevins and others within two or three generations of the conquest and settlement of England. The law of free inheritance was becoming more defined; by the end of Henry's reign the flexible inheritance customs within the family that had previously existed were moving decisively towards primogeniture for military tenures in England, and in Normandy towards a *droit d'aînesse* with its rule that fiefs were impartible. There was enough similarity for cases involving cross-Channel lordships to be settled in the *curia regis* in the king's presence. And similar instruments were used; the sealed writ and the inquest at the king's command were ubiquitous in the Anglo-Norman realm.

At times from the reign of the Conqueror onwards justices were sent out with special commissions; Henry I sometimes appointed justices or justiciars to hear pleas in several counties. They dealt with cases initiated by writ, and the forms of judicial writs were multiplying. These writs, which appeared in both England and Normandy, were specifically designed for a particular set of circumstances. The cases, however, were still heard in the local courts and judgement was pronounced in the traditional way even when a royal officer presided; the fundamental change whereby the officers themselves gave judgement did not come until the reign of Henry II. Although the germ of later developments may now be seen in the language of the writs and in the widening sphere of action of the justices, this did not imply an inevitable development towards the methods of dispensing justice which took a much clearer shape in the later reign.[19]

---

[18] Le Patourel (1976), p. 223.   [19] Brand (1990).

In many cases brought to his notice Henry insisted that the proper place for them to be heard was in the lord's court, where land pleas between vassals were dealt with and feudal dues were enforced. Where the competence of these courts failed, perhaps because men held of different lords, or if justice was denied, he was prepared to have cases transferred to the county courts in England, or ultimately to hear them in his own presence in the *curia regis*. Some, arising out of financial disputes revealed in the audit, were heard by the barons of the Exchequer. The initiative normally lay with the plaintiff. The king did not go out to seek justice, but he offered it widely and the profits of justice and jurisdiction were, after land, one of the most important sources of revenue. Below the king's court there were some differences in the administration of justice in England and Normandy. Tenants-in-chief held their own feudal courts for their own barons, and these interlocked with the king's court in different ways. Little is known of the functioning of the early *vicomtes'* courts in Normandy; they certainly never had the communal element of the county courts to which, in England, some cases found their way. The *vicomtes*, like Landry of Orbec, appear to have brought criminal cases into their courts by impleading suspects *ex officio*.[20] It was an intensely unpopular practice which easily led to extortion, and though used occasionally for a short while under Henry I it had no future in England. The organization of the county courts lent itself to the initiation of criminal prosecutions through juries of presentment which were to become general under Henry II.

Bishops, in so far as they were barons, were liable to come under the same jurisdiction as the lay magnates, though they fought hard to limit their secular liabilities. Their position in both England and Normandy was similar. Ecclesiastical patronage and the control of appointments was equally important to the king in both. The early recognition in Normandy that investment by the duke with the temporalities did not involve spiritual investiture, which was performed by a prelate, meant that in the Anglo-Norman realm the investiture contest never had the same violence as in the empire even after the spread of ecclesiastical reform. The struggle came with the increasing formalities involved in the feudal relationships of prelates as great tenants-in-chief; it was resolved in time by agreeing that homage might be performed before consecration. Election did not become a major problem until later; the kings usually succeeded in having their nominee accepted in a technically correct formal election, or at least reached a working agreement without open conflict. The extent of royal influence appears in the large number of bishoprics held by clerks who had served in the royal household; promotion to a bishopric was a

---

[20] Van Caenegem (1976), pp. 61–70.

valuable form of patronage at a time when patronage helped to guarantee the devotion of the king's servants at every level. The experience of these men in ecclesiastical business made up a part of their training for more secular duties when they served on judicial commissions. John, archdeacon of Sées, had had long experience of judicial business in church courts before Henry made him bishop of Lisieux in 1107, and he became the key figure in the development of a Norman Exchequer.

Henry I, up to his death, maintained his rights of regale. Complaints, when they came, were less about elections and more about sees being left vacant for long periods while the king's officers collected the revenues. New strains were beginning to appear when Stephen succeeded with a doubtful title and needed papal backing just when reformers were demanding a stricter application of canon law. As far as the spiritual jurisdiction of the church courts went, it was slowly being disentangled from temporal business, with a good deal of confusion in areas of overlapping jurisdiction. The question of the activities of bishops in the shire courts was naturally peculiar to England. In the main, problems arising from the increasing activities of the archdeacons' courts and the strengthening of the hierarchy, which led to appeals, were broadly similar in all parts of the realm and routine appeals to Rome had not yet become a bone of contention.

It was still possible in 1137, when the struggle between Stephen and Matilda entered a new phase, for a ruler to hold together, in a single realm, many different provinces with considerable variations in custom. Boundaries might vary as frontier provinces changed hands. In the north of England the claims of the kings of Scotland were tenacious; it would have been possible for Cumbria and perhaps Northumberland to be drawn into their kingdom. The Channel was not an insuperable barrier, and Henry I may have believed that Normandy could in time be brought fully under his royal authority. Nevertheless, the claims of the kings of France were ancient and were never abandoned. An important change in the nature of fealty worked to their advantage. As the concept of liege homage replaced the looser bonds of loyalty that had once prevailed, Louis VII showed clearly that he would be satisfied with nothing less than homage performed in Paris by the duke of Normandy in person, not in the marches by his son as previously. Possibly the struggle between Stephen and Matilda made the break-up of the realm inevitable; possibly it merely hastened the change that drew Normandy decisively away from England into the kingdom of France. The work of the first three Norman kings established a realm bound together by personal ties, with many common instruments of government and a powerful central nucleus in the king's court and household. At the same time, any increase in the establishment of local courts for the king's business and localized finance would be likely to enhance regional divisions.

The permanent establishment of individual branches of cross-Channel families in England tended to break family ties faster than cross-Channel marriages could strengthen them. Paris was too near not to be a threat and the kings of France were constantly vigilant for any weakening of Anglo-Norman power. They seized each opportunity when it came, as it did with the outbreak of civil war.

CHAPTER 8

THE BYZANTINE EMPIRE, 1025–1118

Michael Angold

I

BASIL II died on 15 December 1025 after a reign of almost fifty years. He left Byzantium the dominant power of the Balkans and Near East, with apparently secure frontiers along the Danube, in the Armenian highlands and beyond the Euphrates. Fifty years later Byzantium was struggling for its existence. All its frontiers were breached. Its Anatolian heartland was being settled by Turkish nomads; its Danubian provinces were occupied by another nomad people, the Petcheneks; while its southern Italian bridgehead was swept away by Norman adventurers. It was an astonishing reversal of fortunes. Almost as astonishing was the recovery that the Byzantine empire then made under Alexios I Komnenos (1081–1118). These were years of political turmoil, financial crisis and social upheaval, but it was also a time of cultural and intellectual innovation and achievement. The monastery churches of Nea Moni, on the island of Chios, of Hosios Loukas, near Delphi, and of Daphni, on the outskirts of Athens, were built and decorated in this period. They provide a glimmer of grander monuments built in Constantinople in the eleventh century, which have not survived: such as the Peribleptos and St George of the Mangana. The miniatures of the Theodore Psalter of 1066 are not only beautifully executed but are also a reminder that eleventh-century Constantinople saw a powerful movement for monastic renewal. This counterbalanced but did not necessarily contradict a growing interest in classical education. The leading figure was Michael Psellos. He injected new life into the practice of rhetoric and in his hands the writing of history took on a new shape and purpose. He claimed with some exaggeration to have revived the study of philosophy single-handed. His interest in philosophy was mainly rhetorical. It was left to his pupil John Italos to apply philosophy to theology and to reopen debate on some of the fundamentals of Christian dogma.

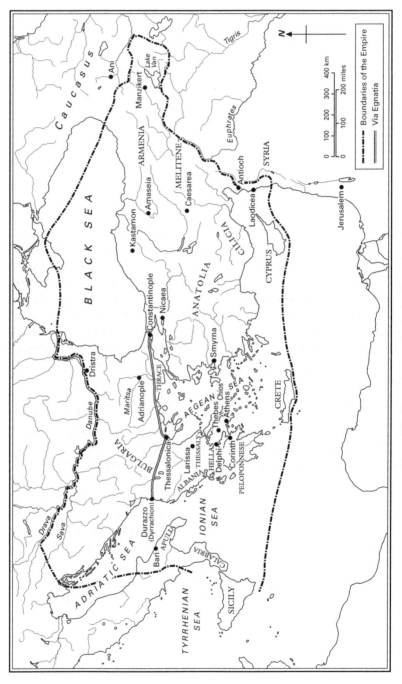

Map 5 The Byzantine empire in the eleventh century

Modern historiography has singled out the period from 1025 to 1118 as the watershed of Byzantine history. G. Ostrogorsky has provided the classic interpretation.[1] He saw the eleventh century as the beginning of Byzantium's inexorable decline, which he attributed to the triumph of feudalism. Private interest gained at the expense of the state. Without effective central institutions it was impossible to mobilize the resources of the empire or provide any clear direction. Symptomatic of the decline of central authority was the struggle for power between the civil and military aristocracies. The latter emerged victorious with the accession to the throne of Alexios I Komnenos. But his success was limited and his restoration of the empire superficial, because 'the Empire was internally played out'. Ostrogorsky meant by this that the peasantry and their property were coming increasingly under the control of great landowners. He believed that this compromised the economic and demographic potential of the empire.

Ostrogorsky's presentation of the history of the Byzantine empire in the eleventh century has been attacked from two main directions. P. Lemerle doubted that the eleventh century was a period of absolute decline at Byzantium.[2] There is too much evidence of economic growth and cultural vitality, which he connects with 'le gouvernement des philosophes'. The tragedy was Alexios I Komnenos's seizure of power, which substituted family rule for the state. R. Browning would add that Alexios damped down the intellectual and religious ferment of the eleventh century through the deliberate use of heresy trials.[3]

A. P. Kazhdan takes a rather different view.[4] He agrees that in the eleventh century Byzantium prospered. He attributes the political weakness of the empire to reactionary elements holding back the process of 'feudalization'. A. Harvey presses this approach to extremes.[5] He insists that the advance of the great estate was essential for economic and demographic growth. Kazhdan is also struck by the buoyancy and innovation of Byzantine culture. He connects this with a growth of individualism and personal relations. It was a victory for progressive elements, which were promoted rather than hindered by the Comnenian regime.[6]

Such a bald presentation does not do justice to the subtleties and hesitations displayed by the different historians nor to their skilful deployment of the

[1] G. Ostrogorsky, *A History of the Byzantine State*, trans. J. Hussey, Oxford (1968), pp. 316–75.

[2] P. Lemerle, *Cinq études sur le XIe siècle byzantin* (Le Monde Byzantin), Paris (1977), pp. 249–312.

[3] R. Browning, 'Enlightenment and repression in Byzantium in the eleventh and twelfth centuries', *PaP* 69 (1975), 3–22.

[4] A. P. Kazhdan and A. W. Epstein, *Change in Byzantine Culture in the Eleventh and Twelfth Centuries*, Berkeley, Los Angeles and London (1985), pp. 24–73.

[5] A. Harvey, *Economic Expansion in the Byzantine Empire 900–1200*, Cambridge (1989), pp. 35–79.

[6] A. P. Kazhdan and S. Franklin, *Studies on Byzantine Literature of the Eleventh and Twelfth Centuries*, Cambridge (1984), pp. 242–55.

evidence. It makes their views far more schematic than they are, but it highlights differences of approach and isolates the major problems. They hinge on the effectiveness of the state. Was this being undermined by social, economic and political developments? Though their chronology is different Ostrogorsky and Lemerle are both agreed that it was. They assume that the health of Byzantium depended on the centralization of power. By way of contrast Kazhdan believes that imperial authority could be rebuilt on a different basis and this is what Alexios Komnenos was able to do. The nature of Alexios's achievement becomes the key issue.

A weakness of all these readings of Byzantium's 'eleventh-century crisis' is a willingness to take Basil II's achievement at face value; to see his reign as representing an ideal state of affairs. They forget that his iron rule represents an aberration in the exercise of imperial authority at Byzantium. His complete ascendancy was without precedent. In a series of civil wars in the early part of his reign he destroyed the power of the great Anatolian families, such as Phokas and Skleros, but only thanks to foreign aid. He used his power to straitjacket Byzantine society and subordinate it to his autocratic authority. To this end he reissued and extended the agrarian legislation of his forebears. Its purpose was ostensibly to protect peasant property from the 'powerful' as they were called. It was, in practice, less a matter of the imperial government's professed concern for the well-being of the peasantry; much more a way of assuring its tax revenues. These depended on the integrity of the village community which was the basic tax unit. This was threatened as more and more peasant property passed into the hands of the 'powerful'. Basil II followed up this measure by making the latter responsible for any arrears of taxation which had till then largely been borne by the peasantry. Control of the peasantry was vital if Basil II was to keep the empire on a war footing, while keeping the empire on a war footing was a justification for autocracy. The long war he waged against the Bulgarians only finally came to an end in 1018. It exploited the energies of the military families of Anatolia. It cowered the aristocracy of the Greek lands. They were terrified that they would be accused of cooperating with the Bulgarians. The war with the Bulgarians was bloody and exhausting, but it was a matter of recovering lost ground, not of gaining new territory. The Bulgarian lands had been annexed by John Tzimiskes in the aftermath of his victory over the Russians in 971. It was only the civil wars at the beginning of Basil II's reign and the emperor's own ineptitude that allowed the Bulgarians to recover their independence. Basil II's triumph over the Bulgarians gave a false impression of the strength of the empire.

In part, it depended on an absence of external enemies. Islam was for the time being a spent force; thanks to Byzantium's clients, the Petcheneks, conditions on the steppes were stable; the Armenians were hopelessly divided;

and western Christendom was still dazzled by Byzantium. The Russians officially converted to Orthodoxy in 989. This confirmed their passage into the Byzantine orbit. The Russians were essential to Byzantine greatness under Basil II. They provided Byzantium with soldiers and sailors. Their merchants made Constantinople the entrepôt for the products of the Russian steppes and forests and stimulated its commercial role. This was complemented by the growing presence of Venetian merchants at Constantinople. In 992 Basil II encouraged their activities by reducing the tolls on their ships paid for passage through the Hellespont to Constantinople. The effect was to favour Constantinople's role as the clearing house of Mediterranean trade. It underlined Constantinople's position as the cross-roads of the medieval world. This brought the Byzantine empire great opportunities. Constantinople was, however, disproportionately large and gave a false impression of Byzantine strength. It drew its wealth and population from well beyond the political frontiers of the Byzantine empire. Under different circumstances this might leave it vulnerable.

If forced to rely entirely on its own demographic and economic resources, Byzantium would have been condemned to the role of a regional power, at best. But it did not have to do so. The Armenian highlands were always an important recruiting ground for the Byzantine armies, but it went further than this. The Byzantine conquests in the east were followed under Byzantine auspices by Armenian colonization of Cilicia, the Euphrates provinces and northern Syria. The Russians provided another recruiting ground. Basil II relied heavily on the Varangian guard, which not only formed a *corps d'élite* but was also an instrument of his political ascendancy. Reliance on foreigners was a two-edged sword. In the course of the eleventh century relations with the Armenians deteriorated, while those with the Russians began to cool. In 1043 for reasons that must remain obscure Jaroslav the Wise, prince of Kiev, sent an expedition against Constantinople. It was easily defeated, but thereafter the Russians played a less prominent role in the affairs of the Byzantine empire. In due course, the Varangian guard would be recruited not from Russians but from exiled Anglo-Saxons. The imperial government at Constantinople lost a source of strength, which went beyond the purely military. Commercial ties with Rus' grew slacker.

When pondering the collapse of the Byzantine empire in the eleventh century, it must be remembered that Basil II left his successors a poisoned legacy. The apparent strength of the empire depended on circumstances that were beyond its control. Conditions along its frontiers might change radically. Basil II's policy of annexing the buffer territories of Bulgaria and Armenia suited his own time, but would produce real difficulties for his successors. His greatest failure, however, lay elsewhere; he neglected to make adequate provision for his succession. This was to mean that there was no settled succession to the

Byzantine throne for some seventy years until Alexios I Komnenos was securely in control.

II

Basil II never married. The understanding was that the succession would pass to his younger brother Constantine VIII, but he never produced a male heir, only daughters, of whom Zoe was Basil II's favourite. It was clear for many years before his death that succession to the Byzantine throne would go with the hand of Zoe. He considered various matches, but all were rejected, so that when he died Zoe was still a spinster. She was in her early forties and unlikely to bear children. Why Basil II was so negligent about the succession is hard to fathom. It may be that the short-term advantages of leaving the succession in doubt were too tempting. Constantine VIII (1025–8) seemed in no more of a hurry than his brother to marry off Zoe. It was only on his deathbed that he married her to Romanos Argyros (1028–34) who then succeeded in the right of his new wife. He was already somewhat elderly and unlikely to satisfy Zoe's hopes for children. Increasingly frustrated Zoe took a young lover Michael the Paphlagonian who happened to be the brother of John the Orphanotrophos, one of Basil II's eunuch ministers. Romanos died in his bath in suspicious circumstances. Michael married Zoe and duly succeeded to the throne. He was remembered as an effective emperor, but he soon fell sick. His brother John therefore sought to keep the throne within the family by persuading Zoe to adopt one of his nephews, also called Michael, as her son. He came to power in 1041, but he had no intention of being beholden to his uncle. He wished to rule as an autocrat in the style of Basil II. He drove out John the Orphanotrophos and other members of his family. He then packed Zoe off to a convent. This produced a spontaneous uprising on the part of the people of Constantinople. They did not want to be deprived of their 'Mother', as they called Zoe. The emperor was cornered and blinded. Zoe was brought back in triumph to the capital. For a few months she ruled jointly with her younger sister Theodora, who had been at the centre of opposition to the coup. She then married again, this time to Constantine Monomachos, who became the new emperor. Zoe died around 1050, so Theodora succeeded on Monomachos's death in 1055. With her death in the following year the Macedonian line came to an end, complicating the succession still further.

There is no *prima facie* reason for supposing that a troubled succession would necessarily weaken the fabric of the Byzantine state. After all, the succession was in doubt on many occasions in the tenth century, but this did not prevent Byzantium from going from strength to strength. It might be argued that frequent change of the imperial regime was a positive benefit because it made for a greater flexibility and ability to meet critical situations. The rise to power of Romanos Lecapenus (920–44) against a background of the threat from the Bulgarian tsar Symeon or the spectacle of Nikephoros Phokas (963–9) and of John Tzimiskes (969–76) holding the throne in trust for the young Basil II are cases in point. They gave clear direction to imperial government, as did Basil II.

His death, however, was followed by a spate of conspiracies. The uncertainty of the succession provides only a partial answer. They had more to do with a rapidly changing elite. The tensions created found some release in plots against the throne. In the early tenth century the Byzantine elite was a less complicated social group than it was to become. It was divided into a military and a civilian establishment. The former was dominated by the great military families of Anatolia, while the latter could boast a handful of civil service families whose members had held office over a number of generations. The great military families went into decline from the end of the tenth century. The family of Phokas, for example, virtually disappears, but others were more fortunate: that of Skleros kept estates in Anatolia, but transferred its centre of operations to Constantinople and gradually abandoned its military traditions. Basil II relied on other families for his commanders, such as those of Dalassenos, Diogenes and the Komnenos. The fortunes of these families were made under him. The military aristocracy was becoming wider and more diffuse. The same could be said of the civilian elite. Alongside the old civil service families, there were others which had made their fortunes in trade, but had converted their wealth into status through education and the purchase of honours. There were many interests to be satisfied. Conspiracy and revolt might become necessary to satisfy supporters and clients or might simply be a gesture of political credibility.[7]

Thus instability came to be built into the political structure. Some modern historians would like to see this as a struggle between the military and civilian elites. There is some contemporary support for this interpretation, but it was a matter of continuing to apply the political divisions of a previous age, which had largely disappeared. The politics of the eleventh century were instead dominated by families that transcended these divisions. They drew their support from the whole spectrum of political society. They were often old military families that had transferred their centre of operation to Constantinople. It comes as no surprise that Romanos Argyros emerged as the successful claimant for Zoe's hand and the imperial throne. His age apart he was eminently well qualified. He came from one of the most ancient of the Anatolian military families, but one which had long been resident in Constantinople. Romanos Argyros made a career and a name for himself within the capital. He became the prefect of the City. He was also related to many of the great families of the

---

[7] J.-C. Cheynet, *Pouvoir et contestations à Byzance (963–1210)*, Paris (1990), pp. 157–98.

capital. These included the Monomachoi. Constantine Monomachos came from a very similar background to Romanos Argyros and was an obvious candidate for the hand of Zoe and the imperial office. He had already plotted to seize the throne from Michael IV, who was regarded as an upstart, being one of those newcomers who had recently risen to prominence. His brother a trusted agent of Basil II. There were connections with the Komnenoi. A sister married into the new wealth of Constantinople. Her husband made a fortune out of shipbuilding. It was their son who succeeded as Michael V. He was known contemptuously as the 'Caulker' by way of reference to his father's activities. The snobbery of the Constantinopolitan crowd told against him. The citizens of Constantinople brought about his downfall. Their rising may have been spontaneous, but it taught them how powerful a force they were. Thereafter emperors had to placate Constantinopolitan opinion. This was another factor making for political instability in the eleventh century. In the tenth century internal tensions could be absorbed through a policy of conquest and expansion. It became less easy after Basil II's death.

III

Basil II's immediate successors attempted to pursue his policy of expansion and annexation, but with precious little success. Large and expensive expeditions were mounted against Sicily, Syria and even Egypt. All there was to show for this costly effort was the annexation of Edessa in 1032 by George Maniakes. Against this, there was a serious revolt by the Bulgarians in 1040. Even if it was suppressed, it suggested that Basil II's conquest was not that securely based. It was a watershed: the period of expansion was over. The empire was beginning to turn in on itself. In these circumstances internal divisions would only be magnified.

Keeping the empire on a war footing may explain why after Basil II's death the imperial government was faced with increasing financial difficulties. Tax revolts were a feature of this phase of Byzantine history.[8] Basil II must bear some of the blame. At the end of his life as an act of charity he remitted two whole years' taxation. His generosity was more than his brother could afford. The new emperor was forced to rescind the measure and collected five years' taxation within the space of three years. This caused hardship and sparked off at least one tax revolt. The next emperor Romanos Argyros instituted a laxer and more humane fiscal regime. The opening years of his reign coincided with drought and a plague of locusts in Anatolia, which forced the peasants off their land.

---

[8] They are attested at Naupaktos, Nikopolis and Antioch. The Bulgarian uprising of 1040 began as a tax revolt.

They swarmed towards Constantinople. To get them to return to their native villages Romanos Argyros provided each with a donative of three *nomismata:* the rough equivalent of the tax on a substantial peasant holding. He also abandoned Basil II's practice of forcing the 'powerful' landowners to pay any arrears of taxation. Instead he farmed these out, which hints at financial difficulties. His successor Michael IV seemed equally in need of ready cash. He forced the Bulgarians to pay their taxes in coin, despite Basil II's promise that they would be taxed in kind. This action sparked off the Bulgarian revolt. Michael IV was also accused of tampering with the currency, while his brother John the Orphanotrophos exploited the state's right of monopoly over the corn trade.

Modern numismatists have reluctantly exonerated Michael IV from the charge of debasement. It was left to Constantine Monomachos to carry out a controlled debasement of the Byzantine gold coinage. It was done quite openly and deliberately. The fineness of the gold coinage was lowered by stages from twenty-four carats to eighteen. Each stage of the debasement was clearly signposted by the issue of different types of coin. This debasement of the coinage is a feature of the history of eleventh-century Byzantium which has attracted a great deal of attention from modern historians, because it seems to provide a key to the economic developments of the time. There are two major interpretations. The first is straightforward: debasement was a solution to a budget deficit and was a way out of the long-standing financial difficulties of the Byzantine state. The other interpretation is more sophisticated: it sees debasement as a reaction to the problems of rapid economic growth which the Byzantine empire was supposed to be experiencing in the early eleventh century.[9] The argument goes that the Byzantine economy was as a result facing a liquidity crisis: there was not enough coinage in circulation to meet demand. Given the inelasticity of the supply of precious metals, the only solution was to debase. Admittedly, some Byzantine civil servants displayed a surprisingly advanced grasp of economics. However, even if they had an inkling that an inelastic money supply was a barrier to economic growth, they were not likely to consider this sufficient justification for debasing a coinage that had remained more or less unchanged since the days of Constantine the Great. Budgetary difficulties are surely the only explanation for the debasement carried out by Constantine Monomachos. The emperor could cite as a precedent the temporary debasement carried out by Nikephoros Phokas in the tenth century. However unpopular at the time, it had eased a period of financial embarrassment.

Even if budgetary difficulties are the explanation, debasement may still have helped to ease a liquidity problem. But was there economic growth in

[9] C. Morrisson, 'La Dévaluation de la monnaie byzantine au XIe siècle: essai d'interprétation', *TM* 6 (1976), 3–48.

the early eleventh century on a scale sufficient to create a liquidity problem? There are certainly signs of economic growth, but they mostly relate to the Greek lands, where towns were prospering and becoming centres of trade and manufactures. Thebes, for example, became a major producer of silk, which in the tenth century had been a monopoly of the capital. There are indications that coastal trade round the Aegean was prospering and that the population of the region was growing. But this scarcely represents growth of such an order that it would have induced the imperial government to debase the gold coinage in order to increase the circulation of coinage.

In any case, it would be hard to square the financial difficulties that the imperial government faced from the death of Basil II onwards with a period of rapid economic growth. Would the state not have been the chief beneficiary, given that it imposed a VAT of 10 per cent on every commercial transaction? This ought to have gone some way towards balancing the budget. Admittedly, the continuing growth of population was not matched by a corresponding increase in the basic tax yield, since the the agrarian legislation of the tenth century was applied less stringently. As significant was the extension of tax exemptions for the great estates. Blanket immunities were probably less important than preferential rates of taxation, such as those enjoyed in the eleventh century by the Athonite monasteries for their estates. This was all part of the creation of a dependent peasantry, which paid taxes and owed labour services to a lord. Ostrogorsky connected this manorialization of rural society with economic decline. He was certainly wrong, but he was correct to see it as a drain on imperial revenues.

It seems safe to assume that there was economic and demographic growth in the early eleventh century, but scarcely on a scale to create liquidity problems. Debasement was a response to the government's financial problems. Tax exemptions were partly to blame, but these were symptomatic of financial mismanagement on the part of the imperial government. Michael Psellos blamed the government's financial difficulties on the extravagance of Zoe and her consorts. This may have been a little unfair on Zoe. Dabbling in perfumes and alchemy may have been unnecessary, but was unlikely to bankrupt the state. It was at best a reflection of lax government. Zoe was not a great builder, unlike her husbands who expended colossal sums on their building activities. Romanos Argyros erected the monastery of the Peribleptos to serve as his last resting place and a memorial of his reign. Michael IV was a patron of the monastery of SS. Cosmas and Damian at Kosmidion, outside the walls of Constantinople, which he rebuilt on a lavish scale. Constantine Monomachos added the church of St George and other buildings to the Mangana complex. Accounts by later travellers provide an impression of the magnificence and scale of these churches. None of them survives; only St George of the Mangana has been partially excavated. Its dimensions were imposing. The dome had a diameter of approximately ten metres. It therefore rivalled in size some of the Justinianic foundations.[10] One of Constantine Monomachos's foundations does survive, however. This is the monastery of Nea Moni on the island of Chios. Its intricate planning and rich mosaics provide some idea of the care and money lavished on these imperial foundations. But the costs did not end with construction. Nea Moni, like St George of the Mangana, was generously endowed by the emperor.

There had not been building on this scale in the Byzantine empire since the sixth century. Emperors had mostly been content to restore the public monuments and churches inherited from the fifth and sixth centuries and to add to the Great Palace of the emperors. Basil II's main contribution had been the repair of St Sophia in 989 after it had suffered damage in an earthquake. The emperors of the eleventh century in good aristocratic fashion wanted to leave their mark on the capital through their monuments and used state revenues to this end. Again building even on the grand scale was unlikely by itself to bankrupt the state, but taken in conjunction with an extravagant court life it placed a substantial extra burden on the state's revenues. They were in any case likely to be declining because of Romanos Argyros's decision to abandon Basil II's strict control over the arrears of taxation.

Government expenditure was rising for quite another reason: the civil list was increasing dramatically as more and more honours were granted out. Michael Psellos was of the opinion that the honours system had been one of Byzantium's strengths, but was now being abused. This he singled out as one of the fundamental causes of the decline of the Byzantine state. Byzantium had developed a complicated system of honours with a double hierarchy of office and dignity. Both brought with them pensions and salaries. While sale of office was rare, sale of dignities was an accepted part of the system. If a dignity was purchased, then the holder received a pension at a standard rate. It has been calculated that this brought a return of around 3 per cent, but it was also possible to purchase at an augmented rate which brought a rather higher rate of up to 6 per cent. The state was creating a system of annuities. It almost certainly worked very well as long as it was properly supervised. The potential cost to the state was also limited by the relatively restricted number of dignities on offer. But this changed rapidly in the eleventh century as new orders of dignities were created to meet a growing demand. It was also the case that they might pass under the control of individuals who could distribute them as they saw fit. They were regarded as an investment which a father might make for

---

[10] C. Mango, 'Les Monuments de l'architecture du XIe siècle et leur signification historique et sociale', *TM* 6 (1976), 351–65.

his sons. Imperial largesse to monasteries sometimes took the form of a grant in perpetuity of the pensions attached to dignities. It is tempting to connect the debasement of the coinage with the inflation of honours, all the more so because of contemporary criticism of Nikephoros Phokas's earlier debasement of the coinage. One of his purposes was apparently to pay salaries and pensions in debased currency and to collect taxation in the old coinage. The temptation to debase would be all the stronger in the eleventh century as the honours system got out of hand.

However, it is difficult, if not impossible, to establish such a connection on a valid statistical basis. The evidence we have is anecdotal. J.-C. Cheynet discounts such evidence as unreliable.[11] He contends that the rate of pension for each dignity is a better guide to the costs of the honours system. The very highest dignities were always granted out sparingly. The inflation of honours affected the lesser dignities from spatharocandidate to vestarch, their pensions ranging from 36 *nomismata* to 1,008 *nomismata* or £14 of gold, which was a considerable sum, but here the argument breaks down: there is simply no way of computing the numbers of office holders. All that remains is the anecdotal evidence. Contemporaries were adamant that by the reign of Nikephoros Botaneiates (1078–81) the honours system had broken down, because the state was unable to meet the cost of the pensions involved. The honours system had bankrupted the state. Alexios I Komnenos's reform of the honours system was equally seen as an essential step towards restoring soundness to the body politic. It has to be admitted, however, that complaints about the failure of the honours system coincide with, rather than antedate, the debasement of the coinage. The two worked together to undermine the fabric of the state. The inflation of honours combined with other items of unnecessary expenditure and with other fiscal measures to cause budgetary difficulties, which led on to debasement under Constantine Monomachos. Thereafter the combination of debasement and a galloping inflation of honours ensured that the financial position would continue to deteriorate. It meant that well-conceived measures of reform had little chance of success.

IV

In the twenty-five years following Basil II's death the Byzantine empire had lost direction and momentum. The policy of military expansionism inherited from Basil II had little to commend it. Keeping the empire on a war footing was expensive. Cutting back on the armed forces was the simplest way of reducing expenditure. The Bulgarian rebellion followed almost immediately

[11] J.-C. Cheynet, 'Dévaluation des dignités et dévaluation monétaire dans la seconde moitié du XIe siècle', *Byzantion* 53 (1983), 453–77.

by the 1042 uprising of the citizens of Constantinople against Michael V were urgent reminders that a new approach to government was needed. The new emperor was Constantine Monomachos. He had an agenda. Military expansionism seemed out of place at a time when the empire appeared to have secure frontiers. Monomachos wished to cut back on the military establishment. To carry out his programme of reconstruction he turned to Constantine Leikhoudes and the team of clever young men he had assembled about him. These included Michael Psellos, the future Patriarch John Xiphilinos and their teacher John Mauropous. The thrust of their reforms was to strengthen the civil administration of the empire and to simplify the military organization.[12] In frontier regions the local levies were stood down and defence was left to professional troops stationed at key points. The armies of the themes continued to exist but largely on paper. Provincial administration passed increasingly from the military commander or *strategos* to a civilian governor known as the judge or the *praitor*. This had been an *ad hoc* development over the preceding fifty odd years. Constantine Monomachos regularized it by creating a new ministry at Constantinople under the *epi ton kriseon*, to which the civilian governors were now responsible. It completed a process of demilitarizing provincial government.[13]

Constantine Monomachos's propagandists presented his reforms in the guise of a *renovatio* of the empire. Imperial revivals punctuated Byzantine history. Normally, they centred on a new codification of the law. The Isaurians issued the Eclogues; the Macedonians the Basilics. Constantine Monomachos judged the Basilics to be more than adequate. What was lacking was an effective legal education. This was either picked up informally or was in the hands of the guild of notaries. Constantine Monomachos therefore instituted as the centrepiece of his reforms an imperial Law School. He placed it under the direction of a new official called the *nomophylax* and appointed John Xiphilinos as the first holder of the office. It was opened in 1047 and attached to the Mangana complex. Constantine Monomachos also created the post of Consul of the Philosophers for Michael Psellos. His duties included supervision of the schools of Constantinople. This measure was designed to bring educational establishments in the capital under more effective government control. Education was at the heart of Constantine Monomachos's reforms.[14]

However admirable, Constantine's reform programme had to be abandoned. It offended too many existing interests. John Xiphilinos found himself

---

[12] J. Lefort, 'Rhétorique et politique: trois discours de Jean Mauropous en 1047', *TM* 6 (1976), 265–303.

[13] N. Oikonomides, 'L'Evolution de l'organisation administrative de l'empire byzantin au XIe siècle (1025–1118)', *TM* 6 (1976), 125–52.

[14] W. Conus-Wolska, 'Les Ecoles de Psellos et de Xiphilin sous Constantin IX Monomaque', *TM* 6 (1976), 223–43.

under pressure from the legal establishment and preferred to retire to monastic seclusion on Bithynian Olympus. John Mauropous was appointed bishop of Euchaita in deepest Anatolia. He treated this as a form of exile, which indeed it was. At the same time, the political conditions along Byzantium's borders were changing rapidly. The Petcheneks were dislodged from the Russian steppe by Uze tribesmen from further east. In the winter of 1046/7 the main body of Petcheneks crossed the Danube, seeking refuge on Byzantine soil. It was reminiscent of the Visigoths seven centuries earlier. The settlement of the Petcheneks was equally mishandled. Constantine Monomachos was forced to send out a series of expeditions to pacify them. They had little success. The upshot was that the Petcheneks were left in possession of large tracts of the Balkans. At almost exactly the same time the Seljuq Turks began to make their presence felt along the eastern frontier. In 1048 they laid siege to Ani, the Armenian capital, which had recently been annexed by the Byzantines. The Turks might have been thwarted on this occasion, but it was a taste of things to come. The tide was also turning against Byzantium in southern Italy, as Norman freebooters harried Byzantine territories from their base at Melfi where they had established themselves in 1041.

The rapidly changing conditions in the empire's frontier provinces meant that Constantine Monomachos had to improvise. Experience had taught him that they were danger zones. They had been the launching pad for the two most serious revolts he had to face. The first came early in his reign and was the work of George Maniakes who had been sent as viceroy to Byzantine Italy by Michael V. He was suspicious of the new regime, if only because his great enemy Romanos Skleros was close to Constantine Monomachos. He crossed over to Albania in 1043 and advanced on Thessalonica down the Via Egnatia. His troops brushed aside the imperial armies sent to oppose him, but in the hour of victory he was mysteriously killed and the revolt fizzled out. The centre of the other revolt was Adrianople, which was the major military base of the southern Balkans. Its leader was Leo Tornikios, a nephew of the emperor. In the autumn of 1047 he advanced on Constantinople. It was only the emperor's coolness which saved the day. There are good reasons to suppose that underlying this revolt was dissatisfaction on the part of the military families of Adrianople with Constantine Monomachos's policies. The emperor was cutting back on military expenditure at a time when he was recruiting detachments of Petcheneks to serve on the eastern frontier.

Constantine Monomachos had to devise some way of neutralizing the danger from discontented generals. In southern Italy he turned to a local leader called Argyros, who despite his Greek name was a Lombard. He had seized the city of Bari in 1040 and had proclaimed himself 'prince and duke of Italy', but he had opposed Maniakes's rebellion. Constantine Monomachos was grateful and brought him and his family to Constantinople. Argyros again proved his loyalty to the emperor in 1047 when he helped defend Constantinople against Tornikios. In 1051 Monomachos sent him to Italy as viceroy. This appointment showed that Monomachos was willing to work through the local elites, rather than rely on Byzantine governors. This seemed to offer two advantages. It should have reconciled local opinion to rule from Constantinople. It should also have led to some relaxation of the grip exerted by the imperial administration. This may have been deliberate. The changing political conditions along the Byzantine frontiers would have alerted the imperial government to one of the disadvantages of the military expansionism espoused by Basil II. Byzantium was left exposed to new forces gathering strength beyond its frontiers. It would have underlined the value of creating buffer states. Byzantium had been more secure when protected by independent territories in Bulgaria and Armenia, however irksome they could seem at times. By working through Argyros, Monomachos seems to have been trying to shed some of the responsibilities for frontier defence which now burdened the imperial government at Constantinople. He seems to have been trying to do something of the same kind in the Balkans and Anatolia with his attempts to settle Petcheneks and Armenians. But these efforts were mismanaged and only produced friction with the local population. Disengagement is always one of the most difficult political feats to carry off.

Constantine Monomachos's reign was pivotal. It is scarcely any wonder that later contemporaries unanimously blamed him for the disasters suffered by the empire later on in the eleventh century. He had a programme for the restoration of the empire and it failed. The programme was well conceived, but was not able to survive a combination of internal opposition and changes occurring along the empire's frontiers. Its failure left the empire adrift. Monomachos dismissed Leikhoudes, the architect of his reforms. His last years were characterized by an oppressive fiscal regime in a vain effort to restore the empire's financial situation.

v

In modern historical writing the schism of 1054 dominates the end of Monomachos's reign. It had little impact at the time, but it was important for the future, because it underlined the unbridgeable gulf that was developing between Byzantium and the west. The background to the schism was paradoxically an alliance between the Byzantine emperor and Pope Leo IX (1049–54). It was directed against the Normans and had been engineered by Argyros. There was an assumption on the part of the papacy that this alliance would promote its claims to jurisdiction over the church in Byzantine Italy. In 1053 the papal forces made contact with the Normans near Civitate. They were expecting to link up with a Byzantine army under Argyros, but it failed to appear. The Normans trounced the papal army and captured Leo IX. This did not prevent him from despatching a delegation to Constaninople in the autumn of 1053 to renew the Byzantine alliance. It was headed by Humbert, cardinal priest of Silva Candida, chief ideologue of the reformed papacy and Leo IX's trusted adviser. By the time the papal legation reached Constantinople the pope was dead, but its members carried on regardless, acting as though their commissions were still valid.

Constantine Monomachos gave them much encouragement: the alliance with the papacy remained vital for his Italian policy. Cardinal Humbert followed the instructions he had received from Leo IX. The alliance was to be cemented by a regularization of relations between the two churches, which had not been in communion for nearly half a century. For once the discussion did not revolve around the addition of the *filioque* to the Latin creed, but around the Latin use of unleavened bread or azymes in the communion service. The patriarch of the day Michael Keroularios condemned it as a Jewish practice and argued that the Byzantine use of leavened bread had the support of the gospels. Leo IX took exception to this and wanted the question resolved. Cardinal Humbert tried to carry out his wishes, but it was difficult because Keroularios refused to acknowledge his presence. Humbert treated this as contumacy. On 16 July 1054 he entered St Sophia with the other papal legates and deposited a bull of excommunication directed at Michael Keroularios on the altar. The patriarch in his turn placed Humbert and the rest of the papal delegation under anathema. It confirmed an already existing state of schism between the two churches.

What stance did Constantine Monomachos adopt? From the outset he worked for an accord between the two churches. The papal legates came under his protection. He organized two debates between Humbert and a representative of the Orthodox church, designed to clarify the issues separating the two churches. They were conducted in an irenic fashion. Constantine Monomachos was as frustrated as the papal legates by Keroularios's lack of cooperation. This does not mean that he would have encouraged Humbert to excommunicate the patriarch. The legates' hasty departure from the city suggests that Constantine Monomachos had not approved their action. Michael Keroularios insisted that the papal legates should be brought back to Constantinople. The emperor demurred, but the patriarch used popular indignation to get his way. The legates were reprimanded, but punishment was reserved for the interpreters and members of Argyros's immediate family, who happened to be resident in the capital. Michael Keroularios blamed the incident on Argyros who was a personal enemy. He accused him of deliberately misinforming the papacy. By singling out Argyros as the main culprit, Keroularios played down the religious issues. There were still hopes that the differences between the two churches might be solved, or so it seemed to one of the legates, Frederick of Lorraine, who in 1057 became Pope Stephen IX. He almost immediately despatched a delegation to Constantinople to repair the damage, but it never reached its destination because he died soon after it set out. Other counsels prevailed at Rome. In 1059 the new pope Nicholas II turned for support to the Normans. By this time the events of 1054 had forced a reassessment of papal interests. These were now seen to be better served by an alliance with the Normans rather than with the Byzantines. It was a momentous change which profoundly affected western relations with Byzantium.

VI

At Byzantium the events of 1054 gave Michael Keroularios a prominence which up until then he had neither enjoyed nor sought. His understanding with the people of Constantinople gave him immense power. He was on bad terms with the empress Theodora. He openly objected to a woman ruling the empire. On her deathbed she nominated Michael Stratiotikos to succeed her. He came from a distinguished civil service family.[15] He was old and was intended as a figurehead for a faction among the bureaucracy which had come to power with Theodora. The new government dealt generously with potential supporters in the capital, but pleaded poverty when the generals Isaac Komnenos and Kekavmenos Katakalon came seeking promotion and donatives. They were sent packing to their estates in Anatolia. They raised the standard of rebellion and defeated the imperial forces sent against them in a particularly bloody encounter not far from the city of Nicaea. The rebels advanced on Constantinople. Within the capital there was a struggle for power between various factions. Michael Stratiotikos hoped to keep the throne by using the good offices of Constantine Leikhoudes and Michael Psellos, who had been absent from the political scene and had not crossed the generals. The emperor sent them to the rebels' camp. They were to offer Isaac Komnenos the rank of Caesar and eventual succession to the throne. But Michael Keroularios had already taken things into his own hands by having Isaac Komnenos proclaimed emperor in St Sophia. Michael Stratiotikos backed down. He was not willing to turn Constantinople into a bloodbath by opposing the entry of Isaac Komnenos's troops. Isaac Komnenos owed the throne to Michael Keroularios. The patriarch's reward was the right to appoint to the two most senior posts of the patriarchal administration: those of the *oikonomos* and the *skeuophylax*, appointments which in the past had been

---

[15] Bringas.

in the imperial gift. It marked an important stage in the emancipation of the patriarchal administration from imperial control.

Isaac Komnenos did not wish to be beholden to the patriarch. He had been impressed by the way Michael Psellos had conducted negotiations, even if they had had no concrete result. He struck him as a man he could trust! He needed an experienced minister to supervise his plans for financial retrenchment. Arrears of taxation were chased up; pensions paid to officials were reduced; grants of property made from the imperial demesne were revoked; and there were restrictions on grants to monasteries in line with the anti-monastic legislation of Nikephoros Phokas. Isaac Komnenos's intentions were made plain by the iconography of his coinage. It showed the emperor holding an unsheathed sword. He had come to restore the military might of the empire. The essential first step was to impose order on the state's finances. In theory, Michael Psellos approved, but he thought that Isaac Komnenos acted too abruptly. His harshness alienated too many vested interests.

It aroused the opposition of the patriarch Michael Keroularios. Isaac Komnenos chose to see this as a challenge to his imperial authority. Michael Psellos claimed that 'the patriarch kept insisting on the superiority of the patriarchal dignity'. The clash of Michael Keroularios and Isaac Komnenos was a *cause célèbre* of the eleventh century. It did raise constitutional issues. Keroularios assumed the role of the moral arbiter, who could discipline emperors if they failed to protect orthodoxy or who could decide the succession when this was in doubt. He had popular support which he exploited. This laid him open to the charge that he was flirting with democracy. This accusation reflected the uncertainties created by the end of the Macedomian line and for the time being of dynamic succession. This produced a debate on the constitutional niceties of selecting an emperor. Michael Psellos looked back to the Augustan settlement for guidance. He recognized that imperial authority rested on three factors: the people, the senate and the army. He objected to the accession of Michael Stratiotikos on the grounds that he only obtained the consent of the people and the senate, but not that of the army. His charge against Michael Keroularios was that he was using the voice of the people to transfer power from one emperor to another. The constitutional role of the people of Constantinople – the New Rome – was never very clear. Their acclamation of a new emperor was one – some would claim, in accordance with Roman practice, the most important – of the constitutive acts in the making of an emperor. The people might on occasion rise up against an emperor, as happened with Michael V. This could be construed as a right to remove tyrants. Another constitutive act was the coronation, which in a period of great political confusion gave the patriarch considerable leverage. Keroularios exploited the constitutional difficulties produced by the end of the Macedonian dynasty; he sought to turn the patriarch into the arbiter of the constitution. This was seen by Michael Psellos as a threat to imperial authority. Under his prompting Isaac Komnenos exiled Keroularios from Constantinople. Michael Psellos was put in charge of the prosecution, but his speech against Keroularios was never delivered, because the patriarch died before he could be brought to trial.[16]

Psellos's evident dislike of the patriarch was something more than a clash of personalities. The two men stood for very different ways of life. Psellos accused the patriarch of being an adept of the mysticism which was then fashionable in some Constantinopolitan circles. It centred on the cult of St Symeon the New Theologian.[17] Its promoter was Niketas Stethatos, a future abbot of the monastery of St John Stoudios. Keroularios supported his campaign for the canonization of St Symeon the New Theologian. His teachings provided some of the inspiration behind the monastic revival, now associated with the monastery of the Theotokos Euergetis, which was gathering strength at Constantinople.

Psellos spelt out the dangers of mysticism. It exalted ignorance and denied human reason. It was divorced from everyday life. Psellos, for his part, gloried in his own humanity: 'I am an earthly being', he told the patriarch, 'made of flesh and blood, so that my illnesses seem to me to be illnesses, blows blows, joy joy.'[18] Psellos came close to admitting that he believed that 'man was the measure of all things'. He certainly emphasized the primacy of human experience. He saw no contradiction between Christianity and life in society. Had not Christ often frequented the market places and much less frequently the mountains? Psellos was preaching a Christian humanism. Society was held together by the bonds of a Christian faith, friendship and reason. It possessed its own logic and justification. However, it was shaped and guided by the 'philosopher' Psellos set his authority as 'philosopher' on the same level as that of the patriarch. If he did not challenge imperial authority quite so directly, his *Chronographia* dwells on the human frailties of individual emperors. Its message is that without the wisdom of a 'philosopher' to guide him an emperor was incapable of living up to the responsibilities of his office. Niketas Stethatos was less circumspect in his promotion of the mystic. He exalted the primacy of the mystic over 'emperor, patriarch, bishop, or priest'.[19]

The emphasis on the role of the mystic and the 'philosopher' devalued traditional authority at Byzantium. They had access to 'knowledge' that was of immediate benefit to a Christian society. Mystical experience opened up direct access to the Godhead. St Symeon the New Theologian saw this as a guarantee that Christ's ministry was ever present and not set in some distant past. Psellos

---

[16] Died 21 January 1059.   [17] Died 12 March 1022.
[18] K. N. Sathas, *Mesaionike Bibliotheke (Bibliotheca graeca medii aevi)*, v, Venice and Paris (1876), p. 232.
[19] I. Hausherr, *Un grand mystique byzantin: vie de Syméon le Nouveau Théologien (949–1022) par Nicétas Stéthatos*, Rome (1928), p. lxxvi.

had the harder task of explaining the relevance of classical learning in a Christian society. He was not simply content with the traditional justification that it was an educational tool: one that provided a means of cultivating human reason. Learning made possible an understanding of the natural world, which offered clues to God's existence and purpose. Psellos sought to build on the classical heritage and bring it up to date. His letters and rhetorical works are not redolent of the drab encyclopaedism of the previous century, but are full of emotion and concrete detail. Unlike earlier Byzantine histories, his *Chronographia* is not dominated by the workings of Divine Providence, but emphasizes instead the human element as a decisive historical factor. Psellos did not see any contradiction between Christianity and the classical tradition; to his way of thinking the former fulfilled the latter. He liked to think of himself as in the tradition of the Cappadocian Fathers who used their profound knowledge of Greek philosophy to deepen understanding of their Christian faith. Psellos never grappled with theology in any systematic way. This task was left to his pupil John Italos, who reopened many of the basic questions of Christian dogma.

The work of John Italos was just one more sign of the cultural vitality of the eleventh century. Its origins lie in a reaction to the repressive official culture of the tenth century. The decline of imperial prestige raised basic questions about the ordering of a Christian society. The rivalry of mystic and humanist will sometimes have sharpened the edge of debate, but not all agreed with Michael Psellos that they were diametrically opposed. Most saw their approaches as complementary.[20] They gave a new breadth to Byzantine culture. Equally, the claims of mystic and humanist were subversive of traditional authority at Byzantium. Some of the strongest social ties were those that formed around them among their followers. In this way, they gave a Christian society a degree of independence of the hierarchical authority exercised by emperor and patriarch. The exchanges between Michael Psellos and Michael Keroularios revealed how traditional assumptions about the ordering of Byzantine life were being reassessed. They raised constitutional, political, social and intellectual issues. Cultural flux mirrored political uncertainties.

VII

The attack on Michael Keroularios lost Isaac Komnenos a good deal of support. Michael Psellos saw which way the wind was blowing. He persuaded the emperor to resign at a time when a bout of illness had left him in a state of depression. The new emperor was Constantine Doukas who happened to be married to a niece of the patriarch. It was an admission among other things that the

[20] J. M. Hussey, *Ascetics and Humanists in Eleventh-Century Byzantium*, London (1960).

reforms initiated by Isaac Komnenos and supervised by Michael Psellos were not working. Constantine Doukas immediately repealed them. He restored honours to those who had been deprived of them. Constantine Doukas set out his programme in a speech he delivered before the guilds of Constantinople. He emphasized that truth and justice, and not the sword, were to be the keynotes of his reign. It was a return to the policies that had been tried at the beginning of Constantine Monomachos's reign. Constantine Doukas was sensible enough to dispense with Michael Psellos's political services. Less wise was his decision to appoint Psellos tutor to his son and heir Michael Doukas. Contemporaries were unanimous that this rendered the latter unfit to rule!

Constantine X Doukas (1059–67) had to all appearances a remarkably successful reign. He was well fitted to be emperor. He had good connections with both the military families of Anatolia and the great families of Constantinople. He also anticipated the future in the way he associated his family in government. He relied heavily on the support of his brother John, whom he raised to the rank of Caesar. He was later criticized for the overgenerous way in which he distributed honours and pensions to the people of Constantinople and for the way he allowed the military establishment to run down. There was increasing pressure on the frontiers of the empire. The Normans made significant advances in the south of Italy in the wake of their alliance with the papacy in 1059, but Constantine Doukas reacted energetically: he despatched a number of expeditions to secure the main Byzantine bases along the Adriatic coast. He himself led the army that mopped up a Uze invasion of the Balkans. Less was done on the eastern frontier. The defences of Melitene were rebuilt in 1063, but Ani – the Armenian capital – was lost to the Seljuqs the next year. Its importance was always more symbolic than strategic. Constantine Doukas will not have heard of the sack of Cappadocian Caesarea and the desecration of the cathedral of St Basil which occurred around the time of his death in May 1067. Only an emperor as securely in control as he was could adopt the strategy he did in the east. It was a war of attrition. He aimed to hold the key positions and allow the eastern provinces to absorb Turkish pressure. There was increasing agitation for a more aggressive policy.

In the normal course of events Constantine Doukas would have been succeeded by his son Michael, who was aged about sixteen, but he was already seen as something of a liability. Constantine therefore left the regency to his empress Eudocia Makrembolitissa.[21] But she was forced to swear on oath never again to marry. She also undertook to rule with the aid of the Caesar John Doukas, until Michael Doukas was capable of carrying out the duties of an emperor. In good

[21] N. Oikonomides, 'Le Serment de l'impératrice Eudocie (1067): un épisode de l'histoire dynastique de Byzance', *REB* 21 (1963), 101–28.

dynastic fashion Constantine Doukas was trying to safeguard the succession for his family. The oath was administered by the patriarch John Xiphilinos. He was soon persuaded that the common interest required that Eudocia should be released from her oath. This allowed her to marry Romanos Diogenes, who was the head of a powerful Anatolian family. He came to the throne on the understanding that he would respect the eventual succession of Michael Doukas.

The chances of this happening became increasingly remote as Eudocia bore her new husband two sons in quick succession. Romanos needed a decisive victory in order to establish himself and his line in power. His efforts to search out and destroy the Turkish bands of marauders left him open to ridicule. They were far too nimble for the lumbering and badly trained troops that he had at his disposal. He changed his strategy. Instead of waiting for the Turks to invade the Byzantine provinces, he decided to engage them at their major point of entry into Byzantine territory. This was the bottleneck to the north of Lake Van, which was commanded by the fortress of Manzikert. In the summer of 1071 Romanos Diogenes led all the troops he could muster to Lake Van. He recovered possession of Manzikert and other strategic points which had been lost to the Turks. The emperor appears not to have known that the Seljuq sultan Alp Arslan was also operating in the area. Once he had learned of the sultan's presence he determined to engage him in battle. It was an opportunity too good to miss. The battle lasted two days. The Byzantines fought with surprising tenacity and discipline. They had the better of the battle until towards evening on the second day a rumour started to spread that Romanos had fallen. This was the work of Andronikos Doukas, a son of the Caesar John Doukas. His motives were political. If Romanos emerged from the battle with credit, the Doukas cause was doomed. Andronikos Doukas was in command of the rearguard and in a position to do maximum damage. He abandoned the field leaving Romanos and his elite troops unprotected. They had fought bravely, but they were now quickly surrounded by the Turks and the emperor was captured.

In military terms Manzikert was not a disaster.[22] The Byzantine casualties were relatively slight. It should only have confirmed Turkish domination of the Armenian highlands, not that almost the whole of Anatolia would be over-run by the Turks within ten years. Early Turkish settlement was concentrated a thousand miles to the west of Manzikert along the northern and western rims of the Anatolian plateau. Why should a defeat at the extreme limit of Byzantium's eastern frontiers have opened up Anatolia to Turkish settlement? Part of the answer is weight of numbers. The Turks were a people on the move seeking new

[22] J.-C. Cheynet, 'Mantzikert: un désastre militaire?', *Byzantion* 50 (1980), 410–38.

pastures. But their penetration of the Byzantine empire was facilitated by the civil wars sparked off by the defeat at Manzikert. Partisans of the Doukas cause at Constantinople, including Michael Psellos, seized control of the government for Michael Doukas. Romanos had not, however, been killed in the battle, as rumour suggested. He was soon released by the sultan. He made his base at Amaseia and rallied his supporters. Defeated by an army despatched from Constantinople, he retreated to Antioch. The next year 1072 he was again defeated by an army sent out from the capital. It was commanded by Andronikos Doukas and consisted largely of Frankish mercenaries. Romanos was captured and taken back under safeconduct. As they were approaching Constantinople the order came that he was to be blinded. This was done so savagely that he died a few weeks later on 4 August 1072. The year of civil war had given the Turks an opportunity to exploit their victory, but it did not end there.

Russell Balliol, a Norman mercenary in Byzantine service, seized the main chance. He had taken part in the opening stages of the Norman conquest of Sicily. He recognized a similar opportunity in the confusion produced by the aftermath of Manzikert. He made Amaseia his centre of operations and soon brought most of the old theme of Armeniakon under his control. Local people welcomed his presence because he offered some protection from the marauding Turks. The government at Constantinople took the threat from Russell Balliol much more seriously than that presented by the Turks. Its apprehension increased when Balliol captured the Caesar John Doukas who had been sent with an army against him. Balliol proclaimed the Caesar emperor and advanced towards Constantinople. The Doukas government brought in Turks as the only way of combating the Norman. In the short term it worked. Balliol was defeated, but managed to get back to Amaseia, where he retained his independence. In retrospect, the use of Turks was a miscalculation on the part of the Byzantine government, but at the time the Turks seemed no kind of threat to Constantinople. Cocooned in the capital, Michael Doukas and his advisers may well have felt that the Turks could be treated like the Petcheneks in the Balkans: given lands and a degree of tribal autonomy and in due course absorbed within Byzantine government and society.

Eventually the young Alexios Komnenos was sent to deal with Russell Balliol. It was his first major commission. With the help of a local Turkish chieftain he managed to apprehend the Norman and take him back to Constantinople. He acquitted himself with great skill and assurance, but the result was that a large part of northern Anatolia fell under Turkish domination. Alexios Komnenos had the greatest difficulty in extricating himself and his prisoner from Amaseia because the whole country was alive with Turks. He made a detour to Kastamon where he expected a friendly reception, since it was the centre of his family's estates. He found instead his grandfather's palace occupied by Turks and he had to hurry on. This incident reveals how swiftly Byzantine control in the region collapsed. It was largely because of a lack of local leadership.

The story was much the same in other parts of Anatolia. In 1077 Nikephoros Botaneiates – a noted general – abandoned his estates in western Asia Minor and marched on Constantinople with his retinue of 300 men. He left the area unprotected. Still worse he engaged the services of a Turkish chieftain. His name was Suleiman. Botaneiates seems to have been unaware that he was no ordinary warband leader, but a scion of the ruling Seljuq dynasty. He had been sent from Baghdad to take control of the haphazard and quite unexpected Turkish conquest of Anatolia. In return for his aid Botaneiates surrendered into his safekeeping the strongly fortified city of Nicaea, scarcely fifty miles as the crow flies from Constantinople. Suleiman set about turning this city into a centre of Seljuq rule. It was a colossal miscalculation on Botaneiates's part, though he might not otherwise have overthrown Michael VII Doukas and become emperor. He in his turn would have to face a challenge which compounded his own folly. Nikephoros Melissenos raised the standard of revolt on the island of Cos. He too turned to the Turks for support. The price was the surrender of cities along the western coast of Asia Minor, such as Smyrna.

A succession of revolts and civil wars had dragged the Turks westward to the shores of the Aegean and had handed them control of most of the great cities of Asia Minor. Thus was the fate of Byzantine Anatolia sealed! The Turks established themselves in force on the northern and western edges of the Anatolian plateau. It proved impossible to dislodge them. Behind this shield the much slower process whereby Byzantine Anatolia was transformed into Turkey could go on more or less unhindered. In retrospect, the loss of Anatolia to the Turks seems to have been folly on a grand scale.

VIII

The emperor Nikephoros Botaneiates was an old hero, but was incapable of mastering circumstances that were spinning out of control. As if the loss of Anatolia was not bad enough, Robert Guiscard, the Norman leader, was massing his forces in southern Italy for an invasion. The commander of Byzantium's western armies was now Alexios Komnenos, but his abilities, ambition and family connections marked him out as a threat to the regime in Constantinople. The young commander found himself in an impossible position. He struck in the spring of 1081. On 1 April 1081 Alexios with the help of his brother Isaac and the support of the Caesar John Doukas seized Constantinople and overthrew the old emperor.

In the meantime Robert Guiscard and his son Bohemond had crossed to Albania and laid siege to Durazzo at the head of the Via Egnatia. Guiscard justified his actions by proclaiming that he was coming to restore to the throne of Constantinople the rightful house of Doukas. These dynastic pretensions made him all the more dangerous at a time when the new emperor's hold on power was still shaky. Alexios assembled all available forces and made for Durazzo, only to suffer a shattering defeat. His troops were no match for the Normans. In military terms it was a far more serious defeat than Manzikert. While one Norman army advanced down the Via Egnatia to within striking distance of Thessalonica, another under Bohemond headed south into Greece. The key position was Larissa in Thessaly. If it fell to the Normans, then the rich provinces of Hellas and the Peloponnese were lost. With a scratch force of Turkish archers Alexios marched in 1083 to the relief of Larissa. The emperor was careful not to engage the Normans in open battle. He relied instead on skirmishing tactics. He was able to raise the siege of Larissa and forced the Normans to evacuate Thessaly. The Norman threat only ended with the death of Robert Guiscard in 1085, which was followed by a succession crisis in southern Italy and the withdrawal of the Normans from their bases in Albania and the Ionian islands.

More by luck than good judgement Alexios emerged from the first test of his reign with his reputation enhanced. His next task was to restore the Danubian frontier. The key this time was the fortress city of Dristra. This was under the control of the Petcheneks, who in 1087 caught Alexios by surprise. Yet another Byzantine army was lost. Once again Alexios was lucky to escape. The Petcheneks pushed south towards Constantinople. The danger was even more serious because they allied with Tzachas, a Turkish amir who had turned Smyrna into a pirate base. By the winter of 1090–1 Alexios controlled little more than Constantinople itself. He had no army to speak of. The force that he led out against the Petcheneks consisted very largely of the retainers of his relatives and supporters. He headed for the port of Ainos at the mouth of the Hebrus (Maritsa), in the hope of preventing the Petcheneks from linking up with their Turkish ally. The situation was further complicated by the appearance of another nomadic people – the Cumans – who had crossed over the Danube into the Balkans. Their original intention was to cooperate with the Petcheneks. Alexios succeeded in winning them over to the Byzantine side. Thanks largely to their help Alexios crushed the Petcheneks at the battle of Mount Levounion in Thrace. The Petcheneks ceased to count. The Cumans were still a potential threat to Byzantine control of the Balkans, but in 1094 Alexios defeated them outside the walls of Ankhialos on the Black Sea. At long last, Alexios was in full control of the Danubian frontier.

Alexios displayed great tenacity in the face of a series of military defeats. But this cannot disguise the fact that they were often of his own making. It was largely his own foolhardiness which had jeopardized Byzantine control of the Balkans. Without the support of his family it is doubtful whether he could have survived his early years as emperor, so patchy was his military record. Alexios had, however, wisely trusted the running of the government to his mother Anna Dalassena. While he was campaigning she kept control of Constantinople and managed to meet his military requirements. This necessitated a harsh administrative regime.

Alexios's survival also depended on the support of the great families. He came to power as the leader of an aristocratic faction. His overthrow would almost certainly have meant their downfall. The Komnenoi were linked by ties of blood and marriage to all the major aristocratic families. Alexios turned this into a principle of government. He did this very largely through a radical reform of the honours system. His daughter Anna Komnena perceptively singles this out as a major achievement.[23] In the past the honours system had been hierarchical rather than dynastic: membership of the imperial family did not bring rank at court as of right. The inflation of honours over the eleventh century resulted in a collapse of the old honours system. Alexios rebuilt it by creating a series of new ranks that were reserved for members of his family. The imperial epithet *sebastos* was now accorded to the imperial family in its widest sense. The *sebastoi* became a distinct hierarchy with their own gradations. At the top came the rank of *sebastokrator* which was a conflation of *sebastos* and *autokrator*. This Alexios created for his elder brother Isaac who shared the burdens of the imperial office. The rank of *protosebastos* went to one of the emperor's brothers-in-law. It was normally combined with the position of *protovestiarios*. This too marked a profound change in the texture of government. In the past the *protovestiarios* had almost always been a eunuch and one of the chief officers of the imperial household. Alexios did away with eunuchs and created an imperial household staffed very largely by members of his family, while the more menial positions went to retainers of the house of Komnenos. The imperial household had always been the instrument for the exercise of direct imperial authority. Its identification with Comnenian family interest gave it a different quality.

In the past office and rank brought lucrative salaries. One of the attractions of reforming the honours system was that it provided a way of abolishing these profits of office. Alexios found other ways of rewarding members of his family. He granted them administrative and fiscal rights over specific areas. This was the basis of grants that were later known as as *pronoiai*. In the past similar grants had been made out of the imperial demesne, but Alexios extended this principle to state lands. In a sense, he was parcelling out the empire among his family and creating a series of appanages. He rebuilt imperial government as an aristocratic connection; family business might be a more accurate description. It was a radical step which would later create tensions because the theory of

[23] Anna Komnena, *Alexiad*, bk III, ch. iv, para. 3: ed. Lieb and Gautier, I, pp. 114–15.

imperial autocracy was not revised to take account of the transformation that occurred in practice. But it provided Alexios with the strengths necessary to hold on to power during his difficult early years.

IX

There were many great families who were not included in the Comnenian circle. It was from these that the main opposition to Alexios's regime came. Those with most to lose were the senatorial families which had run the administration under the Doukai. The underlying current of hostility that existed between them and the Komnenoi surfaced during Alexios's seizure of Constantinople. We are told that his supporters deliberately set upon any senators they came across in the streets. The patriarch Cosmas forced Alexios and members of his family to do public penance for the violence that was a feature of their seizure of power. It was one more demonstration of the moral authority of the patriarch, which was such a powerful factor in the politics of eleventh-century Byzantium. It was a deliberate humiliation of the imperial family. Alexios's reaction showed his metal: he procured the dismissal of the patriarch and replaced him by Eustratios Garidas, a monk cultivated by his mother. It revealed how ruthless he could be, but it earned him the hostility of a powerful section of the clergy led by Leo, bishop of Chalcedon. Leo objected to the way that Alexios had seized church treasures in order to pay for his first campaign against the Normans. It was an action for which there were good precedents. It was, in other words, chosen as a suitable issue through which to attack the emperor. Garidas was not strong enough to defend either himself or the emperor and was replaced in 1084 by Nicholas Grammatikos. Leo of Chalcedon switched the attack to the new patriarch, but Alexios Komnenos was now sufficiently sure of himself to have Leo exiled.

The emperor's new confidence owed much to the successful outcome of the trial of John Italos on a charge of heresy. John Italos had been a leading figure at the court of Michael VII Doukas, who entrusted him with negotiations with Robert Guiscard. He was also a teacher of note. He had succeeded Michael Psellos as Consul of the Philosophers and took over his responsibilities for the supervision of education in the capital. Unlike Psellos his bias was towards Aristotle rather than Plato. His application of philosophical method to theological questions earned him an enthusiastic following but also laid him open like Psellos before him to charges of heresy. Michael VII Doukas encouraged him to submit a profession of faith to the patriarch Cosmas as a way of exonerating himself. The patriarch demurred; and there the matter rested.

The case was reopened by the Comnenian regime in the winter of 1081–2, when its stock at Constantinople was very low following Alexios's defeat at the hands of the Normans. Italos numbered among his former pupils members of prominent Constantinopolitan families who were seen by the Komnenoi as potential centres of opposition to their rule. If successful, an attack on Italos would help to discredit them. After a preliminary hearing before the emperor Italos was passed over to the patriarch, so that his case could come before the patriarchal synod. It duly convened in the church of St Sophia. There was a good chance that Italos would be acquitted, because feeling among the bishops was beginning to turn against the Komnenoi. Before this could happen a mob broke into St Sophia and hunted Italos down. He escaped by hiding on the roof of the Great Church. The patriarch was out of his depth and handed matters back to the emperor, who had Italos condemned as a heretic. On the feast of Orthodoxy, which in 1082 fell on 13 March, Italos publicly abjured his errors.

The trial of John Italos was a significant episode. It allowed Alexios Komnenos to establish an ascendancy over the Orthodox church. There were three distinct strands to this process. The first was his use of the mob. The Constantinopolitan mob had proved itself over the eleventh century to be a significant political factor. But it was normally mobilized in support of the church. Now Alexios was able to win it over to his side and deploy it against the church. How and why he was able to do this has to remain a matter of speculation. The most likely explanation is that the mob responded to Alexios's pose as the guardian of Orthodoxy. This receives some support from the timing of Italos's condemnation to coincide with the feast of Orthodoxy. This was a celebration of the victory over iconoclasm in 843. It was the occasion on which the *synodikon* of Orthodoxy was read out. This was a statement of faith condemning heresy in general and iconoclasm, in particular. It had remained virtually unchanged from 843 down to the eleventh century. It was Alexios who hit upon the device of bringing it up to date by adding to it the condemnation of John Italos and, as his reign progressed, that of others condemned for heresy. It was a concrete expression of the emperor's role as the guardian of Orthodoxy.

Alexios was not content with the condemnation of Italos alone. He also pursued his pupils. They were forbidden to teach. They remained under the shadow of their master's condemnation for heresy. This had two consequences. The first was that it discredited members of families potentially opposed to the Komnenoi. The second paradoxically was a rapprochement with the clergy of the patriarchal church. Among Italos's most prominent pupils were a number of deacons of St Sophia. Induced to disown their master, they were not only reconciled with the church, but were also permitted to continue teaching. One of them was Eustratios, the future bishop of Nicaea, who was soon to become Alexios's most trusted religious adviser. An understanding with the patriarchal clergy was useful to the emperor because at Synod they constituted a counterweight to the episcopal presence. Alexios acted to guarantee the privileges of the patriarchal clergy. He also issued a chrysobull defining the privileges and role of the *chartophylax* of St Sophia. It upheld the precedence of the *chartophylax* over bishops on the grounds that he was the patriarch's deputy. In practice, the holder of the office came to oversee the patriarchal administration. This was much to the advantage of the emperor because he still retained appointment to this office.

Alexios's measures went a long way towards neutralizing the independence of action which the eleventh-century patriarchs had displayed. They had, for instance, assumed the initiative over marriage legislation and litigation. This produced differences between canon and civil law. Alexios intervened to reestablish imperial control of this important area of law. He reenacted the novel of Leo VI over the age of consent for betrothal and marriage with its important rider that the emperor could use his powers of discretion to ignore the stipulations of the novel. Having regained the initiative over legislation, he then conceded that marriage litigation should in normal circumstances go before the ecclesiastical courts.

Alexios's church settlement is among his greatest achievements – and most neglected. It enabled him to rebuild the moral and spiritual foundations of imperial authority, which had been undermined in the course of the eleventh century. He recovered control over the administration of the patriarchal church and regained the initiative in matters of legislation. He was the guarantor of the privileges or liberties of the church. He assumed the role of *epistemonarkhes* or regulator of the church, even if this title did not enter official usage until the mid-twelfth century.

Above all, beginning with the trial of John Italos he used heresy as a way of establishing his credentials as the guardian of Orthodoxy. Under Alexios the suppression of heresy became an imperial preserve. There were a series of heresy trials. They suited the image that Alexios was endeavouring to project, but there were political undercurrents. They were a means of discrediting potential opponents. The most spectacular trial for heresy was that of Basil the Bogomil and his followers. The date can only be fixed approximately to *c.* 1100. The Bogomil heresy originated in Bulgaria and was a form of dualism. It is impossible to establish any clear connection between the Bulgarian and Byzantine phases of Bogomilism. It is possible that they arose quite separately and spontaneously and that a connection was only perceived in retrospect. Byzantine Bogomilism had its roots in lay piety. It was transformed by Basil the Bogomil's missionary zeal. He organized his followers around his twelve disciples. It was assumed that he aimed to convert the world. It has also been suggested that he was responsible for providing Bogomilism with its theological justification: his dualist teaching transformed unease with the material world into a system of belief. Like other holy men Basil could count some distinguished figures among his followers. He had entrée to the highest circles. There is even a suspicion that Anna Dalassena was a supporter. It would explain that comic scene so graphically sketched by Anna Komnena, which otherwise beggars belief. Alexios Komnenos and his brother Isaac interviewed Basil the Bogomil and pretended to be sympathetic to his teachings. By this means they were able to induce Basil to set out his Bogomil beliefs in full. Behind a screen a stenographer was taking down his words, which were then used against him. What distinguishes Basil from other heretics is that he also possessed a large popular following, which meant that he was doubly dangerous.

Though this was not necessarily Alexios's intention, one of the consequences of Basil's condemnation was to strengthen imperial authority on the streets of Constantinople. This is apparent from the edict Alexios issued in 1107 in the aftermath of the Bogomil trials. Its purpose was to create an order of preachers attached to St Sophia who would tackle the problem of heresy on the streets of the capital and act as the moral policemen of the different neighbourhoods. This edict shows how effective his control over the church had become. The creation of an order of preachers was originally the work of the Patriarch Nicholas Grammatikos. It was now taken over by the emperor, who also took responsibility for reorganizing the patriarchal clergy.

Nicholas Grammatikos accepted imperial ascendancy. He understood that the church benefited from the emperor's benevolent supervision. He also recognized the emperor's piety. This was best seen in his patronage of monks and monasteries. This Nicholas Grammatikos would have appreciated, because he was not only the founder of a Constantinopolitan monastery, but was also famed for his self-denial. Alexios was the heir of his mother's careful cultivation of monks and holy men. Their support had been useful during his difficult early years as emperor. He and members of his family supported the work of monastic figures, such as St Christodoulos of Patmos, Hosios Meletios and St Cyril Phileotes in the provinces. They also founded and refounded monasteries in the capital. Constantinople had been the scene of a strong current of monastic revival from the middle of the eleventh century, associated with the monastery of the Theotokos Euergetis. Its *typikon* or rule provided a guide to a series of Comnenian foundations. Monastic order also provided the inspiration for the reform of imperial court life begun by Anna Dalassena and continued by Alexios's empress Eirene Doukaina. Anna Komnena noted that under their guidance 'the palace assumed the appearance of a monastery'.[24] Alexios and his family became exemplars of a piety that drew its inspiration from the monastic revival that gathered strength at Constantinople from the mid-eleventh century. This went a long way towards reconciling the church to

---

[24] *Ibid.*, bk iii, ch. viii, para. 2: ed. Lieb and Gautier, i, pp. 125.30–1.

the Comnenian ascendancy and gave the new dynasty a moral standing that had been denied to the emperors of the eleventh century.

The monastic revival continued, but under Comnenian auspices. This was typical of Alexios's church settlement. His main purpose was to assert imperial control. He harnessed new forces and ideas that surfaced in the eleventh century and put them at the disposal of the imperial dynasty. Alexios's patronage of monastic leaders does not mean that he was therefore hostile to humanism. If he destroyed John Italos, he rehabilitated his pupil Eustratios of Nicaea, who continued his master's work on Aristotle. The Komnenoi promoted humanist culture. Alexios's daughter Anna Komnena was one of its adornments. The *Alexiad*, her history of her father's reign, owed something to Michael Psellos, whose learning Anna much admired. She was also a patron of Eustratios of Nicaea and Aristotelian scholarship. The *sebastokrator* Isaac Komnenos, who may be a brother, but is more probably a son of Alexios Komnenos, continued Michael Psellos's Neoplatonic interests. Comnenian self-interest meant that the cultural revival of the eleventh century changed its character. It lost much of its effervescence, but it might have fizzled out or the Komnenoi might have repressed it. Instead, they preserved its essentials and ensured that cultural breadth and vitality that characterizes later Byzantine history.

x

Alexios's achievement was to rebuild the Byzantine empire. The new and the traditional were mixed in equal measure. He restored the traditional role of the emperor in ecclesiastical affairs, but took it further. Caesaropapism is an apt description of his supervision of the church. Politically, Byzantium was organized on a dynastic rather than a hierarchical basis. This is perhaps where Alexios was at his most radical because it had far-reaching implications for the organization of government. It meant that the emperor shared power with members of an extended family. There was, on the other hand, no radical restructuring of government. Alexios was more interested in finding ways of exercising control. His solution was to create coordinating ministries. The civil service was now subordinated to the logothete of the *sekreta*, later known as the grand logothete; the fiscal services were placed under the control of the grand logariast.

Alexios inherited a bankrupt state. The coinage was miserably debased. The fineness of the gold coinage had been reduced from twenty-four to eight carats. So desperate was his situation that Alexios had to debase still further, but by 1092 he was able to restore some order to the coinage. He raised the fineness of a standard gold coinage to around twenty carats. He kept the debased electrum (silver/gold alloy) issues, but stabilized them at around six carats. He also kept the debased silver coinage in the form of a billon coin with a minimal silver content. He issued a new copper coinage. Alexius's reform of the coinage was typical of the measures he took to restore the empire. He imposed order and stability, but his measures had radical consequences. Michael Hendy contends that 'the Alexian coinage reform of 1092 attempted and achieved nothing less than a complete reconstruction of the coinage system on an entirely novel basis; . . . only the Diocletianic reform had been on a similar scale.'[25] His innovation was to create a regular coinage based on alloys rather than pure metal. It is likely that the existence of both an electrum and a billon coinage, which took the place of the old silver *miliaresia*, made for a more flexible monetary system. But the greatest service that Alexios's coinage reform did was to reestablish clear equivalences between the different coinages. Their absence had brought chaos to the fiscal system. In the wake of his reform of the coinage Alexios was able to proceed to a thorough-going reform of the collection of taxes – the so-called *Nea Logarike*. It was essentially an adaptation of the taxation system to the reformed coinage. It has been estimated that it was done in such a way as to quadruple the tax rate.

Alexios I Komnenos ended the lax fiscal regime of the eleventh century. There are no signs that the Byzantine economy suffered. It quickly recovered from a period of dislocation which lasted for approximately twenty years from the defeat at Manzikert to Alexios's victory over the Petcheneks in 1091. The manorialization of the countryside continued with largely beneficial results for the peasantry. The towns of Greece and the southern Balkans prospered. Places such as Corinth, Thebes and Halmyros (in Thessaly) benefited from a growing Italian presence. There was an upsurge of local trade around the shores of the Aegean. Constantinople continued to be the clearing house of the medieval world. The empire was far from being 'internally played out'. But there had been a decisive shift in its centre of gravity from Asia Minor to Greece and the southern Balkans, which experienced a period of sustained economic growth. It is not clear, however, that this compensated for the loss of the resources of Anatolia. Its recovery was always Alexios's major task.

XI

By 1095 Alexios had pacified the Balkans, brought peace to the church and restored sound government. He was in a position to contemplate recovering Anatolia from the Turks. He moved troops across the Bosphorus and using Nicomedia as a base created a defensible zone, but it soon became clear that he did not have the resources to effect a reconquest of Anatolia. His preoccupation

[25] M. F. Hendy, *Studies in the Byzantine Monetary Economy c. 300–1450*, Cambridge (1985), p. 513.

with Europe had given the Turks the opportunity to settle vital parts of Anatolia in depth. Alexios had made the situation still worse at the very beginning of his reign by withdrawing the remaining Byzantine garrisons from Anatolia. Paradoxically, the only area where there was potential support for a Byzantine reconquest was in the Euphrates lands and Cilicia where the Armenians had retained their independence.

Alexios needed troops. The Byzantines had long appreciated the martial qualities of the Franks, but had reason to fear their indiscipline and ambition. The main recruiting ground had been among the Normans of southern Italy, but a chance meeting in 1089 opened up a new source of Frankish cavalry. Robert I, count of Flanders, was returning overland from a pilgrimage to Jerusalem. He made a detour to pay his respects to Alexios Komnenos, who was then in winter quarters in Bulgaria. He offered to send Alexios a force of 500 cavalry. He sealed the bargain by taking 'the usual Latin oath' to the emperor. The count was as good as his word and the Flemish cavalry arrived the next year. They were sent to guard the area of Nicomedia, but were then evacuated in 1091 in order to take part in the campaign against the Petcheneks which culminated in the victory at Mount Levounion. They were an important addition to Alexios's forces at a critical moment in his reign. However, Alexios required more than a contingent of 500 Flemish cavalry if he was to have any chance of recovering Anatolia. He turned for help to Pope Urban II, with whom he had been conducting negotiations over the reunion of the churches. Their outcome was inconclusive, but relations remained cordial. Urban II knew that his mentor Gregory VII had tried and failed to organize a papal expedition, which was to go to the rescue of Constantinople and then to press on to Jerusalem. Whether Alexios did too is another matter, but he was well aware of the importance of Jerusalem to Latin Christians. In the spring of 1095 Urban II held a council at Piacenza. Byzantine envoys were present and made a plea for papal aid against the Seljuqs. The exact terms in which this plea was couched cannot now be recovered. Urban II then held a council at Clermont in November 1095, where he made an appeal to the knighthood of France for an expedition to go to the rescue of eastern Christendom. The pope linked this with pilgrimage to Jerusalem and the attendant spiritual rewards. He fixed 15 August 1096 as the day of departure for Constantinople which was to be the point of assembly.

The passage of the crusade was to present Alexios with huge problems. The numbers are not easy to estimate. Modern calculations vary from 30,000 to 70,000 soldiers; over 100,000 if non-combatants are included. The first contingents started to arrive in the early summer of 1096 with Peter the Hermit. They were perhaps less of a rabble than Anna Komnena would have us believe. The swiftness of their arrival took Alexios by surprise. He shipped them over to

Asia Minor, where many of them were killed by the Turks. Alexios was better prepared for the crusading armies that followed in the autumn and winter of 1096. These were under the command of western princes, such as the dukes of Normandy and Lower Lorraine, the counts of Toulouse, Blois, Vermandois and Flanders, and worryingly the Norman Bohemond. Alexios had had time to establish markets along the main routes to Constantinople. As the crusade leaders came one by one to Constantinople he was able to persuade them to take 'the customary Latin oath' to him, as the prospective leader of the expedition against the Turks. Raymond of St-Gilles, count of Toulouse, was the leader who gave him most trouble. He refused to take any oath to the Byzantine emperor. Of all the crusade leaders he was the one closest to Urban II. The pope had consulted him before making his appeal at Clermont. Raymond was the first of the princes to take the cross. He also took a vow never to return from the east. The papal legate Adhemar of LePuy was attached to his contingent. Raymond therefore had some claim to be the military leader of the crusade. The emperor had to be content with an alliance, where each agreed to respect the life and honour of the other.

The first task was the conquest of the Seljuq capital at Nicaea. The Turks preferred to surrender the city to the Byzantines rather than face the fury of the Franks. The fall of Nicaea opened the road leading up to the Anatolian plateau. Alexios had turned down the proposal made by the crusade leaders that he should take personal command of the expedition. But he supplied an important contingent under the command of Taticius, one of his most trusted commanders. Alexios's strategy was straightforward. His aim was to encircle the Turks. The crusaders were to force a passage across Anatolia and to establish control over Cilicia, the Euphrates lands and northern Syria, where there was still a reasonable basis for the restoration of Byzantine rule. To begin with, all went according to plan. The crusaders won a great victory over the Turks on 1 July 1097 at Dorylaion on the edge of the Anatolian plateau. By the end of the summer they were encamped in Cilicia and had started to blockade Antioch. Alexios followed up the victory by conquering large parts of western and northern Asia Minor and pushing the Turks back to the Anatolian plateau.

But the period of cooperation was soon over. Ostensibly the stumbling block was control of Antioch. But it went much deeper than this. The hardships of the passage across Anatolia followed by those of the siege of Antioch transformed the crusade from a joint venture of Byzantium and the west into an ideology that was fixated on Jerusalem. It quickly took on an anti-Byzantine stamp. Such was crusader hostility that the Byzantine commander Taticius abandoned the siege of Antioch. His withdrawal was taken as an act of betrayal. The crusaders' distrust of Byzantine intentions was then reinforced by Alexios's failure to go to their rescue. He had set out and reached Philomelion, a Byzantine outpost

on the Anatolian plateau, but there he was met by two of the leaders of the
crusade who had fled from Antioch in despair. They told the emperor that
all was lost. Alexios therefore turned back. It was the sensible thing to do. In
fact, all was far from lost. Thanks to Bohemond the lower city was secured at
the beginning of June 1098 and on 28 June the crusaders inflicted a crushing
defeat on the Seljuq relief force. Bohemond secured possession of the city for
himself, while the crusade moved on towards Jerusalem.

XII

Antioch was vital to Alexios Komnenos's plans for the recovery of Anatolia from
the Turks. It had traditionally been the main Byzantine centre of operations
in the east. The crusade leaders had given Alexios an undertaking that they
would return Byzantine cities and territories. This Bohemond was refusing to
do. Alexios therefore set about trying to evict him from Antioch. His forces had
some success. They occupied Cilicia but the key point was the port of Latakia.
In 1103 the Byzantines secured the lower city and were endeavouring to dislodge
the Normans from the citadel. Such was the pressure that in 1104 Bohemond
decided to leave his nephew Tancred in charge of Antioch, while he returned
to the west for reinforcements. He won the backing of Pope Paschal II and the
support of the French king Philip I, whose daughter he married. It remains an
open question whether his expedition qualified as a crusade. The final goal was
Palestine. Bohemond was accompanied by a papal legate. The pope presented
him with the banner of St Peter and according to a contemporary[26] appointed
him 'standard-bearer of the army of Christ'. Bohemond's propaganda stressed
the treachery of Alexios Komnenos towards the crusade as just cause for his
invasion. Bohemond's expedition against Byzantium displayed many features
of a crusade, but full recognition would depend on its outcome, simply because
crusading theory was still in its infancy. But for Anna Komnena it was a different
matter. She was clear that Bohemond's invasion not only had papal approval,
but had also been accorded the status of a 'Just War'.[27] It confirmed Byzantine
apprehensions about the dangers that the crusade held in store.

Bohemond landed on the Albanian coast in 1107 and laid siege to Durazzo.
Alexios deployed his forces in the surrounding mountains. Bohemond soon
found himself in an impossible position isolated in front of Durazzo; his escape by sea cut off by the Venetians. Paschal II withdrew his support. In 1108
Bohemond sued for peace. He recognized Alexios as his overlord. He accepted
that he held the principality of Antioch from Alexios. On paper Alexios had

---

[26] Bartolf of Nangis.
[27] Anna Komnena, *Alexiad*, bk XII, ch. viii, para. 5: ed. Lieb and Gautier, III, pp. 80.6–7.

won what he most wanted: recognition of his claims to Antioch. But the treaty remained a dead letter. Bohemond returned to southern Italy. His nephew Tancred continued to rule at Antioch and refused to countenance the concessions made to the Byzantine emperor. Alexios was in no position to enforce them. To meet Bohemond's invasion he had withdrawn his forces from Cilicia and Syria. This allowed the Seljuqs to regain the initiative in western Asia Minor. Alexios was not able to mount an expedition against them until 1116. Its purpose was to evacuate from central Anatolia the Greek populations still living under Turkish rule. It was a tacit admission of defeat.

XIII

Alexios's appeal to Urban II was brilliantly conceived, but Byzantium gained very little from the crusade. In its wake Byzantine forces recovered the rich coastlands of western Anatolia, while they might have reasonably expected to have done anyway. The shadow of 1204 looms over Alexios's achievements and calls in question the success of his restoration of the Byzantine empire. His reputation has also suffered among modern historians because of the *Alexiad*: his daughter Anna Komnena's history of his reign. It is judged to lack objectivity. It is too obviously an exercise in filial piety. It is too much of an idealization. It is all these things, but it also provides a consummate portrait of an age, which, when allowance is made for bias, carries conviction. Anna Komnena's assessment of her father's greatness is borne out by his administrative and fiscal reforms and his church settlement, about which she has relatively little to say. These aspects of her father's reign have to be pieced together from the documentary sources. They provide the best evidence for Alexios's achievement in restoring the empire.

Anna Komnena breathes not a word about her father's appeal to Pope Urban II which triggered off the crusade. This may have been because she did not know about it or because she did not connect her father's appeal with the crusade. But it was more likely done to protect her father's reputation. By the time she was writing – some thirty years after her father's death – it was apparent that the crusade was the cutting edge of western expansion. It was Alexios's task to come to terms with western encroachment, which had begun to make itself felt from the middle of the eleventh century. It took various forms. Least harmful appeared to be the commercial activities of Venetian and other Italian merchants. They offered a solution to Byzantium's need for naval assistance. In order to counter the threat from the Normans at the beginning of his reign Alexios engaged the services of the Venetian fleet. In 1082 in order to pay for them he granted the Venetians special privileges in Constantinople and exemption from the payment of customs duties throughout the empire. It appeared a very good bargain. In 1111 Alexios entered into a similar arrangement with the Pisans. He reduced their customs duty to 4 per cent. He was angling for their support in the plans which he had – but which never came to anything – to bring the crusader states under Byzantine control. Alexios was using the Italians much as the emperors of the tenth century had used the Russians: to strengthen the empire's naval and commercial resources. The appeal to Urban was intended to complement this by harnessing the military potential of the Franks. Alexios could not have imagined that it would trigger off the crusade, nor that the crusade would cease to be a cooperative venture and be turned against Byzantium. Within Byzantium the crusade not only hardened attitudes towards the west, it also created tensions. Opinion polarized between those who favoured continuing cooperation with the west and those who rejected this approach, preferring to fall back on 'splendid isolation'. This put added pressure on the fault lines that existed within the Comnenian settlement: between the emperor and church; between autocracy and aristocracy; between the Comnenian ascendancy and the excluded; between the capital and the provinces. Alexios hoped that an understanding with the west would provide Byzantium with the additional resources needed to restore its position as a world power. He could not have foreseen how it would undermine Byzantium from within. This was the true nature of Alexios's failure. It was counterbalanced by the success he had in restoring the integrity of the imperial office and the soundness of imperial administration. For more than half a century after his death Byzantium remained a great power.

CHAPTER 9

KIEVAN RUS', THE BULGARS AND THE SOUTHERN SLAVS,

c. 1020–*c.* 1200

Martin Dimnik

KIEVAN RUS', 1024–1204

IN 1024 Mstislav of Tmutarakan' defeated his elder brother Jaroslav of Novgorod at Listven north of Chernigov and partitioned Rus' into two autonomous principalities. Jaroslav got Kiev and the right (west) bank of the Dnepr as well as Novgorod; Mstislav kept Chernigov and the left (east) bank in addition to the principality of Tmutarakan' on the north-east shore of the Black Sea. However, after the latter died (1034) Jaroslav appropriated Mstislav's domain and this made him the most powerful ruler in the land. He controlled all of Rus' except for two patrimonies: Polotsk belonged to the family of his elder brother Izyaslav, and Pskov, south-west of Novgorod, was the domain of his brother Sudislav.

Jaroslav established friendly ties with the Poles, the Swedes, the Norwegians, the Germans and the French, but his relations with Byzantium were strained. In 1043 he ordered his eldest son Vladimir of Novgorod to attack the Greeks, but after the expedition failed he restored good relations with them. In 1036 Jaroslav's victory over the Petcheneks secured safe passage for merchants travelling from Kiev to Constantinople. He also helped the Novgorodians to wage expansionist campaigns against the neighbouring Finns and Lithuanians.

Jaroslav's reign was one of the high points in the history of Rus' and his achievements earned for him the sobriquet 'the Wise'. To consolidate his authority, to protect trade routes and to defend the frontiers he established new fortified towns. He helped to lay the foundation for a codified law by issuing 'The Russian Law' (*Pravda russkaya*). He imported Greek craftsmen to build churches and monasteries. He encouraged religious and secular learning by assembling a library and patronizing the translation of Greek and Old Church Slavonic texts. In 1051, wishing to assert the independence of the church in Rus', Jaroslav named the hermit Hilarion as the first native metropolitan.

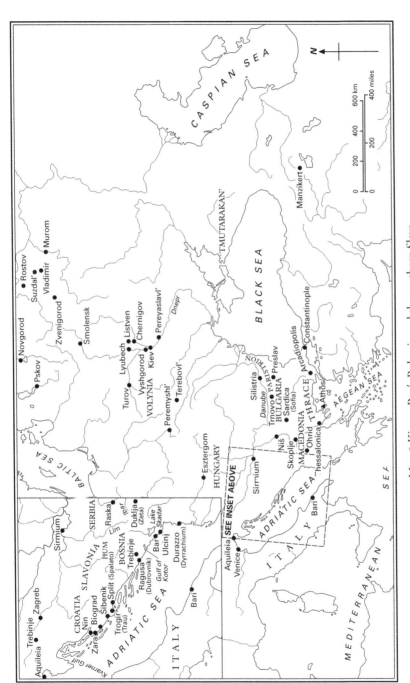

Map 6 Kievan Rus', Bulgaria and the southern Slavs

In imitation of his father Vladimir (d. 1015) and grandfather Svyatoslav (d. 972) Jaroslav allocated towns to his sons before his death (1054); he gave Turov to Izyaslav, Chernigov (along with Murom and Tmutarakan') to Svyatoslav, Pereyaslavl' (and the Rostov-Suzdal' region) to Vsevolod, Vladimir to Igor' and Smolensk to Vyacheslav. The towns were to become their hereditary domains. However, in an attempt to ensure a peaceful transition of supreme power Jaroslav appears to have introduced a new order of succession to Kiev, the capital town of Rus'. To judge from his so-called 'testament', he advocated a system of lateral succession among the families of his three eldest sons; in this way Kiev would never become the hereditary domain of any single family. Accordingly, his eldest son Izyaslav would rule it until his death; the next son Svyatoslav (if he was still alive) would succeed Izyaslav; similarly, Vsevolod would replace Svyatoslav. The two youngest brothers, Igor' and Vyacheslav, and their families were debarred from ruling Kiev.

Izyaslav, Svyatoslav and Vsevolod governed as a triumvirate, so to speak, for almost twenty years and asserted their authority over the other princes. In 1056 and 1060, after the deaths of Igor' and Vyacheslav, they appropriated Vladimir and Smolensk and deprived the deceased princes' sons of their patrimonies. In 1059 they released their uncle Sudislav (whom Yaroslav had incarcerated) from prison and placed him in a monastery after forcing him to forfeit control of Pskov, his patrimony. In 1064 Izyaslav drove out Rostislav, the son of his elder brother Vladimir (d. 1052), from Novgorod, Rostislav's patrimonial domain, and assumed control of it himself. In this way the triumvirate established its authority over all of Rus' except Polotsk. In doing so, it violated the territorial allocations made by Jaroslav 'the Wise'.

In 1068 the nomadic Cumans (Polovtsy) appeared on the steppe south of Kiev for the first time and defeated the forces of the triumvirate. Izyaslav sought safety in Kiev but the citizens forced him to flee when he refused to give them weapons to fight the enemy. They released Vseslav of Polotsk, whom Izyaslav had thrown into prison, and proclaimed him prince. Meanwhile, Svyatoslav sallied forth from Chernigov and scored a brilliant victory over the Cumans. He concluded a peace treaty and established amicable relations with them. In the following year, when Izyaslav marched against to Rus' with Polish reinforcements, Vseslav fled from Kiev and the townsmen asked Svyatoslav and Vsevolod to be their princes. Svyatoslav declined the invitation.

After occupying Kiev the second time Izyaslav waged war against Vseslav but without the support of his brothers; their alliance seemed to be faltering. The three Jaroslavichi demonstrated their solidarity for the last time in 1072 when they met in Vyshgorod, a town north of Kiev. They attended a religious ceremony at which the remains of SS. Boris and Gleb were transferred into the new wooden church built by Izyaslav. The following year Svyatoslav and Vsevolod deposed him and Svyatoslav occupied Kiev. Although Svyatoslav levied what he believed to be just accusations against Izyaslav, his usurpation was a violation of Jaroslav's so-called 'testament' which prohibited a prince from seizing Kiev by force.

Svyatoslav's reign was cut short in 1076 when he died after an unsuccessful operation. However, he was undoubtedly the most gifted of the three brothers and his authority as prince of Kiev surpassed that of Izyaslav whose domains he appropriated. Svyatoslav himself ruled Kiev and Chernigov; his eldest son Gleb governed in Novgorod and his son Oleg administered Vladimir. To his ally Vsevolod of Pereyaslavl' he evidently gave Smolensk and Izyaslav's Turov. German emissaries sent to Kiev on Izyaslav's behalf were impressed with Svyatoslav's immeasurable wealth. He used it to patronize the church and culture; he promoted the cult of SS. Boris and Gleb by beginning to build the first stone church in their honour in Vyshgorod.

After Svyatoslav's death Vsevolod occupied Kiev. However, in the following year (1077) Izyaslav returned from exile and occupied the capital for the third time. Izyaslav formed a pact with Vsevolod and gave him Svyatoslav's patrimonial town of Chernigov in addition to Smolensk and Pereyaslavl'. But the rule of the duumvirate was short-lived. In 1078 Oleg, whom Svyatoslav had evidently designated prince of Chernigov, marched against Vsevolod and drove him out of the town. Later in the year Izyaslav and Vsevolod attacked Oleg and Izyaslav was killed in battle. Oleg himself was defeated and fled to his brother Roman in Tmutarakan'; Vsevolod, the only surviving Jaroslavich, occupied Kiev.

Vsevolod appointed his elder son Vladimir Monomakh to rule Svyatoslav's patrimony of Chernigov, and his younger son Rostislav to govern Pereyaslavl'. Izyaslav's sons Jaropolk and Svyatopolk, who ruled Turov, Vladimir and Novgorod, pledged their fealty to him. However, the sons of his brothers Vladimir, Igor', and Vyacheslav, barred from power, were relegated to positions of political insignificance. Svyatoslav's family suffered a similar fate: in 1078 Gleb was killed in the Novgorod lands; in the following year Roman of Tmutarakan' was murdered by Vsevolod's allies, the Cumans; and in the same year Oleg was exiled to Byzantium apparently with Vsevolod's complicity.

After that Vsevolod's reign was relatively uneventful especially since the Cumans remained at peace. His authority was strengthened in 1086 when Izyaslav's eldest son Jaropolk who ruled Vladimir and Turov was assassinated. Jaropolk's younger brother Svyatopolk vacated Novgorod and moved to his patrimonial domain of Turov. Vsevolod then assumed direct control over Novgorod by appointing his grandson Mstislav, Vladimir's son, to rule it. Towards the end of Vsevolod's reign the princes who had been barred intensified their demands for patrimonies. He therefore granted the descendants of Vladimir of Novgorod the region which later became known as Galicia. Following Jaropolk's murder, Vsevolod allowed Igor's son David to occupy his father's patrimonial domain of Vladimir. In 1093, after Vsevolod's death, his son Monomakh was tempted to occupy Kiev. He did not, the chronicler explains, because Izyaslav's eldest surviving son Svyatopolk had a prior claim since Izyaslav had occupied Kiev before Vsevolod.

Svyatopolk began his twenty-year reign with an act of arrogant stupidity: when the Cumans sent emissaries of peace he threw them into prison. The tribesmen therefore attacked and inflicted a crushing defeat on his and Monomakh's joint forces. Oleg, who had been ruling Tmutarakan' since 1083 when he had returned from Byzantium, took advantage of his cousins' plight: in 1094 he drove out Monomakh from Chernigov with the help of the Cumans. Svyatopolk and Monomakh condemned him for using the Cumans and demanded that he campaign with them against the tribesmen. When he refused, they attacked Chernigov forcing him to flee to Starodub. In 1096 Oleg conducted a series of campaigns against Monomakh's forces hoping to regain his patrimony. In the end, he was defeated by Monomakh's eldest son Mstislav of Novgorod and agreed to attend a meeting of all the princes in order to establish peace in the land.

In 1097 the princes of Rus' met at Lyubech, west of Chernigov, and agreed to honour Jaroslav's original allocation of domains: Svyatopolk would rule Turov (in addition to Kiev); Monomakh got Pereyaslavl'; the three Svyatoslavichi, Oleg, David, Jaroslav, regained Chernigov and Murom. The allocations Vsevolod made to the other princes before his death would also remain in force: Igor's son David kept Vladimir; Volodar and Vasil'ko, the grandsons of Vladimir of Novgorod, retained Peremyshl' and Terebovl' in Galicia. But most important for Svyatopolk and Monomakh, Oleg and the Svyatoslavichi agreed to support their policy against the Cumans.

But even before all the princes returned home from Lyubech the new peace agreement was broken by none other than Svyatopolk. When David of Vladimir convinced him that Monomakh and Vasil'ko of Terebovl' were plotting against them Svyatopolk permitted David to blind Vasil'ko. Monomakh and the Svyatoslavichi, shocked by this unprecedented conduct, marched against Kiev demanding that Svyatopolk punish David. In 1100, at another council of princes held at a place called Uvetichi, David was expelled from Vladimir and relegated to the less important town of Dorogobuzh. After that Svyatopolk, Monomakh, the Svyatoslavichi, and the other princes of Rus' conducted several successful campaigns against the Cumans. By 1111 the tribesmen had been cowed into submission and they remained at peace for over a decade.

In 1113 Svyatopolk died and the Kievans rebelled. Although the unrest was allegedly in response to the injustices committed by Svyatopolk's officials, many of the rioters demanded that Monomakh occupy Kiev. He hesitated. According to Jaroslav's so-called testament, the Svyatoslavichi had a prior claim to Kiev and Monomakh's occupation would be usurpation. Ultimately, the lack of opposition from the Svyatoslavichi and the rioters' threats to inflict violence on his family and possessions if he refused prompted Monomakh to seize power.

His twelve-year rule is generally looked upon as one of the high points in the history of Rus'. Monomakh formed an alliance with the Svyatoslavichi and allowed them to rule their patrimonial lands of Chernigov and Murom. He used his sons to secure control over most of the remaining principalities: Pereyaslavl', Novgorod, Vladimir, Smolensk, Rostov-Suzdal' and Turov. The families of the princes barred from power acknowledged his suzerainty and the Cumans remained at peace. The only principality which continued to remain politically independent of Kiev was Polotsk.

Monomakh was especially renowned for his successful campaigns against the Cumans. After assuming power he also enacted reforms to prevent abuses in interest rates and enslavement. He patronized learning and built many churches. In 1115 he authorized the translation of the relics of SS. Boris and Gleb into the stone church in Vyshgorod begun by Svyatoslav and completed by Oleg. Soon after he composed the autobiographical 'Instruction' (*Pouchenie*) in which he recounted his exploits and gave advice to future rulers.

Before his death in 1125 Monomakh designated his eldest son Mstislav to occupy Kiev and, after him, the next eldest son Jaropolk. He thus attempted to abolish the lateral system of succession advocated by Jaroslav 'the Wise' and to implement a new order which would secure the rule of his descendants in Kiev. Although Mstislav pre-empted the succession right of the Izyaslavichi and the Svyatoslavichi he evidently encountered no opposition from them. Novgorod, Turov, Vladimir and Smolensk which Jaroslav 'the Wise' had bequeathed to four of his sons, but which Monomakh had given to members of his own family, pledged allegiance to Mstislav. In 1127, after Oleg's eldest son Vsevolod (Mstislav's son-in-law) drove his uncle Jaroslav from Chernigov, Mstislav acknowledged Vsevolod's rule and won his support. With the help of his allies Mstislav asserted the authority of the prince of Kiev over Polotsk for the first time. After his death in 1132 his younger brother Jaropolk of Pereyaslavl' succeeded him just as Monomakh had decreed.

Jaropolk's reign was troubled; conflicts arose almost immediately between his brothers the Monomashichi and his nephews the Mstislavichi. Monomakh had intended that the Mstislavichi rather than their uncles occupy the patrimonial domain of Pereyaslavl' after Jaropolk. Monomakh had also designated Mstislav's sons to succeeded Jaropolk to Kiev thereby debarring his own younger sons Vyacheslav, Yury (later known as 'Long Arm' (*Dolgorukiy*)) and Andrey. Yury and Andrey challenged this arrangement, won Jaropolk's support

and forced the Mstislavichi to turn for help to Vsevolod in Chernigov. In this
way the Svyatoslavichi were drawn into conflict with Monomakh's sons. The
two sides clashed on a number of occasions and it appeared that by the time
of Jaropolk's death in 1139 the Monomashichi had won the day. Vyacheslav of
Turov, Jaropolk's eldest surviving brother, succeeded him in Kiev.

Monomakh's plan to make Kiev the patrimony of his family might have
succeeded had it not been for Vsevolod. He immediately challenged Vyacheslav and occupied Kiev. Vsevolod asserted his authority by skilfully breaking
up the princely alliances formed against him. In imitation of Monomakh he
established his jurisdiction over the princes barred from power. He appropriated
Turov and Vladimir; he sent his brother Svyatoslav to rule Novgorod and,
after the latter was driven out, gave it to Mstislav's son Svyatopolk, one of his
brothers-in-law. As the senior prince of the Svyatoslavichi he manipulated his
brothers and cousins by giving them lands in the principality of Chernigov.

Like Monomakh and Mstislav, Vsevolod enjoyed supreme authority in Rus'.
Except for Volodar of Galich who attempted to annex Vladimir, he encountered
no serious threats to his suzerainty. Even Yury of Rostov-Suzdal' realized that
it was futile to challenge him. Before his death in 1146 Vsevolod designated
his younger brother Igor' to succeed him. In imitation of Monomakh who
attempted to make Kiev the patrimonial domain of his family, Vsevolod tried
to secure control of it for the Svyatoslavichi. He was not successful and in the
future the capital of Rus' would become the prize for the strongest contender
from either family. The system of lateral succession advocated by Jaroslav 'the
Wise' had become defunct.

The Kievans refused to accept Igor' as prince and he had insufficient backing
to assert his claim by force. During the uprising that followed Vsevolod's death
the townsmen killed Igor' and turned to Monomakh's descendants for a ruler.
The latter were disunited and a conflict arose between Yury of Rostov-Suzdal'
and Mstislav's son Izyaslav of Vladimir. Yury based his claim on genealogical
seniority according to the customary practice of lateral succession; Izyaslav
demanded Kiev on the ground that his grandfather Monomakh had designated
the Mstislavichi his successors. Izyaslav won the day, in the main because he
had the support of the Kievans.

He ruled from 1146 to 1154. Like Jaroslav 'the Wise' he seemingly attempted,
unsuccessfully, to free the church of Rus' from the direct control of the Greek
patriarch by appointing a native as metropolitan of Kiev. In the political sphere
he exerted much energy in repelling attacks from Yury and his allies, the princes
of Chernigov and the Cumans. In 1155, after Izyaslav's death, Yury finally
occupied Kiev. However, his constant warring, his alliances with the Cumans,
and his oppression made him unpopular; two years after he became prince of
Kiev he was poisoned.

After Yury's death the princes of Chernigov reasserted their supremacy for a short time. Izyaslav, the son of David, occupied Kiev but was overthrown in 1159 when he attempted to impose his rule over Galicia. The Kievans invited Rostislav of Smolensk, Izyaslav's brother, to be their prince. During his reign the Cumans intensified their attacks on trade caravans travelling to Constantinople. Rostislav organized expeditions against the tribesmen but, in the long term, failed to curb their attacks. Evidently, it was during his rule that the so-called expanded version of 'The Russian Law' (*Pravda russkaya*) was completed. After his death in 1167 the unity of the Mstislavichi was broken when his sons objected to the succession of their cousin Mstislav of Vladimir, Izyaslav's son. The balance of power was further disrupted by Yury's son Andrey who sided with the Rostislavichi to pursue his expansionist policies. In 1169, he assembled an enormous army and plundered Kiev.

After that Andrey was recognized as the most powerful prince in the land but he did not occupy Kiev. Since his father had been murdered there he evidently considered it expedient to remain in Rostov-Suzdal'. Moreover, had he moved to Kiev he would have removed himself dangerously far from his centre of power in the north-east. However, as control of Kiev gave its ruler a great military advantage, Andrey could not allow it to fall into the hands of a rival prince. He therefore attempted to control it through an underling. Since the Rostov-Suzdal' district served as the link for the commerce that passed from the Baltic to the Caspian Sea through Novgorod, Andrey also sought to establish his control over that town. In 1170 he failed to capture it by force, but he finally forced the townsmen to capitulate by laying an embargo on all grain shipments to Novgorod.

Andrey attempted to establish absolute rule in his domains by undermining the authority of the citizens in their local assembly (*veche*), by treating his boyars as servitors, and by subordinating all the princes to his control. In order to decrease the influence of the towns – Rostov, Suzdal' and Vladimir on the Klyaz'ma – he moved his court to the village of Bogolyubovo, after which he became known as *Bogolyubskiy*. In an effort to secure greater control over the affairs of the church, he unsuccessfully attempted to create a new metropolitan see in Vladimir on the Klyaz'ma. His autocratic policies evoked much resentment and in 1174 he was assassinated by his boyars.

After that Rostov-Suzdal' was plagued with civil strife until Andrey's brother Vsevolod 'Big Nest' (*Bol'shoe Gnezdo*) asserted his rule over the region. Elsewhere in Rus' the princes of Chernigov, Volynia and Galicia established a balance of power. The Ol'govichi, the descendants of Oleg Svyatoslavich who after the death of Izyaslav Davidovich in 1161 had become the sole rulers of Chernigov, and the Rostislavichi of Smolensk concluded a pact. In 1176 Svyatoslav of Chernigov, Vsevolod's son, occupied Kiev and assumed the office of the most senior prince in the land. He acknowledged Rostislav's son Ryurik from Ovruch, north-west of Kiev, as co-ruler. In Galicia Jaroslav *Osmomysl'*, Vladimirko's son, reigned until his death in 1187; in Volynia the descendants of Izyaslav had firm control.

During the last quarter of the twelfth century the princes of Kiev and Chernigov were primarily concerned with curbing the raids of the Cumans; they had limited success. In 1184 Svyatoslav and Ryurik successfully repelled an attack on Kiev. In the following year one of the minor Ol'govichi, Igor' of Novgorod Severskiy, accompanied by a number of other princelings, led a valiant campaign against the tribesmen. It ended in catastrophe for the princes but it became the subject of the most famous epic poem of Rus', the 'Lay of Igor''s Campaign'.

In 1194 Svyatoslav died in Kiev and was succeeded, evidently according to a previous agreement, by Ryurik. Then, in 1199, Roman of Volynia seized the throne of Galicia with the help of the Poles. He therewith became one of the most powerful princes in the land. In 1202 Roman evicted Ryurik from Kiev but Vsevolod 'Big Nest' of Rostov-Suzdal' came to Ryurik's aid. The following year a coalition of princes and Cumans headed by Ryurik attacked Kiev and plundered it even more mercilessly, according to the chronicler, than Andrey's army had done. Roman and Vsevolod 'Big Nest' reached a compromise and appointed a minor prince to Kiev. In 1205 Roman was killed in battle; his untimely death created a political vacuum in south-western Rus' because his sons, Daniil and Vasil'ko, were still minors. The balance of power now shifted to Rostov-Suzdal' where Vsevolod 'Big Nest' became the most powerful prince in the land. As he was primarily concerned in strengthening his own principality, Vsevolod interfered little in the affairs of the southern princes.

In summary, we have seen that at the beginning of the eleventh century Jaroslav 'the Wise' consolidated his rule over most of Rus' and before his death divided up his realm into patrimonies for his sons. He hoped to ensure a peaceful transition of power to Kiev by instituting a system of lateral succession according to genealogical seniority. It had considerable success until Vladimir Monomakh attempted to secure Kiev as the patrimony for his descendants. In 1139 Vsevolod Ol'govich of Chernigov challenged the Monomashichi and sought to secure Kiev for the Svyatoslavichi. After that, the capital of Rus' became the main object of rivalry between members of the two families as they fought for supremacy in the land.

BULGARIA, 1018–1207

During most of the eleventh and twelfth centuries Bulgaria experienced the so-called period of Byzantine rule. In 1014 Tsar Samuel died after seeing his defeated troops return home blinded at the command of Basil II 'Bulgar-slayer'. Four years later the emperor completed the subjugation of the Bulgarians when he captured Ohrid. He divided up their state into three military themes or provinces: the theme of Bulgaria proper which included most of Macedonia was centred around Skoplje; Silistria was the main town in the theme of Paristrion (Paradunavon) located between the Balkan mountains and the lower Danube; the third theme, situated on the middle Danube and the lower Sava, had Sirmium as its capital. Each was administered by a military governor (*strategos*) who had imperial troops under his command.

To obviate insurrections Basil II transferred the surviving members of the royal family and of the old Bulgarian aristocracy to military outposts in Asia Minor. Whereas he had treated Samuel's defeated soldiers most cruelly, the civil policy he imposed on the vanquished Bulgarians was accommodating: he permitted them to keep the administrative system used by Tsar Samuel. Since they had no coinage he decreed that they would continue to pay their taxes in kind unlike his other subjects who paid in money. He also preserved the Bulgarian Orthodox church but in a weakened form. Although he demoted the patriarch to the status of archbishop, he appointed a Bulgarian, John of Debar, to that post. In the future the archbishop of Ohrid would be named directly by the emperor and thereby kept outside the jurisdiction of the patriarch of Constantinople. The archbishop also retained jurisdiction over all the bishoprics which had belonged to Samuel's kingdom. This and other privileges gave the archbishop a special status within the ecclesiastical structure of the Byzantine church. Basil therewith demonstrated that he was prepared to grant a measure of ecclesiastical autonomy to his new subjects.

After 1025 the successors of Basil II abandoned his reasonable policies in Bulgaria owing, in large part, to the serious military, economic and social crisis which pervaded the empire for the next fifty years. In the 1030s Bulgaria was hit by a series of famines which killed off many of its inhabitants who were, in the main, Slavic peasants. The military units in the themes deteriorated, leaving the Bulgarian themes prey to foreign invaders. The latter pillaged the lands of the peasants inflicting additional hardships on them. The emperor's practice of granting immunities to landowners led to administrative abuses and further weakened the effectiveness of the theme system. What is more, Byzantine tax collectors ruthlessly employed extortionist tactics. Then, in 1040, Emperor Michael IV (1034–41) abrogated the tax system introduced by Basil II and forced the Bulgarians to pay their taxes in cash.

The last measure provoked a major revolt. In the same year Peter Deljan, who claimed to be a grandson of Tsar Samuel, was proclaimed tsar of Bulgaria in Belgrade. Soon after he was joined by a certain Alusianus and the revolt spread over the greater part of the Balkans. Deljan led his troops south and, after capturing the towns of Niš, Skoplje and Durazzo, advanced into northern Greece; but the insurgents failed to take Thessalonica. In 1041 the uprising was suppressed owing to the lack of unity among its leaders. Its temporary success, however, had weakened the structure Basil II had created. It also demonstrated the seriousness of the disaffection which existed not only among the Bulgarians but also among the Serbs, Albanians and Greeks who joined them. Even so, Byzantium's response was merely to tighten its control over the malcontents by replacing whatever Bulgarian officials still remained in administrative posts with Greeks. After that the oppression became even worse.

Other developments were also undermining Byzantine control over Bulgaria. After 1034 the Petcheneks raided the Balkans with increased frequency. In 1064 the Uzes, also of Turkic origin, crossed the Danube into Bulgaria, Thrace and Macedonia. The suffering they inflicted on the Bulgarians nearly forced the latter to emigrate, but an outbreak of plague decimated the invaders. In 1071 the empire appeared to be on the verge of collapse after it had experienced disastrous defeats at Manzikert and Bari.

In the following year the Byzantine government nearly lost the Balkans, the very heart of the empire. The Bulgarians and Serbs rose up in arms and declared Constantine Bodin, the son of King Michael of Duklja (Zeta), tsar of Bulgaria. However, the Byzantines crushed the revolt and took Bodin captive. At the same time the theme of Paristrion, angry at Constantinople's decision to make the corn trade a state monopoly, asserted its autonomy.

It is difficult to determine what role the Bogomils, the dualist heretics named after the priest Bogomil who lived at the time of Tsar Peter (927–69), played in the revolts of the eleventh century. Since the religious dissenters became more active during this period, it is generally believed that they participated in the insurrections and supported the Petcheneks. Although they preached a doctrine of civil disobedience, their social anarchism reflected their moral convictions and not a political programme; shedding blood was contrary to their beliefs. Consequently, even though the Bogomils opposed the established Orthodox church and the Byzantine political structure, it is doubtful that, as a rule, they participated in armed revolts.

During the second half of the eleventh century an economic and political system closely resembling feudalism in the west arose in Bulgaria. It was based on a method of tenure (*pronoia*) according to which the government usually gave land to secular magnates in return for military service. It is difficult to determine how this development influenced the attitude of the Bulgarians towards the Greeks. However, in the light of the peasants' growing distress, the landlords, who were in the main foreigners, were undoubtedly looked upon as imperial exploiters.

The Greeks adopted a policy of cultural assimilation in Bulgaria. John of Debar died in 1037 and after that the archbishop of Ohrid was always a Greek. As an agent of the emperor he had to implement the policy by introducing such changes as the use of Greek in the Bulgarian church. The Greeks also destroyed Slavonic books, but there is little documentation to show the success of this policy. The survival of a number of Old Church Slavonic manuscripts, allegedly copied in the eleventh century by Bulgarian and Macedonian scribes, suggests that the archbishops also condoned the use of such texts. The best evidence that the primate of Ohrid did not attempt to stifle Slavonic traditions is provided by Theophylact (*c.* 1090 – *c.* 1109). For a Greek who allegedly abhorred living in Bulgaria, it is remarkable that he wrote a biography of St Clement of Ohrid which he based on a Slavonic life of the saint. In it he also praised the work of SS. Cyril and Methodius.

In 1185 the Byzantine empire was in serious disarray. The Normans of Sicily had captured Durazzo and Thessalonica. Meanwhile Isaac II Angelus (1185–95) assumed power and imposed a highly unpopular tax to pay for his marriage expenses. In the themes the imperial armies continued to deteriorate and the land fell increasingly into the hands of unscrupulous local boyars. Two such magnates were the brothers Peter (Theodore) and Asen of Trnovo. They were evidently Vlakhs (these were for the most part shepherds descended from the semi-Romanized Dacians who sought refuge in the mountains during the period of Slav invasions) who requested a *pronoia* from the emperor but were rudely dismissed. The insult, in addition to the high taxes, sparked off another insurrection among the Bulgarians and Vlakhs.

In 1187 Isaac II drove the brothers beyond the Danube. But after he returned to Constantinople they regrouped, recruited reinforcements from the nomadic Cumans and seized control of Bulgaria. On this occasion the emperor failed to defeat the upstarts and was forced to conclude a settlement: Peter and Asen agreed to hand over their younger brother Kalojan as hostage – he was to escape from Constantinople two years later – and Isaac II released Byzantium's hold on the territory between the Balkan mountains and the Danube, acknowledging the existence of a new independent Bulgarian state.

The second Bulgarian empire, as it is generally known, was called Bulgarian even though the brothers were Vlakhs. Asen was crowned as ruler and made Trnovo his political capital; Peter governed from Preslav. Spurning the arch-bishopric of Ohrid with its Byzantine loyalties, Asen created an independent one in Trnovo. Most of the boyars in their service no longer came from the old Bulgarian families; many were Cumans who served the brothers as comrades in arms. None the less, the brothers found it useful to retain the Greek ad-ministrative practices that had been introduced during the so-called Byzantine period. After securing their authority Asen and Peter launched new attacks into Byzantine territories; in 1193 they captured Arcadiopolis and with it much of central Thrace.

In 1196 Asen was murdered; Peter occupied Trnovo but suffered a similar fate in the following year. After that Kalojan, their youngest brother, assumed power and intensified Bulgarian attacks against Byzantium. Meanwhile the princes of Kievan Rus' launched a major campaign against the Cumans in the steppes north of the Black Sea. Many Cumans in Kalojan's service (he himself was married to a Cuman princess) sallied forth to the defence of their compatriots. Their exodus seriously weakened his military resources and in 1201 he was forced to conclude a treaty with the empire and cede control of Thrace. Despite this setback Kalojan successfully expanded his domains to the confluence of the rivers Morava and Danube.

In 1199, wishing to obtain ecclesiastical recognition for his rule, Kalojan began negotiating with Pope Innocent III for a crown. After the Fourth Crusade captured Constantinople, a papal legate arrived at his court, crowned him king and recognized Archbishop Basil of Trnovo as primate of Bulgaria. Kalojan pledged his loyalty to Rome but acted as if the pope had granted him an imperial title and had accorded patriarchal status to his archbishop. The ecclesiastical union with the Holy See was a purely political act and evidently had no doctrinal or administrative consequences for the inner life of the Bulgarian church. Kalojan's state lacked strong central institutions. It was a federation of local lords who supported him because they hoped to profit from his raids or because they feared reprisals if they refused to support him.

In summary, we have seen that after Basil II imposed Byzantine rule over Bulgaria his successors failed to absorb it into the empire's political structure. The oppression the Bulgarian peasants suffered at the hands of local Byzantine magnates, the extortionist practices of tax collectors, the rapacious taxation policies and devastating foreign invasions all alienated the Bulgarians from their Byzantine overlords. In 1187, after a number of unsuccessful attempts, they won their independence and created the second Bulgarian empire.

THE SOUTHERN SLAVS

The Serbs (1018–1196)

In 1018 when Basil II conquered Bulgaria a number of Serbian principalities also fell under Byzantine rule. These included Raška, or Rascia, located between the rivers Lim and Ibar, Duklja, or Dioclea, later known as Zeta, located around Lake Skadar (Scutari) and the Gulf of Kotor, Trebinje, or Travunia, located between Kotor (Cotarro) and Ragusa (Dubrovnik), Zahumlje, later known as Hum, located between Ragusa and the River Neretva, and Bosnia, located between the upper Neretva, the Drina and the Sava. Basil II evidently allowed the local county lords (*župans*) to remain in power after they submitted to Byzantine suzerainty. The Serbs were the empire's most important but insubordinate subjects in the western Balkans.

The sources tell us nothing about Byzantine Serbia until the 1030s when a certain Stephen Vojislav rebelled against Constantinople. Imperial troops attacked him, took him captive and placed his domain of Duklja under the jurisdiction of the military governor (*stratatos*) of Durazzo. Around 1039 Vojislav regained control of Duklja and, three years later, inflicted a crushing defeat on the *stratatos* and his client *župans* of Raška, Bosnia and Zahumlje. Vojislav therewith secured the independence of his domain and control over the neighbouring territories of Trebinje and Zahumlje. Duklja, the first of the South Slav territories to break away from imperial rule, became the leading Serbian state until the twelfth century. Vojislav died around 1043 and bequeathed his lands to his five sons. The empire, however, attempted to regain its influence over Duklja by fomenting dissension among them and the nobles of the Serbian territories annexed by Vojislav tried to secede. In the end, the brothers joined forces against their common enemies and, around 1046, Michael assumed the title of king.

Byzantium remained Duklja's most powerful enemy. To obviate any attack from that quarter and to deny his brothers the opportunity of using such a crisis to rebel against him, Michael made peace with Emperor Constantine IX Monomachos. The latter recognized the king's independence and Michael returned to Byzantium some of the territories his father Vojislav had seized from Durazzo. After that Michael set out to consolidate his control over the Serbian lands by strengthening the power of his sons. He increased their territorial holdings by granting them newly conquered territories or lands appropriated from his own brothers.

In 1072 George Vojteh of Skoplje rebelled against Constantinople and asked the king of Duklja to send troops. Ignoring his peace treaty with the Greeks, Michael dispatched an army under the command of his son Constantine Bodin. The insurgents crowned Bodin tsar of the Bulgarians but Bodin's aspirations came to naught when the Byzantines suppressed the revolt. Bodin was captured and remained a prisoner for some six years.

Michael also attempted to undermine the empire's ecclesiastical influence on the south Adriatic coast. As the Orthodox metropolitanate of Durazzo had helped to Christianize Duklja, it vied with the archdioceses of Ohrid and Split to assert its jurisdiction over the Serbian churches. Around 1066, at Michael's request, Pope Alexander II purportedly created the Latin metropolitan archdiocese of Duklja at Bar (Antibari). Its jurisdiction was to extend over Trebinje, Bosnia and Raška, in addition to the churches formerly subordinate to Byzantine Durazzo and Latin Split. In practice, Raška and Bosnia retained their Orthodox affiliations and, even on the littoral, Latin and Byzantine practices continued to overlap. Nevertheless, the creation of the archbishopric in Bar bound Duklja closer to Rome; in 1077 Pope Gregory VII sent a royal crown to Michael and he, in return, pledged loyalty to the Holy See.

But Michael had not renounced his affiliation to the empire completely. In 1081, when the Normans attacked Durazzo he sent an army under Bodin's command to help defend the town. Bodin, for his part, approached the conflict with divided loyalties because, it appears, he had married a Norman woman from Bari a year earlier. He withdrew his troops from battle at a critical moment and thereby helped the Normans capture Durazzo. His betrayal would inevitably bring retribution from Byzantium.

Around 1082 Michael died. Bodin succeeded him and soon faced revolts in the *županijas* his father had annexed to Duklja. Zahumlje seceded. Bodin crushed the revolt in Zeta where his uncle Radoslav ruled and when Raška attempted to break away he asserted his control over it and part of Bosnia. He allowed each region to keep its local nobility but appointed a member of the royal family of Duklja to rule it. Thus, around 1084 he appointed Vukan (Vlkan) and Marko, perhaps the sons of his brother Petrislav to whom Michael had given Raška, as *župans* of Raška. Bodin also maintained close relations with the Latin church. In 1089 the antipope Clement III evidently reaffirmed the metropolitan status of Bar and placed all the churches in Bodin's realm under its control. In the main, the churches on the littoral remained loyal to Rome while those located inland continued to acknowledge the jurisdiction of Orthodox bishops.

In 1085, Emperor Alexios I Komnenos defeated the Norman invaders at Durazzo and reasserted the empire's rule over the south Adriatic region. Soon after Byzantine troops captured Bodin and restored imperial rule over Duklja. This gave rise to a period of anarchy and the state disintegrated as local *župans* fought for the right of succession. Bosnia broke away from Duklja, drew closer to Croatia, and with it became part of the Hungarian state. Raška successfully asserted its independence under Vukan's leadership and became the leading Serbian opponent of Byzantium. Indeed, during the twelfth century Raška and Serbia became synonymous.

Vukan assumed the title grand *župan* and established his capital at the fortress of Ras after which Raška was named. In the early 1090s he initiated an expansionist policy against the empire by marching eastward towards Niš and south-eastward into Macedonia. In 1095 the Byzantines retaliated and forced him to send his son Uroš to Constantinople as a hostage. But this did not deter Vukan. He renewed his incursions into Macedonia. The Greeks finally brought him to heel in 1106, but he had set the example for his successors. They would advance steadily into Macedonia for the next 200 years and establish ever closer contacts with Byzantine administration and culture.

The rulers of Raška were appointed and deposed from Constantinople. Their revolts were looked upon as treason and reprisals were severe. Around 1126 Uroš I, who succeeded his father Vukan as grand *župan*, asserted his independence. The Byzantines defeated him and deported many Serbs to the region of Nicomedia in Asia Minor. Four years later, in order to strengthen his position against the empire, Uroš I formed an alliance with Hungary: he gave his daughter Jelena in marriage to King Béla II, the Blind (1131–41). The latter relied heavily on his wife and her brother Beloš to help him administer his realm. Béla was succeeded by his son Géza II (1141–62), a minor, for whom Beloš became regent.

In 1149, when Emperor Manuel I Komnenus was preparing to launch an attack against the Normans in Italy, the Serbs, Normans and Hungarians formed a pact and the Serbs revolted. Uroš II, who had succeeded his father as grand *župan* of Raška, threatened the emperor's supply base near Durazzo. He also captured much of Duklja and Trebinje. An imperial force was sent against him which devastated much of Raška and again transferred many Serbs to Byzantine territories. Except for a short interval in 1155, the Greeks allowed Uroš II to remain grand *župan* until 1161, at which time his brother Desa was reappointed.

Manuel I crushed many revolts in Raška but he could not put an end to them even by replacing disloyal *župans*. This remained the case even after the dynasty of Nemanja, a new line of princes which ruled Serbia until the second half of the fourteenth century, assumed power. Around 1166, after subduing yet another Serbian revolt, Manuel appointed a certain Tihomir as grand *župan*. He shared authority with his younger brothers Stephen Nemanja, Miroslav and Straçimir. Around 1171 Nemanja deposed Tihomir, who was later killed in battle, and the three remaining brothers divided up Raška among them. In the long term, Nemanja's usurpation inaugurated two centuries of greatness; in the short term, it was the newest Serbian challenge to Byzantine overlordship. In 1172 Manuel defeated Nemanja who was brought before the emperor barefooted, with a rope tied round his neck, and forced to throw himself in submission at Manuel's feet. Later, he was degraded further by being exhibited as a conquered rebel in the emperor's triumphal entry into Constantinople. After the humiliation Nemanja was reinstated in Raška; he remained a loyal vassal until 1180, the year of the emperor's death when he repudiated imperial rule once again. Taking advantage of Byzantium's conflicts with the Normans and the Hungarians he initiated a policy of expansion: he appropriated territories in northern Macedonia and the Kosovo region; he seized Zeta (the name usually given to Duklja after this time) and pressed on to the Dalmatian coast to capture the towns of Ulcinj (Dulcigno), Bar and Kotor; he annexed territories to the east as far as Serdica (modern Sofia). Nemanja also supported the Bulgarian rebels Peter and Asen when they declared their independence. In 1189 he expressed an interest in occupying the imperial throne itself when he met the western Emperor Frederick I Barbarossa in Niš and unsuccessfully attempted to form a coalition with him against Byzantium.

In 1190, after Frederick I had crossed the Bosphorus, Emperor Isaac II Angelus marched against Nemanja, defeated him on the River Morava, and forced him to make peace. The terms of the agreement suggest that the Byzantine victory had been indecisive: the emperor acknowledged Raška's independence and allowed Nemanja to keep many of the Serbian and Bulgarian lands he had seized. Isaac also concluded a marriage alliance with the Serbs: Nemanja's son Stephen married Eudoxia, the niece of Isaac and daughter of the future Emperor Alexios III Angelus. A few years later the latter conferred on Stephen the title of *sebastokrator*. The marriage alliance and the title, it could be argued, were Byzantium's recognition of the fact that Raška had come of age as an autonomous state in the Balkans.

Serbian ties with Byzantium were strengthened through the bishopric in Ras. After the conquest of Basil II the Serbians had been placed under the ecclesiastical jurisdiction of the Bulgarian archbishopric of Ohrid which supplied them with Slavonic Orthodox texts and Byzantine spirituality. Nevertheless, during the twelfth century Rome continued to exert a strong influence over the churches of Raška through the Latin bishoprics on the Adriatic coast such as Bar, Ragusa and Kotor. The ecclesiastical dualism of Serbia was exemplified in the case of Nemanja himself who was allegedly baptized first in his native Zeta by a Latin priest and later by an Orthodox bishop in Ras. Nemanja was not only tolerant of Latin Christians but also patronized churches under Rome's jurisdiction. However, by the end of the twelfth century he had committed himself to the Orthodox church. His youngest son Rastko followed his example. Impressed by the life and teaching of the monks of Mount Athos who frequented his father's court, Rastko ran away to the Holy Mountain, became a monk in the Greek monastery of Vatopedi and adopted the name Sava.

Nemanja's religious inclinations were fortified by his son's example. In 1196 he abdicated in favour of his second son the *sebastokrator* Stephen, the son-in-law of Emperor Alexios III. Earlier, he had given his eldest son Vukan, whose wife was a relative of Pope Innocent III and who probably espoused the Latin rite, control of the less important regions of Zeta and Trebinje. Nemanja entered the monastery of Studenica which he had built and took the monastic name Symeon. Soon afterwards he followed Sava to the Holy Mountain. Alexios III granted him the derelict monastery of Chilandar where he and Sava founded a Serbian monastic community which was to become the leading centre of Serbian culture and spirituality in the middle ages. Nemanja died on 13 February 1199 and was canonized soon after.

In summary, we have seen that after 1018 Duklja asserted itself over the Serbian territories but failed to win independence from Byzantium. Raška replaced Duklja in importance at the beginning of the twelfth century. During the second half of the century, Stephen Nemanja won Raška's independence and founded a new dynasty which would rule the Serbian lands until 1371.

The Croats (1018 – c. 1200)

At the beginning of the eleventh century the Croats lived in two more or less clearly defined regions. Pannonian Croatia constituted the interior region between Hungary in the north, Bosnia centred on the valley of the River Bosna in the east, and the Dalmatian littoral in the south. Dalmatian Croatia constituted most of the Dalmatian coast including such towns as Nin (Nona), Biograd and Sebenico (Šibenik). Within this region, however, Byzantium also controlled a number of towns, including Zadar (Zara), Trau (Trogir), Split (Spalato) and Ragusa (Dubrovnik). These formed the Byzantine theme of Dalmatia. Croats, along with Serbs, also lived in Bosnia which at times came under the control of Croatian kings.

There is little information concerning the history of either Pannonian Croatia or Dalmatian Croatia before the Byzantine conquest. In 1000, King Svetoslav of the Trpimir dynasty was deposed by his brothers, Krešimir III (1000–30) and Gojislav (1000 – c. 1020). He therefore arranged for his son Stjepan to marry the daughter of the doge of Venice whom Byzantium had recently recognized as the imperial agent in Dalmatia. Stjepan's alliance posed a serious threat to his two uncles as the Venetians gradually imposed their control over the Croatian littoral. However, in 1019 the emperor Basil II reasserted Byzantine rule over Dalmatia after he defeated Samuel of Bulgaria.

Krešimir III (Gojislav is no longer mentioned by the sources) acknowledged Byzantium's overlordship and Basil allowed him to rule Croatia as an imperial client. In 1025, after the emperor's death, Byzantine suzerainty became tenuous as the civil bureaucracy which assumed the leading role in Constantinople became less concerned with Dalmatia. Krešimir III declared independence but had to cede territory to his nephew Stjepan. In 1024, the latter had fled strife-torn Venice and sought sanctuary at the court of King Stephen I in Hungary. The king seized Slavonia, as the Croatian territory between the Rivers Drava and Sava was known, and gave it to Stjepan as an appanage.

Krešimir III's son and successor Stjepan I (1030–58) expanded Croatian territories to the north-west and scored military successes against the Venetians and the Greeks. His son Peter Krešimir IV (1058–74) reestablished cordial relations with Byzantium. As it was threatened by the Seljuqs from Asia Minor, the Normans from Italy and Venice on the Adriatic the empire was unable to maintain control over its Dalmatian theme. In 1069, it ceded control over its coastal towns (except Ragusa) to Krešimir IV but retained its nominal overlordship. He respected the autonomous status of the Byzantine towns and made Biograd, a Croatian town, his capital.

There is little information for the ecclesiastical history of Pannonian Croatia where the church was Latin. More is known about the church in Dalmatian Croatia. Despite Byzantium's political control over the coastal towns, the churches there remained under the jurisdiction of the pope. The most powerful prelate was the archbishop of Split but it is not known how much authority he wielded over the Croats living on the coast. From the beginning of the ninth century the patriarch of Aquileia, an agent of the Franks, had conducted missionary activity among Slavs living in northern and central Dalmatia. The centre of his activity was Nin, the princely residence north of Zadar where, around 850, the pope had established a bishopric for the Dalmatian Croats. The bishop of Nin championed the use of Slavonic as a liturgical language unlike the archbishop of Split who advocated Latin.

During Krešimir's reign the Slavonic liturgy, written in the Glagolitic script, became an issue of controversy. It was especially popular in northern Dalmatia on the islands in the Gulf of Kvarner. At the time when the papacy was implementing general reforms in the church, many prelates of the Byzantine towns attempted to prohibit the use of the Slavonic liturgy and to standardize church practices. In 1060 a synod held in Split and attended by all the Dalmatian bishops and a papal legate prohibited clergy from wearing long hair and beards as was customary in the Byzantine church; it also announced that Slavs aspiring to the priesthood had to learn Latin. Three years later Pope Alexander II confirmed the decisions of the synod, but the decrees were most unpopular with the lower classes of Croats who looked upon them as measures designed to suppress the Slavonic liturgy. In 1064 a rebellion broke out on the island of Krk where proponents of the Slavonic liturgy unsuccessfully attempted to establish their own bishopric. Some three years later another synod divided the Dalmatian coast into two archbishoprics: that of Split extended northwards from the River Cetina (located south of Split), and that of Duklja extended southwards from the river Cetina to Durazzo (where Ragusa and Bar vied for ecclesiastical jurisdiction). In 1075 a synod held in Split confirmed this reorganization; it also reiterated the edicts of 1060 against Glagolitic and reaffirmed the use of Latin. But the synodal decrees proved to be ineffective. The Slavonic liturgy was retained in many Croatian communities which either preferred the Slavonic language or could not find priests who knew Latin.

During Krešimir's reign Croatia was made up of three banates: Slavonia, Bosnia and a coastal banate which existed from 1060 to 1069 under the rule of a certain Gojčo. Little is known about the latter two, but Slavonia was governed by the autonomous *ban* Zvonimir, son-in-law of King Béla I of Hungary. In the late 1060s Zvonimir and Kresimir reached an agreement. The former accepted Krešimir's overlordship as a result of which Slavonia, while retaining its autonomy, became part of the kingdom of Croatia. Krešimir, for his part, designated Zvonimir his successor should he die heirless.

Krešimir IV died around 1075 and Zvonimir was crowned king near Split. The ceremony was performed by the legate of Pope Gregory VII to whom Zvonimir pledged fealty. This was a significant step in Croatia's orientation towards the west. Thereafter the king's loyalty to the pope and his success at taking politically independent action reduced Byzantine suzerainty over Croatia to a mere formality. Zvonimir died around 1089 and was succeeded by his son who died soon after. He was evidently the last of the Trpimir dynasty; his death initiated a civil war during which many of the hereditary nobles whose autonomy Zvonimir had curtailed reasserted their traditional rights.

King Ladislas I of Hungary, claiming the succession through his sister Helen, Zvonimir's widow, occupied much of Pannonian Croatia. In 1091 he created a special Croatian banate (*banovina*) between the river Drava and the Gvozd Mountain south of Zagreb and placed it under the command of his nephew Almos. Three years later he also removed the churches in the banate from the jurisdiction of the archbishop of Split and placed them under the newly created bishopric of Zagreb (Agram). The latter was made subordinate to the archbishop of Esztergom (Gran) in Hungary.

A certain Peter (1093–7), evidently from the region of Knin, assumed the title of king and occupied Dalmatian Croatia and those areas of Pannonian Croatia which Álmos did not control. In 1095 he also attempted to expel Álmos from his banate. King Coloman (Kálmán) came to Álmos's assistance and Peter, the last independent Croatian king, was killed in the ensuing conflict. After recapturing Pannonian Croatia Coloman marched into Dalmatia and occupied Biograd. In 1102 he renewed his annexation of Croatian territories but, on reaching the River Drava, was allegedly met by local nobles who negotiated a settlement known as the *Pacta Conventa*. The terms of the settlement are unclear. Allegedly, the nobles elected Coloman king of Pannonian Croatia and Dalmatian Croatia. Henceforth, Croatia and Hungary shared a common king but remained distinct realms. The king of Hungary had to be crowned a second time as the king of Croatia. Coloman promised to defend Croatia but demanded military service from its nobles. However, he granted them local autonomy and exempted them from taxes; he also permitted them to retain their lands and their administrative privileges. This was important because kings like Zvonimir had attempted to curtail these rights. In this way the kingdom of Croatia continued to exist, albeit under a Hungarian dynasty. Except for a brief interlude in the second half of the twelfth century, Croatia never again fell under Byzantine control.

The Croatian lands were now divided into three districts: Croatia, which was bounded by the Adriatic from the Gulf of Kvarner in the west to the River Neretva in the south, the River Vrbas in the east, and the Rivers Sava and Kupa in the north; Slavonia, situated more or less between the Rivers Sava and the Drava; and Bosnia, located to the east of the River Vrbas encompassing, in the main, the valley of the River Bosna.

Hungary's control of Dalmatia was frequently challenged by Venice and Byzantium. Following Coloman's death in 1116 Venice, with Byzantium's backing, occupied Zadar, Split, Trogir, Biograd and the surrounding territories. In 1117 and 1124 the Hungarians failed to regain control of the littoral and it was not until 1158 that King Géza II recaptured Zadar for a few years. In 1167 the emperor Manuel I took advantage of internal unrest in Hungary to assert imperial control over the former Byzantine towns once again, but for the last time. In 1181, the year following the emperor's death, King Béla III regained possession of the coastal towns to the dismay of the Venetians. Hungary remained in control of the littoral until the Fourth Crusade.

For most of the twelfth century after 1102, Croatia and Slavonia were ruled by the king's viceroy (ban). During the reign of King Emeric (Imre) his younger brother Andrew demanded Croatia as his appanage. The king agreed and, in 1198, Andrew became duke of Croatia and Slavonia. Although Andrew remained the king's vassal and had to supply him with troops, he governed the domains as an independent ruler. As duke he had the right to coin money, to appoint bishops, to allocate land and to arbitrate between his nobles. He had residences in Zagreb, Knin and Zadar.

Croatia and Slavonia were subdivided into many *županijas*. In Croatia the *župans* were local nobles, but in Slavonia they were usually of Hungarian origin and Slavonia's political structure reflected that of the Hungarians more than that of the Croats. Furthermore, the church in Slavonia was placed under the archbishop of Kalocsa in Hungary whereas the church in Croatia remained under Split's jurisdiction. During Hungary's overlordship Croatia experienced much political unrest as some *župans* attempted to secede while others living near Bosnia attempted to transfer their allegiance to rulers in that district.

After Coloman annexed Croatia in 1102 he also asserted his rule over Bosnia, but little is known about its history for the next sixty years. In 1167, when the Hungarians were defeated by Manuel I, Bosnia also fell under imperial control. After the emperor's death in 1180 Béla III reclaimed it for Hungary, but his control over much of it was nominal at best, and the central regions of Bosnia, for all practical purposes, remained independent. In the 1180s and 1190s a certain *ban* Kulin arose as the most powerful ruler in Bosnia. Although Hungary evidently exerted no control over his banate, it is doubtful that Kulin himself had any significant sway over the *županijas* surrounding his domain. The mountainous terrain of Bosnia fostered localism and the *župans* opposed any centralizing authority. In 1189 Kulin successfully concluded a treaty with the merchants of Ragusa who established their commercial enterprises and opened silver mines in his banate. Kulin also granted sanctuary to Bogomils who had fled from Serbia and the Dalmatian towns (notably Split and Trau) where they were persecuted.

During the eleventh and twelfth centuries the inhabitants of Bosnia espoused different Christian traditions. The Orthodox faith was predominant in the eastern districts near Serbia and the River Drina; Latin rite Christianity was prevalent in the west, the north and in central Bosnia. In the late twelfth century the Latin Christians, including those in Kulin's banate, fell under the jurisdiction of the archbishop of Ragusa. They had one bishop, known as the bishop of Bosnia, who was selected locally and sent to Ragusa to be consecrated. Although the Latin Christians were affiliated to Rome they continued to celebrate the liturgy in the Slavonic language even after its use had been condemned by the synod in Split in 1060. Moreover, in 1192 when Béla III persuaded the pope to place the Latin Christians of Bosnia under Split's jurisdiction, they ignored the pope's directive and retained their ecclesiastical association with Ragusa. In 1199 Vukan of Zeta denounced Kulin to the pope as a heretic. He also claimed that Kulin was harbouring Bogomils from Dalmatia and that some 10,000 Bosnians professed the heretical faith. Vukan's accusations were reiterated by the archbishop of Split and the king of Hungary. Believing the accusations to be true, the pope called upon Hungary to lead a crusade against the alleged Bosnian heretic. Kulin, professing to be a faithful Christian, countered the threat of war with Hungary by summoning a church council. In 1203 the Bosnians renounced a series of errors in practice, promised to reform their church and reaffirmed their loyalty to the pope. The pledges, plus the presence of an official church representative, even though he was from Ragusa rather than from Split, assuaged the pope's concerns. By giving lip-service to his allegiance to Hungary, Kulin also defused the threat of war. What is more, he secured his church's continued affiliation with Ragusa and continued Bosnian commercial relations with Ragusan merchants. He evidently died in the following year, but despite his assurances to the pope, the alleged heresy flourished after his death.

In summary, we have seen that during the eleventh and twelfth centuries the Croats were never unified under a strong central government. They lived in different areas – Pannonian Croatia, Dalmatian Croatia, Bosnia – which were at times ruled by indigenous kings but more frequently controlled by agents of Byzantium, Venice and Hungary. Even during periods of relatively strong centralized government, local lords frequently enjoyed an almost autonomous status.

CHAPTER 10

POLAND IN THE ELEVENTH AND TWELFTH CENTURIES

Jerzy Wyrozumski

BY the eleventh century the formation of a strong monarchy on the compact territory of the Odra and the Vistula river-basins, extending south as far as the Sudetes and the Carpathian Mountains, and north as far as the Baltic Sea, had been completed; the process of Christianization was well advanced, and Poland could already boast her own saint in the person of Bishop Wojciech (Adalbert) of Prague, who had been exiled from Bohemia; the Polish rulers had established good relations with the western empire and had developed contacts with distinguished personages of the time. In the year 1000 the emperor Otto III arrived in Poland to elevate Gniezno (Gnesen) to the level of archbishopric, thus creating the first Polish ecclesiastical province, to which the apostolic see had given its consent earlier. The ruler of Poland, Prince Boleslaw Chrobry (Boleslaw the Brave) of the Piast dynasty, managed to win Otto's trust by supporting his project of the 'revival of the Roman empire' and was called 'an aide' (*cooperator*) of the empire, in which, it seems, he stood a good chance of representing one of its four basic territorial parts (*Roma, Galia, Germania, Sclavinia*). But the death of Otto III in 1002 and the changes in German policy under Henry II on the one hand and Boleslaw's expansive plans towards Milsko (Milzi), Łużyce (Lusatia) and Bohemia on the other led to a long Polish–German war, which was fought in three stages (1003–5, 1007–13, 1015–17) and ended with a peace treaty in Budziszyn (Bautzen) in 1018.

Apart from seizing the Bohemian throne for a short time in the years 1003–4, Boleslaw the Brave aimed at a partial subordination of Kiev Ruthenia. First he wanted to secure his own influence in the region; then he helped his son-in-law Prince Svatopolk to remain in power against the prince's brother, Jaroslav the Wise. His two expeditions to Ruthenia (1013 and 1018) and a secret diplomatic mission of Bishop Reinbern of Pomerania brought only the reoccupation of the castle-towns of Czerwien, which had been lost to Ruthenia in 981. The final success of his reign, however, was his coronation in 1025. In the same year he died, leaving three sons: Bezprym, Mieszko and Otto. He designated

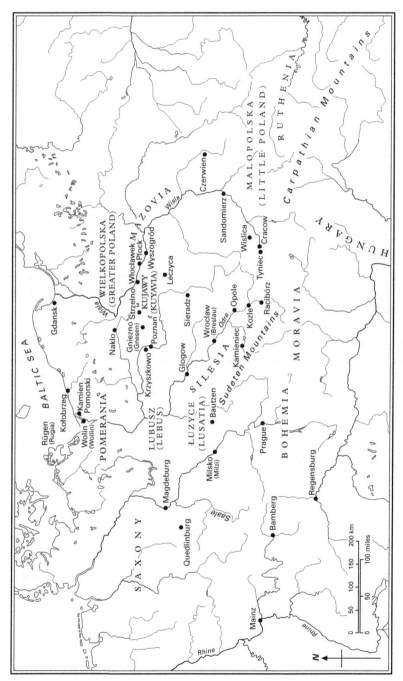

Map 7 Poland

Mieszko, who was to become the second Piast ruler of the name, to be his heir. Mieszko had been educated and introduced in the affairs of the state under his father's supervision. Married to Richeza, niece of Otto III, he tried to continue Boleslaw's work. At the same time entangled in his wife's political and family connections, however, Mieszko II became engaged in the dispute over the German throne between Conrad II of the Salian dynasty and his nephew Conrad the Younger. He supported the latter, as is testified by a letter from Mathilda, mother of Conrad the Younger, sent to Mieszko together with a gift of the book *Ordo Romanus*. Mieszko's two expeditions to Germany aimed towards the Saale (1028 and 1031) may have been intended as diversionary raids in aid of Conrad the Younger, while an expedition of Conrad II against Poland did not succeed.

The newly formed Piast state was racked by a political disaster in 1031. This was due to the simultaneous incursions by Conrad II in the west and by Jaroslav the Wise in the east, to the claims of Mieszko's brothers to the Polish throne and to the fact that his wife left him taking both his and her royal crowns to Germany. Mieszko sought refuge with the unfriendly Bohemian ruler Udalric. According to unreliable tradition, he was supposedly castrated by the Czechs. In the course of these events Poland lost Milsko and Łużyce to Germany, Czerwien to Ruthenia, and Moravia to Bohemia. Pomerania was the last province to win independence from the Piast state. Bezprym, Mieszko's brother, took over the throne, but was soon assassinated, and on his return to Poland, Mieszko had to accept the emperor's suzerainty; Conrad II divided Poland among Mieszko, Otto, his younger brother and Dytryk, their relative. Soon afterwards Otto was also assassinated. Mieszko succeeded in reuniting the state for a short time. In 1034 he was murdered as well and the state fell into chaos caused by a popular rebellion against oppression and heathen uprising. At this time Mieclaw, a lord who did not belong to the dynasty, may have usurped ducal power over Mazovia.

The course of events after Mieszko's death and their chronology remain so obscure that they could not be properly identified by medieval chroniclers and annalists. It is a matter of controversy whether Mieszko had one son, the well-documented Kazimierz (Casimir), or whether he had another son Boleslaw, either older or younger.

Among all these obscurities it seems most likely that Kazimierz took over the power immediately after his father's death but a rebellion of the nobles forced him to flee the country. He went to Hungary, and then to Germany, where he was not only granted a fief but also won knightly fame. Meanwhile Bretislav I, duke of Bohemia, raided the country torn by internal conflicts (1038 or 1039). He carried off from Gniezno the relics of St Wojciech (Adalbert), of Radzim-Gaudenty, his brother and the first archbishop of Poland, and of the Five Martyr

Brothers together with many valuables. He seized prisoners, pillaged and looted the country and annexed Silesia to Bohemia. Soon afterwards Kazimierz, supported by a party of German knights, returned to a devastated country. Basing himself on Cracow, which had apparently been least affected by the recent events, he undertook the reconstruction of the state. This was already acknowledged by his contemporaries, who called him the Restorer (Odnowiciel).

The territory of the Polish state, the ecclesiastical organization and the military power-base needed reconstruction. His marriage to Dobronega, sister of Jaroslav the Wise of Rus', secured Kazimierz Ruthenia's help in the struggle for Mazovia, which lasted for several years. He ultimately defeated Mieclaw in 1047. He may have restored Polish suzerainty over Pomerania, although that did not last. In 1050 he annexed Silesia, which Henry III had already recognized as a Bohemian province. In 1054 at a meeting in Quedlinburg, Kazimierz had to accept the conditions of imperial overlordship over Silesia and to pledge to pay a considerable tribute to Bohemia. He reconstructed the ecclesiastical organization thanks to the substantial aid of the Benedictines, one of whom named Aaron, who had most likely been consecrated bishop in Cologne (Koln), acquired metropolitan power in Poland as an archbishop with his see in Cracow. The Benedictines based, as it seems, first in Cracow, after Kazimierz's death found their lasting home in Tyniec near Cracow. In rebuilding the military basis of the state, Kazimierz probably abandoned the outdated idea of *druzyna*, or the princely 'bodyguard', and systematically created a warrior class holding land in return for service. The financial system did not undergo any essential changes; it consisted of the system of autarchical princely estates, where ancillary settlements fulfilled numerous productive and service functions, often with a high degree of specialization.

There is no indication that Kazimierz Odnowiciel tried to obtain a royal crown. He died in 1058, leaving three sons: Boleslaw, Wladyslaw Herman and Mieszko. The eldest, Boleslaw called the Munificent or the Bold (Szczodry), took over the power after his father's death, although he may, at least originally, have shared it with his brothers. Mieszko died in 1065; Wladyslaw Herman's strong links with Mazovia seem to indicate that this province was his domain, though certainly under his elder brother's suzerainty.

Boleslaw Szczodry's reign lasted for twenty-four years. It was marked by very active Polish policy against the empire and its vassal Bohemia, in spite of the fact that Boleslaw's sister was married to the Czech Prince Vratislav. Boleslaw took a bold step of ceasing to pay tribute for Silesia. In 1068 this led to an open military conflict with Bohemia, which lasted for several years.

In the great political dispute which divided the Latin world at the time into the supporters of Pope Gregory VII and King Henry IV of Germany, Boleslaw Szczodry joined the Gregorian party and played a considerable role in it. He supported the Saxons in their rebellion against the king and he created a diversion against the Czech Prince Vratislav, who belonged to Henry IV's followers. He also actively participated in the struggle over the Hungarian throne, which was a reflection of this great European conflict. He opposed Solomon, who was a supporter of the German party, and effectively backed his rivals: Béla in 1060 and Géza in 1074; and he helped enthrone Géza's son, Vladislav, in 1077. He fervently advocated Ruthenia's rapprochement with the western church, which was initiated by the Russian Prince Izyaslav, related to the Piasts through his wife Gertrude (Boleslaw's aunt). He introduced the Gregorian ecclesiastical reforms in Poland, strengthening the organization of the Polish church.

Boleslaw Szczodry's support for the Gregorian party resulted in him being granted a royal crown by the apostolic see, a title which was not to be achieved by any Polish ruler for the next 220 years. None the less, he did not manage to avoid internal conflicts in his realm, as Henry IV's camp was bound to have some supporters there. Boleslaw's brother, Wladyslaw Herman, was likely to be one of them, at least in the later stage of this ecclesiastical and political dispute, as he married Vratislav's daughter, Judith, in *c.* 1080 and then in 1089 a sister of Henry IV himself, Judith Maria. The king's dispute with Bishop Stanislaw of Cracow overlapped with the obvious tensions reflecting the divisions of contemporary Europe. Its background was left obscure by a chronicler close to the times of Boleslaw; 100 years later a biased tradition attributed the conflict to the king's cruelty and the bishop's attempts at appeasing it. Whatever the case, Bishop Stanislaw was sentenced to death by dismemberment and executed. The archbishop of Gniezno at the time may have participated in the trial. According to the above mentioned tradition, the bishop was supposedly murdered at the altar by the king himself. Such circumstances of death imposed on it the features of martyrdom, important for the canonization of Bishop Stanislaw, which was achieved in 1253.

If Boleslaw Szczodry had opponents as the proponent of the Gregorian reforms and Gregorian political line, the severe punishment of the bishop of Cracow, who must have had numerous family and political connections, was bound to cause further opposition. It may have been the direct cause of the rebellion against the king, which broke out in 1079 and forced him promptly to leave the country with his family. He died in exile in unexplained circumstances, and his son Mieszko, treacherously persuaded to return, was murdered.

Meanwhile Boleslaw Szczodry's brother, Wladyslaw Herman, took over the power in Poland. He was never to be so politically active as Boleslaw, although his marriages seem to have opened various chances of political manoeuvres to him. The revindication of Pomerania was the only concern in his external policy, and he undertook some military steps in this direction. The internal policy was controlled by his palatine Sieciech, who, according to an almost contemporary chronicler, more closely collaborated with Judith Maria, Wladyslaw Herman's wife, than with the king himself. His contemporaries accused him of the merciless policy towards his opponents, who sought refuge in exile, mainly in Bohemia, or were banished from the country. In this situation the conflict within the very family of Wladyslaw Herman acquired a special significance.

Wladyslaw Herman had a son Zbigniew from his obscure first marriage. When he married Judith of Bohemia and his son Boleslaw called the Wrymouthed (Krzywousty) was born, Zbigniew was put in wardship and then promptly sent abroad. It was a common practice aimed at securing the throne for the son from the new, more prestigious marriage. Sieciech's political opponets, however, took advantage of these circumstances. Zbigniew had become for them a convenient pretender and they offered him their support. A bloody contest for power followed, lasting from 1093 to 1099, as a result of which Sieciech had to leave the political stage and the country was divided among the father and his two sons. Wladyslaw Herman retained Mazovia, his favourite province, and held suzerainty over his sons; he made Plock his capital. His elder son, Zbigniew, received the province of Wielkopolska (Greater Poland) with Poznan and Gniezno, and possibly Kujawy (Kuyavia) as well. The younger son, Boleslaw, received all of the south (Malopolska – Little Poland – and Silesia), apart from the main castle-towns, such as Cracow, Wroclaw (Breslau) and Sandomierz.

After Wladyslaw's death in 1102, Mazovia went to Zbigniew, whereas the three castle-towns so far excluded from Boleslaw's power fell to him. Until 1106 the Polish territory had actually been divided into two duchies, probably independent from each other. Yet the two rulers' interests were soon to clash. According to the contemporary tradition connected with the court of Boleslaw Krzywousty, Zbigniew, who maintained peaceful relations with Pomerania, prevented Boleslaw from carrying out their father's plans of the revindication of Pomerania for Poland. He also tried to normalize the relations with Bohemia, while Boleslaw, whose territory directly bordered with the Czechs, was subject to enmity on their part. The imputations against Zbigniew were certainly not groundless, yet the main source of the original conflict between the brothers lay in their different temperaments, aspirations and political visions. The peacefully inclined Zbigniew and the bellicose Boleslaw were bound to clash, especially as the latter appealed to the emerging warrior class attracted by the legends of Pomeranian wealth.

In 1106 Boleslaw Krzywousty attacked his brother's territory, drove him out of Wielkopolska and allowed him to stay only in Mazovia 'as a knight, not as a prince'. Yet already in the following year Zbigniew was removed from Mazovia and had to leave Poland. He found support with King Henry V of Germany, who started a military expedition against Poland in 1109. Yet Boleslaw Krzywousty's military skills, his skilful appealing to patriotic moods, together with his alliance with Ruthenia, based on his marriage with Zbyslawa, daughter of the prince of Kiev, and a temporary alliance with Hungary, which involved a diversionary raid on Bohemia, provided Poland with support. The determined defence of Glogow, the serious defeat of the German troops in the battle of Psie Pole near Wroclaw and the defiant attitude of Boleslaw, who would not give up under Henry V's threat of marching toward Cracow, the capital at the time, contributed to the failure of the expedition. Three years later Boleslaw allowed his brother to return, but, on the pretext of his arrival having been too ostentatious, had him blinded, thus causing his death.

Despite Boleslaw's family ties through his mother with the Czech dynasty of Przemyslids, his relations with Bohemia were tense. This was due to the Czech attempts to win control over the Silesian frontier castle-towns (Racibórz, Kozle, Kamieniec), to Bohemia's continuing vassal dependence on Germany, with which Boleslaw was at war, and finally to Boleslaw's attempt to interfere in the disputes over the Bohemian throne. These conflicts ceased in 1114 and the peace treaty with Bohemia was made in 1137.

The question of Pomerania took priority in Boleslaw Krzywousty's policy. By 1106 he had already led several plundering raids into this province, which Zbigniew must have been trying to hinder. After Zbigniew's banishment, he launched the plan of the conquest of Pomerania. In 1113 he won definite control of the frontier castle-towns, Naklo and Wyszogrod; by 1119 he had subjugated Gdansk-Pomerania (Pommerellen), and he then conquered western Pomerania, reaching Rügen (Rugia) in 1123. In 1121 he imposed feudal overlordship over Prince Warcislaw of western Pomerania; in 1124 he eased the rigorous conditions of this suzerainty. Boleslaw Krzywousty's undeniable success was the second Christianization of Pomerania. The earlier attempts by Poland in the late tenth century had no lasting effect, and the bishopric of Kolobrzeg (Kolberg), founded in the year 1000, disappeared. The missionary efforts of the hermit Bernard the Spaniard in 1123 did not succeed. The next attempt was made under Boleslaw's auspices by Bishop Otto of Bamberg. His success encouraged him to form a new missionary expedition, which he led on his own behalf in 1128. The posthumous achievement of Boleslaw Krzywousty was the fact that his chaplain Wojciech (Adalbert) was to become the first bishop of the newly founded bishopric in Wolin, which was moved to Kamien Pomorski in the second half of the twelfth century. The establishment of the bishopric of Lubusz (Lebus), bordering on western Pomerania, in the 1120s and the establishment or perhaps reestablishment of the bishopric of Wtoctawek, neighbouring Gdansk-Pomerania, were likely to be linked to this plan of Christianization. All these bishoprics were subordinate to the archbishopric of Gniezno.

Boleslaw achieved another success in the area of ecclesiastical organization, essential for the integrity of the state. It was during his reign that Norbert of Xanten (later to be canonized), who was archbishop of Magdeburg, again put forward Magdeburg's claims to the Polish ecclesistical province. The archbishopric of Magdeburg had been established in the time of Otto I (968) in order to convert the Slavs across the German border. The plan did not originally succeed since Poland under the rule of Mieszko I had managed to anticipate it and to embrace Christianity (966) through the mediation of the Bohemian court, from the bishopric of Regensburg and the archbishopric of Salzburg. The skilful use made by Boleslaw Chrobry (the Brave) of the death of Bishop Wojciech of Prague on his mission to Prussia (997) and his canonization by the apostolic see combined with this ruler's good relations with Otto III resulted in Poland being granted its own archbishopric with a see in Gniezno, as mentioned above. Magdeburg tried to impose its supremacy at least over the bishopric of Poznan (Pozen). It actually resorted to forging some documents. Eventually in 1131 and in 1133, respectively, St Norbert managed to obtain two papal edicts of Innocent II, subjugating the Polish ecclesiastical province to Magdeburg. By the skilful withdrawal of his support for the pretender to the Hungarian throne, who was opposing German political interests, Boleslaw Krzywousty won the support of Emperor Lothar, who had good relations with the apostolic see, and thanks to his help managed to achieve Innocent II's withdrawal of the papal edicts.

Boleslaw Krzywousty died in 1138. He left five sons: Wladyslaw from his marriage with Princess Zbyslawa of Russia; Boleslaw called Kedzierzawy (the Curly), Mieszko called the Old (Stary), Henryk and Kazimierz later named the Just (Sprawiedliwy) from his marriage with the German princess Salomea. Wishing to provide each of them with an appropriate appanage and at the same time to ensure the unity of the state, he designed with the help of his advisers a hereditary statute, often associated with the beginning of political fragmentation of Poland, which was to prevail till the early fourteenth century. Boleslaw Krzywousty's hereditary statute has not been preserved and we have to reconstruct its contents on the basis of the later tradition and allusions to it in foreign sources. Yet it is so significant both in its consequences and its Slavonic relevance that one has to aim at its reconstruction. It has been the subject of many conflicting interpretations.

This statute, erroneously called testament, had the character of a public act and was pledged to by the nobles at an assembly; it may also have been sanctioned by the apostolic see. It was probably written in *c.* 1133 when only one of Boleslaw Krzywousty's sons had come of age, two were minors, one might have been an infant and one was not yet born. Hence they could not have been treated in exactly the same way. The statute provided for the supreme rule of the grand duke (principate), which, according to the principle of seniority, was to pass to the eldest of the Piast dynasty. Younger princes were to hold their own appanages and owe allegiance to the senior prince, who was to possess the highest attributes of public power over the entire Polish territory. The territorial basis for the power of the grand duke consisted of the province of Cracow as well as the dependent Gdansk-Pomerania and of suzerainty over western Pomerania and several castle-towns on the route from Cracow to Pomerania, especially Gniezno, the see of archbishop, who was appointed by the ruler in Poland at the time. The dominion of the grand duke was not hereditary and was not meant to be divided but to be ruled by the senior prince of the dynasty. After Boleslaw Krzywousty's death (1138), each of his adult sons received his own hereditary duchy; the eldest son Wladyslaw Silesia, Boleslaw Kedzierzawy (the Curly) Mazovia and Mieszko Stary (the Old) Wielkopolska, possibly with a part of Kujawy. By the introduction of certain revisions into the original statute, Henryk received the area of Sandomierz, extracted from the province of Cracow, but only for life. It implied that in case of his death it was to return to the dominion of Cracow. Boleslaw's youngest son, Kazimierz, did not receive his own appanage because on his father's death he was only an infant or might even have been born posthumously. Hence he remained under his mother's care, who received as her widow's portion a substantial province in central Poland with the main castle-towns of Leczyca and Sieradz, extracted from the dominion of the grand duke.

The hereditary order broke down quite soon after Boleslaw Krzywousty's death as a result of a family dispute between the senior prince Wladyslaw, born of a Russian mother, and his junior stepbrothers, born of a German mother. Wladyslaw's wife, Agnes of the Austrian house of Babenberg, was not popular. The conflict, which was imminent already in 1141, led to a civil war and to the banishment of Boleslaw Krzywousty's eldest son in 1146. Yet neither the principle of seniority nor the 'principate' associated with it was abolished, which guaranteed Polish political unity. The power of the grand duke was taken over by Boleslaw Kedzierzawy, the next son of Krzywousty according to the seniority principle. The junior princes' position was strengthened by the support of the archbishop of Gniezno, the head of the Polish church. Emperor Conrad III supported the exiled Wladyslaw and actually organized an expedition to Poland, but on receiving a promise of allegiance on the part of the victorious Polish princes, he turned back from the Odra (1146). The international situation at the moment was clearly auspicious for the junior princes. It involved preparations for a crusade to the Holy Land and simultaneous plans for a crusade against the European pagans, Obodrits and Prussians, resisting Christianization. The

Polish princes supported these plans. In 1147 Mieszko took part in a Saxon expedition against the Obodrits and Boleslaw Kedzierzawy, together with the Russian princes, participated in an expedition against the Prussians. But the political consequence was that Poland ultimately lost her influence in western Pomerania.

Soon, with the changing situation in Europe, the apostolic see supported the claims of the exiled Prince Wladyslaw. The papal legate Guido on his arrival in Poland pronounced the excommunication on the junior princes, and cast an interdict on the country. He called upon the secular power, the empire, to enforce Wladyslaw's rights, and, with papal support, Emperor Frederick Barbarossa launched a campaign against Poland, reaching Poznan; at Krzyszkowo he received from Boleslaw Kedzierzawy a pledge of fealty and a promise to restore his exiled brother Wladyslaw.

Boleslaw Kedzierzawy did not fulfil the conditions, and Wladyslaw called the Exile (Wygnaniec) died in 1159. The question of the restoration of his three sons emerged. In 1163 they were received by Boleslaw, this time at the emperor's request, and established in Silesia, which they had inherited from their father. Probably they ruled this province jointly. In 1166 Boleslaw Krzywousty's son Henryk, who held the province of Sandomierz for life, died without an heir. The province was divided among the three remaining sons of Boleslaw Krzywousty. The eldest son Boleslaw Kedzierzawy, who was the grand duke, incorporated the largest part of his brother's dominion into the duchy of Cracow, which was the basis of his power; the younger son Mieszko, duke of Wielkopolska, seized an unidentified fragment, and the youngest, Kazimierz, a single castellany (Wislica).

Grand Duke Boleslaw Kedzierzawy died in 1173. The Cracow power elite tried to replace him with Kazimierz, neglecting Mieszko, the eldest of the dynasty, and undeniably trying to break the principle of seniority established by Boleslaw Krzywousty's statute. Mieszko managed to control the situation and to get hold of Cracow. Distrusting the inhabitants, however, he brought with him his own officials. This was to become a source of trouble.

In c. 1177 the whole country was shaken by the rebellion of the younger sons. Boleslaw Krzywousty's youngest son Kazimierz took arms against his brother and Grand Duke Mieszko Stary, the Silesian junior prince Mieszko Platonogi against his elder brother Boleslaw Wysoki, and Mieszko Stary's son Odon, based in Wielkopolska, against his own father. Kazimierz entered an alliance with the Silesian senior prince and together they found an ally in Odon. Grand Duke Mieszko had to leave Poland and returned only after several years. Kazimierz took over the power of grand duke. In order to win over the Silesian junior prince, he gave him the western part of the province of Cracow. His brother gave him the castellany of Raciborz, and in this way a new duchy emerged, to which in 1201 Opole was added. Its ruler, Mieszko Platonogi, started a new line of the Piasts (of Opole and Raciborz). Boleslaw Wysoki began the line of the Silesian Paists. The fate of Konrad, the third son of Wladyslaw the Exile, remains obscure. He may have ruled over Glogow for a short time.

In 1180 Kazimierz named the Just (Sprawiedliwy) called a general meeting in Leczyca (central Poland). It is known that it was attended at least by all the bishops including the archbishop of Gniezno. The meeting recognized Kazimierz as the grand duke. The recognition by the papacy followed; Kazimierz may also have been recognized by the emperor Frederick Barbarossa. It would have implied that Kazimierz at least formally accepted the emperor's suzerainty. Thus the principle of seniority was broken, but the 'principate' was preserved. When Mieszko Stary returned in 1181, he had to accept the new *status quo*. In the 1990s he attempted to regain the throne three times. He managed to recapture it briefly in 1191 when the lords of Cracow rebelled against Kazimierz because of his acquiescence towards the empire. Yet after Kazimierz's death in 1194, when Mieszko arrived in Cracow, he was severely defeated in the military confrontation with the grand-ducal power elite. In *c.* 1197 he managed to win control over Cracow in collaboration with Kazimierz Sprawiedliwy's widow, Helena, who together with the palatine and the bishop of Cracow held the regency over the province during the minority of her sons, Leszek and Konrad. However, he was again expelled, to return again shortly before his death in 1202.

Although a fierce supporter of the principles of his father's hereditary statute, Mieszko Stary contributed to its abolition. When he returned to Cracow in *c.* 1197, he pledged to make Leszek, Kazimierz Sprawiedliwy's son, still a minor at the time, his successor. Thus he agreed to the abolition of the 'seniorate' and to the actual transformation of unihereditable grand-ducal dominion into a hereditary province of Kazimierz Sprawiedliwy's line. It resulted in the legal disintegration of the unity of Poland, actually already fragmented, which entered the next century as a group of independent Piast principalities. There remained a sense of dynastical bond among the 'natural lords' of Poland as the Piasts viewed themselves and were recognized to be, as well as the common tradition of 'the Poland of the Boleslaws' (Boleslaw Chrobry, Boleslaw Szczodry and Boleslaw Krzywousty) and a common ecclesiastical organization.

Summing up this epoch politically, one has to note a fact with lasting implications for Poland, the subjugation of western Pomerania first by the Henry the Lion in 1164, and then in 1181 by Frederick Barbarossa. Another political factor with long-term consequences was Kazimierz Sprawiedliwy's influence over Halicz and Vladimir Ruthenia, which gradually strengthened and led to the incorporation of this part of Ruthenia to Poland in the fourteenth century.

In spite of the unfavourable political developments after Boleslaw Krzywousty's death in 1138, the country developed properly both economically and culturally. The system of closed economy based on productive and various services within the princely estate was extended by a new form of settlement of the lease-holding type; there appeared foreign settlers: Walloons, Flemings and soon also Germans, though mainly in the west of Poland. The existence of numerous trade settlements, confirmed by various sources, testifies to the growth of exchange. The role of money increased, and during the reign of Mieszko Stary (the Old) his mint issued numerous coins with Hebrew inscriptions.

After a short period under the influence of the Carolingian-Ottonian style, Romanesque architecture developed, which required a new art of working stone. The works of art were products of collaboration between foreign masters and local artisans. Among these are the bronze doors of Gniezno Cathedral from the second half of the twelfth century, which depict the life and martyrdom of St Wojciech (Adalbert). Similar doors made in Magdeburg for the cathedral of Plock unfortunately never reached their destination, but decorated the church of St Sophia in Great Novgorod in Ruthenia, where they found their way via Sweden. The magnificent floor of the collegiate church in Wislica, depicting three praying figures; the tympana of St Mary's church in Wroclaw (na Piasku), the collegiate church in Tuma near Leczyca and the church of the Norbertine nuns in Strzelno; and the beautifully sculptured columns of the same church, prove that Poland was assimilating western European artistic styles rapidly in this period.

It is also noteworthy that writing became widespread at the time. At the time of Boleslaw Chrobry at least two lives of St Wojciech (Adalbert) were written as well as the life of the Five Martyr Brothers by Bruno of Querfurt; annals were also kept. These were all written by foreigners. But already in the eleventh century Mieszko II's daughter and Kazimierz Odnowieciel's sister, Gertrude, wrote a series of prayers, some of them highly personal. In the early twelfth century an anonymous visitor from western Europe wrote the first chronicle of Poland, recording for the future generations the deeds of Boleslaw Krzywousty and the tradition of his court. In the mid-twelfth century another visitor named Maurus described in rhyme the deeds of Piotr Wlostowic, magnate and first lord of the state during the reign of that prince, and of his son Wladyslaw. According to an inventory from 1110, the cathedral of Cracow possessed quite a considerable library. Liturgical books were to be found in the possession of other cathedrals. Documents were becoming more common, though mostly charters of endowment for the church. In the second half of the twelfth century, and perhaps even earlier, travelling for study abroad began. Educated at one of the oldest universities, Wincenty Kadlubek, the chancellor to Kazimierz Sprawiedliwy, and later the bishop of Cracow, proved to be a talented and learned writer. In the thirteenth century he was to write a chronicle of Poland, which was a major work of literature.

CHAPTER II

SCANDINAVIA IN THE ELEVENTH
AND TWELFTH CENTURIES[1]

Peter Sawyer

IN the eleventh century the northern and central parts of the Scandinavian peninsula were occupied by a people who are often called Lapps but who called themselves Saami. They were ethnically distinct from the Scandinavians who lived in the coastal regions and southern part of the peninsula and in Denmark, but centuries of contact and intermarriage had resulted in some assimilation of these two peoples. The Saami, who spoke a form of Finnish, supported themselves mainly by hunting, trapping and fishing. Despite their isolation many Saami were forced to render part of their catch, in particular furs, to their Scandinavian neighbours. The Scandinavians spoke various dialects of a common Germanic language known as Old Nordic. At the beginning of the eleventh century they were predominantly pastoral farmers but 200 years later there had been a huge extension of arable cultivation at the expense of woodland and pasture in many parts of Scandinavia.

Contemporaries distinguished four main groups of Scandinavians: Danes, *Götar*, *Svear* and Norwegians or Northmen (a name that foreigners sometimes used to describe all Scandinavians). These collective names were used for the inhabitants of distinct regions. The Danes occupied Jutland and the neighbouring islands but their territory was considered to include areas that they had long dominated in what is now the west coast and southern part of Sweden. The *Götar* (Old Norse *Gauti*, Latin *Gothi*) occupied the plains of central southern Sweden, separated from Danish territory by forest. Lake Vättern divided the east from the west *Götar* (Modern Swedish *Östgötar*, *Västgötar*) after whom the medieval provinces of Östergötland and Västergötland were named.

---

[1]The most recent general accounts of medieval Scandinavian history are Helle (2003) Sawyer and Sawyer (1993 and 2002). The exhibition catalogue Roesdahl and Wilson (1992) covers most aspects of Scandinavian history in this period; the book also has an up-to-date bibliography. For more detailed discussions see: for Denmark, Sawyer (2002) and Fenger (2002); for Iceland, Thorsteinsson (1985) and Byock (1988); for Norway, Andersen (1977), Helle (1974) and Krag (2000) for Sweden, Sawyer (1991a).

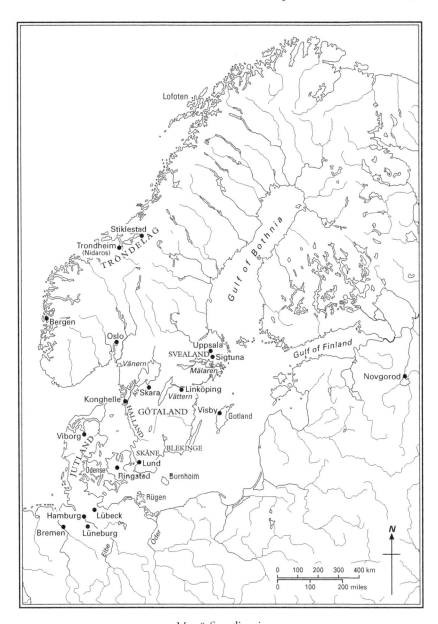

Map 8 Scandinavia

Another, wider, belt of forest lay between the *Götar* and the *Svear* (Old Norse *Sviar*, Latin *Suiones*, *Sueones*) who lived in the region around Lake Mälaren and along the east coast of Sweden. The Norwegians were named after the 'North Way', the Atlantic coast of the Scandinavian peninsula, but the name was also used for people living along the extension of the coast as far as Oslo Fjord, and for those living in the valleys of rivers that flow into that fjord. Extensive forest separated the Norwegians from both the *Götar* and the *Svear*.

By the year 1200 most of the territory occupied by these Scandinavians had been incorporated in the three medieval kingdoms. The Danish kingdom was the first to be firmly established. At the beginning of the eleventh century Sven Forkbeard, who had succeeded his father, Harald Bluetooth, as king of the Danes in 987 after a rebellion, ruled a large territory from Jutland to Skåne. The medieval Danish kingdom at its fullest extent was not much larger; the only additions, made by 1150 at the latest, were Halland, Blekinge and the island of Bornholm. Sven was also widely acknowledged as overlord in other parts of Scandinavia.

There had been attempts to create a Norwegian kingdom based on the west coast but these had failed and in the first decade of the eleventh century Norway was under Danish overlordship. It was in the eleventh century that the Norwegian kingdom was firmly established and by 1100 it extended from Lofoten in the north to the estuary of Göta Älv. Norwegian kings then had authority in many inland areas of Norway but the territorial consolidation of the kingdom was not complete until the early thirteenth century.

The Swedish kingdom was formed by the unification of the *Götar* and the *Svear*. This was a slow process. The first ruler to be called *rex Sweorum et Gothorum* was Karl Sverkersson – he was entitled thus in the papal bull creating the archbishopric of Uppsala in 1164 – but the first Swedish king who is known to have granted land and privileges in most parts of the kingdom, and who struck coins in both Götaland and Svealand, was Knut Eriksson, who died in 1195 or 1196 after a reign of a little more than three decades. There is no reliable evidence that there was ever a kingdom of the *Götar* before the twelfth century, but the *Svea*-kingship is well attested as an ancient institution, closely linked with the pagan rituals celebrated at Uppsala, a famous cult centre north of Mälaren. During the eleventh and twelfth centuries several kings of the *Svear*, including Karl Sverkersson and Knut Eriksson, were *Götar*. The *Svear* seem to have been willing to accept outsiders rather than promote one of themselves. The willingness of the *Svear* to accept kings who were *Götar* was a key factor in forming the medieval kingdom. The process of unification was, however, hindered by the physical barrier of forest dividing the two peoples and by religious disunity; pagan rituals continued to be publicly celebrated at Uppsala for most of the eleventh century.

The earliest Scandinavian historians, writing in the twelfth and thirteenth centuries, believed that the Danish kingdom had existed since time immemorial and that the kingdoms of Norway and Sweden were relatively recent creations formed by the unification of many small kingdoms. It is possible that there were some unrecorded petty kingdoms, but in the first decade of the eleventh century the only Scandinavian kingdoms mentioned in reliable sources were those of the Danes and the *Svear*. They were very different. The territory under the direct control of the Danish king and his agents had recently been greatly enlarged but many of his predecessors had, since the eighth century or earlier, dominated southern Scandinavia. The kingship of the *Svear* was, in contrast, predominantly cultic. Effective power was in the hands of the *Svea*-chieftains, whose wealth depended on their ability to exact tribute, in particular furs, from the peoples living round the Gulfs of Bothnia and Finland and in north Russia. Furs from these northern regions had for centuries been in demand in Europe, and during the ninth and tenth centuries in the Islamic world too. As they were of little value unless they could be sold, merchants had to be encouraged and the peace of markets assured. It appears that the *Svear* tried to achieve the stability they needed by acknowledging a king whose functions were supernatural rather than military.

The king of the *Svear* contemporary with Sven Forkbeard was Olof, who succeeded his father Erik in about 995. He was a Christian and was therefore unable to fulfil the traditional role of the *Svea*-king. He seems only to have had direct authority over the *Svear* living in the vicinity of Sigtuna, a royal centre founded in about 975, probably by Erik, as a base from which a new Christian form of kingship was gradually extended over the region.[2] Whatever success Erik and Olof had, their authority was much less than that of their Danish contemporaries. That is clearly shown by the progress of conversion in the two kingdoms. In Denmark Harald Bluetooth was converted and baptized in about 965, and by the end of the century the process of Christianization was well advanced; pagan rituals were no longer celebrated in public and pagan forms of burial had been abandoned. In contrast, although most of the eleventh-century *Svea*-kings and many of the *Svear* were Christian, the pagan rituals at Uppsala continued until about 1080. By 1060 when the diocesan organization of Denmark was complete, there was only one Swedish bishopric, in Västergötland. It owed its foundation to Olof who, despite being king, was unable to establish a bishopric in the Mälar region. The fact that he was able to do so in Västergötland is one of several indications that he was himself from that region.

In most parts of Scandinavia power was not in the hands of individuals ruling well-defined territories, but was shared between, and contested by, lords or

---

[2] Tesch (1990); Malmer, Ros and Tesch (1991).

chieftains each with his own band of men. That was the pattern of government
the Norwegian emigrants took to Iceland in the ninth century. Power in that
Scandinavian colony 200 years later was still divided between some three dozen
chieftains called *goðar* (singular *goði*), a title that also occurs on three tenth-
century runic inscriptions on the Danish island of Fyn. A *goði* was a lord
of men, not territory, and he exercised authority publicly together with other
goðar in assemblies or things, supported by his thingmen. The number of *goðar*
was gradually reduced by conquests or more peacefully by marriage alliances,
and this led to a territorialization of their power. By the thirteenth century a
district in which a *goði* claimed authority over everyone could be called a *ríki*.[3]
A similar process in Scandinavia may have produced small kingdoms that are
unmentioned in contemporary sources, but in some regions the older structure
with multiple lords survived until the thirteenth century, as it did in Iceland.

In Scandinavia, as in Iceland, the population was grouped in numerous local
communities that regulated their own affairs in regular assemblies that were
as much religious and social as legal and political occasions. Some communities, especially in inland regions, occupied territories that were well defined
by natural boundaries, forest being the most effective barrier, but in coastal
districts or in the relatively open landscapes of Denmark and central Sweden,
where most Scandinavians lived, local communities were not so isolated. Many
were, nevertheless, still largely independent in the early eleventh century, and
retained responsibility for their own affairs after they were incorporated in the
emergent kingdoms. Their assemblies, with some reorganization, were indeed
the main institutions through which royal government was extended in all
three Scandinavian kingdoms.

The assemblies were meetings of the freemen of the community, but in practice they tended to be dominated by the leading men. Competition between
such men led to some of them being recognized as overlords by those who were
less powerful, or lucky. In the late tenth century Håkon of Lade, now a suburb
of Trondheim, was said by a contemporary poet to have been the overlord of
sixteen 'jarls,' a term that was later interpreted as meaning a tributary ruler.[4]
Håkon was himself known as a 'jarl' for he had acknowledged the Danish king
Harald as his overlord.

The Danish overlordship of Norway was interrupted in 995 by Olav
Tryggvason, a Norwegian adventurer, whose attempt to revive an independent
Norwegian kingdom was initially successful, largely thanks to the elimination
of Jarl Håkon, but Olav's triumph was short-lived. In 999 he was defeated and
killed in battle against Sven Forkbeard who thus restored Danish hegemony

[3] Sigurðsson (1999).
[4] Einarr Helgason, *Vellekla*, str. 37; Jonsson (1912–15), I, Ap. 131, B p. 124.

over coastal Norway, with Håkon's sons, Erik and Sven, as his jarls. Sven Forkbeard was also acknowledged as lord by many leading *Götar* and by some *Svear*
too.

The success of the Danish kings Harald and Sven in extending Danish
hegemony in Scandinavia was not welcomed by all, and some men who were
unwilling to submit went into exile as Vikings. Successful Vikings could challenge Danish power, as Olav Tryggvason did. To meet that threat Sven himself
led raids on England to gather plunder and tribute with which he could reward
his supporters and the warriors on whom his power largely depended. Sven's
attacks on England culminated in his conquest of the kingdom in 1013. For
most of his reign Sven Forkbeard was the most powerful ruler in Scandinavia.
He had many advantages. He could not only draw on the resources of the
most fertile and densely populated region of Scandinavia, but also controlled
the entrance to the Baltic and could, therefore, profit from the flourishing trade
between the lands round that sea and western Europe. The Danes had long
benefited from this traffic but the extension of the Danish kingdom in the
latter part of the tenth century to span Öresund enabled Harald and Sven to
control it more effectively than their predecessors. This provoked opposition
and, significantly, the first information about relations between the Danes and
the *Svear* in the tenth century is the report that Erik, king of the *Svear*, formed
an alliance against the Danes with Mieszko, the Polish ruler, whose daughter he
married. Adam of Bremen, whose *Gesta Hammaburgensis Ecclesiae Pontificum*,
written in the 1070s, is the main source of information about Scandinavia at
that time, claimed that Sven was defeated and driven into a prolonged exile. That was a wild exaggeration. Whatever success the allies had, the tables
were soon turned, and Sven marked his triumph by marrying Erik's Polish
widow and then rejecting her after she had given birth to two sons, Harald and
Knut, and a daughter, Estrid. By the end of the century Erik's son Olof had
acknowledged Sven as his overlord, and supported him in battle against Olav
Tryggvason. Olof's subordination is reflected in his nickname *Skotkonungær*
(Mod. Swedish *Skötkonung*). This was first recorded in the thirteenth century
but it was probably given at an early date and meant, according to Snorri
Sturluson, 'tributary king', and was equated by him with 'jarl'.[5]

After Sven's death in February 1014 his empire disintegrated. His son Knut,
who had taken part in the English campaign, was elected king by the army,
but when the English refused to accept him Knut was forced to return to
Denmark. He apparently expected to be recognized as king by the Danes, for
he had some coin dies giving him that title made by English craftsmen.[6] The
Danes had, however, chosen Harald as their king. In 1015 Knut returned to

[5] Sawyer (1991b), pp. 27–40.   [6] Blackburn (1990).

England and by the end of 1016 he had reconquered it. It was, therefore, as king of the English that, after the death of his brother, he was elected king by the Danes, probably in 1019.

By then Olav Haraldsson, another Viking adventurer, had been recognized as king by the Norwegians, who once again rejected Danish authority. It was not until 1028, when he succeeded in driving Olav into exile, that Knut was able to make good his claim to have inherited the kingship of Norway from his father. He planned to revive the custom of ruling through a native jarl. Håkon, grandson of the jarl of Lade who had submitted to Harald Bluetooth, was the ideal choice but he was drowned in 1029. Olav Haraldsson seized the opportunity to return from exile in Russia but as he approached Trondheim Fjord overland from Svealand he was met by enemies and killed in battle at Stiklestad on 29 July 1030. Knut then made the mistake of attempting to impose his own son Sven as king of Norway under the tutelage of the boy's English mother, Ælfgifu. This was unpopular and the short period of Ælfgifu's rule was remembered as a time of harsh and unjust exactions. The Norwegians soon rebelled and expelled Sven and his mother, perhaps even before Knut died in 1035. Olav Haraldsson was soon and widely recognized as a martyr. His young son Magnus was brought from exile in Russia and acknowledged as king.

Sven's death also gave the *Svear* an opportunity to escape Danish overlordship. Olof *Skötkonung* demonstrated his independence in several ways. He arranged the marriage of one daughter to Knut's enemy Olav Haraldsson and of another to Jaroslav, prince of Kiev. These alliances were clearly directed against the Danes. It was as much in the interest of the Russians as of the *Svear* to undermine Danish control of the route from the Baltic to the markets of western Europe, and it was Jaroslav who gave refuge to Olav Haraldsson in 1028. Olof *Skötkonung* further defied Knut by inviting Unwan, archbishop of Hamburg-Bremen, to send a bishop to Sweden at a time Knut did not accept the archbishop's authority.

After Olof *Skötkonung*'s death in 1022 his son and successor, Anund, continued to be hostile to the Danes, and in 1026 he and Olav Haraldsson attacked Denmark but without success. Although these kings of the *Svear* refused to submit to Knut some *Svear* and *Götar* did recognize him as their overlord and Knut was therefore able to claim, in 1027, to be king of some of the *Svear* (*partes Suanorum*).[7]

Knut died in England in 1035 and was succeeded as king of the Danes by his son Harthaknut. There was an influential group in England, including his mother, Emma, who considered that he was Knut's lawful heir there too. Harthaknut was, however, unable to leave Denmark for fear of a Norwegian

[7] Sawyer (1989).

invasion and in his absence the faction that preferred Harald, Knut's other son by Ælfgifu, triumphed. It was only after Harald's death in 1040 that Harthaknut succeeded his father as king in England. After his death two years later the Norwegian king Magnus was recognized as king by the Danes; and there are some indications that this happened while Harthaknut was still alive. The English feared that Magnus would go further and attempt to emulate Knut by recreating a North Sea empire, but the expected attack on England did not happen. Magnus's hold on Denmark was challenged by Sven Estridsen who, after the death of Harthaknut was the oldest male representative of the Danish royal family. He was Knut's nephew, and had spent the last part of Knut's reign in Sweden as an exile. His father, Ulf, had fallen out of favour with Knut; according to some accounts he was killed on the king's orders. Sven's attempts to displace Magnus had little success; he only gained control of Skåne shortly before Magnus died in 1047. His name then began to appear on coins minted in Lund, but not as king, while Magnus continued to issue coins as king of the Danes in Odense and elsewhere in western Denmark.[8] It was only after the death of Magnus that Sven was accepted as king by the Danes.

For the last two years of his life Magnus shared the kingship of Norway with his father's half-brother Harald, known as *Hardrada* 'hard-ruler.' Harald had returned to Norway in 1045 after serving the Byzantine emperor for more than ten years in the Varangian Guard. After 1047 he was sole king in Norway. He too attempted to recreate a North Sea empire but he failed to dislodge Sven from Denmark and was himself killed at Stamford Bridge in 1066 when he attempted to conquer England. He was, however, successful in extending the Norwegian kingdom to include Bohuslän, and founded a new centre of royal power at Konghelle on Göta Älv, which then formed the boundary with the Danish kingdom.

By the end of the eleventh century it was the accepted rule in both Norway and Denmark that only members of the royal families could become kings. All Danish kings after Sven Estridsen were his descendants, and he himself was grandson of Sven Forkbeard. It has been claimed that the hereditary principle was accepted even earlier in Norway and that all Norwegian kings were descendants of Harald Fine-hair. That is, however, a fiction.[9] Harald's dynasty ended with the death of his grandson in about 970 and neither Olav Tryggvason nor Olav Haraldsson were his descendants. The founder of the medieval Norwegian dynasty was Harald Hardrada.

The limitation of kingship to members of the royal families did not eliminate the need to make a choice. This was normally done by the leading men, sometimes after a fight, but the successful claimant had to be recognized in public assemblies. Sometimes different assemblies chose different candidates

---

[8] Becker (1981).   [9] Krag (1989).

and there were numerous occasions when joint kings were chosen, either by agreement or in rivalry. There was no tradition of primogeniture; all the sons of a king had a claim to succeed. After the death of Sven Estridsen in 1074 some of his numerous sons thought they should rule jointly. That did not happen and five of them succeeded in turn. It was in the next generation that the succession was more violently disputed between the sons of the last two, Erik and Niels. For a short while there were three kings but the conflict ended in 1157 when Erik's grandson Valdemar emerged as victorious. He restored stability for a while and was succeeded in turn by his two legitimate sons, Knut (1182–1202) and Valdemar II (1202–41).

Norway was far more extensive than Denmark and had a much shorter tradition of unity. After Harald Hardrada the normal pattern was for the sons of the last king to rule jointly. They apparently did so in relative peace until the death of King Sigurd 'the Crusader' in 1130. Civil war then broke out and continued, with intervals, until 1208. In the 1160s the faction led by Erling Skakke gained the upper hand for a while. His wife was King Sigurd's daughter and their young son Magnus was elected king in 1161. Two years later an attempt was made to regulate the order of succession, but these rules were not respected and kings continued to be chosen by different assemblies for the next sixty years.

Magnus was opposed by several rivals who claimed to be the sons of previous kings but most were defeated by his father. The most serious challenger was Sverri who arrived in 1177 from the Faeroes claiming to be the son of a Norwegian King. He was soon recognized as king in Tröndelag and by 1184 he had defeated and killed both Erling and Magnus. Many Norwegians nevertheless would not recognize him as their king and Øystein, archbishop of Nidaros, refused to crown him. Instead Bishop Nicholas of Oslo did so in 1194, but shortly afterwards Nicholas joined and became one of the leaders of a newly formed opposition group. Conflict between the two factions continued after Sverri's death in 1202, and it was not until 1217 that Sverri's grandson Håkon was recognized as king throughout Norway.

Sweden was the last kingdom to be established and it was not until the latter part of the twelfth century that Swedish kings had to be members of a royal family. Before that the *Svear* elected, or recognized, several kings who were not of royal descent, including Sverker, who was king from about 1132 to his assassination in 1156, and his successor Erik who was killed in 1160. For 100 years all Swedish kings were descendants of these two men and both were *Götar*. Sverker was from Östergötland and Erik from Västergötland.

The linkage of the two peoples was powerfully reinforced in 1164 by the creation of the archiepiscopal province of Uppsala, which included the Götaland sees of Skara and Linköping as well as three in Svealand. Provincial councils summoned by the archbishop of Uppsala, or by papal legates, were the first national councils of Sweden. The same is true of Norway, where the archbishopric of Nidaros was established in 1152 or 1153. That province was the precursor of the Norwegian kingdom at its fullest extent for in addition to the five Norwegian sees it included the sees that had been established in Iceland, Greenland and other Norwegian colonies. It was, however, a century before Iceland and Greenland were incorporated in the kingdom.

The church contributed to the consolidation of the kingdoms in many other ways. The clergy were literate and were members of an international organization based on written law, with a relatively elaborate machinery to implement it. The role of kings as upholders of justice was emphasized by churchmen who also encouraged kings to act as law-makers, in the first place in the interest of the clergy and their churches.

In Norway special assemblies known as law-things were beginning to make or change law by the tenth century. Their early history is obscure but by the thirteenth century there were four. There were similar assemblies in other parts of Scandinavia. Some met in places such as Viborg or Odense that had been the sites of assemblies in pre-Christian times and later became episcopal sees. The creation of these law-making assemblies was an important stage in the formation of the kingdoms. The laws made in them were influenced by kings as well as churchmen, but kings ruled by consent and had to respect existing rights. There were, consequently, in each kingdom significant differences in the law of different provinces when written versions were produced between the twelfth and fourteenth centuries. It was not until the thirteenth century that Scandinavian kings began to issue law codes for their entire kingdoms.

The earliest of the provincial laws, for the west Norwegian province known as Gulating, survives in a twelfth-century version. It shows how magnates acted as royal agents, leading military levies, supporting stewards of royal estates, arresting wrong-doers and choosing representatives to attend the annual law-thing. It also has provisions designed to prevent such men abusing their authority by interfering in the legal process. Clergy, in particular bishops, were also important royal agents. Their influence is manifest in attempts to limit the number of potential claimants to succeed as king by excluding illegitimate sons. That doctrine was only accepted slowly – in Norway not until 1240s; and even then illegitimate sons were not completely excluded from the order of succession. Churchmen, as well as kings, favoured hereditary succession, but this was only made law in Norway. In Denmark and Sweden the magnates were powerful enough to retain the right to elect their kings on most occasions. Churchmen also attempted to strengthen the position of kings against the claims of potential rivals by the ceremony of coronation. There must always have been inauguration rituals but little is known about them before the twelfth century when ecclesiastical coronation, on the model developed in tenth-century Germany, was introduced. The first Scandinavian coronation was of Magnus Erlingsson in 1163 or 1164. His rival and successor, Sverri, attempted to secure his position by coronation but he and his supporters argued that he was king by God's grace which was bestowed directly, not mediated by the church. This view triumphed in Norway and was well expressed in the *King's Mirror*, a treatise on kingship written in the 1250s that reflects a political ideology that may be described as almost absolutist, with the king ruling by divine right as God's representative, chosen not by human electors but by inheritance. The first Danish coronation ceremony was in 1170 on the initiative of Valdemar I, whose attitude seems to have been very much the same as Sverri's. He had his eldest son designated and crowned in a ceremony at Ringsted. In Sweden, where the first recorded coronation was in 1210, the claims of rival dynasties made such ecclesiatical confirmation all the more valuable.

The interaction of the church and kingship was also displayed in the recognition of royal saints. By 1200 each kingdom had at least one. Olav Haraldsson in Nidaros; Sven Estridsen's son Knut, who was killed in Odense in 1086; Valdemar I's father, Knut Lavard, who was murdered by a rival in 1134, and whose sanctity was proclaimed during the coronation ceremony at Ringsted in 1170. In Sweden Erik, killed at Uppsala in 1160, was soon treated as a martyr, but his cult developed slowly.

Despite the efforts of kings and churchmen to ensure stability there were frequent and violent conflicts in most parts of Scandinavia during the eleventh and twelfth centuries. This was partly because kings were not rich or powerful enough to overawe or decisively defeat rivals and rebellious magnates. By the end of the eleventh century Scandinavian rulers could not realistically hope to gather wealth in Russia, the Byzantine empire or in England. They were forced to rely on their own resources, together with what they could gather as plunder or tribute from each other or from the peoples living round the Baltic. It is significant that the periods of stability coincided with the reigns of kings who were able to enlarge their kingdoms. Thus, Norway was relatively peaceful after the death of Harald Hardrada; his son and successor was indeed known as Olav *Kyrre* 'the peaceful'. This may have been in part due to the death of many magnates alongside Harald in England but another factor was the success of Harald and his successors in extending the kingdom. By the end of the century Norwegian kings could draw on the resources of the whole coast at least as far north as Lofoten, and in the south to Göta Älv. The Arctic region was particularly valuable for, as explained below, there was a growing demand in western Europe for its produce at that time. Similarly, Valdemar I and his son Knut owed much of their success in Denmark to their conquest of Slav territory. By 1169 Valdemar had conquered Rügen and in 1185 the prince of the Pomeranians submitted to Knut, who was well placed to take advantage of the dispute over the imperial succession that broke out in 1197. For a while the Danes were the dominant power in the western Baltic and in 1201 even Lübeck, which had been founded by Henry the Lion in 1158, acknowledged Knut as its protector and lord. A year later his brother, Valdemar II, recognized Frederick II as emperor and was rewarded in 1214 by a Golden Bull granting him all the territory that the Danes had won from the Elbe to the Oder; he then adopted the title 'king of the Danes and the Slavs'. Kings were not the only beneficiaries of such territorial expansion. Much of the land and revenues acquired had to be given to the church, to lay supporters or to local rulers who submitted.

Military adventures could be rewarding, but their outcome was uncertain; a more stable basis of royal power in the early middle ages was the yield of royal estates. Royal landholding could be enlarged in several ways other than conquest: by marriage settlements, as penalties to regain the king's favour after an offence or by confiscating the property of rebels. Kings could also claim land for which there was no known heir.

Even in the early middle ages kings were not solely dependent on the land they owned. There was a general obligation to contribute food and materials needed by the royal household as it travelled from place to place. It was in effect one of the earliest taxes and by the thirteenth century had become a regular demand regardless of the king's itinerary, although extra demands might be made when the king did visit. Another obligation was to contribute when defence against invasion was needed. Until the twelfth century offensive operations against enemies abroad were undertaken by royal armies that included the king's own retainers, some of whom had their own retinues, together with warriors supplied by allies and tributary rulers. When defence was needed all able-bodied men could be called on to fight or help in some other way; food and other materials had to be supplied and transported. In the twelfth century cavalry began to play a decisive role in the struggles for power in Denmark and Sweden where the landscape was suitable. Kings and magnates then recruited professional warriors, mainly Germans, to fight on their behalf. By the end of the century most people were no longer required to perform military service but had to pay tax instead. Even in Norway, where the landscape made cavalry warfare difficult if not impossible and royal armies were still based on local levies of amateurs in the fourteenth century, tax was demanded when the levies were not mustered.

During the eleventh and twelfth centuries tolls and rents from towns were increasingly important sources of royal revenue. At the beginning of the eleventh century there were only ten towns in Scandinavia, seven of them being very recent foundations; 200 years later there were twenty-seven (fifteen Danish, eight Norwegian, four Swedish). These included all the medieval towns of Norway, and most of the Danish ones. In Sweden urbanization proceeded more slowly. It was royal power that made these towns possible. Kings could best provide the protection that traders and craftsmen needed and they could grant the privileges that enabled the embryo urban communities to flourish. In the eleventh century kings established episcopal sees in some of them, and endowed churches in others. There were royal residences in some and most of the mints in which coins were struck in the names of kings were located in towns. The inhabitants of towns were, in effect, royal tenants and paid rent to royal agents who also collected tolls and other dues.

This urban expansion reflected not only the growth of royal power, but also economic changes. Scandinavia as a whole was largely self-sufficient; the needs of one region could be met by the produce of another, distributed by itinerant traders, in seasonal fairs or later in town markets. There was, however, some demand for imports. Cloth from Flanders and England was of better quality than that produced in Scandinavia, and in the twelfth century Norwegians supplemented their inadequate supply of cereals by imports from England. Many church furnishings, such as crosses, statues and altar panels, were also obtained abroad. These imports were paid for by Scandinavian produce. Scandinavia had, for centuries, exported furs. Some came from Scandinavia itself but already by the eighth century the *Svear* were gathering large quantities as tribute in Finland and in north Russia to sell to western European or Muslim merchants. By the eleventh century most of the furs reaching western markets came from Russia, but Scandinavians could no longer roam as freely there as they had done earlier; the Russians themselves had by then gained more effective control of their territory. Novgorod in particular made great efforts to monopolize supplies from Karelia, the richest fur-producing region. Merchants who wanted to obtain large quantities of high-quality furs had to buy them in Novgorod. They took their purchases directly to England, Flanders or France or to Slav, later German, trading places in the west Baltic, such as Lübeck, with good land routes into Germany. As a result the importance of trading places around Lake Mälaren declined at the expense of Gotland. There had earlier been several small trading places on the coast of that island, but in the eleventh century one of them, Visby, began to grow rapidly to become one of the major towns of northern Europe. It was visited by merchants from many parts of Scandinavia and from western Europe as well as from the Baltic towns. During the twelfth century Baltic trade was mainly in the hands of Scandinavians but the Germans took an increasing share and by 1225 the Germans in Visby were sufficiently important to be granted special privileges by the bishop of Linköping, whose diocese included Gotland.

Scandinavia's share of the fur trade declined but there were other things, notably falcons and walrus ivory, much of it from Greenland, that they could supply better than anyone else. There were also less exotic exports: horses, timber, tar, goat skins and cowhides, sulphur from Iceland and lamp oil obtained from fish, seals and whales. These and many other goods were shipped from Scandinavian ports, but by the end of the thirteenth century, and probably much earlier, they accounted for only a small part of Scandinavian exports whether measured by volume or value; preserved fish were far more important.

In medieval Europe there was a general need for preserved food that could be eaten in winter and spring. The need was most acute in the towns that were rapidly growing in number and size in many parts of western Europe in the eleventh and twelfth centuries. There were four main methods of preserving food: smoking, fermentation, salting or drying. The simplest and cheapest was drying, which is best done in a cold climate; in warm weather food tends to rot before it is dry. North Norway was ideal; it had an arctic climate, strong winds and fish, especially cod, were abundant in the coastal waters around Lofoten and further north. The main production centre was in Lofoten and dried cod, known as stockfish, from the whole of north Norway was collected there to be shipped south in the spring, initially to Trondheim, which probably owed its rapid development in the eleventh century largely to this traffic. Many towns in England, Flanders, the Rhineland and elsewhere were already large in the eleventh century and stockfish would have been as welcome then as they were in 1191 when Bergen, which had by then become the main export market for this produce, was, according to a contemporary account, 'visited by ships and men from every land; there are Icelanders, Greenlanders, Englishmen, Germans, Danes, Swedes, Gotlanders and of other nations too numerous to mention'.

By the thirteenth century Scandinavia was also supplying western Europe with salt herring from Öresund, where huge shoals arrived in the late summer. Until the end of the twelfth century production was on a small scale, limited by the shortage of salt, but shortly before 1200 Lübeck merchants began to obtain large quantities from the salt deposits at Lüneburg, about forty-five miles away, and that made it possible to process more fish. Merchants came from many parts of Europe, by ship or overland, to collect supplies and sell their wares, making the Skåne Fair, that opened annually on 15 August, one of the major fairs of medieval Europe. Lübeck's control of the salt supply on which the Skåne Fair depended was an important factor in its later domination of Scandinavian trade. The Skåne Fair also led to significant political changes for it was the ambition of several later Norwegian and Swedish kings and of some north German princes, to gain control of Öresund and its approaches, or at least to profit from the wealth that the Fair generated.

CHAPTER 12

HUNGARY IN THE ELEVENTH AND TWELFTH CENTURIES

Nora Berend

THE kingdom of Hungary was formed and consolidated as a part of Latin Christendom during the eleventh and twelfth centuries. Hungary was at the intersection of three cultures: the Roman Christian, Byzantine and nomad; and its development was influenced by each. The Hungarian tribal confederation, which included Finno-Ugric and Turkic groups, moved into the Carpathian basin in the late ninth century, mixing with the local Slavic population. Their culture was that of a nomad steppe people. In 1000, Hungary was not yet unified and its people were mostly pagans, whose chiefs had given up raiding neighbouring countries for plunder barely fifty years before. By 1200, social and economic structures had radically changed, and Hungary was a united and powerful kingdom, with ambitions of and modest successes in expansion. A latecomer to Christendom, Hungary was integrated by the end of the twelfth century. The two main elements of this process of transformation were Christianization and the building of royal power and government. Hungary's development fits into the pattern of emerging Christian states in the Scandinavian and east-central European region.

Until the early fourteenth century, the dynasty that ruled Hungary was the house of Árpád, whose first Christian king was Stephen I (István, 997–1038). Christianization and royal power were linked from the beginning. Stephen's father Géza had invited missionaries to convert the population of the country and had strengthened his power at the expense of clan leaders. Stephen continued these policies, extending royal power eastward, and created both an ecclesiastical and a royal territorial organization. The strong ties between clerics and royal power were evident during the reigns of Stephen and his successors: ecclesiastics filled important roles in the royal council and diplomacy. Stephen was anointed and crowned king in 1001. Contrary to later assertions, he did not receive his crown from the pope; that claim was part of a twelfth-century

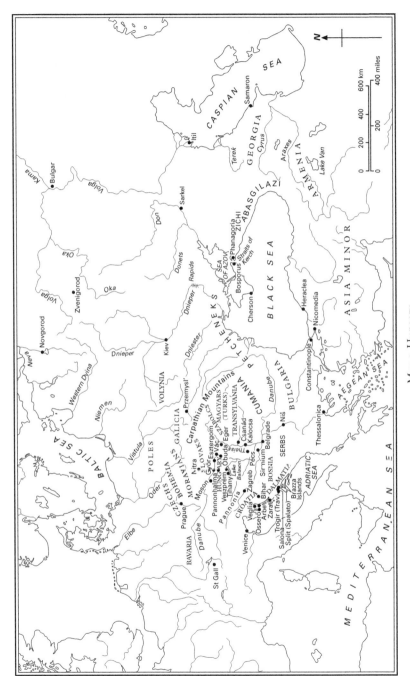

Map 9 Hungary

political construct (see below).[1] His marriage to the Bavarian Gisela, sister of the future Emperor Henry II, was the first among many dynastic marriages that the Árpáds made in order to promote their security and create political alliances. Stephen unified the kingdom, defeating the remaining territorial lords (Koppány in 997, the *gyula* in Transylvania in 1003, Ajtony in 1027–8). Occasionally the king took part in wars against his neighbours, in order to prevent them from backing opponents to his rule in Hungary; he was on the German side in the war against Poland in 1015–18 and on the Byzantine side against the Bulgars (probably in 1018). He enforced the conversion of the people to Christianity, promulgating strict laws to ensure compliance: 'If someone neglects a Christian observance and takes pleasure in the stupidity of his negligence, he shall be judged by the bishops . . . If he rebelliously objects . . . he shall be subject to the same judgement seven times over. If . . . he continues to resist . . . he shall be handed over for royal judgement.[2] For example, commoners who were inattentive during mass were to be 'punished by whipping and by the shearing off of their hair'.[3] Churches were built and the ecclesiastical tithe was introduced. Royal policy imposing adherence to Christianity is also discernible in the art of the period. Objects imitating Carolingian and Ottonian art rapidly replaced the earlier pagan Hungarian styles that had characterized grave-goods of the Conquest period.

Christianization proceeded following tenth-century precedents (both Roman and Byzantine). While monastic communities conforming to the Greek rite flourished in Hungary until the thirteenth century, the missionaries and priests who gathered at Stephen's court were westerners (especially from the German empire) and Roman Christianity became the majority religion. The eastern regions of the kingdom were first influenced by Byzantine Christianity; territorial lords relied on these ties as well on as paganism to oppose the establishment of royal power. Pagan revolts broke out in 1046 and 1061, and pagan practices persisted in Hungary. The synod of Szabolcs (1092) mentioned the punishment of those who made 'a sacrifice next to wells' or gave 'offerings to trees, fountains, and stones according to heathen rites' and included decrees against those not observing Sunday.[4] Pagan rituals had still to be condemned at the synod of Esztergom between 1105 and 1116.

---

[1] Gerics and Ladányi (1996), pp. 12–17; Váczy (1994), pp. 77–93.
[2] *The Laws of the Medieval Kingdom of Hungary*, I, p. 4. 'Si quis observatione christianitatis neglecta et negligentie stoliditate elatus, . . . ab episcopo . . . iudicetur, si vero rebellitate instructus rennuerit sibi inpositum eque sufferre, iterum eodem iudicio restringatur et etiam usque septies. Tandem super omnia si resistens . . . invenitur, regali iudicio . . . tradatur.'
[3] *The Laws of the Medieval Kingdom of Hungary*, I, p. 5. . . . 'corripiantur flagellis et cesura capillorum'.
[4] *The Laws of the Medieval Kingdom of Hungary*, I, p. 58. 'Quicumque ritu gentilium iuxta puteos sacrificaverint, vel ad arbores et fontes et lapides oblationes obtulerint.'

Stephen I laid the groundwork for Hungary's ecclesiastical organization, establishing bishoprics. According to tradition, their number was ten (Veszprém, Győr, Esztergom, Pécs, Eger, Transylvania, Kalocsa – which became an archbishopric during the eleventh century – Csanád, Bihar, Vác); the last two of these, however, were created by his immediate successors.

During the late eleventh and twelfth centuries, the seat of the bishopric of Bihar was moved to Várad, and new bishoprics were created in Zagreb and Nitra. Stephen established an independent Hungarian archbishopric at Esztergom, with the result that the kingdom did not become an ecclesiastical province of the German empire. By the end of the eleventh century, an ecclesiastical network of archdeaconries, churches, monasteries and chapters attached to cathedrals or collegiate churches was developing. The Latin foundation charter of the monastery of Tihany (1055) included the first vernacular Hungarian sentence to be preserved in documentary record.

Stephen also initiated a territorial organization of the kingdom. To protect Hungary, tracts of land were left uninhabited at the borders, followed by an inner ring of obstacles and settlements of guards (*gyepű*). Stephen followed the German model in adopting the system of counties along with its name (*comitatus*); the first counties appeared in western Hungary. Unlike German counts, however, the administrators (*ispán*) appointed by Stephen and his successors could not turn the counties into their hereditary possessions. They remained representatives of the king; throughout the eleventh and twelfth centuries the *ispánok* were members of the royal court appointed as officials of a county. The attachment of one *ispán* exclusively to one county only developed gradually from the late twelfth century. The *ispán* led the army levied from the county, had juridical rights and collected taxes.

The county included royal, ecclesiastical and noble estates. The basis of royal power was land. The king was the largest landlord in Hungary throughout the first two centuries; even Béla III (1172–96) retained about two-thirds of the entire territory (including uninhabited land). Thus initially most of the land in the counties belonged to the king, and these lands were organized into castellanies (*várispánság*). The centre of both the county and castellany was the castle (constructions made of wood and earth, built from the turn of the tenth and eleventh centuries onwards). The castellan – the same *ispán* who administered the county – represented the king as landlord on the royal estates. Officials who were appointed to the castellanies also participated in the administration of the counties. The exact number of either the counties or castellanies established by Stephen himself is not known. Stephen's successors extended both systems, and by the late twelfth century, there were seventy-two castellanies; the number of counties was smaller, perhaps around forty-five. The two types of organization became increasingly distinct from each other;

in the thirteenth century, castellanies disintegrated, while the counties were transformed from being the basis of royal power to juridical organizations of the nobility. Throughout the period, royal and ecclesiastical territorial structure was linked. By the end of the eleventh century, priests of the castle-chapels acquired administrative functions and the archdeaconries developed. Their territories corresponded to those of counties or castellanies.

Kings travelled around the kingdom together with the court, setting up certain royal centres without creating a stable 'capital'. Esztergom, by the late twelfth century housing Hungary's largest lay and ecclesiastical building complex (royal and archiepiscopal palaces and cathedral), became the centre for the collection of taxes and minting. Fehérvár was the sacral centre of the dynasty, the site of royal coronations and many royal burials. Councils and assemblies for royal judgements took place both in Fehérvár and Óbuda.

Stephen followed German models in initiating minting (which remained a royal prerogative throughout the period), as well as in introducing Latin written culture to Hungary. Scribes from the German imperial chancery settled at Stephen's court, allowing Stephen to issue the first charters and the first lawbooks. The *Institutiones morum*, a work on good government and conduct, addressed to Stephen's son Emeric (Imre), attributed to Stephen I, but written by a cleric of the royal court, provides evidence of ideas about government. The Venetian Gerard, bishop of Csanád, wrote an exegetical work on *The Song of the Three Children*, the only theological work to survive from Hungary's first Christian centuries.

Stephen I had no surviving son, and prior to his death appointed his nephew, Peter Orseolo as his successor. Peter's rule was the beginning of wars of succession. There was no single order of succession in Hungary. Several principles of inheritance coexisted: seniority (the heir would be the eldest male member of the dynasty), primogeniture (inheritance of the first-born son), *idoneitas* (the most capable person who to rule) and election could all justify throneworthiness as long as the king was a member of the Árpád dynasty. In fact, the strongest pretender could claim 'his inheritance' on the basis of the most suitable principle. Those nobles who had important positions at the court supported one or another pretender according to their interests, even instigating the succession wars. Despite these struggles, the institution of kingship remained stable, and the kingdom never fell apart into independent principalities. King Peter ruled only a few years (1038–41) when the dissatisfied Hungarian lay and ecclesiastical elite revolted against him and put Samuel Aba – a relative, probably another nephew of Stephen I – on the throne (1041–4).

Peter turned to Emperor Henry III for help. German emperors repeatedly attempted to extend their rule to Hungary. King Stephen successfully defeated the first attack (in 1030). Beginning in the 1040s, German emperors took advantage of succession wars, backing one or another pretender, occasionally even obtaining oaths of fidelity from their candidate. Henry III sent his armies against Hungary in 1042, 1043 and 1044 to back Peter Orseolo against Samuel Aba. Peter was reinstalled in 1044, but in 1046 two sons of Vazul – a cousin of King Stephen, whom Stephen had had blinded to exclude him from the succession, while his sons escaped abroad – returned from Kiev, and, aided by a pagan rebellion, defeated and blinded Peter. One of them, the Christian Andrew I (Endre or András, 1046–60) became king of Hungary, suppressing the pagan revolt. His pagan brother Levente died soon afterwards.

Andrew I recalled his younger brother Béla from Poland and set up a territory approximately one third of the kingdom as a duchy (*ducatus*) under Béla's rule. The *ducatus* functioned between 1047–8 and 1107 and was briefly resurrected in 1162–3. It was always under the rule of a prince of the dynasty, often the reigning monarch's younger brother. At the time of its establishment, this territory was in the area most recently subjugated to royal power, thus on the peripheries of the kingdom. It was organized into a duchy partly in order to establish control over it. The duchy provided a power-base for pretenders to the throne, but no prince tried to turn it into an independent kingdom. From the end of the eleventh century a new system increasingly replaced it; princes gained authority over newly conquered territories or those parts of the kingdom that had a separate administration.

As Peter Orseolo had taken an oath of fidelity to Henry III in 1045, Henry tried to enforce this dependence, attacking Hungary in 1051–2 without success. Fights for the succession continued as Béla I (1060–3), Andrew's brother, seized the throne, although Andrew had appointed his son Solomon as his heir. Béla attacked his brother with the help of the Polish ruler Boleslaw II, and Andrew died of his wounds. Then Solomon (1063–74) asserted his claim to the throne, assisted by the armies of Henry IV. It may have been during Solomon's reign (in any case between the mid-eleventh and the early twelfth century) that the oldest Hungarian *gesta*, the history of the Hungarians, was composed. It has survived in a revised form: subsequent authors made additions and alterations according to the needs of the branch of the dynasty that was then in power.

The sons of Béla I first forced Solomon to cede the duchy to the elder of them, Géza, then defeated him. By the time Solomon took an oath of fidelity to Henry IV in 1074, he was king in name only. Some skirmishes in border areas followed in 1079, but German emperors gave up the attempt to attach Hungary to the empire. (The last intervention, in 1108, when Henry V attacked Hungary to help Álmos wrest the kingdom from his brother Coloman, was a brief, unsuccessful episode.) After Solomon's defeat, first Géza I (1074–7), then after his death Ladislas I (László, 1077–1095) became king of Hungary. Géza I and Ladislas I ascended the throne while the kingdom already had a crowned and anointed king, Solomon, who, marginalized, forced to renounce the throne (1081) and imprisoned, was none the less a constant reminder that Béla I's sons were not legitimate rulers of Hungary. The brothers resorted to practical as well as ideological means to offset their disadvantage. As Solomon possessed the crown, Géza I used a Byzantine crown (perhaps that of his Byzantine wife) which later became the lower part of the 'Holy Crown' of Hungary, which still exists. Because Emperor Henry IV backed Solomon, Ladislas became an ally of Rudolf of Swabia. In addition to creating a system of alliances, Ladislas sought new forms of sacral legitimization. This led to the creation of an ideology centred on the 'holy lineage' of Hungarian kings. Ladislas, probably inspired by Czech and Kievan examples, initiated the canonization of Stephen I. During 1083 (when Solomon was allowed to leave his prison and Hungary), a Hungarian synod declared the bishop-martyr Gerard (killed in the pagan revolt of 1046), Stephen I and his son Emeric, and two hermits (Andrew-Zoerard and Benedict) saints. Ladislas, in turn, was canonized in 1192 at the initiative of Béla III, an act linked to a rising culture of chivalry, and the holy predecessors became a standard reference for Hungarian kings.

Ladislas I innovated in his expansionist policies as well. Although Hungarian kings had participated in wars against neighbouring areas before, their aim from 1091 became the extension of the kingdom's territory through conquest. The results of this policy were modest; the only areas that were more or less durably attached to the kingdom were Croatia, which provided access to the Adriatic Sea (from 1091, although not continuously throughout the middle ages), and Bosnia (from 1136–7). Because the pope refused to acknowledge Ladislas's right to Croatia, claiming it as a papal fief, Ladislas sided with Emperor Henry IV and the antipope Clement III. Two other main areas of – mostly unsuccessful – expansion in the twelfth century were Dalmatia and Galicia. At the same time, the kingdom had to be defended from recurring nomad (Petchenek, Oguz, then Cuman) raids from the east. The main components of the royal army were the soldiers from the castellanies and counties, with special light cavalry units of nomads who settled in the kingdom.

Ladislas died without a male heir, and Géza's two sons reached a compromise. Coloman (Kálmán, 1095–1116) became king, and his younger brother Álmos received the duchy, reviving the territorial division that had ceased to exist during Ladislas's reign. Álmos repeatedly made attempts to oust Coloman and gain the throne; therefore in 1107 Coloman abolished the duchy, and in 1115 ordered the blinding of Álmos and his son.

Coloman continued the expansionist policy of Ladislas I. From his reign onward, Hungarian kings competed with Byzantium and Venice for the Dalmatian coastal cities. In 1097 the Byzantine emperor appointed the Venetian doge to defend the Dalmatian coast. In 1105 King Coloman attached the middle part of Dalmatia (Zadar, Sebenico, Trau, Split, the islands of Brazza, Veglia, Osero and Arbe) to Hungary. In 1115–18 Venice recaptured Dalmatia, and this state of affairs was accepted in the peace treaty of 1119. Venice and Hungary continued to struggle for Dalmatia, while Dalmatian towns bestowed their loyalty according to political needs (Hungarian victories in 1124, 1135–6; Venetian in 1125). In 1167 Dalmatia was ceded to Byzantium together with Croatia, Bosnia and Sirmium. In 1180–1 these territories were once again attached to Hungary.

Beginning with King Coloman in 1099, Hungarian kings also intervened in the civil wars between Rus' principalities. Coloman backed Svyatopolk of Kiev against several other Rus' princes and was defeated. In 1123 Stephen II backed Jaroslav of Volynia, and in 1127 Vladimir prince of Zvenigorod against the prince of Przemysl. In 1138 Béla II sent armies against Chernigov on the side of the princes of Przemysl and Kiev. In 1144 Géza II helped to defend Galicia against Vsevolod of Kiev, and in 1148–52 he intervened in Rus' affairs six times, mostly on the side of Volynia against Galicia. A turning point came in 1188, when Béla III conquered Galicia and made his son Andrew (Endre, the future Andrew II) ruler over it, but a Galician revolt soon ousted the Hungarian prince. Coloman occasionally also participated in wars against other neighbouring countries: for example, in 1107 he backed Svatopolk in his fight for the Bohemian throne, and Boleslaw III against Zbigniew in Poland. One of the main successes of his diplomacy was the marriage of Ladislas I's daughter Eirene (Piroska) to John, heir of the Byzantine Emperor Alexios in 1105–6.

The First Crusade confronted Coloman with a novel problem. Pilgrims to the Holy Land had crossed Hungary since Stephen I had opened the pilgrimage route across the kingdom. At the time of the First Crusade, the armies took the same road. As the crusaders marched through the kingdom in 1096, the armies of Peter the Hermit, Folkmar and Gottschalk began pillaging in Hungary, while Emich of Flonheim, not accepting Coloman's refusal to allow him access through the kingdom, besieged the castle of Moson on the western border. Coloman dispersed and defeated the various bands, but mistrust towards crusaders proved hard to eradicate. Coloman held Godfrey of Bouillon's brother hostage while Godfrey's armies passed through the kingdom, and the passage of subsequent crusading armies through Hungary (in 1147 the German Conrad III and French Louis VII, in 1189 Emperor Frederick Barbarossa) was always accompanied by tension.

The work of devising a theoretical justification for royal power was carried forward during Coloman's reign. In the eleventh century German emperors as well as Pope Gregory VII, who maintained that Stephen I had offered the kingdom to St Peter, claimed suzerainty over Hungary. The Hungarian counter-claim was soon launched, in a *Life* of St Stephen written in the late eleventh century. In this, Stephen offered the kingdom to the Virgin Mary who then saved Hungary from a German attack; the author thus argued against both the imperial and the papal claims.[5] Moreover, Stephen's baptism was attributed to St Adalbert, bishop of Prague, while Bruno of Sankt Gallen, the missionary-bishop who began the conversion of Hungary in the 970s and probably baptized the ruler's family, and Bavarian missionaries were not mentioned at all. Bishop Hartvic elaborated the Hungarian royal position in his *Life* of St Stephen, which was commissioned by King Coloman in the early twelfth century, and subsequently became the official text. Hartvic invented the story of the papal origin of Stephen's crown, according to which a divine vision directed the pope to agree to Stephen's request. Moreover, in this *Life*, the pope called Stephen 'Christ's apostle' and acknowledged that he ruled 'according to both [temporal and spiritual] laws'.[6]

This was a justification for the existing situation; during the whole period, the church in Hungary was under strong royal control. The 'Gregorian re-form' barely affected Hungarian royal rights. Kings presided over ecclesiastical synods, appointed bishops and moved them to different sees. Recent research has questioned the claim, based on late twelfth- and thirteenth-century texts, that King Coloman gave up the right of investiture in 1106, and it has been argued that these texts reflect ecclesiastical constructions, not real events.[7] Late twelfth-century clerics complained that in Hungary, the episcopal pallium was conferred by the king and royal approval was necessary for the clergy to ap-peal to the pope. The system of *ecclesia propria* prevailed, kings and other lay founders retained their rights in appointing priests. 'Gregorian' ideals in general spread very slowly; clerics became exempt from lay jurisdiction, but celibacy did not become universal in the twelfth century even among the higher clergy.

After Coloman's death, his son Stephen II (1116–31) became king. As he left no heir, Álmos's son Béla II (the Blind, 1131–41) was crowned. In revenge for the blinding of his father and himself, he caused many nobles to be massacred. He attached Bosnia to the kingdom, and kept Hungarian interests alive in Dalmatia and various Rus' principalities. From the 1130s Coloman's alleged son Boris (from the king's second marriage to Euphemia of Suzdal') made several unsuccessful attempts to gain the Hungarian throne: he attacked with the help of a Polish army in 1132, with the aid of a Bavarian-Austrian one in 1146 and finally hoped to rouse his followers to revolt when he crossed Hungary in the retinue of Louis VII en route to the Holy Land. After Béla's death, his son Géza II (1141–62) inherited the throne. Hungarian kings took sides in mid-twelfth-century conflicts, bearing in mind the threat posed by the power

---

[5] *Scriptores rerum Hungaricarum*, II, p. 390.

[6] *Scriptores rerum Hungaricarum*, II, p. 414. '... ego sum apostolicus, ille vero merito Christi aposto-lus ... dispositioni eiusdem ... ecclesias simul cum populis utroque iure ordinandas relinquimus'.

[7] Szovák (1996), pp. 23–7.

and ambitions of the Byzantine and German emperors. Géza II sided with the Norman-French alliance, and finally chose to support Pope Alexander III in the schism of 1159. Wars against Byzantium were launched in 1127 at Hungarian initiative. During 1127–9 and 1149–55 the Hungarian aim was the conquest of the territory between Belgrade and Niš, and the weakening of the Byzantine empire through support for Serbian revolts.

By the twelfth century, landed property was becoming the basis of Hungarian society, with groups of different legal status living on royal, ecclesiastical and noble estates. The previously more independent border areas were incorporated into the system of counties during the twelfth century. While Stephen I's laws differentiated only between free and unfree, social stratification during the eleventh century created differences among the free that were soon mirrored in legal terminology. Many of the impoverished freemen settled on royal, then noble estates; they had to provide food, various goods and services, and could not leave the estates. The laws of Ladislas I already distinguished between nobles and 'commoner' freemen. On royal estates, people were divided into groups according to the services they owed. Registers of certain royal manorial (*udvarnok*) estates that were donated to ecclesiastical institutions such as Dömös, belonging to the abbey of Pécsvárad, described people who belonged to royal manor houses as divided into three categories: the free soldiers, the serving-people (*udvarnokok*), who owed specified goods and services, and the unfree (including tillers and other labourers). Others belonged to the castellanies. The elite (*iobagiones castri*) were soldiers, had land, paid no taxes and filled official positions, while the rest owed specified goods or services, such as agricultural labour, produce, pottery and so on, as well as military service, paid taxes and could be donated along with the land. Serving-people were organized into hundreds and tens. The estates were self-sufficient. The *familiae* of ecclesiastical estates also formed groups according to their occupations: officials and soldiers formed the highest ranking group, craftsmen and labourers the lower ranks. On nobles' estates, the main differentiating factor among the inhabitants was legal; *servi*, who were directly under the command of their lord, differed sharply from *libertini* who farmed lands in their own use, and had the right to procure their freedom. The laws of Ladislas I and Coloman reflected the new developments and decreed punishments for those who resisted integration into the new order.

Foreign settlers (*hospites*) arrived in Hungary throughout the period. Until the mid-twelfth century, they settled exclusively on royal lands, then on the estates of nobles as well. From the time of Stephen I, immigrants from western lands included clerics, knights, craftsmen, traders and peasants. Jews also came from Slavic and German areas; they were merchants and farmers. Muslims arrived from Khwarizm and Volga Bulgaria; they acted as traders, royal officials and soldiers in Hungary. Muslim archers were recruited by Géza II from the east. Nomads from the east, especially the Petcheneks, also settled in the king-dom, often as soldiers and border-guards. The number of newcomers increased during the twelfth century; the most numerous groups being the Walloon, French, Italian, Flemish and south and north German settlers. *Hospites* had a privileged status, but the varied groups of immigrants were regarded as fully part of the kingdom. The *gens Ungarorum*, 'the Hungarian people', during this period included the whole population, of whatever origin.

The culture and art of the late eleventh and early twelfth centuries are known mostly from ecclesiastical sources. Schools based in chapter-houses provided training, and clerics transmitted written culture. A late eleventh-century list of the eighty volumes of the library of Pannonhalma, the most important Bene-dictine monastery in Hungary, shows that apart from the Bible, such works as Pope Gregory I's *Moralia in Job* and Sulpicius Severus's *Life* of St Martin were known. The turn of the century also brought a change in building style. Earlier Byzantine-influenced motifs on ecclesiastical buildings (both royal and lay foundations) gave way to the figural representations of Romanesque art, the most important example being the sculpture at the cathedral of Pécs. Twelfth-century buildings and sculptures included work by Italian masters, while liturgical objects in Byzantine, south German, Saxon and Flemish styles existed side-by-side with those produced locally. Coloman's laws provide a glimpse of the types of dress worn by the elites, such as 'fur cloak', 'boots', 'fur cap', 'silken footwear and shirts', 'fibulae'.[8] During the twelfth century, several of the newly founded religious orders made their way to Hungary. Premon-stratensians arrived in the early twelfth century, Cistercians, Hospitallers and Templars in the middle of the century. Recently, some scholars have argued that Géza II founded a Hungarian Order, the Stephanites.[9]

Géza II's son Stephen III (1162–72) was crowned king upon his father's death, but Byzantine intervention resulted in the accession of Béla II's other sons, first Ladislas II (1162–3), then after his death Stephen IV (1163). Byzantine models and influence were important throughout the period, but came to the fore at certain times. For a few years from 1162 Byzantine intervention and influence in Hungary was at its height, with the aim of controlling strategically important borderlands.[10] After defeating Stephen IV, Stephen III came to an agreement with Manuel Komnenos, the Byzantine emperor. In exchange for Manuel's support, Stephen's younger brother Béla (the future Béla III) was sent to Byzantium in 1163, and grew up at the court of Manuel. Stephen also handed over Dalmatia and Sirmium to the emperor.

---

[8] *The Laws of the Medieval Kingdom of Hungary*, I, p. 31. 'utatur pellicio... caliga... cappa... calceo... sericato,... camisia... et serico... fibulis'.

[9] Boroviczényi (1991–2); Puskely (1996), pp. 927–8.   [10] Stephenson (1996).

Béla III's reign (1172–96) marked one of the high points of medieval Hungarian history. Engaged to Manuel's daughter, he was heir to the Byzantine throne, but when Manuel's son was born, Béla lost this position. Soon afterwards, upon Stephen III's death, he returned to Hungary. The archbishops of Esztergom traditionally crowned the kings of Hungary, but Archbishop Lucas refused to accept him as king, possibly because he feared that Béla's accession would enhance Byzantine influence. The archbishop of Kalocsa crowned Béla with papal permission. The king continued the expansionist policies of his predecessors. He regained Croatia, Dalmatia and Sirmium from Byzantium, and in the 1180s attempted to conquer Byzantine areas south of Belgrade. He also tried to establish his son as ruler of Galicia.

Béla reorganized the royal chancery and, detaching it from the royal chapel, turned it into an independent body. The number of charters issued increased; besides royal and ecclesiastical matters, charters detailing transactions and rights of laymen also appeared. The chancery was staffed by high-ranking ecclesiastics, many of whom had studied in Paris. Throughout the middle ages, foreign-born ecclesiastics often filled high positions in the kingdom. From the twelfth century, Hungarian clerics started to study in international centres of learning, and were then appointed to bishoprics and positions in the chancery. In the late twelfth century, and especially from around 1200 onwards, ecclesiastical written culture began to have an impact on lay culture through the *loca credibilia*, ecclesiastical institutions which issued authenticated charters and also provided safekeeping for such documents. These served the needs of local elites. At the same time, a notary in the royal chancery – the Hungarian Anonymous – wrote the first *Gesta Hungarorum* that survives in its original form (although some scholars date the work to the late thirteenth century). At the end of the twelfth century, a codex made for a Hungarian Benedictine abbey (*Codex Prayanus*) included, besides Hungarian synodal decrees, ecclesiastical canons and the texts of masses, the earliest extant vernacular Hungarian text, a burial speech. Early Parisian gothic appeared in Esztergom; the rebuilding of the royal palace, and the portal (*Porta Speciosa*), and incrusted marble ornaments of the cathedral followed the most recent artistic trends.

Otto of Freising and Muslim travellers and geographers described Hungary's rich natural resources in the mid-twelfth century, although Otto also depicted the kingdom as sparsely inhabited, wild and undeveloped. The population of the kingdom at the end of the twelfth century has been calculated as between 1 and 2.2 million. Silver and salt mines contributed to the riches of the king. Trade connections existed between Hungary and the German empire, Rus' and Constantinople. Livestock played an important role besides cultivation, which depended on plots being farmed then abandoned and on the light plough. Twelfth-century settlers, especially German peasants, cleared new lands, bringing them under cultivation according to field-systems. Villages (between sixteen and sixty-five families) consisted of wooden houses often partially dug into the ground. The cities were settlements around the castles and comprised the quarters of craftsmen and foreign settlers. They included centres of ecclesiastical and lay administration, and of commerce if they lay on major routes. They mostly lacked walls as well as autonomy. The few exceptions were communities of French and Walloon settlers, notably Fehérvár and Esztergom which were walled cities with charters of privileges dating back to before 1200. A list of royal revenues prepared on Béla's orders around 1195 indicates the beginnings of a money economy, as well as a reduction in the almost exclusive importance of the revenues from the king's private domains. The list includes returns from yearly coin exchange (new coinage was issued and the previous coins had to be exchanged at a fixed rate), customs and fairs, salt production and sale, two-thirds of the income of the castellanies and gifts from the counties, taxes, often in kind, of privileged groups such as the Saxons of Transylvania.[11]

This list of revenues presented King Béla III as one of the richest and most powerful monarchs of his time; the value of his total income according to the list surpassed that of the English of French king. This was certainly exaggerated, but Béla's strong regime and major reforms made Hungary an international power. Hungary's social and economic structure underwent radical changes during the two centuries considered in this chapter. In place of a country under many territorial lords, with a pagan population whose leaders had barely given up nomad raiding, a strong Christian kingdom emerged, landed estates becoming the basis of social organization, where the beginnings of money economy, chivalry and early Gothic appeared. Béla's death was the end of an epoch. During the thirteenth century, royal power and Hungarian society were to be radically transformed.

[11] *Rerum Hungaricarum Monumenta Arpadiana*, p. 245.

CHAPTER 13

THE PAPACY, 1122–1198

I. S. Robinson

YOU ought to bear in mind that you are the model of righteousness, the mirror of sanctity, the pattern of piety, the declarer of truth, the defender of the faith, the teacher of the nations, the leader of Christians, the friend of the Bridegroom, the Bridesman, the ordainer of the clergy, the shepherd of the people, the master of the simple, the refuge of the oppressed, the advocate of the poor, the hope of the wretched, the protector of the orphans, the judge of the widows, the eye of the blind, the tongue of the dumb, the support of the old, the punisher of crimes, the dread of the wicked, the glory of the good, a rod for the powerful, a hammer of tyrants, the father of kings, the moderator of the laws, the dispenser of the canons, the salt of the earth, the light of the world, the priest of the Most High, the vicar of Christ, the Lord's anointed: finally, the God of Pharaoh.[1]

This influential description of the spiritual, judicial and charismatic elements of the pope's authority is found in the treatise *De consideratione* (1148/9–1152/3) which Bernard of Clairvaux addressed to his former pupil, Pope Eugenius III. The author drew especially on the language of the Old Testament, including his favourite imagery from the Song of Solomon: 'the Bride' of that book was Bernard's most frequent image for the church; 'the friend of the Bridegroom' (that is, of Christ) was his characteristic term for the pope. The Old Testament prophets and patriarchs also inspired him with striking images of papal intervention in the church and the world, notably that final designation in his list of papal titles, which would so much preoccupy the theologians and canonists of the later middle ages. As 'the God of Pharaoh' (the allusion is to Exodus 7:1), the pope must, like Moses, wield his awesome power against tyrants who tried to hinder the progress of God's people along the way of righteousness. While later medieval theologians and jurists thought of these Bernardine titles as designating the rights and prerogatives of the papacy, for Bernard himself they signified the *duties* of the pope, who must always be active in exhorting and correcting the people of Christendom.[2]

---

[1] Bernard of Clairvaux, 'De consideratione' IV. 7.23.
[2] Rivière (1924), p. 278; Congar (1955), p. 85.

Bernard linked the title 'vicar of Christ' with the universal authority of the pope over both the secular and the spiritual sphere. In his allegorical interpretation of the story of St Peter walking on the sea (Matthew 14:29), noting that 'the sea is the world, the ships are the churches', he wrote that 'by walking on the waters in the manner of the Lord, he designated himself the unique vicar of Christ, who ought to rule not over one people but over all'.[3] The extraordinary influence of Bernard's work ensured that this became the standard meaning of the ancient title *vicarius Christi*, just as it also guaranteed the survival of his version of the 'doctrine of the two swords'. The Gospel text Luke 22:38 – 'And they said, "Lord, behold, here are two swords." And He said to them, "It is enough"' – had since the ninth century been interpreted as referring to the 'material sword' of secular coercion and the 'spiritual sword' of excommunication. Bernard's decisive addition to the traditional interpretation of the text was his claim that both these swords belonged to the pope, as the successor of Peter, the prince of the apostles. Addressing Eugenius III, he wrote:

If [the material sword] did not belong to you, when the apostles said, 'Behold, here are two swords', the Lord would not have replied, 'It is enough', but 'It is too much'. Therefore both the spiritual and the material sword belong to the church; but while the former is unsheathed by the church, the latter is unsheathed for the church.[4]

Bernard's interpretation of the 'two swords' sprang from his preoccupation with the specific issue of the pope's responsibility for launching a crusade. 'Put forth both swords, now that Christ is suffering again where he suffered before', he exhorted Eugenius III in 1150. 'Both are Peter's, the one to be unsheathed at his nod, the other by his hand, whenever necessary.'[5]

The claim that the material sword belonged to the church – that secular power was to be exercised at the pope's command – had implications of universal papal lordship which are never discussed in Bernard's writings. Throughout the twelfth century scholars debated the meaning of the allegory of the two swords and the precedents for the papal deposition of kings inherited from the Gregorian papacy of the late eleventh century. For Paul of Bernried, writing his biography of Pope Gregory VII in 1128, the political authority claimed by that pope was still the most vital aspect of the papal primacy: the Roman church is 'the head and mistress of all religion . . . whose prerogative it is to correct the powerful of the world before all others'.[6] This Gregorian notion of the papal duty of *correctio*, inspired by the conduct of the Old Testament prophets, assumed that the pope must supervise the conduct of secular princes, rebuking the disobedient and deposing and replacing those who were not 'suitable' (*idoneus*). The Gregorian view is reflected in Bernard of Clairvaux's idea of the

---

[3] Bernard, 'De consideratione' II.8.16.   [4] *Ibid.* IV. 3. 7. See Stickler (1951); Kennan (1967).
[5] Bernard, 'Epistola' 256.1.   [6] Paul of Bernried, 'Vita Gregorii VII papae' c.61, p. 507.

pope as 'a rod for the powerful, a hammer of tyrants' and 'the God of Pharaoh'. It is also echoed in a passage of Hugh of St Victor's treatise on the sacraments (*c.* 1134) which papalists in the later middle ages would cite in defence of papal supremacy in secular affairs.

As the spiritual life is more worthy than the earthly and the spirit is more worthy than the body, so the spiritual power is superior to the earthly or secular power in honour and dignity. For the spiritual power must establish the earthly power in order that it may exist and must judge it if it has not been good.[7]

The most influential canon lawbook of the twelfth century, the *Decretum* of Master Gratian of Bologna (*c.* 1140), devotes little space to the relations of the papacy and the secular power. True to the dialectical method followed throughout his work, Gratian cited 'authorities' both for and against the Gregorian view of papal supremacy over secular affairs. The only personal opinion which the canonist was willing to give on this subject was that 'there are two persons by whom this world is ruled, namely the royal and the priestly. Just as kings are pre-eminent in the affairs of the world, so priests are pre-eminent in the affairs of God.'[8] Gratian here adopted not the Gregorian view of the relations of the two powers, but the traditional view that the Gregorian papacy had contradicted: the doctrine enshrined in the famous letter of Pope Gelasius I to Emperor Anastasius I (494), that the spiritual and the secular powers were both divinely ordained to govern, neither being subject to the authority of the other.[9] Elsewhere in the *Decretum*, however, Gratian cited Gregorian material under a rubric which paraphrased Gregory VII's own view of the supremacy of the spiritual power: 'Priests are considered the fathers and masters of kings and princes.'[10] Consequently the 'Decretists', the legal experts who composed commentaries on the *Decretum* during the second half of the twelfth century, could develop from their master's text either a 'Gelasian' or a 'Gregorian' view of the relations of the two powers.

Two famous Decretists writing not long after the publication of Gratian's work chose to elaborate the Gregorian materials in the *Decretum*. The researches of Master Roland of Bologna (who has often, although on insufficient evidence, been identified with Roland Bandinelli, the future Pope Alexander III) uncovered claims of Gregory VII concerning the deposition of kings that were more sweeping than was evident from Gratian's selection of Gregorian

---

[7] Hugh of St-Victor, 'De sacramentis Christiane fidei' II.2.4, p. 418. See Kempf (1963), p. 33; Ullmann (1970), pp. 440–1.

[8] Gratian, 'Decretum' c.2 q.7 *dictum Gratiani post* c.41. See Kempf (1963), p. 27.

[9] Gelasius I, *Epistola* 12 (JL 632), ed. A. Thiel, *Epistulae Romanorum pontificum genuinae*, I (Braunsberg, 1868), p. 350. See Ullmann (1981), pp. 198–212.

[10] Gratian, 'Decretum' D.96 c.9–10 (paraphrasing Gregory VII, *Register* VIII.21).

material. Roland drew from his findings the conclusion that 'the pope may
transfer the kingship and may depose the emperor'.[11] Rufinus of Bologna (later
bishop of Assisi and archbishop of Sorrento) in his *Summa decretorum* (1157–9)
concluded that

> the supreme pontiff, who is the vicar of blessed Peter, holds the rights of the earthly
> kingdom. But it must be noticed that the right of authority is one thing and the
> right of administration another... The right of administration is like the function of
> a steward [employed by a bishop], who has the right of administration but lacks the
> authority of command: whatever orders he gives to others, he imposes by the authority
> of the bishop [who employs him]. The supreme patriarch holds the right of the earthly
> empire in respect of authority, in the sense that, firstly, he confirms the emperor in the
> earthly kingdom by his authority when he consecrates him and subsequently by his
> sole authority he punishes both the emperor and other secular rulers if they abuse their
> secular power and he absolves them after they do penance. The secular prince indeed,
> after [the pope], possesses the authority to rule secular men and he holds the office of
> administration apart from [the pope].[12]

Rufinus attributed to the pope 'authority' over 'the earthly empire', based on
the long acknowledged right of the pope to officiate at the imperial coronation
and on the Gregorian idea of the papal *correctio* of delinquent secular rulers.
He used the striking analogy of the secular ruler as a steward, as the agent
of the pope, 'after' whom he governs his subjects. The canonist's distinction
between 'the right of authority' and 'the right of administration' corresponded
to that made in scriptural language by Bernard of Clairvaux: the material
sword is 'to be unsheathed at [the pope's] nod', but unlike the spiritual sword
of excommunication, it cannot be unsheathed by the pope's own hand.

Decretist opinion in the later twelfth century, however, seems more frequently to have inclined towards the 'Gelasian' view of the relations of the
two powers. In his *Summa* (*c.* 1170) the illustrious canonist Stephen of Tournai
ascribed to the pope a 'spiritual empire' (*imperium spirituale*) but did not claim
for him the authority to institute secular monarchs and to supervise their government. According to tradition the pope sanctified the new emperor through
the ceremony of the imperial coronation but he did not create the authority
of one who was 'king by election, emperor by unction'.[13] The Decretist Simon
of Bisignano quoted in his *Summa* of 1177–9 the opinion of an earlier master,
'Cardinal Albert' (who has sometimes been identified as Albert of Morra, the
future Pope Gregory VIII): 'the emperor does not hold the power of the sword
from the pope'. Simon added his own, similarly Gelasian, view of the 'two

---

[11] Roland, 'Stroma ex decretorum corpore carptum' D.96 c.10, pp. 11–12. See Kempf (1963), p. 34;
Noonan (1977).
[12] Rufinus, *Summa Decretorum* D.22 c.1, p. 47. See Benson (1968), pp. 74–5.
[13] Stephen of Tournai, *Summa* D.22 c.1, p. 32.

swords': the emperor received 'the power of the sword' from God and was 'greater than the pope in temporal matters'.[14] By the time that the great Master Huguccio of Pisa restated the Gelasian doctrine in his *Summa* (*c.* 1190), he was representing the view of many canonists. 'Both powers, namely the apostolic and the imperial, were instituted by God; neither depends on the other and the emperor does not hold the sword from the pope. The emperor holds power in temporal affairs and the pope in spiritual affairs from God alone and it is thus that authority is separated.'[15]

One aspect of the Gregorian political claims at least had left a permanent mark on the twelfth-century papacy. 'The imitation of the empire', deriving from the Gregorians' preoccupation with the 'Donation of Constantine', continued to influence the ceremonial life of the pope. That fictional donation had conferred on the pope 'the various imperial ornaments and every procession of the imperial majesty' and it permitted him to 'use the tiara (*phrygium*) in processions in imitation of our imperial power'.[16] Abbot Suger of St-Denis witnessed such a procession at the council of Liège in March 1131, when the entourage of Pope Innocent II, 'preparing themselves in the Roman manner, surrounding themselves with great and admirable splendour, placed on [the pope's head] a tiara, an imperial ornament like a helmet, rounded by a gold circlet, and led him, mounted on a white horse, covered with a blanket'.[17] On this occasion, to mark his first meeting with the king of the Germans and future emperor Lothar III, Innocent II revived a ceremony recorded in the Donation of Constantine: the king performed the functions of a groom (*stratoris officium*) for the pope, as Constantine had allegedly done for Sylvester I. To Abbot Suger it appeared that Lothar behaved 'as if [Innocent] was his lord'.[18] It was presumably this implication of papal lordship over the emperor that disturbed Frederick I Barbarossa when he was invited to perform the *stratoris officium* for Pope Adrian IV in June 1155. Only after a day spent consulting 'old records' and seeking the advice of those princes old enough to remember the events of 1131 was Frederick willing to enact the ceremony.[19]

The papal 'imitation of the empire' inspired Bernard of Clairvaux's famous rebuke to Eugenius III, comparing the mid-twelfth-century papacy with the condition of the primitive church. 'Peter is not known ever to have gone in procession adorned in jewels and silks nor crowned with gold nor mounted

[14] Gloss of 'Albertus', quoted by Pacaut (1956), pp. 355–6. Simon of Bisignano, *Summa* D.96 c.6, quoted by Pacaut (1956), p. 356.
[15] Huguccio, *Summa* D.96 c.6, quoted by Pacaut (1956), p. 365. See Watt (1965), pp. 23–5.
[16] *Constitutum Constantini* c.14, p. 88; c.16, pp. 92–3.
[17] Suger of St-Denis, *Vita Ludovici grossi regis* c.32, p. 262. See Klewitz (1939), p. 56; Stroll (1987), p. 122.
[18] Suger, *Vita Ludovici* c.32, p. 262. Cf. *Constitutum Constantini* c.16, p. 92.
[19] Boso of S. Pudenziana, 'Vita Hadriani, IV', II, pp. 391–2.

on a white horse nor surrounded by knights nor encircled by clamouring servants . . . In these respects you are the heir not of Peter but of Constantine.'[20] Bernard himself had witnessed the triumphant return of Innocent II to Rome at the end of the papal schism of 1130–8 and his remarks may have been a response to an intensification of the *imitatio imperii* during these years, inspired by Innocent II's struggle against his rival, Anacletus II. 'The church has both elected and consecrated you as Caesar and ruler of the whole world', Innocent was told in 1137 by Cardinal Gerard of S. Croce (the future Pope Lucius II).[21] It has been suggested that it was Innocent who installed at the entrance of the Lateran palace, as symbols of the imperial authority of the papacy, the two thrones with panels of porphyry described in the *Ordines Romani* (*c.* 1188). Certainly he was aware of the symbolic character of porphyry, the purple stone associated with the Roman emperors, since he was the first pope to choose a porphyry tomb for his own burial (a sarcophagus believed to have been that of Emperor Hadrian). His example was followed by Adrian IV, Lucius III and Urban III.[22] To this same context of the imperial papacy of the 1130s belonged the controversial mural in the St Nicholas chapel of the Lateran palace in which Innocent II commemorated the imperial coronation of Lothar III. The German accounts of this mural (written after Frederick Barbarossa had demanded its removal in 1155) emphasize the feudal theme of the picture and its tendentious inscription. The picture showed Innocent 'seated on the papal throne and Emperor Lothar in his presence with hands folded, bowing down to receive the crown of the empire'; while the inscription read: 'The king . . . becomes the vassal of the pope and takes the crown which he gives.'[23] That the emperor ought to hold his empire by feudal tenure as the vassal of the pope had been the most radical of the political ideas of Gregory VII.[24]

The Gregorian doctrine of the supremacy of the papacy over the empire was enunciated in the papal curia of Eugenius III – who declared that Christ 'gave to St Peter the keys of the kingdom of heaven, the power of both the earthly and the heavenly empire'[25] – and of Adrian IV. The last official appearance of this doctrine during our period was at the imperial assembly of Besançon in October 1157. On this occasion Emperor Frederick I and his princes were outraged by the terminology both of a letter of Adrian IV and of the papal legate who delivered the letter to the assembly. The papal letter spoke of the

---

[20] Bernard, 'De consideratione' IV.3.6.

[21] Gerard of S. Croce, panegyric in Schramm (1968–71), IV, p. 183 n. 26. See Stroll (1987), p. 124.

[22] Deér (1959), pp. 144–53.

[23] *Chronica regia Coloniensis*, p. 93. Rahewin, *Gesta Friderici imperatoris* III.10, p. 141. See Ladner (1935); Kempf (1963), pp. 23–5; Frugoni (1967); Heinemeyer (1969).

[24] Gregory VII, *Register* IX.3. See Robinson (1990), pp. 410–11.

[25] Eugenius III, JL 9149, col. 1285A.

pope 'conferring' the *beneficium* of the empire on Frederick, which, in his German translation of the letter, the imperial chancellor rendered as meaning that Frederick had 'received the imperial crown as a fief from the lord pope'. The uproar caused by this translation was aggravated by the remark of the papal legate: 'From whom does he hold the empire, if not from the lord pope?'[26] Adrian was obliged to pacify the emperor with a non-feudal interpretation of his original letter: 'Among us *beneficium* means not a fief but a good deed.'[27] During the eighteen-year conflict between empire and papacy which followed the election of Pope Alexander III in 1159 the language of papal supremacy in secular affairs disappeared from the curia. Gregorian language might be used by Alexander III's supporters – by the poet Walter of Châtillon, declaring that 'Caesar receives the temporal power from him who possesses the pastoral care',[28] and by John of Salisbury, urging the precedent of Gregory VII's conduct towards Henry IV[29] – but it was not used by Alexander's curia. The pope excommunicated his enemy, Frederick Barbarossa, and denounced him as a tyrant, but he did not claim to be able either to depose him from his office or to possess a general right of *correctio* in secular affairs. Dependent as he was for his survival on the financial and political aid of the Sicilian, French and English kings, Alexander III could not afford to alienate them by claims of papal superiority over secular rulers. Similarly during the two decades following the schism of 1159–77 the papal curia, bankrupt and war-weary, made no attempt to claim temporal supremacy.

While the idea of papal authority over 'the earthly empire' waxed and waned, the Gregorian conception of the papal primacy in the church was enthusiastically developed and consolidated by the theologians and canonists of the twelfth century. Once more the contribution that was to prove most influential was that of Bernard of Clairvaux in his treatise *De consideratione*, in which he informed Eugenius III that he had 'no equal on earth' and that to his care had been committed 'the universal church spread throughout the world, made up of all the churches'.[30] 'The fullness of power (*plenitudo potestatis*) over all the churches of the world has been given as a unique privilege to the apostolic see', wrote Bernard in 1135. His interpretation of the ancient term *plenitudo potestatis* was adopted by the papal chancery at the end of the century as the

---

[26] Rahewin, *Gesta Friderici imperatoris* III. 10, pp. 141, 140. The letter in question was Adrian IV, JL 10304: Rahewin, *Gesta Friderici imperatoris* III.9, pp. 139–40. See Ullmann (1954) and (1955), pp. 243–4; Heinemeyer (1969); Munz (1969), pp. 140–5.

[27] Adrian IV, JL 10386: Rahewin, *Gesta Friderici imperatoris* III.22, pp. 156–7.

[28] Walter of Châtillon, 'Carmina' II, p. 560.

[29] John of Salisbury, *Letters* 236, 239, 240, 242, 272–4, 298, pp. 446, 454, 458, 474, 553, 572, 574, 690. See Reuter (1984), pp. 416–18.

[30] Bernard, 'De consideratione' II.2.4; II.8.16. See *NCMH*, IV, Part 1, ch. 11.

standard expression for the pope's supremacy over the ecclesiastical hierarchy.[31] As 'declarer of truth' and 'defender of the faith'[32] the pope used his 'unique monarchy of all churches'[33] to preserve doctrinal purity and to achieve the reform of individual churches and of the universal church. It was to the papal curia that the enemies of Peter Abelard appealed in June 1140 to secure the condemnation of 'the heretic'.[34] It was to the curia that the theologian Gerhoch of Reichersberg addressed his treatises calling for the reform of the church in 1142, 1151 and 1156[35] and Henry of Marcy, abbot of Clairvaux, addressed his appeals for the defence of the church against the heretics in southern France.[36]

'It is understood that we have been promoted to the government of the apostolic see in order to increase religion', declared Calixtus II, 'and to establish by the authority of our office whatever is right and whatever is done for the salvation of souls.' This statement of the papal duty to promote and order the religious life appears in the papal privilege conferring protection on the 'New Monastery' of Cîteaux.[37] Calixtus II's privilege of 1119 for Cîteaux illustrates the papacy's principal preoccupation in its relationship with monastic reform during the twelfth century. The privilege confirmed 'certain chapters concerning the observance of the Rule of St Benedict and other matters that seem necessary in [the Cistercian] order': namely the Cistercian constitution, *Carta Caritatis*, and the original statutes guaranteeing the uniformity of the order.[38] The papacy had intervened in order to ensure that Cistercian monasticism was an authentic expression of *regularitas*, the correct observance of the Benedictine Rule. 'First and foremost', begins Innocent II's privilege of 1131 for the canons regular of Auxerre, 'we command that the canonical order according to the Rule of St Augustine shall be preserved in perpetuity in that church.'[39]

The 'new orders' of the early twelfth century – the religious of Chartreuse, Cîteaux, Fontevrault, Savigny, the Knights of the Temple and of the Hospital, the canons of St Ruf in Avignon, Prémontré, Arrouaise and St Victor in Paris – were the product of local reforming initiatives, claiming to restore the ancient forms of religious life. The pope's role was not to initiate but to authenticate. Papal recognition of these experiments, in the form of a privilege granting the protection of St Peter, confirmed that they were genuine expressions of the ancient Rules by which they claimed to have been inspired. Such papal privileges were an important demonstration of the papacy's power of legitimation. The twelfth-century papal chancery was well aware of this and provided each

[31] Bernard, 'Epistola' 131. See *NCMH*, IV, Part 1, ch. 11.   [32] Bernard, 'De consideratione' IV.7.23.
[33] Rufinus of Assisi, 'Sermo habitus in Lateranensi concilio', p. 117.
[34] Bernard, 'Epistola' 188. See Little (1973); Zerbi (1975).   [35] Classen (1960), pp. 181–4, 234–7.
[36] Henry of Marcy, abbot of Clairvaux, 'Epistola' 11.   [37] Calixtus II, JL 6795, col. 1147B.
[38] Calixtus II, JL 6795, col. 1147C. See Lefèvre (1954).
[39] Innocent II, JL 7486, col 1011C. See Dubois (1968), pp. 285–6.

privilege with an impressive 'primacy arenga', a protocol that reminded the recipient of the unique authority of the donor.[40] 'The holy Roman church, which holds from God a principate over all the churches', proclaims a 'primacy arenga' of Adrian IV, 'like a diligent mother provides for the individual churches with constant vigilance: all must have recourse to her, as to their head and origin, to be defended by her authority, to be nourished by her breasts and freed of their oppressions.'[41]

A series of papal interventions during the twelfth century demonstrated that the popes were as ready to correct deviations from *regularitas* as they were to confirm the rights of monasteries. For the generality of monasteries papal policy was stated in the First Lateran Council (1123): 'monks are to be subject to their own bishops with all humility and are to show due obedience and devout subjection in all things to them'.[42] The council restated the ruling of the council of Chalcedon (451), curbing those aspirations for monastic liberty encouraged by the Investiture Contest. Calixtus II and the fathers in the council took seriously the charges against insubordinate monks, who 'hunger insatiably for the rights of bishops' and 'strive by fair means and foul to destroy what belongs to bishops'.[43] Those privileged monasteries that had been exempted from the authority of their diocesan and subjected directly to the Roman church were to understand that 'not only the correction of the persons [of the monks] but also the care and disposal of the whole monastery are [the pope's] concern'.[44] In a striking demonstration of this power of *correctio* Honorius II deposed the heads of the two monasteries that had been closest to the Gregorian papacy, on the grounds of their disobedience (1126). Abbot Pons of Cluny had fallen foul of faction-fighting in his abbey; Oderisius II of Monte Cassino was perhaps the victim of the personal enmity of the pope.[45] Innocent II demanded from the monks of Monte Cassino an oath of fidelity and obedience, which the monks declared to be contrary to their Rule (1137).[46] Eugenius III (the former Cistercian abbot of Trefontane in Rome) ordered the reform of the abbey of Fleury by the monks of Cluny.[47] He punished the disobedience of the abbey of Baumes-Les-Messiers by reducing its status to that of a priory of Cluny(1147).[48]

[40] Fichtenau (1957), pp. 101–12.
[41] Adrian IV, *Papsturkunden in England*, III, p. 234.   [42] Concilium Lateranense I, c.16.
[43] *Chronica monasterii Casinensis* IV.78, p. 542. Cf. Council of Chalcedon, c.4, 8. See *NCMH*, IV, Part I, ch. 9.
[44] Alexander III, JL 12631, *Acta pontificum Romanorum inedita*, III, p. 242. See Maccarrone (1980), pp. 59–60.
[45] Tellenbach (1963); Hoffmann (1971); Zerbi (1972); Cowdrey (1978), pp. 181–268.
[46] *Chronicon monasterii Casinensis* IV.108, p. 572. See Schmale (1961b) p. 172.
[47] Eugenius III, JL 9632, *Epistolae pontificum Romanorum ineditae*, p. 110.
[48] Eugenius III, JL 9061, col. 1227BC. The abbey had failed to obey a papal legate. The sentence was confirmed by Adrian IV, JL 10053, cols. 1415C–1417C.

Alexander III deposed Abbot Hugh III of Cluny for the offence of supporting Emperor Frederick I and his antipope and suspended the monks' right of free election (1161).[49] Lucius III, Urban III, Clement III and Celestine III all intervened in the order of Grandmont to end the schism caused by the rebellion of the lay brothers (1185–8).[50]

The twelfth-century papacy was often obliged to rely on the practical assistance of members of the religious orders to no less a degree than the Gregorian papacy in the late eleventh century. The victory of Innocent II in the schism of the 1130s owed much to the efforts of Bernard of Clairvaux and to other representatives of the new orders, like Peter the Venerable, Norbert of Xanten and Gerhoch of Reichersberg.[51] If Innocent II, 'although expelled from the city, was supported by the world',[52] it was the indefatigable lobbying of Bernard that had helped to rally this support.[53] Bernard's interventions in controversial episcopal elections, his efforts to secure the condemnation of the teachings of Peter Abelard and Gilbert of la Porrée and his role in preaching the Second Crusade all bear witness to his continued influence in the curia.[54] During the schism of 1159–77 Alexander III was indebted to the Cistercian order for their diplomatic efforts to secure for him the recognition of the French and English kingdoms.[55] Alexander was similarly beholden to the order of the Knights Templars, who raised loans for the impoverished papal curia, as well as helping to administer the papal finances.[56] During the last quarter of the twelfth century a central figure in the execution of papal policy was Henry of Marcy, abbot of Clairvaux, who organized the suppression of heresy in southern France, negotiated peace between the French and English kings and preached the Third Crusade.[57]

Throughout the century the papacy recruited members of religious orders to the curia to serve and advise the pope. The eight Cistercian cardinals of the twelfth century, all former monks of Clairvaux, were the legacy of Bernard's influence.[58] The houses of regular canons, S. Frediano in Lucca and S. Maria in Rheno, Bologna, seem each to have provided five cardinals during the

---

[49] Alexander III, JL 10660, 10661, cols. 112AD, 113A–114C. See Maccarrone (1980), pp. 85–6.
[50] Foreville-Rousset de Pina (1953), pp. 303–4.
[51] Klewitz (1957), pp. 210–11, 254–5; Classen (1960), pp. 81–2; Schmale (1961b), pp. 56–7, 77–80, 253–79; Schmale (1961a); Reuter (1983); Stroll (1987), pp. 169–78.
[52] Bernard, 'Epistola' 124 c.2.   [53] Ibid. 124–6.
[54] Constable (1953), pp. 244–7, and (1957); Häring (1965), (1966a) and (1967). See also above p. 324 n. 34.
[55] Preiss (1934), pp. 28–36; Mahn (1945), pp. 142–7. On the persecution that the Cistercian order suffered in the imperial territories as a consequence of their support for Alexander III see Reuter (1976).
[56] Jordan (1933–4), p. 77; Geisthardt (1936), pp. 78–9.   [57] Congar (1958), pp. 45–55.
[58] Jacqueline (1953), p. 29; but see also Zenker (1964), pp. 21, 40, 55, 96, 133, 148, 184.

century.[59] The popes of the period 1124–59 were themselves representatives of the new religious orders of *c*. 1100, with exceptions of the secular clerks Celestine II and Anastasius IV.[60] By the middle of the century the papacy was 'already on the threshold of the period in which the lawyers . . . overtook the religious in the curia'.[61] The popes of the period 1159–98 were former secular clerks, except for Gregory VIII.[62] The cardinals attempted to elect a monk in October 1187, but their chosen candidate, Henry of Marcy, abbot of Clairvaux and cardinal bishop of Albano, declined the honour.[63] The alliance between the papacy and monastic reform was as strong in the later twelfth century as it had been in the later eleventh century. The active role of the religious as agents of the papacy in the schism of 1159–77, in the preaching of the crusade and in the suppression of heresy was as much at odds with ancient canon law and the principle of *regularitas* as had been the role of monks in the Investiture Contest. The papacy's relationship with the religious orders was a constant reminder that the laws of the church 'are in the heart of the lord pope and he may interpret them as he pleases': 'the making, interpreting and abrogating of the canons is in his power'.[64] In cases of *necessitas* and in the interests of reform the pope could adapt existing institutions to meet the ever changing circumstances of the church.

The papal programme for the reform of the universal church and Christian society during the years 1122–98 can be most easily studied in the canons of the 'general councils' of this period. The term *concilium generale* was first used by the papal curia to describe Calixtus II's council of Rheims (1119) and his First Lateran Council (1123). The same term (or the synonymous terms *concilium magnum* or *synodus plenaria*) was subsequently used by the curia to designate

---

[59] S. Frediano in Lucca: Zenker (1964), pp. 41, 129–31, 132, 144; Pfaff (1955), p. 89. See also Schmidt (1972), pp. 199–221. S. Maria in Rheno, Bologna: Brixius (1912), pp. 65–6; Zenker (1964), pp. 41, 107, 112, 142, 149.

[60] Honorius II was a former canon of S. Maria in Rheno, Bologna: Schmale (1961b), p. 140; Hüls (1977), p. 106. Innocent II was perhaps a former canon of St John Lateran: Schmale (1961b), pp. 39–40; but see also Maleczek (1981), p. 33. Lucius II was a former canon of S. Frediano in Lucca: Zenker (1964), p. 129. Eugenius III was a former monk of Clairvaux and pupil of Bernard: Zenker (1964), pp. 185–6. Adrian IV was a former canon of St Ruf in Avignon: Zenker (1964), p. 36. Classen (1968), pp. 36–63, refutes the suggestion that Anastasius IV was also formerly a canon of St Rufus in Avignon.

[61] Classen (1968), pp. 38–9.

[62] Gregory VIII was formerly a canon of St Martin in Laon: Kehr (1924), p. 250. Alexander III has been identified as a former regular canon: Zenker (1964), pp. 86, 210n; but see Noonan (1977) on the problem of establishing the details of Alexander's early career. Lucius III has been identified as a former Cistercian monk on the grounds of his close association with the order during his pontificate: Brixius (1912), p. 43; Pfaff (1981), p. 173; but see Wenck (1926), pp. 421–2; Zenker (1964), p. 23.

[63] Peter of Blois, letter to Archbishop Baldwin of Canterbury, *Epistolae Cantuarienses*, pp. 107–8. See Wenck (1926), pp. 428–9.

[64] Peter the Chanter, '*Verbum abbreviatum*' c.53. See *NCMH*, IV, Part 1, ch. 11.

Innocent II's councils of Rheims (1131) and Pisa (1135) and his Second Lateran Council (1139), Eugenius III's council of Rheims (1148) and Alexander III's Third Lateran Council (1179).[65] At no subsequent period of its history did the papacy assemble so many 'general councils'. These papal councils were called 'general' because they were attended by clergy from every part of Christendom and because their conciliar decrees were binding on the whole church.[66] According to the official language of the curia, the pope summoned to the council 'churchmen from the various regions, whose presence and counsel will permit the taking of sound decisions'.[67] The language of the conciliar decrees similarly suggests consultation and shared decision-making: 'we have decreed on the advice of our brethren and with the approval of the sacred council'.[68] In practice, however, growing procedural sophistication, involving preliminary investigations and commissions of experts (*viri periti*), meant that the role of the majority of participants was simply to approve the decrees prepared beforehand by the curia.[69] The 'general councils' of the twelfth century served mainly to demonstrate the unique authority of the Roman church 'to assemble a universal council, to make new canons and to obliterate old ones'.[70]

The First Lateran Council of 1123 saw the last appearance of the Gregorian reform programme that had preoccupied the papacy for the past fifty years. The decree prohibiting lay investiture figured for the last time in a papal council, as did the decree requiring the canonical election of bishops.[71] The familiar Gregorian decree prohibiting clerical marriage continued to be promulgated after 1123. The version issued by Innocent II's council of Rheims (1131) and Second Lateran Council (1139) had a markedly Gregorian flavour. 'Adhering to the footsteps of our predecessors, the Roman pontiffs Gregory VII, Urban and Paschal, we command that no one is to hear the masses of those whom he knows to have wives or concubines.'[72] By the middle of the century, however,

[65] E.g. Calixtus II, JL 6977, 6995, 7028, 7031, 7034, 7037, 7056, 7075, 7144, 7147; Innocent II, JL 8007, 8016, 8017; Alexander III, JL 13070, 13097-9. The term *concilium generale* was not used by the curia in the case of Calixtus II's council of Toulouse (1119) or Innocent II's council of Clermont (1130), which were attended only by bishops and abbots from southern France. In the narrative sources, although not in the official papal sources, the term *concilium generale* is used of Alexander III's council of Tours (1163), attendance at which was on the same scale as in the 'general councils' of the twelfth century. See Schmale (1974), pp. 37-8.

[66] On the meaning of 'general' as a synonym for 'Catholic' in patristic usage see, for example, Isidore of Seville, *De ecclesiasticis officiis* I.3, *PL* 83, col. 740A: 'Catholica autem ideo dicitur, quia per universum mundum est constituta, vel quoniam catholica, hoc est, generalis in ea doctrina est.' See Fuhrmann (1961), pp. 682-3.

[67] Alexander III, JL 13097, col. 1184D.   [68] Concilium Lateranense III c.1.

[69] Schmale (1974), p. 29. See also *NCMH*, IV, Part 1, ch. 11.

[70] Rufinus of Assisi, 'Sermo habitus in Lateranensi concilio', p. 119.

[71] Concilium Lateranense I, c.1, 3.

[72] Council of Rheims (1131) c.5; Concilium Lateranense II c.7.

the reiteration of this prohibition seemed to some contemporaries to be superfluous. When it was restated at the council of Rheims in 1148, 'it seemed to some to be a futile and ludicrous decree; for who does not know that this is unlawful?'[73] Subsequent councils nevertheless considered it necessary to repeat the demand for a celibate clergy, using the sanction of the loss of the benefice.[74]

Meanwhile a reform programme with a new emphasis, building on the achievements of the Gregorian papacy, had been introduced in the five councils of Innocent II – Clermont (1130), Rheims (1131), Piacenza (1132), Pisa (1135) and the Second Lateran (1139) – and elaborated in the councils of Eugenius III and Alexander III. The new reform programme assumed that the Gregorian battle to protect the church from the encroachments of the secular power had now been won. The purpose of this programme, developed during the papal schism of the 1130s, was to enhance the dignity and sacrosanct character of the clerical estate and to impose Christian standards of conduct on the laity. The clergy was to be recruited only from properly qualified candidates, 'wise and religious persons' of mature age. (The Third Lateran Council emphasized the additional qualification, 'knowledge of literature'.)[75] Neither clerks nor religious should follow 'the wicked and detestable custom' of studying 'secular law and medicine for the sake of worldly lucre' lest they neglect the cure of souls.[76] The clerical order must be distinct from the laity in the style of their dress. 'Both bishops and clerks ... shall not, by the superfluity, cut or colour of their clothes nor by their tonsure, offend the sight of observers, to whom they ought to be a model and example.'[77] To these requirements Alexander III's Third Lateran Council (1179) added a prohibition of pluralism. Clerks who were led by avarice to 'acquire various ecclesiastical dignities and many parish churches against the statutes of the holy canons' were to lose these benefices and their patrons were to lose the right of presentation.[78]

The Third Lateran Council also ruled on a much debated aspect of the problem of the demarcation of the spiritual and the secular spheres. 'No clerk is to presume to take up ... the administration of secular judgement under any princes or secular men, so as to become their justiciars.' Clerks who served as officials in secular courts acted contrary to the teaching of the apostle, 'No soldier of God is to entangle himself in secular affairs' (II Timothy 2:4). They

---

[73] John of Salisbury, *Historia pontificalis* c.3, p. 8.

[74] E.g. Concilium Lateranense III (1179) c.11; Concilium Lateranense IV (1215) c.14.

[75] Council of Clermont (1130) c.11; Rheims (1131) c.8, 15; Pisa (1135) c.9; Concilium Lateranense II (1139) c.10, 16. Cf. Concilium Lateranense III (1179) c.3.

[76] Council of Clermont (1130) c.5; Rheims (1131) c.6; Concilium Lateranense II (1139) c.9; see Kuttner (1964) pp. 237–46; Somerville (1976), pp. 105–44.

[77] Council of Clermont (1130) c.2; Rheims (1131) c.2; Concilium Lateranense II (1139) c.4. See John of Salisbury, *Historia pontificalis* c.3, p. 8, for a protest on this subject in the council of Rheims of 1148.

[78] Concilium Lateranense III c.13. See Baldwin (1970), p. 119.

'neglect the clerical office and plunge into the tempests of the world in order to please the powerful of this world'.[79] The service of clerks as officials of secular courts (*curiales*) was a widespread phenomenon and important source of ecclesiastical advancement, which found eloquent defenders in the later twelfth century.[80] Alexander III himself had condoned Hugh of Champfleury's continuing to serve as chancellor of King Louis VII of France after being elected bishop of Soissons in 1159.[81] King Henry II of England, knowing that 'the archbishop of Mainz claimed the title of arch-chancellor in Germany under the king, as did the archbishop of Cologne in Italy under the emperor', desired that his servant Thomas Becket should similarly add to his office of chancellor that of archbishop of Canterbury 'to promote the interests of the kingdom and the peace of the church'. Becket's resignation of the chancellor's office on becoming archbishop (1162) was not the least of the factors that provoked conflict between archbishop and king.[82] The decree of the Third Lateran Council was a reminder that secular administrations imposed judicial sentences involving bloodshed and that, according to ancient canon law, clerks who were implicated in these 'blood judgements' could not administer the sacraments.[83]

The twelfth-century reform programme emphasized that the persons and the property of the clergy were sacrosanct. So heinous was the offence of the man who 'at the devil's persuasion incurred the guilt of the sacrilege of laying violent hands on a clerk or a monk', that the resultant anathema could be lifted only by the pope.[84] Innocent II's councils condemned the 'right of spoil' (*ius spolii*). 'The goods of deceased bishops should be seized by no man but should remain in the possession of the steward and the clergy for the use of their churches and their successors.'[85] The Third Lateran Council condemned secular rulers who imposed taxation on church property (over and above the

---

[79] Concilium Lateranense III c.12.

[80] Most famously the defence of the life of a clerical *curialis* by Peter of Blois, 'Epistola' 150. See Southern (1953), pp. 212–13. But see also Peter of Blois's letter repenting the ambition that had led him to a career in secular government: 'Epistola' 14. See also Baldwin (1970), pp. 178–9.

[81] Alexander III, JL 10711, 10743, cols. 137C–138C, 162AB (to Bishop Hugh of Soissons). The pope hoped that Hugh of Champfleury would use his influence at the French court to keep Louis VII loyal to the Alexandrine cause in the papal schism. See Foreville and Rousset de Pina (1953), p. 69.

[82] Ralph of Diceto, 'Ex ymaginibus historiarum' 1162, I, p. 308. See Smalley (1973), p. 119; Barlow (1986), p. 67.

[83] Gratian, 'Decretum' C.23 q.8 c.30; cf. D.50 c.8; John of Salisbury, *Policraticus* VII.20, II, pp. 182–90. See Baldwin (1970), p. 178; Smalley (1973), pp. 100–1.

[84] Council of Rheims (1131) c.13; Pisa (1135) c.12; Concilium Lateranense II (1139) c.15. See Kuttner (1935), pp. 68–9. On this *privilegium canonis* see *NCMH*, IV, Part I, ch. 11.

[85] Council of Clermont (1130) c.3; Rheims (1131) c.3; Concilium Lateranense II (1139) c.5. This conciliar legislation extended the decree of the Council of Chalcedon (451) c. 22, concerning the *ius spolii* in the case of bishops, to all *presbyteri vel clerici*.

conventional obligations of the *regalia*). Modern princes were worse than the godless pharaoh, who at least 'left his priests and their possessions in their ancient freedom and gave them sustenance from public resources' (Exodus l: 18–12). The council excommunicated princes who taxed the church 'unless the bishop and clergy perceive that so great an emergency exists that, without compulsion, they consider that (the resources of the laity being insufficient) subsidies ought to be granted by the churches to relieve the general need'.[86] This decree, the earliest conciliar legislation on a subject that was to have so great an impact on the relations of *regnum* and *sacerdotium* in the following century, conceded that ecclesiastical property was subject to secular taxation in a case of *necessitas*. It was, however, left to churchmen to decide whether the emergency claimed by the secular power was genuine.[87]

As for secular society, the twelfth-century reform programme condemned the practice of usury and sought to regulate the warfare and the war-games of the military ruling class. Canon law had long been preoccupied with usury, but the principal emphasis was on usurious clergy. They were to be punished with suspension or degradation.[88] In 1139 the Second Lateran Council turned to the question of eradicating usury among the laity. The council condemned 'the insatiable rapacity of usurers, detestable and shameful, rejected by Scripture in the Old and New Testaments'. Usurers were to be excluded from 'all ecclesiastical comfort'; they were 'to be regarded as infamous as long as they lived and, unless they came to their senses, they were to be deprived of Christian burial'.[89] Forty years later the Third Lateran Council noted that 'the crime of usury has become so deeply rooted in almost every region that many men have given up other businesses in order to practise usury as if it was legal'. As an additional sanction the council decreed the suspension of any clerk who gave Christian burial to a 'manifest usurer'.[90]

The papal councils of the 1130s were the first to prohibit 'those detestable fairs or holidays on which knights are accustomed to assemble by agreement and fight to demonstrate their strength and their rash audacity, from which the deaths of men and the peril of souls often results'.[91] These 'holidays' were tournaments, an aristocratic pastime so important by the end of the twelfth

[86] Concilium Lateranense III c.19. The decree drew attention in particular to the demands of *rectores et consules civitatum*, that is, of the Italian city-republics. See Baldwin (1970), p. 218.
[87] The Fourth Lateran Council (1215), c.46, added the further condition that the local clergy before consenting to pay tax 'Romanum prius consulant pontificem, cuius interest communibus utilitatibus providere' (COD, p. 255). On the contemporary debate in the schools about secular taxation see Baldwin (1970), pp. 218–20.
[88] Gratian, 'Decretum' D.47 c.1–5. See McLaughlin (1940), pp. 1–22; Baldwin (1970), pp. 296–311.
[89] Concilium Lateranense II c.13. See McLaughlin (1940), p. 4.
[90] Concilium Lateranense III c.25.
[91] Council of Clermont (1130) c.9; Rheims (1131) c.21; Concilium Lateranense II c.14.

century that in some parts of France they were held every fortnight during
late autumn.[92] Eugenius III and Alexander III, conscious that these war-games
seriously affected recruitment for the crusade, confirmed Innocent II's denial
of Christian burial to those who met their death in tournaments.[93] In an
attempt to reduce casualties in war the Second Lateran Council forbade the
use of crossbows and catapults in warfare against Christians.[94] In particular
the councils of the 1130s anathematized 'the most wicked, destructive and
horrendous crime of arson': 'this plague and inimical devastation surpasses all
other kinds of depredation.' Those who used arson as an instrument of war or
revenge should be denied Christian burial. Penitent incendiaries might expiate
their offence by a full year's service in the holy war in Jerusalem or Spain.[95]

Finally, in 1179 the Third Lateran Council excommunicated certain notorious groups of 'routiers', professional warriors who were hired as mercenaries in
the armies of princes and resorted to brigandage when they could not find employment. The council denounced them as heretics because 'they wrought such
cruelty against Christians that they respected neither churches nor monasteries,
neither widows and orphans nor old people and children and spared neither
age nor sex, but destroyed and laid waste everything, like pagans'. Those who
employed them were to be denounced publicly in the churches and were to
share the anathema of their employees. The faithful who took arms against
these 'heretics' were promised the rewards of the participants in a holy war.[96]
The twelfth-century papal councils, therefore, extended the scope of ecclesiastical supervision of secular conduct. The Gregorian reform had been concerned
above all with the defence of the *sacerdotium* from the encroachment of the
laity. The twelfth-century reform programme, while accentuating the separateness and privileged status of the clergy, made a series of precise demands
(generally ignored) requiring the laity to conform to the values of a Christian
society.

In addition the papal councils of these years promoted the role of the pope
as the protector of the Catholic faith from heresy, the role described by Bernard
of Clairvaux as 'the defender of the faith, the teacher of the nations'.[97] This role
was of crucial importance for the two popes whose legitimacy was challenged
by rivals in the schisms of 1130–8 and 1159–77. The victors in these conflicts,

---

[92] Baldwin (1970), pp. 224–6; Keen (1984), pp. 84, 94, 96; Barker (1986), pp. 70–1, 73–4.

[93] Council of Rheims (1148) c.12; Concilium Lateranense III c.20.

[94] Concilium Lateranense II c.29. See Fournier (1916), pp. 471–9. The lethal character of the crossbow
greatly preoccupied the moralists of the twelfth-century schools: Baldwin (1970), pp. 223–4.

[95] Council of Clermont (1130) c.31; Rheims (1131) c.17; Concilium Lateranense II c.18.

[96] Concilium Lateranense III c.27. On the identity of 'the Brabançons, Aragonese, Navarese, Basques,
Cottereaux and Triaverdini' see Boussard (1945–6), pp. 189–224; Baldwin (1970), pp. 220–3; Hehl
(1980), pp. 245–6.

[97] Bernard, 'De consideratione' IV.7.23.

Innocent II and Alexander III, represented themselves as triumphing over heresy as well as schism. Innocent II, exiled from Rome by the allies of his rival, Anacletus II, used his councils as much to demonstrate the legitimacy of his own cause as to publicize his reform programme. His council of Clermont (18 November 1130) was held soon after he had been assured of the support of King Louis VI and the French kingdom. The attendance of churchmen from the provinces of Lyons, Bourges, Vienne, Arles, Tarentaise, Narbonne, Auch and Tarragona demonstrated the rapid growth of the Innocentine obedience.[98] The council of Rheims (18–26 October 1131) was attended by numerous French, German, English and Spanish bishops. It witnessed both the coronation of the future King Louis VII of France and an embassy from the German king Lothar III, promising an expedition against the antipope.[99] The council of Pisa (May 1135) was a similar demonstration of the widespread acceptance of Innocent's claims. The council was attended by 126 archbishops and bishops from the kingdoms of Italy, Germany, France, England, Spain and Hungary and witnessed the excommunication of the antipope and his adherents.[100] The Second Lateran Council (3–8 April 1139) celebrated Innocent's victory in the schism.[101] The opening sermon preached by the pope declared the theme of this 'general council': the unity of the Catholic church was guaranteed solely by the Roman primacy. 'Rome is the head of the world' and it is the business of her bishop alone 'to order according to his wisdom whatever is in confusion'.[102] The council obediently declared unlawful the ordinations performed by the antipope Anacletus II 'and the other schismatics and heretics' and invalidated all their actions.[103]

Similarly, the theme of Alexander III's councils was the defence of Catholic unity against the schismatics. The subject of the opening discourse of his council of Tours (19 May 1163), pronounced by Bishop Arnulf of Lisieux, was the unity and freedom of the church.[104] The council solemnly recognized the legality of the election of Alexander III and excommunicated his rival, the antipope 'Victor IV'.[105] The participation in these proceedings of 124 archbishops and bishops and more than 400 other churchmen from France, Italy, Sicily, Spain, England, Ireland, Scotland and the Latin kingdom of Jerusalem together with messages of support from prelates in central Europe, demonstrated the strength

[98] Mansi 21, cols. 437–40. See Foreville (1965), p. 75.
[99] Mansi 21, cols. 453–72. See Foreville (1965), p. 75; Somerville (1975), pp. 122–30.
[100] Mansi 21, cols. 485–8 (here wrongly dated 1134). See Foreville (1965), p. 77; Somerville (1970), pp. 98–114.
[101] For the date of the council see Foreville (1965), p. 78, who differs from *COD*, p. 195.
[102] *Chronicon Mauriniacensis monasterii* III.   [103] Concilium Lateranense II c.30.
[104] Arnulf of Lisieux, *Sermo*, Mansi 21, cols. 1167–75.
[105] Council of Tours, *ibid.*, col. 1179. See Somerville (1977), pp. 14–18.

of the Alexandrine obedience. Like Innocent II's councils of 1130–5, the council of Tours was a propaganda exercise in the midst of a bitterly fought schism. The papal council that followed Alexander's victory, the Third Lateran Council (5–19 March 1179), like its predecessor, declared invalid the ordinations of 'the heresiarchs', the antipopes of the preceding schism.[106] The subject of the opening discourse, preached by the distinguished canonist Bishop Rufinus of Assisi, was (as in the Second Lateran Council) the Roman primacy. 'The holy Roman church, since she is the apex of all episcopal thrones and since she is the mother of all churches and the mistress of all, has most worthily deserved to obtain a unique monarchy of all churches.'[107]

The papal role of 'defender of the faith' derived from the scriptural text Luke 22:32, one of the traditional 'authorities' for the Petrine primacy. It was to this text, for example, that Innocent II referred when announcing the condemnation of Peter Abelard (1141): 'we, who, although unworthy, are seen to sit on the seat of St Peter – to whom the Lord said, "and when you have turned again, strengthen your brethren" – have condemned ... all the teachings of Peter ... together with their author'.[108] The same 'authority' provided the starting-point for Gratian's argument that the Roman church was the guarantor of orthodoxy. Christ 'bore witness that he had prayed especially for [Peter's] faith and enjoined him to strengthen the other [apostles]'. Consequently the Roman church had never erred: 'in the apostolic see the Catholic religion has always been preserved without a blemish'. By means of his authority as supreme judge the pope could resolve questions of doctrine and condemn heretics.[109] Hence the Decretist Huguccio included the resolution of 'a question of the faith' (quaestio fidei) among the maiores causae reserved to the judgement of the pope.[110]

In the course of the century papal councils became increasingly preoccupied with suspected heretics and suspect theologians. Already in 1119 Calixtus II's council of Toulouse concerned itself with unnamed heretics 'who, claiming the pretext of religion, condemn the sacrament of the Lord's body and blood, the baptism of children, the priesthood and the other ecclesiastical orders and contracts of lawful matrimony': 'we condemn them as heretics and expel them from the church of God'.[111] This decree was reissued almost verbatim by the Second Lateran Council (1139).[112] In 1135 the wandering preacher Henry of Lausanne was brought before Innocent II's council of Pisa by the archbishop of Arles, condemned for his notoriously heretical teachings and punished by

[106] III Lateran (1179) c.2. (that is, the antipopes Victor IV, Paschal III and Calixtus III).
[107] Rufinus, 'Sermo habitus in Lateranensi concilio', p. 118.   [108] Innocent II, JL 8148, col. 517A.
[109] Gratian, 'Decretum', D.21 ante c.1; C.24 q.1. c.11. See Tierney (1972), pp. 33–4.
[110] Huguccio, Summa ad D.17 c.3, quoted by Watt (1965), p. 84.
[111] Council of Toulouse c.3.   [112] Concilium Lateranense II c.23.

being made a monk of Clairvaux.[113] The Second Lateran Council investigated the case of the reformer Arnold, prior of the house of regular canons in Brescia. He was deprived of his office for the offence of fomenting rebellion against the bishop of Brescia.[114]

The concern with heresy was particularly pronounced in Eugenius III's council of Rheims in 1148, perhaps reflecting the anxiety of the pope's mentor, Bernard of Clairvaux. It was indeed Bernard who brought the case against Gilbert of la Porré, bishop of Poitiers, that was heard by members of the council. Gilbert was saved from condemnation by cardinals and prelates suspicious of Bernard's motives and determined that the bishop of Poitiers should escape the fate of Peter Abelard.[115] The Breton heretic Eon de l'Etoile was brought before the council, which, concluding that he was mad, sentenced him to imprisonment. Eon's followers who had been captured with him were, however, handed over to the secular authorities, who caused them to be burned. The contrast between the fate of the Eonites in 1148 and that of the formidable heretic Henry of Lausanne in 1135 suggests that by the middle of the century the ecclesiastical authorities, alarmed by evidence of the spread of heresy, were ready to use harsher measures.[116] The council of Rheims was also keenly aware of the problem of heresy in southern France, decreeing (without identifying the heretics) that 'no one is to maintain or defend the heresiarchs or their followers who dwell in the regions of Gascony and Provence and elsewhere and no one is to offer them refuge in his land'.[117]

'It is safer and less wicked to absolve the guilty and deserving of condemnation than to condemn with ecclesiastical severity the lives of the innocent.' This was the judgement of Alexander III in 1162 on a group of Flemish burghers who, being accused of heresy by the archbishop of Rheims and his brother, the king of France, had appealed their case to the pope: the first known instance of an appeal in such a case.[118] Five months later Alexander III's council of Tours (May 1163) pronounced in very different language against 'the damnable

---

[113] Godfrey of Auxerre, *Epistola, RHGF*, XV, p. 599; *Gesta pontificum Cenomannensium* 1134, *RHGF*, XII, p. 554. See Grundmann (1961), p. 45; Moore (1977), pp. 90, 253–4.

[114] John of Salisbury, *Historia pontificalis* c.31, pp. 63–4; Otto of Freising, *Gesta Friderici imperatoris* II.28, pp. 133–4. See Foreville (1965), pp. 85–7; Moore (1977), pp. 116–17.

[115] John of Salisbury, *Historia pontificalis* c.8–11, pp. 15–25. See Häring (1966a), pp. 39–59, (1966b), pp. 3–83, and (1967), pp. 93–117.

[116] *Continuatio Chronici Sigeberti* 1148, *MGH*, VI, pp. 389, 390; William of Newburgh, *Historia rerum anglicarum*, pp. 60–4. See Moore (1977), pp. 69–71. Moore suggests (p. 254) that the Eonites' attacks on ecclesiastical persons and property and their refusal to express repentance sealed their fate.

[117] Council of Rheims c.18. See Moore (1977), p. 256.

[118] Alexander III, JL 10797, col. 187 CD (to Archbishop Henry of Rheims). See Grundmann (1961), pp. 55–6. The pope's statement seems to echo Gratian, 'Decretum' c.23 q.4 c.10: see Walther (1976), p. 122.

heresy that has recently appeared in the region of Toulouse and, gradually
spreading like a cancer to neighbouring regions through Gascony and other
provinces, has already infected very many people'. The heretics were to be
prevented from holding their meetings (*conventicula*). They were to be subject to a social and economic boycott 'so that they may be forced through
the loss of human comfort to repent of the error of their way of life'.[119] The
Third Lateran Council (1179) anathematized 'the heretics whom some call
"Cathars", some "Patarines", some "Publicani" and others by other names',
together with those who sheltered and defended them.[120] The council had received a dossier on these heretics from the papal legates returning from southern
France, Cardinal Peter of S. Grisogono and Henry of Marcy, abbot of Clairvaux.
Henry of Marcy was one of the papal advisers who had most vehemently urged
the summoning of this council, seeing its principal function as the eradication of heresy. He warned the pope that 'heretics dispute publicly against the
faith' in southern France. Alexander III must 'brandish the sword of the priest
Phineas' against those embracing false gods (Numbers 25:1–8). After his victory over the schismatical antipopes, Alexander must 'lay the heretics to rest
likewise'.[121]

The Third Lateran Council was also faced with the new religious movement
of the Waldensians. Having fallen foul of the archbishop of Lyons, the Waldensians sought the pope's recognition for their way of life (like the Flemings who
had appealed to Alexander III in 1162). The chronicler of Laon believed that
their leader himself came to the council: 'the pope embraced Waldes and approved the vow of voluntary poverty that he had made'. The report of a member of the commission of experts who investigated the Waldensians' beliefs
suggests a cooler response. The commission ridiculed the lack of theological
training of these *idiotae et illiterati* and forbade them to preach.[122] Alexander
III's councils were also preoccupied, like those of Innocent II and Eugenius
III, with hunting for academic heresies in the schools. In both the council of
Tours and the Third Lateran Council the pope's experts (*viriperiti*) investigated the teachings of Peter Lombard, the most influential master of the Paris
schools in the mid-twelfth century. The recommendation of the papal expert
that the Third Lateran Council should condemn the 'christological nihilism'
of Peter Lombard was defeated by the master's adherents among the cardinals

[119] Council of Tours c.4. On heresy as a cancer see Moore (1976).
[120] Concilium Lateranense III c.27.   [121] Henry of Marcy, 'Epistola' 11 (to Alexander III).
[122] *Chronicon universale anonymi Laudunensis*, p. 29. No other source mentions the presence of Waldes
    at the council. The expert entrusted by the council with the examination of the delegation referred
    only to two prominent Waldensians, 'Valdesii, qui sua videbantur in secta precipui', saying nothing
    of Waldes's presence: Walter Map, *De nugis curialium* 1.31, p. 60. See Grundmann (1961), pp. 57–61;
    Moore (1977), p. 229.

and prelates in the council in a rare instance of conciliar opposition to the pope.[123]

The twelfth-century papal councils gradually developed the legislative framework for the practical coercive measures against heretics that would be compiled in the decree *Excommunicamus* of the Fourth Lateran Council (1215). This process began with Calixtus II's council of Toulouse in 1119, which commanded that heretics should 'be coerced by external powers'.[124] The same phrase was used in the decree against heresy in the Second Lateran Council (1139).[125] The councils of Alexander III, faced with a dangerous outbreak of heresy in southern France, were obliged to be more specific about the practical measures to be used. The council of Montpellier (1162) assumed that the ecclesiastical authorities in the region affected by heresy would admonish the local secular prince 'to exercise his temporal jurisdiction against the heretics'. The council threatened with anathema any prince who failed to obey such an admonition.[126] The council of Tours (1163) decreed that the secular powers must dispossess heretics of their lands.[127] The Third Lateran Council commanded that the faithful 'for the remission of their sins . . . take up arms to protect the Christian people' against heretics. 'Let [the heretics'] property be confiscated and let princes be free to reduce such men to slavery.' The faithful who responded to this appeal were accorded the same status 'as those who journey to the Lord's Sepulchre'.[128] The role of the secular power in the eradication of heresy was confirmed in the code of practice drawn up by Lucius III's synod of Verona (4 November 1184), the decree *Ad abolendam*. This was the first papal document to speak of heretical movements not as individual regional phenomena but as a universal problem. It was issued 'to abolish the wickedness of the various heresies that have begun to increase in most regions of the world in modern times' and began with a catalogue of the heresies currently known to the curia: 'the Cathars and Patarines and those who deceitfully go by the false name of the Humiliati or the Poor Men of Lyons [Waldensians], the Passagians, Josephines, Arnoldists'. The decree anathematized all those who denied the sacraments of the church and unlawfully claimed the right to preach.[129] The decree was issued jointly by the pope and Emperor Frederick I, symbolizing the church's dependence on the assistance of the secular power in removing this threat to her authority.

---

[123] The expert's report: John of Cornwall, 'Eulogium ad Alexandrum Papam tertium'. See de Ghellinck (1948), pp. 260–1; Foreville (1965), p. 145; Somerville (1977), pp. 56, 60–1, 98.

[124] Concil of Toulouse c.3.   [125] Concilium Lateranense II c.23.

[126] Council of Montpellier (1162) c.4. See Somerville (1977), p. 54.

[127] Council of Tours c.4. See Somerville (1977), pp. 50, 53.   [128] Concilium Lateranense III c.27.

[129] Lucius III, JL 15109, cols. 1297C–1300A. See Grundmann (1961), pp. 67–9; Walther (1976), pp. 124–6; Moore (1977), pp. 257–8.

The basis of this legislation was the doctrine of 'righteous persecution' which Gratian had absorbed from the Gregorian canon law collections of the late eleventh century.

That statement of Jerome, according to which the church is not to persecute anyone, must not be understood as meaning that in general the church persecutes no one but rather that she persecutes no one unjustly. For not every persecution is blameworthy: rather it is reasonable for us to persecute heretics, just as Christ physically persecuted those whom He drove out of the Temple [Matthew 21:12].[130]

To this *dictum* the Decretist Master Roland added that 'to kill wicked men for the sake of correction and justice is to serve God'.[131] Master Huguccio emphasized that the church can practise persecution if the motive is 'love of correction and of justice'.[132] According to Gratian, this 'righteous persecution' must be carried out by the secular powers, under the direction of the *sacerdotium*. 'Although priests must not take up arms in their own hands, nevertheless they are empowered by their authority to persuade those to whom such functions are committed and to command any of them to take up arms.'[133] Secular princes have a divinely ordained duty of defending the church against her enemies: if they fail to come to her assistance, they must be excommunicated.[134] Rufinus was the first canonist (1157–9) to derive from these statements the idea of military intervention against heretics, which eventually formed part of the legislation of the Third Lateran Council: 'heretics are to be compelled by arms to return to the Catholic faith'.[135] The Decretists deduced from Gratian's opinions that, where the defence of the faith was concerned, secular princes were to be regarded as the servants of the church. Huguccio concluded that 'secular [princes] were established for this purpose, that whatever the church is unable to achieve by her own means, should be executed by them as if they were servants so that through their means she may have protection and power and peace'. 'If she wishes to use the secular arm, he from whom help is sought is bound to obey her and defend her.'[136]

Huguccio was one of the earliest authors to use the term 'secular arm' (*seculare brachium*) to describe the lay power when cooperating with the church. As we have already seen, Huguccio adopted the 'Gelasian' rather than the 'Gregorian' view of the relations of the two powers. 'Both powers, namely the apostolic and the imperial, were instituted by God; neither depends on the other and the

---

[130] Gratian, 'Decretum' c.23 q.4 *dictum ante* c.37. See Walther (1976), pp. 113–18. For the Gregorian doctrine of 'righteous persecution' see Erdmann (1935), pp. 212–49.
[131] Roland, *Summa* ad c.23 q.5, p. 93.
[132] Huguccio, *Summa* ad dictum Gratiani ante c.1, c.23 q.3, quoted by Walther (1976), p. 127 n. 90.
[133] Gratian, 'Decretum', c.23 q.8. *dictum post* c.18.   [134] *Ibid.*, c.24 q.1 c.11, 14; c.23 q.5 c.18–45.
[135] Rufinus, *Summa decretorum* ad dictum Gratiani ante c.23 q.1, p. 403.
[136] Huguccio, *Summa* ad D.96 c.16, quoted by Watt (1965), p. 31 n. 43. See Stickler (1947), pp. 1–44.

emperor does not hold the sword from the pope.'[137] Nevertheless Huguccio considered that when the church and the Catholic faith were in danger, secular princes were obliged to obey the ecclesiastical authorities 'as if they were the servants' of the church. He identified two circumstances in particular in which secular assistance was obligatory: when ecclesiastical authority was undermined by delinquent clergy and when the church was threatened by heretics. In the first instance, if clerks 'are utterly incorrigible and cannot be disciplined by the church, then by the church's permission the secular judge can arrest and coerce [them]'.[138] In the second instance, 'note that princes are understood to be defenders of the church . . . and if, on being admonished to do so, they refuse, they can be excommunicated'.[139] This Decretist conception of the duty of the secular princes to engage in wars of 'righteous persecution' against the heretics at the command of the church completed the twelfth-century vision of Latin Christendom as a compulsory society. Membership of this society depended on adherence to the orthodox religion defined by the Roman church. 'The faith of the Roman church has destroyed every heresy.' Consequently 'it is not permitted to think or teach other than the Roman church thinks and teaches'.[140] The touchstone of orthodoxy in the compulsory society of the twelfth-century canonists was obedience to the Roman church and her bishop.

His role as the unique guarantor of Catholic orthodoxy gave the pope the authority to declare holy wars not only against the heretics within but also against *pagani* outside Christendom. It was the undisputed power of the pope to launch a crusade that (as we have already seen) inspired Bernard of Clairvaux to attribute to him possession of the 'two swords', the 'material sword' of lay coercion and the 'spiritual sword' of excommunication. Bernard urged Eugenius III to launch a crusade with the words, 'put forth both swords . . . Who should do so, if not you? Both are Peter's, the one to be unsheathed at his nod, the other by his hand, whenever necessary.'[141] The principal concern of twelfth-century canonists dealing with the subject of holy war was to emphasize that clerks themselves must not be directly involved in the conflict. 'The church does not recognize the use of weapons by her ministers, but recognizes their use by others.'[142] Huguccio concluded that it was 'lawful for clerks in Outremer and in Spain to go into battle and carry the Lord's cross so that the Lord may protect the Christians and terrify the pagans'. These clerks were permitted to defend themselves against attack but if they killed an attacker, they must be

---

[137] Huguccio, *Summa* ad D.96 c.6: see above p. 321 and n. 15.
[138] Huguccio, *Summa* ad C.11 q.1. c.18, quoted by Watt (1965), p. 31 n. 45.
[139] Huguccio, *Summa* ad D.63 c.22, quoted by Stickler (1947), p. 217. See Hehl (1980), p. 232.
[140] Gratian, 'Decretum' ad C.24 q.1. c.10–15.   [141] Bernard, 'Epistola' 256.1. See above p. 318.
[142] *Summa Parisiensis* ad C.23 q.8. c.7, p. 184. This anonymous Decretist *Summa* was perhaps compiled as early as *c.* 1160.

deposed from their office: 'for it is better to suffer death than to inflict death in order to escape'.[143]

The twelfth-century Decretists asked whether the pope, a churchman to whom weapons were forbidden, could authorize others to resort to arms. Master Gratian had supplied them with the 'authority' of Alexander II's letter (1063) to those engaged in warfare against the Spanish Muslims 'who persecute the Christians and drive them out of their cities and their own dwellings'.[144] The Decretists concluded from this 'authority' that papal holy wars were justified by the fact that they were wars of self-defence.[145] Thus the cautious Huguccio defended the war against Saladin on the grounds that 'he now holds Christians captive and defiles and takes tribute from the Holy Land where Christ died'.[146] His fellow Decretist, Sicardus of Cremona, however, was prepared to approve aggressive as well as defensive holy wars: 'it is permissible for the pope and other prelates on his authority to request princes and exhort others to defensive and aggressive measures against the enemies of the holy faith and of the peace of the church and the fatherland'.[147] Sicardus based his opinion on the confident pronouncements of the twelfth-century papacy on the subject of the crusade. By the end of the century most learned men accepted that it belonged to 'the privilege of the apostle Peter and to the general authority of the church' to launch a holy war.[148]

'Recognizing its duty', the apostolic see has proclaimed a crusade, declared Celestine III in 1193.[149] The preaching of a crusade was now a *duty* in the eyes of the late twelfth-century papal curia because crusading had assumed such importance in the penitential system of the church. As Peter of Blois explained in his treatise appealing for a crusade (1188/9), the papal holy war was urgently needed by the laity because it provided a unique 'remedy of penitence' and 'spiritual medicine' for their sins.[150] This was a view of the crusade formulated by Bernard of Clairvaux, preaching the Second Crusade in 1146–7. 'What is [the crusade] but an opportunity for salvation, carefully considered and such as God alone could devise, which the Almighty uses to summon from their servitude murderers, robbers, adulterers, oath-breakers and men guilty of other crimes, as if they were righteous people?'[151] The influence of this vision of the

---

[143] Huguccio, *Summa* ad D.50 c.5, quoted by Hehl (1980), p. 237; ad D.50 c.60, *ibid.*, p. 236.

[144] Gratian, 'Decretum', C.23 q.8 c.11 (Alexander II, JL 4528). Gratian also provided the historical *exemplum* of Leo IV's expedition against Muslim pirates (849): C.23 q.8 c.7 and *dictum post* c.20.

[145] E.g. *Summa Parisiensis* ad D.45 c.3, p. 40.

[146] Huguccio, *Summa* ad C.7 q.1. c.47, quoted by Hehl (1980), p. 237.

[147] Sicardus of Cremona, *Summa* ad C.23 q.8, quoted by Hehl (1980), p. 247. Sicardus cited Concilium Lateranense III c.27 in defence of his argument.

[148] Peter of Blois, 'De Hierosolymitana peregrinatione', col. 1061A.

[149] Celestine III, JL 16944, col. 971A.

[150] Peter of Blois, 'De Hierosolymitana peregrinatione', col. 1065C.   [151] Bernard, 'Epistola' 363.

crusade is apparent in the legislation of the papal councils which prescribes as a penance for arson (the worst imaginable crime in the opinion of the twelfth-century papacy) that the offender spend 'a full year in the service of God in Jerusalem or in Spain'.[152] The importance of the crusade lay in the spiritual reward that the pope alone could confer on the crusader. 'Take the sign of the cross', explained Bernard of Clairvaux, 'and this full indulgence of all the offences that you have confessed with contrite heart is offered to you by the supreme pontiff, the vicar of him to whom it was said, "Whatever you loose on earth will be loosed in heaven" [Matthew 16:19].'[153]

The First Lateran Council in 1123 explained the spiritual reward of crusaders in the words: 'To those who journey to Jerusalem and give effective help in defending the Christian people and in conquering the tyranny of the infidels, we grant remission of their sins.'[154] Similar language is used in Eugenius III's crusading letter of 1 December 1145, *Quantum praedecessores*, which promised

remission of sins and absolution according to the ordinance of [Urban II], . . . so that whoever begins and completes such a holy journey in a spirit of devotion, or dies during the journey, may obtain absolution from all the sins of which he has made confession with a contrite and humbled heart, and may receive the fruit of eternal recompense from Him who rewards all goodness.[155]

Both the First Lateran Council and Eugenius III identified the spiritual reward of the crusaders as 'remission of sins' (*remissio peccatorum*): that is, full remission of all the divinely imposed temporal penalties for sin.[156] In conferring this reward both referred to the precedent of Urban II. In fact the few surviving statements of Urban II describe the crusaders' reward not only as 'remission of sins' but also as a commutation of penance, a more conventional exercise of the church's penitential discipline: 'we release them from all penance for those sins for which they make a true and perfect confession'.[157] The early twelfth-century chroniclers of the First Crusade, however, wrote confidently of the 'immediate remission of sins' promised to the crusaders.[158] It has been suggested that the evidence of these chroniclers (who reflected the views of the crusaders themselves) shows that 'popular crusading propaganda at once went unhesitatingly far beyond the more limited formula' used by Urban II

---

[152] Concilium Lateranense II (1139) c.18. Cf. Council of Clermont (1130) c.13, Rheims (1131) c.17, Rheims (1148) c.15. See above p. 332.

[153] Bernard, 'Epistola' 458.

[154] Concilium Lateranense I c.10. Cf. Calixtus II, JL 7116, col. 1305C.

[155] Eugenius III, JL 8876, in Caspar and Rassow (1924), pp. 304–5.

[156] Paulus (1922), p. 199; Poschmann (1930), pp. 225–7; Constable (1953), pp. 249–52.

[157] Urban II, JL 5670, *PL* 151, col. 483D. Cf. Somerville (1972), p. 74. See Brundage (1969), pp. 139–58; Mayer (1972), pp. 25–40; Riley–Smith (1977), pp. 57–62, and (1986), pp. 27–30.

[158] Fulcher of Chartres, *Historia Hierosolymitana* I.3, p. 324. Cf. Balderic of Dol, 'Historia Ierosolimi-tana', I.4, pp. 14–15; Guibert of Nogent, *Dei gesta per Francos* II.4, p. 138.

and that the papal curia subsequently adopted the 'popular' interpretation of the crusaders' spiritual reward.[159]

This interpretation was certainly known to Eugenius III. 'We have learned from the accounts of writers of former times', declares his letter *Quantum praedecessores*, 'and we have found written in their *Deeds* how much our predecessors the Roman pontiffs laboured for the liberation of the eastern church.'[160] Eugenius III here made clear that he owed his knowledge of Urban II's crusade not to that pope's letters but to the chronicles of the First Crusade. His promise of 'remission of sins and absolution' must have been influenced by the chroniclers' interpretation of Urban II's promise to the crusaders. Bernard of Clairvaux, the official preacher of the Second Crusade launched by Eugenius, explained the message of *Quantum praedecessores* to the laity: 'take the sign of the cross and simultaneously you will obtain indulgence for what you have confessed with a contrite heart'.[161] The crusade, Bernard declared, was 'a day of abundant salvation' and 'a time rich in indulgence' for the laity.[162] The novelty of this language has been underlined by historians.[163] The term *indulgentia* – meaning the remission by the church of the temporal penalties for sin, guaranteed by the treasury of the spiritual merits of the church – was to have a long and controversial history.

It is certain, however, that at the time of the Second Crusade *indulgentia* had not yet acquired the technical meaning that it would be given in the later thirteenth century in the writings of Bonaventura and Thomas Aquinas: scholastic theologians had not yet begun to develop the doctrine of indulgences.[164] Lacking the precise terminology of thirteenth-century theologians, the curia of Eugenius III may have perceived no difference between the 'remission of sins and absolution' of *Quantum praedecessores*, the 'indulgence' of Bernard's recruiting propaganda and the commutation of penance promised in 1095. That is indeed the impression conveyed by Alexander III's crusading letter of 29 July 1169, which reviewed the promises of his predecessors. 'We make that remission of penance imposed by the priestly ministry that our predecessors, the Fathers of happy memory Urban and Eugenius are known to have instituted, so that ... he who undertakes the penance and remains there for two years to defend the land ... shall rejoice in the acquisition of remission of the penance imposed on him.'[165] Placing the spiritual reward of the crusader

---

[159] Mayer (1972), p. 33.   [160] Eugenius III, JL 8876, in Caspar and Rassow (1924), p. 302.

[161] Bernard, 'Epistola' 363. See Constable (1953), p. 247.   [162] Bernard, 'Epistola' 363.

[163] E.g. Gottlob (1906), p. 105: 'The transcendental efficacy of the indulgence was emphasized for the first time in the Second Crusade.'

[164] That development began with Hugh of St-Victor (*c.* 1150). See Gottlob (1906), pp. 270–88; Anciaux (1949), pp. 295–302.

[165] Alexander III, JL 11637, cols. 600D–601A.

firmly in the framework of the church's penitential discipline, Alexander III promised no more than commutation of penance and assumed that Urban II and Eugenius III had done likewise.

This letter of 1169 bears witness to the greater complexity and caution of the formulas used by the curia in the later twelfth century. Alexander III's first crusading letter in 1165 was simply a reissue of Eugenius III's *Quantum praedecessores*.[166] His last crusading letter in 1181 contained an elaborate scale of different spiritual rewards. For two years' service crusaders obtained 'absolution of all their offences for which they have made confession with contrite and humbled heart'; for one year's service they obtained 'indulgence of half the penance imposed on them and remission of sins'.[167] The misleading terms *indulgentia* and *remissio peccatorum* recur but the central message is clear enough: one year's service earned commutation of half the crusader's penance; two years' service earned the commutation of all his penance. Gregory VIII's letter *Audita tremendi* of 29 October 1187, launching the Third Crusade, contained the same message. Crusaders who 'depart as a penance for their sins and in right faith' were assured 'release from the satisfaction imposed for all their sins which they have rightly confessed'.[168] Celestine III's letter of 25 July 1195, the last crusading bull of the twelfth century, combines the formulas of Alexander III's letter of 1169 and Gregory VIII's of 1187. 'We make that remission of penance imposed by the priestly ministry that our predecessors are known to have instituted in their day, so that those who . . . depart as a penance for their sins and in right faith, shall have full indulgence of their crimes and eternal life.'[169] These more detailed papal promises of the last third of the twelfth century, variations on the theme of 'remission (indulgence) of penances', suggest an increasing caution, even a growing uncertainty, in the curia, responding to the elaboration of the doctrine of indulgences in the schools.

The papacy not only offered the spiritual reward that was the *raison d'être* of the crusade but also provided the disciplinary and organizational framework that made the crusade effective. First, papal legislation concerning the crusading vow (*votum crucis*) enabled the fleeting lay enthusiasm inspired by the preaching of the crusade to be transformed into a commitment to join the expedition. Before the formulation of the *votum crucis* canonists accepted that vows (such as the vow to enter the religious life) belonged purely to the realm of private morality. The vow was a voluntary obligation (*votum voluntarium*), the sanction being that the individual staked his salvation on the fulfilment of his promise to God. Papal legislation concerning the *votum crucis*, however, made the

[166] Alexander III, JL 11218, cols. 384B–386C.
[167] Alexander III, JL 14360, col. 1296AB. Cf. JL 11637, 601A.
[168] Gregory VIII, JL 16019, col. 1542C.   [169] Celestine III, JL 17270, col. 1109C.

crusader's vow an obligation in the public sphere, enforceable by legal sanctions in this world as well as the next.[170] The First Lateran Council (1123) used the sanction of the interdict against reluctant crusaders.

We command by apostolic authority that those who are known to have placed crosses on their garments for the expedition to Jerusalem or to Spain and afterwards to have abandoned them, are to take up the crosses again and to complete the journey between this Easter and the next. Otherwise thenceforward we deny them admission to a church and we forbid the divine offices in all their lands except for the baptism of infants and the confession of the dying.[171]

Alexander III and Celestine III issued similar decrees.[172] Simultaneously the formalization of the rite for taking the cross (in which the votary received a cross of cloth symbolizing the *votum crucis*) underlined the gravity of the vow.[173] In 1177, for example, a papal legate described to Alexander III the ceremony in which Count Henry of Champagne made the crusading vow, 'most devoutly receiving the sign of the life-giving cross from the hand of your legate'.

The papacy also promoted the crusade by granting the temporal privileges that encouraged crusaders to absent themselves from their homeland. The First Lateran Council in 1123, summarizing the measures of Urban II, received 'the houses, households and all the property [of crusaders] under the protection of St Peter and of the Roman church'.[174] Eugenius III confirmed this protection in 1145, in terms that were to be repeated by Alexander III and Gregory VIII. 'We decree that [crusaders'] wives and children and also their property and possessions are to remain under the protection of holy church and of us, of archbishops, bishops and other prelates of the church of God.'[175] Eugenius III's letter *Quantum praedecessores* also conferred financial and judicial privileges not previously mentioned in papal documents concerning the crusade. The papal measures to assist crusaders in financing their expedition had the effect of depriving third parties of their rights. First, 'those who are burdened with debt to others and begin the holy journey with a pure heart, are not to pay interest for time past'.[176] Secondly, 'if their kinsmen or the lords to whom their fiefs belong either will not or cannot lend them money, after due warning they may pledge their lands or other possessions, freely

[170] It was perhaps the formulation of the *votum crucis* during the First Crusade that inspired canonists and thaologians to elaborate a coherent doctrine of the vow in the twelfth century. See Brundage (1968) and (1969), pp. 33–7.

[171] Concilium Lateranense I c.10. Noth (1966), p. 138, regarded this as the first formal papal statement of the sanctions that enforced the *votum crucis*. His view was contested by Brundage (1971) pp. 334–43.

[172] Alexander III, JL 14077, Mansi 21, col. 1098; Celestine III, JL 17307, col. 1135BD.

[173] Brundage (1966), pp. 289–310.   [174] Concilium Lateranense I c.10.

[175] Eugenius III, JL 8876, in Caspar and Rassow (1924), p. 304. Cf. Alexander III, JL 11218, 11637, 14360, cols. 385D, 601B, 1295D; Gregory VIII, JL 16019, col. 1542C.

[176] Eugenius III, JL 8876, in Caspar and Rassow (1924), p. 304.

and without any appeal, to churches or churchmen or any other of the faithful'.[177] This innovatory papal interference into secular affairs enabled crusaders to pledge their family lands or fiefs, while depriving their kindred or feudal lords of their customary rights over the crusaders' lands. Finally, *Quantum praedecessores* delayed all judicial proceedings affecting the interests of absent crusaders.[178] All these temporal privileges were confirmed in later crusading bulls, transforming the crusaders into an elite, quite distinct from the rest of the laity.[179] Eugenius III indeed envisaged crusaders claiming the *privilegium fori*, the right to trial in the ecclesiastical rather than the secular courts.[180] This was a privilege, however, which his successors were more anxious to curtail than to confirm.[181]

When secular princes went on crusade, the pope placed their lands under the protection of St Peter. During the absence of the kings of France and Germany on the Second Crusade, for example, Eugenius III guaranteed the security of their kingdoms. The pope's biographer described how in the abbey of St-Denis he 'placed on the king the sign of the cross ... and at his request received the kingdom into his hands and into his power'.[182] Abbot Suger of St-Denis, appointed by Louis VII as regent, was simultaneously acknowledged by the pope as the guardian of the interests of the absent crusader. (This was the papal office known later as *conservator crucesignatorum*.) Suger's biographer underlined the two aspects of the abbot's authority. 'The new ruler was immediately girded with twin swords, one material and royal, the other spiritual and ecclesiastical, but both from heaven and committed to him by the supreme pontiff.'[183] The German kingdom, entrusted to Henry, the ten-year-old son of King Conrad III, was likewise accorded apostolic protection. Eugenius III's privilege declared that 'the honour' of the young king must 'suffer no damage or diminution in his father's absence, under the protection of St Peter'.[184] When Count Henry I of Champagne took the cross and departed for the east (1179),

---

[177] *Ibid.*

[178] The crusader's right to a delay in judicial proceedings appears under the technical name of 'essoin' in the late twelfth-century English treatise on secular law, 'Glanvill' or *Tractatus de legibus et consuetudinibus regni Anglie* II.29, pp. 16–17: the 'essonium de esse in peregrinatione' is here limited to one year.

[179] Alexander III, JL 11218, 11637, 14360, cols. 386AB, 601BC, 1295D–1296A; Gregory VIII, JL 16019, col. 1542D.

[180] Eugenius III, JL 9166, ed. S. Loewenfeld, *Archives de l'Orient latin* 2 (1884), p. 253 (Count William II of Ponthieu should appear in the ecclesiastical court in a case involving title to property); JL 8959, *Epistolae pontificum Romanorum ineditae*, pp. 103–4 (English barons who had lost their lands in the civil war could not claim the *privilegium fori* because their complaint predated their taking the cross).

[181] E.g. Alexander III, JL 14002, *Decretales Gregorii IX* IV. 17.7. See Brundage (1969), p. 171.

[182] Boso, 'Vita Eugenii III', II, p. 387. Cf. Eugenius III, JL 9345, col. 1394D. See Fried (1980), pp. 110–11.

[183] William of St-Denis, 'Vita Sugerii abbatis' III.2. See Grabois (1964a).

[184] Eugenius III, JL 9214, col. 1321A. See Fried (1980), pp. 111–12.

Abbot Henry of Clairvaux petitioned Alexander III on his behalf that his land should be 'fortified and defended by apostolic protection, so that anyone who plots any harm to it in the prince's absence may be in no doubt of incurring your indignation'.[185] The most controversial case involving papal protection of the lands of an absent crusading prince was that of King Richard I of England. When the returning crusader was imprisoned in Germany by his enemy Emperor Henry VI (1193–4), Celestine III came under strong pressure from Richard's supporters to use ecclesiastical sanctions to secure his release.[186] The pope was moved to excommunicate Richard's younger brother, John, who was plotting against the absent king, giving as his justification the papal protection for the property of crusaders. The absent king had 'left the concerns of his kingdom under apostolic protection'.[187] His own precarious political situation, however, inhibited Celestine III from excommunicating Emperor Henry VI: he chose to blame 'the excesses of [the emperor's] vassals'.[188]

The special status and temporal privileges granted to the crusaders in the east were also accorded to those who fought the Muslims in Spain. In Calixtus II's letter of 1123 the papacy for the first time promised to knights engaged in a Spanish expedition 'the same remission of sins that we have made for the defenders of the eastern church'.[189] The First Lateran Council in 1123 and the Second Lateran Council in 1139 similarly equated the war in Spain with that in Outremer: both were crusades.[190] Ecclesiastical politicians in Spain emphasized the connection between these two holy wars. 'Just as the knights of Christ and the faithful sons of holy church have opened up the route to Jerusalem with much labour and at the cost of great bloodshed', declared the papal legate, Archbishop Diego Gelmírez of Compostela, in 1124, 'so we also shall be made knights of Christ and by subduing His enemies, the evil Saracens, we shall open up to the same Sepulchre of the Lord, with His help, a route through the Spanish territories that is shorter and much less laborious.'[191] In the years 1147–8 the two crusades did indeed coincide. An Anglo-Flemish-German

---

[185] Henry of Clairvaux, 'Epistola' 1. Cf. Alexander III, JL 13445, for the regent, Countess Marie of Champagne (*Epistolae pontificum Romanorum ineditae*, p. 179), the only extant personal papal letter of protection of the twelfth century: see Fried (1980), pp. 115–16.

[186] Peter of Blois, 'Epistolae' 144–6 (on behalf of Eleanor, the queen-mother); *ibid.* 64, PL 207, cols. 187A–190A (on behalf of Archbishop Walter of Rouen).

[187] Celestine III, JL 16765, col. 899C. See Foreville (1943), p. 355; Brundage (1963), pp. 448–52; Gillingham (1978), pp. 217–40; Fried (1980), pp. 117–18.

[188] Celestine III, JL 17226, col. 1089C. The pope excommunicated Duke Leopold of Austria, who had taken Richard I prisoner and subsequently surrendered him to Henry VI. See below p. 383.

[189] Calixtus II, JL 7116, col. 1305C. See Fletcher (1984), pp. 297–8.

[190] Concilium Lateranense I c.10; Concilium Lateranense II c.18.

[191] Diego Gelmírez, archbishop of Compostela, address to the legatine council of Compostela, 1124, *Historia Compostellana* II.78. See Villey (1942), p. 199; Fletcher (1984), pp. 298–9.

naval expedition bound for the Second Crusade in Palestine was persuaded to participate in the conquest of Lisbon in October 1147. Simultaneously 'the Genoese were admonished and summoned by God through the apostolic see' to assist Count Ramón Berenguer IV of Barcelona in the siege of Tortosa.[192] The military religious orders, the Templars and Hospitallers, founded for the defence of the crusader kingdom of Jerusalem, accumulated extensive estates in Spain and became involved in their defence against the Muslims. The Spanish kings, notably King Alfonso I of Aragon, envisaged their playing a major part in the wars of the 'Reconquest'.[193] This role was eventually to be shared with the new Spanish military orders of Calatrava and Santiago, the foundation of which 'represented an institutionalization of the war against the Muslims'.[194] It was Alexander III who conferred legitimacy on these new institutions, approving the rules of the new orders in 1164 and 1175 respectively and placing them under papal protection.[195]

Of the popes of our period it was Celestine III who most consistently interested himself in the holy war in Spain. As Cardinal Deacon Hyacinth of S. Maria in Cosmedin, he had been the curia's expert on Spanish affairs, undertaking two lengthy legations (1154–5 and 1172–5). At his legatine council of Valladolid (1155) he had called for an expedition against the Saracens, promising the same indulgence that Urban II had formerly granted the crusaders.[196] In 1172 he had participated in the attempt of King Alfonso VIII of Castile to organize an expedition.[197] As pope he issued in 1193 a crusading bull for Spain, offering Spanish crusaders the spiritual reward and the temporal privileges of 'those who have journeyed to the Lord's Sepulchre'.[198] Celestine III promoted the holy war in Spain by forbidding Spanish knights to participate in the crusade to the east.[199] By his authority, knights from Bordeaux who had bound themselves by a crusading vow to Jerusalem were permitted instead to fight in Spain.[200] Celestine's legatine experience had shown him how much the Spanish crusade was impeded by the rivalries of the Christian rulers. One of his principal preoccupations as pope was, therefore, to compel the reluctant

---

[192] Caffaro di Caschifellone, 'Annales Ianuenses' 1147, p. 36. See Constable (1953), pp. 227–33; O'Callaghan (1975), pp. 230–2.

[193] Alfonso I of Aragon bequeathed his kingdom to the military orders of the Holy Sepulchre, the Hospital and the Temple (1131). His will was ignored by his subjects after his death (1134) but upheld by Innocent II. See Forey (1973), pp. 17–20; Lourie (1975), pp. 635–51; O'Callaghan (1975), pp. 222–6.

[194] Lomax (1978), p. 109.

[195] Alexander III, JL 11064, 12504, cols. 310C–312A, 1024D–1030C. See O'Callaghan (1959), (1960) and (1962).

[196] Erdmann (1928), p. 55, appendix v; Säbekow (1931), pp. 48–51.   [197] Säbekow (1931), pp. 53–5.

[198] *Papsturkunden in Spanien*, II, p. 200.   [199] Villey (1942), p. 200.

[200] Celestine III, JL 17539, *Neues Archiv* 6 (1880), p. 369.

kings and princes of Spain to unite against the Muslims. In 1195, calling for peace among Christians, he threatened with excommunication those Spanish princes who made war on neighbours who were engaged in the crusade.[201] When in 1196 King Alfonso IX of León made an alliance with the Almohads, Celestine excommunicated him, declaring that if Alfonso made use of Muslim troops, 'the vassals of his kingdom would be absolved from his fealty and lordship by the authority of the apostolic see'.[202]

Before the pontificate of Celestine III Spanish princes had figured in papal records mainly as a source of financial support. A number of the Christian rulers of the Iberian peninsula made an annual payment of *census* to the apostolic see. The count of Barcelona had begun to make such a payment when Berenguer Ramón II became a vassal of the Roman church, surrendering his city of Tarragona (1090).[203] There is, however, no reference in twelfth-century papal documents to this feudal relationship. Adrian IV recorded in 1158 that the person and lands of Count Ramón Berenguer IV were 'under St Peter's and our protection' because he was engaged in 'subduing the barbarous peoples and the savage nations, that is, the fury of the Saracens'. The count of Barcelona now enjoyed the status of a crusader.[204] The king of Aragón paid to St Peter an annual *tributum* of 500 *mancusi* and each of his vassals paid an additional *mancusus*. This substantial tribute was paid not because he was the pope's vassal, but because he enjoyed the protection of St Peter.[205] His status was analogous to that of a monastery on which the pope had conferred St Peter's *patrocinium*.[206] (Hence the papacy's interest in Aragonese affairs, such as, for example, Innocent II's preoccupation with the testament of King Alfonso I.)[207]

Afonso I Henriques of Portugal acquired a status analogous to that of the king of Aragon when, in the words of Lucius II's privilege of 1144, he 'offered to St Peter the land committed to [him] by God . . . and committed [his] person and land to his protection'.[208] Afonso Henriques had assumed the title of 'king of the Portuguese' (*rex Portugalensium*) after his great victory over the Muslims

[201] Celestine III, JL 17265, *ibid.*, p. 369.

[202] Celestine III, JL 17433, *Regesta pontificum Romanorum*, II, p. 626.

[203] Jordan (1933–4), p. 79, Fried (1980), pp. 87–101.   [204] Adrian IV, JL 10419, col. 1570CD.

[205] This relationship dated from the pilgrimage to Rome of King Sancho Ramirez of Navarre and Aragon (1068): see Fried (1980), pp. 63–87. The *mancusus* was an Arab gold coin regarded as equal to the more frequently used *marabotinus*. For the purposes of comparison it should be noted that the average annual *census* paid by monasteries enjoying the protection of St Peter was two *marabotini*: see Jordan (1933–4), p. 72; Pfaff (1956), p. 7. The annual *census* paid by the papal vassal kingdom of Sicily in 1139 was the equivalent of 1,200 *marabotini*, raised in 1156 to the equivalent of 2,000 *marabotini*: see below p. 367.

[206] Tellenbach (1950), p. 53.

[207] *Papsturkunden in Spanien*, I, p. 318 (no. 50). See Kehr (1928), pp. 46–7; Lourie (1975); Fried (1980), pp. 189–90.

[208] Lucius II, JL 8590, cols. 860D–861A.

on 25 July 1139. His assumption of the royal title and his request for the *patrocinium* of St Peter were equally intended to secure the independence of the county of Portugal from the kingdom of León. The papacy initially ignored the royal title: Lucius II's privilege called Afonso Henriques 'duke' (*Portugalensium dux*). In 1179, however, Alexander III acclaimed him as 'the intrepid destroyer of the enemies of the Christian name and the energetic defender of the Christian faith'. Afonso I had earned the title of king and the pope declared that his kingdom 'belongs to the jurisdiction of St Peter'.[209] The practical significance of this change for the papal government was that, while as *dux* Afonso I Henriques had paid an annual *census* of four ounces of gold, as *rex* his *census* increased fourfold and moreover he sent a gift of 1,000 gold pieces to the pope.[210]

The case of Portugal was characteristic of the relations of the peripheral lands of western Christendom with the papacy in the twelfth century. Secular rulers desired the pope to use his unique authority to legitimize their political aspirations and they would pay generously for papal support in the form of the *patrocinium* of St Peter. The papacy meanwhile wished to promote reform in the churches of the peripheral lands, gaining access for papal legates and promoting the reorganization of ecclesiastical structures. The mutual benefits of these relationships are illustrated by the papacy's interventions in Scandinavia. The key event was the legation of Cardinal Nicholas of Albano (the future Adrian IV) in 1152–3. According to his biographer, he brought 'peace to the kingdoms, law to the barbarians, tranquillity to the monasteries, order to the churches, discipline to the clergy and a people pleasing to God, devoted to good works'.[211] Arriving in Norway, he reconciled the feuding dynasts and underpinned the authority of King Inge. His legatine council strengthened the economic position of the church and the social status of the clergy. Most importantly he established Nidaros (Trondheim), the centre of the cult of St Olaf, as the metropolitan church of Norway.[212] Cardinal Nicholas's attempt to create a metropolis for the Swedish kingdom failed because he could not find a location acceptable to both the mutually hostile peoples inhabiting Sweden, the Goths and Swedes. As pope, Adrian IV continued to press the case for a Swedish metropolis, authorizing the archbishop of Lund 'to appoint a metropolitan in that kingdom with the consent of the king, the bishops and the princes of that land'.[213] Eventually the inhabitants of the kingdom agreed on the site of Uppsala and in 1164 Alexander III responded to their petition by conferring the metropolitan dignity.[214]

---

[209] Alexander III, JL 13420, col. 1237B, 1237D. See Erdmann (1928), pp. 29–32, 49–50; O'Callaghan (1975), pp. 226–7, 241; Fried (1980), pp. 125, 140–2.
[210] Erdmann (1928), p. 49; Jordan (1933–4), p. 80.   [211] Boso, 'Vita Hadriani', II, p. 388.
[212] Seegrün (1967), pp. 146–70.   [213] Adrian IV, JL 10454, in Seegrün (1967), pp. 174–5.
[214] Alexander III, JL 11047–8, cols. 301C–303D.

The papacy recommended the creation of a separate metropolitan dignity because in a land so far from Rome and 'not long converted to the faith', an authoritative figure was needed who could 'more frequently and more usefully take care of what concerns the salvation of the faithful'.[215] The new metropolis, however, also had a political significance that would not be lost on the Scandinavian kings. In Norway, torn by dynastic disputes, and Sweden, divided by the hostility of Goths and Swedes, the new metropolis was a valuable symbol of unity and political stability.[216] In return, the Norwegian and Swedish kings were willing to pay an annual *census* in order to be bound more closely to the Roman church. This payment (analogous to that paid by the Danish kingdom since the early eleventh century) seems to date from the legation of Nicholas of Albano.[217] In the case of Sweden at least the papal curia linked the payment of *census* directly with the *patrocinium* of St Peter. 'We demand this [*census*]', wrote Anastasius IV, 'assuredly not so much for our own benefit as for the salvation of your souls, since we desire that through the service of inward devotion you obtain St Peter's protection.'[218]

It was not only the Scandinavian kings, however, who desired a closer relationship with Rome. Churchmen also realized that papal patronage might promote the aspirations of their churches or protect them from secular interference. The first important adherent of the papacy in Scandinavia was Archbishop Eskil of Lund, friend of Bernard of Clairvaux and responsible for introducing Cistercian monasticism into Denmark and Sweden. Eskil came to Rome in 1157 seeking papal protection against his enemies King Swein of Denmark and the latter's supporter and kinsman, Archbishop Hartwig of Bremen. Adrian IV defended Eskil from Hartwig's scheme to subject Lund to the jurisdiction of Bremen by granting his protégé the office of papal legate and conferring on Lund a primacy over the Swedish and Norwegian churches.[219] Hartwig's plan was supported by his lord, Emperor Frederick I (who had assisted the efforts of Swein, his vassal, to obtain the Danish crown). The papacy's championing of Eskil's cause, therefore, contributed to the deterioration of papal–imperial relations in the later 1150s.

A similar enthusiast for papal authority was Eysten Erlendsson, whom Alexander III consecrated as archbishop of Nidaros in 1161. Archbishop Eysten brought about the election in 1163 of King Magnus Erlingsson, claiming a role for the episcopate in king-making for the first time and performing the first consecration and coronation of a Norwegian king. On this occasion he obtained

[215] Adrian IV, JL 10454, in Seegrün (1967), p. 174.
[216] Seegrün (1967), p. 203: 'For the Scandinavian kings the papal policy, contact with the popes in general, always meant a strengthening of their power.'
[217] *Ibid.*, pp. 154–5, 167, 169–70. See *NCMH*, IV, Part I, ch. II.
[218] Anastasius IV, JL 9938, col. 1088B.   [219] Seegrün (1967), pp. 171–7.

from the boy king an oath of fidelity and obedience to the Roman church. Magnus swore to observe the reforming legislation of Cardinal Nicholas of Albano, to pay the annual *census* to the papacy and to show 'due reverence and obedience' to the church in Norway. This unconventional royal promise was evidently modelled on the oath sworn to the pope by metropolitans.[220] After attaining his majority King Magnus, still under the influence of Archbishop Eysten, confirmed the bishops' role in the election of the king and freed episcopal elections from secular control. The adventurer who defeated Magnus and usurped his throne (1180), Sverri Sigurdsson, strove to recover control over the election of bishops and ecclesiastical property. Archbishop Eysten's successor, Eric Ivarsson, driven into exile, appealed to Rome against the usurpation and the attack on the church's rights. Celestine III's sentence of excommunication against the king and his adherents (1193) unleashed a protracted struggle between *regnum* and *sacerdotium*, culminating in the papal interdict imposed on Norway in 1198.[221]

The peripheral land that offered the greatest challenge to papal diplomacy was the English kingdom. The record of the papal revenues compiled in 1192, the *Liber Censuum*, suggests that, of the contributions of the western kingdoms to the annual income of the pope, the largest was that made by England. The English payments exceeded even that of the papal vassal kingdom of Sicily.[222] The most important element in the English contribution was 'Peter's pence', the pious offering contributed annually by the churches in each diocese. The king played an important role in the collection of Peter's pence and was responsible for its despatch to the papal curia. 'No one in the kingdom would have considered paying us for an instant, if the king had not given his general command,' Bishop Gilbert Foliot of London informed the pope in 1165. For 'according to ancient custom it is collected at a fixed time by [the king's] command'.[223] The king was therefore in a position to withhold this valuable donation in order to put pressure on the papal curia. This was the strategy of King Henry I in defence of the 'customs' of the Anglo-Norman kings – that is, their control of ecclesiastical affairs in their dominions – against the reforming legislation of the Gregorian papacy.[224] There is no evidence of the royal manipulation of Peter's pence from the 1120s to the early 1160s; but in the years 1166–9 there

---

[220] Holtzmann (1938), pp. 376–7. See Seegrün (1967), pp. 154, 187–99.

[221] Innocent III, *Register* 1.382 (Potthast 386), *PL* 214, cols. 362A–363A. See Foreville and Rousset de Pina (1953), pp. 265–7.

[222] Pfaff (1953), p. 114.

[223] Gilbert Foliot, bishop of London, *Letter* 155, p. 206. This payment is described in the *Liber censuum*, I, p. 226, as 'denarius beati Petri'. The curia also called it 'census beati Petri' and 'eleemosyna beati Petri': Paschal II, JL 5883, 6450, *PL* 163, cols. 81A, 377C. See Jordan (1933–4), pp. 77–8; Lunt (1939), pp. 3–34 and also *NCMH*, IV, Part I, ch. II.

[224] Eadmer, *Historia novorum* III, p. 132. See Lunt (1939), pp. 36–7, 47.

is evidence that King Henry II resorted to his grandfather's tactics. In the interests of preserving Henry I's 'customs' Henry II seems to have used the threat of withholding Peter's pence in his negotiations with the impoverished and beleaguered Alexander III.[225] The twelfth-century papacy faced no more delicate operation than that of balancing their need for good relations with the English king with their wish to protect the liberty of the English church.

In their conduct towards the papacy the twelfth-century English kings adopted the model of King Henry I, who, as his grandson is alleged to have boasted, was 'king, apostolic legate, patriarch, emperor and everything he wished to be, in his own land'.[226] Henry I was accused by Paschal II of neglecting the rights of the papacy in that he ignored the canon law principle that the greater ecclesiastical cases (*maiores causae*) must be referred to the judgement of Rome. 'You settle the affairs of bishops without consulting us . . . You take away from the oppressed [the right of] appeal to the holy see.'[227] In fact during Henry I's reign four *maiores causae* brought English churchmen to the papal curia: the dispute over the papal decree against the investiture of bishops by kings; the claim of the archbishop of Canterbury to be primate of the kingdom of England and indeed of all Britain; the claim of the archbishop of York to be the metropolitan of the Scottish bishops; the appeal of the bishop of Llandaff against the encroachments of his neighbours, the bishops of Hereford and St Davids. Even the lesser clergy of the English kingdom were beginning to appeal to Rome against the judgements of the ecclesiastical courts in England.[228] King Henry I was aware that, thanks to the vision and energy of the Gregorian papacy, the curia had become an inescapable fact of the life of western Christendom. Rome was now exercising its centripetal attraction on English churchmen as on churchmen everywhere, as appellants sought to enlist papal authority in the interests of securing their own rights. Henry I himself saw the value of seeking St Peter's confirmation for his royal rights. When he met Calixtus II in Gisors in 1119, he asked the pope to grant him 'all the customs that his father had possessed in England and Normandy'.[229]

Henry I seems to have been determined not that papal authority should be totally excluded from his territories but that it should be admitted only on his terms and with his consent. Thus in his conversation with the pope

---

[225] Gilbert Foliot, *Letter* 177, p. 250 (1166/7); royal constitutions concerning the church, 1169, *Councils and Synods*, p. 936: see Knowles, Duggan and Brooke (1972), pp. 757–71. Cf. William fitz Stephen, *Vita sancti Thomae* c.65, *Materials*, III, p. 74; Edward Grim, *Vita sancti Thomae* c.56, *ibid.*, II, p. 406. See Lunt (1939), pp. 49–50.

[226] John of Salisbury, *Letter* 275, p. 580. See Deér (1964), pp. 168–81.

[227] Paschal II, JL 6453: Eadmer, *Historia novorum* v, p. 233. See Brett (1975), pp. 36–7. On the *maiores causae* see *NCMH*, IV, Part 1, ch. 11.

[228] Brett (1975), pp. 50–7.

[229] Eadmer, *Historia novorum* v, p. 258. Cf. Hugh the Chanter, *History of the Church of York*, pp. 126–32.

in 1119 he specifically identified the sending of papal legates to England as a practice contrary to the royal 'customs'. His objection to legates was shared by the church of Canterbury, which claimed for the archbishop the status of permanent legate in the kingdom.[230] Nevertheless in 1124 the papal legate John of Crema, cardinal priest of S. Grisogono visited Normandy and in 1125 he 'travelled throughout almost the whole of England, venturing nearly to Scotland, and celebrated a council in London, . . . something that no Roman legate had ever done in the time of the two Williams'. This legation, unlike others during the reign, was opposed neither by the king nor by the archbishop of Canterbury, William of Corbeil, and it demonstrated how useful papal authority could be to both of them. First, John of Crema annulled the marriage between Henry I's nephew and rival William Clito and the daughter of the count of Anjou, Henry's principal enemy in France. The legate thus removed a dangerous threat to Henry's hold over Normandy.[231] Secondly, John of Crema had instructions from the pope to investigate the contentious claim of the archbishop of Canterbury to primatial jurisdiction over York. William of Corbeil believed that such an investigation in an English council (in which the archbishop of York's supporters would be in a minority) would vindicate the claims of his church.[232] In 1126 Honorius II further conciliated King Henry I by granting a legatine commission to Archbishop William of Canterbury 'in England and Scotland'.[233] This was compensation for the pope's refusal to recognize Canterbury's primatial claim. The Canterbury–York dispute continued to surface throughout the twelfth century and the papacy continued to use the same compromise solution, granting a legatine commission to Archbishop Theobald of Canterbury (1150) and to his successors, Richard (1174), Baldwin (1185) and Hubert Walter (1195).[234]

The reign of King Stephen provided unusual opportunities for papal intervention in the English church and kingdom. First, the disputed succession to the English throne was referred to the judgement of the papacy; secondly, the dominant figure in the English church was an enthusiast for papal authority. Henry of Blois, bishop of Winchester, brother of King Stephen, enjoyed a papal legation in England (1139–43) thanks to his friendship with

[230] Southern (1963), pp. 130–42; Brett (1975), pp. 35–41.
[231] Hugh the Chanter, *History of the Church of York*, p. 204. Cf. Orderic Vitalis, *Historia aecclesiastica* XI. 37 (VI, pp. 164–6) (the divorce of William Clito). See Tillmann (1926), p. 28; Schieffer (1935), pp. 215–16, 225; Brett (1975), p. 45.
[232] Nicholl (1964), pp. 93–5; Brett (1975), pp. 45–7.
[233] Honorius II, JL 7284, *Councils and Synods*, p. 743. See Tillmann (1926), pp. 30–3; Dueball (1929), pp. 99–100; Nicholl (1964), pp. 96–7; Bethell (1968), pp. 156–7.
[234] Tillmann (1926), pp. 33–6; Saltman (1956), pp. 30–1; Cheney (1967), pp. 119–22; *Councils and Synods*, pp. 820, 966, 1022, 1042.

Innocent II.[235] English polemicists portrayed him as an ecclesiastical tyrant who sacrificed English 'customs' to Roman influence. 'In England appeals [to Rome] were not in use until Bishop Henry of Winchester in his wickedness cruelly intruded them while he was a legate.'[236] Henry certainly concerned himself with the rights of the papacy[237] and he was not loath to exploit the precedence over Canterbury that the legatine commission gave him. Nevertheless his legatine councils demonstrated his genuine preoccupation with reform and his determination to defend the freedom of the church against the king.[238]

It was perhaps Henry of Winchester who had played the decisive role in negotiating the church's support for his brother's accession on the death of their uncle, King Henry I, in 1135. Stephen's usurpation of the English throne was legitimized by the English church and the papacy, as the new king declared in the opening clause of his charter of liberties for the church (1136). This royal promise of ecclesiastical liberty was the price of papal support for his accession. 'I Stephen, by the grace of God elected king of England with the assent of the clergy and people and consecrated by William, archbishop of Canterbury and legate of the holy Roman church and afterwards confirmed by Innocent, pontiff of the holy Roman see,... grant that holy church shall be free and confirm the reverence due to her.'[239] The disputed succession to the English throne continued to preoccupy the papal curia in the following two decades. During the Second Lateran Council (1139) Matilda, daughter and designated successor of King Henry I, challenged Stephen's usurpation and claimed the English throne by hereditary right. Innocent II adhered to his former decision in favour of Stephen. 'Against the advice of certain cardinals, especially Guido, cardinal priest of S. Marco, he accepted King Stephen's gifts and in a friendly letter confirmed his possession of the kingdom of England and the duchy of Normandy.'[240] Soon after this confirmation of his title, however, Stephen began to alienate the church by his efforts to regain his predecessor's control over the episcopate. When Cardinal Guido succeeded to the papacy as Celestine II, 'he wrote to Archbishop Theobald of Canterbury, forbidding any innovation to be made in the kingdom of England concerning the crown, which was the subject of a lawsuit and the transfer of which was forbidden by law. His successors, Pope Lucius [II] and Eugenius [III], repeated

[235] Tillmann (1926), pp. 41–50; Voss (1932), pp. 22–38, 41–53; Knowles (1951), pp. 33–7.
[236] Henry of Huntingdon, *Historia Anglorum* x.31, p. 757.
[237] E.g. Henry of Winchester concerned himself with the collection of Peter's pence, which seems to have fallen out of royal control: Brooke (1931), p. 182 n. 1; Voss (1932), p. 49; Lunt (1939), pp. 41–2.
[238] *Councils and Synods*, pp. 781–810; Schnith (1976), pp. 103–15.
[239] *Councils and Synods*, p. 764. See Davis (1967), pp. 18–20; Cronne (1970), pp. 30, 87, 125–6.
[240] John of Salisbury, *Historia pontificalis* c. 42, p. 84. Cf. Gilbert Foliot, *Letters*, pp. 60–6; Peter the Venerable, *Letters*, II, 2, pp. 252–6. See Davis (1967), p. 18; Cronne (1970), pp. 89–90; Chibnall (1991), pp. 75–6.

the same prohibition.'[241] In practice, this prohibition of any *innovatio* meant that Stephen could not proceed with his plans to have his son crowned king. The change in papal policy made possible the succession of King Henry II, son of Stephen's rival, Matilda.

The first five years of Henry II's reign coincided with the period in which English influence was strongest in the papal curia, the pontificate of Adrian IV, the English pope. (As Cardinal Bishop Nicholas of Albano he had been the second Englishman to be promoted to the cardinalate, the first being the theologian Robert Pullen, cardinal priest of SS. Martino e Silvestro, who had filled the important office of chancellor in 1145–6.)[242] Adrian IV's attachment to his homeland was demonstrated above all by his devotion to the cult of St Alban.[243] He also promoted the insular and continental ambitions of Henry II in various ways. The pope supported Henry's plan to give Brittany a separate ecclesiastical organization, independent of the archbishopric of Tours, with a series of privileges for the church of Dol, reversing the policy of his immediate predecessors.[244] In the case of England Adrian managed to support the interests of both the rival archbishops. He renewed the legatine commission of Theobald of Canterbury, even though he felt obliged to rebuke the archbishop for conspiring with Henry II to block appeals to Rome by English churchmen.[245] To Archbishop Roger of York Adrian granted a privilege confirming his metropolitan authority over the bishops of Scotland in terms more specific than any predecessor had been prepared to concede.[246] Adrian IV's most striking concession to Henry II was recorded by the English emissary to the papal curia in 1156, John of Salisbury, clerk in Archbishop Theobald's household. 'At my request [Adrian] conceded and gave Ireland as a hereditary possession to the illustrious king of the English, Henry II.' John of Salisbury linked this grant with the claim that 'all islands are said to belong to the Roman church by ancient right, according to the Donation of Constantine'.'[247] This was the only occasion during the twelfth century on which the Donation of

---

[241] John of Salisbury, *Historia pontificalis* c. 42, pp. 85–6.

[242] Poole (1934), pp. 287–91; Zenker (1964), pp. 89–92; Smalley (1973), pp. 41–2.

[243] Poole (1934), pp. 291–7; Sayers (1971b), pp. 58–60. On the Breakspear family connection with the abbey of St Albans see Southern (1970), pp. 234, 249. Nicholas Breakspear may have taken his papal name in honour of Adrian I, who was believed to have shown particular reverence to St Alban: see *Councils and Synods*, p. 830.

[244] Adrian IV, JL 10063–5, 10102–3, 10362, 10367, 10504. See Foreville and Rousset de Pina (1953), p. 36; Warren (1973), p. 561.

[245] Adrian IV, JL 10128, *Historia monasterii sancti Augustini Cantuariensis*, pp. 411–13.

[246] Adrian IV, JL 10000, cols. 1391C–1392A. See Somerville (1982), pp. 40–2, 47–8, and also *NCMH*, IV, Part I, ch. 11.

[247] John of Salisbury, *Metalogicon* IV.42, pp. 217–18. Giraldus Cambrensis, *Expugnatio Hibernica* II.5, pp. 144–6 (and also *De rebus a se gestis, Opera*, V, pp. 317–18, and *De instructione principum, ibid.*, VII, pp. 196–7), preserved a papal letter recording this grant: Adrian IV, JL 10056 (*Laudabiliter*).

Constantine (so important to the Gregorian papacy) was cited in support of papal territorial jurisdiction.[248]

Henry II expected to find Adrian IV's successor equally accommodating, given Alexander III's need for secular allies during his struggle against Emperor Frederick I in the schism of 1159–77. When in 1161 the king requested the canonization of King Edward the Confessor, the pope was given to understand that Henry considered this favour an appropriate reward for his supporting Alexander in the schism.[249] Henry's willingness to permit the English bishops to attend Alexander's council of Tours (1163) was acknowledged by the pope with the promise that 'no new custom would be introduced into his kingdom and the dignity of his kingship would not be diminished'.[250] A year later the king turned to the pope for support when challenged by his new archbishop of Canterbury, Thomas Becket, on the question of the punishment of felonious clergy. Henry II requested the papal confirmation of the 'customs' of his kingdom, just as his grandfather had done at his meeting with Calixtus II in 1119. Unlike Henry I, however, Henry II caused his 'customs' to be set down in writing. When the archbishop brought a copy of these 'Constitutions of Clarendon' to the papal curia, he was able to represent them as 'the customs of the king of the English, opposed to the canons and decrees and even to the laws of secular princes, on account of which [Becket was] forced to endure exile'.[251] Alexander III felt compelled to condemn ten of Henry II's sixteen 'ancestral customs'.[252]

Alexander was in an unenviable position, faced with appeals for support both from the king, on whose support he depended, and from the king's opponent, a vociferous champion of the liberty of the English church. Becket's supporters feared that Henry II would succeed in exploiting the pope's current poverty. He was alleged to have offered to increase the annual payment of Peter's pence by 1,000 pounds of silver in return for Becket's deposition.[253] Henry certainly threatened to renounce his obedience to Alexander and to acknowledge the imperial antipope. Alexander could not ignore the king's 'terrible threats' and was well aware that he might 'seem to have acted negligently in [Becket's] cause and

The authenticity of this letter was questioned by Scheffer-Boichorst (1903), pp. 132–57, and Bémont (1925), pp. 41–53, and defended by Sheehy (1965), pp. 15–16; Watt (1970), pp. 35–40; Warren (1973), pp. 194–7.

[248] The Donation of Constantine had last been cited in support of a territorial claim by Urban II, JL 5449, PL 151, cols. 330D–331A. See Laehr (1926), p. 34, and also NCMH, IV, Part 1, ch. 9.
[249] Gilbert Foliot, Letter 133, p. 177. See Kemp (1948), pp. 82–3.
[250] Alexander III, JL 10834, Materials, V, p. 33. See Somerville (1977), pp. 8–9.
[251] Roger of Pontigny, Vita sancti Thomae c.60, Materials, IV, p. 62. See Warren (1973), pp. 490–1; Barlow (1986), pp. 122–3; Councils and Synods, pp. 894, 915.
[252] Constitutions of Clarendon (1164), Councils and Synods, p. 877. The customs condemned by the pope (nos. 1, 3–5, 7–10, 12, 15): ibid., pp. 878–83.
[253] William Fitzstephen, Vita sancti Thomae c.65, Materials, III, pp. 73–4.

that of the English church'.[254] Thomas Becket, who as Henry II's chancellor had been an energetic defender of the royal rights, had been converted by his appointment as the successor of St Augustine of Canterbury into an equally zealous defender of the rights of his patron saint.[255] Incurring the enmity of the king and facing certain destruction, he became (like Eskil of Lund and Eric Ivarsson of Nidaros) an enthusiast for papal authority, seeking to enlist the pope's protection for his cause. This apparent opportunism contributed to the ambiguous reputation of Becket in the immediate aftermath of his murder (1170).

Some said that he was condemned as a traitor to the kingdom, others that he was a martyr, since he was a defender of the church. The same question was debated in Paris among the masters. For Master Roger swore that he had been worthy of death, albeit not such a death, judging the constancy of the blessed man to be obstinacy. Master Peter the Chanter swore on the contrary that he was a martyr worthy of God, since he was killed for the sake of the freedom of the church.[256]

In the settlement that followed the death of Becket the papal legates required the king to 'abjure all the customs against the churches of his kingdom that seem to have been introduced in his time' (1172).[257] Such customs, Henry II opined, were 'few or none'.[258] The papacy made no attempt to identify the offending customs; there was no reference to the Constitutions of Clarendon. All that the papal legates stipulated was that the king should 'permit appeals of ecclesiastical cases to be made freely to the lord pope, to be handled by him and settled by his judgement'.[259] It was the same demand that Adrian IV had made of Henry II. Provided that the proper channels of communication to Rome were left open, Alexander III was prepared to treat the king generously. He acclaimed Henry as 'a devoted son of the church' in the context of his intervention in Ireland.[260] He supported the king in the dangerous rebellion of 1173.[261] He allowed Henry to fill vacant bishoprics with royal servants who

---

[254] Alexander III, JL 11397, col. 483B; JL, 11832, col. 699C (to Thomas Becket). See Barlow (1986), pp. 143–4, 177–8.

[255] Brooke (1931), pp. 192–5; Knowles (1963), pp. 98–128, and (1970), pp. 165–71; Smalley (1973), pp. 115–21; Warren (1973), pp. 450–1; Barlow (1986), pp. 88–98.

[256] Caesarius of Heisterbach, *Dialogus miraculorum* VIII. 69, ed. Strange, II, p. 139. The question was settled, Caesarius concluded, by the miracles at Becket's tomb. 'Magister Rugerus' was perhaps Master Roger the Norman, canon of Rouen: see Baldwin (1967).

[257] Theoduin, cardinal priest of S. Vitale and Albert, cardinal priest of S. Lorenzo (the future Gregory VIII), letter to the archbishop of Sens, *Councils and Synods*, p. 954.

[258] Henry II, letter to Bishop Bartholomew of Exeter, *ibid.*, p. 955.

[259] Theoduin and Albert, letter, *ibid.*, p. 954.

[260] Alexander III, JL 12163, col. 885A (to the kings and princes of Ireland).

[261] Henry II's son, the young King Henry, sought to enlist the pope's support by representing himself as the champion of ecclesiastical liberty and denouncing his father's episcopal appointments: *RHGF*, XVI, pp. 643–8. Cf. Henry II's letter to Alexander III: *ibid.*, pp. 649–50. See Foreville and Rousset de Pina (1953), pp. 119–20; Warren (1973), pp. 312, 536.

had aided him in the persecution of Becket.[262] Henry II continued (like his grandfather) to maintain that contacts between his dominions and the papal curia required his explicit consent. The legate Hugh Pierleone, cardinal deacon of S. Angelo, came to England in 1175 at the king's request, as did Octavian, cardinal deacon of SS. Sergio e Baccho in 1186.[263] When, however, in 1176 Vivian, cardinal priest of S. Stefano in Celio Monte, entered the kingdom, having a legatine commission for Scotland and Ireland, 'without the king's permission', he was detained by Henry II's command. The legate was granted leave to continue his mission after he swore 'that he would do nothing hostile to [the king] or his kingdom'.[264] Henry II's successor, Richard I, long obstructed the legation of John of Anagni, cardinal priest of S. Marco (1189). The new king forbade the legate to attend his coronation, lest the papacy in future exploit his attendance as the basis of some novel claim.[265] The English episcopate was equally suspicious of Roman innovations. The bishops insisted that only four of their number should attend the Third Lateran Council in 1179 (apparently for reasons of economy).[266] In 1184, when Lucius III requested financial aid from the English church, the bishops warned the king that this 'could be turned into a custom, to the detriment of the kingdom'.[267]

Nevertheless, there is considerable evidence that links between the English church and the papal curia were intensified in the second half of the twelfth century. For in many areas of ecclesiastical life the assistance of Rome had come to seem indispensable. The protection of St Peter was more eagerly sought than ever before. The abbey of St Albans, for example, obtained 100 papal letters between 1159 and 1197, which was five times the number of papal privileges in the abbey's possession before the mid-twelfth century.[268] An increasing number of lawsuits were brought to the curia by English churchmen. The most famous was 'the Canterbury case', the attempt by the monks of Christ Church, Canterbury, to prevent Archbishop Baldwin and later Archbishop Hubert Walter from endowing a collegiate church, first at Hackington, subsequently at Lambeth. The case lasted with intervals for fifteen years.[269] The unusually abundant documentation of the English church shows that many churchmen served as judges

[262] Foreville (1943), p. 380; Mayr-Harting (1965); Duggan (1966), pp. 1–21; Warren (1973), pp. 534–6.

[263] Ralph of Diceto, 'Ex ymaginibus historiarum' I, pp. 402–3; Roger of Howden (?), *Gesta regis Henrici II*, II, pp. 3–4. See Tillmann (1926), pp. 74, 80–1.

[264] Roger of Howden (?), *Gesta regis Henrici II*, I, p. 118. See Tillmann (1926), p. 77; Warren (1973), p. 537.

[265] *Epistolae Cantuarienses* 315, p. 300. See Tillmann (1926), p. 84; Cheney (1956), p. 93.

[266] Roger of Howden, *Chronica* 1179, II, p. 171. See Cheney (1956), p. 92.

[267] Roger of Howden (?), *Gesta regis Henrici II*, I, p. 311. See Lunt (1939), pp. 175–6.

[268] Cheney (1956), p. 85.

[269] It is documented in the 571 letters of the *Epistolae Cantuarienses*. See Cheney (1956), pp. 3–4, 73–4, 85, 90–2; Mayr-Harting (1965), pp. 45–6; Cheney (1976), pp. 5–8, 208–20.

delegate (local judges appointed by the pope to investigate cases in their locality on behalf of the curia).[270] The great variety of legal problems arising from such delegated cases involved the judges delegate in correspondence with the pope, who alone could give an authoritative ruling. The pope's answers to these enquiries (*consultationes*) account for a large part of the *decretales epistolae* issued by the papacy from the pontificate of Alexander III onwards. These papal letters were in turn the raw materials of the decretal collections compiled by canonists for the use of the schools of canon law and the ecclesiastical courts. English canonists were the most numerous and the earliest compilers of decretal collections (beginning in the early 1170s), which explains why so large a proportion of the extant decretals (approximately one half) referred to English churchmen.[271] English intellectuals contributed greatly to that respect for the legislative authority of the pope that characterized later twelfth-century canonist thinking.

With the kingdom of France the papacy enjoyed for most of the twelfth century a much easier relationship. It was during this period that the foundations were laid for the Franco-papal alliance that was so significant in the thirteenth and fourteenth centuries. Several popes had connections with France that predated their pontificates. The Burgundian Calixtus II, formerly Archbishop Guido of Vienne, had served as Paschal II's permanent legate in eastern France and Burgundy.[272] There, 'wherever [he] went as a legate, [he] found scarcely any one of note who was not [his] nephew or close kinsman or [his] vassal'.[273] Innocent II, as Cardinal Deacon Gregory of S. Angelo, had twice visited France as a legate (on both occasions coinciding with Peter Pierleone, cardinal priest of S. Maria in Trastevere, his future rival in the disputed papal election of 1130).[274] Celestine II, the former Guido of Castello, had studied in the schools of Paris. The pupil of Peter Abelard, he was one of the most learned men of his generation and the first clerk with the title of *magister* to be promoted to the college of cardinals (1128).[275] The future Celestine III, Hyacinth Bobo, had also been a pupil of Abelard, whom he had defended against his opponents in the curia.[276] Three popes had formerly made their profession in religious houses in France: Eugenius III (as a monk of Clairvaux), Adrian IV (as a regular canon of St Ruf in Avignon) and Gregory VIII (as a regular canon of St-Martin in Laon).[277]

[270] Morey (1937), pp. 44–78; Cheney (1941), pp. 180–1; Morey and Brooke (1965), p. 243; Sayers (1971a), pp. 9–10. See *NCMH*, IV, Part 1, ch. 11.

[271] Brooke (1931), pp. 212–14; Holtzmann (1945), pp. 16, 34; Duggan (1963), pp. 66–117.

[272] Schieffer (1935), pp. 195–8.

[273] Hugh the Chanter, *History of the Church of York*, p. 118.

[274] Schieffer (1935), pp. 214–15.

[275] Zenker (1964), pp. 83–4; Luscombe (1969), pp. 20–2; Classen (1974), p. 433, and (1983), pp. 129–30.

[276] Zenker (1964), pp. 162–3; Classen (1974), p. 433, and (1983), pp. 130, 133, 150. Cardinal Hyacinth of S. Maria in Cosmedin was also a legate in France in 1162: see Janssen (1961), pp. 80–1.

[277] Zenker (1964), pp. 36, 185–6; Kehr (1924), p. 250.

Many prominent figures in the papal curia were similarly connected with France. The papal chancellor Haimeric was a Burgundian[278] and his successor, Robert Pullen, had taught theology in the schools of Paris.[279] The Frenchman Cardinal Bishop Matthew of Albano, the tireless defender of the cause of Innocent II during his legation in France, had been prior of the monastery of St-Martin-des-Champs,[280] where one of his monks was Imar, later cardinal bishop of Tusculum.[281] The most travelled of the papal legates of the mid-twelfth century, Cardinal Bishop Alberic of Ostia, had also come from St-Martin-des-Champs.[282] During Innocent II's pontificate the college of cardinals contained nine Frenchmen, eight of whom were directly linked with Bernard of Clairvaux, Innocent's most important supporter in France.[283] The papal chamberlain Jordan, cardinal priest of S. Susanna was originally a Carthusian in Le Mont-Dieu near Rheims.[284] On the eve of the Third Lateran Council Alexander III requested the names of suitable French recruits to the college from his expert on French affairs, the legate Peter, cardinal priest of S. Grisogono, who had been bishop of Meaux before entering the college and who ended his life as archbishop of Bourges. This initiative resulted in the appointment to the college of two French abbots, Henry of Clairvaux (cardinal bishop of Albano) and Bernered of St-Crépin, Soissons (cardinal bishop of Palestrina).[285] Such promotions ensured that the influence of French monastic reform and the French schools continued to be felt in the papal curia.

Of the twelve papal councils celebrated in the period from the pontificate of Calixtus II to that of Alexander III, seven took place on French soil. Three of these councils were held in Rheims (1119, 1131 and 1148). This city was chosen partly because the archbishop, enjoying the office and revenues of the count of Rheims, could afford the cost of accommodating the papal curia and partly because the proximity to the imperial territories facilitated the attendance of imperial bishops.[286] Most importantly France provided a refuge for the papal curia when Rome became too dangerous. Calixtus II was elected pope in the abbey of Cluny by the cardinals who had accompanied Gelasius II into exile in

---

[278] Schmale (1961b), pp. 97–8.   [279] Poole (1934), pp. 287–91; Smalley (1973), pp. 40–1.

[280] Berlière (1901); Janssen (1961), pp. 15–18, 30–4; Zenker (1964), pp. 32–4.

[281] He subsequently entered the abbey of Cluny. See Zenker (1964), p. 44.

[282] He was entrusted with legations in England, Scotland, the crusader principality of Antioch and France: see Tillmann (1926), pp. 38–40; Janssen (1961), pp. 39–40; Zenker (1964), pp. 15–20.

[283] The cardinal bishops Drogo and Alberic of Ostia, Stephen of Palestrina, Imar of Tusculum, the cardinal priests Baldwin of S. Maria in Trastevere, Ivo of S. Lorenzo in Damaso (Master Ivo of Chartres), Chrysogonus of S. Prassede, Luke of SS. Giovanni e Paolo. See Zenker (1964), pp. 13–14, 19–20, 40–1, 45, 55, 78–9, 117, 136.

[284] Zenker (1964), pp. 104–6. See also Jacqueline (1953), pp. 31–2.

[285] Peter of S. Grisogono, *Epistola* (to Alexander III), *PL* 200, cols. 1370D–1372A. On Peter's career see Pacaut (1955), pp. 835–7; Janssen (1961), pp. 61–9, 92–3, 104; Zenker (1964), pp. 162, 165–6.

[286] Graboïs (1964b), p. 9.

France (2 February 1119).[287] Calixtus remained in France for eleven months and it was there that he held his first two councils (Toulouse and Rheims) in 1119.[288] Innocent II fled to France in the seventh month of the papal schism of 1130, his destination perhaps suggested by his principal advisers, the Burgundian Haimeric and Matthew of Albano (born in Rheims). On Innocent's arrival in France (September 1130) the attitude of King Louis VI towards his claims was not yet known and the pope took up residence in Cluny. Once informed by Abbot Suger of St-Denis that the royal council in Etampes had recognized his title, Innocent entered the jurisdiction of the Capetian king.[289] He remained in France for seventeen months and here he celebrated his councils of Clermont (November 1130) and Rheims (October 1131), which were triumphs for his cause.[290] Eugenius III, escaping from the political turbulence of Rome, spent nine months in France in 1147–8. Except for a fortnight in Champagne, he remained in the Capetian sphere of influence, where he celebrated his council of Rheims (March 1148).[291] The longest papal visit was the period of three years and five months that Alexander III spent in France (1162–5). He stayed first in Montpellier, in the county of Melgueil, a vassal principality of the Roman church where the pope could raise feudal revenues.[292] After holding his council of Tours (May 1163) on the Capetian–Plantagenet frontier, he moved into the Capetian heartland and settled in Sens, where the curia remained from October 1163 until April 1165.[293]

It is not surprising, therefore, to find the Capetian kings eulogized in papal documents and in the writings of papal supporters. Innocent II 'chose the most noble kingdom of the French as a safe and proven refuge, after God, for the defence of his person and of the church', wrote Suger of St Denis.[294] Alexander III acclaimed King Louis VII as a 'praiseworthy imitator of [his] forebears', with whom persecuted popes had 'always found a haven of longed-for peace and a timely refuge'.[295] King Louis VI had in fact been denounced to the pope as 'the new Herod' by Bernard of Clairvaux in 1128 because of his assertion of his royal rights over the churches in his jurisdiction.[296] Honorius II, however,

[287] Meyer von Knonau (1909), pp. 108–9; Robinson (1990), pp. 63–5.

[288] *Regesta pontificum Romanorum*, I, pp. 782–93; Graboïs (1964b), p. 7.

[289] Suger of St-Denis, *Vita Ludovici grossi regis* c.32, pp. 258–60. See Graboïs (1981), p. 600.

[290] *Regesta pontificum Romanorum*, I, pp. 844–54; Graboïs (1964b), p. 7.

[291] *Regesta pontificum Romanorum*, II, pp. 40–57; Gleber (1936), pp. 83–102; Graboïs (1964b), p. 8.

[292] The county had been a vassal principality of the Roman church since 1085. See Pacaut (1953), p. 18; Fried (1980), pp. 72–3, 130. For Alexander III's council of Montpellier (May 1162) see Somerville (1977), p. 7.

[293] *Regesta pontificum Romanorum*, II, pp. 157–95; Pacaut (1953), pp. 18–23.

[294] Suger, *Vita Ludovici grossi regis* c.32, p. 258.   [295] Alexander III, JL 10644, col. 100BC.

[296] Bernard, 'Epistola' 49. Louis VI was opposed to the plans of Bishop Stephen of Paris to reform the chapter of Notre Dame, Paris, and was involved in disputes with the archbishops of Sens and Tours: see Luchaire (1890), pp. clxxv–clxxviii.

reprimanded Bernard for his attack on the king and in his own correspondence with Louis VI assured him of his paternal affection.[297] Innocent II's concern to associate his cause with that of Louis VI and his dynasty was apparent when, during his council of Rheims, he anointed the young Louis VII to the kingship in the presence of his father. The coronation was a celebration of both the Capetian and the papal monarchy, the pope being 'clad in all his insignia and, as [was] his custom on great and holy festivals, crowned with the *phrygium*'.[298]

Louis VII in fact began his reign with a quarrel with Innocent II. In 1137, failing to secure the election of his chancellor Cadurc as archbishop of Bourges, the king refused to acknowledge the successful candidate, Peter de la Châtre. Innocent II vigorously intervened in favour of Peter, who was the nephew of the papal chancellor, Cardinal Haimeric, and placed the king's lands under an interdict.[299] The interdict was raised only when Innocent was succeeded by the more diplomatic Celestine II.[300] It was Louis VII's recruitment for the Second Crusade that transformed the king's relationship with the papacy. The transformation began when Louis welcomed Eugenius III to Dijon and 'embraced the pope's foot, covering it with kisses and tears' (30 March 1147)[301] and when, on his departure for the east, the king 'left his kingdom under [the pope's] protection and that of holy church'.[302] He returned from the crusade unvictorious but with the reputation of a champion of the Christian faith, 'always making God the beginning and end of his doings'. 'Generous as a king, courageous as a prince, spirited as a knight', wrote the historian of his crusade, 'through his probity he acquired the favour of men, through his piety he obtained divine grace.'[303] To this he added the reputation of a protector of the church's liberty. Henceforward he exercised influence on French ecclesiastical affairs in a subtle manner: there was no repetition of the confrontation at Bourges.[304] Louis's support, at considerable risk to himself, for Alexander III during the schism of 1159–77 and for Thomas Becket during the latter's dispute with Henry II of England completed the image of the saintly king. Alexander III in 1161 contrasted Louis VII's conduct with that of Emperor Frederick I, who failed to fulfil the traditional imperial duty of protecting the pope. 'Frederick, whose office requires him to be the advocate and defender of the church, rages cruelly

---

[297] Honorius II's rebuke was contained in a letter (not extant) of the chancellor Haimeric. The contents can be deduced from Bernard, 'Epistola' 51. See Vacandard (1920), I, pp. I. 277–81.

[298] *Chronicon Mauriniacensis monasterii* II. See Klewitz (1941), p. 105; Schramm (1960), p. 120.

[299] *Chronicon Mauriniacensis monasterii* III. See Pacaut (1957), pp. 94–9, and (1964), pp. 42–3, 68.

[300] Pacaut (1957), pp. 99–100, and (1964), pp. 68–9.

[301] *Chronicon de Ludovico Francorum rege, fragmentum, RHGF*, XII, p. 91.

[302] Eugenius III, JL 9345, col. 1394D.

[303] Odo of Deuil, *De profectione Ludovici VII in orientem* VII, p. 142.

[304] Pacaut (1957), pp. 103–4, 147–8.

against her; while you, as a most Christian prince, love and honour her and revere her with a sincere affection.'[305]

The straitened circumstances of the Capetian king often caused him to make financial demands on the churches within his jurisdiction. When requested to aid the refugee papal curia, cut off from its conventional revenues in Rome and the patrimony, the material support that the king offered usually took the form of permission to share in his exploitation of the wealth of the French church.[306] The traditional right of hospitality (later known as *procuratio canonica*) could be demanded by the pope from any church, but it was a right that could only be enjoyed *in situ*.[307] The curia improvised two further demands from the French church: *subsidia* and 'provisions'. *Subsidia* or 'alms' were emergency supplies which the curia begged from churches where it was not practicable for the pope to seek hospitality. In the case of 'papal provisions', the pope requested the king or a bishop to confer a French benefice on a member of the papal curia, who would then draw the salary of that benefice while continuing to serve the pope in the curia. These emergency measures of the papal exile in France were to became a permanent part of the papal financial system which was to be the cause of such hostility towards the later medieval papacy.[308]

Even after the return to Rome negotiated by Clement III (1188) the popes continued to depend on the financial measures to which the papal curia had resorted during the schism. This dependence helps to explain why the curia avoided conflict with the new French king Philip II Augustus during the 1190s. Philip II antagonized the papacy in two ways: he threatened the French possessions of the absent crusader, King Richard I of England, and he obtained a controversial divorce from a council of French bishops and magnates. Celestine III refrained from taking the decisive measures that would characterize the conduct of his successor, Innocent III, towards the Capetian king.[309] A former student in the Paris schools, who during his long career in the curia had experienced two papal exiles in France, Celestine's natural inclination was to conciliate the French kingdom.[310] The vulnerability of the papacy and the growing power of Emperor Henry VI served to remind the curia of the value of maintaining good relations with the French king.

The political relationships which most closely affected the security of the twelfth-century papacy were, first, that with the pope's subjects in the city of Rome; secondly, that with the pope's traditional protector, the western emperor; thirdly, that with the pope's vassals, the Norman princes of southern Italy and Sicily. All three relationships were turbulent and sometimes threatened

[305] Alexander III, JL 10644, col. 100BC.   [306] Pacaut (1964), pp. 91–117.
[307] Berlière (1919), pp. 510–11; Brühl (1974), pp. 426–7.
[308] Lunt (1934), p. 77; Graboïs (1964b), pp. 15–17.
[309] Baldwin (1986), pp. 83–7, 88–9.   [310] Pfaff (1961), pp. 124–5.

the independence of the papacy. The difficulty of deciding how to respond to such threats was often exacerbated by differences of opinion among the pope's advisers. The cardinals had since the beginning of the twelfth century successfully laid claim to the role of advisers to the pope and it is evident that in times of crisis popes were careful to consult their brethren.[311] What is known of the internal history of the college suggests the existence of rival factions of cardinals eager to influence papal decision-making. Popes seem sometimes to have attempted to use their power of appointing cardinals to control this factionalism and to have recruited cardinals whom they believed to be in sympathy with their own views. This was perhaps the reason for the appointment of papal kinsmen to the college in the pontificates of Lucius II, Clement III and Celestine III.[312]

In particular, three large-scale creations of cardinals during the twelfth century have been interpreted as papal attempts to introduce reliable supporters into the college. First, in the aftermath of a deadly epidemic (September 1121) Calixtus II was compelled to recruit sixteen new cardinals. Those of his appointees who can be identified were northern Italian and French.[313] This has prompted speculation that the pope desired a counterweight to the Roman and southern Italian cardinals whom he inherited from Paschal II and who were unsympathetic to his own aims.[314] Secondly, Innocent II, who at the outbreak of the schism of 1130 was supported by less than half of the college, made fifty appointments in the course of his pontificate. His identifiable appointees consisted of four Romans, seven northern Italians, one Lorrainer and nine Frenchmen. Innocent's appointments, many of which were made in exile in France or Tuscany, have been interpreted as a deliberate intensification of the trend apparent in Calixtus II's pontificate.[315] Thirdly, in 1187 Clement III inherited a greatly diminished college, perhaps only eighteen cardinals and certainly too few to perform the regular duties of the cardinalate. Between 1188 and 1190 Clement appointed approximately thirty cardinals, of whom the majority were (like the pope himself) Romans, including members of the great families – the Malabranca, de Papa, Bobone-Orsini, Conti-Poli, Cenci, Pierleoni, Crescentii – who dominated Rome. Clement III, the pope who made peace with the city of Rome after forty-five years of conflict, consolidated this peace by means of his appointments to the college.[316] Our information about individual cardinals is not full enough to pronounce confidently on any aspect

[311] See *NCMH*, IV, Part 1, ch. 11.   [312] Zenker (1964), pp. 41, 132; Pfaff (1955), pp. 86, 91, 92.
[313] Hüls (1977), pp. 142–3, 162, 164, 193, 220, 236, 238.
[314] Klewitz (1957), pp. 372–412; Schmale (1961b), pp. 31–57, 79–80.
[315] Zenker (1964), pp. 13–14, 19–20, 40–1, 45, 55, 78–9, 117, 136, 202; Tillmann (1972), pp. 336–44; Maleczek (1981), p. 57.
[316] Wenck (1926), pp. 440–1; Pfaff (1955), pp. 84–93, and (1980), pp. 269, 280.

of the politics of the sacred college. It seems plausible, however, that popes would use their right of nomination to create a compliant college, seeking to present a united front to the dangers that threatened them.

In the case of the city of Rome, the independence of the papacy was threatened during the early twelfth century by the ambitions of the noble families. No Roman family of the twelfth century was powerful enough to dominate the papacy in the manner of the 'aristocratic papacy' of the tenth and early eleventh centuries. The danger was that rival factions inside the college of cardinals would use their allies among the Roman nobility to control papal policy-making. The papal elections of 1124 and 1130 both took place against the background of the power-struggle of the two great Roman clans, the Frangipani and the Pierleoni. The election of Honorius II (16 December 1124) was the work of a faction of cardinals led by the papal chancellor Haimeric, who used the might of the Frangipani to achieve his purpose.[317] On the death of Honorius II Haimeric's opponents in the college, led by Peter Pierleone, cardinal priest of S. Maria in Trastevere, relied on the support of the latter's family, the Pierleoni, to frustrate Haimeric's second attempt at pope-making.[318] The reign of Cardinal Peter Pierleone as the antipope Anacletus II gave his family a temporary ascendancy over Rome. They attempted to regain influence in the city by identifying themselves in the mid-1140s with the demands of the Roman citizens for self-government. When the Romans established a commune, 'they appointed as their patrician Jordan, a very great man of the Pierleone family. In order to injure the lord pope they destroyed the palace of Cencius Frangipane, whose family always assisted the church in her hour of need.'[319]

During the years 1143–88 the popes found that the Roman commune was a more formidable enemy than the great Roman families. Developments in Rome parallelled those in the cities of Lombardy and Tuscany, which threw off the government of their bishops and feudal lords, created autonomous city-republics and extended their jurisdiction over the surrounding *contado*. In 1143 the Romans determined to conquer Latium as the Roman *contado* and when Innocent II opposed their ambitions, they rebelled against him, rejecting the papal claim to exercise secular government over the city. They seized the Capitol and set up a senate, whose members exercised executive and judicial authority, declared war and made treaties.[320] Forty-five years of

[317] Klewitz (1957), pp. 243–7; Schmale (1961b), pp. 120–3; Stroll (1987), pp. 11–12, 82, 140–1, 156–7; Robinson (1990), pp. 65–9. See also below p. 373.

[318] Klewitz (1957), pp. 209–29; Schmale (1961b), pp. 145–61; Stroll (1987), pp. 82–90; Robinson (1990), pp. 69–75. See also below p. 373.

[319] John of Salisbury, *Historia pontificalis* c.27, p. 59. See Palumbo (1942), pp. 198, 291.

[320] Halphen (1907), pp. 53–7; Rota (1953), pp. 41–63; Partner (1972), pp. 178–81; Benson (1982), pp. 340–59.

sporadic hostilities between pope and commune (intensified during the papal schism of 1159–77, when the Romans sided with the emperor)[321] demonstrated that the pope had not the power to abolish the senate. Eugenius III was the first to accept that the pope must reach a compromise with the Romans. In 1145 he made peace on the basis 'that the senators should hold their office by [the pope's] authority'.[322] This compromise was also the basis of the treaty made by Clement III with the senate (31 May 1188), which enabled the pope once more to reside peacefully in Rome. Every year the senators must swear fealty to the pope; but in return the pope must abandon his resistance to the territorial ambitions of the Roman commune.[323]

The hostility of the Romans during most of the twelfth century made the papacy more dependent on the aid either of his traditional defender, the emperor, or on his more recently acquired protectors, the Normans of southern Italy and Sicily. The relationship of the popes with the Norman princes was that of lord and vassal: the princes took an oath to be 'faithful to blessed Peter and to the holy Roman church and to my lord the pope'.[324] Southern Italy was the only region outside the Patrimony of St Peter where the papal claim to feudal suzerainty could be of direct practical significance. This feudal relationship with the papacy had legitimized the building of the Norman principalities in the eleventh century. It subsequently involved the papacy in the construction of a single Norman kingdom of Sicily in the twelfth century. At the beginning of our period Calixtus II and Honorius II enjoyed a close friendship with Duke William of Apulia (1111–27), a loyal vassal and pious prince, whose coins bore the head of St Peter.[325] The popes readily intervened in Apulia on the duke's behalf to restrain his rebellious vassals; they received oaths of fealty from the Apulian counts and barons in the interests of preserving peace. They also tried to protect William from his predatory kinsman and vassal, Count Roger II of Sicily (1105–54), who had extorted the territory of Calabria from him after four years of warfare.[326] On the death of the childless William (1127) the heir to the duchy of Apulia was this same Roger, whom the papal curia had so often vainly reproved for his tyrannical conduct towards the Sicilian church.

The prospect of the succession of so unsympathetic a vassal prompted the curia to impose its own highly anachronistic interpretation of the feudal relationship. The southern Italian fiefs were held by the Norman vassals solely by the pope's permission: it was not hereditary succession but papal investiture

---

[321] Petersohn (1974), pp. 308–16.

[322] Otto of Freising, *Chronica* VII. 34, p. 367. See Rota (1953), pp. 93–101; Partner (1972), p. 182.

[323] Treaty of 1188, *Liber censuum*, I, pp. 373–4. See Petersohn (1974), pp. 289–337; Pfaff (1980), pp. 263–5.

[324] Oath of William II of Sicily: *MGH Constitutiones* I, p. 592. Cf. oath of Tancred: *ibid.*, pp. 592–3.

[325] Deér (1972), p. 45.   [326] Kehr (1934), p. 26; Deér (1972), pp. 162–3.

that gave legal title to the fief.[327] Underpinning this theory was the political idea (inherited from the Gregorian papacy) of *idoneitas*, 'suitability': secular government could be exercised only by a ruler 'suitable... for the honour of holy church'.[328] When Roger II pressed his hereditary claim, Honorius II excommunicated him 'because he seized the title of duke, to which he had no right, without consulting the Roman pontiff'.[329] Both Honorius II (1127–8) and Innocent II (1137–9) organized coalitions of Roger's enemies to expel him from the Italian mainland. Both were defeated by Roger when they tried to impose their conception of the pope's rights over southern Italy.[330] The customary papal political strategy of dividing and ruling the Norman princes was rendered irrelevant by Roger II's triumphant unification of the Norman principalities under his own government. Innocent II was compelled in 1139 to legitimate Roger's achievements by recognizing him as the lawful possessor of 'the kingdom of Sicily, the duchy of Apulia and the principality of Capua'.[331] Even in this moment of defeat, however, the papal curia clung to the notion of *idoneitas* as the qualification for secular rule: Roger deserved the kingship because he was 'adorned with prudence, fortified with justice and suitable to rule the people'.[332] After seventeen years of further Norman expansion and encroachment on the Patrimony of St Peter Adrian IV was compelled to conclude the treaty of Benevento (1156), acknowledging Roger's son, William I (1154–66), as the ruler of the whole southern Italian mainland and despoiling the papacy of considerable income and rights of jurisdiction.[333]

The papal defeat of 1156, however, inaugurated three decades of harmonious cooperation between the papacy and the kingdom of Sicily. During the conflict with the empire in the years 1159–77 Alexander III's survival depended in part on the military and financial aid of William I and his successor, William II (1166–89). Hence the eulogies of the Norman kings in Cardinal Boso's biography of Alexander: William I was a 'faithful and devout son of the Roman church'; William II shared his father's 'fidelity and devotion'.[334] This harmony ended with the premature death of William II. In 1189, as in 1127, the death of a childless ruler threatened the papacy with the succession of a far less 'suitable' heir. The hereditary claimant was William's aunt, Constance, who was the

[327] Deér (1972), pp. 51–106, 126–63.
[328] Gregory VII, *Register* ix.3, *MGH Epp. sel.* ii, p. 575. See Robinson (1990), pp. 312–16.
[329] Romuald of Salerno, 'Annales' 1127, p. 418.   [330] Deér (1972), pp. 175–230.
[331] Innocent II, JL 8043, col. 479B. See Kehr (1934), p. 42; Deér (1972), pp. 223–30.
[332] Innocent II, JL 8043, cols. 478C–479D.
[333] Concordat of Benevento, *MGH Constitutiones* i, pp. 588–91 (nos. 413–4). See Kehr (1934), p. 46; Deér (1972), pp. 247–53, 258–9. See also below p. 378.
[334] Boso, 'Vita Alexandri III', ii, p. 414. See Chalandon (1907), pp. 301, 375.

wife of Henry VI, king of the Germans and future emperor. Faced with the
dreadful prospect of 'the union of the kingdom with the empire' (*unio regni
ad imperium*), the papal curia once more invoked the principle of *idoneitas*.
Like Honorius II and Innocent II, Clement III and Celestine III countered the
claim of hereditary right with the claim of the suzerain to choose his own vassal.
The pope rejected Constance and invested her illegitimate nephew, Tancred,
with the kingdom.[335] The papal strategy was foiled by the premature death of
Tancred and the subsequent conquest of Sicily by Henry VI (1194), who finally
accomplished 'the union of the kingdom with the empire'.[336]

According to tradition, the protection of the pope and of the Patrimony of
St Peter was the first duty of the emperor: 'the lord emperor, by virtue of the
duty which belongs to his dignity, is the advocate and special defender of the
holy Roman church'.[337] Henry V (1106–25), who concluded the Concordat of
Worms with the papacy, signally failed to fulfil this function. His successor,
Lothar III (1125–37), was the only emperor of the twelfth century to perform
his duties as protector to the satisfaction of the papal curia. Lothar himself
on the eve of his imperial coronation (1133) described the emperor's duties in
the language traditionally used by the papacy. Since God had appointed him
'patron and defender of the holy Roman church', he was obliged 'to labour
the more willingly for her liberation'.[338] Cardinal Boso represented him as 'the
most Christian emperor, fired with zeal for God and the Christian faith, like
a Catholic advocate of the church'. The Monte Cassino chronicler applied
to him the Gregorian language of *idoneitas*: Lothar was 'useful and suitable
for the honour of the empire'.[339] Lothar's successor, Conrad III (1138–52), was
exhorted to play a similar role – Bernard of Clairvaux, for example, reminded
him that the defence of the church was his duty as *advocatus*[340] – but he
was prevented from performing this duty by the civil war in Germany which
continued for the greater part of his reign. (Conrad III was the first German
king since the mid-tenth century who failed to receive imperial coronation
in Rome.) Conrad's nephew and successor, Frederick I Barbarossa (1152–90),
proved to be the opposite of the *advocatus, patronus* and *defensor* of the Roman
church of whom the curia was in such great need. 'From the time of . . . Pope
Adrian and from the inception of his [imperial] dignity [in 1155], he began,
like a tyrant, to oppress and greatly to injure the holy Roman church.'[341] The

[335] Chalandon (1907), pp. 121–3; Kehr (1934), pp. 51–2; Deér (1972), pp. 260–1.
[336] Chalandon (1907), pp. 443–91; Robinson (1990), pp. 395–7, 515–16.
[337] Alexander III, JL 10597: Boso, 'Vita Alexandri III', II, p. 401. See Ullmann (1970), pp. 121, 198, 217,
    223.
[338] Lothar III, *Encyclica, MGH Constitutiones* I, p. 167.
[339] Boso, 'Vita Innocentii II' II, p. 383. *Chronica monasterii Casinensis* IV.87, p. 548.
[340] Bernard, 'Epistola' 244 c.3.   [341] Alexander III, JL 10627–8, cols. 89BC, 91AB.

conflict of papacy and empire in the years 1159–77 forced the pope to seek help throughout Christendom: from the Sicilian king and the cities of northern and central Italy, fleetingly from the Byzantine empire and from the French church and kingdom.

This period of papal history, which ended in four decades of conflict or uneasy truce with the Staufen emperors Frederick I and Henry VI, had begun with the promise of peace between papacy and empire. The concordat of Worms (September 1122) ended what William of Malmesbury in 1125 called 'that chronic dispute concerning investiture between the kingship and the priesthood which had caused turmoil for more than fifty years'.[342] Writing in the midst of the later conflict of papacy and empire (perhaps in 1162) Gerhoch of Reichersberg recalled that happier time when 'after the great tempest . . . peace was made. Thus through God's grace the church, which since the time of Gregory VII had seemed split by the investiture dispute, was united.'[343] From the papal point of view the concordat was an imperfect solution. As Calixtus II explained to his critics at the First Lateran Council (1123), it was a compromise which the papacy was compelled 'not to approve but to tolerate', 'in order to restore peace'.[344] The papal privilege of 1122 was a temporary expedient, 'given for the sake of peace to [Henry V] alone and not to his successors', to be renegotiated with a future more satisfactory emperor.[345]

The two popes of the second quarter of the twelfth century who, as cardinals, had been responsible for negotiating the Concordat of Worms, Honorius II and Innocent II, seized opportunities to intervene in the affairs of the German church in ways unforeseen in the concordat. Honorius's legate approved the election of Norbert, abbot of Prémontré, to the archsee of Magdeburg, rejecting the claim of a royal kinsman.[346] Innocent was ready to exploit the central ambiguity in the text of the concordat. The papal privilege permitted the emperor to grant the *regalia* (the proprietary and governmental rights attached to a bishopric) to the bishop elect before the latter was consecrated by his metropolitan. Did this mean that by withholding the *regalia* from a candidate, the emperor could veto his election? Alternatively, did the 'free consecration' conceded in the imperial privilege mean that the metropolitan could consecrate a bishop elect on whom the emperor had refused to confer the *regalia*?[347] In 1132, adopting the latter interpretation, Innocent consecrated the archbishop elect of Trier, who had not received the *regalia*. His example was followed by

---

[342] William of Malmesbury, *De gestis regum Anglorum* v.435 (I, p. 780). See Schieffer (1981), p. 3 n. 7.
[343] Gerhoch of Reichersberg, 'Commentarius aureus in psalmos', 33. See Classen (1960), p. 27 n. 5.
[344] Gerhoch of Reichersberg, 'Libellus de ordine donorum Sancti Spiritus', p. 280. See Benson (1968), pp. 229–30; Wilks (1971), pp. 77–9; Classen (1973), pp. 413–22.
[345] Otto of Freising, *Chronica* VII.16, p. 331. [346] Hauck (1952), pp. 126–33.
[347] Concordat of Worms, *MGH Constitutiones* I, pp. 159–60 (imperial privilege) 161 (papal privilege).

Archbishop Conrad of Salzburg in consecrating the bishop elect of Regensburg.[348] It was presumably in response to these cases that Lothar III raised the
question of his rights in episcopal elections on the occasion of his imperial coronation in June 1133. He obtained from Innocent (who depended on imperial
help for the defeat of his rival in the papal schism) a privilege confirming 'the
due and canonical customs', the last papal–imperial agreement on the subject
of investiture.[349]

The papal privilege of 1133 removed the ambiguity in the Concordat of
Worms which Innocent had exploited the previous year. The bishop or abbot
elect was forbidden 'to dare to usurp or seize the *regalia* before requesting them
from [Lothar] and performing to [him] what is rightfully owed to [him] in
respect of them'.[350] Hence the historian Otto of Freising, describing in 1156 the
rights of the German crown in the case of a disputed episcopal election, could
confidently ascribe a veto to the emperor. 'It belongs to the monarch's authority
to appoint the bishop whom he wishes, on the advice of his magnates, and no
elect is to be consecrated before he receives the *regalia* from his hand by the
sceptre.'[351] Otto was describing the practice of the Staufen kings – his own half-
brother, King Conrad III, and his nephew, Frederick I – who, insisting on the
observance of all the customs conceded to the emperor in 1122, exacted from
prelates the performance of homage, which the pious Lothar III had waived.[352]
Their contemporary, the theologian Gerhoch of Reichersberg, continued to
hope for a revision of the concordat in the sense desired by Calixtus II's critics
at the First Lateran Council: 'we hope that in the near future that evil [of
homage] may be removed from our midst'.[353]

Such hopes were frustrated by the firm lordship that Frederick Barbarossa
achieved over the German church. Frederick indeed strove to impose the
German customs on the bishops of his Italian kingdom in a notable extension of the imperial rights conceded by the concordat.[354] By the end of the
twelfth century it was the imperial, rather than the papal version of the Concordat of Worms that was generally accepted by German churchmen. Intervening in the disputed election of the archbishop of Trier in 1186, the truculent
Urban III consecrated Folmar, the candidate opposed by Frederick I. It was a
demonstration of papal authority over the German church intended to provoke confrontation with the emperor. The pope's action inspired reproofs from
the German episcopate, who claimed that 'the most careful record of former
times never mentions that this was done by any of your predecessors to any

---

[348] Hauck (1952), pp. 149–52.   [349] Innocent II, JL 7632, *MGH Constitutiones* I, p. 168.
[350] *Ibid.*, pp. 168–9. See Benson (1968), pp. 256–63.
[351] Otto of Freising, *Gesta Friderici imperatoris* II.6, pp. 85–6.   [352] Classen (1973), p. 433.
[353] Gerhoch, 'Libellus de ordine donorum Sancti Spiritus' p. 280.
[354] Benson (1968), pp. 284–91; Classen (1973), pp. 436–7, 442–3.

of [the emperor's] predecessors'.[355] Innocent II's attempt in 1132 to reinterpret the concordat was now forgotten. Urban III's successors prudently abandoned his support of Folmar and the resolution of the Trier dispute left the emperor firmly in control of the German church.[356]

The twelfth-century papacy continued to be preoccupied by a second question left unresolved at the end of the Investiture Contest: that of the lands of Countess Matilda of Tuscany. That faithful and energetic ally of the Gregorian papacy had willed her extensive allodial lands in Tuscany to St Peter. Such an inheritance, a second 'Patrimony of St Peter' in Tuscany, promised a great accession of power and prosperity to the papacy. On Matilda's death (1115), however, her kinsman, Emperor Henry V, seized these lands, claiming to be her heir, and the papacy was unable to gain possession of its inheritance.[357] Early in the reign of Lothar III the interests of both empire and papacy were threatened when Lothar's rival, the anti-king Conrad of Staufen, attempted to seize the Matildine lands as a base for his war against Lothar.[358] This common danger prompted Lothar and Innocent II to reach a settlement of their claims to the Tuscan inheritance. On 8 June 1133, two days after crowning Lothar emperor, Innocent invested him with the Matildine lands in return for the payment of an annual census of 100 pounds of silver, on condition that on the emperor's death the lands should revert to the Roman church. The fief was then regranted to Lothar's son-in-law, Henry the Proud, duke of Bavaria, who was required to perform homage and fealty to St Peter and Innocent.[359] This settlement made an important contribution to the stability of papal finances in the mid-twelfth century.[360]

During the papal schism of 1159–77 and the war with Frederick Barbarossa the exiled pope once more lost control of the Matildine lands. After the defeat of the emperor by the papal allies, the Lombard cities, at the battle of Legnano (29 May 1176) the initial peace negotiations offered the prospect of the restoration of the prosperity of the mid-century. The imperial negotiators at Anagni (November 1176) conceded the restoration of the papal patrimony and the Matildine lands. Subsequently, however, in negotiating the peace of Venice (July 1177) the emperor was able to exploit the war-weariness of the pope and his allies and to concede far less than his representatives had promised at Anagni. In return for accepting Alexander's proposals for peace with the pope's allies, Frederick successfully demanded the revenues of the Matildine lands for

[355] Archbishop Wichman of Magdeburg, letter to Urban III, *MGH Constitutiones* I, p. 445. Cf. the letter of Archbishop Adalbert of Mainz and his suffragans, *ibid.*, p. 447. See Hauck (1952), pp. 319–21.

[356] Zerbi (1955), pp. 22–8; Pfaff (1980), pp. 275–6.

[357] Overmann (1895), pp. 143–4; Servatius (1979), pp. 100–4.

[358] Bernhardi (1879), pp. 206–7, 481–5.   [359] Innocent II, JL 7633, *MGH Constitutiones* I, pp. 169–70.

[360] Overmann (1895), p. 51; Pfaff (1927), pp. 4–5; Jordan (1933–4), p. 70.

fifteen years.[361] The peace of Venice left the question of the ownership of the Matildine lands unresolved, as did a further conference between Lucius III and Frederick I in Verona (1184). The pope rejected the emperor's preferred solution, which was that the papacy should renounce all claim to the inheritance in return for an annual payment to the pope of one tenth and to the cardinals of one ninth of all the imperial revenues from Italy.[362] Only at the end of the century in the will of Henry VI in 1197 (supposing this document to be authentic) did the papacy obtain the promise of the restoration of its Tuscan inheritance.[363]

The premature death of the formidable Emperor Henry VI (1197) removed a serious threat to the independence of the papacy and gave the pope an unprecedented freedom of action. For the past three-quarters of a century the papacy had sought to maintain its independence and to secure control of Rome and the Patrimony of St Peter by means of alliances. In the years 1122–56 the papacy saw in an alliance with the emperor the only safeguard against the encroachments of the Norman ruler of Sicily; while in the years 1156–97 alliance with the emperor's enemies, including the king of Sicily, was the sole means by which the pope could withstand the Staufen threat to the independence of the church. Unfortunately for the stability of the papal regime, the personnel of the curia had rarely been unanimous in adopting either of these strategies. The faction struggles that were so important a feature of the history of the twelfth-century college of cardinals seem to have been intimately linked with the difficult choices faced by the papacy in determining its political strategy.

The strategy of alliance with the emperor developed at a moment of transformation in the college of cardinals. In 1121, a year before concluding the Concordat of Worms, Calixtus II went to the fortress of Rocca Niceforo to negotiate with Roger II of Sicily, who had invaded the duchy of his cousin William of Apulia. While Roger prevaricated, the papal entourage was struck by an epidemic which killed a number of cardinals and almost killed the pope himself. It was this disaster that forced Calixtus to reconstruct the college by creating sixteen new cardinals in the years 1121–3. Since those of his appointees whose background is known were Frenchmen and northern Italians, historians have suggested that his purpose was to counter the influence of the Romans and southern Italians who hitherto had formed the majority in the college.[364]

---

[361] Pact of Anagni c.3, 6, *MGH Constitutiones* I, p. 350. See Kehr (1888); Leyser (1982), pp. 259–61.

[362] Frederick I, letter to Lucius III, *MGH Constitutiones* I, pp. 420–1. See Pfaff (1981), pp. 164–5.

[363] Henry VI, 'Testament', *MGH Constitutiones* I, pp. 530–1. This document survives as a quotation in the *Gesta Innocentii III*. For a negative assessment of its authenticity see Pfaff (1964).

[364] Klewitz (1957), pp. 209–59; Schmale (1961b), pp. 31–57, 79–80; Deér (1972), pp. 172–4; Hüls (1977), pp. 142–3, 162, 164, 193, 220, 236, 238.

A similar interpretation has been suggested for the appointments of Calixtus's successor, Honorius II.[365] The most important of Calixtus's appointees was Haimeric, cardinal deacon of S. Maria Nuova, who held the office of chancellor from 1123 to 1141, during which time he became the dominant politician in the curia. Haimeric has been identified as the leader of a faction in the college, composed mainly of the 'new' cardinals appointed after 1121. It was he who on the death of Calixtus masterminded the election of Cardinal Bishop Lambert of Ostia as Honorius II (16 December 1124). This was achieved by means of the armed might of the Frangipane family, after other members of the college had already elected Cardinal Theobald of S. Anastasia and clad him in the purple mantle of the pope.[366]

The disputed papal election of 1130 was similarly the result of a bold initiative of Haimeric. Shortly before the death of Honorius II, the cardinals, fearing unrest in the city, entrusted the election of a successor to an electoral commission of eight cardinals, including Haimeric. Immediately after Honorius's death and hurried burial, Haimeric hastened the election of his own candidate, Gregory, cardinal deacon of S. Angelo, a member of the electoral commission, despite the absence of two other members of the commission. Gregory was enthroned as Innocent II in the early hours of 14 February. When the majority of the cardinals heard of this, they held a new election, considering Haimeric's actions to be illegal. Their pope, Anacletus II, was Peter Pierleone, cardinal priest of S. Maria in Trastevere, a member of the Pierleone family, the rivals of Haimeric's allies, the Frangipani.[367] The power of the Pierleoni enabled Anacletus's supporters to enthrone their pope, secure control of the city and expel Innocent II and his adherents. By midsummer, however, the exiled Innocent had been acknowledged as pope by many influential reforming circles, notably by Bernard of Clairvaux and the Cistercians. Before the end of 1130 he had been acknowledged by both the French and German kings and their churches. 'Although he was expelled from the city, he is supported by the world', wrote Bernard, his principal apologist. 'Do not all the princes know that he is truly the elect of God?'[368] Nevertheless, Anacletus II remained in control of Rome until his death (1138) because he had the support of Roger II of Sicily. Since the days of Count Roger I of Sicily the Pierleoni had enjoyed close links with the Sicilian Norman dynasty. That alliance now culminated in the papal privilege of 27 September 1130 which elevated Count Roger II to the kingship of Sicily, Apulia and Calabria. The papal privilege creating the new

[365] Schmale (1961b), pp. 52–6; Zenker (1964), pp. 83–4, 157; Hüls (1977), pp. 96–7, 239, 243.
[366] Klewitz (1957), pp. 243–7; Schmale (1961b), pp. 120–3.
[367] Schmale (1961b), pp. 145–61; Pellegrini (1968), pp. 265–302; Stroll (1987), pp. 82–90.
[368] Bernard, 'Epistola' 124. See Graboïs (1981); Reuter (1983); Stroll (1987), pp. 91–101, 169–78.

kingdom was subscribed by nine members of the Pierleone family and by only one other witness.[369]

Historians have offered conflicting interpretations of the schism of 1130 and the division in the college of cardinals which produced it. The rivalry of the Frangipani and the Pierleoni for control of Rome, the determination of Haimeric to dominate the papal curia, the struggle of two factions of cardinals to determine the reforming aims of the papacy have variously been detected behind the events of February 1130.[370] In particular Haimeric and Peter Pierleone have been identified as the leaders of parties in the college of cardinals with totally opposed views of papal policy. Haimeric acted in 1130, as he had previously acted in 1124, to ensure the continuity of the strategy of Calixtus by ensuring the election of candidates sympathetic to that strategy. The fact that Innocent II was the candidate of the more recent appointees to the college and his rival was the choice of the older cardinals suggests that Peter Pierleone represented the conservative interest in the college.[371] What then were the differences in policy that divided them? There is a clue, first, in the identity of Haimeric's papal candidates in 1124 and 1130 – two cardinals responsible for negotiating the settlement of the investiture question in 1122 – and, secondly, in the opposition of hard-line Gregorians to that settlement in the First Lateran Council in 1123. The division in the college in 1130 may have originated in Calixtus II's recruitment of new cardinals as a counterweight to those veterans who resented the abandonment of the Gregorian reforming and political strategy. One central aspect of that strategy was the friendship with the Normans of southern Italy which was increasingly threatened during the 1120s by the aggression of Roger II of Sicily. Haimeric may well have wished to terminate the Norman alliance, which Peter Pierleone would certainly have wished to continue.[372]

Another significant clue may be the friendship of Haimeric with Bernard of Clairvaux. The most debated interpretation of the schism attributes the division in the college to the impact of the 'new spirituality' of c. 1100: that is, the spirituality of the new orders of the Cistercians, the regular canons and the Premonstratensians. According to this view the Innocentine supporters were predominantly 'new' cardinals from France and northern Italy, the regions most influenced by this 'new spirituality', while the Anacletans were 'old' cardinals mainly from Rome and southern Italy, associated with the older Benedictine

---

[369] Deér (1959), pp. 121–2, and (1972), pp. 212–14.

[370] For summaries of this debate see Schmale (1961b), pp. 1–6, 29–31; Palumbo (1963); Maleczek (1981), pp. 28–30; Stroll (1987), pp. 1–9, 179–81.

[371] Klewitz (1957), pp. 211, 213–21; Schmale (1961b), pp. 34–79; Hüls (1977), pp. 150–2, 186–7, 206–7, 221–2, 227.

[372] Chodorow (1972), pp. 30–40.

monasticism and with Gregorian ideas.[373] More recent analysis of the college on the eve of the schism, however, suggests that there were no homogeneous parties among the cardinals until Haimeric's actions during the night of 13–14 February 1130 polarized opinion, creating an open division between those who supported and those who deplored the chancellor's conduct. Haimeric and his closest adherents may have had a clear-cut purpose, either to perpetuate the chancellor's own influence in the curia or to continue the policies of the popes whom he had served in the years 1123–30. But there was no similar clarity of purpose on the part of those cardinals who elected Anacletus II in reaction to the election of Haimeric's candidate. The electors of Anacletus were a cluster of different interest groups, including veteran Gregorians opposed to the Concordat of Worms, partisans of the Norman alliance and those cardinals who simply resented the chancellor's dominance.

The sharp contrasts in strategy that have been detected between the two rival curias after 1130 may well have been accidental rather than a reflection of fundamental policy differences. After the double election the two popes, left with half a college of cardinals each, made new appointments which were markedly different in character. Those appointees of Anacletus who can be identified were subdeacons of the Roman church, while Innocent's appointees were in many cases drawn from northern Italy and France. While this might suggest a 'conservative' recruitment policy on the part of Anacletus, an 'innovatory' policy on the part of Innocent, it is more probable that the appointments of both popes were governed by necessity. The lesser Roman clergy chose to remain in Rome with Anacletus, who was thus able to draw on their expertise in his curia. Innocent, forced to look elsewhere for recruits, found them in the areas in which he spent most of his exile.[374] Anacletus's pontificate was devoted to furthering the interests of the papacy in southern Italy and to promoting the papal alliance with the Normans. He pursued a 'Gregorian' policy, therefore; but this may have been the result not so much of his conservatism as of his dependence on Roger II of Sicily. Innocent II's strategy was determined by the friensdhip network of proponents of the 'new spirituality' – Bernard of Clairvaux, Peter the Venerable of Cluny, Archbishop Norbert of Magdeburg, Archbishop Walter of Ravenna, Gerhoch of Reichersberg – to whose influence he owed the general recognition that he eventually received everywhere outside Rome and the dominions of Roger II.[375] This may mean that Innocent himself was a proponent of the 'new spirituality' or it may mean that the exiled pope sought help wherever he could find it and that Bernard's

---

[373] Klewitz (1957), pp. 210–11, 255; Schmale (1961b), pp. 43, 56–7, 124–44, 272–9. See the criticisms of Tellenbach (1963); Classen (1968); Maleczek (1981).

[374] Elze (1950), p. 166; Zenker (1964), p. 202; Tillmann (1972), pp. 336–44; Maleczek (1981), p. 57.

[375] Klewitz (1957), pp. 210–11, 254–5; Schmale (1961b), pp. 56–7, 77–80, 253–79.

friendship network contained the most effective propagandists in western Christendom.[376]

The political strategy of Innocent II's reconstructed papal curia centred on cooperation with the emperor. Lothar III of Germany, whom Innocent had crowned emperor in the Lateran basilica in Rome on 4 June 1133, was revered in Innocentine circles as 'a God-fearing emperor, a vigorous warlord, distinguished in arms, prudent in counsel, terrible to the enemies of God, the friend of justice, the enemy of injustice'.[377] He was long remembered in the papal curia as the model prince whose Italian expedition of 1136–7 had defeated the pope's enemy, Roger II, and driven him from the Italian mainland.[378] What was carefully concealed in the papal version of these events was that this triumph had immediately exposed a sharp difference of opinion between pope and emperor about their respective rights over the duchy of Apulia. The papal view was that Lothar had intervened as the advocate of the Roman church to vindicate the territorial rights of St Peter. The imperial view was that 'Apulia and Sicily belonged to [Lothar's] imperial jurisdiction.'[379] Innocent wished to invest Count Rainulf of Alife (Roger II's ambitious vassal) with Apulia as a demonstration of the favourite papal political idea of *idoneitas* rather than hereditary right as the appropriate qualification for secular office. Lothar, however, was determined to invest the new duke of Apulia in order to demonstrate his jurisdiction over the duchy. 'As they were both travelling and neither party had access to documents or proofs, this disagreement could not be settled . . . So they jointly invested Count Rainulf with the duchy of Apulia, the pope holding the standard at the top, the emperor holding it below.'[380] Despite this quarrel, however, Lothar was indispensable to Innocent's war against Roger II. When after the emperor's death (1137) Innocent himself led a coalition of Roger's enemies against the king of Sicily, he was defeated at Galluccio (22 July 1139) and taken prisoner. The victor of the papal schism was forced to issue a privilege containing all the concessions that Roger's ally, Anacletus II, had made nine years before.[381]

The new German king, Conrad III, detained in Germany by his war against the Welfs, was incapable of imitating his predecessor's example. It was in vain that Bernard of Clairvaux exhorted him to perform the role of 'the advocate of the church.'[382] Meanwhile during the fifteen years that followed the defeat of

[376] Reuter (1983); Stroll (1987), pp. 169–78.
[377] 'Vita Norberti archiepiscopi Magdeburgensis' c.21, p. 702.
[378] See, for example, Innocent III, *Registrum de negotio imperii* c.32, *PL* 216, col. 1035C.
[379] Romuald of Salerno, 'Annales' 1136, p. 421; cf. p. 422. See Deér (1972), pp. 42–3.
[380] Romuald, 'Annales' 1137, p. 422.
[381] Innocent II, JL 8043, cols. 478C–479D. See Deér (1972), pp. 224–30.
[382] Bernard, 'Epistola' 244 c.3. Cf. *ibid.* 183.

Galluccio the papal curia was unable to resist Roger II's encroachments on the southern and eastern parts of the Patrimony of St Peter. The papal misfortunes were compounded by the Roman revolution of 1143, which created a commune hostile to the papal government. It had been insecurity in Rome which had prompted the eleventh-century papacy to negotiate a Norman alliance. The creation of the Roman commune seemed likely to compel Innocent II's successors to seek the protection of the king of Sicily. It proved impossible, however, to negotiate a permanent peace with Roger II during the 1140s 'because of the opposition of the cardinals'.[383] The antagonism of the 1130s lived on in the college. Celestine II (1143–4), Lucius II (1144–5) and Anastasius IV (1153–4) had been among Innocent's electors and Haimeric's supporters in 1130. Lucius II indeed, the former Gerard, cardinal priest of S. Croce in Gerusalemme, had served both Honorius II and Innocent II as their expert on German affairs and had been the architect of the alliance with Lothar III, undertaking six legations to Germany between 1125 and 1136.[384] When he became pope, Lucius 'sent a humble letter to King Conrad . . . summoning him to the defence of the Roman church'.[385] Eugenius III (1145–53) was the only pope of the second quarter of the twelfth century who had not previously been a member of Cardinal Haimeric's party; but the influence of his mentor, Bernard of Clairvaux, and probably also the strength of anti-Norman sentiment in the curia perpetuated the desire for an imperial alliance during his pontificate. Eugenius achieved this objective during the first year of the reign of the new German king, Frederick I. According to the treaty of Constance (23 March 1153) Frederick undertook, in return for receiving the imperial crown, to restore the temporal power of St Peter, to protect the *honor* of the papacy and to make no peace with the Romans or the king of Sicily without the pope's approval. Eugenius undertook to increase the *honor* of the empire and to excommunicate the king's enemies.[386]

It was in the pontificate of Adrian IV (1154–9) that the imperial alliance of the papacy was finally abandoned. Initially the new pope adopted the strategy of his predecessors, being hard pressed both by the Romans and by the new king of Sicily, William I. Adrian renewed the treaty of Constance and performed the imperial coronation of Frederick Barbarossa in Rome (June 1155). As a gesture of goodwill towards the pope Frederick captured the leader of the Roman commune, Arnold of Brescia, the reforming preacher and critic of the papacy, and delivered him to the Roman prefect for execution. The emperor

---

[383] Romuald of Salerno, 'Annales' 1143, p. 424.   [384] Bachmann (1913), pp. 10–49.
[385] Otto of Freising, *Chronica* VII.31, p. 358.
[386] Treaty of Constance, *MGH Constitutiones* I, pp. 201–3. See Maccarrone (1959), pp. 50–1, 79–80; Rassow (1961), pp. 60–5; Munz (1969), pp. 64–5; Engels (1987).

then returned to Germany without taking any further action against the pope's enemies in Rome and the kingdom of Sicily.[387] The breach between pope and emperor was caused partly by Frederick's failure to fulfil the terms of the treaty of Constance in 1155 and partly by Adrian's measures to defend himself, which ultimately involved him in breaking the terms of the treaty. The pope allied himself with prominent Norman rebels against King William I of Sicily, who were in turn supported by the forces of the Byzantine emperor, Manuel I Komnenos. The beleaguered William I offered generous terms to the pope in return for peace: the performance of homage and fealty, reparation for the recent encroachments on the papal patrimony, help against the Romans, freedom from royal control for the Sicilian church. According to Adrian's biographer, Cardinal Boso, the pope was in favour of accepting this offer, but 'the greater part of the brethren' opposed him.[388] The pope was obliged, therefore, to reject the Sicilian offer and he made war on William, only to be defeated and forced to make peace on the king's terms. The Concordat of Benevento (18 June 1156) settled the territorial disputes between the pope and the Sicilian king entirely to the latter's advantage.[389] Adrian stumbled towards a new papal strategy against the will of a majority of his cardinals, who still clung to the treaty of Constance. Cardinal Boso claimed that the pope 'sent the greater part of his brethren into the Campagna', so that the concordat was negotiated by the minority among the cardinals who shared his idea of the necessity of a Sicilian alliance.[390]

This reversal of papal strategy in June 1156 contributed directly to the disputed papal election of 4–7 September 1159, when Alexander III and 'Victor IV' were elected by rival groups of cardinals. The electors of 'Victor IV' regarded both the concordat and the election of Alexander as the work of a 'Sicilian party' in the college, led by Adrian IV's chancellor, Cardinal Roland of S. Marco (the future Alexander III).

From the time when friendship was established in Benevento between the lord Pope Adrian and William of Sicily, contrary to the honour of God's church and of the empire, great division and discord have arisen (not without cause) among the cardinals. We... in no way consented to the friendship, ... but others, blinded by money and many promises and firmly bound to the Sicilian, wickedly defended the treaty... and attracted very many others to share their error.[391]

---

[387] Ullmann (1955), pp. 239–42; Munz (1969), pp. 78–88.
[388] Boso, 'Vita Hadriani IV', II, p. 394. See Rowe (1969), pp. 9–12.
[389] Concordat of Benevento, *MGH Constitutiones* I, pp. 588–91. See Clementi (1968), pp. 192–7; Deér (1972), pp. 247–53.
[390] Boso, 'Vita Hadriani IV', II, p. 395.
[391] Letter of the cardinals of 'Victor IV' in Rahewin, *Gesta Friderici imperatoris* IV.62, p. 241.

According to an imperial manifesto of 1160,

during the lifetime of Pope Adrian, the chancellor Roland and certain cardinals . . . conspired with William the Sicilian . . . and with other enemies of the empire,
the men of Milan, Brescia and Piacenza and lest [their] evil faction should perhaps van-
ish because of the death of Pope Adrian, they imposed an oath on each other that on the
death of the pope, no other should replace him except a member of their conspiracy.[392]

The manifesto alludes here to the meeting in Anagni (July 1159) of Adrian IV,
his chancellor and twelve other cardinals with envoys of the Lombard cities
which were currently resisting Frederick's imposition of imperial control.[393]
The influence of this 'Sicilian party' in the college was countered by a group
of imperial supporters. Their leaders were the two curial experts in German
affairs, Octavian, cardinal priest of S. Cecilia, and his kinsman, Guido of
Crema, cardinal priest of S. Maria in Trastevere, both destined to become in
turn the antipopes of Frederick Barbarossa: 'Victor IV' (1159–64) and 'Paschal
III' (1164–8).[394] The divisions among the cardinals were intensified by the
'incident' at the imperial assembly of Besançon (October 1157), provoked by
the papal letter which appeared to refer to the imperial dignity as a 'fief'
(*beneficium*) 'conferred' by the pope. While the 'Sicilian party' represented the
incident as evidence of imperial hostility towards the Roman church, their
opponents in the college 'favoured the party of the emperor and blamed the
negligence and inexperience' of the papal legates at the assembly of Besançon,
the chancellor Cardinal Roland and Bernard, cardinal priest of S. Clemente.[395]
   In the election that followed the death of Adrian IV (1 September 1159) the
thirteen cardinals of the 'Sicilian party' of 1156 seem to have attracted ten more
cardinals to their side. Their opponent, Cardinal Octavian (Victor IV), was
supported initially by nine cardinals, but his following rapidly diminished to
five. Octavian's electors, supported by an armed band, resorted to violence to
prevent the installation of Roland-Alexander III as pope.[396] The presence of
Frederick Barbarossa's envoy, Otto of Wittelsbach, in Rome ensured the loyalty
of the city to 'Victor IV' and forced Alexander into exile.[397] Frederick's conciliar solution to the papal schism – the council of Pavia (5–11 February 1160),
which recognized the title of 'Victor IV', having heard no detailed defence of

---

[392] Rahewin, *Gesta Friderici imperatoris* IV. 79, p. 263.
[393] The thirteen cardinals in Anagni are identified in two papal privileges: Adrian IV, JL 10577, 10579,
        cols. 1636, 1637. See Madertoner (1978), pp. 37–47.
[394] Zenker (1964), pp. 56–9, 66–70; Madertoner (1978), pp. 90–108, 111–14.
[395] Rahewin, *Gesta Friderici imperatoris* III.16, p. 147. For the 'incident' at Besançon see above pp. 322–3
        and nn. 26–7.
[396] Madertoner (1978), pp. 48–52, 120–8.   [397] *Ibid.*, pp. 131–41.

Alexander's claim – persuaded no one outside the imperial territories.[398] Four months after the decision in favour of the antipope Louis VII of France and Henry II of England formally recognized Alexander III at a conference in Beauvais.[399] The widespread acceptance of Alexander throughout Christendom left the emperor with a formidable diplomatic and military task: to detach the kings of France and England from the Alexandrine obedience and to defeat the pope's allies in Italy, the Lombard cities and the king of Sicily. For eighteen years Frederick tried in vain to achieve these aims.

Meanwhile Alexander III, in exile and lacking the conventional resources of the papacy, was acutely aware that his survival depended on the victory of the emperor's enemies, who must at all costs be kept faithful to the papal cause. Hence during the schism of 1159–77 the most important institution of papal government was the papal legation. The two circumstances of a wandering papal curia and a volatile political situation increasingly placed detailed policy-making in the hands of cardinal legates. Perhaps the most important contribution to the survival of the Alexandrine cause was that of the five legates who negotiated and maintained the alliance between the curia and the Lombard League, founded to destroy the system of government introduced by Frederick in 1158. Cardinal William of S. Pietro in Vincoli, the cardinal deacons Odo of S. Nicola in Carcere and Manfred of S. Giorgio in Velabro, Archbishop Galdin of Milan and Hildebrand, cardinal deacon of S. Eustachio, were commissioned 'to strengthen and preserve the unity' of the League and keep open the lines of communication between the curia and the Lombard cities.[400]

The end of the conflict of 1159–77, wrote Cardinal Boso, witnessed 'Emperor Frederick prostrate at the feet of Pope Alexander and the evil of schism entirely extinguished by the divine power'.[401] The peace of Venice indeed obliged Frederick to break the oath which he had sworn at the imperial assembly of Würzburg (1165) never to acknowledge Alexander as pope.[402] He remained, however, master of the German church and no German prelate was disciplined for having sided with the emperor during the schism. Moreover, the conflict had bankrupted the papal curia. It was poverty and war-weariness that compelled the papacy to conclude a peace that left unsettled the important questions of papal lordship over the Patrimony of St Peter and the Matildine lands. The preservation of the hard-won peace with the empire was the central

---

[398] Council of Pavia, *MGH Constitutiones* I, pp. 260–3. See Madertoner (1978), pp. 142–82.

[399] Barlow (1936); Cheney (1969), pp. 474–97.

[400] Alexander III, JL 12737, col. 1082B. See Dunken (1931), pp. 70–1, 79–80, 83–4, 110–11, 166, 168–71; Pacaut (1955), pp. 832–5.

[401] Boso, 'Vita Alexandri III' II, p. 445.

[402] Peace of Venice, *MGH Constitutiones* I, pp. 360–4. The oath at the assembly of Würzburg: *MGH Constitutiones* I, pp. 314–21. See Hauck (1952), pp. 276–82.

preoccupation of the last years of Alexander III's pontificate and the policy of conciliating Frederick I survived his death (1181). Of Alexander's five successors in the years 1181–98 only one had not been a member of the Alexandrine college, that closely knit body of advisers on whom (according to Cardinal Boso) Alexander had so much depended. The exception was Urban III (1185–7), Hubert Crivelli, formerly archbishop of his native Milan. Urban III was a bitter enemy of the emperor and his brief pontificate witnessed a renewal of the conflict of the papacy with Frederick Barbarossa. Urban attempted to revive the Lombard League and strove, by raising the issue of the freedom of the German church, to sow dissension among the ecclesiastical princes in the German kingdom.[403]

This bellicose stand for the freedom of the church by a pope who during the schism had been a member of the circle of the exiled Archbishop Thomas Becket of Canterbury was in marked contrast to the strategy of his predecessor and his successors. Lucius III (1181–5) was a former member of the 'Sicilian party' and, as Cardinal Hubald of Ostia, the most influential figure in the Alexandrine curia.[404] At the conference of Verona (1184) he attempted to settle with the emperor all the questions left unresolved in 1177, succeeding in agreeing at least on the necessity of a new crusade and on new measures against the spread of heresy.[405] Lucius had no choice but to be conciliatory towards Frederick Barbarossa. Exiled from Rome by yet another dispute between the curia and the senate, he found himself observing the dismantling of the alliances which had achieved the Alexandrine victory. The emperor negotiated in Constance a permanent peace with the Lombard cities (1183) and arranged a marriage alliance between his son, Henry VI, and the Sicilian princess Constance, daughter of Roger II and aunt of William II.[406] The successor of the aggressive Urban III was Gregory VIII (1187), the former chancellor of Alexander III with the reputation of being well-disposed towards Frederick.[407] His election immediately brought an end to the conflict that Urban III had provoked with the emperor. The aims that Gregory VIII pursued during his short pontificate were the reform of the church and the launching of a crusade and for both of these peace with the empire was the prerequisite. When Gregory's crusading plans were realized by his successor, Clement III, Frederick Barbarossa was the first monarch to pledge his participation in the Third Crusade. The emperor took the cross in 'the diet of Christ' (*curia Christi*) which he summoned to

[403] Wenck (1926), pp. 425–7; Hauck (1952), pp. 319–22; Pfaff (1981), pp. 175–6.
[404] Zenker (1964), pp. 22–5, 153; Pfaff (1981), pp. 173–4.
[405] Foreville and Rousset de Pina (1953), pp. 191–2; Pfaff (1981), pp. 164–5.
[406] Peace of Constance, *MGH Constitutiones*, I, pp. 408–18. On the papacy and the marriage of Henry VI and Constance see Baaken (1972).
[407] Robert of Auxerre, 'Chronicon', p. 252; Gervase of Canterbury, *Chronica* 1187, p. 388.

Mainz (27 March 1188), together with the papal legate and official crusading preacher, Cardinal Henry of Albano.[408]

The pontificate of Clement III (1187–91) was a period of momentous change in the curia and in the political situation of the papacy. Clement concluded the treaty with the Roman senate (31 May 1188), which restored papal lordship over Rome after forty-five years of intermittent conflict with the commune.[409] Between March 1188 and October 1190 he appointed approximately thirty cardinals, the majority of whom were connected with the great Roman families.[410] It was during this period of radical change in the character of the college that the curia was thrown into confusion by the death of the papal vassal, King William II of Sicily (18 November 1189). The premature death of the childless king threatened the papacy with the succession of his aunt Constance, wife of Henry VI, who in June 1190 was to succeed his father to the German throne. For the rest of the century the papal curia was preoccupied with the problem of 'the union of the kingdom with the empire' and with plans to prevent the kingdom of Sicily from falling into the hands of Henry VI.[411] The cardinals, however, did not approach this problem in a spirit of unity. Events were to demonstrate that Clement III's enlargement of the college had introduced cardinals with attitudes towards the Sicilian succession and towards Henry VI as sharply divided as those of the 1120s and 1150s. Not only had he, for example, recruited Peter, cardinal priest of S. Cecilia, a prominent supporter of Henry VI. He had also appointed Albinus, cardinal bishop of Albano, who was the close friend of Tancred, count of Lecce, the illegitimate cousin of William II, who was elected as their king by Sicilians rebelling against Queen Constance.[412]

These divisions seem to be reflected in the constantly shifting papal policy of both Clement III and his successor, Celestine III (1191–7). Clement was alleged to have recognized the claim to the Sicilian throne of Tancred of Lecce in preference to that of Constance;[413] but he also promised to crown Henry VI emperor and received him with honour when he entered Italy.[414] Celestine III performed the imperial coronation promised by his predecessor (15 April 1191); but he also recognized Tancred as king of Sicily (spring 1192). (The decision to recognize Tancred was taken when Cardinal Peter of S. Cecilia and other supporters of the emperor were absent from the curia.)[415] Celestine gave support to princes rebelling against Henry VI in Germany;[416] but he failed to adopt strong measures against the emperor in the case of King Richard I of England

---

[408] Friedländer (1928), p. 39; Congar (1958), pp. 49–50.

[409] *Liber censuum*, I, pp. 373–4. See above p. 366.   [410] See above p. 364 and n. 316.

[411] See above p. 368.   [412] Friedländer (1928), pp. 119–23; Pfaff (1974a), p. 360.

[413] Richard of S. Germano, 'Chronica regni Siciliae' 1190, p. 324; Arnold of Lübeck, 'Chronica' v.5, p. 182.

[414] Pfaff (1980), p. 278.   [415] Pfaff (1966), pp. 342–4.   [416] Zerbi (1955), pp. 98–9.

(spring 1193). Henry VI had invited excommunication by holding Richard to ransom, although the latter's status as a crusader placed him under the papacy's special protection. When the pope debated this case with the cardinals, however, the majority – consisting of imperial supporters and moderates fearing an escalation of the quarrel with the emperor – opposed excommunication.[417] This paralysis of the curia came to an end with the sudden death of Henry VI (28 September 1197). The flurry of purposeful activity in the last three months of Celestine III's pontificate revealed that the imperial sympathizers had lost their influence. The opponents of the late emperor now enjoyed the support of a majority in the college in their determination to exploit the opportunities of the interregnum.[418] At the moment of Celestine's death (8 January 1198) the papacy unexpectedly enjoyed a political situation more favourable than at any moment in the twelfth century: a situation that was the fortunate inheritance of Innocent III.

---

[417] Pfaff (1966), pp. 347–50; Gillingham (1978), pp. 217–40. See also above p. 346.
[418] Wenck (1926), p. 464; Pfaff (1974b).

CHAPTER 14

THE WESTERN EMPIRE, 1125–1197

Benjamin Arnold

IN 1122 the peace arranged at Worms between Pope Calixtus II and Emperor Henry V was designed to bring an end to the ecclesiastical, political and military emergencies which had disturbed the western empire since the 1070s, the series of confrontations called with hindsight the War of Investitures. The papal curia was enabled to return its attention to the programme of religious reform, and the First Lateran Council was celebrated in 1123. The emperor was freed from the incubus inherited from his excommunicated father Henry IV, and the preliminaries of the Worms *pax* committed the princes to assist the emperor in maintaining the authority and dignity of imperial rule. But the outcome of such intentions was problematical given the ingrained enmities, especially between Saxony and the royal court, caused by the War of Investitures. In any case the restoration of royal authority for which Henry V had striven since 1105 was called into question because the emperor, still a youngish man, died at Utrecht in May 1125. His marriage to Matilda of Normandy had proved childless, so it was necessary for the princes of the empire to set about electing a new king.

ELECTORAL PROCEDURES IN THE TWELFTH CENTURY

In the early summer of 1125 the German bishops and secular magnates who had gathered in Speyer for the obsequies of Henry V sent letters to the other princes of the empire inviting them to Mainz in August for the election of the next king. A surviving version, to Bishop Otto I of Bamberg, requested him to pray for a candidate who would liberate church and empire from the oppression under which they had laboured hitherto. Such explicit criticism of the two preceding emperors was undoubtedly the work of Archbishop Adalbert I of Mainz, whose office traditionally conferred upon the incumbent the leading voice in German royal elections. As royal chancellor and favoured counsellor, Adalbert had been promoted to the see of Mainz by Henry V, but subsequently they had quarrelled about the respective rights and properties of the archbishopric and the crown, and the archbishop had been arrested and imprisoned. Upon his release he continued to make trouble for Henry V, and the form of expression in the letter to the bishop of Bamberg was probably intended as a warning against Duke Frederick II of Swabia, the deceased emperor's nephew and nearest male relative, who confidently expected to be elected to the vacant throne. It was Duke Frederick who had acted as the emperor's representative in the Rhineland during the feuds with Archbishop Adalbert, even besieging him in his cathedral town.

The chronicler Ekkehard of Aura reports that upon his deathbed at Utrecht, Henry V 'gave advice as far as he was able about the state of the realm and committed his possessions and his queen to the protection of Frederick as his heir'.[1] In this attempt to designate the duke of Swabia as successor to the western empire, the best that the emperor could hope for was Frederick's success at the election. But the duke's younger half-brother, Bishop Otto of Freising, explained a generation later that 'the high point of the law of the Roman empire is that kings are made not by descent through blood ties but in consequence of election by the princes'.[2] Duke Frederick II nevertheless had powerful pretensions, and his previous enmity with Archbishop Adalbert need not have prevented a rapprochement over his election to the throne. However, the principal sources for the 1125 election, the anonymous *Narratio de electione Lotharii* and Otto of Freising's *Chronica* or *History of the Two Cities*, indicate that Margrave Leopold III of Austria, a price noted for his personal sanctity, was put forward as a compromise candidate. Like the duke of Swabia, the margrave stood close to the previous ruler through his marriage to Henry V's widowed sister Agnes of Swabia, Duke Frederick II's mother. Leopold III's election would have fulfilled the desire expressed to the bishop of Bamberg that a man of peace and a friend of the church should be elected.

A candidate with much more formidable political pretensions in the empire, Duke Lothar of Saxony, was also acceptable to the most influential electors, yet there were also grounds for distrusting him. The duke's high-handed methods had posed a real threat to the see of Mainz's extensive possessions in Saxony and Thuringia, and the other prince whose dignity also conferred great electoral influence, Archbishop Frederick I of Cologne, was frightened of Duke Lothar's authority over the see's suffragans in Westphalia. So the archbishop of Cologne put forward Count Charles the Good of Flanders as a candidate. In the end the archbishop of Mainz appears to have conceded that the Saxon duke's promotion would be the safest means of excluding Frederick of Swabia, and the majority in a college of forty princes duly elected him as Lothar III. Although Archbishop

---

[1] Ekkehard, 'Chronicon universale' for 1125.   [2] Otto of Freising and Rahewin, *Gesta Friderici* II, 1.

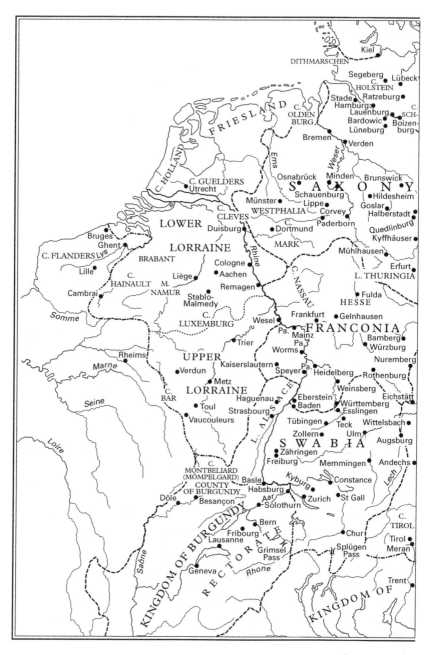

Map 10 Germany under

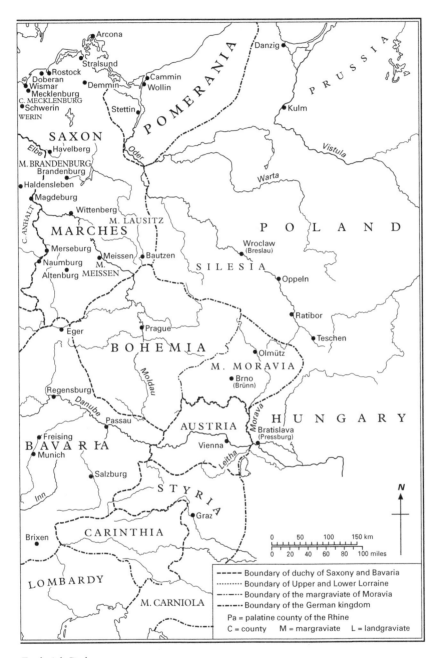

Frederick Barbarossa, *c.* 1190

Adalbert had succeeded in depriving his chief enemy of the throne of Germany and the empire, the author of the *Narratio* was more interested in proclaiming that the outcome of the election was the will of God rather than a political manoeuvre. In twelfth-century political parlance such an explanation could be taken seriously because the empire was held to exist under the especial protection of heaven. In 1157, for example, Emperor Frederick I Barbarossa was to issue a circular in which he appealed to just such principles against the supposed claim by the papacy to possess the authority to confer the imperial office as if it were a papal fief:

And since, through election by the princes, the kingdom and the empire are ours from God alone, who at the time of the passion of his son Christ subjected the world to dominion by the two swords, and since the apostle Peter taught the world this doctrine: 'Fear God, honor the king', whosoever says that we received the imperial crown as a benefice (*pro beneficio*) from the lord pope contradicts the divine ordinance and the doctrine of Peter and is guilty of a lie.[3]

When Lothar III died late in 1137, the difficult electoral circumstances of 1125 were repeated. The Saxon emperor left no son, but his son-in-law Duke Henry the Proud of Bavaria took custody of the imperial insignia and appears to have been confident of winning the election to the empire. However, two reports from the pen of Bishop Otto of Freising suggest that Henry the Proud was even more widely distrusted as a candidate than Frederick II of Swabia had been in 1125. Since the see of Mainz was now vacant and the new archbishop of Cologne was not yet consecrated, Archbishop Albero of Trier emerged as chief elector, and he permitted Duke Frederick's younger brother to be elected as Conrad III at an assembly hastily convened at Coblenz in March 1138. Several princes including the distinguished reformer Archbishop Conrad I of Salzburg objected to these proceedings, but the new king successfully outfaced his opponents at a court held at Bamberg in May. The Saxon and Bavarian princes were possibly persuaded by Lothar III's widow Empress Richenza to accept Conrad III for the sake of peace. Not long afterwards Duke Henry the Proud surrendered the insignia, and the claims of the Swabian house to the kingdoms of Henry V were vindicated after all.

Although the elections of 1125 and 1138 were tense, they need not be interpreted as constitutional crises since they reveal that the procedure of the princes alighting upon a new king by electoral choice was in working order. If Conrad III's election at Coblenz was judged by the Saxons and Bavarians to have been conducted in an underhand manner, then the Swabians and others held Archbishop Adalbert I's domination of the assembly at Mainz in 1125 to have been

---

[3] *MGH Diplomata*, Frederick I, no. 186, p. 315. The translation is by Mierow and Emery (1953), pp. 185–6.

improper. Since they had sons, the new Staufen royal dynasty was enabled to revert to the method preferred by their Salian and Ottonian predecessors, election of the successor during the reigning king's lifetime. Conrad III's son Henry Berengar (d. 1150) was elected upon the eve of his father's departure for the Second Crusade in 1147; Frederick Barbarossa's son Henry VI was elected in 1169 at the age of three; and the latter's infant son Frederick II was elected in 1196.

Upon his death in 1152 Conrad III left a son, Frederick of Rothenburg born in 1144 or 1145, but it was the king's nephew Frederick Barbarossa, duke of Swabia since 1147, who was elected. According to Otto of Freising, Conrad III had 'judged it more advantageous both for his family and for the state if his successor were rather to be his brother's son, by reason of the many famous proofs of his virtues'.[4] Since this passage occurs in a biography designed to promote the reputation of the brother's son in question, the argument is a little suspect. On the other hand, Conrad had not pressed for Frederick of Rothenburg's election after the early death of Henry Berengar either. The bishop of Freising plausibly pointed out that since the new king's mother had been a sister of Henry the Proud, the princes gathered for the election of 1152 'foresaw that it would greatly benefit the state if so grave and so long-continued a rivalry between the greatest men of the empire for their own private advantage might by this opportunity and with God's help be finally lulled to rest'.[5] In fact the problems of regional rivalry between prominent princes were much more complex than the bishop indicates, but he was right to foretell that Frederick Barbarossa would bring about an effective compromise with Duke Henry the Lion, Henry the Proud's heir and his own first cousin, by 1156.

Although the elections of 1125 and 1138 had provided cliques with opportunities to display and perhaps to abuse their power, kings do not appear to have feared the electoral procedure as such. When Henry VI proposed in 1196 to abolish it in favour of a hereditary empire, his principal motive seems to have been an almost eschatological belief that as the true line descended from the Salians and the Carolingians, the Staufen simply constituted the indubitable imperial house destined to rule the Roman empire until the end of human history. Hereditary descent would deftly have incorporated such convictions into the law of the empire. More than one source suggests that with less haste the proposal might have been accepted by the princes of Germany because hereditary right was familiar to them in France and other kingdoms. But while the princes ruminated the emperor was in a hurry to leave for Sicily in order

[4] Otto of Freising and Rahewin, *Gesta Friderici* I, 71. The translation is by Mierow and Emery (1953), p. 111.
[5] Otto of Freising and Rahewin, *Gesta Friderici* II, 2. The translation is by Mierow and Emery (1953), p. 116.

to prepare for the recently proclaimed crusade, so he settled for a traditional election of his young son instead.

Upon election kings adopted the title *Romanorum rex*, 'king of the Romans', one of their tasks then being to undertake the *expeditio Romana* or march to Rome in order to receive the imperii crown at the hands of the pope. But the pope did not thus confer *imperium* upon the German king, as Frederick Barbarossa was at pains to point out during his altercation with the papal curia and its legates in 1157 and 1158. The election in Germany counted as election to the empire in addition to the thrones of Germany, Italy and Burgundy, but it was not the custom to adopt the style of emperor until the Roman coronation had taken place. However, royal intitulation often included the imperial adjective *augustus*, implying that promotion to the superior title was only a question of time. The title was improved by Conrad III's chancery to *rex et semper augustus*, 'king and ever Augustus'.[6] Conrad III never was crowned emperor, but in his correspondence with the court of Constantinople his chancery entitled him 'Emperor Augustus of the Romans' in any case.

THE MEANING OF EMPIRE AND THE PURPOSE OF IMPERIAL RULE

When Bishop Otto of Freising wrote that Lothar III reigned as ninety-second ruler since Augustus, he intended to portray the venerable monumentality of Roman imperial rule which had supposedly descended lineally to the German kings. In the twelfth century their version of *imperium* was being redefined in its several aspects. *Imperium* or imperial rule was the personal right of governance and justice which the king exercised in his three kingdoms. To take examples from Germany, Lothar III, Conrad III and Frederick Barbarossa in turn referred to 'the authority of our *imperium*', 'our imperial authority' and 'authority of empire' when confirming rights for the monasteries of Münchsmünster, Volkenroda and Wessobrunn respectively.[7] If *imperium* was the protective legal authority of the king, then the autocratic potential of such jurisdiction was again made apparent by students of Roman Law in the twelfth century, the lawyers of Bologna advising that *imperium* was in principle limited solely by divine and natural law. However, a letter of 1158 to the pope indicates that Frederick Barbarossa took a cautious view of applying autocratic rights consequentially, at least in Germany: 'There are two things by which our empire should be governed, the sacred laws of the emperors and the good practices of our predecessors and ancestors. We neither desire nor are able to exceed those

---

[6] E.g. *MGH Diplomata*, Conrad III, no. 184, p. 332, 1147.

[7] *Ibid.*, Lothar III, no. 54, p. 86, 1133, has 'imperii nostri auctoritate'; *ibid.*, Conrad III, no. 33, p. 54, 1139, has 'nostra imperiali auctoritate'; *ibid.*, Frederick I, no. 125, p. 210, 1155, has 'imperiali auctoritate' and 'imperatoria auctoritate'.

limits; we do not accept whatever is not compatible with them.'[8] According to Rahewin, Otto of Freising's secretary and the continuator of the bishop's biography of Frederick Barbarossa, the cultivation of *imperium* as protective judicial authority was the emperor's constant concern. As the ruler travelled through the lower Rhineland in 1158, he

let no days pass in idleness, thinking those lost on which he had not made some enactment to the advantage of the empire, for the preservation of law and justice among all peoples. That was the reason why he had so consistently striven for so strong an empire on this side of the Alps, had calmed the spirits of such strong peoples by great discretion, without warfare, and . . . was now regarded not as the ruler of the realm, but as father and governor of one home, one state.[9]

Imperium was an office taken to have been endowed with the power of one of the two swords mentioned to Christ at the Last Supper, this power also being interpreted in medieval times as needful for the defence of the church. As a letter of Frederick Barbarossa's expressed the idea in 1170, ironically at a time when the papacy under Alexander III regarded him as a persecutor, 'It is the duty of imperial majesty to provide for peace and justice in the empire's affairs according to the established laws and canonical decrees, and above all for the church of God, by whose intercessions and prayers we hope to be advanced and to reign more confidently in the Lord.'[10] In spite of perceiving Emperors Henry IV and V as enemies of the church, imperial protection of religion was still accepted as normal by the twelfth-century papacy, including the specific guardianship or advocacy of the papal see at Rome, however differently the papal and imperial courts preferred to interpret the scope and limits of this advocacy. Once Henry V and Pope Calixtus II had offered peace to one another in 1122 over the questions of episcopal election and investiture and of ecclesiastical property in Germany and Italy, the defensive duty of the imperial sword could be resumed with propriety. From enemies such as Roger II of Sicily and the Roman commune of 1143 to 1155, the papacy was eager to be rescued by the military assistance of Lothar III, Conrad III and Frederick Barbarossa in turn. In 1149 Conrad III assured Pope Eugenius III that he was vexed by whatever threatened the pope's person and the Roman church, 'of which we are appointed the defender by God'.[11]

In the convention drawn up at Constance in 1153 between this pope's legates and Frederick Barbarossa, the latter committed himself to preserve and to defend 'the honour of the papacy and the secular properties of St Peter as the

---

[8] *MGH Constitutiones* I, no. 167, p. 233.
[9] Otto of Freising and Rehewin, *Gesta Friderici* III, 17. The translation is by Mierow and Emery (1953), p. 189.
[10] *MGH Diplomata*, Frederick I, no. 568, p. 39.   [11] *Ibid.*, Conrad III, no. 216, p. 386.

devoted and particular advocate of the holy Roman church'.[12] But when the aims of the papal and imperial courts were no longer aligned, these imperial powers of protection and advocacy began to look like a threat. In 1159 for example, Frederick Barbarossa made it clear that the schism which had just occurred in the papacy was to be settled by a council to be convened under his own auspices at Pavia early in 1160. Pope Alexander III was informed that 'since we are obliged to protect all churches established in our empire, we ought so much the more readily to provide for the most sacred Roman church, because the care and defence of it are believed to have been more particularly committed to us by divine providence'.[13] But the bishops assembled at Pavia declared against Alexander III, and his rival Victor IV, who was more solidly in favour of the emperor's anti-Sicilian diplomacy, was proclaimed pope instead. It is not therefore surprising that many churchmen shared reservations about the supposed benefits of imperial defence of the church. But not until the papacy could make *plenitudo potestatis*, 'plenitude of power', truly effective in the secular sense, that is, in the thirteenth century, would it prove possible to circumvent the real presence of the German emperor and his representatives as protectors of the Holy See and of the patrimony of St Peter.

Imperium also signified a geographical space called the Roman empire, occasionally rendered inaccurately as 'the German empire' by the imperial chancery simply because that reflected the realities of rule. A letter from Conrad III mentioned France, Spain, England and Denmark as adjacent to the empire in this geographical sense, and Otto of Freising listed France, England and Hungary in the same mode. In an interesting letter of 1155 to the Pisans, Frederick Barbarossa praised them for terrifying the peoples of Asia and Africa by land and sea, thereby defending 'the borders of Europe within which we occupy the seat and domicile of empire'.[14] More often the texts conceive of *imperium* as a species of terrestrial authority permitted by God for the discipline of the nations, a power transmitted in history from the ancient empires of the east to the Romans. Twelfth-century historiography took great interest in this phenomenon and in its biblical proof-texts, mainly from the Book of Daniel. Learned opinion argued that the Roman *imperium* represented the fourth and last of such empires before the end of political history. According to Abbot Rupert of Deutz (d. 1129), *imperium* would thereafter belong to Christ alone. Bishop Otto of Freising was satisfied that the German kings would be custodians of Rome's *imperium* until the last days, Otto the Great's reception of the title *imperator et augustus* at Rome in 962 having been the final confirmatory act, 'and thus the Roman *imperium* was devolved upon the Germans'.[15] This

[12] *Ibid.*, Frederick I, no. 51, p. 86.   [13] *Ibid.*, no. 285, p. 97.   [14] *Ibid.*, no. 119, p. 201.
[15] Otto of Freising, *Chronica sive Historia* VI, 22.

Roman *imperium* as the last universal empire was held to constitute some form of dominion over the other Christian kingdoms, if not the entire world. In 1137 Wibald of Stablo expressed the idea to Lothar III when he wrote: 'For just as amongst all the stars it is certain that the sun rules in first place in the heavens, so the Roman *imperium* indisputably surpasses all the powers in the world.'[16]

Possession of the city of Rome was held to symbolize this universal dominion, so the German princes received letters in 1157 from the emperor explaining that 'by divine and provident clemency we hold the governance of the city and the world'.[17] In the following year papal legates soothingly addressed the emperor as 'lord and emperor of the city and the world'.[18] 'Lord of the World' was not a title adopted by the imperial chancery but it did enjoy some literary currency. Vincent of Prague referred to Frederick Barbarossa as 'the lord emperor, lord of the world's lands',[19] and the author known as Archipoeta, who belonged to the entourage of the imperial chancellor and archbishop of Cologne, Rainald of Dassel, addressed the emperor as follows:[20]

> *Salve mundi domine*   *cesar noster, ave.*
> *Cuius bonis omnibus*   *iugum est suave.*
> *Princeps terre principum*   *cesar Frederice . . .*
> Greetings to the lord of the world, Hail, our Caesar.
> For the good of all, his yoke is light.
> Prince of the princes of the land, Caesar Frederick . . .

Henry VI's eulogist Peter of Eboli in his *Liber ad honorem Augusti* referred to that emperor as prince of the world and lord of the world, and an aspect of this rhetorical style was taken up by the chancery to proclaim the pre-eminence of the empire over all the powers, peoples and kingdoms of the Christian world. A diploma of 1174, for example, elevates Frederick Barbarossa's clemency and imperial majesty above the nations and the kingdoms. Another consequence was the designation of other kings as *reguli* or kinglets, although this demeaning description was never used officially. However, John of Salisbury reported that Louis VII of France was enraged with the archbishop of Cologne for referring to him as a *regulus*, and the pro-Staufen author of the *Chronica regia Coloniensis* was scornful of provincial kinglets and peoples who were supporting Alexander III during the papal schism.

A letter from Henry II of England, who was on good terms with the imperial court, does contain what looks like an explicit admission of Frederick Barbarossa's supposed world authority; 'We lay before you our kingdom and

[16] *Codex epistolae Wibaldi*, no. 12, p. 92.   [17] *MGH Diplomata*, Frederick I, no. 163, p. 280.
[18] Otto of Freising and Rahewin, *Gesta Friderici* III, 25.
[19] Vincent of Prague, 'Annales', 1163 (actually 1162).   [20] Archipoeta, *Carmina* VII.

whatever is anywhere subject to our sway and entrust it to your power, that all
things may be administered in accordance with your nod, and that in all respects
your imperial will may be done.'[21] Such expressions belonged to a formal language of diplomatic courtesy although one of Henry II's subjects, Stephen of
Rouen, did consider the emperor to be Charlemagne's proper heir and that in
consequence the Capetians had usurped his right to the sovereignty of France.
John of Salisbury was disgusted by German pretensions to world dominion. At
the time of the council of Pavia he wrote with indignation to Ralph of Sarre:

Who has appointed the Germans to be judges of the nations? Who has given authority
to brutal and headstrong men that they should set up a prince of their own choosing
over the heads of the sons of men? In truth their madness has often attempted to do
this; but by God's will, it has on each occasion been overthrown and put to confusion,
and they have blushed for their own iniquity.[22]

To support the last assertion, John of Salisbury offers no proof whatever.

Apart from taking homage from kings of Denmark and England, from dukes
of Poland, Pomerania and Silesia and from counts of Flanders, did the rulers
of twelfth-century Germany entertain concrete plans to transform *imperium*
into an institutional reality beyond the confines of the German, Burgundian
and Italian kingdoms? In alliance with the papacy, Lothar III, Conrad III and
Frederick Barbarossa did in turn propose to conquer the upstart kingdom of
Sicily proclaimed in 1130, but it is not clear what the status of the Regno would
then have been. When they invaded the south in 1137, Lothar III and Pope
Innocent II avoided a confrontation about this issue. Together they invested
Count Rainulf of Alife with the duchy of Apulia, implying joint imperial and
papal lordship over the Sicilian lands, for which homage had intermittently
been offered to the papacy ever since 1059. The problem revived when William
II of Sicily died in 1189. Henry VI regarded himself as the heir in right of his wife,
Constance of Sicily, the last legitimate member of the Sicilian royal house. But
the barons of the Regno elected the illegitimate royal scion, Count Tancred of
Lecce, instead and he was recognized as king by the pope in 1192. In 1191 Henry
VI inconsistently claimed that Sicily should devolve to the empire both by ancient imperial right and as the inheritance of his consort. After he had seized the
kingdom in 1194, he avoided offering the customary homage for it to the pope.
But in apparently rejecting Sicily's status as a papal fief, it is not clear that he really regarded Sicily as a fourth kingdom of the western empire either, although
he did designate its capital, Palermo, to be an imperial as well as a royal town.

[21] Otto of Freising and Rahewin, *Gesta Friderici* iii, 8. The translation is by Mierow and Emery (1953),
p. 179.
[22] Letter 124 (1160) ed. and trans. in *The Letters of John of Salisbury*, i: *The Early Letters (1153–1161)*, ed.
Millor, Butler and Brooke, pp. 206–8.

In its attitude towards the eastern Roman empire, its rival in claims to world dominion, the western imperial court oscillated between formal alliances and covert hostility. Although the western court accepted that the Comnenians were true emperors, the chancery was careful to deny the name of Roman to the eastern empire and invented circumlocutions for its rulers such as king of the Greeks or Constantinopolitan emperor. If theories of world dominion had not assisted Frederick Barbarossa in his efforts to solve the papal schism of 1159 to 1178, then it does appear to have confirmed his desire to take overall military command of the Third Crusade. Henry VI's ambitions to make the claim to universal dominion more realistic were certainly suspected by foreign observers such as Roger of Howden and Niketas Choniates. But no one knows whether the crusade which the emperor was preparing in 1196 and 1197 was partly intended for the conquest of Constantinople or not. This was certainly a strategic option considering what the Fourth Crusade achieved in 1204. A German chronicler, the well-informed monk Otto of St Blasien, thought that Henry VI did intend to take advantage of the prostration of Byzantium and to subject it to his own western *imperium*. Henry VI's acceptance of homage from the new kingdoms of Cyprus and Cilician Armenia can be interpreted as pointing in this direction, because these provinces had until very recently been possessions of the eastern Roman empire. Whatever Henry VI's plans may have been, they died with him in 1197.

Since the 1030s the western empire had consisted geographically of three kingdoms: Germany, sometimes called 'the Roman kingdom' to establish consistency with the title king of the Romans; Italy, sometimes called 'the kingdom of Lombardy', its designation when conquered by Otto the Great; and Burgundy, whose southern portion bordering the Mediterranean was occasionally distinguished as 'the kingdom of Provence'.[23] Election to the German kingdom validated title to the other two thrones, and it is recorded that certain barons from Italy came to Frankfurt to observe Frederick Barbarossa's election in 1152. In 1085 the title of king had been granted on a personal basis to the duke of Bohemia, and in 1158 the emperor repeated the honour for Wladislav II. But Bohemia was not permanently accounted a kingdom in its own right until 1212. It is often held that neither the western empire nor its constituent kingdoms had capitals, and following modern administrative language this is an accurate judgement. To the twelfth-century mind, however, the empire certainly possessed capitals, places associated with the sacred regnal authority conferred by unction and coronation. The gold seals of Conrad III, Frederick

---

[23] E.g. *MGH Diplomata*, Conrad III, no. 4, p. 7, 1138, and no. 50, p. 84, 1140, have 'Romanum regnum' for Germany; *ibid.*, Lothar III, no. 103, p. 167, 1136, has 'cum in regno Longobardiae fuerimus'; *ibid.*, Conrad III, no. 132, p. 240, 1145, has 'in toto regno nostro Provincie'.

Barbarossa and Henry VI were inscribed ROMA CAPVT MVNDI REGIT ORBIS FRENA ROTVNDI, 'Rome, head of the Earth, governs the reins of the round world,'[24] and in 1159 Frederick Barbarossa described Rome as the city 'which is the head of our empire'.[25] He claimed that the papal schism of 1159 threatened to wrest the capital from his jurisdiction; 'For since, by divine ordinance, I am emperor of Rome and am so styled, I have merely the appearance of ruling and bear an utterly empty name lacking in meaning if authority over the city of Rome should be torn from my grasp.'[26]

The same emperor set about revising and extending the official association of certain capital towns with imperial power. During the festivities of December 1165 and January 1166 for the canonization of Charlemagne, Barbarossa declared Aachen to be a holy city and the chief of cities, 'the head and seat of the German kingdom', a place of kings which, as 'the royal seat in which the Roman emperors are first crowned', outshone all other places in dignity and honour.[27] In the theoretical language of imperial ideology, Aachen was thus seen as the capital of Germany, and in the other kingdoms certain towns were distinguished in the same manner. For Italy the emperor had already marked out Monza in 1159 to the detriment of Milan and Pavia as 'head of Lombardy and seat of that kingdom', and built a palace there in 1163. He claimed that 'our predecessors were accustomed to be crowned there [Monza] by the law of the kingdom',[28] but this was deliberate misinformation. The motive may have been to legitimate the only coronation which had actually taken place there, that of his uncle as anti-king Conrad III in 1128. In similar style Arles was declared head of Provence and a principal seat of the empire in 1164, and Vienne was declared the seat of the Burgundian kingdom in 1166.

THE APPLICATION OF LAW AND JUSTICE

When diplomas of Lothar III record 'the authority of the Roman empire' and of Conrad III 'the authority of our power',[29] what methods and resources were available to German rulers to make this authority manifest? The foremost

---

[24] Haussherr (1977), nos. 29, 31, 34, pp. 21–5, and *MGH Diplomata*, Conrad III, p. 241, n. 1 (1145). The inscription goes back to Conrad II's seal; *ibid.*, Conrad II, p. xxvi.

[25] *Ibid.*, Frederick I, no. 285, p. 97, has 'status urbis, quae caput imperii nostri est'.

[26] Otto of Freising and Rahewin, *Gesta Friderici* IV, 35. The translation is by Mierow and Emery (1953), p. 271.

[27] *MGH Diplomata*, Frederick I, no. 502, p. 433, has 'que caput et sedes regni Theutonici est', and no. 503, p. 434, has 'pro sede regali, in qua primo imperatores Romanorum coronantur'.

[28] *Ibid.*, no. 253, p. 53, 1159, has 'que caput Lombardiae et sedes regni illius esse dignoscitur, in qua etiam nostri antecessores de iure regni coronari consueverant'. See Peyer (1951), p. 457.

[29] E.g. *MGH Diplomata*, Lothar III, no. 57, p. 90, 1134, has 'auctoritate Romani imperii'; *ibid.*, Conrad III, no. 79, p. 141, 1142, has 'auctoritatis nostre potestate'.

royal duty was to provide justice. In 1129 Lothar III spoke of having been raised by the grace of God to the royal office in order to provide justice for the church and for all men, an idea expressed with the same dignity by Conrad III in 1141. As the Lord's anointed, he owed judgement and justice against all wrong-doing, and protection for everyone's rights. The rulers of the twelfth-century empire took these ancient formulas and their programme as a serious religious obligation. Quoting Psalm 98, one of Conrad III's diplomas opens with 'The king's honour is to cultivate judgement as King David attests.'[30] Added together, the realms of the western empire were too large for the royal court to be capable of supervising travelling assizes or permanent tribunals in the various regions. The itinerant royal household was itself the highest court of law, its procedures being simple and speedy. For 1151, for example, we possess the record for the archbishop-elect of Cologne, Arnold II, bringing a case before the king to ask for the restoration of episcopal possessions alienated under his predecessor. As usual the king required the princes present to assist him to consider the case, to deliberate the issues and to deliver the judgement.

Ideally the law upheld by the royal court was the will of heaven found out during the hearings and recorded in the findings or *sententiae*. However, the latter did not constitute a code of law which could be consulted. For the *placita* or law courts of dukes, counts and ecclesiastical advocates, the records sometimes refer to the custom of the Bavarians or the Franconians or the Saxons. But after the preservation of ancient regional codes in Carolingian times, no such custom was written down in any detail until Eike von Repgow's *Sachsenspiegel* in the thirteenth century. Writing about German legal practices of the twelfth century, Provost Burchard of Ursberg complained that the lack of written law was a great inconvenience. But one reason why written codes were not widely perceived to be necessary was that many German magnates drew up and operated rules of their own for their households, manors, villages, towns and retinues. Notable twelfth-century examples include Bishop Otto II of Bamberg's regulations for his Bavarian manors; Archbishop Rainald of Cologne's rules for his extensive retinue of *ministeriales*; the duke of Zähringen's regulations for the town of Freiburg im Breisgau founded in 1120 and the bishop of Strasbourg's for his cathedral town, promulgated in 1130 or 1131; and the rules of the bishops of Hildesheim for the rural immigrants to their diocese.

In the twelfth century, concepts of law in Germany were being transformed by three different types of legal endeavour: the study of Roman Law, the establishment of the *pax* or peace-keeping association known as the *Landfriede* and the uses made of feudal law or *feodalis ius*. Since the eleventh century imperial diplomas had quoted from Justinian's legislation, a practice reinforced

---

[30] *Ibid.*, no. 56, pp. 94–5, 1141.

in Conrad III's chancery by Wibald of Stablo, abbot of Corvey. The presence of
Bolognese lawyers at Frederick Barbarossa's court in Italy lent an authoritarian
tone to the ordinances issued at Roncaglia in 1158. Two of this emperor's acts,
Sacramenta puberum on oaths and *Habita* on the privilege of students, were
boldly inserted as *authentica* into the Codex of Roman Law. Bishop Otto of
Freising explicitly referred to the principle of kings standing above the law
when he sent a copy of his *History of the Two Cities* to the emperor in 1157, and
a paragraph from Justinian's legislation stood behind the following passage in a
charter for the town of Speyer issued in 1182: that just as it was up to the emperor
'to create laws, so it is for us to elucidate benevolently things which are unclear'.[31]

A significant example of emperors making law in this sense of *leges condere*
concerns Frederick Barbarossa's edict issued at Osimo in 1177 which forbade
the plunder of wrecks and shipwrecked persons. This was confected by Italian
lawyers, but Henry VI's edict of 1196 on the same subject appears to have been
composed by his chancery. Barbarossa's edict against incendiarism issued at
Nuremberg in 1186 or 1188 also had the character of law made by imperial
authority, but legal scholars today are not agreed as to whether the sworn
associations for enforcing the peace known as *Landfrieden* count as consented
custom or newly made law. For the earliest imperial *Landfriede*, Henry IV's
issued at Mainz in 1103, only a report of the oath sworn has survived. For
Henry V's *Landfrieden* (1119, 1122, 1125), Lothar III's (1125, 1135) and Conrad
III's (1147), the texts have perished. Frederick Barbarossa's *Landfriede* of 1152
survives in the form of twenty rules circulated to the princes of Germany,
conveying the impression of a code in the making. Its justification was set out
in the preface; peace was proclaimed by royal authority in order to maintain
divine and human laws, to defend the church, to guarantee everyone's rights
and to repair the unsettled state of the empire. His *Landfriede* of 1179 was,
on the other hand, a regional association confined to Rhenish Franconia. The
Pöhlde annals report that when the emperor visited Wallhausen in 1169 he
had renewed the *pax*, but it is not known whether this too was a local Saxon
Landfriede or an ordinance for the whole empire.

Although the peace-keeping associations did not work well as a curb upon
feuds, they had great influence upon judicial practice in twelfth-century
Germany in that the princes and their own law courts were involved by the
crown in the tasks of preserving law and order. In the legislation against arson
(1186 or 1188), for example, it was explicitly stated that the dukes, margraves,
counts palatine, landgraves and counts must do justice over incendiaries on
their own authority. But Burchard of Ursberg asserted with reference to this
ordinance that the emperor 'assembled a meeting of princes at Nuremberg

---

[31] *Ibid.*, Frederick I, no. 827, p. 34.

where he made arrangements for peace over the land and ordered it to be set out in writings which the Germans until today call *fridebrief*, that is, letters of peace, nor do they employ any other laws; but they do not obey them properly, being such a wild and unruly people'.[32]

The royal court did not intend to replace older custom in the provinces where it could be effective against crime, and a picturesque example of provincial custom preceding the *Landfrieden* was preserved by Otto of Freising in his report of Frederick Barbarossa's visit to Worms for Christmas in 1155. Archbishop Arnold of Mainz and Count Palatine Hermann of Stahleck were brought to trial for devastating the land during their feuds:

Now an old custom has gained the status of a law among the Franks and the Swabians, that whenever a noble, a *ministerialis* or a peasant (*colonus*) has been found guilty by his judge of such offences, before he is punished by sentence of death the noble is obliged to carry a dog [and] the *ministerialis* a saddle . . . from one county into the next in token of his shame. The emperor, observing this custom, compelled that count palatine, a great prince of the realm, together with ten counts, his accomplices, to carry dogs the distance of a German mile.[33]

The study of law and legal practice in the twelfth-century empire as they affected politics is a complex subject. Nevertheless, renewed interest in Roman Law, the need perceived for *Landfrieden* and the German king's position as overlord of vassal princes who included all the bishops made a deep impression without essentially changing the ruler's traditional role as protector of old custom to that of creator of new law. As a diploma issued by Lothar III judiciously recorded in 1132, 'custom is by long usage transformed into the character of law'.[34]

THE ROYAL CHANCERY

With the itinerant royal court travelled the clerical personnel who staffed both the royal chapel and the chancery. The production of numerous privileges, letters and other written instruments while on the move was one of the remarkable achievements of royal governance in the medieval empire, as the volumes of diplomas edited in the *Monumenta Germaniae Historica* series show. In normal times the chancery was directed by a *cancellarius* or chancellor under the formal obedience of the archbishop of Mainz, and the royal chapel doubling as a chancery was, as part of the royal court doubling as a law court, the principal organ of government in the twelfth-century empire. In 1125 Lothar III

---

[32] Burchard of Ursberg, *Chronicon* for 1186.
[33] Otto of Freising and Rahewin, *Gesta Friderici* II, 48. The translation is by Mierow and Emery (1953), p. 163.
[34] *MGH Diplomata*, Lothar III, no. 41, p. 68.

disbanded the staff of Henry V's chapel and chancery and appointed new men, Saxons for the most part, as the chaplains and notaries. He agreed with Archbishop Adalbert I of Mainz not to appoint a chancellor at all, probably so that the archbishop might enjoy the emoluments normally attached to the chancellor's office as part of his reward for permitting Lothar's election. This unusual arrangement made little difference in practice to the work of the chancery in producing diplomas and other materials. As soon as Conrad III was elected in 1138, he reverted to Salian tradition and appointed Arnold of Wied, cathedral provost of Cologne, as his chancellor. After the latter's promotion to the archbishopric of Cologne in 1151, the king appointed his longest serving chaplain, Arnold of Selehofen, as chancellor. He continued to direct the writing office for Frederick Barbarossa until his elevation to the see of Mainz in 1153.

It can be perceived that the chancellors, chaplains and notaries were bound to wield great influence at the heart of imperial affairs. Wibald of Stablo was taken up by Conrad III as his most creative notary. His advice was heeded at court, and he was further distinguished by receiving the abbacy of Corvey in 1146. He was also employed as an envoy in France and Italy; he continued to work in Frederick Barbarossa's chancery; and in the 1150s he was twice sent as ambassador to the Byzantine emperor. Through his reworking of older charters and through new diplomatic expression, Wibald of Stablo paved the way for the style of Frederick Barbarossa's flamboyant chancellor Rainald of Dassel, appointed in 1156. The third of Barbarossa's nine chancellors, he was rewarded with the see of Cologne in 1159. In the chancery he employed Henry of Würzburg as protonotary, thus confirming a new title invented by Wibald in 1150 and possibly indicating an elaboration of business. Henry was also employed as an envoy, to France, Italy and Byzantium. Rahewin considered him a person fit to judge the literary worth of his work as the continuator of Otto of Freising's biography of Barbarossa. Other notable chancellors were Christian of Buch, a man fluent in several languages, who was promoted to the archbishopric of Mainz in 1165; and Philip of Heinsberg who received the see of Cologne in 1167. Henry VI's capable chancellor Conrad of Querfurt was, like Rainald of Dassel, a Saxon. In 1194 he became bishop of Hildesheim and was later appointed to the see of Würzburg as well. He was assassinated in Würzburg in 1202.

The majority of the extant products of the chancery are grants or confirmation of rights, possessions and imperial protection to the churches and towns of Germany and Italy, diplomas or their copies which have survived the centuries in reasonably well-protected ecclesiastical and urban archives. A number of letters have also survived which are mandates to secular princes, churchmen or *ministeriales* to carry out a particular function in the near future, or to desist forthwith from some species of misdemeanour. It is thought that the chancery may have sent out far more mandates than the residue would indicate, the argument being that they tended not to be preserved because their value, unlike that of diplomas confirming privileges, was transitory. Since the chancery perambulated with the court, its paraphernalia had to be economical. There is no trace of any official register of royal charters. However, when Conrad III was at Aachen for Christmas in 1145, he was able to inform the archbishop of Vienne that the town of Vienne belonged to the crown, information 'which is preserved in the archives of our empire'.[35] So it is possible that there was a muniment box or room in the palace at Aachen, and there are other references to rulers consulting old documents and proofs. The chancery certainly consulted formularies on style, form and content. Wibald of Stablo, abbot of Corvey, kept his own book of records, examples and other materials now known as the *Codex epistolae Wibaldi* which is one of the principal sources for the diplomatic history of the empire in the twelfth century. Another informally used letter-book was the *Codex Udalrici* drawn up by 1125 for didactic purposes at Bamberg. The promotion of this codex from schoolbook to formulary testifies to connections between the imperial notaries and certain episcopal writing offices.

One of the most talented chaplains recruited by Conrad III was an Italian, Godfrey of Viterbo, who had been sent as a child to the cathedral school of Bamberg. Influential at court throughout Barbarossa's reign, he may have acted as tutor to Henry VI who was, unlike his father, literate. Godfrey was a voluminous and imaginative writer on imperial affairs, and left a fine account, perhaps exaggerated, of his busy experiences as an imperial notary, chaplain and envoy. He complained that it was hard to find time and place for his own compositions, which nevertheless fill almost a whole volume in the *Monumenta* series of *Scriptores*, because he had to compose

in the nooks of the imperial palace or on horseback on the road, under a tree or deep in the forest, whenever time permitted, during the sieges of castles, in the dangers of many a battle. I did not write this in the solitude of a monastery or in some other quiet place, but in the constant restlessness and confusion of events, in war and warlike conditions, in the noise of such a large court. As a chaplain I was occupied every day around the clock in the mass and all the hours, at table, in negotiations, in the drafting of letters, in the daily arrangement of new lodgings, in looking after the livelihood for myself and my people, in carrying out very important missions: twice to Sicily, three times to the Provence, once to Spain, several times to France, forty times from Germany to Rome and back. More was demanded of me in every exertion and restlessness than from anyone else my age at the court. The more extensive and difficult all this is, the more miraculous it is that in such hustle and bustle, amidst such great noise and disquiet, I was able to create this work.[36]

One can only agree with him.

[35] *Ibid.*, Conrad III, no. 145, p. 265, has 'quod in archivis imperii nostri continetur'.
[36] Godfrey of Viterbo, 'Memoria seculorum', p. 105. The translation is in Bumke (1991), pp. 460–1.

FINANCES AND THE IMPERIAL FISC

Although there are references in the twelfth century to an imperial treasury or *camera* with its chamberlains, it is difficult to discern whether there was a permanent treasury at court or whether *camera* is a synonym for the fisc, the chamberlains acting as revenue officials. Nothing identifiable as treasury documentation has survived from the twelfth century in Germany. The imperial court must have travelled with strong boxes (examples of which survive from the thirteenth century) for holding the imperial insignia, relics and other valuables such as gold seals and cash. It is known that the small but well-sited castle on the rock of Trifels not far from the Rhine was used as a depository for royal treasure. Already described as the strongest of Henry V's castles, the crown jewels were more than once sent there for safekeeping. Henry VI employed Trifels as a gaol for Richard I of England and other prisoners. Several sources remark upon the astonishment caused in Germany by the richness of the Sicilian royal treasure seized during the occupation of the Regno in 1194 and taken to Trifels. Some of the articles, notably Roger II's crimson and gold mantle, are still to be seen in the Vienna *Schatzkammer*. But like the archive of Aachen, the treasury of Trifels as a possible institutional embryo of imperial governance leaves no more than a shadow in the sources.

Since its virtual expulsion from Saxony in the 1070s, the crown had come to rely heavily upon its possessions in southern Germany, including the lands in Alsace and on the middle Rhine where, according to Bishop Otto of Freising, 'the principal strength of the realm is known to lie'.[37] The crown experienced difficulty in restoring its position as a landowner on the substantial scale enjoyed before the War of Investitures. Upon Henry V's death in 1125 Duke Frederick II of Swabia had occupied as much of the Salian fisc as his agents could hold, claiming it as his rightful inheritance as Henry V's nephew. It took Lothar III and his allies several years of campaigning before the duke and his brother, the anti-king Conrad, would give these resources up to the crown. By the time that Conrad III succeeded in 1138, it is thought that his holdings as king were surpassed by the enormous inheritances collected by the Welf family in Swabia and Saxony. Frederick Barbarossa began his reign with similar disadvantages because he relinquished his Swabian ducal title and lands which he had inherited from his father in 1147 to his cousin Duke Frederick of Rothenburg in 1152 or 1153. Then the emperor's marriage to Beatrice of Burgundy brought her large inheritance to the Staufen dynasty in 1156. Upon the Roman campaign of 1167 so many German princes died of malaria that the emperor was able to initiate a major programme of inheritances and reversions for himself and for his sons.

---

[37] Otto of Freising and Rahewin, *Gesta Friderici* I, 12.

We know that portions of the fisc were entrusted to *ministeriales* enfeoffed with castles from which to protect it, but very little specific information about the fisc's administration in the twelfth century has survived. The most significant source is a list of royal manors in Germany and Italy entitled *Iste sunt curie que pertinent ad mensam regis Romanorum*, 'These are manors which pertain to the sustenance of the king of the Romans',[38] the disparate parts of which must therefore date from the years 1125–33 or 1138–55 or 1169–91 when there were kings of the Romans. Substantial renders in kind from certain manors in Saxony, Lotharingia, Franconia and northern Bavaria and in cash from manors in Lombardy are scheduled, but in spite of a large scholarly literature, it is not known for which king the list was drawn up, or for what purpose the selection of manors and incomes may have been made in the first place.

THE PERIPATETIC ROYAL COURT AND ITS PALACES

The German court had no fixed residence, but the royal *iter* or perambulation around the provinces and dioceses of the empire was in itself a method of governance serving several purposes. It was the means for exposing royal justice in the regions, as we saw in the cases of Frederick Barbarossa's visits to Worms in 1155 and to the lower Rhineland in 1158. It exposed assemblies of princes to the sternness of the royal eye and involved them through the duty of *consilium* or offering counsel in the political and judicial issues of the moment. Between 1178 and 1181 the removal of Henry the Lion as duke of Saxony and Bavaria was worked out during court meetings of this kind. In November 1178 at the court in Speyer the emperor failed to reconcile the duke with his enemies, Archbishop Philip of Cologne at their head. In January 1179 the court held in Worms required the duke to answer charges of having broken the peace. In June 1179 the court at Magdeburg proscribed him for refusing to answer the charges, and proceedings against him as a contumacious vassal were opened by the court at Kayna in August. In January 1180 the court at Würzburg deprived him of his fiefs, and at the courts held in April at Gelnhausen and in September at Altenburg, the fiefs were reapportioned to his rivals. After campaigns against him in 1180 and 1181, the duke made his submission to the emperor at the court held in Erfurt in November 1181, and he was sent into exile.

The royal *iter* was also a progress between various castles and palaces belonging to the fisc, although the theory of routes deliberately patterned to enable the court to take up successively the renders from its own possessions is no longer widely current. The *iter* was a resourceful method for exploiting the court's ancient rights to hospitality from the cathedral churches and from

---

[38] Brühl and Kölzer (1979), p. 53.

some of the abbeys of the empire, hospitality making up one component of the *servitia* or services owed by the imperial church in return for its temporalities. These rights relied upon the legal argument that most of the temporalities of the church pertained ultimately to the crown, and had been enfeoffed or otherwise entrusted to prelates for the mutual benefit of the parties, church and empire. Lothar III, Conrad III and Frederick Barbarossa followed the practice of their Salian predecessors by staying more often in episcopal towns and in royal abbeys than in their own palaces and castles. Of the latter, Lothar III understandably favoured Goslar in Saxony as well as the imperial palace in Aachen. Conrad III preferred Nuremberg and Frankfurt, possibly because he had been well liked in their regions when he was anti-king. Frederick Barbarossa favoured all four, as well as frequently visiting Altenburg in the Saxon marches, Gelnhausen in Franconia, Kaiserslautern west of the Rhine, Hagenau in Alsace and Ulm in Swabia.

Although Henry VI paid more visits to the episcopal towns of Worms and Würzburg than to any single palace of his own, during his reign the royal residences for the first time housed the court more often than the abbeys and the cathedral towns. This reflects not only that the ambitious programme of palace building initiated by Conrad III and Frederick Barbarossa was coming to fruition, but also that the fisc had expanded phenomenally since the late 1160s, thus leaving Henry VI economically less reliant upon ecclesiastical hospitality. No doubt this was a relief to the bishops, because the royal entourage was large. A reliable source reveals that when a cathedral town was the site of a plenary session of the royal court, the crown's officials commandeered the bishop's principal revenues for the two weeks in which the meeting fell.

The royal *iter* was also designed to accommodate the ideological function of displaying the power and the glory of the ruler through the ceremony of wearing a crown before the court, usually coinciding with the major festivals of the church. As Frederick Barbarossa put it in 1158, 'we wear a crown and diadem of glory, namely at Christmas, at Easter and at Pentecost'.[39] Such ceremonies served the explicit purpose of presenting the ruler as a sacred personage under the express protection of Christ, *summus rex et sacerdos*, 'highest king and priest', as Otto of Freising described him in relation to Frederick Barbarossa's first coronation and unction at Aachen in 1152. The bishop drove this point home by explaining that another Frederick, the bishop of Münster, was consecrated by the same bishops who had sanctified the king, so that 'in one church the same day saw the consecration of the only two persons who are sacramentally anointed according to the procedures of the New and Old Testaments and are

---

[39] *MGH Diplomata*, Frederick I, no. 201, p. 337.

solemnly called the Lord's anointed'.[40] The subsequent crown-wearing festivals carried political as well as religious and psychological messages. Meeting with strong resistance at some point during his Lombard campaigns, for example, Barbarossa vowed not to wear his crown until the affront to his majesty had been avenged. By contrast the Whitsun crown-wearing ceremony at Mainz in 1182 was explicitly related by the author of the Worms annals to the victorious outcome of the long effort to topple Henry the Lion. In the summer of 1178 on their way back through Provence and Burgundy from Italy, the imperial tourists took the opportunity to stage new coronations; Frederick Barbarossa was crowned at Arles and Empress Beatrice at Vienne.

Modern scholarship has not come to agreement about the constitutional classification of such ceremonies of coronation subsequent to the initial rites at Aachen for the German kingdom and at Rome for the empire, and precision is perhaps inappropriate. The purpose of an unusual triple coronation carried out at Milan in 1186 was to promote the honour of the empire by a ceremony combining the court's ambition of the moment with the religious and hierarchical values of that age. With considerable sang-froid the emperor had come to Milan to celebrate the marriage of his son Henry VI to Constance of Sicily in the city he had levelled to the ground in 1162. After the wedding ceremony in San Ambrogio all three were crowned, Barbarossa by the archbishop of Vienne, Henry VI by the patriarch of Aquileia and Constance by a German bishop; 'And from that day,' reports the principal source, 'he [Henry VI] was called Caesar.'[41] Since the papal curia had recently refused the emperor's application for his son's imperial coronation, the first time that such an arrangement had been proposed since Otto II's imperial coronation during his father's lifetime in 967, the most plausible explanation is that the 1186 coronations were planned and executed as a substitute.

Although the cathedral towns of the empire were so significant for the royal *iter*, the pattern of journeys was revised in the twelfth century in relation to the castles, palaces and towns situated upon the royal fisc. Upon some of the ancient possessions of the crown mentioned in the twelfth-century list of the king of the Romans' *curiae* such as Nimwegen, Ingelheim, Frankfurt and Kaiserslautern, Conrad III and Frederick Barbarossa undertook reconstruction of the royal palaces. Rahewin preserves a valuable description of one of these projects, which were designed in part to display the glory of the dynasty and the honour of the empire:

In Kaiserslautern he [Frederick I] built a royal palace of red stone and adorned it quite lavishly. On one side he surrounded it with a very strong wall, the other side is enclosed

---

[40] Otto of Freising and Rahewin, *Gesta Friderici* II, 3.
[41] Ralph of Diceto, 'Ex ymaginibus historiarum' for 1186.

by a lake-like fishpond, which contains for the delectation of the eyes and the palate all delicacies of fish and fowl. An adjoining park offers nourishment to a wealth of stages and deer. The royal splendor of all these things and their abundance, which is greater than one could describe, strikes all who see it with amazement.[42]

Another residence belonging to the Staufen family and much visited by Frederick Barbarossa and Henry VI was Hagenau in Alsace. Adjacent to it a town was founded early in the twelfth century, and the emperor granted it a detailed privilege in 1164. Godfrey of Viterbo wrote of the castle's sumptuously painted and gilded apartments, and of the towers which adorned it. Apparently it contained a well-stocked library. Something of the magnificence of the new building programme can be inferred from the royal chapels, halls, arcades and sculptured remnants at Gelnhausen, Nuremberg, Eger, Frankfurt and Wimpfen. From surviving letters and inscriptions we learn a little about the purpose of palaces for promoting imperial prestige. Having repaired the palace at Kaiserswerth upon its island in the Rhine, Frederick Barbarossa installed an inscription over the gateway in 1184 referring to the restoration of justice and peace which the court meetings held in such palaces were intended to sustain. After he had left Germany upon the Third Crusade, the emperor wrote back to Henry VI to remind him not to neglect completion of the projects at Nimwegen and Kaiserswerth since they had been residences of their Carolingian and Salian predecessors, and were therefore valuable in underlining the significance of their own house. The ambitious construction of palaces indicates a reasonably prosperous imperial dynasty in the last third of the twelfth century, and this impression is borne out by the acquisition of so many new assets after 1167 to make up a fisc consisting of ample forests, profitable jurisdictions, hundreds of manors, scores of towns and monasteries and, according to the chronicler Arnold of Lübeck, 350 castles.

THE CROWN AND WARFARE

The resources of the crown, the court's relationship with the church and the ceaseless process of the *iter* also sustained one of the ruler's most demanding tasks, that of making war. As Wibald of Stablo, abbot of Corvey, reminded the bishop of Hildesheim in 1149, the *servitia* owed by the church consisted not only in attending the royal court and in providing hospitality for it, but also in assisting the king's military expeditions. The royal *expeditio* or armed campaign conducted within the borders of the western empire was itself an administrative method of last resort. Quoting the Second Book of Kings, Rahewin thought it obvious that there was a proper time for kings to go forth to war, and applied the

---

[42] Otto of Freising and Rahewin, *Gesta Friderici* IV, 86. The translation is in Bumke (1991), p. 125.

commonplace to Barbarossa's second Italian expedition planned for 1158. He also took it for granted that the bishops would be consulted and one of them, Otto of Freising, wrote to the emperor that it was right to chastise the Milanese for the honour of the empire. In the twelfth century the term *honor* was much used by the imperial chancery to indicate both the dignity of the empire and specific rights belonging to the crown. It was also employed to justify wars 'for the glory and honour of the Roman empire' as Frederick Barbarossa expressed it to Wibald of Stablo, abbot of Corvey in relation to the expedition against Poland in 1157.[43] In Germany itself war or *guerra* was sometimes justified on the same grounds. In 1166 the emperor enjoined Counts Leopold and Henry of Plain in Bavaria to attack the Alexandrine see of Salzburg 'for the honour of the empire', adding that 'our honour depends upon this war'.[44] The means for war were provided chiefly by the armed retinues of the crown, the secular princes and the church, although mercenaries were employed for the empire's wars during the twelfth century and the larger towns of Germany also contributed contingents. Military retinues were normally sustained by fiefs granted to knights by their lords, which is why Lothar III forbade the alienation of fiefs without consent in 1136 since the consequence was that 'our princes are hardly able to make their knights contribute to the success of the expeditions undertaken in our name because of their being so short of fiefs'.[45] Frederick Barbarossa repeated this legislation in 1154 and 1158.

Although many royal monasteries and a handful of bishoprics such as Constance, Bremen and Chur were exempted from military service, the imperial court normally expected all ecclesiastical and secular princes to be prepared to send their militias on campaign, to attend in person when requested to do so and to take the oaths customarily demanded for the purpose. Military obligation in Germany did not run to specified numbers of knights, but ambitious princes close to the court were willing to provide them in some number. In 1161, for example, Archbishop Rainald of Cologne, Duke Frederick of Rothenburg, Count Palatine Conrad of the Rhine and Landgrave Louis II of Thuringia provided more than 1,100 knights to reinforce the army besieging Milan. Many bishops suffered severe financial strain in supporting the high cost of the empire's wars. In addition to the injunctions about preserving fiefs for their proper purpose, several other sources have survived which indicate the scale of organization behind the movement of large armies from Germany to Italy: a statute of 1158 for the conduct of the army and the camp; an edict confected at Reichenau Abbey about 1160 and ascribed to Charlemagne, explaining military obligations, personnel and equipment in considerable detail; and rules

[43] *MGH Diplomata*, Frederick I, no. 181, p. 304, has 'quantave gloria et honore Romanum imperium'.
[44] *Ibid.*, no. 508, p. 442.   [45] *Ibid.*, Lothar III, no. 105, p. 170.

from different parts of Germany about the military conduct of the retinues of knightly *ministeriales*. Several of the campaigns in Lombardy and against the kingdom of Sicily as well as the German military contributions to the Second and Third Crusades were failures. Nevertheless, it is apparent that German armies were formidable and widely feared instruments in the twelfth century, more than one author testifying to their fury and impetus, although some of the language is borrowed from classical usage recording Rome's suspicion of Germanic barbarians.

THE *DE FACTO* INDEPENDENCE OF SAXONY, AND ITS EXPANSION TO THE EAST

The virtual independence of Saxony from the authority of the crown was one result of the War of Investitures which was confirmed by the defeat in 1115 of Henry V's invasion of Saxony at the battle of Welfesholz. Although the crown was not totally bereft of political support and material possessions in Saxony and its marches, the autonomy for which the Saxon aristocracy had striven ever since 1073 was a reality of twelfth-century German politics. In 1125 it was the highest representative of this group, the Saxon duke Lothar, who was himself elected king. The ascendancy of Saxony which this betokened proved transitory when Lothar III's son-in-law, Henry the Proud, failed to secure the succession in 1138. But by this time Saxony was in the grip of a social phenomenon of the utmost significance for its future. By means of force and colonization, missionary zeal and diplomacy, the Saxon frontier of the western empire was extended far to the east in the twelfth and thirteenth centuries. Here we need to consider the political implications and results for northern Germany.

As Saxony's preoccupation with the issues of the War of Investitures receded during the second and third decades of the twelfth century, so it became possible to use the resources of the duchy as well as those of the highly populated Netherlands for a renewed attempt to dominate the adjacent lands of the Slavs by conquest and settlement. Lothar III as duke of Saxony and emperor, and his grandson Duke Henry the Lion, proved adept at choosing commanders and churchmen with the military and organizational talents necessary for annexing and settling the Slav regions. Lothar was responsible for installing the resolute Saxon dynasties of Schauenburg in Holstein (1110), of Ballenstedt in the North March later called Brandenburg (1134) and of Wettin in the marches of Meissen (1123) and Lusatia (1136), with enormous consequences for the consolidation of these vast territories as provinces of the German realm. From the earliest years of the century a plentiful supply of colonists from the Netherlands and Westphalia had been ready to emigrate to the east, but in practice the conversion of the country across the River Elbe into a Germanized landscape was a relatively slow-moving affair due in part to Slav resistance and in part to the rivalries of the Saxon princes.

In 1143 or 1144 Count Adolf II of Schauenburg and Holstein founded the river port of Lübeck which was important because it gave Germany a practical outlet to the Baltic for the first time since the losses of territory to the Slavs during the rising of 983. But the settlement was destroyed in 1147 in an attack by Niklot, prince of the Obodrites, and had to be founded anew by Henry the Lion in 1159. In the meantime the archbishop of Bremen had reestablished the sees destroyed by the Slavs in the eleventh century, Oldenburg, Ratzeburg and Mecklenburg, although his enemy Henry the Lion insisted, as Saxon duke, upon the right of investiture and protection. This was conceded by the royal court in 1154. Some time later the see of Oldenburg was transferred to Lübeck and that of Mecklenburg to Schwerin. Two circumstances ensured the future of German authority in the east. The first was the decision by Slav princes themselves to submit to imperial suzerainty. The second was the influx of German settlers whose utility is attested in the charters of their ecclesiastical lords, and in the chronicle of the settlement composed by Helmold, the parish priest of Bosau in Holstein. The impartiality of Helmold's work will always be a matter for some doubt, but his picture of the conquest and colonization (since it is not the only source from which the story can be constructed) carries reasonable conviction:

As the land was without inhabitants, he [Count Adolf II of Holstein] sent messengers into all parts, namely to Flanders and Holland, to Utrecht, Westphalia and Frisia, proclaiming that whosoever were in straits for lack of fields should come with their families and receive a very good land – a spacious land, rich in crops, abounding in fish and flesh and exceeding good pasturage... An innumerable multitude of different peoples rose up at this call and they came with their families and their goods into the land of Wagria to Count Adolf that they might possess the country which he had promised them.[46]

The initial settlement of Holstein, Stormarn and Wagria was followed by Henry the Lion's venture, the Wendish Crusade of 1147 designed to coincide with the Second Crusade to Jerusalem. In military terms the Saxons did badly, but in the following years the Slav leadership came to realize that Saxon power was in the ascendant and that the Christian faith and German settlement would have to be accommodated in the interests of their own people. For such reasons Pribislav of Brandenburg, who died in 1150, appointed Margrave Albert the Bear as his heir, and the restored sees of Havelberg and Brandenburg were

---

[46] Helmold of Bosau, *Chronica Slavorum* cap. LVII. The translation is by Tschan (1935), p. 168.

rapidly occupied by colonists from the Netherlands. According to Helmold, using somewhat exaggerated expression,

The bishopric of Brandenburg, and likewise that of Havelberg, was greatly strengthened by the coming of the foreigners, [i.e. Netherlanders] because the churches multiplied and the income from the tithes grew enormously . . . the Slavs have been everywhere crushed and driven out. A people strong and without number have come from the bounds of the ocean, and taken possession of the territories of the Slavs. They have built cities and churches and have grown in riches beyond all estimation.[47]

In 1163 the Piast princes Boleslaw of Wroclaw (Breslau) and Mieszko of Racibórz were installed as dukes in Silesia, to be tributaries of the western empire while remaining vassals of the duke of Poland. Silesia had long been converted to Christianity and was not in danger of German invasion, but now the land was opened to German immigration and to eventual incorporation into the empire in the thirteenth century. After another long military campaign initiated in 1158, Henry the Lion installed new counts in the lands of Obodrites, Gunzelin of Hagen in Schwerin and Henry of Schooten in Mecklenburg. In spite of further Slav resistance to these measures, the duke restored the Obodrite prince Pribislav to his principality in 1167 to rule alongside his previous appointees.

The initial conversion of Pomerania had been undertaken as early as the 1120s by Bishop Otto I of Bamberg as the principal missionary. A bishopric set up at Wolin in 1140 as an exempt see under direct papal authority was moved to Kammin in 1174. Bogislav of Stettin, prince of Pomerania who submitted to Henry the Lion in the 1160s, was in 1181 after Henry's fall given the title of duke with the status of vassal immediate to the empire. Pomerania was thus opened to German immigration. In a summary about what had been achieved by the end of the 1160s, Helmold claimed that

all the country of the Slavs, beginning at the Eider which is the boundary of the kingdom of the Danes, and extending between the Baltic Sea and the Elbe River in a most lengthy sweep to Schwerin, a region once feared for its ambuscades and almost deserted, was now through the help of God all made, as it were, into one colony of Saxons. And cities and villages grew up there and churches were built and the number of the ministers of Christ multiplied.[48]

The conquest, conversion and colonization of the vast lands east of the Elbe by the Saxons were challenged by the rising might of Denmark, since the Danish crown was Henry the Lion's rival for dominion over the southern coast of the Baltic and managed intermittently to occupy Holstein, Mecklenburg and Pomerania. Not until the battle of Bornhöved in 1227 could this phase of Denmark's interest in the western empire's lands be brought to an end.

---

[47] Helmold of Bosau, *Chronica Slavorum* cap. LXXXIX. The translation is by Tschan (1935), pp. 235–6.
[48] Helmold of Bosau, *Chronica Slavorum* cap. CX. The translation is by Tschan (1935), p. 281.

THE RESTORATION OF IMPERIAL GLORY IN
THE TWELFTH CENTURY

From the Salian past the rulers of the twelfth-century western empire inherited
a set of institutions, methods and resources which sustained their governance
and authority: the services of the church and the wealth of the fisc, the prestige of
God-guarded law and an itinerant court with its multiple functions as chancery,
source of justice, military command centre and meeting place of princes and
bishops. In spite of the damage inflicted by the War of Investitures, these
institutions remained in good working order. Henry I of England did suggest
to Henry V that regular royal taxation in the Anglo-Norman mode might
profitably be introduced into Germany, but sources from within the western
empire do not complain that the relative paucity of governing institutions as
a consequence of itinerant kingship was a disadvantage. Instead, it was held
that the virtues of the rulers themselves ought to be adequate for solving the
perceived problem of the twelfth century: to restore the honour and glory
of the empire after the disordered years of enmity with the papacy, and the
concomitant 'reformation' of peace, justice and religion. A letter from Conrad
III to Pope Eugenius III in 1150 looks forward to 'the people of Christ living
in peace and in the fear of God, and the Roman empire being restored to the
vigour of its pristine dignity',[49] ideas emphasized again and again in the royal
diplomas.

Although he disliked Saxons and said so, Bishop Otto of Freising thought
that Lothar III was a ruler with the requisite virtues: 'Had he not been forestalled by death he might have been the man to restore, by his ability and energy,
the imperial crown to its ancient dignity.'[50] The Saxon sources obviously gave
him good obituaries, the Hildesheim annals calling him *pater patriae*, father
of the country, for his services in peace and war. The chanceries of Frederick
Barbarossa and Henry VI perfected the technique of presenting royal acts as
necessary for the programme of imperial renewal, but this had been of genuine concern to Conrad III's court as well. Conrad III was not the subject of
panegyric resources such as Gunther devoted to Barbarossa in his *Ligurinus*
or Peter of Eboli to Henry VI in the *Liber ad honorem Augusti*. In his *History
of the Two Cities*, Conrad III's half-brother Otto of Freising gave a decidedly
pessimistic account of the reign down to 1146, largely because Conrad's be-
stowal of the Bavarian ducal title upon his other half-brothers, the margraves
of Austria, had caused war and destruction in the bishopric of Freising and
elsewhere in Bavaria. On the other hand, Godfrey of Viterbo, who was taken on
as a royal chaplain towards the end of the reign, ascribed the conventions and

[49] *MGH Diplomata*, Conrad III, no. 222, p. 395, 1150, has 'et populus christianus in pace et timore dei
vivere et imperium Romanum in pristine dignitatis robur reformari'.
[50] Otto of Freising, *Chronica sive Historia* VII, 20. The translation is by Mierow (1966), p. 428.

attributes of kingliness to Conrad III: wisdom, a fine appearance and martial prowess; and what is more, so did sources from Saxony, a province hostile to the king.

Writing to the pope just after Frederick Barbarossa's election in 1152, Wibald of Stablo, abbot of Corvey, inaugurated the encomiast tradition about this ruler which has gone on ever since: 'of penetrating ability, ready understanding, fortunate in war, eager to embark on difficult and glorious tasks, altogether intolerant of insults, affable and generous, and shiningly eloquent in the native idiom of his language. The Lord increases the nourishment of all the virtues in him so that he may carry out judgement and justice in the land.'[51] All this may be a reconstruction from the abbot's biblical and classical learning, but the bishop of Freising was also enthusiastic about his nephew's abilities. Abandoning his customary sobriety, he applied to Barbarossa a verse lifted from the infancy story of Christ: 'What manner of child shall this be?' (Luke 1:66). Helmold of Bosau who disliked the Swabians was nevertheless struck by Barbarossa and also adapted biblical phrases in praise of him: 'His throne was raised above the throne of the kings that had been before him many days; and he grew in wisdom and in fortitude above all the inhabitants of the land.'[52] Apart from his German panegyrists such as Gunther and Rahewin, the emperor also impressed Italians other than Godfrey of Viterbo. Otto Morena of Lodi and his continuators wrote laudatory history of Barbarossa's warlike deeds in Lombardy, and an anonymous north Italian got as far as 3,343 lines of a heroic *Carmen* on the theme. No doubt such persons were motivated by their own hatred for Milan, the emperor's principal enemy in Lombardy. The Third Crusade inspired new eulogistic literature about Frederick Barbarossa. Henry VI's principal panegyrists were Italians, Godfrey of Viterbo and Peter of Eboli, although some of the German chroniclers were also impressed by his energy in attempting to fulfil the ruler's duty of providing peace and justice in his realms.

LOTHAR III, CONRAD III AND THE PROBLEMS OF REGIONAL RIVALRY

The political language of the twelfth century adopted classical terminology in regarding the empire as a body in which the emperor was head and the princes the obedient members. The arenga of a diploma for Archbishop Rainald of

---

[51] *MGH Constitutiones* I, no. 138, p. 193, has 'fuit antehac ingenio acer, consilio promptus, bello felix, rerum arduarum et gloriae appetens, iniuriae omnino impatiens, affabilis et liberalis, et splendide disertus iuxta gentile idioma linguae suae. Augeat in eo Devs omnium virtutum nutrimenta, ut faciat iudicium et iusticiam in terra'.

[52] Helmold of Bosau, *Chronica Slavorum* cap. LXXII. The translation is by Tschan (1935), p. 197.

Cologne in 1166 proclaimed that nothing could be more fitting and glorious than the emperor assembling and cherishing his *fideles* like members under a head from which the merits of the members would be properly rewarded. In reality it was a difficult task to keep unruly members submissive to the court. Much of Lothar III's reign was taken up with armed confrontations against Frederick II of Swabia and his brother, who found widespread support in the Rhineland, Franconia and Bavaria as well as in their Swabian homeland. Having lost the election of 1125, Duke Frederick did homage to Lothar III but felt unable to accept a ruling made at Regensburg late in the year denying him the lion's share of Henry V's possessions. The Staufen brothers regarded the lands of the Salian dynasty as theirs by hereditary right, but the annals of Disibodenberg reveal that at the Regensburg court, royal property was declared to pertain to regimes rather than to persons, and must therefore pass under Lothar III's *regiminis ditio* or authority of government, not in itself a new principle. But when the Swabian duke refused to accept this, he was declared an outlaw and an excommunicate, and war began. At this time the duke's brother Conrad was absent upon the Venetian crusade of the 1120s. When he returned in 1127, he was proclaimed anti-king at Nuremberg by a small gathering of Staufen supporters. Why Frederick of Swabia as the elder brother did not himself claim the crown is not known. It is possible that his rejection at the election of 1125, his oath to Lothar III and his excommunicate status rendered him less eligible than his brother. At some time in his adventurous career, the duke is known to have lost an eye, and if this happened in 1126 or 1127, then his lack of bodily perfection as future *rex et sacerdos* in the image of Christ may also have stood in the way of his accepting kingly office.

The Staufen brothers had a case strong enough to give them realistic support in southern Germany. In 1128 Conrad III left for Italy to secure coronation from the archbishop of Milan and to attempt to gain possession of the Matildine lands which had passed to Henry V's use in 1115. In Germany Archbishop Adalbert of Mainz and Bishop Embrico of Würzburg were able to hold their cathedral towns for Lothar III, but the Salian strongholds of Speyer and Nuremberg had opted for the Staufen. In order to gain a more secure position in southern Germany, Lothar III married his daughter and heiress Gertrude to Duke Henry the Proud of Bavaria in 1127. The duke's chief residence was Regensburg, and therefore outflanked Nuremberg in the rear. But the main motive may simply have been to find the most suitable match for the greatest heiress in Germany. As head of the Welf dynasty and son of Wulfhild Billung, the duke of Bavaria was exceedingly rich in Swabian and Saxon lands, as well as holding on to much of Bavaria for the king. However, Henry the Proud's sister was married to Frederick II of Swabia, so it is legitimate to infer that Lothar III would have been aware of a possible mode of reconciliation with the Staufen through Gertrude's marriage. Otto of Freising reports that such a rapprochement was proposed in 1129, but the actual meeting of Dukes Henry and Frederick at Zwiefalten Abbey misfired. In 1142 Gertrude's second marriage, to Conrad III's half-brother Margrave Henry II Jasomirgott of Austria, was openly motivated by just such hopes of reconciliation, as we shall see.

The Saxon court of Lothar III thus looked to traditional methods to extend its influence: by arranging marriages, through the services of bishops, and in the cultivation of good relations with other duchies. Duke Simon I of Upper Lotharingia was Lothar III's half-brother, and in Burgundy Duke Conrad of Zähringen was appointed imperial rector in 1127. Relations between Archbishop Adalbert I of Mainz and the king suffered when Louis I of Thuringia was created a landgrave in 1131, because the archbishop perceived this appointment as a threat to his possessions in Hesse and Thuringia. But Lothar III was shrewd in judging which magnates best served his rule. As we have seen, he chose capable margraves to undertake the consolidation of Saxony's renewed expansion into Slav lands. Under the influence of Norbert of Xanten, archbishop of Magdeburg, the king accepted Innocent II as pope in the schism of 1130 and received him at a court held at Liège in 1131. The pope gratefully confirmed the ambitious claims of the Saxon archbishoprics of Magdeburg and Bremen to authority over the churches of Poland and Scandinavia respectively, claims going back to the tenth century. Nothing was to come of this, but nostalgia for the dignity of the Ottonian and Salian past, much of it mythical, continued to colour the political outlook of the court, the bishops and the secular aristocracy throughout the twelfth century in Germany.

Although the anti-king Conrad's challenge to his very title seemed no nearer to a solution, Lothar III was able to leave for Italy upon the prescribed *expeditio Romana* in 1132 and was crowned emperor in Rome in 1133. Nevertheless, the Staufen brothers did eventually submit to the emperor, although there is no entirely satisfactory explanation given their commitment to their legitimacy as heirs not only to the crown but also to the estates of the Salian house. When agreement was reached, it was complete. Frederick of Swabia, by then a widower, married Agnes of Saarbrücken, the niece of his greatest enemy, Archbishop Adalbert I of Mainz. Conrad gave up his royal claims in 1135 and submitted to Lothar III. In 1136 the emperor was able to take him as a commander upon his second Italian campaign, intended to crush the new Sicilian kingdom. Late in 1137 Lothar III died on his way back from this expedition. Given that as duke of Saxony from 1106 to 1125 he had done everything in his power to preserve Saxony from almost any form of authority exercised by the royal court, it is remarkable how he had imposed recognition of himself as king throughout Germany by 1135. But this was not enough to secure his son-in-law's succession. A neutral source, Sigebert of Gembloux's continuator, claimed that 'after the death of King Lothar the princes of the German kingdom, not bearing to be ruled over by anyone not of the royal line, set up Conrad as a man from the family of kings'.[53] Not that this consideration had prevented them from electing Lothar in 1125. However, Conrad III's legitimacy as Salian heir did strengthen his hand, particularly since the remarks of another commentator, Abbot Berthold of Zwiefalten, can be given credence. Of Henry the Proud he wrote that as 'the most powerful amongst all the princes of the realm at that time, he inconsiderately counted upon the succession, but he was truly abominated by everyone for his pride'.[54]

Although Henry the Proud recognized Conrad III's title, the new king considered that the duke represented a threat to his rule. A credible explanation is provided by a source hostile to Conrad III, Helmold of Bosau: 'When King Conrad was raised to the throne of the realm, he tried to establish Albert [the Bear] in the duchy [Saxony], asserting that it was not right that any prince should hold two duchies. Henry [the Proud] claimed for himself the two duchies, Bavaria and Saxony. Therefore these two princes, the sons of two sisters, carried on their civil war, and all Saxony was in turmoil.'[55] Like Henry the Proud, Margrave Albert the Bear was a grandson of the last Billung duke of Saxony, and once Lothar III was gone, the parity of Albert's own claims to the ducal title of Saxony gained effect. Helmold did not find Conrad III's fear of Henry the Proud's double title unreasonable, and repeated the explanation without comment when Henry the Lion as Henry the Proud's heir claimed both duchies early in the 1140s and was refused Bavaria. There were, of course, precedents for princes holding two duchies, but Conrad III and Helmold of Bosau may not have been aware of them. Where the king overshot the mark was in endeavouring to confiscate two duchies from Henry the Proud at the same time. Possibly he desired vengeance upon the man who had burned Ulm, one of the principal residences of the Staufen, to the ground in 1134. In 1139 the king appointed his half-brother Margrave Leopold IV of Austria to the duchy of Bavaria, and after Leopold's death the next brother, Margrave Henry II Jasomirgott, in 1143.

Fortunately for Conrad III, Henry the Proud died late in 1139 but the Saxon aristocracy supported his son Henry the Lion's claim to the Saxon ducal title as better than Albert the Bear's. In May 1142 the king came to terms. Henry the Lion was confirmed duke of Saxony and the boy's mother dutifully married Henry Jasomirgott who could thus be accepted as next duke of Bavaria by the Saxon party early in 1143. Just as Lothar III had been able to settle personal

[53] Sigebert of Gembloux, 'Continuatio' for 1138. [54] Berthold of Zwiefalten, 'Chronicon' cap. 35.
[55] Helmold of Bosau, *Chronica Slavorum* cap. LIV. The translation is by Tschan (1935), p. 163.

rivalries by 1135, so the compacts of 1142 and 1143 might have held up had not Gertrude of Saxony died in childbirth in April 1143. Henry the Lion, assisted by his Swabian uncle Welf VI, then decided to repudiate recognition of his step-father's Bavarian title, and the war dragged on until the Second Crusade provided the opportunity for another solution. Conrad III, Duke Henry Jasomirgott, and Welf VI agreed to leave Germany for Jerusalem; Henry the Lion would place his claim to Bavaria in abeyance and launch the Wendish Crusade on the Saxon frontier; and the king's son Henry Berengar was elected as next king of the Romans. Although the Second Crusade was a failure, it raised the status of the empire which had been unable, under an excommunicate ruler, to participate in the First. But it did not solve the problem of Germany's internal rivalries because Conrad III, upon his return from crusade, still would not accept the combination of Saxony and Bavaria upon which Henry the Lion insisted as his right, and the question was no nearer to a resolution when Conrad died in 1152.

FREDERICK I BARBAROSSA AND THE FORTUNES OF THE EMPIRE

Although Henry the Lion's claim to Bavaria took some time for the new ruler to settle, Frederick Barbarossa's previous tenure of the Swabian ducal title (1147–1152/3) provides the clue to the solution he negotiated. Ever since 1098, when three ducal authorities had been recognized in Swabia by the crown, it was potentially possible to subdivide duchies to accommodate competing claims. Probably Conrad III was not willing to apply this to Bavaria because he did not appreciate the stubbornness of Henry the Lion's character, but in 1156 Barbarossa adopted the Swabian solution of 1098 for Bavaria. Henry the Lion was confirmed duke, Henry Jasomirgott was created duke of Austria and another Bavarian magnate, Count Conrad of Dachau, was recognized as duke of Merania on the Adriatic. Considering the intensity and destructiveness of regional rivalries in Germany stretching back to the War of Investitures, it is not surprising that Otto of Freising, who witnessed the agreement, reported of Barbarossa that 'the prince prized this more highly than the successes of all his other undertakings: the fact that, without the shedding of blood, he was able to bring to friendly relations princes of the realm so mighty and so closely related to himself'.[56]

Since the integrity of the large German duchies had crumbled during the War of Investitures, the creation of more dukes, margraves and landgraves was thus perceived by the crown as a successful method for managing the princes.

---

[56] Otto of Freising and Rahewin, *Gesta Friderici* II, 49. The translation is by Mierow and Emery (1953), p. 164.

Lothar III had already appointed new landgraves and margraves, and endorsed Bishop Embrico of Würzburg's claims to be duke of eastern Franconia. Then in 1151 Conrad III had granted the archbishop of Cologne ducal status over the country between the Rhine and the Meuse. Apart from the division of Bavaria in 1156, Barbarossa created his half-brother Conrad count palatine of the Rhine in the same year, and commissioned Bishop Herold of Würzburg as duke of Franconia in 1168. The creation of more duchies followed the fall of Henry the Lion in 1180, by which time the court regarded the bishops and the senior secular magnates as an order of *principes imperii*, princes of the empire standing in immediate vassal relation to the crown (*Reichsfürstenstand*). As the emperor wrote to the church of Salzburg in 1177 on the subject, he desired to collect these princes around him and to benefit from their counsel, just as the pope was served by the college of cardinals. But it must be said that the emergence of the *Reichsfürstenstand* is a controversial question in modern scholarship. The label *princeps imperii*, 'prince of the empire', was in regular use long before 1177, and the *pax* of Worms in 1122 had already implied that the German episcopate constituted something like an ecclesiastical *Reichsfürstenstand* of vassals immediate to the crown.

Frederick Barbarossa thought highly of Henry the Lion, and already in 1154 had confirmed his rights of investiture in the three bishoprics recently restored in Saxony's colonial territory, as we have seen. Thereafter the Saxon duke, however much he was hated for his arrogant methods by the bishops and nobility of Saxony and the Rhineland, proved a reliable supporter of court policy down to 1176. This policy was primarily concerned with furthering the crown's rights, that *honor imperii* adumbrated in the convention agreed with the papacy at Constance in 1153. Between 1154 and 1178 Barbarossa conducted five expeditions to Italy in pursuit of such *honor*, but although so many German princes devoted their time and resources to these campaigns, the emperor's achievements in renewing his control of Italy were limited. The prominence of Italian affairs in Frederick Barbarossa's reign is in part to be explained by the success of the measures taken in Germany in the 1150s. This was called into question after the council of Pavia in 1160, for when Pope Alexander III excommunicated the emperor, the archdiocese of Salzburg repudiated the council's pope, Victor IV; Archbishop Conrad of Mainz had to be driven from his see for supporting the Alexandrine cause; and Duke Berthold IV of Zähringen wrote to the king of France to complain of the emperor as the destruction of the church and the law. Archbishop Rainald of Cologne as the principal adviser at court was nevertheless confident that Alexander III could be outfaced and negotiated an alliance with Henry II of England for the purpose. In Germany the imperial cause was sanctified by the canonization of Charlemagne in 1165 and reinforced by oaths taken from the church and aristocracy.

In spite of the failure of the siege of Rome in 1167, the late 1160s were still a time of success for the emperor. In 1168 he was able to enforce a reconciliation between Henry the Lion and the other Saxon princes, and in 1169 he secured the future of his dynasty by the election and coronation of Henry VI, the fifth of the eleven or twelve children born to him by Beatrice of Burgundy. The catastrophe before Rome turned out to be of benefit to the imperial house because the emperor was able to secure the rich inheritances of many princely families which had lost their heirs in the malarial infection: the reversion of the vast lands in Swabia from his uncle Welf VI; the titles and lands of Duke Frederick IV of Swabia, the emperor's cousin; the advocacy of the see of Augsburg; the huge fiefs held by the counts of Sulzbach from the bishop of Bamberg; and the possessions of Count Rudolf of Pfullendorf and Bregenz, to list only the most notable. In 1174 the emperor marched south once more against the Lombard cities and Alexander III but this Italian expedition, his fifth, also proved a failure upon his defeat at the battle of Legnano in 1176. However, Barbarossa's subsequent negotiations and his reconciliation with the pope at Venice in 1177 were prompt and successful, suggesting that the emperor was prepared for compromises even before losing the day at Legnano. Escorted by German forces, Alexander III returned to Rome to organize the Third Lateran Council and the emperor returned to Germany to cope with Henry the Lion, who was on the verge of repudiation by the majority of the north German bishops and lay princes for his cruel bellicosity.

Forty years before, in 1138 and 1139, it was the royal court which had planned the expulsion of Henry the Proud from Saxony and Bavaria, but now the Saxons themselves initiated the removal of his son. Although Gislebert of Mons described Henry the Lion as 'the mightiest of all dukes and almost the proudest and cruellest man ever',[57] the duke represented no threat to Frederick Barbarossa's rule, and previously the emperor had supported him against his enemies. Later sources did suggest that Frederick Barbarossa conceived a grudge against the duke for refusing further assistance to the imperial army in Italy in 1176, and that the duke resented Welf VI's preference for the emperor rather than himself as heir to the Welf lands in Swabia. Such ideas appear to be rationalizations, influenced by the conflict of the Welf and Staufen dynasties between 1198 and 1214, and then read back by chroniclers to explain Barbarossa's actions against the duke. However, it is also clear that by 1179 the emperor was obliged to change his attitude to Henry the Lion, and was forced to accept the argument that Henry the Lion was a peace-breaker. The duke was outlawed, and since he refused to answer the charges, he was deprived of all his fiefs early in 1180. The charter issued at Gelnhausen which reapportioned the Saxon fiefs

---

[57] Gislebert of Mons, *Chronicon Hanoniense* cap. XLVIII.

is the only source to set out the legal foundation for Henry the Lion's deposition in any detail. His oppression of the church and nobility broke the law of the land or *Landrecht*, and this, coupled with his contempt of repeated citations before the imperial court, raised the spectre of a treason accusation against him. However, the main proceedings were taken against him *sub feodali iure*, under feudal law, leading to the confiscation of his duchies which he held as fiefs from the empire.

After his submission in 1181 the duke legally retained the Saxon allodial possessions inherited from his grandparents, so that upon his return to Brunswick in 1184 he still figured as a formidable prince. For itself the crown acquired nothing from Henry the Lion's losses, for as the emperor explained to the bishop of Lübeck in 1181, he did not accept personal responsibility for Henry the Lion's humiliation and had saved what he could for his cousin. Frederick Barbarossa was, however, enabled to extend his conciliatory policy of the 1150s by granting more ducal titles upon the ruins of Henry the Lion's authority: Count Bernhard of Anhalt, Albert the Bear's son, became duke of Saxony; Archbishop Philip of Cologne became duke of Westphalia; Count Palatine Otto of Wittelsbach became duke of Bavaria; Margrave Otakar of Styria was promoted to duke, and Bogislav I of Stettin became duke of Pomerania. Apart from the archbishop, all these princes had been Henry the Lion's vassals. The duke's fall originated in his armed confrontation with the Saxon and Rhenish princes late in the 1170s and was not motivated by the court. Not until Otto IV, Henry the Lion's second surviving son, was elected king by a minority of princes in 1198 is it possible to demonstrate that the Welf family, however rich and powerful it may have been, presented a distinct institutional challenge to Staufen rule.

In spite of the peace between church and empire sworn at Venice in 1177, the last years of Barbarossa's reign as well as the reign of Henry VI were punctuated by quarrels with the papacy over their respective rights and resources in Italy. Nevertheless, that quest for the honour and glory of the empire which had so preoccupied the court throughout the twelfth century seemed to have been vindicated. In Germany Barbarossa issued new peace-keeping legislation in 1179 and in 1186 or 1188, as we have seen, and at Constance in 1183 he and Henry VI successfully concluded the negotiations opened in 1177 with the cities of Lombardy, which again accepted imperial sovereignty and paid tribute, although their affairs were to be administered by their own councils. In 1184 a magnificent assembly at Mainz celebrated the knighting of Henry VI and his brother Duke Frederick V of Swabia, and in 1186 the former was married, as we have seen, to Constance of Sicily as part of a diplomatic plan to confirm peace for good between the Normans, the papacy and the empire.

Upon the fall of Jerusalem to Saladin in 1187 the papacy preached a new crusade. At Mainz in 1188 the emperor therefore convened the German princes

to what was designated the *curia Ihesu Christi*, the court of Jesus Christ, took
the cross and proclaimed himself secular commander of the Third Crusade.
Princes at odds with the imperial court dutifully submitted. Henry VI was
appointed regent of the empire and since Henry the Lion was not prepared
to join the expedition, he agreed once more to go into exile. In spite of its
hazardous nature, this crusade raised Barbarossa to the height of his prestige,
inspiring new literary memorials to his glory and piety. He never reached the
Holy Land which he had last seen upon the Second Crusade as a young duke.
While conducting his army through Asia Minor, he was drowned in the River
Saleph in June 1190.

IMPERIAL DESTINIES UNDER HENRY VI

In some quarters the talented new ruler enjoyed an unenviable reputation for
cruelty. Several hostile sources credit Henry VI with arranging the assassination
in 1192 of Albert of Louvain, bishop-elect of Liège, the candidate confirmed by
the papacy, in order to secure the installation of his own nominee, Lothar of
Hochstaden. However, a careful examination of the material has shown that
there is no substance to the story of the emperor's involvement, although he did
very little to prosecute the assassins. There is not much doubt that Henry VI
was a capable guardian of imperial prerogatives and of the interest of his own
house. He held the papal curia in low esteem and his agents occupied the best
part of the Patrimony of St Peter and the Matildine lands, which the papacy
claimed as its own. So great was Henry VI's authority that he could incarcerate
the king of England, extract homage from him and glean a huge ransom which
paid for the conquest of Sicily in spite of the fact that, as a crusader, Richard
I stood under the personal protection of the pope. When William II of Sicily
died unexpectedly in 1189 the barons elected Tancred of Lecce as their king, but
Henry VI claimed the Sicilian crown in right of his wife, as we have seen. The
German invasion of 1191 was a failure, but in 1194 the kingdom was conquered
and Henry VI was crowned king of Sicily at Palermo.

After initial regional opposition to his rule in Germany inspired largely by
the disputed election of Liège, he was well served by churchmen, lay princes
and his own brothers with their commands in Swabia, Tuscany and Burgundy,
although his most capable generals were two of the imperial *ministeriales*,
Marshal Henry of Kalden and Seneschal Markward of Anweiler, who was
rewarded with an Italian dukedom. The emperor brought to a conclusion his
father's efforts to expand the royal fisc by taking possession of the march of
Meissen in 1195, although this acquisition was to prove temporary. The crown
had not possessed such extensive holdings since the tenth century, and the rise

of the agrarian and urban economies of twelfth-century Germany made such assets far more valuable to landowners than ever before.

Henry VI may have contemplated incorporating the Sicilian kingdom into the empire; in Germany in 1195 he styled himself 'by the grace of God emperor and always Augustus of the Romans and of the kingdom of Sicily and Apulia'.[58] As we have seen, he certainly desired to abolish royal election in favour of a hereditary empire, and it is possible that the crusade planned for 1197 and 1198 was intended to conquer the Byzantine empire on the way to Jerusalem so that one Roman emperor would reign both in the west and the east. The imperial chancery continued to proclaim, in language which the emperor himself could read, the honour and glory of the Roman empire which he and his predecessors were committed to defend and to improve. However, the stability of Staufen rule was suddenly undermined by Henry VI's unexpected death in September 1197 in his thirty-second year. In Germany a small but influential party of princes instigated by Archbishop Adolf I of Cologne's ambition to wrest the leading voice in royal elections from the see of Mainz rejected the Staufen succession apparently secured by Frederick II's election in 1196 and offered the crown to Duke Bernhard IV of Saxony and to Duke Berthold V of Zähringen who in turn prudently declined it, and then to Henry the Lion's second surviving son Otto of Brunswick, count of Poitou, who accepted. But the majority of influential princes had already decided to elect Henry VI's brother Duke Philip of Swabia in lieu of the infant Frederick II who was absent in Sicily and thereupon, as the Cologne annalist reported, 'A great war and exceedingly fearful dissension arose amongst the German princes about the empire',[59] justifying the sorrowful epitaph for Henry VI by Vincent of Prague's continuator: 'Upon the emperor's death, justice and peace in the empire also perished.'[60]

---

[58] *MGH Constitutiones* I, no. 367, p. 516.　　[59] *Chronica regia Coloniensis* for 1198.
[60] Gerlac of Milevsko, 'Chronicon' for 1198.

NORTHERN AND CENTRAL ITALY
IN THE TWELFTH CENTURY

Giovanni Tabacco

THE KINGDOM OF ITALY AND THE PAPAL STATES IN THE
TIME OF LOTHAR II AND CONRAD III

The Salian dynasty died out in 1125 and Lothar of Supplinburg, duke of Saxony, came to the throne, in accordance with the wishes of both the German episcopate and Pope Honorius II. However the election in Germany of an anti-king in 1128, in the person of Conrad of the Swabian Staufen, involved Italy, for Conrad sought support there against Lothar, succeeding in having himself crowned with all solemnity by Archbishop Anselm of Milan, then in disagreement with Honorius II for ecclesiastical reasons. As a member of the house of Swabia Conrad considered himself heir, through kinship, to the allodial patrimonia which had belonged to Henry V. He also claimed lands which Henry had occupied in Italy as heir to Matilda of Canossa, a claim destined to give rise to conflicts with the Roman church, to which Matilda had given her possessions before the agreement drawn up with Henry V in 1111. Neither the coronation in Italy nor his claims to Matilda's estates strengthened Conrad's cause during these years and in 1130 he returned to Germany, where he engaged in a fruitless quarrel with Lothar.

Honorius II died in the same year, giving rise to a papal schism between Innocent II and Anacletus II. This schism reflected disagreement among the cardinals, although by this time they had all moved towards the idea of a reforming pontificate, and disagreement between the two families which had now become the most powerful in Rome, the Frangipani, who supported Innocent, and the Pierleoni, who upheld Anacletus. Anacletus prevailed in the city itself and Innocent took refuge in France, where a council pronounced in his favour, in part because of the eloquence of Bernard of Clairvaux. Lothar then overcame his own irresolution and descended into Italy in support of Pope Innocent. He stayed in Lombardy, divided between the hostility of Milan and Crema and the allegiance of Pavia, Cremona, Piacenza and other cities.

Accompanied by Innocent, he pushed on to Rome where he was crowned emperor in 1133, while much of the city remained in the hands of Anacletus, who was supported by the Norman Roger II of Sicily and Apulia. The understanding between Lothar and Innocent also involved the problem of the allodial lands which had belonged to Matilda. The emperor recognized the rights of the church of Rome to these properties, but obtained the usufruct against the payment of an annuity and was recognized by Matilda's vassals.

In the years following Lothar's return to Germany the Tuscan march and the allodial lands of Matilda were placed under the supervision of the emperor's representatives, until in 1136 Lothar, entreated by Pope Innocent to take action against the menacing power of Roger II, once more crossed into Italy. He took upon himself the function of judge and arbiter in the disputes between the Lombard cities and found against Cremona and Milan, which had been reconciled with Innocent II. In a diet held at Roncaglia, in the middle of the Po valley, he promulgated a feudal law to regulate relations between client vassals and their lords, stressing the rights of the latter over their vassals and the obligations of these lords towards the empire. After having thus exercised his power as king of northern Italy with remarkable authority, he organized the expedition agreed upon with the pope against Roger II, under his own command and that of the duke of Bavaria, his son-in-law Henry the Proud, of the powerful house of Welf. The invasion of the kingdom took place in 1137, but led to dissension between papacy and empire, over the legal problems of southern Italy and the abbey of Monte Cassino. Above all Innocent II was concerned at Henry the Proud's power in Germany and Italy; Henry was duke of both Saxony and Bavaria, and he had been granted the Tuscan march as well as the usufruct of the allodial lands of Matilda.

The expedition into southern Italy was interrupted. Lothar returned to Germany, where he died at the end of 1137, after having designated Henry the Proud his successor. Nevertheless, papal concern about Henry's power, combined with that of the German electors, led to the choice of Conrad of Swabia, who years earlier had been anti-king in both Germany and Italy. The subsequent break between Conrad III and Henry, who was formally stripped of his German duchies, and the sudden death of Henry himself, made it possible for the king to maintain his position in Germany and to reclaim it in Italy, by virtue of the inheritance which had come to him from Henry V of Franconia and the allodial lands of Matilda. He was still not in effective control of the kingdom, however. The Tuscan march entrusted by the king to Ulric of Attemo was not a success, as Ulric acted autonomously, allying himself with first one then another of the city communes. Nor was the march of Verona, entrusted to Herman, margrave of Baden. Conrad III, deeply involved as he was in the problems of Germany, never went to Italy after succeeding Lothar to the German throne, although he seriously entertained the idea of an Italian campaign, either to obtain the imperial crown or oppose Roger II of Sicily as an ally of the Byzantine empire. The arduous and unfortunate crusade against the Muslims in the east kept him far from the European theatre during 1147 and 1148. On his return to Germany he made preparations for the Italian expedition, but death struck him down in February 1152 before his plan could be put into effect.

If German control over the kingdom of Italy declined rapidly after the time of Lothar III, this was even more the case in the regions which were theoretically papal – from the regions of Ferrara and Ravenna to Lazio. Political forces sprang into action everywhere from the Alps to the borders of the Norman kingdom in the south, in the form of innumerable noble dynasties and city communes.

The hegemony of the city of Milan over Lombardy increased both at the economic and the commercial level as well as in the military and political sphere, through control of communications. The wars it waged against Como in the north, in the lake region, and Pavia, the old capital of the kingdom, almost at the confluence of the Ticino and the Po to the south, and above all against powerful Cremona in the south-east, made clear the extent of its ascendancy over a region, by this time divided into communal republics, that stretched from the lakes in the foothills of the Alps to the middle of the Po. The government of each of the cities in this region, hinged on the institution of the consul, took precedence over the rural lordships with their dynastic structure, whether episcopal, monastic or canonical, which in their turn, dispersed as they were throughout the countryside, were superimposed on rural groupings in the process of communal organization. City government often cooperated with the remaining temporal powers of the resident bishop. The supremacy of Milan over its neighbouring city communes, sometimes, as in the case of Lodi, bitterly contested, created a wider territorial coordination with an extended field of action.

In eastern Lombardy, from Bergamo to Mantua, between the region of Milanese predominance and the marches of Verona, the autonomy of the communes over the cities and their surrounding rural areas coexisted with the temporal power of the bishops. Brescia took on a particular prominence, for there the political rivalry between the city and the bishop was complicated by the preaching of Arnold of Brescia, who was in rebellion against ecclesiastical authority. The power of the counts in the territory of Brescia and Mantua died with the passing of Countess Matilda and in the district of Bergamo was transformed into a seigneurial power exercised in conjunction with the inherited estates of the various branches of the Giselbertini counts.

Similarly, the march of Verona saw the authority of the marquesses weaken in favour of that of the city, the powerful churches and the families descended from the counts. The counts of Vicenza, Padua and Treviso, and in the Verona region the counts of San Bonifacio and those of Gandolfingi took on the character of noble dynasties prevailing over certain regions of old districts which had had a public tradition. In the southern part of the territory of Padua and the neighbouring lands of Ferrara, the dominion of the Este developed. The name belongs to an eastern and independent branch of the great family of the marquesses of Obertenghi, of Ligurian origin but present particularly in the north-west Apennines through both their inherited estates and their jurisdictional powers. The ecclesiastical entities also preserved full legal and military force where their holdings were especially dense: in particular the bishopric, cathedral chapter and monastery of San Zeno at Verona, the bishopric of Vicenza, the bishopric and cathedral chapter of Padua, the bishopric of Treviso, which was endowed with an exceptionally powerful apparatus of vassals and officials, and the bishopric of Belluno. The cities, meanwhile, increased their autonomy, in the midst of all these very conspicuous seigneuries, both ecclesiastical and secular and interwoven both with them and with the lesser nobility, although often in conflict with them. Verona in particular emerged, distinguished by its economic power, for there a rich merchant class operated in conjunction with the military caste.

To the north and east of the Veneto the ecclesiastical principalities of Trento and Aquileia maintained and indeed consolidated their positions in the Trentino and Friuli respectively, supported by an apparatus of vassals and officials. The bishopric of Trento remained under the influence of the German crown, while the patriarchate of Aquileia was under that of both Germany and the pope. In the Lagoon of Venice, Venice itself, governed completely independently by its doge with his lifetime rule and by its merchant princes, allied with the Byzantine empire and opposed to the aspirations of the Norman kingdom of the south, monopolized trade between the Adriatic and Europe, strengthening its own political presence on the Istrian and Dalmatian coasts and defending itself against the kingdom of Hungary's penetration into Dalmatia and its interference in the lives of the Italian coastal cities on the opposite side of the Adriatic.

A political fabric analagous in its composition to that of eastern Lombardy and the Verona march, with a similar tendency to develop from a predominantly urban area into territorially based principalities with feudal structures, was found to the west of the preponderantly Milan-influenced region, corresponding to present-day Piedmont: from the Ticino to the western Alps. North of the Po, the communes of Novara and Vercelli and – more timidly – Ivrea coexisted with the powerful dominion of the bishops, based upon the cities. Within the territory of Novara, the counts of Biandrate were also vigorously active, and in that of Ivrea, the many branches of the family of the counts of Canavese. They were descendants of families who originally held title to public districts, but their vigour was by this time largely the result of the castles and vassals subjected to them in the rural world. On the Po, the commune of Turin asserted its autonomy at the expense of the temporal power of the bishop resident in that city. Similarly, to the south of the Po, the flourishing commune of Asti, then expanding commercially particularly in its relations with France, coexisted with the great territorial dominion of the bishop. From 1135, it felt threatened by the expansionism of the Marquess William V of Montferrat, who had become the most noteworthy among the numerous representatives of the great Aleramici family. In the tenth century this family had held a march which extended from Savona, on the shores of the Ligurian Sea, all the way to the Po, but the march was subsequently broken up into several marquisates, whose fortunes were changing and various.

The Aleramici had also penetrated the march of Turin, dissolved in 1091 on the death of Countess Adelaide. In it a branch of the family was by this date building up what came to be known as the marquisate of Saluzzo. On this side of the Alps there remained in the possession of the descendants of Adelaide of Turin and her husband Odo, count of Maurienne in Burgundy – the line afterwards known as Savoy – only the valleys of Aosta and Susa. From the plains of Piedmont and the Ligurian coast, across the mountainous band of the Ligurian Alps and Ligurian Apennines there lay, in the Obertenga march from west to east, a succession of Aleramici marquisates. But on the coast, the city-communes of Albenga, Savona and Genoa were now acting with remarkable freedom, in spite of some disagreements among themselves. These conflicts arose from the attempt by Genoa, which originally belonged to the march of the Obertenga, to control both the cities and the nobles who for the most part bore the titles of counts or marquesses, throughout the whole coastal region. The city needed to create a secure hinterland for its economic life and commercial expansion on the seas, an expansion which also gave rise to conflict with Pisa over the control of Corsica. Genoa's prestige and influence were increased by its being raised to the seat of an archbishopric with the consequent diminution of the ecclesiastical province of Milan, following the papal and royal schisms and the related dispute between Innocent II and the archbishop of Milan.

Thus, throughout the whole of north-west Italy the relationship between episcopal and dynastic seigneuries and city-republics was becoming clear, with ruling families prevailing in the harsh and economically backward areas and cities on the plain and along the coast. The same pattern occurs south of the middle course of the Po and along the Emilian Way, where the cities of Piacenza, Parma, Reggio and Modena asserted their own communal governments in the face of the temporal authority of the bishops and the nobility in the rural areas. Among the latter should be numbered, at least as regards the territories of Reggio and Modena, the numerous vassals, clients of the Countess Matilda, who were now claimed by the German kings and by the papacy. In the high valleys of the Tuscan–Emilian Apennines but also continuing on as far as the sea and the plain, various branches of the Obertenghi held sway; foremost among them the Malaspina.

Similar complexities are also to be found in the Tuscan march, again related to the degree of economic development. Pisa, seat of an archbishopric from 1092, held first place on the Tyrrhenian coast as a city-commune with a complex network of ties between clergy and laity. In the north it came into conflict with Lucca, the old capital of the march, and in Corsica with Genoa; it penetrated Sardinia, using the Tyrrhenian Sea as a base from which it spread both its commercial and military activities throughout a large part of the Mediterranean – even, in conjunction with the crusades, to the Orient. Inland, economic and political supremacy in Tuscany was held by the commune of Florence, alternately the ally and adversary of other city-communes such as Pisa, Lucca and Pistoia, as far as Siena and the predominantly episcopal city of Arezzo. At the same time Florence was in competition – as were the other cities – with various noble dynasties. These dynasties were rooted in regions which were harsh and wild in terms of both landscape and population, from the slopes of the Apennines to the areas of transition between one urban district and the next. From north to south, the Guidi counts in the Romagna Apennines and the Casentino were succeeded by the Ubaldini of the Mugello, the Alberti counts of Prato, the Ubertini of the upper Valdarno, the Berardenghi, Ardengheschi and Scialenghi in Sienese territory and, finally, the powerful Aldobrandeschi counts of southern Tuscany.

Even the lands which were theoretically papal witnessed the coexistence of a number of heterogeneous political entities, mostly autonomous and in competition with each other. In Bologna, in full economic and cultural expansion as a centre for legal studies, the authority of the counts waned to the advantage of the commune and its expansion along the Emilian Way, giving rise to conflict with Modena to the west and Imola to the east, as well as with the emperor Lothar. Bologna attracted into its political sphere the famous abbey of Nonantola and certain elements from among the client vassals of the late Countess Matilda. Further to the north, the commune of Ferrara, its autonomy consolidated after the death of Matilda and operating in collaboration with the bishop of the city, found itself in conflict with the claims of the archbishop of Ravenna and the papacy, who claimed – although also in mutual disagreement – ultimate temporal jurisdiction over the whole territory of Ferrara and Romagna as well. The commune of Ravenna, under the hegemony of urban military families owing their origin in part to ancient links with the administration and bearing ducal names, operated for the most part in agreement with the prevailing power of the archbishop, but at the same time took an extremely lively share, by means of both law and force, in the activities of the other cities of Romagna. The presence of noble families, often bearing the titles of counts and holding an independent position within the life of the episcopal and communal cities of Romagna and the surrounding countryside, is to be found again in an analogous fashion in the march of Ancona and the duchy of Spoleto. There march and duchy were elements within the imperial framework, but functioning fairly weakly when faced with the usual interweaving of local aristocracy and city.

In Lazio, the papal schism, which lasted from 1130 to 1139, jeopardized the gradual political recovery which the reforming papacy was bringing about vis-à-vis the noble families and the city-states from the borders of the duchy of Spoleto all the way to Terracina. With the end of the schism, the process of recovery was resumed, as can be clearly seen in the case of Tivoli, which yielded to Innocent II in 1143. But the most serious problem for the papal domination was to be the city of Rome itself, which just then, deluded by the insufficiently severe conditions imposed upon Tivoli by Innocent at its pacification, rose in its turn against the pope and organized its own senate. From 1147, during the pontificate of Eugenius III, political activity in the city also took on a religious hue, thanks to Arnold of Brescia. The high-sounding letters addressed to the German king Conrad III, who aspired to the emperor's crown, bear witness to the high conceit in which the Romans then held the universal significance of their city. But the king acted prudently and the Roman commune was compelled to become reconciled with Eugenius. These developments in Rome were the most striking indication of the changes which were taking place throughout central and northern Italy to the advantage of the city-states.

FROM THE COMING OF BARBAROSSA TO THE PEACE OF COSTANZA

After the death of Conrad III in 1152, his nephew Frederick of Swabia was chosen to succeed him to the throne. He was descended, on his mother's side, from the house of Welf and was thus in a position to conciliate the two great rival lineages. Among Frederick's first actions was the allotment of the Tuscan march, the duchy of Spoleto and the allodial lands which had belonged to the Countess Matilda, to Welf VI, his maternal uncle. This meant that the house of Welf was granted political dominance, under royal aegis, in central Italy. Meanwhile, requests for the king's immediate presence came from the people of Rome and from Eugenius III, who were competing to offer him the imperial crown, and from Lombardy, where the predominance of the Milanese limited the independence of the other cities and led to disputes, particularly in Lodi. It seemed, after so many absences and misadventures, that the royal and imperial authority of the German monarchs was now becoming no more than an element in the political games played among the local powers in Italy, which all tried to make use of the empire in their quarrels. And since, in this closely played game, Milan was emerging as the centre of attraction and organization in northern Italy, the centrifugal forces, faced with its predominance, saw in the new king, who had a high opinion of his own dignity in Germany and had succeeded in balancing noble forces, a reference point around which their own interests crystallized.

Among these essentially centrifugal forces, there were also some dynasties with extensive fields of action; in the first place, the Aleramica marquisate of Montterrat and the counts of Biandrate. The marquess of Montferrat, William V, a close relative of Barbarossa, and Count Guido of Biandrate, his brother-in-law, were constantly with the king in 1154, when he visited Italy for the first time. They contributed towards inclining him against the cities of Chieri and Asti, which opposed the territorial ambitions of the Biandrate and the Montferrats and were consequently proscribed by the empire and ruined. The king formally conferred upon the marquess rights and supremacy over Asti and the neighbouring fortress of Annone in the heart of the region over which William wished to exert his supremacy. As regards Count Guido, he had been in Germany even before Frederick's descent into Italy and had obtained confirmation of a large number of holdings he possessed in northern Piedmont, in particular between the Rivers Sesia and Ticino, as well as revenues from seigneurial income and rights of a public nature. But it should be mentioned that if the Marquess William was acting in a geographical region that was relatively backward in comparison to powerful Milan and was thus freer in his political and military movements and in furthering the anti-Milanese policies of the king, Count Guido was, on the other hand, operating on the margins and within the large area under Milanese domination. He therefore maintained an uncertain balance between adherence to the king and the respect demanded by that great urban centre, the major driving force behind Lombard activity. One can say that Guido most clearly represented the state in which the more evolved parts of the kingdom of Italy found themselves, economically and politically, uncertain. They were divided between the defence of local interests, the lure of an ancient urban centre, with its basic structures strengthened and renewed and well aware of its real function as a regional fulcrum, and the opposite appeal of a prince, foreign to the very distinctive culture of Italy, but cloaked in a royal title and with imperial expectations, surrounded by the noblest representatives of the aristocracy of his kingdoms and supported by an armed force which moved with him; consecrated in Germany and reconsecrated in Italy, at Pavia and Rome, as the legitimate and supreme guarantor of justice among his subjects.

At the end of 1154, in a great diet of the Italian kingdom held at Roncaglia, Frederick promulgated a feudal law, following the example of Lothar III in 1136. Fiefs illegitimately transferred to vassals were returned to the lord and the rules for hereditary transmission were to be rigorously respected. It was an attempt to integrate the itinerant forces of the king, restoring the efficiency of a politico-military organization operating throughout the length and breadth of the kingdom, by means of a hierarchy of allegiances involving the nobles, ecclesiastics and their vassals. The question of the cities seemed equally basic, but in the royal policies it was considered apart, fundamentally in terms of general submission and respect for the hierarchy of the nobility, and of a balance between the cities themselves. The coronation at Rome, on the other hand, was an urgent matter and it was performed in 1155 by the new Pope Adrian IV, in compliance with an agreement drawn up two years earlier at Costanza between the representatives of Frederick and Eugenius III for mutual protection against the dynamism of the Normans and Byzantines in Italy and the agressiveness of Rome and her senate. The most illustrious victim of this agreement was Arnold of Brescia, who fell into the hands of Frederick, was handed over to the representatives of Adrian IV and put to death.

The exiguousness of the military forces available to Frederick when he first entered Italy did not prevent him from taking punitive and destructive action against the cities of Chieri, Asti, Tortona and Spoleto, but did not allow him to take action against the Norman south. For this reason, Adrian IV, after the emperor's return to Germany, reached the Concordat of Benevento with William I of Sicily in 1156. In 1158, under the auspices of the pope, there was a rapprochement between King William and the Byzantine emperor Manuel Komnenos. These were changes prompted by the absence of the Germans and it was this same absence which allowed Milan to prevail once again over Lodi, fight Pavia, foster the rebuilding of Tortona and prevent William of Montferrat from opposing the enterprise of Asti, notwithstanding the charter issued in his favour by the king in 1154. Barbarossa's second entry into Italy took place in the summer of 1158, with military forces considerably greater than those employed four years earlier and subsequently augmented by contingents sent by the great Italian lords of numerous cities. At the end of a month-long siege, Milan surrendered. At the succeeding diet of Roncaglia, a catalogue of royal rights was drawn up, with the aid of the greatest jurists of Bologna. The list went from the appointment of magistrates, both in the cities and the provinces, to the collection of taxes on roads, water, ports, markets, coinage, the contributions levied to provide for the transfer of the king and his army to Italy and fines for infractions of laws. All the rights of the sovereign were declared imprescriptible, with no regard, therefore, being paid to the time-honoured customs of Italy, except where their precise content was explicitly granted in royal confirmatory charters.

This was not a matter of simple theoretical formulae, as was shown most signally by Frederick's intervention in the affairs of numerous cities to influence the choice of a *podestà* responsible for the communal government and faithful to the empire. The emperor, however, in his pursuit of general political control over northern Italy, was forced to accept many compromises, in his relationships with both lords and cities, granting privileges to those entities reliably effective in their offers of support. This is what happened to the commune of Asti at the beginning of 1159. Having succeeded, by its energetic action, in demonstrating the discrepancy between the ambitions of the marquess of Montferrat, nurtured by imperial favour, and his effective political and military capacity, the city was received back into the emperor's favour and obtained confirmation of its civil jurisdiction over a large number of the surrounding villages. At this point it became clear even to Barbarossa that what counted above all in the Po valley were the cities and that an understanding with them was essential. Faced, however, with the persistent reluctance of Milan to accept the heavy conditions imposed upon it, the imperial struggle against this city and its allies flared up once again and continued until the destruction of Milan in the spring of 1162. These events took place against the background of the complications caused by the papal schism, which had dragged on since 1159. With the defeat of Milan, Frederick reached the height of his predominance in northern Italy. His inability to follow a coherent policy with the well-established princes of the kindom of Italy is very obvious from the range of conditions negotiated with the cities, always relating to interests contingent on the imperial power. A particularly striking example is the vast concessions made to Genoa and Pisa all along the Tyrrhenian coast, when Frederick hoped to make use of their navies against the kingdom of Sicily, the main obstacle to his supremacy in Italy.

In actual fact, Barbarossa found himself faced with too many problems at the same time. The development of the papal schism in favour of Alexander III in various regions of western Europe led him in the summer of 1162 to defer the expedition against the Normans and to leave Italy for the kingdom of Burgundy. He sent Rainald of Dassel, the most commanding and energetic of his counsellors, to Italy. Rainald, who had been elected archbishop at Cologne, broadened the empire's field of direct action in central Italy, depriving Welf VI and his son Welf VII of authority in the Tuscan march and the duchy of Spoleto and uniting himself with the local lords and cities in these regions, as well as in the march of Ancona and in Romagna, while making considerable use of German functionaries. When the emperor returned to Italy for the third time in the autumn of 1163, dissatisfaction with these imperial officers was already spreading throughout northern Italy, until in the following spring rebellion broke out among the cities of the Veneto, closely united in a league drawn up at Verona and much encouraged by the support of Venice. The military reaction of the emperor was unsuccessful and he returned to Germany to seek reinforcements.

In Germany, however, Frederick found himself involved in both local and European problems. Moreover, the ideological climate fed by the events of the papal schism induced him to promote the commemorative rites for Charlemagne, declared a saint very obviously with a view to obtaining the supremacy of the empire throughout Christendom. When in the autumn of 1166 he returned for the fourth time to Italy, his mind was dominated by the problem of the persistent papal schism. After some months of political and military preparations, he headed for Ancona, confederate of the emperor Manuel Komnenos and in rebellion, and then to Rome, from which Alexander III was forced to flee. Meanwhile, in 1167 the Lombard League was formed and spread, born in imitation of, and developed from, the League of Verona of 1164. Frederick's move south made possible a full-scale rebellion in the Po valley. Milan was rebuilt and with this event, Lombardy vigorously returned to the line of regional political development, which Milan's rivals had tried for a number of years to counter by coordinating their forces around Barbarossa. The alternative failed on account of the disillusion felt everywhere at the corruption of the German officials.

Frederick's expedition in central Italy failed on account of an epidemic which broke out in his army. In 1168, he returned to Germany. Meanwhile the Lombard League, from the Veneto to western Emilia and eastern Piedmont, organized itself into a sworn alliance of free cities – although the marquess Obizzo Malaspina soon joined it too. This alliance was allied to Alexander III, in honour of whom the name Alexandria was given to a new city founded in eastern Piedmont to resist the marquess of Montferrat. Pope Alexander did his best in his turn to help the united cities to act conjointly, threatening anyone who wished to secede from the league or disobey its governors with interdicts and excommunication. The league in fact served not only as a military alliance, but also as an association – *societas* – directed by a college of rectors. Its aim was to obtain from the empire recognition of the political, administrative and jurisdictional conditions which individual members of the league had arrived at through long tradition and which had remained in force all the way up to the new decrees promulgated at Roncaglia in 1158. Thus the absolute and indefeasible sovereignty of the empire, which Frederick had claimed on the authority of Roman Law up-dated by the researches of the Italian jurists, found itself under challenge.

Problems in Germany and central Europe kept Frederick at home for six years. His fifth expedition to Italy in 1174 led to an unsuccessful siege of Alexandria, unsuccessful negotiations with the rebel cities and the celebrated military engagement at Legnano, between Milan and the Ticino, in 1176. The defeated emperor again began negotiations and, since the cities had no wish to forsake the cause of Alexander III, solemnly met with Alexander at Venice in 1177 and put an end, at least as far as he was concerned, to the schism. A truce was arranged with the Lombard League, until the peace of Costanza, on the Reno, was agreed in 1183. During the long wait, the league showed signs of disintegrating and Frederick signs of a resigned moderation.

The peace treaty confirmed the profound changes which had come about in the relationship between the rival parties. It was presented formally as a privilege granted in perpetuity by the emperor, who in this way confirmed his position as the supreme source of legitimation. In the actual content, however, rights born of custom – implying a broad autonomy for the communes, with urban jurisdiction in general extending also over the surrounding countryside and sometimes over an even wider area – were tempered by norms which ensured the ruler ultimate political and jurisdictional control. The right of the cities to choose their consuls as heads of the commune was recognized, but it was anticipated that the consuls would receive their investiture from the sovereign or his representative, swearing loyalty to him, except where the custom of certain cities demanded that he be placed under the temporal power of the bishop. It was established that in the exercise of justice, appeals against the sentences of city bodies should, in matters of greater importance, be referred to the emperor, but that the emperor was to delegate the actual judgement to his own representative in the city or within the bounds of the diocese, who would be under the obligation to pass judgement according to the city's laws and customs. The right of the cities to erect fortifications and make pacts was recognized and their duty to help the empire preserve and recover its rights and possessions in Lombardy and to subsidize the sovereign on his visits to the region were established. The position of the emperor at the head of the feudal hierarchy was confirmed and the duty of loyalty towards the empire on the part of all citizens was specified.

The resolutions taken at Costanza give an over-view of the orderly state that the kingdom of Italy was beginning to assume after decades of tension and struggle between Frederick and the Lombards and years of wearisome negotiations for a balanced peace. Fundamental was the treatment by the empire of feudal lords and city-republics as parallel. It must be made clear above all that the legally established feudal seigneuries with a certain degree of political and jurisdictional independence originated to some extent in the functions of count or marquess exercised for more than a century by the great families of the kingdom, by their individual branches or by their vassals, and in part in the allodial seigneuries. Already in the period before Barbarossa there had been a certain spontaneous tendency to turn these allodial seigneuries into feudal ones by taking on the obligations of vassalage towards a lord dominant in territorial terms, or directly towards the empire. Subsequently, Frederick's chancery was apt to distinguish between the allodial possession of seigneurial holdings and the exercise of powers of jurisdiction, which were considered to be of a public nature and susceptible to legitimization and inheritance only if conferred by the ruler, directly or indirectly, through feudal investiture. In this way the whole varied political world of the nobility tended to organize itself into that feudal hierarchy culminating in the sovereign which the edict on fiefs, promulgated in Italy by Conrad II, had postulated as early as 1037 and which Lothar III in 1136 and Frederick in 1154 had tried to consolidate. But henceforth the noble world of the kingdom of Italy was to become ever more limited and controlled and indeed often actually incorporated into the communal republics. This occurred not only as a result of the spontaneous economic and territorial development of the city-states, but also to some extent through the military solidarity widely established in 'Lombardy' in reaction to the centralization which Barbarossa obstinately insisted upon. Hence the fundamental importance of the parallelism which came to be established between the self-governing cities and the independent seigneuries.

It is true that the terms of investiture and fealty no longer had a technically feudal value except where they existed in conjunction with the relationship of vassalage or that of beneficiary. The importance conferred by the imperial investiture of the consuls and the swearing of allegiance by consuls and citizens in the negotiations which led to the peace of 1183 revealed an intention to provide a substantial juridical equivalence which represented for the cities the guarantee of a stable autonomy and which also acted as a guarantee for the empire, under the hierarchic profile of subordination. Everything naturally depended on the real possibility that the equilibrium of forces postulated by the peace of Costanza should function, with a notable difference in political weight and position among the cities which had subscribed to it. This was an equilibrium which needed, as fulcrum of the new Italian situation, collaboration between the itinerant curia of the emperor and Milan's restored centrality in Lombardy. The problem of central Italy in any case remained open, since the peace of Costanza only dealt with relations between Frederick and the members of the Lombard League.

THE DECLINE OF BARBAROSSA AND THE AGE OF HENRY VI

In central Italy, from the time when Rainald of Dassel developed direct relations between the empire and the nobility and cities in 1163, the imperial organization was maintained with noteworthy stability, above all through the long period of activity of the imperial legate in Tuscany, Christian, archbishop-elect of Mainz. This was obviously only a relative stability because of the disturbances the papal schism continued to provoke, more directly in central Italy than elsewhere. Small nuclei of German troops were permanently stationed in many fortified places in Tuscany, under the command of castellans and counts appointed by the empire, who could be removed from their posts by the emperor. They should not therefore be confused with those counts and lords of the feudal and dynastic tradition who made up the regional aristocracy and were endowed with the usual autonomy, although these too were often linked to the imperial authority, as were the larger monastic bodies. The most important German military centre was at San Miniato, near the Arno between Pisa and Florence. This system of imperial political control normally had the support of the powerful republic of Pisa, which unlike the other city-communes of Tuscany often obtained from the empire liberal recognition of its freedom of action and territorial expansion. Conflicts between Pisa and the empire did take place, but they occurred for the most part when tensions between Genoa and Pisa involved the empire, which needed the fleets of both republics, as for example in 1164 over the question of Sardinia, when Genoa, through rivalry with Pisa in the Tyrrhenian Sea, induced the emperor to concede official recognition of the title to rule and supremacy over the island to a local dynasty. The empire thus found itself in conflict with Pisa, which in the end obtained a reversal of the imperial mandate and recognition of its own supremacy over the island. This was in any case in greater conformity with the real situation in Sardinia, although it was contested by Genoa afterwards and led to further imperial involvement.

Parallel to what was taking place in Tuscany, a strong imperial presence was developing in these same years – the 60s and 70s – in the neighbouring regions which were theoretically papal. In Romagna relations with the archbishop and individual cities were close. In the march of Ancona a marquisate was created for the whole region under imperial nomination. Similarly, in the duchy of Spoleto the imperial legate ended by formally taking the title of duke. In Lazio the activity of Barbarossa and his representatives assumed the character of sovereign protection of the nobles and citizens, which was also extended, accompanied by grave conflict, to the city of Rome. The peace of 1177 with Alexander III gave rise to papal protests against persistent imperial intrusions, but produced no noteworthy consequences on the political and territorial plane, except for the city of Rome, which the empire renounced and which alternated between submission to the papacy and renewed attempts at civic autonomy and territorial expansion.

These various developments in central Italy were not interrupted in the years following the peace of Costanza, which therefore implies that the profound adjustment in imperial political policy applied only to Northern Italy. In 1184 Frederick visited Italy for the sixth and last time, after a six-year absence, and acted in close unison with Milan in Lombardy. At the beginning of 1185 he took part in a meeting of the rectors of the Lombard League at Piacenza. The league was by then in decline, but it was still a symbol of Lombard autonomy, against which the emperor had fought with such tenacity for decades. This was followed by the recognition of the formal right of the commune of Milan to exercise jurisdiction over a series of countships from Lake Maggiore and the Ticino to the basin of the Adda. In exchange, the Milanese undertook to support the rights of the empire, especially over those allodial estates which had previously belonged to the Countess Matilda and which Barbarossa, disregarding papal claims, had granted to Welf VI in 1152; Welf had renounced them. At the beginning of 1186 there were celebrated in Milan both the marriage of Henry VI to Constance of Altavilla, with a view to the possible succession to the kingdom of Sicily, and Henry's solemn coronation as king of Italy by the patriarch of Aquileia. The double ceremony celebrated in the Lombard capital served, as it were, to consecrate the political link established between the Staufen and their destiny in an Italian context and the restored and consolidated supremacy of Milan from the Alps to the Apennines. Similarly, the operations conducted in June by the German forces, together with those of Milan and other 'Lombard' cities against Cremona, once most faithful to Barbarossa and always a more or less stubborn rival of Milan, sealed their military collaboration.

Set against this situation in northern Italy was the German dynamism in central Italy. Here the leading role was now entrusted to the daring and tenacity of Henry VI, the new king of Italy. His father continued to try in vain to induce the papacy to add the imperial crown to the rule of Germany and Italy, for the greater security of Henry's future succession as supreme political leader of Christendom. While Frederick was taking action against Cremona, Henry was undertaking military operations in Tuscany against the expansion of the commune of Siena and in support of the autonomy claimed by noble dynasties in Sienese territory. This harmonized with a recent decision taken by Frederick: to remove from the Tuscan cities, with the exception of Pisa and Pistoia, public jursidiction over the lands they had conquered.

In the summer of 1186, after the surrender of Siena and while the emperor was on his way back to Germany, Henry VI broadened his political and military operations, carrying them out of Tuscany into the lands formerly belonging to the papacy, and entered into negotiations with the aristocracy of Rome. This corresponded with his unswerving concept of a supreme imperial responsibility, even in the regions depending on the papacy; but it also arose from the disagreements between Pope Urban III and the empire over a number of serious ecclesiastical questions. After the death of Urban III and the news of the fall of Jerusalem to the Muslims, papacy and empire drew together under the aegis of preparations for the Third Crusade, which also enabled Henry VI to leave Italy to join his father in Germany, where, in March 1188, the great assembly of Mainz was held and Barbarossa took the cross. Henry VI then assumed the regency of the whole empire.

After the death of the king of Sicily, William II, in the autumn of 1189, a few months before Barbarossa himself perished in the east, Henry claimed the succession to the kingdom of Sicily, both in the name of his wife Constance and in order to restore, as he himself said, 'the ancient right of the Empire', based on his universal claims and, more specifically, on the concept of an Italian kingdom extending over the whole peninsula, following a tradition going back to the Lombards and the Franks. The conquest of the south thus appeared to be the logical conclusion of the German ascendancy in Italy and turned imperial ambitions towards the Mediterranean. The control of central and northern Italy took on a fundamental importance in the vast political context which resulted from this, as an essential bridge, territorial and ideological, between the military force of the German kingdom and the new Mediterranean horizons of Swabian power. And in this ancient Italian link between the north and the south of Europe, the fleets of Genoa and Pisa acted in their turn as a fulcrum, when in 1194 Henry VI's conquest of the south attained its end. It was not indeed easy to make use of this fulcrum, because, although powerful, it was split by rivalries between the two very active sea-faring republics both in the Tyrrhenian Sea and in the east and by each city's internal dissensions. Henry had to confirm all the jurisdictional and territorial privileges which Barbarossa had already granted to both cities in Tuscany and in the Tyrrhenian islands and he was generous with contradictory promises regarding their commercial and political establishments in the kingdom to be conquered. The promises were not subsequently honoured, to the great disappointment of the two cities. This was an indication of the difficulties which imperial expansion created in the course of maintaining German control over central and northern Italy, difficulties which were further exacerbated by its new orientation towards Milan as a power.

In fact, from 1190 on, as soon as the death of Barbarossa in the east became known and Henry made preparations to return to Italy to claim the imperial crown, the problems of Lombardy and Tuscany once again became matters of prime importance for the German kingdom. Faced with the tangled rivalries of the city-communes, the king abandoned the position adopted by Barbarossa after the peace of Costanza. Instead of accepting Milanese superiority and associating it with the imperial interests in central Italy, Henry attempted a freer form of political action along the road which led to Rome, seeking support and financial aid for his expedition. He favoured Piacenza against Parma, conceded privileges to Como, Cremona and Bologna, made an agreement with Pisa and procured possession of Tuscolo for the city of Rome. After his coronation at Rome in 1191 and an unsuccessful expedition to the south, his renewed activity in Lombardy took on a decidedly anti-Milanese flavour and hinged on the alliance with Cremona. The result was that the cities marshalled themselved into two opposing camps: one closely bound to Milan in the tradition of the Lombard League, the other involving a union of Cremona, Parma, Pavia, Lodi, Como, Bergamo and the marquess Boniface of Montferrat, the son and successor of William V. During Henry VI's stay in Germany, the struggle between the two factions resulted in the Milanese victories of 1193. The respite caused in the following year by the emperor's return to Italy and the conquest of the south did not alter his anti-Milanese bias which ended, in the summer of 1195, by provoking the city – still the most important in Lombardy – into open rebellion and an understanding with Genoa, recently deceived by the emperor in Sicily.

In central Italy, German control proved more successful and in the spring of 1195 it was reinforced by the elevation of Markward of Anweiler, the powerful and faithful minister of the Staufen, to the duchy of Ravenna and Romagna. He was also made duke of Ancona and count of Abruzzo. Similarly, the duchy of Tuscany and the allodial estates of the countess Matilda were assigned to Philip, Henry VI's energetic brother, whose political activities extended into Perugian territory and into Lazio as far as Rome. The strategic points occupied by German forces were firmly held and the aristocratic and ecclesiastic seigneuries were favoured, in order to balance the vigour of the communal republics. This balance was extremely difficult to achieve, in view of the variety of forms of economic and civil development then evolving between the autonomous noble estates and the prosperous world of the cities. In any case, Henry VI's empire did not last long enough to inflict any serious check on the expanding power of the communal republics of central Italy. The death of the emperor on 28 September 1197 not only brought to an end his great plans to restructure and expand the empire and to crusade in the east, but also freed urban Italy from outside constraints and made possible the process whereby the church of Rome once again rebuilt its position of territorial domination.

The so-called testament of Henry VI, which was in fact the declaration of his intentions as sovereign when faced with death, already represented a compromise between the situation arising from the intense imperial activity in central Italy and papal aspirations, for long frustrated. In it were set down the renunciation of the allodial estates of the countess Matilda and also the recognition of the dependence of the duchy of Ravenna and the march of Ancona, although in the possession of Markward of Anweiler, on the church of Rome. The testament also forecast the papal claims – made at the end of the pontificate of Celestine III and during that of Innocent III – to all the places and regions deemed essential for the territorial security of the church of Rome. Thus in 1198 the papal intention of succeeding to the empire throughout central Italy, taking advantage of the anti-German risings which occurred in many places on the news of the death of Henry VI, became clear. But the plan only succeeded in a fairly limited way. It succeeded principally in Lazio and the duchy of Spoleto, but only because of the respect accorded to local autonomies by the papacy and through agreements and the control of certain fortresses. In Romagna and the Marche, Markward of Anweiler tried to continue operations until the autumn, when he moved on to the kingdom of Sicily. The pope, however, had the cooperation of the archbishop of Ravenna in Romagna and in both regions the cities, which in the Marche had formed a close league and in Romagna were even encroaching on the allodial estates of the countess Matilda, for the most part recognized papal sovereignty, although in an essentially formal way. Such recognition did not occur in Tuscany, where political control lay in the hands of a powerful league of cities, with Florence increasingly to the fore. To that league also attached themselves the archbishop of Volterra and the Counts Guidi, Alberti and Aldobrandeschi, while the republic of Pisa stood aside in proud independence.

The twofold royal election of Philip of Swabia and Otto of Brunswick in Germany in 1198 prevented any effective imperial presence in Italy. In Lombardy, the Lombard League revived, from Vercelli to Verona, with Milan as its axis, still in conflict with Cremona and its allies. Throughout the areas of Italy in which communes existed, the independent government of each city continued to improve its internal structure and in the process the rule of the consuls was often flanked, or substituted, by the authority of a *podestà*, following a pattern which had already been established at the time of Barbarossa. The need for a strong single authority, like that of the *podestà*, became all the more urgent in these various cities, in that their economic and social development was reducing the importance of the major families who during the twelfth century had monopolized power, competing among themselves. This was a time of crisis for the so-called consular aristocracy. The entry of new and energetic social groups into the political arena and their progress led to rivalry between those described as noble on account of their traditional political superiority and those known as popular. This continuing development of the cities took place in symbiosis with events in the countryside and in spite of the political preferences of the Swabian dynasty, which aimed to break up concentrations of power and frequently suggested a balance either among the most enterprising cities or between the cities and the rural aristocracy. The process of integrating these aristocrats with their lands and castles into the sphere of the major cities was never actually halted, as was clearly seen at the death of Henry VI.

The most obvious exceptions to this process took place in the areas along the edge of the Po valley. It is true that the house of Savoy, after having succeeded in 1131 in crossing the valley of Susa and reaching Turin, had been driven back by the bishop of Turin, acting in collaboration with the city commune and the German emperors. But Piedmont's interest remained intact, despite the far-flung and complicated political activities of the dynasty, and it was the prelude to a future expansion. Meanwhile, among the various marquisates, the territorial domination of the marquess of Montferrat, Boniface, had been consolidated. He was a faithful ally of Henry VI and took part in his various enterprises, but in Piedmont along the Po and the Tanaro he was tenacious in opposing the communal republics of Asti, Alessandria and Vercelli, whose dynamism he was able to cope with, even after the death of the emperor, adapting himself prudently to the dominance of the resuscitated Lombard League. To the south of the region dominated by this great league, which was in fact tormented within and beset without by Cremona and its allies, the Malaspina had emerged from among the various Obertenghi marquisates, heavily fortified in their strongholds in the Apennines, between the republics of Genoa and Piacenza, as had the Este, ever more attracted by Ferrara, which was destined to become the fulcrum of their power.

To the east of the Lombard League, the communal republics in the hinterland of the Veneto reacted to the disappearance of the imperial threats by achieving complete control of the various rural districts and absorbing their ruling houses into the lives of the cities. Venice, meanwhile, was strengthening her character as an aristocratic and mercantile republic by developing the administration of the city and defining the powers of the doge and the organs of the city-commune. She also consolidated her power over the Lagoon, the Istrian coast and the islands off Dalmatia and spread her influence both through the hinterland, with the support of the commercial privileges granted by the German empire, and on the seas, going as far as to threaten the very survival of the Byzantine empire. North of the Lagoon, Friuli, known as an ecclesiastical duchy, was still under the sway of the patriarch of Aquileia. It gradually evolved a legal constitution based on the consolidation of customary law, but suffered political interference by some of its powerful neighbours – the counts of Gorizia, on account of their having the sympathy of the patriarchate in this matter, and the cities of Treviso and Venice. North of the Veneto, the princely bishopric of Trenta persisted with a ducal dignity in maintaining its feudal structures and exemptions, with a complete lack of uniformity, maintaining a juridically ambiguous position between the kingdoms of Italy and Germany.

The failure of the imperial policies of Frederick I and Henry VI resolved itself at the end of the twelfth century in an exuberant activity in the most varied centres of political activity, from the Alps to the borders of the kingdom of the south. It was not, however, a chaotic anarchy, since there were no areas which failed to organize themselves, but rather a perpetual state of conflict, social and regional, around the centres of greatest economic initiative or military capacity, with a tendency to arrange themselves into a kind of fluid hierarchy of power, as a result of constant bargaining. Each of these innumerable entities saw the progressive strengthening of the institutional order, which was intimately linked to the fluctuations of the various social groups and was accompanied both in the dominant cities and the courts of the noble houses and of the prelates who had survived at a high political level, with cultural and urban development of incomparable intensity.

NORMAN SICILY IN THE TWELFTH CENTURY

G. A. Loud

THE settlement and, eventually, conquest of southern Italy by the Normans during the eleventh century had greatly altered both its society and its political structures, above all by the conquest of Muslim Sicily. What it had not done was to unite the region. Indeed by *c.* 1100 the new principalities which the conquerors had created were already fragmenting, and the maintenance of authority, and law and order, was becoming increasingly difficult. This fragmentation was to be abruptly reversed by the unification of southern Italy and Sicily under the rule of Count Roger II of Sicily in the years 1127–30, and the creation of the new kingdom of Sicily in the latter year. This process was by no means painless; indeed the coronation of 1130 was to usher in nearly a decade of civil war on the south Italian mainland, but it did in the end lead to the unification of the whole area for the first time since the age of Justinian. The kingdom created in 1130 was to last, albeit with many vicissitudes, until 1860. The imposition of strong central government, and the challenges that this government faced, form the central theme of south Italian history in the twelfth century.

AUTHORITY AND CHALLENGE BEFORE 1127

Roger II's contemporary biographer, Abbot Alexander of Telese, claimed that, in 1127, 'If God had not preserved a scion of the Guiscard's lineage through whom the ducal power might quickly be revived, almost the whole country . . . would have rushed headlong to destruction.'[1] Given that Alexander was writing a work of propaganda, justifying Roger's takeover of the mainland and the often drastic methods which his hero used to reduce his new dominions to obedience, such an opinion on his part was hardly surprising. The problem is to

---

[1] 'Nisi Deus guiscardine pertinens prosapie reliquisset semen, per quod cito ducatus recuperaretur monarchia, omnis pene siquidem terra . . . precipituim riutura periret', Alexander Telesinus, *Ystoria Rogerii regis Siciliae* lib. I c.I, p. 6.

estimate how far the disintegration of authority in southern Italy had actually gone by 1127. An objective assessment is not helped by the paucity of source material for this period, which was extremely ill-served by contemporary historians. For much of the time before 1127 one must rely on charter evidence and very sketchy local annals, whose authors' interests rarely extended very far from the town in which they were writing. But enough evidence survives to suggest that, while Alexander of Telese's opinion was undoubtedly exaggerated, the problems of central authority were serious enough.

Both in the duchy of Apulia and the principality of Capua the ruler's effective command became confined to part only of his nominal dominions. After 1090 the authority of the prince of Capua was, except for rare moments, exercised only in the southern part of his principality, in the plain surrounding Capua itself. The nobles of the northern and eastern parts of the principality (the dukes of Gaeta, the counts of Aquino, Fondi, Boiano and Caiazzo) were to all intents and purposes independent of princely authority. Their charters ceased to be dated by the regnal years of the prince. Indeed the latter's cousin Count Robert of Caiazzo (d. *c.* 1116) vaunted his status by having his diplomas drawn up in imitation of the style of the princely *scriptorium*, using the same formulae indicating divine favour as did the prince.[2] When the prince intervened in the north of the principality, as he did for example in what was a virtual civil war raging in and around Gaeta in 1105, he did so rather as one among a number of contending parties than as the ruler. Even in the heartland of his power the prince faced problems, for the city of Capua itself was intermittently in revolt in the 1090s.

Much the same situation prevailed in the duchy of Apulia. Dukes Roger Borsa (1085–1111) and William (1111–27) lost control of the coastal regions of Apulia, and found it increasingly difficult to exercise authority in inland Apulia and northern Calabria. In this last region Duke Roger's authority had only been maintained in the 1080s and 1090s thanks to military assistance from his uncle, Count Roger I of Sicily. In return for this aid he had had to make territorial concessions, including giving his uncle a half-share in the city of Palermo, which Robert Guiscard had kept in his own hands after its capture in 1072. Amalfi was apparently in rebellion against the duke in 1088, and again from 1096 to 1100.[3] However Roger Borsa was no cipher, and did his best to maintain ducal power and authority. He retained his control over the principality of Salerno on the west coast, and never abandoned his claims in Apulia. He even succeeded, in return for his and Count Roger's aid to Prince Richard II in the recovery of his capital in 1098, in securing the fealty of the prince of Capua, something which his father had never achieved. How far this gained him anything more than prestige is a good question, but at least

---

[2] Loud (1981), pp. 200–4. [3] For the dating, Schwarz (1978), pp. 250–3.

relations between duke and prince ran a great deal more smoothly than they had in the 1070s and 1080s. Robert I of Capua (1106–20) was to be found at Salerno in 1116, attending what was probably a meeting of the ducal court, and in 1119 a charter of Duke William referred to the prince as 'our most beloved relative and baron'.[4] Duke Roger was also able to recover control over Amalfi in 1100, and that important port henceforth acknowledged ducal rule without, seemingly, further problems. In 1101 Roger furnished an army which enabled Paschal II to regain Benevento which had thrown off papal overlordship.

Duke Roger was thus, to some extent anyway, an effective ruler. The participation by his half-brother Bohemond in the First Crusade, and the latter's continued absence thereafter in Syria and on campaign against Byzantium, removed probably the most dangerous single threat to his power. But he and his son were unable to enforce their rule, or indeed even overlordship, over the nobility and cities of coastal Apulia. The counts of Conversano, Canne and Monte Sant'Angelo, and further north in the Capitanata/Abruzzi borderland the counts of Loritello, remained independent. Robert of Loritello marked his status by use of the proud title 'count of counts' (*comes comitum*). Documents issued by the counts of the Apulian coast frequently recognized the overlordship of the Byzantine emperor; not through any attachment to Byzantine interests but because he was sufficiently far away to be powerless to affect their *de facto* independence.[5] Duke Roger was not necessarily disposed to accept this state of affairs, and did on occasion intervene in Apulia. He besieged and captured Canosa in 1100 and Monte Sant'Angelo in 1104, and at some point in his last years established his illegitimate son William as lord of Lucera, which had previously belonged to the counts of Monte Sant'Angelo. His influence in southern Apulia was also assisted by the continued loyalty and alliance of his cousin, Richard the Seneschal, lord of Mottola (to the west of Taranto).[6] But, while the authority of Duke Roger may have been enhanced in the later part of his reign, he was at best able to intervene in Apulia, and was never able to enforce his rule effectively. The centre of his activities, and his effective capital, was Salerno on the west coast. When he died in 1111 he was buried in Salerno Cathedral, as was his son sixteen years later, whereas the mausoleum of his father and uncles had been at Venosa in Apulia. This change was a symptom of the geographical shift of ducal interests.

Ducal authority was further undermined by the minority of Duke William, as was the lordship of Bohemond by that of his son (also Bohemond), who was

---

[4] Loud (1987), pp. 166–7, 176–7. *Normannische Herzogs- und Königsurkunden aus Unteritalien und Sizilien*, pp. 28–9 no. 16.

[5] Chalandon (1907), I, p. 208; Cahen (1940), p. 98.

[6] For his continued acknowledgement of ducal rule see *Codice diplomatico Barese*, pp. 102–3 no. 57 (1110), and Cava dei Tirreni, Archivio dell'abbazia di S. Trinità, Arm. Mag. E.39 (1115).

only three when his father died a few weeks after Duke Roger. Furthermore central authority was also undermined by the rise of independence movements in a number of important south Italian towns. Allusion has already been made to the revolts in Capua, Gaeta, Amalfi and Benevento in the 1090s. From 1115 Bari was convulsed by strife between pro- and anti-Norman factions in the city, and from *c.* 1118 the rule of Bohemond's widow Constance (in the name of her son) was no longer recognized there. The new ruler of Bari was one of the city's urban patriciate, Grimoald *Alferanites*, who by 1123 was describing himself as 'prince by the grace of God and St Nicholas' (the city's patron).[7] Duke William's death in 1127 was to be followed by revolts at Salerno itself, Troia and a number of other Apulian towns, and in 1128 the inhabitants of Benevento, who had been growing increasingly restive under papal rule, murdered the pope's rector of the city and founded a commune.

The growing instability in southern Italy can be graphically illustrated by the problems of the Benevento region in the second decade of the twelfth century. Not only was the city itself riven by faction, and under threat from the Norman nobles round about, but from 1118 onwards its environs were the scene of a bitter conflict between Count Jordan of Ariano and Count Rainulf of Caiazzo, both ambitious nobles seeking to extend their lands and power, and to dominate the *Terra Beneventana*. The duke of Apulia was conspicuous by his absence.

With lay authority weak, the papacy attempted to step into the breach. Following the example of Urban II, Pope Paschal proclaimed the Truce of God at Troia in 1115, and Calixtus II, again at Troia, in 1120, at a council where Duke William was also present. But the papacy clearly recognized the realities of the situation, that power in southern Italy had decentralized. When in 1118 Gelasius II received the fealty of Duke William (and probably that of the prince of Capua as well) he also received that of a number of other barons (though exactly whom is unknown). In 1120 Calixtus did the same, receiving fealty and homage (the latter apparently an innovation) from the duke, and Counts Robert of Loritello, Jordan of Ariano and Rainulf of Caiazzo. This was an unprecedented step, for hitherto the territorial rulers, the dukes of Apulia and princes of Capua, had alone been papal vassals.[8] What the papacy was trying to do was not to undermine the latter's rule, but to recognize that it was no longer effective. In the autumn of 1121 Calixtus was forced to intervene in southern Italy once again, to try to protect Duke William's lands in northern Calabria from attack by Count Roger of Sicily.

[7] 'Grimoaldus Alfaranites gratia dei et beati Nicolai princeps', *Codice diplomatico Barese*, pp. 121–2 no. 69.
[8] D'Alessandro (1978), pp. 169–73; Loud (1985), pp. 106–7.

The county of Sicily was very much the exception to the fragmentation affecting the rest of southern Italy. Despite two successive minorities after the death of Roger I in 1101 (his younger son Roger II did not come of age until 1112), strong and effective government was preserved under the regency of his widow, Countess Adelaide. We have no detailed knowledge of the years of the minority, and one tantalizing reference in a later charter suggests that there may have been some problems with Sicilian and Calabrian nobles.[9] But if so, these were overcome. On coming of age Roger II pursued a vigorous and effective policy, not least with regard to the church in his dominions, taking advantage of the privilege granted to his father by Pope Urban II in 1098 in which the pope promised not to appoint a legate for the island of Sicily without the count's agreement, and in the absence of such legate allowed the count to act in his place. Indeed so high-handed were his actions in ecclesiastical matters that Paschal II was moved to a vigorous protest in 1117. At the same time Roger launched a series of naval raids against the North African coast, and from 1121 attempted to consolidate his rule over Calabria, at the expense of his cousin Duke William. He succeeded fairly rapidly in this, though by more indirect means than those he had originally chosen. In return for substantial military assistance and a financial subsidy, which enabled the duke to dispossess the rebel count of Ariano of most of his lands, the duke ceded Count Roger the half-shares he and his father had retained in Palermo and Messina, and the half-share of Calabria (seemingly the northern part) inherited from Robert Guiscard. By 1127 therefore Roger of Sicily was the undisputed ruler of the whole of Calabria as well as Sicily, was possessed of powerful military and naval forces, substantial financial reserves, and was undoubtedly the most powerful, indeed the only effective, ruler in southern Italy.

THE UNIFICATION OF SOUTHERN ITALY UNDER ROGER II

Duke William of Apulia died childless in July 1127, and Roger II promptly claimed the duchy as his nearest heir. It was to take a year for him to make his claim to the ducal title a reality, and it took a further eleven before his rule over the whole of southern Italy was uncontested. The political fragmentation of the region over the previous forty years largely explains this long and fraught process, although from 1130 onwards the fortunes of southern Italy became increasingly involved in wider political and ecclesiastical rivalries in Christendom as a whole.

---

[9] *Diplomi greci ed arabi di Sicilia*, pp. 532–5. Matthew (1992), pp. 20–1, is disposed to doubt how effective comital rule in Sicily was after 1101, but his argument is at best speculative. The subject does, however, need fuller investigation.

In 1127–8 Roger faced opposition from four different sources. First, there were the more powerful among Apulian nobles, afraid that Roger's rule would curtail the effective independence they had hitherto enjoyed from ducal authority. Secondly, a number of towns were equally anxious to preserve or secure the right of self-government – these included the important city of Troia in the Capitanata, and even Salerno, whose inhabitants were only prepared to acknowledge Roger's rule if he left the citadel above the town in their hands. Thirdly, there was Prince Robert II of Capua who clearly did not relish the potential threat the new duke posed to the independence of his principality. He was supported by his cousin and nominal vassal Count Rainulf of Caiazzo, despite the fact that the latter was married to Roger of Sicily's sister.[10] Finally, there was Pope Honorius II.

The pope was the unifying, if not the motivating, force behind the south Italian coalition against Roger II in 1127–8. His involvement stemmed in part from the increasing intervention of the papacy in south Italian affairs in the years immediately preceding, especially after the conclusion of peace with the western empire in 1122. With their position at Rome no longer under threat, the popes no longer needed military assistance from southern Italy, and could therefore afford to take a much tougher line with its rulers. It has also been suggested that the pope's opposition to Roger's claims in 1127–8 resulted from the curia's refusal to treat the duchy, a papal fief, as in any way a hereditary possession. Hence Roger's claim to be Duke William's heir both by blood and by designation infringed papal rights of overlordship.[11] Such a theory is not entirely convincing, and there were other and more immediate reasons why the pope did not wish to see Apulia and Sicily united. The papacy's growing influence in southern Italy would undoubtedly be seriously affected, and the principality of Capua could no longer be considered an effective counterweight to the new duke, as it had been, at least to some extent, in the time of Robert Guiscard. In addition, Roger II's high-handed control over the church within his dominions had already vexed the papacy, and raised fears as to the sort of rule he would impose in the duchy. Paschal II had voiced his disapproval of the count's interference with the church in 1117. The 'Romuald' chronicle (here incorporating contemporary annalistic material, even if itself compiled nearly fifty years later) recorded that Honorius had already excommunicated the count for refusing to allow Sicilian bishops to go to Rome, before the clash over the Apulian succession.[12]

---

[10] Modern scholars habitually refer to him as 'count of Alife', but his few surviving charters call him 'count of the Caiazzans and of many others', *Le Pergamene dell' archivio vescovile di Caiazzo*, pp. 46–8 no. 7, pp. 57–9 no. 13, pp. 463–8 nos. I–III.

[11] Deér (1972), pp. 175–202.

[12] Romuald of Salerno, *Chronicon sive Annales*, pp. 214–15. For this work, Matthew (1981).

The opposition to Roger II was, however, both in 1127–8 and later, merely a loose coalition, and was fatally weakened by the disunity and self-interest of its members. When a major military clash threatened in 1128, first the Capuan forces, whose pay had run out, and then many of the Apulian barons deserted the pope. Deprived of his allies, he was forced to come to an agreement with Roger. In August 1128, outside Benevento, Honorius invested him as duke of Apulia. In the summer of 1129 the new duke crushed any vestiges of resistance in Apulia. In September, at an assembly of Apulian nobles at Melfi, Roger promulgated a comprehensive land peace, forbidding private warfare, which all those present swore to observe, 'that from this time and henceforth they would keep the peace and maintain justice, and assist in its maintenance'.[13] Soon afterwards the prince of Capua agreed to become Roger's vassal (despite the express protection of Capuan independence in Roger's agreement with the pope the previous year).

From the autumn of 1129 therefore southern Italy was at least technically united. That in practice this took a further ten years of warfare to consolidate is testimony to how deep-rooted the opposition to centralized authority on the south Italian mainland was. The creation of the Sicilian monarchy in 1130 had no real effect on this process, except to embroil the domestic disputes of southern Italy in wider conflicts involving the whole of Christendom. Whether without the papal schism of 1130 Duke Roger would have sought a royal crown cannot be known. But the schism did not create domestic conflict in southern Italy, it only exacerbated it.

Roger was granted a royal crown as king of Sicily in a bull of Anacletus II in September 1130 – in return (though this was not expressly stated) for his recognition of Anacletus as the rightful pope and support for his cause against his rival Innocent II – both popes having been elected after a split in the college of cardinals in February of that year. At the same time a carefully stage-managed assembly of magnates and churchmen at Salerno endorsed this proposal, on the ostensible (and historically erroneous) grounds that Sicily had once been ruled by kings and should be so again.[14] Roger was duly crowned king in Palermo Cathedral on Christmas Day 1130.

The coronation not only involved Roger in the schism, which was eventually to be resolved in Innocent's favour after the death of Anacletus in 1138; but by infringing in the most provocative way the claims of the western emperor to rule, or at least to be the overlord, of southern Italy, he incurred the hostility of

[13] 'ab ipsa hora, et in antea, justitiam et pacem tenerent, et adiuvarent tenere', Alexander Telesinus, *Ystoria Rogerii regis Siciliae* 1.21, p. 18. Roger II may have been following the example of his father, who imposed a land peace in Sicily in the 1090s, Jamison (1913), p. 239; Cahen (1940), p. 107.

[14] For this, Alexander Telesinus, *Ystoria Rogerii regis Siciliae* II.1–2, pp. 32–5, who very pointedly ignored all papal involvement.

the German monarch Lothar III, and as it turned out of Lothar's successors up to the conclusion of the treaty of Venice in 1177. Kingly status also helped to develop the absolutist ideology, derived from Roman Law, which characterized Sicilian government in the twelfth century. But it provided little or no material advantage for the suppression of the revolt on the south Italian mainland which broke out in 1132, and which was to take seven years to stamp out. Here the financial and military strength of the king, derived from his existing dominions in Calabria and Sicily (and including the use of Muslim troops from Sicily), and the disunity of his opponents, were paramount.

If the campaigns of 1127–9 can be seen as the first stage of the process which consolidated the unified kingdom of Sicily, three further phases followed. First, in 1132–4 the king and his generals eliminated resistance in Apulia – in two campaigns in the summers of 1132 and 1133 – and, despite the setback of a serious defeat at Nocera in July 1132, forced the submission of the principality of Capua, which was achieved by the autumn of 1134. The prince himself, who was then in Pisa seeking external assistance, did not surrender, but his chief ally within the principality, Rainulf of Caiazzo, and his neighbour Duke Sergius VII of Naples, did. Of the leaders of the Apulian resistance, Grimoald of Bari and Counts Godfrey of Andria and Tancred of Conversano were captured and imprisoned in Sicily; Tancred's brother, Alexander of Gravina, fled into exile in Byzantium.

The king was seriously ill in the winter of 1134–5, and a false rumour of his death led to renewed revolt in the principality of Capua early in 1135, headed once again by Count Rainulf. But prompt action by the king's mainland commanders very swiftly recovered almost all the principality, and confined the rebels to Naples, where they remained blockaded for the next eighteen months. That this was not the end of internal conflict within southern Italy was due to the external assistance the rebels secured, first in the resupply of Naples by the Pisan fleet, whose assistance had been secured by Robert of Capua, and secondly by the invasion of southern Italy by the Emperor Lothar in 1137, which ushered in the final phase of the conflict.

Lothar's army marched down into Apulia as far as Bari, which was captured in May 1137, and then into Lucania. For a time this incursion might have seemed to have doomed King Roger's mainland rule, particularly since a second German force under the emperor's son-in-law Duke Henry of Bavaria overran the principality of Capua and restored Prince Robert. In fact the impact of the invaders was purely transient. Key fortresses remained in the hands of garrisons loyal to King Roger, and by September the German troops were withdrawing, leaving their local allies to face a royalist counter-attack. Lothar and Pope Innocent had installed Count Rainulf as their duke of Apulia, and a number of Apulian towns, under royal control since 1133, were prepared to support him even after the German withdrawal. But, despite a further defeat at Rignano in October 1137, the king held the advantage, and in 1137–8 the rebel forces steadily lost ground. Rainulf's death in April 1139 removed the principal opposition leader, and the capture of Pope Innocent in July led to the recognition of Roger as king by the now-undisputed pope. The remaining rebels, including Robert of Capua, fled into exile, and the surrender of Naples, Troia and Bari (the last after a short siege) ended the last vestiges of resistance.

During this long and bitter conflict the king's treatment of those who opposed him changed dramatically. To begin with he had often been merciful, even to outright rebels, and had been prepared to negotiate with both hostile nobles and towns to secure their submission, if need be on terms favorable to them. An example of this was his agreement with the city of Bari in June 1132. The king's representatives swore to respect the city's churches and the rights of its archiepiscopal see, not to take revenge on its inhabitants for their previous opposition, to respect their property and existing judicial and fiscal immunities, not to impose fresh military obligations upon them, nor to take hostages or to build a citadel within the town.[15] In the end renewed revolt led to much heavier terms being imposed, and when the city surrendered for a fourth and final time in October 1139 the king had Prince Jacquintus (who had replaced the imprisoned Grimoald) and a dozen other notables hanged, and others mutilated or imprisoned. But to begin with at least the king was prepared to act leniently, not least to avoid stirring up unnecessary resistance. In Apulia the watershed was the campaign of 1133. The king made deliberate examples of towns still in revolt, which were brutally sacked by his troops, and of rebel leaders, a number of whom were hanged. He was, said Alexander of Telese, 'so greatly angered that he was hardly willing to spare any count, magnate or even knight who had raised his head in perjury against him'.[16] But in the principality of Capua the king was still prepared to compromise in 1134 when he accepted the surrender of Rainulf of Caiazzo and Count Hugh of Boiano, and also that of Sergius of Naples. He was too ready to come to terms with Prince Robert, and it was the prince who refused them. However, faced with renewed revolt in 1135 he was uncompromising. Aversa, the most important town in the principality after Capua itself, was quite deliberately destroyed and its inhabitants dispersed. Roger's third son, Anfusus, was appointed as the new prince. At the same time royal officials were installed to administer the principality, although two of these, Aymo of Argentia, who was appointed one of the two justiciars of the principality, and the chamberlain Joscelin, were in

---

[15] *Rogerii II regis diplomata Latina*, pp. 54–6 no. 20. Martin (1980), pp. 88–93.

[16] 'tantoque mentis erupit furore, ut non comiti, non magnati, non etiam militi, qui ita periurantes in eum colla erexerant, penitus parceret', Alexander Telesinus, *Ystoria Rogerii regis Siciliae* II.37, p. 41.

fact Capuans who had defected from the prince to support the king, and remained loyal to him. The new administrative arrangements for the principality were to be the model for the local administration of the mainland as a whole after 1139.[17]

Another significant aspect of the consolidation of royal authority was a considerable reorganization of landholding in both Apulia and Capua, with the replacement of rebel nobles by men loyal to the king. Both Counts Rainulf of Caiazzo and Hugh of Boiano had to surrender part of their lands to secure the king's pardon in 1134, and the property confiscated from Count Hugh and his comital title were subsequently granted to a royalist supporter, Robert son of Richard. After 1139 the counties of Caiazzo and Ariano were suppressed and the lands of the former counts remained in the king's hands.[18] In other cases new counts were appointed to replace those imprisoned or exiled, as occurred with the counties of Boiano, Conversano, Manopello and (somewhat later) Andria. Often these new incumbents were royal relatives, or came from the king's hereditary dominions of Calabria and Sicily. The county of Conversano was given to the king's brother-in-law Adam in 1135, and soon afterwards (probably because of Adam's death) to another brother-in-law Robert of Bassonville. Similarly in 1140 the king gave the frontier county of Manopello to a Calabrian baron Bohemond of Tarsia. Strategic centres were also retained in the king's hands, like S. Agata di Puglia, which was confiscated from the former ducal constable Richard son of Hoel, in 1133, although in this case, since he was not in open rebellion against the king, its lord was compensated with lands elsewhere. This process continued for some years after 1140. In a few cases exiled rebels managed to make their peace with the king and had their lands and titles restored, as was the case with Hugh of Boiano, who recovered his county in the early 1140s. (His supplanter Robert son of Richard was transferred to the county of Civitate).[19] The county of Andria was not revived until *c.* 1147, and that of Loritello not until 1154, when it was given to Robert II of Bassonville, to hold along with Conversano. Indeed *c.* 1142 a number of new counties were created, as part of a wholesale reorganization of the defence of the mainland provinces. The role of the counts after 1140 was primarily military.[20] But the changes among the nobility stemmed from the resistance to the king in the mid-1130s.

---

[17] Jamison (1913), especially pp. 279–80, 306–7, remains fundamental, despite some modifications by more recent scholars such as Caravale (1966), especially pp. 222–39. Joscelin had been the prince's chamberlain before 1130.

[18] The later Count Malgerius of Alife, found in the *Catalogus Baronum*, held only a part of the former possessions of Count Rainulf, and was not in any direct sense his successor.

[19] Count Hugh and his successors were henceforth known as counts of Molise, a title which was derived from his family name. His restoration probably occurred before 1142, Jamison (1929), p. 53.

[20] See Cuozzo (1989), especially pp. 105–20.

From 1139 onwards the mainland provinces remained peaceful. But despite the treaty of Mignano of 1139 relations with the papacy had not been entirely settled. Not only had Innocent II's recognition of Roger as king been extorted from him by *force majeure* – something which some at least of the cardinals very much resented – but a number of other problems remained outstanding, not least the reorganization of the episcopal structure on the island of Sicily, sanctioned by Anacletus but rendered abortive by his rival's victory in the schism. Above all, in the early 1140s King Roger's sons extended the Sicilian frontier in the Abruzzi region northwards into papal territory, and by 1144 had overrun the whole area (known to contemporaries as Marsia) from the River Sangro northwards as far as Pescara. Not surprisingly relations with the papacy were to remain strained, if not entirely sundered, until a settlement was finally reached in 1156.

The expansion of the kingdom's northern frontier was part of a generally aggressive foreign policy pursued in the 1140s. The Muslim cities of Tripolitania and Tunisia were already heavily dependent on Sicilian grain supplies; now King Roger turned what was already a virtual protectorate into direct rule. Sicilian expeditions captured Tripoli in 1146, and Mahdia, Sfax and Sousa in 1148, thus securing both sides of the central Mediterranean 'narrows', and being in a position to control or interdict the trade of the entire region. The motives for this may well have been primarily economic, but the north African conquests served also to protect the coast of Sicily from Islamic piracy and to prevent outside subversion among the island's still largely Muslim population.[21] The motives for the attack launched against Byzantium in 1147 are more difficult to discern. The Byzantine chronicler John Kinnamos implied that it was the Emperor Manuel's refusal during diplomatic negotiations in the mid-1140s to recognize Roger's royal title that led to this attack.[22] The capture of Corfu in 1147 provided the Sicilians with a base from which they could launch an offensive against the European provinces of the empire along the Via Egnatia, as Robert Guiscard had done in the 1080s (and indeed he had secured Corfu as the essential preliminary to his attack). But in addition it gave the Sicilians control of both sides of the mouth of the Adriatic. This, combined with their hold over the 'narrows', ensured them a potential stranglehold over the trade of the north Italian maritime cities, and could hence discourage these cities from providing naval aid to the German emperor, without which any attack on the Sicilian kingdom would be much less likely to succeed.[23]

---

[21] Abulafia (1985) provides a most valuable discussion.

[22] John Kinnamos, *Deeds of John and Manuel Komnenus*, p. 75.

[23] Admittedly the Venetians aided the Byzantine emperor against Sicily in 1148, probably precisely because they wanted to break the Sicilian stranglehold on the mouth of the Adriatic. But they later (in 1155–6) showed themselves equally hostile to the Byzantines' attempt to control both sides of the Adriatic coast, Abulafia (1984), p. 198.

Naval raids on the Byzantine empire proper, on Thebes, Corinth and even into the Bosphoros, were perhaps primarily spoiling operations, intended to discourage the enemy and throw him off balance by demonstrating the power of the Sicilian fleet. It may be too that with the breakdown of diplomatic negotiations King Roger anticipated and wished to forestall a Byzantine attack on Apulia, over which the Byzantines had never relinquished their claims.

Such wide-ranging strategic considerations were undoubtedly important, for though internally peaceful the kingdom of Sicily was still, in the last years of King Roger's reign, very much under threat from its external foes. While Conrad III of Germany's participation in the Second Crusade removed the most significant of these threats for a time, the alliance against Roger concluded between him and Manuel Komnenos in 1147 put the kingdom into a potentially very fraught position, and the presence of Sicilian exiles such as Prince Robert of Capua at Conrad's court and Count Alexander of Gravina at Manuel's cannot have made the king any happier. Two important counter-measures were undertaken. In 1150 the king met Pope Eugenius at Ceprano on the border between the kingdom and the Papal States, and an accord was concluded which, for a time at least, restored good relations between king and pope. Secondly, at about the same time a register was prepared of the military strength of the kingdom, in preparation for any potential invasion, and reflecting the reorganization of fiefs and military obligations which had taken place in the 1140s. The main part of this register, covering Apulia and the principalities of Salerno and Capua, survives today in the text known as the 'Catalogue of the Barons'.[24]

A PERIOD OF INSTABILITY, 1154–1168

The reign of William I (1154–66) and the early years of that of his son, William II (1166–89), were marked by internal instability and external threat. The most detailed contemporary chronicle, the *History* of the so-called 'Hugo Falcandus', ascribed the problems of these years largely to the incapacity, sloth and suspicion (seemingly verging on paranoia) of the king himself. Too idle to take an active role in government, William I allowed himself to be manipulated by his Svengali-like minister, Maio of Bari, and the revolts within the Regno were, so 'Falcandus' suggests, largely directed against Maio, until the latter was murdered in November 1160. Thereafter it was as much fear of the king's vengeance as any other factor which prolonged the immediate domestic crisis

---

[24] *Catalogus Baronum*. For its purpose, Jamison (1971), especially pp. 3–7. Whether Calabria and Sicily were also covered is not certain.

for some months more.[25] William II's minority was riven by factional dispute, and similar dislike of another over-powerful chief minister, Stephen of Perche.

William I's posthumous reputation was certainly poor, and even a more balanced contemporary than the prejudiced 'Falcandus' described him on his death as 'hateful to his kingdom and more feared than loved, very active in collecting money but not very generous in dispensing it'.[26] He was to go down to posterity as 'King William the Bad', although this nickname was only coined some centuries later. But one might suggest that many of the problems affecting the kingdom of Sicily in these years were in fact a legacy from the time of Roger II, and indeed the circumstances in which the kingdom was created. King Roger left his successor serious and unresolved difficulties.[27] The kingdom was faced with the hostility of both eastern and western empires, and (once again) of the papacy; for the accord patched up with the latter had not survived the coronation, without papal agreement, of William as king and co-ruler at Easter 1151. Furthermore, the events of 1155–6 showed how fragile the unity of the kingdom still was. The nobility of the frontier provinces – the principality of Capua and the Abruzzi borderlands conquered in the 1140s – for the most part rose in revolt. The towns of Apulia were also still restive under royal control. The citizens of Bari, for example, demolished the hated royal citadel there. And King Roger had also left the problem of the exiles, who looked to the two empires, but especially to the western emperor Frederick Barbarossa, to support their cause. According to 'Falcandus' King Roger had 'made efforts to administer justice in its full rigour on the grounds that it was particularly necessary for a newly established realm'.[28] But the harshness of his rule, however necessary it may have been, led to a reaction after his death.

Rebellion on the mainland was sparked off by the march of Frederick Barbarossa to Rome in the spring of 1155 for his imperial coronation, and by the defection, at the same time, of the king's cousin Robert, created count of Loritello only a year earlier. Robert's revolt was probably motivated by jealousy of the influence of Maio at the centre of government. If we are to believe 'Falcandus', the king was also very suspicious of his relatives and ready to believe the worst about them.[29] A bungled effort to arrest the count at Capua (c. May

[25] *La Historia o Liber de regno Sicilie di Ugo Falcando*. The author's alleged name, 'Hugo Falcandus', in fact stemmed from a misreading by a Renaissance editor, Jamison (1957), pp. 191–6. The unknown author was, however, almost certainly a member of the royal court, although none of the attempts to identify him have been convincing, Loud and Wiedemann (1998), pp. 28–42.

[26] 'regno suo odibilis et plus formidini quam amari, in congreganda pecunia multum sollicitus, in expedenda non adeo largus', Romuald of Salerno, *Chronicon sive Annales*, p. 253.

[27] Enzensberger (1980), pp. 386–96; Loud (1999a).

[28] 'postremo sic iustitie rigorem ut novo regno perneccessarium studuit exercere', *La Historia o Liber de regno Sicilie*, p. 6 (English translation, Loud and Wiedemann (1998), p. 58).

[29] *La Historia o Liber de regno Sicilie*, pp. 12–13, Loud and Wiedemann (1998), pp. 64–5.

1155) was the last straw which drove him into rebellion. Certainly the arrest soon afterwards of the master constable of Apulia, Count Simon of Policastro, another cousin of the king, was to have grave consequences on the island of Sicily.

However, the seriousness of the rebellions in 1155–6 was largely due to two factors beyond the control of the Sicilian government: the presence in Apulia from the autumn of 1155 of a powerful Byzantine expeditionary force, and the king's illness at the same period, which not only incapacitated him for some months but also spread rumours of his death which encouraged rebellion on the mainland, just as the illness of King Roger had done in 1134–5. After his recovery, the king's presence was still required for some time in Sicily owing to the rebellion which had broken out in the south-east of the island. The mainland revolt flourished in the king's absence, and collapsed once he took charge on the mainland.

Revolt in Sicily itself was a new development – and of the various problems which beset William I's government this was the one for which the king and his minister were largely to blame. The centre of the revolt was Butera, which was the *caput* of the Sicilian lordship of the imprisoned Count Simon of Policastro. The rebels professed themselves loyal to the king but opposed to Maio, whom they alleged to be a traitor.[30] The government found it necessary to release Count Simon and offer lenient terms to secure Butera's surrender. However, once the Sicilian rebellion was quashed, it was relatively easy to re-store royal authority on the mainland, even though, while the king had been detained in Sicily, the Byzantine troops and their local allies had taken over most of the coastal towns of Apulia, and Prince Robert and his cousin Andrew of Rupecanina had, with papal backing, recovered most of the principality of Capua. However, a number of important towns, including Naples, Amalfi and Salerno, remained loyal to the king – or had been sufficiently well garrisoned to prevent their defection – and in others, notably Brindisi, royal troops held out in the citadel even if the town had been captured or had revolted. Further-more, just as in the 1130s, the king's opponents were divided and pursued their own ends rather than combining effectively against him. Barbarossa provided little or no effective support and speedily withdrew to northern Italy after his coronation. The Byzantines soon alienated Robert of Loritello and the other rebel barons. When the royal army confronted the Byzantines outside Brindisi in May 1156 the Apulian rebels abandoned the Greeks and fled. Outnumbered, the Byzantines were then catastrophically defeated. The Capuan rebellion col-lapsed without a battle, and the prince was captured and subsequently blinded.

---

[30] *La Historia o Liber de regno Sicilie*, pp. 18–19, Loud and Wiedemann (1998), pp. 71–2. 'Falcandus' alleged, with a wealth of circumstantial (but unlikely) detail, that Maio was plotting to murder the king. His account should be treated with scepticism.

Pope Adrian IV, hitherto intransigent, abandoned the contest and came to an agreement with the king at Benevento only three weeks after the latter's victory at Brindisi.

Most of the counts installed by King Roger remained loyal in 1155–6. Richard of Andria was, for example, killed fighting the Byzantines in September 1155. Only the counts of Loritello, Civitate, the Principato and Avellino seem to have taken part in the revolt, and the count of Avellino was subsequently pardoned for betraying the exiled prince of Capua to the king.[31] The speedy victory achieved once the main royal field army arrived on the mainland was a testimony to the basic strength of the regime. Furthermore the government moved effectively to defuse the threat from its external foes. A peace had been agreed with Venice during the first year of the new reign, and a treaty was concluded with Genoa in 1156. The treaty of Benevento settled almost all the issues which had hitherto prevented agreement with the papacy, including the recognition of the quasi-legatine rights of the king on the island of Sicily and his rule over the disputed Abruzzi borderlands. Early in 1158 peace was settled with Byzantium too. The international situation of the kingdom of Sicily was thus much more secure than it had been at King Roger's death. However, internal problems continued, despite the harsh repression which followed the revolt in 1156 (including the wholesale and deliberate destruction of the rebel city of Bari). In part this was the product of the continued pressure from those exiled. Andrew of Rupecanina penetrated deep into the principality of Capua in 1158, and both he and Robert of Loritello took advantage of the domestic problems in Sicily to launch a further invasion in 1161. But the crisis of the Sicilian monarchy in 1160–1 was fundamentally the product of factional dispute in Sicily itself, centred around the royal court.

The exaggeration and slanders of 'Falcandus' (by far the most detailed source for these events) must clearly be treated with caution, but none the less it seems very clear that, as the chronicler alleged, the root of the trouble lay in the pre-eminent position at court of Maio of Bari. That this was no mere invention of 'Falcandus' is shown by the treaty of Benevento, where Maio was described as the king's *familiarissimus*.[32] From early in 1158 onwards the two master captains of Apulia and Terra di Lavoro (the royal governors on the mainland) were his brother Stephen and his brother-in-law Simon the Seneschal (the latter had been in office from the summer of 1156). Potential rivals like Simon of Policastro and the chancellor Asclettin had been disgraced and imprisoned. Furthermore, Maio's dominance represented the triumph of the bureaucrats of the royal administration, whose influence as a group entirely outweighed

[31] *La Historia o Liber de regno Sicilie*, p. 22, Loud and Wiedemann (1998), pp. 74–5.
[32] William I of Sicily, *Guillelmi I regis diplomata*, p. 34 no. 12. Loud and Wiedemann (1998), p. 249.

that of the nobility and was correspondingly resented. The nobles were also threatened by the suspicions which King William exercised towards those related to him, several of whom, like his illegitimate half-brother Simon and his nephew Tancred, had also been imprisoned.

In November 1160 Maio was murdered by a group of conspirators headed by a Sicilian noble, and erstwhile protégé of his, Matthew Bonellus. So unpopular was he that the king did not dare to revenge himself on the murderers, although their fears that he would do so when the time was more favourable played their part in the attempted coup which followed in March 1161.[33] The prisoners in the dungeons of the royal palace, headed by the king's relatives Simon and Tancred, escaped, took over the palace and arrested the king, intending to replace him by his eldest son Roger, a child of perhaps twelve. They were, however, too few to resist the populace of Palermo who forced them to release the king; and their fellow-conspirators from eastern Sicily never arrived in the capital to reinforce them. The coup was speedily suppressed, and this time Butera, once again the centre of the Sicilian rebellion, was destroyed. The leaders were exiled or executed, and the king then speedily suppressed the revolt on the mainland, once again driving out Robert of Loritello and his associates.

None the less, even though the attempted coup of 1161 quickly collapsed and the exiles' invasion of the mainland was defeated without serious fighting, royal rule had been gravely threatened by these events. Not only had the king himself been in imminent danger of assassination (and his son Roger had been killed by a stray arrow during the fighting in Palermo), but his over-reliance on Maio, and the diversion of patronage to Maio's family and associates, had alienated a substantial section of the nobility, including a number of counts who had remained loyal during the earlier revolt of 1155–6. Furthermore, the domestic problems of the Regno made it impossible to protect the Sicilians' North African colonies against the Almohads of Morocco, who reconquered Tripoli for Islam in 1158 and Mahdia in 1160.[34] During the disturbances of 1161 relations between Christians and Muslims on the island of Sicily had also deteriorated, and both the Christians of Palermo and settlers from northern Italy in the east of the island had taken advantage of the temporary slackening of central authority to massacre their Muslim neighbours. Nor did the defeat of the rebels necessarily ensure the safety of the kingdom. The German empire remained hostile, and during 1163–4 Barbarossa was negotiating with both Pisa and Genoa to secure naval aid for an attack on the kingdom of Sicily. The northern border of the kingdom remained vulnerable to attacks by the exiles. In October 1163 Pope Alexander III asked his ally the French king to warn William I to be on his guard, 'since his enemies are preparing themselves and

[33] Romuald of Salerno, *Chronicon sive Annales*, p. 246.   [34] Abulafia (1985), pp. 41–4.

devoting their whole purpose towards entering his lands and wearing him out with their continual harassment'.[35]

To judge by the absence of recorded incident in the chroniclers, the kingdom seems to have remained internally peaceful during the later years of William I.[36] But on his sudden death in May 1166 his eldest surviving son, also called William, was still a child, just short of his thirteenth birthday. For some years thereafter the boy's mother, Queen Margaret, acted as regent. While the country as a whole was relatively stable – aided by the regent's conciliatory policy of releasing political prisoners, recalling exiles and revoking the punitive fines levied on a number of mainland towns in the wake of the 1161 rebellion – the court was riven by faction. Nor for a while was the kingdom's external situation any less threatening, particularly with Barbarossa's march on Rome in 1167. 'Falcandus' recorded how, probably some months earlier, Count Gilbert of Gravina, the master captain of Apulia and Terra di Lavoro, was forced to leave the court at Palermo and hurry to the mainland after a rumour (in the event false) had been spread by his political opponents that the emperor was about to invade the kingdom. He was instructed not only to raise an army, but also to ensure the continued loyalty of the mainland towns, something which clearly could not be taken for granted.[37]

During William I's later years the administration had been directed by a triumvirate of *familiares*: Matthew of Salerno, a former royal notary and protégé of Maio; Richard Palmer, the bishop-elect of Syracuse, an English immigrant; and a senior financial official and convert from Islam Caid (Qa'id) Peter; and their position was confirmed by the king's will. (In a Sicilian context the word *familiaris* should be translated as 'minister' and not merely 'courtier' or 'favourite'.) But Queen Margaret subsequently favoured Peter above his colleagues, and doing so unleashed a series of factional disputes so virulent that within a few months he fled for his own safety to North Africa. Thereafter the court polarized between the two erstwhile *familiares*, Matthew, allied with a group of bishops (hitherto largely excluded from the centre of power) and Bishop Richard, aided by the powerful count of Gravina. To escape this dispute the queen first turned to the royal constable, Richard of Mandra (who was granted the vacant county of Molise), and then invited her cousin, Stephen of Perche, to her court, and appointed him in rapid succession to be chancellor and archbishop of Palermo. But while, to begin with at least, his rule was well received by the populace, his pre-eminence alienated both the administrators of the court and the nobility. In part this was because of his attempts to control abuses by officials, and

---

[35] *PL* 200, col. 269.

[36] This silence does not just apply to the chroniclers either. Only three charters of William I survive from the years 1161–6, Enzensberger (1981), pp. 111–12.

[37] *La Historia o Liber de regno Sicilie*, p. 101, Loud and Wiedemann (1998), p. 149.

in part the result of the diversion of patronage to his allies and the members of his (largely foreign) household. According to 'Falcandus': 'the magnates of the court...saw that all the material advantages of the court were going to the chancellor and his friends, and that from this wealth of gifts only a trickle was left over for them'.[38] But fundamentally Stephen's problem was the same as that of Maio. The diversion of authority to one all-powerful minister inevitably created resentment, and this became more acute when, feeling himself under threat, he had potential rivals (including Richard of Molise and Matthew of Salerno) arrested. In the spring of 1168 a popular revolt in Messina, sparked off by the excesses of one of Stephen's officials, led to a coup. Stephen was forced into exile in the Holy Land where he died soon afterwards. His principal ally, Gilbert of Gravina, was also exiled and dispossessed. The governing council set up in the wake of the coup drew on all three of the chief parties in the kingdom, the bishops, the court bureaucrats and the nobility. To assure continued stability, the most prominent of the exiles from William I's reign, Count Robert of Loritello, was recalled in 1169 and restored to his former position.

This policy of accommodation appears to have been entirely successful. The direction of the government was fairly soon limited once again to a group of three, or later four, *familiares*: Walter, the new archbishop of Palermo, Matthew of Salerno and one (or from *c.* 1184 two) other bishops, but any rivalries within this group were kept within bounds and did not de-stabilize the kingdom's government.[39] The external threat was also much diminished after Barbarossa's withdrawal from Rome in 1167. William II's reign was indeed remembered as a period of enviable stability and good government; a thirteenth-century chronicler (conscious of the disorders after his death) recalled that 'during his lifetime such peace and justice existed in the kingdom that the like was not recorded before or after him'.[40]

THE STRUCTURES OF GOVERNMENT

Outside observers were prone, like 'Falcandus', to describe the king of Sicily as a tyrant, though this observation had as much to do with the dubious circumstances of the acquisition of the royal title in 1130 – and hence the presumed illegitimacy of the king's rule – as the style of government. Such an accusation was of course particularly levied by writers from the German empire, which maintained its claims over southern Italy right through the twelfth century.[41]

---

[38] *La Historia o Liber de regno Sicilie*, p. 118, Loud and Wiedemann (1998), p. 169.

[39] For details, Takayama (1989), especially pp. 365–8.

[40] 'Tanta Pax et iustitia extitit, eo vivente, in regno suo, quanta non recordatur fuisse ante eum nec actenus post eum', *Chronicon Ignoti monachi Cisterciensis sanctae Mariae de Ferraria*, p. 32.

[41] See Wieruszowski (1963) here.

None the less, the kings of Sicily faced a long and difficult task in imposing their rule on the mainland, and resorted to harsh measures to make it effective. But they also needed to create a viable and efficient administrative structure, both to consolidate their rule in the newly acquired mainland dominions and to govern and exploit their ancestral lands, Calabria and Sicily, to provide the wealth which underpinned their rule, and for which they were generally renowned.

In both Calabria and Sicily there seems to have been a fair degree of administrative continuity from the pre-Norman period. The Byzantine and Arabic administrations in the two regions were appreciably more sophisticated and bureaucratic than those in the contemporary west, and the Norman conquerors continued to employ indigenous officials and their existing records, particularly cadastral surveys. As early as 1087 a charter of Count Roger I made a grant 'according to the old boundaries of the Saracens'.[42] Up to 1127 the comital chancery issued charters almost exclusively in Greek (only seven comital charters in Latin are known from this period) – though administrative documents, notably the *plateae* or lists of serfs, might also be written in Arabic, and Arabic land surveys were almost certainly revised and kept up to date. The majority of officials in Sicily and Calabria at this period were, however, Greeks, as were Roger II's two successive chief ministers, Christodoulos (up to *c.* 1122) and George of Antioch.

The extension of Roger's rule to Apulia and Capua led to a number of administrative developments. From 1127 onwards the chancery issued many more documents in Latin, primarily for mainland recipients, although the Latin section of the chancery only became the dominant one in the 1150s with the rule of Maio of Bari, himself a former chancery official. In addition a proper administrative structure had to be developed for these new provinces, to bind them firmly under royal rule. The disparate nature of these provinces, and particularly the fragmentation of Apulia before 1127, meant that this governmental apparatus had largely to be created *de novo*. The 'Romuald' chronicler reported that in 1140 King Roger 'instituted chamberlains and justiciars throughout the land to preserve the peace [and] promulgated laws which he had newly drafted'.[43] The chronicle's dating is only approximate; the first installation of justiciars and chamberlains came with the takeover of the principality of Capua in 1135, and royal *justificatores* (an early title for justiciars) can also be found in Apulia in 1136, though it may have taken several years for the full extension of a network of royal officials over the mainland as a whole. (Hostilities after all continued

---

[42] 'secundum antiquas divisiones Saracenorum', *Diplomi della cattedrale di Messina*, pp. 2–3 no. 2.

[43] 'pro conservanda pace camerarios et iusticiarios per totam terram instituit, leges a se noviter condidatos promulgavit', Romuald of Salerno, *Chronicon sive Annales*, p. 236.

until the summer of 1139.) Similarly, while King Roger promulgated some laws, especially relating to the coinage, at an assembly at Ariano in 1140, it is by no means clear that either of the two surviving texts detailing different versions of King Roger's legislation is to be connected with that assembly, although this legislation probably does date from the 1140s.[44]

The legislation ascribed to King Roger was derived, indeed usually *verbatim*, from Roman Law, and it reflected the exalted view of the sovereign which that law embodied. But the preface to the earlier text of this code (if it may be described as such) said that the customs and laws of the different peoples under his rule should be maintained unless they were in direct contravention of royal law. For most purposes therefore Lombards (i.e. native Italians), Greeks, Muslims and French remained under the sway of local customary law, administered by their own local judges (especially in the towns) or by aristocrats who possessed judicial authority in their own lands. Royal justiciars dealt with serious criminal offences (particularly those to do with public order), important property disputes – principally those involving fiefs, and cases referred to them from other tribunals by the royal court because of 'defect of justice' – they presided therefore over a court of appeal. Such cases were often the result of pressure from below, with a dissatisfied plaintiff going to the royal court to secure a mandate for a case to be tried before the justiciars.

The mainland justiciars were drawn from the lesser nobility, and very occasionally the knightly class, and often held office for long periods. They were usually landowners in the area in which they officiated. From the first there would appear to have been fixed areas of jurisdiction, even though express territorial titles ('Justiciar of the Terra di Bari' etc.) do not appear in the sources until the 1170s. Usually a pair of justiciars officiated together in each circuit. The rewards of long service as a justiciar could be considerable. For example Henry of Ollia was one in the Monte Gargano region of northern Apulia from c. 1141 until 1153; his son Geoffrey was granted the county of Lesina, forfeited by its previous incumbent, in 1155.

The chamberlains were primarily financial officials who supervised crown lands and royal revenues on the mainland, and oversaw other more minor officers such as local bailiffs and *portulani*. They also presided over some legal cases in what the thirteenth century would have called 'civil' issues.[45] They could too exercise a supervisory role over local judges, and it is in fact probable

---

[44] Ménager (1969) is (rightly) very critical of the supposed 'Assizes of Ariano', but his suggestion that neither of these codes should in fact be attributed to the Rogerian period is very controversial. See now Houben (2001), pp. 135–47.

[45] How far there was an express distinction between civil and criminal law in the twelfth century is disputed; see Caravale (1966), pp. 263–4 *contra* Jamison (1913), pp. 322–30, but in practice the limitation of the chamberlains' judicial competence is clear.

that there was no hard and fast distinction between their judicial competence and that of the justiciars, although the latter dealt with the more important cases. In Calabria and Sicily (where local justiciars are found from the beginning of William I's reign) the justiciars seem sometimes to have performed purely administrative tasks, which they apparently did not in Apulia and Capua where their duties remained exclusively legal. However, a number of mainland justiciars also functioned as royal constables, responsible for the levying and organization of troops. While as time went on the competence of various officials doubtless became more closely defined, there would seem therefore to have been some overlap of functions. Furthermore, the jurisdiction of the justiciars did not extend to the lands of the mainland counts, who themselves exercised criminal justice and acted as the royal legal officers within their counties. What is significant, however, is that they did this not as an exercise of their proprietary right but as the delegated officers of the king, acting in effect as justiciars. Indeed there are instances of men of comital rank describing themselves expressly as 'count and justiciar'. Furthermore, the 'counties' were often very disparate collections of lands, and not coherent territorial units. (The county of Andria is a particular case in point.) In addition, legal immunities in the kingdom of Sicily, even to the most favoured churches, did not extend to the 'pleas of the crown', those cases involving violence or treason, which were reserved to the royal prerogative and to be judged only by royal officials. Similarly in 1144 there was a major investigation of privileges throughout the kingdom. These were in future to be valid only if expressly confirmed by the king.

Under Roger II the overall supervision of the mainland was vested, at least nominally, in the king's sons as duke of Apulia and prince of Capua, although in practice their role seems to have been mainly military and there is no evidence that they took any active part in administrative or judicial matters. In the 1140s the king himself still frequently visited the mainland, and the royal chancellor Robert of Selby (d. 1151) seems also to have been actively involved in mainland administration, though not necessarily on any continuous basis. Under Maio of Bari, from 1155–6 onwards, more systematic arrangements for the supervision of the mainland administration and the command of its defence were created, with overall control being invested in two 'master captains of Apulia and Terra di Lavoro' (i.e. the principality of Capua), and a similar official being appointed for Calabria. A master chamberlain was appointed for each of these two regions to oversee financial matters and the operations of the chamberlains. From the death of Maio onwards the master captains (after 1170 master justiciars) were invariably mainland counts. In the 1170s Robert of Caserta (d. 1183), held office in Apulia and Terra di Lavoro with, as his colleague, first Richard of Gravina, and then (from 1176) Tancred of Lecce, the king's cousin. Count Hugh of

Catanzaro was the master justiciar of Calabria from 1163, and would seem to have been succeeded by Richard of Gravina (d. 1177/8). In the 1180s Tancred and Count Roger of Andria were in office together in Apulia and Terra di Lavoro.

The administration of Sicily itself was kept separate from that of the mainland and run directly from the royal court, although, as said, justiciars were appointed on the island from *c.* 1154. The chief administrative office was known by the Arabic name of *diwan*, and many of its officials were indeed converted Muslims. ('Falcandus' alleged that they were only nominally converted.) From *c.* 1145, when there was a substantial reorganization of the Sicilian central administration, there were two separate sections – the *ad-diwan al-maʿmur* – the general administrative and financial office, which also administered the crown lands, and the *dīwān at-tahqīq al-maʿmur* or (Latin) *Duana de Secretis*, which was the land registry, keeping details of fiefs, boundaries and transfers of ownership. The functions of these two offices were clearly distinct, but in practice there was a considerable interchange of personnel. And, rather than it being simply a development of existing practice, the inspiration for the administrative reorganization of the 1140s probably came from Fatimid Egypt, with which the Sicilian administration, and in particular George of Antioch, was in close and friendly communication during the 1130s and 1140s.[46]

Under Maio of Bari the judicial activity of the royal court was put on a more professional footing with the appointment of three master justiciars permanently attached to it. The royal court in formal session, with one or more of these specialist judges present, acted as the court of appeal for Sicily, dealt with cases involving royal officials, defect of justice or failures in enforcing judicial decisions (sometimes on the mainland too) and conducted political trials such as that of Count Richard of Molise in 1168. One of the master judges in the 1160s was a Greek called Tarentinus.[47]

The most significant administrative change thereafter came *c.* 1168 when the mainland financial administration was brought more closely under the supervision of the central government, with the abolition of the two master chamberlains' posts and the creation of a branch office of the *diwan* on the mainland, known as the *Duana Baronum* and based at Salerno. Its competence was limited to Apulia and Capua, and the chamberlains of Calabria were henceforth under the direct administrative control of the *diwan* at Palermo. It was probably in connection with the setting up of the new *Duana Baronum*,

---

[46] Johns (1993), pp. 138–9, 145–7. For the administration generally, Takayama (1985) and (1993). Jamison (1913) is still fundamental for the government of the mainland.

[47] See Jamison (1967) here.

which like the *Duana de Secretis* kept registers of fiefs, that a revision of the 'Catalogue of the Barons' was put under way *c.* 1168, to update the government's list of landholders and military obligations in the mainland provinces at a time when the kingdom was still facing a significant (if perhaps diminishing) external threat.

The officials of the central government remained mainly of Greek and Arabic origin until the death of Roger II. The rise of Maio of Bari led to much greater influence by the Latin element. The majority of royal charters were henceforth written in Latin, and Latin bishops, hitherto largely excluded from the direction of affairs, provided the majority of *familiares* after 1166. But converted Muslims still fulfilled important roles, notably Caid Peter as a *familiaris* in the 1160s and Caid Richard, the master chamberlain of the royal palace, who directed the *Duana de Secretis* throughout the reign of William II. If anything the growth of Latin influence was at the expense of the Greek officials who had been most important under King Roger. Nevertheless Greeks too still held important posts, notably the judge Tarentinus as a legal expert, Eugenius, one of the masters of the *Duana Baronum* from 1174 onwards (and later head of King Tancred's administration), and Margaritus of Brindisi, commander of the fleet from the late 1180s.

By the time of William II the kingdom of Sicily had therefore a complex and sophisticated administrative system, which functioned efficiently under the overall direction of the *familiares* in Palermo. The king himself, even after he grew to manhood, was much less active than his grandfather had been, and spent most of his time in Palermo, only occasionally visiting the mainland. But the structure of government had evolved sufficiently to allow this. Furthermore the great wealth which contemporary commentators attributed to the king of Sicily – while it was a product of the scale of the crown lands, especially in Sicily itself, and of the island's position at the centre of Mediterranean trade routes – was also the result of the king having an efficient administration through which he could exploit his dominions. The relatively small number of known royal documents (only 66 from the reign of William I and 240 from that of his son) in no way reflects the scale of governmental activity, although the increasing proportion of mandates (that is, executive orders) known from the time of William II *is* certainly a sign of an increasingly active central government.[48] The king of Sicily was no tyrant, but he did rule a strong and centralized kingdom.

---

[48] The full texts of only 35 charters of William I now survive; of the 240 documents of William II known (103 of which are mandates) the texts of 156 now survive (55 of which are mandates), Enzensberger (1981), pp. 111–13. 72 documents of King Tancred are known, of which the texts of only 35 now survive. Brühl (1978), p. 35, suggests that the 166 surviving Latin charters of Roger II represent perhaps only 10 per cent of the total written.

KING, POPE AND CHURCH

The kingdom of Sicily was technically a papal fief, as the duchy of Apulia and principality of Capua had been from 1059 onwards. Roger II's royal title had been granted by Anacletus II in 1130; he did homage to Innocent II in 1139, as did William I to Adrian IV in 1156, and both kings agreed to pay an annual *census* to the papacy in return for their fief. But in practice this 'feudal' relationship was of very little importance; nor did it enhance papal authority within the kingdom.

Admittedly, relations between king and pope remained uneasy between 1139 and 1156. But this stemmed not so much from differing interpretations of the vassalic relationship as from the continued dislike among many at the papal court for a kingdom created by a bull from the antipope Anacletus, the existence of which Innocent II had been forced to recognize in 1139, and from a number of unresolved territorial and ecclesiastical disputes. The conquest of Marsia by Roger's sons in the early 1140s encompassed territory claimed by the papacy, as well as being a potential threat to the security and communications of Rome itself. The control exercised by the king over the church was an infringement of ecclesiastical liberty. The reorganization of the episcopal structure on the island of Sicily undertaken at Roger's behest by Anacletus in 1130–1 was by definition unacceptable to his successful rival in the schism. The well-informed English commentator John of Salisbury alleged that because of these disputes the papacy had forbidden the consecration of bishops-elect within the Sicilian kingdom.[49] But even in the 1140s relations were never entirely severed; there was for example something of a thaw during the brief pontificate of Lucius II (1144–5), in 1148 Roger sent troops to assist Eugenius III against the rebellious Romans, and in 1150 the meeting between pope and king at Ceprano led to a rapprochement and the consecration of the Sicilian bishops-elect. Admittedly, relations collapsed once again less than a year later after the coronation of the king's son as co-ruler without consultation with the papacy (almost the only evidence of the pope's role as overlord being of any significance), and Adrian IV was a party to the attacks on the kingdom in 1155–6. But the treaty of Benevento of June 1156 marked a definitive end to this period of hostilities. It saw the full recognition of the kingdom of Sicily, including the Marsian territories, and the definition of the special ecclesiastical privileges claimed by the king in virtue of Urban II's privilege to Roger I of 1098 (the right to control appeals to Rome and legations was recognized, but only for the island of Sicily and not for the mainland). The royal right of veto in episcopal elections throughout the kingdom was also tacitly allowed.[50] Only the status of the Sicilian bishoprics

---

[49] John of Salisbury, *Historia pontificalis*, pp. 65–6.
[50] There is an English translation of the treaty in Loud and Wiedemann (1998), pp. 248–52.

remained unresolved; and indeed it was not until 1166 that Alexander III agreed that Messina should become a metropolitan see and that bishops should be consecrated for the sees at Lipari and Cefalù – as Roger and Anacletus had intended in 1131.

In practice not only were nearly all the problems settled at Benevento in 1156, but thereafter both sides worked together in amity. The popes only rarely exercised their rights to send legates to the mainland of southern Italy, and the scanty evidence suggests that such legations actually did very little. The king secured the appointment of *curiales* to some of the Sicilian sees and a few key archbishoprics on the mainland such as Salerno and Capua. But, although the king's permission was required before the election of a new bishop or abbot could take place, in most cases the choice of a new prelate was then left to the canonical electors. Indeed, given how numerous the kingdom's bishoprics were (some 144 in all), and also how poor many of them were, the king had little motive for interference, except in the case of a very few wealthy or strategically important sees.

The amicable relations between king and pope after 1156 were of course fostered by their political alliance. With the papal schism of 1159 and the existence of an imperially sponsored antipope, the king of Sicily became the principal lay ally of the papacy, furnishing diplomatic, financial and, when the papal state was threatened, military support – as William I did against the forces of Christian of Mainz in 1165. Indeed, with the pope remaining in exile from Rome for almost a decade and the administration of the papal lands in ruins, the annual *census* paid by the king of Sicily, which had been increased in return for the Marsian lands in 1156, provided a very important part of Alexander III's income. Furthermore, for three and a half years, from August 1167 to February 1171, Alexander was living at Benevento, the papal enclave within the boundaries of the kingdom of Sicily, and thus under the direct protection of the king.

In these circumstances it was not surprising that the papacy was prepared to tolerate the control exercised by the Sicilian monarch over the church in his dominions – a control which was for the most part benevolent, and which, through the reassertion of law and order, was very much in the interests of local churchmen, and infinitely preferable to the disorder which had prevailed before 1127. One of King Roger's laws stated unequivocally that 'we shall defend and guard inviolate all the property and possessions of the holy churches which have been entrusted to our custody'.[51] That the bishoprics on the island of

---

[51] 'sacrarum ecclesiarum res omnes et possessiones . . . custodia collocatas atque commissas . . . defendimus et inviolatas custodimus'. Assize 2 of the Vatican MS, ed. F. Brandileone, *Diretto romano nelle legge normanne*, p. 96.

Sicily and a number of the most important sees on the mainland derived much of their income from direct subventions from royal revenues, rather than from their own lands, also predisposed Sicilian churchmen to acquiesce in this royal control.[52] The relative unimportance of the vassalic relationship can be seen from the fact that the king's oath of fealty was not renewed until 1188 – and that it was then may well have been dictated more by Clement III's desire to establish a precedent for the future, given that William II's marriage was childless and his designated heiress the wife of the heir to the German empire, than to any wish to interfere directly with the kingdom.

There does seem to have been rather more papal activity concerning the day-to-day workings of the south Italian church in William II's later years, and the papacy may never have been entirely reconciled to the authority claimed by the king over the church – certainly in 1192 Celestine III took advantage of King Tancred's need for external support, given his disputed title to the crown, to renegotiate the terms of the treaty of Benevento and diminish royal powers. But while William II lived this control remained an unchallenged reality.

ECONOMY, DEMOGRAPHY AND SOCIAL STRUCTURE

The wealth which contemporaries attributed to the king was derived in part from sales taxes and tolls on trade, but to a large extent from a flourishing and expanding agrarian economy.[53] Although parts of southern Italy were mountainous and infertile, other areas, notably the Campania, the coastal plain of Apulia and (with the aid of irrigation) much of Sicily itself, were agriculturally very productive. In the twelfth century the population was expanding, and areas hitherto only lightly settled, such as the Tavoliere of Apulia between Bari and Monte Gargano, were being cleared and opened for cultivation. The kingdom became a major source of food exports, especially grain, both for northern Italy and North Africa, as well as an important staging-post for trade between northern Italy and the Levant. The development of the agricultural sector can be seen for example in the spread of olive cultivation in central Apulia. (By the late twelfth century olives had become the principal crop in this region, and a major export commodity.) Vegetable cultivation was also introduced to Apulia, and in the Campania new types of cereals appeared and arboriculture spread, with the domestication of hitherto wild species.

The development of the kingdom's external trade was encouraged by treaties with the commercial powers of northern Italy such as that with Genoa in 1156, though here there was clearly a political element as well, to try to deprive

---

[52] Usually a tenth of royal revenues from within the diocese. See Kamp (1980), pp. 104–5, 118.
[53] See here Abulafia (1983), and for what follows Martin (1987), (1992) and (2002).

Frederick Barbarossa of naval aid for a potential invasion. Such trade directly benefited the ruler, not just because of commercial taxes – where the north Italians were given preferential treatment – but because much of the produce exported came from the extensive royal demesne, especially in Sicily itself. Extensive royal ownership of salt pans was also very profitable, although there was at this period no formal royal monopoly as there was later to be under Frederick II. The numerous tunny fisheries off the coast of Sicily and mining rights were, however, reserved to the crown. A favourable balance of trade with North Africa explains the import of gold from which the Sicilian rulers continued to mint tari (in origin gold Islamic quarter-dinar coins) as the centrepiece of their currency. Sicily was the only western European kingdom to have a gold coinage in the twelfth century. The German chroniclers of Henry VI's takeover in 1194 were to comment in amazement at the profusion of precious metals, jewels and textiles among the booty captured.[54] Although some raw silk was produced in Calabria and woven in Sicily, the other valuables were imported.

However, the growth of this trade did not necessarily benefit the towns of the Regno as much as it did the ruler. Commercial concessions to the north Italians placed the native merchants at a disadvantage from which they never really recovered. Furthermore, Amalfi, the chief mercantile city of the south in the early middle ages, was greatly harmed when it was sacked by a Pisan fleet in 1134, and Bari, the principal port of the Adriatic coast, was destroyed by William I in 1156 and for a time deserted. Nor were the kings prepared to concede more than very limited legal privileges or autonomy to the towns, whose commercial interests were thus subordinated to the political and financial concerns of the ruler.

The expansion of external trade did play a significant part in the development of Messina, which became the key commercial entrepôt within the kingdom. By the late twelfth century colonies of both Genoese and Pisan merchants had been established there. Under Muslim rule Messina had been relatively unimportant; by the 1180s it was, in the words of the Spanish Muslim pilgrim Ibn Jubayr, 'the mart of the merchant infidels, the focus of ships from all over the world . . . teeming with worshippers of the Cross'.[55] But the growth of Messina was also part of a significant change in the balance of population in Sicily. Immigration greatly increased the Christian population of the island, and by c. 1200 the Muslims, who a century earlier had comprised at least two-thirds of its inhabitants, had become a minority. Some of the immigrants may well have been Greeks from Calabria, although the scale of any such movement is by no means certain. Messina was considered to be a primarily Greek city by the English chroniclers of the Third Crusade in 1190; charters

---

[54] Loud (1999b), p. 818.   [55] Ibn Jubayr, *The Travels*, p. 338.

from the city were still written almost exclusively in Greek until *c.* 1200, and some documents from eastern Sicily continued to be written in Greek as well as Latin for a century after that. But the foundation of Greek monasteries on the island ceased after 1130, and a number of those previously founded were later abandoned or converted to the Latin rite, which suggests that the Greek population had already reached its peak. The majority of the immigrants were Lombards (i.e. native Italians), both from the southern mainland and from northern Italy. The south-east of the island was colonized by northern settlers under the aegis of King Roger's maternal uncle Count Henry of Paterno. 'Falcandus' considered Butera, Piazza Armerina and Vizzini to be 'towns of the north Italians' (*oppida Lombardorum* – as opposed to the *Longobardi* or south Italians), and recorded that in 1168 these *Lombardi* offered to provide 20,000 men to aid the chancellor Stephen of Perche against the rebels in Messina.[56] This figure was probably an exaggeration, but the scale of their immigration was undoubtedly considerable. By this time Palermo had become a largely Christian city, and here, and indeed elsewhere on the island outside the south-east, the bulk of the new settlers were from the mainland parts of the Regno. There were, for example, a number of natives of Bari resident in Palermo in the last years of Roger II,[57] and towns like Cefalù were overwhelmingly Latin by the late twelfth century.

The population of the interior of western Sicily, including the great tract of royal demesne given by William II to his new abbey of Monreale in the 1170s, was still almost exclusively Arabic, and very largely Muslim. But by this time the Muslims were beginning to feel threatened. A prominent royal official of Arabic extraction called Philip of Mahdia, a Muslim convert to Christianity, was executed in 1153 for apostasizing back to Islam. The attempted coup against William I in 1161 saw attacks by Christians on Muslims, which occurred once again after the death of William II in 1189. The sense of unease which permeated the Muslims, or at least those living in the towns of western Sicily, despite their apparent prosperity, was vividly conveyed by Ibn Jubayr's account of his visit to the island in 1184. He was told that they were under considerable pressure to convert to Christianity (does this reflect the growing influence of churchmen in the government of William II?), and that many of them wanted to emigrate to Muslim countries.[58] One cannot be certain how far the rural population of the interior felt the same pressure. Onomastic evidence suggests that there were already some Christians of Arabic extraction among the inhabitants of western Sicily, as for example among those serfs listed in the Monreale *plateae* of the

---

[56] *La Historia o Liber de regno Sicilie*, pp. 70, 155, Loud and Wiedemann (1998), pp. 121, 208.
[57] *Codice diplomatico Barese*, pp. 170–3 no. 100 (1146), p. 183 no. 107, pp. 185–6 no. 109 (both 1154).
[58] Ibn Jubayr, *The Travels*, pp. 348–9, 357–60.

1180s – at Corleone they formed almost 20 per cent of the total population.[59] But Muslims remained very much in the majority on the Monreale lands, as they were also in the region of Agrigento. The riots in Palermo in 1189 were the trigger for a widespread Muslim revolt in western Sicily, which was to smoulder intermittently for more than thirty years until its suppression by Frederick II and the removal of many of the surviving Muslims to his military colony at Lucera in northern Apulia.

By the end of the twelfth century therefore the Latin element in the kingdom was dominant, to a much greater extent than it had been in the early years of Roger II. Immigration and a slow process of acculturation were weakening the Muslims in Sicily, and to a lesser extent the Greek population in Calabria. Nevertheless, this process should not be exaggerated. The Greeks were certainly under no overt pressure after 1100, and arguably not even before then in the immediate wake of the Norman conquest. Furthermore the Latin element, at least in the upper class, was far from being homogeneous. Romuald of Salerno recorded that King Roger attracted and rewarded 'virtuous and wise men, whether from his own land or born elsewhere',[60] and high-status immigrants continued to be absorbed, if not always without tension, by the ruling class in both church and state. From the Anglo-Norman realm there was Roger II's chancellor Robert of Selby, the *familiaris* Richard Palmer, bishop of Syracuse from 1157 and then archbishop of Messina (1183–95), and Herbert of Middlesex, archbishop of Conza (1169–81).[61] The lay aristocracy in the 1160s included two Spanish relatives of Queen Margaret, Counts Gilbert of Gravina and Henry of Montescaglioso, and a French immigrant, Hugh Lopinus, count of Catanzaro.

Above all, the upper class on the mainland was an amalgam of the descendants of the Norman conquerors of the eleventh century and of the indigenous Lombards. The larger towns remained the preserve of the Lombards, and Lombard aristocrats remained powerful in a number of areas, especially in the border regions and in the principality of Salerno. Admittedly the distinction between Lombard and Norman became politically less and less significant as time went on. However, it left its mark on the institutions and law of southern Italy. The Normans had, for example, introduced both the fief and the ceremony of homage. But it was only with King Roger in the 1140s that a universal structure of military obligation was imposed *from above*; and even then, while most men owed service because of the fiefs they held, some still

---

[59] Metcalfe (2002), pp. 309–16.

[60] Romuald of Salerno, *Chronicon sive Annales*, p. 234, cf. *La Historia o Liber de regno Sicilie*, p. 6, Loud and Wiedemann (1998), pp. 58, 220.

[61] However, Archbishop Walter of Palermo (1168–90) and his brother Bishop Bartholomew of Agrigento (1171–91), who succeeded him as archbishop (and died 1199), were not Englishmen, as once was supposed. See Loewenthal (1972).

had a personal duty to serve, irrespective of their property, as their ancestors had done in the days of the Lombard princes. Normans and Lombards differed too in their customs governing inheritance, marriage and the status of women. Partible inheritance remained the norm among those of Lombard descent, primogeniture ruled among those from Norman and French antecedents. In Lombard law women were always legally minors, who needed the consent of a male guardian before undertaking any legal transaction. Women living under French or Roman law were freer to act on their own behalf.

Thus while the kingdom of Sicily had by the late twelfth century become an accepted part of the European political scene, and possessed an effective system of government, it was unified, but remained far from uniform. In this it reflected the diversity of its origins, and the cosmopolitan society at the crossroads of the Mediterranean which the Normans had conquered in the eleventh century, and which a great ruler had welded forcibly together after 1130. But the years after 1189 were to see the unity of the kingdom under threat, and it was ultimately unable to resist the renewed attack of the German empire.

SICILY, THE MEDITERRANEAN AND THE WESTERN EMPIRE

The nostalgic reminiscences of later writers, who saw the reign of William II as a golden age of peace and prosperity, were conditioned by later events. William died childless on 17 November 1189, at the age of thirty-six. The result was five years of conflict before the kingdom was conquered by the German emperor Henry VI, and after his equally premature death, aged thirty-two in 1197, there was more than twenty years of intermittent anarchy. But this was by no means inevitable, nor does it suggest that the Sicilian kingdom was intrinsically flawed.

William II's later years saw the kingdom internally at peace, but deploying an increasingly ambitious foreign policy. His envoys at the peace conference at Venice in 1177, where a fifteen-year truce was agreed with the German empire, proclaimed that it was his wish to live at peace with all Christian rulers, but to attack the enemies of the cross.[62] The Sicilian fleet attacked Muslim Alexandria in 1174 and the Balearic Islands in 1182 (this latter operation probably in response to Muslim piracy). In 1185 a full-scale assault was mounted on the Byzantine empire, which under the incompetent and unpopular rule of Andronikos Komnenos seemed to be on the verge of collapse. In the event, despite the capture of Thessalonica, this attack failed. But it certainly showed the determination of William II to be one of the leaders of western Christendom. So too did his prompt despatch of naval aid to the crusader states after the fall

---

[62] Romuald of Salerno, *Chronicon sive Annales*, p. 290. Cf. Houben (1992), especially pp. 124–8.

of Jerusalem to Saladin. The high status of the king of Sicily was confirmed by two diplomatic marriages, that of the king himself to Joanna, the daughter of Henry II of England, in 1176, and of his aunt Constance, Roger II's daughter, born in 1154 just after her father's death (and thus a year younger than her nephew the king), with Henry, the heir to the German empire, in 1186.

Frederick Barbarossa had first suggested a marriage alliance with the Sicilians as early as 1173, though papal opposition had ensured that this proposal was stillborn. But by the conclusion of such a marriage the intrinsic legitimacy of the Sicilian kingdom was at last recognized by the German empire, its principal external enemy since Roger II's coronation in 1130, and thus it is not difficult to see why William II was prepared to permit it. The price to be paid was the acknowledgement of Constance as the designated heir to the childless king. But the significance of such a move should not be over-estimated. William was still a relatively young man in 1186, his wife was only twenty; he is unlikely to have abandoned hope of future offspring, and these would have automatically invalidated Constance's claim. However, the king did die young, and without a direct heir.

His death was followed by a split within the kingdom. The claims of Henry and Constance had a number of prominent supporters, including Archbishop Walter of Palermo and Count Roger of Andria, one of the two master justiciars of Apulia. But a group of prominent court officials, led by the *familiaris* Matthew of Salerno, moved swiftly to elect their own candidate, the other master justiciar, Count Tancred of Lecce, William II's cousin (who had been the commander of the army which had captured Thessalonica in 1185). Tancred was crowned king on 18 January 1190, a move which had the covert support of the papacy, anxious to avoid the union of Sicily and the empire.

Although hampered by the Muslim rebellion, Tancred was from the first in control of Sicily and Calabria. He did, however, face widespread opposition from the mainland nobility, especially from the principality of Capua and the Abruzzi, and to a lesser extent from Apulia. He did, however, also have a number of advantages. Henry VI was preoccupied with domestc affairs in Germany, and this gave the king time to establish his rule. Most of the higher clergy (apart from those in the principality of Capua) and the more important towns supported him, and the latters' loyalty was made more secure by privileges and fiscal concessions. His brother-in-law, Count Richard of Acerra, proved an able lieutenant on the mainland, and his support gave Tancred immediate control of much of the principality of Salerno. Furthermore, nine of the twenty-eight counties in Apulia and Capua were vacant, and thus under the administration of royal officials, in 1189, giving the king a strong foothold in the mainland provinces, especially in Apulia, and the means to reward potential supporters. And in November 1190 his chief domestic opponent, Roger of Andria, was captured and put to death. When Henry VI finally launched his invasion in the spring of 1191 his army became embroiled in a fruitless siege of Naples and fell victim to an epidemic, while his naval forces, recruited from Pisa and Genoa, arrived too late to be of help and proved no match for the Sicilian fleet.

The withdrawal of the German army allowed Tancred to consolidate his rule. By 1193 only the Abruzzi region on the frontier held out. The mainland counts who had opposed him had either gone over to his side (as did the counts of Molise, Carinola and Caserta), or had been exiled (those of Tricarico, Gravina, Fondi and the Principato). If the Abruzzi was still a problem, and a base for German forces to raid into the kingdom proper, his position appeared relatively secure. That the kingdom's defences collapsed before a second invasion in 1194 was due almost entirely to two factors. Tancred himself died in February 1194, leaving a small boy as his heir (William III) and his supporters seem to have lost heart. And the ransom exacted from King Richard of England gave Henry VI the wealth he needed to launch another, better organized and coordinated invasion. This time there were no delays for long sieges, areas of potential opposition were bypassed, and the fleet arrived in time. Many of Tancred's erstwhile supporters immediately submitted, as did the strategic city of Naples. Messina surrendered to the Pisan and Genoese fleet in September, Palermo in November, Tancred's widow abandoned the struggle, and Henry was crowned king of Sicily on Christmas Day 1194.

Henry's coronation was followed almost immediately by the arrest of his erstwhile rival, the unfortunate William III, and a number of prominent nobles and royal officials, including the sons of Matthew of Salerno, the amir Eugenius and the admiral Margaritus of Brindisi, all of whom were sent to prisons in Germany. Despite, or perhaps because of, this brutal action, resistance on the mainland was not finally extinguished until the capture and execution of Richard of Acerra in 1196. A further revolt in Sicily was brutally suppressed in the summer of 1197. Although some south Italians who had supported Henry were favoured – Bishop Walter of Troia was, for example, made chancellor – the chief beneficiaries of the new regime were his German commanders, men like Conrad of Lützelinhard, made count of Molise, and Diepold of Schweinspunt, the new count of Acerra. Tancred's government was regarded as illegitimate and its acts, including the concessions made to the papacy at Gravina in 1192, of no legal standing. But if Henry regarded himself as the conqueror of Sicily, ruling it by right of his imperial title, Constance represented the continuity of the royal dynasty. In October 1195 she wrote to the pope complaining about various infringements of the crown's ecclesiastical rights, including the appointment of a general legate for the mainland provinces: 'such things', she claimed, 'were never attempted in the kingdom by the Roman Church under our father the lord king Roger and then under the other kings, our brother and nephew'.[63] After Henry's sudden death in September 1197 she did her best to diminish the German role in the kingdom. In the years after her death (in November 1198), with the new king a child and the Regno a prey to the rivalries of local nobles, German adventurers, Pisans and Genoese, Muslim revolt and papal interference, it was the court officials who had served William II who represented the principal force for stability and order, and who maintained the government as best they could through the difficult years of the early thirteenth century.[64] It was on their work that Frederick II was ultimately to build.

[63] 'sub domino patre nostro rege Rogerio . . . et deinceps sub aliis regibus, fratre et nepote nostro . . . numquam in regno talia per sanctam Romanam ecclesiam fuerint attentata', *Constantiae imperatricis et reginae Siciliae diplomata*, pp. 12–13 no. 3. Loud (2002), pp. 180–1.

[64] Jamison (1957), pp. 146–74, argued that the amir Eugenius was a key figure in this administrative continuity, up to his death *c.* 1202, though this has been disputed. For continuity in the chancery, Schaller (1957), pp. 207–15.

CHAPTER 16

SPAIN IN THE TWELFTH CENTURY

Peter Linehan

THE death of Alfonso VI of León on the last day of June 1109 brought a woman to the throne of 'all Spain' for the first time in its history. Or so three weeks later Queen Urraca described the extent of her authority. 'All Spain' in that summer comprised the area from the Atlantic in the west to the Ebro in the east and to the north of a line running from Coimbra by way of Toledo to Medinaceli and the border of the kingdom of Saragossa (the northernmost of the formally independent taifa kingdoms into which the caliphate of Córdoba had disintegrated in the previous century), beyond which lay the kingdom of Aragón and the county of Barcelona. Yet within ten years this description of the area between the Pyrenees and the sierras of the centre would no longer apply, and within sixty it would be unrecognizable. By then the north of the peninsula would be occupied by the five kingdoms of Portugal, León, Castile, Navarre and Aragón which endured until the end of the century and beyond, and by the end of this chapter further kaleidoscopic transformations will have occurred. The history of twelfth-century Spain was enacted on constantly shifting foundations.

This was the case with the reign of Urraca herself (1109–26), one of whose first acts after her father's death was to marry Alfonso I, the Battler, of Aragon (1104–34). This she did 'during the vintage time', according to the chronicle of Sahagún, in fulfilment of arrangements made by Alfonso VI in the last year of his life. But as well as being uncanonical, the match was unsuitable. Too nearly related for the pope's liking, in all other respects the couple were re-mote. On their wedding night it hailed, the rabidly anti-Aragonese chronicler reported with satisfaction. (Apart from being dangerously close to the best wine-growing areas along that stretch of the Duero, Monzón, where apparently the marriage was celebrated, was a place of no ecclesiastical significance: a doubly inauspicious venue therefore).[1] And, sure enough, worse followed.

---

[1] Reilly (1982), p. 59.

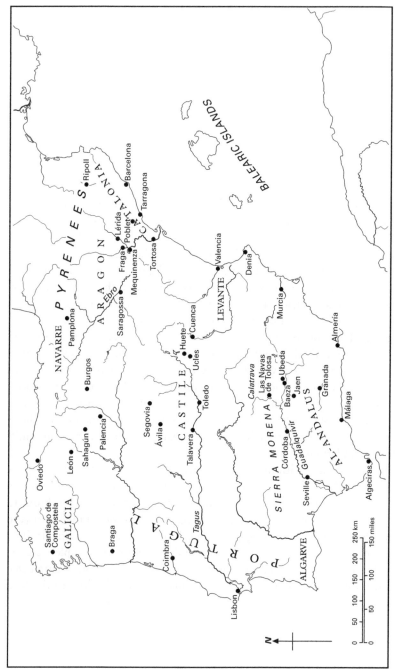

Map II Spain

Within the year the pair were at odds, and the inhabitants of the regions around the rivers Miño, Duero and Ebro found themselves being fought over by their coreligionists with a degree of ferocity which, according to the same writer, far exceeded anything ever experienced there at the hands of the Muslims. Urraca's marriage was the first of a series of dynastic alliances across the century whose evident potential for disaster from the outset serves notice on the historian of the otherness of the world into which he is entering.

Our knowledge of Urraca's reign derives from two contemporary sources: the aforementioned chronicle of the Leonese monastery of Sahagún, which has survived in a much later, and possibly much revised, Spanish translation, and the *Historia Compostellana*, a work commissioned by an actor in the ensuing drama, Bishop (subsequently Archbishop) Diego Gelmírez of Santiago de Compostela, who had even less cause to recall the Aragonese with affection.[2] We do not have a pro-Alfonsine corrective. We altogether lack an account addressed from the point of view of the king whose Christian zeal would inspire him in 1131 to nominate the Order of the Temple as one of his heirs.[3] By way of compensation we are well supplied with charters. However, because so many of these are fabrications or have been tampered with, the history of the reign remains riddled with uncertainties. As does that of the entire twelfth century. Indeed, in comparison with its second half the age of Urraca and Alfonso VII is well catered for. Even so, those acquainted with countries rich in chronicles must allow for the fact that Spain is not.[4] They will look in vain for those little vignettes which elsewhere reveal more than a hundred charters can. They will find nothing to match the glimpse of Henry II of England wielding his darning needle for example. The rulers of twelfth-century Spain come across as irredeemably two-dimensional figures.

The reign of Urraca was overshadowed by Alfonso VI's various failed attempts to provide for the succession, and its course largely determined by the personalities brought in by that much-married monarch to compensate for his remarkable inability to beget a male heir capable of surviving him. As count of Galicia, Urraca's first husband, the Burgundian Raymond of Amous had had his centre in the remote north-west, where (with the assistance of his brother Archbishop Guy of Vienne) he secured in 1100 the election of his protégé Diego Gelmírez as bishop of Compostela. His death in September 1107 left Urraca a widow of twenty-seven with a one-year-old child, Alfonso Raimúndez, the

[2] 'Crónicas anónimas de Sahagún'; *Historia Compostellana*.

[3] García Larragueta (1957), II, p. 16: 'qui ad defendendum Christianitatis nomen ibi vigilant'.

[4] Sánchez Alonso (1947), pp. 119–25, 137–48; Linehan (1993), chs. 7–9. For the sequence of events related in what follows I am indebted to the works of Soldevila (1962), Valdeavellano (1968) and Serrão (1979), but have not thought it necessary to provide repeated footnote references either to them or to Bishko (1975) where further bibliographical guidance will be found.

future Alfonso VII, in her care. Since 1097 Count Raymond had been scheming to succeed Alfonso VI himself: the Pact of Succession which, with the
assistance of Abbot Hugh of Cluny, he had made in that year with his cousin,
Henry of ducal Burgundy, husband of Alfonso VI's bastard daughter Teresa,
had promised Henry a share of a divided kingdom. In 1109 Henry, one of a
number of entrenched interests dismayed by Urraca's Aragonese marriage, was
firmly installed as count of Portugal, the territory between the rivers Miño and
Tagus.[5]

By the terms of their marriage settlement (Dec. 1109) Urraca and any child
of the marriage were to inherit the kingdom of Aragon if Alfonso died first.
If Urraca predeceased him he and the child would acquire Urraca's lands, and
when Alfonso died they would revert to Alfonso Raimúndez. The settlement
was a recipe for disaster; resistance had already begun in Galicia, led by the
count of Traba, Pedro Froilaz, the guardian of Alfonso Raimúndez. But the
settlement proved a nullity because there was no child. Whereas Urraca bore
Count Pedro González of Lara two bastards in the years that followed, Alfonso
may have been either impotent or uninterested. Moreover, developing mutual
antipathy between the couple was not diminished by the Aragonese monarch's
need to attend to the defence of his kingdom against the Muslim ruler of
Saragossa. On Teresa's behalf, Henry of Portugal fomented trouble between
1110 and his death in May 1112, regularly shifting his support from the king to
the queen and back. But the situation was transformed in late 1111 by Urraca's
recovery of Alfonso Raimúndez, the symbol of legitimacy, and by mid-1112 the
marriage was finished.[6] Not until the 1470s would the opportunity of achieving
Christian unification across the Ebro recur.

Urraca spent the rest of her reign striving to recover the authority which
Alfonso VI had bequeathed to her. In February 1117, at the council of Burgos
held under the presidency of the papal legate Cardinal Boso of S. Anastasia,
the canonical rules relating to consanguineous marriage were reiterated, rules
of which neither party had been unaware in 1109 but with which it now suited
both of them to conform. On the same occasion a truce of a sort appears to
have been reached whereby each undertook to leave undisturbed the other's
conquests, Alfonso's in Castile and Urraca's in Vizcaya and Rioja. However,
the queen had not only her former husband to contend with but her half-
sister Teresa and Diego Gelmírez (raised to metropolitan rank in 1120) as
well, and above all Alfonso Raimúndez, the election of whose uncle Guy of
Vienne as Pope Calixtus II in 1119 provided an ally even more powerful than the
prelate of Santiago. In 1120–1 Cardinal Boso returned to Spain with instructions
either to constrain Urraca to liberate the archbishop and restore his castles and

---

[5] Reilly (1982), pp. 3–62.   [6] *Ibid.*, pp. 63–86.

extensive territorial 'honour' or to impose sentences of excommunication and general interdict on her and her kingdom. By then the focus of Alfonso the Battler's attention had anyway shifted to his own kingdom and to the Almoravid presence in the Ebro valley. Here he was assisted by contingents of Gascons and Normans, notably Count Gaston V of Béarn and Count Rotrou of Mortagne (Perche), whose numbers were greatly swollen in 1118 when Gelasius II issued crusading indulgences at the council of Toulouse. The capture of Saragossa (Dec. 1118), the greatest feat of Christian arms since the reconquest of Toledo, was largely due to these trans-Pyrenean warriors, and notably to the count of Béarn and the experience of siege warfare he had acquired at Jerusalem in 1099.[7]

At Jerusalem the Muslim defenders had been massacred. At Saragossa they were permitted either to leave or to remain on terms. Alfonso the Battler was overstretched. The ambitions of the victor of Saragossa extended to all parts of the taifa kingdom, as far as Tudela and Calatayud in the west and Lérida in the east. In 1125–6, at the urging of Mozarabic Christians of the deep south, he led an army as far as Granada, defeated the forces of the governor of Seville near Lucena and returned to Saragossa bringing with him thousands of Christian families to settle his new territories in the Ebro valley. But in order to be able to afford such forays, economies had to be made elsewhere and in 1122–3 Alfonso relinquished the hold which he had fitfully exercised over Toledo since 1111, thereby enabling the Leonese to exploit Almoravid weakness and launch an attack on the city of Sigüenza, which fell to them at the beginning of 1124. Significantly it was not with Urraca but with Alfonso Raimúndez that his agreement to withdraw from Toledo was reached. The queen's political initiative after 1117, in reconciling her son to herself and making him the agent of her authority in the trans-Duero and Toledo, has been acclaimed for its brilliance.[8] This is perhaps excessive: from what can be inferred from the as ever patchy evidence it would appear that Alfonso Raimúndez was determined to be neither his mother's man nor the archbishop of Santiago's, but his own. On 8 March 1126 Urraca died in adulterous childbirth. She was forty-six.

Alfonso Raimúndez, who succeeded her as Alfonso VII (1126–57), had served a long and tough apprenticeship and alone of his line had his exploits recorded in a contemporary chronicle, the 'Chronica Adefonsi Imperatoris'.[9] Even in his mother's lifetime Alfonso had used the imperial title. He appears to have done so for the first time in 1117, shortly after entering Toledo;[10] which, if so, was not fortuitous for the Leonese monarch was strongly attached to the

[7] *Ibid.*, pp. 87–204; Lacarra (1971), pp. 59–68.   [8] Reilly (1982), pp. 173–80, 360.
[9] The most recent study of the reign is that of Recuero Astray (1979).
[10] Reilly (1982), p. 126; García Gallo (1945), p. 227 n. 94.

old Visigothic capital. Historians have long debated the question of the use
of imperial nomenclature by the kings of León from the 910s onwards. For
Alfonso VI the idea of empire was associated with Toledo. For Alfonso VII,
however, committed as he was to the city in which he would be buried (as
Alfonso VI had not been), the idea of empire represented something else: not
an evocation of the past history but the acknowledgement of present politics. At
Whitsun 1135 it was not Toledo, it was León that hosted his imperial coronation,
thereby proclaiming the fact that 'King García [Ramírez] of Navarre and King
Zafadola of the Saracens [Abu Ja'far Ahmad ibn Hud, ruler of Rueda] and
Count Ramón [Berenguer IV] of Barcelona and Count Alphonse of Toulouse
and many counts and dukes of Gascony and France were obedient to him in all
things (*in omnibus essent obedientes ei*).'[11] The twelfth-century peninsular ruler
to whom Spanish posterity would refer simply as 'the emperor' adopted the
imperial title in order to express the extent of his feudal authority either side
of the Pyrenees and either side of Spain's religious divide. Though he was only
nine years into it in 1135 his thirty-one-year reign is perhaps best approached
by treating that occasion as its central event.

During those first nine years Alfonso VII was occupied in undoing the damage of the previous seventeen. On his accession in 1126 even León, the capital
of his ancestors, offered resistance. To the east there were Aragonese garrisons
at Burgos and beyond. However, having brought the Leonese to order, his first
move was westwards for discussions with Countess Teresa of Portugal. With her
and her paramour the king 'made peace . . . until the appointed time' (*usque
ad destinatum tempus*).[12] And so he did with others. But what, if anything,
would these arrangements be worth? As soon as the king was out of sight his
sword counted for no more than a knife that had passed through warm butter.
Following the chronicler's account (on which for these years we are wholly
dependent) we turn east. From Carrión and Burgos the locals sent the king ('of
León') friendly signals 'because he was their natural lord' (1, p. 8). The Aragonese
custodian of Burgos was loath to surrender, whereupon the Christians and Jews
of the place turned him out and handed him over to Alfonso. When he heard of
this the king of Aragón was furious. But the game was up, the Battler knew it,
and with a sudden crescendo the ordinarily flat prose of the chronicle records
the fact. Messengers were sent through Galicia, Asturias, León and Castile summoning a great army, and the king of Aragón bowed to the inevitable, at Támara
tamely pleading for just forty days in which to withdraw his troops (1, pp. 9, 10).

From other evidence, however, it appears that the chronicler's account of
the 'Peace of Támara' is less than entirely credible, and that far from returning
empty-handed the Aragonese envoys brought back with them Alfonso VII's

---

[11] *Chronica Adefonsi imperatoris*, bk 1, ch. 70.   [12] *Ibid.*, bk 1, ch. 5. i. 5.

agreement to surrender territory in Vizcaya, Alava and Guipúzcoa which had been annexed by Alfonso VI when the kingdom of Navarre had been partitioned between Castile-León and Aragón after the murder of Sancho IV Garcés in 1076. Moreover, Alfonso I did not surrender to Alfonso VII all the lands stipulated in the Rioja and eastern Castile. Nevertheless, the effect of the 'Peace of Támara' was to extend Leonese influence into areas where it had been ineffective since before 1109, a development confirmed in 1127 when Alfonso VII took as his wife Berenguela, daughter of the count of Barcelona, Ramón Berenguer III: his lovely, albeit little bride, as the author of the 'Crónica' describes her.[13]

Throughout the previous half-century, during which Aragón had been colonizing the Ebro valley, the kingdom of Navarre had remained in a state of suspended animation, attached as a county to the kingdom of Aragón. The consequences for its future were far-reaching. Hemmed in between its mightier Christian neighbours, Navarre was thereafter denied the opportunity of colonizing Muslim territory: its expansion would have to be either at the expense of the kingdoms of Castile and Aragón, which regularly conspired to squeeze it out of existence, or otherwise into Gascony. For the county of Barcelona, by contrast, these had been years of growth. While consolidating his hold over the historic ninth-century heartland, acquiring the counties of Besalú and Cerdanya (1111, 1117), Ramón Berenguer III (1096–1131) extended Catalan influence northwards across the Pyrenees, by his marriage and acquisition of the title of count of Provence in 1113 confronting the counts of Toulouse with a potent rival. In 1114–15, in concert with the Pisans and Genoese, he led a briefly successful expedition against Almoravid Majorca. In the city of Barcelona Ramón Berenguer possessed a thriving commercial centre unequalled elsewhere in Christian Spain. Yet, formally at least, the hegemony he exercised was constrained by the past, in this case by the Frankish past: ecclesiastically his territories remained subject to the see of Narbonne. Allied to the availability of land-hungry crusaders from the north, however, the geographical advantage he enjoyed over the other Christian leaders which enabled him to prosecute the struggle against Islam by sea as well as land provided a remedy. To the extent that its Muslim garrison had been dislodged, the ancient metropolitan see of Tarragona had been reconquered in 1096, the first year of Ramón Berenguer's rule, and already (in the jurisdictional aftermath of the reconquest of Toledo) Urban II had decreed its restoration. But the realization of this outcome, and the reconstruction of the place, was due to the combined efforts of Archbishop Oleguer and the Norman Robert Burdet who, having left the service of the king of Aragón, was in 1128 established by Oleguer as 'prince of Tarragona'. The terms of the agreement between the archbishop and the warrior, which

---

[13] 'puellam paruulam, totam pulchram et decoram nimis' (*ibid.*, bk 1, ch. 12).

extended to the latter's descendants, were exceptionally favourable: Burdet was to have 90 per cent of the profits of the place. The Tarragona settlement demonstrated the richness of the opportunities that twelfth-century Spain was capable of offering adventurers from the north. Equally, the strained relationship which developed between the successors of the parties to it, culminating in 1171 in the murder in his cathedral of Archbishop Hugo de Cervelló by one of Burdet's sons, epitomized the difficulties that tended to arise one generation on as appreciation dawned of the full implications of the transfer of residual (in this case comital) authority in a corner of Europe in which human assistance on any terms had once been welcome.[14] In England in the 1170s only the king could have had an archbishop killed. But Spain was different, and there the *costa del crime* was already establishing its ground-rules, which then as now were dictated by riff-raff from the foggier north. We shall return later to their exploits elsewhere in the peninsula.

Meanwhile, by the extent of their activities the kings of Aragon and León had been defining the perimeters within which they were able to operate. In 1130 Alfonso I of Aragon was at Bayonne, besieging the city in support of Gaston of Béarn, the vassal to whose skills he was beholden for Saragossa and who was now at odds with Duke William of Aquitaine. And three years later he was engaged in riparian warfare up the Ebro as far as Tortosa,[15] while Alfonso VII had struck as far as Cadiz. From Cadiz on a fine day Africa is visible, but in the early 1130s such expeditions south were nevertheless possible. The Almoravids, who had annihilated the armies of Alfonso VI at Zalaca in 1086 and as recently as 1118 had had to be beaten off from Saragossa, were themselves being pressed from behind. In Morocco sometime in 1121 Ibn Tumart had declared himself mahdi. A Berber from those parts noted for extreme asceticism, he rejected Almoravid doctrine as altogether too literal and at the same time too anthropomorphic in its interpretation of the koran, favouring instead an interpretation of the prophetic text more in tune with the sense of the Muslim community. The name of his followers, *al-Muwahhidun*, has been transliterated as Almohad.[16] Of the fury of the zeal with which they would pursue the heretic Almoravids, climaxing in the weltering bloodbath at Marrakesh in 1147 (and *a fortiori* the even more benighted Christians), Alfonso VII was almost certainly not yet aware as he peered across the straits in 1133. He soon would be.

The following year presented the Christian kingdoms with a crisis nearer home. At Fraga in July 1134 Alfonso I of Aragon fought and lost his last battle against the Almoravids, and two months later died childless. Despite

---

[14] Soldevila (1962), pp. 136–8; *La documentación pontificia hasta Inocencio III*, no. 32; Villanueva (1851), pp. 155–60, 289–90; Defourneaux (1949), pp. 224–30.
[15] Lacarra (1971), pp. 102–24.   [16] Le Tourneau (1969), pp. 25–41; Lomax (1989), pp. 38–40.

the fact that his experience of Urraca provides sufficient explanation of his lack of interest in procreation, Alfonso I's childlessness continues to fascinate historians and to foster speculation at a number of levels. At the time, however, it was his will's consequences rather than its causes that counted, for Alfonso had named as his heirs the Orders of the Temple and St John of Jerusalem and the Holy Sepulchre.[17] Conjecture regarding that has been rampant too. Was his will a subtle ploy, intended to provide breathing space by involving the papacy on behalf of the military orders, thereby keeping Alfonso VII at bay? Or did the king of Aragon really mean it to be effective?[18]

Whatever he may have meant, events took their course. In Aragon the late king's younger brother was called upon to do his dynastic duty. Ramiro was a monk; he had been an abbot and at one time or another bishop-elect of at least three sees. On the question of whether he was also either a priest or a deacon, opinions have differed. But Ramiro II (as briefly he counted) selflessly coupled with Agnes of Poitiers, a lady known to be reliable for the purpose, and she promptly bore him a daughter. Named Petronilla, her mother's milk scarce dry upon her lip, the infant was betrothed to the new count of Barcelona, Ramón Berenguer IV (1131–44). This singular sequence of events, dynasty's triumph over humanity, marked the foundation of the 'Corona de Aragón'. Meanwhile Navarre had seized the opportunity of escaping Aragonese tutelage. Amidst the confusion an illegitimate member of the Navarrese royal house was acclaimed king at Pamplona: García Ramírez (1134–50). The kingdom of Aragon and the county of Barcelona had been yoked together, and the kingdom of Navarre had been resuscitated. In a matter of months the political profile of northern Spain had changed out of all recognition.[19]

The inhabitants of Saragossa, fearful of a repetition of the disaster at Fraga, welcomed Alfonso VII into the city (Dec. 1134) and the monk-king Ramiro 'gave' the place to him to be held by him and his forever. Shortly afterwards the count of Barcelona and Count Alphonse of Toulouse came to León, promised Alfonso VII obedience and 'were made his knights', Ramón Berenguer receiving Saragossa from him 'in honorem'. The new king of Navarre likewise became Alfonso's vassal. So extensive was the throng of warriors, so numerous the array of noble sons from Gascony, France and Poitou who received money fiefs from the king of León that his chronicler felt able to describe him as ruling from the Atlantic to the Rhône.[20] It was this new prestige that Alfonso VII's imperial coronation proclaimed in May 1135, fifty years and a day after the reconquest of Toledo.

[17] García Larragueta (1957), II, no. 10.   [18] Lourie (1975); Forey (1980–1); Lourie (1984–5).
[19] Soldevila (1962), pp. 147–69; Lacarra (1972), I, pp. 330–3.
[20] *Chronica Adefonsi imperatoris*, bk I, chs. 64, 67; Bonnassie (1980), pp. 38–9.

Or so Alfonso's chronicler wished it to be believed. In fact, at the level of peninsular power politics, the advantage which Alfonso VII had derived from the death of Alfonso of Aragón had been far less than had been hoped for, and actually represented a serious reverse. This his chronicler contrived to disguise by reshuffling the order of events. Thus, Ramón Berenguer IV's receipt of Saragossa from the king of León occurred not in 1134–5, as the 'Crónica' records, but in 1137, and signified the failure of an alternative dynastic settlement involving the marriage of Petronilla to the Infante Sancho, Alfonso VII's heir, a match which, had it occurred, must have taken the history of medieval Spain on a wholly different course. Certainly there would have been no 'Corona de Aragón'. Instead of combining with the county of Barcelona, the fate of the kingdom of Aragón would have been unification with Castile-León. Navarre's fate would have been sealed, and García Ramírez (who had already broken with the emperor) acknowledged as much by making common cause with Afonso Henriques the master of Portugal.[21]

But the bid for Leonese hegemony foundered on a combination of Aragonese intransigence and papal insistence that the terms of Alfonso I's will be honoured. The kingdom of Aragón was a papal fief and Innocent II was insistent that the military orders should not be deprived of their inheritance. Yet Alfonso I's provisions were both impracticable and incompatible with law and custom. Ramón Berenguer, whose father had died a Templar,[22] was best qualified to provide an escape from the impasse, and although it was not until 1158 that Adrian IV confirmed the terms of compensation to the orders and recognized the count of Barcelona's title,[23] by 1137 the latter (henceforth styling himself *princeps* not king of Aragón) was already master of the north-east.

The resolution of the succession crisis in Aragon was not the only setback suffered by Alfonso VII in these years, despite his chronicler's proud boast that his rule reached the Atlantic. While his schemes to drive a territorial bridgehead across the Ebro were meeting with failure, to his rear control of the old county of Portugal was slipping from him fast.[24]

The death of the ambitious Count Henry in 1112 had left his widow with a son of about five, a political inheritance which despite Urraca's preoccupations elsewhere was as delicate as it was dangerous, and an empty bed. Teresa, however, was in all matters resourceful, and moreover was sustained by Count Pedro Froilaz, guardian of the still young Alfonso Raimúndez, and (at least for the time being) by Bishop Diego Gelmírez of Santiago. But the latter's promotion to metropolitan rank in 1120 inevitably affected his attitude to

[21] Valdeavellano (1968), ii, p. 438.
[22] There appears to be no warrant for the regularly repeated assertion that he himself was a member.
[23] Forey (1973), pp. 17–21.
[24] Serrão (1979), i, pp. 77–86; Livermore (1966), pp. 46–9.

Portuguese affairs and brought him into contention with the see of Braga just as Braga's prestige had been besmirched by the appointment of its archbishop, Maurice Bourdin, as the Emperor Henry V's antipope, Gregory VIII (1118–21).[25] However, the consolations of religion having been compromised, by then Teresa was otherwise sustained. Pedro Froilaz had sent his son, Fernando Peres, to be her military adviser. Their relationship developed along other lines, however, and by 1121, when she and 'comes Fernandus' began to attest diplomas together, it was generally assumed that his services to her were not principally strategic, and for all that her lover's (or husband's) Galician connections were to Teresa's advantage, south of the Miño his influence was widely resented.

By 1126–7 when Alfonso VII first visited her as king, not only was his aunt describing herself as queen,[26] opposition to her was forming around the adolescent Afonso Henriques, and in the summer of 1128 he got the better of his mother in pitched battle at São Mamede[27] and sent her and her consort packing to Galicia where she died (?1130).

For the emergent kingdom of Portugal the next ten years were critical. Afonso Henriques had to have eyes everywhere. J. Veríssimo Serrão refers to the necessity of his maintaining a 'double policy', to the need for him to keep his frontier under surveillance while not losing sight of developments on his doorstep.[28] But this understates the extent of his problem. Afonso Henriques had three frontiers to patrol: Galicia north of the Miño, where Fernando Peres was now active in the service of Alfonso VII; Alfonso VII himself to the east; and the south where he had to prove his worth to the political community by masterminding profitable raids into Almoravid territory. Until 1136 the sea to the west was his only ally. In that year, however, the promotion of João Peculiar to the metropolitan see (for which he had lobbied earnestly) provided him with another. As archbishop of Braga for the next thirty-seven years João Peculiar steered the infant kingdom through innumerable perils. Much maligned, to the extent of being charged with having trampled the sacred host underfoot and of castrating a cleric with his bare hands, and not unjustly criticized for the directness of his methods, it is to him after Afonso Henriques himself that the kingdom of Portugal owed its existence. It was he above all who successfully countered Alfonso VII's various attempts to invoke arguments from *Hispania*'s ecclesiastical past, dodging and parrying the primate of Toledo's shafts when Leonese arms and diplomacy had failed.[29]

[25] David (1947), pp. 489–99; Fletcher (1984), pp. 197–206; Vones (1980), pp. 365–427.
[26] As the daughter of Alfonso VI. Thus *Chronica Adefonsi imperatoris*, bk 1, ch. 5.
[27] On 24 June or 24 July; authorities vary. It is to be noted that the later date is the eve of the feast of Santiago.
[28] Serrão (1979), 1, p. 81.   [29] Erdmann (1928), pp. 54–5; Ferreira (1928), pp. 284–319.

Which by 1140 they had. By the treaty of Tuy (July 1137) Afonso Henriques had again acknowledged Alfonso VII's authority. But in April 1140 he began to describe himself as king, *rex*.[30] Just like that. And three years later the emperor accepted the fact. In return for his cousin's renunciation of his claims in Galicia, by the treaty of Zamora (1143) Alfonso VII tacitly acknowledged the new kingdom's existence, whereupon Afonso Henriques commended his kingdom to the Roman church and declared himself a vassal of the pope. The scarcely perceptible nature of this development continues to intrigue historians. Why 1140? Why was the break not made sooner? By 1140 Afonso Henriques had been securely established at Coimbra for ten years, and in 1135 had been conspicuous by his absence from Alfonso VII's imperial coronation. Posterity would not be satisfied by a mere absence however. A military achievement was required, a great display, a Portuguese Covadonga, a foundation myth.[31]

By about 1300 it was believed that it was as a result of his victory over the Moors at 'Erich' that Afonso I assumed the royal title. Later the story was embellished: at the battle of Ourique (25 July 1139) Christ Himself had taken the field and assisted him in putting the 'innumerable armies' of no fewer than five Moorish kings to flight. As with Covadonga there are problems about Ourique however. One is its date, the feastday of Santiago suggesting a concerted attempt to appropriate the mystique associated with Castile-León's patron saint. Another is the scale of an encounter which to judge by the earliest accounts of it was no more than a skirmish of the sort in which Christian raiding parties regularly engaged all along the frontier in these years. Finally, there is that of the location of the chroniclers' *Oric* or *Ouric*: the modern Ourique in the Lower Alentejo, only fifty miles from the coast of the Algarve, was far beyond the range of the northerners at this date. Amongst other possible identifications, even the castle of *Aurelia* (Colmenar de Oreja, near Toledo), currently being besieged by Alfonso VII has been suggested![32]

Of greater significance than the legend of Ourique is the near-contemporary evidence for the existence of a distinctive historiographical tradition, associated with the Augustinian house of Santa Cruz de Coimbra. Established by about 1130, with João Peculiar as one of its co-founders, in June 1139 Santa Cruz received extensive territorial endowment from Afonso Henriques. Thereafter it provided the young monarchy with unwavering ideological support, a historical identity and a sense of nationhood, a service similar to that rendered to the counts of Barcelona by the monks of Ripoll,[33] and an advantage which the contemporary kings of León and Castile did not enjoy. According to the so-called 'Annals of Alfonso I', written there before the end of the century, that

[30] Feige (1978), p. 245.   [31] See *NCMH*, II, ch. 11, pp. 272–89.
[32] Herculano (n.d.), II, note XVI; Lindley Cintra (1957).
[33] Mattoso (1986), II, pp. 205–6; Bisson (1984a), pp. 462–5.

king's reign had commenced not in 1139–40 but in 1128 with his defeat of Teresa and her 'foreign' confederates.[34]

The new kingdom's credibility was finally established in October 1147 when, after a seventeen-week siege, the city of Lisbon was taken. The conquest of Lisbon was described with great élan by an English participant, one of a large force of northerners *en route* to the Holy Land for the Second Crusade whose fleet had put in at Oporto for supplies. There they were learnedly harangued by the local bishop, Pedro Pitões. However, his listeners were unmoved by his discourse on the canon law of the just war and by appeal to their Christian sentiment. What persuaded them to stay and fight were the king's written promises of material benefits, and what spurred them to action was indignation when the enemy unsportingly attacked a group of them out fishing.[35] The Tagus valley was now secure. Santarém had surrendered earlier in the year, Sintra and Palmela soon followed.

These successes were facilitated by the disarray of the Almoravids whose military inability to recover Toledo or Saragossa from the Christians and increasing religious laxity provoked a series of risings in the cities of the south from the Algarve to Cordoba and Valencia (1144–5), largely inspired by Abu-l-Qasim, a sufi demagogue and Ibn Tumart's successor as mahdi. In 1146 Abu-l-Qasim persuaded the Almohad caliph, 'Abd al-Mu'min, who was engaged in destroying the Almoravid amirate in the Maghreb, to send troops across the straits where early in 1147 they gained control of Seville. However, the taifa rulers of al-Andalus had not rid themselves of the Almoravids in order to submit to new masters, and an influential anti-Almohad movement now developed, the leading spirit of which was Muhammed ibn Mardanish, ruler of Valencia, Murcia and the Levante. Known to the Christians as King Lobo, Ibn Mardanish claimed to be of pure Arab descent, but his lifestyle was emphatically Spanish – it has been conjectured that his strange name was a corruption of the Romance 'Martínez' – and his guiding principle was self-preservation: a reverse Cid in short. Ibn Mardanish preferred to recruit his troops from amongst the Christians of the north, and accordingly in 1147 he allied himself with Alfonso VII, García Ramírez of Navarre and Ramón Berenguer IV for the siege of Almería, Muslim Spain's principal port and link with Africa and the east.[36]

Almería was captured on 17 October 1147, just six days before Lisbon surrendered. It was a gala event, attended by contingents from every region of Christian Spain, William of Montpellier and the Pisan and Genoese as well as the Catalan navies, and celebrated in Latin hexameters in the (incomplete) 'Poem of Almería' attached to the chronicle of Alfonso VII.[37] 'Terror of the

[34] Blöcker-Walter (1966), p. 152.   [35] *De expugnatione Lyxbonensi*, pp. 141; Hehl (1980), p. 259.
[36] Lacarra (1952); Le Tourneau (1969), pp. 48–55.
[37] *Prefatio de Almeria*.

Ishmaelites', the chronicler had just called Alfonso VII (II, p. 107), and the Castilian historian Valdeavellano describes the conquest of Almería as 'his most brilliant achievement'.[38] In fact, the initiative for the campaign seems to have originated with the count of Barcelona and the Italians, Almería having long provided the pirates of the Mediterranean with a safe haven. In the autumn of 1147 the reign of the emperor still had ten years to run, though for this period our information is meagre: the emperor's chronicler fell silent at this point. To a degree these were years of disappointment and unfulfilment. In the south the Almohads were consolidating their power; in 1157 they recovered Almería. The secession of Portugal was definitive and signalled the end of Leonese hegemony in the peninsula. There are signs that Alfonso VII retained hopes of compensating for the political reverses he had suffered and, by appealing to the past and to other traditions, of maintaining the possibility of eventual peninsular reunification. It was now that he was to be found seeking to manipulate Toledo's ecclesiastical primacy for secular ends, and assuming certain of the imperial trappings of Frederick Barbarossa.[39] But these new departures led nowhere.

The fate of Almería serves to explain why they led nowhere. As an episcopal chronicler a century later remarked (though whether in respect just of Almería or in general is unclear), Alfonso VII was more successful in capturing places than in keeping them. The emperor's reign was full of spectacular sorties south and sieges successfully completed. But he was overstretched, his lines of communication were too extended. Places taken were soon lost again. The extent of his operations was beyond the capacity of his resources, necessitating devolution of his authority. Thus, for example, in the last year of his reign Manrique de Lara, Alfonso's *tenente* at Baeza, was authorizing diplomas issued in the emperor's name.[40]

The contrast with Ramón Berenguer IV is striking. The places reconquered by him – in 1148–9 Tortosa, Lérida, Fraga and Mequinenza, although far to the north of Uclés and Cordoba where Alfonso VII was actively engaged at the time – remained reconquered. Hence the real significance of the treaty of Tudellén, agreed by the two monarchs in January 1151. Ostensibly this agreement confirmed the traditional pan-peninsular authority of the kings of León. The emperor and the 'prince of Aragon', who were currently contemplating the partition of the kingdom of Navarre on the death of García Ramírez, used the opportunity to look further forward to the reconquest of the Levante. The regions of Valencia, Denia and Murcia were to be the responsibility of Ramón Berenguer. In accordance with ancient expectations, they were to be held by him

---

[38] Valdeavellano (1968), II, p. 454.   [39] Linehan (1993), ch. 9.

[40] 'Felix siquidem in acquirendo, sed minus discretus in retinendo': 'Chronique latine inédite', c. 5; Sánchez Belda (1951).

as the emperor's vassal. But he was to have them: the principle of peninsular partition had been surrendered.[41] Ninety years on, another constructive antiquarian would similarly seek to ignore the ineluctable consequences of several centuries, invoking the evidence, such as it was, of the Visigothic councils to establish Toledo's claim to exercise ecclesiastical jurisdiction in Valencia.[42] For the moment, the hopelessness of that procedure was demonstrated on the legitimists' own terms. On the death of Alfonso VII (Aug. 1157) his realms were divided between his two sons. In the thirteenth century the dismemberment of Alfonso VII's realms was widely deplored, an episcopal chronicler of the 1240s attributing it to human sinfulness. In fact it was strictly in accordance with the same principles of dynastic legitimacy that had governed events on the deaths of Sancho III of Navarre in 1035 and Fernando I in 1065 that Castile should pass to the elder son, Sancho (since although Castile was the junior kingdom it comprised the family's patrimonial lands), and that the younger, Fernando, should receive León.[43]

The death of Alfonso VII left Ramón Berenguer IV the peninsula's senior ruler and, despite his Provençal preoccupations, also its most effective one. Less than thirty years before, his father had been informed by the count of Montcada, Berenguer Ramón I, that 'for all I hold from you, I would not thank you with one fart'. Four generations on, in 1227, Count Guillem III acknowledged to the then king of Aragon 'the debt that I hold to you . . . , for your lineage, that of the count of Barcelona by name, has made our very lineage'. But by 1157, in less than a third of a century, the relationship of the parties had been more than half transformed. For more than a century the lords of Montcada, with their patrimonial lands situated just to the north of Barcelona, had possessed the title of seneschal of Barcelona, and while periodically bickering with the counts whose seneschals they were had striven to establish hereditary title to the office. They thus typified the dynasties and vested interests with which Ramón Berenguer had to contend, dynasties and vested interests which since the 1070s had encountered and succeeded in containing the forces unleashed by Pope Gregory VII and his satellites.[44] By about 1150 Ramón Berenguer had mastered them. The *Usatges of Barcelona*, the regalian code which he issued at this time, purporting to date from the time of Ramón Berenguer I (d. 1076), not only vested ultimate judicial authority in the count-prince but also stated his right to the service of all men within his jurisdiction when necessity demanded, a claim not asserted in Castile until

[41] *Colección de documentos inéditos del archivo de la corona de Aragón*, p. 168; Soldevila (1962), pp. 186–7; Lacarra (1976), pp. 209–10.

[42] Linehan (1993), pp. 344–8.

[43] 'Chronique latine inédite', c. 7 ('permittente Deo propter peccata hominum'); Lacarra (1976).

[44] Shideler (1983), pp. 38, 155; Freedman (1983), pp. 45–67.

1166. In 1151–2 he followed this with a survey of peasant tenures and obligations in the county of Barcelona and the regions surrounding it, which its recent historian has described as 'virtually a "Domesday" for Catalonia'. Aragon seems to have been spared such scrutiny. Not until the compilation of the *Libros de las Behetrías* 200 years later would Castile experience the like.[45]

The division of Alfonso VII's realms in 1157 points a crucial truth about twelfth-century Spain which the most celebrated event of Alfonso's reign, his imperial coronation, tends to obscure. The peninsula accommodated what one recent historian has described as a veritable 'throng of kings'. Aragón, Navarre, Portugal after 1139, León again after 1157, each had its own king as well as Castile; kings who, for all their dedication to the cause of peninsular unity, did not hesitate to subscribe documents recording their children as 'regnante' or 'rex similiter' (as Sancho III was with Alfonso VII in the 1150s), or to leave their inheritance to be partitioned when they died, in accordance with family tradition, as Alfonso VII did in 1157. There was no even approximate correlation between 'rex' and 'regnum'. In accordance with this 'principle of fragmentation', kings were kings 'not of a kingdom but of a space', a space the extent of which was capable of measurement by reference to the summary which the dating clauses of the king's own charters contained of the segments of the notional whole over which he currently claimed to exercise control.[46]

The emperor's death provides a convenient opportunity to attempt a lateral survey of the peninsula at mid-century and a rough description of these 'spaces' and of the human supplies which fed and maintained the political structures outlined in the preceding pages.

Christian Spain was subject to forces exerted by two different systems of coordinates, creating a two-dimensional complex which greatly complicates the describing of it. At the time, the author of the chronicle of Alfonso VII met the difficulty by dealing with the emperor's activities to east and west in the first book of his work, and his forays against the peninsular Muslims separately in the second. The course of the reconquest was determined by geo-physical characteristics aeons older than the peninsula's religions.[47] Impassable mountain ranges separated the northern nodes of Christian reconquest from one another: then as now, for Oviedo and Barcelona communication with Córdoba and Valencia respectively was easier than it was with each other. And the climatic shock administered to the northerner on reaching the Meseta was made all the more severe by the absence of safety and shade in the vast frontier area over which armies and raiding parties passed and repassed, burning crops

[45] Bisson (1986), pp. 31–5; Soldevila (1962), pp. 170–97; *Usatges de Barcelona*; I, Bisson (1984b) p. 25, II, pp. 3–29.
[46] Maravall (1964), pp. 359, 366 ('pululación de reyes en un mismo ámbito'), p. 369.
[47] Vicens Vives (1967), pp. 22–4.

and vines. Though Castilians mocked the Frenchmen who returned home before the battle of Las Navas in 1212,[48] the heat which drove them had proved the Muslims' most reliable ally throughout the previous century and as unfamiliar an experience to the foreign recruits of the Christian rulers as the camels in the enemy army which the chronicler so regularly mentioned.[49]

Foreign warriors were preceded by foreign pilgrims. For well over a century already Santiago de Compostela had been attracting Christians from far afield; by 1105 the earliest recorded English pilgrim, the Yorkshireman Richard Mauleverer, had been there. But, despite the fact that at mid-century another Englishman did not think the place worth commenting on, by the time Louis VII of France made the journey in 1154, Santiago's fame and prestige who established. This transformation was due above all to Diego Gelmírez during whose pontificate (1100–40) the see was raised to metropolitan status (1120) and the mighty romanesque cathedral and the vast complex of buildings associated with it was largely completed.[50]

The guidebook for pilgrims which comprised the fifth and final book of the contemporary work *Jacobus* (the so-called *Liber Sancti Jacobi*) described the four major routes along which pilgrims travelled from France, converging at Puente la Reina and continuing by way of Estella, Logroño and Burgos (where it was joined by the road from Bayonne), Sahagún, León, Astorga and Ponferrada before entering Galicia. The guidebook is full of essential information concerning both the necessities of life – bread (excellent at Estella, but then Estella was French), rivers (poisonous in most parts of Navarre, safer further west), fish and meat (fatal everywhere) – and the inhabitants of the region whom the traveller would encounter: the barbarous Basques with their terrifying language; the Navarrese with their particularly disagreeable habits, whose name betrayed the malignity of their origins (*Nauarrus*: *non verus*) and who ate like pigs and sounded like dogs; the Castilians, a people as vicious as their land was fertile; and at the end of the journey the Galicians, bad-tempered and litigious.[51]

Jacobus was not a guidebook in any ordinary sense of the word, and its widespread dissemination after about 1170 was moreover something of an accident.[52] Even so (and whether these sentiments merely reflected their author's personal prejudices or were an expression of common opinion), the effect of their publication ought to have been to have discouraged foreigners from

---

[48] Below, p. 507.   [49] *Chronica Adefonsi imperatoris*, bk II, chs. 23, 27, 33, 52, 73, 92.

[50] Vázquez de Parga, Lacarra and Uría Ríu (1948–9), I, pp. 51, 64; Fletcher (1984), p. 96; Miret y Sans (1912). It was Oviedo that possessed 'the most precious relics of all Spain' according to the chronicler of the siege of Lisbon: *De expugnatione Lyxbonensi*, pp. 63–5.

[51] *Libri sancti Jacobi*, pp. 349–60; Vázquez de Parga, Lacarra and Uría Ríu (1948–9), I, pp. 202–15; Defourneaux (1949), pp. 102–6.

[52] Hohler (1972), pp. 55, 69.

venturing to Spain at all. Yet still they came, and all along the road, and to the north and the south of it, towns and settlements responded to their presence. The *camino francés*, Christian Spain's main economic artery, supplied the peninsula with the commodity which it needed most: people. With the *parias* they had received from the Muslim south the eleventh-century rulers of the Christian north had been able to afford to smooth the pilgrim way, mending bridges and deterring brigands, and by providing security and *fueros* which exempted them from tribute had persuaded the men and women who came to pray to stay to trade and fight. Though no longer in receipt of the *parias* themselves, their twelfth-century successors reaped the human reward.[53]

They also imitated their predecessors' techniques. To the episcopal city of Pamplona, the first place of any consequence on the road from Roncesvalles, Frenchmen came in ever-increasing numbers during the pontificate of its French bishop Peter of Rodez (1083–1115). In 1129 Alfonso I of Aragon granted those of them ('totos francos') who settled in the region of San Saturnino de Iruña the *fuero* that Pyrenean Jaca had received from his father Sancho Ramírez in 1063.[54] The effect was to establish a highly favoured mercantile 'burgo', physically and juridically separate from the existing city, where the *franci* were allowed to choose their own judge ('alcaldus') as well as monopolize the trade with pilgrims, and the native Navarrese were excluded. Accordingly, a double city was created, and a seedbed of strife prepared which would flourish until the fifteenth century. The same form of apartheid existed at Estella, a French new town created in 1090 by diverting the pilgrim road from its former course, though here the harshness of division was mitigated when in 1187 Sancho VI extended the *fuero* of the French to its other inhabitants.[55] Meanwhile the 'Pseudo-Turpin', the spurious memoirs of Archbishop Turpin of Rheims (one of the casualties of Roncesvalles according to the *Song of Roland*), attributed the discovery of Santiago's tomb to Charlemagne, and spread the story that as well as establishing the church of Compostela and decreeing that 'all prelates, princes and Christian kings both Spanish and Galician' should thereafter be subject to its bishop, the Frankish emperor had reconquered the entire peninsula not just once but three times, on each occasion the feckless locals losing the initiative again as soon as he left them to their own devices.[56] In the form in which it was incorporated as the fourth book of *Jacobus*, having originated as a book for teaching Parisian schoolboys grammar, the 'Pseudo-Turpin' seems to

---

[53] Valdeavellano (1969), pp. 103–76; Gautier Dalché (1979), pp. 67–85.

[54] The *fuero* granted to Jaca was adopted further afield than Pamplona; details in *Fueros de Navarra*.

[55] Valdeavellano (1969), pp. 136–40; Defourneaux (1949), p. 250.

[56] *Libri sancti Jacobi*, pp. 306, 325–6 (Santiago as 'sedes secunda' after Rome, St James having been *maior* amongst the apostles after St Peter, 'et in celis primatum super eos tenet'); Defourneaux (1949), pp. 82–90.

date from the middle years of the century. But well before this francophobia found expression in both word and deed. No one from abroad had ever come to Christian Spain's assistance, the Leonese author of the so-called *Historia Silense* insisted, putting the historical record straight, least of all Charlemagne who 'in the manner of the French' had been corrupted by gold and at Roncesvalles had been defeated by the Navarrese.[57] And meanwhile a counter-legend was developing, that of Bernardo of Carpio, the 'anti-Charlemagne' who worsted the emperor at Roncesvalles.[58]

At Sahagún, however, where a contemporary's list of those who had responded to Alfonso VI's appeal for settlers 'from foreign nations, from my own kingdom and from various other parts' (1085) included Gascons, Bretons, Germans, English, Burgundians, Normans, Provençaux and Lombards, the violence that erupted during the civil wars of Urraca's reign (1110–16) was not directed against the foreigners, but organized by them and the locals together, who made common cause against the abbatial jurisdiction under which the king had placed them, formed themselves into a *concejo* and appealed to Alfonso of Aragón for assistance. The looting of the royal monastery was undertaken by the latter's brother, Ramiro, the future saviour of the Aragonese dynasty. In the disturbed conditions of the 1110s such resentments were the more easily manipulated. At Santiago in 1116–17, having stirred up Bishop Diego Gelmírez's enemies against him, Urraca came close to suffering the consequences herself.[59]

The brotherhood formed by those who seized power at the end of the pilgrim road demonstrated the potential of the forces brought in to colonize and trade all along its length, notwithstanding the fact that the 'germanitas' (as an unsympathetic contemporary described it) which has created so much excitement amongst some social historians seems to have been largely composed of Galicians.[60] It also demonstrated the need to maintain control over these forces and to ensure that they were directed where they really were needed. Fear of social anarchy was never far away. The chronicler of Alfonso VII told the story of the 'optimates' of Salamanca who resolved to raid towards Badajoz in order to 'make a name for themselves and not let any prince or duke enjoy the credit', and in consequence suffered a crushing defeat.[61] Only after they

---

[57] Hohler (1972), pp. 33–40; *Historia Silense*, pp. 129–30.

[58] Défourneaux (1949), pp. 302–16. Bernardo of Carpio seems to have been a creation of the second half of the century. There is no mention of him in *Historia Silense* despite the fact that the date assigned to that work, 1110–20, may well be too early: Canal Sánchez-Pagin (1980), pp. 101–2; Linehan (1993), ch. 5.

[59] Défourneaux (1949), pp. 232–8; Fletcher (1984), pp. 185–9.   [60] Pastor de Togneri (1973), pp. 13ff.

[61] 'Eamus et nos in terram Badalioz et faciamus nobis nomen grande et non demus nomen glorie nostre ullo principi aut duci.' 'Who is your leader?', the Moorish king asked them, and on hearing from them that they all were concluded that they were mad: *Chronica Adefonsi imperatoris*, bk II, chs. 27–8.

had done penance, paid the church their tithes and first fruits and submitted to the emperor's commanders did God give them victory again, and profit (II, p. 29). The moral of the chronicler's story was clear. The interrelationship of the parties whose complementary activities constituted the code of the frontier was vindicated. The sin for which the warriors had had to do penance was the social sin of insubordination.

Although not all the towns along the pilgrim road were exclusively mercantile in character,[62] those south of the Duero ('Extremadura') and further still beyond the mountain range of the *cordillera central* ('Transierra') were principally military. Toledo on the Tagus marked the southernmost extent of an area stretching from Lisbon to Tortosa: rough and inhospitable country only lately (and indeed still) the haunt of bears and boars, as Alfonso VI described the region of Segovia in 1107. In recent years a series of pioneering studies has almost entirely transformed our knowledge of the processes of resettlement of the area after 1085 and of the role of fighting families organized by national groupings in the occupation of strategically situated walled cities to each of which was attached an area of open land running down to the Tagus. The example of Ávila, with its massive fortified cathedral, revealed the ability of these groupings to retain their own identity while collaborating in the common task. The Arab geographer al-Idrisi describes the city as a cluster of small villages. Around such places livestock was kept, to be brought within the walls at the approach of the enemy. At such times the countryside was evacuated, obliging the raiders from the south either to remain for only a single day or to bring all necessary provisions with them.[63] The effective limit of the Christian reconquest at any time was determined by the furthest pasture south in which sheep might safely graze. There could be no question of agriculture: standing crops were a standing invitation to enemy arsonists. Animals can be moved, vines cannot.[64] For the same reason monasticism did not flourish on this frontier, as it had in earlier times further north and as it continued to do in Catalonia under the auspices of the monks of Poblet (founded 1150–3). It was in Galicia that the cloistered Cistercians made their mark, infilling the Galician hinterland. In Castile they served a different function, not on the Christian frontier with Islam (where their warrior brethren were active), but on Castile's with its Christian neighbours. During the 1170s, at Alfonso VIII's behest, the communities of Bujedo, Herrera, Rioseco and Benavides were all relocated for this purpose.[65]

[62] Gautier Dalché (1979), p. 74.
[63] Barrios García (1983–4); Portela (1985), pp. 94–115; Powers (1988), pp. 93–205; García de Cortázar (1990), pp. 55–121; *Chronica Adefonsi imperatoris,* bk II, chs. 47, 84.
[64] García de Cortázar (1990), pp. 62–3.
[65] McCrank (1983); Pallares Méndez and Portela Silva (1971), pp. 69ff; Alvárez Palenzuela (1978), pp. 83, 90–1, 103, 121–32; Moxó (1979), pp. 269ff.

Those who undertook the task, coming from other parts of the peninsula or further afield, were induced to do so by terms such as those of the *fuero* which Alfonso VI had granted to Sepúlveda in 1076, a code subsequently adopted as far afield as Morella in Aragon (1233) and Segura de León to the south of Badajoz (1274). Sepúlveda provided immunity for all-comers: even murderers were assured of refuge once they had crossed the Duero.[66] On his way to seek monastic sanctuary at Cluny 'because there was nowhere for him to stay' in Alfonso VII's kingdoms, the treacherous Count Gómez Núñez would have passed streams of aspiring frontiersmen travelling south for precisely the same reason, the ruthlessness of whose exploits on arrival bore witness to the ruggedness of their origins.[67] Here the quality most admired was vigour (*strenuitas*), and the most reprehensible failing its opposite, that 'negligence' in maintaining arms and equipment which according to the chronicle of Alfonso VII led to the loss of Mora and was only to be expiated by a series of acts of conspicuous bravery against the enemy resulting in much carnage and booty.[68] Eternal vigilance was the rule: at Plasencia when fire broke out the first duty of the citizens was to secure the city walls. But offensive warfare as well as defence was the business of members of the non-noble municipal militia (*caballería villana*), and in pursuit of it they regularly travelled prodigious distances, striking deep into Muslim territory.[69]

With them often went churchmen. Many of these were foreigners too, men of the stamp of Bishops Peter of Osma, 1101–9, who had come there from Bourges, or his contemporary Jerome of Valencia who explains in the 'Poem of The Cid' that he had come from France to the frontier 'because of the urge he had to kill a Moor or two' and had since lost count of his tally. An episcopal formulary of the early thirteenth century contains a letter from the bishop of Zamora enquiring of the king of León when the fighting was to start,[70] Quite how distinctively religious the motives were of the likes of Bishop Ramón of Palencia – a Catalan monk who was reported to have enfeoffed his church's possessions, let his episcopal palace go to rack and ruin and gone off to live in a hut near the front line – we have little means of knowing and none at all of judging. The commitment of the chronicler of Alfonso VII, for example, was rather more tepid. Though he may have been a bishop too, he describes a treaty between his hero and Afonso Henriques as 'apparently useful' because

[66] Sáez (1953), pp. 46 ('Et si aliquis homo de Sepuluega occiderit alium de Castella et fugier usque ad Duero, nullus homo persequatur eum', c.13), 190, 200.
[67] *Chronica Adefonsi imperatoris*, bk I, ch. 87 ('quia nusquam erat ei locus ad habitandum').
[68] *Ibid.*, bk II, chs. 46–9.
[69] *Ibid.*, bk II, chs. 2, 18; Blöcker-Walter (1966), p. 151; Linehan (1993), ch. 9; Lourie (1966), p. 59; Powers (1988), p. 1.
[70] Linehan (1993), ch. 8.

'good for Christians'.[71] And it was not concern for Christendom that weighed with the crusaders who allowed themselves to be sidetracked to Lisbon in 1147; it was the fine print concerning spoils. By the terms in which they bid for volunteers for the Almería campaign that same year, 'all the bishops of León and Toledo' who unsheathed both swords, the divine and the earthly, in the cause confirmed that from one side of the peninsula to the other it was the rewards of 'both lives' that mattered.[72]

The circumstances which prompted Spain's rulers to grant *fueros* such as that of Sepúlveda – little money, fewer men, abundance of territory theoretically at least theirs to dispose of – and the calculating spirit in which the warriors at Lisbon and Almería discharged their Christian duty, together provided ideal conditions for the making of agreements which historians of other parts of twelfth-century Europe are accustomed to describing as 'feudal', though to their Spanish colleagues while General Franco was alive the concept of feudalism seemed ideologically difficult and tended to be rejected as altogether too European (and therefore too alien) a proposition. Since the mid-1970s, however, feudalism has been fiercely embraced for the reassurance it provides that, as well as approximating to European norms, medieval Spain may even have measured up to Marxist requirements. Recent historical literature on the subject is very slippery therefore, certainly more so than the twelfth-century evidence itself. The statement in the 'Historia Roderici', for example (which can hardly be later than the 1140s), that Alfonso VI granted the Cid and his heirs lands to be held in perpetuity, is unequivocal. And similar grants which Alfonso VII made to lesser folk during the last years of his reign provide confirmation.[73]

The reign of Sancho III of Castile, which lasted just a year (1157–8), was notable for the foundation of the first of the Spanish military orders by Raimundo the Cistercian abbot of Fitero. Alfonso VII had entrusted the Templars with custody of Calatrava, the fortress at the gateway to Andalucía which he had conquered in 1147, but being unable to provide for its defence after his death they had returned it to Sancho III. Raimundo's confraternity followed the Cistercian rule but when in 1164 the friars of Calatrava were admitted to that order its rigour was modified so that they could engage in military activity. The order of Santiago, established by Fernando II of León in 1170 to serve the same purpose,

---

[71] *Chronica Adefonsi imperatoris*, bk II, ch. 87 ('quia bona Christianis, utilis uisa est').

[72] 'Mercedem uite spondent cunctis ruriusque. / Argenti dona promittunt cumque corona/ Quicquid habent Mauri rursus promittitur auri': *Prefatio de Almeria*, lines 43–5.

[73] 'Insuper autem talem dedit absolutionem et concessionem in suo regno sigillo scriptam et confirmatam, quod omnem terram uel castella, que ipsimet [*sic*] posset adquirere a Sarracenis in terra Sarracenorum, iure hereditario prorsus essent sua, non solum sua uerum etiam filiorum suorum et filiarum Suarum et tocius sue generationis': 'Historia Roderici', c. 26. Cf. Smith (1983), pp. 57–8; *Los cartularios de Toledo*, p. 81; Linehan (1993), ch. 7.

differed to the extent that its rule allowed its knights, who were lay brothers, to marry. As the Almohad danger increased, responsibility for the defence and re-settlement of the vast area between the Tagus and the Sierra Morena was vested in them. In Portugal the order of Évora (later of Avis) was founded soon after 1166. In Aragón, however, the Templars and Hospitallers were dominant.[74]

Sancho III's premature death in August 1158 left Castile with a three-year-old ruler, Alfonso VIII, and by the terms of Sancho's will Gutierre Fernández of Castro as his tutor until he reached the age of fifteen. Gutierre's tutorship immediately provoked the opposition of the Lara family, who (1160–1) secured custody of the child-king, occasioning the invasion of Castilian territory by Sancho VI of Navarre and Alfonso's uncle, Fernando II of León. By 1162 Toledo, which had successfully resisted the forces of Islam since 1085, was in Leonese hands with Fernando Rodríguez of Castro installed as governor. In August of that year Ramón Berenguer IV died, leaving as his heir another small Alfonso, the four-year-old Alfonso II, and rendering the already precarious situation of the peninsular Christians even more perilous. Its survival until 1170, when to the inconvenience of two royal minorities was added that of Afonso of Portugal's broken leg, was certainly not due to the exertions of Fernando of León. The *mêlée* at the gates of Badajoz in which Afonso I's limb was crushed, thereby preventing him from ever riding again, involved not the enemies of the cross but his Leonese son-in-law who in order to protect his interests in that region of the south-west now proceeded to make a treaty with the Almohad caliph Abu Ya'qub Yusuf (1163–84).[75]

In September 1162 Fernando II, having assumed the title 'king of Spain' or 'of the Spaniards', had taken Alfonso of Aragón under his protection and in the following July all but succeeded in seizing the person of his nephew, Alfonso of Castile. Meanwhile, Ibn Mardanish, who since 1159 had extended his rule from the Valencia–Murcia area as far west as Jaén, Ubeda and Baeza, suffered defeat at the hands of the Almohad army outside Granada (1162), and when the same fate again befell him at Murcia (Oct. 1165) the kings of Aragón and Navarre combined to oust him.[76] After 1166, while the Aragonese were preoccupied with recovering the county of Provence, which in 1131 had passed to Ramón Berenguer III's younger son, Berenguer Ramón, Christian achievements in the south-west were due to Geraldo sem Pavor ('the Fearless'), the Portuguese Cid, as he is regularly described on account of his having been exiled by his king and ending his days in Almohad Seville, but whose feats of derring-do at Trujillo, Évora, Cáceres and Montánchez (1165–6) equally entitle him to be remembered as the Portuguese Scarlet Pimpernel.[77]

---

[74] Lomax (1978), pp. 107–11.   [75] Valdeavellano (1968), pp. 561–2.
[76] Lacarra (1952).   [77] Cabestany (1960), pp. 63–73; Lopes (1941), pp. 93–4.

Either in 1169 or in the following year Alfonso VIII, now aged fifteen, began his effective reign, a rite of passage marked by two developments of great significance: an alliance of peace and friendship with Alfonso II of Aragón (Sahagún, 1170), sealed in 1174 by the latter's marriage to his aunt Sancha of Castile and his own to Eleanor, daughter of Henry II of England. How he had managed to survive his stormy minority is unclear: our knowledge of events in Castile during these years is more than usually sketchy, with not a single chronicle to enlighten us. However, it appears that the year 1166 marked a turning-point and that a crucial part was played by the city of Toledo and its archbishop John of Castellmorum (1152–66). At the synod of Segovia in March 'all the bishops of the kingdom of King Alfonso' under the archbishop's presidency invoked canonical penalties to ensure that those who held any *honor* of the king within the kingdom did him homage as his vassals, and declared those who did not to be under equal obligation to defend the kingdom from attack. And in the autumn Toledo was again reconquered, this time from the Leonese invader. As in 1085, an important role was again played by the city's Mozarabs, this time under the leadership of their *alguacil* (chief of police), Esteban Illán. On this occasion, however, they received their due reward. For eighty years they had been excluded from high office both civil and ecclesiastical. Now the French archbishop, whose pontificate witnessed the establishment of the so-called Toledo school of translators in which Mozarabs were much involved, lifted the embargo. By 1164 one of their number, Domingo Alpolichén, had been appointed urban archpriest of Toledo. And soon after, perhaps, the policy of conciliation was furthered when Alfonso VIII unified Toledan law by extending the Mozarabs' distinctive *fuero* to all its citizens.[78]

By whatever means, by the end of the 1160s Castilian morale had been sufficiently restored to ensure that neither the arrival of the caliph Yusuf in the south in 1171, nor even his alliance with both the king of León and Fernando Rodríguez of Castro and the death of Ibn Mardanish and the surrender of his kingdom to the Almohads in the following year, precipitated the catastrophe that had seemed inevitable as recently as five years before. Though Yusuf's armies penetrated as far north as Talavera, forcing both Castile and Portugal to make truces (1173), the failure of their siege of Huete in the previous year had already testified to the strength of Castilian resolve and to the increasing effectiveness of the military orders. In 1177, moreover, a year after the caliph's return to Tunisia, Alfonso VIII captured Cuenca. For this, the first significant military achievement of his reign, Alfonso was greatly obliged to Alfonso of Aragón and in return for his assistance at the siege the latter was released

[78] Linehan (1980), pp. 34–6; Hernández (1985), pp. 79–82; d'Alverny (1982), pp. 445–6; García Gallo (1975), pp. 361–2, 438–45, 480; Linehan (1993), ch. 9.

from the homage which the kings of Aragón had owed for the kingdom of Saragossa since 1136. The Castilian's concession acknowledged new peninsular realities. In the judgement of the Catalan historian Soldevila, however, it was achieved at exorbitant cost. Scrupulous regard for feudal niceties had prejudiced the interests of the Corona de Aragón in an area in which it had legitimate ambitions of its own. And the same verdict has been given of the treaty of Cazola (March 1179) the terms of which reiterated those of Tudellén, but with two significant variations. At Cazola Castile abandoned its claim to fealty in respect of future conquests within Aragón's sphere of influence, and Aragon ceded to Castile the kingdom of Murcia.[79] On the same occasion the two rulers concluded a pact of alliance and friendship against all other rulers, Moorish and Christian alike, 'but most particularly against the king of Navarre'. Two months later by the bull *Manifestis probatum* (23 May 1179) Alexander III ratified Afonso of Portugal's conquests, and recognized his royal title and the rights of his successors.[80]

These events gave formal effect to a severing of links with the past of which the late 1170s provided various other indications. One of these was the repudiation of the Leonese ancestry of the king of Castile's grandfather Alfonso VII, and hence of his links with the rulers of Visigothic Spain, in favour of an alternative genealogy which traced his descent from Nuño Rasura, the champion of tenth-century Castilian independence from León.[81] Another was the terminology adopted by the Castilian chancery. After 1168, as royal authority began gradually to be reasserted, Alfonso VIII was regularly presented in majestic terms. Throughout the 1170s the theme of *regia maiestas*, with its Romanist connotations imitative of contemporary German usage, was dominant. After 1180, however, quite suddenly the tone changed. While in Aragon the royal chancery finally abandoned the practice of dating documents by the regnal year of the French kings, in Castile Christianity displaced majesty. After his capture of Cuenca and the self-determination in different senses of the kingdoms of Aragón and Portugal, the ruler of Castile assumed the new role of champion of *christianitas*, and on the gold *maravedís* he issued from 1172 in replacement of the interrupted supplies of Almoravid dinars, Alfonso VIII figured as 'the prince of the Catholics'.[82]

Circumstances in the south of the peninsula and further afield conspired in the king of Castile's favour, providing him with a stage on which to act out this

---

[79] Soldevila contrasts Catalonia's high-minded, Christian, Hispanic idealism with the unscrupulous nationalist realism of Castile which had never observed the terms of its own vassalge to León. The sacrifice of Aragonese rights in Murcia in exchange for the renunciation of a purely nominal overlordship he describes as 'disastrous' (*funesta*): (1962), pp. 208–11.

[80] Lacarra (1972), II, pp. 74–8; Feige (1978), pp. 300–12.

[81] *Crónica general de España*, pp. liii–lv.   [82] Linehan (1993), ch. 9.

exalted role. By 1182 he was able to attack Córdoba and wreak havoc along the coast from Málaga to Algeciras. In July 1184 Yusuf died of a wound received while besieging Santarém. When in the following year death also removed both Afonso I of Portugal and Fernando Rodríguez of Castro, the latter's son Pedro Fernández surrendered to Alfonso the lordship centred on Trujillo which his father had held of the caliph. Castile and the order of Santiago, which Alfonso established there, were thus provided with both extensive territory at the expense of León and a strategically significant bridgehead in the south-west for attacks into Andalucía. Fernando II of León's removal from the scene in January 1188 left the king of Castile as the peninsula's senior ruler while in the aftermath of the catastrophe suffered by the Latin kingdom of Jerusalem at Hattin Christian Europe was scouring the horizon for effective military leaders. Two developments of these years confirmed the extent of Alfonso's pre-eminence. One was his foundation in 1187 of a dynastic pantheon in the 'capital of Castile' such as the church of San Isidoro had provided in the previous century: the Cistercian nunnery of Las Huelgas at Burgos where later he chose to be buried, rather than with his father and grandfather at Toledo. The other was the informal acknowledgement of his hegemony by the other peninsular rulers implicit in the series of alliances against him into which they entered culminating in the Pact of Huesca between Sancho I of Portugal, Alfonso IX of León and Alfonso of Aragón (May 1191), with which Sancho of Navarre associated himself two months later.

The late 1180s were also notable for a series of supposedly new departures which in the modern period have been adjudged constitutionally significant. In his old age Fernando II of León had married his long-time mistress Urraca López of Haro, a lady to whom he had paid tribute in 1183 for the good service which she had done him 'with her body, her castles and her men'.[83] Fernando's successor, Alfonso IX the child of his father's earlier uncanonical union with Urraca of Portugal, therefore had a scheming stepmother to contend with on his accession. The uncertainty of the seventeen-year-old's situation in the first summer of his reign accounts for two events of July 1188 which were to determine the course of the rest of it. At the curia of Carrión sometime between the 4th and the 28th of that month, the European ascendancy which Alfonso VIII now enjoyed was manifested by his knighting of Conrad of Hohenstaufen, the son of Frederick Barbarossa, and the giving to him in marriage of the eight-year-old heiress of Castile, Berenguela. On the same occasion, a few days earlier, the king of León was also knighted and kissed the hand of his Castilian cousin in token of vassalage.[84] As time passed the indignity which this act of submission represented bore ever deeper on Alfonso IX. His alliance with the Almohads

---

[83] González (1944), I, p. 35.   [84] Rassow (1950); Procter (1980), p. 75; Martínez Díez (1988), p. 142.

in 1196 was attributed to it, and although in 1197 he would reknight himself before the altar of Santiago Cathedral, as though to remove the stain, the sense of slight remained and fuelled feelings of resentment which ultimately were responsible for his notable absence from the battle of Las Navas de Tolosa in 1212. And either shortly before or soon after[85] he convened a curia of his own kingdom at León.

The curia of León of 1188 is renowned as an occasion of exceptional significance because, it is claimed, 'for the first time in medieval European history the sovereign recognized and accepted that power be shared directly and fully with the bishops, nobles and "good men" of the cities'. 'There can be no doubt (it is alleged) that the decisions taken [there] were intended to create a new political constitution for the country', no less. This is 'demonstrated clearly', for example, by 'the undertaking given by the king to follow the counsels of his bishops, nobles and wise men in all circumstances in matters of peace and war'. Moreover, these were not simply 'good men'; they were *elected* 'good men': 'cum electis civibus ex singulis civitatibus' as is stated in the decrees presumed to have been issued on that occasion.[86] In fact, the authenticity of the 'decrees of 1188' is highly questionable. In the late manuscript in which they occur they are undated, and the only authority for ascribing them to León in 1188 is the aprioristic conviction of the nineteenth-century liberal Muñoz y Romero that that was a fitting occasion for their enactment. The credentials of the so-called 'Leonese Magna Carta', and of Alfonso IX's undertaking only to make war and peace 'with the counsel of bishops, nobles and good men *per quorum consilium debeo regi*' (c. 3), are therefore distinctly unimpressive.[87]

However, there were representatives of the *concejos* present at Alfonso IX's curiae of Benavente and León (1202, 1208), thereby qualifying them to be described by historians as 'Cortes' (though they were absent from the León assembly of 1194),[88] and despite the fact that the Castilian curia of Carrión is if not the last then certainly the last-but-one such meeting of Alfonso VIII's reign of which record survives, and that in Navarre, Portugal and the crown of Aragón the 'third estate' did not figure before 1200, their growing involvement in the management of public affairs in the last years of the century has to be allowed for. In the judgement of some historians it was the reception of Roman Law in the peninsula in these years that provided a 'theoretical justification'

[85] 'Chronique latine inédite', c. 14; Palacios Martín (1988), p. 171. On the crucial question of the precise date of the León curia, whether before or after that of Carrión, consensus is lacking. González (1944), II, no. 12, O'Callaghan (1989), p. 17, and Pérez-Prendes (1988) p. 514, opt for April. For the reasons adduced by Estepa Díez (1988), p. 28, July seems altogether likelier.

[86] Marongiu (1968), pp. 32, 62. Cf. O'Callaghan (1975), p. 242; *Córtes de León y de Castilla*, I, p. 39.

[87] Arvizu (1988) p. 48; Pérez-Prendes (1988), pp. 512–13; Estepa Díez (1988), p. 28.

[88] Estepa Díez (1988), pp. 82–103.

for this development.[89] This appears fanciful. The hard-headed veterans of the *concejos* did not need sapient jurists from abroad to teach them that *quod omnes tangit ab omnibus debet approbari*. Nor did a king with his stepmother in hot pursuit, for whom representative propositions would not have constituted the most attractive feature of Romanist ideology anyway.[90]

Nevertheless, sapient jurists from abroad were indeed a feature of Alfonso VIII's Castile. In the next century Archbishop Rodrigo of Toledo reported their arrival in great numbers from France and Italy, 'masters of all faculties' attracted thither by the *magna stipendia* proffered by the king.[91] Their destination was Palencia, whose cathedral chapter had contained a Catalan contingent ever since the restoration of the church there in the 1030s, and where from the late 1170s Italians were increasingly in evidence. Though it is difficult to imagine a more unsuitable time and place for the establishment of an academic foundation, in 1177 Alfonso is alleged to have instituted a *studium* in the Uclés garrison of the order of Santiago.[92] But the king certainly had Romanists in his entourage. One was the Catalan Pere of Cardona, a luminary of Montpellier and Alfonso's chancellor from 1178 to 1181/2 when Lucius III spared him promotion to the see of Toledo by appointing him a cardinal. Also prominent were Ardericus, a Milanese appointed bishop of Sigüenza in 1178/9 and translated to Palencia in 1184 (d. 1206) and Ugolino da Sesso, author of a number of procedural treatises, who hailed from Reggio Emilia.[93] While scientists of the calibre of Gerard of Cremona flocked to Toledo,[94] it was to Palencia that the jurists came. So did the young Domingo of Guzmán, between 1185 and 1195, to study arts and theology, and it was at Palencia during that decade that the peninsula's first *studium* can be said to have been established by Alfonso VIII, the process being completed, according to the testimony of Lucas of Tuy, sometime between 1208 and 1214.[95]

The foundation of Castile's first university perhaps represented a bid to monopolize the talents of the peninsula's increasingly cosmopolitan clergy, hence doubtless Alfonso IX of León's establishment of a rival seat of learning at Salamanca late in his reign. Evidence of links between the university and the court has been discerned in the development by the royal chancery of

[89] O'Callaghan (1989), p. 15.
[90] In the 1110s, for example, the citizens of Sahagún and Santiago had not needed Justinian to tell them that the shoe pinched, while in 1185 (or shortly before) dissidents at Vic, where Pere of Cardona (next paragraph) had been active before he came to Castile, found that Justinian's Code was against them: Freedman (1983), pp. 86–7.
[91] Rodrigo of Toledo, *Historia de rebus Hispanie*, bk VIII, ch. 34.
[92] Beltrán de Heredia (1935), p. 216.
[93] García (1985), p. 49; Linehan (1993), ch. 9; Maffei (1990). [94] D'Alverny (1982), pp. 452–4.
[95] Maffei (1990), pp. 18–20; Lucas of Tuy, *Chronicon mundi*, p. 109; Beltrán de Heredia (1970), pp. 37–53.

sets of rules and conventions for the writing of documents in the vernacular (first adopted in 1206, treaty of Cabreros with León).[96] The increasing sense of national differentiation implied by this development is confirmed by evidence that by 1200 the Portuguese were already accustomed to regarding inhabitants of other areas of the peninsula as 'foreigners'.[97]

Meanwhile, in April 1196, Alfonso II had died aged thirty-nine, his thirty-four-year reign having witnessed the continuation of his father's policy of internal consolidation. 'For the public utility of all my land', at Fondarella in 1173 Alfonso decreed the extension as far as Lérida and Tortosa of the Peace and Truce of God which since the 1020s had supplemented the guarantees of vassalic conventions in the cause of law and order thoughout Catalonia. Vicars were instituted as secular judges of the peace to assist the diocesan bishops, and under the direction of Ramón of Caldes, dean of Barcelona, control over comital bailiffs was tightened, culminating in the compilation of the *Liber feudorum maior*, the 'Great Book of Fiefs', in 1194.[98] However, progress was neither steady nor uninterrupted. Deprived of the measure of outdoor relief which campaigns against the Moorish south had previously afforded, in the mid-1170s the military elite of Old Catalonia, to whom Alfonso's activities in Provence and Navarre offered few prospects of profit, found a focus for their frustrations and a symbol of their desire for a return to the expansionist policies of the previous generation in the person of a pseudo-Alfonso the Battler, and proceeded to conspire against the implementation of the count-king's Peace in their territories. Their protest at Gerona in 1188 that the statutes of Fondarella were in breach of the *Usatges* forced Alfonso to abandon these measures and to reissue them in 1192 in a revised form addressed to the 'good men and people of the cities and towns' as well as to the military establishment of Catalonia.[99] But tensions remained. The year in which the *Liber feudorum maior* was completed was also marked by the hacking to death of the archbishop of Tarragona, Berenguer of Vilademuls, an act performed with such deliberation that the dying man was able to record his last will and testament between blows. He was the second prelate of that church to be butchered during Alfonso's reign, but whereas in 1171 the assassin had been an immigrant, this time it was a local, Count Guillem Ramón I of Montcada. Whether or not, as Pope Celestine III insisted, all Christendom was aghast at the outrage, Catalan society was evidently in need of the means of sublimating the violent instincts that were endemic there.[100]

In the following year the train of events began which in 1212 would provide just that opportunity and establish the king of Castile as both the peninsula's

[96] Rico (1985), pp. 6–15; Wright (1982), p. 283.   [97] Mattoso (1986), II, p. 205.
[98] Soldevila (1962), pp. 198–216; Bisson (1977), pp. 297–8, and (1986), I, pp. 78–121.
[99] Bisson (1986), pp. 52–7.   [100] Villanueva (1851), pp. 169, 305–8; Shideler (1983), pp. 124–6.

senior monarch and the champion of Christendom. After the disappointments
of the Third Crusade observers abroad viewed with increased dismay the divisions of Christendom's leaders on its western frontier. As in 1147, Portugal had
benefited from the crusading fervour of the late 1180s, a fleet of northerners
assisting in the capture of Silves on the Algarve (Sept. 1189) and providing
Sancho I – a king given to melancholy according to a contemporary source –
with the first military success of his reign (1185–1211).[101] But in 1191 the caliph
Ya'qub not only recovered Silves but also seized Alcácer do Sal, Palmela and
Almada, leaving the Christians with Évora as their only stronghold in the
Alentejo. Meanwhile the anti-Castilian coalition of 1190 held. Not until 1194
was a breach created, facilitated by the death of Sancho VI of Navarre and the
efforts of Celestine III's legate Cardinal Gregory of S. Angelo. But the treaty
of Tordehumos (April 1194) between Castile and León, whereby it was agreed
that if Alfonso IX died sonless his kingdom would be incorporated with Castile
and Alfonso VIII undertook to restore to him various disputed territories,[102]
failed to provide a basis for Christian cooperation against the Almohads and,
indeed, was followed in July 1195 by the worst disaster that the Christians had
suffered since 1086, the rout of Alfonso VIII and his army at Alarcos.

   Alarcos revealed the full extent of Christian Spain's divisions in the face of a
determined foe. Rather than await the arrival of Leonese and Navarrese contingents (the latter under the command of Sancho VII *el Fuerte*, 1194–1234), the
king of Castile chose to engage the enemy alone but for the assistance of a token force of Portuguese. After the annihilation of the Christian army, of which
apart from Alfonso there were only twenty survivors, the surrender of the castle
of Alarcos by Diego López of Haro was taken by Pedro Fernández of Castro
who had fought alongside Ya'qub. The baneful consequences of the Haro–Lara
rivalry, medieval Castile's Montagues and Capulets, were never more plainly
demonstrated. In seeking to apportion blame for the defeat, Spanish writers
of the next generation perpetuated the memory of these divisions.[103]

   And while Christian Europe looked on aghast, and the troubadovr Peire
Vidal castigated Spain's kings for failing in its defence, Spain's kings looked to
their own advantage. Despite the earnest efforts of Alfonso of Aragon to forge
an effective defensive alliance, the high point of which was the dinner party
held between Agreda and Tarazona in March 1196 at which, tradition had it, he

---

[101] 'Narratio de itinere navali'; 'Chronique latine inédite', c. 2.   [102] González (1944), II, no. 79.

[103] Thus the Leonese Lucas of Tuy charged the Castilian with impetuousity for failing to await
reinforcements, claiming that Alfonso IX had already reached Toledo (*Chronicon mundi*, p. 108),
whereas the Castilian Rodrigo of Toledo alleged that the assistance of the Leonese and Navarrese
kings was a sham ('cum uenire simulassent': Rodrigo of Toledo, *Historia de rebvs Hispanie*, bk VII,
ch. 30) and that at the time of the battle they had only reached the Castilian frontier: *ibid.*, p. 252.
Cf. Huici Miranda (1956), pp. 137–69.

and the kings of Castile and Navarre ate from the same table while seated each within his own kingdom, León and Navarre preferred to collaborate with the caliph at the expense of Alfonso VIII[104]. The effects of the intervention of Celestine III (the extent of whose anxiety at last resulted in papal recognition of the Navarrese royal title in April 1196) were offset by the death of Alfonso of Aragon three days later. In 1197 events moved from tragedy to folly in the shape of a Castilian–Leonese marriage alliance which, even allowing for the relaxed attitudes current south of the Pyrenees regarding such matters, was singularly ill-advised.

For although they were not uncle and niece (as the papal chancery seems to have supposed), Alfonso IX and the Infanta Berenguela, Alfonso VIII's eldest daughter, whose Hohenstaufen prospects had withered on the birth of her brother Fernando, as descendants of a common great-grandfather were plainly within the limits. Otherwise, the match had everything to recommend it. Moreover, by the time that the knot was tied (?Oct. 1197) Alfonso VIII had agreed a truce not only with the Almohads but even with the king of Navarre. In England Roger of Howden heard that Celestine III had approved the match as expedient (*pro bono pacis*), also that Alfonso IX had offered Celestine's successor and his cardinals 20,000 marks of silver and 200 men for a year 'for the defence of the Christians against the pagans' if only they would allow Berenguela to stay with him until she had given him an heir – 'or for three years, say'.[105]

But the cure proved worse than the disease, for unfortunately Celestine III's successor was Innocent III, with whom arguments from expediency cut as little ice as hard cash. For their effrontery in suggesting that there were worse things than incest (*item* Muslims, heretics, Jews, priests on the streets, all of which were rife on account of the papal interdict imposed on the kingdom of León), in May 1199 a deputation led by the archbishop of Toledo and containing at least one canonist of note experienced a pontifical roasting of an intensity sufficient to cause Spanish bishops to give the papal curia a wide berth until well into the next century.[106] When in the same year Pedro II, the new king of Aragon, having agreed with Alfonso of Castile to partition the kingdom of Navarre (treaty of Calatayud, May 1198), declared his intention of marrying the king of Navarre's sister, the pope forbad it, the king of León invaded Portugal and by the grace of the Christian God the caliph Yu'qub died (Jan. 1199). By occupying the Basque provinces of Alava and Guipúzcoa, Alfonso VIII, now with French rather than Aragonese assistance, while Sancho VII enjoyed the support of John of England, dealt Navarre the most serious blow it had suffered

---

[104] Avalle (1960), pp. 70, 325.
[105] 'Vel saltem per tres annos': Roger of Howden, *Chronica*, iii, p. 90, iv, p. 79.
[106] Innocent III, *Register*, pp. 130–1; linehan (1993), ch. 8.

since the restoration of the kingdom in 1134. In the spring of 1204 Alfonso IX bowed to papal pressure and, the father now of four children including the future Fernando III, separated from Berenguela and resumed hostilities against Castile.[107]

Although in the will he made in December 1204 Alfonso VIII acknowleged the injustice of his seizure of Navarrese territory, not until October 1207 (treaty of Guadalajara) did hostilities cease and even then he did not surrender his recent conquests. But at Cabreros in the previous year he had reached a new truce with León, and at Monteagudo in February 1209 the rulers of Navarre and Aragón were also reconciled. For the first time since Alarcos a Christian alliance against the Almohads seemed feasible, the Infante Fernando of Castile was anxious for battle, and in February 1210 Innocent III directed the archbishop of Toledo, Rodrigo Jiménez of Rada, and his suffragans to urge Alfonso VIII to imitate the example of the king of Aragón and take the fight to the enemy.[108] We have it on his own authority, from the *De rebus Hispanie* written under his supervision in the 1240s, that the archbishop did so. In 1218 his admirer, the chancellor of Castile, Diego García, would pay the archbishop the very same compliment that the Arab writer Ibn Bassam had once paid the Cid: the damage that one Rodrigo had caused Spain (in 711) another of the same name had now repaired.[109] A native of Navarre, Rodrigo had already been involved in the peninsular diplomatic round and on his appointment to the primatial see in 1209 he immediately emerged as the impresario of the coming conflict.

Events moved swiftly. In May 1211 Alfonso VIII raided as far as the Mediterranean coast at Játiva to the south of Valencia while the king of Aragon successfully laid siege to Moorish castles to the north. The Almohad response came in the following month. A huge army led by the caliph Muhammad al-Nasir (known to history as 'Miramamolín') invested Salvatierra, the stronghold of the order of Calatrava high in La Mancha not far from Alarcos. 'The king of Castile's right hand' as the caliph described the place, Salvatierra seemed of all places the most impregnable. Its significance was as much symbolic as strategic, and its capture by the enemy in September, followed by the death of Alfonso's heir the Infante Fernando in the following month, sent shock waves across Europe and the archbishop of Toledo to France (and according to some historians to Italy and Germany too, which seems scarcely possible), and other envoys in all directions from Portugal to Constantinople, allegedly to encourage recruits to come to Castile ready for battle at Pentecost 1212. To the churches of France and Provence Innocent III wrote offering plenary indulgences as inducement, issued fierce inhibitions directed especially at the

---

[107] Lacarra (1972), II, pp. 93–8.   [108] *La documentación pontificia hasta Inocencio III*, no. 416.
[109] Alonso (1943), p. 181; Menéndez Pidal (1969), pp. 413, 573.

king of León, and ordered solemn processions to be held at Rome to coincide with the muster at Toledo.[110]

By June 1212, vast numbers of volunteers had crossed the Pyrenees to present themselves for action: by Alfonso's reckoning, up to 2,000 knights with their attendants, 10,000 mounted men and as many as 50,000 infantry. But most soon deserted on account of the sheer slog and the heat – and, true, it was 'a bit hot', the king informed the pope. He also implied that they had done so despite his having acquiesced in the demands of the king of Aragon and the *transmontani* that he permit the Moors ensconced at Calatrava to surrender, thus providing them with rich pickings, rather than raze the place to the ground. (The truth was probably the opposite, the foreigners with no stake in the future insisting on the papal injunction of 'no quarter', and the king, conscious of rebuilding costs and with an eye to the future, preferring terms of surrender.)[111] Anyway, only 150 of the tens of thousands remained, together with the papal legate, Arnaud Amaury (archbishop of Narbonne, ex-abbot of Cîteaux). At this point the Castilians pressed on while Pedro of Aragon awaited the arrival of Sancho of Navarre. Alfonso made a point of stressing how small the contingents were that his 'illustrious friends and relations' brought with them *cum potentatu suo* 'in the assistance and defence of the Catholic faith'. He refrained from mentioning either the new ruler of Portugal, Afonso II, whose corpulent frame was not designed for such exertions, or Alfonso IX of León, for whom the inexperience of his Portuguese neighbour offered opportunities requiring his urgent attention.

Moving south across the Sierra Morena the Christians encountered the enemy encamped on the plain of Las Navas de Tolosa to the south of the (later entitled) Despeñaperros pass. Barring a miracle, there seemed no way forward. A miracle was duly vouchsafed however. 'A certain rustic', later confidently identified as St Isidro the patron of Madrid, came forward and indicated a path unknown even to the locals, thus enabling the Christians to adopt the position from which on Monday 16 July they dealt the caliph and his forces a crushing and decisive blow.[112]

Never before had the Christians defeated the caliph in pitched battle, Alfonso's daughter Berenguela informed her sister Blanca (Blanche of Castile, wife of the future Louis VIII of France). And where had the French been that

---

[110] *La documentación pontificia hasta Inocencio III*, nos. 465, 470–2; Goñi Gaztambide (1958), pp. 110–30. Alfonso's letter to Innocent after the battle mentions only legates 'ad partes Francie': González (1960), III, p. 567. One of these was his physician Master Arnaldus ('Chronique latine inédite', c. 21) whom he sent to Poitou and Gascony. Was Arnaldus one of the king's celebrated foreign recruits?

[111] González (1960), III, p. 568; Huici Miranda (1956), p. 246.

[112] González (1960), III, pp. 569–71; Huici Miranda (1956), pp. 219–327, Lomax (1978), pp. 124–8.

day? By means of Archbishop Arnaud's report to the Cistercian general chapter, news of the victory spread as far and as fast as that of Salvatierra. Spain had saved not only itself, the bishop of Cremona recorded, 'but Rome too and indeed the whole of Europe'. And when he said Spain what he really meant was Castile, he explained.[113]

Later ages would agree. Las Navas was 'the greatest battle ever fought between the Moors and the Christians'.[114] And at the time the triumphalism engendered by victory echoed and re-echoed within Castile itself in the works of canonists as well as in the chronicles. So much for Charlemagne! Frenchmen had a lot to say. But it was Spaniards who got things done, the canonist Vincentius Hispanus tartly observed in a gloss. It was *Spanish* kings who fought for the Faith, Lucas of Tuy insisted after the event.[115] And before Las Navas too perhaps. There is, for example, the intriguing possibility that the *Poema de mio Cid* was in some sense a piece of Alfonsine propaganda intended to galvanize Castile into action, 'a sort of recruiting poster' for the Las Navas campaign, perhaps that it was even commissioned by the king who had attracted to Palencia the best scholars of law and theology that money could buy.[116] Certainly the vernacular poem presents a very different Cid from that of the earlier Latin Life in which the late eleventh-century warrior figures as a mercenary no less willing than the kings of Christian Spain themselves until the early 1200s to collaborate with the Muslim. Now he is a born-again Christian crusader, the inveterate enemy of Islam, Castile incarnate. In this connection, scholarly attention in recent years has centred on the significance of the date May 1207 when, according to the unique manuscript of the work, the poem was 'written' by 'Per Abbat'; the nature of the latter's links with the royal court and Archbishop Rodrigo; and the relationship of the fictional cortes of Toledo at which the poetic hero was finally vindicated to what appears to have been an authentic assembly there in 1207 itself.[117]

The contrast between the highly charged *Poema de mio Cid* and the chronicler of Alfonso VII's bathetic 'it seemed useful' would suggest that the emergence of a 'crusading ideology' in the peninsula occurred later rather than earlier in the century.[118] Whether that spirit of exultation accurately reflected a widespread consensus, however, it is impossible to determine. Doubtless degrees of intensity of feeling regarding the confessional foe were at least partially

[113] González (1960), III, pp. 572–4; Linehan (1971), p. 5; Lomax (1988), pp. 39–41.
[114] Gibbon (1972), p. 179.
[115] 'Facto, ut ispanus, non autem uerbis, ut francigena': Post (1964), p. 485; 'Pugnant Hispani Reges pro fide': Lucas of Tuy, *Chronicon mundi*, p. 113.
[116] Smith (1983), pp. 97ff.   [117] Duggan (1989); Hernández (1988); Michael (1991) Linehan (1992), ch. 10.
[118] Above, n. 71 Cf. Fletcher (1987), pp. 42–6. The tone of the poem of Almería might seem to indicate otherwise – if, as is universally assumed, the poem is indeed a work of the late 1140s.

determined by distance from the front line, making *convivencia* easier to maintain in the hinterland than at Salvatierra, for example. Thus at Tudela in Navarre the prosperous Mudejar community continued to enjoy the considerable advantages which it had been granted, by Alfonso the Battler incidentally, in 1118. And the reason was Christian self-interest, just as it was for the converse phenomenon of refusing Muslims baptism, reported from Ávila in 1185.[119] Yet there are no clear signs that *convivencia* was a casualty of these years. At the highest level popes continued to rail against the likes of Alfonso IX for allying themselves with the enemy. But it was the Christian hero of Las Navas who favoured the orderly capitulation of Calatrava, it was in his foundation at Las Huelgas that the nuns were ministered to by Jewish physicians and Mudejar servants who had their own mosque, and it was he who in 1205 had to be reprimanded by Innocent III for infringing the liberty of the church and appearing rather to extol the synagogue and the mosque.[120] Likewise, although Alfonso VI reportedly attributed the defeat of his army at Sagrajas in 1086 to his soldiers' taking too many baths, in the togetherness of various municipal bath houses across the land over the next century cleanliness, godliness, Muslims, Jews and Christians all shared the same installations, and to that extent bathed in the same water. Albeit with racial as well as sexual segregation rigidly enforced, here, at least, 'some degree of acculturation clearly took place'.[121] The 'society organized for war' had not altogether forgotten how to relax.

[119] García-Arenal (1984), pp. 15–16; *Documentos medievales de la catedral de Ávila*, pp. 22, 24.

[120] Torres Balbás (1954), pp. 78–9; *La documentación pontificia hasta Inocencio III*, no. 312.

[121] Powers (1979), p. 665, noting a greater degree of permissiveness in Aragonese towns whose *fueros* were based on that of Teruel than in Castilian places whose regulations were modelled on that of Cuenca; Dillard (1984), pp. 151–2. Cf. Lucas of Tuy, *Chronicon mundi*, p. 102, and (another century on) Alfonso X, *Las siete partidas*, pp. 673 ('And we forbid any Jew to bathe together [*de bañarse en baño en uño*] with any Christian').

CHAPTER 17(a)

CROWN AND GOVERNMENT

John W. Baldwin

FROM the death of Philip I in 1108 to that of Philip (II) Augustus in 1223 the Capetian monarchy made steady progress in asserting its authority over France. This secular rise levelled off in the second half of the twelfth century, but concluded with a dramatic upswing after the Third Crusade in 1190. Early accessions combined with congenital longevity produced lengthy reigns (Louis VI, 1108–37, Louis VII, 1137–80 and Philip Augustus, 1179–1223), but these regnal dates are of little import in charting the evolution of government. More significant is the punctuation introduced by military campaigns. By removing the monarchs from their realm, the Second (1147–9) and Third Crusades (1190–1) induced administrative innovations in the king's absence. After Philip Augustus's return in 1191 governmental tempo accelerated, marking the Norman invasion in 1202/3 and the victory at Bouvines in 1214 as the chief transitions.

FROM THE ACCESSION OF LOUIS VI TO THE SECOND CRUSADE (1108–1147)

History is little more than a function of its sources. As medieval governments began to generate their own documentation, these written sources subsisted in symbiosis both as products and evidence of the institutions that produced them. Louis VI inherited two genres of sources, charters and chronicles, from the first Capetians. Royal charters were written declarations of the king's actions addressed to designated parties. Transcribed on parchment either by clerics working for the royal chancellor or by those employed by the recipients, they were authenticated by a wax seal. Since the royal household took few pains to copy these documents, their survival depended on their preservation or recopying by recipients, for the most part monasteries and churches. A good sign of the progress of royal activity is the rapidly increasing number of these extant charters from 5.7 per annum during Philip I's reign to 14.0 under Louis

VI, to 19.1 under Louis VII, and finally to 28.1 under Philip Augustus.[1] The contemporary chroniclers were chiefly monks or clergymen, like the Norman Or deric Vitalis or the Flemish Galbert of Bruges, whose horizons were limited to the provinces where they lived or to events that caught their attention. Few chroniclers, however, took note of the French king except when he intruded upon their limited worlds. The Capetians none the less found their own spokesmen at the royal abbey of St-Denis to the north of Paris where the monks began compiling a short chronicle, the *Gesta gentis Francorum* during the reign of Louis VI. In the succeeding reign the influential Abbot Suger, confidant and adviser to Louis VI and Louis VII, wrote a *Life of Louis VI*. Neither a full biography nor a regnal history, this work rhetorically shaped the activities of the king around symbolic and often sacred images. Both the extant royal charters and the historiography of St-Denis therefore offer a perspective on the Capetians that was highly configured by ecclesiastical concerns.

During the first half of the twelfth century the leading barons of northern France began to consolidate their hold on their principalities. This can be seen in Blois and Anjou, but especially in Flanders and the Anglo-Norman realm, where, in the last case, Henry I was unusually effective. Parallel efforts were undertaken by Louis VI and Louis VII to exploit the two fundamental resources of land and men. Louis VI inherited from his father a royal domain consisting of a conglomerate of lands, revenues and rights productive of income, the extent of which is known chiefly through charters. Restricted in scope, it was centred on Paris and Orleans but extended to the north-east to Laon and to the south-west towards Sens. Interlaced with these royal holdings were those of local lords who possessed castles that dominated the vicinities. So powerful were these castellans that, for example, it was difficult for the king to travel safely from Paris to Orleans. Suger depicted scores of Louis's campaigns against powerful castellans such as Thomas of Marle and Hugh of Le Puiset who besieged and subjugated troublesome castles such as Montaigu, Montlhéry, and Le Puiset. Although often frustrated in these endeavours, by his death Louis VI had succeeded in pacifying most of the royal domain, a programme brought to completion by his son.

To manage and collect income from the royal domain Philip I had created local officials called *prévôts* who were retained by the two Louis not only as

---

[1] These statistics are calculated from the *Recueil des actes de Philippe Ier* and the *Recueil des actes de Philippe Auguste* and from the estimates kindly furnished by Jean Dufour and Michel Nortier, editors responsible for the editions of the charters of Louis VI and Louis VII respectively. The figure of 28.1 for Philip Augustus is based on the years 1179 to 1203, before the registers were compiled. (See Baldwin (1986), p. 403.) If the charters preserved in the registers are included, the figure jumps to 41.1 per annum. The annual figures (increasing from 5.7 to 28.1) are statistically comparable because they are essentially compiled from the same collections of sources.

domanial agents but also as royal officials to guard castles and administer justice. Because of the domain's diminutive size, transversable in a matter of days,
the king travelled about to supervise the *prévôts* and receive the revenues. It
was easier to bring the government to the countryside than the contrary. The
Capetian court, like that of all early medieval monarchs, was therefore ambu-
latory, transported in baggage wagons and halting at the chief centres of Paris
and Orleans as well as at dispersed castles, monasteries and royal residences.
The king's companions can be ascertained from the royal charters. In Philip
I's reign these documents contained extensive lists of witnesses who constituted the royal entourage, but under Louis VI the charters began to change.
The multiple witnesses were replaced by five household officers who by mid-
century became the sole personages to co-sign the kings' acts. Reminiscent of
the Carolingian household, these officers were named for their domestic duties:
the seneschal supplied the household, the butler the drink, the chamberlain
cared for the bedroom, the constable for the horses and the chancellor supervised the chapel and eventually the secretariat. Their exclusive place on the
royal charters indicated that their domestic tasks were giving way to responsibilities as royal counsellors and governmental agents, since the great magnates
of France, with few exceptions, rarely attended court. The household officials
were recruited from the principal castellan families of the royal domain, three
of whom, the Rochefort-Montlhérys, the Garlandes and the Senlis, competed
with each other to monopolize the offices and to make them hereditary. When
the Garlandes finally took over three of the offices, and Stephen of Garlande
held the position of seneschal and chancellor simultaneously, Louis VI was
compelled to dismiss them in 1127 and to leave the principal posts of seneschal
and chancellor vacant. Thereafter vacancy became a technique aimed at curbing over-ambitious officials. Despite the formalized charters that obscured the
royal entourage, it becomes none the less apparent that Louis VI and Louis VII
increasingly relied on the services of lesser men for the routine operations of central government. This personnel consisted of chamberlains, knights and clerics
drawn from the castles and towns of the royal domain. Although most are mere
names in the documentation, one, a monk with the eccentric name of Suger,
appeared frequently within this group. Originating most likely from a family of
small knights, he benefited from the patronage of the Garlande clan. Selected
by Louis VI to become abbot of St-Denis in 1122 because of his demonstrated
talents as a domanial administrator for the abbey, he joined the magnates of the
realm as head of this influential monastery. After the Garlandes' disgrace, he
swiftly assumed the responsibilities of chief counsellor, familiar and functionary
for both Louis VI and Louis VII, as well as historian of the Capetian monarchy.

   In the deployment of lands and men to enhance power Louis VI and Louis
VII acted no differently than the contemporary magnates. Unlike the others,

however (with the exception of the duke of Normandy, also king of England), the Capetians were likewise kings, a dignity that offered incalculable advantages. From their Robertian origins the Capetians proclaimed their dynastic rights to the crown. With other lords they realized that patrilineal succession assured the integrity of their lands. The chief patrimony went customarily to the eldest son, while cadets were supported by tangential holdings, marriages to heiresses and positions in churches. Hereditary succession to the crown was reinforced by the Carolingian precedent of anticipatory association whereby the eldest son was designated or consecrated king during his father's lifetime. Louis VI was already *rex designatus* by 1100; his son Philip was consecrated in 1129 at the age of thirteen. When he died in an accident two years later, the second son Louis (age eleven) was immediately consecrated. At Louis VI's death in 1137 Suger remarked how smoothly the royal succession had proceeded in France in contrast to the disputed successions in the German empire and England. The Capetian dynastic right to the French throne was serenely recalled in their naming patterns. Queen Anna (of Kiev) had undoubtedly chosen Philip's name from Macedonian traditions in her Russian family. Philip I in turn adopted a Carolingian name for his firstborn son Louis VI. Thereafter and into the fourteenth century the Capetians (with only one exception) alternated the pattern Philip–Louis and Louis–Philip for their first two sons. Whenever the same name repeated itself in succession, it denoted the death of an older brother.

A change of dynasty, however, always underscored the need for an ecclesiastical consecration at the king's coronation. Following the Carolingian example of 751, the Capetians were careful to have themselves anointed by the archbishop of Rheims in 987, and they continued the practice thereafter with few modifications. Merely designated king at the death of his father in 1108, Louis VI was quickly consecrated at Orleans by the archbishop of Sens. (The see of Rheims was disputed at the time by rival candidates.) Philip was consecrated in 1129, and after his unexpected death Louis VII likewise in 1131, this time with full ceremony at Rheims by Pope Innocent II. These consecrations undoubtedly adhered to the protocol of Philip I in 1059 (of which a report has survived) which, in turn, was based on *ordines* dating from the tenth century. According to this tradition, after the king promised to defend the church and to enforce justice and peace throughout the realm, he was anointed with holy oil and invested with the royal insignia including crown, sword, sceptre and rod. Thus consecrated as a sacred personage he could thereafter rule as 'king by the grace of God' (*rex Dei gratia*) as was proclaimed by his title and on his seal.

During the coronation ceremonies churchmen offered the king consecration in exchange for the promise of protection from enemies. Suger underscored this bargain both at Louis VI's coronation in 1108 and throughout his narrative. Unlike his father Philip, who had abused the church, Louis had fully deserved anointing because already at the age of twelve he had protected churches by defending St-Denis, Rheims and Orleans against local predators, a service which his son performed with equal zeal. If the two Louis accepted the responsibilities as guardians of the church, in return they asserted rights over regalian churches. These churches consisted of cathedrals and monasteries whose temporal properties or *regalia* were held by the king during the vacancy, that is, between the death of the last prelate and his successor's accession. Regalian rights further implied that the choice of successor belonged to the king. In 1122, for example, when the monks of St-Denis selected Suger as their abbot without royal approval, they provoked Louis VI's anger, although their particular choice indubitably was acceptable to the king. In 1141 Louis VII became embroiled in a conflict with Bourges when the canons refused to accept the royal chancellor Cadurc as archbishop. Regalian cathedrals numbered nearly twenty and monasteries more than thirty. Although concentrated in the Ile-de-France (in the province of Sens), important regalian churches were also located in the provinces of Rheims and Bourges. As far distant as Tournai and Arras in the north, for example, as well as Rheims and Châlons-sur-Marne in the east, and Mende and Le Puy in the south, the king's influence thereby exceeded the actual royal domain. Regalian collegiate churches like St-Martin of Tours, St-Aignan of Orleans and St-Frambaud of Senlis also supplied benefices to clerics who staffed the royal entourage.

In addition to distant bishops and abbots the Capetians, as kings of the Franks, also claimed suzerainty over the great magnates which further extended their influence beyond the royal domain. Such claims implied fealty and homage, but the practical effectiveness depended on the king's enforcement. Rights of suzerainty, for example, permitted Louis VI to intervene in the affairs of the lords of the Bourbonnais and the counts of Auvergne to the south, but both Louis found it difficult to assert authority over the great principalities since they were likewise consolidating their powers. Even the royal panegyrist Suger was unable to conceal Capetian weakness when the king confronted great vassals. During a border dispute Henry, duke of Normandy, but also a king, refused to do homage to the French king. In the resulting warfare Louis lost a pitched battle at Brémule in 1119. Throughout these hostilities Henry was usually supported by his nephew Theobald, count of Blois, who intermittently interfered with Louis's pacification of the royal domain. Louis VII intensified this conflict in 1142 with a full-scale, but ultimately ineffectual, invasion of Blois and Troyes-Champagne. Throughout the rivalry between the Capetians and the Norman–Champenois party the counts of Flanders and Anjou usually supported the king. Louis VI asserted suzerainty over Flanders when he sought to regulate the succession after the assassination of Count Charles the Good in 1127, but again with little success. When Henry I married Matilda, his only legitimate heir, to Count Geoffrey of Anjou in 1127 and the latter conquered Normandy for his wife by 1144, this union between Normandy and Anjou offered new challenges to the Capetian suzerainty. With French over-lordship resisted from all sides, it came as a surprise that William X, duke of Aquitaine, offered his only heir, Eleanor, as ward to Louis VI, who promptly married her to his heir. Louis VII therefore succeeded his father in 1137 not only as king of the Franks but also as duke of Aquitaine, although the vast and unruly southern duchy was held separately by marriage and was never integrated into the royal domain.

Dynastic claims, ecclesiastical consecration, authority over regalian churches and suzerainty over great vassals were all traditional rights of the Frankish crown. The charters of Louis VI and Louis VII, however, announced a new policy towards the commercial groups who converged upon towns in northern France spurred by the revival of trade at the turn of the eleventh century. To separate themselves from the peasant servitudes in the countryside the townspeople sought written definition of the customs or liberties that regulated their civil, commercial and political affairs. To reinforce these privileges they occasionally established sworn associations called communes. Not without ambivalence, the two Louis responded to their demands by issuing charters that defined customs and recognized communes in bishoprics outside the royal domain such as Laon, Amiens and Rheims, particularly when they were vacant. Orleans and Poitiers at the centre of Louis VII's lands, however, were denied such privileges in 1137 when Louis became king and duke. At the very heart of the royal domain Paris was never granted a charter. Charters confirming urban liberties none the less became a standard Capetian practice that sought both to reinforce royal authority in the domain and to extend the king's influence beyond.

Not long after the accession of Louis VII in 1137 Suger articulated the salient ideology of the Capetian monarchy in his *Life of Louis VI*. True to his coronation promise, Louis was pictured repeatedly as defending churches throughout his kingdom. To this religious responsibility Suger added an analysis of suzerainty that shaped it in the form of a hierarchy of vassals requiring two components: the gradation of vassalage and the positioning of the king at the apex. When Louis intervened in the affairs of Auvergne, for example, he thereby recognized an ascending chain of vassals from the count of Auvergne to the duke of Aquitaine to the king. When Louis acquired the county of the Vexin from St-Denis, he further asserted that he could not do homage to the abbey because he was king, thus suggesting his ultimate suzerainty over all vassals. Despite the particular features of this case, Suger none the less placed St-Denis at the

centre of royal ideology. As the traditional necropolis for the Frankish kings and
the repository for the royal crown and insignia, the abbey and its patron saint
were designated the special patrons and protectors of the entire kingdom. In
1124 when the emperor Henry V, seconded by Henry I of England, threatened
France from the east with a massive army recruited from the German principalities, Louis took the banner of St-Denis from the abbey's altar and hastened
to Rheims to meet the invasion. Magnates as far distant as Burgundy, Brittany
and Aquitaine, as well as from northern France, rallied to the saint's standard,
and their spontaneous show of force deterred the attack. Suger concluded that
this triumph over a Roman emperor and an English king was the most glorious
event France had witnessed in ancient and modern times.

Except for new attention to townspeople and Suger's ideological formu-
lations Louis VI and Louis VII introduced few governmental innovations.
Rather, they inherited from the first Capetians and transmitted to their successors the components of landed domain, administrative personnel and traditional royal rights over churches and lords. These elements remained the basis
of government throughout the Capetian era upon which all further change proceeded without abolishing the foundations. Such was the nature of medieval
reform.

FROM THE SECOND TO THE THIRD CRUSADE (1147–1190)

In 1146 Louis VII announced an intention that he had long kept secret. At
the urging of Pope Eugenius III he would take the cross and depart for the
Holy Land, joined by Conrad of Germany and many magnates, all inspired by
the preaching of Bernard, abbot of Clairvaux. Following his father's gesture,
he received the banner of St-Denis from the abbey's altar and left the realm
from 1147 to 1149. The regency was committed to the royal cousin Ralph,
count of Vermandois, Samson, archbishop of Rheims, and Suger, the old royal
confidant. Reinforcing his appointment by a papal commission, the abbot of
St-Denis quickly assumed leadership. Although he had to deal with political intrigues from the king's brother Robert, count of Dreux, and to handle
the affairs of the regalian churches, Suger's great expertise lay in the field of
administration, as he had recently demonstrated in a treatise *De administra-
tione* relating to St-Denis. What survives of his correspondence allows a brief
glimpse into the two chief concerns of government, justice and finance. One
letter suggests that Suger was holding regular pleas at Paris to hear cases of
justice in the king's place. Another indicates that local royal agents were rendering their accounts before the regent at a financial bureau. Suger personally
assured the king that the royal income from justice, tallages, relief of fiefs and
domanial income was kept intact. Of particular concern to Louis, the royal

treasury was moved to the house of the Knights Templars, members of a military order, who as bankers transferred money directly overseas. Throughout his correspondence Suger employed the term *corona regni* (the crown of the kingdom) to symbolize the royal administration that transcended the king's person during his absence. When Louis returned in 1149 to resume charge, however, whatever administrative innovations had been created disappeared from sight.

The documentary sources of the next half-century remain of the same nature as in the preceding era. Suger began a history of Louis VII which was finished in an abbreviated fashion by a monk of St-Germain-des-Prés. At St-Denis Abbot Odo of Deuil also wrote on Louis VII but restricted his attention to the crusade. It was not until 1196 that Rigord, a doctor turned monk of St-Denis, resumed Suger's tradition and wrote a regnal history of the opening decade of Philip Augustus. Towards the close of the century, however, Anglo-Norman chroniclers such as Roger of Howden were inspired by the governmental innovations of King Henry II of England and the extent of his continental dominions to include the political activities of the Capetians in their narratives. Louis VII and the young Philip Augustus continued to issue charters modelled on those of Louis VI, but at an accelerating rate. In 1172 the royal chancellor Hugh of Champfleuri, bishop of Soissons, made a private collection of incoming letters to the king, but since these were of a more personal nature, they were of less concern to government.

Throughout the second half of the twelfth century Louis VII and the young Philip retained the basic framework of inherited governmental power. The royal domain, administered by local *prévôts*, increased only incrementally but continued to supply the major income, except in 1180 when Philip exploited his authority over the Jews in his domain by confiscating their property in a one-time windfall. As the king's court peregrinated through the royal lands, it was composed of the traditional household officers and lesser *familiares* consisting of chamberlains (Walter), knights (Adam of Villeron) and clerics (Barbedor and Master Mainerius). Increasingly these lesser names were identified as counsellors (*consiliarii*) who constituted a more or less permanent council/counsel (*consilium*) for routine business. Upon Philip's accession many towns hastened to have their customs and privileges reconfirmed in charters of the new king.

When Louis VII returned from the crusade in 1149, his marital life was in disarray. Not only had the king and queen become personally estranged, but, what was more important, Eleanor had failed to deliver the requisite son for the Capetian dynasty. (In fact, she gave birth to two daughters.) Louis obtained an annulment of his marriage on the grounds of consanguinity and married Constance, a Spanish princess, who also produced girls. When she died in 1160, within the month Louis married Adela from the family of the counts of Troyes-Champagne. Although Louis VI had had seven legitimate sons, the vaunted Capetian fertility in males was rapidly approaching a crisis. Five years later when the queen finally gave birth to a male child, Paris celebrated with relief and joy, and Philip acquired the sobriquet *Dieudonné* (given by God). In 1179 the king, bedridden from a stroke, continued Capetian tradition by having the fourteen-year-old boy crowned and anointed at Rheims before his own death. The next year Philip married Isabella, daughter of the count of Hainault. Unlike his father, he refused to depart on a crusade until a male heir, Louis, was born (1187). When he did take leave of the realm, his son was as yet unconsecrated. Never again was a Capetian to repeat the traditional practice of anticipatory association, a sure sign that after seven unbroken generations the Capetians finally felt secure in their dynastic right.

In addition to his marital woes Louis VII returned to France with the failure of the crusade on his conscience. Despite the efforts of two monarchs and many lords the expedition had achieved few of its goals. Perhaps this was evidence of divine displeasure that was provoked by the king's violation of ecclesiastical freedom when he took violent measures to enforce candidates on regalian sees such as Bourges. Thereafter Louis made few overt attempts to interfere in church elections. His policy was summarized in his son's ordinance of 1190 which stated that the clergy of a vacant see were to seek a licence to choose a new prelate from the king who, in turn, accorded a free election. Such cooperation was designed to produce prelates 'who were both pleasing to God and useful to the kingdom'.[2] In fact, regalian bishoprics and monasteries rewarded the king's restraint by electing candidates generally favourable to the king. Benefiting from this harmony, Louis began to issue royal charters of protection to monasteries and bishoprics in distant provinces, especially in the south of France. These documents had little practical effect, but they embellished the king's image as defender of the church.

Although deemed necessary for the survival of the dynasty, Louis VII's separation from Eleanor in 1152 came at the worst possible moment for upholding his suzerainty over the great magnates. By this time it had become clear that Matilda's Anglo-Norman realm and Count Geoffrey's Anjou would be united in their son Henry. When the young Angevin quickly married Eleanor, heiress of Aquitaine, and ascended the English throne as King Henry II in 1154, he had become lord of the entire western half of France through inheritance and marriage. To assist him in the government of this vast conglomeration he divided his titles among his sons, the young Henry, Richard and Geoffrey. In face of this formidable accumulation of land the Capetians' only recourse was to react in indirect and complex ways. As suzerains they were able to require

---

[2] 'qui Deo placeat et utilis sit regno'. *Recueil des actes de Philippe Auguste*, I, no. 345.

homage from Henry and his sons for their various continental fiefs, chiefly because they, too, as great lords also depended on homage from their vassals. In
addition, Louis reinforced these ties of vassalage by marrying his two daughters
from Constance to the young Henry and Richard. Nevertheless, the Capetians
encouraged insubordination among Henry's sons and vassals whenever opportunity presented itself. Louis VII, for example, supported the rebellion of
Henry's sons in 1172–3, fomented by Eleanor now disaffected with her second husband. Philip Augustus sought to fuel the discontent of young Henry,
Geoffrey and Richard against their father, but at no time did the Capetians
seriously threaten Henry's authority. More effective was Louis's deployment
of marriages to forge new alliances against the Anglo-Norman-Angevins. The
heir to Flanders was given a daughter from the royal cousins of Vermandois,
but, equally importantly, Louis married his two daughters by Eleanor to the
brothers, counts of Blois and Troyes-Champagne, and he himself, as we have
seen, wedded Adela, their youngest sister. Flanders was thereby neutralized,
and the great complex of Champagne was detached from its traditional ties to
the Anglo-Normans and allied closely to the Capetians.

These manoeuvres and marriages among the great lords reinforced corresponding alterations within the composition of the central court. In the
preceding era the magnates were largely absent, except for the solitary figures
of the abbot of St-Denis and the count of Vermandois. As Louis became involved in the summons for the crusade, more great vassals attended his court
and remained after his return. Theobald, count of Blois, became seneschal of
the royal household, Matthew, count of Beaumont, chamberlain, and Hugh,
bishop of Soissons, chancellor. A mixture of lords and prelates along with the
chamberlains, knights and clerics, the Capetian court resembled the large and
heterogeneous entourages of the Anglo-Normans. The infiltration of leading
magnates into the Capetian court can best be seen at the coronation of the
young Philip Augustus at Rheims in 1179. The ceremony was presided over
by William, archbishop of Rheims, who was brother of the counts of Troyes
and Blois and Queen Adela. The count of Flanders carried the king's sword in
the opening procession and performed the duties of steward at the subsequent
banquet. The Anglo-Norman-Angevin house was represented by the young
King Henry who bore Philip's crown, prominently accompanied by his brothers. All parties who counted most in the kingdom were present, exhibiting
their rivalries at the centre of the king's court.

When Rigord, historian and monk of St-Denis, surveyed the first decade
of Philip's reign, he reverted to the two traditional ideologies of birthright
and sanctity. By his belated birth Philip had demonstrated not only that he
was *Dieudonné* but also that the Capetian dynastic right was reconfirmed,
having persisted for seven generations. This success encouraged a search for

origins. Rigord was the first to discuss the Capetian dynastic right within royal circles. While others outside the court had proposed Carolingian connections by blood descent through female lineage, Rigord ignored these theories for the more ancient myth of Trojan origins. This was a foundational myth inspired by Virgil's *Aeneid* that accounted for the origins of both Rome and the barbarian kingdoms as successors of the Trojans who had abandoned Troy in flames. According to the Frankish version adopted by Rigord, the descendants of the eponymous Francio, grandson of King Priam, eventually settled in France thus establishing the Merovingians, who, in turn, produced the Carolingians and finally the Capetians. By ignoring the genealogical discontinuities Rigord could assert that Philip was directly descended from ancient Trojan roots. Equally significant was the sanctity conferred by consecration with sacred oil at Philip's coronation in Rheims. As Suger had depicted the king's grandfather and father, Rigord envisaged Philip as defending churches from local predators in fulfilment of his coronation promises. His holy zeal for the church, however, was most fully expressed when he, too, took the cross to recover the Holy Land in 1190. For Philip's faithful defence of the church Rigord revived a traditional epitaph that the popes had accorded Frankish kings since Carolingian times. Philip had once again earned the title of *christianissimus*, 'the most Christian king' of the French.

FROM THE THIRD CRUSADE TO THE CONQUEST OF NORMANDY (1190–1203)

Overshadowed by the might of the Anglo-Norman-Angevins, Philip Augustus was reluctant to respond to the call for the Third Crusade. When he could be assured that King Richard (who had succeeded Henry II) would depart simultaneously, he took the banner from St-Denis and left his kingdom in 1190 for eighteen months, confiding the regency to William, archbishop of Rheims, and Adela, the queen-mother, both of the house of Champagne. For their guidance he drew up an ordinance in the guise of a testament that decreed provisional measures during his absence, confirmed older practices such as regalian elections, but, most importantly, announced radical innovations in justice and finance. New local officials called *baillis*, who had surfaced shortly before the ordinance, were instituted throughout the royal domain with wide-ranging duties. Circulating in teams of two or three, they held monthly assizes in which they heard the judicial pleas of the inhabitants of the domain and from which they transmitted appeals to the regents at Paris three times a year. On these triennial occasions Philip commanded that his revenues also be brought to Paris to be accounted in writing by a cleric. A record of these periodic exercises has survived for the fiscal year 1202/3. In this document we can see the *prévôts* acknowledging the regular income and expenses of the domain, while the *baillis* accounted for the profits of justice and other occasional finances. They deposited their monies at the house of the Knights Templars, which, as under Louis VII, served both as a bank to transmit funds for the crusade and as a permanent royal treasury. Although other provisions of the ordinance of 1190 disappeared when the king returned, the innovations of the *baillis* dispensing justice and the accounting bureau operating on a triennial schedule in Paris remained permanent features of royal government. Unlike Suger's earlier experiments, Philip Augustus's ordinance-testament effected lasting change. It initiated a reversal in the flow of governmental operations. Although the king continued to travel widely, the trennial visits of scores of *prévôts* and *baillis* increasingly drew representatives from the domain to Paris. To enhance the appearance of the city Philip paved the chief squares and roads and issued the command for encircling it with walls before his departure in 1190. By that year, therefore, Paris was finally designated as the centripetal capital of the Capetians.

Included with these innovations were new royal documents. The king's absence had occasioned the first constitution or description of the royal government and the first series of periodic fiscal accounts, but upon his return Philip added a new royal archive. In the fighting of 1194 he fell into an ambush prepared by Richard at Fréteval where he lost baggage that contained treasure, the royal seal and documents. While the nature and the extent of the losses cannot be fully known, it is clear that thereafter Philip established at Paris an archive that preserved incoming correspondence for safekeeping in a collection subsequently known as the Trésor des Chartes. The historian Rigord who had copied the ordinance of 1190 was equally aware of the contents of this collection. Once again, these series of written sources appeared symbiotically as products of and testimony to new institutions. For the first time the royal administration can be viewed from the inside as it was perceived by the king's entourage and not exclusively transmitted through ecclesiastical channels.

The new fiscal accounts indicate that the royal domain had begun to grow at an accelerating rate during the first two decades of Philip's reign as a result of dynastic crises in the houses of Flanders and the Anglo-Norman-Angevins. The marriage alliance between the royal cousins of Vermandois and the counts of Flanders was reinforced by Philip's own marriage to Isabelle of Hainault (also related to the Flemish house) and the birth of their son Louis. When it became apparent that Philip of Alsace, count of Flanders, would die without heir, these alliances promised significant gains to the Capetians. Through complex negotiations, the king acquired Amiens, Montdidier and Roye in 1185, and after the death of the childless Flemish count in 1191, Péronne and the county of Artois in the name of Louis. King Richard's death without direct heir in 1199 caused similar difficulties for the Anglo-Norman-Angevin succession. When Richard's brother John's claim was disputed by a nephew Arthur, Philip Augustus was able to exact from the former the Norman territory of Evrecin and parts of the Vexin as the price of confirming John's succession. The value of these acquisitions may be calculated from the fiscal accounts. The number of *prévôtés* (circumscriptions headed by *prévôts*) in the royal domain increased from forty-one in 1179 to fifty-two in 1190 to sixty-two in 1202/3, but the increase in domanial revenues was even more striking: 22 per cent by 1190 and 50 per cent by 1203. On the eve of the Capetian conquest of Normandy, therefore, Philip Augustus's regular domanial income had increased by almost three-quarters. In 1196 Rigord encapsulated the significance of the growing domain when he entitled Philip as *Augustus* because, like the Caesars, he augmented (*auge[bat]*) the *respublica* by adding Vermandois.[3]

The new governmental sources also reveal a notable shift in the personnel of the royal entourage. Philip Augustus insisted that all his great vassals accompany him on the crusade, allowing no important personage to remain behind to cause the mischief that had plagued his father. As he had probably calculated, the rigours of the expedition took their toll on the magnates of his father's generation. An unusual number died, including the counts of Flanders and Blois at the siege of Acre in 1191. The crusade, therefore, provided the youthful king with an opportunity to restaff his entourage afresh. Although the regent, William, archbishop of Rheims, lingered into the next decade, no great lord achieved prominence at the royal court. After the death of Theobald, count of Blois, Philip revived the tactic of vacancy and neglected to refill the post of seneschal as he had done for the chancellor in 1185. Since the two chief household offices were thereby suppressed, the other officers were reduced to honorific status. In their place he continued his grandfather's and father's policy of relying on lesser men. The central court recruited chamberlains, including Louis VII's faithful Walter, now accompanied by his two sons, Urso and Walter the Young, knights such as Bartholomew of Roye and Henry Clément, and clerics such as Brother Guérin and Brother Haimard. The *prévôts* were joined at the local level by at least a dozen new *baillis* on circuit throughout the domain. To the titles of chamberlains, knights, clerics and *baillis* was added the distinctive sobriquet 'of the king'. The salient characteristics of these men were obscurity of origins, youth and faithfulness. Bartholomew of Roye, for example, came from the petty knights of Vermandois, and the family of Brother Guérin has not yet been identified. In all likelihood Philip discovered him while on the crusade. With one exception the *baillis* were drawn from the same level as the royal knights. None were promoted above their origins into the baronage; only Brother Guérin became a magnate by election to the bishopric of Senlis.

---

[3] Rigord, *Gesta*, in *Œuvres de Rigord et de Guillaume le Breton*, I, p. 6.

All outlived their youthful master, except Henry Clément who died of battle wounds. Only a single *bailli* was dismissed in disgrace from service.

As each new set of royal records appeared, the diverse duties of these men were revealed. Brother Guérin first emerged in the royal chancery in 1201–2 when he began annotating royal charters with the inscription 'given by the hand of Brother Guérin'.[4] Thereafter the fiscal accounts show him disbursing monies widely throughout the domain. In the judicial rolls surviving after the conquest of Normandy he is seen presiding over the exchequer sessions at Falaise. The archives and subsequent collections reveal him active in judging, holding inquests, executing commands and serving on missions. He was in attendance at virtually all recorded meetings of the royal court. As he became better known to chroniclers, he was identified as 'second only to the king'.[5] Functioning as Guérin's lay counterpart, Bartholomew of Roye's activities replicated his colleague's in diversity, intensity and ubiquity, except for chancery service which was reserved for clerics. Like Louis VII, Philip relied on the lesser chamberlains, knights and clerics both for routine business and for advice in the inner council. Unlike the entourage of his father and the Anglo-Norman-Angevins, however, his was not large and heterogeneous, mixing magnates with lesser men, but was limited to a small number of intimates composed of Guérin, Bartholomew, Henry Clément and Walter the Young. When the chroniclers first took notice of them, they were advising the king in the military campaign leading up to Bouvines in 1214 and remained close by his side at the battle itself. From governmental documentation, however, they can be observed having worked together since 1195. In the words of a royal chronicler, 'these were the only people to whom the king was accustomed to open his soul and reveal his secret thoughts on all occasions'.[6]

Beyond the innovations in justice, finance and personnel, accompanied by new documentation, Philip continued with the traditions of his predecessors. Returning from the crusade a widower and debilitated by sickness, the king was forced to recognize the fragility of his lineage, especially after his infant son had barely escaped severe illness as well. One of his preoccupations, therefore, was to remarry and reinforce the royal lineage with additional sons. Only this long-range goal remains clear; the means to achieve it defy explanation. It is difficult to comprehend his choice of the Danish princess Ingeborg, because her political assets were minimal, but his sudden aversion to her on their wedding night of 14/15 August 1193 can only be laid to personal neuroses. Obtaining a separation on the grounds of consanguinity, as his father had secured from

---

[4] 'data... per manum fratris Garini'. *Recueil des actes de Philippe Auguste*, II, no. 688 (first instance).

[5] 'secundus a rege'. William the Breton, *Gesta*, in *Œuvres de Rigord et de Guillaume le Breton*, I, p. 256.

[6] 'His etenim solis re confidenter in omni / Enucleare animum secretaque vota solebat.' William the Breton, *Philippidos* vv. 536–7, in *Œuvres de Rigord et de Guillaume le Breton*, II, p. 271.

Eleanor of Aquitaine, Philip found a personally congenial bride in Agnes from the Bavarian nobility of Andechs-Meranien. When she died in 1201, she had given the king a daughter and a second son. Philip's shuffle of one spouse for another might have succeeded like his father's were it not for the accession in 1198 of a new pope, Innocent III, who was ambitious to secure ecclesiastical jurisdiction over all matters related to marriage. Since the claims to consanguinity were patently specious, the king dared not hazard his matrimonial project to a papal judgement. Willing to endure papal interdict on his lands in 1200, Philip kept the pope at bay with legal manoeuvres, until after Agnes's death when he obtained papal legitimation of his children in exchange for dubious diplomatic offers. Although still legally wed to Ingeborg, whom he stubbornly refused to see, he had none the less obtained the dynstic objective of a second son.

The great interdict that threatened to close churches throughout the king's lands for nine months in 1200 severely strained the ties between Philip and the regalian churches. Bishops and abbots were compelled to choose between two masters, the spiritual head of the universal church or their temporal protector. The papal registers and chronicles divulge the decisions of nineteen of some twenty-five regalian sees. A clear majority of thirteen (as well as the influential abbeys of St-Denis and St-Germain-des-Prés) sided with the king and disobeyed the pope. This victory encouraged Philip to renew the traditional Capetian policy of liberty and cooperation. When he acquired the bishopric of Evreux from King John in 1200, he declared that the bishop would be freely chosen 'just as the other canons of French churches have the power to elect bishops'.[7] Since Evreux was not vacant at the time, the proclamation sought to contrast French liberties with former ducal oppression of the Norman church. In addition, Philip began to enlarge ecclesiastical liberty by renouncing his regalian rights altogether in 1203 on the eve of the military campaign against Normandy. These privileges were granted to Langres and Arras on the kingdom's borders and extended to Auxerre, Nevers, Troyes and Mâcon during the next six years. Since the king's return from the crusade the chapters of regalian churches continued to elect candidates who could be considered in the main favourable to the king. The freedom of elections reformulated in the ordinance of 1190 evidently continued to produce prelates 'pleasing to God' and, of equal importance, 'useful to the kingdom'.

Except for the Ingeborg scandal, the contemporary chroniclers were generally silent on Capetian governmental affairs; rather their attention was absorbed with the mounting military hostilities between Philip and the

---

[7] 'sicut et alii canonici ecclesiarum Francie liberam habent eligendi sibi episcopum potestatem'. *Recueil des actes de Philippe Auguste*, II, no. 637.

Anglo-Norman-Angevins. Richard did not return to his lands until 1194, because of unfinished business in the Holy Land and his capture and imprisonment on his journey back through Germany. Needless to say, Philip lost no opportunity to prolong the imprisonment while preying on Richard's lands. By 1198, however, Richard's superior military skill had recovered his losses in France and his celebrated generosity won him new allies, including the count of Flanders. During the nearly continuous fighting Philip not only lost his baggage but was also entrapped by the count of Flanders and humiliated by Richard at Gisors. While the Anglo-Norman chroniclers recorded these defeats in minute detail, Rigord attempted to minimize their effect. Richard's string of victories, however, was cut short by his unforeseen death in 1199. Against this redoubtable adversary Philip's only recourse had been the traditional Capetian tactic of pitting one member of the Anglo-Norman-Angevin family against the other. During Richard's absence Philip conspired with John, Richard's younger brother, and at Richard's death Philip supported Arthur, John's nephew. A treaty was finally negotiated at Le Goulet in 1200 in which John secured recognition as successor to his brother in exchange for land (Evrecin and Vexin), a large sum of money, and the acknowledgement of Capetian suzerainty over John's continental holdings. With John formally established as vassal, Philip had only to wait for John's caprice to provide further opportunity for action. True to character, John soon outraged the Aquitainian house of Lusignan by abducting and marrying the heiress of the neighbouring barony of Angoulême, who had been affianced to a Lusignan. When John refused to hear the Lusignans' complaint, the latter appealed to Philip, John's overlord. Summoned as duke of Aquitaine in 1202, John failed to appear before the royal court and was summarily adjudged forfeit of his lands for neglect of service.

Having assured legal authority, Philip now required the military and financial means to enforce the sentence. The fiscal accounts of 1202/3 also reveal financial preparations for warfare. In addition to the reports of *prévôts* and *baillis* were triennial accounts of specially designated war treasurers who supervised groups of castles along the Norman border. From these accounts military movements can be observed, especially of an army composed of some 2,300 troops, of which 250 were knights, amassed on the west bank of the Seine and poised to invade Normandy. At the same time the fiscal document included a separate accounting of a war tax, called the *prisée des sergents*, assessed on towns and abbeys. Its total was sufficient to pay the annual wages of the troops at the Norman border, thus enabling Philip to create a permanent and salaried nucleus for his military force. Beyond this war tax the *prévôts* and *baillis* were reporting substantial surpluses of receipts over expenditures. On the eve of the attack against Normandy in 1203, therefore, Philip's finances were in excellent condition to mount an attack against the Anglo-Norman-Angevins.

FROM THE CONQUEST OF NORMANDY TO THE BATTLE OF BOUVINES AND ITS AFTERMATH (1204–1223)

Normandy rapidly succumbed to two campaigns waged in the spring and summer of 1203 and 1204. When John precipitously abandoned the duchy in December 1203, after refusing to engage in combat, and when Richard's great fortress, Château Gaillard, fell in March 1204, the Normans found little hope for further resistance. After the key castles of Chinon and Loches likewise capitulated in the spring of 1205, the Loire valley was no longer defensible. These astounding losses were due both to John's desertion and to Philip's financial strength. The dismantling of Henry II's great conglomeration in north-western France prompted new manoeuvrings among the great barons. During the next decade John, like Richard before him, reopened his purse to enlist new allies, including the counts of Boulogne and Flanders, as well as his nephew Otto of Brunswick, who aspired to the imperial crown of Germany. By 1214 John had devised a grand strategy to recover his losses by attacking Philip from opposite sides. If the two thrusts could be coordinated, the Capetian armies could be split and annihilated. John himself approached from the south-west where Philip's son Louis met him at La Roche-aux-Moines near Angers. Although John quickly withdrew, he none the less had divided the Capetian forces at the crucial moment. Philip Augustus was therefore left alone to face a coalition from the north composed of Otto, the counts of Boulogne and Flanders and others from the Low Countries. The two armies met on a Sunday, 17 July 1214, on the fields of Bouvines near Lille. Forcing battle before the allied lines could be fully formed, Philip gained the advantage and won the victory. Otto barely escaped the debacle, but the counts of Boulogne and Flanders were among the numerous captives. After this spectacular defeat, further efforts to recover the Anglo-Norman-Angevin territories north of the Loire were futile, and John set sail for England, never to return.

Although Philip Augustus retained the existing local administration in his new conquests, he none the less introduced a fundamental division between Normandy and the Loire fiefs of Anjou, Maine and Touraine. As early as 1202 the king announced his intention to separate Normandy and hold it directly as royal domain. The local Norman officials, called *vicomtes* and *baillis* (corresponding to the Capetian *prévôts* and *baillis*), were replaced with personnel recruited from the royal lands, but they continued to report twice a year to a central exchequer that supervised their financial and judicial affairs. The exchequer was moved to Falaise closer to Paris and was presided over by a pair of delegates (usually Brother Guérin and Walter the Young) from the king's entourage. In the Loire fiefs Philip inherited a regime based on local seneschals under the jurisdiction of the chief seneschal of Anjou. Even before the conquest the king had accepted William of Les Roches, the former seneschal of Anjou, for this post. It appears that the king was not yet prepared to absorb the Loire fiefs into the royal domain because he permitted the seneschal unusual authority over local administration. These new territories undoubtedly increased Capetian revenues, but perhaps not as much as historians have previously imagined. The discovery of a new financial account from 1221 suggests that Normandy and the Loire fiefs raised Philip's ordinary income by 70 per cent, an increase within the same order of magnitude as the annexations before 1200.

The acquisition of new lands also prompted new collections of governmental documents. Unlike the accounts of 1202/3 which were devised to supervise and control the financial operations of the local *prévôts* and *baillis*, the newly discovered accounts of 1221 recapitulated general categories of income and expenses and calculated balances. For the first time, therefore, the government possessed a budget to assess its fiscal position. From the Norman exchequer Philip further inherited the tradition of keeping plea rolls or brief records of cases heard. The survival of such a roll (beginning in 1207) from the exchequer at Falaise constitutes the earliest judicial collection of the Capetian monarchy. The most important collections, however, to appear in this period were the registers. In 1204, 1212 and 1220 three separate codices were compiled, one from the other, by scribes in the royal chancery, most likely under the direction of Brother Guérin. Over half of their contents consisted of charters and letters, not only the incoming materials collected in the archives, but especially the king's outgoing charters. For the first time, therefore, the Capetian monarchy kept at least a partial record of its own acts comparable to contemporary enrollments and registers in England and at the papal court. In addition, the registers contained heterogeneous inquests, inventories, accounts and varied lists concerning the domain, forests, finances, fiefs and much more. In short, they served as handbooks of useful information on governmental routine that could be easily transported by the chancery during the king's habitual displacements.

Shortly after Philip took the Norman city of Caen he had copied into his first register of 1204 a survey of fiefs of the duchy of Normandy undertaken by Henry II in 1172. From the beginning the Capetians had asserted their rights as suzerains over the great magnates of the kingdom and the lesser vassals of the royal domain. These rights included the traditional obligations of fealty, homage, marriage, wardship and especially knight service, but they were only vaguely defined and rarely recorded. From the Anglo-Normans, therefore, Philip inherited the technique of inventorying the vassals of their domain. In 1207 and 1220 the Norman surveys were continued and revised in the registers and extended to other sections of the royal domain. As an effort to record and thereby to supervise royal rights of suzerainty, these inventories contributed to Philip's general programme of reducing the obligations of all his vassals to writing. As early as 1180, for example, Henry II's homage for his lands was recorded in a charter, as was that of the new count of Flanders in 1196. Such charters were carefully preserved in the registers or archives. A traditional means for enforcing these obligations was the requirement of pledges to guarantee the service of the vassal. Philip's registers contain over eighty lists of such pledges. The ultimate enforcement of suzerainty, however, was a judgement in the royal court. Until the Capetians could summon a great vassal and execute the sentence, their suzerainty over the great baronage was only theoretical. The turning-point therefore came in the summons and condemnation of John as duke of Aquitaine in 1202. Since 1194 John's obligations as a vassal had been meticulously recorded and preserved in the archives. When Philip Augustus was able to execute the sentence by dispossessing John of his fiefs, his suzerainty over the great lords was significantly reinforced.

As an aftermath of Bouvines the last decade of Philip's reign may be characterized by the expected fruits of victory: peace, prosperity and the re-expression of ideology. The two military campaigns of the period were conducted by Louis and removed military operations far from the France north of the Loire. An expedition to England (1216–17) ended in failure, and crusades against the heretics in southern France (1215, 1219) brought inconclusive results. These campaigns apparently placed little strain on the royal finances because the budget of 1221 shows a balance of one third the revenues remaining in the treasury, a surplus that continued through the next reign. Philip's own testament in 1222, moreover, bequeathed an extraordinary sum equivalent to nearly four times the annual royal income. This impression (if not the details) of the king's prosperity was confirmed by an eyewitness who reported hearsay from royal officials at Philip's funeral in 1223.

The victory at Bouvines inspired one of the participants, a chaplain of the king named William the Breton, to bring Rigord's prose chronicle up to date and to transform it into verse in a second work entitled the *Philippidos*. The latter was modelled on Walter of Châtillon's epic poem, the *Alexandreis*, which was deemed appropriate for a panegyric devoted to a king who like Alexander bore a Macedonian name. Throughout both works Philip was no longer entitled *Augustus*, redolent of Roman connotations, but *magnanimus*, the well-known sobriquet of the Macedonian conqueror. Although William the Breton assumed the tasks of Suger and Rigord, he was not a monk of St-Denis, but a royal cleric who enjoyed the direct patronage of the king and his chief minister, Brother Guérin. His versions may therefore be considered the first 'official' history of the Capetian monarchy. As William reflected upon the battle, he discerned three underlying messages of significance for the Capetian ideology. In the first place the capture of five counts, including the powerful count of Flanders and the rebellious count of Boulogne, guaranteed the supremacy of royal suzerainty over the great lords. Throughout William's narratives all the major barons were meticulous in doing homage to the king. When John was finally summoned before the royal court in 1202, William has him explicitly acknowledge Philip's ultimate jurisdiction. Bouvines, in the second place, represented a victory of a Capetian king of the Franks over a Roman emperor. Reminiscent of the summons of 1124, the simple silk banner of St-Denis had once again triumphed over the terrifying eagle, the ancient emblem of Roman ambition to dominate the world. To justify the claim that the Franks were *franci*, that is free from the Roman yoke, William revived the foundational myth of the Trojan origins that saw the Frankish kings, like the Roman, descending in full equality from common ancestors at Troy. For that reason also the pre-Roman Alexander and not Caesar (nor Augustus) was the appropriate exemplar for Philip. Finally, standing directly behind the king before battle, William heard the king's harangue in which he reminded his troops that Otto's forces were under ecclesiastical excommunication, but they, although sinners, were in communion with God and fought to protect the clergy. Once again, William returned to the hallowed theme, reiterated at each coronation, that it was the Capetian duty to defend the liberties of the church. Philip's death in 1223 presented William the Breton with one last opportunity to return to this traditional theme. Not only was the king *christianissimus* for defending the church, but he was also personally a saint. William asserted that Philip's death was presaged by portents, that the funeral cortege to St-Denis was attended by miracles, and that visions were reported in which the king was conducted directly into the divine presence by his patron saint. Despite these efforts to demonstrate Philip's sanctity after his death, the marital scandal and evident shortcomings of his life were too recent to allow a viable campaign for his canonization, but the Capetians had only to wait for two generations before a credible saint did appear in Louis IX.

THE SEIGNEURIES

Michel Bur

SEIGNEURIE (lordship) was a system of government in which the seigneur or lord (*dominus* in Latin) exercised for his own profit powers that were regalian in origin, that is, powers of a public character. It was accompanied by the territorial fragmentation of the kingdom and a more-or-less pronounced crumbling of authority, which was none the less offset by a general and traditional sense of belonging to the *regnum Francorum* (kingdom of the Franks) and also, juridically, in a system of feudal relations that culminated in the king. Seen from this angle, the lord was not called *dominus* in Latin, but *senior* and his men *vassi*.

LORDSHIPS AND PRINCIPALITIES

The formation of lordships resulted in a parcelling-out of the kingdom which gave birth to great principalities, baronies or castellanies, those cells of local life generated by a castle. The chapter in Philip Augustus's registers headed *Scripta de feodis* bears witness to this hierarchy: archbishops, bishops, abbots of great monasteries, dukes and counts are ranked among the princes; then come the barons, castellans, vavassours or sub-feudatories (*arrière-vassaux*) and, finally, the recently established category of the communes. These last have to be treated as a special case. Thirty or so communes had been set up in the north of the kingdom in the twelfth century. They had benefited from a transfer – often very incomplete – of seigneurial powers to the urban community represented by a mayor and *jurés*. Other towns, with no history of conspiracy or revolt, bought liberties from their lord that were sometimes more extensive than those of communes; and even villages, such as Beaumont-en-Argonne, assumed full responsibility for their own administration. However, numerous settlements were satisfied with judicial and economic privileges and left the task of governing them to their lord. At Paris the bourgeoisie very soon realized that it was more worthwhile to feed off the avenues of power than to demand its exercise. There was thus in both town and country a very broad range of constitutions, conspicuous among them the very exceptional instance of the urban republic, a status enjoyed at the beginning of the thirteenth century only by Tournai, on the border of France and the county of Flanders.

Besides these collective lordships, called 'communes', the lay and ecclesiastical principalities demand attention first. A slow process of simplification and stratification led to the disengagement of a group of twelve princes distinguished by the title of *pairs* (peers). The formalization of this title seems to date from the coronation of Philip Augustus in 1179, in the spirit of a return to the Carolingian tradition, with six ecclesiastical peers (the archbishop of Rheims and the bishops of Beauvais, Noyon, Laon, Châlons-sur-Marne in Belgica secunda, and the bishop of Langres, suffragan of the archbishop of Lyons, in Lugdunensis prima), and six secular peers (the dukes of Burgundy, Aquitaine and Normandy, and the counts of Flanders, Toulouse and Troyes, that is, the future count of Champagne).

The ecclesiastical peers were always chosen from among the twenty-six prelates who owed direct allegiance to the king. They all held sees on a curving frontier which, north-east of Paris, separated the Capetian domain from Angevin Normandy, Flemish Amiénois and Vermandois, imperial Lorraine and Burgundy. In a kingdom in which for more than a century foreign relations had been the concern of the great feudal lords, it was to the king's advantage to favour bishops who contrived for him opportunities for intervention outside the Paris Basin.

The ecclesiastical lordships were, without exception, gradually constructed on the basis of a vast temporal power in town and country by the extension of the privilege of immunity, to which were added economic concessions related to market and minting rights. When the civil wars of the tenth century handed over to the bishops the keys of the gates and the defence of the ramparts, it was clear that the most powerful among them were equal to many of the great secular lords. At Châlons-sur-Marne, episcopal power was exercised over an eight-league radius, that is, for twenty kilometres around the town. At the end of the twelfth century, the area around Rheims subject to the archbishop's jurisdiction was bounded by the five fortresses of Courville, Cormicy, Bétheneville, Sept-Saulx and Chaumuzy.

It was not surprising that at the same period some prelates began to assert that they held the *comitatus* of their city. Indeed, from 1015 at Beauvais, 1023 at Rheims and *c.* 1065 at Châlons-sur-Marne, the bishops had succeeded in removing from the secular counts the last remnants of their power within the city (*intra muros*), with the support of the king, who encouraged a similar transfer at Mende in 1161, Le Puy in 1169 and Langres in 1171. One consequence of Gregorian reform was the imposition of an increasingly clear distinction between the temporal and the spiritual and, in the person of prelates, between bishop and lord, the first holding his religious office by election and ordination, the second his powers of justice and command by investiture. This dichotomy made it easier for the upper clergy to acknowledge their feudal dependence on the king, but it was difficult to live out in practice, and equilibrium between the two offices remained precarious. A bishop of Beauvais like Philippe of Dreux left the memory of a warrior fighting with a mace at the battle of Bouvines rather than that of a churchman. In the thirteenth century the bishop's house was transformed into the episcopal palace. Soon the bishops of Rheims, Laon and Langres were to call themselves dukes and those of Noyon, Beauvais and Châlons counts!

The secular peers had older roots. The duchies of Aquitaine and Burgundy were former Carolingian kingdoms. They had contracted in the tenth century as a result of the emancipation of their border areas, which had been transformed into feudal dependencies. The ducal domain was henceforth limited to a few counties, for example that of Poitiers in the case of Aquitaine. To the north of the Loire, the *ducatus Franciae* experienced the same evolution. The Capetians held only the heart of the Paris Basin, between Paris and Orleans, with extensions towards Bourges, Sens and Laon, while vassals were solidly installed at Blois, Tours and Angers. Two blocks had been separated from the former *Francia* – the county of Flanders (which experienced significant territorial fluctuations before being driven back to the Germanic-speaking areas by the conquests of Philip Augustus) and Normandy, clearly included in the ecclesiastical province of Rouen, whose seven bishops were held reliably in check by the duke who had, furthermore, achieved the feudal subjugation of Brittany.

Territorial contraction on one hand, fragmentation on the other. But there was a third way in which principalities were formed, illustrated by Champagne, since at the time when (in 1152) the eastern possessions of the house of Blois achieved autonomy it had no name. It was a slow process of the addition of counties, churches and landed domains which, little by little, merged into a coherent and well-structured whole, the fruit of the patient labour of a lineage outside every political framework (*regnum*, *ducatus*, *marca*) and every ecclesiastical framework then extant. Champagne was a recent creation, born from favourable contemporary conditions. The mark of its success was the entry of the count of Troyes into the college of the twelve peers, admittedly assisted by the double marriage of Count Henry the Liberal to Marie, the daughter of Louis VII and Eleanor of Aquitaine, and of Louis VII to Henry's sister, Adela.

Finally, there were the Occitanian lands, with the county of Toulouse, stretching to Quercy and the Rouergue, and its vast feudal dependency which resulted from the splitting-up of the former duchy of Gothia or Narbonne. Its entry into the peerage was explained by the king's concern to reaffirm his authority over a great fief threatened by the Plantagenets and also against the influence of Aragón: through Catalonia which since 1180 showed more marked secessionist tendencies from the kingdom of France.

After the great secular and ecclesiastical principalities, the *Scripta de feodis* placed groupings which stemmed directly from Carolingian counties, such as Boulogne, Guines, Dreux, Clermont-en-Beauvais, Brienne, Roucy, Joigny, Chalon-sur-Saône and Foix, as well as baronies produced by the bringing together of several castles: Lusignan, Coucy, Bourbon, Beaujeu. Finally, on a lower level, came simple castellanies like Joinville or Vignory and, a consequence of the rupture of castle households in *c.* 1150 and the dispersal of the *milites* who comprised them, a host of village lordships based on moated residences, fortified manor houses, which were to grow in number in the thirteenth century with another still greater disintegration of the judicial system, or *ban*, a phenomenon which led to an examination of the exact content of seigneurial powers.

There was to be no question here of the landed basis of lordship, that is, the system by which the land was worked, nor of its officers or profits, but – to express it in contemporary terms – of upper, judicial lordship, the lordship of the *ban*, in other words that which derived from an appropriation of public powers. At the highest level this was exercised over the churches: twenty-seven bishoprics in the Angevin empire, only one in the county of Champagne (Troyes). Gregorian reform put an end to the most glaring abuses. The right of spoliation retreated and even disappeared and, if the prince unduly prolonged the vacancy of a see in order to collect the revenues, he could no longer impose his own candidate and had to be content with instigating the electoral procedure by the grant of *licentia eligendi*. The same applied to monasteries, long considered as simple properties, which were released from the *ditio* or domination of their holder in order to benefit from his protection or *tuitio*.

The right to order, constrain and punish – this was the definition of the *ban* – the right of executing high criminal justice, of summons to the feudal host, or of building fortifications (a monopoly generally little respected), of maintaining order and keeping the peace in all public places and on the main roads, of striking and recalling coin, of levying personal taxes (*chevage*), occasional taxes (mortmain, levies on marriage or remoal), exceptional taxes (the *aide* and the *taille*) on the inhabitants of his lands: these were the regalian prerogatives concentrated in the hands of the great lords and unequally distributed among the lesser. In addition, there were rights of an economic nature that bore heavily on markets and fairs, the circulation of goods, the maintenance of roads and bridges, the authoritarian organization of trades and the control of money-changing, the exploitation of rivers and mills, not forgetting (above all in ecclesiastical lordships) the profits drawn from parish churches and their operation.

Frequently moving from castle to castle, the lord – and especially the great lord – was served by several officers, first among them the seneschal, who supervised at the table and at uproarious gatherings in the hall, stored up the domanial produce with the assistance of the butler and cellarers, commanded the army with the aid of the marshals responsible for mounting the cavalry and the provision of forage, inspected castle garrisons and, in his master's absence, presided over court sessions. For his part, the chamberlain, custodian of the private apartments (*camera*) and of the treasure stored there, directly administered the revenues from trade and tolls and extended his jurisdiction over trades guilds. Finally, a clerk, half-notary, half-chaplain, held the office of chancellor, sealed documents and saw his role grow with the renewed use of written legal instruments in the law courts. In ecclesiastical lordships, justice and the *ban* were delegated to the *vidame* (the bishop's secular deputy).

Because of their size, principalities were divided into smaller administrative units usually called by the generic term, provostships (*prévôtés*). Assisted by sergeants, administrators, deputies and foresters, the provost (*prévôt*) rendered justice, exacted military service and collected revenues. There were provostal families, but the office, which was paid, remained revocable. At the end of the twelfth century the *baillis* appeared, a form of special commissioners who took over justice, leaving the subordinate prerogatives of domanial administration to the provosts.

Leaving generalities behind, we must now analyse particular cases, especially the great principalities whose historical destiny was bound in part to their capacity for organization and structuring.

ECCLESIASTICAL LORDSHIPS

It was a long way from the *comitatus* claimed by the bishop of Noyon in 1193, and the similar episcopal claim acknowledged by the canons of Beauvais in 1212, to the inferior lordship of their fellow ecclesiastical peer of Troyes. Here it was the count who, following the Gregorian reform, had established immunities to the benefit, not only of the prelates and canons, but also of numerous abbeys, in order to ensure them a certain autonomy, granting genuine exemptions to houses, a street or a little neighbourhood, and personal exemptions to ecclesiastical office holders, their household (*familia*) and sergeants, even when they were involved in trade. Thus the abbess of Notre-Dame-aux-Nonnains had at her disposal the criminal justice over four houses, three ovens (for baking) and one court. The bishop was master of a small quarter of the town (*bourg*); his sergeants were exempt from comital authority (*potestas*), his men likewise, except when it was a case of flagrant dereliction; but in all circumstances and throughout the town, the count reserved to himself the *exercitus*, that is, the right of levying soldiers, and the execution of all criminals.

At the other end of the spectrum there was Rheims, the most significant and prestigious of the ecclesiastical lordships. The archbishop governed a town of 10,000 inhabitants crammed together in 60 hectares within the city walls, whose rapid growth was revealed in the appearance of suburbs in front of the gates. From 1160 onwards, a policy of allocation and settlement led to the demarcation of territorial *bans* held principally from three lords: the archbishop, the chapter and the abbey of St-Rémi. The archbishop's *ban* was the most extensive. It included the whole of the fortified town and three artisanal suburbs, La Couture, Le Jard and Venise. Confined in their cloister, the canons extended their power over the little quarter of Vesle, while the abbey of St-Rémi began belatedly to group round its tenth-century walls the families which were to multiply in the thirteenth. Monopoly over the coinage, with an exchange rate aligned to that of Paris, was retained by the archbishop as an expression of his quasi-regalian prerogative. He could demand armed aid from men from all the *bans*. The execution of those condemned to death was his by right, as was the collection of all tolls except those in the quarter of St-Rémi where he shared them with the abbot.

Rheims had a heterogeneous population, composed of groups with divergent interests: clerics of all ranks, enfeoffed knights responsible for the gates of the city, citizens (*bourgeois*) who frequented the bishop's household (*familia*) and supplied the bishop with his chamberlains, toll-collectors and his provosts, integrating themselves as much as possible into both the echevinal law court and local administration; but it was a population which had been subject for fifty or so years to upheavals comparable to the communal agitation so widespread in the towns between the Rivers Seine and Meuse in the twelfth century. In 1182 the archbishop, William of Champagne, decided to grant the men of his *ban* the so-called 'Wilhelmine Charter', by which he not only confirmed the customs relative to *chevage* and mortmain, but surrendered the annual election of the *échevins* to the citizens, reserving for himself only the right to invest them and receive their oaths of loyalty. Moreover, these *échevins* saw themselves entrusted with substantial judicial competence from which only murder, theft and treason were exempted. Although the charter by no means recognized the existence of the population as an urban body, the town henceforth had real representation at its disposal, a privilege which the abbot of St-Rémi refused to concede in his *ban* and, at a greater distance, the bishop of Châlons in his city.

In the countryside a comparable development occurred, sanctioning the grant in 1182 of a charter of privileges to the village of Beaumont-en-Argonne. By this document, William handed over to the mayor and *jurés* elected by the peasant community all powers in matters of justice, taxation and defence. This ordinance conferring autonomy seemed so enviable that it spread in the thirteenth century, admittedly with considerable modifications required by the lords, to more than 500 villages in Lorraine. Notwithstanding, in 1197 the archbishop submitted all his temporal power to the high jurisdiction of a *bailli*.

There is no need to labour the point further to demonstrate the originality and flexibility of William's policy. It contrasts markedly with the highly violent procedure of Roger of Rozoy, bishop of Laon who, at the same period, bloodily put down the claims of the rural communes of the Laonnois. The episcopacy of William of Champagne at Rheims marked simultaneously the apogee of seigneurial prerogative and the start of its decline, accelerated in the thirteenth century by the encroachments of the king.

SECULAR PRINCIPALITIES

In this section, I shall place more emphasis on what differentiates the secular principalities than on what makes them similar, given the general development which imposed common characteristics upon them.

The comté *of Champagne or of Troyes*

Having become the dominant fief in relation to the other possessions of the family of Blois (Blois, Chartres, Châteaudun, Sancerre and so on) in 1152, Champagne, as has already been observed, was an agglomeration of *comtés* held from the king, the duke of Burgundy, the emperor, the archbishop of Rheims, the bishop of Langres and the abbot of St-Denis, to name but a few, constituting a whole sufficiently coherent to withstand Louis VII's attempt to dissolve it in 1142–3.

Its stability resulted first from the comital domain, densely spread over central and southern Champagne. In the mid-twelfth century the fifteen provost-ships were administered by temporary officers, while the twenty principal fortresses were defended by hereditary enfeoffed castellans. At a higher level, the count could rely on his great officers, among whom the seneschal was pre-eminent. Organized in *c.* 1100 on the English model, the chancery was at first no more than a writing-office held by a clerk or chaplain skilled in law. It grew after 1150. Although the church in Troyes (that is, the bishopric) aimed to break free from comital power – which it succeeded in doing, with the aid of the king, in *c.* 1170 – and although the monasteries were subject only to the protection of the prince, Henry the Liberal (1152–81) compensated for this weakness by founding the great secular collegiate churches at Bar-sur-Aube, Sézanne and Provins, which supplied him with administrative personnel, and, in his palace chapel of St-Etienne at Troyes, a repository for archives and books, as well as his tomb.

The means available to the count, the revenues – thanks to which (as in Flanders) he outstripped all his vassals – enabled him to enforce the latter's obedience. In *c.* 1170 registers of fiefs were drawn up and deposited in St-Etienne, just as the great cartularies of the *comté* were to be at beginning of the thirteenth century. With Henry the Liberal, and as a consequence of a fraternal agreement between Henry and Archbishop William of Rheims, feudal dependency was very extensive in northern Champagne.

Since the earliest times, the counts had been in evidence on the frontier with Lorraine and the empire. The son of Theobald II and Matilda of Carinthia, Henry the Liberal maintained close relations with Frederick Barbarossa, then very active in the *comté* of Burgundy. He made closer ties with him, which all but rebounded on Louis VII at St-Jean-de-Losne in 1162. This active frontier policy only confirmed the inclination of the principality of Champagne to extend eastwards.

But the most original feature of the period is to be found in the economic take-off, less in production than in distribution, a phenomenon linked to the voluntarist policy of the princes, in particular Theobold II (1107–52). By creating a second fair in Champagne at Provins, fixing the cycle of exchange both geographically and chronologically, by the authoritarian concentration of international trade (and especially the sale of cloth) in a few well-chosen centres, by agreement with Flanders, he had prepared the ground for the rise of one pole of the world-economy, as F. Braudel put it, the only one that the kingdom of France was to know in the middle ages. Such success was made possible by the extent of the principality, stretching out like a frontier from Montereau on the Seine to Vaucouleurs on the Meuse, by civil order and peace which 'softened the warriors' (Suger) but favoured the merchants, by the creation of a policing system for the fairs – the watches announced in 1174 – and by the extension of comital safeconduct outside the bounds of the principality, the count taking full responsibility for merchants injured on the great roads leading to his towns with fairs. The effect of this policy was quick and dazzling. It can be summed up as the seizure of the commercial currents crossing western Europe from the Mediterranean to the North Sea, the desertion of the old route of Agrippa via Rheims and Châlons-sur-Marne, the development of the four transit towns of Bar-sur-Aube, Lagny, Provins and Troyes, and also of textile production in the last two. This new road-axis, around which the *comté* of Champagne and Brie was structured, also deflected international trade from the Capetian domain; the king reacted to the competition of Champagne and Normandy by reserving the monopoly of river-traffic on the Seine to the association of merchants at Paris.

Finally, there was one last sign of this success: the construction of an exclusively comital zone of monetary circulation. While to the north of the Marne, the *deniers* of Rheims, Châlons and Paris circulated, all with the same value in the twelfth century, the south was the realm of the Provins *denier*, on which that of Troyes was aligned and, after 1158, the coins struck by the bishop of Meaux. At about this date, the coinage of Provins started to push back that of Châlons, penetrated the royal zone in the Laonnois and the Beauvaisis, and invaded Lorraine. Its circulation was such that in Italy its type was imitated by the Roman Senate.

The comté *of Flanders*

As Champagne blocked Capetian expansion to the east, so did Flanders to the north. This principality similarly presented an internally unbalanced structure, with the bulk of the domain gathered north of a line between Lille and St-Omer, while the French-speaking south was given over to the sphere of action of fief (Boulogne) and rear-fief (St-Pol). Again like Champagne, it had a territorial extension in the empire, to such an extent that in 1125 Count Charles the Good could be put forward as successor to the Emperor Henry V, and in 1185 Philip of Alsace, warring against Philip Augustus, had no hesitation in doing homage for all his possessions to Henry VI, an extreme attitude which seems to have similarly tempted Henry the Liberal at St-Jean-de-Losne in 1162.

In 1163 the *comté* of Flanders was enlarged as a consequence of Philip of Alsace's marriage to the heiress of the Vermandois, the Amiénois and the Valois. It then stretched from the Scheldt estuary to the banks of the Marne. Tutor to King Philip Augustus, the count married his pupil to his niece, Isabelle of Hainault, to whom he promised Artois as a dowry. In the absence of a direct heir and also as a result of this promise, the southern possessions of Flanders were soon lost and the *comté* drawn back within more limited dimensions with a preponderantly Flemish-speaking population. This loss, which included the largest town, Arras, was not acknowledged by Philip of Alsace's successors, who hurled themselves headlong into the coalition annihilated by the French king at Bouvines in 1214.

The hereditary succession to the *comté* of Flanders followed the rule of male primogeniture. Thus the absence of a direct male heir inevitably posed serious problems. At the beginning of the twelfth century, the counts, bound in other respects very closely to the kings, to whom they were closely related, had imposed public order by executions and hangings. The unruly vassals bowed to this, but in 1127 a reaction set in and Charles the Good was assassinated. As he had relied on the support of the towns to govern, they – speaking through the men of Ghent and of Bruges – demanded to be involved in the choice of his successor; then, in 1128, when they had rejected William Clito in favour of Thierry of Alsace, they asserted that it was the right of the assembled clergy, barons and citizens to judge and depose the count, before choosing another. Throughout Galbert of Bruges's account of these events, a doctrine of national sovereignty is being sketched. The Alsace dynasty (1128–91) understood this and endeavoured to check claims of this kind, but Philip had to concede the participation of the *échevins* of Flanders in the most important deliberations.

The *comté* of Flanders was characterized by stable central institutions, in particular a comital court of unlimited judicial powers, which in the second half of the twelfth century strove to its utmost to reserve high justice to itself. As in the Capetian entourage, the great officers were constantly present: seneschal, butler, chamberlain, constable and, above all, chancellor. This last office had devolved on the provost of the church of St-Donatien in the castle at Bruges, and he was the head of the domanial administration, keeper of the seals since before 1084. Every year he had his notaries draw up the *Gros Brief*, a summary of the accounts provided by the forty receivers of the castellany, of which the oldest surviving dates from 1187. Just as early as the chancery office, the receipt of finances was organized at the end of the twelfth century to constitute the court of the *Rennenghe* with its high-ranking *Renneurs*, accounting officers always placed under the chancellor's control. In this respect Flanders was competing with the Anglo-Norman administration, which also had a sophisticated central accounting system at a very early date.

Local institutions functioned within the sole framework – at once military, administrative, judicial and domanial – of the castellany, the castellan being re-munerated with a fief which was not the castle. In *c.* 1130 the urban *échevinages* were separated from the law courts of the castellany, while the penal law writ-ten down in the *Keures* (charters) developed with some degree of uniformity, according to the will of the count (in particular, Philip of Alsace). Given the tendency of the castellans to hereditary self-perpetuation, in *c.* 1170 the count created *baillis* entrusted with a watching brief over his rights in matters of justice and of public peace. He appointed them, paid them, transferred them dismissed them. Among their other duties, they had to preside over the castel-lany's feudal court, established to reduce the burden on the comital court. At the end of the century war and fortification – the corollary of public peace – became a monopoly of the prince.

Swept on by powerful social forces, the counts of the house of Alsace par-ticipated in the economic development of the region by relying on their right to exploit uncultivated land, marshes, turf moors and dunes. Philip created the ports of Gravelines (1163), Nieuwpoort, Damme (1180), Biervliet, Dunkirk and Mardijk on the coast, while his brother Matthew of Boulogne laid the foundations of Calais. Just inland a policy of land development was undertaken at the initiative of the chancellor, Robert of Aire (who died in 1174). This aimed to drain the waters of the mainland, especially in the marshes of the Aa near Gravelines. The public service of the *Wateringues* was established for the health of the region. Elsewhere, the count had peat extracted to save timber. He protected afforested regions and controlled forest clearances. From the 1130s onwards, six fairs were organized in the towns of Ypres, Bruges, Torhout, Lille and Messines. As in Champagne, the prince understood that his superiority was conditional on his wealth.

The duchy of Burgundy

Not all principalities had the same structure or vigour. In Burgundy, the duke fell back upon a territorial core dominated by Autun, Beaune and Dijon, with a surrounding penumbra of fiefs, strengthened by marriages and by the performance of liege homage for castles. Beyond these began the theoretical sphere of authority of the *comté*s of Nevers, Auxerre, Tonnerre, Troyes, Chalon and Mâcon, coincidentally reinvigorated by mutual oaths of non-injury and non-aggression pacts. Ducal protection was maintained over numerous monasteries, but the bishoprics – free from this – had become royal. It was at the expense of that of Langres that the duke had acquired Dijon in 1137 and Châtillon-sur-Seine between 1162 and 1192.

Inspired at first by resentment at seeing the count of Chalon in 1166 and the count of Mâcon in 1172 paying homage to the king, then by his marriage to the heiress of the Viennois, Duke Hugh III pursued an active frontier policy, which drew him close to Frederick Barbarossa. Philip Augustus, aided by the count of Flanders, forced him into greater fidelity as a result of a war unleashed by an appeal of the lord of Vergy (1183–6). Taken prisoner, but released through the intervention of the emperor, Hugh had formally to acknowledge himself the vassal of the crown of France.

With a strong dynastic succession and younger sons established in bishoprics, a ducal court furnished with permanent officers and a primitive chancery administered by an ordinary chaplain, the duchy cut a good figure without having the more sophisticated framework of Flanders or Normandy. Moreover, in imitation of his uncle Henry the Liberal, Duke Hugh III founded a palace chapel at Dijon before 1184 in order to furnish himself with more and abler administrators.

In each castellany, a *prévôt de justice et d'armes* controlled the working of the domain with his subordinates. At the end of the twelfth century the 'great provosts' *(grands prévôts)* appeared, who took charge of several provostships. Urban growth was evident in Dijon with the building of a new, extended town wall. In 1185 the commune obtained a charter on the model of that of Meaux and Soissons. A mayor and elected *prudhommes* exercised justice in the name of the duke, who succeeded in recovering the policing of the highways.

THE GREAT TERRITORIAL CONCENTRATIONS

Powerful and compact, the principalities we have just considered were like that of the Capetians. In this respect they were distinct from the great territorial concentrations, a phenomenon both typical of the twelfth century and nevertheless exceptional.

The first unsuccessful attempt at a vast territorial agglomeration was the Anglo-Norman-Blois-Champagne empire. Through his mother, Theobald II of Blois was the oldest of Henry I ('Beauclerk') of England's nephews, to whom he should have succeeded in 1135. The Norman aristocracy had received him as heir to the throne when they learnt that, on the other side of the Channel, the great lords of England had rallied to his brother Stephen and proclaimed him king at Westminster. In order to preserve their interests in the English kingdom, the Normans abandoned their candidate. The law of primogeniture was flouted. Theobald withdrew, letting his brother reign in his stead, but he gave him no help when the Empress Matilda, daughter of Henry I, and her husband, Geoffrey, count of Anjou, succeeded in vindicating the rights of their young son, Henry II Plantagenet, who succeeded Stephen in 1154.

Another instance of the failure to build up a large, looser territorial principality was the union of Aquitaine and the royal principality in the person of Eleanor and Louis VII. The annulment of the marriage celebrated at Bordeaux in 1137 made the duchess Eleanor free once more and in 1152 she was married again, to Henry II Plantagenet. Thus was born what historians have called 'the Angevin empire'. This empire encompassed the patrimonial holdings of the counts of Anjou (Anjou, Touraine, Maine), augmented, by right of conquest, with Normandy in 1144, with Aquitaine and Gascony through marriage in 1152 and, through Henry's accession to the throne, with England in 1154. This agglomeration of territories remained fragile. Henry II himself provided for its division between his sons in 1169–70. Crowned king at Westminster in 1170 and at Winchester in 1172, the oldest, Henry fitz Henry was to reign over England, Anjou and Normandy; the second, Richard, was to inherit from his mother Aquitaine, under the direct suzerainty of the king of France; the third, Geoffrey, was to be, by marriage, duke of Brittany, under Norman suzerainty; and the last, John 'Lackland', was to remain just that – landless. The death of

Henry fitz Henry made Richard the heir to the whole empire and holder of the two peerages of Normandy and Aquitaine.

Normandy

In this vast empire Normandy was the keystone. Henry I 'Beauclerk', who had recovered it in 1106, endeavoured to revive the *Consuetudines et justicie* attributed to his father. He presented himself as the holder of public authority, the guarantor of peace, master of forests and rivers, highways and roads, having monopoly of the coinage and fortifications. Throughout the duchy, he delegated *juges enquêteurs* to investigate misdeeds. Their 'assises' suspended private jurisdictions. Barons and freemen had to appear there. Anyone who wanted could place himself under the prince's protection. The authority thus restored blossomed after 1135 in legislation independent of the traditional conciliar framework.

Local administration was provided by twenty-two *vicomtes*, flexible and revocable appointments, remunerated out of ducal revenues. Their role declined towards the middle of the twelfth century with the institution by the Plantagenets of the *baillis*, whose scope did not coincide with the former divisions. There were twenty-eight in 1172 and they commanded the vassals in the feudal host. Elsewhere enfeoffed sergeanties evolved who supervised forests, markets and prisons. On a higher level, the increasingly specialized ducal court was presided over by the justiciar in the absence of the king-duke. From 1176 onwards, this great officer became a kind of universal agent in administrative and judicial matters. An embryonic budget was worked out in the second half of the twelfth century. Receipts were centralized at the exchequer at Caen. Expenditure could only be initiated by ducal writ. All these operations were recorded on rolls of parchment, of which the oldest extant go back to 1180.

In Normandy, the feudal hierarchy tended henceforth to incorporate the commoners. It bound to the duke the barons who were his tenants-in-chief, the titular vassals of a knight's fee and the vavasseurs, with reservation of fealty to the *dominus Normanniae* imposed on all, including rear-vassals. *Enquêtes* such as that of 1172 fixed the level of services, aids and relief due to the suzerain who was always the guardian of orphans. In 1181 by the Assise of Arms, from ulgated in England and then probably applied on the continent, it was decided that everyone with movables worth 100 *livres angevines* should have the equipment of a knight; with movables worth 40, 30 or 25 a haubergeon (i.e. coat of mail), lance, sword or a bow and arrows. Henry II sometimes replaced military service by the payment of a levy (*l'écuage*), exacted by the *baillis*, which allowed him to recruit mercenaries and pay knights. Of course, every castle could revert to the prince on simple requisition.

From the end of the eleventh century a royal style of government became more pronounced in the duchy. The name of the king of France began to be omitted from the dating clauses of charters from 1087 onwards. After 1176, the king of England issued general ordinances in Normandy which applied to all his dominions.

Aquitaine

In contrast with this solid territorial core, springing up on the ruins of the former Neustria, the huge duchy of Aquitaine, enlarged since the second half of the eleventh century with the addition of Gascony, was always trying to strain in all directions. In *c.* 1100, William IX sought by right of his wife to seize the *comté* of Toulouse and its feudal dependencies. He narrowly failed in 1119. In his turn Henry II Plantagenet fixed his sights on the shores of the Mediterranean in 1159. He had some success in 1167 and, in 1170, he claimed all the territories within the ecclesiastical province of Bourges. The background to this dream of hegemony was the memory of the ninth- and tenth-century *regnum Aquitaniae* encompassing, among other lands, Berry, the Auvergne, the Velay, the Albigeois and the Toulousain – a good fifteen *comtés* in all.

Capable of magnificent feats in order to achieve expansion, the dukes had poor control over a vaguely defined area, subject to anarchic forces. The collapse of Carolingian structures had given way to a whole system of relations, more or less binding, based on temporary *convenientiae*. Ducal suzerainty was inconsistent, clientage many-layered and unstable, castellanies virtually independent. All this was further aggravated by ecclesiastical privileges and a rapid decline in the public peace.

The duke could only count on his own resources, which came to him essentially from Poitou and Gascony, where provosts administered his domains and castellans (often hereditary) defended his castles. Thanks to his wealth, he was in a position to build fortresses, pay wages to mercenaries and reward loyalty. Thus he began to restore his pre-eminence, first in the Charente region. Turning succession disputes to his own advantage, he ruined several powerful lords (the house of Châtelaillon) and marked his victory with the foundation of La Rochelle. He was always conscious of his own position in the feudal hierarchy. Suger recounts the famous episode in which the duke intervened between Louis VI and the count of Auvergne, promising to make the latter appear before the royal court on condition that he was acknowledged as the duke's vassal. This policy bore fruit from before 1137. At that date, William X delivered, unopposed, with his daughter Eleanor, an indivisible duchy to the king, Louis VII.

Louis immediately furthered his predecessors' policy towards greater administrative centralization and a more robust structuring of feudal ties. The ducal

court was organized on the French model, with the principal office devolved
to the seneschal who, in 1147, had the entire duchy under his authority, both
Aquitaine proper and Gascony. The Second Crusade gave Geoffrey of Rancon
the position of a vice-regent.

Under Henry II, Eleanor's second husband, the Anglo-Norman model was
imposed. From 1156 several seneschals were set over the eleven ducal provost-
ships. There were six in 1174 to collect taxes, render justice and command the
army. In fact periods of rebellion required better control of the population.
Under Richard, the great seneschal reappeared, but the presence of the duke at
Poitiers – a duke with the ring of St Valery on his finger as a sign of his wedding
to his duchy – prevented him from acquiring his former stature. Finally, from
1180 to 1216, the region was divided into two *sénéchaussées*: on the one hand
Poitou, on the other Gascony and Périgord; a prophetic division, for Philip
Augustus was soon to seize the first, leaving the second – the future Guyenne –
to the Plantagenets.

Elsewhere in the duchy the quickening pace of feudalization resulted in the
formation of a true territorial principality. The prince encroached on the affairs
of his vassals when there was a disputed succession, relying with increasing insistence upon the force of the law. He demanded homage and, in order to obtain
it, confiscated – provisionally at least – Limoges in 1139 and Angoulême in 1181.
This attitude provoked six revolts in twenty-one years, especially between 1173
and 1183. Incapable of coordinating their efforts – the Gascons knew nothing
of the Aquitanians and vice versa – the rebels finally failed. Their castles were
razed or lost their allodial status, becoming fiefs. Broken, the nobles themselves
drew the ties that bound them more tightly by making appeals to the suzerain.
The latter benefited from these circumstances to impose liege homage in a
region which did not know it. When Philip Augustus conquered Poitou, the
intermediate (ducal) level which separated him from his rear-vassals collapsed.
Henceforth, the count of La Marche and the *vicomtes* of Thouars or Limoges
would become the direct vassals of the king.

Toulouse and the Mediterranean coast

An aggregate of territories acquired at the end of the eleventh century by Raymond of St-Gilles, the principality of Toulouse (consisting of the Toulousain,
Quercy and Rouergue), embraced a vast dependency originating in the break-
up of the former march of Gothia. The *vicomtés* of Albi and Carcassonne were
attached to the Toulousain and Quercy, those of Narbonne, Béziers and the
Gévaudan to the Rouergue. Moreover, in 1125 the comital domain was enlarged
by the marquisate of Provence, between the Isère and the Durance, with its
extension into the Velay. Established on both sides of the frontier, the count
of Toulouse could intervene in the empire at his pleasure.

As has just been observed, the domanial core of this principality was clearly off-centre, west of the dependencies along the Mediterranean coast and the lands closely bordering it: an unbalanced situation which we have already seen elsewhere, in Champagne and in Flanders. Some great families, comparable to the *vicomtes* of Poitou or the counts of Angoulême, held the *vicomtés* of the Languedoc, the most powerful of them being the Trencavels of Albi, Carcassonne and Béziers. In a region which was witnessing the rebirth of Roman customary law in written form, where the allod was an impediment to enfeoffments, where fevdal obligations proceeded from oaths without homage, and where castles, even held as fiefs, were not liable to be surrendered to a lord, the prince was powerless before a prosperous aristocracy who possessed minting, judicial and economic rights. The most common coins were those struck by the count of Melgueil, the direct vassal of the pope since 1085.

The ecclesiastical lordships, strengthened by the Gregorian reform, were another outpost of resistance: at Narbonne power was divided between the *vicomte* and the archbishop; the *vicomté* or *comté* was transferred to the bishops at Albi, Lodève and Mende with the support of Louis VII in *c.* 1160. A degree of weakness in Raymond of Toulouse's edifice was accentuated still further by the fact that the counts were very involved in the crusades.

Their successes should also be stressed. They had succeeded in imposing primogeniture as the rule for succession, whereas the Trencavels continued to divide their goods between their sons. The comital court eventually had a monopoly of judicial appeals, with the chancellor operating like the president of a law court at the end of the twelfth century. At local level, domanial administration was entrusted to *bayles* and justice to provosts (*viguiers*). Finally, the count – who had founded the *ville neuve* of Montauban in 1144 and feared the independence of the urban communes – was able to tame the burgeoisie of Toulouse. He granted the city a consulate in 1152 and connected the burghers more closely with the administration of the city in 1189. The counts' achievement was positive, although the threats they faced included the proximity of Barcelona and the development of the Cathar heresy.

Catalonia

Master of Barcelona and Gerona, then through default of heirs of Cerdanya and the Besalú, and lastly of Roussillon in 1172, the count of Barcelona held all the *comtés* that constituted the new ecclesiastical province of Tarragona restored by the pope at the beginning of the twelfth century, apart from the Ampurias and Haut-Pallars. It was then (in 1178, to be exact) that the term 'Catalonia' appeared in documents to designate a territory undergoing religious, customary and monetary unification. To this old Catalonia was gradually added a new one, resulting from the *Reconquista* of the lower valley of the Ebro, with Tortosa falling in 1148 and Lérida in 1149. The military government necessitated by the war against the Muslims facilitated the consolidation and extension of feudal bonds and the appearance (under the name of *solidantia*) of liege homage to the prince. The important achievement of classifying the archives by lineage and castle which was undertaken by the dean of Barcelona Cathedral, Ramón of Caldes, resulted in the drawing-up of the *Liber feodorum major* in 1194.

Running alongside this attempt at feudal organization was a strengthening of administrative systems, with judicial *viguiers* and domanial *bayles* at local level, as in the Toulousain, and, in the central administration, a court that was still rudimentary and incapable of drawing up a budget, but where great officers like the seneschal gradually gave way to a more competent personnel of knights and secular clergy, some of whom constituted the secret council. These men were always concerned to base their activities on written authority. In *c.* 1150 they compiled the *Usages of Barcelona*, erroneously attributing them to Ramón Berenguer I, the founder of Catalan power in *c.* 1060, to establish more securely, as we have seen, the regalian prerogative in the *comté* in matters of public peace, fortification, coinage and criminal justice, to detach sovereignty from suzerainty and force the recalcitrant barons to submit to princely ordinances.

This development should be linked to the count of Barcelona's marriage to the heiress of the crown of Aragón and in 1152 the birth of Alfonso I, who was to be simultaneously count and king. Official acknowledgement of the term 'Catalonia' to signify the young prince's patrimonial possessions followed, and in 1180 the decision of the council of Tarragona to suppress in documents all reference to the regnal years of the king of France. It was thus debatable whether or not the territories recently conquered from the Muslims were held from the Capetian king at all.

In the face of this affirmation of the sovereignty of the count-kings, the barons attempted resistance by invoking the Carolingian origin of their autonomy. It took Alfonso I and his son Pedro II twenty-five years to subdue them. The ordinances of Fondarella were issued in 1173. The former diocesan peace was transformed into the king's peace, which the *viguiers*, with the bishops, were to enforce. Similarly, a new tax was introduced, the *bovatage*, to support the war against the Muslims. The discontent of the aristocracy was so great that in 1205 Pedro II had to accept the terms of a great charter restoring ancient customs. More fortunate than John 'Lackland' of England slightly later, he was not forced to promulgate it. He ducked and dived skilfully on other issues. Against the barons he placed the representatives of towns summoned to sit in the plenary courts. Above all, outside the limits of his territories, he followed

a brilliant and risky policy of expansion northwards, towards the former ecclesiastical province of Narbonne (from which the province of Tarragona had
been sliced off), a region that spoke the same language and where it was easy
to extend his feudal domination at the expense of the count of Toulouse.

With this policy the counts could lend a helping hand to the younger
members of their family who occupied Lower Provence in the empire and
who also claimed rights of suzerainty over the Gévaudan, Millau and half of
the Carladès. Independently of this support, the count endeavoured in 1150 to
secure the fealty of the Trencavels for Carcassonne, the Razès and the Lauragais
but, in 1163, the count of Toulouse reversed the situation with Carcassonne,
Narbonne and Montpellier once again submitting to his authority. His Catalan
rival retaliated in Béarn in 1170, Bigorre in 1175, Béziers in 1179; moreover, Pedro
II married the Montpellier heiress. Although the count of Toulouse took the
initiative in 1197 at Nîmes, the *comtés* of Comminges and Foix slipped in 1213
to the side of Barcelona.

In this competitive climate, Catharism made continual advances. The progressively impoverished lower aristocracy refused to hand over the tithes the
church demanded and turned towards heresy. The crusaders led by Simon of
Montfort attacked the dissidents. On 12 September 1213, at Muret, they annihilated the troops of Pedro II, who had decided to aid the Toulousains in order
to preserve the territorial *status quo*. Soon afterwards the barons of the north
imposed the law of the king of France upon the south.

CULTURAL AND POLITICAL LIFE: THE WORLD OF THE PRINCELY IMAGINATION

There is one last principality to consider, that of the Capetians. Neither its
size nor its resources differentiated it from the others until the beginning of
the thirteenth century, but its prince was also the suzerain of all the lords of
the kingdom and virtual sovereign over all its inhabitants. The subject need
not detain us here, since it is treated elsewhere. It would also have been illuminating to have analysed an instance of micro-lordship. The same structures
would have been observed functioning at local level, the same characters would
have been involved, diminished in proportion to their resources but proud of
their real or fabled ancestors (a Danish adventurer for the Guines, for instance)
or, thanks to several clerics in their entourage, artfully provided, like guy of
Bazoches with the same genealogy as the count of Champagne and linked
through the female line to Charlemagne and even Clovis. Grafted on to royal
stock, the minor lords portrayed the nobility as a great society of cousins.
Unfortunately, there is no scope to pursue this subject here.

In twelfth-century France, the rise of the principalities followed, accompanied or even preceded that of the royal domain. The twelfth century was a period of equilibrium between king and princes. Everywhere more land was cultivated and there was more settlement, towns grew, commerce accelerated, production increased and building renewed the environment in which people lived. Everywhere, too, the princes provided themselves with a better administration in order to benefit from demographic and economic growth. A court culture which had been born in the Occitanian lands gained ground northwards and flourished between the Loire and the Meuse. Courtly poetry, *chanson de geste* and Breton romance were appreciated at Poitiers and Troyes even more than at Paris: Chrétien of Troyes was the protégé of Marie of Champagne and Philip of Flanders. What is more, some princes sought in history and legend arguments which could be used for augmenting their prestige or consolidating their rule. As a consequence of the *Reditus ad stirpem Caroli*, the Capetians purloined to their advantage the memory of Charlemagne, hitherto preserved by the counts of Boulogne and Hainault. Henry II Plantagenet asked Wace and Benedict of Ste-Maure to glorify his mother's Norman ancestors while, in reaction to the Normans, Duchess Constance of Brittany called her son Arthur to associate him with the Bretons. As for the count-king of Catalonia, he scored an anti-Frankish point with his *Gesta comitum Barcinonum*.

It was thus a many-faceted society, often divided against itself, but one in which the members shared in the same world of the imagination. Charlemagne was always accompanied by the twelve peers and Arthur by his knights. The Round Table, which abolished hierarchies, represented the political ideal of the twelfth-century aristocracy. In this perspective the role of king, *primus inter pares*, is to inspire prowess and put it at the service of right. None the less, all the would-be Percevals and Gawains would have been mistaken if they believed that King Arthur would remain imprisoned for long in this enchanted circle. At the beginning of the thirteenth century, the peers of France, doubtless influenced by events in Germany, attempted to create a kind of *Reichfürstenstand*, but the endeavour was unsuccessful and from 1216 onwards their college had to open itself to officers of the Palais. In 1226 Louis VIII rejected without hesitation the countess of Flanders's request to be judged exclusively by her peers. Without anyone really realizing it, the victory of Bouvines (1214) had put an end to the aristocracy's egalitarian dream.

CHAPTER 18

ENGLAND AND THE ANGEVIN
DOMINIONS, 1137–1204

Thomas K. Keefe

ON a November night in 1138, Count Geoffrey of Anjou and his men spent part of the evening feasting in the burghal houses of the Norman coastal town of Touques. The experience, no doubt, was exhilarating. This was the first occasion since King Stephen's leaving the duchy a year earlier that the count had managed on his own to occupy a major town beyond his wife's properties along the Maine–Norman border. But the revelry was premature. The castellan at nearby Bonneville, having been left alone, secretly dispersed 'poor boys and common women' throughout all quarters of the town in a plan to burn the Angevins out. Forty-six fires were set in all. The amount of smoke and flames made it impossible for either side to engage in combat. Geoffrey and some of his men found refuge in a local cemetery where they waited out the horrific night.[1] Few who waited with him could then have imagined that within six years their lord would become master of Normandy, or that his son, Henry of Anjou, yet a child, would someday reunite the kingdom of England with the duchy of Normandy, joining them in a larger Angevin dominion.

The way to the future lay not with the count's further campaigns in the duchy, which ended with the Bonneville-sur-Touques debacle, but with the strategic thinking and enterprise of Robert, earl of Gloucester, perhaps the most powerful, certainly the ablest, member of the Anglo-Norman landowning aristocracy. His stature, experience and involvement in the fight of his half-sister, the empress Matilda, countess of Anjou, and her husband for Normandy and England gave the Angevin cause more than hope – it gave it a chance.

The tangible assets Earl Robert brought to the Angevins were the city and stronghold of Bristol in England, the county of Glamorgan in Wales, numerous other castles and properties in the south-west and elsewhere in England, together with Bayeux and Caen in Normandy, and a network of loyal Anglo-Norman and Welsh allies and vassals. One glaring weakness of King Henry

---

[1] Orderic Vitalis, *Historia aecclesiastica*, VI, pp. 526–8.

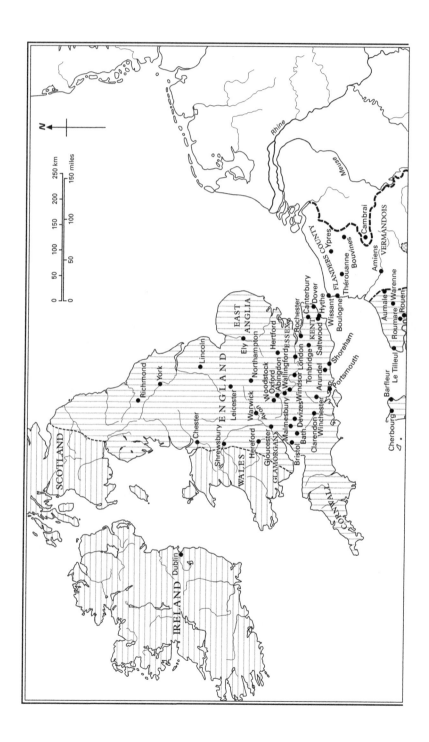

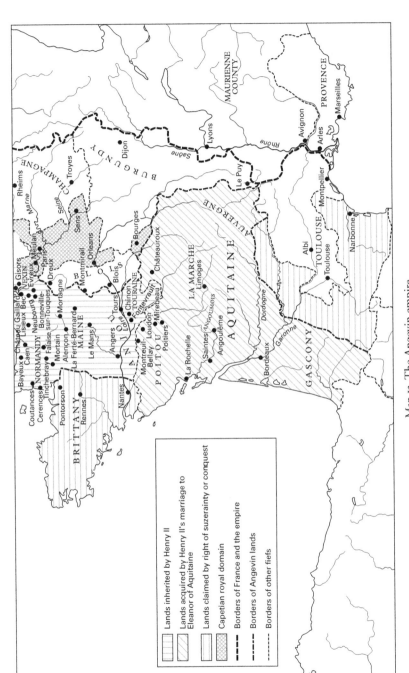

Map 12 The Angevin empire

Lands inherited by Henry II

Lands acquired by Henry II's marriage to
Eleanor of Aquitaine

Lands claimed by right of suzerainty or conquest

Capetian royal domain

Borders of France and the empire

Borders of Angevin lands

Borders of other fiefs

I's plan for his grandson and namesake to succeed him, if necessary, following a regency of Matilda and Geoffrey, was that no English castles or towns were assigned to the couple for a base of operations against the chance of a fight for the succession, which, of course, happened. Matilda and Geoffrey had to rely on great magnates like Robert, especially in Britain.

All the reasons for Earl Robert choosing to remain behind in Normandy after Stephen's departure in November, 1137, then, formally to renounce his allegiance to the king in May 1138, may never be known. Surely, he recognized the child Henry, his nephew, as the only legitimate Anglo-Norman ruler in spite of Stephen's anointing, but Henry was too young to rule, his mother's gender posed a serious barrier to her rule, even to a prolonged regency, while her husband's descent from the Normans' age-old Angevin enemies made his overlordship out of the question. If Robert thought of the future, he worked in the present. His family ties with Matilda and Geoffrey always would be a cause for suspicion. Stephen's Flemish mercenary captain, William of Ypres, had devised at least one attempt on the earl's life already. And the earl's influence at the royal court had been steadily undermined in countless ways by the Beaumont group, most notably the king's confidant, Count Waleran of Meulan. The earl in the end acted while he was still free to do so and in some measure by serving his sister he served himself.

In June 1138 Count Geoffrey invaded Normandy. Now with Bayeux and Caen being held for Matilda by her brother, and Stephen facing rebellion and a Scottish invasion in England, the expectation must have been to take Normandy finally. It was not to be. Waleran of Meulan and William of Ypres, coming from England, blunted the Angevin advance with the support of Count Ralph of Vermandois and French troops. Earl Robert was forced to find security behind the strong walls of Caen, where he remained inactive for months, while Count Geoffrey found sanctuary in Argentan after his near disaster at Bonneville-sur-Touques. Angevin partisans in England fared little better.

In the winter of 1138 King David of Scotland, Matilda's uncle, had invaded northern England reaching the River Tyne before being chased back into Scotland by a determined Stephen, who clearly saw the Scottish advance as a serious challenge to his kingship and ability to protect the north. In April David crossed the border once again with a large army, espousing the right of his niece to the English throne, while taking advantage of the unsettled situation to press age-old Scottish territorial ambitions in Northumbria and beyond. Stephen could not meet this second challenge in person. By chance or design, rebellion had broken out along the Welsh march, in the south-west, and in Kent where Earl Robert's supporters and castles were situated. Bristol, Hereford and Shrewsbury, to name the principal places, were all in rebel hands. So too was the pivotal fortress of Dover which was held for Earl Robert by his

castellan, Walchelin Maminot. Stephen concentrated his forces on the march
and Bristol. Queen Matilda, his wife, was sent against Dover supported by
ships from her county of Boulogne. The northern barons, under the guidance
of Archbishop Thurstan of York, had to fend for themselves. Angevin tactics,
if there was an overall strategy, seemed aimed at spreading the royal forces in
England as thinly as possible with the bonus of preventing significant reinforcements from reaching Normandy, where Count Geoffrey's invasion through the
centre of the duchy was in progress, and Reginald of Dunstanville, another
of Matilda's half-brothers, Baldwin of Redvers, and Stephen of Mandeville,
a Gloucester ally, were reeking havoc in the Cotentin. Earl Robert himself
curiously remained at Caen.

The strategy failed. Count Waleran of Meulan and others were dispatched,
as we have seen, to Normandy with substantial effect. In England, Stephen
first made an attempt on Bristol, but found the stronghold too formidable
and dangerously protected from siege by a broad arc of outlying castles in the
earl's hands. The king then concentrated on taking Hereford, an effort which
lasted five weeks. A second try at Bristol proved equally fruitless. After a string
of successes with smaller castles in the region, Stephen invested Shrewsbury,
taking the town and castle in little over a week. It was late August. About
this time, Dover capitulated to Queen Matilda, and within days the Scots
were resoundingly defeated by the northern barons near Northallerton at the
battle of the Standard. For the moment serious fighting in England ceased. By
November the Angevin progress in Normandy, too, had been stalemated.

If the Angevin revanche of 1138 failed to produce any immediate territorial
gains, it did shake the foundations of the Anglo-Norman world, bringing to
the fore the weaknesses of Stephen's kingship and the many dangers of the
current political situation. In spite of the year's string of royal victories, with
towns and castles taken or retaken and invasions repelled, the Angevin group's
leaders remained at large and unreachable. For all the expense, for all the hard
campaigning, nothing had been decided. Continued conflict was certain, and
Stephen most likely had exhausted the treasure left the monarchy by Henry I.
Normandy was beyond Stephen's or anyone's control, as its barons fought each
other as vigourly as they fought the Angevins. In England and Wales, Stephen's
failure to invest methodically or reduce the greatest of the rebel strongholds –
Bristol and Wallingford stand out – meant that civil war could continue seemingly without end; it did.

On 30 September 1139, Earl Robert and Matilda landed at Portsmouth
with a body of knights and made their way safely to Arundel Castle. Stephen,
having had notice of their coming, had ordered watches day and night over
the harbours along the southern shores. He was no doubt furious that Robert
had managed his entry undetected, and more furious still when he arrived at

Arundel with his army only to learn that the earl had slipped away in the night
with a bodyguard of twelve knights in an attempt to cross the south of England
and reach his men at Bristol. All the by-roads had been blocked by guards at
the first notice of the landing and it is even rumoured that Henry of Blois,
bishop of Winchester and papal legate, had actually caught up with the earl
but let him go in peace. The story may be fanciful, though the bishop had
reason enough to spite his brother, since Stephen had recently connived with
the Beaumonts to deny Henry election to the archbishopric of Canterbury
and had arrested three curial bishops, stripping them of their castles, again at
the suggestion of the Beaumonts. Court politics and rivalries played no small
part in allowing the Angevins to gain a necessary foothold in England. The
empress Matilda (the title she continued to use after the death of her first
husband, preferring it to the lesser title of countess), the legitimate heir to
the English throne according to the professed oaths of the barons taken on
several occasions during Henry I's lifetime, was now in England to claim her
inheritance. Equally importantly, Earl Robert, the natural military leader of the
Anglo-Normans among the Angevin group, had reached Bristol unmolested,
bringing over such powerful magnates as Miles of Gloucester and Brian fitz
Count to the Angevin side.

Arundel Castle held two women of royal rank, the empress and her protec-
tress, the queen dowager, Adeliza, widow of Henry I. Adeliza's second husband,
William of Albini *pincerna* and loyal to the king, was also in the castle, but decisions rested with Adeliza for Arundel was hers through dower. To begin what
would be a lengthy siege had drawbacks for Stephen, who was encamped outside, beyond allowing Earl Robert the freedom to rally his forces uncontested.
Public opinion, never to be discounted, might swing dramatically away from
Stephen if the king led a brutal assault on the castle holding these two high-
born women. After all, only a few months had passed since he had shocked
the clergy and many courtiers outside the Beaumont affinity with the arrest
of the bishops. On the other hand, if Stephen tried and did not capture the
castle, his reputation might not easily recover from the embarrassment of being
defeated by a female-commanded garrison. Besides the military threat lay with
Robert, not with Matilda. What would Stephen do if he took her? Send her
back to Normandy, imprison her? Never known as a deep thinker, the king's
problem was resolved for him by his brother, Henry bishop of Winchester,
who advised that it would be wiser to let Matilda go unharmed to the earl;
they could be contained and attacked all the more easily in one part of the
country. And so the empress Matilda was escorted by the Beaumont, Waleran
of Meulan, and Bishop Henry himself all the way to Bristol. Reflecting on this
unusual sequence of events, the contemporary historian Orderic Vitalis vented
his exasperation over this chivalric act: 'the king showed himself very guileless

or very foolish, and thoughtful men must deplore his lack of regard for his own safety and the security of the kingdom'.[2] The match for the English throne hardly was over, yet in the last months of 1139 an end game had indeed begun.

But neither the king, nor the Angevins, were strong enough to gain a meaningful advantage over the other as they played siege and run. Many must have felt, as William of Malmesbury did, the insecurity and anxiety of not knowing what might happen next or who would protect them. In William's word's, 'there were many castles all over England, each defending its own district or, to be more truthful, plundering it'.[3] As the end game progressed, an offer of mediation came from an unlikely source, King Stephen's own brother Henry, bishop of Winchester, the papal legate. Somehow Henry arranged a meeting at Bath in May 1140 between Robert, earl of Gloucester, as the empress's representative, and Matilda, Stephen's queen and a practised negotiator. Theobald of Bec, archbishop of Canterbury, attended along with Bishop Henry, making the church the primary go-between in seeking a resolution to the spreading civil war. Details of the discussions are lost to us, although they must have been promising enough for Bishop Henry to set out in September for France where he consulted with his eldest brother, Count Theobald of Blois, the head of the family, and King Louis VII of France whose obvious political interest in the outcome of the struggle for Normandy and England was newly bound up with familial concern: his sister had just married Stephen's son and heir, Eustace. Later in November Bishop Henry returned to England with a suggested solution, again unknown, acceptable to the empress and her party, but not to Stephen. The proposed solution very probably was some variation on what would come to pass years later: Stephen was to remain king for his lifetime, while Matilda's and Geoffrey's son, Henry, would inherit the kingdom his grandfather had intended for him. Clearly, Stephen meant to concede nothing without a fight. He got his wish, although he might have thought twice about tempting fortune. As one contemporary warned: 'Let no one . . . depend on the continuation of Fortune's favours, nor presume on her stability, nor think that he can long maintain his seat erect on her revolving wheel.'[4] On Sunday 2 February 1141, King Stephen was taken prisoner by the Angevins at Lincoln.

The battle of Lincoln was one of those rare occasions in Anglo-Norman experience, like Tinchebray, where opposing forces risked everything in a single encounter. That the battle took place at all was chance, the result of a quarrel between the king and two brothers, Ranulf, earl of Chester, and William of Roumare, who were upset by the king's mismanagement of patronage. They sought, as did so many others during the civil war, their own self-interest, in

[2] *Ibid.*, VI, p. 534.   [3] William of Malmesbury, *Historia novella*, ch. 483.
[4] Henry of Huntingdon, *Historia Anglorum*, pp. 266–7.

this instance mastery of a block of territory stretching from Cheshire beyond Lincoln to the eastern coast. Shortly before Christmas 1140 the two brothers tricked the royal garrison at Lincoln and seized its castle, with which went the town and the surrounding region. Winter did not deter Stephen from reacting quickly to an appeal from the bishop of Lincoln and townspeople for aid. On the night of 6 January, he entered the town so unexpectedly that several of Ranulf's men were taken captive returning to the castle from an evening's revelry. Earl Ranulf somehow managed to escape, leaving behind his wife, Robert of Gloucester's daughter, and brother. The earl of Chester, who had never shown sympathy for the empress's cause before, now sent messengers to Robert of Gloucester, his father-in-law, pledging support if Robert would help rescue those, including his daughter, who were in danger of captivity. The earl of Gloucester, putting aside resentment towards his son-in-law for having remained neutral up to this point, seized the moment and gathered together a large army of his own vassals, Welsh allies and those disinherited by Stephen. He moved on Lincoln from Gloucester, taking an indirect route, and on the way joined up with Ranulf coming from Chester with another body of Welsh troops in his command. The Angevin army arrived at the outskirts of Lincoln early on the morning of 2 February. Surprised, many of those with the king argued against risking battle, suggesting instead that he withdraw to some safer quarter to marshal a larger army, while a small detachment defended themselves in Lincoln as best they could. Stephen would listen to none of this talk of withdrawal. His advisers were ridiculed by younger knights as being 'battle-shy boys'.[5] What went through Stephen's mind in deciding on battle only can be guessed at. Count Geoffrey of Anjou had eluded him in Normandy; Earl Robert to this point had avoided any direct confrontation. The kingdom was suffering more and more from this civil war and flight now would invite comparison with his father, who, after having run away from Antioch during the First Crusade, later died in ignominy. On this day the Blois's family past coloured Stephen's judgement. He stayed; he fought; he was captured. What the king had not foreseen was the treachery of his own greater supporters, many of whom, including six earls, abandoned the battlefield at the outset of combat. Taken first to a meeting with the empress at Gloucester, Stephen found himself within a fortnight imprisoned in the earl of Gloucester's castle at Bristol.

Fortune's wheel continued its wild spin through the remainder of 1141. The taking of the king did not end the game after all. In a process which rewarded speed, the empress's party moved too slowly. By summer, Matilda's own mismanagement of the political situation had cost her the support of the Londoners and Bishop Henry of Winchester, who, again in his comfortable role

[5] John of Hexham in Simeon of Durham, *Opera omnia*, II, p. 307.

of power-broker, had smoothed the way for her coronation at Westminster. On 24 June she was forced to flee London in a general uprising, not yet a queen. Another Matilda, Stephen's queen, entered the city the same day in triumph backed by a loyalist army. For their revenge, the Angevins sought out the bishop of Winchester. The bishop, having changed sides once more, now was in agreement with his sister-in-law that his brother should be restored to the throne by any means possible. As the empress's troops besieged the episcopal palace at Winchester, Queen Matilda came down in relief with her considerable army and a host of Londoners. With much of the city burnt and supplies dwindling, the Angevins decided upon withdrawal before being completely encircled. Withdrawal turned to rout. The empress made it to safety, but Robert of Gloucester was taken prisoner defending her escape. With the earl in captivity at Rochester Castle, with members of their party scattered far and wide, the Angevins agreed to the only workable solution: an exchange of king for earl. The exchange took place in the first week of November. What had been done at the battle of Lincoln seemed undone by the rout of Winchester, but not quite.

News of King Stephen's capture at Lincoln had sent a seismic wave through Normandy. What once had seemed insurmountable, now came about. Count Geoffrey of Anjou broke the Normans' defence. And his relentless, if slow, conquest of Normandy led to the ultimate success of the Angevin party. In March when Geoffrey called upon the barons to surrender their castles, a group met at Mortagne and made another offer to Count Theobald of Blois to become their duke. Not only did the count of Blois refuse the offer, he countered with an offer of his own to Geoffrey. He would give up any claim to the Anglo-Norman inheritance in return for Stephen's release, the restoration of his personal estates and the small favour of Tours. The court of Anjou cleverly met this bid with silence. Nor was help forthcoming at this time from Stephen's ally, King Louis VII of France. Unfazed by the prospect of a union of England and Normandy with Anjou, the French king took an army south during the spring of 1141 to press his wife's claims to Toulouse. In despair, Norman towns, among them Lisieux and Falaise, began their submissions. By autumn, even Waleran, count of Meulan, had joined the Angevin court. With this, Count Geoffrey was in control of central Normandy.

In the summer of 1142, while Geoffrey contemplated how to consolidate and extend his gains, Robert of Gloucester arrived in Normandy and urged him to come to England with an army large enough to confront Stephen's revitalized forces. Stephen, no longer trusting the great magnates, many of them earls of his own creation, after the experience at Lincoln, had surrounded himself with a new court and household troop made up of men dependent upon him and not likely to measure every move against their own territorial self-interest. Since the Angevin party in England saw no hope of overcoming this leaner, more dogged, royal force on their own, they feared for their cause, and, in truth, for their lands. Now more than ever Geoffrey's help was needed in securing the English inheritance of his wife and their children. The count's perspective was much different. He had never been to England. He knew neither its people, nor its geography. Why risk the future on a gamble across the Channel when Normandy finally lay open to conquest? Besides, who would guard Anjou in his absence or for that matter Angevin-held Normandy? In a turn about, Geoffrey enlisted Robert in the winning of western Normandy. Perhaps this was in the count's mind all along. The earl's presence in the count's vanguard, his prestige within Anglo-Norman society, his military acumen, all would contribute to further successes. The main target was King's Stephen's county of Mortain. First Tinchebray fell, then Mortain itself, followed by Le Teilleul, Pontorson and Cerences. The lesson for the Norman barons still holding out in the west was clear: submit – no one could possibly save them; even King Stephen was powerless to retain his Norman lands – submit. And the submissions came. With the fall of Cherbourg in the autumn of 1143, virtually all of Normandy west and south of the Seine was in Geoffrey's hands.

Meanwhile the situation in England had deteriorated in Earl Robert's absence, forcing his return in November 1142, half-way through the campaign for western Normandy. Let down by the men left to protect her, and besieged in Oxford Castle, the empress was in imminent danger of being taken prisoner by Stephen. Once again fate intervened. Matilda miraculously escaped the trap on her own a few days before Christmas, walking five to six miles in the night through snow and ice to Abingdon, then riding with her small escort to the safety of Wallingford Castle, where Earl Robert found her. Although not known at the time, this proved to be the last in a series of remarkable adventures and near misses for the empress, which left at least one contemporary, the author of the *Gesta Stephani*, astonished:

I do not know whether it was to heighten the greatness of her fame in years to come, or by God's judgement..., but never have I read of another woman so luckily rescued from so many mortal foes and from the threat of dangers so great; the truth being that she went from the castle of Arundel uninjured through the midst of her enemies and escaped without a scratch from the midst of the Londoners..., stole away alone in wondrous fashion, from the rout of Winchester, when almost all her men were cut off; and then, when she left besieged Oxford, came away, ... safe and sound.[6]

From Wallingford, Robert took the empress to the greater security of Devizes Castle, where she stayed until finally leaving England in 1148. Travelling with them was her eldest son Henry, a boy of nine.

[6] *Gesta Stephani*, p. 144.

That Henry, not Count Geoffrey, had been brought back to England with the earl of Gloucester was significant. Here was the future, the true heir to the Anglo-Norman dominion of his grandfather, Henry I, and perhaps as a male, the individual and symbol to rekindle the hopes of the Angevin party in England. Henry remained at Bristol with his uncle's household until being recalled to Normandy shortly before the fall of Rouen in April 1144 and his father's investiture as duke. As Count Geoffrey took over the governance of the whole of the duchy, and set about restoring order, it must have been understood by the Normans that for their cooperation, Henry, who was being raised as an Anglo-Norman, would be made their duke as soon as he came of age. This may well have been King Louis VII's understanding too when he recognized Geoffrey's title (in exchange for the Norman Vexim) and helped the duke put down the last of the Norman resistance.

In and after 1144, events outside the Anglo-Norman world counted, perhaps more than at any other time, towards Angevin success. One barrier to the Angevin cause in England had always been papal recognition of Stephen's proper, and thus sacred, anointing. This recognition, given by Pope Innocent II in 1136, was reaffirmed in 1139 when the same pope set aside Empress Matilda's appeal for Stephen's deposition as an oath-breaker and a usurper without the curia voting or otherwise reaching a final decision. The election of Pope Celestine II in 11in 1143, following Innocent's death, was a boon for the Angevins. As a cardinal, Celestine had heard the 1139 debate and had developed a sympathy for the empress's case, which later evolved into a friendship with the empress herself. Although Celestine's pontificate lasted only a few months (September 1143 to March 1144), it was time enough to influence the next English succession. As it happened, Archbishop Theobald of Canterbury was in Rome on other business during early 1144 and was told by Celestine in no uncertain words that no innovation should be allowed regarding the throne, since its transfer, justly disputed, had never been resolved. Here was an opening worth exploiting. Many within and without the church from the mid-1140s onwards increasingly saw young Henry Plantagenet, heir to Normandy, as the logical and rightful heir to England as well.

In 1147, Henry revealed himself at the age of fourteen to be an intrepid warrior in the making by mounting an expedition of like adventurers on England without anyone else's knowledge, his parents included. However, the bond formed about this time with the powerful Cistercians, and their leader Bernard of Clairvaux, by Geoffrey and Matilda was far more important for the future. The amalgamation of the Cistercians with Norman Savigny conpregation and its daughter houses in England no doubt raised the level of Bernard's interest in the progress of Anglo-Norman affairs. A personal involvement is suggested by the presence of Bernard's brother, Nivard, in Normandy during the final negotiations with the Savignacs and then in south Wales at the inauguration of Margam Abbey, founded by Robert of Gloucester. Nivard conferred with Matilda on his journey. Meanwhile, Geoffrey met Bernard himself in Paris. Also in Paris were Archbishop Theobald of Canterbury and Pope Eugenius III, Bernard's protégé. This coming together of the greatest Cistercian abbot and the primate of England, occasioned by King Louis VII's departure on the Second Crusade, gave Geoffrey the opportunity to cultivate all three, to turn them to the Angevin viewpoint regarding the English succession, or at least to try to do so. Certainly, Matilda and Robert, for their part, must have said something to Nivard of Angevin intentions, something of the benefits of mutual cooperation.

The bond with the Cistercians helped the Angevin party survive the twin shocks of Robert of Gloucester's death in October 1147 and the empress's departure from England shortly thereafter in January 1148. Any advantage Stephen might have won from these events was lost in his clash with Bernard and the pope over the archiepiscopal election to the see of York and the attendance of English bishops at the council of Rheims. Stephen's brother the bishop of Winchester was of little use, since he had been suspended from office and called to Rome for absolution for his role in the war. Following Rheims, the bishop of Thérouanne went to England at Duke Geoffrey's urging and denounced Stephen as an usurper. The stage was being set. In Rome Eugenius III gathered the cardinals to hear once again the case of the English succession. Then fate intervened. News of the terrible defeat of the crusading armies reached Rome; overwhelmed with emotion, the papal curia quit its deliberations. The case went unresolved. Nevertheless, the real casualty of Stephen's embroilment with the church was his son Eustace's chance of being crowned co-king. As long as his annointing was prevented, as long as the Angevin party maintained a foothold in England, hope prevailed. In October 1148 Empress Matilda, Duke Geoffrey and their three sons gathered in Rouen to map out the next move.[7]

The plan, as it evolved, called for Henry to go to England, where he would be knighted by his uncle the king of Scotland, take the homage of Angevin supporters and afterwards return to Normandy for his formal investiture as duke, all accomplished by March 1150. This simplified many matters. Henry at the age of sixteen entered his inheritance with the boundless energy and excitement of youth, revitalizing the Angevin party. Matilda, long used to living independently without her husband, stayed in the Norman environment of Rouen as an adviser to her eldest son, assisting him in the governance of the duchy. Geoffrey, true to his bargain in giving the Normans a duke whom they could call their own, refocused his attentions on keeping peace in Anjou, always

---

[7] Chibnall (1991), p. 153.

a difficulty and recently made more difficult by the short-lived, yet troublesome, rebellion of his brother, Elias. Most of all, the spectre confronting Stephen now was not one of a woman trying to rule in a man's world, nor of an alien Angevin trying to conquer the Anglo-Norman world, but of Henry himself, Norman duke, grandson and namesake of Henry I. Both Stephen and Eustace, realizing that the stakes were changing, tried desperately to capture the newly knighted youth in 1149 while he was in England.

Still, the political situation remained fluid. If Pope Eugenius continued to be unmovable on the question of Eustace's anointing, Louis VII's coming home from the crusade brought promise of a renewed alliance. The French king was at odds with Count Geoffrey over his treatment of their vassal Giraud Berlai, the seneschal of Poitou. Throughout 1150 diplomatic missions were sent by the English, Normans and Angevins to Paris, each vying for Louis's support. The death of Abbot Suger, Louis's chief adviser, who favoured supporting the Angevins, and Geoffrey's pressing of the siege of Giraud's castle of Montreuil-Bellay led the French king in 1151 to join his brother-in-law Eustace in an attack on Normandy. Momentarily the Angevin cause was in jeopardy. Louis had yet to recognize Henry as duke. If Normandy were overrun, perhaps Eustace might claim the title. In any event, attacking Normandy kept Henry out of England. It was a good strategy.

Count Geoffrey remained in Anjou during the crisis just long enough to bring about a successful conclusion to his three-year siege of Montreuil-Bellay (a feat which much impressed contemporaries), and then moved with an Angevin army up into Normandy where he joined his son. Few in the French camp were comfortable with the thought of an attack on the combined Norman–Angevin armies, least of all Louis VII himself who, feeling ill, withdrew to Paris. There, in August 1151 a complex process of disengagement followed in which Eustace's interests proved expendable. Geoffrey, Henry and Louis VII met for a peace conference under the guidance of Bernard of Clairvaux. In the outcome, Geoffrey made amends for his harsh treatment of the Berlai family, while Louis accepted Henry's homage as duke of Normandy, the price for which was the duke's agreement to the surrender of the Norman Vexin. Norman–Angevin arms, skilled diplomacy and luck, with able assistance from the Cistercians, had carried the day. Son and father finally were freed to concentrate their energies on helping the Angevin party in England without compromising the security of Normandy or Anjou.

Whatever frustrations Eustace felt with his brother-in-law's about-face have been lost to us; the Normans on the other hand were elated. Within days of the peace conference, a war council was called to Lisieux on 14 September to make ready the invasion of England. Count Geoffrey, having wisely stayed behind in 1139, 1142 and 1149, now, in 1151, was prepared to leave Normandy and Anjou for England and fight for his son's right to the throne. The humiliation of Bonneville-sur-Touques lay in the distant past. The conquest of Normandy, the winning over of the Cistercians and the papacy, the siege of Montreuil-Bellay, the facing down of the French king, had erased all that. Patience and forethought had brought success. Then the unexpected happened. Geoffrey died after a brief illness. The catch on Fortune's Wheel once more released. At the age of eighteen, Duke Henry became count of Anjou, Maine and Touraine. The English invasion would have to wait while he took control of his father's county. It was precious time to lose.

Even with Henry on the continent, Stephen's position in England was becoming more desperate. Lately, magnates on both sides in the civil war had adopted a policy of 'wait and see'. They entered into private agreements with one another intent on limiting the scope of war and protecting their territorial interests. The son and heir of Robert of Gloucester, for example, married the daughter of the Beaumont, Robert, earl of Leicester, joining in some degree of friendship the two principal rival baronial houses in the kingdom. Stephen's latitude for action against the Angevin party was becoming increasingly limited. The idea that he was rightfully king, but that Henry, not Eustace, was rightfully heir, had gained ground among the magnates, as it had among the church. That Stephen never tried to have the magnates swear fealty to Eustace as heir, or perform homage, shows how little store he put on the mechanism Henry I used to ensure his succession plan. After all, Stephen himself had shown how chancy a mechanism it could be. Stephen had only one recourse left, force. Rebuffed again by Pope Eugenius on the question of his son's anointing, the king gathered together all the English bishops in London in March 1152 and demanded their blessing and acquiescence in Eustace's anointing. To a man, the bishops refused. Since Stephen had gained the throne through perjury, they said, the son could not inherit. These were Eugenius's words, but they were Angevin sentiments, planted in minds long ago. Frustrated and outraged, Stephen imprisoned his bishops, but Archbishop Theobald escaped to the continent. Faced with the hopelessness of trying to bully a unified English episcopate, the king released the others.

Henry, on the other hand, had a decisively better spring. In March, Louis VII divorced his wife, Eleanor of Aquitaine, and foolishly let the ex-queen return on her own to Poitou. In May, 'either suddenly or by design', Eleanor married Henry, whom she had met the previous August in Paris.[8] The events, which in a matter of months had made Henry overlord of virtually all of western France, left observers astonished. Within weeks of the marriage, he was at Barfleur ready to sail for England.

[8] Robert of Torigny, *Chronica*, p. 165.

Louis VII's response to his ex-queen's remarriage, however, ended any chance for an English expedition in the summer of 1152. Instead, Henry found himself facing the other way, fighting for all his possessions, including Normandy and Anjou. Louis wanted to ruin his vassal, to confiscate his lands and redistribute them among a coalition expressly formed for this purpose. The coalition was made up of Eustace, count of Boulogne, who had rushed over from England with renewed hopes, Henry, count of Champagne, the betrothed of the eldest daughter of Louis and Eleanor, who had been declared legitimate before the divorce and promised part of Aquitaine as her inheritance, Robert, count of Perche, Louis's brother, and Geoffrey of Anjou, Duke Henry's brother. Robert of Torigny gives the details of the fighting, reporting that the duke's masterful defence of his possessions won him praise, even from his enemies.[9] In a little more than two months, by early September, Henry had secured the Norman frontier from attack and crushed his brother's rebellion in Anjou. This was the first of many similar victories to come as Henry fought great coalitions over long distances in protecting his Angevin dominions. The year 1152 not only brought him great resources, it also fixed his reputation. Here was a man who would be king. Finally, in January 1153, braving winter seas, he sailed for England – a new end game had begun.

On a bitter January morning, Duke Henry and King Stephen, each at the head of his troops, met face to face near Malmesbury, separated only by the River Avon, swollen by winter rains. Torrents of rain and sleet poured down upon the two armies. Yet, it was not adverse weather conditions which prevented the all-out battle the duke and king sought as the moment of final reckoning. Magnates on both sides, like the church, desired peace, not wanting to engage further in the risks of war. Stephen lost confidence in the lords serving him, agreed to a truce and withdrew to London. For the next six months it seemed as if both men intentionally avoided one another in their campaigns. Stephen still held the loyalty of the major towns, like London, with their resources of money and manpower. Henry moved about, making grants and concessions to churches and magnates. Rewards were given to longtime supporters, such as the fitz Hardings of Bristol, while enticements for defection were offered to royalists. When the dominant magnate in the midlands, the Beaumont, Earl Robert of Leicester, openly declared for the duke, the strength of the king's cause suffered measurably. And when in late July or early August Henry finally marched to relieve the Angevin outpost of Wallingford, which had held out under siege even after the death of Brian fitz Count, Stephen had to react. However, their confrontation at Wallingford ended in the same fashion as it had at Malmesbury: the opposing armies refused to fight.

[9] *Ibid.*, pp. 165–6, 169.

Peace negotiations, which had been progressing behind the scenes through-out the year, now were conducted in the open. Archbishop Theobald of Canterbury took part with Bishop Henry of Winchester and others in fix-ing the terms. The basic idea went back to the early 1140s: Stephen was to remain king as long as he lived, Henry would inherit after his death. Feeling betrayed, Eustace left his father's court for East Anglia in a destructive rage. His sudden death on 17 August 1153 ended any hesitation Stephen might have had about concluding the negotiations. He seemed most concerned about se-curing and enlarging the inheritance of his youngest son, William, still a boy. In the first weeks of November, Stephen and Henry met at Winchester where the king took Henry as his adoptive heir. William was well provided for by being assured of his mother's extensive lands in England (she had died in May 1152), the Anglo-Norman estates conferred on his father by Henry I, the cross-Channel lands of the earls of Warenne which were to come to him through marriage, and other significant properties, towns and castles in England. If William was not to inherit the kingdom, he would be its greatest magnate, and would rule independently, as his brother had done in Boulogne. By this arrangement Stephen preserved his family's honour and future power as best he could under the circumstances. From Winchester king and duke went on to London, where during the Christmas holidays a formal treaty was prepared and witnessed at Westminster.

No one at the outset of 1154 could easily have predicted how long the treaty would hold or whether the civil war in England truly was finished. Powerful forces had combined to put a stop to the war, not the least of which was pressure from the papacy, skilfully brought to bear by the Angevins. But Bernard of Clairvaux and Eugenius III had died in the summer of 1153 along with Count Eustace, whose coronation they had helped prevent. The Angevin victory, if it was to be maintained, would have to depend after all upon Stephen's continued cooperation and the goodwill of the magnates themselves. And when Duke Henry hastily quit England for the continent in April after a plot against his life by Flemish mercenaries had been uncovered, it could not have been foreseen that Stephen, even at the age of sixty, would die only months later in October, and that Duke Henry would become king on 19 December 1154 within a year of the treaty's signing unopposed. Looking back, the events of 1151–4 were extraordinary. They brought into being an Angevin dominion scarcely imaginable in the 1140s centred on the older Anglo-Norman state, but including much of central and southern France. It would take four more years, however, for the young king Henry II to secure this vast dominion. With this, the history of these regions was changed for generations to come.

The flight of Henry of Blois, the bishop of Winchester, into self-imposed exile at Cluny in the autumn of 1155 was a clear signal that no resistance to

Henry II's rule in England was possible after the king's methodically decisive actions in breaking the power of the few barons who defied him following his coronation. If anything, Henry II's most serious challenge in his first year as king arose on the continent, not in England, and came from his own brother, Geoffrey. In December 1155 Geoffrey raised a revolt in Anjou calling for the fulfilment of their father's will: that when and if Henry gained England, he should turn over the Touraine, Anjou and Maine to Geoffrey to complete his inheritance, which in 1151 had included the strategically located castles of Chinon, Loudun and Mirebeau.[10]

At word of the revolt, Henry II crossed from Dover to Wissant on the coast of Boulogne in January 1156 and reached Rouen by 2 February. In the next weeks a family conference was held in the Norman capital to discuss the dispute. Several Angevin family members directly or indirectly affected gathered there: Henry II, William his youngest brother, Matilda his mother, Sibylla countess of Flanders his aunt, and Geoffrey. Henry saw to Geoffrey's diplomatic isolation by securing papal and Capetian assent to his retention of Anjou. Indeed, he performed homage to Louis VII for Normandy, Anjou and Aquitaine the very week before the conference began, and had sent an embassy to the English pope Adrian IV months earlier with a request to be released from his oath to uphold the will because he had sworn it under duress. Perhaps this isolation, or the promise of a fair hearing by the family in the presence of Empress Matilda, is what drew Geoffrey away from his Angevin strongholds to Rouen. Whatever the case, a peaceful resolution of the conflict could not be agreed upon. When Geoffrey withdrew from Rouen into Anjou, Henry followed.

Not until summer, 1156, did Henry finally force his brother into submission. Later in that same year, after Geoffrey had renounced his claims to their father's lands in favour of an annuity and the possession of a single castle (Loudun), Henry helped him become the new count of Nantes, extending Angevin power along the Loire and into Brittany. With Anjou firmly in hand, Henry, joined now by Eleanor, journeyed to Aquitaine where he punished the *vicomte* of Thouars for supporting his brother's revolt. And if any lingering doubt over the propriety of Henry's overlordship of Anjou remained, it was removed with Geoffrey's unexpected death a short time later, in 1158. By this date England, Normandy, Anjou and Aquitaine were all under control, and Henry, at the age of twenty-five, stood foremost among the princes of western Christendom.

Henry II's success in governing his vast dominions with their varied populations and frontiers rested, in part, on his boundless energy and pragmatism.

---

[10] William of Newburgh, *Historia rerum Anglicarum*, I, pp. 112–14; Hollister and Keefe (1973); and Keefe (1974). Compare Le Patourel (1984); Flanagan (1989), pp. 273–6; and Chibnall (1991), p. 155 n. 65.

His energy is seen in his constant travels, his pragamatism in his selection of advisers. Among a group of ten or so of the king's most influential advisers during the late 1150s and 1160s were his uncle, Reginald earl of Cornwall; his mother, Empress Matilda; William of Aubigny earl of Arundel, Queen Adeliza's widower; the justiciars Robert earl of Leicester and Richard of Lucy; the king's brother William fitz Empress; the English chancellor Thomas Becket; the Norman constable Richard of Hummet; and the Archbishops Theobald of Canterbury, Roger of York and Rotrou of Rouen. These individuals, with few exceptions, came from an older generation, one divided by civil war, yet now working largely in harmony with their ruler. Of this group, only Becket would prove a disappointment. Too late, Henry II recognized the mistake of changing his once faithful chancellor into the primate of all England. The lesson would be a harsh one.

In July 1163 at the council of Woodstock, Archbishop Thomas Becket infuriated Henry II by attacking a crown project to turn the annual aid paid to sheriffs into royal revenue. Henry II shouted, 'By the eyes of God, it shall be given as revenue and entered in the royal rolls: and it is not fit that you should gainsay it, for no one would oppose your men against your will.' To which Becket responded, 'By the reverence of the eyes by which you have sworn, my lord king, there shall be given from all my land or from the property of the church not a penny.'[11] W. L. Warren sees in this exchange a 'unilateral declaration of independence by Becket'.[12] If so, the archbishop was playing a most dangerous game. His behaviour in 1163, and in the coming years as his quarrel with Henry II intensified, was conditioned in part by his choice of a role model, Anselm of Bec, archbishop of Canterbury and defiant opponent of Kings William II and Henry I. A month or so before the Woodstock confrontation, Becket had lobbied, albeit unsuccessfully, at the council of Tours for Anselm's canonization. A biography of Anselm, now lost, had been prepared by John of Salisbury in support of canonization. As R. W. Southern remarked, 'Henry II might have noted an ominous significance in his [Becket's] admiration for Anselm.'[13]

When Henry promoted Becket to the see of Canterbury, he was expecting a Lanfranc, a Roger of Salisbury. What he got instead was a reincarnated Anselm, and an imperfect copy at that. Becket, unlike Anselm, proved to be an inept politician whose defiance, often miscalculated, hopelessly alienated the king and his closest advisers. One such series of miscalculations, which began in 1163 with Becket's attempt to restore, as Anselm had done, tenures lost by the archiepiscopal see, climaxed in January 1164 with the death of Henry II's brother, William fitz Empress, and ended with the archbishop's own murder in

---

[11] Edward Grimm, 'Vita S. Thomae', pp. 373–4.
[12] Warren (1973), p. 459.   [13] Southern (1966), p. 337.

1170 at the hands of, among others, a former member of William's entourage. It is a story of struggle for castles, baronies and political influence, a story of two individuals, Thomas Becket and William fitz Empress, tied together by fate in death, deaths which left their imprint on the remainder of Henry II's reign.

Prior to the 1163 Woodstock confrontation, Becket had petitioned the crown for the restoration of certain tenures which had once belonged to the see of Canterbury. He sought from Henry himself the return of the Kentish castles of Rochester, Saltwood and Hythe together with the barony of William of Ros, and demanded from Roger of Clare, earl of Hertford, homage for Tonbridge Castle and its town. According to the *Actus pontificum*, Henry and his courtiers were angered by the suits.[14] Becket's contemporary biographer, William fitz Stephen, suggests as much, saying that the dispute with the earl seriously hurt the archbishop's standing at court because nearly all of the English aristocracy were related to the Clares in some degree.[15]

The suits, however, were not without legal basis. Canterbury's lordships over Hythe, Saltwood and Tonbridge can be traced back to the eleventh century. The other claims were of more recent origin. In 1127, King Henry I had granted to Canterbury control of Rochester Castle in perpetuity, while King Stephen had made a similar gift of the Ros barony in 1136. If successful in pressing these suits, Thomas Becket, as archbishop of Canterbury, would become a dominant force in Kent. Possession of the castles of Rochester, Tonbridge, Saltwood and Hythe would go far to give the archbishop baronial power and independence to match his spiritual power and independence as head of the English church. Becket's actions, as it turned out, were ill-advised but his motives were natural enough. The former chancellor, who had aided his monarch in recovery of alienated estates, set out on a duplicate course upon entering his own realm. After the confrontation at Woodstock, though, the studied opinion of the royal judges hearing the suits, no doubt with some prompting, was a complete denial. Henry was not about to alienate the families of Clare and Ros or reward defiance with grants of castles and knight service. It would have been foolish on his part to do so.

Following Woodstock the quarrel became more a test over church–state issues: the archbishop's right to excommunicate tenants-in-chief without first consulting the king, the king's right to try criminous clerks in secular courts. In the autumn of 1163, alarmed by Becket's behaviour and potential for troublemaking, Henry pressed the English bishops to recognize certain customs governing the interaction of church and state. Predictably, Becket refused to

---

[14] Gervase of Canterbury, *Historical Works*, ii, p. 391.
[15] William fitz Stephen, *Vita sarcti Thomae Cantuariensis*, in *Materials*, p. 43.

assent to any customs that would weaken church prerogatives. Henry then played trumps, stripping the archbishop of the castles and baronies of Eye and Berkhampstead, which he had held since his days as chancellor. All that Becket would be left with now was Canterbury itself.

Hurt by the king's move, Becket lost little time repaying in kind. He used his office to ruin Henry's plans for the marriage of his brother, William fitz Empress. After the death of Stephen's son, William of Blois, in 1159, Henry planned to marry his widow, Isabella of Warenne, to his brother. This Becket now prohibited on the grounds of consanguinity and it was within his right to do so since the two were distant cousins. For the moment, Becket had his revenge. Henry kept the game and the rivalry alive by selecting Berkhampstead as the site for his Christmas court. Perhaps it was here, in apartments the archbishop had built for his own pleasure, that the council of Clarendon, where Henry forced the bishops to agree to his customs, was planned.

Angered, William sought consolation and advice in Normandy from his mother, Empress Matilda. What soothing words she had for her youngest son are unknown. William died on 30 January 1164, just two days after the conclusion of Clarendon. Henry was distraught over the news of his brother's death. More than that, he held Becket directly responsible.[16] The quarrel now was more than a fight over castles or church independence; it was personal. In the years to come, members of the dead prince's household nursed a deep-seated hatred for the archbishop. They too would have revenge. Richard le Bret, one of Becket's murderers in 1170, was heard to cry out as he swung his sword: 'Take this for the love of my lord William, the king's brother.'[17]

Henry employed all his diplomatic skills and resourcefulness to distance himself from Becket's murder. In time he recovered, reaching a rapprochement with the papacy and outraged clergy. While these delicate negotiations were underway, the king kept out of the eye of the storm, first disappearing into Brittany, then intervening in the affairs of Ireland. This unsettled period, however, brought to the surface a new problem Henry II never proved able to manage: the disaffection of his queen, Eleanor, and their sons. Empress Matilda's death in 1167 had removed an experienced voice whose wise counsel may have prevented the coming family crisis. Where before Henry had been the master of his success, he now became its uncertain prisoner.

Queen Eleanor had borne Henry II eight children, all but one of which survived infancy. In 1170, their four sons and three daughters ranged in age from fifteen to three years old. The eldest daughter, Matilda, was wed to Henry the Lion, duke of Saxony, one of Germany's great lords. Her sister,

---

[16] Stephen of Rouen, 'Draco Normannicus' II, p. 676.
[17] William fitz Stephen, *Vita sancti Thomae Cantuariensis*, in *Materials*, p. 142.

Eleanor, was betrothed to King Alfonso of Castile. The eldest son, Henry, was married to Margaret, daughter of King Louis VII of France and his second wife Constance of Castile, while another son, Richard, was bethrothed to her uterine sister, Alice. Their brother, Geoffrey, was betrothed to the heiress of Brittany, Constance, in whose name Henry II had taken over governance of the duchy from her father, leaving the youngest children Joanna and John as yet without provision. After two marriages and four daughters, Louis VII finally had had a son and heir, Philip, by his third wife Adela of Blois, whose own brothers, the counts of Champagne and Blois, had been married to Louis VII's eldest daughters by Eleanor in the early 1160s. The French king may well have envisioned the day when his son and heir would rule over a kingdom whose prominent barons were his brothers-in-law. Certainly, it was in Louis VII's mind that the Angevin dominions be broken into their constituent parts in the next generation. Under the treaty of Montmirail in 1169, Henry II had agreed to as much by formally designating his son Henry as the heir to England, Normandy and Anjou, Geoffrey as the heir to Brittany and Richard as the heir to his mother's Aquitaine. Again in 1170, a few months before Thomas Becket's murder, while Henry II lay seriously ill at a small castle near Domfront on the Norman frontier with Maine, he made out a will reaffirming the above inheritance scheme. More importantly, he had engineered the anointing of his son and namesake as co-king of England that summer, fixing the English portion of the inheritance in a fashion which had eluded Stephen. But there were two absences from the anointing, the archbishop of Canterbury, whose right it was to crown the kings of England, and the younger Henry's wife, Margaret, who should have been made a queen. No doubt, Henry II calculated the effect of the anointing on Louis VII and Becket, hoping that the French king would persuade the archbishop to quit his exile, return to England and redeem both their honour by a second crowning, which would include the French princess. The calculation worked. Becket did return, but the consequences were tragic. In his manipulations, Henry II snared himself, giving Louis VII the advantage of playing off his sons against him.

In May 1172 Henry II returned to Normandy, having spent seven months in Ireland, to receive absolution from the papal legates awaiting him there for his complicity in Thomas Becket's murder. Once reconciled with the church, he was willing to accede to Louis VII's wish for a recrowning of young Henry with Margaret's inclusion as his queen. This was done at Winchester in August. Earlier that summer Richard had been formally installed as duke of Aquitaine in separate ceremonies at Poitiers and Limoges in the presence of his mother, Eleanor. So, the inheritance scheme worked out in 1169 was taking on a greater reality, although Henry II never intended to give up any of his authority at this stage; if anything he was intent on maintaining his 'old path of family politics and territorial expansion'.[18] He had been working on a marriage proposal with Count Humbert of Maurienne since 1171. The count's lands controlled all the passes through the western Alps. Since Humbert had two daughters but no sons, Henry II was willing to pay up to 5,000 marks to secure his youngest son, John's, marriage to the count's heir, whichever daughter it might turn out to be. A meeting took place at Montferrat in early February 1173 to draw up an agreement. Later in the month the court moved to Limoges where Count Raymond of Toulouse, with the kings of Navarre and Aragon looking on, performed homage in turn to Henry II, Henry the young king and Richard. It was a splendid display, one far removed from the necessary penitential humiliation of his scourging by the papal legates months before. The young king had watched that scene. When his father, at Count Humbert's urging, agreed to give the Angevin castles of Chinon, Loudun and Mirebeau to the five-year-old John to finalize the marriage arrangement, he exploded in anger. Louis VII already had pointed out to his son-in-law that he was twice crowned, but lord of nothing in any real sense. The young Henry now demanded that his father hand over any one of his inheritances: England, Normandy or Anjou. After all he was within days of his eighteenth birthday, about the same age as Henry II was when Count Geoffrey released Normandy. The demand was promptly refused. It is hard to imagine that what occurred next was completely spontaneous. Eleanor, Henry II found out, was plotting against him with their sons. And, behind the plotting, stood his overlord, the king of France.

In the civil war which consumed the next two years, Henry II once again proved himself the luckiest and most resourceful of princes. With the kings of France and Scotland, the counts of Boulogne, Flanders, Dreux and Blois all arrayed against him, with his wife and sons in rebellion, with their rebellion supported by numerous magnates throughout the Angevin dominions, he triumphed. And he triumphed from a distance. The count of Boulogne's death from a chance crossbow shot in the summer of 1173 ended his brother the count of Flanders's campaign deep into Norman territory that year, while Eleanor's capture and imprisonment as she tried to leave Poitou to join he sons in Paris prevented her involvement in the war. Similarly, the capture by the king's men of the earl of Leicester in the autumn of 1173 and of the king of Scotland in the summer of 1174 broke the back of the rebellion in England. On each of these occasions Henry was elsewhere. He effectively managed his men and resources from afar, trusted his subordinates to perform their tasks and chose the right moments to intervene in person. The size of the Angevin dominions was never an important factor in their defence. What was important was the

---

[18] Gillingham (1984a), p. 62.

sheer talent of the administrators and barons upon whom Henry relied: their capacity to take charge, the protection and control of transportation routes – both land and sea – the loyalty of churchmen and townsmen, the ready wealth used to hire mercenaries, and Henry II's own renowned defensive genius and quick-strike ability. Even so, the problems which had brought about the civil war remained.

First, the estrangement between Henry and Eleanor offered no ready resolution. Whatever the motives for her rebellion – anger at her husband's affair with Rosamund Clifford, a longing for real political power away from her husband's shadow, fear of the permanent vassalage of Aquitaine to the English kings, which all have been suggested – Henry blamed her for the civil war and never again trusted her, never forgave her. In 1175 he tried to talk a papal legate visiting England or other business into annulling their marriage. After the annulment, she was to be placed in seclusion in the nunnery of Fontevrault. Later in 1176, the younger Henry, Richard and Geoffrey vigorously protested against their father's intentions. Even Rotrou, archbishop of Rouen, one of Henry's closest advisers, refused to sanction such an idea. Family and court opinion aside, only Pope Alexander III's rejection of the proposal ended the initiative. What Henry decided upon instead was Eleanor's continued imprisonment, keeping open the wound occasioned by her rebellion. Secondly, Henry was unable, or unwilling, to accommodate the reasonable expectations of his eldest son. Where after 1174 Richard was allowed a certain freedom as duke of Aquitaine, and Geoffrey, following his marriage to Constance of Brittany (1181), much the same in Brittany, Henry III, as the younger king was sometimes called, was never given a territory of his own to rule. He died in 1183, at the age of twenty-eight, while in rebellion against his father, having recently asked for Normandy and having been denied it one last time.

The young king's death, far from settling matters, threw the Angevin dominions into yet another succession crisis. It had been easy for the kingdom of France. When Louis VII became incapacitated in 1179, his only son Philip, a youth of fifteen, succeeded him. Henry II, as fortune would have it, had too many sons. And their hostility towards their father and one another had become a common feature of Angevin politics by the 1180s. Even if Henry had resigned one or more of his territories, there is little evidence that Richard, Geoffrey and John could have co-existed for long in peaceful cooperation. Before Henry would name Richard as his heir to England, Normandy and Anjou, he wanted Aquitaine for John. Richard saw no real usefulness in giving up real power over his duchy for the empty mantle of his elder brother, so he balked. Henry could have gone ahead and declared Richard his heir anyway. The implication of a permanent union of Aquitaine with Anjou, Normandy and England, though, might have threatened the French monarchy, possibly leading to war, and certainly would have alienated Geoffrey and John. John had been promised the county of Mortain and the earldoms of Cornwall and Gloucester. Geoffrey was earl of Richmond by right of his wife and had designs on Normandy. Making Richard heir to England and Normandy without adequate compensation for the other sons would only lead to trouble. Not making Richard heir would lead to trouble too. Besides this, there was the issue of Richard's bethrothal to King Philip's half-sister Alice. On several occasions the French king pressed for the marriage to take place. She had been at the Angevin court since 1169 and the delay was scandalous. Yet beyond Henry's own rumoured affection for Alice, he had reason enough for putting off this marriage. He did not want Richard falling in with Capetian in-laws as the young king had done. The effect, however, of keeping Philip and Richard apart was to bring Philip and Geoffrey closer together. Just before Geoffrey's accidental death at a Parisian tournament in August 1186 he had been boasting that he and the French king were going to devastate Normandy. And although death removed another son from the equation, the year ended with the succession question unresolved.

While Geoffrey's departure from the stage of Angevin family politics closed one door for King Philip, another was opened to him. He claimed the wardship of the eldest of Geoffrey's two daughters and, with her, custody of the whole of the duchy of Brittany. Henry II was not about to compromise the Angevin lordship of Brittany in any way, especially since he knew that Geoffrey's widow, Constance, was in the early stages of pregnancy (she gave birth to a son, Arthur, in March 1187). The future of the Breton inheritance too was uncertain. The English king employed the favourite tactic of medieval politics – the delay – to put Philip off. In early October 1186 an embassy of his closest advisers – William of Mandeville earl of Essex and count of Aumale, the English justiciar Ranulf of Glanville, and the former vice-chancellor Walter of Coutances archbishop of Rouen – was dispatched to the French court to request a truce regarding this matter, to last until mid-January. When they returned to England and announced their success, William and Walter were sent back again to ask for an extension of the truce until Easter, about the time Constance was due to give birth. This embassy met with a cool reception. Earl William was in charge of castle defences in Upper Normandy. It seems that a kinsman of his, Henry of Vere constable of Gisors, had found the French building a castle in the vicinity and had attacked the workers, killing the son of an important nobleman. Outraged, Philip had arrested all the king of England's subjects on the French side of the border. In retaliation French subjects found on the Norman side of the border had also been arrested. Although all those who were arrested were shortly released, tensions remained high.

Henry expected a full-scale war. In December Ranulf of Glanville went into Wales to recruit mercenaries for a campaign in Normandy. Welsh mercenaries had been used with great effect in the 1173–4 civil war and Henry had come to rely upon them. By January 1187 Philip was attacking in the area of Gisors and Henry had begun to collect his forces for a massive movement of supplies and personnel from England to the continent. One group who attempted the winter crossing from Shoreham in Sussex to Dieppe was lost at sea with a large part of the king's treasure. In late February Henry himself crossed from Dover to Wissant, where he was met by the counts of Flanders and Blois, who escorted him to Normandy. The French magnates, it appears, were not seeking the battle King Philip apparently wanted. A meeting in April between the two kings ended without any reconciliation. Henry then divided his army into five groups: one under his command, the others under the commands of Earl William of Mandeville, his sons Richard and John, and his natural son Geoffrey, since 1182 the chancellor of England. Richard and John took their groups into Berry where in June they were besieged by Philip's forces at Châteauroux. Upon learning this, Henry marched with a great army to their relief. Philip was caught, his prestige at risk. This was his first open attack on the Angevins. His father had tried on numerous occasions to defeat his Angevin counterpart and had faltered. Philip decided to risk all in a pitched battle. Henry showed himself equally determined.

Every morning for the next fortnight the two opposing armies, separated by the Indre, arrayed themselves in battle formation, while individuals from both sides, well acquainted with the dangers of pitched battle, sought a settlement. Rumours flowed back and forth. Troops from the county of Champagne were said to have been bought off by the English, causing much concern among the French. Henry became worried when he found out that Richard, swayed by the count of Flanders, was meeting in secret with Philip. Somehow Richard persuaded Henry to agree to a truce and promptly left with Philip for Paris. The armies rejoiced in the peace. Alarmed, Henry sent messengers to recall Richard; he had been down this path before.

Henry and Richard were reconciled in time, though the succession issue still divided them. Philip kept the pressure up by massing an army on the Norman border and threatening an invasion if Henry, among other things, did not proceed with Richard's marriage to Alice. At this point international events further complicated the problem. In the summer of 1187 news of the losses at the battle of Hattin in the Holy Land shocked and depressed westerners. The fall of Jerusalem to Saladin in October of the same year made the need for a crusade all the more urgent. At a conference on 21 January 1188, the kings of England and France, and a host of French magnates, Richard included, took the cross. Later that month the famous Saladin Tithe was proclaimed at a conference in Le Mans. While Henry II proceeded to England to oversee the collection of the tithe, Richard was drawn to Aquitaine to suppress a revolt.

After this, he became embroiled in a fierce war with the count of Toulouse. His successes in this war caused King Philip to invade Berry, hoping to attract Richard's attention away from Toulouse. The fighting brought Henry II out of England. He landed back in Normandy in July with a large force of Welsh and English troops. Battles erupted all along the frontiers of the Angevin and French dominions; towns were burnt, villages destroyed. With no end to the fighting in sight, and pressure for a crusade continuing to build, a preliminary peace was agreed upon in November, but only after the counts of Flanders, Blois and others had refused to participate any further in the hostilities. As details of peace were being worked out in a meeting between the two kings, Philip asked for Richard's marriage to Alice to take place and for the barons of England and the rest of the Angevin dominions to swear an oath of fealty to Richard as Henry's heir. More importantly, in front of those present, Richard asked if his father would recognize him as heir. Henry, trapped by the young king's legacy, kept silent. In a startling move, Richard then knelt before Philip and rendered him homage for Normandy, Anjou and Aquitaine. All that Henry had sought to avoid had come to pass.

There was little room for negotiations. While truces were agreed upon, the first lasting through Christmas, another extending through March, then Easter, nothing could bring Richard to depart on crusade now without having secured his inheritance, and nothing could bring Henry publicly to recognize Richard as his heir. King Philip was the pivot; his interests lay in causing the Angevins as much trouble as possible, although he might be turned if a suitable arrangement was devised for his sister. In a parley at La Ferté-Bernard on the Maine–Blois border in the last week of May 1189, Henry tested Philip's attachment to Richard by offering to settle a long-standing dispute over the Vexin with Alice's marriage to John. The offer also played against Richard's fears of losing the major part of the Angevin dominions to his younger brother. Behind the scenes, Henry had been preparing for war. Mercenaries had been recruited again from among the Welsh, troops brought over from England, and an army readied in Normandy at Alençon. Instead of leaving the area after the parley, Philip and Richard caught Henry unaware by overrunning local castles and marching on Le Mans. On 12 June with the city on fire, Henry was forced to flee for his life, narrowly escaping capture by Richard. Inexplicably he stopped only hours short of the safety of Alençon where his army awaited him and slipped back into Anjou, going on some two hunderd miles to Chinon. The king's health had been failing for several months, and this last exertion in the summer's heat caused his illness to become all the more intense. Unable to prevent the continuing collapse of Anjou's defences, Henry was persuaded by the counts of Flanders and Burgundy to reach a settlement. On 4 July near Azai-le-Rideau, a visibly ill Henry II listened as conditions were read out to him in the presence of Philip and Richard. Added to the old demands of Alice's marriage and Richard's recognition were a £20,000 indemnity, the surrender of key castles, and a willingness to follow Philip's pleasure in all things. Henry agreed, but defiantly whispered in Richard's ear: 'God grant that I may not die until I have my revenge on you.'[19] Too weak to ride back to Chinon, he was carried there on a litter, where he died two days later. With this the family quarrels ceased and the Angevin dominions passed intact to the next generation. Ironically, for all of Philip's machinations, Richard carefully stepped into a position of power as great as, perhaps even greater than, his father.

Queen Eleanor was released from her captivity in England immediately upon news of Henry II's death and burial in the abbey of Fontevrault. Aged sixty-eight, her re-entry into public life was marked by energy and intelligence. Much like the empress Matilda before her, Eleanor took part in the political affairs of her son. Richard departed on crusade in July 1190, having carefully provided for the governance of the Angevin dominions and negotiating in secret a marriage alliance, his own, with the royal house of Navarre. Eleanor was intimately involved with both projects, accompanying Berengaria of Navarre, Richard's intended bride, in the winter of 1191 to meet her fiancé at Messina on way to the Holy Land. She was back in Normandy by October 1191, where her stature and acumen quickly became of use. She knew how to play the spins of Fortune's Wheel, perhaps better now than any other Angevin family member.

While Normandy and the Angevin continental dominions kept stable during Richard's absence, English political life slipped into chaos. Castles and administrative posts in England had been split between the nobles, clergy and royal officials so that no particular group or faction exercised overwhelming power. What upset the balance was the supercilious manner of the chancellor-justiciar, William of Longchamp, bishop of Ely and for a time papal legate. Richard got enough complaints about the chancellor's conduct to send Walter archbishop of Rouen home from Messina with Queen Eleanor with letters empowering him to take over the government if the need arose. And there was danger in the way that the disaffected English lords were looking to the king's brother John as their champion. John's resources were substantial. In addition to the county of Mortain in Normandy, he had been given two English earldoms, seven other major baronial honors, lordship over seven counties and interests in at least two royal forests. He naturally believed himself heir to the Angevin dominions in the event of misfortune befalling Richard, even though in a treaty with Tancred of Sicily the king recently had designated their four-year-old nephew, Arthur of Brittany, as his successor. Until Richard had

---

[19] Gerald of Wales, *Opera*, VIII, p. 296.

a true heir of his own body, the circumstances which had plunged the Anglo-Norman world into the civil war following Henry I's death always existed. Even though John, with Archbishop Walter's help, managed to oust William of Longchamp from office in October 1191 and took on a greater political role himself, his insecurity got the better of him. When King Philip of France, back early from the crusade and angry over Richard's marriage to Berengaria, invited John to marry Alice instead and seize his brother's possessions, he started off for Southampton without much hesitation. Only Eleanor's arrival in England in February 1192 prevented him from joining Philip on the continent. In a series of councils called by her at Windsor, Oxford, London and Winchester, the justiciars and barons agreed to confiscate all John's lands and revenues if he should attempt to leave.

Without John, Philip gained little from his attacks along the Norman frontier. This was due as much to the strength of the duchy's defences and the resolve of its seneschal, William fitz Radulf, as it was to the lack of enthusiasm by the French king's vassals for the invasion of a crusader's lands. Meanwhile, an attack on Gascony by the count of Toulouse was turned back by Sancho of Navarre, Berengaria's brother, proving the utility of Richard's alliance. In England, Eleanor attempted the reconciliation of Archbishop Walter of Rouen and the barons with the chancellor William of Longchamp, whom she invited to return. She was unable to bring it off. The barons allied themselves with John against the chancellor, who, with Eleanor's acquiescence, was sent into a second exile. For some time William of Longchamp had been trying to get the pope to intervene in his case and uphold his excommunication of the archbishop of Rouen and the others who had forced him from office. When papal legates on their way to mediate the dispute were stopped at the Norman border, they promptly excommunicated the seneschal and placed the duchy under interdict. The sentences were lifted a few months later. Then, a most difficult year ended with the shocking news of King Richard's capture and imprisonment in Germany as he made his way home from the crusade.

In January 1193 John surfaced in Paris, performed homage to Philip for his brother's dominions, promised again to marry Alice (although he was already married to his cousin, Isabel of Gloucester) and came back to England with a story of Richard's death. No one was fooled. Eleanor and Archbishop Walter swiftly set in motion a counter-offensive of diplomacy and arms aimed at Richard's release and the protection of his lands. John's castles in England, where he attracted few followers beyond his own men, were put under siege. The closing of the Channel ports and the arrest of an advance party of Flemish mercenaries eliminated the prospect of John receiving relief. Philip's attack on Normandy floundered at the walls of Rouen, just as Louis VII's had nearly twenty years before. All the while a large amount of money for a ransom was being collected throughout England, Normandy, Anjou and Aquitaine. If anything, the experience of 1193 proved the loyalty of the Angevin dominions to Richard, the strength of the Angevin defensive system and the competence of the agents, Eleanor included, whom the king had left in charge.

In February 1194, one year, six weeks and three days after his capture, Richard was set free at Mainz. Eleanor had gone to accompany him home, while John and Philip, who had come together in one last attempt to take Normandy, overran Evreux, Neubourg and Vaudreuil. As Richard approached, the two nervously withdrew to Paris. The king landed in England on 13 March; within a month the kingdom was pacified. By May Richard was back on the continent and never returned to England again. The kingdom's governance was entrusted to Hubert Walter, a relative and former protégé of Henry II's justiciar, Ranulf Glanville. Hubert had been promoted to the see of Salisbury in 1189 and had accompanied Richard on crusade. He had been translated to the see of Canterbury in 1193 at the king's insistence and later took over the office of justiciar from Archbishop Walter of Rouen. Not since Roger of Salisbury in Henry I's day had the kingdom had so willing and able a prelate-administrator. Indeed, what Henry II had wished for in Becket, Richard found in Hubert, whose loyal service brought him and his see the Kentish tenures Becket had sought in 1163: Rochester, Saltwood, Hythe, Tonbridge and the Ros barony. With England at peace and in capable hands, all of Richard's attention could be focused on throwing back the French from their foothold in Normandy. To this end, the better part of the next five years and considerable treasure were spent on wars with the king of France.

In the last months of Richard's reign, all the varied elements of past Angevin politics seemed to replicate themselves. In December 1198 a new pope, Innocent III, anxious for a crusade, tried to negotiate a peace between the warring kings of western France. Richard refused anything more than a truce as long as King Philip still held Norman territory, especially the castle of Gisors, taken during his German captivity. With Gisors went domination of the Vexin, the strategic region on the Franco-Norman frontier protecting the eastern approaches to Rouen and Upper Normandy on the one side, and the French royal domain on the other. The Vexin had long been a zone of conflict between the Norman dukes and Capetian kings. Henry I and Louis VI fought over its control. Count Geoffrey Plantagenet pledged the region to Louis VII in 1141 for recognition as duke of Normandy. Henry II was compelled to do the same in 1151. It formed the dowry of Margaret, Louis VII's daughter, who married Henry the younger in 1160. Their early marriage and Henry II's subsequent occupation of the Vexin caught Louis VII by surprise. Louis felt betrayed and never ceased trying to recover his daughter's dowry. After the death of the young king, Henry II allowed the Vexin to be counted in Alice's dowry in order to avoid its return becoming a cause of war for Philip. Gisors fell into Philip's hands in 1193 when its castellan Gilbert of Vascoeuil turned it over without a blow having been struck. Its loss forced Richard to counter with the building of Château-Gaillard in 1196–8 at enormous cost. Alice mercifully was removed as the bride-pawn in the struggles for the Vexin through her marriage in 1195 to William of Ponthieu. Under the truce of 1198, however, it was stated that Gisors should become the marriage gift of Philip's son, Louis (VIII), and one of Richard's nieces, a daughter of Eleanor of Castile. If so, a source of conflict for almost a hundred years might continue for another generation without closure. That was the Angevin fate. No matter how much power the house of Anjou amassed, no matter how often or cleverly they defeated their enemies, conflicts were never resolved completely. They were never at peace, save for the few years following Henry II's triumph in 1174. Perhaps Richard could have changed this, but he died at the siege of Chalus-Chabrol on 6 April 1199, struck down by a cross-bow bolt. And when he died at the age of forty-one, he left no children by Berengaria, his wife of seven years.

Eleanor had been summoned to Richard's bedside from her retirement at Fontevrault. She arrived only hours before his death. She concurred with his wishes for the disposition of England and the Angevin dominions. They were to pass intact to John, with whom Richard had been fully reconciled. The succession itself was not quite this simple. At word of Richard's death, Constance of Brittany entrusted the twelve-year-old Arthur, son of Geoffrey, John's elder brother, to King Philip and moved with a Breton army to claim Maine, Anjou and Touraine in his name. After the Bretons took Angers, the local barons declared Arthur their count. As a French army came in to support the Bretons, John, who was in the area on his way to Normandy from Richard's funeral and burial at Fontevrault, barely avoided capture. He found safety in Normandy, where the leading men of the duchy, unable even to consider having a Breton, a child at that, as their duke, invested him with the duchy at Rouen on 25 April. He then took a Norman army into Maine and flattened the castle and city walls of Le Mans for failing to support him. The need he felt to take this brutal action against the city beloved by Henry II and the burial place of Count Geoffrey Plantagenet, together with the declaration on Arthur's behalf at Angers, show how distant the Angevin house had become from its roots.

The English, like the Normans, found it difficult even to conceive of a Breton on the throne, although Hubert Walter at first is said to have preferred Arthur to John.[20] Indeed, a baronial council at Northampton held a lengthy debate before finally agreeing to John's coronation, which took place at Westminster on 27 May, two days after he had landed in England. Meanwhile, Eleanor went

---

[20] *Histoire de Guillaume le Mareschal*, III, pp. 159–60.

on a political tour of her own dominions of Poitou and Aquitaine, travelling from Loudon to Poitiers and on to Saintes and Bordeaux. With great wisdom and awareness of the dangers of the moment, she granted charters of liberties to cities and towns along the way, making the townspeople responsible for their defence and creating a militia.[21] In mid-July she met King Philip at Tours and did homage to him for her lands. What feelings swept over her as she kissed in submission the hand of this man, the son of her first husband, who had done so much, and would do more, to destroy Angevin fortunes, are lost to us. Her homage protected Aquitaine, and that was what was important. For his part, Philip was probably relieved not to have to occupy himself with Aquitaine just yet.

In September 1199 Angevin fortunes changed for the better. A dispute between King Philip and his ally the seneschal of Anjou led Constance and Arthur to seek a peace with John. A few months later the prospect of a papal interdict on the French kingdom, stemming from a dispute with Innocent III over Philip's repudiation and treatment of his second wife, caused him to recognize John as Richard's heir. For this important recognition John in May 1200 ceded Philip by the treaty of Le Goulet the Norman Vexin, much of the county of Evreux and a number of frontier castles already in French possession. The treaty was solemnized by the wedding of Blanche of Castile, recently brought from Spain by her grandmother, Eleanor, and the young Capetian prince, Louis. A few months afterwards, John himself wed, having had his marriage to the countess of Gloucester annulled. His new wife was the youthful heiress to the county of Angoulême, Isabel. While this alliance could have strengthened John's feudal hold over his mother's Aquitainian duchy, it alienated the powerful Lusignan family, a member of which had been betrothed to Isabel. Their appeal for justice to Philip as John's overlord in 1202 gave the French king just the opportunity he was looking for to renew the war. He summoned John to Paris in April and when John failed to appear the French court declared all his continental fiefs forfeit. In the war that followed Arthur of Brittany besieged his grandmother, Eleanor, at Mirebeau, only to be captured by John. It was the most fateful sequence of events in Angevin history. For the Angevins to fight among themselves was nothing unusual, in fact it had become normal. But no one was prepared for what occurred next. Arthur was murdered while in custody and everyone thought John responsible. Suspicion of Arthur's death gave the Bretons and French a certain moral justification for their attacks on John's lands. Worse, Norman and other barons began to desert him and castles capitulated. Fearing treachery, John left Normandy for England in December 1203.

[21] Pernoud (1967), p. 250.

John, like Stephen after he had abandoned Normandy in 1137, never returned. The Angevin loss of Normandy is usually marked by the surrender of the fortress of Château-Gaillard, which took place in March 1204, after a five-month siege by Philip. However, it is arguable that the real end came with the capitulation of Rouen in June, as it had in 1144 when Count Geoffrey Plantagenet conquered the duchy. Eleanor, one of the few who could recall that conquest first hand, died in April and was buried alongside her husband, Henry II, and her son, Richard, in the abbey church of Fontevrault. Count Geoffrey lay at le Mans, William fitz Empress and the young king at Rouen, and the empress Matilda close by at Bec-Hellouin. What had happened to their world? Born in a time of civil war, it had been torn apart by succession disputes and family rivalries. Fortune's Wheel had come full circle.

CHAPTER 19

SCOTLAND, WALES AND IRELAND
IN THE TWELFTH CENTURY

Geoffrey Barrow

FOR all three of the countries whose development is reviewed in this chapter, a leading theme was provided by the continuing after-effects of the Norman Conquest of England, which made themselves felt far into the twelfth century and beyond. The Norman conquerors and colonizers who flocked to England in the forty years separating the battles of Hastings and Tinchebray hardly raised their sights sufficiently to take in southern Scotland and showed almost no interest in Ireland. There was already in 1066 a lengthy history of close relations, friendly and unfriendly, between Wessex and Mercia on the one hand and the Welsh kingdoms or principalities on the other. Even if the Norman kings had been willing to stand aloof from the situation in Wales the aggressive and acquisitive conduct of some of their closest followers would have compelled them to intervene if only to prevent the creation of dangerously independent lordships on their western frontier. The expansion policy pursued successfully before 1100 in the north and mid-Wales, and only to a slightly lesser extent in the south, meant that not only the incoming conquerors but also the Welsh princes were brought ineluctably within the political segment of north-west Europe which it is convenient to think of as Anglo-Norman. Moreover, by seizing the English kingship Duke William automatically became heir to a tradition, reaching back at least to the tenth century, of English claims to exercise some kind of lordship over the kings of Scots. Ireland was a different matter, yet although the Conqueror in 1081 stopped short at St David's and demanded no tribute from Irish kings or trading towns the fact that both Lanfranc and Anselm, as archbishops of Canterbury, laid claim to an ecclesiastical hegemony over the Irish bishops, together with the occasional freelance venture into Irish affairs by Norman settlers in Wales such as Arnulf of Montgomery, lord of Pembroke, kept Ireland in focus as it were, to remain until the 1170s the greatest single imponderable in English royal policy.

The gradation of dependency in political and military matters set up by the Norman Conquest, with Wales being brought most closely into the English

ambit, Scotland somewhat less so and Ireland scarcely at all, was not reflected
in the social organization, languages and customs, or religious life of the
three countries under review. Despite the lightning military successes of the
first Normans to penetrate Wales, and the inextricable links forged between
Wales and England by Anglo-Norman settlement, the whole process of castle-
building and colonization suffered major setbacks of long duration, especially
in the reign of Stephen. There is little if any sign that the Welsh language, Welsh
law and custom, or the basic ways in which Welsh society was organized, were
seriously affected, still less threatened, by Anglo-Norman pressure and incursion. Only in the structure, personnel and external relations of the church can
we see specifically English and continental influences being gradually brought
to bear. In Scotland, by contrast, a much more complex situation prevailed.
Wales, politically fragmented to an extraordinary degree, was culturally and
socially remarkably homogeneous. Scotland, politically speaking, formed a
recognizably single entity, a kingdom with a history of some three to four centuries. This kingdom, which had not yet taken the geographical shape familiar
since 1266 (save for the important addition of the Northern Isles two centuries
later), was composed of elements diverse in language, law and social organization, although not differing significantly in general culture. The south-east part
of Scotland, especially Lothian, Tweeddale and Teviotdale, together with certain districts of the middle south, notably Clydesdale, Annandale and Eskdale,
shared many features of social organization, as of basic pastoral economy, with
what are now the northernmost regions of England, especially Cumberland,
Westmorland, Northumberland and County Durham. As these northern areas were brought more firmly under the control of the English crown, feudal
nobility and church hierarchy, the common features which they shared with
southern Scotland to some extent diminished in importance. But at the same
time (essentially in the twelfth century) many of the innovative features of post-
Conquest English government and social order, especially military feudalism,
were deliberately introduced into Scotland by a line of strong kings. Consequently we have the seeming paradox that *c.* 1200 Scotland was in important
respects less different from England than Wales was, despite the closer dependence of the Welsh princes upon the English crown. Ireland, in comparison
with both Scotland and Wales, seems to pass from one extreme to the other.
Until 1171 the Irish kings and the trading communities founded by the 'Ostmen'
or Norse-speaking Scandinavians enjoyed somewhat restricted relations with
the new political forces east of the Irish Sea but were in no way subordinate to
them. After the Henrician conquest a large part of Ireland suddenly became an
Angevin province, more tightly controlled in the name of the English crown
than almost any part of Wales. Nevertheless, save in the towns such as Dublin,
Waterford and Limerick which had never known a predominantly Irish form

of society, the island as a whole had, like Wales, a remarkably homogeneous social system. Despite an influx of Anglo-Norman – by 1171 it would be more accurate to call them 'English' – settlers, barons, knights, esquires, freeholding yet dependent tenants, as well as of vitally important merchants, craftsmen and clergy, the vast majority of the population continued to owe their first loyalty to kings of various grades whose power and prestige cemented the immemorial kin-based character of Irish society. The strength of traditional custom and the autonomous nature of Irish law, administered almost independently of the kings by a hereditary caste of *breamhan* (judges), made Irish society even more impervious to external influences than was Welsh society, although it may readily be recognized that the systems of both countries had much in common.

It has long been usual for historians to sum up and explain the common features observable in Welsh, Irish and at least northern Scottish society by classifying them as 'Celtic'. This practice rests on a fundamental truth, namely that the peoples who used one or other of the Celtic languages – Irish and its Scottish derivative, in the twelfth century only just becoming distinctively 'Scottish Gaelic', the closely related Manx form of Gaelic, Cumbric (so far as it still survived after *c.* 1100) and Welsh – did also hold fast to social customs and modes of organization, and to legal concepts and practices, for which there was almost a common Celtic vocabulary. Nevertheless, the blanket word Celtic ought to be used with caution and discrimination. In the first place, the use of a particular language or family of languages does not necessarily imply adherence to any particular pattern of social customs. Secondly, there is the implied assumption that the patterns of marriage, inheritance and landholding familiar in Celtic kin-based society had been frozen at some remote period and remained almost immutable throughout the middle ages. Finally, to explain the persistent features of Welsh, Irish and Scottish society solely in terms of a Celtic kin-based system is to underestimate the extent to which several of these features – the importance of agnatic relationships, for example, or the concept of the honour price and man-price (*wergild*), or fosterage – were common to many of the barbarian peoples of northern Europe. To adapt a phrase made famous by F. W. Maitland, 'We must be careful how we use our Celt.' The one certainty which may be affirmed is that, by comparison with Norman-conquered England, Ireland, Wales and Scotland – especially the first two – displayed a remarkable degree of social and legal conservatism.

SCOTLAND

Only five kings reigned over Scotland in the twelfth century, and the last three of these ruled from 1124 to 1214. As in England, long reigns made for political

Map 13 Scotland

stability, strengthened by the fact that the five rulers represented only two different generations. Three brothers, Edgar (1097–1107), Alexander I (1107–24) and David I (1124–53), were followed by David's two older grandsons, Malcolm IV (1153–65) and William I 'the Lion' (1165–1214). The dynasty to which they belonged was held to be in direct succession to the Cenél nGabráin which had held the kingship of Scottish Dalriada until the eighth century. Their undoubted ancestor was Kenneth Mac Alpin (d. 858). Rightly or wrongly he was believed to have inherited the royal authority not only of Dalriada but also of the old Pictish kingdom of Alba (Scotland north of the Forth–Clyde isthmus and east of Argyll). Consequently, the twelfth-century kings enjoyed a native and traditional prestige and respect which did not depend on the military power at their disposal.

It was the royal house which imposed and encouraged such unity as existed in the Scottish realm. Alba, together with mainland Argyll, was relatively homogeneous: Gaelic in speech and, largely, in culture, composed of ancient territorial divisions ruled by mormaers (essentially provincial governors, yet having some kingly quality attaching to them), served by a church which, in spite of continental and English influences operating from the eighth to the eleventh century, still possessed many features characteristic of the Irish church, strongly kin-based in its social organization which (as in Ireland) penetrated the clergy as well as the laity. Only in two important respects may any sign of a fundamental break with tradition be seen before 1100 – both attributable to continental and English influence. The older practice of royal succession whereby an adult collateral – brother or cousin – was preferred to a son was defied when a rebellion in favour of Donald Bán, Malcolm III's brother, was finally defeated in 1097 and the throne was taken by Edgar, Malcolm's fourth son. Native sensitivities may have been allayed by the succession in turn of Edgar's two younger brothers, but in 1153 the profoundly important switch to linear parent-to-child succession was highlighted by the acceptance (with seemingly only minor resistance) of David I's eldest grandson, Malcolm IV. His Gaelic name (the last ever borne by a king of Scots), and the fact that he was followed by his brother, may again have appeased the conservative nobility, who gave only half-hearted support to collateral rival claimants for the kingship under William the Lion; but some faint hankerings after the old custom can still be seen even in the thirteenth century.

The second significant change discernible before 1100 was the advent of military feudalism, that is to say the granting of land (in the first instance by the crown) on privileged terms, usually with jurisdiction and the right to build castles, in return for the performance of military service with horses trained for warfare and with expensive armour and weaponry. Under Malcolm III and Edgar the impact of feudal lordships held for knight-service was slight and chiefly confined to Lothian. But the process had come to stay and, quickening appreciably under Alexander I, became the predominant fashion of landholding across much of southern Scotland in the reign of David I. Large estates were created in this way in the period *c.* 1120– *c.* 1170, and although the impetus behind feudalization hardly slackened before Alexander II's reign the emphasis shifted to smaller fiefs (parish or village sized) and towards the country north of the Forth, at least as far as the Moray Firth.

The patchy advance of military feudalism underlines the geographical divisions which retained both social and political importance at least until the thirteenth century. South-eastern Scotland still bore many traces of its earlier history as part of Bernicia or northern Northumbria. The northernmost version of English speech was standard from Annandale eastward to Berwickshire, and had long since obtained a firm hold upon Mid and East Lothian, where it had been marginally challenged by Gaelic since the mid-tenth century. Below the crown, whose demesne lands were very extensive, a native aristocracy of service and status ('thegns' or 'thanes') held sway over a semi-free or even free peasantry whose obligations to their lords took the not notably onerous form of occasional labour service, especially at harvest time, seasonal renders of food and hospitality and here and there money rents. Below this class of substantial 'husbandmen' there were poorer but not invariably less free 'cottars' and grazing tenants ('gresmen') whose name reminds us of the strongly pastoral nature of even south-eastern Scotland.

West of Lothian and the border river systems, the twelfth-century Scottish kingdom embraced the Clyde valley – politically an important remnant of the old Cumbric kingdom of Strathclyde, and thoroughly feudalized by the crown in the period 1150–70 – the Ayrshire littoral, of which the two northern districts (Cunningham and Kyle) were either royal demesnes or feudal tenancies by 1165, and the highly distinctive region of Galloway, consisting of the southernmost district of Ayrshire (Carrick) and the valleys flowing into the Solway Firth, especially those of Bladnoch, Cree, Dee and Nith. Before 1162 Galloway was recognized, at least by its own ruling dynasty, as a kingdom, owing only the most tenuous obedience to the king of Scots. The prevailing Gaelic language and culture of twelfth-century Galloway was in no sense a contradiction of this fact, for multiplicity of kingship was the norm throughout Ireland and at least the western seaboard of Scotland. The reduction of Galloway to the status of political, though never feudal, subordination was to take the Scottish crown many years and cost it much in terms of military expeditions, abortive experiments in feudalization and recognition of Gallovidian separateness. The whole process began in earnest under Malcolm IV and was not completed till 1235.

Of the remaining regions making up modern Scotland the northern isles of Orkney and Shetland, subject to dense Norwegian settlement since the early ninth century, did not become part of the Scottish realm until 1468–9. The western isles and the westernmost districts of the mainland (including what medieval people called the 'Isle of Kintyre') formed a complex area in which cultures clashed and intermingled and political claims were a bone of contention between Scottish and Norwegian rulers. An agreement between Edgar and Magnus 'Barelegs' stipulated that the western isles (including Man but perhaps excluding the islands in the Firth of Clyde) should be subject to Norwegian rule while the mainland seaboard acknowledged Scottish sovereignty. Although not unworkable (the agreement was only cancelled by the treaty of Perth in 1266), it was unsatisfactory because actual lordship – often seen as 'kingship' in the Irish sense – in the west crossed interregnal boundaries and embraced both mainland and insular territories. Thus many local lords, and particularly the powerful family of Somerled 'king' of Argyll, held sway, with the help of fast galleys, over groups of islands where they were nominally lieges of a remote Norwegian king and districts such as Lorn and Cowal where, again somewhat nominally, they were subjects of the king of Scots. David I exercised some measure of royal authority in the west and could even call out troops from this region in time of emergency. Malcolm IV's forces repulsed an invasion by west highlanders and islesmen in 1164 in which Somerled was slain. During the long reign of William the Lion the west remained comparatively peaceful, yet there is little doubt that dynastic rebellions against William's rule, notably in 1187 and 1212, drew their military support from the isles and the western seaboard.

Neither geographical and cultural diversity nor lingering provincial separatism should obscure the strong currents flowing throughout the twelfth century in the direction of political and national unity. The introduction of feudalism at the crown's behest proceeded apace from *c.* 1120 to *c.* 1220, and with remarkably little friction. In origin partly functional and partly social, the Scottish brand of feudalism promoted by David I and his grandsons laid the foundations not only of the dominant class of 'lairds' (tenants-in-chief of the crown or substantial tenants of the greatest feudatories), who were to wield decisive power in Scotland until the eighteenth century, but also of Scottish land law, which remains markedly 'feudal' to the present day. The crown also encouraged the concept of the *regnum Scotorum*, a kingdom of the Scots which embraced an extent of territory much wider than Alba or Scotia, taking in Lothian, Strathclyde and Galloway and until 1157 including the country stretching south from the Solway Firth as far as Stainmore on the northern edge of Yorkshire. On occasion (e.g. in the later 1130s, in 1163, between 1174 and 1189, and again in 1209 and 1212) the relationship between the Scots and the English crowns was challenged by English rulers who sought to reestablish the hegemony which William the Conqueror and his sons had appeared to enjoy in respect of the Scottish monarchy. David I refrained during Henry I's

lifetime from striking an independent pose save in the matter of ecclesiastical
autonomy – he would not allow his bishops to acknowledge the supremacy
of either York or Canterbury. On the accession of Stephen David refused
any kind of homage involving his kingdom, while allowing his son Henry to
swear fealty for the earldom of Northumberland and honour of Huntingdon.
Henry II may have attempted in 1163 to impose some degree of lordship over
Malcolm IV, but it was not until William the Lion was captured by the English
eleven years later, having ill-advisedly supported the Young King's unsuccessful
revolt, that the king of Scotland, by the treaty of Falaise, was forced to become
the liege man of the English crown 'for Scotland and his other lands'. This
explicit feudal subjection lasted till 1189, when on Henry II's death William
bought his release, and restoration of the king of Scots' position to what it
had been under Malcolm IV, from Richard I. Friendly relations prevailed until
John succeeded his brother in 1199; for the remaining fifteen years of William's
reign there was mutual suspicion and mistrust between the realms, accompanied by two attempts by John (1209 and 1212) to revert to something like the
Henrician overlordship. Paradoxical as it may seem, the lengthy period during which William the Lion was either formally subject to the English crown
or at least under threat from aggressive English royal policy saw the Scottish
king strengthen his political grip upon the more outlying regions, especially
in the highlands and Galloway. The high-handed manner in which Henry II
and John treated William may actually have excited some sympathy among
his own lieges, and there is no doubt that the concept of a Scottish kingdom
whose people owed a special, overriding loyalty to the crown had grown into
a reality by the end of the twelfth century.

The population of Scotland, perhaps approaching 350,000 by the end of
the twelfth century, earned its living chiefly by pastoralism and fishing. Cattle
and pigs were owned by all but the poorest families, and the herds kept by the
greatest magnates, for example the lord of Galloway, the earls north of the Forth
or the bishops of St Andrews and Glasgow, would be counted in many hundreds. Sheep too were reared, and their numbers must have increased steadily
through the century as newly founded religious houses began to specialize in
meeting the needs of the Flemish wool markets and the fleece became more
valuable than the flesh. Both cows and ewes were of course bred for their milk
and the butter and cheese to be made from it. Goats were common, valued
for their milk and their skins. Horses – to judge from Pictish sculpture – must
have been familiar long before the Norman adventurers rode into Scotland on
their war-trained destriers, but as with sheep, equine numbers would surely
have risen markedly between 1100 and 1200, and Clydesdale's reputation for
breeding versatile horses may well date from this period. As for fishing, the
species most frequently appearing in contemporary record are salmon, herring

and eels. Herring in particular was an estuarine fish in this period (and for many centuries longer), and fishermen from as far afield as the Low Countries were visiting the Firth of Forth by the 1150s. A pastoral way of life, with fisheries forming a significant supplement to food supplies along the sea shore, as well as by the numerous rivers and lochs, seems to go naturally hand in hand with hunting. Much of the land above 400–500m was either too rugged or too remote for the summer pasturing in 'shielings' (transhumance) which was standard practice throughout Scotland. Nevertheless, such areas carried in the summer months a sizeable population of red deer, which could normally find adequate winter shelter in lower-lying woodland, considerably more extensive than in later centuries. Although in later Scots law, following Justinian, wild animals were regarded as *res nullius*, fair game for all, in medieval practice the pursuit of red deer was a jealously guarded royal right which was extended, not over-generously, to the higher nobility. Earls and certain of the bishops enjoyed hunting preserves, as did such notable magnates as the hereditary steward (Stewart) and constable or the lord of Annandale (head of the Scottish branch of the Bruce family). Many tracts of upland and well-wooded ground in the south and middle parts of Scotland, especially along the 'highland line', were designated forest, in which hunting was controlled and through which passage was restricted to permitted routes, probably sign-posted. A corollary of the protection of wild game was the prohibition of tree-cutting and destruction of undergrowth and of the eyries of falcons and other birds of prey. For kings and nobles hunting was undoubtedly a sport, but venison probably made a significant contribution to the general diet, and it would be naive to suppose that unprivileged folk, especially in the remoter hill country, did not poach the occasional salmon or deer. Foxes, wild cat, wild boar and wolves were also hunted, the last two species to the point of extinction in the sixteenth or seventeenth centuries.

The predominance of pastoralism in highlands and lowlands alike did not mean that cereal growing was unimportant. Across much of the flatter or lower-lying territory of south-eastern Scotland, and along the eastern littoral as far north as Stonehaven, agriculture in the strict sense had been practised immemorially. In the course of the twelfth century the area of land brought into cultivation by ox-drawn ploughs and harrows increased very substantially. In this period the valley of the Clyde, the Ayrshire coastal strip and sizeable pockets of favourable terrain along the shores of the Moray Firth witnessed an extension of arable or its introduction for the first time. The customary manner of quantifying land in Lothian and Tweeddale was by the ploughgate (*carucata*) of 104 acres, made up of eight 13-acre oxgangs (*bovatae*). This usage was shared with the northernmost part of England, indicating perhaps an Anglian origin. Whatever its roots, the system emphasized the vital role of the

plough and plough-team of eight oxen in the rural economy. North of Forth
and Clyde, and in earlier periods in the far south-west also, habitable land
was generally divided into davochs (Gaelic *dabhach*, 'vat', 'tub'), terminology
which may suggest delving with a spade rather than ploughing, or which might
possibly point to a levy of corn for purposes of rent or tax. Again, the cereal
element is important, yet the emphasis is not on the plough. Crops were
cultivated whenever soil and climate allowed, but the share of rural income
derived from corn was obviously larger in the more favoured lands of southern
and eastern Scotland, smaller in the north and west. Some wheat was grown,
for example in East Lothian and the Carse of Gowrie, but the standard cereals
were rye (perhaps winter sown) and the spring-sown oats and bere, the six-
rowed northern barley preferred until modern times. There is no record of peas
or beans before the thirteenth century, but here and there some flax may have
been cultivated. The typical peasant farmer of the south, the husbandman or
bonder, held a 'husbandland' consisting of 26 acres of arable (two oxgangs),
together with a proportional share of hay meadow and pasture in the common
grazing possessed by every permanent settlement. In good years such a holding
might provide a reasonable livelihood for a peasant upper class, but below the
husbandmen were numerous cottars and landless families from whom either
permanent or seasonal labour could be recruited. It is harder to discern a typical
peasant in northern Scotland, yet safe to assume that he kept cattle or pigs and
held only a modicum of arable. Although servitude of a fairly thoroughgoing
nature was by no means unknown in southern Scotland, it seems clear that the
peasantry of Alba were subject to even more oppressive restrictions upon their
freedom than their southern counterparts.

Self-sufficient as the rural communities of twelfth-century Scotland were in
many respects, they needed to sell some of their surplus production and import
goods made in other parts of Scotland or imported from England, Ireland and
the continent of Europe. The aristocracy required fine cloth, jewels, weaponry
and wine, none of which could be produced at home. In times of dearth the
common people might need corn. Trade must have been immemorial, yet the
twelfth century saw two innovations which gave a revolutionary boost to mercantile activity and to general prosperity. The twelfth-century kings – perhaps
beginning with Edgar and Alexander I, certainly maturing with David I –
instituted the earliest explicitly privileged trading communities or 'burghs' in
Scotland. Most of the early burghs were on or close to the east coast – Berwick,
Roxburgh, Haddington, Edinburgh, Linlithgow, Stirling, Dunfermline, Perth,
Dundee, Montrose and Aberdeen. Secondly, David I, around 1136, authorized
the first issue of Scottish silver coins, pennies modelled precisely on the sterlings
of English kings but bearing the name and image of the king of Scots. Even
though these new coins were insufficient for Scottish needs their issue ushered

in a new era in which the Scottish economy, backward as it might seem from a continental European viewpoint, was ultimately money-based. The combination of small trading centres, whose inhabitants enjoyed 'first-come first-served' privileges of trading within carefully demarcated zones, with the regular issue of silver pennies exchanging at par with English-minted sterlings, gave a boost to Scottish economic activity which can scarcely be exaggerated. Wool clipped from increased lowland flocks was sold to Flanders, cow-hides and deerskins from the highlands went to Germany and France, pearls from Tay and Dee were sought after by continental jewellers. The trading towns ('burghs' is the Scottish version of English 'boroughs') attracted immigration from England, the Low Countries and Germany as well as from the Scottish hinterland. Even the highlands were involved in urban development, for although none of the new burghs was strictly within the highland line, settlements such as Inverness, Forres, Elgin, Perth, Stirling and Dumbarton lay along that invisible boundary and served as centres for the exchange of highland produce for foreign manufactures. By 1200, when upwards of thirty burghs had been created, mostly by the crown, the urban trading centre, with its weekly market and quarterly or half-yearly fair, had become an integral feature of the country's social and economic fabric.

Burghs played a political and administrative as well as an economic role. It was normal for a royal castle to be sited beside a burgh, and for this castle to serve as headquarters for a sheriff who acted as the chief agent of royal government in the district associated with burgh and castle – the sheriffdom or shire. Smaller and much more ancient districts known as shires, administered by thanes or sheriffs, still persisted in many parts of twelfth-century Scotland, but the grander and more powerful sheriffs established by David I were a conscious imitation of the practice of Norman England. By 1200 the geography of royal government bore a strong though perhaps superficial resemblance to the English pattern, with sheriffdoms or 'counties' filling almost the whole of southern and eastern Scotland as far north as Inverness. As yet Galloway and the highlands were not 'shired', but royal authority and the crown's role in administering justice did not depend exclusively on the sheriff. David I's sheriffs and their successors were drawn mainly from the baronial class, the new feudal nobility. It was from their ranks, but also from among the older territorial aristocracy – earls and provincial lords – that the kings appointed their highest administrative officers, the justiciars. Normally there was one justiciar for the country north of Forth (Scotia) and one for the south (Lothian), but the later practice of having a third justiciar for Galloway may have been briefly anticipated in the 1190s.

In Scotland – contrasting markedly in this respect with twelfth-century England – the king's hand did not lie heavy on his lieges year after year in terms of taxation or military service or hunting reserves or judicial decrees. Scottish royal government was no less real for being much less centralized, much less bureaucratic, than English. It may be no coincidence that the major officers of the royal household, derived from Anglo-Norman and Capetian models, especially the steward, constable and marischal, quickly came to fill a public position within the community of the realm as a whole, taking their style (though not before the thirteenth century) from the country rather than merely from the king.

The profound transformation undergone by government and society in twelfth-century Scotland was matched by a far-reaching reform of the church. In 1100 a tiny handful of Scottish clergy had attained to the grade of bishop and there was no territorial diocesan system. There were monasteries north of the Forth of a decidedly Irish type, in particular communities of *célidé* (culdees), 'clients of God', who practised an asceticism derived from an eighth- and ninth-century reformation of Irish monasticism. Ill-defined *clerici*, some probably in priests' orders, were attached to churches and chapels which served the spiritual needs of widely scattered rural communities but were not parochial as that word was understood in most of western Christendom. South of the Forth a markedly Northumbrian situation prevailed, with quasi-parochial churches – some of them classifiable in Anglo-Saxon terms as old minsters – served by priests who were virtually hereditary proprietors; having succeeded their fathers in the benefice they would in turn expect to pass it on to a chosen son or grandson. In the view of this somewhat inward-looking and tenuously organized church the pope was little more than an object of vague and remote veneration. By 1200 the self-consciously styled *ecclesia Scoticana* consisted of eleven territorial dioceses each ruled by a bishop who since 1192 had had to visit the papal curia to be confirmed in his office. The faithful were allocated to parishes with fixed boundaries. Groups of parishes formed 'deaneries of Christianity', and in each of the two largest bishoprics of St Andrews and Glasgow groups of deaneries constituted two archdeaconries. Marriage among the lesser clergy, and heritable livings, had not yet been eliminated, but the end of these practices was in sight. Parochial incumbents were supposed to be priests and the crown ensured the effectiveness of a parish system by enforcing the payment of teinds or tithes, the tax of 10 per cent of the annual increase of domesticated plants (corn, hay etc.) and animals. Already by the middle of David I's reign the pope's commands were being taken seriously by clergy and laity; by the 1160s Scottish bishops were being appointed papal legates; and in 1192, by the bull of Celestine III known as *Cum universi Christi*, the entire Scottish church (save for the diocese of Galloway, attached by ancient tradition to York) was uniquely made the 'special daughter' of the Roman see, with no ecclesiastical authority holding an intermediate role between the pope and the Scottish bishops.

Dramatic as these changes were – and they amounted to nothing less than the gathering of isolated Scottish Christianity within the fold of the papal-dominated western Catholic church – they probably came second in the popular mind to the introduction of Benedictine monasticism and other continental forms of conventual life. This was overwhelmingly the work of the monarchy, inspired by the example of Queen Margaret who had brought the first Benedictine monks to Scotland, from the cathedral monastery of Canterbury, in the 1080s. The church she founded at Dunfermline, which became an abbey in 1128, was the inspiration rather than the model for the religious communities established by Margaret's sons Alexander I and especially David I. They favoured newer 'reformed' orders such as the Augustinians, Tironensians and Cistercians, and by the end of Malcolm IV's reign (1165) a score of monasteries had been founded by the crown and a few great magnates from the English border to the Moray Firth. Monks and canons regular acquired vast landed estates and applied advanced techniques to their management and exploitation. Arable cultivation, fisheries and the production of salt and coal were all given a powerful boost by monastic enterprise. But what the Cistercians of Melrose and Newbattle, the Tironensians of Kelso and the Augustinians of Jedburgh and Holyrood especially excelled in was the breeding and rearing of sheep whose fleeces were of sufficient quality to sell to advantage on the Flemish market.

It can hardly be doubted that twelfth-century Scotland gained in peace and stability from the good fortune of a largely undisputed succession of strong kings. The shocks and strains consequent upon the Norman Conquest of England were cushioned by the native Scottish dynasty, and more profoundly it may be argued that the heterogeneity of Scotland even before the Norman advent made it easier, not harder, for the dynasty to encourage so much drastic innovation and at the same time keep its sights fixed steadily on the target of a unified *regnum Scotorum*. However strange it may seem, William the Lion died in the odour of sanctity. Thirty-five years later the canonization of his great-grandmother Margaret set the seal of religious respectability upon the labours of the twelfth-century monarchy.

WALES

In many fundamental respects, Wales resembled Scotland. Innumerable kindred groups governed by agnatic relationships composed the dominant class to which the words 'free' and 'noble' could be applied indistinguishably. Along with their slaves and dependent peasantry or bondmen, the communities of

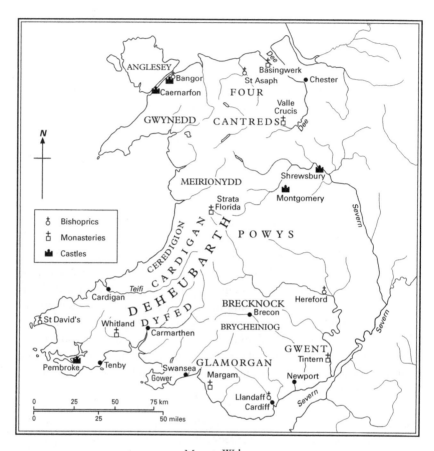

Map 14 Wales

free kindreds lived in scattered townships established across the limited areas of lowland plain (Anglesey, Glamorgan and parts of the south-western peninsula) and in the sheltered valleys of the hillier or mountainous country which made up the rest of Wales. The typical basic unit of settlement was the *tref* or homestead, usually consisting of a permanent nucleus of dwellings, byres, a mill and perhaps a chapel sited on lower or sheltered ground, where humans and stock would over-winter, together with an area of upland grazing occupied, especially by women, children and older men, in the summer months so that cattle, sheep and pigs could get the fullest benefit of the short growing season for hill grass. The permanent valley settlement was the *hendref* ('old homestead'), while the hill shieling, where structures for habitation might be temporary, was called *hafod* or *hafoty*. A larger unit, implying lordship over free and unfree was the *maenol* or *maenor*, composed of around a dozen *trefi*, while a dozen *maenolau* would make up a *cantref* (Anglicized as cantred), the standard district throughout most of Wales for the purposes of royal or princely government. In the twelfth century, however, Wales did not form, and indeed never had formed, a single kingdom. Wales, after all, was simply the largest area (others were English and Scottish Cumbria and Cornwall) from which the Anglo-Saxon invaders of the fifth and sixth centuries had failed to dislodge and supplant the existing Brittonic population. The Welsh were acutely conscious of constituting, with a few other groups, the last of the Britons, preserving and handing down traditions of Christianity and even of *romanitas* which long antedated the culture of the barbarian and hated *Saeson* or Saxon. But in reality there was nothing in Wales of *romanitas* save the surviving remains of Roman fortresses, towns and roads.

It is conceivable that in one or two places (e.g. Old Carmarthen, east of the medieval borough) the site of a Roman town had continued as a place for trade or seasonal fairs. But in general the organization of Welsh society was hostile to the formation of genuinely urban communities. Such settlements, formally definable as boroughs, inhabited by burgesses enjoying trading privileges and the protection afforded by a castle and perhaps an earthwork or stone *enceinte*, can only be seen to emerge in Wales from the end of the eleventh century. They were the work of 'English' invaders and colonizers, and for long were regarded with suspicion and even hatred by the Welsh, even though in periods of peace they took advantage of the trading opportunities provided. Thus in the south such boroughs as Brecon and Newport, both on the River Usk, Cardiff on the Taff, Swansea on the Tawe, Carmarthen on the Tywi and (probably) Tenby came into being through the deliberate planning of incoming Anglo-Norman feudatories such as Braose, fitz Hamo, Beaumont or Clare. The urban element in twelfth-century Wales should not be underestimated, although for long the boroughs remained small, inward-looking and markedly on the defensive.

The Welsh, united culturally by their use of a P-Celtic version of the common Celtic family of languages, were a pastoral people organized in clans, recognizing the superior chiefship or lordship of a number of warring dynasties each of which would claim the right to provide a king or prince over a distinct *gwlad* ('country'), a term difficult to define but most easily understood when applied to the best-known and longest enduring of such territories, Mon (Anglesey), Gwynedd, Powys, Brycheiniog (Brecknock), Morgannwg (Glamorgan), Ceredigion (Cardigan) and Dyfed. These geographical divisions reflected the fact that Wales is composed of big mountain massifs, hill plateaux and spiny ridges intersected by many river valleys and long tidal estuaries. A ruler powerful enough to command a *gwlad* or group of *gwladoedd* in the north – Anglesey, Gwynedd and the 'Four Cantreds' further east, for example – could seldom hope to assert any permanent lordship over the south of Wales, with which his lines of communication were very poor. And vice versa: a warlord dynasty might rise to power in Deheubarth ('the southern part') but could make no impression on the north. The most that northern or southern princes could normally hope to achieve was to exert control over the middle countries of Meirionydd, Ceredigion or Powys, and for this control they were frequently rivals.

To a much greater degree than Scotland, Wales had felt the impact of the Norman invasion of England. Within ten years of the battle of Hastings Norman warriors had established powerful lordships and built massive castles along the uncertain border between Wales and England and had penetrated far into indisputably Welsh territory. By 1102, the three buffer-states created by William the Conqueror to guard against Welsh attacks – and also as springboards from which a Norman advance into Wales could be launched – had been reduced to one: Hereford and Shrewsbury had been eliminated, leaving only Chester as the principal bastion of English royal aggression. On the southern march of Wales, in Gwent and Glamorgan, lesser barons and feudatories held lordships below the level of earldom, and pushed on steadily and unobtrusively with foreign settlement. Robert fitz Hamo laid claim to Glamorgan, Bernard of Neufmarché to Brycheiniog, and Gilbert fitz Richard of Clare to Ceredigion far in the west. In mid-Wales the lesser followers of the great family of Montgomery, disgraced and dispossessed in 1102, held fast to their frontier castleries and penetrated into Welsh cantreds on the upper Severn and Dee. From Chester Hugh of Avranches (d. 1101) followed up the pioneering conquests of his cousin Robert 'of Rhuddlan' and built castles as far west as Bangor and Caernarfon. At the outset of the twelfth century it must have seemed that Wales was poised on the brink of a thoroughgoing and permanent Norman conquest.

It was not to be. In some ways the twelfth century may be seen as an heroic age for Wales, and in respect of cultural and national identity it was unquestionably an age of great achievements. At least three Welsh rulers of the century, Gruffydd ap Cynan and his son Owain (Owain Gwynedd) in north Wales and Rhys ap Gruffydd (usually known as the Lord Rhys) in the south, achieved a measure of independence vis-à-vis English kings and Anglo-Norman marcher lords. Their kingly status was admittedly not to be compared with that of Henry I or Henry II, or even with the status of the kings of Scots in this period. Yet the ascendancy they established in Gwynedd and Deheubarth pointed the way for the more spectacular achievements of Llywelyn ab Iorwerth ('the Great') and Llywelyn ap Gruffydd in the thirteenth century. At the very least they made it clear that in the absence of notable advances in technology no English conquest of Wales would succeed without a massive concentration of energy and resources.

Although Henry I spent much time and effort in order to assert his authority over the border lordships initiated by his father and over the Welsh princes, he achieved little more than an uneasy peace. The fall of the house of Bellême or Montgomery in 1102 created a dangerous vacuum in mid-Wales (Powys) which was filled partly by the promotion of the native ruling dynasty to a short-lived ascendancy, partly by appointing an able Norman administrator, Richard of Belmeis, as, in effect, warden of the Middle March – supported, rather oddly, by appointment as bishop of London. In southern Wales English power was exerted even more effectively, partly because of the persistent pressure of Anglo-Norman, Flemish and Breton adventurers, partly because Henry I took care to appoint men of outstanding military ability such as Gerald of Windsor to key positions, among which was the custody of Pembroke Castle, first built by Arnulf of Montgomery in the later eleventh century. On the west coast, the *gwlad* of Ceredigion was in 1110 bestowed by the English king upon Gilbert fitz Richard of Clare, who proceeded to allocate the constituent cantreds to 'Norman' followers, each securing his position as settler in hostile territory by building his own castle. Gilbert himself built the earliest motte-type fortresses near Llanbadarn (Tanycastell, south of Aberystwyth) and at Din Geraint (Cardigan), at the mouth of the Teifi. He was succeeded in 1117 by his son Richard who held Ceredigion until the death of Henry I prompted the most successful Welsh revolt since 1094.

Even a strong king such as Henry I could not impose calm upon the Welsh situation for more than a few months at a time. In 1114 Henry found it necessary to lead an expedition to north Wales where Gruffydd ap Cynan, scion of the ancient dynasty of Rhodri Mawr (d. 878), was steadily building up a kingship to rival that of his great eleventh-century namesake Gruffydd ap Llywelyn. The English king himself advanced through Powys while the earl of Chester and Alexander I of Scotland (clearly acting on this occasion as Henry's vassal) led a force along the northern coastal route. Although there were no open hostilities, the Welsh rulers submitted and Gruffydd was forced to pay a heavy fine to be restored to Henry I's peace. Seven years later Henry again invaded mid-Wales and subdued Maredudd ap Bleddyn upon whom the English king imposed the severe penalty of 10,000 head of cattle. By dint of maintaining peaceable relations with the English crown while at the same time taking advantage of strife and rivalries among the neighbouring Welsh rulers, Gruffydd, who died in 1137, was able to hand over a substantially enlarged kingdom of Gwynedd to his heirs, especially to his eldest son Owain, known simply (to distinguish him from a contemporary prince of Powys of the same name) as Owain Gwynedd.

The English (by 1135 it makes little sense to call them 'Normans' or even 'Anglo-Normans') seem to have been completely unprepared for what happened in Wales as soon as the news came of Henry I's death. On New Year's day 1136 a native prince from Brycheiniog inflicted a startling defeat upon the English settlers in Gower. This was a signal for a general uprising. The ruler of

Deheubarth, Gruffydd ap Rhys, appealed to Gwynedd for aid to rid the south of foreign oppressors. Richard fitz Gilbert lord of Ceredigion was slain in ambush and the forces of Gwynedd over-ran Richard's lordship and razed the castles of himself and his supporters. Stimulated by these successes the Welsh from almost every *gwlad* joined the revolt. The decisive engagement took place at Crug Mawr north of Cardigan early in October. A well-armed English army recruited from south Wales and led by the sons of Gerald of Windsor was routed with great slaughter by the native levies under Owain Gwynedd. Inept fumbling by Stephen and those he deputed to restore English royal authority allowed the Welsh to consolidate the gains they had made. Gruffydd ap Rhys died in 1137 leaving young sons. In consequence the initiative passed to Owain Gwynedd who took Ceredigion into a northern ambit. From north to south the marcher lords who represented the front line of English settlement fell back, losing castles and territory. The outbreak of war in England towards the end of 1139 did not complicate matters as much as might have been expected. Most of the marcher lords took their cue from the most powerful magnate among them, Robert earl of Gloucester, who was the Empress Matilda's half-brother and principal supporter. In the later 1140s there had been some modest recovery of English positions, especially in the middle marches and in Dyfed (the region around Carmarthen). But by and large a revived Welsh ascendancy, under the aegis of Owain Gwynedd, prevailed throughout much of Wales – save for Glamorgan and the south-east – until the early years of Henry II's reign.

In some respects the spirit of independence which swept through the Welsh ruling classes in 1136 also took hold among the clergy. Claims were put forward vigorously in the 1140s for St David's, the oldest of the Welsh bishoprics and the principal church of south-west Wales, to be recognized by the papacy as metropolitan, on a footing of equality with Canterbury and York. The efforts of Bishop Bernard (1115–48) failed, but claims for Demetian primacy were to be revived at the end of the twelfth century by Gerald of Wales (Giraldus Cambrensis), a direct descendant of Gerald of Windsor. Welshmen were appointed as bishops in the dioceses of Bangor and even Llandaff, but the newly created see of St Asaph, serving north-east Wales, may be seen as a deliberate extension of English influence. The Cistercian Order took root in Wales during the period when national revival was at its height. Although several of the Order's houses, for example Tintern, founded from L'Aumône as early as 1131, or Basingwerk (also 1131 and originally Savignac), were always very closely under marcher influence, many others, especially the family branching out from Whitland (1140), a daughter house of Clairvaux, quickly became identified with Welsh culture and aspirations. The family of Whitland was the most widely ramified throughout Wales, offshoots being established at Cwm

Hir, Strata Florida, Strata Marcella, Cymer, Llantarnam, Aberconwy and Valle Crucis, while Margam (1147) was Whitland's sister house.

The second half of the twelfth century saw the establishment of a north Welsh dominance which was to persist until the overthrow of independent Welsh rule in the later thirteenth century. The pre-eminence of the southern prince Rhys ap Gruffydd ('the Lord Rhys') from 1170 to 1197 may appear to contradict this statement. Rhys's power, however, was personal and owed much to the trust placed in him by Henry II. After his death the marcher lords were able to reassert their domination of Gwent, Glamorgan, Gower and Pembroke. In so far as Welsh national aspirations had a focus it was to be found in Gwynedd and specifically in the dynasty of Gruffydd ap Cynan.

Northern Welsh power had been built up during the 'Anarchy', helped by a vacillating English king and an earl of Chester far more interested in his English ambitions than in his Welsh frontier. With Henry of Anjou firmly in the saddle Owain Gwynedd was forced to adopt a different strategy. It is true that the English royal expedition against him in 1157 went badly wrong, but Owain prudently did homage, surrendered hostages and, more seriously, gave up his control of Tegeingl (Flint). Henry's next attempt to assert English authority in Wales, in 1163, was directed against mid- and south Wales. By 1155, one son alone, Rhys, survived of the offspring of Gruffydd ap Rhys of Dyfed, and he had succeeded in expanding the lordship of southern Wales until it reached from the Bristol Channel to the River Dovey. But in 1158 he had accepted English overlordship and surrendered much conquered territory, including Ceredigion which was reclaimed by the house of Clare. In 1163 Henry advanced through south Wales to the borders of Ceredigion where Rhys ap Gruffydd submitted and was led into England virtually as Henry's prisoner. In July he did homage to Henry at Woodstock, along with Owain of Gwynedd and Malcolm IV of Scotland. The long quarrel between Henry and Thomas Becket allowed the Welsh to throw off Angevin control. In 1165 Gwynedd and Deheubarth combined in a full-scale revolt against crown and marcher lords alike. Henry II's army entered Wales in early August north of the Severn valley and struck westward towards the Berwyn range. The weather proved appalling, the heavily armed horse and more lightly equipped infantry floundered in impassable bogs and ran perilously short of food. The king withdrew with his host to Shrewsbury and never again attempted to subdue the Welsh by military force.

Until his death in 1170 Owain Gwynedd pursued a statesmanlike policy, acknowledging Angevin overlordship yet keeping it at a distance by refusing to carry out provocative strikes against the English crown or sensitive marcher baronies. The full measure of his achievement was only to show itself at the end of the century, when his grandson Llywelyn ab Iorwerth ('Llywelyn the Great') successfully asserted his claim to rule over the enlarged Gwynedd built up by

Owain and went on to create the closest approximation to a native kingdom of Wales which there was ever to be. For almost thirty years after Owain's death, however, ascendancy among the Welsh passed to the south. In the later 1160s Rhys ap Gruffydd was shrewd enough to take full advantage of the situation unfolding in Ireland. The king of Leinster's appeal to Henry II for military help against his Irish enemies opened the way for many marcher lords in southern Wales to try their luck across the sea. They hoped to compensate themselves for the loss of territory they had suffered in Wales since the beginning of Stephen's reign. For his part Henry II was content to make an apparently loyal Rhys the English crown's chief supporter in south Wales. On his way to Ireland in autumn 1171 Henry confirmed Rhys in possession of the extensive territories (especially Ceredigion) which the Welsh had recovered in 1165. On his return to Britain, in 1172, he appointed Rhys 'justiciar of south Wales' effectively placing him in charge of all the lesser princes of Deheubarth. The Lord Rhys repaid the king's favour by supporting him loyally in the great rebellion of 1173–4. The relative peacefulness of Wales was demonstrated at Christmas 1176 when an *eisteddfod* was held at Rhys's newly built castle at Aberteifi (Cardigan) to which poets, singers and musicians were invited not only from Wales but also from England, Scotland and Ireland. Rhys's ascendancy was to last for another two decades, but his last years were darkened by strife among his own sons and by a marked deterioration in his relations with the English crown. Nevertheless, it has to be said that in Wales, scarcely less than in Scotland, the twelfth century saw the arrest, and in some important ways the reversal, of a major historical process. From 1066 individuals and families of continental (especially Norman) origin had penetrated far into the island of Britain, acquiring kingship, lordship and land. From 1169 they were to repeat the process in Ireland. In Scotland the development of a strong feudally organized kingdom had retarded and radically modified this process. In Wales a succession of outstandingly able native rulers, supported by a powerful and articulate resurgence of national feeling and culture, had likewise been able to apply a brake to the 'Norman' tide. The result was to be two countries, marcher Wales and Welsh Wales (*pura Wallia*), producing consequences which have lasted to our own times.

IRELAND

In Irish history the twelfth century must always be the age of conquest, the momentous turning-point when English adventurers, mostly belonging to families of Norman, Flemish, Breton or other continental background, exploited their military skills and techniques to acquire kingdoms and trading towns in the south of Ireland. Their freelance attempts gave the monarchy of Henry II the opportunity, seized without delay, to assert an explicit claim to suzerainty in

Map 15 Ireland, *c.* 1160

Ireland. This in turn led to the establishment by 1185 of an Angevin lordship of Ireland, nominally held by Henry II's youngest son John, and in principle embracing the entire island. The Angevin or (as it would better be called) English conquest of Ireland ought not to obscure the fundamental process of reorientation which Irish society had begun to experience by the third quarter of the eleventh century and which continued during the twelfth. The isolation of Ireland must not be exaggerated. In the Viking era the island had been plundered again and again by Scandinavian raiding parties. In the course of

time a few carefully selected coastal sites at the mouths of important rivers –
Dublin, Wexford, Waterford, Cork and Limerick – were permanently settled
by 'Ostmen', Danes and Norwegians for the most part, whose careers as part-
time merchants, part-time pirates led them to establish small trading towns of a
type previously unknown in Ireland. The Ostmen communities represented a
significant element of foreign influence and provided an avenue through which
alien ideas, commodities, fashions and individuals could gain a foothold in a
country noted for its social conservatism.

Ireland, lying on the north-western edge of Christian Europe, was in many
respects favoured by nature. Abundance of pasture for cattle and sheep, abundance of peat for fuel, abundance of oak and other woods to provide pannage
for pigs, abundance of game (even though wolves and foxes were not uncommon), abundance of salmon and trout in lochs and rivers, a sufficiency in many
regions of land fit for tillage – all this, with a population scarcely pressing at the
margins of survival, made for an internally self-sufficient, prosperous economy.
A prevailing mild climate admittedly went hand in hand with a high average
rainfall, and the country was certainly not free from visitations of disease af-
flicting humans and animals alike. But although luxuries such as wine, fine
cloth and precious metals had to be imported, Ireland possessed the resources
necessary to support comfortably, in most years, a simple and healthy way of
life. Human fertility seems to have been at a high level, the universal practice
of polygamy producing an endless supply of male and female offspring. It may,
indeed, be no exaggeration to say that the ruling order in Ireland, a warrior
aristocracy not far removed from the later Iron Age in its culture and outlook,
had too easy a time of it, and were too ready to indulge in inter-tribal warfare
and competition for cattle, slaves, land and prestige.

It was particularly in matters relating to the church and especially to ecclesiastical organization that Ireland became receptive to external influences by the
middle of the eleventh century. Irish notables had gone to Rome as pilgrims,
Irish clerics had corresponded with the churches of Canterbury and Worcester.
Significantly, there were links between Canterbury and the episcopal see established at Dublin by one of the Ostmen kings who had travelled to Rome as a
pilgrim. A priest named Patrick had been consecrated bishop of Dublin in 1074
by Lanfranc, the archbishop appointed by William the Conqueror. His two
successors had been monks at English Benedictine monasteries, the second of
them consecrated by Archbishop Anselm. It is evident that as far as Britain and
Ireland were concerned the church of Canterbury, secure in its possession of
the primacy of 'all Britain', was more consciously and consistently imperialist
than the post-Conquest English monarchy. The church of York, with its claims
to supremacy over the Scottish sees, was hardly less imperialist in its outlook.
The problem for Irish bishops and other clergy who had personal experience

of the papacy and the church of western Christendom generally, including England, was that they earnestly wished to carry through a drastic reform and reorganization of their own church without simultaneously paving the way for an intrusive domination by English archbishops.

As it was, both Lanfranc and Anselm urged reform upon high kings of Ireland, respectively Toirdelbach (Turlough) Ua Briain and his son Muirchertach, of one of the royal lines of Munster. It was the latter who convened the first of a series of councils intended to reform the Irish church along Gregorian lines. It met in 1101 at Cashel, an ancient royal site which was solemnly handed over to the church by King Muirchertach free of all secular burdens. Maolísu Ua hAinmire 'chief bishop of Munster' presided over the council explicitly as papal legate. The business embraced the liberation of the clergy from lay control, clerical celibacy and privileges, the de-tribalizing of the ancient monasteries and an attack, which was to prove quite unsuccessful, upon the immemorial and clearly un-Christian Irish marriage customs, which permitted concubinage, wife-swapping and easy divorce. A dramatic consequence of the council of Cashel was the decision of Cellach, hereditary coarb ('heir' of St Patrick) of the monastery of Armagh, to become ordained and consecrated as priest and bishop in 1105–6. Because of its traditional associations with St Patrick, Armagh had long enjoyed pre-eminence among Irish churches. The conversion of its hereditary leader to the reform programme was thus of the greatest significance.

Ostmen and purely Irish strains mingled when the Ua Briain dynasty of Munster made Limerick their chief place about the turn of the century. A see was established whose first holder, an Irishman named Gilla Espuic (englished as Gilbert), threw himself vigorously into the cause of reform. He acted as papal legate for over a quarter of a century and wrote a treatise on ecclesiastical order. He was a friend of Anselm without allowing his church to become subordinate to Canterbury. Under his direction the clergy of all Ireland, north and south, met at Rathbreasail, near Cashel, in 1111, and promulgated legislation which inaugurated a fundamental restructuring of the Irish church. Traditionally, Ireland had been divided into two parts, north ('Conn's Half', *Leth Cuinn*) and south ('Mogh's Half', *Leth Moga*), the notional boundary running approximately from Galway Bay across to Dublin. Armagh was indisputably the chief church of the northern province and Cashel now took the leading place in the south. To Armagh were assigned twelve bishoprics, in addition to its own, and to Cashel ten. Because of its close link with Canterbury the status of the see of Dublin was left in the air. Twenty-five dioceses (soon to be twenty-six when Clonmacnoise was added) were clearly too many, yet the figure represented a drastic reduction from the total in earlier times. Archbishop Cellach of Armagh died in 1129 and was succeeded not by the candidate put forward by

his own clan, Ui Sinaich, who had monopolized the church since 996, but by
the learned monk and teacher Maol Maodoc Ua Morgair (St Malachy), who
was passionately committed to the cause of reform. For almost twenty years,
till his death in 1148, Malachy steered the Irish church by example and exhor-
tation, introducing at Armagh the use of liturgical music, regular confession,
confirmation and marriage as a religious sacrament. As bishop of Down and
Connor before 1129 Malachy had already reformed the old monastery of Bangor
as an Augustinian house; in 1140 he paid a visit to Rome, travelling by way
of Clairvaux and becoming the firm friend of St Bernard. The introduction
of the Cistercian order into Ireland, of the utmost importance for the success of church reform, resulted from this journey. Mellifont, beside Drogheda,
founded in 1142, was the first of a family of no fewer than twenty-one Cistercian
abbeys spread across Ireland mainly in Meath, Leinster and Munster, but also
appearing in Ulster and Connacht, all founded before 1230. Until the thirteenth century the order played a notable part in furtherance of ecclesiastical
reform. Mellifont itself, consecrated in 1157, when it was the largest church
so far to be built in Ireland, represented the outward and physical aspect of
reform and innovation. Malachy's zeal for reform, however, did not confine
itself to Cistercian channels. He grasped the relevance of the Augustinian way
of life for Irish society, and under his auspices old churches were turned over
to communities of Augustinian canons, and new houses were founded, so that
over sixty monasteries of this order had come into existence before the English
invasion. All this reforming activity brought foreign influences into the island,
pointing church and clergy, if hardly yet the laity, in a markedly more Roman
direction. One fascinating example of foreign influence was the decision by
Irish monks in some of the *Schottenklöster* ('Irish monasteries') in southern
Germany to come back to their homeland and bring Benedictine monachism
with them. Thus in the 1130s monks from Würzburg established a house at
Cashel.

The culminating point in the movement of church reform came in 1151–2,
some years after Malachy's death but very much under his impetus. A papal
legate, Cardinal John Paparo, came to Ireland in response to a request sent
to the papacy by the kings and clergy, and convened a great synod which
held sessions in Meath at Kells and, probably, at Mellifont. A comprehensive
programme of reforming legislation was promulgated, addressed mainly to
the issues of simony, the law of marriage and sexual irregularities and the
payment of tithes, which was an essential precondition for an effective parochial
system. But the synod of Kells is chiefly remembered for establishing the
provincial and diocesan system which prevailed until the sixteenth century
and later. Cardinal Paparo brought no fewer than four *pallia* (the strips of
cloth symbolizing metropolitan authority). There were to be archbishops at

Armagh (for Ulster and Meath, but also, as primate, for all Ireland), Cashel (for Munster), Tuam (for Connacht) and, somewhat controversially in view of Armagh's claim, Dublin (for Leinster). Altogether, some thirty-seven sees were homologated by Kells, and although the next half-century saw a number of modifications to the pattern, the diocesan structure of the Irish church remained broadly that which the synod accepted. The addition of Tuam took account of the power enjoyed by the Ua Conchobair dynasty in Connacht, while Dublin's promotion recognized the importance of the Ostman city and the Leinster kingship, and was made more acceptable to conservative Irish clergy by the consecration as second archbishop (1162) of Lorcan Ua Tuathail (St Laurence O Toole) who has been called 'a prelate in the Malachian mould', and who happened to be the king of Leinster's brother-in-law.

A small number of highly placed clergy were sufficient to steer the Irish church as a whole in the direction of the Gregorian reforms, in particular the separation of the clerical from the lay elements in society, the liberation of the church from secular control and the establishment of an orderly ecclesiastical hierarchy. No parallel development of any significance took place within the ruling orders of secular society. In the century following the Norman Conquest of England the Irish warrior aristocracy remained largely impervious to external influences. In Ireland (as in Wales) a large class of free or noble lineages, closely bound by ties of agnatic kinship, competed for land, power and prestige. It has been estimated that around 170–80 nobles in twelfth-century Ireland could claim the style of *rígh*, 'king'. In the case of the vast majority this meant no more than that individuals so styled were recognized as chiefs of their lineage, at best exercising some political authority over a small district which might represent the *tuath* or 'tribe' of more remote periods. Their own lineage did not necessarily monopolize the territory of such a district, but every king was expected to defend the interests of his own clan, and if a lineage expanded a king's grandsons and great-grandsons might well elbow out any rival freeholders who did not belong to the clan, even if they were dependants and adherents. A militarily successful king at the head of a rapidly growing clan might well seize fresh territory from his neighbours or from further afield; and all the more powerful kings were expected as a matter of course to undertake great 'hostings' or plundering raids, often traversing many miles of country and penetrating deep into the territory of a rival ruler in search of cattle, pigs and slaves.

The ruling order was supported by an underclass, of indeterminate size, consisting of peasants actually holding land, serfs living very much at the will of their lords and outright slaves, often bought from markets such as Bristol. Just as, in a society so highly compartmentalized as that of Ireland, there were hereditary castes of kings, clerics, judges, learned poets and historians, so also there were hereditary castes of bondmen, tied for ever to a monastic church or royal house. Some of these *biataigh* ('food providers'), as they were known, were substantial enough to have their own plough teams and to be burdened with relatively light labour services in addition to the inevitable food renders and forced hospitality. But the chief occupation of the peasantry must have been the tending of cattle, pigs and sheep, the staple of Irish food production. The *biataigh* survived recognizably until the fourteenth century, but long before that the English invaders had brought in a peasant class from Wales and England, whose function was to intensify the arable cultivation of large areas of Meath and the lowland parts of Leinster and Munster.

At the summit of the shallow broad-based pyramid of kings were some six or seven rulers whose lineages had acquired dominant positions in the ancient provincial divisions of Ireland. Since there were traditionally five of these provinces, Ulster, Connacht, Meath, Leinster and Munster, there should have been no more than five provincial royal lineages, the 'five royal bloods (races)' as they were known in later times. But splitting and rivalry had led to two competing families claiming chief place in both Ulster and Munster, while there were dynasties in kingdoms of somewhat less than provincial standing, such as Breifne (Leitrim and north-west Cavan), Airgialla (Monaghan and Armagh), or Tir Conaill (Donegal), which if opportunity offered might make a bid for higher kingship. The relationship of these royal houses at the top of Irish society might be said to have been characterized by a stable state of flux. At the outset of the twelfth century a degree of supremacy throughout Ireland was enjoyed by the Ui Briain (O Brian) kings of Munster, two of whom, Toirdelbach (d. 1086) and his son Muirchertach, held the high kingship in succession. After the latter lost his kingly power in 1116, the chief of the branch of the Northern Ui Neill (O Neills) ruling over Aileach (north Donegal), Domnall MacLochlainn, briefly became high king, but by 1122 the king of Connacht, Toirdelbach Ua Conchobair (O Connor), rose to power after a period of destructive raids against his neighbours both south and north and, quite exceptionally, held the high kingship 'without opposition' for thirty-four years. For the next ten years (1156–66) the position reverted to the Ui Lochlainn of the north, in the person of Muirchertach MacLochlainn. On the eve of the English invasions Muirchertach was brought low and finally slain as a result of his own treachery and cruelty, and the chief of the Ui Conchobair, Ruaidri (Rory), made himself high king, but only 'with opposition'.

High kingship was essentially a matter of prestige; the position conferred hardly any concrete powers on its holder, save that deference would be shown, and if any decisions affecting the whole island were required (including its defence from external attack) it would be expected that the high king would take the initiative. Power was acquired by great 'hostings'; it was maintained by the immemorial custom of keeping hostages, usually the sons or other kindred of potentially hostile kings. Rulers who persisted in being recalcitrant might be blinded or otherwise mutilated, and the same cruelties were often practised upon brothers or cousins of a reigning king. Traditionally, it was the high kings who convened the famous Fair of Táiltiu (Teltown in Meath), a great gathering of all Ireland where bardic poetry and song mingled with barter and trade and where important judgements were pronounced and irregular marriages were entered into.

The elevation of MacLochlainn to the high kingship (consolidated in 1161) strengthened the position of his ally the king of Leinster, Diarmaid MacMurchada (Dermot Macmurrough). Between them they established the saintly Lorcan Ua Tuathail, Diarmaid's brother-in-law, in the archdiocese of Dublin. Dublin, under its own petty ruler, acknowledged Diarmaid as 'over king' and MacLochlainn as even higher. Inspired by tales of ancestral prowess preserved in the great story-cycles in whose collection Leinster's learned men were especially active, Diarmaid sought to exalt the position of his kin and province. He successfully attacked Ostmen seaports such as Waterford and rival but subordinate kings in north Leinster. Aware that his strongest enemies were the kings of Connacht and their dependants, the rulers of Breifne, he allied himself to MacLochlainn: in 1152 the beautiful wife of the king of Breifne, Dervorguilla, had arranged for Diarmaid to carry her off to Leinster as his mistress, a grave affront to the dignity of her husband Tighernan Ua Ruairc (O Rourke).

The hatred which Muirchertach MacLochlainn aroused among lesser northern rulers in Ulaidh or Ulidia (north-east Ulster) and Airgialla led to his overthrow and death in battle in 1166. The Connacht star was now in the ascendant, and although Dervorguilla had long since returned to Ua Ruairc, Tighernan seized the opportunity to attack Leinster in force, assisted by Diarmaid Ua Maelsechlainn (O Melaghlin) king of Meath. Diarmaid MacMurchada's chief seat at Ferns was devastated, and Diarmaid himself, despairing of finding any allies in Ireland, fled to Bristol where he was befriended by the chief burgess Robert fitz Harding. The king of Leinster sought out Henry II in Gascony, did homage and requested assistance to recover his inheritance. Henry had harboured thoughts of Irish conquest since the beginning of his reign when Pope Adrian IV had authorized an English conquest of Ireland in the famous bull *Laudabiliter*, accompanied by a symbolic emerald ring. In 1166, however, Henry merely issued letters inviting his lieges to come to Diarmaid's succour. A year after fleeing Ireland Diarmaid returned with a mere handful of Flemish adventurers from Pembrokeshire. But he had made a fateful bargain with the earl of Pembroke, Richard fitz Gilbert of Clare, known as 'Strongbow', whereby the earl would bring an army to conquer Leinster, receiving Diarmaid's daughter Aoife (Eva) to wife and with her – quite improperly in terms of Irish law – the succession to the kingdom of Leinster.

Another year passed before Diarmaid's plans began to mature. In May 1169 a substantial force of 'Norman' feudatories from south Wales, led by Maurice of Prendergast and Robert fitz Stephen, sailed to Bannow Bay between Waterford and Wexford, promptly capturing the latter town. They then secured most of Leinster for Diarmaid but had to confront a great hosting by Ua Conchobair, who was anxious to assert his overlordship and also to rid Ireland of the dangerous foreigners. The high king made Diarmaid promise to bring over no additional troops and to repatriate those already in Ireland as soon as Leinster was fully under Diarmaid's control. Thus matters rested until the spring of 1170, when Maurice fitz Gerald (fitz Stephen's half-brother) and Raymond 'le Gros' of Carew came over with reinforcements, as an advance party for Strongbow. The earl himself, with a much larger force of knights, men-at-arms and archers, landed near Waterford in August, took the city by storm and soon afterwards married King Diarmaid's daughter. The English conquest may be dated from these events, although it still had a long way to go. Dublin was seen by the invaders as an essential goal. Not only was it the chief urban settlement of Ireland, it had acquired some of the characteristics of a capital; and it has been remarked that no one made himself high king without securing the loyalty and support of the men of Dublin. Strongbow and Diarmaid (aspiring to the high kingship) accordingly laid siege to Dublin, evading the sprawling, undisciplined army brought to its rescue by Ruaidri Ua Conchobair. The city fell to a surprise attack (21 September 1170) and in the following summer the tables were turned as an immense host, drawn by the king of Connacht from almost every part of the island, encamped to the west of Dublin, awaiting a sea-borne attack upon the English garrison by Scandinavians from the isles rallying to the cause of their Ostmen kindred. Against all the odds Strongbow's knights and archers put the Irish host to flight with great slaughter and also destroyed the much better-disciplined and better-equipped Norse army. With these victories the earl of Pembroke and his followers had effectively conquered Ireland, not for Diarmaid, who died in May 1171, and not even for themselves, but for their lord, Henry II.

The king crossed to Waterford on 17 October 1171 with some 4,000 troops, including 500 cavalry. No native Irish host could have withstood such a force, but Henry's purpose seems rather to have been a public assertion of sovereignty. Many kings and lesser chiefs submitted, following the lead given by the two kings of Munster, MacCarthy of Desmond and Ua Briain (O Brien) of Thomond. Strongbow had prudently surrendered all his conquests. He received Leinster back as a fief, not a kingdom, to be held for 100 knights' service, and without the Ostmen cities of Dublin, Wexford and Waterford which with their hinterlands were kept as crown demesne. Meath was given to Hugh of Lacy for fifty knights, along with the office of justiciar. No attempt was made to enforce the submission of Ua Conchobair the high king, or of the north-western potentates Ua Neill of Aileach, and Ua Domhnaill of Tir Conaill (Donegal). In 1175 Ua Conchobair agreed to the treaty of Windsor, which placed him in a clearly subordinate position, holding Connacht for annual tribute. He was allowed an ill-defined lordship over such Irish kings as were not already subject to English rule, making himself responsible for the regular payment of their tribute.

Henry II spent the winter of 1171–2 in Ireland, entering Dublin at Martinmas (11 November) and lodging in a 'palace' built of wattle and thatch in the Irish style. He was open-handed towards the Irish kings and suspicious of the free-lance adventurers who had preceded him. Delayed by stormy weather, he eventually returned to Britain on 17 April 1172. His most enduring achievement had been to give a decisive change of direction to the reform movement in the church. A synod assembled at Cashel while Henry was still in Ireland. It reiterated and confirmed reform measures agreed by earlier councils, but significantly concluded with an undertaking to adopt the church in England as the model for Irish religious life. From 1181 the archbishops of Dublin were invariably English and the see itself, though unable to oust Armagh from its primacy, came increasingly to assume an ecclesiastical status parallel to the secular role of Dublin as the seat of Angevin royal government. A series of powerfully worded letters from Pope Alexander III reinforced *Laudabiliter* and set the church's seal of approval on the Henrician conquest.

Three themes predominated in Irish history from the Conquest till the end of the twelfth century and, indeed, till the end of King John's reign (1216). First, the Angevin monarchy sought to establish an administration for Ireland, based on Dublin and modelled on English (rather than continental) lines. In 1177 Henry II's youngest son John was made 'lord of Ireland'. Hugh of Lacy would govern in his name, as justiciar, supported by Meath which he was now to hold feudally for 100 knights' service. John visited his lordship in person in 1185, replacing Hugh of Lacy by John of Courcy and making many land grants to his followers. After John succeeded Richard I on the throne Ireland was assimilated more decisively to the English model. Dublin Castle was built as government's headquarters, royal courts and a fiscal and financial system were established, while a reproduction of English law came into force, soon to be known as the 'Customs of Ireland'. A second theme, closely connected with the first, was provided by the crown's suspicion and jealousy of the nobler English settlers, towards whom it pursued an ambivalent policy of encouragement by land grants and discouragement through confiscation or overt support for native Irish rulers against their would-be supplanters. Certainly the English conquest proceeded inexorably despite the treaty of Windsor. In Munster MacCarthy of Desmond and Ua Briain of Thomond were displaced with the English crown's connivance. In eastern Ulster the whole structure of native kingship was toppled by the startlingly rapid free-lance conquest carried out in 1177 by John of Courcy, who held on to his huge gains till 1205 and showed some signs of turning himself into a potentate of thoroughly indigenous type. To offset these private conquests (of which John of Courcy's was merely the largest and most dramatic), the crown appointed a series of non-settler officials, justiciars, sheriffs and the rest, who were intended to counterbalance the power of settled feudatories. The flaw in this policy lay in the fact that officials who spent more than a brief period in Ireland became effectively settlers themselves and quickly developed settler interests. The final and, as it proved, perpetual theme to dominate the history of Ireland in this period was provided by the Irish, and especially by the survivors of the ruling lineages. In the earlier 1170s the tribal kings failed to grasp the implications of Angevin overlordship. Foreigners in mail hauberks could be absorbed and assimilated, and the English crown would defend the Irish kings against further encroachment. After Strongbow's death in 1176 came severe disillusionment, as Ulster was overrun and the newcomers took over large areas of Munster, while the lower-lying and more fertile parts of Leinster and Meath become intensively feudalized. Even Connacht was attacked, though here – for almost the first time – the English were defeated and driven back. Ruaidri Ua Conchobair lived until 1199 and was buried at the monastery of Cong, near Tuam, for which the great craftsman Maelisa son of Bratan had fashioned the beautiful cross of Cong on the orders of his father Toirdelbach Ua Conchobair. At the time of Ruaidri's death, the old highly privileged, easy-living, warrior aristocracy of Ireland survived intact only in Connacht, Tir Conaill and parts of Tyrone (Cenél Eoghan). Elsewhere, power at the top had passed to foreigners, who imported their own freeholders from England and Wales, and even, in Leinster and Meath, their own peasantry. The kin-based Irish tribal groupings lived on in Leinster, Munster and eastern Ulster, but in a depressed condition and confined largely to the hillier or less fertile districts. As in Wales, so now in Ireland, Plantagenet England had succeeded only in bringing into existence two societies and cultures in the same country.

CHAPTER 20

THE BYZANTINE EMPIRE, 1118–1204

Paul Magdalino

BETWEEN the death of Alexios I and the establishment of the Latin empire of Constantinople, eight emperors ruled in the eastern Roman capital. Their reigns were as successful as they were long. Under John II (1118–43) and Manuel I (1143–80) Byzantium remained a wealthy and expansionist power, maintaining the internal structures and external initiatives which were necessary to sustain a traditional imperial identity in a changing Mediterranean world of crusaders, Turks and Italian merchants. But the minority of Manuel's son Alexios II (1180–83) exposed the fragility of the regime inaugurated by Alexios I. Lateral branches of the reigning dynasty seized power in a series of violent usurpations that progressively undermined the security of each usurper, inviting foreign intervention, provincial revolts and attempted *coups d'état*. Under Andronikos I (1183–5), Isaac II (1185–95), Alexios III (1195–1203), Alexios IV (1203–4) and Alexios V (1204), the structural features which had been the strengths of the state in the previous hundred years became liabilities. The empire's international web of clients and marriage alliances, its reputation for fabulous wealth, the overwhelming concentration of people and resources in Constantinople, the privileged status of the 'blood-royal', the cultural self-confidence of the administrative and religious elite: under strong leadership, these factors had come together to make the empire dynamic and great; out of control, they and the reactions they set up combined to make the Fourth Crusade a recipe for disaster.

The Fourth Crusade brought out the worst in the relationship between Byzantium and the west that had been developing in the century since the First Crusade; the violent conquest and sack of Constantinople expressed and deepened old hatreds, and there is clearly some sense in the standard opinion that the event confirmed beyond doubt how incompatible the two cultures had always been. Yet the Fourth Crusade also showed how central Byzantium had become to the world of opportunity that Latin Europe was discovering in the east, and how great an effort its rulers had made to use this position to advantage. Growing estrangement came from growing involvement; the

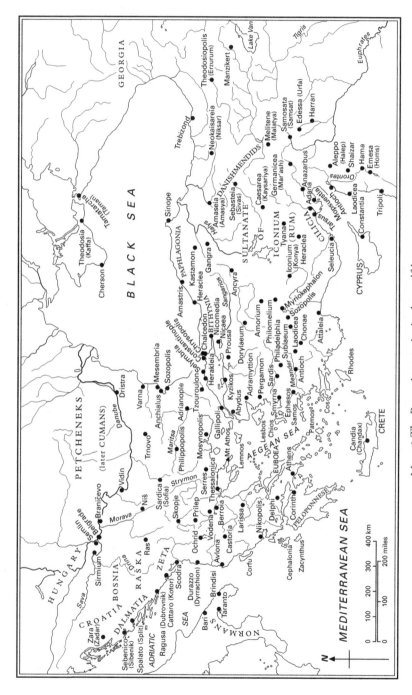

Map 16 The Byzantine empire in the twelfth century

xenophobia which manifested itself in the 1182 massacre of the Latins in Constantinople was the reverse side of the accommodation of westerners and their values taking place at all social and cultural levels. Both sides of the coin are reflected in the main source for the period, the *History* of Niketas Choniates, which combines impassioned outbursts against the Latins with idealization of individual western leaders and disapproval of his own society in terms which echo criticism of Byzantium.

SOURCES

Choniates's *History* covers the years 1118–1206. The author was a contemporary of most of the events he relates, and from about 1175 he was an increasingly close eyewitness of developments at the centre of power, first as a student and clerk in government service, then as a rising government official involved in the making and presentation of imperial policy. Such credentials, together with the power, the nuance, the acuity and the high moral tone of his narrative, make it difficult to resist seeing the period through his eyes. However, there is a growing recognition that the very qualities which make Choniates a great literary commentator on his age also make him a sophisticated manipulator of the facts to fit his picture of a decadent society being punished by Divine Providence for the excesses of its rulers and the corruption of their subjects. For the period 1118–76 his account can be balanced by the *History* of John Kinnamos, which is slightly more critical of John II and much more favourable to Manuel I, whom the author served for most of his reign. Otherwise, as for earlier and later periods of Byzantine history, the picture has to be supplemented and corrected by a wide range of other material – literary, legislative, archival, epigraphic, visual. The balance of this material partly reflects and partly determines what makes the twelfth century look distinctive. It is richer than the preceding century in high-quality information from Latin chronicles, in rhetorical celebration of emperors and in canon law collections which preserve a wealth of imperial and patriarchal rulings. The flow of documentation from Patmos and Mount Athos dries up for much of the period, though some material has been preserved from other monastic archives in Asia Minor and Macedonia, and the archives of Venice, Pisa and Genoa begin to yield substantial evidence for the movement of their merchants into Constantinople and other markets throughout the empire.

JOHN II

Alexios I left his successor with a state in good working order. Territorially it was smaller, especially in the east, than the empire of the early eleventh century, but thanks to Alexios's reforms and good management over a long reign, it was once more an effective financial and military power, and as a result of Alexios's controversial family policy, it had a structural coherence which was largely new to Byzantium. After the failure of numerous conspiracies against Alexios, the ruling family of Komnenos had established itself not only as the unchallenged source of the imperial succession, but also, in association with the Doukai, as the centre of a new princely aristocracy in which wealth, status and military command depended on kinship to the emperor and were reflected in a hierarchy of titles all of which had originally applied to the emperor. The emperor's kinsmen were in such a dominant position, and so widely connected, that for almost the first time in the empire's history the threat to the ruling dynasty from a rival faction was entirely eliminated. Instead, competition for power had moved inside the family circle. The weakness of the system was that it gave the whole imperial family a share and a stake in the imperial inheritance without providing any firm rules of precedence. Thus John II, though Alexios's eldest son and crowned co-emperor in 1092, had to contend with a serious effort by his mother Eirene to exclude him from the succession in favour of his sister Anna and her husband Nikephoros Bryennios. Only by building up his own group of loyal supporters, inside and outside the family, and making a pre-emptive strike while Alexios lay on his deathbed did John secure his claim, and only by putting those supporters into key positions did he prevent a conspiracy by Anna within a year of his accession. To gain and maintain power, the emperor had had to create his own faction. He was well served by the members of this faction, especially by John Axouch, a Turkish captive with whom he had grown up and whom he entrusted with the supreme command of the armed forces. But the promotion of these favourites played a part in causing the growth of an opposition at court. Anna and Nikephoros were no longer a threat; Nikephoros served the emperor loyally until his death in 1138, leaving Anna to nurse her grievances in writing the epic biography of her father, the *Alexiad*. However, their place as a magnet for the disaffected was taken by John's brother, the *sebastokrator* Isaac, who had supported John at their father's death, but in 1130 sought the throne for himself. When his plot was detected, he fled with his son John into exile among the empire's eastern neighbours, moving from court to court until he sought reconciliation in 1138. But his son again defected to the Turks in 1141, Isaac remained a prime political suspect and his other son, Andronikos, would later inherit his role.

John's power base in Constantinople was secure enough to allow him to leave the city on campaign year after year, but this ceaseless campaigning, in which he surpassed most of his imperial predecessors, including his father, is indicative of his need to command the loyalty of the army and to prove himself worthy of his inheritance. It was rarely necessitated by emergencies as serious as those Alexios had faced for most of his reign, and it was not clearly dictated by any pre-existing strategy of territorial expansion. Certainly, the recuperation of lost territory was high on the agenda which John took over from his father. The First Crusade had originated in a Byzantine attempt to reverse the Turkish occupation of Asia Minor and northern Syria, and for the last twenty years of his reign Alexios I had expended great military and diplomatic energies in pressing his claims to Antioch and other territories which the crusaders had appropriated. Yet over the same twenty years, the empire had learned to live with the eastern borders which Alexios had established in the wake of the crusade, and with the new Turkish dynastic states, of the Danishmendid amirs and the Seljuqid sultans, which had formed in the lost territories of central and eastern Anatolia. The empire was left in control of the coastal plains and river valleys which were the most valuable parts of Asia Minor to a ruling elite based, more than ever, on Constantinople; the loss of the Anatolian plateau and the frontier regions of northern Mesopotamia, which had been the homeland of many military families, greatly facilitated the integration of the aristocracy into the Comnenian dynastic regime. Alexios's successor thus had to strike a balance between the completion of unfinished business and the consolidation of such gains as had been made. Either way, he was expected to produce victories, and these John delivered consistently. Their propaganda value was their most lasting result, and possibly their most important objective.

The year after his accession, John took and fortified the town of Laodicea in the Meander valley; the next year he captured and garrisoned Sozopolis, on the plateau to the east. This might have been the beginning of a campaign of reconquest against the Seljuqid sultanate of Rum; on the other hand, both places lay on the land route to Attaleia, and John's later interest in this area suggests that he might have been securing his lines of communication for an expedition to Antioch. Yet if Antioch was the goal, it is surprising that John did not simultaneously revive the negotiations for a dynastic union which Alexios had been conducting at the end of his reign, especially since the disaster of the battle of the Field of Blood (1119) provided an ideal opportunity for John to offer imperial protection in return for concessions. There is no evidence that John tried to take advantage of the crisis in the Latin east, as Venice did by joining the crusading movement. Indeed, the fact that John initially refused to renew his father's treaty with Venice, and did not change his mind even in 1122, when a Venetian armada passed through Byzantine waters on its way to Palestine, suggests that the new emperor was pursuing a policy of deliberate isolationism with regard to the Latin world. Only when the Venetian fleet ravaged Chios, Samos and Modon on its return journey in 1125 did John agree to renew the treaty. This he did in 1126, acceding to two further Venetian demands.

Meanwhile, he had been forced to turn his attention from Asia to Europe by an invasion of the Petcheneks which caused great alarm but which he defeated by resolute military action in 1122. No campaigns are recorded for the next five years, during which John became occupied by diplomatic relations not only with Venice but also with Hungary, where he was connected through his wife to the ruling Árpád dynasty. In 1125 he welcomed her kinsman Almos as a refugee from the king of Hungary, Stephen II. Stephen took offence at this support for a political rival, and he may have felt threatened by the Byzantine rapprochement with Venice, which disputed Hungary's dominion over the cities of the Dalmatian coast. There followed a two-year war, in which Stephen attacked the imperial border fortresses and stirred the Serbs into revolt, while John retaliated by leading two expeditions to the Danube to restore the *status quo*.

When in 1130 he returned to campaigning in Asia Minor, it was with a new objective: the northern sector of the frontier, where the imperial position in Bithynia and along the Black Sea was being eroded by the aggressive Turkish amirate of the Danishmendids, and by the defections of the Greek magnates who controlled much of the littoral. For six years the emperor led expeditions into Paphlagonia. The Byzantine sources highlight the successful sieges of Kastamon (twice) and Gangra, thus giving the impression that this was a war of reconquest. But these and other gains in the area were soon retaken after the emperor's departure and it is difficult to believe that John realistically expected to be able to hold them with the modest garrisons that he could afford to leave behind. On balance, it seems clear that the aim was also to make a show of force, to raid the flocks of the Turkish nomads in retaliation for past depredations and to impress all in Constantinople and in the imperial entourage whose loyalty was wavering. For John's first campaign against the Danishmendids was cut short by the conspiracy of his brother Isaac, and it was to the Danishmendids that Isaac fled to avoid arrest in 1130. A year or two later, John abandoned another campaign in order to deal with a plot to put Isaac on the throne. In the circumstances, it is not surprising that the emperor's subsequent successes were advertised to maximum effect and that he celebrated the taking of Kastamon by a triumphal entry into Constantinople, to the accompaniment of panegyrical songs and speeches (1133). These celebrations set the tone for the extravagant glorification of imperial achievements that was to characterize the imperial image for the rest of the century.

Isaac's movements in exile, which took him from Melitene to Armenia, Cilicia, Iconium and Jerusalem, help to explain why, from 1135, John made larger plans for political and military intervention further east. The opportunity arose when Alice, the widow of Bohemond II of Antioch, offered their daughter Constance in marriage to John's youngest son Manuel. The offer was a desperate and doomed attempt to prevent Constance from marrying Raymond of Poitiers, to whom she had been promised, but it encouraged John to focus on Antioch as the key to the strategy for dealing with all the empire's eastern neighbours, Muslim and Christian. Raymond's marriage to Constance in 1136 provided a justification for military action in support of imperial claims to Cilicia and Antioch. An imperial expedition in 1137 succeeded in reconquering Cilicia from the Armenian Rupenid prince Leo, who held the mountainous areas, and the Latins who held the cities of the plain, Adana, Mopsuestia and Tarsus. John also compelled the new prince of Antioch to become his vassal, to allow him right of entry into the city, and to hand it over in return for investiture with the cities of the Syrian interior – Aleppo, Shaizar, Homs and Hama – once these were recaptured from the Muslims. The subsequent campaign to take them failed, and so did the emperor's attempt to use the excuse to take possession of Antioch. But overall, the performance of the imperial army and the deference showed by all the local rulers were a triumphant demonstration of the empire's and the emperor's power. According to Choniates, it had the effect of making John's exiled brother Isaac seek a reconciliation, 'for lacking money, and seeing the emperor John universally renowned for his feats in battle, he found no one who would fall in with his ambitions'.[1] During the following years, John returned to Asia Minor, to strengthen the frontier defences in Bithynia, to strike at Neokaisareia, the town from which the Danishmendids threatened the eastern section of the Black Sea coastal strip, and to secure and extend imperial control in the southern sector of the frontier in western Asia Minor. Yet these last operations, in the area where he had conducted his earliest campaigns, were clearly a prelude to the new expedition to Syria which he launched at the end of 1142. He wintered in the mountains of Cilicia, preparing to strike at Antioch in the spring and from there to go on to Jerusalem.

The emperor's death from a hunting accident in February 1143 aborted what looks like the most ambitious attempt at restoring the pre-Islamic empire that any Byzantine ruler had undertaken since the tenth century. John was finally making up for Alexios's failure to take personal command of the First Crusade. With the wisdom of hindsight, we may question whether the course of history would have been very different if John had lived. His constant campaigning and drilling had made the Byzantine field army into a superb expeditionary force with an unrivalled siege capability, but he had pushed its performance to the limit. It had consistently run into problems when operating beyond the empire's borders and rarely held on to its acquisitions. In addition to the standard logistical constraints of medieval warfare, there was the basic problem that the empire was frequently unwelcome in many of its former territories,

[1] Niketas Choniates, *Historia*, p. 32

even among the Greeks of Turkish-occupied Asia Minor. John had, moreover, developed the army at the expense of the navy. However, Cilicia had remained in imperial control since 1138. If John had succeeded in his aim of welding Antioch and Cilicia together with Cyprus and Attaleia into a kingdom for his son Manuel, the benefits to the empire and to the crusader states would have been enormous; at the very least, if the imperial army had remained in Syria throughout 1143, the emperor would have formed a coalition of local Christians that would have checked the Islamic counter-crusade of Zengi and thus postponed, or even prevented, the fall of Edessa and the calling of the Second Crusade.

The revival of imperial interest in the crusader states had permanent consequences in that it led to a renewal of Byzantine links with western Europe. During the first half of his reign, John had retreated from the active western diplomacy that Alexios had conducted. But this changed in 1135, when John revived imperial claims to Antioch and sought to cover his back against interference from Roger II of Sicily, who also had an interest in the principality. He renewed the empire's treaty with Pisa, negotiated alliances with the German emperors Lothar and Conrad, and sent a very conciliatory letter to Pope Innocent II on the subject of church union. Most importantly for the future, the alliance with Conrad III was sealed by the betrothal of Conrad's sister-in-law Bertha to John's youngest son Manuel. Manuel not only happened to be available; he had also been proposed as a husband for the heiress to Antioch, and was the intended ruler of the projected kingdom of Antioch, Cilicia, Cyprus and Attaleia.

Apart from the conspiracies of his sister and brother, the internal history of John's reign looks conspicuously uneventful. On the whole, it seems fair to conclude that the paucity of documentation generally reflects a lack of intervention or of the need for it. As with the frontiers, it was a case of maintaining internal structures that had stabilized in the last ten years of the previous reign. John's most significant policy change was to reduce expenditure on the fleet, on the advice of his finance minister John of Poutza. Although he looked outside his family for individual support, John upheld the ascendancy of the Komnenos and Doukas kin-groups, and continued to consolidate their connections by marriage with other aristocratic families. In the church, he was by Byzantine standards remarkably non-interventionist, apparently because church affairs had settled down after the disputes of Alexios's reign. He left his mark on them principally through his generous benefactions to churches and monasteries, above all through his foundation of the monastery of Christ Pantokrator. The foundation charter and the church buildings provide the best surviving picture of the appearance, the organization and the wealth of a great metropolitan monastery and its annexes, which included a hospital.

MANUEL I

For most of his reign, John had managed to prevent his own children from being divided by the sibling rivalries which had bedevilled his own succession. Yet in the months before his death, his arrangements were thrown into confusion when Alexios, his eldest son and co-emperor of long-standing, fell ill and died, followed shortly by the next son, Andronikos. This left John, on his deathbed, with a highly invidious choice between his older surviving son, Isaac, who was in Constantinople, and the youngest, Manuel, who was with him in Cilicia. John no doubt voiced many of the arguments for Manuel's superiority which the Byzantine sources put into his mouth, but it is hard to fault the explanation of William of Tyre that Manuel was chosen in order to ensure the army's safe return. Prompt action forestalled any attempt by Isaac to take advantage of his presence in the capital. Manuel was thus able to enter Constantinople and have himself crowned without opposition. As the winner, he was able to command or commission the propaganda which represented his election as providential and inevitable. Yet Isaac nursed a legitimate grievance, and his sympathizers included his father's right-hand man, John Axouch. Isaac was not the only one who coveted his brother's throne: their brother-in-law, the caesar John Roger, attempted a *coup*, backed by a faction of Norman exiles, and their uncle Isaac was believed to be still awaiting his opportunity. Even apparently innocuous female relatives, Manuel's aged aunt Anna and his widowed sister-in-law Eirene, were treated as political suspects. The new emperor was unmarried and therefore without immediate prospect of legitimate issue. All in all, the circumstances of his accession put him under intense pressure to prove himself by emulating his father's achievements without putting his inheritance at risk.

The immediate priority was to bring the unfinished foreign business of John's last years to an honourable conclusion. There could be no question of the emperor leading another grand expedition to Syria, so Manuel contented himself with sending an army and a fleet to ravage the territory of Antioch. This and the fall of Edessa to Zengi in 1144 obliged Raymond of Antioch to come to Constantinople and swear obedience, while Manuel promised to come to the prince's aid. There was also the matter of the German alliance. Manuel's marriage to Bertha of Sulzbach had been negotiated and she had come to Constantinople, before he had any prospect of becoming emperor. It was probably to extract more favourable terms from Conrad III that Manuel put off the marriage and exchanged embassies with Roger II of Sicily, against whom the alliance with Conrad had been directed. When he finally married Bertha, who adopted the Greek name Eirene, in 1146 he had evidently won some sort of unwritten promise from Conrad, possibly to guarantee Manuel a free hand in the east, but more likely to give him a share of the conquests from his planned invasion of southern Italy.

These treaties opened up commitments and prospects which Manuel did not, however, immediately pursue. Instead, he used the security they gave him to revert to the limited-objective campaigning against the Turks which had characterized his father's reign, with even more emphasis on military victory for its own sake. The expedition which he led as far as Iconium in 1146 was ostensibly in retaliation for the capture of a border fortress in Cilicia. In effect, however, it was a display of the emperor's prowess in leading his army up to the walls of the sultan's capital and then fighting heroic rearguard actions in the retreat. This gratuitous heroism was intended to vindicate Manuel's youthful heroism in the eyes of his critics. It may also have been meant to impress the Latins with the emperor's zeal for holy war. But it did nothing to help the crusader states, and that help now came in a form which exposed Manuel's lack of a strategy for dealing with the fall of Edessa and the repercussions that this was bound to have in the wider world of Latin Christendom. The fact that the Byzantine sources fail to mention the event which provoked the Second Crusade suggests that they seriously underestimated its importance.

The Second Crusade would have been a major military and political crisis even if it had been confined to the expedition of Louis VII, as Manuel was originally led to expect. The size of Louis's army, his royal status, which precluded any oath of vassalage to the emperor, and the ties which bound him and his entourage to the nobility of the Latin east were sufficient to thwart any effective concordance between Byzantine claims and crusader objectives. The problem was more than doubled by the unexpected participation of Conrad III with an equally huge army and an even touchier sense of sovereign dignity. His arrival in the east strained their alliance almost to breaking point, since it brought the German emperor-elect where Manuel least wanted him from where he needed him most, namely as a threat to Roger II of Sicily. Roger now took advantage of the situation to seize the island of Corfu and to launch raids on the Greek mainland, whose garrisons had been redeployed to shadow the crusading armies. It was alarmingly reminiscent of earlier Norman invasions of Epiros, and Manuel, like Alexios I in 1082, responded by calling on Venetian naval help, in return for which he renewed Venice's trade privileges and extended the Venetian quarter in Constantinople.

In these circumstances, it is understandable that Manuel moved the crusading armies as quickly as possible across the Bosphoros into Asia Minor, where the treaty of peace that he had signed with the sultan of Iconium may well have contributed to the appalling casualties they suffered at the hands of the Turks. These casualties, which rendered the armies largely ineffective by the time they reached Syria and Palestine, earned Manuel a lasting reputation as the saboteur of the Second Crusade. However, they did lead eventually to a renewal of the alliance with Conrad III, who, when he fell ill at Ephesus in December 1147, accepted Manuel's invitation to come and recuperate in Constantinople. Manuel then provided ships and money for Conrad to continue to Palestine and recruit a new army. On his return to Europe late in 1148, the two monarchs met at Thessalonica to agree on a joint invasion and partition of southern Italy and Sicily. The Byzantine share was to count as the dowry owing to Manuel from his marriage to Bertha-Eirene. The alliance was sealed by the marriage of Manuel's niece Theodora to Conrad's cousin Henry of Babenberg.

The renewal of the German alliance determined the principal orientation of Manuel's foreign policy for the rest of his reign. For the next twelve years he remained committed to a partnership with the Hohenstaufen which he hoped would bring substantial territorial gains in Italy. He pursued this goal despite setbacks and distractions, and despite the gradual divergence of interests between the two empires after Conrad III died and was succeeded by Frederik Barbarossa (1152). As soon as he had recovered Corfu from its Sicilian garrison in 1149, he planned to carry the war into Italy. The invasion plan was frustrated, first by bad weather, and then by wars in the Balkans which were stirred up by the disruptive diplomacy of Roger II. Thus the campaigns which Manuel led from 1150 to 1155 against the Serbian *župans* of Raška and King Géza II of Hungary were essentially diversions, for all the energy he put into them and the considerable publicity they generated. However, the war at sea continued, and at the death of Roger II (1154) Manuel moved to take advantage of the insecurity and unpopularity of the young William I, reviving the invasion plan of 1149. Without German participation, the campaign eventually came to grief at Brindisi in 1156, and Frederick disowned it as a Greek initiative which interfered with his own programme of Roman imperial renewal. Yet for a time, the Byzantine agents had enjoyed great success, receiving the co-operation of disaffected Norman lords and the submission of many towns throughout Apulia. Manuel did not act as if either the German alliance or the prospect of a Byzantine revival in Italy had been destroyed by the defeat. His agents returned to sow disaffection against William I in 1157, and he continued to seek collaboration with Frederick Barbarossa even after he had concluded a peace treaty with William in 1158. In 1160, they were still exchanging embassies to discuss joint action against Sicily, and a Byzantine request for a share of imperial dominion in the Italian peninsula.

Manuel's basic and consistent objective was the acquisition of the coastal towns of Apulia: they had a Greek population, they had belonged to the imperial province of Longobardia before 1071, and control of them would prevent the recurrence of invasions like those of Robert Guiscard, Bohemond and Roger II. Beyond that, Byzantine territorial aims in Italy were flexible, and by 1160 it seems that Manuel had traded his empire's historic claims to Calabria and the Naples area in return for the recognition of a right to the Pentapolis, the area comprising the city of Ancona and its hinterland. Ancona was the Byzantine base of operations in 1155–6, and it had been chosen for this purpose in 1149. It may well, therefore, have been designated in the treaty of 1148 between Conrad and Manuel as belonging to the Byzantine sphere of influence. Justification for the Byzantine claim could have been found in the fact that the Pentapolis had been part of the old exarchate of Ravenna. While the coastal towns of Apulia were ruled by the king of Sicily, Ancona was the only alternative to Venice as a gateway for Byzantine agents, envoys, troops and subsidies to reach the empire's Italian and German allies – and Venice was basically opposed to any Byzantine revival in Italy. Once the coastal towns of Apulia also reverted to Byzantine rule, possession of the Pentapolis would have given Manuel control of almost the entire east coast of Italy.

The failure of his negotiations with Frederick Barbarossa in 1160 caused Manuel to try an alternative to the German alliance, which was coming under strain for other reasons. Frederick's increasingly strident imperialism made him less receptive to the idea of sharing sovereignty in Italy with the Greek empire. Indeed, his programme of reclaiming imperial rights, which he had stated at the diet of Roncaglia (1158) and showed every sign of enforcing, threatened to change the balance of power in Italy and make the Hohenstaufen empire the main danger to Byzantium's western flank. At the same time, his quarrel with Pope Adrian IV, and his refusal to recognize the canonical election of Adrian's successor, Alexander III, made him an embarrassment for Manuel's relations with other parts of Latin Christendom, particularly the crusader states. Above all, the bond of kinship between the two emperors was severed when Manuel's German wife Bertha-Eirene died in 1159.

From 1161, Manuel aligned himself with Pope Alexander III and all who took his side against Frederick and the antipope elected by Frederick's council of Pavia (1160). Thus relations between Byzantium and Alexander's main European supporter, Louis VII of France, began to improve for the first time since the Second Crusade. Manuel's main diplomatic priority, however, was to cultivate close relations with all those in the Italian peninsula who, like Alexander, felt threatened by Frederick's expansionism. Chief among them was the king of Sicily, and Manuel twice entered into negotiations with a view to marrying his daughter to William II, who succeeded his father, William I, in 1166. But Manuel also poured money into creating an extensive web of potential supporters among the towns and the aristocracy throughout Italy. Byzantine money helped to rebuild the walls of Milan, razed at Frederick's orders in 1162. To the pope himself, Manuel not only gave material support but offered the prospect of reuniting the Greek and Roman churches, and several discussions were held. In return, the pope gave Manuel to understand that he would consider recognizing him as sole Roman emperor.

This ambition seems like a vastly unrealistic escalation of Manuel's previous aims, but it is unlikely to have involved any major political changes, other than excluding Frederick Barbarossa from Italy and giving Manuel the senior place among the rulers of Christendom. For the pope to entertain the notion, it must have been predicated on a guarantee to maintain the *status quo* in Italy: the continued existence of the communes in the north, the papal lordship in the centre and the kingdom of Sicily in the south. It is far from certain that the arrangement would have involved any territorial concessions such as Manuel had sought from the Hohenstaufen. The ulterior aim of Manuel's diplomacy after 1160 may have been to pressurize Frederick Barbarossa into renewing the alliance. The prospect of renewing it in 1170–2 was certainly enough to make Manuel pull out of a marriage treaty with William II of Sicily for what he thought was a better offer from Frederick. The offer did not materialize, and the 'cold war' resumed, but the episode demonstrated that what Manuel sought above all was a partnership with the sovereign powers of the Christian west that would guarantee security for his empire within negotiated territorial limits. In the papal alliance as in the Hohenstaufen alliance, Italy was the focus for negotiation, and Ancona remained the Byzantine gateway to Italy.

The peace of Venice in 1177, in which Frederick Barbarossa and Alexander III settled their differences and Italian affairs without reference to Manuel, put an end to the latter's hopes of either territorial gains in Italy or a western imperial crown. However, it was not the end of his diplomacy, or of his deeper ambition to align his dynastic programme of imperial restoration with the power structure of Latin Christendom from which his empire had been perilously excluded at the time of the Second Crusade. That ambition was as close to being realized at his death in 1180 as it would ever be. He had failed to secure a working relationship with Frederick Barbarossa, but he remained on good terms with Alexander III, his daughter had married Renier of Montferrat, from the major magnate family of north-western Italy, and his son was betrothed to the daughter of the king of France.

On other fronts, while Manuel did not neglect the security and the extension of the empire's borders, his initiatives were ultimately shaped by the aim of being taken into partnership by the great powers of the west. The crusader states provided an ideal opportunity for him to enhance his credentials in western eyes. The disaster of the Second Crusade had left them increasingly vulnerable to Zengi's successor, Nur al-Din, who had taken over Damascus following the failed crusader offensive, and had made the kings of the west wary of getting involved in a major new expedition to the Holy Land. Although they were

responsive to the plight of the Latin settlers, their own domestic problems and
mutual rivalries kept them in Europe, while the armed pilgrimages undertaken
by some of their vassals did not properly compensate for the lack of a general
crusade. In the circumstances, the princes of Outremer turned increasingly to
Byzantium for military and financial aid and the Byzantine emperor was only
too pleased to avoid the recurrence of a general crusade.

Soon after the Second Crusade, the northern principalities suffered a crisis
when Raymond of Edessa was killed in battle (1149) and Joscelin II of Edessa was
captured (1150). Manuel bought the remaining castles of the county of Edessa
from Joscelin's wife and attempted to persuade Raymond's widow Constance
to marry his recently widowed brother-in-law, the half-Norman caesar John
Roger. However, the castles soon fell to the Muslims, and Constance rejected
John Roger in favour of Reynald of Châtillon, a recent arrival from France.
Neither these failures nor Reynald's subsequent raid on Byzantine Cyprus, in
conjunction with Thoros, the Armenian prince of Cilicia, drew an immediate
response from Manuel, who was occupied with the war with Sicily. Only when
this was over did the emperor intervene personally with a show of force. Moreover, his expedition to Cilicia and Syria in 1158–9 was not, despite superficial
resemblances, a repeat of those conducted by his father. It followed the conclusion of a marriage alliance with King Baldwin III of Jerusalem, who in 1157
broke with crusader precedent and sought a bride from the Byzantine imperial
family. Thus the reassertion of imperial supremacy in Cilicia and Antioch,
and the humiliation of Reynald and Thoros, were performed with the full
cooperation of the senior potentate in Outremer, who accepted them as the
ritual price the Latin settlers had to pay for Byzantine material aid, and as the
necessary prelude to joint military action against Nur al-Din by all the local
Christian powers. Although this action was cut short when Manuel was recalled to Constantinople by news of a conspiracy, he continued to work closely
with the crusader states. It was to Tripoli, and then to Antioch, that he looked
for a new bride after the death of Bertha-Eirene in 1100. He married Maria of
Antioch, daughter of Raymond and Constance, in 1161, and some fifteen years
later strengthened his connection with her brother, Prince Bohemond III, by
providing the latter with a Comnenian bride. The connection with Jerusalem
was briefly interrupted at Baldwin III's death in 1163, but it resumed when
the king's brother and successor, Amalric, decided he could not do without
Byzantine aid and negotiated a marriage to another imperial relative (1167).
Following a treaty in 1168, a Byzantine naval force joined Amalric in an invasion of Egypt (1169), and the king came to Constantinople to negotiate a
fresh agreement in 1171. The resulting plans for further joint operations against
Egypt were halted at Amalric's death (1174), but were back on the agenda in
1176–7, when a Byzantine fleet was despatched to Palestine.

These ventures came to nothing militarily, but they proved that the empire would deploy impressive resources in offensive as well as defensive support of its Latin allies, and thus undoubtedly helped to impede the counter-crusade of Nur al-Din and Saladin. Manuel further bolstered the Latin settlements both by providing their princes with generous subsidies, and by ransoming their knights who were captured in battle. In return, the emperor asked only for due recognition of his overlordship, and for fulfilment of the long-standing treaty agreement to appoint a Greek patriarch in Antioch.

Despite his considerable investment in Latin Syria, Manuel did not revisit the area after 1159. On the other hand, he returned more than once to the Danube frontier after King Géza II of Hungary died in 1161, leaving a disputed succession. The position of Hungary between the German and Byzantine empires, and adjacent to the empire's Serbian vassals, gave it a strategic importance in Manuel's growing conflict of interest with Frederick Barbarossa, which increased his concern to ensure that it was in friendly hands. His kinship with the Hungarian royal dynasty via his mother, and the empire's historic claim to certain frontier areas of the kingdom, also incited his intervention in Hungarian affairs. Although Manuel initially failed to instal his first candidate, Stephen IV, repeated campaigning from 1162 to 1167 ensured the future succession of his next protégé, Béla III, and the cession to the empire of Béla's patrimony, consisting of the central Dalmatian coast and an area south of the middle Danube known as Frangochorion, which included the old Roman frontier capital of Sirmium. Béla III lived in Constantinople from 1164, where he was betrothed to Manuel's daughter Maria and regarded as heir apparent to the throne until the birth of the emperor's son Alexios (1169). He took power in Hungary at the death of his brother Stephen III (1172) and served the empire loyally while Manuel was alive.

On the empire's other land frontier, in Asia Minor, Manuel's preferred policy was similarly one of trying to maintain and improve the *status quo* by drawing the main regional power, the sultanate of Iconium, into the imperial orbit. After some fighting in 1159–60, Manuel welcomed the sultan, Kilic Arslan II, to Constantinople in 1161. The two rulers concluded a treaty whereby the emperor ritually adopted the sultan as his son and undertook to subsidize his wars against his Turkish rivals; in return, any important cities recovered from the latter were to be surrendered to the emperor, and the sultan promised to prevent raids on the empire's territories. Kilic Arslan did not keep his side of the treaty, which effectively allowed him to unify Turkish Asia Minor under his rule. But it brought peace to western Anatolia for fourteen years, and it set up an effective Islamic rival to the rising power of Nur al-Din, which helped the crusader states. Only when the death of Nur al-Din (1174) changed the configuration of power in the Islamic world did Manuel adopt a policy of confrontation with Kilic Arslan, building fortresses on the Anatolian plateau to control the routes to the east (1175), and then mounting a major expedition to conquer the sultan's capital of Iconium (1176). It is also clear from the publicity surrounding this offensive that it was not only a belated move from appeasement to reprisal, but also a holy war intended to restore Asia Minor to imperial rule and open up the land route for pilgrims to Palestine. The grand expedition of 1176 was thus, above all, the culmination of Manuel's long attempt to redeem the failure of the Second Crusade which had come to grief in the borderlands of Asia Minor. It was meant to finish, under imperial leadership, the business that had got out of imperial control in the First Crusade. The resounding defeat which the expedition suffered at Myriokephalon was correspondingly a devastating setback to Manuel's attempt to take over the crusading movement and to reverse a century of Turkish occupation in Asia Minor. Yet the empire's army, finances and borders were intact; its power in the Balkans and its influence in eastern Europe had never stood higher. Louis VII of France gave a big vote of confidence by sending his daughter Agnes as a future bride for the young Alexios II. There is no knowing how things would have developed if Manuel had not died only four years after the battle.

Manuel conducted his warfare and his diplomacy with lavish ceremony and rhetorical publicity which explicitly recalled Constantine and Justinian. This and the autocratic style which he adopted in his legislation and in his regulation of church doctrine led Choniates to assert, and modern scholars to accept, that Manuel dreamed the impossible dream of restoring the Roman empire in all its ancient glory. Careful attention to the reality behind the rhetorical and ceremonial image reveals that Manuel's Roman imperialism was more concerned with security than with expansion. It is true that at different times he sought the elimination of the two main neighbouring states, the Norman kingdom of Sicily and the Seljuqid sultanate of Rum, which had recently been founded at the empire's expense. However, he did not do so consistently, and he did so only within the framework of an alliance. His imperialism only began to depart from tradition after 1160, when he was obliged to seek an alternative to the German alliance. The main departure (though even this had precedents) was that instead of following the time-honoured practice of weakening the empire's neighbours by setting them against each other or destabilizing their regimes, he sought to establish a ring of reliable satellite kingdoms which he strengthened against their enemies in return for their support. The kingdom of Jerusalem, Hungary, the sultanate and the kingdom of Sicily were all tried in this role to a greater or lesser extent.

In general, it seems clear that Manuel sought allies and clients more than he sought territories. As we have seen, he hoped that the German alliance would give him control over the Adriatic coast of Italy, while from Hungary he gained

Frangochorion and the Dalmatian coast. Otherwise, apart from his rather belated crusade of reconquest in Asia Minor, his main identifiable objective was the coastal area of Egypt, which was to be the Byzantine share in the partition of the country agreed between Manuel and Amalric in 1168 and, presumably, in later renewals of their treaty. This was hardly a programme to restore the empire of Justinian. At the same time, it was more than random opportunism. The Egyptian coast, including the ports of Alexandria and Damietta, was the most sought-after trading destination in the Mediterranean. Possession of the east coast of Italy together with possession of the Dalmatian coast would have given the empire control of the Adriatic and thus of the access to eastern markets from Venice, the main trading city in the Mediterranean. Realization of all these territorial goals would have allowed the empire to dominate the commerce of the eastern Mediterranean and thus to renegotiate its treaties with the Italian maritime republics. That this was indeed Manuel's aim is suggested, first, by his considerable investment in the Byzantine navy, and, secondly, by the evolution of his policy towards Venice, an evolution which parallels his adoption of a less indulgent line in dealing with the Byzantine church, the other main beneficiary of economic privilege. In 1148, during the crisis of the Second Crusade, he had extended the already exceptional privileges enjoyed by Venetian merchants throughout the empire, but in 1171 he ordered their arrest and the confiscation of their goods. The Pisans and Genoese to some extent took their place, but not with the same exemption from the 10 per cent sales tax. Pisa was unable to negotiate an improvement to the terms of its original treaty with Alexios I, which had allowed a total exemption only on bullion exports, and a 6 per cent reduction on imports of other goods. The Genoese were originally admitted on the same basis in 1155, but had to accept further restrictions on the 6 per cent concession in 1169.

In the light of recent work on Byzantium in the eleventh and twelfth centuries, it is clear that Manuel's power was more impressive and his ambitions more moderate than used to be thought. However, his achievements still fell short of his ambitions, and his military failures against Sicily and the Turks were spectacular, perhaps more so than his successes against Hungary. The empire declined so rapidly after his death that historians from Choniates onwards have sought, and continue to seek, the seeds of its decline in his reign and in his policies. Modern commentators have also looked for structural weaknesses in the imperial regime of the Comnenian dynasty.

THE LEGACY AND THE SUCCESSORS OF MANUEL I, 1180–1204

Choniates believed that the empire and its rulers had incurred God's displeasure by their impious behaviour, and he identified the beginnings of this sinfulness in Manuel – in the emperor's belief in astrology, in his jealousy of popular and talented nobles, in his extravagant expenditure, in his favouritism of kinsmen and foreigners and in his assumption of authority in church matters. These were flaws that Manuel could be seen, with hindsight, to have shared with the emperors who reigned after him with obviously disastrous effect. But in picking on these characteristics, Choniates also undoubtedly echoed criticisms which had surfaced during Manuel's lifetime. His military failures in Italy and Asia Minor, together with his failure to produce a male heir by his first wife or in the first eight years of his second marriage, must have led to speculation that he had offended God by his style of government, and the speculation would have been encouraged by those male relatives, notably Manuel's cousin Andronikos, who were suspected of harbouring designs on the throne. Thus the insecurity which Manuel had faced at his accession stayed with him throughout his reign, and the soundness of his imperial edifice was already under scrutiny during his lifetime. The imperial image projected by the voluminous court rhetoric of his reign seems altogether too confident to be plausible.

Yet on the whole the image commanded respect from foreigners and subjects alike. Manuel controlled his subjects, his resources and his policies as well as any of his imperial predecessors or royal contemporaries. What he did not control was beyond the control of any ruler: the tender age at which his son succeeded him. The crisis of Byzantium after 1180 was in a very obvious way the familiar story of a monarchy thrown into disarray by a minority.

However, Byzantium had experienced minorities in the past without falling apart and falling prey to foreign conquest. Is there a case for thinking that the disasters of the period 1180–1204 were waiting to happen, inherent in the structure of the empire of the Komnenoi?

Thirty years ago, the view prevailed that although the Comnenian emperors gave the empire a temporary reprieve by their vigorous military leadership, their aristocratic dynastic priorities undermined the efficacy of the state system that had made Byzantium great in the 'imperial centuries'. According to the classic formulation of George Ostrogorsky,

> in structure the Empire now differed considerably from the rigid centralized state of the middle Byzantine period. The age of the Comneni saw an intensification of the feudalizing process and those very feudal elements in the provinces, against which the tenth-century emperors had battled with such insistence, were to become the mainstay of the new state... Byzantium had thrown over its once solid foundations and its defences, and its economic and financial strength were greatly diminished. This is the explanation why the successes of the Comneni were not enduring and were followed by the collapse of the Byzantine state.[2]

---

[2] Ostrogorsky (1968), pp. 374–5.

Recently, this view has been replaced by the realization that the privileges and immunities bestowed by the Comnenian emperors did not in themselves de-centralize, weaken or impoverish the machinery of government and warfare. The Comnenian empire had all the apparatus of a fully developed pre-industrial state: a standing army and navy, regular monetary taxation and an elaborate bureaucracy. The armed forces performed indifferently, the taxation was op-pressive and iniquitous and the bureaucracy often inefficient and corrupt, but under strong leadership the apparatus worked. Moreover, the resource base on which it worked was not obviously diminished by either the loss of territory in Asia Minor or the granting of exemptions. Rather, all the indications from written and material evidence are that agricultural production and trade inten-sified throughout the twelfth century, and that the government was reaping the benefits as well as the aristocracy, the monasteries and the Italian merchants.

The most eloquent testimony to the wealth of Byzantium in the late twelfth century comes from the observation of an Anglo-Norman writer, Gerald of Wales, that the revenues of the German and English monarchies were as nothing compared with those of the kingdom of Sicily and the Greek empire before these were destroyed 'by the Latins'; the yearly income from Palermo alone (a smaller city than Constantinople) exceeded that from the whole of England.[3] Interesting here is the coupling of Byzantium and Sicily as wealthy states which were destroyed by northern European conquest. Gerald goes on to recall a remark of Louis VII of France, reported somewhat differently by Walter Map,[4] contrasting the great resources of other kingdoms with the simple self-sufficiency of his own. The king of Germany had many armed men but no wealth, the rulers of Sicily and Greece were rich in gold and silk, but had no men who could do anything but talk, and the king of England had something of both. In the perception, and the reality, of statehood in twelfth-century Europe, strong finances and a strong war machine did not necessarily go together.

Byzantium's problem was one of survival in a world where weak, wealthy Mediterranean societies were in the way of northern warrior aristocracies with slender means and big appetites. Survival lay in the effective use of wealth to manage the bonds which kept the empire together and free from confronta-tion with potential aggressors. These bonds consisted in three characteristic features of the Comnenian empire which had either not existed or been less pronounced before 1081: the deep involvement of the empire with the Latin west, the centralization of power and resources in Constantinople and the em-phasis on family, lineage and kinship as the defining elements in the Byzantine political system. The unravelling of all three features is clearly visible in the disintegration of imperial power at the end of the twelfth century.

---

[3] Gerald of Wales, 'De principis instructione', III, pp. 316–17.
[4] Walter Map, *De nugis curialium*, p. 451.

BYZANTIUM AND THE WEST

The empire's involvement with the west derived partly from its historic interest in the Italian peninsula, and partly from the consequences of its attempt to use western military power to restore its position in Asia. The relationship set up by the First Crusade persisted and intensified throughout the twelfth century, tying the empire's eastern interests to its western relations, and making the viability of its traditional role in the Christian Orient dependent upon its standing among the powers of the Latin west. The Second Crusade confirmed what John II had belatedly begun to realize in the 1130s: that to succeed, and even to survive, Byzantium needed to keep one move ahead of the crusading movement in preserving the Latin settlements in Syria; it needed to participate as an inside player in the power politics of western Christendom. In the thirty years following the crusade, Manuel had done all in his power to make the involvement inextricable and irreversible. The proliferation of ties with the Latin world which he cultivated so assiduously at all levels was a natural response to the growing volume of western business and religious interests in the eastern Mediterranean. These would have affected Byzantium regardless of imperial policy.

Yet the period following Manuel's death and the overthrow of the regency government of Alexios II saw reversion to something like the isolationism of John II's early years. Under Andronikos I, Isaac II and Alexios III, Byzantium opted out of the crusading movement at a time when crusading activity was intensifying, and abandoned the search for a high-level European entente with one or more of the major western powers. To some extent this was the result of a backlash against Manuel's expensive Latinophilia, which was carried to even greater excess by the regency government of Maria of Antioch; it proceeded inexorably from the massacre of the Latins in Constantinople, mostly Pisans and Genoese, which accompanied the seizure of power by Andronikos Komnenos in 1182, as well as from his liquidation of the key members of Manuel's family through whom dynastic links to the west had been forged: Manuel's widow Maria of Antioch, Manuel's daughter Maria and her husband Renier of Montferrat, and the young Alexios II himself. That Andronikos, who was probably older than Manuel, did not murder Alexios's child fiancée, Agnes of France, but forced her to marry him, can hardly have made her family warm to him. In the circumstances, it is not surprising that when he was threatened with invasion by the king of Sicily, the only western power prepared to ally with him was Venice, whose citizens had been unaffected by the massacre of 1182 and were only too glad to take advantage of the removal of the Pisans and Genoese. Nor is it surprising that Andronikos considered that imperial interests in the east were better served by alliance with the growing power of Saladin rather than with the beleaguered Latin princes of Outremer, who no doubt remembered Andronikos's scandalous sexual adventures in Antioch and Jerusalem in 1166–7.

It is perhaps more remarkable that no realignment was attempted after 1185 by Isaac II Angelos, who otherwise had every reason to reject his predecessor's reign as a tyrannical deviation from the normal course of imperial policy. Isaac was not anti-western. Soon after his accession he took as his second wife Margaret, a daughter of Béla III of Hungary, and he invited Conrad of Montferrat, brother of the murdered Renier, to Constantinople, where he played a large part in defeating a major revolt (1187). Yet despite receiving the title of caesar, which Renier had held, and the hand of the emperor's sister in marriage, Conrad became dissatisfied and moved on to Syria, where he joined in the defence of Tyre against Saladin and became a candidate for the throne of Jerusalem. Isaac's renewal of Andronikos's alliance with Saladin may have been a factor in Conrad's disenchantment; what is certain is that Saladin's conquest of the Holy Land and the subsequent mobilization of the Third Crusade only confirmed Isaac in the alliance, from which he hoped to gain some sort of Byzantine dominion in Palestine, including the occupation of all the episcopal sees and the Holy Places, in return for obstructing the crusaders' advance. The rapprochement with Saladin should also be seen in the context of Isaac's treaties with Venice, which also took no part in the Third Crusade and stood to gain at the expense of Genoa and Pisa from either a Byzantine or a Muslim occupation of the coast of Palestine. In both alliances, one may detect the influence of Isaac's spiritual mentor, Dositheos, a Venetian-born monk who had predicted Isaac's rise to power and was rewarded accordingly by being appointed patriarch, first of Jerusalem, and then of Constantinople.

This disengagement from the Latin west – which was not total, since it gave the Venetians an even more privileged position in Byzantine society than they had enjoyed before 1171 – may have seemed more true to the 'national' interest, which was increasingly being seen in terms of Greek as well as Orthodox identity, than Manuel's costly commitments to allies with no love for the empire. Indeed, the process of dissolution had been started by one of those allies, Manuel's brother-in-law Bohemond III, who put aside his Comnenian wife well before Andronikos's usurpation. However, the empire paid dearly for its withdrawal. The pirates who terrorized the shipping and the coastal settlements of the Aegean world in the 1180s and 1190s came mainly from Pisa and Genoa, the cities which had suffered most from the massacre of 1182. The Sicilian invasion of 1185, which took Durazzo and went on to sack Thessalonica, could have been prevented if Andronikos had had firm alliances, or at least a proactive diplomacy, in the west. By failing to anticipate the Third Crusade, and by allying with Saladin instead of supporting the crusaders, Isaac II weakened

his moral claim for the restitution of the island of Cyprus when Richard I of
England conquered it from its self-proclaimed emperor, Isaac Komnenos, in
1191: Cyprus was too important a source of supplies for the crusaders to entrust
it to an unfriendly power. Isaac II also entered into a damaging confrontation
with Frederick Barbarossa when the latter came through Byzantine territory
on the overland route to Palestine (1189–90). The damage was not so much
in the humiliating defeats inflicted by the German army, or in its systematic
plundering of much of Macedonia and Thrace from its base at Philippopolis, as in the manifest contrast between Isaac's inability to obstruct a crusade
which he wrongly assumed to be directed against Constantinople and Frederick's ability to threaten Constantinople if Isaac persisted in obstructing him.
The contrast was painfully apparent to Niketas Choniates, who was assigned
to Philippopolis at the time, and it was much appreciated by the Serbs and
Vlakhs, then in revolt against Byzantine authority, who offered to join forces
with the Germans. Nor was the significance of the episode lost on Frederick's
son Henry VI, whom Frederick had charged with collecting money and ships
from Italy in preparation for an assault on Constantinople. When Henry succeeded as emperor after Frederick's tragic death by drowning in Cilicia, he
inherited Frederick's unfulfilled crusading ambitions and placed them high on
his agenda, along with his claim to the throne of Sicily which he derived from
his marriage to Constance, the aunt of William II, who died childless in 1189.
The danger from Henry VI spurred Isaac II into diplomatic action. In 1192,
he negotiated the renewal of the empire's commercial treaties with Pisa and
Genoa, the two cities which Henry relied on to provide him with ships for his
conquest of Sicily. He also married his daughter Eirene to Roger of Apulia, the
son of Tancred of Lecce, who had occupied the Sicilian throne in defiance of
Henry's claim. But Eirene was widowed a year later, and in 1194 she was among
the spoils which fell to Henry VI in his violent occupation of the Sicilian
kingdom. He married her to his brother Philip of Swabia, thus making her an
instrument in his policy of aggression against Byzantium.

It is uncertain whether Henry VI of Hohenstaufen really intended to take
over the Byzantine empire by force, but he threatened to do so, and he used
the threat, first against Isaac II, and then against Alexios III, to try and extort
money and ships for his forthcoming crusade. Alexios accordingly levied an
extraordinary tax, the *alamanikon,* to pay the tribute. He was saved by Henry's
sudden death in 1197. Yet the episode showed that however much Byzantium
wanted to opt out of the crusading movement, the crusading movement would
not leave it alone. It had relinquished the initiative, but was still expected to
pay the bill. On this point, the western empire and the papacy, although in
all other respects implacable enemies, were in agreement. Pope Innocent III
insisted on it in his letters to Alexios III: Alexios ought to model himself on

Manuel, whose devotion to the cause of the Holy Land and the unity of the church had been exemplary.

Isolationism still might have worked, and the Byzantine empire might just have been allowed to find a niche as a neutral regional power, if the Fourth Crusade, preached in 1198, had gone according to its original plan of sailing directly against Egypt. The crusade seems to have been intended to bypass Byzantium completely, and the conquest of Egypt would not only have liberated the Holy Land, but made the crusader settlements materially self-sufficient. But the leadership failed to communicate its strategic vision to the majority of crusaders. The army which assembled in Venice was well below the numbers which the Venetians had estimated in building and equipping the fleet. A detour via Byzantium thus seemed an irresistible option, indeed, the only option for keeping the crusade on course, when a pretender to the imperial throne conveniently turned up with a promise of rich rewards if the crusaders restored him to what he plausibly claimed was his rightful inheritance. The pretender was Alexios, son of the deposed Isaac II, who had escaped from custody in Constantinople and gone to join his sister Eirene and her second husband, Philip of Swabia; the promise, no doubt formulated on Philip's advice and calculated partly on the basis of the demands made by Henry VI, was to place the empire under the obedience of the Roman church, to pay 200,000 silver marks and supply provisions for every man in the army, to send 10,000 men with the expedition to Egypt and to maintain 500 knights for the defence of Outremer for the duration of his lifetime. As Isaac II later remarked, 'this is a big commitment, and I do not know how it can be kept',[5] especially since Byzantium was to get no share in the conquest of Egypt. Whether or not the crusade leaders knew that the offer was too good to be true, the diversion to Constantinople attracted them for other reasons. It appealed to Boniface of Montferrat, who saw a chance to claim the Byzantine inheritance of which his brothers Renier and Conrad had been cheated. It appealed to Enrico Dandolo, the doge of Venice, which stood not only to recover the costs of the fleet, but also to improve its trading position in Constantinople from the restoration of Isaac II, a much better friend than Alexios III, who had tended to favour Genoa and Pisa despite his confirmation of Venetian privileges in 1198. It could be made to appeal to the crusaders from northern France by reminding them of the generosity with which Manuel had treated their forebears.

The diversion of the Fourth Crusade was thus a reversion to a prevailing tendency. Now, however, Byzantium had to promise much more than it could expect in return, and Byzantium's weakness could not really help the crusading movement. The problem for both the Byzantines and the crusaders was that

[5] Geoffrey of Villehardouin, *La conquête de Constantinople*, 1, §189, p. 192.

the latter came to Constantinople in 1203 at the invitation not of a reigning emperor, but of a rival claimant for power and resources that were dwindling rapidly. In 1197, Alexios III had only just managed to raise the money to buy off Henry VI. By 1203 Alexios IV had a much smaller resource base from which to make good his promises: Alexios III had emptied the treasury on fleeing from Constantinople, and he and his supporters in the provinces naturally denied the government in Constantinople the provincial revenues which they controlled. Alexios IV made himself unpopular in Constantinople by his demands for money, by resorting to the requisitioning of church valuables and by consorting with the crusaders; he then alienated the crusaders by failing to keep up his payments. His overthrow and murder in a palace coup by Alexios Doukas Mourtzouphlos relieved them of the embarrassment of making war on their own protégé and gave their renewed attack on Constantinople the status of a holy war against a traitor and regicide. Alexios V put up a competent defence, but it could not prevent the Venetians from using their ships to storm the low sea walls on the Golden Horn; and when the crusaders entered the city the defence collapsed. The crusaders were thus able to gorge themselves on the riches of Constantinople, set up a Latin regime and divide up the empire on paper. However, making the division a reality proved much harder, and in the end they held on to only a fraction of the twelfth-century empire. The Fourth Crusade never reached Egypt, and the Latin empire of Constantinople operated at a loss.

CONSTANTINOPLE AND THE PROVINCES

The Byzantine state was one of the most centralized in the medieval world, and never more so than in the period 1081–1180, when the loss of central and eastern Anatolia forced the empire's military elite, as well as its bureaucratic elite, to identify with the capital as never before. Territorial contraction thus accentuated the already marked tendency of the Byzantine aristocracy to think fiscally rather than territorially, to invest in office holding rather than land holding. Indeed, it is possible to see a correlation between the centralized structure of the Comnenian empire and its territorial limits, which were essentially those of the area within which expeditionary forces mobilized from Constantinople could operate without allied help, and within which the emperor could safely absent himself from Constantinople. By these criteria, the Danube and the Adriatic were within the range of imperial government from Constantinople, but southern Italy, Iconium and Egypt were not, and the empire was overextended in Dalmatia, Cilicia and Syria. Thus the empire consisted of those territories which a secure, mobile, military emperor could control from Constantinople. Those territories corresponded by and large to the limits of Greek linguistic

culture and Orthodox Christianity. The main exceptions were, first, in the
Balkan interior, where Slavonic, Vlakh and Albanian speakers predominated,
along with a sizeable, non-integrated Armenian population, and, secondly, in
the areas of southern Italy and Asia Minor which had been lost to the empire in
the late eleventh century, and in which Greek-speaking Orthodox Christians
were numerous. Looked at another way, Byzantium, or 'Romania', as its inhabitants referred to it, corresponded to the area needed to support a large standing
army and navy, an expensive international diplomacy and an enormous capital city. There was an outer frontier zone, broad in the Balkans, thin in Asia
Minor, which was partly protective shield and partly forward base for imperial
operations in Italy and Syria. In this zone, direct imperial administration was
limited to a few key strongholds, and local resources were either unexploited
(to starve invading forces), untaxed (to secure local loyalties) or used to pay for
regional defence and diplomacy (notably the case in Cyprus). Surrounded by
this zone, in an area consisting essentially of the Aegean and southern Black
Sea hinterland, the core Comnenian empire existed largely to maintain the
safety, the opulence and the population of Constantinople.

The pull of Constantinople was due not only to its role as the administrative capital, but also to its status as the 'reigning city' of New Rome, an
unrivalled showcase of holy relics, glittering treasures, ancient public monuments and magnificent buildings, a megalopolis with a population somewhere
between 200,000 and 400,000 which appears to have been growing steadily
throughout the eleventh and twelfth centuries, even as the empire contracted
overall in territorial extent. By the late twelfth century, the relationship between the 'reigning city' and the provinces was seen, on both sides, as that
of a metropolis to its satellite tributaries, which were inhabited by culturally
inferior second-class citizens. Ownership of the empire's prime agricultural
land was overwhelmingly concentrated in Constantinople. In the 'outer territories', as opposed to Constantinople, heretics abounded, ignorance of the
law was standard, uncanonical, semi-pagan religious customs were practised,
people spoke bad Greek and there was no protection against corrupt and brutal
officials. Yet this unequal relationship obviously depended on the productivity of the suppliers, on the ability of provincial communities to provide the
metropolis not only with money, foodstuffs, manpower and raw materials,
but also, increasingly, with manufactured goods, such as silks from Thebes
and knives from Thessalonica. It is abundantly clear that Constantinople was
not the only place where urban society was expanding. It is also clear, although documentation is patchy, that revenue could not have been raised or
military defence organized in the localities without the cooperation and participation of the local aristocracy, the *archontes*. In frontier cities, such as Durazzo,
Philadelphia or Trebizond, their loyalty was crucial in keeping invaders out.

Equally, in those parts of Asia Minor which had come under Turkish rule, the attitude of the local notables was crucial in the empire's failure to recover lost territory. The administration of the *pronoia* system, the conditional allocation of state lands and revenues as livings to mounted soldiers, which was greatly extended by Manuel I, must have created opportunities for patronage at the local level. Thus, as Constantinople became more and more self-important, self-centred and exclusive of the 'outer territories', it became increasingly noticeable that Constantinople needed the 'outer territories' more than the latter needed Constantinople. The perception may have existed before 1180, but it found expression, for the first time in the middle ages, in the following years, as central government proved less and less capable of protecting the provinces from raiders and invaders. The period 1180–1204 also saw the resurgence of the populace of Constantinople as a political factor for the first time since 1082, in changes of regime, in anti-government and anti-Latin riots and in opposition to imperial demands for money to buy off Henry VI and the Fourth Crusade.

Under Manuel's successors, the provinces of the Comnenian empire were lost to imperial control or became centres of opposition to the government in Constantinople. The process began, predictably, in areas of the frontier zone where the empire's hold had been short or shaky, and administration largely in the hands of local potentates. Soon after Manuel's death, Béla III of Hungary seized Byzantine Dalmatia and Sirmium, which he considered to be his own patrimony. Next to secede were the Serbs of Raška, and the Armenians of Cilicia, whose princes, Stephen Nemanja and Roupen II, had always been unwilling vassals of the emperor. In the process, Roupen took possession of the last Byzantine cities in Cilicia, capturing their governor, Isaac Komnenos, and then releasing him on payment of a ransom from Andronikos I; this he promptly spent, no doubt with the connivance of Roupen and Bohemond III of Antioch, on making himself lord of Cyprus (1185), where he ruled independently until dispossessed by Richard I and the Third Crusade. At least initially, Isaac had the support of the local aristocracy. The usurpation of Andronikos also provoked rebellions in two major cities of north-western Asia Minor, Nicaea and Prousa, and dissatisfaction with his rule may have contributed to the ease with which the Sicilian army took Durazzo in 1185 and advanced unopposed to Thessalonica.

The most serious and damaging centrifugal movement, however, was provoked not by the 'tyrant' Andronikos, but by Isaac II Angelos, the emperor who delivered the empire from Andronikos's tyranny. This was the Vlakh revolt started by the brothers Peter and Asan and continued by their brother John. As it spread, the revolt came to resemble the other ethnic separatist movements, those of the Serbs and Armenians. Like them, it occurred in a mountainous frontier area, it was boosted by the Third Crusade and it resulted in the formation of a national kingdom, whose ruler received a crown from the pope. Yet there were differences: the revolt of Peter and Asan involved two peoples, the Vlakhs and the Bulgarians, and the kingdom it created was a conscious resurrection of the first Bulgarian empire of the tenth century. Like its predecessor, it was not marginal to the Byzantine heartland, but encroached significantly on the agricultural hinterland of Constantinople and the northern Aegean. Moreover, it originated in what had been, for almost a century, the most trouble-free sector of the frontier zone, where there were no local dynasties with a history of political insubordination, and contacts with the neighbouring nomads, the Cumans, took the form of peaceful commerce in the cities of the lower Danube. The revolt resulted largely from the complacency that is evident, first, in Isaac II's failure to prevent, punish or recompense the rapacity of his officials who seized Vlakh livestock for his marriage feast; secondly, in his rude rejection of Peter and Asan when they requested a modest benefice; thirdly, in his failure to move quickly to deprive the rebels of their military advantages, their mountain strongholds and their Cuman allies. Peter and Asan were thus local chieftains politicized by the carelessness of central government. In this, they may have had something in common with Theodore Mangaphas, a Greek magnate in Philadelphia, who used his proximity to the Turkish frontier to declare independence from Isaac II. Although eventually subdued by Isaac, Mangaphas re-emerged at the time of the Fourth Crusade, as one of several 'dynasts' who took advantage of the changes of regime in Constantinople to seize power in their localities. By then, many other rebels had more or less successfully defied imperial authority from a variety of provincial power-bases.

It is difficult to generalize about the origins and aims of all these figures. Several were from the Comnenian nobility, and ultimately sought power at the centre. Others (Ivanko, Dobromir Chrysos) were by-products of the Vlakh–Bulgarian revolt. A certain Spyridonakes, who followed their example, was a Cypriot immigrant who had worked in the treasury of the imperial household and then been posted as administrator of Smolena in the Rhodope mountains. Aldobrandinus, who ruled Attaleia in 1204, may have been a Pisan pirate. The others must have originated among the provincial *archontes,* and notably among the local cadres of miltary recruitment and defence. They included the least ephemeral of the local lordships to emerge before the formation of the Byzantine successor states: that of Theodore Mangaphas in Philadelphia, the main command centre on the eastern frontier, and those of Leo Sgouros and Leo Chamaretos in the coastal towns of the eastern Peloponnese which contributed contingents to the imperial fleet.

Whatever the specific origins and aims of these individuals, they all shared the conviction that more was to be gained from opposition than from service to central government, and that they could count on provincial support. The trend they represented received a spectacular endorsement in 1203, when it was joined by the emperor Alexios III. Instead of persisting in the defence of Constantinople against the crusaders, he decided to abandon the city to Alexios IV, and to establish his court at Mosynopolis in Thrace, where he drew on the resources of a rich hinterland extending as far as Thessalonica.

THE COMNENIAN FAMILY SYSTEM

The most distinctive, as well as the most fatal, characteristic of the Comnenian empire was the identification of the state with the imperial family: this was the essence of what used to be labelled the feudalism of the Comnenian dynasty. In some ways, Manuel's regime looks less feudal than that of Alexios or John, despite his liking for the culture and the company of western knighthood. As he matured, according to Choniates, 'he ruled more autocratically, treating his subjects not as free men but as if they were servants who belonged to him by inheritance.[6] His reliance on eunuchs recalls the pre-Comnenian period, as do his attempts to cut back on grants of privilege and immunity. Yet the cut-back was mainly at the expense of the church and of the Italian maritime republics. All other indications are that he was at least as indulgent to his extended family as his father and grandfather had been, and that he was scrupulous in maintaining a strict hierarchy by blood-relationship. He created one new title, that of *despotes*, for Béla-Alexios of Hungary, when designating him as his future son-in-law and heir to the throne; the title lapsed at the birth of Alexios II, but it was revived by later emperors, and it remained the most senior of the three titles (the others were *sebastokrator* and caesar) which were reserved for the emperor's immediate family, and carried semi-imperial status, allowing their bearers to wear quasi-imperial insignia and to sit with the emperor on ceremonial occasions. Manuel may also have introduced certain changes to the titulature of the wider circle of imperial relatives. In the earlier years of the dynasty, all relatives by blood or marriage below the rank of caesar had been designated by variants of the title *sebastos*. In the ceremonial lists of Manuel's reign, however, the imperial nephews and cousins, who stand next to the enthroned imperial family, have no titles beyond their kinship designation, with the sole exception of the senior imperial nephew, who is *protosebastos* ('first *sebastos*') and *protovestiarios*, i.e. head of the imperial household. The ranks of the *sebastoi* begin at the next level down, and, among them, those who are designated as the emperor's *gambroi*, that is the husbands of his female nieces and cousins, rank senior to those whose relationship is too distant to be named. Not only are ranks carefully graded by degree of kinship to the emperor, and

---

[6] Niketas Choniates, *Historia*, p. 60.

within each degree according to the seniority of the kinsman through whom the kinship is traced, but kinship designations begin to take the place of titles.

In addition to this continual articulation of the imperial family system, Manuel's reign witnessed its further extension downwards from the military to the bureaucracy, and outwards into the sphere of foreign relations. As the Comnenian aristocracy proliferated, more of its members came to hold civilian office, while others married into the more illustrious civilian families, one of which, the Kamateroi, was already connected with the Doukai and well on the way to establishing its later ascendancy in the church and the bureaucracy. The marriage diplomacy of Alexios I and John II had created blood lines leading from the Komnenoi to ruling dynasties in Russia, the Caucasus, Hungary and Germany. Manuel more than doubled the network with marriage alliances that related the imperial family in Constantinople to royal and princely families in Austria, Jerusalem, Antioch, Tuscany, Piedmont, northern France and Languedoc. Marriage alliances were also discussed with Henry II of England and William II of Sicily. This was perhaps the closest Byzantium came to being at the centre of an international 'family of kings': even the sultan of Iconium was included by virtue of his ritual adoption as the emperor's son. That Manuel saw a close connection between his internal and external families is evident in the way he interfered with the church's marriage legislation on the forbidden degrees of kinship and punished men from undistinguished bureaucratic families who threatened to devalue the status of Comnenian brides by attempting to marry into noble families.

In 1180, then, the political existence of the Byzantine empire was governed by kinship and lineage to an unprecedented degree. The future of the system consisted as never before in the cohesion of the extended imperial family. For a century that cohesion had been managed by the emperor as head of the family, but now that the emperor was an eleven-year-old, it depended on a consensus of loyalty to the young Alexios II among the Comnenian nobility. Manuel did what he could to create a framework of collective patriotic and familial responsibility: he set up a regency council, perhaps based on his inner circle of advisers, comprising his widow, the patriarch and a number of relatives. The latter were presumably selected on the basis of seniority, although Choniates indicates that they participated on a basis of equality. At the same time, he obtained guarantees from the sultan, the prince of Antioch, the king of Jerusalem and possibly other members of the external 'family of kings' that they would defend Alexios's inheritance.

With hindsight it seems clear, and contemporaries seem to have sensed, that these measures were doomed to failure. The Comnenian family had been prone to factionalism from the time of Alexios I, and its solidarity inevitably weakened with every generation that multiplied the number of household units

(*oikoi*) with which the imperial *oikos* at the heart of the kin-group (*genos*) had
to share the finite resources of an empire which all continued to regard as the
Comnenian family patrimony. The accessions of John and Manuel had not
gone unchallenged, and although Manuel saw off his original challengers, the
sebastokrators Isaac, his brother and uncle, the latter's place was taken by his
son Andronikos, while the former's supporters seem to have gravitated towards
Alexios Axouch, the husband of Manuel's niece by the emperor's late brother
Alexios. Axouch's 'conspiracy' in 1167 was quickly disposed of, but Andronikos
was a constant worry to Manuel from 1154, almost as troublesome during his
long spells in prison, from which he escaped twice (1159 and 1164), and in exile
among the empire's eastern neighbours (1167–80), as he was during his brief
period of liberty. After his return and rehabilitation in Manuel's final year,
he was understandably sent – like his father before him – into a comfortable
internal exile on the Black Sea coast. But this exclusion from Constantinople
played into Andronikos's hands, by giving him a provincial power-base where
he could recruit supporters, and by casting him as an impartial outsider to
the selfish intrigues which divided the regency council of Alexios II, to the
gross neglect of the boy's upbringing and the public interest. According to
Choniates, there were those who lusted after the widowed empress and sought
to seduce her, those who lusted after money and appropriated public funds
to meet their growing expenses and those who lusted after imperial power.[7]
Elsewhere he describes them in somewhat different terms: 'Some of his noble
guardians winged their way repeatedly like bees to the provinces and stored
up money like honey, others like goats hankered after the tender shoots of
empire which they continually longed to crop, while others grew fat like pigs
on filthy lucre.'[8] The emphasis on money-making is interesting, particularly
the implied distinction between the misappropriation of tax revenue from the
provinces, and the sordid enrichment from the profits of trade, and possibly of
prostitution, in Constantinople. It shows that the search for funds to maintain
an aristocratic lifestyle was a constant motivating factor in political loyalty.

His enforced isolation thus put Andronikos in an ideal position, which he
exploited masterfully, to pose as the champion of Alexios II's best interests,
which the boy's guardians were patently neglecting, and to win the sympathies
of the many noble figures in Constantinople, including Manuel's daughter
Maria, who resented the dominance which one of the regency council, Manuel's
nephew the *protosebastos* Alexios, acquired over the young emperor by forming
an amorous liaison with the dowager empress. After the tension between Maria
and the *protosebastos* broke out in armed conflict, Andronikos's intervention
became inevitable.

[7] *Ibid.*, pp. 223–4.   [8] *Ibid.*, pp. 227–8.

If Andronikos, once in power, had kept his election promises and formed a genuinely inclusive regency government for Alexios II, it is possible that he might have held the Comnenian nobility together. His programme of administrative reform, admirable in itself, could have won him support even among his peers if he had treated them fairly and generously. But by instituting a reign of terror against all potential rivals for the regency, including the emperor's sister and mother, he provoked a serious revolt in Asia Minor; then, by going on to eliminate Alexios II and settle the succession on his son John, he removed the only focus of consensus among the Comnenian kin-group, and committed himself to dependence on a faction bound to him by self-interest. The terror continued, and those who could escaped it by fleeing abroad, to the courts of rulers who had had ties or treaties with Manuel and Alexios II. Thus the sultan, the prince and patriarch of Antioch, the king of Jerusalem, the pope, Frederick Barbarossa, the marquis of Montferrat, the king of Hungary and, above all, the king of Sicily were approached by refugees imploring their intervention. It was at the insistence of Manuel's great-nephew, the *pinkernes* Alexios Komnenos, that William II of Sicily sent the invasion force which took Durazzo and Thessalonica in 1185. The stated aim of the expedition was to replace Andronikos with a young man claiming to be Alexios II: Pseudo-Alexioi were the inconvenient but inevitable consequence – for later emperors as well – of the fact that Andronikos had sunk Alexios's body in the Bosphorus. The Sicilian invasion thus not only recalled the past invasions of Rober Guiscard, Bohemond and Roger II; it also set a precedent for the diversion of the Fourth Crusade, both by the damage and humiliation it caused, and in the way it involved the external 'family of kings' in the politics of the Comnenian family.

Andronikos would probably have succeeded eventually in repelling the Sicilian invasion, as he succeeded in quelling every organized conspiracy against him, but the very diligence of his agents in hunting down potential conspirators led, quite unpredictably, to the spontaneous uprising which toppled him. When his chief agent went to arrest a suspect who had given no cause for suspicion, the suspect slew the agent in desperation, and then did the only thing he could do in order to avoid immediate capital punishment: he rushed for asylum to the church of St Sophia. A crowd gathered, Andronikos – evidently feeling secure – was out of town and, St Sophia being also the imperial coronation church, one thing led to another. So Isaac Angelos became emperor because he was in the right place at the right time, and this had a decisive effect on the course of his reign. His propagandists claimed, and he firmly believed, that his accession was providential, that he was the Angel of the Lord sent by heaven to end the tyranny, so that his whole reign was ordained, blessed and protected by God. He considered his power irreproachable and untouchable, and he exercised it with a mixture of grandiosity and complacency which was quite inappropriate to the situation. For other important people did not share his belief. His miraculous elevation was not enough to convince Isaac Komnenos in Cyprus, Peter and Asan in Bulgaria, Theodore Mangaphas in Philadelphia and Basil Chotzas at Tarsia, near Nicomedia, that they owed loyalty to Constantinople, or to prevent two young men from raising rebellions by pretending to be Alexios II. Among his own close family, it did not make up for his lack of seniority, or his military incompetence: he was challenged by his uncle John and his nephew Constantine. The Comnenian nobility as a whole were not impressed, because many of them had equally good, if not better, dynastic claims in terms of the hierarchy of kinship which had operated under Manuel: Isaac was descended from Alexios I's youngest daughter, but others could trace their descent through the male line, and some could count John II among their ancestors. For several of them, Isaac's success was only an incentive to follow it and turn up at St Sophia in the hope of being acclaimed. The first to try this was Alexios Branas, the general who had halted the Sicilian invasion. Having failed in this first attempt, he waited until he was put in command of the army sent to quell the Vlakh revolt. What made his rebellion so dangerous was the fact that he combined good Comnenian lineage with military expertise and strong family connections among the military aristocracy of Adrianople. Isaac was saved only by the loyalty of the people of Constantinople and a bold sortie by Conrad of Montferrat.

During ten years in power, Isaac II faced at least seventeen revolts, a number exceeded in the eleventh and twelfth centuries only by the twenty-one plots that are recorded for the thirty-nine-year reign of Alexios I. Isaac undoubtedly saw something providential in the fact of his survival, but repeated opposition took its toll on the effectiveness of his rule, by making it virtually impossible for him to delegate important military commands to highly competent noble commanders. This was probably decisive for the outcome of the rebellion of Peter and Asan. Lack of support among the Comnenian nobility may have prompted what was seen to be Isaac's excessive favouritism to his chief bureaucrat, his non-Comnenian maternal uncle Theodore Kastamonites, and to the latter's successor in office, Constantine Mesopotamites. It certainly drove the members of five leading Comnenian families, Palaiologos, Branas, Kantakouzenos, Raoul and Petraliphas, to mount the coup in 1195 which replaced Isaac with his elder brother Alexios III.

Sibling rivalry had, as we have seen, threatened to destroy the Comnenian system in the past, but it had been kept under control, and its eruption into successful usurpation sealed the fate of the system in its twelfth-century phase. Choniates saw the overthrow of brother by brother as the supreme manifestation of the moral depravity for which the fall of Constantinople was just retribution.[9] From the deposition of Isaac II proceeded the escape of his son Alexios to the west just when the Fourth Crusade needed an excuse for a detour via Constantinople. In their comeback, the internal and external dimensions of the system fatally converged. Choniates, perhaps looking back to Andronikos and even to his father, saw a pattern:

> If anything was the supreme cause that the Roman power collapsed to its knees and suffered the seizure of lands and cities, and, finally, itself underwent annihilation, this was the members of the Komnenoi who revolted and usurped power. For, dwelling among the nations which were unfriendly to the Romans, they were the bane of their country, even though when they stayed at home they were ineffectual, useless and incompetent in anything they tried to undertake.[10]

This retribution apart, however, Alexios III faced relatively little opposition from the Komnenoi. In 1200–1 there were provincial revolts led by his cousins Michael Angelos and Manuel Kamytzes, and a one-day occupation of the Great Palace in Constantinople by a son of Alexios Axouch, John Komnenos the Fat. But otherwise, Alexios had fairly good support in the bureaucracy and the church through his connection by marriage into the Kamateros family, and the consortium of Comnenian families which brought him to power appear to have been satisfied with his laissez-faire regime, and with his adoption of the name Komnenos in preference to Angelos. All five families flourished after 1204; four were to be prominent after 1261 in the restored empire of the Palaiologoi, and the Palaiologoi gained a head start in their future ascendancy from the marriage which Alexios III arranged between his daughter Eirene and Alexios Palaiologos.

The marriage of another daughter, Anna, to Theodore Laskaris laid the dynastic basis for the empire of Nicaea, the most successful of the three main Greek successor states after 1204. Cousins of Isaac II and Alexios III established the western state which enjoyed brief glory as the empire of Thessalonica and then survived in north-western Greece as the despotate of Epiros. The empire of Trebizond, which lasted until 1461, was ruled by a dynasty calling themselves the Grand Komnenoi, who were descended from Andronikos I.

Under the successors of Manuel I, the Comnenian system, centred on Constantinople, was programmed for self-destruction. Relocated to the provinces after 1204 through the leading families of the last twelfth-century regimes, it ensured the survival of the Byzantine empire for another two and a half centuries, while losing none of its divisive potential.

---

[9] *Ibid.*, pp. 453–4, 532.   [10] *Ibid.*, p. 529.

CHAPTER 21

THE LATIN EAST, 1098–1205

Hans Eberhard Mayer

THE First Crusade ended with the conquest of Jerusalem on 15 July 1099, resulting in the foundation of the Latin kingdom of Jerusalem. This was to become the biggest and most important crusader state but others had been established while the crusade was *en route*. From the autumn of 1097 to March 1098 Baldwin of Boulogne occupied the country west and east of the Euphrates, finally taking over Edessa where he set up the county of Edessa which protected the other crusader states in the north-east. Latin rule was imposed on a predominantly Armenian population. Following the conquest of Antioch in June 1098 Bohemond I of Taranto who had been the leading figure in the long and bitter siege of the town succeeded in having his claim to Antioch recognized by the leaders of the crusading army before the crusade started to move again. Provençal attempts to curb Norman ambitions had been thwarted. Neither Baldwin nor Bohemond participated in the rest of the crusade and neither one of them adhered to a promise made earlier to the Byzantine emperor that all conquests of formerly Byzantine territories would be restored to Byzantium. Bohemond now established the principality of Antioch where a distinctly Norman ruling class governed a population partly Muslim, partly Greek. He gained legitimacy when he was invested with the principality by the patriarch of Jerusalem on Christmas 1099.

When the crusaders had reached Ramla, the old capital of Palestine, they appointed a Latin bishop there without any participation of the Greek church. In retrospect this was to become the starting-point of a Latin church in Palestine. After a siege of nearly six weeks Jerusalem was stormed and its population massacred in a blood bath. On 12 August this success was consolidated when an Egyptian army was beaten near Ascalon. Three years had passed since Godfrey of Bouillon had set out from Lorraine. Organizing the success was more difficult. After Raymond of Toulouse had rejected a half-hearted offer to rule over Jerusalem, Godfrey of Bouillon, duke of Lower Lorraine, was brought to power by the army but refused the kingship and continued under the title of

Map 17 The Latin east

duke. In Jerusalem he was king in fact but not in name. The relations between state and church remained undefined not only because of the ambiguity of Godfrey's position but also because the patriarchate of Jerusalem could not, at first, be adequately filled. The Greek patriarch had died on Cyprus, but the able Fleming Arnulf of Chocques, who was placed over the church of Jerusalem, was so objectionable in terms of canon law that he was not consecrated and was, in fact, soon removed.

In September 1099 most crusaders made for home. Raymond of Toulouse was driven by Godfrey first from Jerusalem, later out of south-western Palestine, and went to Syria and Lebanon. Godfrey, who died on 18 July 1100, had had only one year in which to rule. He had not enough fighting power left to do more than hold Jerusalem, Jaffa, Lydda and Ramla, Bethlehem and Hebron. These were islands in a sea of hostile Muslims. Yet when Bohemond's nephew Tancred subjected large parts of Galilee to Christian rule Godfrey could persuade him to hold them in fief from him. The demographic structure was totally unsatisfactory and remained so, more or less, at all times. The largest elements in the population were the Muslims and the Syro-Christians but it is impossible to know which of the two were more numerous in the open country whereas in the cities the Syro-Christians certainly outnumbered the Muslims who, like the Jews, were totally barred from Jerusalem. The term 'Syro-Christians', the *Suriani*, very often met with in crusader documents, is vague and it meant different things at different times and in different places. Generally speaking it lumped together all Christians 'not of the law of Rome'. For most purposes this was enough in a country where the deepest social gap was between Frank (i.e. crusaders or their offspring) and non-Frank. The vagueness appears when we try to differentiate. Inasmuch as the sources allow a generalization the term referred to eastern Christians with Arabic language and – in most cases – Syriac liturgy, more particularly, and following a rough geographical distribution of predominant creeds from north to south, to heretical Monophysite Jacobites in the north, heretical (until 1181) Monothelite Maronites in Lebanon and schismatic Greek Orthodox in the south. Above them the European ruling class of Catholic creed, known as Latins or Franks and divided into clergy, nobility and personally free burgesses, remained numerically very small, but this *Staatsvolk* monopolized all political rights although in very different degrees.

To make things worse, the Franks were very unevenly distributed throughout the country. There was a heavy concentration in the cities; in fact the nobility was largely absent from their landed estates which were run by native administrators. Contrary to received opinion it has recently been shown that the Franks in the open country did not live in total segregation from the native Syro-Christians but that they rather settled in areas where Syro-Christians had already lived in pre-crusade days and continued to live together with the Franks in the same villages. The Frankish population was thinnest where, for security reasons, it was most badly needed, namely on the desert fringe east of Galilee, of the Jordan river and the Dead Sea. Given this deficiency in an adequate defence it was of vital importance that the supply lines from Europe be kept open at least during the shipping season from spring to autumn. This required the conquest of the coast. Godfrey clearly recognized this problem and, in order to buy Pisan naval support, he had to give in to the unrelenting pressure of the church now under the rule of Daimbert, a former archbishop of Pisa, and make over to him a principality in successive stages.

After Godfrey's death his vassals, originating mostly from Lorraine and northern France, prevented the implementation of these donations and successfully invited Godfrey's brother Baldwin to come from Edessa. On Christmas Day 1100 he was crowned as the first Latin king of Jerusalem. His solemn behaviour contrasted sharply with his scandalous married life in three marriages. An incessant warrior, he ruled his vassals with an iron fist and became the true founder of the Latin kingdom of Jerusalem. With the church he dealt in pre-Gregorian fashion attributing to himself the control of ecclesiastical revenues and riding rough-shod over several patriarchs. But he also energetically supported the endeavours of Arnulf of Chocques, canonical patriarch after 1112, to reform the church of Jerusalem. In 1101 he consolidated the predominantly Lorraine–northern French character of the kingdom by pushing the Norman Tancred out of Galilee. By 1110, when he took Beirut and Sidon, he had conquered most of the coast. In these two towns the Muslim inhabitants were, for the first time, given a choice between emigration and remaining under Frankish rule, a remarkable change, dictated by necessity, of the previous policy of extermination. Particularly important was the conquest of Acre in 1104. It gave the kingdom the first safe harbour and the town grew quickly into the economic centre of the kingdom; by 1120 it had spilled over the city walls into a suburb. By 1105 King Baldwin I had stopped the threat of an Egyptian reconquest in a series of battles near Ramla.

Indecisive fighting in the regions east of the Sea of Galilee came to an end in 1108–10 when Baldwin and Damascus set up a kind of no-man's land with a condominium over the northern Transjordan, the Jaulan and the Lebanese plain of Biqa' in which the revenues squeezed from the peasants were divided. In spite of temporary violations this system lasted until 1187, although neither side had considered it as final. From 1110 to 1113 Baldwin successfully opposed a great Muslim coalition seriously menacing his kingdom. He was saved by the death of his leading opponents. This gave him the chance in 1115 and 1116 to intervene seriously for the first time in the southern Transjordan, which he secured by building the great castle of Montréal.

The price for these startling successes was heavy. Following precedents already discernible under Godfrey, Baldwin embarked on a policy of buying the necessary naval support, which only the Italian maritime republics could give, by grants which not only gave them freedom from, or large reduction of, taxes and customs but also quarters of their own which, at least from 1124, became increasingly autonomous from state intervention in which they enjoyed their own consular jurisdiction over everything apart from certain crimes, the most offensive of which normally reserved for royal jurisdiction.

In 1113 Baldwin concluded a very valuable alliance with Sicily by marrying Adalasia, the mother of Roger II, who also brought much desperately needed money. But the marriage contract envisaged the succession of Roger in Jerusalem should there be no children and Baldwin never had any. In 1117 the church and the vassals, using the fact, formerly conveniently overlooked, that Baldwin's former wife was still alive and the marriage undivorced, forced him to repudiate Adalasia, thus revoking the Sicilian alliance. It was the first sign that the king had become politically vulnerable. In the following year the vassals forced him to abandon a campaign to Egypt which he refused to conduct according to their wishes. On the way back he died from an old wound.

He was succeeded by his kinsman Baldwin II. But part of the nobility at first offered a stiff opposition to this and attempted to place Baldwin I's brother Eustace III of Boulogne on the throne. Civil war was barely averted. Internal consolidation now followed the political expansion of the previous reign. The king quickly made peace with the church at the council of Nablus in 1120, releasing ecclesiastical tithes from royal and baronial control.

The king's main concern was the Syrian north. He himself had been appointed count of Edessa from 1100 onwards. The Franks had been weakened by a series of misfortunes. Bohemond I of Antioch was a Muslim prisoner from 1100 to 1103 and his nephew Tancred became his regent. He secured Antiochene possession of Cilicia and permanently added the port of Latakia in 1108. After Bohemond's release in 1103 an attempt by the united Frankish north to cut off Aleppo from the Seljuq bases in Mesopotamia was stopped short by the Frankish defeat at the Balikh river in 1104, which destroyed the legend of Frankish invincibility and brought Baldwin of Edessa into Muslim captivity. Edessa became for a time a dependency of Antioch and Tancred once more took the regency of Antioch when Bohemond went to Europe in 1105 to enlist support against growing Byzantine pressure on his principality from the north. But his crusade against Durazzo on the Adriatic coast ended in utter failure and with such a humiliating peace treaty, never in fact enforced, that Bohemond did not dare show his face again in Antioch and died in 1111 in his native Apulia, a forgotten man.

When Baldwin of Edessa regained his liberty in 1108 Tancred hesitated to hand back Edessa. A war between inter-religious coalitions now ensued, Tancred and Aleppo fighting against Edessa and Mosul: the crusaders had quickly been integrated into the bewildering Syro-Mesopotamian political scene. King Baldwin I was asked to come from Jerusalem to act as arbitrator of the Frankish east. He did so in camp before Tripoli, which had been under siege since 1103, first by Raymond of Toulouse, who had died there in 1105, leaving behind a succession dispute. In 1109 Baldwin I worked out a compromise which for a short time split the old count's Lebanese possessions in two under the influence of Antioch and Jerusalem respectively. Soon, however, death, or perhaps murder, reunited the county which then became a fief of the kings of Jerusalem although it was not formally united with the kingdom and was often ready to cut these ties. Antioch, in 1109, was left under Tancred's rule, its independence from Jerusalem guaranteed. An alternative for Tancred was provided in Galilee, should Bohemond I return, but Tancred had to give up his claims to Edessa. Then the siege of Tripoli was pressed and the city capitulated in July 1109. This completed the foundation of the last crusader state, the county of Tripoli, which was Provençal in character.

It was of the greatest importance that the settlement of 1109 established a precedent for the kings of Jerusalem to be the supreme arbiters of the whole Latin east. When King Baldwin I fought against Damascus and Mosul (1110–13), he was acting as much in the interest of the north as in that of his own kingdom. More or less by coincidence he was not present when Antioch and Edessa, now assisted by Aleppo and Damascus, defeated the Seljuqs at Tall Danith in 1115, which meant the end of the attempts by the Seljuq sultans to reconquer Syria.

No king of Jerusalem became more involved in Antioch affairs than Baldwin II. Tancred officially ruled Antioch as regent until he died in 1112. His successor Roger was formally only regent for Bohemond II, the minor son of Bohemond I, who was in Apulia. Hardly had Baldwin II become king and had given his former county of Edessa to his kingmaker Joscelin I of Courtenay, previously lord of Galilee, when he had to go north, following an appeal for help from Roger of Antioch, who foolishly joined battle with the Muslims before Baldwin's arrival. His army was annihilated in 1119 in what justly became known as the 'Field of Blood' and he himself was killed. Baldwin II now had to shoulder the regency of Antioch, which he could not shed until Bohemond II arrived in 1126. On the whole he did well for the north but he paid heavily for it. The regency was unpopular in Jerusalem from the beginning. The vassals had to go through interminable wars against Aleppo but were excluded by a formal regency contract from being rewarded with fiefs in the north. As early as 1120 the king had difficulties in obtaining the chief war relic of the True Cross for a campaign to the north. In April 1123 he was captured by the Aleppans and did not permanently regain his liberty until the summer of 1124. Even then he stayed in the north until 1125. During his captivity he had been replaced in Antioch by the patriarch, in Jerusalem by a council of three regents. That there had not been a constitutional crisis testifies to the solidity of monarchical institutions in Jerusalem, but the population may, in fact, have preferred the regency to the rule of a king forever absent.

The regents scored a considerable success when they conquered the important port town of Tyre in July 1124 with naval support from Venice. But this indispensable help had to be bought with enormous concessions. In addition to the usual privileges Venice obtained its own court over all cases involving Venetians, except mixed cases with a Venetian plaintiff which were reserved to the king. Venice also received one third of the town's *contado*. A standard of Italian accomplishment had been set by which other Italian maritime republics would measure their own success. But these grants seriously affected the jurisdictional, in fact even the political, coherence of the state.

In 1126 Baldwin II could at last surrender his regency in the north, but he had to resume it in 1130 when Bohemond II was killed in battle, leaving behind an infant daughter Constance. On the Muslim front Baldwin's last years, although troubled by internal revolt, were uneventful after an expedition against Damascus had failed miserably in 1129. At this time, after a precarious existence of nearly ten years, the military order of the Knights Templar gained recognition by the church, although it took another decade until its organizational framework was complete. The Templars' future rivals, the Knights Hospitallers, were older and went back to an Amalfitan hostel in Jerusalem of pre-crusade days. While the Templars were warriors from the beginning, the Hospitallers, who never gave up their charitable functions, took on military duties in the Holy Land from 1136 on; by 1154 their organization was complete. Both orders could soon draw on large revenues in Europe and added a very useful new element to the kingdom's fighting power both in men and in maintenance of many big castles.

The king died in 1131. There being no sons he had provided for his succession by creating a system of joint rule for his eldest daughter Melisende and Count Fulk of Anjou, her husband since 1129.

Responsibility for the north rested on Fulk just as it had done on the two Baldwins. Repeatedly he had to ward off attempts by the dowager princess Alice of Antioch, another of Baldwin's daughters, to establish herself as ruler at the expense of her own daughter Constance. In the course of these machinations Alice was not above seeking, or flirting with, allies wherever she could find them: Edessa, Tripoli, the patriarch, but, more dangerously, Byzantium and even Mosul. These troubles so weakened Antioch that Cilicia was lost first to the Armenians, later to Byzantium. In 1136 Fulk installed Raymond of Poitiers as Constance's husband and prince of Antioch. This was the end of Norman predominance there.

Great difficulties now arose from renewed Byzantine designs on Antioch as a former Byzantine possession. When Emperor John Komnenos himself appeared before Antioch in 1137 both Prince Raymond and King Fulk had to accept terms which made Antioch a Byzantine fief. It was hoped that Byzantium would provide decisive help against 'Imad al-Din Zengi, a formidable foe who had united Mosul and Aleppo in 1127–8. But such help did not come. Emperor John refrained from entering Antioch until 1138 when he was driven out by a popular riot because his army was still campaigning further east. Zengi now had designs on Damascus. This led Damascus to an alliance with Jerusalem in 1139 which became the backbone of Jerusalem's foreign policy until 1154. No matter how severe the strain under which it came from time to time, it held. In 1140 Fulk conquered Banyas. It controlled the headwaters of the Jordan and fertile lands in upper Galilee and was also important as a principal Muslim gateway into the kingdom's north. In the same year a papal legate deposed Patriarch Ralph of Antioch who had been the last one to dream of an autocephalous Latin church in the east. In the south-west Fulk contained the Egyptian outpost of Ascalon by building a ring of fortresses around it and much was done in his days for the Transjordan. In 1142 Emperor John Komnenos once more marched into Cilicia and Syria. This time he even contemplated an armed 'pilgrimage' to Jerusalem. The project greatly alarmed Fulk who dissuaded him with some difficulty. Antioch was saved by the emperor's sudden death in April 1143, followed in November by that of Fulk.

Fulk was succeeded by his minor son Baldwin III for whom his mother acted as regent. The most pressing problems were, again, in the north. The history of the county of Tripoli had been more or less uneventful since 1109 except for a rapprochement in 1112 between Tripoli and Antioch which ended the Provençal–Norman antagonism that had arisen in 1098. Early in Fulk's reign, there had also been a Tripolitan attempt to throw off Jerusalem suzerainty. But the pressure from the lesser amirates on the upper Orontes river who successively came under Zengi's control grew to a point where the counts of Tripoli had doubts about holding their own. In order to protect their eastern frontier they established two important and virtually independent frontier marches, one in 1144 by giving the castle of Crak des Chevaliers near Homs to the Knights Hospitallers, who much enlarged it, the other from 1152 when the Knights Templar took over most of Tortosa, adding in the course of time the mighty castle of Chastel Blanc. Both marches faced the Syrian branch of the Assassins, an unruly and extremely dangerous Shi'ite sect which, between 1132 and 1141, had established itself in the mountains east of Tortosa. Whereas the

Hospitallers constituted a real threat to them, the Templars by 1173 protected them in return for an annual tribute. In 1152, in one of their spectacular political murders, the Assassins murdered Count Raymond II of Tripoli: it was the first time that they had struck out at the Franks.

The fate of Edessa was more dramatic. The energetic count Joscelin I, from the house of Courtenay, who had come to the east in 1101, had died thirty years later, leaving his county to his son and namesake, an indolent *débauché* who indulged in luxuries and carried on interminable intrigues against Raymond of Antioch, his feudal overlord from 1140. East of the Euphrates the county had so often been ravaged by the Turks that it had become impoverished. In the capital the stocks of food and arms had been allowed to fall below the critical level. The Frankish element in the population was even smaller than in the other crusader states and the city was defended by Armenian mercenaries who were only irregularly paid. When Zengi laid siege to Edessa at the end of 1144 it was too late. After the death of the Byzantine emperor in 1143 the Byzantine army had evacuated Syria. Antioch now had to look after herself and her prince was in no mood to do much for Edessa. Jerusalem, after King Fulk's death, was politically unstable. Queen Melisende did send an army of relief but before its arrival Edessa fell on Christmas 1144, the event sparking off the Second Crusade. It was only a matter of time before the rest of the county should fall.

A reconquest of Edessa after Zengi's death in 1146 lasted only a few days and led to the town being pillaged and burnt and the Christian population being enslaved and murdered. Edessa never fully recovered from this blow and ceased to be an attractive target for the Franks. From a new capital further west Joscelin II could hold the line of the Euphrates until he was captured in 1150, never to be set free again. What was left of the county now lay open to Seljuq attacks from Anatolia. Neither Antioch, where Prince Raymond had been killed in 1149, nor Jerusalem, where there was bitter internal strife, were able to do more than cover the retreat. Consequently, and with Baldwin III's approval, the countess of Edessa sold the remaining six fortresses west of the Euphrates to Byzantium in 1150, although they were lost to the Muslims within a year. Edessa, the first crusader state to have been founded, was the first to fall after only half a century of a precarious Latin rule.

When Zengi was murdered in 1146 his dominions were divided between his two sons, one of them, Nur al-Din, receiving Aleppo. He was to become an even more redoubtable enemy for the Franks than his father had been. Unlike Zengi, Nur al-Din was not occupied by Mesopotamian affairs and could concentrate on fighting Damascus and the Franks. Following the sack of Edessa, he took from Antioch most of her possessions east of the Orontes in 1147–8, reducing the principality to a stretch of territory wedged in between the Orontes and the Mediterranean. The coming of the Second Crusade in 1148 forced him to march to the relief of Damascus. Owing to a rift which had occurred between Louis VII of France and Raymond of Antioch, the principality kept aloof from the crusade, as did Tripoli for other reasons. But after the crusade Nur al-Din returned. In June 1149 he joined battle with the Franks at Inab east of the Orontes and won his finest victory against them. Prince Raymond was killed. The government of Antioch was placed in the hands of Raymond's widow Constance but was, in effect, exercised by the patriarch Aimery of Limoges who, for much of his long pontificate of fifty-three years, was the *éminence grise* of Antioch politics. What had remained of the principality east of the Orontes was now lost but to the west of it the immediate effects of the battle were negligible. However, it established Nur al-Din as the champion of Sunnite Islam and of the Holy War against the Franks. Muslim propaganda supported his religious and political aims and the reconquest of Jerusalem became a political programme.

In the south the kingdom of Jerusalem was badly split by internal strife and it served King Baldwin III's purposes that he had gained some prestige as a military leader by campaigns in support of the northern crusader states as well as by a successful expedition to Petra in the Transjordan. Warfare was one field in which his mother could not compete with him, because in every other respect she did.

It is not clear how, after initial difficulties, the joint rule initiated in 1131 had worked under Fulk. After 1134 the consent of his queen Melisende was included in Fulk's charters but it is not certain to what extent this reflected a real share in government. What is easier to see is that Patriarch William of Jerusalem (1130–45) had a more direct influence on royal government than any other patriarch before or after him. Joint embassies attest to this. In a unique exception from Jerusalem chancery usage William sealed a royal charter jointly with the king and, even more significantly, once issued a charter in his name but at the king's command and concerning royal business. Melisende's hour came when Fulk died. Her son, King Baldwin III, was a minor and until 1145 Melisende was his regent. When Baldwin came of age Melisende continued in her government as if nothing had happened, because as co-ruler she had, already in Fulk's days, held a (territorially undefined) share in the kingdom which remained hers. For the kingdom this meant trouble.

By 1149 the chancellor, the very able Englishman Ralph, had to leave his office and failed in a bid for the archbishopric of Tyre. For several years mother and son failed to agree on a new chancellor and the royal charter business was transacted in rival personal *scriptoria* by their respective chaplains. This collapse was the most visible sign of the deep rift between mother and son splitting the whole kingdom. Melisende had the support of the church. She controlled Jerusalem and Judaea and also Samaria and Galilee. Except for the chancery she succeeded in creating her own household officials. The kingdom's chief military officer, the constable Manasses of Hierges, was a relative of hers. The king only very gradually succeeded in turning the royal domain around Tyre and Acre into a power-base. He was also successful in securing the loyalty of the lords of Beirut and Toron in the north, and the lord of Toron also held Hebron in the south for him as castellan.

Early in the crisis the Second Crusade gave Baldwin III a chance against his mother. Given the fact that the alliance with Damascus was essential for the peaceful development of Jerusalem, the plan to besiege it has baffled historians as much as the execution of the siege. An explanation may be found in the power-struggle going on in Jerusalem. There are signs in the sources that Baldwin intended to give Damascus to the lord of Beirut, which would decisively have swung the balance of power in his favour. Owing to treasonable manoeuvres by the Jerusalem nobles the siege had to be abandoned and, among others, Elinand of Galilee who, as lord of Galilee and as a partisan of Melisende, would have been doubly affected by the king's designs, was held responsible for this.

From 1150 onwards a showdown was likely. The king had to rely for support on the dispossessed and the disgruntled. The queen-mother had created vassals of her own who claimed to owe allegiance only to her and who, in 1150, refused to answer the king's summons to serve in the army, arguing that they were from Melisende's portion of the kingdom. This was tantamount to a division of the kingdom, but after the Second Crusade Melisende's position began to weaken. Galilee changed sides. She was able to offset this by creating her younger son Amalric count of Jaffa in 1151. But she made a serious mistake when, in 1150 or 1151, she arranged a marriage between her constable Manasses, still a landless newcomer, and a very rich widow. This antagonized the old families in general and the widow's sons from the rapidly climbing powerful Ibelin clan in particular. Baldwin III struck at Easter 1152. He petitioned the patriarch to crown him in the absence of his mother. When, predictably, the patriarch refused, the king marched through the capital wearing his crown. It was a declaration of war. An immediate formal division of the kingdom was ineffective and in a three-week civil war the king dislodged his mother from power and brought down the unpopular Manasses, who had to return to Europe. As a last remnant of her former share in the kingdom Melisende (d. 1162) was able to retain the royal domain in Samaria with a promise of non-interference by the king. Occasionally she emerged from her retreat at Nablus to exercise ecclesiastical patronage and even to voice opinions on policy, when the king was out of the country. Otherwise the joint rule was dead. The former chancellor Ralph was reappointed and rose to be bishop of Bethlehem in 1156.

Only the most prominent supporters of Melisende re-entered royal service quickly. Others were never readmitted or were kept on the sidelines for a long time.

With his rule now secure Baldwin III looked for political success. In 1153, after a siege of nearly seven months, during which seasonal pilgrims were pressganged into the army and the king was brought to the brink of bankruptcy, he conquered Ascalon, the last Muslim stronghold on the coast. He was now strong enough to restore his brother Amalric, a strong supporter of Melisende, to his graces by creating him count of Jaffa-Ascalon (1154).

The spectacular success at Ascalon may have made people forget that further north things were not going at all well. Since 1149 Damascus had been internally weak following the death of Unur, its able Turkish commander, who had struck the alliance with Jerusalem in 1139. From 1150 onwards Nur al-Din of Aleppo increased the pressure on Damascus while his propagandists denounced the treaty with the Franks. The king tried to bolster the defence of Antioch in 1150 by finding a new husband for Constance, the widow of the last prince. Although he proposed candidates of convincing reputation she rejected all of them and, in fact, all idea of a new marriage. Subsequent events demonstrated that this was a mere pretext caused by a political impasse since, in 1150, the king and his mother had been unable to agree on a suitable candidate. But within a year of Melisende's political fall Constance, in a move which took her vassals totally by surprise but for which she had obtained the king's approval, married Reynald of Châtillon, a reckless dare-devil from Burgundy who, having lost his French patrimony, was serving as a penniless mercenary at Ascalon. Peter of Blois later beatified him, mostly because of his undeniable bravery, and in doing so he missed the mark. Reynald may have been helped by his claim to an illustrious ancestry reaching back to a Gallo-Roman senatorial family but Baldwin III should never have approved the marriage. From now on Reynald made eternal trouble wherever he went. Hardly was he in office at Antioch when he rid himself of the political influence of Patriarch Aimery by driving him into an exile which lasted until 1159 through an act of extravagant brutality.

It is true that warriors were needed after the people of Damascus had opened the gates of the city to Nur al-Din in 1154. Jerusalem had lost the relative security enjoyed under the alliance of 1139. But with Aleppo and Damascus now united against Antioch and Jerusalem, with Emperor Frederick Barbarossa busy in Italy and with England and France eternally locked in their conflict of interests, it was clear that the only power capable of supporting the Franks was Byzantium. That alliance required a diplomatic skill which Reynald sadly lacked. Fortunately, King Baldwin III was more skilful. He began negotiations with Byzantium in 1157, trying to offset the very bad impression Reynald had made in the previous year when, in cooperation with an Armenian prince from Cilicia, he had sacked the rich Byzantine island of Cyprus. The new alliance between Jerusalem and Byzantium was concluded in September 1158 when Baldwin married a Byzantine princess. In political terms it was agreed that Emperor Manuel Komnenos would bring help against Nur al-Din, and Baldwin would acquiesce in the humbling of Reynald. In 1158 Manuel marched into Syria with a well-trained army. Reynald submitted quickly, recognized the emperor's suzerainty and promised to install a Greek patriarch in the city. But for the time being Manuel did not press this point.

In 1159 he concluded a truce with Nur al-Din which set up a system of balance of power for north Syria which was to last until the Byzantine position in Anatolia, and consequently in Cilicia and Syria, collapsed in 1176 in the battle of Myriokephalon. While no direct Byzantine administration was set up in Antioch, the principality came under heavy Byzantine influence. However, this *pax Byzantina* meant security for the Franks. Nur al-Din understood that Manuel was capable and willing, if need be, to intervene decisively on their behalf. Conversely, Nur al-Din could rest assured that the Franks would not engage in a full-scale war against his bases in Damascus and Aleppo.

For a decade, the Franks directed their war efforts towards Egypt. In one of the skirmishes in the north Prince Reynald was captured (in 1161, rather than 1160) and remained imprisoned at Aleppo for sixteen years. No one troubled to ransom him. When he was finally released from prison he was more violently anti-Muslim than ever before. Following his capture, there was a governmental crisis in Antioch in which both Constance and Patriarch Aimery, who was supported by Baldwin III, claimed the rulership. Constance sought to improve her position by marrying her daughter Maria to Emperor Manuel but this led to accusations that she was inviting a Byzantine garrison to be stationed in Antioch. Her own barons now drove her out and installed as prince Bohemond III (1163–1201), her son by Raymond of Poitiers. Bohemond was captured by the Muslims in 1164 and set free in 1165 but his ransom had been set at an amount he was unable to pay without Byzantine help. In exchange he had to accept a Greek patriarch in Antioch, the first since 1100, who was killed in 1170 by his cathedral collapsing on him in the great earthquake which also turned Tripoli into a ghost town. The Latin patriarch was then restored.

In 1163 Baldwin III died without offspring and his widow was soon to elope with a Byzantine adventurer. Baldwin was succeeded by his brother Amalric who could only become king, however, after he had separated from his wife, whom he had taken away from his principal vassal to whom she had been married at the time. Amalric left a record of being an outstanding law-maker, even though Baldwin II and Baldwin III had set fine precedents. He is best remembered in this field for his *Assise sur la ligece* (below, p. 672) and for his creation of special courts dealing with commercial and maritime cases.

The pact with Byzantium remained the backbone of Amalric's foreign policy even though he placed increasing strains upon it. But in its shadow, and protected by it on his northern flank, he embarked on an ambitious policy to conquer Egypt. The door had been opened by the conquest of Ascalon but the lure had always been there because Egypt, under the last Fatimid caliphs, was politically weak and in the grip of competing viziers and corrupt Coptic bureaucrats. It was, however, a country rich through trade and productivity: in 1168 it was seriously believed that the grant of the city of Bilbais and its *contado* would provide the Knights Hospitallers with annual revenues of 100,000 gold pieces. Since 1156 King Baldwin III had taken a hard line, trying to hit the Fatimid navy by enforcing an embargo on shipbuilding materials and in 1159 he had discussed the conquest of Egypt with the Byzantine emperor.

But it was Amalric who seriously attacked Egypt. He invaded the country in 1163, 1164, 1167, 1168 and 1169. This aggressive policy, together with the internal weakness of Egypt, was bound to attract Nur al-Din's attention, and he sent troops to Egypt. In 1164 he also put the pressure on Amalric by launching, in spite of the *pax Byzantina*, a short but dangerous campaign against Antioch and Tripoli, capturing the rulers of both. Raymond III of Tripoli (1152–87) remained in prison for ten years while King Amalric took over his county as regent. Worse than this, Nur al-Din reconquered Banyas at the same time. This caused the Franks a profound shock and it forced Amalric out of Egypt. In 1167 he was obliged to return to the Nile to offset the effects of another army which Nur al-Din had sent there. He and his Egyptian allies forced the Syrian army to leave the country and a Frankish garrison was installed in Cairo to supervise the collection of an enormous annual tribute to be paid to Jerusalem.

But Amalric was not satisfied. He now planned to conquer Egypt with Byzantine help and strengthened his alliance by marrying a great-niece of Emperor Manuel immediately after the campaign of 1167. In 1168 a formal treaty on the conquest of Egypt was concluded. Byzantium was to provide the naval support indispensable for blockading the Nile delta. But a war party persuaded the king to commence the camapaign prematurely without Byzantium. Syria and Egypt now formed a common front. Nur al-Din's Kurdish general Shirkuh made himself vizier of Egypt and, after his death in 1169, was succeeded in this post by his nephew Saladin, the fifth vizier in only six years. Saladin came from a Kurdish military family in Nur al-Din's service and was to become the founder of the great dynasty of the Ayyubids. He was obliged to bide his time as master of Egypt under Nur al-Din's formal overlordship even after he had abolished the Shi'ite caliphate of the Fatimids in 1171.

By that time he had beaten off Amalric's last assault on Egypt in 1169, this time launched against Damietta with the active support of a Byzantine fleet. The understanding was that, in the event of a conquest, Jerusalem would

receive the interior with Cairo and Bilbais and a port at Rosetta while the
rest would go to Byzantium. When the Byzantines sent an armada of 200
ships, Amalric had second thoughts and made a secret deal with Damietta
leading to the evacuation of Egypt. For the remainder of the twelfth century
this meant the end of the Frankish assault on Egypt. Nothwithstanding initial
successes Amalric's Egyptian policy had ended in disaster. It had been very
costly to finance because the vassals had to be paid in cash when they were
called to serve outside the kingdom: the campaign of 1164 had been paid for
by an Egyptian ally, who put up generous *per diems*; in 1167 an extraordinary
10 per cent tax was levied on the vassals remaining at home; in 1168 lavish
promises in Egypt were made to the participants; while in 1169 Byzantium was
the paymaster. Except for the short-lived tribute of 1167 the gains which had
been hoped for had not materialized nor had the country been occupied.

On a royal visit to Constantinople in 1171 Amalric was treated with lavish
magnificence but this probably covered up the acceptance of some son of feudal
dependence on Byzantium by the king. The result was a growing influence of
the Byzantine emperor in the kingdom of Jerusalem. The Greek church could
emerge more freely than before into the open. For the first time since 1099 a
Greek patriarch of Jerusalem was able to reside in Palestine for eleven months
in 1177–8. Greek painters and mosaicists embellished, at Manuel's expense,
not only small crusader churches like the one at Abu Ghosh near Jerusalem
but also the principal shrines of the Nativity at Bethlehem and of the Holy
Sepulchre at Jerusalem. To the latter the crusaders had added a large choir
which had been completed in the days of King Fulk, although consecration
had been postponed to coincide with the fiftieth anniversary of Jerusalem's
conquest on 15 July 1149. In Bethlehem Manuel was remembered in a bilingual
inscription. His portrait was painted in the church and a mosaic showing the
ecumenical council of 381 spoke, albeit in Greek, of the procession of the Holy
Spirit without reference to the *filioque* clause which had later been added to
the conciliar creed in the west. It seems that the bishop-chancellor Ralph of
Bethlehem truly merited William of Tyre's verdict that he was utterly worldly.

Help from Europe, although constantly requested, did not come. Saladin
in Cairo was not idle. In 1170 he recaptured Gaza and drove the Latins out
of Aqaba on the Red Sea, thus reopening the land route between Egypt and
Mecca and threatening the Frankish Transjordan from the south. His political
power in Egypt grew steadily. Following the restoration of Sunnism there, he
came to be considered as the champion of Islamic orthodoxy by the Sunnites.
This led to an increasing estrangement between him and his Syrian master after
1171. He was rescued from these difficulties by the more or less simultaneous
deaths of Nur al-Din and Amalric in 1174. In 1175 he was recognized by the
caliph as overlord of Egypt and most of Syria.

Over the years Saladin became increasingly committed to destroying the crusader states and it is for his overwhelming success on this score that his name has gone down all through history, but he was not admired by everyone. Over the centuries he has sometimes been forgotten in Islam and his renewed fame only dates from 1898 when the German emperor William II extolled his fame in a dinner speech in Damascus. William also restored Saladin's mausoleum in which consequently the Prussian eagle, sculptured in wood, is seen rising to the skies.

Although Saladin did not neglect the war against the Franks, he was not above concluding truces with them to gain time to advance his career in the Islamic world. This, and the fact that in 1177 he suffered a crushing defeat at the hands of the Franks, may have deceived some people in Jerusalem as to his actual strength. The truth was that after 1183 the Franks were caught, as if in a pair of tongs, by one man who ruled from Aleppo to Cairo.

Saladin's rise accelerated the decline of the Franks. King Amalric was succeeded by his minor son Baldwin IV who was afflicted by leprosy. Imperceptibly his legs became paralysed and he had to change from horse to litter. By the time he was twenty-one years of age he was a living corpse. He was beginning to lose his eyesight and his face was now so disfigured that in public he had to hide it behind a veil. As leprosy, in principle, rendered a king unfit for office, and as he could not marry and have children, his succession became a cause for concern in the east and in Europe. A regime of regents was not sufficient to prevent the rapid disintegration of the kingdom at the hands of greedy and opposing factions. In the beginning he had been under the thumb of his late father's favourite, the seneschal Miles of Plancy, who established an unconstitutional regime and interrupted the normal contacts between the king and his barons. It seems that it was the nobility which removed Miles by murder. He was accused of having plotted to supplant the king, but so did everyone else prominently in power in those years, including Count Raymond III of Tripoli after 1184.

Raymond had been released from Muslim captivity in 1174 and had not only regained his county but had also married the heiress of Galilee, which made him one of the greatest magnates in the kingdom. During his two regencies (1174–6 and 1184–6), and always in close cooperation with Bohemond III of Antioch, he conducted a cautious policy aiming at truces rather than battles. He headed one of the rival parties in the kingdom, and the view of the disintegration of the kingdom under the influence of rival factions in the decade before 1187 should, I believe, be retained, although it has recently been questioned. Raymond, who represented the interests of the old baronial families, was supported by the chronicler William of Tyre, who had had close affiliations with the royal family since his return from long studies in Europe in 1165. King Amalric had entrusted the education of his son to him and had commissioned him to write his famous chronicle of the crusader states. Raymond appointed him royal chancellor in 1174 and archbishop of Tyre in 1175. Until 1180 he was the chief foreign policy adviser of the king and consistently advocated the alliance with the Byzantines.

The opposing faction, today mostly referred to as the 'court party', was actually a mixed bag of people. Most prominent among them was Agnes of Courtenay, the mother of the king. Banished from the court and separated from her children in 1163, she had made a return in 1175. After Raymond's regency had ended when the king reached his majority in 1176, she became the dominant influence on the king and very skilfully built up a camarilla which shamelessly enriched itself. In 1176 she bought the release of her brother Joscelin III from Muslim captivity, where he had been since 1164. This titular count of Edessa was appointed to direct the king's financial administration.

On the same occasion Reynald of Châtillon regained his liberty after sixteen years of prison. He was a prince without a principality who could not return to Antioch. His claims there had rested on his marriage to Princess Constance, who had been replaced by her son Bohemond III in 1164. In 1177 Reynald received the hand of Stephanie of Milly, one of the richest heiresses in the land. This made him lord of the Transjordan. Two Poitevin brothers, Aimery and Guy of Lusignan, added their ambitions to those of the others. Aimery became the king's constable in 1181, after the towering figure of Humphrey II of Toron, constable since 1152 and a fine soldier, had died in 1179. It was Agnes who secured Aimery's appointment, just as it was she who, in 1180, obtained the election of an old favourite, Archbishop Eraclius of Caesarea, to the patriarchate of Jerusalem. Eraclius was not, perhaps, the ideal candidate but certainly better than his extremely poor medieval reputation made him out to be.

The loser on this occasion was William of Tyre. From 1180 onwards he lost more and more of his former influence. He saw others preferred to him on important foreign missions and his political strategy of leaning on Byzantium collapsed two years after the death of Emperor Manuel Komnenos when, in a reaction to the regency of Maria of Antioch, the Latins in Constantinople were massacred in 1182. One year later William resigned from the chancellorship. In 1184, worn down by the deepest pessimism, he was ready to end his chronicle and could only with difficulty be persuaded to record future events of which he hoped in vain *utinam fausta feliciaque*. When he died in September 1186 he had written only one additional chapter, but at least his death spared him the grief of witnessing the total collapse of the kingdom only nine months later. While William remained at Raymond's side, most of the clergy were brought over to the 'court party'; they were followed in 1186 by the Templars.

The deteriorating state of the king's health sparked off many debates on his succession. In the absence of any children his closest heirs were his sister Sibyl and, failing her, his half-sister Isabella. This made their marriages state business of the first order. Sibyl was married to the marquis of Montferrat in 1176 but he died after one year, leaving her pregnant with the future Baldwin V. Various projects to find husbands for her had foundered before 1176; others met with the same fate afterwards. She had been born from an illicit union and had expressly been legitimized by the church but from 1183 at the latest doubts were being expressed about this. The debate was a delicate one because what applied to her applied equally to her brother on the throne. If she had no claim to his succession, he was the wrong man to wear the crown. In 1180 the prince of Antioch and the count of Tripoli were approaching from the north, apparently to talk with the king about Sibyl's re-marriage. By now illness had turned Baldwin IV into a man desperately clinging to his office and suspecting almost everyone of designs to supplant him. He quickly married Sibyl to Guy of Lusignan, thus making Guy count of Jaffa-Ascalon, Sibyl's inheritance.

He was to regret his choice which was a triumph for the 'court party'. The kingdom would, after the king's death, go to Sibyl and Guy. They and Agnes's party controlled the royal domain as well as the lordships of Jaffa-Ascalon, the Transjordan and Hebron, adding Toron in the north, when it was given to Agnes in *c.* 1183. Sidon was neutral after 1183. Only Galilee, under Raymond III of Tripoli, Ramla, Ibelin and Nablus under various members of the Ibelin family, and, perhaps, Caesarea were likely to put up any opposition. In fact, Raymond inspired such panic in the king and the court that in 1182 he was formally forbidden entry into the kingdom. In 1183 Baldwin IV abdicated *de facto* when he appointed Guy of Lusignan to be his regent on condition, characteristically, that he promise that he would not formally supplant him. For himself Baldwin only kept Jerusalem and a substantial annuity in cash. But in the same year the king had a change of heart for reasons which are not entirely clear. He dismissed his regent and reverted to a personal rule which he was less and less capable of discharging. In a last-ditch attempt to prevent a new regency by Raymond, Agnes of Courtenay tabled a motion which was carried after much debate. The king would continue to rule personally which meant that the 'court party' would remain in power. The succession problem was 'solved' by the coronation of Baldwin V, a boy of six, as king while his predecessor was still alive. It was hoped that this would mean the exclusion of Guy from the throne and make the deal acceptable to Baldwin IV.

But the king was not satisfied. In 1184 he tried to bring Guy down completely by having his marriage to Sibyl ended. This drove Guy into open disobedience. The king now confiscated his county and appointed Raymond to the kingdom's regency, in spite of the latter's hard conditions. This regency continued beyond

the old king's death in 1185 but at the end of the summer of 1186 the child-king
also died suddenly. Raymond tried to promote Sibyl's half-sister Isabella as
queen, but her husband went over to Guy's side and in September 1186 there
was a spectacular *coup d'état* by the 'court party'. Joscelin III of Courtenay
seized the royal domain of Acre and Beirut and even prevented Raymond from
attending the funeral of Baldwin V. To bar Guy from the kingship Sibyl was
divorced from him under pressure from the patriarch and Reynald of Châtillon.
She agreed to this only on the condition that after her coronation as queen
of Jerusalem she should be entirely free to choose her new husband and after
she had received the crown she caused general consternation by selecting Guy
from whom she had just been divorced. Guy had to be crowned.

The country was now on the brink of civil war between Raymond and Guy,
who lavishly compensated Joscelin III, and doubtless others, for their support.
Bohemond III of Antioch and Raymond III of Tripoli entered into truces
with the Muslims for their northern possessions and in Galilee Raymond even
accepted armed support from Saladin. Reynald of Châtillon now did in the
Transjordan as he pleased. In 1179, 1182 and 1186, in spite of prevailing truces,
he fell upon Muslim caravans and never made amends. The systematic attacks
were probably aimed at wresting from the crown the last right it held there,
that of taxing peaceful Muslim caravans. When Guy complained, Reynald
answered that he was *sires de sa terre* in the same way as Guy was king in
his kingdom and that truces between the kingdom and the Muslims did not
concern him. He thus declared himself virtually independent. In 1183 he had
shocked the Muslim world by a spectacular maritime invasion of the Red Sea
and had been a target for Saladin ever since. Saladin, therefore, was ready to
strike. In 1187 Reynald gave him the desired *casus belli* by ambushing another
Muslim caravan. Saladin now invaded the country. Both sides pulled together
all the troops they had. But in the middle ages pitched battle was always a risky
business. Raymond of Tripoli, reconciled to the king, strongly advised against
leaving good water supplies in Galilee. The master of the Templars changed
the king's mind, perhaps because, contrary to the will of Henry II of England,
he had opened the large treasure which Henry had laid up as a frozen account
in the east, to be spent only with his permission, and was now condemned to
success to justify his action. On 3 and 4 July 1187 the Frankish army was cut
to pieces on the hills of Hattin near Lake Galilee in the worst defeat ever to
befall the crusader states. The relic of the True Cross was lost for ever. The
king was captured. The army was either slain or taken prisoner. Most Templars
were killed in captivity and Saladin in person struck off the head of Reynald of
Châtillon. Within a matter of months Saladin took the rest of the country. Acre
fell at once, Jerusalem followed in October. The great castles in the Transjordan
surrendered in 1188 and 1189. It was the end of Frankish rule there, although in

1217 a German pilgrim still found a French widow in Montréal who showed him the way to Sinai. Beaufort in Lebanon capitulated in 1190.

In 1188 it was the turn of the north. Tripoli and the castles of the military orders in the county held out. The castles around Antioch fell, but the city bought a truce. One year before this Raymond III had died childless in Tripoli, after having arranged for the succession to his county by a son of the ruler of Antioch, but Antioch faced problems stemming from the rise of Lesser Armenia in Cilicia under Leon II (1187–1219). Tensions began to mount in 1191, coming to a head in 1194 when Bohemond III became Leon's prisoner. An Armenian takeover of Antioch failed, however, in the face of resistance offered by the urban commune. Jerusalem intervened on behalf of Bohemond who had to renounce his loose feudal suzerainty over Cilicia. Lesser Armenia now took advantage of German imperial politics and in 1198 Leon did homage to the emperor and was crowned king by the archbishop of Mainz. The death of Bohemond III in 1201 triggered a bitter war of succession between Tripoli and Lesser Armenia which lasted for fifteen years and eventually led to Antioch's union to Tripoli in 1219.

All that remained of the Latin kingdom of Jerusalem in 1187 was the port-city of Tyre. It was valiantly defended by Conrad of Montferrat who had just arrived in time and set up another urban commune according to Italian fashion. Conrad had designs on the crown from the moment he arrived. Saladin could not wrest Tyre from him and made a considerable mistake when he failed to raze the chief port of Acre to the ground. When King Guy had been set free in 1188, in a situation to try the stoutest heart, he showed his mettle and in August 1189 set down to besiege Acre. He was insufficiently equipped for the siege, particularly since he received little or no help from Tyre, where Conrad refused to recognize him as king. The two contenders now dissipated what was left of the royal domain on an unprecedented scale, by their grants to their supporters. But, helped by growing arrivals from Europe, Guy kept the siege going until the coming of the Anglo-French armies of the Third Crusade which forced Acre to capitulate in July 1191.

The crusade saved the country. In September 1192 it was reconstituted, on a smaller scale and excluding Jerusalem, by the truce between Saladin and Richard I of England, which also covered Antioch and Tripoli. Before Richard left in October for Europe he had settled the problem of who was to rule the Latin kingdom, or thought he had. Up to this time he had supported Guy of Lusignan against Conrad, who relied on the French. He now dropped Guy who was compensated by becoming the ruler of Cyprus. The law of the country, in fact, favoured Conrad because Queen Sibyl had died, while Conrad had married her half-sister Isabella in 1190. But before Conrad could be crowned he was struck down by two Assassins in April 1192.

Within days his widow was married to Henry of Champagne, the count palatine of Troyes, who ruled for five years without ever being crowned. Gaining a respite when Saladin died in 1193, Henry ruled from Acre which was now the capital. Not only Jerusalem was lost but also Nazareth and the natural frontier along the Jordan river. The coast from north of Tyre to south of Jaffa was Frankish but, close to the coast, Lydda and Ramla were partitioned between the Franks and the Muslims. Land connections between the kingdom of Jerusalem, a name which persisted, and the county of Tripoli were broken by Muslim possession of Sidon and Beirut whereas a Muslim Latakia separated the county from the principality of Antioch. The old nobility had been decimated at Hattin, and the survivors had become impoverished by the loss of fiefs now in Muslim territory. There was emigration to Cyprus, now under Latin rule, and, after 1204, to the new crusader states in Frankish Greece. There were newcomers but the future among the nobles belonged to the Ibelin family, in the country since a little before 1115.

Henry of Champagne was an able ruler who tried to reconstruct the kingdom. Occasionally he resorted to high-handed measures, as when he imprisoned the canons of the Holy Sepulchre because, in 1194, they elected a patriarch without his knowledge instead of presenting him with a choice of two as had been the custom formally abolished by Pope Celestine III in 1191. Henry had to give in quickly. He also had his share of troubles, with the Pisans plotting against him on behalf of Guy of Lusignan. They were Guy's natural allies because both he and Conrad had made enormous concessions to them in Acre, giving them the waterfront on both sides of the old city including the whole port. They had made vain attempts to take over large parts of the Seigneurie de Joscelin (below, p. 669). This would have made them crown vassals. They had also briefly succeeded in subjecting their scattered holdings in the royal part of Acre to their own consular jurisdiction, now extended to cover everything except feudal tenures, and to have them taxed by Pisa rather than the king. This policy had a certain *grandeur* but challenged the rulers. Henry bluntly presented them with a choice of surrendering their holdings in the royal part of the city if they wished to keep their privileges or, like others, to hold them on his conditions. He cut the Pisan quarter back to its previous size; in any case the donation of the waterfront had not been implemented after the reconquest of Acre. But Henry overreacted when he drove the Pisans completely from the mainland and arrested the constable Aimery, Guy's brother. In the end he needed the naval squadron which Pisa was the only Italian city to maintain permanently in the Levant at that time and he had to readmit them in 1194.

Aimery of Lusignan preferred to join his brother in Cyprus, succeeding to him there in 1194. Faced by a Greek-speaking and Orthodox population, Guy had distributed lands on a reckless scale to prospective vassals ready to come to

Cyprus from the mainland or establish a second foothold there. Aimery, who became the first king of Cyprus in 1197 after performing homage to the emperor Henry VI, reduced this to proportions, ensuring a financial preponderance for the Cypriot kings. With the able help of Alan of Lydda, now the first chancellor of Cyprus and archbishop of Nicosia, he organized the Latin church on Cyprus by despoiling, it must be admitted, the Greek church. The ritual differences could never be solved and much work in organizing the hierarchy and the distribution of revenues was left to the thirteenth century.

Henry of Champagne died in 1197 during the emperor Henry VI's crusade. Under German pressure the hand of Henry's widow Isabella was now given to King Aimery of Cyprus who thus also became king of Jerusalem. Jerusalem was not an imperial fief but Aimery's election opened a long period of Hohenstaufen influence in the east. Its chief instrument was the order of the Teutonic Knights, formally founded in March 1198 in Acre but having its origins in a German field hospital established during the Third Crusade and, even further back, in a German hospital in twelfth-century Jerusalem. In electing Aimery the barons of the kingdom had hoped for a united kingdom of Cyprus and Jerusalem, but Aimery kept the two strictly apart in a purely personal union. He thus saved the wealth of Cyprus from being depleted on behalf of the mainland. In 1197 he occupied Beirut, thus restoring the land connection with Tripoli. In 1198 he renewed a truce with the Muslims which had been broken by the arrival of the German crusade. When he renewed it again in 1204 the terms were surprisingly advantageous, the Christians receiving the Muslim half of Sidon and Ramla and all of Jaffa, which had been lost in 1197.

It used to be believed that among the great tragedies on 1187 had been the loss of the *Lettres de Sépulcre*, the collection of royal laws enacted since 1099 and deposited as individual charters in the church of the Holy Sepulchre and that in an attempt to replace them Aimery issued a codification of feudal law known as the *Livre au Roi*. The text of the *Livre* is preserved and reveals the king's intentions in reflecting at least some of the rights of the stronger twelfth-century monarchy. But it has recently been proven that the *Lettres* had never existed but were only a myth fabricated by thirteenth-century feudal lawyers. The *Livre* was not likely to make the king popular with his vassals. Neither was the fact that, for lack of revenues, he curtailed their money fiefs, even if for this purpose he relied on the help of two commissioners elected by them. All this may have been behind the spectacular attempt on the king's life by four German knights in 1198 from which he only very narrowly escaped. He took a considerable time to recover from his wounds. It was the one and only Christian attempt to murder a king of Jerusalem, although previous kings had repeatedly feared for their lives. Aimery fixed the blame on Ralph of Tiberias, who had competed with him for the crown in 1197. He survived the German swords but in Lent 1205 (1 April) he died from over-indulging in fish which may not have been fresh and his queen Isabella soon followed him to the grave. After a century of kings the stage was set for a century of the aristocracy.

This feudal nobility was already, of course, of great importance in the twelfth century but so little is known about the feudal society in the northern crusader states that the discussion must here be limited to the kingdom of Jerusalem and must, for lack of space and knowledge, be confined to the Latin *Staatsvolk*, to the exclusion of the Muslims and Syro-Christians, not to mention the minorities of the separated eastern churches or, even smaller in number, the Jews.

Roughly speaking, the Latin kingdom consisted of royal domain, lordships and church lands, leaving aside the exempt Italian concessions in the port cities. Church properties, owing little or no service or payments, were scattered throughout both the royal domain and the lordships. In the thirteenth century this became a serious problem but it is difficult to contend that in the twelfth century this impoverished the lords, and if the kings were poor – and they frequently were – it was certainly not a result of an alienation of royal lands to the church. Such alienation by the magnates was frequently the result of their need for ready cash, and of this the kings, even when poor, had more than their vassals. Often enough, giving lands to a religious corporation was a cheap way for the vassals to settle wastelands and make them economically more profitable in the first place. It is true that the lords thus lost revenues, but the kingdom gained settlers, alleviating thereby the most pressing problem of the crusader states: manpower shortage. Also, the secular and the regular church, at least in times of need, carried a heavy burden of footsoldiers maintained at their expense, with the patriarch of Jerusalem and his chapter owing 500 each. Certainly, the military orders successfully claimed full exemption from services to the king or the lords for whatever they owned, but they added their considerable fighting power and the castles built or enlarged by them to the kingdom's strength and fought, more often than not, without direct financial reward. It is true that in the Egyptian campaign of 1168 the Hospitallers presented a very heavy bill but so did everyone else because military service outside the kingdom had to be paid for directly; and the king did not seal the respective diploma. There was, in the twelfth century, only one big defensive frontier march in the hands of a military order on the borders of the Latin kingdom, around the Templar castle of Safad in Galilee, while the much smaller county of Tripoli had two of them. The other castles of the orders were sometimes strong (Belvoir) but did not control extensive marches.

The royal domain was the greatest block of lands owned by any one person. At least according to the feudal jurists of the thirteenth century, the king could do in his domain as he pleased: he could freely alienate royal lands to the

church, he could create allodial lands or fiefs without service, he could relieve
vassals of their service or fully acquit them of it, he could create as many
vassals as he pleased, while they were bound not to sub-infeudate more land
than they themselves retained. Conversely, he could not do anything in the
lordships without the lord's consent, nor could he make a donation or create
a rear-vassal at a lord's expense. Whether the feudal practice was ever that
strict is open to conjecture, although the kings seem to have refrained from
interference in the lordships unless called upon to redress patent wrong-doings
against rear-vassals. There is, with regard to the domain, a particular lack of
sources because within it the kings made extensive use of the money fief. To
estimate the extent of this we would need to have the lost records of the royal
secrète, the king's exchequer so to speak. As the century proceeded, the domain
was subject to great fluctuations in size and, hence, in revenue. The kingdom
expanded up to 1153 and so did the domain. But the expansion of both was
quicker at the beginning of the century than towards the middle. The domain
also grew from confiscation of fiefs following revolts but, although there was
no *Leihezwang* preventing the king from keeping such acquisitions, such fiefs
sooner or later were used again to provide for family or vassals. Occasionally,
the king adroitly exploited a vassal's financial difficulties such as when he cut
off a debt-ridden lord of Beirut in *c.* 1166 from all credit until he was forced
to trade his lordship to the king for a money fief. The king did allow him to
marry the very rich heiress of the Transjordan but after her death he lost the
lordship and found himself very insufficiently compensated with the tiny one
of Blanchegarde. In 1180 Humphrey IV of Toron, the heir of the Transjordan,
had to surrender to the king his patrimony at Toron, which he had inherited
in the previous year, as part of a deal which gave him a king's daughter for a
bride.

But these gains through conquest, confiscation and manipulation were offset
by the constant demand on the king to pay his vassals and mercenaries, to
reward his supporters and to provide for members of the royal family. The last
was done on a lavish scale. Acre and Tyre, the economic centres of the kingdom,
had to provide for the king's son-in-law Fulk of Anjou 1129–31. The county of
Jaffa–Ascalon was an appanage first for Amalric, the brother of King Baldwin
III, then for Sybil, the sister of King Baldwin IV. The county was a true fief
only in *c.* 1108–34, 1191–3 and 1197, but was an appanage in 1151, 1154–63 and
1176–86. Nablus with most of Samaria was given to Queen Melisende 1152–62
and to Queen Maria Komnena from either 1167 or 1174 to 1187.

The king administered and exploited his domain, including its towns,
through the viscounts as the principal crown agents, who had judicial, administrative and financial functions. King Baldwin I originally had only one
viscount for the whole of the kingdom, but as the kingdom grew this became

impractical and in 1115 there was a major administrative reform which broke up the kingdom into several vicecomital districts (Jerusalem with Judaea, Nablus with Samaria, Acre, later also Tyre). This office was so successful that many lordships began to have viscounts of their own.

Since after 1115 the royal viscounts were restricted to their respective districts, their office was ill suited to help the king in ruling his kingdom as opposed to administering his domain. Government was carried out by the king in person acting in council with the advice of his barons. With them, and often with the episcopate, he debated and formulated government policies and with them he sat in supreme judgement on feudal matters pertaining to crown fiefs. This body, known in the twelfth century as the *curia regis*, became known later as the *Haute Cour*. It had its smaller counterparts in the seigneurial courts. In the task of government the king was helped by his great household officials. As these offices were lucrative and of considerable political weight, they were often in the hands of the landed aristocracy, although royal favourites not from this privileged class might be appointed through royal patronage. An exception was the chancellor because he had to be a literate ecclesiastic. At first he actually composed the royal charters but as time wore on, he withdrew from this daily business retaining, however, the formal direction of the chancery and keeping and controlling the seal. In the second half of the twelfth century he was the principal foreign policy adviser of the king, and from early on his office quite naturally was a springboard for an episcopal career. The kingdom's military establishment was under the direction of the royal constable and the royal marshal, whereas the seneschal, to whom the viscounts accounted financially, directed the king's financial affairs through a separate office known as the *secrète*, perhaps more departmentalized than the chancery but still rudimentary when compared, for example, with England's exchequer. The greater lordships who could afford it emulated the royal household for their own administrative purposes.

With the exception of most church lands, the properties of the military orders and the autonomous quarters of the Italian communes, the kingdom became, for practical purposes, fully feudalized. At the source of this process was, of course, the king. In the early days he occasionally signed away whole conquered towns and their districts as fiefs (Haifa 1100–1, Sidon and Beirut 1110). In 1100 Tancred accepted Tiberias and Bethsan as a fief from Godfrey, and Tiberias grew into a very large fief, the principality of Galilee. But most of the lordships originated in royal castellanies (Tiberias 1099, Hebron and Jaffa 1100, Arsuf and Caesarea 1101, Ramla 1099–1102, Toron *c.* 1105, Scandalion 1117, Ibelin and Blanchegarde *c.* 1142, Mirabel before 1150). The only lordship to have neither a town nor a castle as a nucleus was Transjordan, which slowly grew from 1115 onwards.

Occasionally whole towns given in fief became lordships from the beginning. Taking as points of reference the years of death of the kings, the lordships of Haifa, Sidon and Beirut existed by 1118. By then some castellanies had also risen to this status (Tiberias 1100, Caesarea by 1110, Jaffa 1108–10, Toron *c.* 1115). By 1131 one of the kingdom's two ecclesiastical lordships had been added to the seigneurial map, that of the archbishop of Nazareth (before 1121), while Bethsan had been elevated by 1129, both in unknown circumstances. By 1143 Ramla and the ecclesiastical lordship of the bishop of Lydda (a vassal of the ruler since 1099) had become lordships. Both had been created before 1138 in the wake of the revolt of Count Hugh II of Jaffa in 1134. By the end of the following reign in 1163 there were three new lordships (Scandalion before 1148, Mirabel by 1162, Arsuf *c.* 1163, at the latest by 1168). By 1174 Ibelin (1163–7) and Blanchegarde (1174) had acquired seigneurial status. The last castellany to become a lordship was Hebron (1177; at least this seems more probable than 1161 which has also been argued). To these must be added the quasi-seigneuries which were lordships in fact, or even in name, but not in law, such as Nablus, which after 1177 developed out of the dowry for a former queen, and the Seigneurie de Joscelin, a conglomerate of lands, revenues, wardships and other rights which Joscelin III of Courtenay, uncle and seneschal of King Baldwin IV, obtained for himself from 1179 onwards in the royal domain of Acre.

This account is, to some extent, deceptive. While it demonstrates that most of the big lordships go back to the early days of the kingdom, it does not reveal that some developed only very gradually or that others gained and lost their status as they drifted out of, and into, the royal domain. Examples must suffice. Jaffa, for instance, was a royal castellany until *c.* 1107. Between 1108 and 1110 it became a county under the Le Puiset family until 1134, when the king confiscated it. It remained royal domain until 1151 when it became the appanage of the king's brother, Amalric. He lost it in the civil war of 1152, regained it in 1154 and was able to add Ascalon to it, to which the Le Puisets had laid proleptic claims as early as the 1120s. When he rose to be king in 1163, Jaffa-Ascalon returned to the royal domain and left it, once more, in 1176 as an appanage for the king's sister. When she, in turn, rose to be queen in 1186, the double county became royal domain again, was a fief in 1191, domain in 1193 and again a fief when it fell to the Muslims in 1197. Its checkered history continued in the thirteenth century. These changes in status had their repercussions among the vassals of the counts, particularly at Ramla which started out as a royal castellany. It became a fief of the counts of Jaffa but by 1120 had an unofficial quasi-seigneurial status. Shortly after the county reverted to the royal domain in 1134, Ramla was officially recognized as a lordship, but it lost this status in the 1150s, when there was a count again. Hugh of Ramla then used his grandfather's seal, although when his count was present he used the comital seal, claiming that he had no seal of his own. After the count had become king, Ramla was again ranked as a lordship.

The most striking example of a gradual growth was Transjordan. After campaigns from 1100 to 1115 which brought the country north of the Yabbok river into the principality of Galilee, the former Viscount Pisellus was established as lord south of the Yabbok. In the same year (1115) the king, further south, built the strong castle of Montréal (Shaubak) which was not joined to the Transjordanian lordship until the early 1130s; only around this time was Frankish rule extended as far as Petra and Aqaba. But this most southern part continued to be a royal holding until 1161, when the region south of Petra was made part of the lordship which now, after nearly half a century, finally reached its greatest extension, from the Yabbok to the Red Sea.

In theory this feudal map did not change when most lordships were wiped out in 1187. Only some of them could be regained, but on paper they all continued in being. A text of 1239 enumerating land occupied by the Muslims carefully listed the pretender to Transjordan, who was already four generations removed from the last Frankish holder, although Transjordan was never returned to the kingdom. Until recently it was believed that after *c.* 1130, and except for the most major upheavals in feudal revolts, there was security of possession for feudal tenures big and small. This is, indeed, true if we think in medieval fashion in terms of *lignages*, of families firmly rooted in their lordships and fiefs. Putting down such roots was facilitated by legislation. It is true that an old rule that fiefs could be inherited not only by direct offspring but also by collateral heirs was changed before 1150, but the 'old fiefs' could successfully defend themselves against it. Another law preventing the accumulation of fiefs by one man also disappeared. This was to the benefit of all fiefholders but, more particularly, to that of the small baronial group, which, through carefully arranged marriages, concentrated more and more feudal lands in the hands of a very small group of families steadily growing in status, richness and power. It was obviously difficult to dispossess such *lignages*. We used to believe that a law promulgated by King Baldwin II set down twelve crimes which entailed royal confiscation of fiefs without trial by peers but this view has successfully been challenged. Rather, the law laid down fixed penalties which were at the king's disposal, but only after a vassal had been pronounced by his peers to be guilty.

In the thirteenth century the inheritance of fiefs was rigidly governed by the theory of the *plus dreit heir aparant*, that is the nearest relative to the last in possession of a fief, present in the east and capable of performing the services due. But it seems that twelfth-century practice was less rigid and protected more the *lignage* than the individual. For the latter the wheel of fortune could turn very quickly and there were more conflicts between the kings and their vassals than our principal chronicles reveal at first sight. These men rose not only by the fortune of their swords but also by royal patronage, by faithful royal service, by shrewdly planned marriages which, however, needed the king's approval. But they could fall from grace very suddenly and when there was a change of king they often fell because the new king felt the need for a *clientèle* of his own.

Again examples of such vicissitudes must suffice. In Beirut the first lord from the Brisebarre family was driven into exile in the wake of the revolt of Hugh II of Jaffa (1134) and was succeeded by his brother Guy, a particularly faithful supporter of King Fulk. Soon after Fulk's death he had to relinquish the seigneurie to his brother Walter, now back from exile (1144), as Queen Melisende was in power as regent. But Guy, again on the king's side, made a come-back after King Baldwin III had attained his majority in 1145. He had regained his fief by 1147. He now maintained himself in Beirut until his death, whereas Walter embarked on a distinguished career as a Knight Templar. This reconstruction is more plausible than the older Beirut genealogies with their constant changes of Guys and Walters from seemingly different generations.

The most spectacular fall was that of Count Hugh II of Jaffa. He had successfully claimed Jaffa as his inheritance shortly before 1120. In 1123 he married Emma, the widow of Eustace I of Caesarea-Sidon. In addition to his county of Jaffa he now administered the rich oasis of Jericho belonging to Emma and the lordships of Caesarea and Sidon on behalf of Emma's two minor sons. He controlled the coast from its then most southerly point at Jaffa almost to Haifa and, again, from north of Tyre almost to Beirut. He had to surrender Caesarea when Eustace's son Walter reached his majority in 1128, but he seems to have held Sidon until his fall in 1134. Hardly had King Fulk ascended the throne when Walter of Caesarea put in an unsuccessful claim to Sidon. Fulk decided to finish with Hugh. His *de facto* accumulation of fiefs was without precedence and made him a potential danger. As a second cousin of Queen Melisende Hugh resented and opposed Fulk's attempt to upset, in his early years, the joint rule which guaranteed Melisende a share in the government and the kingdom. As one of the greatest vassals he was a natural leader of those among the nobles who were angered by the disconcerting way in which Fulk had changed the trusted servants of Baldwin II for his own men, many of them upstarts. Above all, Hugh was a Norman by upbringing, although he came from a Chartrain family, since he had been born and raised in Apulia. He was, in fact, the head of the Norman party which was Fulk's favourite target.

Fulk found a willing tool in the disgruntled Walter of Caesarea, who coveted Sidon. In 1134, at Fulk's instigation, he rose in the king's court accusing his stepfather Hugh of having plotted against the king's life. A judicial duel was to be held but Hugh failed to appear and preferred to enlist the help of the Muslims at Ascalon. This was open treason. Hugh was now left by his own vassals who went over to the king's side. He was finished and was banished from the kingdom for three years. He went to Apulia never to return. Melisende was associated with Fulk's government and to that extent Fulk had lost. But in all other respects he was the winner. The Norman party was finished and the vassals had been tamed. The king confiscated not only the county of Jaffa but certainly Jericho and very likely Sidon, which Walter did not get, and where a new lord, from a different family, is not found until 1147.

In 1161 Gerald, this new lord, was briefly banished from the kingdom because he had arbitrarily dispossessed one of his vassals. The king intervened *manu militari* and re-instated his rear-vassal and drawing on this incident, the next king, Amalric, promulgated the *Assise sur la ligece* which brought all rear-vassals into direct contact with the king by making him liege lord for vassals and rear-vassals alike. This may have been intended to increase the power of the king by letting him interfere directly in the lordships and by providing him, in his *Haute Cour*, with support against the barons from the far more numerous small rear-vassals who now obtained a voice. If this was the purpose it miscarried. The *Assise* did ease changing the status of a vassal. As recently as 1161 the king, when transferring the service of a royal vassal to a seigneur, had specified that homage would continue to be rendered to the king. This safeguarded this man's social status when, for all practical purposes, he became a seigneurial vassal. Such complicated solutions were no longer necessary after the *Assise* had placed the rear-vassals on an equal footing with even the greatest magnates. Parity between the different strata of vassals, however, remained purely fictitious. The small rear-vassals, equipped as they were with only a money fief of between 300 and 1,000 gold pieces per annum, were no match for the magnates and quite simply did not have the money to attend the king's court. Through the *Assise* the king did not gain in power. It did not prevent the steady decline of the monarchy after 1174 and we never hear of it being applied by the king in his interests or against the magnates. On the contrary, in the thirteenth century the *Assise* became the Magna Carta of the nobility against arbitrary rule by the king or his regent. This belongs to another chapter even though the first instance of such an interpretation belongs to the late twelfth century.

Apart from the Frankish barons and knights there were also Frankish *bourgeois*, a relatively large group comprising all non-noble Franks. The Frankish peasants in the small settlements and in the manor houses in the countryside were included in this class, but most were concentrated in the towns, where they engaged in various artisanal productions or trade. Some of them also served as minor officials of a king or a lord in town and country or as jurors in the *Cour des Bourgeois*, which declared the law in all civil and criminal cases pertaining to the burgesses and also exercised blood justice over the non-Franks. Petty commercial cases were heard in special courts composed of more Syro-Christians than Franks, but major ones were transferred to the *Cour des Bourgeois*, which also was an appeals court for these special courts in cases of less value. As the *Cour des Bourgeois* was exclusively composed of Franks and had such a wide competence, the jurors were quite an influential group of people whose office frequently ran in the family. The king or respective lord retained his influence through his viscount, whose chief duty it was to preside over the burgess court. Inevitably, therefore, burgesses rose from the jury to be viscounts now and then. But the jurors were local *notables* rather than veteran politicos. The political influence of the burgesses as a coherent social group was insignificant. In the thirteenth century a law was thought to be unconstitutional because it had been passed without the assent of the *bourgeois*, but the significant fact is that in the twelfth century it had been enacted.

The *bourgeois* had their own non-feudal land tenures held either from the king or one of his feudatories or an ecclesiastical corporation. These holdings, mostly but not exclusively urban, were known as *héritages* or *tenures en bourgeoisie*. They were hereditable properties, mostly real estate, for which the tenant answered to the *Cour des Bourgeois*, normally paid a *cens* and provided other burgess services about which we know little except for the duty to serve as footsoldiers in emergencies. As opposed to fiefs, the sale of which was very restricted, *héritages* could be freely sold or partitioned. This made them attractive even to the nobles, although this was largely a thirteenth-century phenomenon. *Bourgeois* belonged to the Latin ruling class and were, even when poor, socially superior to, and more privileged in law than, rich Syro-Christians; even as peasant settlers they were personally free and therefore better off than most of their European counterparts. But as a political class they do not seem to have had any consciousness of their own in the twelfth century. They did not form craftsmen's guilds which might have become the nucleus of urban autonomy and they did not acquire a law code of their own until the thirteenth century, but were content to live in the rudimentary political and social framework of limited self-government which the *Cour des Bourgeois*, based on orally transmitted customary law, provided. It is hardly surprising, therefore, that the urban commune so powerful in Italy and France never played a significant role in the Latin east except when such organizations sprang up temporarily to defend the community in times of need. Even then they were dominated by the nobles and are to be found only towards the end of the twelfth century. In the thirteenth century, when Acre was not only the capital but very often all that was left of the state, the *bourgeois* made themselves politically more felt. But in the twelfth century they were not a match for either the king or the nobility.

It may look as if the nobles were not a match for the kings up to 1174. It is only in careful retrospect that we notice the signs that from 1143 onwards, imperceptibly at first, a very small group of baronial clans were beginning to impose checks on the monarchs. After 1174, they increasingly turned the kingdom into a self-service store for their *lignages*. These magnates were very able men and later produced some of the finest feudal lawyers anywhere. But they were too egocentric. The crusader states had great kings and great barons, but they never had a Simon of Montfort. As the twelfth century gave way to the thirteenth they were not only encircled and endangered. They were also inwardly unhealthy.

CHAPTER 22

'ABBASIDS, FATIMIDS AND SELJUQS

Michael Brett

THE FATIMID EMPIRE

In the year 1000, in the midst of the so-called Shi'ite century of Islam, the Sevener Shi'ite imam and caliph al-Hakim bi amr Allah, 'He Who Rules in Accordance with God's Command', had his tutor and regent, the white eunuch Barjawan, assassinated in the royal palace city of al-Qahira, 'the Victorious', from which Cairo takes its name. From then until his disappearance in 1021, he presided over an empire intended to restore the religious and political unity of the Muslim community under its true leaders, the descendants of Muhammad, of his cousin and chosen successor 'Ali, and his daughter Fatima, divinely appointed to the imamate or supreme authority for the faith, and destined to the caliphate or lieutenancy of God and His Prophet as commanders of the faithful. In the course of the tenth century, his Fatimid dynasty had risen to power, first in North Africa and then in Egypt and Syria, while the original Arab empire under the older 'Abbasid dynasty of caliphs had finally disintegrated under the weight of its own excessive taxation.[1] The 'Abbasids themselves had survived at Baghdad, but as the purely nominal rulers of the Muslim world, traditionally recognized but no longer obeyed by the independent princes of their former provinces. At Baghdad itself, moreover, they were under the protection of the Buyid or Buwayhid dynasty of western Iran and Iraq. Like the Fatimids, the Buyids were also Shi'ites or partisans of the fourth caliph 'Ali, in preference to the 'Abbasids who claimed descent from the Prophet's uncle. They did not therefore recognize the Fatimids as true heirs to the empire of the faith, but rather the Hidden Imam of the Twelver Shi'ites, who had vanished into *ghayba* or supernatural occlusion in 874. Together with the Fatimids, the Buyids nevertheless ensured that the heartlands of the Islamic world in the Near and Middle East were ruled by monarchs whose political and religious

---

[1] See Kennedy (1986), pp. 187–99.

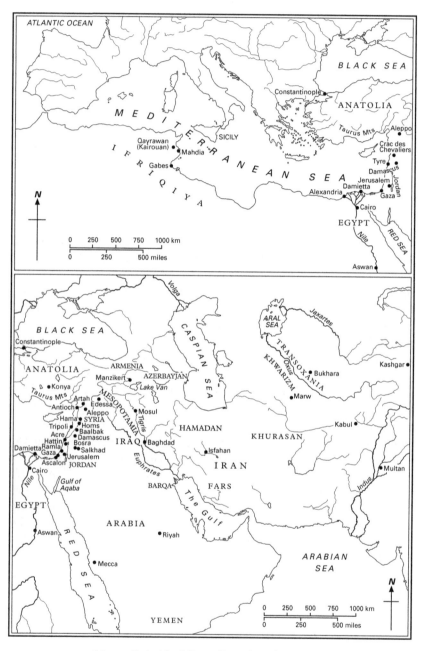

Map 18 Fatimids, Seljuqs, Zengids and Ayyubids

authority had wholly or partially superseded that of the previous sovereigns of Islam.

Despite this Shi'ite supremacy, the Shi'ite victory was precarious. Shi'ism itself had barely emerged as a religious doctrine out of widespread political loyalty to the 'Alids or 'Alawis, the descendants of 'Ali who laid claim to rule as the Prophet's closest kin. In so far as it had done so, it was riven by the disagreement of the Seveners and the Twelvers over the identity of the imam whose religious authority was central to their faith. The Fatimids' impressive rise from revolution to empire had convinced a variety of Shi'ites right across the Islamic world of the truth of their claim to the imamate in line of descent from 'Ali's younger son Husayn, through the figure of Muhammad ibn Isma'il, the Seventh Imam with whom the line had passed into *satr* or concealment at the end of the eighth century, before its reappearance in the person of the Fatimid mahdi in North Africa in 910.[2] But this claim was disputed by the Twelvers, who did not recognize the imamate of Muhammad ibn Isma'il, and by many 'Alids who challenged the whole of the Fatimid genealogy. While Shi'ites thus divided their loyalties between alternative, even multiple claimants to the authority of God on earth,[3] their opponents not only included established monarchs threatened by the principle of 'Alid rule, beginning with the 'Abbasids but extended to dynasties on the periphery of the Islamic world, most notably the Umayyads in Spain and the Ghnaznavids in eastern Iran. The majority of the men of religion objected less to Shi'ite claims to power than to Shi'ite claims to authority over the Shari'a or Islamic Law. Whereas most jurists claimed to follow the Sunna or exemplary custom of the Prophet as preserved by the collective scholarship of successive generations of students and teachers, Shi'ites had come to regard their chosen imam as the sole guarantor of the authenticity of this Prophetic tradition from generation to generation. When, as in the case of the Fatimids, the chosen imam who laid down the Law was also the monarch who enforced it, the conflict between Shi'ites and the Sunni majority, who relegated the ruler to the executive arm of the Law, was not only doctrinal but political.[4] It was made all the more acute by the Mahdism of the Fatimids, by their belief in their messianic mission to revive the faith after its lapse into ignorance on the part of the faithful, which had brought their dynasty to power in North Africa and Egypt. The Buyids, who laid no claim to religious authority themselves, were more modest, seeking only a niche for themselves as barbarian intruders upon the imperial Arab scene. The lines of battle were nevertheless sharply drawn; and despite the political success of Shi'ism, the obstacles to its

---

[2] See Brett (1994a).

[3] See, for Twelver Shi'ism, Momen (1985), and for Sevener Shi'ism, Daftary (1990).

[4] For the relationship between government and the Law in Sunni jurisprudence, and the distinctive difference from Shi'ism, see Coulson (1964), ch. 9, pp. 120–34 and pp. 106–7.

further empire building were formidable, and in the end, insuperable. Hakim himself was to prove the point.

By the time he came to power any aspiration the Fatimids may have had to reconstitute the old Arab empire by conquest had been effectively abandoned, as the dynasty settled firmly into the pattern of states created by the break-up of the 'Abbasid empire in the tenth century. Their state in Egypt and Syria was none other than the empire of the Ikhshidids, who had carved it out of the 'Abbasid dominions in the 930s and 40s; and it suffered the same limitations. During the reign of Hakim's father 'Aziz, 975–96, the North African territories of the dynasty in Ifriqiya, that is, Tunisia with eastern Algeria and Tripolitania, had become a hereditary monarchy under their Zirid viceroys, who ruled in the name of the caliph but no longer at his command. The failure of the dynasty to retain control of its original base for the conquest of Egypt in 969 was matched by the difficulty of annexing Syria, the necessary base for any advance into Iraq to eradicate the 'Abbasids and their authority entirely. By the death of 'Aziz in 996, the Fatimids were in control of the former Ikhshidid province of southern and central Syria from a capital at Damascus, but Aleppo under the Hamdanids had eluded them, not least because its independence was championed by Byzantium, which feared for its hold on Antioch, captured in 969 as the Fatimids marched triumphantly into the Nile valley. 'Aziz had died in the midst of hostilities between the two empires, which had allowed him to pose as the champion of Islam in the holy war upon the infidel, but little more.[5] The Syrian desert, meanwhile, was in the hands of three large, and militant, tribal Arab groups – the Kilab in the north, the Kalb in the centre and the Tayy in the south – which had threatened the security of the country for the past century. During the thirty years that had elapsed since their arrival in Egypt, the inability of the Fatimids to alter the political pattern of the Muslim world by force of arms was only matched by their inability to overcome the religious divisions of the community by persecution or persuasion. Out of the general revolutionary atmosphere at the beginning of the tenth century, the da'wa or call of the dynasty had condensed its respondents into a sectarian minority of Isma'ilis, whose revolutionary appeal was either limited or localized. Despite their high profile, the popularity of the 'Alid cause and the widespread Shi'ite sympathies of Iraq and Syria, which favoured their recognition as caliphs in the Friday prayer, the Fatimids had no mass following of believers to advance their claim to speak for Islam as a whole, or to promote their imperial cause. The empire over which Hakim ruled was thus of a different kind from that which the 'Abbasids had lost.

---

[5] When Basil II unexpectedly invaded Syria in 995 to relieve the Fatimid siege of Aleppo, 'Aziz had summoned the faithful to the holy war, but sat in camp for weeks outside Cairo until the emperor withdrew at the end of the season: Maqrizi, *Itti'az*, I, pp. 287–8.

It was an empire which continued to be predicated upon the divine mission of the Fatimid imamate to bring the whole of Islam into its fold. The fold in question embraced the state or Dawla proper in Egypt and Syria, where the Fatimid imam ruled as well as reigned in the capacity of caliph or deputy of God on earth, and what might be termed the Dawla by courtesy, where he reigned but did not rule. The chief example of such a state was that of Ifriqiya under the Zirids, together with Sicily under the Kalbids and the Hijaz, the Holy Places, of which the Fatimid caliph was the protector as well as the supplier with grain. Despite the failure of 'Aziz to take Aleppo in 995, the city with its mainly Shi'ite population became a Fatimid dependency in 1002, when the Hamdanids were dispossessed by their army commander Lu' lu', who was succeeded in 1008 by his son Marwan. Outside the fold, meanwhile, was what might be termed the Dawla Irredenta, the rest of the Muslim world, where the imam–caliph neither ruled nor reigned, but which he would have to redeem in God's good time if the mission of the dynasty were to be accomplished. Here, therefore, conquest was never excluded, but diplomacy was more characteristically employed to win friendship and possible recognition from dynasties such as the Kurdish Marwanids of Mayyafariqin in the hill country of the upper Tigris, and the Arab bedouin 'Uqaylids of northern Iraq. Behind the diplomacy lay the propaganda, systematically put out to maintain the cause of the dynasty and promote local revolutions, whether by violence or persuasion, which would draw the states in question, under a pro-Fatimid prince, into the inner circle of the Dawla by courtesy. The propaganda was directed on the one hand at the Isma'ili faithful, stretching across the Islamic world as far as India and central Asia, to encourage their missionary activity, and on the other hand at princes like the Buyids, who might be willing to convert. The great achievement of Hakim's reign was to develop this propaganda from the personal task of the imam in Ifriqiya, followed by that of the chief *qadi* in Egypt, into the work of a college responsible for the teaching and training of *du'at* (sing. *da'i*), 'missionaries' under the direction of a chief *da'i*.[6] At the same time, this teaching provoked the greatest controversy of the reign.

THE REIGN OF HAKIM AND ITS OUTCOME

For the reign was nothing if not controversial. When Hakim so ruthlessly took power, he did so with one eye upon his imperial mission, and the other on the servants of his household, his secretariat and his army, which had quarrelled over the regency during his minority, and threatened to rule in his name. The threat was symptomatic of the evolution of the Fatimid regime from the 'patriarchal',

[6] See Assaad (1974).

household government of the dynasty in Ifriqiya to the grander 'patrimonial' style of the caliphate in Egypt, to borrow Weber's terms. The Fatimids in fact provided Weber with important examples of the 'routinization of charisma' on the one hand, whereby the monarch's God-given right to rule became institutionalized, and 'patrimonialism' on the other, whereby the monarch's authority was delegated to his servants, to the detriment of his ability to rule.[7] The evolution of such a regime in Egypt was theatrical, governed by the need to emulate all rivals with a show of power and authority in the manner of the time. It centred therefore on the great new palace city of al-Qahira outside the civilian metropolis of Fustat, where government was conducted with all due pomp and ceremony.[8] That government rested upon the fiscal bureaucracy of Egypt, whose largely Coptic Christian personnel supplied the secretarial skills required throughout the administration. Increasingly, however, the Copts were joined by secretarial families from Iraq in search of employment after the collapse of the 'Abbasid Dawla,[9] and by Jews, one of whom, the convert Ya'qub ibn Killis, had become the first Fatimid wazir, the servant who 'lifted the burden' of government from the shoulders of the sovereign.[10] His appointment by 'Aziz was a significant step away from the personal control of the administration by the caliph in Ifriqiya, towards government by an army of clerks distinct from the royal household, directed by a minister rather than the monarch. Meanwhile, the single most important task of that clerical army was to pay the army proper, which in the course of the warfare in Syria had grown from a corps of Berber cavalry into a composite force of Turkish as well as Berber cavalry, and black Sudanese and Daylami (that is, Iranian) infantrymen, together with white slave guardsmen in the palace itself. Jealousy of the Turkish Mashariqa or easterners by the Kutama Berber Maghariba or westerners, who had brought the Fatimids to power in North Africa and been rewarded with the title of awliya' or friends of the dynasty, lay behind the struggle for power during the minority of Hakim, when the Kutama had been defeated in their attempt to monopolize the government. When Hakim disposed of his regent Barjawan, he took in hand this burgeoning army of secretaries and soldiers.

How he did so is obscured by his reputation for madness. His madness rests upon the opinion of his physician, reported by the Christian chronicler Yahya ibn Sa'id al-Antaki,[11] and the evidence of his many cruelties and apparent eccentricities.[12] The black legend of the monster is expounded with relish by

[7] See Turner (1974), pp. 75–92.
[8] For al-Qahira and its ceremonies, see Lane-Poole (1906), pp. 118–34; Raymond (1993), pp. 53–65; Canard (1951, repr. 1973), and (1952, repr. 1973); Sanders (1989) and (1994).
[9] See Ashtor (1972), repr. (1978).   [10] See Lev (1981).
[11] See Yahya ibn Sa'id al-Antaki, 'The Byzantine-Arab Chronicle'.
[12] For the list, see Encyclopaedia of Islam (1954–), s.v. 'al-Hakim bi-amr Allah', art. Canard.

Lane-Poole.[13] But a clinical diagnosis of madness cannot be accepted at this distance in time and the symptomatic evidence is quite unclear. Attempts to explain his actions have identified him as a man of sound political and economic sense, who either believed or disbelieved in his theocratic role.[14] Alternatively his more peculiar acts and excesses have been considered to have been those of a madman and his insanity has been treated as an aggravating influence upon essentially rational behaviour.[15] Bianquis presents him as a frightened tyrant, executing his wazirs on the least suspicion, and perpetually afraid of the *wasita* or 'middleman', the representative of the military who from time to time was entrusted with the duties of wazir.[16] But there was evidently also a religious dimension to the reign, in which Hakim appears in the role of the ideal ruler. Unfolding in three stages out of the dynasty's doctrine of the imamate, this dimension allows his policies to be periodized and thus rationalized without recourse to psychology.

Some features remained constant, beginning with the edicts which eventually prohibited, not only wine and beer, but nakedness in bathhouses, women leaving the house and idle amusements including chess, together with the biblical shellfish and fish without scales, and less obviously, the vegetable *mulukhiyya*; dogs were to be killed. So too were officials accused of corruption, beginning almost immediately with the *muhtasib* or inspector of markets Ibn Abi Najda, and extending to the chief *qadi* Husayn.[17] Since the use of office for personal enrichment was systematic and ineradicable,[18] the entire army of office holders fell under suspicion, and succumbed throughout the reign to executions and mutilations motivated either by the caliph's zeal for justice or fear of his servants. Among the victims were the descendants of the principal officers of Hakim's grandfather, the great Mu'izz li-Din Allah, who had brought the dynasty in from the periphery of the Muslim world in Ifriqiya to its centre at Cairo: on the one hand the *qadi* al-Nu'man, the canonical exponent of the doctrine of the imamate,[19] and on the other Jawhar al-Siqlabi, the conqueror of Egypt in 969. Great families of jurists and generals, the aristocracy of the regime, their sons and grandsons, had been put to death by the middle of the reign. Wazirs like the Christian Fahd ibn Ibrahim lost their lives; other aspirants to office survived precariously, like the Iraqi al-Jarjara'i, whose hands

---

[13] Lane-Poole (1914), pp. 123–34. The account of al-Maqrizi, *Khitat*, is extensively translated by Lewis (1974), I, pp. 46–59.

[14] See Vatikiotis (1957); Shaban (1976), pp. 206–10.   [15] See e.g. Bianquis (1978).   [16] *Ibid.*

[17] Al-Maqrizi, *Itti'az* II, p. 59; al-Maqrizi's chronicle, derived from lost contemporary sources largely through the late thirteenth-century writer Ibn Muyassar as well as non-Egyptian authors like Ibn al-Athir, is the principal source for the history of the dynasty.

[18] See Bianquis (1992).

[19] Most notably in al-Nu'man, *Da'a'im al-islam*, or 'Pillars of Islam'; see Poonawala (1977); Daftary (1990), pp. 249–53; Gottheil (1906).

were both cut off, but who lived to become a leading figure in government by the time of Hakim's disappearance in 1021. From this point of view, the regime conformed nicely to Weber's description of a patrimonial society 'characterised by rapid turnover and instability of personnel but great stability of social structures', under a ruler living by 'the fiction that he is benevolent and concerned for the welfare of his subjects', who looked to the monarch as the fount of justice.[20]

The system, however, was not static. For the first seven years after his assumption of power, Hakim enforced the Fatimid doctrine of the imamate established by Mu'izz and the *qadi* al-Nu'man, ordering the cursing of Abu Bakr, 'Umar and 'Uthman, the three predecessors of 'Ali in the caliphate, as usurpers, and insisting on Isma'ili forms of worship. It was a symbolic gesture, designed to hold up to respect the example of the true faith, rather than seeking to convert the whole of Islam to Fatimism by imposing a single comprehensive doctrine of the Shari'a upon the various schools of Law – a task far beyond the capacity of any government. As caliph or commander of the faithful, however, he upheld Islam as a whole by obliging Christians and Jews to wear distinctive dress, thus putting them conspicuously in their rightful place. These policies changed after the Mahdist rebellion of the pretender Abu Rakwa at the head of the bedouin of the western desert in 1005–6, an apocalyptic event which gave Hakim a God-sent trial and triumph. Discrimination against non-Muslims became active persecution, culminating in the destruction of the Church of the Holy Sepulchre in Jerusalem during the years 1009–11. On the other hand, the cursing of 'Ali's predecessors was forbidden and Sunnis were placed on a par with Isma'ilis as good Muslims over whom the imam presided as the caliph or deputy of God on earth. The persecution of the Copts, which drove many into exile and others to convert to Islam, led once again into revolt, this time by the Tayy bedouin of Palestine in the name of the *sharif* of Mecca, who represented the lineage of 'Ali's elder son Hasan; and this second seven-year period ended with yet another change, when Hakim's nephew 'Abd al-Rahman ibn Ilyas was invested as Wali 'Ahd al-Muslimin, as heir to the throne but not the imamate. This separation of functions, emphasized by the designation of a nephew rather than a son, was against the whole principle of the dynasty, and it may be that Hakim had conceived of himself prophetically as the ninth and last imam in line from Muhammad ibn Isma'il, whose successors would be no more than leaders of the Muslim community.[21] The final seven years of the reign, when Hakim took to the life of a reclusive ascetic, were certainly the most controversial. The persecution of Jews and Christians was reversed, but extremist Persian Isma'ilis, Hamza and al-Darazi, made their appearance

---

[20] Turner (1974), pp. 80–1.   [21] See Makarem (1970).

to claim that Hakim was divine. Rioting against such blasphemy in Fustat led to the burning of much of the city. Hodgson has argued that Hakim approved of their preaching, Assaad that he did not, inviting the philosopher al-Kirmani to explain that the ways of the imam might be unaccountable, but were fully in accord with the doctrine of the dynasty.[22] The fact remains that the sources for this period are defective, perhaps officially destroyed;[23] that Hakim mysteriously disappeared in the desert in 1021; and that the dynasty moved swiftly to install his son in place of his nephew under the significant title al-Zahir li-I'zaz Din Allah, 'He Who Appears Openly to Strengthen the Religion of God', a clear affirmation of the recognized doctrine of the imamate promulgated by Hakim's grandfather Mu'izz in the works of the *qadi* al-Nu'man.

The result was twofold. The government at Cairo was assumed by a cabal of leading officers in alliance with the princesses who now controlled the palace: first Hakim's sister Sitt al-Mulk, and after her death the queen-mother Ruqiyya, until in 1027 the leader of the cabal, the immigrant Iraqi 'Ali ibn Ahmad al-Jarjara'i, became wazir. From then until his death in 1045, Jarjara'i al-Aqta', 'the Handless', who dictated his letters to a secretary, ruled as head of a party of clients in control of the army of secretaries and soldiers, the Men of the Pen and the Men of the Sword. This party became so deeply rooted that the wazir survived the death of Zahir in 1036, and the appearance of a powerful enemy in the shape of Rasad, mother to the new, infant Caliph Mustansir. In Syria Jarjara'i's ally, the Turkish general Anushtakin al-Dizbiri, defeated the Mirdasids, the bedouin Arabs of Kilab who had captured Aleppo in 1023, together with their ally Ibn Jarrah in command of the Tayy of Transjordan, at the battle of Uqhuwana in northern Palestine in 1029, and went on to annex the city to the province of Damascus in 1038. In the course of protracted negotiations,[24] good relations were restored with Constantinople and confirmed by a treaty of 1036 or 1038; by 1048 the Byzantines had rebuilt the Church of the Holy Sepulchre at Jerusalem after permission was given by Hakim in his final years. Despite, and probably because of, the notoriously 'rapid turnover and instability of personnel' in the previous reign, the personnel in question had combined in this way to form a government whose members could enjoy the fruits of office without interruption by the monarch. The power and authority of the imam–caliph remained intact, but was effectively smothered by the collusion

---

[22] Hodgson (1962); Assaad (1974).

[23] See Bianquis (1978). The departure from Egypt of the Christian author Yahya ibn Sa'id al-Antaki, which brought his chronicle of events in Egypt to an end in 1014, may have been coincidental, but seven years of the contemporary court chronicle of al-Musabbihi, the principal source for subsequent writers, were evidently missing from the copies at the disposal of subsequent generations.

[24] See Canard (1961).

of his servants, much as Hakim had feared. The result was a conservative regime content to consolidate the position of the dynasty in Egypt and Syria without enthusiasm for its manifest destiny in the world at large.

If the Dawla had fallen into the hands of ministers from outside the royal household and the adepts of the sect, the *daʿwa* or missionary doctrine of the dynasty was nevertheless summed up in a grand synthesis which presented the Muslim world with a challenge it could not ignore. The doctrinal uncertainty which culminated in Hakim's acclamation as a divine being by Hamza and Darazi may have killed off a certain enthusiasm for Ismaʿilism in evidence in Egypt at the beginning of the reign. In the end, however, it served to complete rather than destroy the doctrinal achievement of his ancestors.[25] The preaching of Hakim's divinity by the Iranian *duʿat* was the final outburst under the Fatimids of that *ghuluww* or religious extremism which had entered into the origins of the dynasty as the eschatological expectation of the mahdi, the bringer of a final revelation.[26] At the death of Hakim, the followers of Hamza and Darazi were driven from Egypt to establish themselves, after twenty years of proselytism among Ismaʿilis all over the eastern Islamic world, as the Druzes of Mount Lebanon and the Hawran, believing in the eternity of Hakim and his eventual return.[27] In Egypt itself, the religious establishment created by Hakim had already turned to the Iranian al-Kirmani to refute such dangerous delirium. Al-Kirmani did so not simply by reaffirming the divinely inspired appointment of the imam in succession to Muhammad as the supreme authority for the holy Law revealed in the Qurʾan and the Sunna of the Prophet. He brought about the final abandonment of the cabbalistic number mysticism common to *ghuluww* and earlier Fatimid writing,[28] and the final replacement of its myths of creation by a comprehensive Neoplatonic cosmology, in which the imam of the time represented the creative principle of the Active Intellect or Eternal Imam. Not only, therefore, was the imam the authority for the patent Revelation, the Zahir or Open doctrine of Islam; he was also the supreme authority for the Batin, the Hidden meaning of the Qurʾan, now defined as the universe of Reason to which the imam was the only sure intellectual guide as keeper of God's Word. A vast *summum theologicum* was thereby offered to the Muslim world, in which the Fatimid imamate was cast in the role later proposed for itself by the thirteenth-century papacy. The Fatimid cause was equipped with a formidable intellectual case, maintained by the teachings of the Bab, the Door through which the imam spoke to the world, and promoted by Ismaʿilis throughout Islam, irrespective of the domestic preoccupations of the regime.

---

[25] See Walker (1993).   [26] See Daftary (1990), pp. 64–5; Brett (1994a).
[27] See Daftary (1990), pp. 195–200; Hodgson (1962); Bryer (1975–6).   [28] See Halm (1978).

THE 'ABBASID RESPONSE

Like the Fatimids, the Buyids had come to power in the tenth century on the strength of an army of mountain tribesmen, in their case from the region of Daylam to the south of the Caspian Sea. Like the Kutama of the mountains of Kabylia in eastern Algeria, the Daylamis were one of many such peoples embraced by the Arab conquests but largely independent of the Arabs, for whom Islam was either foreign or a weapon to be used against the conquerors. Drawn into the politics of the empire from the ninth century onwards, they were the principal agents of the Shi'ite revolution of the tenth century which ushered in the century of Shi'ite hegemony in the Near and Middle East. The Daylamis had a long history of support for militant 'Alid pretenders to the throne; but the Buyids themselves were not 'Alids. In origin they were freelance captains, who had established themselves in command of the southern Iranian province of Fars, the central Iranian province of Rayy and Isfahan, and finally central and southern Iraq. Unlike the Fatimids, therefore, they formed what Kennedy calls a family confederation centred upon Fars and its capital Shiraz, with no pretensions to caliphate or imamate, but rather to the old Persian title of *shahanshah*, 'king of kings'. This claim to independence of existing political authority in Islam was nevertheless prudently reinforced by their patronage of Twelver Shi'ism, whose Hidden Imam posed no threat to their power, but enabled them to keep their distance from the third source of their legitimacy, the 'Abbasids, in whose name they ostensibly ruled as 'Imad al-Dawla, Rukn al-Dawla, Mu'izz al-Dawla, 'Adud al-Dawla, etc., Pillars and Buttresses of the ('Abbasid) State, as well as from the Fatimids with their pretensions to the sovereignty of the world. This was especially the case in Baghdad, where they were opposed by the Turkish militias who briefly expelled them from the city in 974, and by the 'Abbasid caliphs, who identified themselves firmly with Sunnism in an attempt to regain a measure of independence. By the end of the tenth century, the religious factionalism they had encouraged in the population of Baghdad had grown to the point of entry into the wider world of Islam.[29]

Despite the inevitable family quarrels over the succession at Rayy, Shiraz and Baghdad, the Buyid hold upon western Iran remained firm down to the middle years of the eleventh century. The Buyids of Rayy remained in close contact with their Daylami homeland to the north-west, to the extent of permitting the establishment of a related Daylami dynasty, the Kakuyids, at Hamadan, while relying for cavalry upon the Kurds of the Zagros to the west, under their Hasanuyid leaders. The Buyids of Shiraz were less happily dependent upon expatriate armies of Daylami infantry at odds with the squadrons of Turkish cavalry who had originally been recruited from central Asia by the 'Abbasids

---

[29] See Kennedy (1986), pp. 212–36.

in the ninth century. These had since become a self-perpetuating caste of warriors raised from boys imported as slaves for training as *ghilman* (sing. *ghulam*), 'youths', in the warbands of their commanders.[30] The Buyid solution to the problem of paying such troops was the *iqta* or apportionment, loosely rendered as 'fief', a grant of particular revenues to particular warriors or groups of warriors in return for their military service. In a highly centralized state such as Fatimid Egypt, this need be no more than an accounting device on the part of the Treasury to ensure the proper payment of the troops on parade;[31] but where the fisc was less developed, as in Iran, the soldiers might be allowed to collect such revenues for themselves. Buyid practice came increasingly to involve such a devolution of authority, with all its dangers.[32] Central government nevertheless remained largely in the hands of able wazirs, usually of Persian origin, who possessed the political as well as administrative skills to contain the quarrels of the dynasty and the military, and preside over a long period of comparative peace and prosperity, with local affairs in mainly local hands.[33] The rationale of such a state in the eyes of contemporaries was the *shawka* or thorn of the ruler, the terrible might of which the subject went in fear and dread about his lawful business;[34] or as the saying ascribed to the 'Abbasid Caliph Ma'mun went: 'The best life has he who has an ample house, a beautiful wife, and sufficient means, who does not know us and whom we do not know.'[35] The combination of royal courts, literate ministers and the revival of Persian in addition to Arabic meanwhile encouraged the proliferation of literatures and sciences that contributed to what Mez called 'the renaissance of Islam',[36] of which Iran in the Shi'ite century was the centre.

In the third Buyid realm of Iraq, following the death of the great 'Adud al-Dawla in 983, and the separation of the province from his seat of power in Fars, it was a different story. By the time the last of 'Adud al-Dawla's sons came to power at Shiraz in 998 with the title of Baha' al-Dawla, 'Splendour of the State', the bulk of Iraq was in the hands of the bedouin Arab 'Uqaylids to the north of Baghdad, the Mazyadids to the south, and the Kurdish 'Annazids to the east. These tribal dynasties had all arisen under Buyid patronage, and came to power through Buyid quarrels over the succession to 'Adud al-Dawla. Their dominions were not so much administrative units as tributary regions, whose cities, like Mosul, paid for their protection.[37] When Baha' al-Dawla moved to reoccupy Baghdad in 1002, he took over little more than the city

---

[30] See *ibid.*, pp. 206–11.   [31] See Brett (1995a).

[32] See Cahen (1953); *idem*, in *Encyclopaedia of Islam* (1954–), s. v. 'Ikta'; Lambton (1965); Al-Duri (1969); Sato (1982).

[33] See Kennedy (1986), pp. 236–49.   [34] See Mottahedeh (1980), pp. 175–90.

[35] Quoted by Von Grunebaum (1955), p. 26.   [36] Mez (1937).

[37] See Kennedy (1986), pp. 210, 253–4, 292–302.

itself. The competent regime which he reinstated survived his death in 1012, but ended with the execution of his governor in 1016, leaving Baghdad a prey to communal violence: fighting between Shi'ites and Sunnis merged into gang warfare and brigandage, which left great tracts of the city desolate. Crippled by poverty, the Buyid regime in the city was powerless; the Turks who upheld the rule of Shiraz, followed by that of the Buyid prince Jalal al-Dawla in Baghdad itself, represented yet another faction. Only the 'Abbasids in their palace not merely survived but prospered as the champions of the Sunni cause, aided by the longevity as well as the ability of the two caliphs al-Qadir, 991–1031, and al-Qa'im, 1031–75. The claims of the Fatimids, from which the Buyids had distanced themselves through their patronage of the doctrine of the Hidden Imam, were now exploited by the 'Abbasids to win the support of the Twelver Shi'ites of the city as well, through the denunciation of the Fatimids as impostors which was drawn up by the Shi'ites of Baghdad and promulgated by al-Qadir in 1011.[38] This declaration that the Fatimids were not of 'Alid descent touched a raw nerve, in that their genealogy was in fact far from clear, more a matter of faith than general knowledge;[39] and it prepared the way for a positive restatement of the 'Abbasid position, which became a new and comprehensive theory of the caliphate. This was the work of the 'Abbasid jurist and spokesman al-Mawardi (d. 1058), who composed his *Ahkam al-sultaniyya* or Rules of Government for al-Qadir's successor al-Qa'im.

Al-Mawardi's was a specifically Sunni theory of the caliphate, in that succession to the throne was declared to be by election of the community rather than by designation by the previous imam, as in Shi'ism, and that the principal duty of the ruler was to enforce rather than authorize the Shari'a. It was the first time that such a formula, implicit in the jurisprudence of the Sunni schools of Law, had been explicitly enunciated in the literature or explicitly accepted by the dynasty, with the qualification that the caliph now deputized for the Prophet in his capacity of ruler of the community, rather than God as ruler of the world. The Fatimids were left alone to maintain the original claim of the rulers of Islam to the caliphate of Allah.[40] As described by Mawardi, the offices of this caliphate were essentially those of the patrimonial state in the days of its glory in the eighth and ninth centuries, now sanctified as the ideal of government in accordance with the Law.[41] The irony that the empire to be governed in this way had ceased to exist became instead the justification for the caliphate to exercise its authority rather than its power, pronouncing in favour of true as against false doctrine, and conferring legitimacy upon actual

---

[38] See *ibid.*, pp. 241–2; Daftary (1990), pp. 109ff.
[39] See Mamour (1934); Brett (1994a).   [40] See Crone and Hinds (1986).
[41] Most accessible in English in Ibn Khaldun, *The Muqaddimah*, I, pp. 448–65, II, pp. 3–73.

rulers by delegating its powers to them. This was little more than past practice, previously employed by the 'Abbasids to prevent the total disintegration of their empire, and subsequently by the Fatimids as a means of gaining an empire of their own, elevated into a principle of divinely instituted government. Nevertheless, it enabled the 'Abbasids convincingly to carry the ideological war back into the camp of their Fatimid enemies as well as their Buyid protectors. In the first half of the eleventh century, the universal caliphate may have been a fiction, but the fiction was potent, and portentous.[42]

In the old dynastic stamping-ground of the Fertile Crescent, the 'Abbasids had been unable to keep Aleppo under the Hamdanids and Mirdasids from falling into the Fatimid orbit in Syria, but successfully prevented the 'Uqaylids of Iraq, for example, from changing their allegiance from Baghdad to Cairo in 1010. Away to the east of the Buyid dominions, on the other hand, al-Qadir found a powerful ally in Mahmud of Ghazna to the south of Kabul, who between 998 and his death in 1030 created a vast new empire in eastern Iran, from the Oxus and the Aral Sea to the Indian Ocean and the Indus, finally annexing the Buyid principality of Rayy in 1029. The son of a Turkish *ghulam* in the service of the Samanids of Bukhara, who had ruled the eastern Iranian world in the name of the 'Abbasids since the end of the ninth century, he took over the bulk of the Samanid dominions from his former masters in the name of al-Qadir, whose accession at Baghdad the Samanids had refused to recognize. Mahmud was duly rewarded with the titles of Wali Amir al-Mu'-minin or Friend of the Commander of the Faithful, and Yamin al-Dawla wa Amin al-Milla, or Right Hand of the State and Keeper of the Community. Such titles reflected the thinking of Baghdad on the structure of its government in the absence of its empire: they represented a transposition of the office of wazir, the surrogate who 'lifted the burden' of power from the shoulders of the monarch,[43] from a prime minister to a prince whose *shawka* was his own. To Mahmud they meant legitimacy or confirmation of the power he had won by the sword: the justification of his conquests and the commission to enlarge them at the expense of heretical rebels and rebellious infidels. The latter were represented by the Hindu princes of India, the former by the Shi'ite Buyids in western Iran, but also by the Isma'ilis, who upheld the cause of the Fatimid caliph in Mahmud's own dominions.[44]

Unlike the states of the Fatimids and the Buyids, Mahmud's empire was predicated upon continuous conquest, which paid for the large professional Turkish army out of the revenues of plunder, tribute and taxation of the conquered provinces, without the need for *iqta's* or fiefs in the Buyid sense. The

[42] See Gibb (1962), pp. 141–50, 151–65; Rosenthal (1962), pp. 27–37; Kennedy (1986), pp. 241–3.
[43] See above, at n. 8; and Goitein (1942) and (1961), both repr. in (1966).
[44] For Mahmud and his dynasty, see Bosworth (1963) and (1975), ch. 5.

chief function of the large itinerant secretariat that accompanied the sultan on his expensive campaigns was thus to procure the sums required from each district of the immense realm, and keep the district officers themselves under constant scrutiny. When the Buyids of Rayy succumbed in 1029, their administration was left in place, but subjected to the harsh fiscal requirements of the new master. The Isma'ilis presented the Ghaznavid conqueror with a similarly attractive target in the prosperous city-state of Multan in the Punjab, a satellite of Cairo so remote that fifty years earlier, at the time of the Isma'ili conversion of the city (c. 958), the correspondence of the Fatimid Mu'izz reveals mutual ignorance on the part of the imam and his followers in Sind and the Indus valley.[45] Multan under its Isma'ili prince Da'ud ibn Nasr was first made tributary, and then conquered in 1010 with a massacre of the Isma'ilis, considered as vile heretics. Otherwise, Isma'ilism served a propaganda purpose. It was by no means extirpated from India or the rest of Mahmud's empire, but the persecution of its widespread following throughout his reign was a hallmark of his position at home and abroad. It led conspicuously to the execution in 1012–13 of the Fatimid *da'i* al-Taharti, sent by Hakim to woo the sultan, but tried and condemned to death as an agent of the impostor, and eventually to the execution of his wazir Hasanak by Mahmud's Mas'ud, on charges which included the acceptance of a robe of honour from Cairo while on pilgrimage to Mecca.[46] Apart from such dramatic incidents and rhetorical statements, persecution itself seems largely to have been left to local zealots, and, given the nature of the Ghaznavid state, is likely to have been sporadic, intermittent and ineffective in wiping out its victims. Mahmud's stance nevertheless established the Ghaznavids' reputation as militant champions of Sunni Islam and the cause of the caliph. Under his son Mas'ud, their imperial designs upon the territories of the Buyids were extended by pronouncement to encompass the liberation of Baghdad, the reopening of the route across the desert for the pilgrimage to the Holy Places and the assault upon Cairo.[47] Thus it formed the mould into which the Seljuqs poured in the middle of the century.

THE COMING OF THE SELJUQS

The Shi'ite century, which began with the conquest of the Near and Middle East by armies of mountain tribesmen from within the original Arab empire, concluded with the invasion of its territories by tribal nomads from beyond its borders. This extension of the appeal of Islam – religion, way of life and civilization – from peoples left aside to peoples unreached by the Arab conquests,

[45] See Stern (1949) and (1955), both in (1983).
[46] See Bosworth (1963), pp. 51–4, 182–3, 187, 199–200.   [47] See Bosworth (1962) and (1975), p. 189.

bears witness to the spectacular growth of the empire they created into a flourishing commonwealth. The lands through which the Arab armies passed on their outward journey to the periphery of their empire had been drawn together by the elaboration of their creed as a religion of government in every sense of the word. A close cultural and economic relationship was articulated by the long-distance routes of trade and travel along the lines of the conquests in 'the arid zone' to which the Arab expansion was largely confined. 'The arid zone' is Hodgson's expression for the swathe of desert stretching from the Atlantic to central Asia and northern India, punctuated by seas, mountains and river valleys which create oases of fertility separated by huge wastes.[48] Placed in relationship to the Mediterranean by Braudel,[49] and to the Indian Ocean by Chaudhuri,[50] it is celebrated by Lombard as the geographical setting for 'the golden age of Islam', its period of prosperity from the middle of the eighth to the middle of the eleventh century.[51] Hodgson's pessimistic view of the limitation of investment in agriculture and industry, and the consequent weakness of the economic base,[52] is opposed to Lombard's optimistic assessment of the expansion of both in response to consumer demand.[53] Both Hodgson and Lombard agree upon the role of trade centred upon the major cities, larger, fewer and more widely spaced than in Europe, for example, but drawing in commodities not only from the length and breadth of the arid zone itself, the lands of Islam, but from outside: from Europe to the north, tropical Africa to the south, and India and China to the east. The ramifications of this market economy had established the civilization of the Near and Middle East as the central civilization of the known world.

The nomadic populations of the arid zone – Berbers, Arab bedouin and Turks – who flourished on the margins of this civilization had become involved with it in different ways. The Berbers of the western and central Sahara were instrumental in the important gold and slave trades across the desert with the western and central Sudan. The bedouin of Arabia and Egypt were torn between symbiosis with and settlement among the peasant populations and between marauding and military alliances with the rulers of the cities and the greater states, leading in the case of the 'Uqaylids of Iraq and the Mirdasids of Aleppo to petty dynasties. The similar relationship of the Turks of central Asia with the Iranian populations to the south, along the line of the Jaxartes or Sir Darya, was shot through by the trade in Turkish slave boys for the armies of *ghilman*, and overlaid by the import into the Islamic world of silk and porcelain from China and furs from Siberia and Russia. Behind this lurked the historic

---

[48] Hodgson (1974), *passim*.   [49] Braudel (1972), I, pp. 168–230.
[50] Chaudhuri (1985), chs. 1 and 2.   [51] Lombard (1975).
[52] Hodgson (1974), II, pp. 136–8.   [53] Lombard (1975), pp. 161–204.

threat of invasion of the lands on the periphery of the central Asiatic steppe by the horse-riding nomads who had appeared in Europe as the Huns; who had forced the Chinese to build the Great Wall; and whose wars with Iran were the stuff of legend, woven by Firdausi in the reign of Mahmud of Ghazna into the Persian epic of the Shah-nama or Book of Kings, and passing into English literature as the tale of Sohrab and Rustam. In the eleventh century, as Firdausi composed his masterpiece, that threat revived as the Turkish peoples closest to the Muslim frontier, the Qarluq and the Oghuz or Ghuzz, adopted Islam and advanced into Muslim territory.

At the end of the tenth century, as Mahmud of Ghazna seized the bulk of Samanid territory to the south of the Oxus, the Qarluq took over the homeland of the dynasty in Transoxania, and established their own Qarakhanid dynasty at Bukhara, whose power extended eastwards over the mountains to Kashghar in Farghana or Sinkiang.[54] To the west of the Qarluq towards the Aral Sea and the Volga, the Oghuz under their *yabghu* or khan were divided between paganism and Islam, which provided a minority of the chiefly clan with the opportunity to combat their rivals as *ghazis* or warriors upon the infidel. These were the sons of the eponymous chieftain Seljuq, who meanwhile became involved in the wars of the Qarakhanids in Transoxania and were eventually expelled southwards across the Oxus into Ghaznavid Khurasan. In an extraordinary decade following the death of Mahmud in 1030 and the accession of his son Mas'ud, they and their nomadic followers, too elusive to be brought to battle, overran the province. In pursuit, the ponderous Ghaznavid army was deprived of the plunder it was accustomed to win and the revenue it expected to enjoy. Lured out into the desert in 1040, it was routed by the mobile Seljuq horde at the battle of Dandanqan. The harsh and unpopular Ghaznavid regime in Iran collapsed, leaving the dynasty only with its capital at Ghazna and its conquests in India, while the victorious Seljuq brothers, Tughril, Chaghri and Musa Yahghu, divided Iran between them.

Leaving the east to Chaghri and Musa, Tughril, the leader if not the eldest, turned west with his half-brother Ibrahim Inal to occupy the old Buyid kingdom of Rayy in 1041–3. There, they had been preceded by scattered bands of Oghuz who had fled from the wars in Khurasan, only to become embroiled in the warfare attending the efforts of the Daylami Kakuyids of Hamadan to win back the kingdom for themselves from the clutches of Mas'ud. These bands of nomads, seeking pasture for their sheep as much as plunder, were constantly augmented as the victories of the Seljuqs opened the way to a stream of such emigrants out of their homelands into the pastures of northern Iran, from where they moved westwards towards Anatolia. Known as Turkmen or

---

[54] See Bosworth (1967), pp. 111–14, and (1968), pp. 5–7.

Turcomans, they were already into Azerbayjan and in the 1040s spread into Armenia, northern Iraq and northern Syria: Mosul was sacked in 1044. As Tughril moved into Rayy and Ibrahim Inal into Hamadan, they fled away from the Seljuqs' claim to overlordship and obedience. Beneath and ahead of the advance of the new Seljuq empire, a major new element was appearing in the population of the Near and Middle East.[55]

Tughril may have followed the Turcomans westwards quite as much as he led them. What gave his advance its purpose was nevertheless his adoption of the pro-'Abbasid and specifically anti-Fatimid rhetoric of Mas'ud, which brought this extraordinary story of an immigration that became an empire firmly into the context of Islam and its concerns. Whatever the Islam of the Seljuqs may have been at the outset of their career on the frontier, their profession of faith was a prerequisite of their participation in the wars of a Muslim country like Transoxania, and certainly a condition of success in the struggle for Khurasan. Without a cause or religious leader of their own, moreover, it was necessary that this Islam should be not only Sunni but 'Abbasid. Thus the announcement of victory at Dandanqan was sent straight from the battlefield to Baghdad. It is clear that the Seljuqs had already conceived the possibility of power on these terms, and proceeded to claim the mantle of the Ghaznavids for the purpose, no doubt under the strong influence of the Khurasanian secretaries who passed into their service from the Ghaznavids.[56] In choosing the west as his province, Tughril as leader was identifying the ambitions of the Seljuqs with the cause of Sunni empire.

That did not prevent his marriage alliance with the last powerful Buyid ruler of Fars, Abu Kalijar 'Imad al-Din (1024–48), the victor in the long succession dispute following the death of Baha' al-Dawla in 1012, which had thrown the Buyid regime in Baghdad into anarchy. The 1040s were not in fact a time of spectacular advance; the Seljuqs and the Turcomans in western Iran were confronted by a multiplicity of peoples and petty dynasties in the mountainous terrain with whom they were obliged to deal. The cause of empire was not helped by the growing divisions between the Turcomans on the one hand, the Seljuq leadership on the other, and between the leaders themselves. These divisions centred around the figure of Tughril's partner Ibrahim Inal at Hamadan, who sided with the Turcomans in their opposition to Seljuq control, while encouraging and occasionally leading their westward movement towards Anatolia. The growth of Tughril's power may have been steady, but it was consequently slow, and depended for its greatest advance in this period upon the death of Abu Kalijar at Shiraz in 1048 and the struggle over the succession

---

[55] See Bosworth (1975), pp. 187–95, and (1968), pp. 16–23, 23–53 *passim*.
[56] Bosworth (1968), pp. 45–6.

that promptly ensued. The barriers to the Turcoman invasion of Fars then collapsed; meanwhile Tughril, recognized by the Marwanids of Amid or Diyarbakr in 1049–50, took the remaining Kakuyid city of Isfahan as his capital in 1050–1 and proceeded to intervene in the succession at Shiraz, until by 1055 the Buyid kingdom under its new ruler Fulad-Sutun was all but annexed. The way was open to Baghdad, under the ineffective rule of Abu Kalijar's other son al-Malik al-Rahim. Control of the city was disputed between the Turkish commander al-Basasiri and Ibn al-Muslima, the wazir whom the 'Abbasid caliph al-Qa'im had appointed in 1045 as a mark of his increasing independence. In 1055 Tughril assembled his forces for an expedition which, in the manner of the Ghaznavid Mas'ud, looked beyond Baghdad to the pilgrimage to Mecca and a war upon the Fatimids in Egypt. In December he made a processional entry into the city, received by the officers of the caliph though not by al-Qa'im in person, to fulfil the imperial destiny of the new dynasty.

THE APPEARANCE OF THE BANU HILAL

The tribes of bedouin Arabs, collectively known as the Banu Hilal, who made their appearance in North Africa in the middle of the eleventh century, shared with the Seljuqs a similar involvement in the conflict between Cairo and Baghdad, so much so that they are commonly said to have been sent from Egypt by the Fatimids in 1051 to punish the Zirids of Ifriqiya for their desertion to the 'Abbasids. This, however, is a legend rooted in Fatimid historiography,[57] obscuring a different reality. The Banu Hilal belonged to what Ibn Khaldun called 'the Arabs of the fourth age', who had been left behind in the desert by the conquerors belonging to the great third age of the race, to emerge as the modern representatives of the ancient nation and its virtues after the founders of the Arab empire had been swallowed up by the civilization they had created.[58] Not strictly tribesmen from outside the old Arab empire, they nevertheless exemplified the utter savagery of people adapted to a life of utmost hardship, as far as possible from that of settlement and cities, by which they were alternately attracted and repulsed.[59] In the heart of Arabia, they had gone far to make the desert crossing from Iraq to Mecca and Medina impassable since the heyday of the 'Abbasid empire, whence the stated aim of the Ghaznavids and Seljuqs to open the route and make the pilgrimage. On the fringes of the Fertile Crescent, they had revolted unsuccessfully on behalf of the Fatimid mahdi at the beginning of the tenth century, but had subsequently given rise to bedouin dynasties such as the 'Uqaylids and Mirdasids. In Egypt they had

---

[57] See Brett (1982).   [58] See Cheddadi (1986), pp. 135–6, 419–24.
[59] Ibn Khaldun, *The Muqaddimah*, I, pp. 250–2, 306–8, II, pp. 279–80.

spread southwards on either side of the Nile towards Aswan, and wandered westwards out into the territories of the native Berber nomads of the Sahara. In the second half of the tenth century, the Banu Hilal were reported by Ibn Hawqal to frequent the western oases of Kharga and Dakhla.[60] But in the eleventh century, bedouin such as the Banu Qurra of Cyrenaica had shared in the revolt of Abu Rakwa against Hakim and had gone on to take control of Barqa. In 1037–8, the Hilali tribe of the Zughba had killed the Berber prince of Tripoli, Sa'id ibn Khazrun, and ten years later were entering into an alliance with Mu'izz ibn Badis, the Zirid sultan of Ifriqiya.[61] As warrior nomads newly established in the northern Sahara, they entered in this way into the politics of the Fatimid empire in North Africa at a time when it was under great strain, presenting Cairo with a far more immediate problem than the advance of the Seljuqs in the east.

In Cairo, the gap between the affairs of the Dawla proper in Egypt and Syria, and the concerns of the Fatimid empire at large, was slow to close. The 1040s were a decade in which the regime was preoccupied with the succession to the wazirate following the death of al-Jarjara'i in 1045. Ever since the accession of the infant Imam–Caliph al-Mustansir in 1036, this eminently capable politician had been faced with the hostility of the new queen-mother Rasad, who employed her immense personal wealth as Sitt al-Mulk and Ruqiyya had done, to build up a following in the administration, this time in opposition to the old wazir. Al-Jarjara'i was weakened by his distrust of his old ally al-Dizbiri in Syria. In 1041 he engineered a military coup at Damascus which drove Dizbiri, branded a traitor, into exile and death at Aleppo. Aleppo itself was promptly reoccupied by the Mirdasids; the Jarrahids of Palestine were again in revolt; and the new governor of Damascus, Nasir al-Dawla ibn Hamdan, a scion of the old Hamdanid dynasty, was unable to restore the position. In Egypt, the queen-mother's *coterie* was headed by Abu Sa'd al-Tustari, the Iranian Jewish merchant who had purveyed her as a concubine to the caliph al-Zahir, and now served as steward of her estates. When al-Jarjara'i died, his chief lieutenants were the only possible candidates for the succession; but the first, al-Anbari, was almost immediately deposed, and his colleague, the converted Jew al-Fallahi, was appointed on the recommendation of al-Tustari, whose influence was now paramount. Al-Anbari was imprisoned and executed; but in 1047 the new wazir rebelled against his tutelage, and connived at the murder of al-Tustari in the street by Turkish soldiery. For this he too was deposed, imprisoned and eventually executed; al-Tustari's brother Abu Nasr was given charge of the *khizanat al-khass* or 'privy purse' of the caliph, while the stewardship of

---

[60] Ibn Hawqal, *Surat al-ard*, ed. Kramers, p. 155; trans. Kramers and Wiet, p. 153.
[61] See Brett (1974–5).

the queen-mother's estates went to a very different man, the Isma'ili scholar al-Yazuri from Ramla in Palestine. The wazirate itself remained in the hands of the Jarjara'i faction in the person of the great man's nephew, Abu'l-Barakat al-Jarjara'i, whose notorious arrests, banishments and confiscations were presumably intended to secure himself against the fate of his two predecessors. He attempted to remove al-Yazuri from politics by appointing him chief *qadi* and chief *da'i*; but al-Yazuri survived by appointing his son as his deputy over the queen-mother's estates.[62]

The tension was only resolved by a disastrous expedition against Aleppo in 1049, for which Abu'l-Barakat was responsible, and for which he was dismissed. In 1050 al-Yazuri was appointed in his place and the transfer of power within the administration from one party to another was finally complete. His position was by no means so secure as that of al-Jarjara'i, in that the followers of his predecessor remained entrenched in the army of secretaries and soldiers, jealous of his promotion and anxious for their places. Enjoying the confidence of the palace, al-Yazuri was nevertheless able to assert his authority at home and abroad, beginning with Syria, where he and his chief military ally Nasir al-Dawla effected a reconciliation with the Mirdasids. The alliance with Byzantium was confirmed, while to the south, an expedition, sent to Nubia to demand the tribute known as the *baqt* or 'pact', renewed the Fatimids' generally friendly relations with the Christian kingdom.[63] From the Yemen came a bonus in the form of presents sent by the *da'i* al-Sulayhi to announce the progress of the campaign of conquest he had undertaken in 1038.[64] Out to the west, however, the situation was more menacing.

Morally and materially, the position of the Zirids of Ifriqiya had been undermined since the beginning of the century. Their western province in Algeria had been lost to their cousins the Hammadids, while Tripoli had been seized by the Banu Khazrun, Zanata Berber nomads from western Algeria militarized by a century of war between the Fatimids and the Umayyads of Cordoba in the west. Their control of the oases of southern Tunisia was threatened not only by the immigrant Zanata, but by the Berber populations of Djerba, the Jabal Nafusa and the Djerid, the majority of whom were Ibadis, opposed to Shi'ites and Sunnis alike. At Qayrawan itself, the old Arab capital of the

[62] Besides al-Maqrizi's *Itti'az*, the principal sources for the history of Egypt in this period are, in chronological order: Ibn al-Sayrafi, *Al-Ishara* (to 1130); Ibn Muyassar, *Akhbar Misr* (late thirteenth century); and al-Maqrizi, *Khitat* (early fifteenth century); together with Ibn al-Athir, *Kitab* (early thirteenth century).
[63] Al-Maqrizi, *Itti'az*, II, p. 222. For the *baqt* as the basis of Egyptian relations with Nubia in the Muslim period, see *Cambridge History of Africa* (1978), II, pp. 505–6, 565–7, and *passim*; Hasan (1967), pp. 20–8, 90–3.
[64] *Ibid.*

country, the dynasty resident in the old Fatimid palace of Sabra, confronted an unruly populace. The grievances of the citizens were probably economic, in that the prosperity generated by the Fatimids had diminished, while that of Tunis in particular is likely to have increased.[65] But they were made specific by the opposition between the dynasty which ruled in the name of the Fatimid imam and the Sunni *ulama* or jurists of the Malikite school, who had made Qayrawan one of the great seats of Sunni scholarship. Behind their learned objections to Isma'ilism stood a militant zeal which threatened not only riot but revolution. In 1016 or 1017, following the accession of the young sultan Mu'izz ibn Badis, and in the final phase of Hakim's reign, the crowd throughout Ifriqiya turned on the Isma'ilis and massacred them in defiance of the authorities. The long reign of Mu'izz became in consequence a slow movement towards Sunnism, in which the sultan allied with the greater jurists in the hope of isolating and eliminating the more radical preachers. By the 1030s and 1040s, the regime was increasingly embattled, campaigning against the Hammadids on the one hand, the Zanata on the other. Mu'izz nevertheless intervened in the quarrels of Muslim Sicily as the Kalbid dynasty at Palermo weakened, apparently hoping to annex the island; the attempt was a failure, and the Ifriqiyans were expelled, either by the Sicilians themselves or by the Byzantine general George Maniakes in 1038–40. Despite the lack of success, this obscure episode prefigured a grander attempt to revive the fortunes of the dynasty by seizing the initiative at home and abroad.[66]

In 1048, Mu'izz formally abjured his allegiance to the imam–caliph, and transferred it to the 'Abbasids. The date given by the Zirid chronicler Ibn Sharaf[67] is confirmed by the coinage, which in AH 441, 1049–50, changed from the gold *dinar* of the Fatimids to one bearing the Qur'anic legend – 'Whoever chooses a religion other than Islam, it shall not be accepted from him, and in the Hereafter he shall be lost' – a denunciation of the Fatimids and their followers as heretics.[68] Diplomatic relations with Baghdad may have dated from the appointment of Ibn al-Muslima as 'Abbasid wazir in 1045; the Persian al-Darimi, who had served under Mahmud of Ghazna, apparently arrived as 'Abbasid envoy to Qayrawan in 1047–8.[69] A second such envoy was seized by the Byzantines at Antioch in 1051 and sent to Cairo, where the 'Abbasid insignia he was taking to Mu'izz were publicly burnt.[70] It was all that al-Yazuri could do in reply to an opponent who had captured the Sunni cause in North Africa, and set out to create a rival Sunni empire in the west. The Banu Khazrun at Tripoli and the Banu Qurra at Barqa both declared for Baghdad

[65] See Brett (1969).   [66] For exhaustive references, see Idris (1962); Amari (1937–9).
[67] As reported by Ibn 'Idhari, *Al-Bayan al-muqhrib*, pp. 277–9.
[68] See Hazard (1952), pp. 52–5, 90–3.
[69] Idris (1962), pp. 191–2.   [70] See Brett (1982), p. 49.

and Mu'izz. Under their amir Jabbara ibn Mukhtar, the Banu Qurra, who had risen against the Fatimids under Abu Rakwa at the beginning of the century, attacked Alexandria once again in 1052, only to be defeated.

Mu'izz's ambitions, however, came to grief much nearer home. From around the time of his breach with Cairo in 1048, the sultan had allied with the Hilali Arab bedouin tribes of Zughba and Riyah, to whom he had given land in return for military service. The land in question is likely to have been the Jaffara plain between Gabes and Tripoli, a strategic corridor blocked by the Germans in the Second World War at Mareth, and threatened in the eleventh century by the Berbers of Djerba and the Jabal Nafusa. Such an attempt to pacify the region nevertheless failed when the Arabs advanced north of Gabes in search of more land. In 1052 a major expedition led by Mu'izz to reassert his authority over the south was ambushed by the two tribes in hilly county some two or three day's march from Qayrawan, and routed at the battle of Haydaran. With the loss of all his baggage, Mu'izz fled back to his capital, which was promptly besieged as the Arabs overran the countryside. A disaster which might have been remedied was made permanent by the appeal of the Riyah and Zughba to Cairo, and the intervention of Egypt in the following year. While the tribes were encouraged to resume the siege of Qayrawan, al-Yazuri's envoy, the general Amin al-Dawla wa Makinuha Hasan ibn 'Ali ibn Mulhim,[71] appeared at Gabes to receive the submission of the cities of Ifriqiya on the one hand, and the breakaway Hammadids of eastern Algeria on the other, returning to Cairo with a share of the booty taken by the Arabs in the battle.[72] The old state of Ifriqiya, dating back to Byzantine Africa, finally disintegrated. Mu'izz abandoned the inland city of Qayrawan for the more defensible coastal fortress of Mahdia in 1057, while the great metropolis was emptied of its inhabitants. Some jurists remained to preserve the Malikite tradition, but many emigrated, not least to Morocco. At Sijilmasa they handed on the torch of Sunni empire to the Almoravids. This militant Sunni movement, created out of the Sanhaja Berber nomads of the western Sahara by a prophet of the Malikite school inspired from Qayrawan, was at the outset of its career, victorious in the desert and advancing north. The *dinars* first minted by the Almoravids at Sijilmasa in the year of Mu'izz's flight to Mahdia replicated his aggressively Sunni coinage, while at Mahdia itself the Zirids reverted to their Fatimid allegiance and thus to the Fatimid style.[73] It was in the name of Sunni Islam that the Almoravids went on to build an empire of their own in the Muslim west, one that under the Almohads in the following century embraced Ifriqiya itself.

---

[71] Thus in the Fatimid letter which is the fundamental document: Brett (1982), pp. 51–2, but Makin al-Dawla in the chronicles.
[72] See Brett (1974–5) and (1982). [73] See Launois (1964); Idris (1962), pp. 225–6.

The Almoravids effected the third great invasion of the old Arab empire by tribal nomads drawn into Islam by the religious and political quarrels of the Shi'ite century. In North Africa, they represented the same appeal of Islam to the tribal population to make a new submission to God to fight for the faith against His enemies, which had brought the Fatimids to power in Ifriqiya 150 years before and was to culminate in the takeover of their empire by the Almohads 100 years later.[74] Unlike either the Seljuqs or the Banu Hilal, they formed a specifically religious as well as ethnic community, which, although it founded an empire, as did the Seljuqs, was unaccompanied by an influx of nomads who altered the composition of the population in the lands it conquered. The Banu Hilal, on the other hand, founded no empire, despite the favour shown by the Fatimids to leaders like the Riyahid Mu'nis ibn Yahya, who posed in southern Tunisia as the Sahib Ifriqiya or Lord of Ifriqiya, and despite the prominence of the bedouin in the campaigns of the warring princes who ruled the country for the next hundred years. Their failure to rise to the imperial occasion, even in the absence of a religious leader, is all the more remarkable in view of the progressive bedouinization and Arabization of the rural population, which over the centuries has reduced the native Berber element to a minority.[75] The fact remains that even at their kingmaking worst, the Banu Hilal remained as nomads within the framework of the state system.

THE CRISIS OF THE FATIMID EMPIRE

Ironically, the return of the Zirids to Fatimid allegiance in 1057, even at the cost of the disintegration of their dominions, was a triumph for al-Yazuri which he did not live to enjoy. Early in 1058 he was arrested and executed on a charge of treason. Over the two years since the arrival of Tughril Beg in Baghdad at the end of 1055, the internal and external affairs of the Fatimid realm had drawn together with a vengeance to precipitate a crisis at home and abroad. The elements of the crisis had fallen into place over a number of years, beginning with the situation in Baghdad itself, where fighting between Sunnis and Shi'ites accompanied the hostility between the 'Abbasid wazir Ibn al-Muslima and the Turkish commander al-Basasiri, who as the Buyid regime weakened had turned towards Egypt. In Egypt itself, al-Yazuri faced a domestic trial of strength in the form of famine in 1052 and 1054–5. The problem was not so much shortage of grain as hoarding; the difficulty was to force supplies on to the market, since the speculators were not only the merchants but the landholding aristocracy, from the caliph down. The last serious famine, in 1024–5, had provoked disturbances because, in the years leading up to al-Jarjara'i's appointment as wazir, he and his

---

[74] See Brett (1983) and (1994b).   [75] See Brett and Fentress (1995), ch. 4.

colleagues had taken no action in the matter, presumably to avoid antagonizing their backers.[76] Al-Yazuri did so, to the extent of advising the caliph to invest in less publicly harmful activities, as well as ensuring that all grain collected in taxes reached the state granaries for release on to the market;[77] but he cannot have made many friends in high places. More immediately, he sought grain from Byzantium; but the emperor Constantine IX died in January 1055 and the aid was refused by the aged empress Theodora, anxious not to antagonize the Seljuqs pushing into Armenia and eastern Anatolia. Egypt was in consequence unable to supply the Hijaz with the grain on which the pilgrimage depended. Since at the same time the empress had ordered the prayers in the mosque at Constantinople to be said in the name of the 'Abbasids rather than the Fatimids, Egypt declared war, sending Makin al-Dawla ibn Mulhim, returned from his mission to Ifriqiya, to attack both Antioch and Aleppo, where the Mirdasids had allied with the Turcomans. When Tughril Beg finally entered Baghdad, the Fatimids in Syria were in arms.

Ousted by the Seljuqs from Baghdad, al-Basasiri moved up to Rahba on the Euphrates, and appealed to Cairo for aid. Behind al-Yazuri at this juncture stood the distinguished Iranian *da'i* al-Mu'ayyad fi'l-Din al-Shirazi, the last of the great Fatimid philosophers, who, like his predecessor al-Kirmani, hailed from the Buyid realm of Fars. In the 1030s and 1040s he had spent some ten years at the court of Abu Kalijar, who lent a sympathetic ear to his exposition of Isma'ilism until 'Abbasid pressure forced his expulsion to Cairo in 1046–7. At Cairo al-Shirazi was thwarted by the appointment of al-Yazuri as chief *da'i*, who bestowed the post on the descendants of the *qadi* al-Nu'man when he became wazir, but in 1052 took charge of the *diwan al-insha'* or chancellery, the office of state correspondence and diplomacy. Al-Shirazi persuaded al-Yazuri to accede to al-Basasiri's request, and he was duly entrusted with the mission of organizing and financing an Arab tribal coalition in northern Syria and Iraq for the purpose. In 1057, while Makin al-Dawla continued the offensive against Antioch and Aleppo with the help of reinforcements sent under the command of al-Yazuri's son, al-Basasiri defeated the Seljuqs at Sinjar north of Mosul and briefly occupied Mosul itself. In 1058 the effort was crowned with success. At the beginning of the year Makin al-Dawla captured Aleppo, and sent the body of al-Dizbiri, driven into exile by al-Jarjara'i, to Cairo for honourable burial. At the end of the year, while Tughril Beg was drawn away from Baghdad by the revolt of Ibrahim Inal, he occupied the city and proclaimed the suzerainty of the Fatimids. Al-Basasiri's great enemy, the 'Abbasid wazir Ibn al-Muslima, was put to a frightful death, but the 'Abbasid caliph himself was placed under the protection of the 'Uqaylid prince Quraysh. Only the insignia of his caliphate

---

[76] See Bianquis (1980).   [77] Al-Maqrizi, *Itti'az*, II, pp. 224–6; *idem, Traité des famines*, pp. 18–22.

were sent to Cairo, where they were received in triumph by Mustansir in
1059. From the Fatimid point of view, the episode was a crowning victory for
the dynasty's campaign to win the world for the imam by revolution rather
than conquest, especially since the *da'i* al-Sulayhi in the Yemen was on the
verge of complete success. But whereas the campaign in the Yemen was one
of dedication, the league commanded by al-Basasiri was an ephemeral alliance
of the forces of anarchy in late Buyid Iraq. The return of Tughril Beg from
his final victory over Ibrahim Inal at the end of the year drove al-Basasiri
from the city, to die in battle in January 1060.[78] The whole episode had been,
said the Egyptian chronicler Ibn Muyassar, 'the last happiness of the Egyptian
empire'.[79]

The train was laid before ever al-Basasiri entered Baghdad. Whatever the
expectations of Mustansir from his capture of the 'Abbasid city, Egyptian aid to
the enterprise had been cut off since the spring of 1058. At the end of February,
al-Yazuri fell victim to the charge of his opponents that by sending all the wealth
of Egypt for the conquest of Baghdad, he had provoked the wrath of the Seljuqs
and so imperilled the realm. The charge was distorted, and envenomed, by the
accusation of treasonable correspondence with Tughril Beg, and of plans to
flee to Baghdad. The wazir was arrested and executed by order of the caliph. He
was briefly replaced with his close lieutenant al-Babili, until another protégé of
the queen-mother's, al-Maghribi, was promoted from within al-Yazuri's circle
of appointments; the damage, however, was done. The new wazir sought to
disengage the regime from the conflict in Iraq, while returning Nasir al-Dawla
al-Hamdani to Damascus to maintain control of Syria; but the regime itself
had been undermined by the execution of his predecessor. Al-Maghribi fell in
1060 in exactly the same way as his predecessor Abu'l-Barakat in 1049, in the
wake of a major expedition he had sent under Nasir al-Dawla to recapture the
ever-rebellious city of Aleppo, which ended in disaster. But on this occasion no
alternative faction existed within the administration, to whose leader power
could be transferred as it had been from the party of al-Jarjara'i to that of
al-Yazuri ten years previously; and government broke down.

Over the next few years, the wazirate became a merry-go-round of appointments lasting no more than a few months or weeks, as candidates failed to
gain the support of their colleagues or the palace, and lost all credibility. On
the whole, the turnover was not bloody, as it had been under Hakim; many,
beginning with al-Babili, were appointed three or four times. But the political
system built by al-Jarjara'i for the benefit of the Men of the Pen had collapsed

---

[78] For the career of al-Shirazi, see *Diwan*, pp. 259–60; Sirat al-Mu'ayyad, p. 56; 'The Sira'; for that of
al-Basasiri, see *Encyclopaedia of Islam* (1954–), s.v. art. Canard.
[79] Ibn Muyassar, *Akhbar Misr*, p. 21.

under the strain of intrigue. In this second great crisis of the patrimonial state in Egypt the monarchy, far from reasserting its control, merely accelerated the breakdown by placing its trust in those whom Maqrizi contemptuously calls *rijal*, 'men', by whom we are to understand a crowd of favourites who plied the caliph with letters and petitions to the exclusion of the officers of state. The wazirate in consequence was utterly devalued, while the revenues of state were systematically diverted into the pockets of the new men. Maqrizi, who waged his personal campaign for honest government in the fifteenth century, may have written for the sake of effect, to provide a historical example of the faults traditionally exposed in legendary guise in the Mirrors for Princes literature;[80] but the ultimate derivation of his information from Fatimid sources is not in dispute, and the analysis interpolated into his chronicle at this point seems fair comment.[81] In the absence of political direction, the army divided into its own ethnic factions, represented by the Turkish *ghilman* on the one hand and the Black *'abid al-shira'* or 'bought slaves' on the other. These were the product of the trans-Saharan slave trade, whether from Nubia or the central Sudan, who functioned as bowmen and spearmen and had supposedly been acquired in large numbers by Rasad, the Black queen-mother, as a defence against the Turks who had killed her mentor al-Tustari.[82] On parade in 1063 the two sides came to blows; and although they were parted the antagonism remained.

Matters came to a head in 1067 when the Turks at Cairo emptied the treasury and eventually the palace with their demands for pay; the blacks were driven out to brigandage in Upper Egypt; and Nasir al-Dawla al-Hamdani set out to seize and hold the wazirate by force of arms. The *fitna* or strife endured for seven or eight years, accompanied by a prolonged *shidda* or famine throughout the land, less the result of a low Nile than the breakdown of government, law and order. While land went out of cultivation, the taxation and marketing of whatever grain there was disintegrated. Nomads, both Arab and Berber, devastated the Delta and the Valley while the struggle developed between Nasir al-Dawla and the Turks at Cairo for control of the capital. Repeatedly besieged and cut off, the great metropolis was particularly hard hit. The story of the caliph sitting on a mat in an empty palace, fed only by charity, may be a *topos* belied by the equally emblematic tale of the caliph in the depth of despair, shamed into taking effective action to bring grain on to the market by a lady who had exchanged a necklace worth 1,000 dinars for a bag of flour, but which, after she had been robbed on the way home, was only enough for a cake.[83] The extant information, however, is at least partially derived from an eyewitness

---

[80] See e.g. Ibn Khaldun, *The Muqaddimah*, II, pp. 104–6.
[81] Al-Maqrizi, *Itti'az*, II, pp. 262–3; idem, *Traité des famines*, pp. 24–6.   [82] See above, p. 694.
[83] Al-Maqrizi, *Itti'az*, II, pp. 298–9; idem, *Traité des famines*, pp. 25–7.

account.[84] As at Qayrawan ten years earlier, people left the city, in this case for Syria, while the remainder were reduced to eating dogs and, allegedly, each other. The treasure of the dynasty was undoubtedly dispersed, with much, including the 'Abbasid insignia, apparently finding its way to Baghdad. It was an extreme example of the dearth described by Bianquis for the years 1024–5, with valuables sold for food to the point of beggary:[85] a comment on the precariousness of the economy under such a system of distribution, with the difference that on this occasion the famine was real; it affected the countryside and, compounded with plague, led to a drastic fall in the population which affected the country well into the next century.

On the political level, the dynasty itself was threatened with extinction in 1070–1, when Nasir al-Dawla wrote from Alexandria to the Seljuq sultan Alp Arslan, inviting him to send an army to restore Egypt to its 'Abbasid allegiance, while Alp Arslan himself arrived at Aleppo to renew the Seljuq offensive against Cairo. Since the debacle of 1060, the Fatimid position in Syria had crumbled, despite the tenacity of the Fatimid commanders: the Arab Makin al-Dawla followed by the Kutama Berber Haydara ibn Manzu, but notably by the Armenian Badr al-Jamali. Their difficulties centred upon Damascus, where Badr al-Jamali became governor in 1063, only to begin a conflict with the citizens and their notables which forced him from the city in 1064 and finally in 1068, when his enemy Nasir al-Dawla intrigued with the opposition and with the bedouin, who had taken advantage of the growing anarchy to overrun the settled lands. Badr al-Jamali retired to Acre on the coast, while the Syrian capital was torn by fighting between the townsfolk with their *ahdath* or militias, ill-disciplined Fatimid troops under the command of Ibn Manzu's son Mu'alla, and the tribal Arab Kalb: in 1069 the Great Umayyad Mosque was burnt. In 1062, Acre and Tiberias had been entrusted to the safe hands of Makin al-Dawla and with Sidon to the north and Caesarea to the south it became under Badr al-Jamali the bastion of what remained of Fatimid rule in Syria. Between Acre and Sidon, however, Tyre was under the command of its *qadi* Ibn Abi' Aqil, who successfully resisted the siege of the city by Badr al-Jamali in 1070. Further north, Tripoli had likewise gained its independence under its *qadi* Ibn 'Ammar. To the south, Ramla, the Fatimid capital of Palestine, provided Nasir al-Dawla with a centre from which to assemble a tribal coalition out of the bedouin Tayy and Kalb, in the hope of recovering Syria for himself. A mere vestige of Fatimid rule remained at Aleppo, disputed by the princes of the Mirdasid dynasty, who retained the Friday prayer in the name of Mustansir more out of respect for the Shi'ism of the population than obedience to Cairo.[86]

---

[84] Ibn Muyassar, *Akhbar Misr*, Introduction, pp. dh, d, t.   [85] See above, at n. 76.
[86] The obscure and complicated story is documented by Bianquis, (1986), pp. 527–652.

Despite this breakdown of the regime in Syria as well as Egypt, however, the protracted crisis of the Fatimid empire unfolded throughout the 1060s in the absence of either the Seljuqs or the Turcomans. Tughril Beg had died in 1063, to be succeeded by his nephew Alp Arslan as sultan or ruler of the world in the name of the 'Abbasid caliph. 'King of the East and the West', Tughril appears to have been content for the moment with the position he had won as head of a great new family empire. The war against heretics and infidels, which had carried him to Baghdad, was not an overriding imperative, but a posture only to be practised when it coincided with imperial policy. That policy was not necessarily one of conquest. The Seljuqs differed from their predecessors the Ghaznavids, who had campaigned systematically to keep their professional army in plunder and pay. At the same time they differed from their successors the Mongols, whose family empire was based on control of the tribes in their homeland on the steppe. As the conflict with the restless Ibrahim Inal and the adventurous Turcoman chieftains in the west had shown, the Great Seljuq sultan was obliged to fight *against* unlimited expansion in order to assert his authority. Under Tughril's successor Alp Arslan the pattern of the empire became clearer. A growing distinction appeared between the Turcomans and the *ghilman* recruited into the guards of the Seljuq princes; the rebellions of those princes helped to confirm the distribution of their dominions in the east; while the warrior sultan himself favoured peace with the Qarakhanids in Transoxania, the Ghaznavids in Afghanistan and India and the Byzantine empire in Anatolia. This was the region of greatest difficulty, where Turcoman penetration provoked the Byzantine emperor Romanos Diogenes to campaign across the mountains as far as the Euphrates to secure the frontier cities of Antioch, Edessa and Malatya. After his own years of campaigning in Armenia and the Caucasus, it was this confrontation as much as renewed interest in Fatimid Syria and Egypt that brought Alp Arslan to Aleppo in 1071, and gave him a famous victory when he returned northwards to encounter the emperor at Manzikert in Armenia. The battle entailed the historic collapse of the old Roman empire in Asia Minor and a major change in the historical geography of the eastern Mediterranean; but it was no part of the sultan's strategy, and was followed up only by the Turcomans, to whom Anatolia was now completely open. Alp Arslan himself went east against the Qarakhanids, but was killed the following year; and the Seljuq invasion of Syria was again deferred.

The Turcomans were a different matter. From their first appearance at Aleppo in 1065, they entered Syria in the manner of the Banu Hilal in Ifriqiya, as bands of warriors to whom the local princes turned as allies against the native bedouin as well as each other. Warriors, however, they remained, rather than the avant-garde of a nomadic immigration into a land whose pasture was both unfamiliar and subject to the different regime of a different culture. Only on the northern borders of the country beyond Aleppo did they begin to compete with the local populations, including the Arabs of the Mirdasids' own people, the Kilab. Further south, they were invited to help defend Tyre against Badr al-Jamali in 1070, but he may well have called on them himself to dislodge the brother of Nasir al-Dawla from Ramla in 1071.[87] Atsiz, their leader, took not only Ramla but also Jerusalem, and went on to attack Damascus, doggedly held against the citizens on the one hand and the Turcomans on the other by the Fatimid troops of Mu'alla. For several years thereafter, Atsiz returned in spring to devastate the oasis beyond the walls, until he allied with the citizens to dislodge Mu'alla in 1075 and enter the city in 1076. Although he recognized the new caliph al-Muqtadi at Baghdad, he was effectively independent of the new Seljuq sultan Malikshah.

In the meanwhile the crisis in Egypt itself had been resolved. Nasir al-Dawla was murdered by the Turks at Cairo in 1073 and Dakaz or Bildukuz (Ildeguz), their commander, was left aimlessly in charge of the state. But Mustansir sent for Badr al-Jamali at Acre, who arrived by sea with his troops at the beginning of 1074 and within three years had massacred the Turks and cleared the Delta and the Valley of bedouin and brigands. His departure from Syria entailed the loss of Acre to a second Turkish adventurer, but the end of the *fitna* meant the end of the *shidda* and a gradual return to normality. The difference lay in the character of the regime. As wazir, Badr al-Jamali bore the title of *amir al-juyush* or Commander of the Armies. The transition of the patrimonial state in Egypt from direction by the Men of the Pen to direction by the Men of the Sword, so disastrously commenced by Nasir al-Dawla, was complete.

THE RECONSTRUCTION OF THE FATIMID STATE

The revolution was permanent, in that the military remained in charge of the government of Egypt down to the Ottoman conquest in 1517, their dominance never challenged by the secretariat, but only by the Fatimids themselves in the middle of the following century. Badr himself, a convert from Christianity, was in the paradoxical position of depending absolutely on the caliph for his authority while relying on the army for his power, which put him beyond the reach of the palace executioner. At one and the same time, therefore, he identified himself with the monarchy as the Great Lord, Commander of the Armies, Sword of Islam, Giver of Victory to the Imam, the Fortunate Star (Abu Najm), Full Moon of Mustansir (Badr al-Mustansiri), while taking over all the offices of the dynasty, including that of chief *da'i* on the retirement and death of al-Shirazi in 1078. Officially, at least, he enjoyed the confidence of

---

[87] See Cahen (1974), no. 1.

Mustansir, who recommended him to the faithful in the Yemen as the saviour of the state.[88] The defence of the realm was a clear priority, and the military character of his regime was affirmed by the rebuilding of the old brick walls of al-Qahira, the royal city, in stone; with their three great gates of Bab Zawila, Bab al-Futuh and Bab al-Nasr, these represented an extension into Egypt of the castle building that transformed both warfare and society in the Islamic world after the spacious palaces of the Age of the Caliphates. In 1077 Badr repelled an invasion of Egypt by Atsiz, whom he besieged in Damascus the following year, only to be driven back by Tutush, the brother of Malikshah. The city became Tutush's capital, while his lieutenant Urtuq was installed in Jerusalem. With Syria at last in Seljuq hands, however, the new rulers continued to look north rather than south, towards Aleppo and Byzantine Antioch. These they captured in 1085, giving Badr the opportunity for a second attack on Damascus. In 1089 he was more successful in recovering the ports of Sidon, Tyre, Acre and Jubayl, thus recreating for Egypt what was essentially a maritime empire on the Palestinian littoral, maintained from the sea by the surprisingly powerful Fatimid fleet and paying for itself from the revenues of trade. But Badr's most notable achievements were in Egypt itself.

The chronicles are thin on his reign as wazir, and the evidence for his reformation of the provincial administration largely indirect. Lists of administrative districts from various sources at various times show a sharp change in the second half of the eleventh century from 50–70 *kuwar* (sing. *kura*), the units of provincial administration inherited by the Arabs from the Byzantines, to some 26 *a'mal* (sing. *'amal*), or districts. These in turn were grouped into five large provinces: Qus in the south; Middle Egypt with a capital at Asyut or Ashmunayn; Sharqiyya, the eastern Delta; al-Gharbiyya, the western Delta; and Alexandria. We first hear of the province of Qus, whose governor was responsible for the Nubian frontier and for the passage of the pilgrimage up the Nile and then across the desert to the port of 'Aydhab, in 1079–80, which would date the change to the outset of Badr's reign. The five provinces were clearly designed to extend the military regime at Cairo to the country as a whole; the creation of the *a'mal* was probably an overdue recognition of the fact that the governors of the *kuwar* had long lost their original fiscal functions to tax farmers on the one hand and treasury officials on the other, retaining only their responsibility for law and order. While the *kuwar* survived as tax districts, tax collection was now clearly the responsibility of the *musharif* or tax inspector of each province, working with escorts provided by the governors of the new *a'mal*. The production of taxes, on the other hand, was equally clearly the responsibility of tax farmers, in charge of the regulation of the

[88] See al-Mustansir, *Al-sijillat*; described in 'The letters', letter nos. 14–16, 20–2, 32, 34.

Nile flood and the cultivation of the land. Here again Badr introduced a new principle.[89]

With the pacification of Egypt complete in 1076, Badr remitted the *kharaj* or land tax for a period of three years to allow the country to recover. To make good the loss of revenue, on which he depended to pay his troops, he allocated the land tax farms, through whose agency the land would be brought back into production, as *iqta*ʿs to his men for a probable period of thirty years. He thus introduced into Egypt the Buyid practice of assigning particular revenues to individual soldiers at source instead of through the treasury, with this difference, that the 'fiefs' in question remained tax farms, cultivated for their revenue to the state by soldiers whose pay came from the excess profit. An emergency measure modified in the following century, the device nevertheless survived to become the fiscal foundation of the Mamluk army in the later middle ages.[90] As a means to fiscal recovery, it apparently succeeded in restoring the revenues of Egypt to around their normal level of 3 million dinars towards the end of Badr's life.[91] Politically, it gave the troops a vested interest in the regime.

Badr himself endeavoured to perpetuate his relationship to the dynasty by marrying his daughter to the caliph's youngest son Ahmad, while designating his own son al-Afdal as heir to the wazirate. The arrangement barely survived the test, for when Badr died in 1094, Mustansir initially appointed another amir, and was forced to accept al-Afdal by the bulk of the army. When the caliph himself died eight months later, it was the turn of al-Afdal to secure the succession of Ahmad in place of Mustansir's eldest son Nizar, moving rapidly to proclaim him as the designated heir of his father. Nizar, who claimed the designation for himself, fled to Alexandria, where his revolt collapsed and he was captured, to be walled up alive in one of the great new gates of al-Qahira. Against Ahmad, who called himself al-Mustaʿli, 'the Elevated', Nizar had taken the title al-Mustafa, 'the Chosen', a clear indication of the critical importance of the selection of the imam by his predecessor, which on the one hand secured the continuity of divine guidance and on the other had so far preserved the dynasty from the succession disputes which racked so many others: since the arrival of the dynasty in Egypt, all males other than the imam had withdrawn without protest into obscurity. The designation of Ahmad and the legitimacy of his succession as Mustaʿli duly became an article of Fatimid faith; but it was rejected by the Iranian Ismaʿilis, who finally separated themselves from Cairo in the name of Nizar. For al-Afdal, it was crucial to his survival, and the beginning of his own career. Ahmad had no ambitions, and when he died in

---

[89] See Brett (1984), and more generally Rabie (1972).

[90] *Ibid.*, and Brett (1995a). The evidence comes from the time of Badr's son al-Afdal: see below.

[91] See Lane-Poole (1914), pp. 151–2; Maspero and Wiet (1919), pp. 192–3. The reports (*ibid.*) of 1 million dinars under al-Yazuri, and 5 million dinars under Badr's son al-Afdal, are subject to caution.

1101, the wazir became the regent for his five-year-old son al-Amir. In 1110 he moved his residence, and thus the seat of government, out of al-Qahira to a new palace, the Dar al-Mulk or Home of the Kingdom between the imperial city and the old city of Fustat, emphasizing his distance from the caliph while ruling absolutely in his name.

The glory which for ten years he actively sought as the Sword of the Imam nevertheless eluded him. The death of the great Seljuq sultan Malikshah at the end of 1092 precipitated precisely the kind of succession crisis which even at the death of Mustansir the Fatimids avoided. In 1093 Tutush left Damascus to fight for the throne of his family's loose empire, and in 1095 fell in battle; Seljuq Syria was left divided between his rival sons, Ridwan at Aleppo and Duqaq at Damascus, with Antioch under the *ghulam* Yaghisiyan, and Ilghazi and Sukman ibn Urtuq at Jerusalem. Al-Afdal, at the head of a reconstituted state and army, was well placed to exploit their divisions and aspire to the reconquest of the country for the dynasty he represented, especially since the Turks were thrown into confusion in 1097–8 by the victorious advance of the First Crusade across Anatolia to the siege and capture of Antioch. His offer of an alliance rejected by the Franks, he nevertheless besieged Jerusalem in the summer of 1098, expelling the Urtuqids and celebrating his triumph at Ascalon, where he enshrined the sacred head of Husayn, second son of 'Ali and ancestor of the Fatimids, martyred in 680 and revered throughout Islam. The celebration heralded the attempt of the Fatimids in the twelfth century to renew their appeal to the Muslim world on the strength of their descent from 'Ali rather than their controversial imamate. It was al-Afdal's misfortune that the crusaders were in fact bent on the city, and that the speed with which they advanced from Tripoli past the Fatimid cities of the coast left him no time to bring his army back from Egypt before Jerusalem fell to their assault. To add insult to injury, he and his host were promptly attacked and routed by the crusaders at Ascalon. Al-Afdal retired ingloriously to Cairo, never again to campaign in person.[92]

The First Crusade, originating in the appeal of Byzantium for help against the Turks, was the final repercussion of the coming of the Seljuqs, and the opposition which they represented to the Buyids and the Fatimids. Entering the cockpit of the Near East in the aftermath of the great conflict, the crusaders found in Syria a land reverting to the grass roots of castles, cities and diverse communities, to whose number they swiftly added. It was many years before the common Christian action to which the crusaders remained committed, in spite of their quarrels with each other and their pacts with their Muslim neighbours, was reflected in a similar commitment by the Syrians, and parochialism was

---

[92] See Runciman (1951–4), I, pp. 229–30, 275ff; Brett (1995b).

once again overshadowed by imperialism and ideology. The shape of things to come was nevertheless adumbrated at the very beginning of the century by al-Afdal, who over the six years following the creation of the Latin kingdom of Jerusalem, campaigned almost annually against its growing power. The three battles of Ramla, 1101–5, were close-run but inconsequential, in Runciman's view, since although 'the resources of Egypt were enormous' and its armies vast, their quality was poor and their leadership incompetent.[93] Hamblin regards the encounters favourably as attempts by smaller, well-trained forces to relieve the pressure on the Fatimid cities of the coast, such as Acre, which fell in 1104. These attempts failed because, as in 1099, it took so long to bring such forces up from Egypt in response to the crusaders' attacks. They were abandoned either when the cities themselves fell or when it was decided to supply them by sea.[94] Thus Tripoli under the Banu 'Ammar held out until 1109, Sidon till 1110 and Tyre until 1124, while Egypt fell back on the defensive behind the frontier fortress of Ascalon. But the overtures evidently made by al-Afdal to Damascus, to the Seljuq prince Duqaq and to the *atabeg* Tughtigin who succeeded him in 1104, which resulted in a Seljuq contingent at the third battle of Ramla in 1105, strongly suggest that the war that al-Afdal effectively waged for six years was indeed a holy war upon the infidel, in which he represented himself as the champion of Islam and the leader of a united Muslim front. His failure may have entailed the consolidation of the Latin kingdom, cutting the Fatimids off from their Syrian stamping-ground, and reducing them to an Egyptian dynasty; but the success of the crusaders had opened up a new perspective, not only for their caliphate but for government in Islam as a whole.[95]

The war failed at least partly because the resources of Egypt were *not* enormous. In 1107–8, after the end of the war and some thirty years after Badr al-Jamali's initial allocation of the land tax farms as *iqta*'s to his troops, their value was reviewed in the light of complaints from the treasury that the yield of the farms allocated to the higher ranks was higher than their assessment, and complaints from the lesser ranks that the yield of their farms was less, so that while some *muqta*'s (or tenants) paid too little, some paid too much. The farms were thus redistributed, some at auction, to bring their assessment into line with their actual yield, and the results were confirmed for a further thirty years. It would appear that while some of the land had been successfully brought back into production after the great *shidda*, some had not, because the peasant population was still too small to cultivate the whole of the Valley and Delta; for many farms, the troops bid low or not at all, leaving much good land on the treasury's hands. The situation revealed by the Afdali survey may

[93] Runciman (1951–4), II, pp. 74–80, 89–90.
[94] Hamblin (1987), pp. 294–301. [95] See Brett (1995b); and Lambton (1981).

have become even worse when al-Ma'mun al-Bata'ihi, the officer responsible for the reallocation in 1107–8, became wazir himself in 1121, to find that much of the land tax was in arrears, and, moreover, that tax farmers and peasants alike had converted much of the land illegally into personal property on which they grew summer crops such as sugarcane by means of artificial irrigation. Frustrated, but presumably unable to break the thirty-year military contracts, the treasury had meanwhile resorted to auctioning (other?) tax farms, covering bathhouses, bridges and the like, to the highest bidder before the previous contract had expired. The wazir could do little except forbid the practice, and meanwhile remit all arrears on condition that payment would be made in future; land newly brought under cultivation would be exempt from tax for three years.[96] To this unhappy picture of shrunken agricultural revenues must be added the loss of Acre and the commercial revenues of the Palestine littoral.

Al-Afdal was sufficiently concerned with the administration to create in 1107–8 a new office, the *diwan al-tahqiq* or office of inquiry into the affairs of the various financial departments, which under its director Ibn Abi 'l-Layth al-Nasrani, the Christian, became central to the administration. The fleet, repeatedly employed in operations in support of the remaining cities of the Syrian coast, must have been a heavy expense, as was the need to garrison Ascalon, from which occasional raids were made into the Latin Kingdom. In reply, Egypt was invaded and Farama sacked by King Baldwin I in 1118. But the real danger to al-Afdal came not from Jerusalem but from within. In 1121 the ageing wazir was murdered in the street. The finger of suspicion pointed variously at his wazir or lieutenant al-Ma'mun al-Bata'ihi: at the caliph al-Amir, now a man; and at the Iranian Isma'ilis who had left the fold in 1094 in the name of Nizar.

THE ORDER OF ASSASSINS

Both al-Bata'ihi and al-Amir benefited from the great man's murder, the caliph from the treasure he recovered from al-Afdal's residences, the Dar al-Mulk outside and the Dar al-Wizara inside al-Qahira, and al-Bata'ihi from his appointment as wazir, with all the titles of his predecessor. Their coup, if coup it was,[97] transformed the political scene. The caliph was brought out of his seclusion with elaborate public ceremonies, through which the new wazir endeavoured to establish himself as the indispensable agent of the monarchy, while taking control of the administration and army.[98] Such ceremonies were no longer

---

[96] See Brett (1984) and (1995a).   [97] See Ladak (1971).
[98] See Sanders (1989), with ref. to *idem* (1994).

specifically Ismaʿili; ironically, as the servant of the Ismaʿili imam, al-Bataʾihi in fact strove to prevent the entry into Egypt of those Persian and Syrian Ismaʿilis who might assassinate his master as they were accused of murdering al-Afdal. Al-Amir himself was more particularly concerned to heal the rift opened up by the succession of Mustaʿli in 1094. As imam, he had the unquestioned support of the Ismaʿilis of the Yemen under the rule of the Sulayhids, and specifically under their long-lived queen, al-Sayyida Arwa, 1075–1138, who began life as a consort and ended as the supreme representative of the imamate in the country. The relationship had been close since the days of al-Yazuri and al-Shirazi. ʿAli al-Sulayhi, the founder of the dynasty, had achieved the conquest of the Yemen with the occupation of Zabid on the Red Sea coastal plain in 1060 and Aden in 1062. As Egypt moved towards *fitna* and *shidda*, ʿAli himself aspired to the domination of Mecca, but was murdered in 1067, when the prospect of a great Arabian empire evaporated. Saʿda in the north was recovered by the rival ʿAlid Zaydi imams, and the Sulayhids, together with the Zurayʿids whom they installed at Aden in 1083, became a provincial dynasty who needed the Fatimid connection as much as the Fatimids, in their darkest hour, needed them. It was in her capacity as *hujja* or proof of the imam that Sayyida presided for so long over so difficult and diverse a country, staunchly supporting the Mustaʿlian succession, and overseeing the creation of a major tradition of Ismaʿili scholarship rooted in the writings of the *qadi* al-Nuʿman on the *zahir* or open doctrine of the imamate and the Law, and of al-Muʾayyad fiʾl-Din al-Shirazi on the *batin* or 'hidden' cosmological doctrine of the imam. The teachings of this tradition, which preserved those of the Fatimid *daʿwa* at its zenith in the mid-eleventh century, were in stark contrast to those of the Iranians. In seeking to reintegrate these Iranian secessionists by persuading them of the truth of Mustansir's designation of his father Ahmad as the next imam, Amir was appealing in vain to a movement established well before the overt schism, furnished with its own highly developed creed, and actively hostile to him.[99]

Ismaʿilism in the Iranian world had flourished despite the Ghaznavids and the Seljuqs, whose great wazir, Nizam al-Mulk, in the service of both Alp Arslan and Malikshah, had patronized the development of an explicitly orthodox, Sunni scholarship through the foundation of *madrasa*s or colleges called in his honour Nizamiyyas, of which the first was at Baghdad in 1067. The Fatimid *Daʿwa*, headed for twenty years by the Iranian al-Shirazi, continued to base itself at Isfahan, the Seljuq capital, with representatives at Shiraz and Rayy, the old Buyid capitals. It was at Rayy around 1070 that Hasan-i Sabbah was apparently converted from Twelver Shiʿism to Ismaʿilism, yet another success for the determined proselytization of the Buyid dominions from Cairo over the

---

[99] See Stern (1950), and in (1984).

previous century. Promoted by Ibn 'Attash, the *da'i* at Isfahan, he went to Egypt in 1078, returning to Iran in 1081. The death of the great al-Shirazi in 1078, and the assumption of the post of chief *da'i* by the wholly unqualified Badr al-Jamali, may have been the turning-point in the growth of an Iranian Isma'ilism away from direction by Cairo towards independence in both organization and doctrine, of which Hasan took command. In 1090 he declared his mission openly with the seizure of Alamut, a mountain fortress in that historic home of militant Shi'ism, the region of Daylam to the south of the Caspian. The Isma'ilis of Kuhistan in eastern Iran responded with the seizure of several citadels; and when the Seljuq forces retreated at the death of Nizam al-Mulk and Malikshah in 1092, Hasan's followers went on to seize Lamasar and others in the Rudbar district of Daylam; Girdkuh in the eastern Elburz; and points in the southern Zagros as the Seljuq succession crisis worsened and widened. By 1100 Ibn 'Attash's son Ahmad, who had inherited much of his father's authority, was in possession of the fortress of Shahdiz outside Isfahan.

From strongholds such as these, the newly militant Isma'ilis, who have become known in western historiography as the 'Assassins', struck at the Seljuqs and especially their ministers through assassination, although they were not averse to a convenient alliance, or to attacks on the supporters of one prince rather than another. Such terrorism, which famously claimed the life of the great Seljuq wazir Nizam al-Mulk in 1092, induced the fear of a sinister underground, and provoked the massacre of Isma'ilis, real and imagined, at Isfahan and elsewhere; it discredited a movement which seems partly nationalist, in that it was anti-Turk; partly anti-clerical, in that it was hostile to the Sunni establishment; and partly socialist, in that it was egalitarian; but which was first and foremost millenarian in anticipating a new and final dispensation by revolutionary action. When Muhammad Tapar succeeded to the Seljuq sultanate in 1105, and a concerted effort against the Isma'ilis was undertaken, these were forced on to the defensive with the capture of Shahdiz and the killing of Ahmad-i 'Attash in 1107, the loss of the fortresses in the Zagros, and advances into Daylam culminating in the abortive siege of Alamut itself in 1118. The Isma'ili revolution, if that is what it had been, had come to nothing; but the Isma'ili state remained at Alamut, Girdkuh and in Kuhistan under the autocracy of Hasan-i Sabbah, the undisputed representative of the Hidden Imam Nizar. It was futile to expect him to abjure the foundation of his lifetime's authority and power.[100]

It was all the more futile since that authority was grounded in a doctrine which superseded the teachings of the Fatimid *da'wa*, with their panoply of

---

[100] For Hasan-i Sabbah and Nizari Isma'ilism, see Hodgson (1955) and (1968); Lewis (1967), pp. 324–434.

arguments for the necessity of the infallible imam as the linchpin of the relationship of heaven to earth, whether by revelation or by reason. All such
proofs of his infallibility were deemed by Hasan to fail, since they supposed
a higher infallibility on behalf of the evidence and ultimately of the believer
who judged of its credibility. Logically, the imam could only be known by
his absence, when his existence and identity would become self-evident to the
seeker who knew only that he did not know. The doctrine which sprang from
this ontological argument, the *da'wa jadida* or 'new preaching', required none
of the *ta'lim* or teaching of the old doctrine, which it was the responsibility
of the Fatimid imam and his *da'wa* to impart to humanity. *Ta'lim* now meant
command, and by definition required unquestioning acceptance and obedience from the followers of the imam or his representative on earth – a striking
thesis upon which the discipline of the new sect was based, and from which
it took the soubriquet of *Ta'limiyya*. Alternatively it was called the *Batiniyya*,
once again from the old 'hidden' doctrine of the Fatimids, now redefined as
belief in the imam as the absolute source of divine guidance. Both appellations
became names of fear, evoking the obedience and secrecy of the *fida'iyyun*, the
'fedayeen' or 'self-sacrificers' who carried out their assassinations in public, at
the risk of almost certain death. But the significance of the *da'wa jadida* extended far beyond the revolutionary activities of Hasan-i Sabbah's followers to
the doctrines of Islam itself in the works of al-Ghazali, the so-called Mujaddid
or Reviver of Islam at the beginning of the sixth century of the Hijra. Al-
Ghazali was appointed to teach at the Nizamiyya of Baghdad in 1091, as a
polemicist against all such heresy, although in 1095 he abandoned the post for
the life of a wandering ascetic. Challenged by the *da'wa jadida* to refute the
doctrine of the self-evident imam, he did so by proposing the self-evidence of
the Qur'an and the Prophet through whom it had been revealed, turning the
scripture into the perennial source of divine illumination that needed no proof
besides itself.[101] Like the *da'wa jadida*, his work represented an attack on the
Greek philosophical tradition in Islam, subordinating reason to revelation, and
substituting meditation for metaphysical inquiry. Unlike the *da'wa jadida*, it
did not dispense with the obligations of ritual prescribed by the Sunna, but
regarded them as a necessary form of spiritual discipline.[102] Nevertheless it
served to raise the definition of Sunnism from the level of jurisprudence in
which it was grounded, and at which it had been attacked by the Fatimids, to
the level of theology as a definition of faith.

   Although the Isma'ilis of Alamut were driven on to the defensive in Iran
after 1105, their action in Syria developed over a longer period of time with

---

[101] See al-Ghazali, *Al-Munqidh min al-dalal* (1939), p. 132; trans. Watt (1953), pp. 60, *et passim*.
[102] See Watt (1953), pp. 86–152.

the sympathy of Syrian Isma'ilis and the complicity of the Seljuq princes. It began in 1103 with the assassination of the amir of Homs, an enemy of Ridwan at Aleppo, who had allowed the Iranian missionaries of Hasan-i Sabbah to install themselves in the city with its large Shi'ite population. If their aim was revolution, however, it was frustrated by the heterogeneity of the country. As in Iran, the immediate objective of these Hashishiyyun or Assassins, as they came to be known in Syria,[103] was to obtain their own fortress or fortresses, beginning with Afamiya, which they briefly held in 1106. Meanwhile they played a colourful role in Syrian affairs, adding to the complexity of local politics, and guarding against the prospect of intervention from the east by the assassinations of the Seljuq *atabegs* of Mosul, Mawdud at Damascus in 1113 and Bursuqi at Mosul itself in 1126. They were expelled from Aleppo after the death of Ridwan in 1113, and again finally in 1124; however, they established themselves at Damascus under Tughtigin, and proceeded to occupy the castle of Banyas in the Upper Jordan valley until they were driven from both after the death of Tughtigin in 1128. Having revenged themselves upon Tughtigin's successor Buri in 1131, they were sufficiently established in northern Syria to acquire a cluster of fortresses in the range between the Orontes and the sea from 1132 to 1141, of which the last and most important was Masyaf. In this mountain retreat they added to the patchwork of Syria at a time when, to the north, the threat from Mosul was growing with the annexation of Aleppo in 1128 and the conquest of Edessa in 1144 by the *atabeg* Zengi, followed by the occupation of Damascus by his son Nur al-Din in 1154. By the time their most celebrated *da'i* Sinan, 'the Old Man of the Mountain', took command at Masyaf in 1162, the Assassins had been marginalized by the new hegemony of the Zengids.

Sinan had been sent from Alamut as an agent of the new ruler Hasan, who in 1162 succeeded to the headship of the Nizari community. Hasan-i Sabbah had died in 1124, to be succeeded by Buzurgumid, the commandant of the neighbouring castle of Lamasar, and no theologian. Under him and his son Muhammad, 1138–62, the Isma'ili state became dynastic and while fighting off periodic attacks on Kuhistan and invasions of Rudbar settled as in Syria into the political life of the country; even the assassination of the 'Abbasid caliph al-Mustarshid in 1135 may have been connived at by the Seljuq sultan of western Iran and Iraq, Mas'ud, and the great sultan Sanjar in the east, as the caliph endeavoured to exploit the divisions within the Seljuq family by participating in its struggles for power. Muhammad's son Hasan, however, abandoned their

---

[103] The origin of the term, from *hashish*, 'grass' or 'hemp', is unknown, but does not refer to the taking of drugs: cf. Lewis (1967), pp. 11–12; it is, on the other hand, the root of the term 'assassin', 'assassination'.

more humble role of guardians of the faith to return to that of Hasan-i Sabbah as the *hujja* or proof of the imam of the time,[104] with the authority to speak in his name. In 1164 he proclaimed the *Qiyama* or resurrection in a ceremony which symbolized the emancipation of the faithful from the tyranny of the Law by inverting all its rituals, breaking the fast in the middle of Ramadan. While the faithful thus attained the enlightenment promised by the *daʿwa jadida*, Hasan himself emerged as the *Qāʾim*, 'He Who Arises', an apocalyptic figure identical with the mahdi and thus in effect with the imam in whose name he spoke. His own name became both a prayer and a title as Hasan *ʿala dhikrihiʾl-salam*, 'upon the mention of whose name be peace'. In 1166 he was murdered for such blasphemy, but his son Muhammad maintained his doctrine until his own death in 1210. It was then repudiated, whether out of conviction or *taqiyya*, 'prudent hypocrisy', in favour of Sunnism, largely obscuring the doctrinal position of Alamut under Jalal al-Din (1210–21), ʿAla al-Din (1221–55) and Rukn al-Din, who surrendered to the Mongols in the following year. The *Qiyama*, however, survived the fall of the Ismaʿili state to become the basis of Nizari Ismaʿilism, as did the hereditary imamate. With Hasan *ʿala dhikrihiʾl-salam* now unequivocally recognized as the true imam in line of descent from Nizar, the continuity of the apostolic succession to Muhammad and ʿAli was paradoxically reaffirmed on the original principle of transmission from father to son.

In Syria, under the renewed impulsion of the *Qiyama*, Sinan, the Old Man of the Mountain, ruled his state at Masyaf for over thirty years. A prominent feature of the political scene, Masyaf was an important factor in the calculations of the Zengids, the Ayyubids and the Latins down to the defeat of the Mongols at ʿAyn Jalut in 1260 and the creation of the Mamluk empire. Like the Latin kingdom, its independence was then neither tolerable nor tenable and by 1273 it had been suppressed, leaving the Nizaris of Syria to look to the imamate in Iran for spiritual guidance. The guidance in question was sectarian; the *Qiyama*, unlike the *daʿwa jadida* from which it sprang, was for the few rather than the many. Yet it was not wholly peculiar. The sixth Islamic century opened by al-Ghazali rather than by his intellectual opponent Hasan-i Sabbah saw on the one hand the Almohad revolution in the Maghrib, the substitution of al-Ghazali's doctrine of the light of the Qurʾan for the legalism of the Almoravids, which had characterized the Sunni opposition to the Fatimids in the middle of the fifth, and on the other, following the example of al-Ghazali, the rapid rise of Sufism or Islamic mysticism to the surface of Islam as a form of enlightenment under the direction of a spiritual guide. The failure of the *daʿwa jadida* at Alamut to generate a revolutionary movement to compare

[104] See Hodgson (1955), pp. 66–7.

with that of the Almohad mahdi Ibn Tumart led the successors of Hasan-i Sabbah into a doctrine of spiritual resurrection to compare with the 'taste of God', the spiritual illumination sought by al-Ghazali himself and by the great Ibn al-ʿArabi.[105] The teaching that set the Nizaris apart as a community made them otherwise typical of the Islam of their time.

THE LAST OF THE FATIMIDS

Such beliefs were alien to those upheld in principle by the Fatimid imam and caliph al-Amir, and in practice by his followers in the Yemen. In emphasizing his caliphate rather than his imamate as the heir of ʿAli, al-Amir was in fact moving beyond the old doctrines of the dynasty in quite a different way to legitimize the power which he finally resumed in 1125. In that year, he had the wazir al-Bataʾihi arrested and eventually executed on suspicion of a plot against his life and took back the control of affairs which had been abandoned or lost by the monarch since the death of Hakim a hundred years before. It was a testimony to the enduring strength of a dynasty which had retained not only its ultimate authority but its residual powers throughout the rule of its state by its servants. Continuing al-Afdal's policy of rapprochement with the Seljuqs, he sent presents to Bursuqi, the *atabeg* of Mosul, in the year in which he fell victim to the Assassins, and received in return the head of the *daʿi* Bahram when the Nizaris were evicted by Buri from Damascus and Banyas. At home, he dispensed with a wazir, employing the Christian Abu Najah to increase his revenues until he sacrificed him to the fury of his victims, high and low. He is portrayed as a greedy tyrant, not the statesman to refound the monarchy, but he was nevertheless unchallenged until he himself was murdered in 1130, apparently by the Assassins but possibly by his henchmen Hazarmard and Barghash, shortly after the birth of a son, Muhammad. These elevated his cousin ʿAbd al-Majid to the position of wali ʿAhd al-muslimin, the lesser title of the heir apparent, which Hakim had once bestowed upon his nephew Ibn Ilyas. The infant Muhammad disappeared. In the confusion that followed, the wazirate was restored by al-Afdal's son, Ahmad al-Kutayfat ('Little Shoulders') at the head of his father's faction in the army, who ruled first in the name of ʿAbd al-Majid and then in the name of Muhammad al-Muntazar, the Hidden Imam of the Twelvers, until he was killed by the loyal Armenian Yanis in 1131. ʿAbd al-Majid was then restored to the throne as imam and caliph with the title *al-Hafiz li-Din Allah*, 'Keeper of God's Creed'.[106]

---

[105] See *ibid.*, pp. 180–2, and *idem* (1968), pp. 463–6.
[106] See Ladak (1971) and Stern (1951), and in (1984).

The accession of Hafiz to the imamate prompted the secession of the Yemeni *daʿwa*, which had acknowledged the infant Muhammad as al-Amir's heir and would not for the most part accept the irregular succession of his cousin. Muhammad, called al-Tayyib, 'the Good', was deemed to have survived, and subsequently believed to have fathered a line of Hidden Imams in *satr* or concealment, who were represented in the community by a dynasty of *daʿis* with complete authority to speak on their behalf. The decision to reject the succession of al-Hafiz, which gave the Yemenis, like the Iranians, their independence as a sect, was the last achievement of Sayyida before her death in 1138 put an end to the Sulayhid dynasty and its power over central Yemen. While the affiliated dynasties of the Hamdanids of Sanaʿa and the Zurayʿids of Aden clung to power on the strength of their continued loyalty to the Fatimid al-Hafiz and his successors, down to the Ayyubid conquest of the Yemen which began in 1174, the majority of Ismaʿilis in the country abandoned the political for the religious leadership of the Tayyibi *daʿwa*. Unlike the Nizaris, the Tayyibis retained the original emphasis of the Fatimids on the observation of the Law, as well as a cosmogony derived from al-Shirazi, which became still more elaborate. The new sect extended into India, where Ismaʿilism had revived after the Ghaznavid purge as a result of the Sulayhids' missionary activity and where Gujerat eventually became its chief centre.

In Egypt itself, the violent deaths within ten years of three commanders of the armies and the caliph himself threatened a return to the days of the *fitna* in the absence of a single leader able to dominate both the army and the palace. The system nevertheless survived along with the Hafizi succession and along with the newfound ability of the monarchy to play an active role in government. This was partly because the monarchy was now more necessary than ever to the rivalries of its servants, and partly because of the caliph himself. Twenty years older than al-Amir, al-Hafiz had the determination and ability to rule as well as reign, despite the ambitions of his sons and his generals. Twin poles of power thus emerged in the state, on the one hand the palace, where the caliph was defended by his household guards and a corps of several thousand black infantry, and on the other hand the field army of Armenians, Turks and Arabs under the command of the provincial governors created by Badr al-Jamali, who vied with each other for the position of wazir. The troops themselves were mutinous, helping to prevent the clear victory of any one contender for supremacy. In the course of his long reign, al-Hafiz faced three major crises: the rebellion and execution of his son Hasan in 1134 at the demand of the black soldiery; the rebellion of the governor of al-Gharbiyya, Ridwan ibn al-Walakhshi, against the Christian wazir Bahram in 1137, followed by Ridwan's two-year reign as wazir with the title of *malik*, 'king'; and finally the fighting between the black regiments in 1149, in the midst of which the caliph died. Despite such interruptions, his government survived, and during the ten years after the overthrow of Ridwan, when he himself himself ruled through the amir Ibn Masal, was even constructive.

The cult of 'Ali and the 'Alid saints was developed as the caliph made a virtue out of the vice of his succession, by claiming that he had succeeded al-Amir as 'Ali had succeeded the Prophet before ever the principle of descent of the imamate from father to son had been established.[107] In the same way, the ceremonial routine devised for al-Amir by al-Ma'mun al-Bata'ihi was continued, with the elaborate military hierarchy of the court as described by the contemporary Ibn al-Tuwayr.[108] Ibn al-Tuwayr likewise described the administrative practice which so impressed al-Hafiz's fellow-monarch Roger II of Sicily,[109] documents of which have survived from the monastery of St Catherine in Sinai.[110] Underlying such procedures is likely to have been a further revision of the *iqta'* system established by Badr al-Jamali and al-Afdal, some thirty years after the survey of 1107–8, when the contracts issued by al-Bata'ihi should have expired. The evidence is provided by al-Makhzumi, who like Ibn al-Tuwayr produced his account of past Fatimid practice for the benefit of the new ruler Saladin, including a description of the Fatimid *iqta'* which purports to refer to the period preceding Saladin's arrival in 1169. According to al-Makhzumi, the soldier had been paid at a fixed rate by the treasury out of the tax upon his *iqta'*, rather than paying the tax and keeping the excess, as he evidently did under al-Afdal's regime. In the middle of the twelfth century, the *muqta'* (or holder of the grant) nevertheless remained quite clearly the tax farmer responsible for the cultivation of the land and the production of its revenue to the fisc. As a solution to the problems apparent in 1107–8 and again in 1121–2, this bears witness to a high degree of central control, which is reflected in the other arrangements described by al-Makhzumi for the pay of tribal Arab forces, and troops in garrisons. Together they suggest a satisfactory reform of the financial system following the excesses of Abu Najah during al-Amir's personal rule. The state in Egypt was far from breaking down under the strain of disorder, but continuing to evolve as a powerful administrative machine.[111]

Following the death of Hafiz and the accession of his youngest son al-Zafir, disorder at the top nevertheless turned finally to *fitna* or civil war as the monarchs became mere figureheads, and the provincial governors fought each other and the palace for the wazirate. Ibn Masal, the able lieutenant of Hafiz, was immediately swept aside and killed in the rebellion of Ibn al-Salar, the Kurdish governor of Alexandria, who followed the example of Ridwan in

[107] See Sanders (1992); Williams (1983, 1985).
[108] Quoted by al-Qalqashandi (d. 1418), trans. Lewis (1974), I, pp. 201–8.   [109] See Johns (1993).
[110] Published in *Fatimid Decrees*.   [111] See Brett (1995a).

assuming the title of *malik*. Three years later, however, Ibn al-Salar was murdered in a conspiracy between the caliph and the amir ʿAbbas ibn Tamim, who as wazir had al-Zafir himself murdered in 1154, and the five-year-old al-Faʾiz proclaimed. ʿAbbas was promptly expelled by Talaʾiʿ b. Ruzzik, the Armenian governor of Asyut or Middle Egypt, who ruled for seven years, replacing al-Faʾiz at his death in 1160 with his nine-year-old cousin al-ʿAdid. But in 1161 he too was murdered from within the palace, and his son Ruzzik, who succeeded him, was overthrown and put to death in 1163 by the Arab governor of Qus or Upper Egypt, Shawar. Shawar himself was at once driven out by Ibn Ruzzik's Arab general Dirgham, and fled to Damascus to seek the aid of Nur al-Din. The affairs of Cairo thus became a matter of concern not only to Damascus, but also Jerusalem, with consequences fatal to the dynasty.

Throughout the reign of Hafiz, as the power of Zengi and his son Nur al-Din grew in northern Syria, and a united Muslim front against the Latin states began to develop, Cairo had abandoned the approach of al-Amir to the Syrian princes, and contented itself with a strong garrison at Ascalon to keep the frontier. With the Franks threatening an attack upon Ascalon from Gaza, however, the approach was renewed by Ibn al-Salar. Ascalon was in fact lost to a determined attack by King Baldwin in the aftermath of the *malik*'s murder in 1153. Its capture was not, however, followed up. After a victory at Gaza obtained by his commander Dirgham, Talaʾiʿ ibn Ruzzik wrote again to Nur al-Din, whose occupation of Damascus in 1154 had completed the formation of the Zengid empire in Iraq and Syria, once more to little purpose. In 1160 he bought off a threatened Frankish invasion of Egypt with the promise of an annual tribute, whose non-payment became the excuse for an attack by the new King Amalric upon the new *malik* Dirgham in 1163. Dirgham cut the dykes to flood the king out of the siege of Farama, only to be attacked in the following year from Damascus by his deposed rival Shawar with an army led by Nur al-Din's Kurdish general Shirkuh. Dirgham appealed to Amalric for aid, but was defeated and killed before any could be sent. When Shawar promptly renewed the appeal to Jerusalem to rid himself of his Syrian ally, however, Amalric forced Shirkuh to retire. A similarly inconclusive campaign followed in 1167, when Shirkuh, with Nur al-Din's permission, set out to conquer the country, but again was thwarted by the Franks whom Shawar had summoned. In 1168 the aggressor was Amalric, and it was Shirkuh who obliged the army of Jerusalem to retire. Shirkuh's victory proved decisive. Shawar was executed and Shirkuh appointed in his place, to be succeeded after his sudden death in March 1169 by his nephew Saladin with the title *al-Malik al-Nasir*, 'Victorious King'. Yet another ineffective invasion by the Franks in conjunction with the Byzantine fleet was repelled at the end of the year, leaving the new wazir in full, if still precarious, possession.

The motive for what Lane-Poole called this 'race for the Nile'[112] was partly strategic, in that neither Jerusalem nor Damascus could afford to see Egypt in the hands of the other; partly economic, in that the country was a source of wealth to relieve the pressures on the limited resources of the antagonists in Palestine and Syria; and partly personal, in that Shirkuh in particular had the ambition to make his military and political fortune. As far as Saladin was concerned, he was obliged to succeed or perish, moving to take command of his uncle's forces on the one hand, and on the other to neutralize the palace by destroying the black regiments who maintained its independence and its capacity for intrigue. More important still was the imperative to rise above both his troops and the dynasty as a figure in his own right. Putting an end to the ceremonial round of the caliphate, which had sustained the Fatimids since the murder of al-Afdal, Saladin took advantage of the sickness and death of al-'Adid in September 1171 to terminate the caliphate by refusing to proclaim a successor. Instead, in his capacity as *malik* or king, he offered his allegiance to the caliph of Baghdad. The royal family was left helpless in the seclusion to which it was accustomed, while the males were apparently separated from the women to ensure that the line died out. Such an accumulation of power, prestige and wealth, all within the space of two and a half years, meanwhile gave Saladin his effective independence from his original master Nur al-Din in Damascus. As ruler of Egypt, he was able to attract the necessary number of warriors into his service; to keep them with the grant of *iqta*'s; and to employ them as the Seljuqs had always done, to create a fresh empire for himself and his immediate family. Thus in 1174 his brother Turan shah was dispatched by way of Mecca to the conquest of the Yemen. In that same year, the death of Nur al-Din gave Saladin the opportunity finally to establish his monarchy and his dynasty with the occupation of Damascus.[113]

In this way, the political logic of Saladin's position in Egypt combined with the logic of the Fatimid state to complete the work begun by Nasir al-Dawla and Badr al-Jamali a hundred years before, converting the commander of the armies into the wazir, and the wazir or *malik* into a sultan, the independent founder of a new, Ayyubid, Dawla or dynastic state. While the charisma of the Fatimids was spent, their patrimony nevertheless remained intact, to serve as the basis of the patriarchal regime of Saladin and his kinsfolk in Egypt, Syria and the Yemen, and subsequently of the institutionalized empire of the Mamluk sultanate. It did so through the Fatimid *iqta*', the tax farm whose revenues were divided between the soldier and the state in various ways, until eventually the Mamluk *faris* or cavalier was assigned the income from a variety of specified taxes levied on his villagers as his fixed

[112] Lane-Poole (1914), p. 179.   [113] See Lyons and Jackson (1982), chs. 2–6.

reward.[114] The cancellation by Saladin of the *iqta*'s of the Fatimid troops and their allocation to his own followers, on terms that are admittedly obscure, contributed to a brief pro-Fatimid revolt in 1174, but began the transformation of his Turkish and Kurdish warbands from conquistadors into the regular Egyptian army they eventually became.[115] In that longer perspective, the Mamluk warriors who completed the transformation with the establishment of their own monarchy in 1250 were the true successors of the Fatimids in the last century of their reign.

[114] See Rabie (1972), pp. 41, 57, 64, 132.   [115] See Gibb (1962), pp. 74–90.

CHAPTER 23

ZENGIDS, AYYUBIDS AND SELJUQS

Stephen Humphreys

FOR thirty years, from the moment he was made chief minister in 1063 by
the sultan Alp Arslan (regn. 1063–72), Nizam al-Mulk devoted every effort to
shaping the jerry-built Seljuqid political enterprise into a centralized absolutist
monarchy. By the late 1080s, he could claim considerable success, for the sultan
whom he now served (Malikshah, regn. 1072–92) enjoyed uncontested authority from the Oxus to the Mediterranean. After an initial succession struggle
between Malikshah and his uncle Qavurd, there were no further disruptions
which seriously threatened Malikshah's supremacy. Nizam al-Mulk had created
an administrative machinery which allowed him to maintain a fairly effective
control over the flow of revenues and information. It is clear that he wanted
to penetrate the whole apparatus with a network of informers and security
agents, though it is not clear that he was able to achieve this goal. In any case,
he dispersed his relatives and protégés everywhere he could, and even the most
powerful officials in the remotest places had good reason to think that they
were being watched.[1]

Nizam al-Mulk could only use the tools available to him in the world of
eleventh-century Iran and Iraq, of course. For example, he would have preferred
to build a tax system based on salaried officials, but fiscal reality compelled him
to make wide use of the *iqta'*. Even so, he strove to maintain a close supervision
over these *iqta'*s and to limit the powers which their holders could exercise over
the villages assigned to them. By this time, Seljuqid military power was based
increasingly on a standing 'professional' army – an army whose members were
registered by name, paid regular stipends and (in principle) subject to muster
as needed. In these regular forces Turkish slave recruits (*ghulam, mamluk*) from
central Asia played a central role, but there were also soldiers, both slave recruits

---

[1] Nizam al-Mulk has left us a superb statement of his programme: Siyasat-nameh. Nizam al-Mulk
envisions an ideal order, but his frank critiques of current practice tell us much about the realities of
his day. On the Seljuqid vizierate, see Horst (1964); Klausner (1973); Lambton (1968), esp. pp. 247–68,
and (1988), ch. 1.

and free mercenaries, drawn from many other ethnic groups. In addition, the dynasty continued to rely heavily on the nomadic Turcoman tribesmen who had brought it to power a half-century before, but these were increasingly treated as auxiliaries. The tribal chiefs received regular subsidies to ensure their loyalty to the regime, and their followers were recruited and paid on an *ad hoc* basis for particular campaigns.[2]

Nizam al-Mulk's unremitting labours led to the emergence of the best-integrated and most effectively governed large state which the Muslim world had seen since the death of the 'Abbasid caliph al-Mutawakkil (847–861) two centuries before. Even so, he was only able to mask or mitigate the stresses and fracture lines which threatened the great edifice. To begin with, he was never able to eliminate the confederative character of the Seljuqid polity. Like so many dynasties in the eastern Islamic world between 900 and 1500, the Seljuqids always assumed that political authority should be shared among the leading princes of the ruling family.[3] This sharing was typically carried out by carving the empire into a group of territorial appanages, each assigned on a more or less hereditary basis to a sub-lineage within the ruling house. An empire of this sort was thus not a unitary state but a confederation, held together chiefly by the charisma of its founder and solidarity among the members of the ruling family. The largest and richest appanage would be held by the senior prince of the family. (Under the Seljuqids the senior prince typically took the title of *sultan mu'azzam*, 'supreme sultan'; the other princes settled for the more modest titles of sultan, *malik*, or amir.) The senior prince's authority rested in part on the material resources provided by his appanage, but even more on his place within the ruling family: a man who was the father of the other princes could normally get his way, while a mere older brother or nephew had to expect considerable opposition. On a formal level, the senior prince's authority over his colleagues was real but limited. He rarely chose the other appanage princes, but he did formally invest them with their territories. He had the right (not always enforceable, to be sure) to demand their military and political support against rebels or external enemies. He seldom had the power to interfere in the internal affairs of the appanage princes, but his greater financial and military resources gave him a certain paramountcy within the confederation's affairs.

The problem with such family confederations was that they were based on custom and *ad hoc* improvisation. They were not shaped in accordance with any formally articulated principles or institutions. In his famous *Siyasat-nameh*

---

[2] The main studies of Seljuqid fiscal and military administration are by Lambton (1953), (1968), pp. 231–9, and (1988), chs. 3, 4, 6. See also Cahen (1953): old but still penetrating. On the origins of the *iqta'*, see most recently Sato (1997), chs. 1, 2.

[3] This point was first made by Barthold (1968), p. 268; further discussion in Humphreys (1977b), pp. 66–75; see also Bosworth (1995), pp. 939–40.

Nizam al-Mulk does not deign to mention this mode of political organization. Contemporary chroniclers do recognize it, but only in passing; they never treat it discursively. The lack of explicit principles and institutions caused many problems. For example, there was no agreed-upon rule of succession; it was never clear whether rule should be transmitted to the oldest member of the family, to the brother of the previous ruler, or to his son. Hence every succession represented a political crisis and often led to outright warfare. In the final analysis, family confederations were glued together almost solely by loyalty and deference within the ruling house, and those qualities could evaporate in a moment.

Even as Nizam al-Mulk and Malikshah unified the empire, seeds of fragmentation were being sown.[4] In 1078 Malikshah sent his brother Tutush to conquer Syria, but from the outset the latter's ambitions were not easy to restrain. Malikshah only kept him on a leash by his personal intervention in Syria on two occasions (1083, 1086–7), and by the device of assigning Aleppo to a second independent governor. In Iran, Malikshah's uncle Qavurd had been killed early in the former's reign when his thrust for the sultanate fell short; even so, his appanage of Kirman continued in his line without a break, and the region's autonomy was quickly recovered on Malikshah's death. Worst of all, Malikshah had four sons by different mothers, and by the late 1080s the dangers of a succession struggle manipulated by different palace and harem factions were already apparent. Thus the assassination of Malikshah's minister Nizam al-Mulk in 1092, and his own death shortly thereafter at the age of thirty-seven, assured a time of troubles.

One of Malikshah's widows put his youngest son Mahmud on the throne, but he had no chance against his older brothers Berk-Yaruk and Muhammad Tapar and was quickly shunted aside. A more serious contender was Malikshah's brother Tutush, by now the uncontested master of Syria; he was an experienced politician and soldier, and had a plausible claim to succeed his brother as the oldest male of the paramount lineage within the Seljuqid clan. Tutush's initial forays into Mesopotamia and Azerbayjan boded well, but in 1095 he fell in battle against the troops of Berk-Yaruk, and thereafter the struggle would be conducted exclusively among the sons of Malikshah. Berk-Yaruk (regn. 1094–1104) claimed the role of *sultan mu'azzam*, but his position was contested by his half-brother Muhammad Tapar until Berk-Yaruk's death of natural causes. At last a modicum of internal peace and stability was restored, and Muhammad Tapar (regn. 1105–18) was able to assert his authority as supreme sultan in Iraq and Iran relatively uncontested. Khurasan had been assigned by Berk-Yaruk as an

---

[4] There is no book-length western-language study of the Seljuqid empire for the period after Malikshah; see Bosworth (1968), pp. 102–57, 167–84, and (1995).

appanage to his young half-brother Sanjar, and Muhammad Tapar found it expedient to leave him there. Sanjar would ultimately prove an able (and extremely durable) ruler, but during Muhammad Tapar's life he was content to remain under the latter's tutelage.

Though Muhammad Tapar had at last been successful in restoring peace within the ruling family, the structural flaws of the empire that he governed continued to deepen. Malikshah and Nizam al-Mulk had been able to restrict the size and autonomy of *iqtaʿ* holdings; in effect, they had made them units of fiscal administration, subject to a substantial degree of oversight and control by the central ministries. However, the exigencies of the struggle for power had compelled both Muhammad Tapar and Berk-Yaruk to assign larger districts, sometimes whole provinces, in *iqtaʿ*. In these, the *iqtaʿ*-holder was (both in name and in fact) the governor. He would derive his personal revenues from only a portion of the province, but he exercised full governmental powers (taxation, justice, defence and public security) over the whole. In regard to such *iqtaʿ*-governorships, the sultan's only effective means of control was his power to remove governors; the latter could be quite intransigent in the face of such demands, and it often required a major military expedition to enforce them. Indeed, the Seljuqid sultans normally led a migratory existence, as they moved from one city to the next with their household entourage, senior administrators and a substantial military contingent. They could only enforce their authority by being present and by demonstrating their capacity to use force against officials who would otherwise be free to do what they wanted.

Muhammad Tapar (and his successors to a markedly greater degree) also made increasing use of a second device for establishing a visible Seljuqid presence in the provinces. This was the institution of the *atabeg* (lit., 'father-prince', hence 'royal guardian').[5] The *atabeg* was an ancient Turkish institution, whereby a young prince within the paramount clan would be assigned nominal authority over a district or people. Since the prince was too young to rule by himself, he was accompanied by a guardian who would teach him the art of government while administering affairs in his name. Although *atabeg*s can be found in early Seljuqid times, the institution really began to flourish in the twelfth century. The sultan would try to retain his authority over a critical region by naming one of his sons, sometimes even an infant, as its governor; in that way, the sultan himself would be present not only symbolically but virtually in the flesh – or so it was hoped. The actual powers of government of course were assigned to an *atabeg*, who by this time was normally one of the sultan's *mamluk*s. Everything depended on the loyalty and skill of the *atabeg*, of course; many carried out their duties strictly, but the mortality rate among young Seljuqid

---

[5] On the *atabeg* (Ar., spelling *atabak*), see Cahen (1960a); Lambton (1968), pp. 239–44.

princes is suspiciously high. Ultimately (by the 1120s), the office and title of *atabeg* became quasi-hereditary, though the term was also still used in the traditional way down to the mid-thirteenth century. It sometimes became attached to the rulers of a particular city, even when no Seljuqid princes had resided there for decades, and likewise it could be passed on down from father to son. By the mid-twelfth century, the title of *atabeg* often meant only that one was an autonomous territorial ruler whose authority had its origins in the Seljuqid empire.

Muhammad Tapar was an effective and respected ruler, but like his father he died quite young, at the age of thirty-six, and left his empire to five young sons and his brother Sanjar. There was no question of displacing Sanjar, who had had thirteen years to consolidate his position in Khurasan and was far older and more experienced than his nephews. Indeed, he quickly made himself *sultan muʿazzam* and would hold that rank until his death in 1157. Iraq and western Iran remained in the hands of the sons of Muhammad Tapar – though they were now subordinate to Sanjar – and they would dominate the stage there for the next three decades. The oldest, Mahmud (regn. 1118–31), was the most powerful ruler in Iraq and western Iran, though he had to face constant rebellions and demands for autonomy from his four brothers (or, rather, since they were still young children, from the *atabeg*s who guided them). He was never quite able to establish his authority in Azerbayjan, and Syria and Mesopotamia were only tenuously subject to him. He also had to deal with an ever more assertive ʿAbbasid caliphate, which was no longer willing to be dominated by an obviously weakened Seljuqid regime. Mahmud had the better of this contest, but in the following decades the tide would turn and a small but increasingly prestigious caliphal state would reclaim a significant role in the politics of the Muslim world. Concessions in the form of *iqtaʿ*s and hereditary appanages to his brothers, their *atabeg*s, and powerful amirs, which were necessary to maintain a viable basis of political support, inevitably weakened his control over his domains and sapped his fiscal resources.

Mahmud died very young, at the age of twenty-seven, and was succeeded as sultan in Iraq by his brother Masʿud (regn. 1134–52). Masʿud's long reign was not without achievements, but at bottom it was characterized by an intensification of all these trends: the sapping of the sultan's authority and resources, the rise of *atabeg*s and amirs to a degree of power hardly inferior to the sultan's, and a resurgence of caliphal autonomy and prestige under the able and ambitious al-Muqtafi (regn. 1136–1160). After Masʿud died, his successors were never able to re-enter Baghdad (the traditional capital of the western Seljuqids since Tughril Beg had occupied the city in 1055), and direct Seljuqid rule was more and more restricted to north-western Iran. Indeed, the Seljuqid sultans now fell under the domination of the powerful *atabeg*s of this region. The last Seljuqid of Iran, Tughril III (regn. 1176–94), struggled to liberate himself from these warlords and almost succeeded, but fell in battle against the rising power of the Khwarizm Shahs.

The decadence of Seljuqid power in western Iran after the death of Mas'ud coincided with the collapse of Seljuqid rule in the East. At the cost of unremitting labour, Sanjar maintained his authority in Khurasan and Transoxiana, but he was so preoccupied by affairs on his northern and eastern frontiers that, especially after 1130, he was unable to play the supreme sultan's traditional roles of arbiter and commander-in-chief within the empire as a whole. In 1141, even his authority in the east was dealt a severe blow when his forces suffered a crushing defeat at the Qatvan Steppe on the mid-Jaxartes River, at the hands of the Kara Khitay, a pagan nomadic people from the steppes north of China. Sanjar was forced to withdraw south and west of the Oxus River – and fortunately the Kara Khitay had no interest in following him. In spite of this blow, he was able to recover some authority over his remaining dominions. However, he found himself increasingly at loggerheads with the Turcomans of Khurasan; they belonged to his own ethnic group (the Ghuzz or Oğuz) and always recognized him as their sovereign, but at the instigation of his hard-pressed fiscal officials he mounted a series of punitive campaigns to subject them to regular taxation and supervision. These expeditions succeeded only in inciting a powerful revolt in 1153. Sanjar was defeated and taken prisoner, and he spent the next two years in humiliating captivity, as the Turcomans raided cities and agricultural districts throughout Khurasan. Even when he escaped in 1156, he was unable to rebuild his regime, and he died a homeless wanderer in 1157. With his death, the Seljuqid sultanate in eastern Iran disappeared. After some two decades of near-chaos, the region was absorbed within a new empire being erected by former Seljuqid governors in Khwarizm, the rich agricultural basin south of the Aral Sea. But the new Khwarizmian empire was founded more on momentum than on substance, and it was annihilated in the Mongol invasion of 1219–20.

Throughout the slow but inexorable disintegration of Seljuqid power, the crucial events occurred in Iraq, north-western Iran and Khurasan, which had in fact been the traditional focal points of political conflict and change in the Nile-to-Oxus region since the rise of Islam. In this great drama Syria – a term covering the eastern Mediterranean coastlands from Gaza to Antioch and the interior steppe west of the Euphrates from the Gulf of Aqaba to the Taurus mountains – played a very minor role. This is so even though Syria was an integral part of the Seljuqid political system and the struggle for power there was conducted according to Seljuqid rules. Syria's marginality is hardly surprising, since it was only a recently acquired frontier province when the time of troubles began after the death of Malikshah. It was too remote from the major centres of Seljuqid power – Baghdad, Isfahan, Rayy, Marw – to be worth fighting over. Moreover, it possessed such slender resources of money and manpower that it could not serve as a serious power-base. Finally, it was fragmented into a varying number of petty city-states, each jealous and fearful of its neighbours, and none able to assert effective paramountcy over the others. But, ironically, as the Great Seljuqids went into an irreversible decline after the deaths of Mas'ud (1152) and Sanjar (1157), Syria began to acquire a centrality in the politics, economy and culture of the eastern Islamic world which it had not enjoyed since the fall of the Umayyads four centuries earlier. By the end of the twelfth century, it would be linked to Egypt as the core of an empire stretching from Lake Van in the north-east to Aswan and Yemen in the south. Though never a really wealthy region, it had come to enjoy a substantial prosperity. During this same half-century, finally, it emerged from a sleepy provincialism and became a dynamic and influential centre of Islamic religious and intellectual life.

The catalyst for the Syrian renaissance was surely the establishment of the crusader states at the beginning of the twelfth century. The crusades re-energized Syrian political life in at least two ways – both unintended by the crusaders, of course. First, they created a milieu in which an ideology of *jihad* – long dormant in a Syria far removed from the frontiers of the Islamic world – could flourish. Indeed, the crusaders' bloody conquest of Jerusalem in 1099 and their standing threat to every other Muslim city in Syria-Palestine almost compelled such a response. As the *jihad* idea evolved in twelfth-century Syria, it implied the need for Muslim cooperation to ward off the invaders, and ultimately for Muslim unity to expel them. In short, *jihad* against the crusaders legitimized political expansion and consolidation. In principle, the crusades made it possible for a local ruler to claim that his struggles against his rivals were not grounded in selfish ambition, but rather were essential for the vindication of Islam. All that was required was a ruler who knew how to visualize and execute such a policy. In the event several decades passed before the implications of the situation were fully grasped and an effective ideology of unity and *jihad* was articulated, but by the mid-1140s all the elements for such an ideology were at last in place.[6]

The second impact of the crusades was less immediately visible but no less important. The crusader conquest of Syria's port cities (effectively complete with the fall of Tyre in 1124) connected these to the rapidly expanding network of Mediterranean commerce which the Italian communes had begun to construct in the mid-eleventh century. The bulk of this commerce continued to flow through Constantinople and Alexandria, as it always had, but a significant proportion – perhaps ultimately as much as a third – was now directed to Acre,

---

[6] On the evolution of the counter-crusade, Sivan (1968) remains the only comprehensive study.

Tyre and Antioch (the latter through its port of St Simeon/Suwaydiyya). In spite of political barriers, the interior cities, especially Damascus and Aleppo, inevitably became part of this network, and their role in it increased as the volume of trade increased throughout the twelfth and early thirteenth centuries.[7]

It is impossible to quantify the overall economic impact of this commerce, but it is undeniable that Muslim Syria was a more prosperous place by the mid-twelfth century than it had been in the eleventh, or that it continued to flourish until the turmoil of the 1240s and 1250s. The direct fiscal implications of commercial growth are obvious; although most medieval Muslim regimes (like their European counterparts) relied chiefly on agricultural taxes or tax-equivalents, urban tariffs and excises were a very important part of their revenues. Muslim rulers in 1200 simply had more money than their predecessors to spend on their armies, on the construction and endowment of religious institutions, even on infrastructure (irrigation canals, caravanserais and so on). In one of those ironies that enliven the history of every age, the crusaders wound up financing the political and economic revitalization of their opponents. The growth of Mediterranean trade was of course not the whole cause of Muslim Syria's restored prosperity, but it was certainly a significant element in the process.

The processes sketched in the preceding paragraphs only slowly became visible, and they were surely hardly conceivable in 1095 when Tutush was killed trying to seize his brother Malikshah's legacy. Indeed, Tutush's unexpected death echoed Malikshah's in that it ushered in an uncontrolled scramble for power among his sons and officers, albeit within a far smaller domain. But whereas Muhammad Tapar was at last able to restore political cohesion within his vast domains in Iraq and Iran, there was nobody in Syria to play that role. Indeed, twenty years after Tutush's death the Seljuqid lineage in Syria was extinct, its possessions parcelled out among a motley collection of local warlords.

In the framework of a short chapter, it is almost impossible to tell a coherent story of Syrian politics until the late 1120s. Tutush was a heavy-handed ruler, but after the death of Malikshah he was at last able to bring all the interior districts of Syria, from Jerusalem in the south to the Taurus mountains in the north, under his direct authority. (The major port cities south of Latakia, such as Tripoli, Tyre, Acre, Jaffa and Ascalon, had never been subjected to Seljuqid rule. They remained nominally Fatimid possessions, though Tripoli and Tyre were effectively self-governing.) He had apparently made no plans for a succession, but in accordance with the almost universally held principle that his domains should be distributed among his family, Aleppo and Damascus fell to two different sons: the thirteen-year-old Ridwan in Aleppo (regn.

[7] Heyd (1885–6); Schaube (1906); and Labib (1965) remain indispensable repositories of information.

1095–1113) and his somewhat younger half-brother Duqaq in Damascus (regn. 1095–1104).[8]

The transition to a divided principality was not smooth. The older son, Ridwan, initially tried to take direct control of all his father's lands, and, when that failed, to assert some degree of primacy within them. Though he was astute and tenacious, his military talents were modest and his resources exiguous, and these efforts were but delusions of petty grandeur. Jealous of his status and fearful, not always without reason, that his Muslim neighbours were bent on seizing his lands, he devoted the bulk of his reign to blocking every effort at unified action among them.

During his father's lifetime Ridwan had been under the tutelage of an *atabeg* (Janah al-Dawla Husayn, the governor of Homs), but he found this insupportable and quickly drove Janah al-Dawla from Aleppo. For the rest of his eighteen-year reign, he kept affairs in his own hands and suffered no opposition to his authority. He could be vindictive and brutal, but he knew how to find competent officials, and he faced no serious internal challenge during the last decade of his reign. When he died as the result of a hunting accident, the throne passed to his son Alp Arslan without contest. Unfortunately Alp Arslan possessed his father's vices but not his talents. He was assassinated in 1114 and replaced by his *atabeg*, the eunuch Lu'lu'. Lu'lu' was likewise not up to the task and was murdered in 1117. For the next decade Aleppo was the plaything of transitory rulers, often petty warlords invited in from the Turkish principalities of southern Anatolia by the Aleppan notables, who were desperate to find a competent military leader. Among these the most effective was undoubtedly Il-Ghazi of Mardin (regn. 1119–22), who led his forces, made up largely of Turcoman tribesmen hired for the occasion, to a crushing victory at Sarmada (Latin, Ager Sanguinis) over Roger of Antioch in 1119, a victory which undermined Antioch's military power for many years and undoubtedly saved Aleppo from imminent conquest by the Latin settlers. Il-Ghazi's death from a sudden illness in 1122 again threw Aleppo's fate into question. Only in January 1128, when Aleppo was occupied without resistance by the newly installed *atabeg* of Mosul, Zengi b. Aqsunqur, was order restored. Indeed, Zengi's standing as a senior officer and governor in the Seljuqid empire, together with his ability to combine the resources of Mosul and Aleppo, gave him a power-base such as no Syrian ruler had enjoyed since the death of Tutush three decades earlier.

The dynastic history of Damascus was simpler. Ridwan's half-brother Duqaq was too young to rule by himself, but he had the support of an able and loyal *atabeg*, Tughtigin, a former *mamluk* of Tutush's. When Duqaq died in 1104

---

[8] Seljuqid Damascus: Mouton (1994); Yared-Riachi (1997). Seljuqid Aleppo: Eddé (1986). Broader studies by Cahen (1940), pp. 177–307; Elisséeff (1967), II, pp. 277–332.

at roughly the age of twenty, the throne passed to his infant son Tutush II, but Tughtigin continued to be the *de facto* ruler. Tutush II died very soon, and his successor, Duqaq's younger brother Irtash, fled to Mesopotamia within the year. After 1104 Tughtigin ruled alone, as an *atabeg* without a prince.[9] In 1116, Sultan Muhammad in Baghdad finally recognized the reality that there was no longer a prince of the Seljuqid line in Damascus and formally invested Tughtigin as hereditary prince of the city. He reigned there until his death in 1128, having passed a total of thirty-three years at the head of affairs.

The other major cities of Seljuqid Syria – Homs, Hama and Antioch – continued to be governed by amirs who had been appointed (or at least recognized) by Tutush. In principle these men were subordinate to Ridwan or Duqaq, but in fact they acted quite independently and sometimes in open opposition to their overlords. Jerusalem (a city of symbolic rather than strategic or economic importance) was occupied in 1098 by the Fatimid wazir al-Afdal, who thus took advantage of the chaos among the Seljuqids to restore central Palestine to the Egyptian sphere of influence. The question of Antioch was quickly though unhappily resolved by the crusader conquest of the city in the summer of 1098, and Jerusalem suffered a similar fate a year later. Homs and Hama remained in Muslim hands; sometimes autonomous and sometimes controlled from Damascus or Aleppo, they at least continued to be part of the now much-reduced Seljuqid political enterprise in Syria. The progressive fall of the port cities to the crusaders did not affect the structure of Seljuqid rule, of course, since these had been Fatimid possessions.

Whatever the personal qualities of Duqaq and Ridwan, they could not have faced a more difficult situation. Each possessed only a tiny standing army: almost certainly no more than 1,000 men each. These regular forces were made up of the prince's personal *mamluk*s together with whatever number of free mercenaries (usually Turkish, but sometimes Kurdish as well) he could afford to pay and equip on a permanent basis. In the present state of research, it is simply not clear whether or not the amirs who commanded these forces maintained additional troops of their own, paid from the *iqta*'s from which they drew their own salaries and allowances. If there were separate amirs' contingents, we do not know their numbers or what percentage of a whole they represented.

---

[9] Duqaq's mother Safwat al-Mulk was suspected by some of having poisoned him. (She was also the wife of Tughtigin; it was very common for Seljuqid rulers to cement an *atabeg*'s loyalty by having him marry the mother of the prince whom he was to guard.) The evidence for her guilt is vague, however; possibly certain chroniclers confused this Safwat al-Mulk with her namesake Safwat al-Mulk Zumurrud Khatun, the wife of Tughtigin's son Taj al-Muluk Bori, who certainly did arrange the murder of her son Shams al-Muluk Isma'il in 1135. Tutush II's sudden death also raised suspicions, but infant mortality was rampant in premodern times, and the Seljuqids tended to be short-lived in any case.

Ridwan and Duqaq were thus forced to recruit Turcoman or Arab bedouin auxiliaries on an *ad hoc* basis; these could be effective warriors, but neither prince could pay them well enough to keep their services for more than a single battle and they often evaporated into the steppes at the most awkward possible moment. Aleppo and Damascus both had substantial urban militias, made up of young men (*ahdath*) recruited from the poorer social groups in the cities. These militias were of real value in defending a city against sieges, but they were quite useless in the open field. In peacetime, moreover, they often disrupted public order, and within the confines of a walled town they were well able to threaten a prince's ability to police and administer his own capital.

Control over the militias, and indeed any sort of effective governance, required close cooperation with the urban notables, and in particular with a figure called the *ra'is al-balad* (roughly, 'town headman').[10] This latter was sometimes invested with his office by princely decree, and he often had certain administrative and fiscal functions. In the final analysis, however, he normally belonged to an influential and well-established local family. As such, he was the spokesman at court for the interests of all the city's leading families. He was also the man through whom the urban militias were recruited and kept in order. In a very real sense, then, he was not appointed by the prince but recognized by him. Apart from the *ra'is al-balad*, the local notables normally supplied those religious and civil officials without whom a government could not function: judges, mosque functionaries, fiscal agents, sometimes even the prince's chief of administration (the wazir). So long as they had the support of the militias, the urban notables of early twelfth-century Syria were easily a match for the Seljuqid princes and their armies. This was the case until the mid-twelfth century; thereafter the increasingly powerful princes would come to rely more heavily (though never exclusively) on outsiders, on scholars and administrators who did not belong to established local families but were itinerant professionals who had made their careers as members of the ruler's personal entourage.

Finally, Ridwan, Duqaq and their immediate successors had to face the crusaders. With only their own resources, the Syrian princes were barely able to defend their territories. Certainly neither could hope to dislodge the crusaders without strong support from the Seljuqid sultan in Iraq. However, the Great Seljuqids had never abandoned their claim to Syria. In principle, the princes of Aleppo and Damascus were subordinate to the sultans in Iraq and Iran. Seeking their military aid thus entailed considerable political risk. Fortunately,

---

[10] An early but useful study is that of H. A. R. Gibb, in his introduction to his translation of Ibn al-Qalanisi, *Dhayl ta'rikh Dimashq*. See also Ashtor-Strauss (1956), pp. 73–128; Cahen (1958–9); Havemann (1975); Mouton (1994), pp. 231–7.

Syria was only of marginal concern to the Great Seljuqids, with the result that their aid was occasional and often half-hearted. The sultans themselves never led an expedition to Syria. This is quite understandable in the case of the beleaguered Berk-Yaruk, but it was true also of Muhammad Tapar, whose throne was relatively secure. Mahmud and Mas'ud were even less concerned with Syrian affairs. When they did intervene, the Seljuqid sultans assigned full responsibility to their governors of Mosul.[11] Indeed, for the first fifty years of the crusading era – from the siege of Antioch in 1098 down to the death of Zengi in 1146 – Mosul would be the political and military keystone of Muslim resistance to the crusaders.

Ridwan was particularly skittish about military expeditions from the east, and between 1110 and 1113 he consistently sabotaged the far-sighted efforts of the *atabeg* Mawdud of Mosul. In Damascus, Duqaq and and his successor Tughtigin were readier to cooperate, but that only made the enterprise even more dubious in Ridwan's eyes. Possessing few resources and a small territory entirely surrounded by his enemies, Ridwan was determined to retain his throne at any price. He thus pursued a constantly shifting series of alliances, each aimed at the opponent which seemed at the moment to be most dangerous. In this perspective, Latin Antioch was as likely to be a treaty partner as an opponent. Though a Sunni, Ridwan was also happy to ally himself with the Nizari Isma'ilis (the so-called Assassins) to ward off undue pressure, and we find them operating openly in Aleppo as early as 1100. It is likely that he used them to murder his former *atabeg* Janah al-Dawla in Aleppo (1103) and Mawdud of Mosul in Damascus (1113).[12]

In the beginning, the crusader occupation in Edessa, Antioch and especially Jerusalem was a touch-and-go operation. Neither Damascus nor Aleppo was in any immediate danger. But by 1105, with the crushing defeats of an allied Egyptian-Damascene army at Ramla and Ridwan's army at Artah, the Latin settlers had secured a solid foothold. They now embarked on a systematic policy of expansion, a policy which would secure for them every seaport north of Gaza, all Palestine west of the Jordan and parts of southern Transjordan. In the face of this expansion, both Damascus and Aleppo were extremely vulnerable and would remain so for decades to come. Damascus and Aleppo were often compelled to pay a heavy tribute to keep the Latin states of Jerusalem and

---

[11] The governors of Mosul, down to and including Zengi, were *atabeg*s for young Seljuqid princes who were assigned that city as their personal appanage. Even when their wards disappeared from view, the governors retained this title. It thus became customary to refer to the governor as the *atabeg* of Mosul.

[12] The Seljuqid court in Baghdad accused Tughtigin of plotting this murder, but Elisséeff ((1967), II, 308–9) argues that Ridwan was the only one who stood to gain from it. On the Assassins in Syria, see Lewis (1967), pp. 97–124.

Antioch at bay. In addition, both were coerced into sharing the revenues from some of their richest agricultural lands with their Frankish 'neighbours', and this arrangement obviously undermined their fiscal resources. Aleppo suffered far more than Damascus, however; it was a much smaller state and faced a greater military threat on all sides. Indeed, Aleppo and its dependencies seem to have been progressively impoverished throughout Ridwan's reign and the fifteen chaotic years that followed his death in 1113. Ridwan's notorious avarice and tyranny certainly did not help matters, but it must be admitted that his back was to the wall.

Under Tughtigin's aegis (regn. 1104–28), in contrast, Damascus entered a period of modest but growing prosperity. He faced a somewhat more favourable situation than Ridwan, to be sure. He had only one serious enemy, albeit a formidable one – the kingdom of Jerusalem. His domains reached from Bosra and Salkhad in the south to Hama in the north; they included the rich grainfields of the Hawran and the Biqa', and Damascus itself was one of the finest oases in the Middle East. Tribute payments and shared-revenue arrangements were a severe burden but did not destroy the fiscal integrity of his regime. It is also important that he had a long, uncontested reign; the three decades of internal stability which Damascus enjoyed under his aegis stand in sharp contrast to the turbulence of the eleventh century. Finally, he was by all reports a far more equitable ruler than Ridwan – his passing in 1128 was greeted with genuine grief and distress among his subjects – and this too must have helped to reinvigorate the economic life of his principality.

Tughtigin was a cautious man, far more concerned to defend his principality than to try to expand it. A firm advocate of Sunni Islam, he did what he could to protect Muslim Syria from crusader ambitions, and entered into a wide array of alliances with the Fatimids, the Seljuqid *atabegs* of Mosul, even Aleppo. However, he knew how limited his resources and opportunities were. Like Ridwan, albeit more reluctantly, he was willing to enter an alliance with the Latins against Muslim rivals when he felt seriously threatened. More often, he would seek a truce even on unfavourable terms, either to buy off Latin depredations or to give himself the leisure to deal with his Muslim rivals. For this reason, later chroniclers and modern scholarship have treated him rather dismissively, but in fact he laid the foundations for the cultural and political vitality of Damascus in the later twelfth and thirteenth centuries.

The year 1128 marks a watershed: the beginning of the end of Syria's political fragmentation and a rise in Muslim military power sufficient not only to meet the Latins on a more equal footing but even to win victories with permanent consequences. It also saw at least a temporary reversal of fortunes in Damascus and Aleppo. With the death of Tughtigin, the principality of Damascus gradually slid into diplomatic isolation and political marginality for the next quarter century. In contrast, Zengi's seizure of power not only made Aleppo the political centre of Syria for several decades, but opened a century which would witness the restoration of the city's economic fortunes and the rebirth of its cultural and religious life.[13]

To be sure, Damascus did not always lack for effective rulers in these years. Tughtigin's son Taj al-Muluk Böri (regn. 1128–32) was a worthy but tragically short-lived successor to his father. His own sons (three of whom succeeded him as *atabeg* of Damascus) were not of the same metal, but his widow Safwat al-Mulk and then the amir Mu'in al-Din Unur, an old *mamluk* of Tughtigin's, successfully defended the independence of Damascus against both the crusaders and Zengi throughout the late 1130s and 1140s. Upon the death of Unur in 1149, the government reverted to Böri's grandson Mujir al-Din Uvaq (regn. 1140–54), but he was quickly forced to give way before the rising power of Zengi's son and successor in Aleppo, Nur al-Din Mahmud, who occupied Damascus peaceably in April 1154.

Zengi's control of Mosul and Aleppo made him the paramount ruler in Mesopotamia and north Syria.[14] However, he was able to exploit this opportunity in large part because of his uncommon longevity; he reigned for nineteen years, until he was assassinated by a disgruntled page in 1146. Zengi was lauded by Ibn al-Athir (d. 1233), the court historian of the dynasty he founded, as the first real champion of the *jihad* against the crusaders, and this judgement was accepted by western scholars until the 1950s. Since that time, Zengi has usually been dismissed as just another power-seeking warlord, abler and more cunning than his contemporaries, perhaps, but most of all luckier, because in 1144 he seized the great prize of Edessa while its ruler Joscelin II was absent on campaign with most of his army. This judgement understates Zengi's achievement. During his two decades of rule, he built a durable and effective political system which provided at least the basic framework for the more brilliant reigns of his son Nur al-Din Mahmud and the latter's general Saladin.

In spite of the obvious military and strategic benefits that he derived from his control of both Mosul and Aleppo, Zengi faced a difficult challenge in trying to rule two major cities. First, Mosul and Aleppo were separated from each other by twenty days' march. Secondly, each belonged to a distinct if overlapping geopolitical system. Mosul always had to deal with the Great Seljuqids in

---

[13] On Zengi and his era: Cahen (1940), pp. 347–73; Gibb (1969a); Elisséeff (1967), II, pp. 332–87; Mouton (1994), pp. 38–43; Yared-Riachi (1997), pp. 159–207.

[14] Zengi was not *atabeg* in name only: Mosul was the appanage of Sultan Mahmud's infant son Alp Arslan, and Zengi held office as his guardian and tutor. Alp Arslan tried to take advantage of the confusion following Zengi's sudden demise in 1146 to reclaim his principality for himself. He failed, however, and was quickly heard of no more. Alp Arslan was the last Seljuqid prince of Mosul; henceforth, Zengi's heirs would hold it in their own name. Elisséeff (1967), II, pp. 391–4.

Baghdad and north-west Iran, and later on with the reviving ʿAbbasid caliphate. Aleppo was lodged between central Syria, the Frankish-dominated coast, and the Turcoman amirates in upper Mesopotamia. Finally, each had its own political traditions and a jealous local elite. In short, when Zengi took power the two cities were hardly part of a common political system. Indeed, Aleppo (not only its princes but key notables as well) had demonstrated its fear of domination by Mosul many times over the preceding three decades.

Zengi overcame these difficulties by several means. First of all, in the manner of the Seljuqid sultans, he was constantly on the move between his two capitals, something which hindered the emergence of over-mighty viceroys. Equally important, his senior administrative cadre, whose key members usually travelled with him, was recruited from Mosul and the western Seljuqid lands; in this way his chancery and fiscal bureaux were run by men whose talents he knew and whose careers were directly dependent on him. On the other hand, religious officials in the major towns, such as judges, intendants and preachers in the great mosques, were typically recruited among established local families known for their piety and learning. Zengi's army has yet to be studied, but clearly he tried to build a substantial standing army, and relied much less on the Turcoman tribes of Mesopotamia than had his predecessors. Zengi was himself a Turk, the son of a *mamluk*, and for both officers and common soldiers he naturally favoured men like himself: Turkish *mamluks* and their descendants. However, such *mamluks* were scarce and expensive in the region he ruled. To compensate for this lack, he recruited widely among the Kurds who dominated the mountains north of Mosul, a policy continued by his Zengid successors and of course by the Ayyubids, who began as Kurdish officers in the Zengid armies. (The Kurds had long since become Muslims, so they were recruited as free mercenaries rather than *mamluks*, but in terms of their military prowess and the expense of maintaining them, that was a distinction without a difference.) In the time of Nur al-Din and Saladin, the Kurds would be placed in separate regiments organized according to the tribal origin of their members, but it is not clear that this practice was already established under Zengi.

The geographical character of his principality compelled Zengi to be engaged on two widely separated fronts. Both his own origins as a Seljuqid amir and his determination to expand his territories in northern Iraq drew him into an active involvement in Great Seljuqid politics. Indeed, Iraq was the major focus of his concern in the first half of his reign. By 1136, however, it was clear that he had little to gain by continued immersion in Iraqi affairs; likewise, neither Sultan Masʿud nor any other Seljuqid prince had the power or will to threaten Zengi's own territories. He could thus devote much of his later career to Syria. Here he had two goals – to contain or drive back the Latins in north Syria, thereby securing his position in Aleppo, and to seize control of Damascus. In his time few saw these goals as intimately linked. Fighting the Latins was of course meritorious in itself, but the struggle for Damascus was simple empire-building.

However sporadic and self-interested Zengi's campaigns against the Latins may have been, they were undoubtedly effective. His reconquest of Ma'arrat al-Nu'man (1135) not only restored an important town to Muslim rule, but did much to secure the western frontiers of Homs and Hama. He nearly captured King Fulk of Jerusalem at Barin in 1137, and after a stiff siege obtained the surrender of the place on terms. Though he did not directly confront the expedition led by the Byzantine emperor John II Komnenos in 1138, he did shadow it until external pressures compelled John to withdraw. That expedition marked the last serious Christian threat to Aleppo. Zengi's conquest of Edessa in 1144 was no doubt a stroke of luck, not the result of planning and long purpose, but in striking contrast to many of his predecessors he seized the opportunity when he saw it. Edessa was not the first major Muslim victory over the Franks, but it was the first to have irreversible consequences. The route between Mosul and Aleppo was now untrammelled, the Franks' position east of the Euphrates fatally compromised. We should not exaggerate, for the other crusader states were intact and would remain a formidable presence for decades to come. Still, Zengi's victories marked a real shift in the regional balance of power.

Zengi's designs on Damascus had more ambiguous results. In the end, they won him control of Hama, Homs and Baalbak, but also aroused a determined and successful resistance by the people of Damascus. His Syrian conquests reversed the relative political and military weight of Aleppo and Damascus. On the other hand, his repeated treachery toward the Börids of Damascus surely deferred the unification of Muslim Syria for many years. Zengi quickly seized Hama in 1130 by arresting its governor (a brother of Taj al-Muluk Böri of Damascus) after Böri had ordered him to join forces with Zengi in Aleppo. Briefly recaptured by Damascene forces in 1133, Hama was occupied again (this time permanently) in 1135. In the same year Zengi came within an ace of taking Damascus without a struggle. Its prince Shams al-Muluk Isma'il b. Böri (regn. 1132–5), after some striking initial victories against Zengi and the Franks, had become increasingly erratic and tyrannical. Facing open revolt by the Damascenes, he secretly agreed to surrender Damascus to Zengi. Isma'il's mother, the redoubtable Safwat al-Mulk, learned about this in the nick of time and coldly had her son executed, turning the throne over to his younger brother Shihab al-Din Mahmud (regn. 1135–9). Zengi laid siege to Damascus but was not prepared to pursue the matter very long on this occasion, though he kept up unrelenting pressure against Damascus for the rest of his reign. He likewise attacked Homs several times, but the city was always stoutly defended by its Börid governors. He finally obtained it in 1138 through a marriage alliance with the Börids: Shihab al-Din Mahmud of Damascus married Zengi's daughter, while Zengi himself married the prince's mother Safwat al-Mulk, who brought Homs as her dowry. The Damascenes no doubt hoped that this alliance would buy them a respite from Zengi's ambitions, but that was not the case. He took advantage of the murder of his son-in-law Shihab al-Din Mahmud in 1139 to seize Baalbak and besiege Damascus a second time. The garrison of Baalbak was massacred after having surrendered on terms. Zengi's motive for this act is unclear, since he was harsh but not mindlessly brutal, but it made the Damascenes all the more determined to hold out. The amir Mu'in al-Din Unur, then administering the city on behalf of Shihab al-Din's heirs, took the grave but unavoidable step of allying himself with King Fulk of Jerusalem in order to force Zengi to retreat. The strategy was successful, and relations between Damascus and Jerusalem remained uncommonly cordial for nearly a decade, not surprisingly, since both states had every interest in checking the expansion of Zengi's power.

Zengi's skill as an empire-builder, along with the limitations imposed on him by the political world in which he lived, are revealed by the fate of his dominions upon his sudden death at the height of his power in 1146. Assassinated by one of his pages while encamped near Edessa, he had made no plans for the disposal of his lands, and so this task fell to his heirs and high officials. His oldest son Sayf al-Din Ghazi at once took control of Mosul, Zengi's original power-base and still the administrative and military core of his empire. His second son Nur al-Din Mahmud was escorted to Aleppo and quickly enthroned as the autonomous prince of that city and its dependencies. In an instant, the unitary state carved out by Zengi and sustained by his energy and iron will was transformed into a family confederation of the usual Seljuqid type. The new confederation was surprisingly harmonious, partly because Sayf al-Din Ghazi did not try to impose his authority on his younger brother in Aleppo; perhaps he did not reign long enough to pursue such ambitions. He died in 1149 and a third (much younger) brother, Qutb al-Din Mawdud, took the throne of Mosul. Mawdud enjoyed a long reign (1149–70) but always deferred to Nur al-Din.

Under Qutb al-Din Mawdud Mosul receded to the second plane within the Zengid confederation. It maintained a fairly long-lived hereditary succession (until 1234) and of course continued to dominate affairs in northern Iraq.[15] When Nur al-Din died in 1174, Mawdud's two sons (Sayf al-Din Ghazi II,

---

[15] There is no detailed study of the Zengids of Mosul after Zengi's death. See Elisséeff (1967), II, on the period 1146–74. For the Ayyubid period (1174–1260), one must rely on biographies of Saladin (see below); Humphreys (1977b); and Patton (1991).

regn. 1170–80, and 'Izz al-Din Mas'ud, regn. 1180–93) struggled mightily to re-establish Mosul's former paramountcy in north Syria and Mesopotamia. But faced with the ambition, tenacity and astuteness of the usurper Saladin (for so they regarded him), they had all they could do to preserve the independence of their city and its immediate hinterland. A key source of Mosul's weakness, no doubt, is that after Mawdud's death in 1170 the principality was divided into two and sometimes three appanages. As a result, the Zengid prince of Mosul no longer commanded the same resource base as his predecessors. The fate of Zengid Mosul holds few surprises; it was altogether typical of the Seljuqid and post-Seljuqid world of Iraq and western Iran.

Aleppo, however, followed a different path. With the enthronement of Nur al-Din Mahmud (regn. 1146–74), it became the centre of an expanding and relatively centralized state. Even when Nur al-Din's state shrivelled and disappeared in the decade after his death, Aleppo remained both a focal point of Syrian politics and a thriving commercial and cultural centre for another eighty years. Had it not been for the Mongol catastrophe in 1260, Aleppo would no doubt have flourished far longer than that. No doubt Zengi's long reign and his success in containing the Christian threat had done much to restore Aleppo's social equilibrium and frayed economy. Still, it was very much the second city in his empire, being a base for his operations in Syria more than a permanent residence. Under Nur al-Din, however, Aleppo was (with Damascus after 1154) a real capital. It benefited enormously from his benefactions: revamped defences, a plethora of new mosques and colleges, a marked growth in population. Nor was Nur al-Din the city's only patron, for he pressed his amirs and officials to follow his example. After the Ayyubids occupied the city in 1183, they energetically pursued his rebuilding of the city's physical and institutional fabric. As an urban setting, Aleppo became the crown jewel of the Zengid and Ayyubid realms.[16]

Aleppo's renaissance was not the product of some inexorable process; on the contrary, it was grounded in the fortunate accident of its new prince. Nur al-Din was twenty-nine when he mounted the throne, old enough to take personal charge of affairs, and he enjoyed an uncontested reign of almost three decades. More important, he had a rare combination of personal qualities. He combined high ambition with moderation, far-sighted vision with a sense of limits, austere personal piety with moderation and a commitment to justice. He was a competent though not brilliant battlefield commander, but he was an astute negotiator and won some of his most important successes through diplomacy. He quickly mastered the delicate art of obtaining and keeping the

---

[16] Sauvaget (1941), I, ch. 8, pp. 109–54; Elisséeff (1967), III, pp. 750–80, 838–53, 915–18; Al-Tabba (1982), I, pp. 38–65; H. Gaube and E. Wirth, *Aleppo* (Wiesbaden, 1984), *passim*; Tabbaa (1997).

services of able soldiers and officials. These talents allowed him to build on the achievements of his father while rinsing away the bitter aftertaste that Zengi had left with so many. Most importantly, they gave him unparallelled credibility as an advocate of *jihad* against the Franks and hence of the Syrian unity necessary to pursue that goal effectively.[17]

Obviously the struggle against the Franks had been understood as *jihad* from the time of their first appearance. As we have seen, however, the struggle in God's path had been pursued only fitfully by the Muslim rulers of Syria and Egypt, both because it was a chancy and often discouraging business and because the westerners could be very useful allies (on a short-term basis, admittedly) against Muslim rivals. In any event, even the most dedicated men, like Tughtigin of Damascus or Mawdud of Mosul, seemed to visualize only a defensive policy, one of preventing crusader expansion and recovering key frontier zones rather than driving them out altogether. Even the sacred city of Jerusalem did not inspire loftier goals; its loss had been lamented but no one seriously thought of restoring it to Islam.

Nur al-Din quickly moved the meaning and purpose of the *jihad* against the Franks to a higher plane. His propaganda – far more systematic and pervasive than anything which had preceded it – argued four key points: (1) *jihad* was the primary duty of every Muslim ruler; (2) effective *jihad* required unity among the Muslims, under the leadership of that ruler who was best able to vindicate the cause of Islam; (3) *jihad* was a matter of moral rearmament, a struggle not only against foreign invaders but against heresy and corruption within Islam; (4) finally, the goal of *jihad* should be the complete recovery of all Muslim lands seized by the crusaders, the purification of those lands from their pollution, and the highest symbol of this campaign should be the recovery of Jerusalem. It was a programme of genius. It was made up of elements long familiar to Muslims, including key themes articulated by the early Seljuqids, but it combined these into a compelling whole whose innate rightness was irrefutable. Almost from the outset of his reign, therefore, Nur al-Din monopolized the symbols and values of Islam and thereby controlled the ideological discourse of Syria and Mesopotamia.[18]

Nur al-Din opened his career with several spectacular victories against the crusaders. At Inab (1149) he shattered the army of Antioch; among the slain was its prince, Raymond of Poitiers. Nur al-Din's victory left Antioch mired in political crisis for years, but he gained only limited advantages from the situation. In 1164, he won a second crushing victory against a combined Antiochene and

---

[17] A meticulous survey of events in Elisséeff (1967), II, pp. 389–699; see also Cahen (1940), pp. 374–415; Gibb (1969b). Elisséeff (1967), III, contains a wealth of data on fiscal and military administration, economy and society, but these topics merit further analysis.

[18] Sivan (1968), pp. 59–92.

Armenian force at Artah. That battle not only ended any possible military threat from Antioch but also led to the definitive loss of almost all Latin possessions east of the city. Even now, however, Nur al-Din felt unable to mount a siege against Antioch itself, and it remained in Christian hands for another century. Perhaps more important in the long run was his eradication of the county of Edessa, beginning with the bloody suppression of a revolt in the city of Edessa itself in 1146, and ending in 1151 with the occupation (carried out jointly with the Rum Seljuqids of Konya) of every town and fortress still controlled by the city's former ruler. In short, if Nur al-Din's success in restoring north Syria to Muslim rule was not total, it was very impressive; by the end of his reign the kingdom of Jerusalem carried the burden of the crusader enterprise almost alone.

Isolated as Jerusalem may have been, however, he made little direct progress against it. In 1157 he overwhelmed an army led by Baldwin III near Banyas and came within an ace of capturing the king himself. Striking as it was, however, this victory did not seriously threaten the integrity of the kingdom. Thereafter, Nur al-Din fell into a long period of political and military frustration, marked by an extremely destructive series of earthquakes throughout Syria (1157), two grave illnesses (1157, 1158) and a humiliating defeat at the Crac des Chevaliers (1162). He was also mired in a long but rather petty struggle with the Byzantines and the Rum Seljuqids over the northern frontiers of his kingdom. As the 1160s opened, the Christians had good reason to feel that they had won at least a stalemate with their formidable opponent.

It is ironic that after the first five years of his reign, Nur al-Din's truly decisive victories were won against Muslim opponents, and were as much political as military. However, it was these victories over Muslims that fatally undermined the foundations of Frankish rule in Palestine and exposed their lands to Saladin's assaults in the late 1180s. The first of these was his annexation of Damascus in 1154, a victory won by negotiation, though the powerful army encamped outside the walls no doubt made his proposals especially persuasive. This had been his father Zengi's lifelong ambition, but Nur al-Din laid the groundwork with far more care. He saw at the beginning of his reign that the Börid line (now represented by the youthful Mujir al-Din Uvaq) still commanded substantial loyalty among the notables and populace. Thus he bided his time, honeycombing the city with agents and sending substantial subsidies to influential people whom he hoped to win over to his cause. Only when Uvaq had conclusively demonstrated his weakness and ineptitude did Nur al-Din move against the city in a decisive way. By this point most Damascenes were convinced that he alone could save them from imminent conquest by the crusaders, and the city opened its gates to him in May 1154.

The occupation of Damascus reunified Syria for the first time since the death of Tutush sixty years earlier, and the way in which unity was achieved ensured that Nur al-Din could exploit the city's military and fiscal resources with no fear of rebellion or subversion. Indeed, Nur al-Din saw to it that Damascus benefited from the new order of things; it became his second capital, and as with Aleppo he showered benefactions on it, including some of its most characteristic religious monuments.[19] Under his regime, the local notables and the militias lost most of the political power that they had enjoyed under the Seljuqid and Börid princes; Nur al-Din's garrisons were quite able to defend the city and maintain law and order without them. On the other hand, men of religion (some of whom were newcomers, but many of whom belonged to long-established notable families) had ready access to this pious ruler, and their influence extended into many areas of public policy – taxes, relations with the Franks, justice – outside matters of religion narrowly defined. As with Aleppo, the reign of Nur al-Din marked a clear and long-term rise in the political, intellectual and economic importance of the city.

Nur al-Din's second victory was in many ways an accident, created not by any long-term strategic plan but by sheer force of circumstances. Even so, the occupation of Egypt in 1168 and the ending of the 'heretical' Fatimid caliphate of Cairo in 1171 was surely his greatest military achievement.[20] It was a profoundly ironic achievement, to be sure: Nur al-Din never set foot in Egypt, he derived very little military or financial benefit from it during his lifetime, and the victory of his armies there led directly to the ruin of his own dynasty. However, Nur al-Din's conquest of Egypt not only placed the kingdom of Jerusalem in an untenable geopolitical position, it *potentially* more than doubled the financial and military resources at his disposal. He now ruled, or at least exercised unrivalled paramountcy within, a massive realm stretching from Mosul to Cairo. In principle, a grand strategy aimed at the recovery of Jerusalem and the expulsion of the Franks was now possible. On the other hand, developing and executing such a strategy was a very difficult problem, and in the few years remaining to him Nur al-Din made little progress on it.

The fundamental problem which Egypt posed for Nur al-Din was that he did not control the country directly, and he had no effective means of imposing his will on those who did, even though they were his own men. Egypt had fallen into his hands because of the progressive disintegration of the Fatimid regime in mid-century, a process which accelerated after the assassination of the vizier al-Salih Tala'i' b. Ruzzik in 1161. In the mad scramble for power after al-Salih's death, the various contenders sought allies anywhere they could find

[19] Elisséeff (1967), III, pp. 919–30; Al-Tabba (1982), I, pp. 86–138; Ibn 'Asakir, *Ta'rikh madinat Dimashq*, trans. Elisséeff.

[20] Elisséeff (1967), II, pp. 593–690; Ehrenkreutz (1972), chs. 3–6; Lyons and Jackson (1982), pp. 6–69.

them. Inevitably one of them turned to Amalric, the energetic new king of Jerusalem (regn. 1163–74), who saw in this turmoil a chance to add the land of Egypt to his beleaguered realm. Just as inevitably, another rival (the ill-fated Shawar) sought Nur al-Din's support for his ambitions. This three-way struggle between Egypt's rival politicians, Amalric and Nur al-Din wore on inconclusively for five years.

By autumn 1168, however, matters came to a crisis. The Fatimid state had no capacity whatever to defend itself, and Amalric's army was now encamped outside the walls of Cairo and seemed on the verge of taking the city. For the third time, Nur al-Din dispatched a major expeditionary force to Egypt. As in his two previous interventions (1164, 1167), he placed this force under the command of one of his oldest and most trusted amirs, the Kurd Shirkuh, who had helped him gain control of Aleppo at the outset of his reign. As in the two previous campaigns, Shirkuh was accompanied by a favorite nephew who had been part of his military entourage for many years, Salah al-Din Yusuf b. Ayyub (Saladin). This time the outcome was decisive: the Latins were forced to withdraw, and the Fatimid vizier Shawar, whose ceaseless machinations had fuelled the confusion of these years, was seized and executed. The hapless Fatimid caliph al-ʿAdid was compelled to name Shirkuh as his new vizier (January 1169). With that act Egypt became part of Nur al-Din's empire, as a kind of protectorate in which legal sovereignty remained with the Fatimid caliph but all effective political and military power was exercised by Nur al-Din's amirs. Shirkuh died quite suddenly after only two months, however. To the consternation of many in the Syrian expeditionary force, Shirkuh's inner circle swiftly manoeuvred his nephew Saladin into his place. Saladin was at this point thirty-two years old and a veteran of many battles, but he had little senior command or administrative experience. Moreover, as a Kurd he was viewed by the powerful Turkish amirs with some suspicion and disdain. Finally, he had inherited a country in political and fiscal chaos, and the Christian threat to Egypt remained grave.

We cannot follow Saladin's career in detail, but a brief sketch will bring out the key points. His first five years (1169–74) were spent as Nur al-Din's nominal viceroy in Egypt. Among some medieval and modern historians his conduct in this period has earned him a reputation for unbridled opportunism. Nur al-Din certainly found his new viceroy (whom he had had no part in choosing) uncooperative at best. Nur al-Din was eager to use Egypt as a base for large-scale coordinated campaigns against the kingdom of Jerusalem, but Saladin was dilatory about sending money or troops and almost openly sabotaged at least one campaign.

However, Saladin did face very real threats in Egypt, and until those were mastered he had good reason to focus on securing his position there. He took advantage of the death of the Fatimid caliph al-ʿAdid in 1171 (at the age of twenty-three) to terminate that dynasty. In the eyes of Nur al-Din and Saladin, both staunch Sunnis, the Isma'ili interpretation of Islam espoused by the Fatimids was flagrantly heretical. This action therefore fulfilled a crucial demand of Nur al-Din's platform, that the *jihad* against heresy must be pursued as vigorously as the *jihad* against the crusaders. Although the suppression of the Fatimids had gone smoothly, however, pro-Fatimid conspiracies and rumours of conspiracy continued for years. Moreover, Saladin needed to reconstruct the Egyptian fiscal system so that he could replace the large but ineffective Fatimid army with a smaller but more costly cavalry force on the Zengid model. The long-term economic impact of Saladin's reforms in Egypt has been extensively debated, but it is undeniable that he devoted much attention to this problem, and that under his aegis were laid the foundations of an Egyptian military administration which would endure until the end of the Mamluk sultanate in 1517.[21]

Whatever Saladin's excuses, an open rupture with Nur al-Din was almost a certainty; it was avoided only by the latter's death in Damascus in May 1174. Nur al-Din had left but a single heir, al-Salih Isma'il, and for once there should have been no succession crisis. But of course there was: al-Salih was only eleven years old, and the struggle to assert guardianship over him quickly broke up Nur al-Din's inner circle. Al-Salih was spirited off to Aleppo by one faction, while another in Damascus invited Saladin to occupy the city. He did not let the opportunity slip, and by the spring of 1175 he was master of all Muslim Syria except Aleppo itself. Saladin appropriated Nur al-Din's programme of *jihad*, Muslim unity and the expulsion of the Latins, and soon created a propaganda apparatus even more formidable than his mentor's. In so acting he portrayed himself as the sole true heir of Nur al-Din's political legacy. In asserting this role he faced the counter-claims of the Zengid ruler of Mosul, Sayf al-Din Ghazi II b. Mawdud, who was the obvious guardian of the Zengid patrimony. But Nur al-Din's old amirs were jealous of their prerogatives and regarded Sayf al-Din's attempts to intervene in Syria with suspicion. Moreover, Sayf al-Din's army had been shattered at the Horns of Hama in April 1175, and for the rest of his reign he could do nothing to loosen Saladin's grip on Syria. The inability of the Zengid princes to coordinate an effective resistance to Saladin and his successors would in fact be a crucial factor in north Syrian and Mesopotamian history for the next fifty years.[22]

---

[21] Ehrenkreutz ((1972), pp. 172, 187–8, 234–5) is very critical, Lyons and Jackson ((1982), pp. 49–66 and *passim*) are dismissive. The relevant data are presented in Gibb (1962), pp. 74–88; Cahen, (1977); Rabie (1972); Sato (1997), ch. 3.

[22] Saladin's career after Nur al-Din is adequately covered by Gibb (1973), Ehrenkreutz (1972) and Lyons and Jackson (1982). Their interpretations of his goals and achievements differ sharply. For Saladin's ideological programme, Sivan (1968), ch. 4.

For several years after 1175, however, Saladin's advance seemed to stall. In spite of constant pressure against Aleppo, al-Salih Isma'il enjoyed strong support there, and Saladin could not repeat Nur al-Din's peaceful occupation of Damascus in 1154. Likewise, his struggle against the Franks – the supposed *raison d'être* of his empire-building – saw only tactical successes. He did consolidate his early gains on several levels, to be sure. He completed his reform of the Egyptian army and also built a formidable navy, which for more than a decade was able to vie with Italian fleets for control of the south-eastern Mediterranean.[23] No less important, he was able to win over most of Nur al-Din's amirs and high officials in Syria, and he showed himself no less skilful than his mentor in retaining their loyalty throughout his reign.

Between 1181 and 1186, Saladin was finally able to make himself the paramount ruler in north Syria and Mesopotamia. The death of al-Salih Isma'il in 1181 deprived Zengid loyalists in Aleppo of a crucial symbol, and Saladin occupied the city in 1183. Aleppo was not the end of the game, however, for to Saladin Mosul was hardly less vital. As the traditional anchor of Zengid power, Mosul posed a latent threat to Saladin's position in Syria; in addition, its troops would be a valuable addition to his armies. He faced a tenacious opponent in 'Izz al-Din Mas'ud, who (like al-Salih Isma'il in Aleppo) had the firm support of his soldiers and subjects. Two sieges of Mosul (1182, 1185) failed, and Saladin had to be content with 'Izz al-Din's promise to send troops for the war against the infidels upon demand. Though reduced almost to a client-state, Mosul remained a Zengid city, due both to 'Izz al-Din Mas'ud's stubborn resistance and to a near fatal illness in autumn 1185 which forced Saladin to break off his campaign. However, after twelve years of unremitting struggle, Saladin had fulfilled his ambition to reconstitute Nur al-Din's empire. The issue now confronting him was how to use the resources that he had so painstakingly assembled.

Similar to Nur al-Din in his goals and political talents, Saladin nevertheless constructed his new empire along quite new lines. Both Zengi and Nur al-Din had maintained a unitary state during their lifetimes, and the division of Zengi's empire into two autonomous principalities upon his death conformed to Seljuqid political values but was never planned by him. Saladin, in contrast, deliberately set out to distribute his territories to his kinsmen during his lifetime, indeed at the very height of his power.[24] The Ayyubid confederation did not just happen; it was a carefully designed enterprise. No doubt Saladin had observed the agonizing disintegration of the Seljuqid and Zengid empires and hoped to avoid a similar fate for his domains. The complexity of his arrangements reflected his desire to meet the 'legitimate' expectations of his

---

[23] Ehrenkreutz (1955); Pryor (1988), pp. 112–34.   [24] Humphreys (1977b), pp. 52–66.

very large family, as well as his hope of devising a balanced political structure in which the confederation's paramount prince could lead but not not dominate his colleagues.

Saladin had achieved supremacy in Egypt and then Syria in part by using his numerous kinsmen as his chief commanders and governors. These men were exceedingly ambitious, but Saladin was able to control them through generous rewards and by persuading them that they were part of a winning enterprise. Two older brothers, Turanshah and Tughtigin, found it hard to defer to his authority; he soon sent them off to carve out an effectively independent domain in the Yemen. Ayyubid rule there would last until 1229, and it ensured friendly control of the economically vital Red Sea route to India and east Africa. In the late 1170s, he assigned the central Syrian towns of Homs, Baalbak and Hama as *iqta*'s to a cousin and two nephews. When the original assignees died he transferred their *iqta*'s to their sons, thereby confirming that these were hereditary appanages. However, only after the occupation of Aleppo in 1183 did Saladin begin to carve out the major princely appanages within his empire. These were given their definitive form in 1186, after the end of his last campaign against Mosul. Not surprisingly, the settlement of 1186 favoured Saladin's own sons, now approaching adulthood: Damascus went to his eldest, al-Afdal 'Ali; Egypt to al-'Aziz 'Uthman; and Aleppo to al-Zahir Ghazi.[25] He kept no appanage for himself – a clear sign of his confidence in the loyalty of his sons. A few years later, he placed the crucial frontier zones of Transjordan and the East[26] in the more experienced hands of his younger brother al-'Adil Sayf al-Din, for many years an indispensable counsellor and administrator. In spite of the turbulence of Ayyubid dynastic history after Saladin's death, the quasi-hereditary appanages into which he had divided his empire proved highly stable and indeed would constitute the framework of Syrian provincial administration down to the Ottoman conquest.

Up to the end of 1186, Saladin had conducted only occasional campaigns against the kingdom of Jerusalem; the kingdom's frontiers were still stable, its

---

[25] The Ayyubid naming system requires a brief explanation. An Ayyubid princely name consisted of three parts. The first element is a throne name combining *al-malik* (king) with an attribute; thus Saladin's throne name was al-Malik al-Nasir, the Victorious King. In modern scholarship it is normal to omit 'al-Malik' and to cite only the attribute: hence al-'Adil, al-Zahir, etc. The second element – often omitted in modern usage – is an honorific identifying one's service to or standing in the faith: al-'Adil was Sayf al-Din, 'Sword of the True Faith', Saladin was Salah al-Din, 'Integrity of the True Faith'. Finally, there is a personal name, often a Qur'anic prophet: Yusuf (Joseph), Muhammad, 'Isa (Jesus), and so on.

[26] The Arabic sources call the Ayyubid domains east of the Euphrates 'al-Bilad al-Sharqiyya' – 'the Eastern Territories', or simply 'the East'. The portions ruled by the Ayyubids were constantly changing, but they variously included the regions of Diyar Mudar (with its chief cities of Harran and Edessa), Diyar Bakr and Diyar Rabi'a (whose capital is Mosul).

armies and major strongholds intact. Moreover, Saladin was restrained from any
new initiatives by a truce which he had signed in 1185. Then, early in 1187, the
truce was violated by the lord of Kerak, Reginald of Châtillon, who raided an
Egyptian caravan passing near his fortress. Saladin now had a *casus belli* and no
plausible excuse for refusing to act. In the spring of 1187, he mustered the largest
field army he ever led, some 12,000 regular cavalry, plus an unknown number of
auxiliaries and volunteers. (These 12,000 cavalry represented roughly half the
regular forces available to him, including allied contingents supplied by Mosul
and other Mesopotamian client-states.)[27] Until this point, he had suffered
many criticisms of his commitment to the *jihad* against the Franks. But in
the next two years he redeemed them all with a brilliantly conducted series of
campaigns. The kingdom of Jerusalem's army was annihilated at the Horns
of Hattin in July 1187 and Jerusalem itself fell in October. By the autumn
of 1188, every Latin stronghold in the interior had been captured, and every
major coastal city had fallen, with the exception of Tyre, Tripoli and Antioch.
Another season's campaigning would surely finish the task. A more complete
realization of Nur al-Din's old programme can hardly be imagined.

As is so often the case, victory ended in disappointment. Bitter resistance
by the last Latin strongholds, combined with a powerful new crusade led
by a soldier of genius, Richard I of England, wrested back the Palestinian
coast between Ascalon and Tyre, and came close even to reclaiming Jerusalem.
After Richard's arrival, Saladin never won another battle. However, he kept
his exhausted and discouraged forces in the field for three years – no trivial
accomplishment – and in the end he negotiated a truce (September 1192) which
saved most of what he had won. Saladin was now old and tired, and when he
fell ill six months later he no longer had the strength to recover. But as he lay
on his deathbed in Damascus, he could look back on his career with a rare
sense of satisfaction, for he was surely the only monarch in twelfth-century
Egypt and Syria who had achieved almost everything he had set out to do.

On 4 March 1193, Saladin's vast empire passed to his heirs. The head of the
confederation was the prince of Damascus and his eldest son, al-Afdal ʿAli,
now aged twenty-four. In spite of Saladin's careful planning, al-Afdal's position
was a weak one. First, his capacity to obtain deference within the Ayyubid
family was tenuous, for he was only the brother of two major princes (al-ʿAziz
ʿUthman of Egypt and al-Zahir Ghazi of Aleppo) and the nephew of a third
(al-ʿAdil Abu Bakr of Transjordan and the East). Moreover, he had had no
part in creating his father's empire, so that the other princes owed nothing to
him. Likewise, Saladin's amirs regarded him not as a master but as a tool for

[27] For the armies of Saladin and the later Ayyubids, see Gibb (1962); Elisséeff (1967), III, pp. 720–50; Humphreys (1977b), pp. 67–99; Ayalon (1977) and (1981).

their own ambitions. Thirdly, Damascus lay at the heart of the confederation, but it did not have the fiscal and military resources to dominate the other appanages. Egypt in particular was far richer and could support a standing army three or four times larger than that of Damascus.[28] In fact between 1198 and 1250 the ruler of Egypt would always be the head of the confederation for just this reason. Finally, Saladin's brother al-ʿAdil was far more experienced and prestigious than the other princes. He had played a crucial role in building the empire and in the wars against the Franks, and it was hard to imagine him deferring to his nephews.

Under these circumstances, it is no surprise that Saladin's political settlement quickly collapsed.[29] The Ayyubid confederation fell into eight years of political intrigue and civil war. When the dust finally settled in 1201, only al-Zahir Ghazi of Aleppo still retained his patrimony; the rest of the empire was in the hands of al-ʿAdil. He followed Saladin in assigning the major appanages to three of his own sons: Egypt to the eldest, al-Kamil Muhammad; Damascus to al-Muʿazzam ʿIsa; and the East mainly to al-Ashraf Musa. Like his brother, he kept no appanage for himself, but his authority was uncontested. Hama and Homs represented no threat to the balance of power within the confederation and remained in the hands of the princes installed by Saladin.[30] The Ayyubid confederation thus retained the structure that Saladin had given it in 1186, though it was now dominated by a new lineage. This new dispensation would prove more durable than Saladin's, however, for al-ʿAdil's descendants would be the paramount actors within the confederation down to the death of al-Salih Ayyub (regn. 1240–9).

Al-ʿAdil recognized that Aleppo, as the last major appanage held by a son of Saladin, held a special place within the reconstituted Ayyubid order. He asserted his supremacy by having al-Zahir Ghazi (regn. 1186–1216) marry his daughter Dayfa Khatun, and it was the child of that marriage, al-ʿAziz Muhammad, who succeeded al-Zahir in 1216. Otherwise, however, al-ʿAdil interfered little

[28] In the 1220s, the standing forces of Egypt under al-Kamil Muhammad are given by Ibn Wasil as 12,000, those of Damascus under al-Muʿazzam ʿIsa as 3,000 (or 4,000 in another but less reliable manuscript). Each Ayyubid principality had its own army, separately recruited, trained and financed. In periods when there was an effective paramount ruler, as under Saladin and al-ʿAdil, these separate armies could readily be combined. Obviously that was not always the case. The total regular forces – almost entirely heavy cavalry – of the Ayyubid confederation numbered 22,000 to 24,000.

[29] The Ayyubids after Saladin: Gibb (1969d) Cahen (1960b). Rise and domination of al-ʿAdil: Humphreys (1977a), chs. 3–4.

[30] Hama was ruled by the descendants of Saladin's nephew Taqi al-DinʿUmar b. Shahanshah, who had been one of his ablest though most troublesome commanders; Homs by the descendants of his uncle Shirkuh, whose patronage had been crucial in his rise to power in Egypt. Both these appanages would enjoy an unbroken hereditary succession down to the end of Ayyubid rule in Syria: Homs until 1263, Hama until 1328.

in Aleppo's internal affairs. Al-Zahir was thus enabled to build a remarkably stable and centralized state, one able to endure two infant successions to the throne (in 1216 and 1236) without a major political crisis. After the death of al-'Adil in 1218, in fact, Aleppo tended to pursue an independent regional policy, focused chiefly on the Rum Seljuqids, now at the height of their power, and was usually able to keep clear of the rivalries that constantly pitted the other Ayyubid principalities against one another. Only with the grave succession crisis that broke out after the death of al-Kamil Muhammad (regn. 1218–38) was Aleppo dragged back into the thick of things. Though it would take us beyond the chronological limits of this chapter to explore Aleppo's role in these events, we should note the skilful diplomacy of the queen-mother Dayfa Khatun, who was the officially recognized and much-admired regent for her young grandson al-Nasir Yusuf until her death in 1242. Through her the hand of al-'Adil was still felt in the affairs of Aleppo.

The reign of al-'Adil was on the whole one of consolidation rather than dynamic expansion. This may be partly a matter of personality, since throughout his career al-'Adil had more often been an administrator and diplomat than a soldier. He was also in his late fifties by the time he consolidated his power in 1201, and he had been almost constantly at war for two decades. A degree of caution and fatigue seems altogether understandable. His first concern was to rebuild the treasury, left almost empty by his brother's empire-building, the constant full-scale warfare against the Franks between 1187 and 1192 and eight years of intra-dynastic strife after 1193. This policy required an aggressive quest for revenues, and al-'Adil was not beloved amongst his subjects. In the end he was successful, however, and his heirs, faced with the terrible crisis of the Fifth Crusade (1217–21), had good reason to be grateful to him. He also had to reshape the Ayyubid armies in Egypt and Damascus, riven and factionalized by the civil war. This he did with great discretion, often permitting the passage of time to solve the more delicate problems. His skill is shown by the fact that from 1201 to the end of his reign, he faced no significant military unrest. Finally, he undertook a major programme of refortification throughout his domains; among many impressive monuments, the massive citadel of Damascus embodies his goals and achievements with a special power.

Al-'Adil in fact did not lack imperial ambitions, but he focused them on Mesopotamia and south-eastern Anatolia; either directly or through the agency of his son al-Ashraf Musa, he was able to bring most of the old Zengid dominions, apart from Mosul and Sinjar, within his realm, in addition to the region around Lake Van. The goals of this expansion are only partly clear. The Ayyubids had had their eye on Mesopotamia and Mosul since Saladin's time, of course, and in any case it made sense to pre-empt any efforts at a Zengid revanche in Mesopotamia and north Syria. The Lake Van region was remote and poor, however, and it is hard to be sure what al-ʿAdil had in mind when he sent his troops there. It may have been an effort to gain paramountcy within the Ayyubids' old Kurdish homeland, but that is only speculation.

In contrast, al-ʿAdil pursued a very cautious policy in regard to the Latins in Palestine.[31] Far from attempting to finish the job begun by his brother, he took the field only when Christian initiatives compelled him to. He was quite willing to negotiate minor territorial concessions in order to bring things to a prompt conclusion. It is true that he pursued a more active policy against Tripoli and Antioch, but it was intended to restrain them, not to eradicate them. Again we must infer his motives. One surely was the fear of provoking a new crusade like that of 1189–92, which had so nearly ended in disaster. In addition, an aggressive anti-Frankish policy would have undermined his emphasis on administrative consolidation and financial retrenchment. Finally, the ports of Acre and Tyre carried a flourishing commerce in the early thirteenth century. Damascus profited greatly from this commerce, as did Aleppo from the trade through St Simeon and Antioch. War could only have disrupted this useful source of revenues, while producing very uncertain benefits.

Apart from the *jihad* against the Latins, al-ʿAdil and the other Ayyubid princes adhered closely to the ideology which they had inherited from Nur al-Din and Saladin. In particular, they were active patrons of Sunni Islam, and the decades of Ayyubid rule saw an extraordinary profusion of mosques, madrasas, Sufi convents and other religious foundations. It was not merely a question of money and physical infrastructure; the religious and historical scholarship of the Ayyubid period is remarkable both for its quantity and calibre. Damascus may have been the most important centre of Sunni learning in the world in the thirteenth century, and Cairo and Aleppo were not far behind.[32]

In the last year of al-ʿAdil's reign, the struggles of a lifetime almost came to naught. The arrival of a new crusade in Acre in 1217 at first seemed just another passing threat to Muslim Palestine, and a crusader thrust through Galilee was fended off by some hard fighting in the autumn and early winter. But in the spring of 1218, the crusade turned toward Egypt and laid siege to the crucial port city of Damietta. The struggle there would continue for more than three years, and more than once threatened the ruin of Ayyubid political power.

It was no doubt a mercy that the aged al-ʿAdil died in August 1218 while leading his forces from Damascus down to the Delta, but his passing left his sons to manage a difficult succession in the midst of a major military crisis.[33]

---

[31] Sivan (1968), ch. 5; Humphreys (1998).

[32] Religious and intellectual life in Damascus: Pouzet, (1988); Chamberlain (1994). Architectural patronage in Damascus: Humphreys (1988) and (1994). Aleppo: Sourdel (1949–51); Tabbaa (1997), chs. 5–8.

[33] Al-Kamil (regn. 1218–38): Gottschalk (1958); Humphreys (1977b), chs. 5, 6.

As at the death of Saladin, the empire's key appanages were held by three sons roughly equal in age: al-Kamil Muhammad of Egypt, al-Mu'azzam 'Isa of Damascus, and al-Ashraf Musa in the East. Al-'Adil's successor as head of the confederation, al-Kamil Muhammad, could base his leadership within the family only on the fragile authority of an older brother. Moreover, all three were well into their thirties; they had held their appanages for many years, were experienced in battle and administration, and inevitably regarded their standing vis-à-vis one another with some jealousy. Worse, al-Kamil almost at once faced a military coup mounted by a disgruntled Kurdish amir. The grave situation was further compounded by a Rum Seljuqid attack on Aleppo in the spring of 1218. To the astonishment of contemporary observers, the three brothers maintained an effective alliance throughout the bitter years of the Fifth Crusade. The coup against al-Kamil was quickly suppressed, the Rum Seljuqids were driven off by al-Ashraf, and the crusaders, who had twice refused to accept the retrocession of Jerusalem in exchange for the evacuation of Damietta, had to abandon Egypt in total defeat in September 1221.

It was inevitable that the fraternal harmony of the war years would break down once the crusader armies had left Egypt. The events of the next seventeen years are far too complex to chronicle in detail. In essence they can be divided into four unequal periods: (1) 1221–7, which witnessed an ingeniously conducted struggle by al-Mu'azzam of Damascus to defend his principality (and to expand it where possible) against the ambitions of his brothers al-Kamil and al-Ashraf; (2) 1227–9, which saw both the strange episode of the crusade of Frederick II and the doomed effort by al-Mu'azzam's son and successor al-Nasir Da'ud to maintain his father's policy, an effort defeated by al-Kamil's astuteness in manipulating the ambitions of Frederick and al-Ashraf for his own benefit; (3) 1229–36, a period of restored harmony within the confederation, with a kind of dyarchy between al-Ashraf (now the ruler of Damascus) and al-Kamil (very much the senior partner, since he controlled both Egypt and al-Ashraf's former lands in the East); (4) 1236–8, during which the confederation again fell into a period of open civil war, culminating in al-Kamil's conquest of Damascus in January 1238.

It is tempting to interpret al-Kamil's reign as a long struggle not merely to assert his supremacy within the Ayyubid confederation, but to convert it into a unified monarchy. After 1229, al-Kamil certainly controlled more territory than any other Ayyubid prince since Saladin's division of the empire in 1186. Likewise, the lands he ruled directly – Egypt and the East – allowed him to grip the Syrian principalities (Damascus, Homs, Hama and Aleppo) in a vice. In addition to the strategic location of al-Kamil's lands, they supported some 16,000 regular cavalry, a force almost twice as large as the combined armies of Syria. In the final analysis, however, al-Kamil was a conservative; throughout his reign he scrupulously respected the confederate structure of the empire. If he was planning a radical reshaping of this structure, he died before he could take any concrete steps toward that goal. In the siege of 1238 he had even promised to restore Damascus to al-Nasir Da'ud, the nephew whom he had dispossessed nine years before. (We cannot of course be sure that he would have kept his promise; al-Kamil was always a man of flexible principles.) Upon his death in Damascus in March 1238, al-Kamil's personal dominions went to his two sons, al-'Adil II in Egypt and al-Salih Ayyub in the East. Damascus was left to the discretion of his amirs; they assigned it to one of his nephews, al-Jawad Yunus, a prince of surpassing obscurity.

In principle, then, the Ayyubid confederation was still intact, along lines not much different from those laid down by Saladin and al-'Adil. In reality, everything had changed. No one was happy with the new settlement. It would break down almost at once, and the internecine wars of the next decade, far bitterer than any that had preceded them in Ayyubid times, would utterly transform the political system created by Saladin. The dissolution of the Ayyubid confederation led finally to the centralized military autocracy of the Mamluk sultanate, but the analysis of these events must be reserved for another chapter.

The century and a half between the death of Malikshah and al-Kamil Muhammad was clearly a period of intense political decentralization in western Iran and the Fertile Crescent. However, only sporadically was it an era of political chaos. What we observe is a competition for autonomy or paramountcy among local rulers and senior amirs who possessed roughly equal resources. That competition was governed by well-understood if rarely articulated rules of politics. Moreover, it was carried out within a rather stable set of fiscal and administrative practices (the *iqta'*, the *mamluk* system, the *atabeg* and so on).

The dynastic succession, passing from Seljuqids to Zengids to Ayyubids, marked no deep changes in these rules or practices. However, each of these dynastic formations did incorporate them in a distinctive way. The Seljuqid legacy left by Tutush in 1095 was so inchoate that his immediate successors were unable to organize effective states, nor could any one of them hope to impose a lasting order on the whole region from Damascus to Mosul. Zengi, schooled in the Great Seljuqid politics of Baghdad, was no doubt more talented and determined than his predecessors. He was also luckier, because there was almost no one to oppose him between Mosul and Aleppo at the beginning of his career, and because he lived long enough to convert his first acquisitions into a solid political structure. He was also fortunate in his successors, particularly his second son Nur al-Din Mahmud, who knew how to extend and strengthen his father's legacy over a long reign. Nur al-Din created an enduring political framework for his successors; in effect he trained the amirs and administrators who would build the Ayyubid empire. Saladin, finally, began his career as a junior amir at Nur al-Din's court, and clearly acquired an uncommon understanding of the workings of Nur al-Din's political system. What set him apart, excluding his boldness and astonishing good luck in the summer of 1187, was his very conscious political planning, his effort to build a complex confederative structure that could be transmitted from generation to generation. In spite of the lengthy succession crisis of 1193–1201, he succeeded remarkably well. Only half a century after his death did the Ayyubid system of politics begin to disintegrate. This time, however, it was replaced by a new system, based on new administrative institutions and sharply different ways of playing the political game.

APPENDIX: GENEALOGICAL TABLES

.

LEGEND

bp	bishop
c	count
co-k	co-king
ctess	countess
d	duke
dtr	daughter
e	emperor
k	king
m	margrave
p	prince
pcess	princess
q	queen
- - - -	illegimate birth

Table 1 Salian and Hohenstaufen emperors and kings

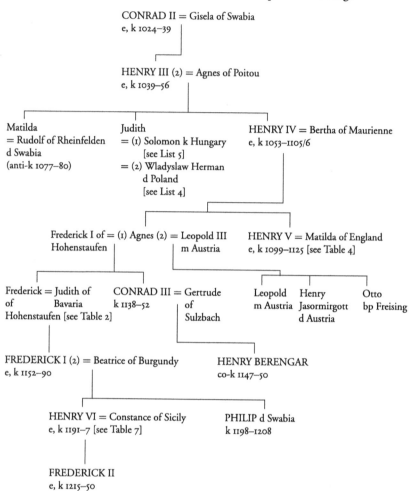

CONRAD II = Gisela of Swabia
e, k 1024–39

HENRY III (2) = Agnes of Poitou
e, k 1039–56

Matilda
= Rudolf of Rheinfelden
d Swabia
(anti-k 1077–80)

Judith
= (1) Solomon k Hungary
[see List 5]
= (2) Wladyslaw Herman
d Poland
[see List 4]

HENRY IV = Bertha of Maurienne
e, k 1053–1105/6

Frederick I of = (1) Agnes (2) = Leopold III
Hohenstaufen   m Austria

HENRY V = Matilda of England
e, k 1099–1125 [see Table 4]

Frederick = Judith of
of   Bavaria
Hohenstaufen [see Table 2]

CONRAD III = Gertrude
k 1138–52   of
                Sulzbach

Leopold   Henry   Otto
m Austria Jasormirgott   bp Freising
           d Austria

FREDERICK I (2) = Beatrice of Burgundy
e, k 1152–90

HENRY BERENGAR
co-k 1147–50

HENRY VI = Constance of Sicily
e, k 1191–7 [see Table 7]

PHILIP d Swabia
k 1198–1208

FREDERICK II
e, k 1215–50

Table 2　Welfs, dukes of the Bavarians and Saxons

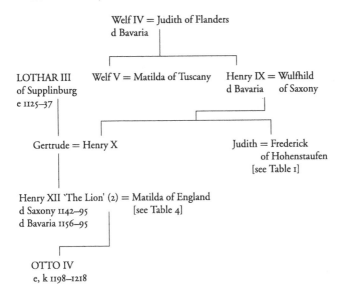

Welf IV = Judith of Flanders
d Bavaria

LOTHAR III　　　Welf V = Matilda of Tuscany　　　Henry IX = Wulfhild
of Supplinburg　　　　　　　　　　　　　　　　　d Bavaria　　of Saxony
e 1125–37

Gertrude = Henry X　　　　　　　　　Judith = Frederick
　　　　　　　　　　　　　　　　　　　　　　　of Hohenstaufen
　　　　　　　　　　　　　　　　　　　　　　　[see Table 1]

Henry XII 'The Lion' (2) = Matilda of England
d Saxony 1142–95　　　　　[see Table 4]
d Bavaria 1156–95

OTTO IV
e, k 1198–1218

Table 3 Capetians, kings of the French

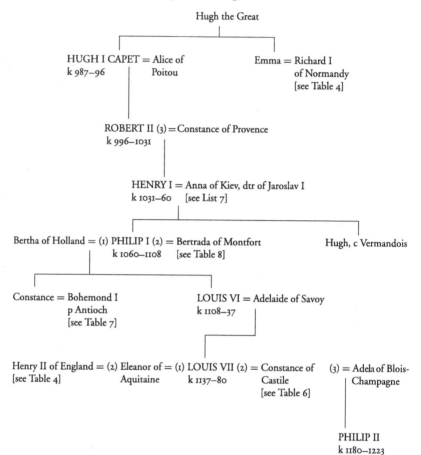

Hugh the Great

HUGH I CAPET = Alice of
k 987–96   Poitou

Emma = Richard I
          of Normandy
          [see Table 4]

ROBERT II (3) = Constance of Provence
k 996–1031

HENRY I = Anna of Kiev, dtr of Jaroslav I
k 1031–60   [see List 7]

Bertha of Holland = (1) PHILIP I (2) = Bertrada of Montfort
                          k 1060–1108   [see Table 8]

Hugh, c Vermandois

Constance = Bohemond I
                p Antioch
                [see Table 7]

LOUIS VI = Adelaide of Savoy
k 1108–37

Henry II of England = (2) Eleanor of = (1) LOUIS VII (2) = Constance of   (3) = Adela of Blois-
[see Table 4]   Aquitaine   k 1137–80   Castile   Champagne
                                                                    [see Table 6]

PHILIP II
k 1180–1223

Table 4 Kings in England, dukes in Normandy

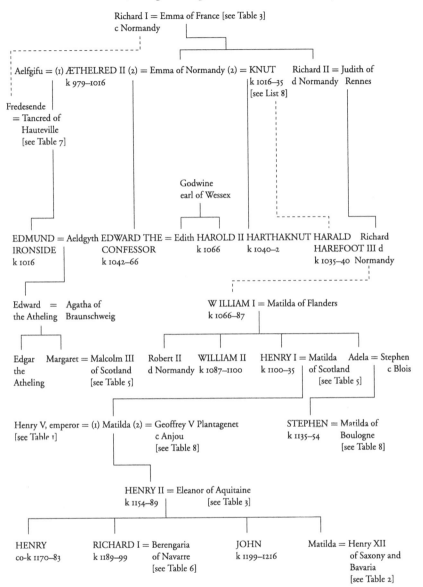

Richard I = Emma of France [see Table 3]
c Normandy

Aelfgifu = (1) ÆTHELRED II (2) = Emma of Normandy (2) = KNUT   Richard II = Judith of
      k 979–1016   k 1016–35   d Normandy   Rennes
                                              [see List 8]

Fredesende
= Tancred of
Hauteville
[see Table 7]

Godwine
earl of Wessex

EDMUND = Aeldgyth EDWARD THE = Edith HAROLD II HARTHAKNUT HARALD   Richard
IRONSIDE   CONFESSOR   k 1066   k 1040–2   HAREFOOT III d
k 1016   k 1042–66   k 1035–40 Normandy

Edward   =   Agatha of
the Atheling   Braunschweig

W ILLIAM I = Matilda of Flanders
k 1066–87

Edgar   Margaret = Malcolm III   Robert II   WILLIAM II   HENRY I = Matilda   Adela = Stephen
the   of Scotland   d Normandy   k 1087–1100   k 1100–35 | of Scotland   c Blois
Atheling   [see Table 5]   [see Table 5]

Henry V, emperor = (1) Matilda (2) = Geoffrey V Plantagenet   STEPHEN = Matilda of
[see Table 1]   c Anjou   k 1135–54   Boulogne
                           [see Table 8]   [see Table 8]

HENRY II = Eleanor of Aquitaine
k 1154–89   [see Table 3]

HENRY   RICHARD I = Berengaria   JOHN   Matilda = Henry XII
co-k 1170–83   k 1189–99   of Navarre   k 1199–1216   of Saxony and
                           [see Table 6]   Bavaria
                                                              [see Table 2]

Table 5 Kings of the Scots

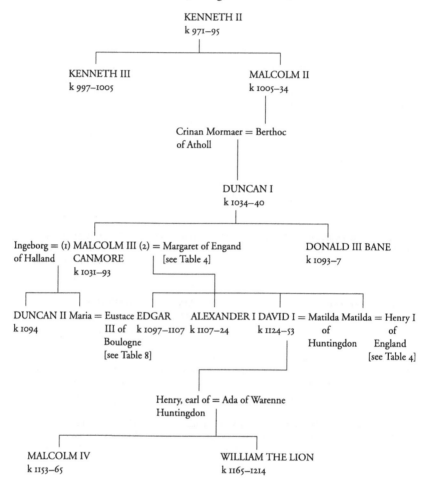

KENNETH II
k 971–95

KENNETH III
k 997–1005

MALCOLM II
k 1005–34

Crinan Mormaer = Berthoc
of Atholl

DUNCAN I
k 1034–40

Ingeborg = (1) MALCOLM III (2) = Margaret of Engand
of Halland   CANMORE   [see Table 4]
              k 1031–93

DONALD III BANE
k 1093–7

DUNCAN II Maria = Eustace EDGAR   ALEXANDER I DAVID I = Matilda Matilda = Henry I
k 1094   III of   k 1097–1107 k 1107–24   k 1124–53   of   of
                Boulogne   Huntingdon England
                [see Table 8]   [see Table 4]

Henry, earl of = Ada of Warenne
Huntingdon

MALCOLM IV
k 1153–65

WILLIAM THE LION
k 1165–1214

Table 6 Kings in the Iberian peninsula

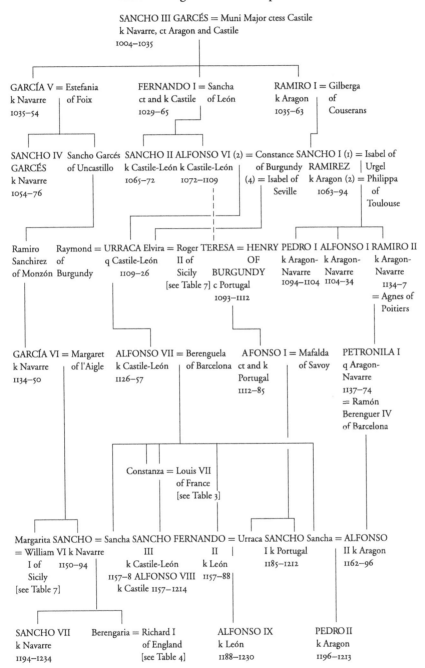

SANCHO III GARCÉS = Muni Major ctess Castile
k Navarre, ct Aragon and Castile
1004–1035

GARCÍA V = Estefania
k Navarre | of Foix
1035–54

FERNANDO I = Sancha
ct and k Castile of León
1029–65

RAMIRO I = Gilberga
k Aragon | of
1035–63 | Couserans

SANCHO IV Sancho Garcés SANCHO II ALFONSO VI (2) = Constance SANCHO I (1) = Isabel of
GARCÉS of Uncastillo k Castile-León k Castile-León | of Burgundy RAMIREZ | Urgel
k Navarre 1065–72 1072–1109 (4) = Isabel of k Aragon (2) = Philippa
1054–76 Seville 1063–94 of
Toulouse

Ramiro Raymond = URRACA Elvira = Roger TERESA = HENRY PEDRO I ALFONSO I RAMIRO II
Sanchirez of q Castile-León II of OF k Aragon- k Aragon- k Aragon-
of Monzón Burgundy 1109–26 Sicily BURGUNDY Navarre Navarre Navarre
[see Table 7] c Portugal 1094–1104 1104–34 1134–7
1093–1112 = Agnes of
Poitiers

GARCÍA VI = Margaret ALFONSO VII = Berenguela AFONSO I = Mafalda PETRONILA I
k Navarre of l'Aigle k Castile-León of Barcelona ct and k of Savoy q Aragon-
1134–50 1126–57 Portugal Navarre
1112–85 1137–74
= Ramón
Berenguer IV
of Barcelona

Constanza = Louis VII
of France
[see Table 3]

Margarita SANCHO = Sancha SANCHO FERNANDO = Urraca SANCHO Sancha = ALFONSO
= William VI k Navarre III II I k Portugal II k Aragon
I of 1150–94 k Castile-León k León 1185–1212 1162–96
Sicily 1157–8 ALFONSO VIII 1157–88
[see Table 7] k Castile 1157–1214

SANCHO VII Berengaria = Richard I ALFONSO IX PEDRO II
k Navarre of England k León k Aragon
1194–1234 [see Table 4] 1188–1230 1196–1213

Table 7 The Hautevilles in southern Italy, Sicily and Antioch

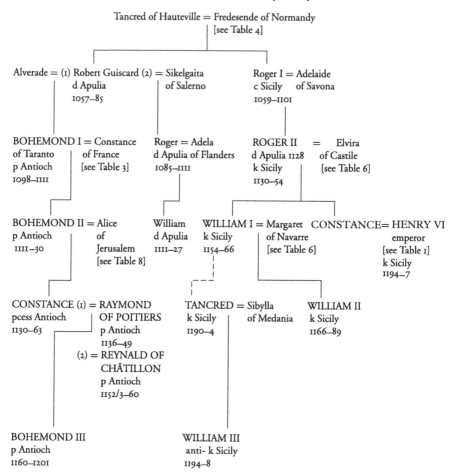

Table 8 Counts of Boulogne and Anjou, kings of Jerusalem

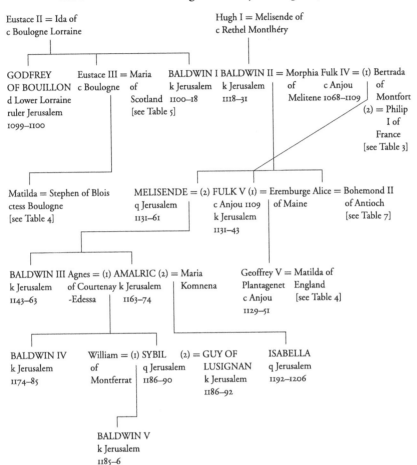

Christian rulers

1 Byzantine emperors, 976–1204

Basil II, 976–1205
Constantine VIII, 1025–8
Romanos III Argyros, 1028–34
Michael IV, 1034–41
Michael V, 1041–2
Zoe and Theodora, 1042
Constantine IX Monomachos, 1042–55
Theodora (again), 1055–6
Michael VI, 1056–7
Isaac I Komnenos, 1057–9
Constantine X Doukas, 1059–67
Romanos IV Diogenes, 1068–71
Michael VII Doukas, 1071–8
Nikephoros III Botaneiates, 1078–81
Alexios I Komnenos, 1081–1118
John II Komnenos, 1118–43
Manuel I Komnenos, 1143–80
Alexios II Komnenos, 1180–3
Andronikos I Komnenos, 1183–5
Isaac II Angelos, 1185–95
Alexios III Angelos, 1195–1203
Isaac II Angelos (again) and Alexios IV Angelos, 1203–4
Alexios V Murtzouphlos, 1204

2 Popes, 1012–1216

Benedict VIII, 18 May 1012; died 9 Apr. 1024
John XIX, Apr. or May 1024; died 20 Oct. 1032
Benedict IX, 1032; resigned Sept. 1044
Silvester III, 20 Jan. 1045; deposed 10 Mar. 1045
Benedict IX, for the second time, 10 Mar. 1045; deposed 20 Dec. 1046
Gregory VI, 5 May 1045; deposed 20 Dec. 1046
Clement II, 25 Dec. 1046; died 9 Oct. 1047
Benedict IX, for the third time, returned 8 Nov. 1047; expelled 17 July 1048
Damasus II, 17 July 1048; died 9 Aug. 1048
Leo IX, 12 Feb. 1049; died 19 Apr. 1054
Victor II, 13 Apr. 1055; died 28 July 1057
Stephen X, 3 Aug. 1057; died 29 Mar. 1058

[anti-pope: Benedict X, 5 Apr. 1058; deposed 24 Jan. 1059]
Nicholas II, 24 Jan. 1059; died 27 July 1061
Alexander II, 1 Oct. 1061; died 21 Apr. 1073
    [anti-pope: Honorius II, 28 Oct. 1061; died late 1072]
Gregory VII, 30 June 1073; died 25 May 1085
    [anti-pope: Clement III, 24 Mar. 1084; died 8 Sept. 1100]
Victor III, 24 May 1086; died 16 Sept. 1087
Urban II, 12 Mar. 1088; died 29 July 1099
Paschal II, 14 Aug. 1099; died 21 Jan. 1118
    [anti-popes: Theoderic, Sept. 1100; expelled Jan. 1101
       Albert, elected and deposed 1102
       Silvester IV, 18 Nov. 1105; deposed 12 Apr. 1111]
Gelasius II, 10 Mar. 1118; died 28 Jan. 1119
    [anti-pope: Gregory VIII, 8 Mar. 1118; deposed Apr. 1121]
Calixtus II, 9 Feb. 1119; died 13 Dec. 1124
Honorius II, 21 Dec. 1124; died 13 Feb. 1130
    [anti-pope: Celestine II, Dec. 1124; died 1125–6]
Innocent II, 23 Feb. 1130; died 24 Sept. 1143
    [anti-popes: Anacletus II, 23 Feb. 1130; died 25 Jan. 1138
       Victor IV, Mar. 1138; resigned 29 May 1138]
Celestine II, 3 Oct. 1143; died 8 Mar. 1144
Lucius II, 12 Mar. 1144; died 15 Feb. 1145
Eugenius III, 18 Feb. 1145; died 8 July 1153
Anastasius IV, 12 July 1153; died 3 Dec. 1154
Adrian IV, 5 Dec. 1154; died 1 Sept. 1159
Alexander III, 20 Sept. 1159; died 30 Aug. 1181
    [anti-popes: Victor IV, 4 Oct. 1159; died 20 Apr. 1164
       Paschal III, 26 Apr. 1164; died 20 Sept. 1168
       Calixtus III, Sept. 1168; resigned 29 Aug. 1178
       Innocent III, 29 Sept. 1179; deposed Jan. 1180]
Lucius III, 6 Sept. 1181; died 25 Nov. 1185
Urban III, 1 Dec. 1185; died 20 Oct. 1187
Gregory VIII, 25 Oct. 1187; died 17 Dec. 1187
Clement III, 20 Dec. 1187; died Mar. 1191
Celestine III, 14 Apr. 1191; died 8 Jan. 1198
Innocent III, 22 Feb. 1198; died 16 July 1216

3 *Doges of Venice, 991–1205*

Pietro II Orseolo, 991–1008
Otto Orseolo, 1008–26
Pietro Centranico (Barbolano), 1026–30

Otto Orseolo, 1030–2
Domenico Flabianico, 1032–43
Domenico Contarini, 1043–70
Domenico Silvio (Selvo), 1070–84
Vitale Falier, 1084–96
Vitale I Michiel, 1096–1101
Ordelafo Falier, 1101–18
Domenico Michiel, 1118–29
Pietro Polani, 1129–48
Domenico Morosini, 1148–55
Vitale II Michiel, 1155–72
Sebastiano Ziani, 1172–8
Orio Mastropiero (Malipiero), 1178–92
Enrico Dandolo, 1192–1205

4 *The Piasts, counts, grand dukes and kings of the Poles, 992–1202*

Boleslaw Chrobry, 992–1025
Mieszko, 1025–34
Kazimierz Odnowiciel, 1039–58
Boleslaw Szczodry, 1058–80
Wladyslaw Herman, 1080–1102
Boleslaw Krzywousty, 1102–38
Wladyslaw, 1138–46
Boleslaw Kedzierzawy, 1146–73
Mieszko, 1177–80, 1194–1202
Kazimierz, 1180–94

5 *The Árpáds, kings of the Hungarians, 997–1204*

Stephen I, 997–1038
Peter Orseolo, 1038–41, 1044–6
Samuel Aba, 1041–4
Andrew I, 1046–60
Béla I, 1060–3
Solomon, 1063–74
Géza I, 1074–7
Ladislas I, 1077–95
Coloman, 1095–1116
Stephen II, 1116–31
Béla II, 1131–41

Géza II, 1141–62
Stephen III, 1162–72
  Ladislas II, 1162–3
  Stephen IV, 1163
Béla III, 1172–96
Emeric, 1196–1204

6 *Kings of the Croatians, 1000–97*

Krešimir III, 1000–30
Stjepan I, 1030–58
(Peter) Krešimir IV, 1058–74
Zvonimir Dmitar, 1075–*c.* 1089
Stjepan II, *c.* 1089–1090/1
Peter, 1093–7

7 *The Rurikids, grand princes of Kiev, 1024–1205*

Jaroslav I, 1024–54
Izyaslav I, 1054–73
Svyatoslav I, 1073–6
Vsevolod I, 1076–93
Svyatopolk II, 1093–1113
Monomakh, 1113–25
Mstislav I, 1125–32
Jaropolk II, 1132–9
Vyacheslav, 1139
Vsevolod II, 1139–46
Izyaslav II, 1146–54
Yury I, 1155–8
Izyaslav III, 1158–9
Rostislav I, 1159–67
Mstislav II, 1167–9
Andrey, 1169–74
Svyatoslav II, 1176–9
Ryurik II, 1194–1202
Roman Mstislavich, 1202–5

8 *Kings in Denmark, 987–1202*

Sven I Forkbeard, 987–1014
Harald, 1014–18

Knut the Great, 1019–35
Harthaknut, 1035–42
Magnus, 1042–7
Sven Estridsen, 1047–74
Harald, 1074–80
Knut II, 1080–6
Olaf I, 1086–95
Erik I, 1095–1103
Niels, 1104–30
Magnus, 1134
Erik II, 1134–7
Erik III, 1137–46
Sven III, 1147–57
   Knut III, co-king, 1154–7
Valdemar I, 1157–82
Knut IV, 1182–1202

9 *Kings in Norway, 1047–1202*

Harald Hardrada, 1045–66
Magnus, 1066–9
Olav, 1069–93
Magnus Barefoot, 1095–1103
Eystein, co-king, 1103–23
Sigurd, co-king, 1103–30
Olav, co-king, 1103–15
Harald, 1130–6
Magnus the Blind, co-king, 1136–9
Sigurd, co-king, 1136–55
Inge, co-king, 1142–61
Eystein, co-king, 1142–57
Haakon II, 1157–62
Sigurd, 1162–3
Magnus, 1161–84
Sverre, 1184–1202

Muslim rulers (with dates of accession)

10 *The 'Abbasid caliphs in Baghdad, 991–1180*

al-Qadir, 991
al-Qa'im, 1031

al-Muqtadi, 1075
al-Mustazhir, 1094
al-Mustarshid, 1118
al-Rashid, 1135
al-Muqtafi, 1136
al-Mustanjid, 1160
al-Mustadi', 1170
al-Nasir, 1180

11　The Fatimid caliphs in Cairo, 996–1171

al-Hakim, 996
al-Zahir, 1021
al-Mustansir, 1036
al-Musta'li, 1094
al-Amir, 1101
al-Hafiz, 1131
al-Zafir, 1149
al-Fa'iz, 1154
al-'Adid, 1160–71

12　The Ayyubids (Saladin and his descendants), 1169–1250

In Egypt
al-Nasir I Salah-al-Din (Saladin), 1169
al-'Aziz 'Uthman, 1186
al-Mansur Nasir-al-Din, 1198
al-'Adil I Sayf-al-Din, 1200

In Damascus
al-Afdal Nur-al-Din 'Ali, 1186
al-'Adil I Sayf-al-Din, 1196

In Aleppo
al-'Adil I Sayf-al-Din, 1183
al-Zahir Ghazi, 1186
al-'Aziz Muhammad, 1216

In Diyarbakr
al-Nasir I Salah-al-Din (Saladin), 1185
al-'Adil I Sayf-al-Din, 1195

al-Awhad Najm-al-Din Ayyub, 1200
al-Ashraf I Musa, 1210

In the Yemen
al-Mu'azzam Shams-al-Din Turan-Shah, 1174
al-'Aziz Zahir–al-Din Tughtigin, 1181
Mu'izz-al-Din Isma'il, 1197
al-Nasir Ayyub, 1202
al-Muzaffar Sulayman, 1214
al-Mas'ud Salah-al-Din, 1215

13 The Almoravids in North Africa and Spain, 1061–1147

Yusuf b. Tashufin, 1061
'Ali, 1106
Tashufin, 1142
Ibrahim, 1146
Is'haq, 1146–7

14 The Almohads in North Africa and Spain, 1130–1214

Muhammad b. Tumart, 1121
'Abd-al-Mu'min, 1130
Abu-Ya'qub Yusuf I, 1163
Abu-Yusuf Ya'qub al-Mansur, 1184
Muhammad al-Nasir, 1199

PRIMARY SOURCES

WESTERN SOURCES

Acta pontificum Romanorum inedita, ed. J. Pflugk-Harttung, 3 vols., Tübingen and Stuttgart (1881–6)

Adalbero of Laon, *Poème au roi Robert*, ed. C. Carozzi (Classiques de l'Histoire de France au Moyen Age 32), Paris (1979)

Adrian IV, 'Epistolae', *PL* 188, cols. 1361–640

Alexander III, 'Epistolae', *PL* 200, cols. 69–1320

Alexander Telesinus, *Ystoria Rogerii regis Siciliae, Calabriae atque Apuliae*, ed. L. de Nava (FSI 112), Rome (1991)

Alfonso X, *Las siete partidas del rey don Alfonso el Sabio*, ed. Real Academia de la Historia, 3 vols., Madrid (1807)

Amatus of Monte Cassino, *Storia de' Normanni*, ed. V. De Bartholomeis (FSI 76), Rome (1935)

Ambroise, *L'Estoire de la guerre sainte*, ed. G. Paris, Paris (1897); trans. M. J. Hubert and J. La Monte as *The Crusade of Richard the Lionheart*, New York (1941)

Anastasius IV, 'Epistolae', *PL* 188, cols. 989–1088

Ancient Laws and Institutes of Wales, ed. and trans. A. Owen, 2 vols., London (1841)

The Anglo-Saxon Chronicle: A Revised Translation, ed. D. Whitelock, D. C. Douglas and S. I. Tucker, London (1965); *The Anglo-Saxon Chronicle*, ed. G. N. Garmonsway, London (1954)

Anglo-Scottish Relations 1174–1328, ed. E. L. G. Stones, London (1965); rev. edn Oxford (1970)

'Annales Beneventani', ed. O. Bertolini, *BISI* 42 (1923), 112–55.

Annales Marbacenses, ed. H. Bloch, *MGH SRG*, IX

Annales monastici, ed. H. R. Luard, 5 vols. (RS 36), London (1864–9)

Archipoeta, *Carmina*, ed. H. Watenphul and H. Krefeld, Heidelberg (1958)

Arnold of Lübeck, 'Chronica', *MGH S*, XXI, pp. 100–250

Árpádkori új okmánytár: codex diplomaticus Arpadianus continuatus, ed. G. Wenzel, 12 vols., Budapest (1860–74)

Az Árpád-házi királyok okleveleinek kritikai jegyzéke: regesta regum stirpis Arpadianae critico-diplomatica, comp. I. Szentpétery and I. Borsa, 3 vols., Budapest (1923–61)

Baldric of Dol, 'Historia Ierosolimitana', *RHC Occ.* IV, pp. 1–111

Baldric of Dol, 'Vita sancti Hugonis Rothomagensis epscopi', *PL* 166, cols. 1163–72

Becerro Gótico de Cardeña, ed. L. Serrano, Valladolid (1910)

Benoît de Sainte-Maure, *Chronique des ducs de Normandie*, ed. F. Michel, Paris (1938)

Bernard of Clairvaux, 'De consideratione', in Bernard of Clairvaux, *Opera omnia*, ed. J. Leclercq, H. M. Rochais and C. H. Talbot, III Rome (1963), pp. 393–493

Bernard of Clairvaux, 'Epistolae', in Bernard of Clairvaux, *Opera omnia*, ed. J. Leclercq, H. M. Rochais and C. H. Talbot, VII–VIII Rome (1974–7)

Berthold of Zwiefalten, 'Chronicon', ed. L. Wallach, 'Berthold of Zwiefalten's Chronicle', *Traditio* 13 (1957), 141–6

Bibliotheca hagiographica latina antiquae et mediae aetatis, ed. Bollandists, 3 parts, Brussels (1898–1911)

Bonizo of Sutri, 'Liber ad amicum', *MGH Libelli* I, pp. 571–620

Boso of S. Pudenziana, 'Vita Alexandri III', in *Liber pontificalis*, II, pp. 397–446

Boso of S. Pudenziana, 'Vita Eugenii III', in *Liber pontificalis*, II, pp. 386–7

Boso of S. Pudenziana, 'Vita Hadriani IV', in *Liber pontificalis*, II, pp. 388–97

Boso of S. Pudenziana, 'Vita Innocentii II', in *Liber pontificalis*, II, pp. 379–84

'Braint Teilo', ed. and trans. W. Davies, *Bulletin of the Board of Celtic Studies* 26 (1974–6), 123–37

Burchard of Ursberg, *Chronicon*, ed. O. Holder-Egger and B. von Simson, *MGH SRG*, XVI

Burchard of Worms, 'Decretorum libri XX', *PL* 140, cols. 537–1058

Caesarius of Heisterbach, *Dialogus miraculorum*, ed. J. Strange, 2 vols., Cologne, Bonn and Brussels (1851)

Caffaro di Caschifellone, 'Annales Ianuenses', in L. T. Belgrano (ed.), *Annali Genovesi*, I (FSI 11), Genoa (1890)

Calixtus II, 'Epistolae', *PL* 163, cols. 1093–338

Cartas de población del Reino de Aragón en los siglos medievales, ed. M. L. Ledesma Rubio, Saragossa (1991)

Cartulario de San Juan de la Peña, I, ed. A. Ubieto Arteta, Valencia (1962)

Cartulario de San Millán de la Cogolla (759–1076), ed. A. Ubieto Arteta, Valencia (1976)

Los cartularios de Toledo: catálogo documental, ed. F. J. Hernández (Monumenta Ecclesiae Toletanae Historica 1.1), Madrid (1985)

Catálogo de documentos del monasterio de Santa Maria de Otero de las Dueñas, comp. R. Rodríguez, León (1949)

Catalogue des actes de Philippe Auguste, ed. L. Delisle, Paris (1856)

Catalogus Baronum, ed. E. M. Jamison (FSI 101), Rome (1972)

Catalogus fontium historiae Hungaricae, ed. F. Gombos, 3 vols., Budapest (1937–8); index ed. Cs. Csapodi (1943)

Celestine III, 'Epistolae', *PL* 206, cols. 867–1262

Les chansons de croisade, ed. C. M. J. Bédier and P. Aubry, Paris (1909)

Chartae Antiquissimae Hungariae ab anno 1001 usque ad annum 1196, ed. Gy. Györffy, Budapest (1994)

The Charters of David I, ed. G. W. S. Barrow, Woodbridge (1999)

The Charters of Gaelic Scotland and Ireland in the Early and Central Middle Ages, ed. D. Broun (Quiggin Pamphlet 2), Cambridge (1995)

Chronica Adefonsi imperatoris, ed. A. Maya Sánchez, in *Chronica Hispana saec. XII* (CCCM 71), Turnhout (1990), pp. 149–248

Chronica monasterii Casinensis, ed. H. Hoffmann, *MGH S*, xxxiv

Chronica regia Coloniensis, ed. G. Waitz, *MGH SRG*, xviii

The Chronicle of Battle Abbey, ed. E. Searle, Oxford (1980)

Chronicles of the Reigns of Stephen, Henry II and Richard I, ed. R. Howlett, 4 vols. (RS 82), London (1884–90)

'Chronicon Compostellanum', ed. E. Flórez, *España Sagrada* 20, Madrid (1765), pp. 608–13

Chronicon Ignoti monachi Cisterciensis sanctae Mariae de Ferraria, ed. A. Gaudenz, Naples (1888)

'Chronicon Mauriniacensis monasterii', *PL* 180, cols. 130–76

Chronicon universale anonymi Laudunensis, ed. A. Cartellieri and W. Stechele, Leipzig and Paris (1909)

'Chronique latine inédite des Rois de Castille (1236)', ed. G. Cirot, *Bulletin Hispanique* 14 (1912), 30–46, 109–18, 244–74, 353–74; 15 (1913), 18–37, 170–87, 268–83, 411

Chronique de Saint Maixent, ed. J. Verdon, Paris (1979)

Chronique de Saint-Pierre-le-Vif de Sens, ed. R.-H. Bautier and M. Gilles, Paris (1979)

Chroniques d'Anjou, ed. P. Marchegay and A. Salmon, Paris (1856)

Chroniques des comtes d'Anjou et des seigneurs d'Amboise, ed. L. Halphen and R. Poupardin, Paris (1913)

Chroniques des églises d'Anjou, ed. P. Marchegay and E. Mabille, Paris (1869)

Chroniques de St Martial de Limoges, ed. H. Duples-Agier, Paris (1874)

Chroniques de Touraine, ed. A. Salmon, Tours (1854); Supplement (1857)

Church Historians of England, ed. J. Stevenson, 5 vols. in 8, London (1853–8)

Codex diplomaticus Caietanus, 2 vols., Monte Cassino (1888–92)

Codex diplomaticus Cavensis, ed. M. Morcaldi *et al.*, 8 vols., Naples (1873–93)

Codex diplomaticus Hungariae ecclesiasticus ac civilis, ed. G. Fejér, 11 vols., Buda (1829–44)

Codice diplomatico Barese, 5 Le Pergamene di S. Nicoa di Bari: periodo normanno 1071–1194, ed. F. Nitti di Vito, Bari (1902)

Colección diplomática de Fernando I (1037–1065), ed. P. Blanco Lozano, León (1987)

Colección diplomática del monasterio de Sahagún (857–1230), iii: *(1073–1109)*, ed. M. Herrero de la Fuente, León (1988)

Colección diplomática de Pedro I de Aragón y de Navarra, ed. A. Ubieto Arteta, Saragossa (1951)

Colección diplomática de Santa María de Otero de las Dueñas (León) (854–1037), ed. G. del Ser Quijano, Salamanca (1994)

Colección documental del archivo de la catedral de León (775–1230), iv: *1032–1109*, ed. J. M. Ruiz Asencio, León (1990)

Colección de documentos inéditos del archivo de la corona de Aragón, ed. P. de Bofarull, iv, Barcelona (1850)

Le colonie Cassinesi in Capitanata, i: *Lesina*, ed. T. Leccisotti (Miscellanea Cassinese 13), Monte Cassino (1937)

Conciliorum oecumenicorum decreta, ed. J. Alberigo, J. A. Dossetti *et al.*, 3rd edn, Bologna (1973)

Constantiae imperatricis et reginae Siciliae diplomata (1195–1198), ed. T. Kölzer (Codex Diplomaticus Regni Sicilae, ser. 2, 1.2), Cologne (1983)

Constitutum Constantini, ed. H. Fuhrmann, *MGH Fontes iuris germanici antiqui*, x, Hanover (1968)

Corpus inscriptionum crucesignatorum terrae sanctae (1099–1291), ed. S. De Sandoli (Pubblicazioni della Studium Biblicum Franziscanum 21), Jerusalem (1974)

Cortes de los antiguos reinos de León y de Castilla, ed. Real Academia de la Historia, i, Madrid (1861)

Crónica general de España de 1344, ed. D. Cátalán and M. S. de Andrés, 2 vols., Madrid (1971)

Crónica Najerense, ed. A. Ubierto Arteta, 2nd edn, Saragossa (1985)

Crónicas anónimas de Sahagún, ed. A. Ubierto Arteta, Saragossa (1987); also ed. J. Puyol, *Boletín de la Real Academia de la Historia* 76 (1920), 7–26, 111–22, 242–57, 339–56, 395–419, 512–19; 77 (1921), 51–9, 151–61

Crónicas asturianas, ed. J. Gil Fernández, J. L. Moralejo and J. I. Ruiz de la Peña, Oviedo (1985)

Councils and Synods with Other Documents relating to the English Church, ed. D. Whitelock, M. Brett and C. N. L. Brooke, i–ii Oxford (1981)

Cyfreithiau Hywel Dda yn ôl Llyfr Blegywryd, ed. S. J. Williams and J. E. Powell, 2nd edn, Cardiff (1961)

Decretales Gregorii IX, in E. A. Friedberg (ed.), *Corpus iuris canonici*, ii, Leipzig (1881)

Decretales Pseudo-Isidorianae et capitula Angilramni, ed. P. Hinschius, Leipzig (1863)

De expugnatione Lyxbonensi: The Conquest of Lisbon, ed. C. W. David, New York (1936)

Deusdedit, *Die Kanonessammlung des Kardinals Deusdedit*, ed. V. W. von Glanvell, Paderborn (1905); repr. Aalen (1967)

Diplomata Hungariae antiquissimae, ed. Gy. Györffy, Budapest (1992)

I diplomi della cattedrale di Messina, ed. R. Starraba (Documenti per Servire alla Storia di Sicilia, ser. 1, 1), Palermo (1876–90)

I diplomi greci ed arabi di Sicilia, ed. S. Cusa, Palermo (1860)

Il diretto romano nelle legge normanne e sueve del regno di Sicilia, ed. F. Brandileone, Turin (1884)

'Divisio regnorum', ed. *MGH Capitularia regum Francorum*, i, Hanover (1883), no. 45, pp. 126–30

Documentación medieval de Leire (siglos IX a XII), ed. A. J. Martín Duque, Pamplona (1983)

Documentación del monasterio de San Juan de Burgos (1091–1400), ed. F. J. Peña Pérez, Burgos (1983)

La documentación pontificia hasta Inocencio III (965–1216), ed. D. Mansilla, Rome (1955)

Documentos medievais Portugueses: documentos regios, ed. R. P. de Azevedo, i, Lisbon (1958)

Documentos medievales de la catedral de Avila, ed. A. Barrios García, Salamanca (1981)

Domesday Book, ed. A. Farley, 4 vols., London (1783–1816)

Eadmer, *Historia novorum in Anglia*, ed. M. Rule (RS 81) London (1884)

Early Records of the Burgh of Aberdeen, ed. W. C. Dickinson, Edinburgh (1957)

Early Scottish Charters prior to AD 1153, ed. A. C. Lawrie, Glasgow (1905)

Early Sources of Scottish History, AD 500–1286, ed. A. O. Anderson, Stamford (1922; repr. 1990)

Edward Grim, 'Vita S. Thomae, Cantuariensis archiepiscopi', in *Materials*, II, pp. 353–450

Ekkehard, 'Chronicon universale', *MGH S*, VI, pp. 33–265

Episcopal Acts and Cognate Documents relating to Welsh Dioceses, 1066–1272, trans. J. Conway Davies, 2 vols., Cardiff (1946–8)

Epistolae Cantuarienses, in W. Stubbs (ed.), *Chronicles and Memorials of the Reign of Richard I*, II (RS 38/2), London (1865)

Epistolae pontificum Romanorum ineditae, ed. S. Loewenfeld, Leipzig (1885)

Eugenius III, 'Epistolae', *PL* 180, cols. 1013–1606

Florence of Worcester, *Chronicon ex Chronicis*, ed. B. Thorpe, 2 vols., London (1848–9); *The Chronicle of Florence of Worcester with Two Continuations*, ed. T. Forester, London (1854)

Fontes Byzantini historiae Hungaricae aevo ducum et regum ex stirpe Árpád descedentium, ed. Gy. Moravcsik, Budapest (1984)

Frederick I, Emperor, *Carmen de gestis Frederici I. imperatoris in Lombardia*, ed. I. Schmale-Ott, *MGH SRG*, LXII

Frederick I, Emperor, *Quellen zur Geschichte des Kreuzzuges Kaiser Friedrichs I*, ed. A. Chroust, *MGH SRG NS*, V

Frederick I, Emperor, *Die Urkunden Friedrichs I*, ed. H. Appelt *et al.*, *MGH Diplomata* X/1–5

Fulbert of Chartres, *The Letters and Poems*, ed. F. Behrends, Oxford (1976)

Fulcher of Chartres, *Historia Hierosolymitana*, ed. H. Hagenmeyer, Heidelberg (1913)

Fueros de Navarra, ed. J. M. Lacarra and A. J. Martín Duque, 2 vols., Pamplona (1969–75)

Geoffrey Malaterra, *De rebus gestis Rogerii Calabriae et Siciliae comitis*, ed. E. Pontieri, *RIS NS* 5/1, Bologna (1927–8)

Geoffrey of Monmouth, *Historia regum Britannie*, I–V, ed. N. Wright and J. C. Crick, Cambridge (1985–91); trans. L. Thorpe, *Geoffrey of Monmouth: The History of the Kings of Britain*, Harmondsworth (1966)

Geoffrey of Vigeois, 'Chronica', in P. Labbe (ed.), *Novae bibliothecae manuscriptorum*, II, Paris (1657), pp. 279–343; *Chronique de Geoffrey, prieur de Vigeois*, ed. F. Bonnelye, Tulle (1864)

Geoffrey of Villehardouin, *La conquête de Constantinople*, ed. E. Faral, 2 vols., Paris (1938; repr. 1973)

Gerald of Wales, *Expugnatio Hibernica: The Conquest of Ireland*, ed. and trans. A. B. Scott and F. X. Martin, Dublin (1978)

Gerald of Wales, *The Journey through Wales and the Description of Wales*, trans. L. Thorpe, Harmondsworth (1978)

Gerald of Wales, *Opera*, ed. J. S. Brewer, J. F. Dimock and G. F. Warner, 8 vols. (RS 21), London (1861–91)

Gerald of Wales, *De principis instructione liber*, ed. G. F. Warner (RS 21.8), London (1891)

Gerald of Wales, *Topographia Hiberniae*, trans. J. J. O'Meara, Dundalk (1951); 2nd edn Harmondsworth (1982)

Gerhoch of Reichersberg, 'Commentarius aureus in psalmos', *PL* 193, cols. 621–1814; 194, cols. 9–998

Gerhoch of Reichersberg, 'Ex commentario in Psalmos', *MGH Libelli*, III, pp. 411–502

Gerhoch of Reichersberg, 'Libellus de ordine donorum Sancti Spiritus', *MGH Libelli*, III, pp. 273–83

Gerlac of Milevsko, 'Chronicon sive Continuatio chronicae Vincentii Pragensis', *MGH S*, XVII, pp. 683–710

Gervase of Canterbury, *The Historical Works of Gervase of Canterbury*, ed. W. Stubbs, 2 vols. (RS 73), London (1879–80)

Die 'Gesta Hungarorum' des anonymen Notars: Die älteste Darstellung der ungarischen Geschichte, ed. G. Silagi and L. Veszprémy (Ungarns Geschichtschreiber 4), Sigmaringen (1991)

'Gesta pontificum Autissiodorensium', ed. L.-M. Duru, *Bibliothèque Historique de l'Yonne*, I, Auxerre (1850)

Gesta regis Henrici Secundi, ed. W. Stubbs, 2 vols. (RS 49), London (1867)

Gesta Stephani, ed. K. Potter, Oxford (1976)

Gilbert Foliot, *The Letters and Charters of Gilbert Foliot*, ed. Z. N. Brooke, A. Morey and C. N. L. Brooke, Cambridge (1967)

Giraldus Cambrensis, *see* Gerald of Wales

Gislebert of Mons, *Chronicon Hanoniense*, ed. L. Vanderkindere, Brussels (1904)

Glanvill, *Tractatus de legibus et consuetudinibus regni Anglie qui Glanvilla vocatur*, ed. G. D. G. Hall, London (1965)

Godfrey of Viterbo, 'Opera', *MGH S*, XXII, pp. 1–338

Les Grandes Croniques de Bretagne, ed. A. Bouchart, Rennes (1886)

Gratian, *Decretum*, in E. A. Friedberg (ed.), *Corpus iuris canonici*, Leipzig (1879)

Gregory VII, *Quellen und Forschungen zum Urkunden- und Kanzleiwesen Papst Gregors VII*, I: *Quellen: Urkunden, Regesten, Faksimilia*, ed. L. Santifaller (Studi e Testi 190), Vatican City (1957)

Gregory VII, *Das Register Gregors VII*, ed. E. Caspar, 2nd edn, *MGH Epp. sel.*, II, 2 Berlin

Gregory VIII, 'Epistolae', *PL* 202, cols. 1537–64

Guibert of Nogent, *Dei gesta per Francos*, ed. R. B. C. Huygens (CCCM 127a), Turnhout 1996

Guy, bishop of Amiens, *Carmen de Hastingæ Prælio*, ed. F. Barlow, Oxford (1999)

Hariulf, 'Vita S. Arnulfi episcopi Suessionensis', *PL* 174, cols. 1367–440

Helmold of Bosau, *Chronica Slavorum*, ed. B. Schmeidler, *MGH SRG*, XXXII; trans. F. J. Tschan, *The Chronicle of the Slavs by Helmold, Priest of Bosau*, New York (1935)

Henry IV, *Die Briefe*, ed. C. Erdmann and N. Fickermann, *MGH Epistolae*, V

Henry of Huntingdon, *Historia Anglorum: The History of the English People*, ed. D. Greenway (Oxford Medieval Texts), Oxford (1996); also ed. T. Arnold (RS 74), London (1879)

Henry the Lion, *Die Urkunden Heinrichs des Löwen Herzogs von Sachsen und Bayern*, ed. K. Jordan, *MGH Die deutschen Geschichtsquellen des Mittelalters*, I, *Urkundentexte*, Stuttgart (1957)

Henry of Marcy, abbot of Clairvaux, 'Epistolae', *PL* 204, cols. 215–52

Histoire de Guillaume le Marechal, ed. P. Meyer, 3 vols., Paris (1891–1901)

Historia Compostellana, ed. E. Falque (CCCM 70), Turnhout (1988)

'Historia dedicationis ecclesiae S. Remigii apud Remos', ed. J. Mabillon, *Acta Sanctorum O.S.B.* 6 (1) (1701), 711–27

La Historia o Liber de regno Sicilie di Ugo Falcando, ed. G. B. Siragusa (FSI 22), Rome (1897)

Historia monasterii sancti Augustini Cantuariensis, ed. C. Hardwick (RS 8), London (1858)

'Historia Roderici', ed. E. Falque in *Chronica Hispana saec. XII* (CCCM 71), Turnhout (1990), pp. 1–102

Historia Silense, ed. J. Pérez de Urbel and A. González Ruiz-Zorrilla, Madrid (1959)

The History of Gruffydd ap Cynan, ed. and trans. A. Jones, Manchester (1910)

Hugh the Chanter, *The History of the Church of York 1066–1127*, ed. C. Johnson, M. Brett, C. N. L. Brooke, M. Winterbottom, Oxford (1990)

Hugh of Fleury, 'Modernum regum Francorum acta', *MGH S*, IX, pp. 376–95

Hugh of St-Victor, 'De sacramentis Christianae fidei', *PL* 176, cols. 173–618

Innocent II, 'Epistolae', *PL* 179, cols. 53–658

Innocent III, *Die Rejister Innocenz' III*, II: *Pratifikatojah 1199/1200*, ed. O. Hageneder *et al.*, Rome and Vienna (197)

Isidore of Seville, *Etymologiarum sive originum libri viginti*, ed. W. M. Lindsay, 2 vols., Oxford (1957–62)

Iter Italicum, ed. J. Pflugk-Harttung, Stuttgart (1883)

Itinerarium peregrinorum et gesta regis Ricardi, in W. Stubbs (ed.), *Chronicles and Memorials of the Reign of Richard I*, I (RS 38), London (1864)

Ivo of Chartres, 'Epistolae', *PL* 162, cols. 11–288

Jocelin of Brakelond, *The Chronicle of Jocelin of Brakelond*, ed. H. E. Butler, London (1949); *Chronicle of the Abbey of Bury St Edmunds*, ed. D. Greenway and J. Sayers, Oxford (1989)

John of Cornwall, 'Eulogium ad Alexandrum papam tertium', ed. N. M. Haring, *Medieval Studies* 13 (1951), 253–300

John of Hexham, 'Historia', in T. Arnold (ed.), *Symeonis Monachi opera omnia*, II (RS 75), London (1885), pp. 284–332

John of Salisbury, *Historia pontificalis*, ed. M. Chibnall, London (1956; repr. Oxford, 1986)

John of Salisbury, *The Letters of John of Salisbury*, I, ed. W. J. Millor, H. E. Butler and C. N. L. Brooke, London (1955; repr. 1986); II, ed. W. J. Millor and C. N. L. Brooke, Oxford (1979)

John of Salisbury, *Metalogicon*, ed. C. J. Webb, Oxford (1929)

John of Salisbury, *Policraticus*, ed. C. J. Webb, 2 vols., Oxford (1909)

John of Worcester, *Chronicle, 1118–1140*, ed. J. Weaver, Oxford (1908)

Jordan Fantosme, *Chronique de la guerre entre les Anglois et les Ecossois en 1173 et 1174*, in R. Howlett (ed.), *Chronicles of the Reigns of Stephen, Henry II and Richard I*, III (RS 82), London (1886), pp. 202–327; *Jordan Fantosme's Chronicle*, ed. R. C. Johnston, Oxford (1981)

Lanfranc, *The Letters of Lanfranc*, ed. and trans. H. Clover and M. T. Gibson, Oxford (1979)

Latin Redaction A of the Law of Hywel, trans. I. F. Fletcher, Aberystwyth (1986)

The Latin Texts of the Welsh Laws, ed. H. D. Emanuel, Cardiff (1967)

The Law of Hywel Dda: Law Texts from Medieval Wales, trans. D. Jenkins, Llandysul (1986)

The Laws of the Medieval Kingdom of Hungary, I: *1000–1301*, ed. and trans. J. M. Bak, Gy. Bónis and J. R. Sweeney, Bakersfield, CA (1989)

Layettes du trésor des chartes, ed. A. Teulet, H.-F. Delaborde, E. Berger, 5 vols., Paris (1863–1909)

Le Liber censuum de l'église romaine, ed. P. Fabre and L. Duchesne (Bibliothèque des Ecoles Françaises d'Athènes et de Rome 2, série 3), 3 vols., Paris (1886–1952)

Liber diurnus Romanorum pontificum, ed. T. E. von Sickel, Vienna (1889)

Le Liber pontificalis: texte, introduction et commentaire, ed. L. Duchesne, 3 vols. (Bibliothèque des Ecoles Françaises d'Athènes et de Rome 2, série 2), Paris (1886–1957)

Libri sancti Jacobi: codex Calixtinus, I: *Text*, ed. W. M. Whitehill, Santiago de Compostela (1944)

Llyfr Cyfnerth: Welsh Medieval Law, ed. and trans. A. W. Wade-Evans, Oxford (1909)

Llyfr Iorwerth, ed. A. Rh. William, Cardiff (1960)

Lothar III, Emperor, *Die Urkunden Lothars III. und die Kaiserin Richenza*, ed. E. von Ottenthal and H. Hirsch, *MGH Diplomata*, VIII

Lucas of Tuy, *Chronicon mundi*, ed. A. Schottus, *Hispania illustrata*, IV, Frankfurt (1608)

Lucius II, 'Epistolae', *PL* 179, cols. 823–936

Lucius III, 'Epistolae', *PL* 201, cols. 1071–1378

Magnum rotulum scaccarii 31 Henry I, ed. J. Hunter, London (1833)

Materials for the History of Thomas Becket, Archbishop of Canterbury, ed. J. C. Robertson and J. B. Sheppard, 7 vols. (RS 67/1–7), London (1875–85)

Medieval Church Councils in Scotland, ed. D. E. R. Watt, Edinburgh (2000)

Miracula sancti Benedicti, Paris (1858)

Monumenta Corbeiensia, ed. P. Jaffé (Bibliotheca Rerum Germanicarum I), Berlin (1864)

Monumenta ecclesiae Strigoniensis, ed. F. Knauz and L. C. Dedek, 3 vols., Strigonii (1874–1924)

'Narratio de electione Lotharii in regem Romanorum', *MGH S*, XII, pp. 509–12

'Narratio de itinere navali peregrinorum Hierosolymam tendentium ad Silviam capientium, AD 1189', ed. C. W. David, *Proceedings of the American Philosophical Society* 81 (1939), 591–671

Normannische Herzogs- und Königsurkunden aus Unteritalien und Sizilien, ed. L. von Heinemann, Tübingen (1899)

Odo of Deuil, *De profectione Ludovici VII in orientem*, ed. V. G. Berry, New York (1948)

Orderic Vitalis, *Historia aecclesiastica*, ed. M. Chibnall, 6 vols., Oxford (1969–80)

Orkneyinga Saga, trans. H. P. Pálsson and P. Edwards, Harmondsworth (1982)

Otto III, *Die Urkunden, MGH Diplomata*, II/1

Otto of Freising, *Chronica sive Historia de duabus civitatibus*, ed. A. Hofmeister, *MGH SRG*, XLV; trans. C. C. Mierow, *The Two Cities: A Chronicle of Universal History to the Year 1146 AD by Otto, Bishop of Freising*, new edn, New York (1966)

Otto of Freising and Rahewin, *Gesta Friderici imperatoris*, ed. B. von Simson, *MGH SRG*, xlvi; trans. C. C. Mierow and R. Emery, *The Deeds of Frederick Barbarossa by Otto of Freising and his Continuator Rahewin*, New York (1953)

Otto Morena, *Das Geschichtswerk des Otto Morena und seiner Fortsetzer über die Taten Friedrichs I. in der Lombardei*, ed. F. Güterbock, *MGH SRG NS*, vii

Otto of St Blasien, *Chronicon*, ed. A Hofmeister, *MGH SRG*, xlvii

Papsturkunden in England, ed. W. Holtzmann (Abhandlungen der Gesellschaft der Wissenschaften zu Göttingen, Phil.-Hist. Klasse), Berlin (1930–52)

Papsturkunden in Spanien, ed. P. F. Kehr (Abhandlungen der Gesellschaft der Wissenschaften zu Göttingen, Phil.-Hist. Klasse), Berlin (1926–8)

Paul of Bernried, 'Vita Gregorii VII papae', ed. J. M. Watterich, *Pontificum Romanorum vitae*, I. Leipzig (1862), pp. 474–546

Pelayo of Oviedo, *Crónica*, ed. B. Sánchez Alonso, Madrid (1924)

Le Pergamene dell'archivio vescovile di Caiazzo (1007–1265), ed. C. Salvati, M. Arpago *et al.*, Caserta (1983)

Peter of Blois, 'Epistolae', *PL* 207, cols. 1–560

Peter of Blois, 'De Hierosolymitana peregrinatione acceleranda', *PL* 207, cols. 1057–70

Peter the Chanter, 'Verbum abbreviatum', *PL* 205, cols. 23–370

Peter Damian, *Die Briefe*, ed. K. Reindel, *MGH Epistolae*, iv, 4 parts

Peter of Eboli, *Liber ad honorem Augusti di Pietro da Eboli*, ed. G. B. Siragusa, FSI, 39 (1906)

Peter the Venerable, *Letters*, ed. G. Constable, *The Letters of Peter the Venerable*, 2 vols. (Harvard Historical Studies 78), Cambridge, MA (1967)

Poema de mio Cid, ed. C. Smith, Oxford (1972)

Prefatio de Almeria, ed. J. Gil, *Chronica Hispana saec.XII* (CCCM 71), Turnhout (1990)

Le Premier Budget de la monarchie française: le compte général de 1202–1203, ed. F. Lot and R. Fawtier (Bibliothèque de l'Ecole des Hautes Etudes, Sciences Historiques et Philogiques 259), Paris (1932)

Radulf Glaber, *Historia*, ed. J. France, Oxford (1989)

Rahewin, *Gesta Friderici imperatoris*, *MGH SRG*, xlvi

Ralph of Coggeshall, *Chronicon Anglicanum*, ed. J. Stevenson (RS 66), London (1875)

Ralph of Diceto, 'Ex ymaginibus historiarum', ed. W. Stubbs, *Radulfi de Diceto decani Londoniensis opera historica*, i–ii (RS 68), London (1876)

Ralph Niger, *Chronica*, ed. R. Anstruther (Caxton Society 13), London (1851)

Recueil des actes de Louis VI, ed. J. Dufour, 4 vols. (Chartes et Diplômes Relatifs à l'Histoire de France), Paris (1992–4)

Recueil des actes de Philippe Auguste, ed. H.-F. Delaborde, C. Petit-Dutaillis, J. Boussard and M. Nortier, 4 vols. (Chartes et Diplômes Relatifs à l'Histoire de France), Paris (1916–79)

Recueil des actes de Philippe Ier, ed. M. Prou (Chartes et Diplômes Relatifs à l'Histoire de France), Paris (1908)

Recueil des chartes de l'abbaye de Cluny, ed. A. Bernard and A. Bruel, 6 vols., Paris (1876–1903)

Recueil des jugements de l'échiquier de Normandie au XIIIe siècle 1207–1270, ed. L. Delisle, Paris (1864)

Regesta pontificum Romanorum ab condita ecclesia ad annum post Christum natum MCX-CVIII, ed. P. Jaffé, 2nd edn, ed. S. Loewenfeld, F. Kaltenbrunner and P. Ewald, 2 vols., Leipzig (1885–8)

Regesta pontificum Romanorum: Italia pontificia, i–iii: (*Roma, Latium, Etruria*), ed. P. F. Kehr, Berlin (1906–8)

Regesta regum Scottorum, ed. G. W. S. Barrow *et al.*, Edinburgh (1960)

Les Registres de Philippe Auguste, ed. J. W. Baldwin, F. Gasparri, M. Nortier and E. Lalou, 1 vol. so far (Recueil des Historiens de la France, Documents Financières et Administratives 7), Paris (1992–)

Rerum Hungaricarum monumenta Arpadiana, ed. S. L. Endlicher, Sangalli (1849)

Richard of Devizes, *The Chronicle*, ed. J. T. Appleby, London (1963)

Richard fitz Neal, *Dialogus de Scaccario*, ed. C. Johnson, Oxford (1983)

Richard of S. Germano, 'Chronica regni Siciliae', *MGH S*, xix, pp. 321–84

Rigord and William le Breton, *Œuvres de Rigord et de Guillaume le Breton*, ed. H.-F. Delaborde, 2 vols., Paris (1882–5)

Robert of Auxerre, 'Chronicon', in *MGH S*, xxvi, pp. 219–76

Robert of Torigny, *Chronica*, in R. Howlett (ed.), *Chronicles of the Reigns of Stephen, Henry II and Richard I*, iv (RS 82), London (1889); *Chronique de Robert de Torigni*, ed. L. Delisle, 2 vols., Rouen (1872–3)

Rodrigo Jiménez de Rada (or of Toledo), *Historia de rebus Hispanie sive Historia Gothica*, ed. J. Fernández Valverde (CCCM 72), Turnhout (1987)

Roger of Howden, *Chronica*, ed. W. Stubbs, 4 vols. (RS 51/1–4), London (1868–71)

(Roger of Howden), *Gesta regis Henrici II*, ed. W. Stubbs (RS 49/1–2), London (1867)

Roger of Wendover, *Flores historiarum*, ed. H. G. Hewlett, 3 vols. (RS 84), London (1886–9)

Rogerii II regis diplomata Latina, ed. C.-R. Brühl (Codex Diplomaticus Regni Siciliae, ser. 1, ii. 1), Cologne (1987)

Roland, 'Stroma ex decretorum corpore carptum', in F. Thaner (ed.) *Die Summa magistri Rolandi, nachmals Papst Alexander III.*, Innsbruck (1874), pp. 1–4

Roland, *Summa*, ed. F. Thaner, *Die Summa magistri Rolandi, nachmals Papst Alexander III.*, Innsbruck (1874)

Romuald of Salerno, 'Annales', in *MGH S*, xix, pp. 387–461; also *Chronica sive annales*, ed. C. A. Garufi (*RIS NS* 7/1), Città di Castello (1909–35)

Rufinus, *Die Summa decretorum des Magister Rufinus*, ed. H. Singer and F. Schöningh, Paderborn (1902)

Rufinus of Assisi, 'Sermo habitus in Lateranensi concilio sub Alexandro papa III', ed. G. Morin, in 'Le discours d'ouverture du concile général de Latran (1179) et l'œuvre littéraire de maître Rufin, évêque d'Assise', *Atti della Pontificia Accademia Romana di Archeologia*, ser. 3, memorie 2, Rome (1928), pp. 113–33

Sacrorum conciliorum nova et amplissima collectio, ed. G. D. Mansi, 31 vols., Florence and Venice (1759–98)

Scotia pontificia: Papal Letters to Scotland before the Pontificate of Innocent III, ed. R. Somerville, Oxford (1982)

Scottish Annals from English Chroniclers AD 500–1286, ed. A. O. Anderson, London (1908; repr. 1991)

'Scripta de feodis ad regem spectantibus et de militibus ad exercitum vocandis e Philippi Augusti registis excerpta', *RHGF*, XXIII, pp. 605–723

Scriptores rerum Hungaricarum, ed. E. Szentpétery, 2 vols., Budapest (1937–8)

Sheriff Court Book of Fife, ed. W. C. Dickinson, Edinburgh (1928)

Sigebert of Gembloux, 'Continuatio', *MGH S*, VI, pp. 375–535

Simeon of Durham, *Opera omnia*, ed. T. Arnold, 2 vols. (RS 75), London (1882–5)

The Song of Dermot and the Earl, ed. G. H. Orpen, Oxford (1892)

Stephen of Rouen, 'Draco Normannicus', in R. Howlett (ed.), *Chronicles of the Reigns of Stephen, Henry II and Richard I*, II (RS 82), London (1885), pp. 585–781

Stephen of Tournai, *Summa*, ed. J. F. von Schulte, Giessen (1891)

Suger, 'Histoire du roi Louis VII', in A. Molinier (ed.), *Vie de Louis le Gros* (Collection de Textes pour Servir à l'Etude et de l'Enseignement de l'Histoire), Paris (1887)

Suger of St Denis, *Vita Ludovici grossi regis*, ed. H. Waquet (Les Classiques de l'Histoire de France au Moyen Age II), Paris (1929; repr. 1964)

Summa Parisiensis, in T. P. McLaughlin (ed.), *The Summa Parisiensis on the Decretum Gratiani*, Toronto (1952)

'The Templars and the castle of Tortosa in Syria: an unknown document concerning the acquisition of the fortress', ed. J. Riley-Smith, *EHR* 84 (1969), 278–88

The Text of the Book of Llan Dâv, Reproduced from the Gwysaney Manuscript, ed. J. G. Evans and J. Rhys, Oxford (1893); trans. W. J. Rees, *Liber Landavensis*, Llandovery (1840)

Urban II, *The Councils of Urban II: Decreta Claromontensia*, ed. R. Somerville, (Annuarium Historiae Conciliorum Supplementum I), Amsterdam (1972)

Usatges de Barcelona i Commemoracions de Pere Albert, ed. J. Rovira i Ermengol, Barcelona (1933)

Vincent of Prague, 'Annales', *MGH S*, XVII, pp. 658–83

'Vita Norberti archiepiscopi Magdeburgensis', *MGH S*, XII, pp. 670–703

Vitae sanctorum Britanniae et genealogiae, ed. and trans. A. W. Wade-Evans, Cardiff (1944)

Vorarbeiten zum Oriens pontificus III: Papsturkunden für Kirchen im Heiligen Lande, ed. R. Hiestand, Abhandlungen der Akademie der Wissenschaften in Göttingen (Philologisch-Historische Klasse, ser. 3, no. 136), Göttingen (1985)

Walter Bower, *Scotichronicon*, ed. and trans. J. and W. MacQueen, Aberdeen (1993–)

Walter of Châtillon, 'Carmina', *MGH Libelli*, III, pp. 555–60

Walter Map, *De nugis curialium*, ed. M. R. James, R. A. B. Mynors and C. N. L. Brooke, Oxford (1983)

The Welsh Law of Women, ed. and trans. D. Jenkins and M. E. Owen, Cardiff (1980)

William I of Sicily, *Guillelmi I regis diplomata*, ed. H. Enzensberger (Codex Diplomaticus Regni Siciliae, ser. I.iii), Cologne (1996)

William of Apulia, *La Geste de Robert Guiscard*, ed. M . Mathieu, Palermo (1961)

William fitz Stephen, *Vita sancti Thomae Cantuariensis*, in *Materials*, III, pp. 1–154; and in *The Life and Death of Thomas Becket*, ed. D. Greenway, London (1961)

William of Jumièges, *Gesta Normannorum ducum*, ed. E. M. C. van Houts, 2 vols., Oxford (1992–5)

William of Malmesbury, *De gestis regum Anglorum*, ed. W. Stubbs, 2 vols. (RS 90), London (1887–9); new edn R. A. B. Mynors, R. M. Thomson and M. Winterbottom, I, Oxford (1998)

William of Malmesbury, *Historia novella*, ed. K. R. Potter, Edinburgh and London (1955)

William of Newburgh, *Historia rerum anglicarum*, in R. Howlett (ed.) *Chronicles of the Reigns of Stephen, Henry II and Richard I*, I–II (RS 82), London (1884–5); *The History of English Affairs, Book I*, ed. P. G. Walsh and M. J. Kennedy, Warminster (1988)

William of Poitiers, *Gesta Guillelmi ducis Normannorum et regis Anglorum*, ed. R. H. C. Davis and M. Chibnall, Oxford (1998)

William of St-Denis, 'Vita Sugerii abbatis', *PL* 186, cols. 1193–1208

Wipo, 'Vita Chuonradi', *MGH S*, XI, pp. 254–75

BYZANTINE SOURCES (INCLUDING RUS', BULGARIA, SERBIA AND EASTERN CHURCHES)

Editions and translations

Alexios Komnenos

Maas, P., 'Die Musen des Alexios I', *BZ* 22 (1913), 348–69

Anna Komnena

Anna Comnena, Alexiad: Anne Comnène, Alexiade, ed. B. Leib and P. Gautier, 4 vols., Paris (1937–76; repr. 1967). Two English translations are by E. A. S. Dawes, *The Alexiad of the Princess Anna Comnena*, London (1928), and E. R. A. Sewter, *The Alexiad of Anna Comnena*, London (1969)

Anonyme Metaphrase zu Anna Komnene, Alexias XI–XIII, ed. H. Hunger (Wiener Byzantinistische Studien 15), Vienna (1981)

Reinsch, D. R., 'Die *editio princeps* eines Auszugs aus den *Alexias* Anna Komnenes aus dem Jahr 1562: ein unabhängiger überlieferungsträger', *BZ* 84/5 (1991–2), 12–16

Anon.

Un traité de vie spirituelle et morale au XIe siècle: le florilège sacroprofane du manuscrit 6 de Patmos, ed. E. Sargologos, Asprovalta and Thessalonica (1990)

Bar Hebraeus

Bar Hebraeus (Gregory Abu'l-Faraj), *The Chronography*, ed. and trans. E. A. W. Budge, 2 vols., London (1932)

Christopher of Mitylene

I calendari in metro innografico di Cristoforo Mitileneo, ed. E. Follieri (Subsidia Hagiographica 63), 2 vols., Brussels (1980)

Cristoforo di Mitilene, Canzoniere, ed. R. Anastasi, Catania (1983)

Die Gedichte des Christophoros Mytilenaios, ed. E. Kurtz, Leipzig (1903)

Eustratios of Nicaea

Joannou, P., 'Die Definition des Seins bei Eustratios von Nikaia', *BZ* 47 (1954), 365–8

Joannou, P., 'Der Nominalismus und die menschliche Psychologie Christi', *BZ* 47 (1954), 369–78

Joannou, P., 'Le sort des évêques réconciliés', *Byzantion* 28 (1958), pp. 1–30

John the Deacon and Maistor

Gouillard, J., 'Léthargie des âmes et culte des saints: un plaidoyer inédit de Jean diacre et maïstor', *TM* 8 (1981), 171–86

John Italos

Gouillard, J., 'Une lettre de (Jean) l'Italien au patriarche de Constantinople?', *TM* 9 (1985), 175–9

Gouillard, J., 'Les procès officiel de Jean l'Italien: les actes et leurs sous-entendus', *TM* 9 (1985), 133–74

Ioannis Itali opera, ed. N. Kechkmadze, Tbilisi (1966)

Quæstiones quodlibertales (ΑΠΟΡΙΑΙ ΚΑΙ ΛΥΣΕΙΣ), ed. P. Joannou, Ettal (1956)

Romano, R., 'Un opuscolo inedito di Giovanni Italo', *Bollettino dei Classici*, ser. iii. 13 (1992), 14–24

John Kinnamos

John Kinnamos, *Epitome*, ed. A Meinecke (Corpus Scriptorum Historiae Byzantinae 9), Bonn (1836)

John Cinnamus, *Deeds of John and Manuel Comnenus*, trans. C. M. Brand, New York (1976)

John Mauropous

Anastasi, R., 'Il "Canzoniere" di Giovanni di Euchaita', *Siculorum Gymnasium*, n.s. 22 (1969), 109–44

Follieri, E., 'Altri testi della pietà bizantina. II. Giovanni Maurope, metropolita di Eucaita: Otto canoni paracletici a N.S. Gesù Cristo', *Archivio Italiano per la Storia della Pietà*, 5 (1968), 1–200

Giovanni Mauropode metropolita di Euchaita, Canzoniere, trans. R. Anastasi, Catania (1984)

The Letters of Ioannes Mauropous, metropolitan of Euchaita, ed. A. Karpozilos (Corpus Fontium Historiae Byzantinae, 34, series Thessalonicensis), Thessalonica (1990)

John Oxites

Gautier, P., 'Diatribes de Jean l'Oxite contre Alexis Ier Comnène', *REB* 28 (1970), 5–55

Gautier, P., 'Jean V l'Oxite, patriarche d'Antioche: notice biographique', *REB* 22 (1964), 128–57

Gautier, P., 'Réquisitoire du patriarche Jean d'Antioche contre le charisticariat', *REB* 33 (1975), 77–132

Leib, B., 'Deux inédits byzantins sur les azymes au début du XIIe siècle', *Orientalia Christiana* 2 (1924), 244–63

Spadaro, M. G., 'Sui ff.174-183 del cod. *Vat.gr.* 840', *Siculorum Gymnasium* n.s. 26 (1973), 363–86

John Skylitzes
Ioannis Scylitzae Synopsis historiarum, ed. I. Thurn (Corpus Fontium Byzantinae 5, series Berolinensis), Berlin and New York (1973); German trans. H. Thurn, *Byzanz, wieder ein Weltreich* (Byzantinische Geschichtsschreiber), Graz, Vienna and Cologne (1983)
Η ΣΥΝΕΧΕΙΑ ΤΗΣ ΧΡΟΝΟΓΡΑΦΙΑΣ ΤΟΥ ΙΩΑΝΝΟΥ ΣΚΥΛΙΤΖΗ (Ioannes Skylitzes Continuatus), ed. E. T. Tsolakis, Thessalonica (1968)

John Zonaras
Jacobs, A., *ΖΩΝΑΡΑΣ–ZONARA. Die byzantinische Geschichte bei Joannes Zonaras in slavischer Übersetzung* (Slavische Propyläen 98), Munich (1970)
John Zonaras, *Epitome historiarum*, ed. M. Pinder and M. Büttner-Wobst, 3 vols., Bonn (1841–97); ed. L. Dindorf, 6 vols., Leipzig (1868–75)
Trapp, E., *Militärs und Höflinge im Ringen um das Kaisertum: Byzantinische Geschichte von 969–1118* (Byzantinische Geschichtsschreiber 16), Graz, Vienna and Cologne (1986)

Kekaumenos
Cecaumeni strategicon et incerti scriptoris de officiis regiis libellus, ed. B. Wassiliewsky and V. Jernstedt, St Petersburg (1896); *Soviety i rasskazy Kevavmena: Sochinenie vizantijskogo polkovodtsa XI veka*, ed. G. G. Litavrin, Moscow (1972). German trans. H.-G. Beck, *Vademecum des byzantinischen Aristokraten: Das sogennante Strategikon des Kekaumenos* (Byzantinische Geschichtsschreiber 5), Graz, Vienna and Cologne (1956)

Leo of Preslav
Poppe, A., 'Le traité des azymes ΛΕΟΝΤΟΣ ΜΗΤΡΟΠΟΛΙΤΟΥ ΤΗΣ ΕΝ ΡΩΣΙΑ(Ι) ΠΡΕΣΛΑΒΑΣ quand, où et par a-t-il été écrit', *Byzantion* 35 (1965), 504–27

Manuel Straboromanos
Gautier, P., 'Le dossier d'un haut fonctionnaire d'Alexis Ier Comnène, Manuel Straboromanos', *REB* 23 (1965), 168–204

Matthew of Edessa
Matthew of Edessa, *Chronique de Matthieu d'Edesse (962–1136) avec la continuation de Grégoire le Prêtre, jusqu'en 1162*, ed. E. Dulaurier (Bibliothèque Historique Arménienne I), Paris (1858)

Michael Attaleiates
Michael Attaleiates, *Historia*, ed. I. Bekker, Bonn (1853)

Michael Cerularius
Darrouzéz, J., 'Un faut ΠΕΡΙ ΑΖΥΜΩΝ de Michael Cérulaire', *REB* 25 (1967), 288–91

Michael Psellos

Agati, M. L., 'Due epistole di Psello a un monaco del Monte Olimpo', in *Studi in onore di G. Valentini*, Florence (1986), pp. 177–90

Agati, M. L., 'Tre epistole inedite di Michele Psello', *Siculorum Gymnasium* 33 (1980), 909–16

Anastasi, R., *Michele Psello, Encomio per Giovanni, piissimo metropolita di Euchaita e protosincello*, Padua (1968)

Criscuolo, U., *Michele Psello, Autobiografia: encomio per la madre*, Naples (1989/90)

Criscuolo, U., *Michele Psello, Epistola a Giovanni Xifilino*, 2nd edn, Naples (1990)

Criscuolo, U., *Michele Psello, Epistola a Michele Cerulario*, 2nd edn, Naples (1990)

Criscuolo, U., *Michele Psello, Orazione in memoria di Constantino Lichudi*, Messina (1983)

Dennis, G. T., *Michaelis Pselli orationes forenses et acta*, Stuttgart and Leipzig (1994)

Dennis, G. T., *Michaelis Pselli orationes panegyricae*, Stuttgart and Leipzig (1994)

Duffy, J. M., *Michaelis Pselli Philosophica minora*, I: *Opuscula logica, physica, allegorica, alia*, Stuttgart and Leipzig (1992)

Dyck, A. R., *Michael Psellus: The Essays on Euripides and George of Pisidia and on Heliodorus and Achilles Tatius* (Byzantina Vindobonensia 16), Vienna (1986)

Feaver, D. D., 'More on medieval poetics', *Classical World* 62 (1969), 14–116

Fisher, E. A., *Michaelis Pselli orationes hagiographicae*, Stuttgart and Leipzig (1994)

Galigani, P., *Il 'De Lapidum virtutibus' di Michele Psello*, Florence (1980)

Garzya, A., 'Un encomio del vino inedito di Michele Psello', *Byzantion* 35 (1965), 418–28

Garzya, A., 'On Michael Psellus' admission of faith', *EEBΣ*, 35 (1966), 41–6

Garzya, A., *Versi e un opuscolo inediti di Michele Psello* (Quaderni di le Parole e le Idee 4), Naples (1966)

Gautier, P., 'Collections inconnues ou peu connues de textes pselliens', *Rivista di Studi Bizantini e Slavi* I (1981), 39–69

Gautier, P., 'La défence de Lazare de Philippoupolis par Michel Psellos', *TM* 8 (1981), 151–69

Gautier, P., 'Deux manuscrits pselliens: le Parisinus graecus 1182 ct le Laurentius graecus 57–40', *REB* 44 (1986), 45–110

Gautier, P., 'Un discours inédit de Michel Psellos sur la crucifixion', *REB* 49 (1991), 5–66

Gautier, P., 'Eloge funèbre de Nicolas de la Belle Source par Michel Psellos moine à l'Olympe', *BYZANTINA* 6 (1974), 9–69

Gautier, P., 'Eloge inédit du lecteur Jean Kroustoulas par Michel Psellos', *Rivista di Studi Bizantini e Neoellenici* n.s. 17–19 (1980–2), 119–47

Gautier, P., 'Lettre au sultan Malik-Shah rédigée par Michel Psellos', *REB* 35 (1977), 73–97

Gautier, P., *Michaelis Pselli Theologica*, I, Stuttgart and Leipzig (1989)

Gautier, P., 'Monodies inédites de Michel Psellos', *REB* 36 (1978), 83–151

Gautier, P., 'Monodie inédite de Michel Psellos sur le Basileus Andronic Doucas', *REB* 24 (1966), 123–70

Gautier, P., 'Un recueil de lettres faussement attribué à Michel Psellos', *REB* 35 (1977), 99–106

Gautier, P., 'Quelques lettres de Psellos inédites ou déjà éditées', *REB* 44 (1986), 111–97

Gemmiti, D., 'Omelia di Psello sull'Annunciazone', *Studi e Ricerche sull'Oriente Cristiano* 7 (1984), 97–164

Guglielmino, A. M., 'Versi di Michele Psello all'imperatore, signore Isaaco Comneno, sulle calende, le none e le idi', *Siculorum Gymnasium* n.s. 27 (1974), 121–33

Joannou, P.-P., *Démonologie populaire – démonologie critique au XIe siècle: la vie inédite de saint Auxence par M. Psellos* (Schriften zur Geistesgeschichte des Östlichen Europa 51), Wiesbaden (1971)

Karpozilos, A., 'ΔΥΟ ΑΝΕΚΔΟΤΕΣ ΕΠΙΣΤΟΛΕΣ ΤΟΥ ΜΙΧΑΗΛ ΨΕΛΛΟΥ', *ΔΩΔΩΝΗ* 9 (1980), 299–310

Littlewood, A. R., *Michaelis Pselli Oratoria minora*, Stuttgart and Leipzig (1985)

Maltese, E. V., 'Epistole inedite di Michele Psello, I, II, III', *Studi Italiani di Filologia Classica*, ser. 3, 5 (1987), 82–98, 214–23; 6 (1988), 110–34

Masullo, R., 'Excerpta neoplatonici inediti di Michele Psello', *Atti Accad. Pontaniana* n.s. 37 (1988), 33–47

Michaelis Pselli Historia Syntomos, ed. W. J. Aerts (Corpus Fontium Historiae Byzantinae 30, series Berolinensis), Berlin and New York (1990)

Michel Psellos, *Chronographie*, ed. E. Renauld, 2 vols., Paris (1926–8; reissued 1967); English trans. E. R. A. Sewter, *Fourteen Byzantine Rulers*, Harmondsworth (1966)

Michele Psello, *Imperatori di Bisanzio (Cronografia)*, ed. S. Impellizzeri, comm. U. Criscuolo, trans. S. Ronchey, introd. D. del Corno, 2 vols., Vicenza (1984)

Musso, O., *Michele Psello, Nozioni Paradossali*, Naples (1977)

Niarchos, C. G., 'John Patricios: Michael Psellos in praise of his student and friend', *BYZANTINA* 11 (1982), 223–42

O'Meara, D. J., *Michaelis Pselli Philosophica Minora*, II: *Opuscula psychologica, theologica, daemonologica*, Stuttgart and Leipzig (1989)

Perusino, F., *Anonimo (Michele Psello?), la tragedia greca*, Urbino (1993)

Pizzari, P., *Michael Psellos, le opere dei demoni*, Palermo (1981)

Snipes, K., 'A letter of Michael Psellos to Constantine the nephew of Michael Cerularios', *Greek, Roman and Byzantine Studies* 22 (1981), 89–107

Snipes, K., 'An unedited treatise of Michael Psellos on the iconography of angels and on the religious festivals celebrated on each day of the week', in *Gonimos: Neoplatonic and Byzantine Studies Presented to L. G. Westerlink at 75*, Buffalo (1988), pp. 189–205

Spadaro, M. D., 'Un chrysobullon Pselliano (Nr. 1023 Dölger)', *Orpheus* 5 (1984), 335–56

Spadaro, M. D., 'Un'epistola di incerta attribuzione (Nr. 202 Sathas) et una semiedita (Nr. 203 Sathas)', *JöB* 30 (1981), 157–67

Spadaro, M. D., 'Un inedito di Psello dal cod.Paris gr.1182', *ΕΛΛΗΝΙΚΑ* 30 (1977–8), 84–98

Spadaro, M. D., *Michaelis Pselli in Mariam Sclerenam*, Catania (1984)

Spadaro, M. D., 'La monodia ΕΙΣ ΤΗΝ ΤΗΣ ΑΓΙΑΣ ΣΟΟΙΑΣ ΣΥΜΠΤΩΣΙΝ atrribuita a Psello', *Siculorum Gymnasium* n.s. 28 (1975), 192–202

Weiss, G., 'Die Leichenrede des Michael Psellos auf den Abt Nikolaos vom Kloster von der Schönen Quelle', *BYZANTINA* 9 (1977), 219–322

Weiss, G., 'Die "Synopsis legum" des Michael Psellos', *Fontes Minores* 2 (1977), 147–214

Westerlink, L. G., *Michaeli Pselli Poemata*, Stuttgart and Leipzig (1992)

Michael the Syrian
Michael the Syrian, *Chronique de Michel le Syrien, patriarche jacobite d'Antioche (1166–1199)*, ed. and trans. J. B. Chabot, 4 vols., Paris (1899–1924)

Nikephoros Bryennios
Nicéphore Bryennios, *Histoire*, ed. P. Gautier (Corpus Fontium Historiae Byzantinae 9, series Bruxellensis), Brussels (1975)

Nikephoros the Chartophylax
Darrouzès, J., 'Une réponse du chartophylax Nicéphore (IXe siècle)', *REB* 22 (1964), 279–80
Gautier, P., 'Le chartophylax Nicéphore: œuvre canonique et notice biographique', *REB* 27 (1969), 159–95

Niketas Choniates
Niketas Choniates, *Historia*, ed. J.-L. van Dieten, 2 vols., Berlin and New York (1975)

Niketas Stethatos
Nicétas Stéthatos, *MYΣTIKA ΣYΓΓΡΑΜΜΑΤΑ*, ed. P. Chrestou, Thessalonica (1959)
Nicétas Stéthatos, *Opuscules et lettres*, ed. J. Darrouzès, Paris (1961)
Nicétas Stéthatos, *Vie de Syméon le Nouveau Théologien (949–1022)*, ed. I. Hausherr (Orientalia Christiana Analecta 14), Rome (1928)

Nicholas Grammatikos
Darrouzès, J., 'L'éloge de Nicolas III par Nicolas Mouzalon', *REB* 46 (1988), 5–53
Darrouzès, J., 'Un faux acte attribué au patriarche Nicolas (III)', *REB* 28 (1970), 221–37
Darrouzès, J., 'Les réponses de Nicolas III à l'évêque de Zeitounion', in J. Chrysostomides (ed.), *KAΘHΓHTPIA*, Camberley (1988), pp. 327–43
Koder, J., 'Das Fastengedicht des Patriarchen Nikolaos III. Grammatikos. Edition des Textes und Untersuchung seiner Stellung innerhalb der byzantinischen Fastenliteratur', *JöB* 19 (1970), 203–41
Papagianne, E. and Troianos, S., 'Die kanonische Antworten des Nikolaos III. Grammatikos an den Bischof von Zetunion', *BZ* 82 (1989), 234–50

Nicholas Kataskepenos
Nicolas Kataskepenos, *La Vie de St. Cyrille de Philéote, moine byzantin (†1110)*, ed. E. Sargologos (Subsidia Hagiographica 39), Brussels (1964)

Nicholas Mouzalon
Doannidou, S., 'Η ΠΑΡΑΙΤΗΣΙΣ ΝΙΚΟΛΑΟΥ ΤΟΥ ΜΟΥΖΑΛΩΝΟΣ ΑΠΟ ΤΗΣ ΑΡΧΙΕΠΙΣΚΟΠΗΣ ΚΥΠΡΟΥ. ΑΝΕΚΔΟΤΟΝ ΑΠΟΛΟΓΗΤΙΚΟΝ ΠΟΙΗΜΑ', *ΕΛΛΗΝΙΚΑ* 7 (1934), 109–50

Nicholas of Andida
Darrouzès J., 'Nicolas d'Andida et les azymes', *REB* 32 (1974), 199–210

Symeon Seth

Sjöberg, L.-O., *Stephanites und Ichnelates*, Stöckholm, Göteburg and Uppsala (1962)

Theodosius Goudelis

Theodosius Goudelis, *The Life of Leontios, Patriarch of Jerusalem*, ed., trans. and comm. D. Tsougarakis (The Medieval Mediterranean 2), Leiden (1993)

Theophylact of Bulgaria

Garton, C., 'Theophylact "On Predestination", a first translation', *Greek, Roman and Byzantine Studies* 14 (1973), 83–102

Gautier, P., 'Le discours de Théophylacte de Bulgarie à l'autocrator Alexis Ier Comnène (6 janvier 1088)', *REB* 20 (1962), 93–130

Gautier, P., *Théophylacte d'Achrida, discours, traités, poésies* (Corpus Fontium Historiae Byzantinae 16/1), Thessalonica (1980)

Gautier, P., *Théophylacte d'Achrida, lettres* (Corpus Fontium Historiae Byzantinae 16/2), Thessalonica (1986)

Timarion

Macleod, M. D., *Luciani Opera*, IV, libellus 86, Oxford (1987)

Romano, R., *Pseudo-Luciano Timarione*, Naples (1974); English trans. B. Baldwin, *Timarion*, Detroit (1984)

Typika

Gautier, P., 'La *diataxis* de Michel Attaleiate', *REB* 39 (1981), 5–143

Gautier, P., 'Le typikon du Christ Sauveur Pantokrator', *REB* 32 (1974), 1–145

Gautier, P., 'Le typikon du sébaste Grégoire Pakourianos', *REB* 42 (1984), 5–146

Gautier, P., 'Le typikon de la Theotokos Evergétis', *REB* 40 (1982), 5–101

Gautier, P., 'Le typikon de la Theotokos Kecharitomène', *REB* 43 (1985), 5–165

MUSLIM (INCLUDING SPANISH) AND ORIENTAL SOURCES

'Abd Allah, *The Tibyan: Memoirs of 'Abd Allah B. Buluggin, Last Zirid Amir of Granada*, trans. A. T. Tibi, Leiden (1986)

Abu Shama, 'Abd al-Rahman ibn Isma'il, *Kitab al-rawdatayn fi akhbar al-dawlatayn al-nuriyya wa l-salahiyya*, 2 vols., Bulaq (AH 1287–92/1871–5)

Abu Shama, 'Abd al-Rahman ibn Isma'il, *Tarajim rijal al-qarnayn al-sadis wa' l-sabi' al-ma 'ruf bi'l-dhal 'ala al-rawdatayn*, ed. M. al-Kawthari, Cairo (1947)

Anonymi auctoris Chronicon ad AC 1234 pertinens, ed. A. Abouna, annotated J.-M. Fiey, Louvain (1974)

al-'Azimi, Muhammad b. 'Ali, 'La chronique abrégée d'al-'Azimi', ed. C. Cahen, *Journal Asiatique* 230 (1938), 353–448; ed. I. Za'rur, *Ta'rikh Halab*, Damascus (1984)

al-Bundari, Fath b. 'Ali, *Zubdat al-nusra wa nukhbat al-'usra*, ed. M. T. Houtsma, *Recueil de textes relatifs à l'histoire des Seljoukides*, II, Leiden (1889)

Christians and Moors in Spain, III: *Arabic Sources (711–1501)*, trans. C. Melville and A. Ubaydli, Warminster (1992)

Fatimid Decrees, ed. S. M. Stern, London (1964)

al-Ghazali, *Al-Munqidh min al-dalal*, Damascus (1939); trans. W. M. Watt, *The Faith and Practice of al-Ghazali*, London (1953)

al-Husayni, Sadr al-Din, *Akhbar al-dawla al-saljuqiyya*, ed. M. Iqbal, Lahore (1933)

Ibn al-ʿAdim, ʿUmar ibn Ahmad, *Bughyat al-talab fi taʾrikh Halab*, ed. Suhayl Zakkar, 11 vols., Damascus (1988)

Ibn al-ʿAdim, ʿUmar ibn Ahmad, *Zubdat al-halab min taʾrikh Halab*, ed. Sami al-Dahhan, 3 vols., Damascus (1951–68)

Ibn ʿAsakir, ʿAli ibn al-Hasan, *Taʾrikh madinat Dimashq*, various editors, 14 vols. so far (Arab Academy of Damascus), Damascus (1951–92); complete edn, ʿAli Shiri, 80 vols., Beirut (1995–8); 1, part 2, trans. N. Elisséeff, *La Description de Damas d'Ibn ʿAsakir*, Damascus (1959)

Ibn al-Athir, *Kitab al-kamil fi ʾl-taʾrikh*, ed. C. J. Tornberg (1851–76); revised edn, Ihsan ʿAbbas, 13 vols., Beirut (1965)

Ibn al-Athir, ʿAli ibn Muhammad, *Al-Taʾrikh al-bahir fi al-dawlat al-atabakiyya*, ed. A. A. Tulaymat, Cairo (1963)

Ibn al-Azraq al-Fariqi, Ahmad ibn Yusuf, *Taʾrikh Mayyafariqin wa-Amid*, ed. and trans. C. Hillenbrand, *A Muslim Principality in Crusader Times: The Early Artuqid State*, Leiden (1990)

Ibn Bibi, *Die Seltschukengeschichte des Ibn Bibi*, trans. H. W. Duda, Copenhagen (1959)

Ibn al-Furat, Muhammad ibn ʿAbd al-Rahim, *Taʾrikh al-duwal waʾl-muluk*, I–III, Vienna, Österreichische Nationalbibliothek, AF 117–119; IV, ed. H. al-Shamma, Basra (1967)

Ibn Hamdun, Muhammad ibn al-Hasan, *Al-Tadhkira al-Hamduniyya*, ed. I. ʿAbbas, 10 vols., Beirut (1996)

Ibn Hawqal, *Surat al-ard*, ed. J. H. Kramers, Leiden (1938–9); trans. J. H. Kramers and G. Wiet, *Configuration de la terre*, Paris (1964)

Ibn ʿIdhari, *Al-Bayan al-mughrib*, ed. G. S. Colin and E. Levi-Provençal, 1, Leiden (1948); trans. F. Maillo Salgado as *La caida del Cóifato de Córdoba y los Reyes de Taifas (al-Bayan al-Mugrib)*, Salamanca (1993)

Ibn al-ʿImrani, Muhammad ibn ʿAli, *Kitab al-anbaʾ fi taʾrikh al-khulafaʾ*, ed. Q. al-Samarraʾi, Leiden (1973)

Ibn al-Jawzi, Abu al-Faraj, *Al-Muntazam fi taʾrikh al-muluk waʾl-umam*, 6 vols., Hyderabad (1938–41)

Ibn Jubayr, Muhammad ibn Ahmad, *Tadhkira li-akhbar ʿan ittifaqat al-asfar*, ed. W. Wright, Leiden (1907); trans. R. J. C. Broadhurst, *The Travels of Ibn Jubair*, London (1952); trans. M. Gaudefroy-Demombynes, *Voyages*, 4 vols., Paris (1949–65)

Ibn al-Kardabus, *Historia de al-Andalus*, trans. F. Maillo Salgado, Madrid (1986)

Ibn Khaldun (1967), *The Muqaddimah*, trans. F. Rosenthal, 2nd edn, New York and London (1986)

Ibn Khallikan, *Wafayat al-aʿyan fi anbaʾ abnaʾal-zaman*, ed. Ihsan ʿAbbas, 8 vols., Beirut (1972); trans. Macguckin de Slane, *Ibn Khallikan's Biographical Dictionary*, 4 vols., Paris (1842–71)

Ibn Manzur, Muhammad ibn Mukarram, *Mukhtasar taʾrikh Dimashq li-Ibn ʿAsakir*, various eds., 29 vols., Damascus (1984–9)

Ibn Muyassar, *Akhbar Misr*, ed. A. F. Sayyid, *Choix de passages de la Chronique d'Egypte d'Ibn Muyassar*, Cairo (1981)

Ibn al-Qalanisi, *Dhayl ta'rikh Dimashq*, ed. H. F. Amedroz, Leiden (1908); ed. S. Zakkar, Damascus (1983); partial trans. H. A. R. Gibb, *The Damascus Chronicle of the Crusades*, London (1932); partial trans. R. LeTourneau, *Damas de 1075 à 1154*, Damascus (1952)

Ibn al-Sayrafi, 'Al-Ishara ila man nala al-wizara', ed. A. Mukhlis, *Bulletin de l'Institut Français d'Archéologie Orientale*, 25 (1924), 49–112; 26 (1925), 49–70

Ibn Shaddad, Baha' al-Din Yusuf, *Al-Nawadir al-sultaniyya wa 'l-mahasin al-yusufiyya*, ed. J. al-Shayyal, Cairo (1962); trans. C. W. Wilson and C. R. Conder, *Saladin, or What Befell Sultan Yusuf* (Palestine Pilgrims Text Society 13), London (1897)

Ibn Shaddad, Muhammad ibn 'Ali, *Al-A'laq al-khatira fi dhikr umara 'al-Sham wa 'l-Jazira*: *Aleppo*, ed. D. Sourdel, Damascus (1953); *Damascus*, ed. Sami al-Dahhan, Damascus (1956); *Palestine, Transjordan and Lebanon*, ed. Sami al-Dahhan, Damascus (1963); 'North Syria', ed. A.-M. Eddé, *Bulletin d'Etudes Orientales* 32–3 (1982–3), 264–402, and trans. A.-M. Eddé, *Description de la Syrie du Nord*, Damascus (1984); *Mesopotamia (al-Jazira)*, ed. Y. 'Abbara, 2 vols., Damascus (1977–8)

Ibn Wasil, Muhammad b. Salim, *Mufarrij al-kurub fi akhbar Bani Ayyub*, ed. J. al-Shayyal, S. A. F. 'Ashur and Hasanayn al-Rabi', 6 vols. so far, Cairo (1963–77)

'Imad al-Din al-Katib al-Isfahani, *Al-Barq al-Shami*, abridged by al-Bundari as *Sana al-Barq al-Shami*, ed. R. Nabarawy, Cairo (1979)

'Imad al-Din al-Katib al-Isfahani, *Al-Fath al-qussi fi al-fath al-qudsi*, ed. Carlo de Landberg, Leiden (1888); trans. H. Massé, *Conquête de la Syrie et de la Palestine par Saladin*, Paris (1972)

al-Maqrizi, *Itti'az al-hunafa*, 3 vols., Cairo (1967–73)

al-Maqrizi, *Le Traité des famines de Maqrizi*, trans. G. Wiet, Leiden (1962)

al-Maqrizi, Ahmad ibn 'Ali, *Kitab al-mawa'iz wa'l-i'tibar bi-dhikr al-khitat wa 'l-athar*, 2 vols., Bulaq (AH 1270/1853–4)

al-Maqrizi, Ahmad ibn 'Ali, *Kitab al-suluk fi ma'rifat duwal al-muluk*, 1, ed. M. M. Ziyada, Cairo (1934); trans. of section on Ayyubids by E. Blochet, *Histoire d'Egypte*, Paris (1908), and by R. J. C. Broadhurst, *History of the Ayyubid Sultans of Egypt*, Boston (1980)

al-Mu'ayyad fi 'l-Din al-Shirazi, 'The Sira', ed. A. Hamdani, PhD, London (1950)

al-Mustansir, *Al-sijillat al-Mustansiriyya*, ms. School of Oriental and African Studies, no.27155, ed. A. M. Magued, Cairo (1954)

al-Mustansir bi'llah, 'The letters', ed. H. F. Hamdani, *Bulletin of the School of Oriental Studies* 7 (1933–5), 307–24

Nishapuri, Zahir al-Din, *Saljuq-nameh*, Tehran (AH 1332/1954)

Nizam al-Mulk, al-Hasan ibn 'Ali, *Siyasat-nameh ya siyar al-muluk*, ed. H. Darke, Tehran (1976); trans. H. Darke, *The Book of Government, or Rules for Kings*, London (1978)

al-Nu'aymi, 'Abd al-Qadir, *Al-Daris fi ta'rikh al-madaris*, ed. Ja'far al-Hassani, 2 vols., Damascus (1948–51)

al-Nu'man (al-Qadi), *Da'a'im al-islam*, ed. A. A. A. Fyzee, Cairo (1951)

Rawandi, Muhammad ibn 'Ali, *Rahat al-sudur wa-ayat al-surur*, ed. M. Iqbal, London (1921)

al-Shirazi, *Diwan*, ed. M. Kamil Husayn, Cairo (1949)

al-Shirazi, *Sirat al-Mu'ayyad*, ed. M. Kamil Husayn, Cairo (1949)

Sibt ibn al-Jawzi, Yusuf b. Qizoghlu, *Mir'at al-zaman fi ta'rikh al-a'yan* – ʿAH 448–480 / AD 1056–1086', ed. Ali Sevim, Ankara (1968); ʿAH 495–654 / AD 1100–1256', as vol. VIII in 2 parts, Hyderabad (1951–2)

Usama b. Munqidh, *Kitab al-i 'tibar*, ed. P. K. Hitti, Princeton (1930); trans. P. K. Hitti, *An Arab-Syrian Gentleman and Warrior in the Period of the Crusades*, New York (1929)

Yahya ibn Saʿid al-Antaki', 'The Byzantine–Arab Chronicle (938–1034)', ed. J. Forsyth, PhD, Michigan (1977); facsimile repr., Ann Arbor (1978)

BIBLIOGRAPHY OF SECONDARY
WORKS ARRANGED BY CHAPTER

2 THE PAPACY, 1024–1122

Barlow, F. (1963), *The English Church, 1000–1066*, London

Becker, A. (1955), *Studien zum Investiturproblem in Frankreich*, Saarbrüken

Blaauw, S. de (1987), *Cultus et decor: Liturgie en architectuer in Laatantick en middeleeuws Rome: Basilica Saluatoris, Sandae Mariae, Sandi Petri*, Delft; traas M. B. Annis, *Cuttus et decor: Liturgia e architectura reda Roma tardoantica e medierale* (studi e testi, 355-6), attá del vaticano, 1994

Blumenthal, U.-R. (1978), *The Early Councils of Pope Paschal II, 1100–1110* (Studies and Texts 43), Toronto

Blumenthal, U.-R. (1986), 'Bemerkungen zum Register Papst Paschalis II', *QFIAB* 66: 1–19

Blumenthal, U.-R. (1988a), *The Investiture Controversy: Church and Monarchy from the Ninth to the Twelfth Century*, Philadelphia

Blumenthal, U.-R. (1988b), 'Papal registers in the twelfth century', *Proceedings of the Seventh International Congress of Medieval Canon Law* (1984), Cambridge, pp. 135–51

Bresslau, H. (1912–31), *Handbuch der Urkundenlehre für Deutschland und Italien*, 2 vols., Leipzig

Bresslau, H. (1918), 'Internationale Beziehungen im Urkundenwesen des Mittelalters', *Archiv für Urkundenforschung* 6: 19–76

Brooke, C. N. L. (1971), 'Gregorian Reform in action: clerical marriage in England, 1050–1200', in C. N. L. Brooke (ed.), *Medieval Church and Society: Collected Essays*, London, pp. 69–99

Brooke, Z. N. (1952), *The English Church and the Papacy from the Conquest to the Reign of John*, Cambridge; repr. 1968

Cantor, N. F. (1958), *Church, Kingship, and Lay Investiture in England 1089–1135*, Princeton

Capitani, O. (1966), *Studi su Berengario di Tours*, Lecce

Caspar, E. (1913), 'Studien zum Register Gregors VII', *NA* 38: 144–226

Chodorow, S. A. (1971), 'Ecclesiastical politics and the ending of the Investiture Contest: the papal election of 1119 and the negotiations of Mouzon', *Speculum* 46: 613–40

Congar, Y. M.-J. (1961), 'Der Platz des Papsttums in der Kirchenfrömmigkeit der Reformer des 11. Jahrhunderts', in J. Danielou and H. Vorgrimler (eds.), *Sentire ecclesiam: das Bewusstsein von der Kirche als gestaltende Kraft der Frömmigkeit*, Freiburg, Basle and Vienna, pp. 196–217

Cowdrey, H. E. J. (1970), *The Cluniacs and the Gregorian Reform*, Oxford

Cowdrey, H. E. J. (1972), 'Pope Gregory VII and the Anglo-Norman church and kingdom', *SG* 9: 79–114

Cowdrey, H. E. J. (1983), *The Age of Abbot Desiderius: Montecassino, the Papacy, and the Normans in the Eleventh and Early Twelfth Centuries*, Oxford

Cowdrey, H. E. J. (1989), 'The Gregorian Reform in the Anglo-Norman lands and in Scandinavia', *SG* 13: 321–52

Dahlhaus, J. (1989), 'Autkommen und Bedenting der, Rota in der Urkuden des Papstes Leo IX; *Archivum Historiae Pontificiae* 27: 7–84

Deer, J. (1964), 'Der Anspruch der Herrscher des 12. Jahrhunderts auf die apostolische Legation', *AHP* 2: 117–86

Ehrle, F. (1910), 'Die Frangipani und der Untergang des Archivs und der Bibliothek der Päpste am Anfang des 13. Jahrhunderts', in *Mélanges offerts à M. Emile Chatelain*, Paris, pp. 448–83

Ehrle, F. (1913), 'Nachträge zur Geschichte der drei ältesten päpstlichen Bibliotheken', *Römische Quartalschrift*, Supplement 20: 337–69

Elze, R. (1952), 'Das "sacrum palatium Lateranense" im 10. und 11. Jahrhundert', *SG* 4: 27–54

Erdmann, C. (1935), *Die Entstehung des Kreuzzugsgedankens*, Stuttgart, trans. M. W. Baldwin and W. Goffart as *The Origin of the Idea of Crusade*, Princeton, 1977

Feine, H. E. (1972), *Kirchliche Rechtsgeschichte: die Katholische Kirche*, Cologne and Vienna

Fichtenau, H. (1957), *Arenga, Spätantike und Mittelalter im Spiegel von Urkundenformeln* (Mitteilungen des Österreichischen Geschichtsinstitut, Ergänzungsband 18), Vienna

Fornasari, G. (1989), 'Le riforma gregoriana nel "Regnum Italiae"', *SG* 13: 281–320

Förster, H. (ed.) (1958), *Liber diurnus Romanorum pontificum* (Gesamtausgabe) Berne

Frenz, T. (1986), *Papsturkunden des Mittelalters und der Neuzeit*, Wiesbaden

Fuhrmann, H. (1954), 'Studien zur Geschichte mittelalterlicher Patriarchate, II.', *ZSSRG KA* 40: 1–84

Fuhrmann, H. (1955), 'Studien zur Geschichte mittelalterlicher Patriarchate, III. (Schluss)', *ZSSRG KA* 41: 95–183

Fuhrmann, H. (1961), 'Das ökumenische Konzil und seine historischen Grundlagen', *Geschichte in Wissenschaft und Unterricht* 12: 672–95

Fuhrmann, H. (1972–4), *Einfluss und Verbreitung der pseudoisidorischen Fälschungen*, 3 vols., Stuttgart

Fuhrmann, H. (1989), 'Papst Gregor VII. und das Kirchenrecht: zum Problem des Dictatus Papae', *SG* 13: 123–49

García y García, A. (1989), 'Riforma gregoriana e idea de la *militia sancti Petri* en los reinos ibéricos', *SG* 13: 341–62

Gottlob, T. (1936), *Der kirchliche Amtseid der Bischöfe*, Bonn

Halphen, L. (1907), *Etudes sur l'administration de Rome au moyen âge 751–1252*, Paris; repr. 1981

Hauck, A. (1958), *Kirchengeschichte Deutschlands*, III, Berlin

Herde, P. (1970), 'Das Papsttum und die griechische Kirche in Süditalien vom II. bis 13. Jahrhundert', *DA* 26: 1–46

Hermann, J.-J. (1973), *Das Tuskulanerpapsttum 1012–1046* (Päpste und Papsttum 4), Stuttgart

Hess, H. (1958), *The Canons of the Council of Sardica*, AD 343, Oxford

Hinschius P. (1869), *System des katholischen Kirchenrechts mit besonderer Rücksicht auf Deutschland (Das Kirchenrecht der Katholiken und Protestanten in Deutschland)*, I, Berlin

Hoffmann, H. (1976), 'Zum Register und zu den Briefen Papst Gregors VII', *DA* 32: 86–130

Huels, R. (1977), *Kardinäle, Klerus und Kirchen Roms 1049–1130*, Tübingen

Jasper, D. (1986), *Das Papstwahldekret von 1059: Überlieferung und Textgestalt*, Sigmaringen

Jordan, K. (1932), 'Das Eindringen des Lehnswesens in das Rechtsleben der römischen Kurie', *Archiv für Urkundenforschung* 12: 13–110

Jordan, K. (1947), 'Die päpstliche Verwaltung im Zeitalter Gregors VII', *SG* I: 111–35

Jordan, K. (1973), *Die Entstehung der römischen Kurie: ein Versuch, mit Nachtrag 1962* (Libelli 91), Darmstadt; appeared originally in *ZSSRG KA* 28 (1939), 97–152

Katterbach, B. and Peitz, W. M. (1924), 'Die Unterschriften der Päpste und Kardinäle in den "Bullae maiores" vom II. bis 14. Jahrhundert', *Studi e Testi* (Miscellanea F. Ehrle 4) 40: 177–274

Kehr, P. F. (1901), *Scrinium und Palatium: zur Geschichte des päpstlichen Kanzleiwesens im XI. Jahrhundert* (*MIÖG*, Ergänzungsband 6), Vienna

Kempf, F. (1969), 'The church and the western kingdoms from 900 to 1046', in F. Kempf, H.-G. Beck, E. Ewig and J. A. Jungmann (eds.), *The Church in the Age of Feudalism*, Handbook of Church History, III, trans. A. Biggs, New York, pp. 194–258; also pp. 320–39: 'Renewal and reform from 900–1050'; and pp. 351–403: 'The Gregorian Reform'

Kempf, F. (1978), 'Primatiale und episkopal-synodale Struktur der Kirche vor der gregorianischen Reform', *AHP* 16: 27–66

Klewitz, H.-W. (1934–5), 'Studien über die Wiederherstellung der römischen Kirche in Süditalien durch das Reformpapsttum', *QFIAB* 25: 105–57

Klewitz, H.-W. (1936), 'Die Entstehung des Kardinalkollegiums', *ZSSRG KA* 25: 115–21

Klinkenberg, H. M. (1955), 'Der römische Primat im X. Jahrhundert', *ZSSRG KA* 72: 1–57

Krause, H. G. (1976), 'Über der Verfasser der Vita Leonis IX papae', *DA* 32: 49–85

Kurze, W. (1990), 'Notizen zu den Päpsten Johannes VII., Gregor III. und Benedikt III. in der Kanonessammlung des Kardinals Deusdedit', *QFIAB* 70: 23–45

Kuttner, S. (1945), 'Cardinalis: the history of a canonical concept', *Traditio* 3: 129–214

Lohrmann, D. (1968), *Das Register Papst Johannes' VIII. 872–882* (Bibliothek des Deutschen Historischen Instituts in Rom 30), Tübingen

Maccarone, M. (1989), 'I fondamenti "Petrini" del Primato Romano in Gregorio VII', *SG* 13: 55–122

Maleczek, W. (1981), 'Das Kardinalskollegium unter Innocenz II. und Anaklet II.,' *AHP* 19: 27–78

Maleczek, W. (1984), *Papst und Kardinalskolleg von 1191 bis 1216* (Publikationen des Historischen Instituts beim Österreichischen Kulturinstitut in Rom 1.6), Vienna

Meulenberg, L. F. J. (1965), *Der Primat der Römischen Kirche im Denken und Handeln Gregors VII*, The Hague

Miccoli, G. (1966), *Chiesa gregoriana: ricerche sulla riforma del secolo XI*, Florence

Minninger, M. (1978), *Von Clermont zum Wormser Konkordat: die Auseineranderstungen um den Lehnsnexus zwischen König und Episkopat*, Cologne

Partner, P. (1972), *The Lands of St Peter*, London

Petrucci, E. (1975), *Rapporti di Leone IX con Constantinopoli*, I: *Per la storia dello scisma del 1054*, Rome

Petrucci, E. (1977), *Ecclesiologia e politica di Leone IX*, Rome

Pfaff, V. (1953), 'Die Einnahmen der römischen Kurie am Ende des 12. Jahrhunderts', *Vierteljahrschrift für Sozial- und Wirtschaftsgeschichte* 40: 97–118

Picasso, G. (1989), 'Gregorio VII e la disciplina canonica: clero e vita monastica', *SG* 13: 151–66

Rabikauskas, P. (1958), *Die römische Kuriale in der päpstlichen Kanzlei*, Rome

Robinson, I. S. (1978a), *Authority and Resistance in the Investiture Contest: The Polemical Literature of the Late Eleventh Century*, Manchester

Robinson, I. S. (1978b), 'Periculosus homo: Pope Gregory VII and episcopal authority', *Viator* 9: 103–31

Robinson, I. S. (1988), 'Church and papacy', in J. H. Burns (ed.), *The Cambridge History of Medieval Political Thought, c. 350–c. 1450*, Cambridge, pp. 252–305

Robinson, I. S. (1990), *The Papacy 1073–1198, Continuity and Innovation*, Cambridge

Ryan, J. J. (1956), *Saint Peter Damiani and his Canonical Sources*, Toronto

Ryan, J. J. (1966), 'Bernold of Constance and an anonymous Libellus de Lite: "De Romani pontificis potestate universas ecclesias ordinandi"', *AHP* 4: 9–24

Santifaller, L. (1940), 'Saggio di un Elenco dei funzionari, impiegati e scrittori della Cancelleria Pontificia dall'inizio all'anno 1099', *BISI* 56: 1–865

Santifaller, L. (1973), 'Über die Neugestaltung der äusseren Form der Papstprivilegien unter Leo IX', in *Festschrift Hermann Wiesflecker*, Graz, pp. 29–38

Santifaller, L. (1976), *Liber Diurnus: Studien und Forschungen*, ed. H. Zimmermann (Päpste und Papsttum 10), Stuttgart

Schieffer, R. (1971), 'Tomus Gregorii papae, Bemerkungen zur Diskussion um das Register Gregors VII', *Archiv für Diplomatik* 17: 169–84

Schieffer, R. (1972), '*Spirituales latrones:* zu den Hintergründen der Simonieprozesse in Deutschland zwischen 1069 und 1075', *Historisches Jahrbuch* 92: 19–60

Schieffer, R. (1981), *Die Entstehung des päpstlichen Investiturverbots für den deutschen König* (*MGH Schriften*, XXVIII), Stuttgart

Schieffer, T. (1935), *Die päpstlichen Legaten in Frankreich vom Vertrage von Meersen (870) bis zum Schisma von 1130* (Historische Studien Ebering 263), Berlin

Schimmelpfennig, B. (1978), 'Zölibat und Lage der "Priestersöhne" vom 11. bis 14. Jahrhundert', *HZ* 227: 1–44

Schimmelpfennig, B. (1984), *Das Papsttum: Grundzüge seiner Geschichte von der Antike bis zur Renaissance*, Darmstadt

Schmale, F. J. (1961), 'Papsttum und Kurie zwischen Gregor VII. und Innocenz II.', *HZ* 193: 265–85

Schmale, F.-J. (1976), 'Synodis – synodale concilium – concilium', *Annuarium Historiae Conciliorum* 8: 80–102

Schmale, F.-J. (1979), 'Die "Absetzung" Gregors VI. in Sutri und die synodale Tradition', *Annuarium Historiae Conciliorum* 11: 55–103

Schmidt, T. (1977), *Alexander II. und die römische Reformgruppe seiner Zeit* (Päpste und Papsttum 11), Stuttgart

Schramm, P. E. (1929), 'Studien zu frühmittelalterlichen Aufzeichnungen über Staat und Verfassung', *ZSSRG*, Germanistische Abteilung 49: 199–218

Schramm, P. E. (1947), 'Sacerdotium und Regnum im Austausch ihrer Vorrecht: eine Skizze der Entwicklung zur Beleuchtung des "Dictatus Papae" Gregors VII.', *SG* 2: 403–57

Schneider, C. (1972), *Prophetisches Sacerdotium und heilsgeschichtliches Regnum im Dialog 1073–1077; Zur Geschichte Gregors VII. und Heinrichs IV.*, Münster

Servatius, C. (1979), *Paschalis II. 1099–1118* (Päpste und Papsttum 14), Stuttgart

Somerville, R. (1989), 'The councils of Gregory VII', *SG* 13: 33–53

Somerville, R. (1990), *Papacy, Councils and Canon Law in the 11th–12th Centuries* (Variorum Collected Studies CS 312), Aldershot

Sydow, J. (1951), 'Cluny und die Anfänge der Apostolischen Kammer', *Studien und Mitteilungen zur Geschichte des Benediktiner Ordens* 63: 45–66

Sydow, J. (1954–5), 'Untersuchungen zur kurialen Verwaltungsgeschichte im Zeitalter des Reformpapsttums', *DA* 11: 18–73

Toubert, P. (1973), *Les Structures du Latium médiéval: le Latium et la Sabine du IXe siècle à la fin du XIIe siècle* (Bibliothèque des Ecoles Françaises d'Athène et de Rome 211) 2 vols., Rome

Valentini, R. and Zucchetti, G. (1940–53), *Codice topografico della città di Roma*, 4 vols., Rome

Vehse, O. (1929–30), 'Die päpstliche Herrschaft in der Sabina bis zur Mitte des 12. Jahrhunderts', *QFIAB* 21: 120–75

Vones, L. (1980), *Die 'historia Compostellana' und die Kirchenpolitik des nordwestspanischen Raumes 1070–1130*, Cologne and Vienna

Winroth, A. (2000) *The Making of Gratian's Decretales*, Cambridge

Zafarana, Z. (1966), 'Sul "conventus" del clero romano nel maggio 1082', *Studi Medievali* 3rd series 7: 399–403

3 THE WESTERN EMPIRE UNDER THE SALIANS

Althoff, G. (1987), 'Der friedens-, bundnis- und gemeinschaftstiftende Charakter des Mahles im früheren Mittelalter', in I. Bitsch, T. Ehlert and X. von Ertzdorff (eds.), *Essen und Trinken in Mittelalter und Neuzeit*, Sigmaringen, pp. 13–25

Althoff, G. (1993), 'Demonstration und Inszenierung: Spielregeln der Kommunikation in mittelalterlicher Öffentlichkeit', *FmaSt* 27: 27–50

Angenendt, A. (1984), *Kaiserherrschaft und Königstaufe. Kaiser, Könige und Päpste als geistliche Patrone in der abendländische Missionsgeschichte*, Berlin and New York

Beulertz, S. (1991), *Das Verbot der Laieninvestitur im Investiturstreit*, Hanover

Blumenthal, U.-R. (1988), *The Investiture Controversy: Church and Monarchy from the Ninth to the Twelfth Century*, Philadelphia

Chazan, R. (1987), *European Jewry and the First Crusade*, Berkeley

Claude, D. (1972), *Geschichte des Erzbistums Magdeburg*, pt 1, Cologne and Vienna

Fenske, L. (1977), *Adelsopposition und kirchliche Reformbewegung im östlichen Sachsen: Entstehung und Wirkung des sächsischen Widerstandes gegen das salische Königtum während des Investiturstreits*, Göttingen

Fried, J. (1973), 'Der Regalienbegriff im 11. und 12. Jahrhundert', *DA* 29: 450–528

Fried, J. (1991), *Die Formierung Europas 840–1046*, Munich

Fried, J. (1994), *Der Weg in die Geschichte bis 1024* (Propyläen Geschichte Deutschlands 1), Berlin

Fuhrmann, H. (1986), *Germany in the High Middle Ages c. 1050–1200*, trans. T. Reuter, Cambridge

Gilchrist, J. (1973, 1980), 'The reception of Gregory VII into canon law', *ZSSRG KA* 59: 35–82; 66: 192–229

Hartmann, W. (1993), *Der Investiturestreit* (Enzyklopädia deutsche Geschichte 21), Munich

Haverkamp, A. (1988), *Medieval Germany, 1056–1273*, trans. H. Braun and R. Mortimer, Oxford

Heidrich, I. (1984), *Ravenna unter Erzbischof Wibert*, Sigmaringen

Heinemeyer, K. (1986), 'König und Reichsfürsten in der späten Salier- und frühen Stauferzeit', *Blätter für Deutsche Landesgeschichte* 122: 1–39

Hoffmann, H. (1993), *Mönchskönig und rex idiota. Studien zur Kirchenpolitik Heinrichs II. und Konrads II.*, Hanover

Jackman, D. (1990), *The Konradiner: A Study in Genealogical Methodology*, Frankfurt

Jakobs, H. (1988), *Kirchenreform und Hochmittelalter 1046–1215* (Oldenbourg Grundriß der Geschichte 7), Munich

Jasper, D. (1986), *Das Papstwahldekret von 1059*, Sigmaringen

Keller, H. (1983), 'Schwäbische Herzöge als Thronbewerber', *Zeitschrift für die Geschichte des Oberrheins* 131: 123–62

Keller, H. (1986), *Zwischen regionaler Begrenzung und universalem Horizont (1024–1250)* (Propyläen Geschichte Deutschlands 2), Berlin

Koziol, G. (1992), *Begging Pardon and Favour: Ritual and Political Order in Early Medieval France*, Ithaca and London

Leyser, K. (1983), 'The crisis of medieval Germany', *PBA* 69: 409–43, repr. in K. Leyser, *Communications and Power in Medieval Europe: The Gregorian Revolution and Beyond*, ed. T. Reuter, London, 1994, pp. 21–49

Leyser, K. (1991), 'The Anglo-Norman succession 1120–1125', *ANS* 13: 225–41

Leyser, K. (1993), 'Am Vorabend der ersten europäischen Revolution: das 11 Jahrhundert als Umbruchszeit', *HZ* 257: 1–28; repr. as 'On the eve of the first European revolution', in K. Leyser, *Communications and Power in Medieval Europe: The Gregorian Revolution and Beyond*, ed. T. Reuter, London, 1994, pp. 1–19

Lynch, J. H. (1985), 'Hugh of Cluny's sponsorship of Henry IV', *Speculum* 60: 800–26

Lynch, J. H. (1986), *Godparents and Kinship in Early Medieval Europe*, Princeton

Mertens, D. (1981), 'Christen und Juden zur Zeit des ersten Kreuzzuges', in B. Martin *et al.* (eds.), *Die Juden als Minderheit in der Geschichte*, Munich, pp. 46–67

Minninger, M. (1978), *Von Clermont zum Wormser Konkordat*, Cologne and Vienna

Reuter, T. (1982) 'The "imperial church system" of the Ottonian and Salian rulers: a reconsideration', *JEH* 33: 347–74

Reuter, T. (1992), 'Unruhestiftung, Fehde, Rebellion, Widerstand', in Weinfurter (1991–2), III, pp. 297–325

Riley-Smith, J. (1986), *The First Crusade and the Idea of Crusading*, London

Rousset, P. (1983), *Histoire d'une idéologie: la croisade*, Lausanne

Schieffer, R. (1972), 'Spirituales Latrones: zu den Hintergründen der Simonieprozesse in Deutschland zwischen 1069 und 1075', *Historisches Jahrbuch* 92: 19–60

Schieffer, R. (1981), *Die Entstehung des päpstlichen Investiturverbots für den deutschen König*, Stuttgart

Schieffer, R. (1986), 'Rechtstexte des Reformpapstums und ihre zeitgenössische Resonanz', in R. Kottje and H. Mordek (eds.), *Überlieferung und Geltung normativer Texte des frühen und hohen Mittelalters*, Sigmaringen, pp. 51–69

Schlesinger, W. (1973), 'Die Wahl Rudolfs von Schwaben zum Gegenkönig 1077 in Forchheim', in. J. Fleckenstein (ed.), *Investiturstreit und Reichsverfassung*, Sigmaringen, pp. 61–86; repr. in W. Schlesinger, *Ausgewählte Aufsätze*, Sigmaringen, 1987, pp. 273–96

Schmid, K. (1983), 'Heinrich III. und Gregor VII. im Gebetsgedächtnis von Piacenza des Jahres 1046', in K. Schmid, *Gebetsgedenken und adliges Selbstverständnis im Mittelalter*, Sigmaringen, pp. 598–619

Schmitt, J.-C. (1990), *Le Raison des gestes dans l'Occident médiéval*, Paris

Southern, R. (1990), *Saint Anselm: A Portrait in a Landscape*, Cambridge

Tellenbach, G. (1988), 'Der Charakter Kaiser Heinrichs IV. Zugleich ein Versuch über die Erkennbarkeit menschlicher Individualität im hohen Mittelalter', in G. Althoff *et al.* (eds.), *Person und Gemeinschaft*, Sigmaringen, pp. 345–67

Tellenbach, G. (1993), *The Church in Western Europe from the Xth to the Early XIth Century* (Cambridge Medieval Textbooks), Cambridge

Vogel, J. (1983), *Gregor VII. und Heinrich IV. nach Canossa: Zeugnisse ihres Selbstverständnisses*, Berlin and New York

Vollrath, H. (1992), 'Konfliktwahrnehmung und Konfliktdarstellung in erzählenden Quellen des 11. Jahrhunderts', in Weinfurter (1991–2), III, pp. 279–96

Vollrath, H. (1993), 'L'accusa di simonia tra le fazioni contrapposte nella lotta per le investiture', in C. Violante and J. Fried (eds.), *Il secolo XI: una svolta?*, Bologna, pp. 131–56

Wendehorst, A. (1996), 'Who could read and write in the middle ages', in A. Haverkamp and H. Vollrath (eds.), *England and Germany in the High Middle Ages*, Oxford, pp. 57–88

Weinfurter, S. (1991), *Herrschaft und Reich der Salier*, Sigmaringen

Weinfurter, S. (ed.) (1991–2) *Die Salier und das Reich*, 3 vols., Sigmaringen

Zimmermann, H. (1975), *Der Canossagang von 1077: Wirkungen und Wirklichkeit*, Mainz

4(a) NORTHERN AND CENTRAL ITALY IN THE ELEVENTH CENTURY

Archetti Giampaolini, E. (1987), *Aristocrazia e chiese nella Marca del centro-nord tra IX e XI secolo*, Rome

Arezzo e il suo territorio nell'alto medioevo (1985), Cortona

Ascheri, M. and Kurze, W. (eds.) (1989), *L'amiata nel medioevo*, Rome

Atti del 9° Congresso internazionale di studi sull'alto medioevo: il ducato di Spoleto (1983) (Congressi del Centro Italiano di Studi sull'Alto Medioevo 9), Spoleto

Atti dell' 11° Congresso internazionale di studi sull'alto medioevo: Milano ed il suo territorio in età comunale (1989) (Congressi del Centro Italiano di Studi sull'Alto Medioevo 11), Spoleto

Bordone, R. (1980), *Città e territorio nell'alto medioevo: la società astigiana dal dominio dei Franchi all'affermazione comunale* (Biblioteca Storica Subalpina 200), Turin

Bordone, R. (1987), *La società cittadina del regno d'Italia* (Biblioteca Storica Subalpina 202), Turin

Bordone, R. and Jarnut, J. (eds.) (1988), *L'evoluzione delle città italiane nell' XI secolo* (Annali dell'Istituto Storico Italo-Germanico 25), Bologna

Boscolo, A. (1978), *La Sardegna bizantina e alto-giudicale*, Sassari

Bosl, K. (1982), *Gesellschaftsgeschichte Italiens im Mittelalter*, Stuttgart

Branca, V. (ed.) (1979), *Storia della civiltà veneziana*, 1: *Dalle origini al secolo di Marco Polo*, Florence

Brancoli Busdraghi, P. (1965), *La formazione storica del feudo lombardo come diritto reale*, Milan

Bresslau, H. (1879–84), *Jahrbücher des deutschen Reiches unter Konrad II* (Jahrbücher der Deutschen Geschichte), 2 vols., Leipzig

Brezzi, P. (1947), *Roma e l'impero medievale 774–1252* (Storia di Roma 10), Bologna

Brezzi, P. (1959), *I Comuni medioevali nella storia d'Italia*, Turin; new edn 1970

Brühl, C. (1968), *Fodrum, gistum, servitium regis* (Kölner Historische Abhandlungen 14), Cologne and Graz

Cammarosano, P. (ed.) (1988), *Storia della società friulana: il medioevo*, Udine

Capitani, O. (1986), *Storia dell'Italia medievale 410–1216*, Rome and Bari

Castagnetti, A. (1979), *L'organizzazione del territorio rurale nel medioevo*, Turin

Castagnetti A. (1985), *Società e politica a Ferrara, sec. X–XIII*, Bologna

Castagnetti, A. (1986), *La marca veronese-trevigiana* (Storia degli Stati Italiani), Turin

Castagnetti, A. (1988), *Arimanni in 'Romania' fra conti e signori*, Verona

Cessi, R. (1944), *Storia della repubblica di Venezia*, 1, Milan and Messina

I ceti dirigenti in Toscana nell'età pre-comunale (1981) (Convegni sui Ceti Dirigenti in Toscana 1), Pisa

Clementi, A. (1988), 'Le terre del confine settentrionale', in *Storia del Mezzogiorno II*, 1: *Il medioevo*, Naples

Cognasso, F. (1952), 'Novara nella sua storia', in *Novara e il suo territorio*, Novara

Comuni e signorie nell'Italia nordorientale e centrale (1987) (Storia d'Italia 7), 2 vols., Turin

Coniglio, G. (ed.) (1958), *Mantova: la storia*, 1, Mantua

Cracco, G. (1986), *Venezia nel medioevo dal secolo XI al secolo XIV*, Turin

Cracco, G. (ed.) (1988), *Storia di Vincenza*, II: *L'età medievale*, Vicenza

La cristianità dei secoli XI e XII in Occidente: conscienza e strutture di una società (1983) (Università Cattolica, Miscellanea del Centro di Studi Medioevali 10), Milan

Darmstädter, P. (1896), *Das Reichsgut in der Lombardei und Piemont 568–1250*, Strasbourg

Davidsohn, R. (1896), *Geschichte von Florenz*, 1, Berlin

De Vergottini, G. (1924–5), *Lineamenti storici della constituzione politica dell'Istria durante il medio evo*, Trieste; repr. 1974

Dilcher, G. (1967), *Die Entstehung der lombardischen Stadtkommune* (Untersuchungen zur deutschen Staats- und Rechtsgeschichte), Aalen

Fasoli, G. (1969), *Dalle 'civitas' al Comune nell'Italia settentrionale*, Bologna
Formazione e strutture dei ceti dominanti nel medioevo: marchesi, conti e visconti nel regno italico, sec. IX–XII (1988) (Nuovi Studi Storici 1), Rome
Formentini, U. (1941), *Storia di Genova dalle origini al tempo nostro*, 1: *Genova nel basso impero e nell'alto medioevo*, Milan
Galassi, N. (1984), *Figure e vicende di una città* (Imola), 1, Imola
Galasso, G. (ed.) (1981), *Storia d'Italia*, IV: *Comuni e signorie*, Turin
Goetz, W. (1944), *Die Entstehung der italienischen Kommunen im frühen Mittelalter* (Bayerische Akademie der Wissenschaften), Munich
Graf, G. (1936), *Die weltlichen Widerstände in Reichsitalien gegen die Herrschaft der Ottonen und der ersten beiden Salier*, Erlangen
Hof, E. (1943), *Pavia und seine Bischöfe im Mittelalter*, 1, Pavia
Hyde, J. K. (1973), *Society and Politics in Medieval Italy 1000–1350*, London
Jarnut, J. (1979), *Bergamo 568–1098*, Wiesbaden
Jenal, G. (1974–5), *Erzbischof Anno II von Köln (1056–75) und sein politisches Wirken* (Monographien zur Geschichte des Mittelalters 8), 2 vols., Stuttgart
Keller, H. (1979), *Adelsherrscraft und städtische Gesellschaft in Oberitalien 9. bis 12. Jahrhundert* (Bibliothek des Deutschen Historischen Instituts in Rom 52), Tübingen
Kretschmayr, H. (1905), *Geschichte von Venedig* (Allgemeine Staatengeschichte), Aalen; repr. 1964
Lane, F. C. (1973), *Venice: A Maritime Republic*, Baltimore and London
Maranini, G. (1927), *La constituzione di Venezia dalle origini alla serrata del Maggior Consiglio*, Venice
Meyer von Knonau, G. (1890–1903), *Jahrbücher des deutschen Reiches unter Heinrich IV und Heinrich V* (Jahrbücher der Deutschen Geschichte), 7 vols., Berlin; repr. 1964–5
Mor, C. G. and Schmidinger, H. (eds.) (1979), *I poteri temporali dei vescovi in Italia e in Germania nel medioevo* (Annali dell'Istituto Storico Italo-Germanico 3), Bologna
Overmann, A. (1895), *Gräfin Mathilde von Tuscien*, Innsbruck
Paschini, P. (1934), *Storia del Friuli*, 1, Udine; new edn 1953
Piemonte medievale: forme del potere e della società (1985), Turin
Pisa nei secoli XI e XII: formazione e caratteri di una classe di governo (1979), (Istituto di Storia dell'Università di Pisa 10), Pisa
Racine, P. (1980), *Plaisance du Xe à la fin du XIIIe siècle*, 1, Lille and Paris
Rauty, N. (1988), *Storia di Pistoia*, 1: *Dall'alto medioevo all'età precomunale 406–1105*, Florence
Renouard, Y. (1969), *Les Villes d'Italie de la fin du Xe siècle au début du XIVe siècle*, 2 vols., Paris
Rösch, G. (1982), *Venedig und das Reich* (Bibliothek des Deutschen Historischen Instituts in Rom 53), Tübingen
Rossi Sabatini, G. (1935), *L'espansione di Pisa nel Mediterraneo fino alla Meloria*, Florence
Salvatorelli, L. (1940), *L'Italia comunale* (Storia d'Italia 4), Milan
Schevill, F. (1936), *History of Florence*, New York; new edn 1961
Schmidinger, H. (1954), *Patriarch und Landesherr*, Graz and Cologne
Schumann, R. (1973), *Authority and the Commune: Parma 833–1133*, Parma
Schwartz, G. (1913), *Die Besetzung der Bistümer Reichsitaliens unter den sächsischen und salischen Kaisern*, Leipzig and Berlin

Schwarzmaier, H. (1972), *Lucca und das Reich bis zum Ende des II. Jahrhunderts* (Bibliothek des Deutschen Historischen Instituts in Rom 41), Tübingen

Sergi, G. (1981), *Potere e territorio lungo la strada di Francia: da Chambéry a Torino fra X e XIII secolo* (Nuovo Medioevo 20), Naples

Sestan, E. (1966), *Italia medievale*, Naples

Settia, A. A. (1983), *Monferrato: strutture di un territorio medievale*, Turin

Settia, A. A. (1984), *Castelli e villaggi nell'Italia padana* (Nuovo Medioevo 23), Naples

Simioni, A. (1968), *Storia di Padova*, Padua

Sorbelli, A. (1938), *Storia di Bologna*, II: *Dalle origini del cristianesimo agli albori del Comune*, Bologna

Steindorff, E. (1874–81), *Jahrbücher des deutschen Reiches unter Heinrich III* (Jahrbücher der Deutschen Geschichte), 2 vols. Darmstadt; repr. 1963

La storia dei Genovesi (1981–2), I–II, Genoa

Storia di Bologna (1978), Bologna

Storia di Brescia, (1963), I, Brescia

Storia di Milano (1954), III, Milan

Storia di Piacenza, II: *Dal vescovo conte alla signoria 996–1313* (1984), Piacenza

Storia di Venezia, II: *Dalle origini del ducato alla IV crociata* (1958), Venice

Structures féodales et féodalisme dans l'Occident méditerranéen, Xe–XIIIe siècles (Ecole Française de Rome 44) (1980), Rome

Studi Matildici, II Convegno (1971), Modena

Studi Matildici, III Convegno (1978), Modena

Tabacco, G. (1966), *I liberi del re nell'Italia carolingia e postcarolingia* (Biblioteca degli 'Studi Medievali' 2), Spoleto

Tabacco, G. (1979), *Egemonie sociale e strutture del potere nel medioevo italiano*, Turin

Toubert, P. (1973), *Les Structures du Latium médiéval: le Latium et la Sabine du IXe siècle à la fin du XIIe siècle* (Bibliothèque des Ecoles Françaises d'Athènes et de Rome 211), 2 vols., Rome

Vaccari, P. (1940), *Profilo storico di Pavia*, Pavia

Valeri, N. (ed.) (1965), *Storia d'Italia*, I: *Il medioevo*, Turin

Vasina, A. (1970), *Romagna medievale*, Ravenna

Vasina, A. (ed.) (1983), *Storia di Cesena*, II: *Il medioevo*, Rimini

La Venezia del mille (1965), Florence

Verona e il suo territorio (1964), II, Verona

Violante, C. (1953), *La società milanese nell'età precomunale*, Bari

Violante, C. (1972), *Studi sulla cristianità medioevale*, Milan

Vittale, V. (1955), *Breviario della storia di Genova*, Genoa

Volpe, G. (1961), *Medioevo italiano*, Florence

Wickham, C. J. (1988), *The Mountains and the City: The Tuscan Appennines in the Early Middle Ages*, Oxford

4(b) SOUTHERN ITALY IN THE ELEVENTH CENTURY

Borsari, S. (1966–7), 'Aspetti del dominio bizantio in Capitanata', *Atti dell'Accademia Pontaniana* n.s. 16: 55–66

Capitani, O. (1977), 'Specific motivations and continuing themes in the Norman chronicles of southern Italy in the eleventh and twelfth centuries', in *The Normans in Southern Italy and Sicily: Lincei Lectures 1974*, Oxford, pp. 1–46

Chalandon, F. (1907), *Histoire de la Domination Normande en Italie et en Sicile*, 2 vols., Paris

Citarella, A. O. (1968), 'Patterns in medieval trade: the commerce of Amalfi before the Crusades', *Journal of Economic History* 28: 531–55

Clementi, D. R. (1982–3), 'Stepping stones in the making of the regno', *BISI* 90: 227–93

Cowdrey, H. E. J. (1983), *The Age of Abbot Desiderius, Montecassino, the Papacy and the Normans in the Eleventh and Early Twelfth Centuries*, Oxford

D'Alessandro, V. (1978), *Storiografia e politica nell'Italia normanna*, Naples

D'Alessandro, V. (1989), 'Servi e liberi', in *Uomo e ambiente nel Mezzogiorno normanno-svevo* (Centro di Studi Normanno-Svevi 8), Bari, pp. 293–318

Deér, J. (1969), *Das Papsttum und die süditalienischen Normannestaaten 1053–1212*, Göttingen

Deér, J. (1972), *Papsttum und Normannen*, Cologne

Deér, J. (1974), *Papsttum und Normannen: Untersuchungen zu ihren lehnsrechtlichen und kirchenpolitischen Beziehungen*, Cologne and Vienna

Dormeier, H. (1979), *Montecassino und die Laien im 11. und 12. Jahrhundert*, Stuttgart

Falkenhausen, V. von (1967), *Untersuchungen über die byzantinische Herrschaft in Süditalien vom 9. bis ins 11. Jahrhundert*, Wiesbaden

Falkenhausen, V. von (1975), 'Aspetti storico-economici dell'età di Roberto il Guiscardo', in *Roberto di Guiscardo e il suo tempo: relazioni e communicazioni nelle prime giornate normanno-sveve*, Bari, pp. 115–34

Falkenhausen, V. von (1977), 'I ceti dirigenti prenormanni al tempo della costituzione degli stati normanni nell'Italia meridionale e in Sicilia', in G. Rossetti (ed.), *Forma di potere e struttura sociale in Italia nel medioevo*, Bologna, pp. 321–77

Feller, L. (1998), *Les Abruzzes médiévales: territoire, économies et société en Italie centrale du IXe au XIIe siècle*, Rome

Fonseca, C. D. (1977), 'L'organizzazione ecclesiastica dell'Italia normanna tra l'XI e il XII secolo: i nuovi assetti istituzionali', in *Le istituzioni ecclesiastiche della 'Societas Christiana' dei secoli XI e XII* (Miscellanea del Centro di Studi Medievali 7), Milan, pp. 327–52

France, J. (1991), 'The occasion of the coming of the Normans to southern Italy', *JMH* 17: 185–205

Gay, J. (1904), *L'Italie méridionale et l'empire byzantin depuis l'avènement de Basile Ier jusqu'à la prise de Bari par les Normands (867–1071)*, Paris

Galasso, G. (1977), 'Social and political developments in the eleventh and twelfth centuries', in *The Normans in Southern Italy and Sicily: Lincei Lectures 1974*, Oxford, pp. 47–63

Guillou, A. (1963), 'Inchiesta sulla populazione greca della Sicilia e della Calabria nel medio evo', *Rivista Storica Italiana* 75: 53–68 (repr. in Guillou (1970))

Guillou, A. (1965), 'La Lucanie byzantine: étude de géographie historique', *Byzantion*, 35: 119–149 (repr. in Guillou (1970))

Guillou, A. (1970), *Studies on Byzantine Italy*, London

Guillou, A. (1974), 'Production and profits in the Byzantine province of Italy (tenth to eleventh centuries): an expanding society', *DOP* 28: 91–109 (repr. in Guillou (1978))

Guillou, A. (1978), *Culture et société en Italie byzantine (VIe–XIe siècles)*, London

Hoffmann, H. (1969), 'Die Anfänge der Normannen in Süditalien', *QFIAB* 49: 95–144

Hoffmann, H. (1978), 'Langobarden, Normannen, Päpste: zum Legitimationsproblem in Unteritalien', *QFIAB* 58: 137–80

Houben, H. (1989), *Tra Roma e Palermo: aspetti e momenti del mezzogiorno medioevale*, Galatina

Houben, H. (1995), *Die Abtei Venosa und das Mönchtum im normannisch-staufischen Suditalien*, Tübingen

Jahn, W. (1989), *Untersuchungen zur normannischer Herrschaft in Süditalien (1040–1100)*, Frankfurt

Joranson, E. (1948), 'The inception of the career of the Normans in Sicily', *Speculum* 23: 353–96

Kamp, N. (1977), 'Vescovi e diocesi dell'Italia meridionale nel passagio dalla dominazione bizantina allo stato normanno', in G. Rossetti (ed.), *Forma di potere e struttura sociale in Italia nel medioevo*, Bologna, pp. 379–97

Loud, G. A. (1981a), 'How "Norman" was the Norman Conquest of southern Italy?', *Nottingham Medieval Studies* 25: 13–34

Loud, G. A. (1981b), 'A calendar of the diplomas of the Norman princes of Capua', *Papers of the British School at Rome* 49: 99–143

Loud, G. A. (1985), *Church and Society in the Norman Principality of Capua 1058–1197*, Oxford

Loud, G. A. (1987), 'The abbey of Cava, its property and benefactors in the Norman era', in R. A. Brown (ed.), *Anglo-Norman Studies 9: Papers from the Battle Conference 1986*, Woodbridge, pp. 143–77

Loud, G. A. (1988), 'Byzantine Italy and the Normans', in J. D. Howard-Johnston (ed.), *Byzantium and the West c. 850–c. 1200: Proceedings of the XVIII Spring Symposium of Byzantine Studies*, Amsterdam, pp. 215–33

Loud, G. A. (1992), 'Churches and churchmen in an age of conquest: southern Italy 1030–1130', *Haskins Society Journal* 4: 37–53 (repr. in Loud (1999b))

Loud, G. A. (1996), 'Continuity and change in Norman Italy: the Campania during the eleventh and twelfth centuries', *JMH* 22: 313–43 (repr. in Loud (1999b))

Loud, G. A. (1999a), 'Coinage, wealth and plunder in the age of Robert Guiscard', *EHR* 114: 815–43

Loud, G. A. (1999b), *Conquerors and Churchmen in Norman Italy*, Aldershot

Loud, G. A. (2000), *The Age of Robert Guiscard: Southern Italy and the Norman Conquest*, Harlow

Loud, G. A. and Metcalfe, A. (eds.) (2002), *The Society of Norman Italy*, Leiden

Martin, J.-M. (1993), *La Pouille du VIe au XIIe siècle*, Rome

Ménager, L.-R. (1958–9), 'La byzantinisation religieuse de l'Italie méridionale (IX–XIIe siècles) et la politique monastique des Normans d'Italie', *RHE* 53: 747–74; 54: 5–40

Ménager, L.-R. (1975a), 'Pesanteur et étiologie de la colonisation normande de l'Italie', in *Roberto il Guiscardo e il suo tempo: relazioni e communicazioni nelle prime giornate normanno-sveve*, Bari, pp. 189–215

Ménager, L.-R. (1975b), 'Inventaire des familles normandes et franques emigrées en Italie méridionale et en Sicile (XIe–XIIe siècles)', in *Roberto il Guiscardo e il suo tempo: relazioni e communicazioni nelle prime giornate normanno-sveve*, Bari, pp. 261–390

Norwich, J. J. (1967), *The Normans in the South*, London

Scaduto, M. (1947), *Il monachismo basiliano nella Sicilia medievale, rinascita e decadenza sec. XI–XIV*, Rome

Schwarz, U. (1978), *Amalfi im frühen Mittelalter (9.–11. Jahrhundert)*, Tübingen

Skinner, P. (1995), *Family Power in Southern Italy: The Duchy of Gaeta and its Neighbours, 850–1139*, Cambridge

Taviani-Carozzi, H. (1991), *Le Principauté lombarde de Salerne (IXe–XIe siècle): pouvoir et société en Italie lombarde méridionale*, 2 vols., Rome

Taviani-Carozzi, H. (1996), *La Terreur du monde: Robert Guiscard et la conquête normande en Italie*, Paris

Tramontana, S. (1970), *I Normanni in Italia: linee di ricerca sui primi insediamenti*, 1: *Aspetti politici e militari*, Messina

Tramontana, S. (1977), 'Populazione, distribuzione della terra e classi sociali nella Sicilia di Ruggero il Granconte', in *Ruggero il Gran Conte e l'inizio dello stato normanno: relazione e communicazioni nelle seconde giornate normanno-sveve*, Bari, pp. 213–70

Tramontana, S. (1983), 'La monarchia normanna e sveva', in G. Galasso (ed.), *Il Mezzogiorno dai Bizantini a Federico II*, Turin, chs. 1–4, pp. 437–562

Travaini, L. (1995), *La monetazione nell'Italia normanna*, Rome

Vehse, O. (1930–1), 'Benevent als Territorium des Kirchenstaates bis zum Beginn der Avignonesischen Epoche. I. Bis zum Ausgang der normanischen Dynastie', *QFIAB* 22: 87–160

White, L. T. (1938), *Latin Monasticism in Norman Sicily*, Cambridge, MA

Wolf, R. L. (1995), *Making History: The Normans and their Historians in Southern Italy*, Philadelphia

5 THE KINGDOM OF THE FRANKS TO 1108

Bloch, M. (1924), *Les Rois thaumaturges: étude sur le caractère surnaturel attribué à la puissance royale*, Strasbourg

Bloch, M. (1961), *Feudal Society*, trans. L. A. Manyon, Chicago

Blumenthal, U.-R. (1988), *The Investiture Controversy: Church and Monarchy from the Ninth to the Twelfth Century*, Philadelphia

Bonnassie, Pierre (1975), *La Catalogne du milieu du Xe à la fin du XIe siècle: croissance et mutations d'une société*, 2 vols., Paris

Bouchard, C. B. (1981a), 'The origins of the French nobility: a reassessment', *AHR* 86: 501–32

Bouchard, C. B. (1981b), 'Consanguinity and noble marriages in the tenth and eleventh centuries', *Speculum* 56: 268–87

Bouchard, C. B. (1987), *Sword, Miter and Cloister: Nobility and the Church in Burgundy 980–1198*, Ithaca

Brown, E. A. R. (1974), 'The tyranny of a construct: feudalism and historians of medieval Europe', *AHR* 79: 1063–88

Bur, M. (1977), *La Formation du comté de Champagne v.950–v.1150* (Mémoires des Annales de l'Est 54), Nancy

Chédeville, A. (1973), *Chartres et ses campagnes, XIe–XIIIe siècles*, Paris

Chédeville, A. and Tonnerre, N.-Y. (1987), *La Bretagne féodale, XIe–XIIIe siècle*, Rennes

Cowdrey, H. E. J. (1970a), *The Cluniacs and the Gregorian Reform*, Oxford

Cowdrey, H. E. J. (1970b), 'The Peace and the Truce of God in the eleventh century', *PaP* 46: 42–67

Dunbabin, J. (1985), *France in the Making, 843–1180*, Oxford

Duby, G. (1968), *Rural Economy and Country Life in the Medieval West*, trans. C. Postan, Columbia, SC

Duby, G. (1971), *La Société aux XIe et XIIe siècles dans la région mâconnaise*, 2nd edn, Paris

Duby, G. (1973), 'Guerre et société dans l'Europe féodale', in V. Branca (ed.), *Concetto, storia, miti et immagini del medio evo* (XIV Corso Internazionale d'Alta Cultura), Venice, pp. 449–82

Duby, G. (1980), *The Three Orders: Feudal Society Imagined*, trans. A. Goldhammer, Chicago

Duby, G. (1983), *The Knight, the Lady, and the Priest: The Making of Modern Marriage in Medieval France*, trans. B. Bray, New York

Fawtier, R. (1960), *The Capetian Kings of France: Monarchy and Nation, 987–1328*, trans. L. Butler and R. J. Adam, London

Fliche, A. (1912), *Le Règne de Philippe Ier, roi de France (1060–1108)*, Paris

Flori, J. (1988), 'Chevalerie, noblesse et lutte de classes au moyen âge', *MA* 94: 257–79

Guillot, O. (1972), *Le Comté d'Anjou et son entourage au XIe siècle*, 2 vols., Paris

Hallam, E. M. (1980), *Capetian France, 987–1328*, London

Head, T. and Landes, R. (eds.) (1987), *Essays on the Peace of God: The Church and the People in Eleventh-Century France* (special issue of *Historical Reflections/Reflexions Historiques* 14 (3))

Hunt, N. (1967), *Cluny under Saint Hugh 1949–1109*, London

Lackner, B. K. (1972), *The Eleventh-Century Background of Cîteaux* (Cistercian Studies Series 8), Washington, DC

Lemarignier, J.-F. (1965), *Le Gouvernement royal aux premiers temps capétiens (987–1108)*, Paris

Lewis, A. W. (1981), *Royal Succession in Capetian France: Studies on Familial Order and the State*, Cambridge, MA

Lot, F. and Fawtier, R. (1957), *Institutions seigneuriales* (Histoire des Institutions Françaises au Moyen Age 1), Paris

Lot, F. and Fawtier, R. (1958), *Institutions royales* (Histoire des Institutions Françaises au Moyen Age 2), Paris

Magnou-Nortier, E. (1969), 'Fidélité et féodalité d'après les serments de fidélité (Xe–début XIIe siècle)', in *Les Structures sociales de l'Aquitaine, du Languedoc et de l'Espagne au premier âge féodal*, Paris, pp. 115–35

Magnou-Nortier, E. (1974), *La Société laïque et l'église dans la province ecclésiastique de Narbonne (zone cispyrénéenne) de la fin du VIIIe à la fin du XIe siècle*, Toulouse

Newman, W. M. (1937), *Le Domaine royal sous les premiers capétiens (987–1180)*, Paris

Petit, E. (ed.) (1885–98), *Histoire des ducs de Bourgogne de la race capétienne*, 6 vols., Paris and Dijon

Poly, J.-P. (1976), *La Provence et la société féodale (879–1166)*, Paris

Poly, J.-P. and Bournazel, E. (1980), *La Mutation féodale, Xe–XIIe siècles*, Paris

Prou, M. (ed.) (1908), *Recueil des actes de Philippe Ier, roi de France, 1059–1108*, Paris

Reuter, T. (ed.) (1978), *The Medieval Nobility: Studies on the Ruling Classes of France and Germany from the Sixth to the Twelfth Century* (Europe in the Middle Ages, Selected Studies 14), Amsterdam

Richard, J. (1954), *Les Ducs de Bourgogne et la formation du duché du XIe au XIVe siècle*, Paris

Searle, E. (1988), *Predatory Kinship and the Creation of Norman Power, 840–1066*, Berkeley and Los Angeles

Soehnée, F. (1907), *Catalogue des actes d'Henry 1er, roi de France, 1031–1060*, Paris

Structures féodales et féodalisme dans l'Orient méditerranéen (X–XIIIe siècles) (1980), Paris

Vajay, S. de (1971), 'Mathilde, reine de France inconnue', *Journal des Savants*: 241–60

6 SPAIN IN THE ELEVENTH CENTURY

Barrios García, A. (1983–4), *Estructuras agrarias y de poder en Castilla: el ejemplo de Avila (1085–1320)*, 2 vols., Salamanca

Bensch, S. P. (1995), *Barcelona and its Rulers, 1096–1291*, Cambridge

Bishko, C. J. (1961), 'Liturgical intercession at Cluny for the king-emperors of León', *Studia Monastica* 3: 53–76; repr. in *Spanish and Portuguese Monastic History 600–1300*, London, 1984

Bishko, C. J. (1965), 'The Cluniac priories of Galicia and Portugal: their acquisition and administration, 1075–c. 1230', *Studia Monastica* 7: 305–56; repr. in *Spanish and Portuguese Monastic History 600–1300*, London, 1984

Bishko, C. J. (1971), 'Count Henrique of Portugal, Cluny, and the antecedents of the Pacto Sucessório', *Revista Portuguesa de Historia* 13: 155–88; repr. in *Spanish and Portuguese Monastic History 600–1300*, London, 1984

Bishko, C. J. (1980), 'Fernando I and the origins of the Leonese–Castilian alliance with Cluny', in C. J. Bishko, *Studies in Medieval Spanish Frontier History*, II, London, pp. 1–136

Bisson, T. N. (1986), *The Medieval Crown of Aragon: A Short History*, Oxford

Bonnassie, P. (1964), 'Une famille de la campagne barcelonnaise et ses activités économiques aux alentours de l'an mil', *Annales du Midi* 75: 261–307

Bonnassie, P. (1975–6), *La Catalogne du milieu du Xe à la fin du XIe siècle: croissance et mutations d'une société*, 2 vols., Toulouse

Bosch Vilá, J. (1956), *Los Almorávides*, Tetuán; repr. Granada, 1990

Buesa Conde, D. J. (1996), *Sancho Ramírez, rey de aragoneses y pamploneses (1064–1094)*, Saragossa

Bull, M. (1993), *Knightly Piety and the Lay Response to the First Crusade: The Limousin and Gascony c. 970–c. 1130*, Oxford

Carlé, M. C. (1973), 'Gran propiedad y grandes proprietarios', *Cuadernos de Historia de España* 57–8: 1–224

Carzolio de Rossi, M. I. (1981), 'La gran propiedad laica gallega en el signo XI', *Cuadernos de Historia de España* 65–6: 59–112

Collins, R. (1990), *The Basques*, 2nd edn, Oxford

Collins, R. (1995), *Early Medieval Spain: Unity in Diversity, 400–1000*, 2nd edn, London

Cowdrey, H. E. J. (1970), *The Cluniacs and the Gregorian Reform*, Oxford

David, P. (1948), 'Le Pacte successoral entre Raymond de Galice et Henri de Portugal', *Bulletin Hispanique* 50: 275–90

Défourneaux, M. (1949), *Les Français en Espagne aux XIe et XIIe siècles*, Paris

Dunlop, D. M. (1942), 'The Dhunnunids of Toledo', *JRAS*: 77–96

Fernández-Armesto, F. (1992), 'The survival of a notion of *Reconquista* in late tenth-and eleventh-century León', in T. Reuter (ed.), *Warriors and Churchmen in the High Middle Ages: Essays Presented to Karl Leyser*, London, pp. 123–43

Fernández del Pozo, J. M. (1984), 'Alfonzo V, Rey de León', in *León y su Historia: Miscelánea histórica*, v, León, pp. 9–262

Ferreiro, A. (1983), 'The siege of Barbastro 1064–65: a reassessment', *JMH* 9: 129–44

Fletcher, R. A. (1978), *The Episcopate in the Kingdom of León in the Twelfth Century*, Oxford

Fletcher, R. A. (1984), *Saint James's Catapult: The Life and Times of Diego Gelmírez of Santiago de Compostela*, Oxford

Fletcher, R. A. (1987), 'Reconquest and crusade in Spain c. 1050–1150', *TRHS* 5th series, 37: 31–47

Fletcher, R. A. (1989), *The Quest for El Cid*, London

Fletcher, R. A. (1994), 'Las iglesias del reino de León y sus relaciones con Roma en la alta edad media hasta el Concilio IV de Letrán de 1215', in *El reino de León en la alta edad media*, vi, León, pp. 459–95

García de Cortázar, J. A. (1985), 'Del Cantábrico al Duero', in J. A. Garciá de Cortázar *et al.*, *Organización social del espacio en la España medieval: la corona de Castilla en los siglos VIII a XV*, Barcelona, pp. 43–83

García Gómez, E. and Menéndez Pidal, R. (1947), 'El conde mozárabe Sisnando Davídiz y la política de Alfonso VI con los taifas', *Al-Andalus* 12: 27–41

Gautier Dalché, J. (1989), *Historia urbana de León y Castilla en la edad media (siglos IX–XIII)*, 2nd edn, Madrid

González Jiménez, M. (1989), 'Frontier and settlement in the kingdom of Castile (1085–1350)', in R. Bartlett and A. Mackay (eds.), *Medieval Frontier Societies*, Oxford, pp. 49–74

Grassotti, H. (1964), 'Para la historia del botín y de las parias en León y Castilla', *Cuadernos de Historia de España* 39–40: 43–132

Hitchcock, R. (1973), 'El rito hispánico, las ordalías y los mozárabes en el reinado de Alfonso VI', *Estudios Orientales* 21: 19–41

Hrbek, I. and Devisse, J. (1988), 'The Almoravids', in M. El Fasi (ed.), *Africa from the Seventh to the Eleventh Century: UNESCO General History of Africa*, iii, Berkeley, pp. 336–66

Huici Miranda, A. (1956), *Las grandes batallas de la Reconquista durante las invasiones africanas*, Madrid

Huici Miranda, A. (1969–70), *Historia musulmana de Valencia y su región, novedades y rectificaciones*, 3 vols., Valencia

Kehr, P. (1945), 'Cómo y cuándo se hizo Aragón feudatario de la Santa Sede', *EEMCA* 1: 285–326

Kehr, P. (1946), 'El papado y los reinos de Navarra y Aragón hasta mediados del siglo XII', *EEMCA* 2: 74–186

Lacarra, J. M. (1951), 'Desarrollo urbano de Jaca en la edad media', *EEMCA* 4: 139–55

Lacarra, J. M. (1975), *Historia del reino de Navarra en la edad media*, Pamplona

Lacarra, J. M. (1981a), 'Aspectos económicos de la sumisión de los reinos de taifas (1010–1102)', in *Colonización, parias, repoblación y otros estudios*, Saragossa, pp. 41–76

Lacarra, J. M. (1981b), 'Dos tratados de paz y alianza entre Sancho el de Peñalén y Moctadir de Zaragoza (1069 y 1073)', in *Colonización, parias, repoblación y otros estudios*, Saragossa, pp. 77–94

Lagardère, V. (1989a), *Les Almoravides*, Paris

Lagardère, V. (1989b), *Le Vendredi de Zallāqa, 23 Octobre 1086*, Paris

Lévi-Provençal, E. (1931), 'Alphonse VI et la prise de Tolède (1085)', *Hespéris*, 12: 33–49; repr. in *Islam d'Occident: études d'histoire médiévale*, Paris, 1948, pp. 109–35

Lévi-Provençal, E. (1944), *Histoire de l'Espagne musulmane*, 1, Cairo

Linage Conde, A. (1973), *Los orígenes del monacato benedictino en la península Ibérica*, 3 vols., León

Lomax, D. W. (1978), *The Reconquest of Spain*, London

López Ferreiro, A. (1898–1911), *Historia de la Santa A. M. Iglesia de Santiago de Compostela*, 11 vols., Santiago de Compostela

Marín, M. (1992), 'Crusaders in the Muslim west: the view of Arab writers', *Maghreb Review* 17: 95–102

Martínez Sopena, P. (1985), *La tierra de campos occidental: poblamiento, poder y comunidad del siglo X al XIII*, Valladolid

Menéndez Pidal, R. (1956), *La España del Cid*, 2 vols., 5th edn, Madrid

Miranda Calvo, J. (1980), *La Reconquista de Toledo por Alfonso VI*, Toledo

Molina, L. (1981), 'Las campañas de Almanzor a la luz de un nuevo texto', *Al-Qantara* 2: 209–63

Molina López, E. (1990), 'Estudio preliminar', in J. Bosch-Villa, *Los Almoravides*, Granada, pp. v–lxxxi

Moralejo, S. (1985), 'The tomb of Alfonso Ansúrez (†1093): its place and the role of Sahagún in the beginnings of Spanish Romanesque sculpture', in B. F. Reilly (ed.), *Santiago, Saint-Denis, and Saint Peter: The Reception of the Roman Liturgy in León-Castile in 1080*, New York, pp. 63–100

Moreta Velayos, S. (1971), *El monasterio de San Pedro de Cardeña: historia de un dominio castellano (902–1338)*, Salamanca

Müssigbrod, A. (1994), 'Die Beziehungen des Bischofs Petrus von Pamplona zum französischen Mönchtum', *RBén* 104: 346–78

Nelson, L. H. (1984), 'Internal migration in early Aragón: the settlers from Ena and Baón', *Traditio* 40: 131–48

O'Callaghan, J. F. (1975), *A History of Medieval Spain*, Ithaca

O'Callaghan, J. F. (1985), 'The integration of Christian Spain into Europe: the role of Alfonso VI of León-Castile', in B. F. Reilly (ed.), *Santiago, Saint-Denis, and Saint Peter: The Reception of the Roman Liturgy in León-Castile in 1080*, New York, pp. 101–20

Pastor, R. (1980), *Resistencias y luchas campesinas en la época del crecimiento y consolidación de la formación feudal: Castilla y León, siglos X–XIII*, 2nd edn, Madrid

Pattison, D. G. (1996), '"¡Dios, que buen vassalo! ¡Si oviesse buen señor!": the theme of the loyal vassal in the *Poema de mio Cid*', in B. Powell and G. West (eds.), *Al que en buen hora naçio: Essays on the Spanish Epic and Ballad in Honour of Colin Smith*, Liverpool, pp. 107–13

Pérès, H. (1953), *La poésie andalouse en arabe classique au XIe siècle: ses aspects généraux, ses principaux thèmes et sa valeur documentaire*, 2nd edn, Paris

Pérez de Urbel, J. (1950), *Sancho el mayor de Navarra*, Madrid

Powers, J. F. (1988), *A Society Organized for War: The Iberian Municipal Militias in the Central Middle Ages, 1000–1284*, Berkeley

Prieto Prieto, A. (1975), 'El conde Fruela Muñoz: un asturiano del siglo XI', *Asturiensia Medievalia* 2: 11–37

Reilly, B. F. (1988), *The Kingdom of León-Castilla under King Alfonso VI, 1065–1109*, Princeton

Reilly, B. F. (1992), *The Contest of Christian and Muslim Spain, 1031–1157*, Oxford

Rivera Recio, J. F. (1966), *La iglesia de Toledo en el siglo XII*, Rome and Madrid

Ruiz Asencio, J. M. (1968), 'Campañas de Almanzor contra el reino de León (981–986)', *Anuario de Estudios Medievales* 5: 31–64

Ruiz de la Peña Solar, J. I. (1993), 'Las colonizaciones francas en las rutas castellano-leonesas del camino de Santiago', in J. I. Ruiz de la Peña Solar (ed.), *Las peregrinaciones a Santiago de Compostela y San Salvador de Oviedo en la edad media*, Oviedo, pp. 283–312

Ruiz Doménec, J. E. (1977), 'The urban origins of Barcelona: agricultural revolution or commercial development?', *Speculum* 52: 265–86

Säbekow, G. (1931), *Die päpstlichen Legaten nach Spanien und Portugal bis zum Ausgang des XII Jahrhunderts*, Berlin

Sáez, E. (ed.) (1953), *Los fueros de Sepúlveda*, Segovia

Salrach, J. M. (1987), 'El procés de feudalització (segles III–XII)', in P. Vilar (ed.), *Historia de Catalunya*, II, Barcelona

Sánchez-Albornoz, C. (1965), 'Notas para el estudio del "petitum"', in *Estudios sobre las instituciones medievales españolas*, Mexico City, pp. 483–519

Sánchez-Albornoz, C. (1966), *Despoblación y repoblación del valle del Duero*, Buenos Aires

Sánchez-Albornoz, C. (1978), *El regimen de la tierra en reino asturleónes hace mil años*, Buenos Aires

Santiago-Otero, H. (ed.) (1992), *El camino de Santiago, la hospitalidad y las peregrinaciones*, Salamanca

Scales, P. C. (1994), *The Fall of the Caliphate of Córdoba: Berbers and Andalusis in Conflict*, Leiden

Seco de Lucena Paredes, L. (1970), 'New light on the military campaigns of Almanzor', *Islamic Quarterly* 14: 126–42

Segl, P. (1974), *Königtum und Klosterreform in Spanien: Untersuchungen über die Cluniacenserklöster in Kastilien-León vom Beginn des 11. bis zur Mitte des 12. Jahrhunderts*, Kallmünz

Slaughter, J. E. (1974–9), 'De nuevo sobre la batalla de Uclés', *Anuario de Estudios Medievales* 9: 393–404

Sobrequés i Vidal, S. (1985), *Els grans comtes de Barcelona*, 4th edn, Barcelona

Tapia Garrido, J. A. (1978), *Historia general de Almería y su provincia*, II, Almería

Terrón Albarrán, M. (1971), *El solar de los Aftásids: aportación temática al estudio del reino moro de Badajoz: siglo XI*, Badajoz

Turk, A. (1978), *El reino de Zaragoza en el siglo XI de Cristo (V de la Hégira)*, Madrid

Ubieto Arteta, A. (1948), 'La introducción del rito romano en Aragón y Navarra', *Hispania Sacra* 1: 299–324

Ubieto Arteta, A. (1981), *Historia de Aragón: la formatión territorial*, Saragossa

Valdeavellano, L. G. de (1968), *Historia de España: de los orígenes a la baja edad media*, 2 vols., 4th edn, Madrid

Valdeavellano, L. G. de (1969), *Orígenes de la burgesía en la España medieval*, Madrid

Vázquez de Parga, L., Lacarra, J. M. and Uría Ríu, J. (1948–9), *Las peregrinaciones a Santiago de Compostela*, 3 vols., Madrid

Viguera Molíns, M. J. (1992), *Los reinos de Taifas y las invasiones magrebíes (Al-Andalus del XI al XIII)*, Madrid

Viguera Molíns, M. J. (ed.) (1994), *Los reinos de Taifas: al-Andalus en el siglo XI*, Madrid

Villar García, L. M. (1986), *La Extremadura castellano-leonesa: guerreros, clérigos y campesinos (711–1252)*, Valladolid

Viñayo González, A. (1961), 'Cuestíones historico-criticas en torno a la traslación del cuerpo de San Isidoro', in M. Díaz y Díaz (ed.), *Isidoriana*, León, pp. 285–97

Wasserstein, D. (1985), *The Rise and Fall of the Party-Kings: Politics and Society in Islamic Spain, 1002–1086*, Princeton

West, G. (1977), 'King and vassal in history and poetry: a contrast between the "Historia Roderici" and the "Poema de Mio Cid"', in A. D. Deyermond (ed.), *'Mio Cid' Studies*, London, pp. 195–208

Whitehill, W. M. (1941), *Spanish Romanesque Architecture of the Eleventh Century*, Oxford

Wright, R. (1979), 'The first poem on the Cid – the *Carmen Campi Doctoris*', in F. Cairns (ed.), *Papers of the Liverpool Latin Seminar*, II, Liverpool, pp. 213–48

7 ENGLAND AND NORMANDY, 1042–1137

Anglo-Norman Studies (1979–), ed. R. A. Brown, M. Chibnall and C. Harper-Bill, Woodbridge and Wolfeboro

Barlow, F. (1970), *Edward the Confessor*, London

Barlow, F. (1983), *William Rufus*, London

Barrow, G. W. S. (1973), *The Kingdom of the Scots*, London

Bates, D. (1982), *Normandy before 1066*, London and New York

Bates, D. (1989a), 'Normandy and England after 1066', *EHR* 104: 851–80

Bates, D. (1989b), *William the Conqueror*, London

Bishop, T. A. M. (1961), *Scriptores regis*, Oxford

Brown, R. A. (1985), *The Normans and the Norman Conquest*, 2nd edn, Woodbridge

Blackburn, M. (1991), 'Coinage and currency under Henry I', *ANS* 13: 49–81

Brand, P. (1990), '"Multis vigiliis excogitatem et inventam": Henry II and the creation of the common law', *Haskins Society Journal* 2: 197–222

Campbell, J. (1987), 'Some agents and agencies of the late Anglo-Saxon state', in Holt (1987b), pp. 201–18

Chaplais, P. (1965–9), 'The Anglo-Saxon chancery from the diploma to the writ', *Journal of the Society of Archivists* 3: 160–7

Chibnall, M. (1986), *Anglo-Norman England 1066–1166*, Oxford

Chibnall, M. (1991), *The Empress Matilda*, Oxford

Clanchy, M. (1979), *From Memory to Written Record*, London

Crouch, D. (1987), *The Beaumont Twins* (Cambridge Studies in Medieval Life and Thought), Cambridge

David, C. W. (1920), *Robert Curthose* (Harvard Historical Studies 5), Cambridge, MA

Davies, R. R. (1987), *Conquest, Coexistence and Change in Wales, 1063–1415*, Oxford

Davis, R. H. C. (1980), 'William of Jumièges, Robert Curthose and the Norman succession', *EHR* 95: 597–606

Davis, R. H. C. (1987), 'Domesday Book: continental parallels', in Holt (1987b), pp. 15–39

Davis, R. H. C. (1990), *King Steven*, 3rd edn, London and New York

Douglas, D. C. (1946), 'The Earliest Norman counts', *EHR* 61: 129–56

Douglas, D. C. (1964), *William the Conqueror*, London

Eales, R. (1990), 'Royal power and castles in Norman England', in C. Harper-Bill and R. Harvey (eds.), *The Ideals and Practices of Medieval Knighthood*, 3 vols., Woodbridge and Wolfeboro

Fleming, R. (1991), *Kings and Lords in Conquest England*, Cambridge

Flori, J. (1986), *L'Essor de la Chevalerie XIe–XIIe siècles*, Geneva

Garnett, G. (1986), 'Coronation and propaganda: some implications of the Norman claim to the throne of England in 1066', *TRHS* 5th series, 36: 91–116

Green, J. A. (1981), 'The last century of Danegeld', *EHR* 96: 241–58

Green, J. A. (1982), '"Praeclarum et magnificum antiquitatis monumentum": the earliest surviving Pipe Roll', *Bulletin of the Institute of Historical Research* 55: 1–17

Green, J. A. (1986), *The Government of England under Henry I* (Cambridge Studies in Medieval Life and Thought), Cambridge

Green, J. A. (1989), 'Unity and disunity in the Anglo-Norman state', *Historical Research* 63: 115–34

Haskins, C. H. (1925), *Norman Institutions* (Harvard Historical Studies 24), Cambridge, MA

Hollister, C. W. (1973), 'The strange death of William Rufus', *Speculum* 48: 637–53

Hollister, C. W. (1975), 'The Anglo-Norman succession debate of 1126: prelude to Stephen's anarchy', *JMH* 6: 289–306

Hollister, C. W. (1976), 'Normandy, France and the Anglo-Norman regnum', *Speculum* 51: 202–42

Hollister, C. W. (1978a), 'The origins of the English treasury', *EHR* 93: 262–75

Hollister, C. W. (1978b), 'The rise of administrative kingship: Henry I', *AHR* 83: 868–91

Hollister, C. W. (1986) *Monarchy, Magnates and Institutions in the Anglo-Norman World*, London and Ronceverte

Hollister, C. W. (1987), 'The Greater Domesday tenants-in-chief', in J. C. Holt (ed.), *Domesday Studies*, Woodbridge and Wolfeboro, pp. 219–48

Holt, J. C. (1972), 'Politics and property in early medieval England', *PaP* 57: 3–52

Holt, J. C. (1984), 'The introduction of knight service into England', *ANS* 6: 89–106

Holt, J. C. (1987a), '1066', in Holt (1987b), pp. 41–64

Holt, J. C. (ed.) (1987b), *Domesday Studies*, Woodbridge and Wolfeboro

Hyams, P. (1987), '"No register of title": the Domesday inquest and land adjudication', *ANS* 9: 127–41

Kealey, E. J. (1972), *Roger of Salisbury*, Berkeley, Los Angeles and London

Keynes, S. (1991), 'The Æthelings in Normandy', *ANS* 13: 173–205

Le Patourel, J. (1976), *The Norman Empire*, Oxford

Lewis, C. P. (1991), 'The early earls of Norman England', *ANS* 13: 207–23

Leyser, K. (1960), 'England and the empire in the early twelfth century', *TRHS* 5th series, 10: 61–83

Leyser, K. (1991), 'The Anglo-Norman succession, 1120–1125', *ANS* 13: 225–41

Loyn, H. R. (1962), *Anglo-Saxon England and the Norman Conquest*, London

Mason, J. F. A. (1963), 'Roger de Montgomery and his sons (1067–1102)', in *TRHS* 5th series, 13: 1–28

Milsom, S. F. C. (1976), *The Legal Framework of English Feudalism*, Cambridge

Musset, L. (1968), 'Gouvernés et gouvernants dans le monde scandinave et dans le monde normand', in *Gouvernés et gouvernants* 2 (Recueils de la Société Jean Bodin), Brussels

Musset, L. (1970), 'Naissance de la Normandie', in Michel de Bouard (ed.), *Histoire de Normandie*, Toulouse, pp. 75–130

Prestwich, J. R. (1954), 'War and finance in the Anglo-Norman state', *TRHS* 5th series, 4: 19–43

Prestwich, J. R. (1981), 'The military household of the Norman kings', *EHR* 96: 1–37

Reynolds, S. (1977), *An Introduction to the History of Medieval Towns*, Oxford

Ritchie, R. L. G. (1954), *The Normans in Scotland* (Edinburgh University Publications, History, Philosophy and Economics 4), Edinburgh

Round, J. H. (1909), *Feudal England*, London

Searle, E. (1988), *Predatory Kinship and the Creation of Norman Power, 840–1066*, Berkeley, Los Angeles and London

Southern, R. W. (1973), *Medieval Humanism and Other Studies*, Oxford

Southern, R. W. (1990), *St Anselm: A Portrait in a Landscape*, Cambridge

Stafford, P. (1989), *Unification and Conquest: A Political and Social History of England in the Tenth and Eleventh Centuries*, London and New York

Stenton, F. *et al.*, (1959), *The Bayeux Tapestry*, London

Stenton, F. M. (1961), *The First Century of English Feudalism*, 2nd edn, Oxford

Stenton, F. M. (1971), *Anglo-Saxon England*, 3rd edn, Oxford

Tabuteau, E. Z. (1988), *Transfers of Property in Eleventh-Century Normandy*, Chapel Hill and London

Van Caenegem, R. C. (1976), 'Public prosecution of crime in twelfth-century England', in C. N. L. Brooke *et al.* (eds.), *Church and Government in the Middle Ages*, Cambridge, pp. 41–76

Van Caenegem, R. C. (ed.) (1959), *Royal Writs in England from the Conquest to Glanvill* (Selden Society 77), London

Van Caenegem, R. C. (ed.) (1990), *English Lawsuits from William I to Richard I*, 1 (Selden Society 106), London

Van Houts, E. M. C. (1988), 'The ship list of William the Conqueror', *ANS* 10: 159–83

Yver, J. (1957), 'Les châteaux forts en Normandie jusqu'au milieu du XIIe siècle', *Bulletin de la Société des Antiquaires de Normandie* 53: 28–115, 604–9

Yver, J. (1969), 'Les premières institutions du duché de la Normandie', in *I Normanni e la loro espansione in Europa nell'alto medioevo* (Centro Italiano di Studi sull'alto Medioevo; Settimana 16), Spolpeto pp. 299–366

8 THE BYZANTINE EMPIRE, 1025–1118

For a full bibliography (to 1962) see J. M. Hussey (ed.) *Cambridge Medieval History*, IV part 1, Cambridge, 1966, pp. 858–67.

Criticism of sources: studies of authors
Anna Komnena
Aerts, W. J. (1976), 'Anna's mirror, attic(istic) or "antiquarian"?', in *XVe Congrès international d'études byzantines: rapports et co-rapports*, II I, Athens

Browning, R. (1962), 'An unpublished funeral oration on Anna Comnena', *Proceedings of the Cambridge Philosophical Society* n.s. 8: 1–12

Buckler, G. (1929), *Anna Comnena*, Oxford

Chrystostomides, J. (1982), 'A Byzantine historian: Anna Comnena', in D. O. Morgan (ed.), *Medieval Historical Writing in the Christian and Islamic Worlds*, London, pp. 30–46

Cresci, L. R. (1993), 'Anna Comnena fra storia ed encomio', *Civiltà Classica e Cristiana*, 14: 63–90

Davlen, R. (1972), *Anna Comnena*, New York

Dyck, A. R. (1986), 'Iliad and Alexiad: Anna Comnena's Homeric reminiscences', *Greek, Roman and Byzantine Studies* 27: 113–20

Ferrari d'Occhieppo, K. (1974), 'Zur Identifizierung der Sonnenfinsternis während des Petschenegkrieges Alexios I. Komnenos (1084)', *JöB* 23: 179–84

France, J. (1983), 'Anna Comnena, the *Alexiad*, and the First Crusade', *Reading Medieval Studies* 10: 20–32

Gouma-Peterson, T. (2000), *Anna Commena and her Times*, New York

Hunger, H. (1978), 'Stilstufen in der byzantinischen Geschichtsschreibung des 12. Jahrhunderts', *Byzantine Studies/Etudes Byzantines* 5: 139–70

Kambylis, A. (1975), 'Zum "Program" der byzantinischen Historikerin Anna Komnene', in *ΔΩΡΗΜΑ, Hans Diller zum 70. Geburtstag*, Athens, pp. 127–46

Kambylis, A. (1970), 'Textkritisches zum 15. Buch der Alexias der Anna Komnena', *JöB* 19: 121–34

Leib, B. (1958), 'Les silences d'Anna Comnène', *BS* 19: 1–10

Lilie, R.-J. (1987), 'Der erste Kreuzzug in der Darstellung Anne Komnenes', in *VARIA II* (Poikila Byzantina 6), Bonn, pp. 49–148

Lilie, R.-J. (1993), 'Anna Komnene und die Lateiner', *BS* 54: 169–82

Ljubarskij, J. N. (1964a), 'Mirovozzrenie Anny Komniny', *Uchenye zapiski Velikolukskogo pedinstituta* 24: 152–76

Ljubarskij, J. N. (1964b), 'Ob istochnikakh "Aleksijady" Anny Komninoj', *VV* 25: 99–120

Loud, A. (1991), 'Anna Comnena and her sources for the Normans of southern Italy', in I. Wood and G. A. Loud (eds.), *Church and Chronicle in the Middle Ages: Essays Presented to John Taylor*, London, pp. 41–57

Maltese, E. V. (1987), 'Anna Comena nel mare delle sventure (Alex. XIV 7,4)', *BZ* 80: 1–2

Reinisch, D. R. (1989a), 'Ausländer und Byzantiner im Werk der Anna Komnene', *Rechtshistorisches Journal* 8: 257–74

Reinisch, D. R. (1989b), '"De minimis non curat Anna?"', *JöB* 39: 129–34

Reinisch, D. R. (1989c), 'Eine angebliche Interpolation in der *Alexias* Anna Komnenes', *BZ* 82: 69–72

Reinisch, D. R. (1990), 'Zum Text der *Alexias* Anna Komnenes', *JöB* 40: 233–68

Reinisch, D. R. (1996), 'Zur literarischen Leistung der Anna Komnene', in J. O. Rosenquist (ed.), *ΛΕΙΜΩΝ: Studies Presented to Lennart Rydén on his Sixty Fifth Birthday*, Uppsala, pp. 113–25

Thomas, R. D. (1991), 'Anna Comnene's account of the First Crusade: history and politics in the reigns of Alexius I and Manuel I Comnenus', *BMGS* 15: 269–312

Christopher of Mitylene
Follieri, E. (1964), 'Le poesie di Cristoforo Mitilenio come fonte storica', *ZRVI* 8/2: 133–48

Digenes Akrites
Angold, M. J. (1989), 'The wedding of Digenes Akrites: love and marriage in the 11th and 12th centuries', in C. Maltezou (ed.), *Η ΚΑΘΗΜΕΡΙΝΗ ΖΩΗ ΣΤΟ ΒΥΖΑΝΤΙΟ*, Athens, pp. 201–15
Beaton, R. (1981a), 'Was *Digenes Akrites* an oral poem?', *BMGS* 7: 7–27
Beaton, R. (1981b), '*Digenes Akrites* and modern Greek folk song: a reassessment', *Byzantion* 51: 22–43
Beaton, R. and Ricks, D. (1993), *Digenes Akrites: New Approaches to Byzantine Heroic Poetry*, Aldershot
Dyck, A. (1983), 'On *Digenes Akrites*, Grottaferrata version Book 5', *Greek, Roman and Byzantine Studies* 24: 185–92
Galatariotou, C. (1987), 'Structural oppositions in the Grottaferrata *Digenes Akrites*', *BMGS* 11: 29–68
Huxley, G. (1974), 'Antecedents and context of *Digenes Akrites*', *Greek, Roman and Byzantine Studies* 15: 317–38
MacAlister, S. (1984), 'Digenes Akrites: the first scene with the Apelatai', *Byzantion* 54: 551–74
Magdalino, P. (1989), 'Honour among Romaioi: the framework of social values in the work of Digenes Akrites and Kekaumenos', *BMGS* 13: 183–218
Oikonomides, N. (1979), 'L'épopée de Digénis et la frontière orientale de Byzance aux Xe et XIe siècles', *TM* 7: 375–97

Eustratios of Nicaea
Giocarinis, K. (1964), 'Eustratius of Nicaea's defense of the doctrine of ideas', *Franciscan Studies* 24: 159–204

George Cedrenus
Maisano, R. (1977–9), 'Sulla tradizione manoscritta di Georgio Cedreno', *Rivista di Studi Bizantini e Neoellenici*, 14–16: 179–201
Maisano, R. (1983), 'Note su Giorgio Cedreno e la tradizione storiografica bizantina', *Rivista di Studi Bizantini e Slavi*, 3: 227–48

John Italos
Clucas, L. (1981), *The Trial of John Italos and the Crisis of Intellectual Values in Byzantium in the Eleventh Century* (Miscellanea Byzantina Monacensia 26), Münich
Kechakmadze, N. (1967), 'Grammatiko-logicheskij traktat Ioanna Itala', *VV* 27: 197–205
Nikolaou, T. (1984), 'Eine quellenkritische Untersuchung des Traktats (87) "de iconis der Quaestiones Quodlibetales" und seine Bedeutung hinsichtlich der Verurteilung

des Johannes Italos', in *MNHMH MHTPOΠOΛITH IKONIOY IAKΩBOY*, Athens, pp. 279–94

John Mauropous

Anastasi, R. (1970), 'Dione Crisostomo e Giovanni di Euchaita', *Siculorum Gymnasium* n.s. 23: 17–39

Anastasi, R. (1972), 'Su tre epigrammi di Giovanni di Euchaita', *Siculorum Gymnasium* n.s. 25: 56–60

Anastasi, R. (1976), 'Su Giovanni d'Euchaita', *Siculorum Gymnasium* n.s. 29: 19–49

Bonis, C. G. (1966), 'Worship and dogma: John Mauropous, metropolitan of Euchaita (11th century): his canon on the three hierarchs and its dogmatic significance', *BF* 1: 1–23

Dyck, A. R. (1993), 'John Mauropous of Euchaita and the "Stoic Etymologikon"', *JöB* 43: 113–40

Follieri, E. (1971), 'Sulla Novella promulgata da Costantino IX Monomaco per la restaurazione della Facoltà giuridica a Constantinopoli (sec. XI med.)', in *Studi in onore di Edoardo Volterra*, 11, Milan, pp. 647–64

Karpozilos, A. (1982), *ΣYMBOΛH ΣTH MEΛETH TOY BIOY KAI EPΓOY TOY IΩANNH MAYPOΠOΛOΣ*, Ioannina

Kazhdan, A. (1993), 'Some problems in the biography of John Mauropous', *JöB* 43: 87–112

Lefort, J. (1976), 'Rhétorique et politique: trois discours de Jean Mauropous en 1047', *TM* 6: 265–303

Mitsakis, K. (1966), 'Problems concerning the manuscript tradition of John Mauropous's work: John and Symeon metropolitans of Euchaita and the question of authorship of the "Letter to John the contemplative monk"', *APXEION ΠONTOY* 28: 191–6

John Skylitzes

Fatouros, G. (1975), 'Textkritische Beobachtungen zu Ioannes Skylitzes', *JöB* 24: 91–4

Ferluga, J. (1967), 'John Skylitzes and Michael of Devoi', *ZRVI* 10: 163–70

Laiou, A. (1992), 'Imperial marriages and their critics in the eleventh century: the case of Skylitzes', *DOP* 46: 165–76

Seibt, W. (1976), 'Ioannes Skylitzes: zur Person des Chronisten', *JöB* 25: 81–5

Shepard, J. (1975–6), 'Scylitzes on Armenia in the 1040s and the role of Catacalon Cecaumenos', *Revue des Etudes Armeniennes* n.s. 11: 269–311

Shepard, J. (1977–9), 'Byzantium's last Sicilian expedition: Scylitzes' testimony', *Rivista di Studi Bizantini e Neoellenici* n.s. 14–16: 145–59

Shepard, J. (1992), 'A suspected source of Scylitzes' *Synopsis Historion*: the great Catacalon Cecaumenus', *BMGS* 16: 171–81

Thurn, I. (1966), 'Zur Textüberlieferung des Skylitzes', *BZ* 59: 1–4

Tsolakis, E. T. (1964), 'TO ΠPOBΛHMA TOY ΣYNEXIΣTH THΣ XPONOΓPAΦIAΣ TOY IΩANNOY ΣKYΛITΣH', *EΛΛHNIKA* 18: 79–83

John Xiphilinos (the Younger)

Halkin, F. (1966), 'Le concile de Chalcédoine esquissé par Jean Xiphilin', *REB* 24: 182–8

Hennephof, H. (1972), 'Der Kampf um das Prooimion im xiphilinischen Homiliar', *Studia Byzantina et Neohellenica Neerlandica* 3: 281–99

Kekaumenos
Bartikian, H. (1965), 'La généalogie du magistros Bagarat, catépan de l'Orient, et des Kékauménos', in *Revue des Etudes Arméniennes* n.s. 2: 261–72
Darrouzès, J. (1964), 'Kekaumenos et la mystique', *REB* 22: 282–4
Lemerle, P. (1960), *Prolégomènes à une édition critique et commentée de Kékauménos*, Brussels
Litavrin, G. G. (1968a), 'Kekavmen i Mikhail Psell o Varde Sklire', *BF* 3: 157–64
Litavrin, G. G. (1968b), 'Ο ΠΑΠΠΟΣ ΤΟΥ ΚΕΚΑΥΜΕΝΟΥ – Ο ΕΧΘΡΟΣ ΤΗΣ ΡΩΜΑΝΙΑΣ', *VV* 28: 151–8

Manuel Straboromanos
Bühler, W. (1969), 'Zu Manuel Straboromanos', *BZ* 62: 237–42

Michael Attaleiates
Amande, C. (1989), 'L'encomio di Niceforo Botaniate nel Historia di Attaliate: modeli, fonti, suggestioni letterarie', *Serta Historica Antiqua* 2: 265–86
Cresci, L. R. (1991), 'Cadenze narrative e interpr etazione critica nell'opera storica di Michele Attaliate', *REB* 49: 197–218
Cresci, L. R. (1993), 'Anticipazione e possibilità: moduli interpretativi della Storia di Michele Attaliata', in R. Maisano (ed.), *Storia e tradizione culturale a Bisanzio fra XI e XII secolo* (ITAΛΟΕΛΛΗΝΙΚΑ Quaderni 3), Naples, pp. 71–96
Kazhdan, A. P. (1976), 'Sotsial'nie vozrenija Mihaila Attaliata', *ZRVI* 17: 1–53
Pertusi, A. (1958), 'Per la critica del testo della "storia" di Michele Attaliate', *JöB* 7: 59–73
Thurn, I. (1964), 'Textgeschichtliches zu Michael Attaleiates', *BZ* 57: 293–301
Tsolakis, E. T. (1965), 'Aus dem Leben des Michael Attaleiates (seine Heimatstadt, sein Geburts- und Todesjahr)', *BZ* 58: 3–10
Tsolakis, E. T. (1969a), 'Ο ΜΙΧΑΗΛ ΑΤΤΑΛΕΙΑΤΗΣ ΩΣ ΚΡΙΤΙΚΟΣ ΤΩΝ ΕΠΙΧΕΙΡΗΣΕΩΝ ΚΑΙ ΤΗΣ ΤΑΚΤΙΚΗΣ ΤΟΥ ΠΟΛΕΜΟΥ', *BYZANTINA* 1: 187–204
Tsolakis, E. T. (1969b), 'Das Geschichtswerk des Michael Attaleiates und die Zeit seiner Abfassung', *BYZANTINA* 2: 251–68

Michael Psellos
Aerts, W. J. (1980), 'Un témoin inconnu de la Chronographie de Psellos', *BS* 41: 1–16
Agati, M. L. (1991), 'Michele VII Parapinace e la Chronographia di Psello', *Bollettino della Badia Greca di Grottaferrata* n.s. 45: 11–31
Anastasi, R. (1966), 'Sull'epitafi di Psello per Giovanni Xiphilino', *Siculorum Gymnasium* n.s. 19: 52–6
Anastasi, R. (1969), *Studi sulla 'Chronographia' di Michele Psello*, Catania
Anastasi, R. (1975a), 'Sugli scritti giurdici di Psello', *Siculorum Gymnasium* n.s. 28: 169–91
Anastasi, R. (1975b), 'Psello e Giovanni Italo', *Siculorum Gymnasium* n.s. 28: 525–38
Anastasi, R. (1976), *Studi di filologia bizantina* (Quaderni di Siculorum Gynmasium 2), Catania

Anastasi, R. (1985), 'Considerazione sul libro VII della "Chronographia" di Michele Psello', *Orpheus* n.s. 6: 370–95

Aubreton, R. (1969), 'Michel Psellos et l'Anthologie Palatine', *L'Antiquité Classique* 38: 459–62

Aujac, G. (1975), 'Michel Psellos et Denys d'Halicarnasse: le traité "Sur la composition des éléments du langage"', *REB* 33: 257–75

Baggarly, J. D. (1970), 'A parallel between Michael Psellus and the Hexaemeron of Anastasius of Sinai', *OCP* 36: 337–47

Benakis, L. (1964), 'Doxographische Angaben über die Vorsokratiker im unedierten Kommentar zur "Physik" des Aristoteles von Michael Psellos', in *XAPIΣ K. I. BOYP-BEPH*, Athens, pp. 345–54

Benakis, L. (1975–6), 'ΜΙΧΑΗΛ ΨΕΛΛΟΥ ΠΕΡΙ ΤΩΝ ΙΔΕΩΝ, ΑΣ Ο ΠΛΑΤΩΝ ΛΕΓΕΙ', *ΦΙΛΟΣΟΦΙΑ* 5/6: 391–423

Benakis, L. (1980–81), 'ΧΡΟΝΟΣ ΚΑΙ ΑΙΩΝ', *ΦΙΛΟΣΟΦΙΑ* 10/11: 398–421

Browning, R. (1963), 'A Byzantine treatise on tragedy', in *ΓΕΡΑΣ: Studies Presented to G. Thomson*, Prague, pp. 67–81

Browning, R. and Cutler, A. (1992), 'In the margins of Byzantium? Some icons in Michael Psellos', *BMGS* 16: 21–32

Bühler, W. (1967), 'Zwei Erstveröffentlichungen (Psellos und Eusathios)', *Byzantion* 37: 5–10

Cameron, A. (1970), 'Michael Psellus and the date of the Palatine Anthology', *Greek, Roman and Byzantine Studies* 11: 339–50

Canart, P. (1967), 'Nouveaux inédits de Michel Psellos', *REB* 25: 43–60

Carelos, F. (1991), 'Die Autoren der Zweiten Sophistik und die *Chronographia* des Michael Psellos', *JöB* 41: 133–40

Chamberlain, C. (1986), 'The theory and practice of imperial panegyric in Michael Psellus', *Byzantion* 56: 16–27

Criscuolo, U. (1982), 'ΠΟΛΙΤΙΚΟΣ ΑΝΗΡ: contributo al pensiero politico di Michele Psello', *Rendiconti dell'Accademia di Archeologia, Lettere e Belle Arti: Napoli* n.s. 57: 129–63

Dagron, G. (1983), 'Psellos épigraphiste', in C. Mango and O. Pritsak (eds.), *Okeanos: Essays Presented to I. Sevcenko*, Cambridge, MA, pp. 117–24

Dakouras, D. G. (1977), 'Michael Psellos' Kritik an den alten Griechen und dem griechischen Kult', *ΘΕΟΛΟΓΙΑ* 48: 40–75

Dakouras, D. G. (1978), 'Die Rehabilitation der griechischen Studien im. XI. Jahrhundert und Michael Psellos', *ΘΕΟΛΟΓΙΑ* 49: 185–98, 392–411

Des Places, E. (1966), 'Le renouveau platonicien du XIe siècle: Michel Psellus et les oracles chaldaïques', *Académie des Inscriptions et Belles-Lettres: Comptes Rendus*, 313–24

Dostálóva, R. (1986), 'Tabula Iliaca (Odysseaca) Ducaena: au sujet d'une épitre de Psellos', *BS* 47: 28–33

Dyck, A. R. (1994), '*Psellus Tragicus*: observations on *Chronographia* 5:26ff', *BF* 20: 269–90

Ebbesen, S. (1973), 'Ο ΨΕΛΛΟΣ ΚΑΙ ΟΙ ΣΟΦΙΣΤΙΚΟΙ ΕΛΕΓΧΟΙ', *BYZA-NTINA* 5: 427–44

Fisher, E. A. (1988), 'Nicodemia or Galatia? Where was Psellos' church of the Archangel Michael?', in *Gonimos: Neoplatonic and Byzantine Studies Presented to L. G. Westerlink at 75*, Buffalo, pp. 175–87

Fisher, E. A. (1993), 'Michael Psellos on the rhetoric of hagiography and the *Life of St Auxentius*', *BMGS* 17: 43–53

Fisher, E. A. (1994), 'Image and Ekphrasis in Michael Psellos' Sermon on the Crucifixion', *BS* 55: 44–55

Gadolin, A. R. (1970), *A Theory of History and Society with Special Reference to the* Chronographia *of Michael Psellus*, Stockholm

Gautier, P. (1976), 'Precisions historiques sur le monastère de Ta Narsou', *REB* 34: 101–10

Gautier, P. (1977), 'Michel Psellos et la Rhétorique de Longin', *Prometheus* 3: 193–203

Gemmiti, D. (1983), 'Aspetti del pensiero religioso di Michele Psello', in *Studi e Ric cordi. sull'Oriente Cristiano* 6: 77–169

Grosdidier de Matons, J. (1976), 'Psellos et le monde de l'irrationnel', *TM* 6: 325–49

Guglielmino, A. M. (1974), 'Un maestro di grammatica a Bisanzio nell'XI secolo e l'epitaphio per Niceta di Michele Psello', *Siculorum Gymnasium* n.s. 27: 421–63

Hohlweg, A. (1988), 'Medizinischer "Enzyklopädismus" und das ΠΟΝΗΜΑ ΙΑΤΡΙΚΟΝ des Michael Psellos', *BZ* 81: 39–49

Johnson, G. J. (1982), 'Constantine VIII and Michael Psellos: rhetoric, reality and the decline of Byzantium A.D. 1025–1028', *Byzantine Studies/Etudes Byzantines* 9: 220–32

Kambylis, A. (1994), 'Michael Psellos' Schrift über Euripides und Pisides: Probleme der Textkonstitution', *JöB* 44: 203–15

Karahalios, G. (1973), 'Michael Psellos on man and his beginnings', *Greek Orthodox Theological Review* 18: 79–96

Kazhdan, A. (1983), 'Hagiographical notes 3: an attempt at auto-hagiography: the pseudo-life of "Saint" Psellus?', *Byzantion* 53: 546–56

Koutsogiannopoulos, D. I. (1965), 'Η ΘΕΟΛΟΓΙΚΗ ΣΚΕΨΙΣ ΤΟΥ ΜΙΧΑΗΛ ΨΕΛΛΟΥ', *ΕΕΒΣ* 34: 208–17

Kriaras, E. (1968), 'Psellos', in *Real-Encyclopädie der classischen Altertumswissenschaft (Pauly-Wissowa)*, Suppl. Bd. 11: 1124–82

Kriaras, E. (1972), 'Ο ΜΙΧΑΗΛ ΨΕΛΛΟΣ', *BYZANTINA* 4: 53–128

Kyriakis, M. J. (1976–7), 'Medieval European society as seen in two eleventh-century texts of Michael Psellos', *Byzantine Studies/Etudes Byzantines* 3: 77–100; 4: 67–80, 157–88

Leroy-Molinghen, A. (1969a), 'Styliané', *Byzantion* 39: 155–63

Leroy-Molinghen, A. (1969b), 'La descendance adoptive de Psellos', *Byzantion* 39: 284–317

Linnér, S. (1981), 'Literary echoes in Psellus' *Chronographia*', *Byzantion* 51: 225–31

Linnér, S. (1983), 'Psellus' *Chronographia* and the *Alexias*: some textual parallels', *BZ* 76: 1–9

Littlewood, A. (1981), 'The midwifery of Michael Psellos: an example of Byzantine literary originality', in M. Mullett and R. Scott (eds.), *Byzantium and the Classical Tradition*, Birmingham, pp. 136–42

Littlewood, A. (1990), 'Michael Psellos and the witch of Endor', *JöB* 40: 225–31

Ljubarskij, J. N. (1977), 'Der Brief des Kaisers an Phokas', *JöB* 26: 103–7

Ljubarskij, J. N. (1978), *Mikhail Psell: Lichnost' i tvorchestvo. K istorii vizantijskogo predgumanizma*, Moscow

Maisano, R. (1987), 'Un nuovo testimone dell'epistola di Psello a Giovanni Kifilino (Paris Gr.1277)', *Byzantion* 57: 427–32

Maisano, R. (1988), 'Varia Byzantina', in F. Sisti and E. V. Maltese (eds.), *Heptachordos lyra Humberto Albini oblata*, Genoa

Maltese, E. V. (1988), 'Osservazioni critiche sul testo delle epistole di Michele Psello', *JöB* 38: 247–55

Maltese, E. V. (1989), 'Il ms. Barocci 131 per l'epistolario de Michele Psello', *Aevum* 63: 186–92

Maltese, E. V. (1991), 'Un nuovo testimone parziale dei *Theologica* di Michele Psello: Vat.gr.409', *Studi Italiani di Filologia Classica* 3rd series 9: 121–5

Maltese, E. V. (1992), 'Michele Psello commentatore di Gregorio Nazianzo: note per una lettura dei *Theologica*', in C. Moreschini and G. Menestrina (eds.), *Gregorio Nazianzeno, teologo e scrittore*, Bologna, pp. 227–48

Maltese, E. V. (1993), 'I *Theologica* di Psello e la cultura filosofica bizantina', in R. Maisano (ed.), *Storia e tradizione culturale a Bisanzio fra XI e XII secolo* (ITAΛOEΛΛHNIKA Quaderni 3), Naples, pp. 51–69

Miller, T. A. (1975), 'Mikhail Psell i Dionisij Galikarnasskij', in *Antichnost i Vizantija*, Moscow, pp. 140–74

Milovanovic, C. (1984), 'Psel i Grigorje, Nona i Teodota', *ZRVI* 23: 73–87

Ronchey, S. (1985), *Indagini ermeneutiche e critico-testuali sulla Cronografia di Psello* (Istituto Storico Italiano per il Medio Evo, Studi Storici 152), Rome

Snipes, K. (1989), 'The *Chronographia* of Michael Psellos and the textual tradition and transmission of the Byzantine historians of the eleventh and twelfth centuries', *ZRVI* 27/8: 43–62

Sophroniou, S. A. (1966–7), 'Michael Psellos' theory of science', *AΘHNA* 69: 78–90

Spadaro, M. G. (1974), 'Per una nuova edizione dell'elogio funebre per Sclerena di Michele Psello', *Siculorum Gymnasium* n.s. 27: 134–51

Spadaro, M. G. (1975), 'Note su Sclerena', *Siculorum Gymnasium* 28: 351–72

Tinnefeld, F. (1973), '"Freundschaft" in den Briefen des Michael Psellos: Theorie und Wirchlichkeit', *JöB* 22: 151–68

Van Dieten, J. L. (1985), 'Textkritisches zu Psellos: Chronographie II 167, 16ff Renauld', *BYZANTINA* 13: 565–88

Vergari, G. (1987), 'Michele Psello e la tipologia femminile cristiana', *Siculorum Gymnasium* n.s. 40: 217–25

Weiss, G. (1970), 'Untersuchungen zu den unedierten Schriften des M. Psellos', *BYZANTINA* 2: 337–78

Weiss, G. (1972), 'Forschungen zu den Schriften des M. Psellos', *BYZANTINA* 4: 9–51

Weiss, G. (1977), 'Die juristische Bibliothek des Michael Psellos', *JöB* 26: 79–102

Westerlink, L. G. (1987), 'Le Parisinus Gr. 1182 and le Vaticanus Gr. 671 de Psellos', in J. Dummer (ed.), *Texte und Textkritik: eine Aufsatzsammlung*, Berlin, pp. 605–9

Nikephoros Bryennios

Carile, A. (1964), 'Il problema della identificazione del cesare Niceforo Briennio', *Aevum* 38: 74–83

Carile, A. (1969), 'La "YΛH IΣTOPIAΣ" del cesare Niceforo Briennio', *Aevum* 43: 56–87, 235–82

Failler, A. (1989), 'Le texte de l'Histoire de Nicéphore Bryennios à la lumière d'un nouveau fragment', *REB* 47: 239–50

Reinsch, D. R. (1990), 'Der Historiker Nikephoros Bryennios, Enkel und nicht Sohn des Usurpators', *BZ* 83: 423–4

Nikon of the Black Mountain

Giankos, T. (1991), *ΝΙΚΩΝ Ο ΜΑΥΡΟΡΕΙΟΤΗΣ. ΒΙΟΣ–ΣΥΓΓΡΑΦΙΚΟ, ΕΡΓΟ–ΚΑΝΟΝΙΚΗ ΔΙΔΑΣΚΑΛΙΑ*, Thessalonica

Grumel, V. (1963), 'Nicon de la Montagne Noire et Jean IV(V) l'Oxite', *REB* 21: 270–2

Nasrallah, J. (1969), 'Un auteur antiochien du xie siècle: Nicon de la Montagne Noire (vers 1025–début du XIIe s.)', *Proche-Orient Chrétien* 19: 150–61

Peira

Oikonomides, N. (1986a), 'Η ΠΕΙΡΑ ΠΕΡΙ ΠΑΡΟΙΚΩΝ', in *ΑΦΙΕΡΩΜΑ ΣΤΟΝ ΝΙΚΟ ΣΒΟΡΩΝΟ*, I, Rethymno, pp. 232–42

Oikonomides, N. (1986b), 'The Peira of Eustathios Romaios: an abortive attempt to innovate in Byzantine law', *Fontes Minores* 7: 169–92

Simon, D. (1986), 'Das Eheguterrecht der Peira: Ein systematischer Versuch', *Fontes Minores* 7: 193–238

Vryonis, S., jnr (1974), 'The Peira as a source for the history of Byzantine aristocratic society', in *Near Eastern Numismatics, Iconography, Epigraphy and History: Studies in Honor of G. C. Miles*, Beirut, pp. 279–84

Weiss, G. (1973), 'Hohe Richter in Konstantinopel: Eustathios Rhomaios und seine Kollegen', *JöB* 22: 117–43

Philip Monotropos

Hörander, W. (1964), 'Die Wiener Handschriften des Philippos Monotropos', in *ΑΚΡΟΘΙΝΙΑ*, Vienna, pp. 23–40

Hörander, W. (1985), 'Notizen zu Philippos Monotropos', *BYZANTINA* 13: 815–31

Theophylact of Bulgaria

Dragova, N. (1992), 'Theophylact of Ochrida's Old Bulgarian sources on Cyril and Methodius', *Etudes Balkaniques* 28: 107–10

Epstein, A. W. (1980), 'The political content of the paintings of St Sophia at Ochrid', *JöB* 29: 315–29

Gautier, P. (1963), 'L'épiscopat de Théophylacte Héphaistos, archevêque de Bulgarie', *REB* 21: 159–78

Iliev, I. G. (1992), 'The manuscript tradition and the authorship of the Long Life of St Clement of Ochrid', *BS* 52: 68–73

Leib, B. (1953), 'La *ΠΑΙΔΕΙΑ ΒΑΣΙΛΙΚΗ* de Théophylacte, archevêque de Bulgarie et sa contribution à l'histoire de la fin du xie siècle', *REB* 11: 197–204

Leroy-Molinghen, A. (1938), 'Prolégomènes à une édition critique des lettres de Théophylacte de Bulgarie', *Byzantion* 13: 253–62

Leroy-Molinghen, A. (1966), 'Du destinaire de la lettre Finetti I de Théophylacte de Bulgarie', *Byzantion* 36: 431–7

Maslev, S. I. (1972), 'Les lettres de Théophylacte de Bulgarie à Nicéphore Mélissénos', *REB* 30: 179–86

Maslev, S. I. (1974a), 'Za roljata i znechenieto na dejnostta na Teofilakt Okhridski kato arkhiepiskop bulgarski', *Izvestija na Instituta za bulg. istorija* 23: 235–47

Maslev, S. I. (1974b), *Fontes graeci historiae bulgaricae IX: Theophylacti Achridensis, archiepiscopi Bulgariae, scripta ad historiam Bulgariae pertinentia. I. Studia in scriptis quibusdam a Theophylacto Achridensi archiepiscopo Bulgariae (1090–ca.1126) relictis*, Sofia

Mullett, M. (1990), 'Patronage in action: the problems of an eleventh-century bishop', in R. Morris (ed.), *Church and People in Byzantium*, Birmingham, pp. 125–47

Mullett, M. (1995), *Theophylact of Ochrid: A Byzantine Archbishop and his Letters*, Aldershot

Obolensky, D. (1986), 'Theophylaktos of Ochrid and the authorship of the *Vita Clementis*', *Byzantion*, 2: 601–18

Obolensky, D. (1988), *Six Byzantine Portraits*, Oxford

Prinzing, G. (1985), '"Contra Judaeos": ein Phantom im Werkzeichnis des Theophylaktos Hephaistos', *BZ* 78: 350–4

Solarino, M. (1991), 'Un intellettuale in provincia: Teofilatto di Achrida', in *Syndesmos: Studi in onore di Rosario Anastasi*, 1, Catania, pp. 63–82

Spadaro, M. G. (1981), 'Un inedito di Teofilatto di Achrida sull'eunuchia', *Rivista di Studi Bizantini e Slavi* 1: 3–38

Spadaro, M. G. (1992), 'Sugli "errori" dei Latini di Teofilatto: obiettività o scelta politica?', in A. M. Babbi *et al.* (eds.), *Medioevo romanzo e orientale: testi e prospettive storiografiche*, Rubbettino, pp. 231–44

Timarion

Alexiou, M. (1983), 'Literary subversion and the aristocracy: a stylistic analysis of *Timarion* chapters 6–7', *BMGS* 8: 29–45

Baldwin, B. (1982), 'A talent to abuse: some aspects of Byzantine satire', *BF* 8: 19–27

Baldwin, B. (1984), 'The authorship of the *Timarion*', *BZ* 77: 233–7

Reinsch, D. R. (1990), 'Zum überlieferten Text des *Timarion*', in D. Harlfinger (ed.), *ΦΙΛΟΦΡΟΝΗΜΑ: Festschrift für Martin Sicherl zum 75. Geburtstag*, Paderborn, pp. 161–70

Reinsch, D. R. (1993–4), 'Zur Identität einer Gestalt im *Timarion*', *BZ* 86/7: 383–5

Romano, R. (1973), 'Sulla possibile attribuzione del *Timarione* pseudo-lucianeo a Nicola Callicle', *Giornale Italiano di Filologia* 4: 309–15

Modern Works

A Byzantine Foreign Relations 1025–1118

1 The Russians

Kazhdan, A. (1963), 'Ioann Mavropod, Pechenegi i Russkie v seredine XI v.', *ZRVI* 8, 1: 177–84

Kazhdan, A. (1977), 'Once more about the "alleged" Russo-Byzantine treaty (ca. 1047) and the Pechenegs' crossing of the Danube', *JöB* 26: 65–77

Kazhdan, A. (1988–9), 'Rus–Byzantine princely marriages in the eleventh and twelfth centuries', *Harvard Ukrainian Studies* 12/13: 414–29

Litavrin, G. G. (1967), 'Psell o prichinakh poslednego pokhoda russkikh na Konstantinopel v. 1043 g.', *VV* 27: 71–86

Poppe, A. (1971), 'La dernière expédition russe contre Constantinople', *BS* 32: 1–29, 233–68

Poppe, A. (1981), 'The building of the church of St Sophia in Kiev', *JMH* 7: 15–66
Shepard, J. (1975), 'John Mauropus, Leo Tornicius and an alleged Russian army: the chronology of the Pecheneg crisis of 1048–1049', *JöB* 24: 61–89
Shepard, J. (1979), 'Why did the Russians attack Byzantium in 1043?', *Byzantinisch-neugriechischen Jahrbücher* 22: 147–212

2 The Danube frontier and Bulgaria
Diaconu, P. (1970), *Les Petchénègues au Bas-Danube* (Bibliotheca Historica Romaniae 27), Bucharest
Diaconu, P. (1978), *Les Coumans au Bas-Danube aux XIe et XIIe siècles*, Bucharest
Laurent, V. (1957), 'Le thème byzantin de Serbie au XIe siècle', *REB* 15: 185–95
Laurent, V. (1969), 'Deux nouveaux gouverneurs de la Bulgarie byzantine: le proèdre Nicéphore Batatzès et le protoproèdre Grégoire', *RES-EE* 7: 143–50
Miltenova, A. and Kajmakanova, M. (1986), 'The uprising of Petar Delyan (1040–1041) in a new Old Bulgarian source', *Byzantinobulgarica* 8: 227–41
Stanescu, E. (1966), 'La crise du Bas-Danube byzantin au cours de la seconde moitié du XIe siècle', *ZRVI* 9: 49–73

3 The Turks and the loss of Anatolia and Armenia
Antoniadis-Bibicou, H. (1964), 'Un aspect des relations byzantino-turques en 1073–1074', in *Actes du XIIe congrès international des études byzantines 1961*, II, Belgrade, pp. 15–25
Cahen, C. (1965), 'La diplomatie orientale de Byzance face à la poussée seljukide', *Byzantion* 35: 10–16
Cahen, C. (1968), *Pre-Ottoman Turkey*, London
Canard, M. (1965), 'La campagne arménienne du sultan seldjuqide Alp Arslan et la prise d'Ani en 1064', *Revue des Etudes Arméniennes* n.s. 2: 239–59
Cheynet, J.-C. (1980), 'Mantzikert un désastre militaire', *Byzantion* 50: 410–38
Eickhoff, E. (1991), 'Zur Wende von Mantzikert', in M. Kitzinger *et al.* (eds.), *Das Andere Wahrnehmen (Festschrift August Nitschke)*, Cologne, pp. 101–19
Felix, W. (1981), *Byzanz und die islamische Welt im früheren 11. Jahrhundert* (Byzantina Vindobonensia 14), Vienna
Friendly, A. (1981), *The Dreadful Day: The Battle of Manzikert 1071*, London
Janssens, E. (1968–72), 'La bataille de Mantzikert (1071) selon Michel Attaliate', *Annuaire de l'Institut de Philologie et de l'Histoire Orientales et Slaves* 20: 291–304
Janssens, E. (1973), 'Le lac de Van et la stratégie byzantine', *Byzantion* 42: 388–404
Kaegi, W. E., jnr (1964), 'The contribution of archery to the Turkish conquest of Anatolia', *Speculum* 39: 96–108
Shepard, J. (1975–6), 'Scylitzes on Armenia in the 1040s, and the role of Catacalon Cecaumenos', *Revue des Etudes Arméniennes* 11: 269–311
Sümer, F. (1967), 'The Turks in eastern Asia Minor in the eleventh century', in *Proceedings of the XIIIth International Congress of Byzantine Studies*, Oxford, pp. 144–6
Toumanoff, C. (1967), 'The background to Mantzikert', in *Proceedings of the XIIIth International Congress of Byzantine Studies*, Oxford, pp. 411–26
Vryonis, S., jnr (1971), *The Decline of Medieval Hellenism in Asia Minor and the Process of Islamization from the Eleventh through the Fifteenth Century*, Berkeley, Los Angeles and London

Yarnley, C. J. (1972), 'Philaretos: Armenian bandit or Byzantine general?', *Revue des Etudes Arméniennes* n.s. 9: 331–53

4 The papacy

Alexander, P. J. (1963), 'The Donation of Constantine at Byzantium and its earliest use against the western empire', *ZRVI* 8, 1: 11–26

Cowdrey, H. E. J. (1982), 'Pope Gregory VII's "crusading" plans of 1074', in B. Z. Kedar, H.-E. Mayer and R. C. Smail (eds.), *Outremer: Studies in the History of the Crusading Kingdom of Jerusalem Presented to Joshua Prawer*, Jerusalem, pp. 27–40

Denzler, G. (1966), 'Das sogennante morgenländische Schisma im Jahre 1054', *Münchener Theologische Zeitschrift* 17: 24–46

Gauss, J. (1967), *Ost und West in der Kirchen- und Papstgeschichte des 11. Jahrhunderts*, Zurich

Kaplan, M. (1993), 'La place du schisme de 1054 dans les relations entre Byzance, Rome et l'Italie', *BS* 54: 29–37

Krause, H.-G. (1983), 'Das *Constitutum Constantini* im Schisma von 1054', in *Aus Kirche und Reich: Festschrift für F. Kempf*, Sigmaringen, pp. 131–58

Leib, B. (1924), *Rome, Kiev et Byzance à la fin du XIe siècle*, Paris

Nasrallah, J. (1976), 'Le patriarcat d'Antioch est-il resté, après 1054, en communion avec Rome?', *Istina* 21: 374–411

Nicol, D. M. (1962), 'Byzantium and the papacy in the eleventh century', *JEH* 13: 1–20

Nicol, D. M. (1976), 'The papal scandal', *Studies in Church History* 13: 141–68

Petrucci, E. (1973), 'Rapporti di Leone IX con Constantinopoli', *Studi Medievali* 3rd series 14: 733–831

Ševčenko, I. (1964), 'The Civitas Russorum and the alleged falsification of the Latin excommunication bull by Kerullarios', in *Actes du XIIe congrès international des études byzantines 1961*, II, Belgrade, pp. 203–12

Smith, M. H. III (1977), *'And taking bread . . . ': Cerularius and the azyme controversy of 1054* (Théologie Historique 47), Paris

Tuilier, A. (1981), 'Michel VII et le pape Grégoire VII: Byzance et la réforme grégorienne', in *Actes du XVe congrès international d'études byzantines*, IV, Athens, pp. 350–64

5 Southern Italy, the Normans and the west

Balard, M. (1976), 'Amalfi et Byzance (Xe–XIIe siècles)', *TM* 6: 85–96

Bibicou, H. (1959–60), 'Michel VII Doukas, Robert Guiscard et la pension des dignitaires', *Byzantion* 29/30: 43–75

Bloch, H. (1946), 'Monte Cassino, Byzantium and the west', *DOP* 3: 165–224

Guillou, A. (1967), 'Recherches sur la société et l'administration byzantines en Italie au XIe siècle', in *Proceedings of the XIIIth International Congress of Byzantine Studies*, Oxford, pp. 391–6

Guillou, A. (1974), 'Production and profits in the Byzantine province of Italy (10th–11th centuries): an expanding society', *DOP* 28: 89–109

Guillou, A. (1976), 'La soie du Catépanat d'Italie', *TM* 6: 69–84

Hanawalt, E. A. (1986), 'Norman views of eastern Christendom: from the First Crusade to the principality of Antioch', in V. Goss and C. C. Bornstein (eds.), *The Meeting of Two Worlds*, Michigan, pp. 115–21

Hermans, J. (1979), 'The Byzantine view of the Normans', *ANS* 2: 78–92

Kolias, G. T. (1966), 'Le motif et les raisons de l'invasion de Robert Guiscard en territoire byzantin', *Byzantion* 36: 424–30

Loud, G. (1988), 'Byzantine Italy and the Normans', *BF* 12: 215–33

McQueen, W. B. (1986), 'Relations between the Normans and Byzantium, 1071–1112', *Byzantion* 56: 427–76

Shepard, J. (1988), 'Aspects of Byzantine attitudes and policy towards the west in the 10th and 11th centuries', *BF* 12: 67–118

Van Houts, E. M. C. (1985), 'Normandy and Byzantium in the eleventh century', *Byzantion* 55: 544–59

Von Falkenhausen, V. (1967), *Untersuchungen über die byzantinische Herrschaft in Süditalien vom 9. bis 11. Jahrhunderts* (Schriften zur Geistesgeschichte des Östlichen Europa 1), Wiesbaden

Wolff, R. L. (1978), 'How the news was brought from Byzantium to Angoulême; or, The pursuit of a hare in an ox cart', *BMGS* 4: 139–89

6 Varangians

Blondal, S. (1978), *The Varangians of Byzantium*, trans. and revised B. Benedikz, Cambridge

Ciggaar, K. (1974), 'L'émigration anglaise à Byzance après 1066: un nouveau texte en latin sur les Varangues à Constantinople', *REB* 32: 301–42

Ciggaar, K. (1976), 'Une description de Constantinople traduite par un pèlerin anglais', *REB* 34: 211–67

Ciggaar, K. (1980), 'Harald Hardrada: his expedition against the Petchenegs', *Balkan Studies* 21: 385–401

Ciggaar, K. (1981), 'Flemish mercenaries in Byzantium: their later history in an old Norse miracle', *Byzantion* 51: 44–75

Ciggaar, K. (1982), 'England and Byzantium on the eve of the Norman Conquest (the reign of Edward the Confessor)', *ANS* 5: 78–96

Godfrey, J. (1978), 'The defeated Anglo-Saxons take service with the eastern Emperor', *ANS* 1: 63–74

Head, C. (1977), 'Alexios Komnenos and the English', *Byzantion* 47: 186–98

Shepard, J. (1973a), 'A note on Harold Hardrada: the date of his arrival at Byzantium', *JöB* 22: 145–50

Shepard, J. (1973b), 'The English and Byzantium: a study of their role in the Byzantine army in the later eleventh century', *Traditio* 29: 53–92

Shepard, J. (1974), 'Another New England? – Anglo-Saxon settlement on the Black Sea', *Byzantine Studies/Etudes Byzantines* 1: 18–39

7 The First Crusade

Abrahamse, D. (1986), 'Byzantine views of the west in the early crusade period: the evidence of hagiography', in V. Goss and C. C. Bornstein (eds.) *The Meeting of Two Worlds*, Michigan, pp. 189–200

Cahen, C. (1974), 'La politique orientale des comtes de Flandre et la lettre d'Alexis Comnène', in P. Salmon (ed.), *Mélanges d'Islamologie: volume dédié à la mémoire d'Armand Abel*, Leiden, pp. 84–90

Cowdrey, H. E. J. (1988), 'The Gregorian papacy, Byzantium and the First Crusade', *BF* 13: 145–69

De Waha, M. (1977), 'La Lettre d'Alexis I Comnène à Robert I le Frison', *Byzantion* 47: 113–25

Ferluga, J. (1961), 'Le ligesse dans l'empire byzantine', *ZRVI* 7: 97–123

France, J. (1970), 'The crisis of the First Crusade: from the defeat of Kerbogah to the departure from Arqa', *Byzantion* 40: 276–308

France, J. (1971), 'The departure of Tatikios from the crusader army', *BIHR* 44: 137–47

France, J. (1994), *Victory in the East: A Military History of the First Crusade*, Cambridge

Ganshof, F. L. (1961a), 'Recherche sur le lien juridique qui unissait les chefs de la première croisade à l'empereur byzantin', in *Mélanges offerts à Paul-Edmond Martin*, Geneva, pp. 49–63

Ganshof, F. L. (1961b), 'Robert le Frison et Alexis Comnène', *Byzantion* 31: 57–74

Kindlimann, S. (1969), *Die Eroberung von Konstantinopel als politische Forderung des Westens im Hochmittelalter: Studien zur Entwicklung der Idee eines lateinischen Kaiserreichs in Byzanz*, Zurich

Lilie, R.-J. (1981), *Byzanz und die Kreuzfahrerstaaten* (ΠΟΙΚΙΛΑ ΒΥΖΑΝΤΙΝΑ 1), Munich; trans. J. C. Morris and J. E. Ridings, *Byzantium and the Crusader States 1096–1204*, Oxford, 1993

Lounghis, T. C. (1979), 'The failure of the Germano-Byzantine alliance on the eve of the First Crusade', *ΔΙΠΤΥΧΑ* 1: 158–67

Pryor, J. H. (1984), 'The oaths of the leaders of the First Crusade to Emperor Alexios I Comnenus: fealty, homage – ΠΙΣΤΙΣ, ΔΟΥΛΕΙΑ', *Parergon* n.s. 2: 111–41

Serper, A. (1976), 'La prise de Nicée d'après la "Chanson d'Antioche" de Richard le Pélerin', *Byzantion* 46: 411–21

Skoulatos, B. (1980), 'L'auteur anonyme des Gesta et le monde byzantin', *Byzantion* 50: 504–32

8 Venice

Antoniadis-Bibicou, H. (1962), 'Note sur les relations de Byzance avec Venise: de la dépendance à l'autonomie et à l'alliance: un point de vue byzantin', *ΘΗΣΑΥΡΙΣΜΑΤΑ* 1: 162–78

Borsari, S. (1964), 'Il commercio veneziano nell'impero bizantino nel XII secolo', in *Rivista Storica Italiana* 76: 982–1011

Borsari, S. (1969–70), 'Il crisobullo di Alessio I per Venezia', *Annali dell'Istituto Italiano per gli Studi Storici* 2: 111–31

Borsari, S. (1976), 'Per la storia del commercio veneziano col mondo bizantino nel XII secolo', *Rivista Storica Italiana* 88: 104–26

Frances, E. (1968), 'Alexis Comnène et les privilèges octroyés à Venise', *BS* 29: 17–23

Gadolin, A. R. (1980), 'Alexius Comnenus and the Venetian trade privileges', *Byzantion* 50: 439–46

Lilie, R.-J. (1984), *Handel und Politik zwischen dem byzantinischen Reich und den italienischen Kommunen Venedig, Pisa und Genua in der Epoche der Komnenen und der Angeloi*, Amsterdam

Martin, M. E. (1978), 'The chrysobull of Alexius I Comnenus to the Venetians and the early Venetian quarter in Constantinople', *BS* 39: 19–23

Martin, M. E. (1988), 'The Venetians in the Byzantine empire before 1204', *BF* 12: 201–14

Nicol, D. M. (1988), *Byzantium and Venice: A Study in Diplomatic and Cultural Relations*, Cambridge

Pertusi, A. (1964), 'L'impero bizantino e l'evolvere dei suoi interessi nell'alto Adriatico', in *Le Origini di Venezia*, Florence, pp. 59–93

Pertusi, A. (1965), 'Venezia e Bisanzio nel secolo XI', in *La Venezia del mille*, Florence, pp. 117–60

Pertusi, A. (1979), 'Venezia e Bisanzio, 1000–1204', *DOP* 33: 1–22

Tuilier, A. (1967), 'La date exacte du chrysobulle d'Alexis Ier Comnène en faveur des Vénitiens et son contexte historique', *Rivisti di Studi Bizantini e Neoellenici* n.s. 4: 27–48

Tuma, O. (1981), 'The dating of Alexius's chrysobull to the Venetians: 1082, 1084 or 1092?', *BS* 42: 171–85

9 Bohemond

Epstein, A. W. (1983), 'The date and significance of the cathedral of Canosa in Apulia, southern Italy', *DOP* 37: 79–90

Gadolin, A. R. (1982), 'Prince Bohemund's death and the apotheosis in the church of San Sabino, Canosa di Puglia', *Byzantion* 52: 124–53

Marquis de la Force (1936), 'Les conseillers latins du Basileus Alexis Comnène', *Byzantion* 11: 153–65

Rösch, G. (1984), 'Der "Kreuzzug" Bohemunds gegen Dyrrachion 1107/1108', *Römische Historische Mitteilungen* 26: 181–90

Rowe, J. G. (1966), 'Pascal II, Bohemond of Antioch and the Byzantine empire', *Bulletin of the John Rylands Library* 49: 165–202

Shepard, J. (1988), 'When Greek meets Greek: Alexius Comnenus and Bohemund in 1097–98', *BMGS* 12: 185–277

Wolf, K. B. (1991), 'Crusade and narrative: Bohemond and the *Gesta francorum*', *JMH* 17: 207–16

B *The Internal History of the Byzantine Empire 1025–1118*
1 Political, legal and administrative

Anastos, M. V. (1993), 'The coronation of Emperor Michael IV in 1034 by Empress Zoe and its significance', in J. Langdon *et al.* (eds.), *To Hellenikon: Studies in Honour of Speros Vryonis Jnr.*, 1, New York, pp. 23–43

Angold, M. J. (1984), *The Byzantine Empire 1025–1204: A Political History*, London

Angold, M. J. (1990), 'The Byzantine empire on the eve of Mantzikert', *BF* 16: 9–34

Angold, M. J. (1994), 'Imperial renewal and Orthodox reaction: Byzantium in the eleventh century', in P. Magdalino (ed.), *New Constantines: The Rhythm of Imperial Renewal in Byzantium*, Aldershot, pp. 231–46

Bompaire, J. (1976), 'Les sources diplomatiques byzantines et, en particulier, les actes de la chancellerie impériale, de 1025 à 1118', *TM* 7: 153–8

Burgmann, L. (1994), 'A law for emperors: observations on a chrysobull of Nikephoros III Botaneiates', in P. Magdalino (ed.), *New Constantines: The Rhythm of Imperial Renewal in Byzantium*, Aldershot, pp. 247–57

Cheynet, J.-C. (1983), 'Dévaluation des dignités et dévaluation monétaire dans la seconde moitié du XIe siècle', *Byzantion* 53: 453–77

Cheynet, J.-C. (1985), 'Du stratège de thème au duc: chronologie de l'évolution au cours du XIe siècle', *TM* 9: 181–94

Cheynet, J.-C. (1990), *Pouvoir et contestations à Byzance (963–1210)*, Paris

Frances, E. (1964), 'La disparition des corporations byzantines', in *Actes du XIIe congrès international des études byzantines 1961*, II, Belgrade, pp. 93–101

Gautier, P. (1977), 'Défection et soumission de la Crète sous Alexis Ier Comnène', *REB* 35: 215–27

Hill, B., James, L. and Smythe, D. (1994), 'Zoe: the rhythm method of imperial renewal', in P. Magdalino (ed.), *New Constantines: The Rhythm of Imperial Renewal in Byzantium*, Aldershot, pp. 215–30

Inque, K. (1993), 'The rebellion of Isaakios Komnenos and the provincial aristocratic *Oikoi*', *BS* 54: 268–78

Kresten, O. and Müller, A. E. (1993–4), 'Die Auslandsschreiben der byzantinischen Kaiser des 11. und 12. Jahrhunderts: Specimen einer kritischen Ausgabe', *BZ* 86/7: 402–19

Leib, B. (1977), *Aperçus sur l'époque des premiers Comnènes: Collectanea byzantina* (Orientalia Christiana Analekta 204), Rome

Lemerle, P. (1967), 'Roga et rente d'état aux Xe–XIe siècles', *REB* 25: 77–100

Lemerle, P. (1977), *Cinq études sur le XIe siècle byzantin* (Le Monde Byzantin), Paris

Lounghis, T. C. (1991–2), 'Un empire romain devant la féodalisation: remarques sur l'emploi du terme EIPHNH au XIe siècle', *ΔIΠTYXA* 5: 87–95

Mullett, M. E. (1984), 'The disgrace of the ex-basilissa Maria', *BS* 45: 202–11

Mullett, M. E. (1994), 'Alexios I Komnenos and imperial renewal', in P. Magdalino (ed.), *New Constantines: The Rhythm of Imperial Renewal in Byzantium*, Aldershot, pp. 259–67

Mullett, M. E. and Smythe, D. (1995), *Alexios I Komnenos*, I: *Papers Given at the Second Belfast International Colloquium* (Belfast Byzantine Texts and Translations 4), Belfast

Oikonomides, N. (1963), 'Le serment de l'impératrice Eudocie (1067): un épisode de l'histoire dynastique de Byzance', *REB* 21: 101–28

Oikonomides, N. (1966), 'The donations of castles in the last quarter of the 11th century (Dölger, Regesten No. 1012)', in *Polychronion: Festschrift F. Dölger*, Heidelberg, pp. 413–17

Oikonomides, N. (1976), 'L'évolution de l'organisation administrative de l'empire byzantin au XIe siècle (1025–1118)', *TM* 6: 125–52

Oikonomides, N. (1978), 'The mosaic panel of Constantine IX and Zoe in St Sophia', *REB* 36: 219–32

Oikonomides, N. (1980–1), 'St George of Mangana, Maria Skleraina and the "Malyj Sion" of Novgorod', *DOP* 34/5: 239–46

Oikonomides, N. (1994), 'La couronne dite de Constantin Monomaque', *TM* 12: 241–62

Scheltema, H. J. (1950), 'Une pétition à l'empereur Alexis Comnène de l'an 1085', *Revue Internationale des Droits de l'Antiquité* 5: 457–63

Seibt, W. (1993), 'APMENIAKA ΘEMATA als terminus technicus der byzantinischen Verwaltungsgeschichte des 11. Jahrhunderts', *BS* 54: 134–41

Sorlin, I. (1976), 'Publications soviétiques sur le XIe siècle', *TM* 6: 367–98

Spadaro, M. D. (1987), 'La deposizione di Michele VI: un episodio di "Concordia discors" fra chiesa e militari?', *JöB* 37: 153–71

Spadaro, M. D. (1991), 'Archontes a confronto nella periferia dell impero sotto la *basileia* di Alessio I Comneno', in *Syndesmos: studi in onore di Rosario Anastasi*, I, Catania, pp. 83–114

Stanescu, E. (1966), 'Les réformes d'Isaac Comnène', in *RÉS-EE* 4: 35–69

Stanescu, E. (1967), 'Solutions contemporaines de la crise: un quart de siècle de réformes et contreréformes impériales (1057–81)', in *Proceedings of the XIIIth International Congress of Byzantine Studies*, Oxford, pp. 401–8

Vryonis, S., jnr (1963), 'Byzantine ΔΗΜΟΚΡΑΤΙΑ and the guilds in the eleventh century', *DOP* 17: 287–314

Vryonis, S., jnr (1982), 'Byzantine imperial authority: theory and practice in the eleventh century', in G. Makdisi, D. Sourdel and J. Sourdel-Thomine (eds.), *Les Notions d'authorité au moyen âge: Islam, Byzance, Occident*, Paris, pp. 141–61

Weiss, G. (1973), *Oströmische Beamte im Spiegel der Schriften des Michael Psellos* (Miscellanea Byzantina Monacensia 16), Munich

2 Prosopography and chronology

Barzos, K. (1984), *Η ΓΕΝΕΑΛΟΓΙΑ ΤΩΝ ΚΟΜΝΗΝΩΝ* (ΒΥΖΑΝΤΙΝΑ ΚΕΙΜΕΝΑ ΚΑΙ ΜΕΛΕΤΑΙ 20), 2 vols., Thessalonica

Cheynet, J.-C. (1984), 'Toparque et topotèrètes à la fin du IIe siècle', *REB* 42: 215–24

Cheynet, J.-C. (1990), 'Thathoul, archonte des archontes', *REB* 48: 233–42

Duyé, N. (1972), 'Un haut fonctionnaire byzantin du XIe siècle: Basile Malésès', *REB* 30: 167–78

Gautier, P. (1967), 'La date de la mort de Christodule de Patmos (mercredi 16 mars 1093)', *REB* 25: 235–8

Gautier, P. (1969), 'L'obituaire de Pantocrator', *REB* 27: 235–62

Gautier, P. (1971), 'Le synode des Blachernes (fin 1094): étude prosopographique', *REB* 29: 213–84

Grierson, P. (1985), 'The dates of Patriarch Sophronius II of Jerusalem (post 1048–1076/83)', *REB* 43: 231–6

Kazhdan, A. (1970), 'Die Liste der Kinder des Kaisers Alexios I. in einer Moskauer Handschrift (ΓΝΜ 53/147)', in *Festschrift F. Altheim*, II, Berlin, pp. 233–7

Kazhdan, A. (1973), 'Kharakter, sostav i evoljutsija gospodstvujushchego klassa v Vizantii XI–XII vv. Predvaritel'nye vybody', *BZ* 66: 47–60

Kazhdan, A. (1974), *Sotsial'nyj sostav gospodstvujushchego klassa Vizantii XI–XII vv.*, Moscow

Kazhdan, A. (1989), 'A date and an identification in the Xenophon No. 1', *Byzantion* 59: 267–71

Kazhdan, A. and Ljubarskij, J. (1973), 'Basile Malésès encore une fois', *BS* 34: 219–20

Leven, K. H. (1988), 'Der Tod des Kaisers Alexios I. Komnenos', in *Actes du XXX Congrès international d'histoire de la médecine 1986*, Dusseldorf, pp. 896–904

Papachryssanthou, D. (1963), 'La date de la mort du sébastokrator Isaac Comnène, frère d'Alexios I, et de quelques événements contemporains', *REB* 21: 250–5

Polemis, D. I. (1965), 'Notes on eleventh-century chronology (1059–1081)', *BZ* 58: 60–76

Polemis, D. I. (1968), *The Doukai: A Contribution to Byzantine Prosopography* (University of London Historical Studies 22), London

Runciman, S. (1949), 'The end of Anna Dalassena', *Annuaire de l'Institut de Philologie et d'Histoire Occidentales et Slaves* 9: 517–24

Shepard, J. (1977), 'Isaac Comnenus' coronation day', *BS* 38: 22–30

Skoulatos, B. (1980), *Les Personnages byzantins de l'Alexiade: analyse prosopographique et synthèse*, Louvain

Tinnefeld, F. (1989), 'Michael I. Kerrullarios: Patriarch von Konstantinopel 1043–1058', *JöB* 39: 95–127

3 Ecclesiastical

Ahrweiler, H. (1967), 'Charisticariat et autres formes d'attribution de fondations pieuses aux Xe–XIe siècles', *ZRVI* 10: 1–27

Angold, M. J. (1995), *Church and Society in Byzantium under the Comneni 1081–1261*, Cambridge

Browning, R. (1975), 'Enlightenment and repression in Byzantium in the eleventh and twelfth centuries', *PaP* 69: 3–22

Darrouzès, J. (1966), 'Dossier sur le charisticariat', in *Polychronion: Festschrift F. Dölger*, Heidelberg, pp. 150–65

Darrouzès, J. (1976), 'Le mouvement des fondation monastiques au XIe siècle', *TM* 6: 159–76

Eleuteri, P. and Rigo, A. (1993), *Eretici, dissidenti, Musulmani ed Ebrei a Bisanzio: una raccolta eresiologia del XI secolo*, Venice

Garsoian, N. G. (1974), 'L'abduration du moine Nil de Calabre', *BS* 35: 12–27

Gautier, P. (1973), 'L'édit d'Alexis Ier Comnène sur la réforme du clergé', *REB* 31: 165–227 (text, 179–201)

Glabinas, A. A. (1972), *Η ΕΠΙ ΑΛΕΞΙΟΥ ΚΟΜΝΗΝΟΥ ΠΕΡΙ ΙΕΡΩΝ ΣΚΕΥΩΝ, ΚΕΙΜΗΛΙΩΝ ΚΑΙ ΑΓΙΩΝ ΕΙΚΟΝΩΝ ΕΡΙΣ (1081–1095)* (BYZANTINA KEIMENA KAI ΜΕΛΕΤΑΙ 6), Thessalonica

Gouillard, J. (1959–60), 'Un chrysobulle de Nicéphore Botaneiatès à souscription synodale', *Byzantion* 29/30: 29–41

Gouillard, J. (1965), 'L'hérésie dans l'empire byzantin dès origines au XIIe siècle', *TM* 1: 299–324

Gouillard, J. (1976), 'La religion des philosophes', *TM* 6: 305–24

Gouillard, J. (1978), 'Quatre procès de mystiques à Byzance (vers 960–1143): inspiration et authorité', *REB* 36: 5–81

Gress-Wright, D. (1977), 'Bogomilism in Constantinople', *Byzantion* 47: 163–85

Jenkins, R. J. H. (1967), 'A cross of the patriarch Michael Cerularius', *DOP* 21: 232–49

Kalavrezou, I. (1982), 'Silvester and Keroularios', *JöB* 32/5: 453–8

Kaplan, M. (1984), 'Les monastères et le siècle à Byzance: les investissements des laiques au XIe siècle', *CCM* 27: 71–83

Laurent, V. (1946), 'Le titre de patriarche œcuménique et Michel Cérulaire: à propos de deux sceaux inédits', in *Miscellanea Giovanni Mercati*, III Rome, pp. 373–86

Lemerle, P. (1967), 'Un aspect du rôle des monastères à Byzance: les monastères donnés à des laics, les charisticaires', in *Académie des Inscriptions et Belles-Lettres: Comptes Rendus*, pp. 9–28

Loos, M. (1967), 'Certains aspects du bogomilisme byzantin des 11e et 12e siècles', *BS* 28: 39–53

Morris, R. (1981), 'The political saint of the eleventh century', in S. Hackel (ed.), *The Byzantine Saint*, London, pp. 43–50

Morris, R. (1985), 'Monasteries and their patrons in the tenth and eleventh centuries', *BF* 10: 185–231

Morris, R. (1992), 'Divine diplomacy in the late eleventh century', *BMGS* 16: 147–56

Mullett, M. and Kirby, A. (1994), *The Theotokos Evergetis and eleventh-century monasticism* (Belfast Byzantine Texts and Translations 6.1), Belfast

Oikonomides, N. (1960), 'Un décret inédit du patriarche Jean VIII Xiphilin concernant l'élection et l'ordination des évêques', *REB* 18: 55–78

Podalsky, G. (1991), 'Religion und religiöses Leben im Byzanz des 11. Jahrhunderts', *Orientalia Christiana Periodica* 57: 371–97

Rigo, A. (1990), 'Messalianismo = Bogomilismo: un equazione della eresiologia medievale bizantina', *Orientalia Christiana Periodica* 56: 53–82

Schmink, A. (1979), 'Vier eherechtliche Entscheidungen aus dem 11. Jahrhundert', *Fontes Minores* 2: 252–67

Spadaro, M. D. (1993), 'Contestazione, fronda e sovversione dei patriarchi di Antiochia alla fine dell'XI secolo', in R. Maisano (ed.), *Storia e tradizione culturale a Bisanzio fra XI e XII secolo*, Naples, pp. 71–96

Thomas, J. P. (1984), 'A Byzantine ecclesiastical reform movement', *Mediaevalia et Humanistica* n.s. 12: 1–16

Tiftixoglu, V. (1969), 'Gruppenbildungen innerhalb des konstantinopolitanischen Klerus während der Komnenenzeit', *BZ* 62: 25–72

Walter, C. (1973), 'Pictures of the clergy in the Theodore Psalter', *REB* 31: 229–42

4 Social, economic and ethnic

Ahrweiler, H. (1976), 'Recherches sur la société byzantine au XIe siècle: nouvelles hiérarchies et nouvelles solidarités', *TM* 6: 99–124

Antoniadis-Bibicou, H. (1965), 'Villages désertés en Grèce: un bilan provisoire', in *Villages désertés et histoire économique, XIe–XVIIIe siècles*, Paris, pp. 343–417

Antoniadis-Bibicou, H. (1972), 'Démographie, salaires et prix à Byzance au XIe siècle', *Annales ESC* 27: 215–46

Argenti, P. (1966), 'The Jewish community in Chios during the eleventh century', in *Polychronion: Festschrift F. Dölger*, Heidelberg, pp. 39–68

Brand, C. M. (1989), 'The Turkish element in Byzantium, eleventh–twelfth centuries', *DOP* 43: 1–25

Dagron, G. (1976), 'Minorités ethniques et religieuses dans l'Orient byzantin à la fin du Xe et au XIe siècle: l'immigration syrienne', *TM* 6: 177–216

Dédéyan, G. (1975), 'L'immigration arménienne en Cappadoce au XIe siècle', *Byzantion* 45: 41–117

Dédéyan, G. (1993), 'Les Arméniens sur la frontière sud-orientale de Byzance: fin IXe–fin Xe siècles', in Y. Roman (ed.), *La Frontière*, Lyons and Paris, pp. 67–85

Harvey, A. (1982–3), 'Economic expansion in central Greece in the eleventh century', *BMGS* 8: 21–28

Harvey, A. (1989), *Economic Expansion in the Byzantine Empire 900–1200*, Cambridge

Harvey, A. (1990), 'Peasant categories in the tenth and eleventh centuries', *BMGS* 14: 250–6

Harvey, A. (1993), 'The land and taxation in the reign of Alexios I Komnenos: the evidence of Theophylact of Ohrid', *REB* 51: 139–54

Hendy, M. F. (1969), *Coinage and Money in the Byzantine Empire 1081–1261*, Washington DC

Hendy, M. F. (1970), 'Byzantium 1081–1204: an economic reappraisal', *TRHS* 5th series, 20: 31–52

Kazhdan, A. (1982), 'Two notes on Byzantine demography of the eleventh and twelfth centuries', *BF* 8: 115–22

Laiou, A. E. (1986), 'The festival of "Agathe": comments on the life of Constantinopolitan women', in *Byzantium: Tribute to Andreas N. Stratos*, I, Athens, pp. 111–22

Morrisson, C. (1976), 'La dévaluation de la monnaie byzantine au XIe siècle: essai d'interprétation', *TM* 6: 3–48

Morrisson, C. (1979), 'La logarikè: réforme monétaire et réforme fiscale sous Alexis Ier Comnène', *TM* 7: 419–64

Mullett, M. E. (1988), 'Byzantium: a friendly society?', *PaP* 118: 3–24

Nesbitt, J. and Wiitta, J. (1975), 'A confraternity of the Comnenian era', *BZ* 68: 360–84

Oikonomides, N. (1990), 'Life and society in eleventh-century Constantinople', *Südostforschungen* 49: 1–14

Svoronos, N. (1959), 'Recherches sur le cadastre byzantin et la fiscalité aux XIe et XIIe siècles: le cadastre de Thèbes', *Bulletin de Correspondance Hellénique* 83: 1–145

Svoronos, N. (1967), 'Société et organisation intérieure dans l'empire byzantin au XIe siècle', in *Proceedings of the XIIIth International Congress of Byzantine Studies*, Oxford, pp. 373–89

Svoronos, N. (1976), 'Remarques sur les structures économiques de l'empire byzantine au XIe siècle', *TM* 6: 49–67

Thomson, R. W. (1967), 'The influence of their environment on the Armenians in exile in the eleventh century', in *Proceedings of the XIIIth International Congress of Byzantine Studies*, Oxford, pp. 138–40

5 Cultural

Anastasi, R. (1974), 'Filosofia e techne a Bisanzio nell'XI secolo', *Siculorum Gymnasium* n.s. 27: 352–86

Anderson, J. C. (1983), 'The date and the purpose of the Barberini psalter', *Cahiers Archéologiques* 31: 35–60

Anderson, J. C. (1988), 'On the nature of the Theodore Psalter', *Art Bulletin* 70: 550–68

Belting, H. (1980–1), 'An image and its function in the liturgy: the Man of Sorrows in Byzantium', *DOP* 34/5: 1–16

Bouras, C. (1982), *Nea Moni on Chios: History and Architecture*, Athens

Conus-Wolska, W. (1976), 'Les écoles de Psellos et de Xiphilin sous Constantin IX Monomaque', *TM* 6: 223–43

Conus-Wolska, W. (1979), 'L'école de droit et l'enseignement du droit à Byzance au XIe siècle: Xiphilin et Psellos', *TM* 7: 1–103

Der Nersessian, S. (1970), *L'Illustration des Psautiers grecs du moyen âge*, II: *Londres Add. 19. 352*, Paris

Hörandner, W. (1976), 'La poésie profane au XIe siècle et la connaissance des auteurs anciens', *TM* 6: 245–63

Kalavrezou, I., Trahoulia, N. and Sabar, S. (1993), 'Critique of the emperor in the Vatican Psalter gr. 752', *DOP* 47: 195–219

Kalavrezou-Maxeiner, I. (1977), 'Eudokia Makrembolitissa and the Romanos ivory', *DOP* 31: 307–25

Kazhdan, A. P. and Epstein, A. W. (1985), *Change in Byzantine Culture in the Eleventh and Twelfth Centuries*, Berkeley, Los Angeles and London

Kazhdan, A. P. and Franklin, S. (1984), *Studies on Byzantine Literature of the Eleventh and Twelfth Centuries*, Cambridge

Ljubarskij, L. (1992), 'The fall of an intellectual: the intellectual and moral atmosphere in eleventh-century Byzantium', in S. Vryonis jnr (ed.), *Byzantine Studies: Essays on the Slavic World and the Eleventh Century* (Hellenism: Ancient, Medieval, Modern, 9), New Rochelle and New York, pp. 175–82

Maguire, H. (1992), 'The mosaics of Nea Moni: an imperial reading', *DOP* 46: 205–14

Mango, C. (1976), 'Les monuments de l'architecture du XIe siècle et leur signification historique et sociale', *TM* 6: 351–65

Mouriki, D. (1980–1), 'Stylistic trends in the monumental painting of Greece during the eleventh and twelfth centuries', *DOP* 34/5: 77–124

Mouriki, D. (1985), *The Mosaics of Nea Moni on Chios*, 2 vols., Athens

Niarchos, C. (1981), 'The philosophical background of the eleventh-century revival of learning in Byzantium', in M. Mullett and R. Scott (eds.), *Byzantium and the Classical Tradition*, Birmingham, pp. 127–35

Papadopoulos, K. (1966), *Die Wandmalereien des XI. Jahrhunderts in der Kirche ΠΑΝΑΓΙΑ ΤΩΝ ΧΑΛΚΕΩΝ in Thessaloniki* (Byzantina Vindobonensia 2), Vienna

Walter, C. (1988), '"Latter-day" saints in the model for the London and Barberini psalters', *REB* 46: 211–28

Weitzmann, K. (1966), 'Byzantine miniature painting in the eleventh century', in *Thirteenth International Congress of Byzantine Studies, Oxford 1966, Main Papers*, VII, Oxford

9 KIEVAN RUS', THE BULGARS AND THE SOUTHERN SLAVS, *c.* 1020–*c.* 1200

1 Kievan Rus'

Dimnik, M. (1987), 'The "Testament" of Iaroslav "the Wise": a re-examination', *Canadian Slavonic Papers* 19: 369–86

Dimnik, M. (2003), *The Dynasty of Chernigov, 1146–1246* Cambridge

Drevnerusskie knyazhestva X–XIII vv. (1975), ed. L. G., Beskrovnyy, Moscow

Hrushevsky, M. (1890), *Ocherk istorii Kievskoy zemli ot smerti Yaroslava do XIV stoletiya*, Kiev

Hurwitz, E. S. (1980), *Prince Andrej Bogoljubskij: The Man and the Myth*, Florence

Kaiser, D. H. (1980), *The Growth of the Law in Medieval Russia*, Princeton

Kuchkin, V. A. (1985), '"Slovo o polku Igoreve" i mezhduknyazheskie otnosheniya 60-kh godov XI veka', *Voprosy istorii* 11: 19–35

Obolensky, D. (1988), 'Vladimir Monomakh', in *Six Byzantine Portraits*, Oxford, pp. 83–114

Oljancyn, D. (1960), 'Zur Regierung des Grossfursten Izyaslav-Demeter von Kiev (1054–1078), *Jahrbücher für Geschichte Osteuropas* n.s. 8: 397–410

Orlov, A. S. (1946), *Vladimir Monomakh*, Moscow and Leningrad

Pashuto, V. T. (1950), *Ocherki po istorii Galitsko-Volynskoy Rusi*, Moscow

Russ, H. (1981), 'Das Kiever Seniorat von 1054 bis 1169', in *Handbuch der Geschichte Russlands*, I, Stuttgart

Solov'ev, S. M. (1959–66), *Istoriya Rossii s drevneyshikh vremen*, 15 vols., Moscow

Stokes, A. D. (1970), 'The system of succession to the thrones of Russia 1054–1113', in R. Auty, L. R. Lewitter and A. P. Vlasto (eds.), *Gorski vijenats: A Garland of Essays Offered to Professor Elizabeth Mary Hill*, Cambridge, pp. 268–75

Stokes, A. D. (1976), 'Kievan Russia', in R. Auty and D. Obolensky (eds.), *An Introduction to Russian History*, Cambridge, pp. 49–77

Vernadsky, G. (1948), *Kievan Russia*, New Haven

2 Bulgaria

Angelov, D. (1967), 'Die bulgarischen Länder und das bulgarische Volk in den Grenzen des byzantinischen Reiches im XI.–XII. Jahrhundert (1018–1185), in *Proceedings of the XIIIth International Congress of Byzantine Studies*, London, pp. 149–66

Browning, R. (1975), *Byzantium and Bulgaria*, Berkeley

Diaconu, P. (1978), *Les Coumans au Bas-Danube aux XIe et XIIe siècles*, Bucharest

Dostal, A. (1967), 'Les relations entre Byzance et les Slaves (en particulier les Bulgares) aux XIe et XIIe siècles du point de vue culturel', *Proceedings of the XIIIth International Congress of Byzantine Studies*, London, pp. 167–75

Dujcev, I. (1956), 'V"stanieto v 1185 g. i negovata hronologija', in *Izvestija na Instituta za B"lgarska istorija*, VI, pp. 327–56

Fine, J. V. A., jnr (1977), 'The size and significance of the Bulgarian Bogomil movement', *East European Quarterly* 11: 385–412

Fine, J. V. A., jnr (1983a), 'Bulgaria', in J. R. Strayer (ed.), *Dictionary of the Middle Ages*, II, New York, pp. 399–414

Fine, J. V. A., jnr (1983b), *The Early Medieval Balkans: A Critical Survey from the Sixth to the Late Twelfth Century*, Ann Arbor

Fine, J. V. A., Jnr (1987), *The Late Medieval Balkans: A Critical Survey from the Late Twelfth Century to the Ottoman Conquest*, Ann Arbor

Gelzer, H. (1902), *Der Patriarchat von Achrida*, Leipzig

Lang, D. M. (1976), *The Bulgarians: From Pagan Times to the Ottoman Conquest*, London

Litavrin, G. G. (1960), *Bolgariya i Vizantiya v XI–XII vv*, Moscow

Mutafciev, P. (1943), *Istorija na bulgarskija narod*, 2 vols., Sofia

Mutafciev, P. (1973), *Izbrani proizvedenija*, II, Sofia

Obolensky, D. (1948), *The Bogomils*, Cambridge

Obolensky, D. (1971), *The Byzantine Commonwealth: Eastern Europe 500–1453*, London

Obolensky, D. (1988), *Six Byzantine Portraits*, Oxford

Ostrogorsky, G. (1970), *Vizantija i Sloveni*, Belgrade

Pundeff, M. (1968), 'National consciousness in medieval Bulgaria', *Sudost-Forschungen* 27: 1–27

Runciman, S. (1948), 'Byzantium and the Slavs', in N. H. Baynes and H. St. L. B. Moss (eds.), *Byzantium*, Oxford

832   *Bibliography of secondary works, chapter 9*

Snegarov, I. (1924), *Istoriya na Okhridskata arkhiepiskopiya*, Sofia
Spinka, M. (1968), *A History of Christianity in the Balkans*, Hamden, CT
Stanescu, E. (1966), 'La crise du Bas-Danube byzantin au cours de la seconde moitié du XIe siècle', *Zbornik Radova Vizantološkog Instituta* 9: 49–73
Vlasto, A. P. (1970), *The Entry of the Slavs into Christendom*, Cambridge
Zlatarski, V. N. (1918–40), *Istorija na bulgarskata durzava prez srednite vekove*, 3 vols. in 4, Sofia

3 Serbia
Ćirković, S. (1964), *Istorija Srednjovekovne Bosanske Države*, Belgrade
Ćirković, S. (ed.) (1981), *Istorija Srpskod Naroda*, I, Belgrade
Dinić, M. (1966), 'The Balkans 1018–1499', in *The Cambridge Medieval History*, IV, I, Cambridge, pp. 519–22
Dinić, M. J. (1978), *Srpske zemlje u srednjem veku*, Belgrade
Fine, J. V. A., jnr (1983), *The Early Medieval Balkans: A Critical Survey from the Sixth to the Late Twelfth Century*, Ann Arbor
Fine, J. V. A., jnr (1987), *The Late Medieval Balkans: A Critical Survey from the Late Twelfth Century to the Ottoman Conquest*, Ann Arbor
Grafenauer, B., Perović, D. and Šidak, J. (eds.) (1953), *Historija naroda Jugoslavije*, Belgrade
Jireček, J. K. (1952), *Istorija Srba*, 2 vols., trans. into Serbo-Croatian and updated by J. Radonić, Belgrade
Melik, A. (1919–20), *Zgodovina Srbov, Horvatov in Slovencev*, 2 vols., Ljubljana
Obolensky, D. (1971), *The Byzantine Commonwealth: Eastern Europe 500–1453*, London
Prelog, M. (1920–1), *Pregled povijesti Južnikh Slavena Srba, Hrvata i Slovenaca*, 2 vols., Sarajevo
Radojčić, B. (1961), 'O hronologiji ugarsko-vizantijskih borbi i ustanku Srba za vreme Jovana II Komnina', *Zbornik radova Vizantološkog Instituta* 7: 177–86
Spinka, M. (1968), *A History of Christianity in the Balkans*, Hamden, CT
Srejović, D. et al. (eds.) (1981–2) *Istorija srpskod naroda*, I–II, Belgrade
Stanojević, S. (1928), *Istorija Srba, Hrvata i Slovenaca*, 3rd edn, Belgrade
Vlasto, A. P. (1970), *The Entry of the Slavs into Christendom*, Cambridge

4 Croatia
Ćorović, V. (1940), *Historija Bosne*, Belgrade
Dabinović, A. (1940), *Hrvatska državna i pravna povijest*, Zagreb
Fine, J. V. A., jnr (1983), *The Early Medieval Balkans: A Critical Survey from the Sixth to the Late Twelfth Century*, Ann Arbor
Fine, J. V. A., jnr (1987), *The Late Medieval Balkans: A Critical Survey from the Late Twelfth Century to the Ottoman Conquest*, Ann Arbor
Ferluga, J. (1957), *Vizantiska uprava u Dalmaciji* (Serbian Academy of Sciences, posebna izdanja, 291, Vizantološki Institut, knj. 6), Belgrade
Ferluga, J. (1990), 'Bizanc na Jadranu (6.–13. stoletje)', *Zgodovinski Časopis* 44: 363–86
Guldescu, S. (1964), *History of Medieval Croatia*, The Hague

Klaić, N. (1971), *Povijest Hrvata u ranom srednjem vijeku*, Zagreb

Klaić, V. (1972), *Povijest Hrvata od najstarijih vremena do susretka XIX stoljeća: Kniga prva: Prvo doba – Vladenje knez va i kraljeva Hrvatske krvi (641–1102); Drugo doba – Vladanje kraljeva Arpadovića (1102–1301)*, Zagreb

Mandić, D. (1963), *Rasprave i Prilozi iz stare Hrvatske povijesti*, ed. D. Lasić and B. Pandžić, Rim

Šišić, F. (1920), *Pregled povijesti hrvatskoga naroda od najstarijih vremena do 1918*, I, izd. 2, Zagreb

Šišić, F. (1925), *Povijest Hrvata u vrijeme narodnih vladara*, repr. Zagreb, 1990

10 POLAND IN THE ELEVENTH AND TWELFTH CENTURIES

Carter, F. W. (1994), *Trade and Urban Development in Poland: An Economic Geography of Cracow, from its Origins to 1795*, Cambridge

Davies, N. (1981), *God's Playground: A History of Poland*, Oxford

Fedorowicz, J. K. *et al.*, (eds.) (1982), *A Republic of Nobles*, Cambridge

Gasiorowski, A. (ed.) (1984), *The Polish Nobility in the Middle Ages*, Wroclaw

Gieysztor, A. *et al.*, (1968), *History of Poland*, Warsaw; 2nd edn 1979

Górecki, P. (1992), *Economy, Society and Lordship in Medieval Poland 1100–1250*, New York

Górecki, P. (1993), *Parishes, Tithes and Society in Earlier Medieval Poland, c. 1100–c. 1250*, Philadelphia

Górski, K. (1976), *Communitas, Princeps, Corona*, Warsaw

Grudzinski, T. (1985), *Boleslaus the Bold, Called also the Bountiful, and Bishop Stanislaus: The Story of a Conflict*, Warsaw

Halecki, O. (1983), *A History of Poland*, London

Halecki, O. (1991), *Jadwiga of Anjou and the Rise of East Central Europe*, Boulder, CO

Hoffmann, R. (1989), *Land, Liberties and Lordship in a Late Medieval Countryside: Agrarian Structures and Change in the Duchy of Wroclaw*, Philadelphia

Kloczowski, J. (1981), *The Christian Community of Medieval Poland*, Wroclaw

Kloczowski, J. (1990), 'The church and the nation: the example of the mendicants in thirteenth-century Poland', in D. Loades (ed.), *Faith and Identity: Christian Political Experience*, Oxford, pp. 47–55

Kloczowski, J. (2000), *A History of Polish Christianity*, Cambridge

Knoll, P. W. (1972), *The rise of the Polish Monarchy 1320–1370*, Chicago and London

Knoll, P. W. (1989), 'Economic and political institutions on the Polish–German frontier in the middle ages', in R. Bartlett and A. MacKay (eds.), *Medieval Frontier Societies*, Oxford, pp. 151–74

Kozlowska-Budkowa, S. (1985), 'The foundation of the university of Cracow', in J. Braun (ed.), *Poland in Christian Civilization*, London, pp. 165–79

Manteuffel, T. (1982), *The Formation of the Polish State (963–1194)*, Detroit

Michael, M. (trans.) (1997), *The Annals of Jan Dlugosz*, Chichester

Polonsky, A. *et al.* (eds.) (1994), *The Jews in Old Poland (1000–1795)*, London

Reddaway, W. F. *et al.*, (1950), *The Cambridge History of Poland*, Cambridge

Vardy, S. B., Grosschmid, G. and Domonkos, L. S. (eds.) (1986), *Louis the Great: King of Hungary and Poland*, Boulder, CO

Wandycz, D. S. (ed.) (1966), *Studies in Polish Civilization*, New York
Zientara, B. (1974), 'Foreigners in Poland 10–15th centuries', *Acta Poloniae Historica* 29: 5–28

11 SCANDINAVIA IN THE ELEVENTH AND TWELFTH CENTURIES

Andersen, P. S. (1977), *Samlingen av Norge og kristningen av landet 800–1130* (Handbok i Norges Historie 2), Bergen, Oslo and Tromsø
Bagge, S. (1986), 'Borgerkrig og statsutvikling i Norge i middelalderen', *Historisk Tidsskrift* 65: 145–97
Becker, C. J. (1981), 'The coinage of Harthacnut and Magnus the Good at Lund c. 1040–c. 1046', in C. J. Becker (ed.), *Studies in Northern Coinages of the Eleventh Century* (Det Kongelige Danske Videnskabernes Selskab: Historisk-filosofiske Skrifter 9: 4), Copenhagen, pp. 119–74
Bengtsson, H. (1999), *Den höviska kulturen: en konsthistorisk undersökning*, Stockholm
Blackburn, M. (1990), 'Do Cnut the Great's first coins as king of Denmark date from before 1018?', in K. Jonsson and B. Malmer (eds.), *Sigtuna Papers: Proceedings from the Sigtuna Symposium on Viking-Age Coinage 1–4 June 1989*, Stockholm and London, pp. 55–68
Breengaard, C. (1982), *Muren om Israels hus: regnum og sacerdotium i Danmark 1050–1170*, Copenhagen
Byock, J. L. (1988), *Medieval Iceland: Sagas, Society and Power*, Berkeley, Los Angeles and London
Christensen, A. E. (1977), 'Tiden 1042–1241', in A. E. Christensen *et al.* (eds.), *Danmarks historie*, 1, Copenhagen, pp. 211–399
Dahlbäck, G. (ed.) (1997), *Kyrka – samhälle -stat: fran kristnande till etablerad kyrka*, Helsinki
Edgren, T. and Törnblom, L. (1992), *Finlands Historia*, 1, Esbo
Fenger, O. (2002), *'Kirker rejses alle vegne' 1050–1250* (Danmarkshistorie, ed. O. Olsen, 4), 2nd ed. Copenhagen
Helle, K. (1974), *Norge blev en stat 1130–1319* (Handbok i Norges Historie 3), Bergen, Oslo and Tromsø
Helle, K. (ed.) (2003), *The Cambridge History of Scandinavia Pre history to 1520*, Cambridge
Jonsson, F. (1912–15) *Den Norsk-Islandske Skaldedigtning*, 1, Copenhagen
Krag, C. (1989), 'Norge som odel i Harald Harfagres ætt', *Historisk Tidsskrift* 68: 288–302
Krag, C. (2000), *Norges Historie gram til 1319*, Oslo
Malmer, B., Ros, J. and Tesch, S. (1991), *Kung Olofs Mynthus i kvarteret Urmakaren, Sigtuna*, Sigtuna
Nilsson, B. (1998), *Sveriges kyrkohistoria*, 1: *Missionstid och tidig medeltid*, Stockholm
Nordal, S. (1990), *Icelandic Culture*, Ithaca
Nyberg, T. (2000), *Monasticism in North-Western Europe, 800–1200*, Aldershot
Roesdahl, E. and Wilson, D. M. (1992), *From Viking to Crusader: The Scandinavians and Europe 800–1200*, Copenhagen
Sawyer, B. and Sawyer, P. (1993), *Medieval Scandinavia from Conversion to Reformation circa 500–1500*, Minnesota
Sawyer, B. and Sauyer, P. (2002), *Die Welt der Wikinger*, Berlin

Sawyer, P. (2002), *Da Danmark blev Danmark: fra ca. ar 700 til ca. 1050* (Danmarkshistorie, ed. O. Olsen, 3), 2nd edn Copenhagen

Sawyer, P. (1989), 'Knut, Sweden and Sigtuna', in S. Tesch (ed.), *Avstamp – för en ny Sigtunaforskning*, Sigtuna, pp. 88–93

Sawyer, P. (1991a), *När Sverige blev Sverige*, Alingsas

Sawyer, P. (1991b), 'Swein Forkbeard and the historians', in I. Wood and G. A. Loud (eds.), *Church and Chronicle in the Middle Ages: Essays Presented to John Taylor*, London, pp. 27–40

Sigurðsson, J. V. (1999), *Chieffains and Power the Icelandic Commonwealth*, Odense

Skyum-Nielsen, N. (1971), *Kvinde og Slave*, Copenhagen

Tesch, S. (ed.) (1990), *Makt och Människor i Kungens Sigtuna: Sigtunautgrävningen 1988–90*, Sigtuna

Thorsteinsson, B. (1985), *Island*, Copenhagen

12   HUNGARY IN THE ELEVENTH AND TWELFTH CENTURIES

Bartlett, R. (1994), *The Making of Europe*, London

Berend, N. (2001), *At, the Gate of Christendom: Jews, Muslims and 'Pagans in Medieual Hungary, c. 1000–c.1300*, Cambridge

Bogyay, T. von, Bak, J. and Silagi, G. (1976), *Die Heiligen Könige* (Ungarns Geschichtsschreiber 1), Graz, Vienna and Cologne

Bóna, I. (1995), *Áz Árpádok korai várairól: 11–12. századi ispáni várak és hátarvárak*, Debrecen

Boroviczényi, K. (1991-2), 'Cruciferi sancti regis Stephani: Tanulmányok a Stefaniták, egy középkori magyar ispotályos rend történetéröl', *Orvostörténeti Közlemények* 133–40: 7–48

Csapodi, Cs. (1979), 'Le catalogue de Pannonhalma, reflet de la vie intellectuelle des Bénedictins du XIe siècle en Hongrie', in P. Cockshaw, M.-C. Garand and P. Jodogne (eds.), *Miscellanea Codicologica F. Masai dicata*, Gand, pp. 165–73

Engel, P. (1990), *Beilleszkedés Európába, a kezdetektöl 1440–ig*, Budapest

Érszegi, G. (1993), *The Deed of Foundation of Tihany Abbey*, Veszprém

Font, M. (1990), 'Politische Bezichungen zwischen Ungarn und der Kiever Rus' im 12. Jahrhundert', *Ungarn-Jahrbuch* 18: 1–18

Fügedi, E. (1969), 'Die Entsehung des Städtewesens in Ungarn', *Alba Regia* 10: 101–18

Fügedi, E. (1974), 'Das mittelalterliche Königreich Ungarn als Gastland', in W. Schlesinger (ed.), *Die deutsche Ostsiedlung des Mittelalters als Problem der europäischen Geschichte* (Vorträge und Forschungen 18), Sigmaringen, pp. 471–507

Fügedi, E. (1986a), *Castle and Society in Medieval Hungary (1000–1437)* (Studia Historica Academiae Scientiarum Hungaricae 187), Budapest

Fügedi, E. (1986b), *Kings, Bishops, Nobles and Burghers in Medieval Hungary*, London

Gerevich, L. (ed.) (1990), *Towns in Medieval Hungary* (East European Monographs 297), Highland Lakes, NJ

Gerics, J. (1984), 'Über Vorbilder und Quellen der Vita Hartviciana S. Stephani Regis', *Acta Antiqua Academiae Scientiarum Hungaricae* 29: 425–44

Gerics, J. and Ladányi, E. (1996), 'A Szentszék és a magyar állam a 11. században', in I. Zombori (ed.), *Magyarország és a Szentszék kapcsolatának 1000 éve*, Budapest, pp. 9–20

Göckenjan, H. (1972), *Hilfsvölker und Grenzwächter im mittelalterlichen Ungarns*, Wiesbaden

Györffy, Gy. (1963–), *Az Árpád-kori Magyarország történeti földrajza*, 3 vols. to date, Budapest

Györffy, Gy. (1976), 'Zur Frage der Herkunft der ungarländischen Dienstleute', *Studia Slavica Academiae Scientiarum Hungaricae* 22: 40–83, 311–37

Györffy, Gy. (1977), *István király és műve*, Budapest

Györffy, Gy. (1983), *Wirtschaft und Gesellschaft der Ungarn um die Jahrausendwende mit einem Anhang Gesetze und Synodalbeschlusse Ungarns aus dem 11. Jahrhundert* (Studia Historica Academiae Scientiarum Hungaricae 186), Budapest

Györffy, Gy. (1990), *A magyarság keleti elemei*, Budapest

Györffy, Gy. (1994), *King Saint Stephen of Hungary* (East European Monographs 403), Highland Lakes, NJ

Heckenast, G. (1970), *Fejedelmi (királyi) szolgálónépek a korai Árpád-korban* (Értekezések a történeti tudományok köréből 53), Budapest

Higounet, C. (1989), *Les Allemands en Europe centrale et orientale au moyen âge*, Paris

Hóman, B. (1916), *Magyar pénztörténet 1000–1325*, Budapest

Jánosi, M. (1996), *Törvényalkotás a korai Árpád-korban*, Szeged

Klaniczay, G. (1990), 'From sacral kingship to self-representation: Hungarian and European royal saints', in *idem, The Uses of Supernatural Power*, Princeton, pp. 79–94

Kristó, Gy. (1974), *A XI. századi hercegség története Magyarországon*, Budapest

Kristó, Gy. (1988), *A vármegyék kialakulása Magyarországon*, Budapest

Kristó, Gy. (1990), 'Die Entstehung der Komitatsorganisation unter Stephan dem Heiligen', in F. Glatz (ed.), *Settlement and Society in Hungary* (Etudes Historiques Hongroises), Budapest, pp. 13–25

Kristó, Gy. (1993), *Die Arpadendynastie: die Geschichte Ungarns von 895 bis 1301*, Budapest

Kristó, Gy. (1997), *A magyar nemzet megszületése*, Szeged

Kristó, Gy. (comp.) (1985), *Saecula Hungariae 1000–1196*, Budapest

Kristó, Gy. (ed.) (1994), *Korai magyar történeti lexikon (9–14. század)*, Budapest

Kumorovitz, B. L. (1960), 'Die erste Epoche der ungarischen privatrechtlichen Schriftlichkeit im Mittelalter (XI–XII. Jahrhundert)', in Gy. Ember, E. Mályusz et al. (eds.), *Etudes historiques*, I, Budapest, pp. 253–90

Lovag, Z. (ed.) (1983), *Insignia regni Hungariae I: Studien zur Machtsymbolik des mittelalterlichen Ungarn*, Budapest

Makk, F. (1989), *The Árpáds and the Comneni: Political Relations between Hungary and Byzantium in the 12th Century*, Budapest

Makk, F. (1993), *Magyar Külpolitika (896–1196)*, Szeged

Mályusz, E. (1966), 'Die Eigenkirche in Ungarn', *Wiener Archiv für Geschichte des Slawentums und Osteuropas* 5: 282–302

Mályusz, E. (1969), 'La chancellerie royale et la rédaction des chroniques dans la Hongrie médiévale', *MA* 75: 51–86, 219–54

Marosi, E. and Wehli, T. (1997), *Az Árpad-kor művészeti emlékei*, Budapest

Mezey, L. (1968), 'Ungarn und Europa im 12. Jahrhundert: Kirche und Kultur zwischen Ost und West', *Vorträge und Forschungen* 12: 255–72

Moravcsik, J. [Gy.] (1934), 'Les relations entre la Hongrie et Byzance à l'époque des Croisades', *Bibliothèque de la Revue des Etudes Hongroises* 9: 1–8

Moravcsik, Gy. (1947), 'The role of the Byzantine church in medieval Hungary', *American Slavic and East European Review* 6: 134–51

Moravcsik, Gy. (1966), 'Hungary and Byzantium in the middle ages', in *The Cambridge Medieval History*, IV, part I, Cambridge, pp. 566–92

Moravcsik, Gy. (1970), *Byzantium and the Magyars*, Budapest

Pálóczi-Horváth, A. (1989), *Pechenegs, Cumans, Iasians: Steppe Peoples in Medieval Hungary*, Budapest

Puskely, M. (1996), *Keresztény Szerzetesség*, Budapest

Stephenson, P. (1996), 'Manuel I Comnenus, the Hungarian crown and the "feudal subjection" of Hungary, 1162–1167', *BS* 57: 33–59

Sweeney, J. R. (1981), 'Hungary in the crusades 1169–1218', *International History Review* 3: 468–81

Szabó, I. (1971), *A falurendszer kialakulása Magyarországon (X–XV. század)*, Budapest

Székely, Gy. (1962), 'Gemeinsame Züge der ungarischen und polnischen Kirchengeschichte des XI. Jahrhunderts', *Annales Universitatis Scientiarum Budapestinensis de Rolando Eötvös Nominatae, Sectio Historica* 4: 55–80

Székely, Gy. (1964), 'Wallons et Italiens en Europe centrale aux XIe–XVIe siècles', *Annales Universitatis Scientiarum Budapestinensis de Rolando Eötvös Nominatae, Sectio Historica* 6: 3–71

Székely, Gy. (1967), 'La Hongrie et Byzance aux Xe–XIIe siècles', *Acta Historica Academiae Scientiarum Hungaricae* 13: 291–310

Székely, Gy. (1969), 'Evolution de la structure et de la culture de la classe dominante laïque dans la Hongrie des Árpád', *Acta Historica Academiae Scientiarum Hungaricae* 15: 223–52

Székely, Gy. (1974), 'Les contacts entre Hongrois et Musulmans aux IX–XII siècles', in Gy. Káldy-Nagy (ed.), *The Muslim East: Studies in Honour of Julius Germanus*, Budapest, pp. 53–74

Székely, Gy. (1984), *Magyarország története: Előzmények és Magyar történet 1242-ig*, Budapest

Szentirmai, A. (1956), 'Der Ursprung des Archidiakonats in Ungarn', *Österreichisches Archiv für Kirchenrecht* 7: 231–44

Szentirmai, A. (1961), 'Der Einfluss des byzantinischen Kirchenrechts auf die Gesetzgebung Ungarns im XI–XII Jahrhundert', *Jahrbuch der Österreichischen Byzantinischen Gesellschaft* 10: 73–83

Szovák, K. (1993), 'The image of the ideal king in twelfth-century Hungary: remarks on the legend of St Ladislas', in A. J. Duggan (ed.), *Kings and Kingship in Medieval Europe* (Kings College London Medieval Studies 10), London, pp. 241–64

Szovák, K. (1996), 'Pápai-magyar kapcsolatok a 12. században', in I. Sombori (ed.), *Magyarország és a Szentszék kapcsolatának 1000 éve*, Budapest, pp. 21–46

Szücs, J. (1972), 'König Stephan in der Sicht der modernen ungarischen Geschichtsforschung', *Südost-Forschungen* 31: 17–40

Szücs, J. (1981), *Nation und Geschichte: Studien*, Budapest

Szücs, J. (1983), 'The three historical regions of Europe: an outline', *Acta Historica Academiae Scientiarum Hungaricae* 29: 2–4, 131–84

Takács, I. (ed.) (1996), *Mons Sacer 996–1996: Pannonhalma ezer éve*, Pannonhalma

Váczy, P. (1994), *A magyar történelem korai századaiból*, Budapest

Waldmüller, L. (1987), *Die Synoden in Dalmatien, Kroatien und Ungarn von der Völkwanderung bis zum Ende der Arpaden* (Konziliengeschichte 21), Paderborn and Munich

Zsoldos, A. (1997), *Az Árpádok és alattvalóik: Magyarország története 1301-ig*, Debrecen

13 THE PAPACY, 1122–1198

Anciaux, P. (1949), *La Théologie du sacrement de pénitence au XIIe siècle* (Universitas Catholica Lovaniensis, Dissertationes in Facultate Theologica, series 2, 41), Louvain and Gembloux

Baaken, G. (1972), '*Unio regni ad imperium*: die Verhandlungen von Verona 1184 und die Eheabredung zwischen König Heinrich VI. und Konstanze von Sizilien', *QFIAB* 52: 219–97

Bachmann, J. (1913), *Die päpstlichen Legaten in Deutschland und Skandinavien 1125–1159* (Historische Studien 115), Berlin

Baldwin, J. W. (1967), 'A debate at Paris over Thomas Becket between Master Roger and Master Peter the Chanter', in *Collectanea Stephan Kuttner* (Studia Gratiana 11), pp. 121–6

Baldwin, J. W. (1970), *Masters, Princes and Merchants: The Social Views of Peter the Chanter and his Circle*, 2 vols., Princeton

Baldwin, J. W. (1986), *The Government of Philip Augustus: Foundations of French Royal Power in the Middle Ages*, Berkeley and Los Angeles

Barker, J. R. V. (1986), *The Tournament in England 1100–1400*, Woodbridge

Barlow, F. (1936), 'The English, Norman and French councils called to deal with the papal schism of 1159', *EHR* 51: 264–8

Barlow, F. (1986), *Thomas Becket*, London

Bémont, C. (1925), 'La bulle *Laudabiliter*', in *Mélanges d'histoire du moyen âge offerts à Ferdinand Lot*, Paris, pp. 41–53

Benson, R. L. (1968), *The Bishop Elect: A Study in Medieval Ecclesiastical Office*, Princeton

Benson, R. L. (1982), 'Political renovatio: two models from Roman antiquity', in R. L. Benson and G. Constable (eds.), *Renaissance and Renewal in the Twelfth Century*, Oxford, pp. 340–59

Berlière, U. (1901), 'Le cardinal Matthieu d'Albano', *RBén* 18: 113–40, 280–303

Berlière, U. (1919), 'Le droit de procuration ou de gîte', *Bulletin de la Classe des Lettres et des Sciences Morales et Politiques de l'Academie Royale de Belgique*: 509–38

Bernhardi, W. (1879), *Lothar von Supplinburg* (Jahrbücher der Deutschen Geschichte), Leipzig

Bethell, D. (1968), 'William of Corbeil and the Canterbury–York dispute', *JEH* 19: 145–59

Boussard, J. (1945–6), 'Les mercenaires au XIIe siècle: Henri II Plantegenêt et les origines de l'armée de métier', *BEC* 106: 189–224

Brett, M. (1975), *The English Church under Henry I*, Oxford

Brixius, J. M. (1912), *Die Mitglieder des Kardinalkollegiums von 1130 bis 1181*, Berlin

Brooke, Z. N. (1931), *The English Church and the Papacy from the Conquest to the Reign of John*, Cambridge

Brühl, C. (1974), 'Zur Geschichte der procuratio canonica vornehmlich im 11. und 12. Jahrhundert', in *Le istituzioni ecclesiastiche della 'societas christiana' dei secoli XI–XII* 1 (Miscellanea del Centro di Studi Medioevali 7), Milan

Brundage, J. A. (1963), 'The crusade of Richard I: two canonical *questiones*', *Speculum* 38: 448–52

Brundage, J. A. (1966), '*Cruce signari*: the rite for taking the cross in England', *Traditio* 22: 289–310

Brundage, J. A. (1968), 'The votive obligations of crusaders: the development of a canonistic doctrine', *Traditio* 24: 77–118

Brundage, J. A. (1969), *Medieval Canon Law and the Crusader*, Madison

Brundage, J. A. (1971), 'The army of the First Crusade and the crusade vow', *Medieval Studies* 33: 334–43

Caspar, E. and Rassow, P. (1924), 'Die Kreuzzugsbullen Eugens III.', *NA* 45: 285–305

Chalandon, F. (1907), *Histoire de la domination normande en Italie et Sicile*, 11, Paris

Cheney, C. R. (1956), *From Becket to Langton: English Church Government 1170–1213*, Manchester

Cheney, C. R. (1967), *Hubert Walter*, London

Cheney, C. R. (1976), *Pope Innocent III and England* (Päpste und Papsttum 9), Stuttgart

Cheney, M. G. (1941), 'The compromise of Avranches of 1172 and the spread of canon law in England', *EHR* 56: 177–97

Cheney, M. G. (1969), 'The recognition of Pope Alexander III: some neglected evidence', *EHR* 84: 474–97

Chibnall, M. (1991), *The Empress Matilda: Queen Consort, Queen Mother and Lady of the English*, Oxford

Chodorow, S. (1972), *Christian Political Theory and Church Politics in the Mid-Twelfth Century*, Berkeley and Los Angeles

Classen, P. (1960), *Gerhoch von Reichersberg, Eine Biographie*, Wiesbaden

Classen, P. (1968), 'Zur Geschichte Papst Anastasius IV.', *QFIAB* 48: 36–63

Classen, P. (1973), 'Das Wormser Konkordat in der deutschen Verfassungsgeschichte', in J. Fleckenstein (ed.), *Investiturstreit und Reichsverfassung* (Vorträge und Forschungen 17), Sigmaringen

Classen, P. (1974), 'La curia romana et le scuole di Francia nel secolo XII', in *Le istituzioni ecclesiastiche della 'societas christiana' dei secoli XI–XII*, 1 (Miscellanea del Centro di Studi Medioevali 7), Milan, pp. 432–6

Classen, P. (1983), *Studium und Gesellschaft im Mittelalter* (*MGH Schriften* 29), Stuttgart

Clementi, D. (1968), 'The relations between the papacy, the western Roman empire and the emergent kingdom of Sicily and south Italy, 1050–1156', *BISI* 80: 191–212

Congar, Y. M.-J. (1955), 'Die Ekklesiologie des hl. Bernhard', in J. Lortz (ed.), *Bernhard von Clairvaux, Mönch und Mystiker, Internationaler Bernhardkongress, Mainz 1953*, Wiesbaden, pp. 76–119

Congar, Y. M.-J. (1958), 'Henri de Marcy, abbé de Clairvaux, cardinal-évêque d'Albano et légat pontifical', in *Analecta Monastica: textes et études sur la vie des moines au moyen âge*, 5th series (Studia Anselmiana 43), Rome, pp. 1–90

Constable, G. (1953), 'The Second Crusade as seen by contemporaries', *Traditio* 9: 213–79

Constable, G. (1957), 'The disputed election at Langres in 1138', *Traditio* 13: 119–52

Cowdrey, H. E. J. (1978), 'Abbot Pontius of Cluny (1109–22/6)', *Studi Gregoriani per la Storia della 'Libertas Ecclesiae'* 11: 177–277

Cronne, H. A. (1970), *The reign of Stephen, 1134–54*, London

Davis, R. H. C. (1967), *King Stephen 1135–1154*, London

Deér, J. (1959), *The Dynastic Porphyry Tombs of the Norman Period in Sicily* (Dumbarton Oaks Studies 5), Cambridge, MA

Deér, J. (1964), 'Der Anspruch der Herrscher des 12. Jahrhunderts auf die apostolische Legation', *AHP* 2: 117–86

Deér, J. (1972), *Papsttum und Normannen: Untersuchungen zu ihren lehnsrechtlichen und kirchenpolitischen Beziehungen* (Studien und Quellen zur Welt Kaiser Friedrichs II., 1), Cologne and Vienna

De Ghellinck, J. (1948), *Le Mouvement théologique au XIIe siècle*, 2nd edn, Bruges

Dubois, J. (1968), 'Les ordres religieux au XIIe siècle selon la Curie romaine', *RBén* 78: 283–309

Dueball, M. (1929), *Der Suprematiestreit zwischen den Erzbistumern Canterbury und York, 1070 bis 1126* (Historische Studien 184), Berlin

Duggan, C. (1963), *Twelfth-Century Decretal Collections and their Importance in English History*, London

Duggan, C. (1966), 'Richard of Ilchester, royal servant and bishop', *TRHS* 5th series 16: 1–21

Dunken, G. (1931), *Die politische Wirksamkeit der päpstlichen Legaten in der Zeit des Kampfes zwischen Kaisertum und Papsttum in Oberitalien unter Friedrich I.* (Historische Studien 209), Berlin

Elze, R. (1950), 'Die päpstliche Kapelle im 12. und 13. Jahrhundert', *ZSSRG KA* 36: 145–204

Engels, O. (1987), 'Zum Konstanzer Vertrag von 1153', in *'Deus qui mutat tempora': Menschen und Institutionen im Wandel des Mittelalters: Festschrift für Alfons Becker*, Sigmaringen, pp. 235–58

Erdmann, C. (1928), *Das Papsttum und Portugal im ersten Jahrhundert der portugiesischen Geschichte* (Abhandlungen der Preussischen Akademie der Wissenschaften, phil.-hist. klasse Jahrgang 1928, no. 5), Berlin

Erdmann, C. (1935), *Die Entstehung des Kreuzzugsgedankens* (Forschungen zur Kirchen- und Geistesgeschichte 6), Stuttgart

Fichtenau, H. (1957), *Arenga: Spätantike und Mittelalter im Spiegel von Urkundenformen*, Cologne and Graz

Fletcher, R. A. (1984), *Saint James's Catapult: The Life and Times of Diego Gelmírez of Santiago de Compostela*, Oxford

Foreville, R. (1943), *L'Eglise et la royauté en Angleterre sous Henri II Plantagenêt*, Paris

Foreville, R. (1965), *Latran I, II, III et Latran IV* (Histoire des Conciles Œcuméniques 6), Paris

Foreville, R. and Rousset de Pina, J. (1953), *Du premier Concile du Latran à l'avènement d'Innocent III* (Histoire de l'Eglise depuis les Origines jusqu'à nos Jours 9), Paris

Forey, A. J. (1973), *The Templars in the Corona de Aragón*, London

Fournier, P. (1916), 'La prohibition par le deuxième concile de Latran d'armes jugés trop meurtrières', *Revue Générale de Droit International Publique* 23: 471–9

Fried, J. (1980), *Der päpstlichen Schutz für Laienfürsten: die politische Geschichte des päpstlichen Schutzprivilegs für Laien (11.–13. Jh)* (Abhandlungen der Heidelberger Akademie der Wissenschaften, phil.-hist. klasse 1980, 1), Heidelberg

Friedländer, I. (1928), *Die päpstlichen Legaten in Deutschland und Italien am Ende des XII. Jahrhunderts (1181–1198)* (Historische Studien 177), Berlin

Frugoni, A. (1967), 'A pictura cepit', *BISI* 78: 123–35

Fuhrmann, H. (1961), 'Das Ökumenische Konzil und seine historischen Grundlagen', *Geschichte in Wissenschaft und Unterricht* 12: 672–95

Geisthardt, F. (1936), *Der Kämmerer Boso* (Historische Studien 293), Berlin

Gillingham, J. (1978), *Richard the Lionheart*, London

Gleber, H. (1936), *Papst Eugen III. (1145–1153) unter besonderer Berücksichtigung seiner politischen Tätigkeit* (Beiträge zur Mittelalterlichen und Neueren Geschichte 6), Jena

Gottlob, A. (1906), *Kreuzablass und Almosenablass: eine Studie über die Frühzeit des Ablasswesens* (Kirchenrechtliche Abhandlungen 30–1), Stuttgart

Graboïs, A. (1964a), 'Le privilège de croisade et la régence de Suger', *Revue Historique de Droit Français et Etranger* 4th series 42: 458–65

Graboïs, A. (1964b), 'Les séjours des papes en France au XIIe siècle et leurs rapports avec le développement de la fiscalité pontificale', *Revue d'Histoire de l'Eglise de France* 49: 5–18

Graboïs, A. (1981), 'Le schisme de 1130 et la France', *RHE* 76: 593–612

Grundmann, H. (1961), *Religiöse Bewegungen im Mittelalter*, 2nd edn, Hildesheim

Halphen, L. (1907), *Etudes sur l'administration de Rome au moyen âge* (Bibliothèque de l'Ecole des Hautes Etudes 176), Paris

Häring, N. M. (1965), 'Das sogenannte Glaubensbekenntnis des Reimser Konsistoriums von 1148', *Scholastik* 40: 55–90

Häring, N. M. (1966a), 'Notes on the council and consistory of Rheims 1148', *Medieval Studies* 28: 39–59

Häring, N. M. (1966b), 'The writings against Gilbert of Poitiers by Geoffrey of Auxerre', *Analecta Cisterciensia* 22: 3–83

Häring, N. M. (1967), 'Das Pariser Konsistorium Eugens III. vom April 1147', *Studia Gratiana* 11: 93–117

Hauck, A. (1952), *Kirchengeschichte Deutschlands*, IV, 6th edn, Leipzig

Hehl, E.-D. (1980), *Kirche und Krieg im 12. Jahrhundert: Studien zu kanonishchen Recht und politischen Wirklichkeit* (Monographien zur Geschichte des Mittelalters 19), Stuttgart

Heinemeyer, W. (1969), '*Beneficium – non feudum sed bonum factum*: der Streit auf dem Reichstag zu Besançon 1157', *Archiv für Diplomatik* 15: 183–97

Hoffmann, H. (1971), 'Petrus Diaconus, die Herren von Tusculum und der Sturz Oderisius II. von Montecassino', *DA* 27: 1–109

Holtzmann, W. (1938), 'Krone und Kirche in Norwegen im 12. Jahrhundert', *DA* 2: 341–400

Holtzmann, W. (1945), 'Über eine Ausgabe der päpstlichen Dekretalen des 12. Jahrhunderts', *Nachrichten der Akademie der Wissenschaften in Göttingen, phil.-hist. klasse*: 15–36

Hüls, R. (1977), *Kardinäle, Klerus und Kirche Roms, 1049–1130* (Bibliothek des Deutschen Historischen Instituts in Rom 48), Tübingen

Jacqueline, B. (1953), 'Saint Bernard de Clairvaux et la curie romaine', *Rivista di Storia della Chiesa in Italia* 7: 27–44

Janssen, W. (1961), *Die päpstlichen Legaten in Frankreich vom Schisma Anaklets II. bis zum Tode Coelestins III. 1130–1198* (Kölner Historische Abhandlungen 6), Cologne and Graz

Jordan, K. (1933–4), 'Zur päpstlichen Finanzgeschichte im 11. und 12. Jahrhundert', *QFIAB* 25: 61–104

Keen, M. (1984), *Chivalry*, New Haven

Kehr, P. F. (1888), 'Der Vertrag von Anagni im Jahre 1176', *NA* 13: 75–118

Kehr, P. F. (1924), 'Papst Gregor VIII. als Ordensgründer', in *Miscellanea Francesco Ehrle: Scritti di storia e paleografia*, II (Studi e Testi 38), Rome, pp. 248–75

Kehr, P. F. (1928), *Das Papsttum und die Königreiche Navarra und Aragón bis zur Mitte des 12. Jahrhunderts* (Abhandlungen der Preußischen Akademie der Wissenschaften, phil.-hist. klasse 1928/4), Berlin

Kehr, P. F. (1934), *Die Belehnungen der süditalienischen Normannenfürsten durch die Päpste 1059–1192* (Abhandlungen der Preußischen Akademie der Wissenschaften, phil.-hist. klasse 1), Berlin

Kemp, E. W. (1948), *Canonization and Authority in the Western Church*, Oxford

Kempf, F. (1963), 'Kanonistik und kuriale Politik im 12. Jahrhundert', *AHP* 1: 11–52

Kennan, E. (1967), 'The *De consideratione* of St Bernard of Clairvaux and the papacy in the mid-twelfth century: a review of scholarship', *Traditio* 23: 73–115

Klewitz, H.-W. (1939), 'Die Festkrönungen der deutschen Könige', *ZSSRG KA* 28: 48–96

Klewitz, H.-W. (1941), 'Die Krönung des Papstes', *ZSSRG KA* 30: 96–130

Klewitz, H.-W. (1957), *Reformpapsttum und Kardinalkolleg*, Darmstadt

Knowles, D. (1951), *The Episcopal Colleagues of Archbishop Thomas Becket*, Cambridge

Knowles, D. (1963), *The Historian and Character and Other Studies*, Cambridge

Knowles, D. (1970), *Thomas Becket*, London

Knowles, D., Duggan, A. J. and Brooke, C. N. L. (1972), 'Henry II's supplement to the Constitutions of Clarendon', *EHR* 87: 757–71

Kuttner, S. (1935), *Kanonistische Schuldlehre von Gratian bis auf die Dekretalen Gregors IX.* (Studi e Testi 64), Vatican City

Kuttner, S. (1964), 'Dat Galienus opes et sanctio Justiniana', in *Linguistic and Literary Studies in Honour of Helmut A. Hatzfeld*, Washington, pp. 237–46

Ladner, G. B. (1935), 'I mosaici gli affreschi ecclesiastico-politici nell'antico palazzo Lateranense', *Rivista di Archeologia Christiana* 12: 281–90

Laehr, G. (1926), *Die Konstantinische Schenkung in der abendländischen Literatur des Mittelalters bis zur Mitte des 14. Jahrhunderts* (Historische Studien 166), Berlin

Lefèvre, J. A. (1954), 'La véritable constitution cistercienne de 1119', *Collectanea Ordinis Cisterciensium Reformatorium* 16: 97–104

Leyser, K. (1982), *Medieval Germany and its Neighbours 900–1250*, London

Little, E. (1973), 'Bernard and Abelard at the Council of Sens', in *Bernard of Clairvaux: Studies Presented to Dom Jean Leclercq* (Cistercian Studies 23), Washington, pp. 55–71

Lomax, D. W. (1978), *The Reconquest of Spain*, London and New York

Lourie, E. (1975), 'The will of Alfonso I *el Batallador*, king of Aragón and Navarre: a reassessment', *Speculum* 50: 635–51

Luchaire, A. (1890), *Louis VI le Gros: annales de sa vie et de son règne (1081–1137) avec une introduction historique*, Paris

Moore, R. I. (1976), 'Heresy as disease', in W. Lourdaux and D. Verhulst (eds.), *The Concept of Heresy in the Middle Ages* (Medievalia Lovaniensia series 1, Studia 4), Louvain, pp. 1–11

Moore, R. I. (1977), *The Origins of European Dissent*, London

Morey, A. (1937), *Bartholomew of Exeter, Bishop and Canonist*, Cambridge

Morey, A. and Brooke, C. N. L. (1965), *Gilbert Foliot and his Letters*, Cambridge

Munz, P. (1969), *Frederick Barbarossa: A Study in Medieval Politics*, London

Nicholl, D. (1964), *Thurstan, Archbishop of York (1114–1140)*, York

Noonan, J. T. (1977), 'Who was Rolandus?', in K. Pennington and R. Somerville (eds.), *Law, Church and Society: Essays in Honour of Stephan Kuttner*, Pennsylvania, pp. 21–48

Noth, A. (1966), *Heiliger Krieg und heiliger Kampf in Islam und Christentum: Beiträge zur Vorgeschichte und Geschichte der Kreuzzüge*, Bonn

O'Callaghan, J. F. (1959, 1960), 'The affiliation of the order of Calatrava with the order of Cîteaux', *Analecta Sacri Ordinis Cisterciensis* 15: 161–93; 16: 3–59, 255–92

O'Callaghan, J. F. (1962), 'The foundation of the order of Alcántara 1176–1218', *Catholic Historical Review* 47: 471–86

O'Callaghan, J. F. (1975), *A history of medieval Spain*, Ithaca and London

Overmann, A. (1895), *Gräfin Mathilde von Tuscien: Ihre Besitzungen*, Innsbruck

Pacaut, M. (1953), 'Louis VII et Alexandre III (1159–1180)', *Revue d'Histoire de l'Eglise en France* 39: 5–45

Pacaut, M. (1955), 'Les légats d'Alexandre III (1159–1181)', *RHE* 50: 821–38

Pacaut, M. (1956), *Alexandre III: étude sur la conception du pouvoir pontifical dans sa pensé et dans sa œuvre*, Paris

Pacaut, M. (1957), *Louis VII et les épiscopales dans le royaume de France* (Bibliothèque de la Société d'Histoire Ecclésiastique de la France), Paris

Pacaut, M. (1964), *Louis VII et son royaume* (Bibliothèque Générale de l'Ecole Pratique des Hautes Etudes 6. Section), Paris

Palumbo, P. F. (1942), *Lo scisma del MCXXX: i precedenti, la vicenda romana e le ripercussioni europee della lotta tra Anacleto e Innocenzo II* (Miscellanea della Deputazione Romana di Storia patria 13), Rome

Palumbo, P. F. (1963), 'Nuovi studi (1942–1962) sullo scisma di Anacleto II', *BISI* 75: 71–103

Partner, P. (1972), *The Lands of St Peter: The Papal State in the Middle Ages and the Early Renaissance*, London

Paulus, N. (1922), *Geschichte des Ablasses im Mittelalter*, 1, Paderborn

Pellegrini, L. (1968), 'La duplice elezione papale del 1130: i precedenti immediati e i protagonisti', in *Raccolta di studi in memoria di Giovanni Soranzo*, II (Contributi dell'Istituto di Storia Medioevale), Milan, pp. 265–302

Petersohn, J. (1974), 'Der Vertrag des Römischen Senats mit Papst Clemens III. (1188) und das Pactum Friedrich Barbarossas mit den Römern (1167)', *MIÖG* 82: 289–337

Pfaff, V. (1927), *Kaiser Heinrichs VI. höchstes Angebot an die römische Kirche (1196)* (Heidelberger Abhandlungen zur Mittleren und Neueren Geschichte 55), Heidelberg

Pfaff, V. (1953), 'Die Einnahmen der römischen Kurie am Ende des 12. Jahrhunderts', *Vierteljahrschrift für Sozial- und Wirtschaftsgeschichte* 40: 97–118

Pfaff, V. (1955), 'Die Kardinäle unter Papst Coelestin III. (1191–1198)', *ZSSRG KA* 41: 58–94

Pfaff, V. (1956), 'Aufgaben und Probleme der päpstlichen Pinanzverwaltung am Ende des 12. Jahrhunderts', *MIÖG* 64: 1–24

Pfaff, V. (1961), 'Papst Coelestin III.', *ZSSRG KA* 47: 109–28

Pfaff, V. (1964), 'Die Gesta Innocenz' III. und das Testament Heinrichs VI.', *ZSSRG KA* 50: 78–126

Pfaff, V. (1966), 'Die Kardinäle unter Papst Coelestin III. (2. Teil)', *ZSSRG KA* 52: 332–69

Pfaff, V. (1974a), 'Das Papsttum in der Weltpolitik des enden 12. Jahrhunderts', *MIÖG* 82: 338–76

Pfaff, V. (1974b), 'Der Vorgänger: das Wirken Coelestins III. aus der Sicht von Innocenz III.', *ZSSRG KA* 60: 121–67

Pfaff, V. (1980), 'Papst Clemens III. (1187–1191): mit einer Liste der Kardinalsunterschriften', *ZSSRG KA* 66: 261–316

Pfaff, V. (1981), 'Sieben Jahre päpstlicher Politik: die Wirksamkeit der Päpste Lucius III., Urban III., Gregor VIII.', *ZSSRG KA* 67: 148–212

Poole, R. L. (1934), *Studies in Chronology and History*, Oxford

Poschmann, B. (1930), *Die abendländische Kirchenbusse im frühen Mittelalter*, Breslau

Preiss, M. (1934), *Die politische Tätigkeit der Cisterzienser im Schisma von 1159–1177* (Historische Studien 248), Berlin

Rassow, P. (1961), *Honor Imperii: die neue Politik Friedrich Barbarossas 1152–1159*, 2nd edn, Darmstadt

Reuter, T. (1976), 'Das Edikt Friedrich Barbarossas gegen die Zisterzienser', *MIÖG* 84: 328–36

Reuter, T. (1983), 'Zur Anerkennung Papst Innocenz II.: eine neue Quelle', *DA* 39: 395–416

Reuter, T. (1984), 'John of Salisbury and the Germans', in M. Wilks (ed.), *The World of John of Salisbury* (Studies in Church History, Subsidia 3), Oxford, pp. 415–25

Riley-Smith, J. (1977), *What Were the Crusades?*, London; 3rd edn 2002

Riley-Smith, J. (1986), *The First Crusade and the Idea of Crusading*, Philadelphia

Rivière, J. (1924), 'Sur l'expression "Papa Deus" au moyen âge', in *Miscellanea Francesco Ehrle*, II, Rome, pp. 276–89

Robinson, I. S. (1990), *The Papacy 1073–1198: Continuity and Innovation*, Cambridge

Rota, A. (1953), 'La costituzione originaria del Comune di Roma: l'epoca del Comune libero (luglio 1143–dicembre 1145)', *BISI* 64: 19–131

Rowe, J. G. (1969), 'Hadrian IV, the Byzantine empire and the Latin orient', in T. A. Sandquist and M. R. Powicke (eds.), *Essays in Medieval History Presented to Bertie Wilkinson*, Toronto, pp. 3–16

Säbekow, G. (1931), 'Die päpstlichen Legationen nach Spanien und Portugal bis zum Ausgang des 12. Jahrhunderts', dissertation, Berlin

Saltman, A. (1956), *Theobald, Archbishop of Canterbury*, London

Sayers, J. E. (1971a), *Papal Judges Delegate in the Province of Canterbury 1198–1254: A Study in Ecclesiastical Jurisdiction and Administration*, Oxford

Sayers, J. E. (1971b), 'Papal privileges for St Albans Abbey and its dependencies', in D. A. Bullough and R. L. Storey (eds.), *The Study of Medieval Records*, Oxford, pp. 57–84

Scheffer-Boichorst, P. (1903), *Gesammelte Schriften*, I, Berlin

Schieffer, R. (1981), *Die Entstehung des päpstlichen Investiturverbots für den deutschen König* (*MGH Schriften* 28), Stuttgart

Schieffer, T. (1935), *Die päpstlichen Legaten in Frankreich vom Vertrage von Meersen (870) bis zum Schisma von 1130* (Historische Studien 263), Berlin

Schmale, F.-J. (1961a), 'Papsttum und Kurie zwischen Gregor VII. und Innocenz II.', *HZ* 193: 265–85

Schmale, F.-J. (1961b), *Studien zum Schisma des Jahres 1130*, Cologne and Graz

Schmale, F.-J. (1974), 'Systematisches zu den Konzilien des Reformpapsttums im 12. Jahrhundert', *Annuarium Historiae Conciliorum* 6: 21–39

Schmidt, T. (1972), 'Die Kanonikerreform in Rom und Papst Alexander II. (1061–1073)', *Studi Gregoriani per la Storia della 'Libertas Ecclesiae'* 9: 199–237

Schnith, K. (1976), 'Zur Problematik englischer Konzilien im Zeitalter der "Anarchie"', *Annuarium Historiae Conciliorum* 8: 103–15

Schramm, P. E. (1960), *Der König von Frankreich: das Wesen der Monarchie vom 9. zum 16. Jahrhundert*, Darmstadt

Schramm, P. E. (1968–71), *Kaiser, König und Päpste: Gesammelte Aufsätze zur Geschichte des Mittelalters*, I–IV, Stuttgart

Seegrün, W. (1967), *Das Papsttum und Skandinavien bis zur Vollendung der nordischen Kirchenorganisation (1164)* (Quellen und Forschungen zur Geschichte Schleswig-Holstein 51), Neumünster

Servatius, C. (1979), *Paschalis II. (1099–1118)* (Päpste und Papsttum 14), Stuttgart

Sheehy, M. P. (1965), *Pontificia Hibernica: Medieval Papal Chancery Documents concerning Ireland 640–1261*, Dublin

Smalley, B. (1973), *The Becket Conflict and the Schools*, Oxford

Somerville, R. (1970), 'The Council of Pisa, 1135: a re-examination of the evidence for the canons', *Speculum* 45: 98–114

Somerville, R. (1972), *The Councils of Urban II, I: Decreta Claromontensia* (Annuarium Historiae Conciliorum, Supplementum 1), Amsterdam

Somerville, R. (1975), 'The canons of Reims (1131)', *Bulletin of Medieval Canon Law* new series 5: 122–30

Somerville, R. (1976), 'Pope Innocent II and the study of Roman Law', *Revue des Etudes Islamiques* 44: 105–14

Somerville, R. (1977), *Pope Alexander III and the Council of Tours (1163)*, Berkeley and Los Angeles

Somerville, R. (1982), *Scotia Pontificia: Papal Letters to Scotland before the Pontificate of Innocent III*, Oxford

Southern, R. W. (1953), *The Making of the Middle Ages*, London

Southern, R. W. (1963), *Saint Anselm and his Biographer*, Cambridge

Southern, R. W. (1970), *Medieval Humanism and Other Studies*, Oxford

Stickler, A. M. (1947), 'Der Schwerterbegriff bei Huguccio', *Ephemerides Iuris Canonici* 3: 1–44

Stickler, A. M. (1951), 'Il "gladius" negli atti dei concili e dei RR. Pontefici sino a Graziano e Bernardo di Clairvaux', *Salesianum* 13: 414–45

Stroll, M. (1987), *The Jewish Pope: Ideology and Politics in the Papal Schism of 1130*, Leiden, New York, Copenhagen and Cologne

Tellenbach, G. (1950), 'Vom Zusammenleben der abendländischen Völker im Mittelalter', in R. Nürnberger (ed.), *Festschrift für Gerhard Ritter zu seinem 60. Geburtstag*, Tübingen, pp. 1–60

Tellenbach, G. (1963), 'Der Sturz des Abtes Pontius von Cluny und seine geschichtliche Bedeutung', *QFIAB* 42–3: 13–55

Tierney, B. (1972), *Origins of Papal Infallibility, 1150–1350* (Studies in the History of Christian Thought 6), Leiden

Tillmann, H. (1926), 'Die päpstlichen Legaten in England bis zur Beendigung der Legation Gualas 1218', dissertation, Bonn

Tillmann, H. (1972), 'Ricerche sull'origine dei membri del collegio cardinalizio nel XII secolo II/1', *Rivista di Storia della Chiesa in Italia* 26: 313–53

Ullmann, W. (1954), 'Cardinal Roland and Besançon', *Miscellanea Historiae Pontificiae* 18: 107–25

Ullmann, W. (1955), 'The pontificate of Adrian IV', *Cambridge Historical Journal* 11: 233–52

Ullmann, W. (1970), *The Growth of Papal Government in the Middle Ages*, 3rd edn, London

Ullmann, W. (1981), *Gelasius I. (492–496): das Papsttum an der Wende der Spätantike zum Mittelalter*, Stuttgart

Vacandard, E. (1920), *Vie de St Bernard, abbé de Clairvaux*, 2 vols., Paris

Villey, M. (1942), *La Croisade: essai sur la formation d'une théorie juridique* (L'Eglise et l'Etat au Moyen Age 6), Paris

Voss, L. (1932), *Heinrich von Blois Bischof von Winchester (1129–1171)* (Historische Studien 210), Berlin

Walther, H. G. (1976), 'Häresie und päpstliche Politik: Ketzerbegriff und Ketzergesetzgebung in der Übergangsphase von der Dekretistik', in W. Lourdaux and D. Verhulst (eds.), *The Concept of Heresy in the Middle Ages* (Mediaevalia Lovaniensia Series 1, Studia 4), Louvain, pp. 104–43

Warren, W. L. (1973), *Henry II*, London

Watt, J. A. (1965), *The Theory of Papal Monarchy in the Thirteenth Century: The Contribution of the Canonists*, New York

Watt, J. A. (1970), *The Church and the Two Nations in Medieval Ireland*, Cambridge

Wenck, K. (1926), 'Die römischen Päpste zwischen Alexander III. und Innocenz III. und der Designationsversuch Weihnachten 1197', in A. Brackmann (ed.), *Papsttum und Kaisertum: Forschungen zur politischen Geschichte und Geisteskultur des Mittelalters Paul Kehr zum 65. Geburtstag dargebracht*, Munich, pp. 415–74

Wilks, M. (1971), '*Ecclesiastica* and *regalia*: papal investiture policy from the Council of Guastalla to the First Lateran Council, 1106–23', in D. Baker (ed.), *Councils and Assemblies* (Studies in Church History 7), Cambridge, pp. 69–85

Zenker, B. (1964), 'Die Mitglieder des Kardinalkollegiums von 1130 bis 1159', dissertation, Würzburg

Zerbi, P. (1955), *Papato, impero e 'respublica christiana' dal 1187 al 1198* (Pubblicazioni dell'Università Cattolica del S. Cuore, n.s. 55), Milan

Zerbi, P. (1972), 'Intorno allo scisma di Ponzio, abate di Cluny (1122–26)', in *Studi storici in onore di Ottorino Bertolini*, II, Pisa, pp. 835–91

Zerbi, P. (1975), 'San Bernardo di Chiaravalle e il concilio di Sens', in *Studi su S. Bernardo di Chiaravalle nell'ottavo centenario della canonizzazione* (Bibliotheca Cisterciensis 6), Rome, pp. 115–80

14 THE WESTERN EMPIRE, 1125–1197

Angermeier, H. (1974), 'Landfriedenspolitik und Landfriedensgesetzgebung unter den Staufern', in J. Fleckenstein (ed.), *Probleme um Friedrich II.* (Vorträge und Forschungen 16), Sigmaringen, pp. 167–86

Appelt, H. (1959), 'Die Erhebung Österreichs zum Herzogtum', *Blätter für Deutsche Landesgeschichte* 95: 25–66

Appelt, H. (1960), 'Der Vorbehalt kaiserlicher Rechte in den Diplomen Friedrich Barbarossas', *MIÖG* 68: 81–97

Appelt, H. (1973), *Privilegium minus: das staufische Kaisertum und die Babenberger in Österreich* (Böhlau Quellenbücher), Vienna, Cologne and Graz

Appelt, H. (1988), *Kaisertum, Königtum, Landesherrschaft: Gesammelte Studien zur mittelalterlichen Verfassungsgeschichte* (*MIÖG* Ergänzungsband 28), Vienna, Cologne and Graz

Assmann, E. (1977), 'Friedrich Barbarossas Kinder', *DA* 33: 435–72

Baaken, G. (1968), 'Die Altersfolge der Söhne Friedrichs Barbarossa und die Königserhebung Heinrichs VI.', *DA* 24: 46–78

Baaken, G. (1978), 'Zur Beurteilung Gottfrieds von Viterbo', in K. Hauck and H. Mordek (eds.), *Geschichtsschreibung und Geistiges Leben in Mittelalter: Festschreib für Heinz Lowe*, Cologne and Vienna, pp. 373–96

Benson, R. L. (1982), '*Political renovatio*: two models from Roman antiquity', in R. L. Benson, G. Constable and C. D. Lanham (eds.), *Renaissance and Renewal in the Twelfth Century*, Cambridge, MA, pp. 339–86

Bernhardi, W. (1879), *Lothar von Supplinburg* (Jahrbücher der Deutschen Geschichte), Leipzig

Bernhardi, W. (1883), *Konrad III.* (Jahrbücher der Deutschen Geschichte), Leipzig

Böhmer, J. F. and Baaken, G. (1972), *Die Regesten des Kaiserreiches unter Heinrich VI. 1165 (1190)–1197* (Regesta Imperii 4, part 3), Cologne and Vienna

Brinken, B. (1974), *Die Politik Konrads von Staufen in der Tradition der rheinischen Pfalzgrafschaft* (Rheinisches Archiv 92), Bonn

Brühl, C. and Kölzer, T. (1979), *Das Tafelgüterverzeichnis des römischen Königs, Ms. Bonn S. 1559*, Cologne and Vienna

Bumke, J. (1991), *Courtly Culture: Literature and Society in the High Middle Ages*, trans. T. Dunlap, Berkeley, Los Angeles and Oxford

Classen, P. (1983), 'Corona imperii: die Krone als Inbegriff des römisch-deutschen Reiches im 12. Jahrhundert', in J. Fleckenstein (ed.), *Ausgewälte Aufsätze* (Vorträge und Forschungen 28), Sigmaringen, pp. 503–14

Colorni, V. (1969), *Die drei verschollenen Gesetze des Reichstages bei Roncaglia, wieder aufgefunden in einer Pariser Handschrift* (Untersuchungen zur Deutschen Staats- und Rechtsgeschichte, n.s. 22), Aalen

Crone, M.-L. (1982), *Untersuchungen zur Reichskirchenpolitik Lothars III. (1125–1137) zwischen reichskirchlicher Tradition und Reformkurie* (Europäische

Hochschulschriften, 3rd series, Geschichte und ihre Hilfswissenschaften 170), Frankfurt am Main and Berne

Engels, O. (1972), *Die Staufer* (Urban-Taschenbücher 154), Stuttgart

Engels, O. (1988), *Stauferstudien: Beiträge zur Geschichte der Staufer im 12. Jahrhundert*, Sigmaringen

Fichtenau, H. (1939), 'Bamberg, Würzburg und die Stauferkanzlei', *MIÖG* 53: 241–85

Fichtenau, H. (1965a), *Von der Mark zum Herzogtum: Grundlagen und Sinn des 'Privilegium Minus' für Österreich* (Österreich-Archiv. Schriftenreihe des Arbeitskreises für Österreichische Geschichte), Vienna and Munich

Fichtenau, H. (1965b), 'Zur Überlieferung des "privilegium minus" für Österreich', *MIÖG* 73: 1–16

Ficker, J. (1862), 'Die Reichshofbeamten der staufischen Periode', *Sitzungsberichte der Phil.-Hist. Classe der Kaiserlichen Akademie der Wissenschaften* 40, part 4: 447–549

Ficker, J. (1911), *Vom Reichsfürstenstande: Forschungen zur Geschichte der Reichsverfassung zunachst im XII. und XIII. Jahrhunderte*, Innsbruck

Fleckenstein, J. (1972), 'Friedrich Barbarossa und das Rittertum: zur Bedeutung der grossen Mainzer Hoftage von 1184–1188', in *Festschrift für Hermann Heimpel*, II (Veröffentlichungen des Max-Planck-Instituts für Geschichte 36/2), Göttingen, pp. 1023–41

Fried, J. (1983), 'Friedrich Barbarossas Krönung in Arles (1178)', *Historisches Jahrbuch* 103: 347–71

Fried, J. (1984), 'Die Wirtschaftspolitik Friedrich Barbarossas in Deutschland', *Blätter für Deutsche Landesgeschichte* 120: 195–239

Fried, J. (1990), 'Die Rezeption bologneser Wissenschaft in Deutschland während des 12. Jahrhunderts', *Viator* 21: 103–45

Geldner, F. (1977), 'Kaiserin Mathilde, die deutsche Königswahl von 1125 und das Gegenkönigtum Konrads III.', *Zeitschrift für Bayerische Landesgeschichte* 40: 3–22

Giese, W. (1978), 'Das Gegenkönigtum des Staufers Konrad 1127–1135', *ZSSRG Germanistische Abteilung* 95: 202–20

Grundmann, H. (1942), 'Rotten und Brabanzonen: Söldner-Heere im 12. Jahrhundert', *DA* 5: 419–92

Grundmann, H. (1959), *Der Cappenberger Barbarossakopf und die Anfänge des Stiftes Cappenberg* (Münstersche Forschungen 12), Cologne and Graz

Haller, J. (1911), 'Der Sturz Heinrichs des Löwen', *Archiv für Urkundenforschung* 3: 295–450

Hausmann, F. (1950), 'Formularbehelfe der frühen Stauferkanzlei: Untersuchungen über deren Herkunft, Verwendung und Verhältnis zur Urkundensammlung des Codex Udalrici', *MIÖG* 58: 68–96

Hausmann, F. (1956), *Reichskanzlei und Hofkapelle unter Heinrich V. und Konrad III.* (*MGH Schriften* 14), Stuttgart

Hausmann, F. (1969), *Die Urkunden Konrads III. und seines Sohnes Heinrich* (MGH Diplomata Regum et Imperatorum Germaniae 9), Vienna, Cologne and Graz

Haussherr, R. (1977), *Die Zeit der Staufer: Geschichte-Kunst-Kultur*, I, Stuttgart

Havercamp, A. (1987), 'Der Konstanzer Friede zwischen Kaiser und Lombardenbund (1183)', in H. Maurer (ed.), *Kommunale Bündnisse* (Vorträge und Forschungen 33), Sigmaringen, pp. 11–44

Heinemann, H. (1983–4), 'Untersuchungen zur Geschichte der Zähringer in Burgund', *Archiv für Diplomatik* 29: 42–192; 30: 97–257

Heinemeyer, K. (1981), 'Der Prozess Heinrichs des Löwen', *Blätter für Deutsche Landesgeschichte* 117: 1–60

Heinemeyer, W. (1969), '"*Beneficium – non feudum sed bonum factum.*" Der Streit auf dem Reichstag zu Besançon 1157', *Archiv für Diplomatik* 15: 155–236

Herkenrath, R. M. (1964), 'Reinald von Dassel als Verfasser und Schreiber von Kaiserurkunden', *MIÖG* 72: 34–62

Herkenrath, R. M. (1969), *Regum et imperium: das 'Reich' in der fruhstaufischen Kanzlei (1138–1155)* (Sitzungsberichte der Österreichischen Akademie der Wissenschaften, phil.-hist. Klasse 264), Vienna

Herkenrath, R. M. (1977), *Die Reichskanzlei in den Jahren 1174 bis 1180* (Denkschriften der Österreichischen Akademie der Wissenschaften, phil.-hist. klasse 130), Vienna

Herkenrath, R. M. (1985), *Die Reichskanzlei in der Jahren 1181–1190* (Denkschriften der Österreichischen Akademie der Wissenschaften, phil.-hist. klasse 175), Vienna

Hildebrand, R. (1937), *Der sächsische 'Staat' Heinrichs des Löwen* (Historische Studien 302), Berlin

Jakobi, F.-J. (1979), *Wibald von Stablo und Corvey (1098–1158)* (Veröffentlichungen der Historischen Kommission für Westfalen 10 / Abhandlungen zur Corveyer Geschichtschreibung 5), Münster

Johanek, P. (1978), 'Zur Geschichte der Reichskanzlei unter Friedrich Barbarossa', *MIÖG* 86: 27–45

Jordan, K. (1939 and 1952), *Die Bistumsgründungen Heinrichs des Löwen: Untersuchungen zur Geschichte der osterdeutschen Kolonisation* (*MGH Schriften* 3), Stuttgart

Jordan, K. (1979 and 1986), *Heinrich der Löwe: eine Biographie*, trans. P. S. Falla, *Henry the Lion: A Biography*, Munich and Oxford

Jordan, K. (1981), 'Heinrich der Löwe und seine Familie', *Archiv für Diplomatik* 27: 111–44

Kaminsky, H. H. (1973), 'Das "Tafelgüterverzeichnis des römischen Königs": eine Bestandaufnahme für Lothar III.?', *DA* 29: 163–96

Koch, G. (1968 and 1982), 'Sacrum imperium: Bemerkungen zur Herausbildung der staufischen Herrschaftsideologie', *Zeitschrift für Geschichtswissenschaft* 16: 596–614; and in M. Kerner (ed.), *Ideologie und Herrschaft im Mittelalter* (Wege der Forschung 530), Darmstadt, pp. 268–302

Koch, W. (1973), *Die Reichskanzlei in den Jahren 1167 bis 1174* (Denkschriften der Österreichischen Akademie der Wissenschaften, phil.-hist. klasse 115), Vienna

Koch, W. (1979), *Die Schrift der Reichskanzlei im 12. Jahrhundert (1125–1190): Untersuchungen zur Diplomatik der Kaiserurkunde* (Denkschriften der Österreichischen Akademie der Wissenschaften, phil.-hist. klasse 134), Vienna

Koch, W. (1980), 'Zu Sprache, Stil und Arbeitstechnik in den Diplomen Friedrich Barbarossas', *MIÖG* 88: 36–69

Koch, W. (1985), 'Die Reichskanzlei unter Kaiser Friedrich I.', *Archiv für Diplomatik* 31: 327–50

Koeppler, H. (1939), 'Frederick Barbarossa and the schools of Bologna: some remarks on the "Authentica Habita"', *EHR* 54: 577–607

Kölzer, T. (1990), 'Sizilien und das Reich im ausgehenden 12. Jahrhundert', *Historisches Jahrbuch* 110: 3–22

Krieger, K.-F. (1970), 'Die königliche Lehnsgerichtsbarkeit im Zeitalter der Staufer', *DA* 26: 400–33

Leyser, K. J. (1988), 'Frederick Barbarossa and the Hohenstaufen polity', *Viator* 19: 153–76

Mariotte, J.-Y. (1963), *Le Comté de Bourgogne sous les Hohenstaufen 1156–1208* (Cahiers d'Etudes Comtoises 4), Paris

Mayer, T., Heilig, K. and Erdmann, C. (1944 and 1952), *Kaisertum und Herzogsgewalt im Zeitalter Friedrichs I. Studien zur politischen und Verfassungsgeschichte des hohen Mittelalters* (*MGH Schriften* 9), Leipzig and Stuttgart

Metz, W. (1964), *Staufenische Güterverzeichnisse: Untersuchungen zur Verfassungs- und Wirtschaftsgeschichte des 12. und 13. Jahrhunderts*, Berlin

Meuthen, E. (1975), 'Barbarossa und Aachen', *Rheinische Vierteljahrblätter* 39: 28–59

Mohrmann, W.-D. (1980), *Heinrich der Löwe* (Veröffentlichungen der Niedersächsischen Archivverwaltung 39), Göttingen

Munz, P. (1969), *Frederick Barbarossa: A Study in Medieval Politics*, London

Opll, F. (1976), 'Das kaiserliche Mandat im 12. Jahrhundert (1125–1190)', *MIÖG* 84: 290–327

Opll, F. (1978), *Das Itinerar Kaiser Friedrich Barbarossa (1152–1190)* (Forschungen zur Kaiser- und Papstgeschichte des Mittelalters 1), Vienna, Cologne and Graz

Opll, F. (1986), *Stadt und Reich im 12. Jahrhundert (1125–1190)* (Forschungen zur Kaiser- und Papstgeschichte des Mittelalters 6), Vienna, Cologne and Graz

Opll, F. (1990), *Friedrich Barbarossa* (Gestalten des Mittelalters und der Renaissance), Darmstadt

Petke, W. (1985), *Kanzlei, Kapelle und königliche Kurie unter Lothar III (1125–1137)* (Forschungen zur Kaiser- und Papstgeschichte des Mittelalters 5), Vienna and Cologne

Peyer, H. C. (1951), 'Friedrich Barbarossa, Monza und Aachen', *DA* 8: 438–60

Probleme des 12. Jahrhunderts: Reichenau-Vorträge 1965–1967 (1968) (Vorträge und Forschungen 12), Stuttgart

Rassow, P. (1961 and 1973), *Honor imperii: die neue Politik Friedrich Barbarossas 1152–1159*, new editions, Munich and Darmstadt

Riedmann, J. (1967–8), 'Studien über die Reichskanzlei unter Friedrich Barbarossa in den Jahren 1156–1166', *MIÖG* 75: 322–402; 76: 23–105

Rörig, F. (1937), 'Heinrich der Löwe und die Gründung Lübecks: Grundsätzliche Erörterungen zur städtischen Ostsiedlung', *DA* 1: 408–56

Schieffer, R. (1990), 'Bleibt der Archipoeta anonym?', *MIÖG* 97: 59–79

Schlunk, A. C. (1988), *Königsmacht und Krongut: die Machtgrundlage des deutschen Königstums im 13. Jahrhundert – und eine neue historische Methode*, Stuttgart

Schmale, F.-J. and Schmale-Ott, I. (1972), *Frutolfs und Ekkehards Chroniken und die Anonyme Kaiserchronik* (Ausgewählte Quellen zur Deutschen Geschichte des Mittelalter. Freiherr vom Stein-Gedächtnisausgabe 15), Darmstadt

Schmandt, R. H. (1967), 'The election and assassination of Albert of Louvain, bishop of Liège, 1191–92', *Speculum* 42: 639–60

Schmid, K. (1954), *Graf Rudolf von Pfullendorf und Kaiser Friedrich I.* (Forschungen zur Oberrheinischen Landesgeschichte 1), Freiburg im Breisgau

Schmid, K. (1986), *Die Zähringer: eine Tradition und ihre Erforschung* (Veröffentlichung zur Zähringer-Ausstellung 1), Sigmaringen

Schmidt, U. (1987), *Königswahl und Thronfolge im 12. Jahrhundert* (Forschungen zur Kaiser- und Papstgeschichte des Mittelalters 7), Cologne and Vienna

Schreibmüller, H. (1955), 'Herzog Friedrich IV. von Schwaben und Rothenburg (1145–1167), *Zeitschrift für Bayerische Landesgeschichte* 18: 213–42

Schubert, P. (1913), 'Die Reichshofämter und ihre Inhaber bis um die Wende des 12. Jahrhunderts', *MIÖG* 34: 427–501

Schwarzmaier, H. (1986), 'Staufer, Welfen und Zähringer im Lichte neuzeitlicher Geschichtsschreibung', *Zeitschrift für die Geschichte des Oberrheins* 134: 76–87

Seltmann, I. (1983), *Heinrich VI. Herrschaftspraxis und Umgebung* (Erlanger Studien 43), Erlangen

Simonsfeld, H. (1908 and 1967), *Jahrbücher des deutschen Reiches under Friedrich I., 1152–1158* (Jahrbücher der Deutschen Geschichte), Leipzig and Berlin

Speer, L. (1983), *Kaiser Lothar III. und Erzbischof Adalbert I. von Mainz: eine Untersuchung zur Geschichte des deutschen Reiches im frühen zwölften Jahrhundert* (Dissertationen zur mittelalterlichen Geschichte 3), Cologne and Vienna

Stelzer, W. (1978), 'Zum Scholarenprivileg Friedrich Barbarossas (Authentica "Habita")', *DA* 34: 123–65

Stoob, H. (1974), 'Zur Königswahl Lothars von Sachsen im Jahre 1125', in H. Beumann (ed.), *Historische Forschungen für Walter Schlesinger*, Cologne and Vienna, pp. 438–61

Toeche, T. (1867 and 1965), *Kaiser Heinrich VI.* (Jahrbücher der Deutschen Geschichte), Leipzig and Darmstadt

Wadle, E. (1969), *Reichsgut und Königsherrschaft unter Lothar III (1125–1137): ein Beitrag zur Verfassungsgeschichte des 12. Jahrhunderts* (Schriften zur Verfassungsgeschichte 12), Berlin

Wadle, E. (1987), 'Der Nürnberger Friedebrief Kaiser Friedrich Barbarossas und das gelehrte Recht', in G. Kobler (ed.), *Wege europäische Rechtsgeschichte: Karl Kroeschell zum 60. Geburtstag* (Rechtshistorische Reihe 60), Frankfurt am Main

Wattenbach, W. and Schmale, F.-J. (1976), *Deutschlands Geschichtsquellen im Mittelalter: vom Tode Kaiser Heinrichs V. bis zum Ende des Interregnum*, I, Darmstadt

Weikmann, M. (1967), 'Königsdienst und Königsgastung in der Stauferzeit', *Zeitschrift für Bayerische Landesgeschichte* 30: 314–32

Werke, H. (1962), 'Staufische Hausmachtpolitik am Rheine im 12. Jahrhundert', *Zeitschrift für die Geschichte des Oberrheins* 110: 241–370

Wolf, G. (1975), *Friedrich Barbarossa* (Wege der Forschung 390), Darmstadt

Wolter, H. (1985), 'Die Verlobung Heinrichs VI. mit Konstanze von Sizilien im Jahre 1184', *Historisches Jahrbuch* 105: 30–51

Zeillinger, K. (1966), 'Die Notare der Reichskanzlei in den ersten Jahren Friedrich Barbarossas', *DA* 22: 472–555

Zeillinger, K. (1970), 'Friedrich Barbarossa, Wibald von Stablo und Eberhard von Bamberg', *MIÖG* 78: 210–23

Die Zeit der Staufer 1977 & 1979, Katalog der Ausstellung im Würtembergischen (1977, 1979), *Landesmuseum*, I–IV (Vorträge und Forschungen 5), Stuttgart

Ziegler, H.-U. (1984), 'Der Kompilator des Codex Udalrici – ein Notar der Bamberger Bischofskanzlei?', *Archiv für Diplomatik* 30: 258–81

15(a) NORTHERN AND CENTRAL ITALY IN THE TWELFTH CENTURY

L'amiata nel medioevo (1989), ed. M. Ascheri and W. Kurze, Rome

Atti del 9° Congresso internazionale di studi sull'alto medioevo (1983) (Il Ducato di Spoleto, Congressi del Centro Italiano di Studi sull'Alto Medioevo 9), Spoleto

Atti dell'11° Congresso internazionale di studi sull'alto medioevo (1989) (Milano ed il suo Territorio in Età Comunale, Congressi del Centro Italiano di Studi sull'Alto Medioevo 11), Spoleto

Beiträge zur Geschichte Italiens im 12. Jahrhundert (Vorträge und Forschungen, Sonderband 9), Sigmaringen 1971

Bernhardi, W. (1879), *Lothar von Supplinburg* (Jahrbücher der Deutschen Geschichte), Leipzig

Bernhardi, W. (1883), *Konrad III* (Jahrbücher der Deutschen Geschichte), Leipzig

Bordone, R. (1987), *La società cittadina del regno d'Italia* (Biblioteca Storica Subalpina 202), Turin

Bosl, K. (1982), *Gesellschaftgeschichte Italiens im Mittelalter*, Stuttgart

Brancoli Busdraghi, P. (1965), *La formazione storica del feudo lombardo come diritto reale*, Milan

Brezzi, P. (1947), *Roma e l'impero medievale 774–1252* (Storia di Roma 10), Bologna

Brezzi, P. (1959), *I Comuni medioevali nella storia d'Italia*, Turin; new edn 1970

Brühl, C. (1968), *Fodrum, gistum, servitium regis* (Kölner Historische Abhandlungen 14), Cologne and Graz

Capitani, O. (1986), *Storia dell'Italia medievale 410–1216*, Rome and Bari

Cardini, F. (1985), *Il Barbarossa*, Milan

Castagnetti, A. (1985), *Società e politica a Ferrara, sec. X–XIII*, Bologna

Castagnetti, A. (1986), *La marca veronese-trevigiana* (Storia degli Stati Italiani), Turin

Castagnetti, A. (1988), *Arimanni in 'Romania' fra conti e signori*, Verona

Cessi, R. (1944), *Storia della repubblica di Venezia*, 1, Milan and Messina

Cessi, R. (1953), *La repubblica di Venezia e il problema adriatico*, Naples

I ceti dirigenti dell'età comunale nei secoli XII e XIII (1982) (Convegni sui Ceti Dirigenti in Toscana 2), Pisa

Clementi, A. (1988), 'Le terre del confine settentrionale', in *Storia del Mezzogiorno*, II, 1: *Il medioevo*, Naples

Cognasso, F. (1952), 'Novara nella sua storia', in *Novara e il suo territorio*, Novara

Cognasso, F. (1968), *Il Piemonte nell'età sveva* (Miscellanea di Storia Patria IV 10), Turin

Comuni e signori nell'Italia nordorientale e centrale (1987) (Storia d'Italia 7), 2 vols., Turin

Cracco, G. (1986), *Venezia nel medioevo dal secolo XI al secolo XIV*, Turin

La cristianità dei secoli XI e XII in Occidente: coscienza e strutture di una società (1983) (Università Cattolica, Miscellanea del Centro di Studi Medioevali 10), Milan

Cultura universitaria e pubblici poteri a Bologna dal XII al XV secolo (1990), ed. O. Capitani, Bologna

Darmstädter, P. (1896), *Das Reichsgut in der Lombardei und Piemont 568–1250*, Strasbourg

Davidsohn, R. (1896), *Geschichte von Florenz*, 1, Berlin

De Vergottini, G. (1924–5), *Lineamenti storici della costituzione politica dell'Istria durante il medio evo*, Trieste; repr. 1974

Dilcher, G. (1967), *Die Entstehung der lombardischen Stadtkommune* (Untersuchungen zur Deutschen Staats- und Rechtsgeschichte 7), Aalen

Falco, G. (1919), *I comuni della campagna e della marittima nel medioevo*, Rome

Formazioni e strutture dei ceti dominanti nel medioevo: marchesi, conti e visconti nel regno italico, sec. IX–XII (1998) (Nuovi Studi Storici 1), Rome

Frugoni, A. (1954), *Arnaldo da Brescia nelle fonti del secolo XII* (Studi Storici 8–9), Rome

Galassi, N. (1984), *Figure e vicende di una città* (Imola), 1, Imola

Haverkamp, A. (1970–1), *Herrschaftsformen der Frühstaufer in Reichsitalien* (Monographien zur Geschichte des Mittelalters 1), 2 vols., Stuttgart

Hessel, A. (1910), *Geschichte der Stadt Bologna von 1116 bis 1280*, Berlin

Hyde, J. K. (1973), *Society and Politics in Medieval Italy 1000–1350*, London

Kauffmann, H. (1933), *Die italienische Politik Kaiser Friedrichs I nach dem Frieden von Constanz*, Griefswald

Keller, H. (1979), *Adelsherrschaft und städtische Gesellschaft in Oberitalien 9. bis 12. Jahrhundert* (Bibliothek des Deutschen Historischen Instituts in Rom 52), Tübingen

Kommunale Bundnisse Oberitaliens und Oberdeutschlands im Vergleich (1987) (Vorträge und Forschungen 33), Sigmaringen

Kretschmayr, H. (1905), *Geschichte von Venedig* (Allgemeine Staatengeschichte), Aalen; repr. 1964

Lamma, P. (1955–7), *Comneni e Staufer* (Studi Storici 14–18, 22–5), Rome

Lane, F. C. (1973), *Venice: A Maritime Republic*, Baltimore and London

Leonhard, J.-F. (1983), *Die Seestadt Ancona im Spätmittelalter* (Bibliothek des Deutschen Historischen Instituts in Rom 55), Tübingen

Ludwig, C. (1973), *Untersuchungen über die frühesten Podestaten italienischer Städte*, Vienna

Luzzati, M. (1986), *Firenze e la Toscana nel medioevo* (Storia degli Stati Italiani), Turin

Maire Vigueur, J.-Cl. (1987), *Comuni e signorie in Umbria, Marche e Lazio* (Storia degli Stati Italiani), Turin

Mantova: la storia (1958), 1, ed. G. Coniglio, Mantua

Maranini, G. (1927), *La costituzione di Venezia dalle origini alla serrata del Maggior Consiglio*, Venice

Moscati, L. (1980), *Alle origini del comune romano*, Naples

Nahmer, D. von der (1965), *Die Reichsverwaltung in Toscana unter Friedrich I und Heinrich VI*, Aalen

Opll, F. (1986), *Stadt und Reich im 12. Jahrhundert (1125–1190)* (Forschungen zur Kaiser- und Papstgeschichte des Mittelalters 6), Vienna, Cologne and Graz

La pace di Costanza 1183: un difficile equilibrio di poteri fra società italiana ed impero (1984), Bologna

Paschini, P. (1934), *Storia del Friuli*, 1, Udine; new edn 1953

Piemonte medievale: forme del potere e della società (1985), Turin

Pisa nei secoli XI e XII: formazione e caratteri di una classe di governo (1979) (Istituto di Storia dell'Università di Pisa 10), Pisa

Popolo e stato in Italia nell'età di Federico Barbarossa (1970), Turin

Potere, società e popolo tra età normanna ed età sveva (1189–1210) (1983) (Quinte Giornate Normanno-Sveve), Bari

I problemi della civiltà comunale (1971), ed. C. D. Fonseca, Milan

Prutz, H. (1871–4), *Kaiser Friedrich I*, 3 vols., Danzig

Racine, P. (1980), *Plaisance du Xe à la fin du XIIIe siècle*, 1, Lille and Paris

Renouard, Y. (1969), *Les Villes d'Italie de la fin du Xe siècle au début du XIVe siècle*, 2 vols., Paris

Rosch, G. (1982), *Venedig und das Reich* (Bibliothek des Deutschen Historischen Instituts in Rom 53), Tübingen

Rossi Sabbatini, G. (1935), *L'espansione di Pisa nel Mediterraneo fino alla Meloria*, Florence

Salvatorelli, L. (1940), *L'Italia comunale* (Storia d'Italia 4), Milan

Scarsella, A. R. (1942), *Storia di Genova III: Il comune dei consoli*, Milan

Schevill, F. (1909), *Siena: The History of a Medieval Commune*, New York and London; new edn 1964

Schevill, F. (1936), *History of Florence*, New York; new edn 1961

Schmidinger, H. (1954), *Patriarch und Landesherr*, Graz and Cologne

Sergi, G. (1981), *Potere e territorio lungo la strada di Francia: da Chambéry a Torino fra X e XIII secolo* (Nuovo Medioevo 20), Naples

Sestan, E. (1966), *Italia medievale*, Naples

Sestan, E. (1989), *Italia comunale e signorile*, Florence

Settia, A. A. (1983), *Monferrato: strutture di un territorio medievale*, Turin

Settia, A. A. (1984), *Castelli e villaggi nell'Italia padana* (Nuovo Medioevo 23), Naples

Simioni, A. (1968), *Storia di Padova*, Padua

Simonsfeld, H. (1908), *Jahrbücher des deutschen Reiches unter Friedrich I: 1152 bis 1158* (Jahrbücher der Deutschen Geschichte), Leipzig

Società e istituzioni dell'Italia comunale: l'esempio di Perugia (1988), Perugia

Spazio, società, potere nell'Italia dei Comuni (1986), ed. G. Rossetti, Naples

La storia dei Genovesi (1981–4), 4 vols., Genoa

Storia di Bologna (1978), Bologna

Storia di Brescia (1963), I, Brescia

Storia di Cesana, II: *Il Medioevo* (1983), ed. A. Vasini, Rimini

Storia della civiltà veneziana, I: *Dalle origini al secolo di Marco Polo* (1979), ed. V. Branca, Florence

Storia d'Italia, I: *Il medioevo* (1965), ed. N. Valeri, Turin

Storia d'Italia, IV: *Comuni e signorie* (1981), ed. G. Galasso, Turin

Storia di Milano (1955), IV, Milan

Storia di Piacenza, II: *Dal vescovo conte alla signoria 996–1313* (1984), Piacenza

Storia della società friulana: il Medioevo (1988), ed. P. Cammarosano, Udine

Storia di Venezia, II: *Dalle origini del Ducato alla IV crociata* (1958), Venice

Storia di Vicenza, II: *L'età medievale* (1988), ed. G. Cracco, Vicenza

Structures féodales et féodalisme dans L'Occident méditerranéen , Xe–XIIIe siècles (1980) (Ecole Française de Rome 44), Rome

Studi sulla pace di Constanza (1984), Milan

Tabacco, G. (1979), *Egemonie sociale e strutture del potere nel medioevo italiano*, Turin

Toeche, Th. (1867), *Kaiser Heinrich VI* (Jahrbücher der Deutschen Geschichte), Darmstadt; repr. 1965

Torelli, P. (1930–52), *Un comune cittadino in territorio ad economia agricola*, 2 vols., Mantua

Toubert, P. (1973), *Les Structures du Latium médiéval* (Ecoles Françaises d'Athènes et de Rome 221), 2 vols., Rome

Vaccari, P. (1940), *Profilo storico di Pavia*, Pavia

Van Cleve, T. C. (1937), *Markward of Anweiler and the Sicilian Regency*, Princeton

Vasina, A. (1970), *Romagna medievale*, Ravenna

Venezia dalla prima crociata alla conquista di Constantinopoli del 1204 (1966), Florence

Verona e il suo territorio (1964), II, Verona

Violante, C. (1953), *La società milanese nell'età precomunale*, Bari

Violante, C. (1980), *Economia, società, istituzioni a Pisa nel Medioevo*, Bari

Vitale, V. (1955), *Breviario della storia di Genova*, Genoa

Volpe, G. (1902), *Studi sulle istituzioni comunali a Pisa*, Florence; repr. 1970

Volpe, G. (1961), *Medioevo italiano*, Florence

Volpe, G. (1964), *Toscana medievale*, Florence

Waley, D. (1969), *The Italian City-Republics*, new edn. London; 1978

Zerbi, P. (1955), *Papato, Impero e 'respublica christiana'* (Università Cattolica, Scienze Storiche 26), Milan; repr. 1980

15(b) NORMAN SICILY IN THE TWELFTH CENTURY

Abulafia, D. S. H. (1977), *The Two Italies: Economic Relations between the Norman Kingdom of Sicily and the Northern Communes*, Cambridge

Abulafia, D. S. H. (1983), 'The crown and the economy under Roger II and his successors', *DOP* 37: 1–14; repr. in Abulafia (1987)

Abulafia, D. S. H. (1984), 'Ancona, Byzantium and the Adriatic, 1155–1173', *Papers of the British School at Rome* 52: 195–216; repr. in Abulafia (1987)

Abulafia, D. S. H. (1985), 'The Norman kingdom of Africa and the Norman expeditions to Majorca and the Muslim Mediterranean', *ANS* 7: 26–49; repr. in Abulafia (1987)

Abulafia, D. S. H. (1987), *Italy, Sicily and the Mediterranean*, London

Bercher, H., Courteaux, A. and Mouton J. (1979), 'Un abbaye latine dans la société musulmane: Monreale au XIIe siècle', *Annales ESC* 35: 525–47

Brühl, C. R. (1978), *Urkunden und Kanzlei König Rogers II. von Sizilien*, Cologne

Cahen, C. (1940), *Le Régime féodal de l'Italie Normande*, Paris

Caravale, M. (1966), *Il regno normanno di Sicilia*, Rome

Chalandon, F. (1907), *Histoire de la domination Normande en Italie et en Sicile*, 2 vols., Paris

Clementi, D. R. (1953–4), 'Some unnoticed aspects of the Emperor Henry VI's conquest of the Norman kingdom of Sicily', *Bulletin of the John Rylands Library* 36: 328–57

Clementi, D. R. (1967), 'The circumstances of Count Tancred's accession to the kingdom of Sicily, duchy of Apulia and principality of Capua', in *Mélanges Antonio Marongiu*, Palermo, pp. 59–80

Clementi, D. R. (1968), 'The relations between the papacy, the western Roman Empire and the emergent kingdom of Sicily and south Italy (1050–1156)', *BISI* 80: 191–212

Cuozzo, E. (1984), *Catalogus Baronum: commentario* (Fonti per la Storia d'Italia), Rome

Cuozzo, E. (1989), *'Quei maledetti normanni': cavalieri e organizzazione militare nel mezzogiorno normanno*, Naples

D'Alessandro, V. (1978), *Storiografia e politica nell'Italia normanna*, Naples

D'Alessandro, V. (1989), 'Servi e liberi', in *Uomo e ambiente nel Mezzogiorno normanno-svevo* (Centro di Studi Normanni-Svevi 8), Bari, pp. 293–318

Deér, J. (1959), *The Dynastic Porphyry Tombs of the Norman Period in Sicily*, Cambridge, MA

Deer, J. (1972), *Papsttum und Normannen*, Cologne

Enzenberger, H. (1980), 'Der "bose" und der "gute" Wilhelm: zur Kirchenpolitik der normannischen Könige von Sizilien nach dem Vertrag von Benevent (1156)', *DA* 36: 385–432

Enzenberger, H. (1981), 'Il documento regio come strumento di potere', in *Potere, società e popolo nell'età dei due Guglielmi* (Atti del Centro di Studi Normanno-Svevi 4), Bari, pp. 103–38

Falkenhausen, V. von (1987), 'Il popolamento: etnio, fedi, insediamenti', in *Terra e uomini nel Mezzogiorno normanno-svevo* (Atti del Centro di Studi Normanno-Svevi 7), Bari, pp. 39–73

Houben, H. (1992), 'Tra vocazione mediterranea e destino europeo: la politica estera di re Guglielmo II di Sicilia', in C. D. Fonseca, H. Houben and B. Vetere (eds.), *Unità politica e differenze regionali nel regno di Sicilia*, Galatina, pp. 119–33

Jamison, E. M. (1913), 'The Norman administration of Apulia and Capua, more especially under Roger II and William I, 1127–1166', *Papers of the British School at Rome* 6: 211–481; repr. as a separate monograph, Aalen, 1987

Jamison, E. M. (1929, 1930), 'The administration of the county of Molise in the twelfth and thirteenth centuries', *EHR* 44: 529–59; 45: 1–34

Jamison, E. M. (1957), *Admiral Eugenius of Sicily, his Life and Work*, London

Jamison, E. M. (1967), 'Iudex Tarantinus', *PBA* 53: 289–344

Jamison, E. M. (1971), 'Additional work on the Catalogus Baronum', *BISI* 83: 1–63

Johns, J. (1993), 'The Norman kings of Sicily and the Fatimid caliphate', *ANS* 15: 133–59

Kamp, N. (1980), 'Der unteritalienische Episkopat im Spannungsfeld zwischen monarchischer Kontrolle und römischer "libertas" von der Reichsgrundung Rogers II. bis zum Konkordat von Benevent', in *Società, potere e popolo nell'età di Ruggero II* (Atti del Centro di Studi Normanno-Svevi 3), Bari, pp. 99–132

Loewenthal, L. J. A. (1972), 'For the biography of Walter Ophamil, archbishop of Palermo', *EHR* 87: 75–82

Loud, G. A. (1981), 'The Norman counts of Caiazzo and the abbey of Montecassino', in *Monastica. I. Scritti raccolti in memoria del xv centario della nascita di S. Benedetto 480–1980* (Miscellanea Cassinese 44), Monte Cassino, pp. 199–217

Loud, G. A. (1982), 'Royal control of the church in the twelfth-century kingdom of Sicily', *Studies in Church History* 18: 147–59

Loud, G. A. (1983), 'The church, warfare and military organisation in Norman Italy', *Studies in Church History* 20: 31–45

Loud, G. A. (1985), *Church and Society in the Norman Principality of Capua, 1058–1197*, Oxford

Loud, G. A. (1987), 'The abbey of Cava, its property and benefactors in the Norman era', *ANS* 9: 143–77

Martin, J.-M. (1980), 'Les communautés d'habitants de la Pouille et leur rapports avec Roger II', in *Società, potere e popolo nell'età di Ruggero II* (Atti del Centro di Studi Normanno-Svevi 3), Bari, pp. 73–98

Martin, J.-M. (1987), 'Le travail agricole: rythmes, corvées, outillage', in *Terra e uomini nel Mezzogiorno normanno-svevo* (Atti del Centro di Studi Normanno-Svevi 7), Bari, pp. 113–57

Martin, J.-M. (1992), 'Les structures économiques du royaume à l'époque normande', in C. D. Fonseca, H. Houben and B. Vetere (eds.), *Unità politica e differenze regionali nel regno di Sicilia*, Galatina, pp. 85–104

Matthew, D. J. A. (1981), 'The chronicle of Romuald of Salerno', in R. H. C. Davis and J. M. Wallace-Hadrill (eds.), *The Writing of History in the Middle Ages: Essays Presented to Richard William Southern*, Oxford, pp. 239–74

Matthew, D. J. A. (1992), *The Norman Kingdom of Sicily*, Cambridge

Ménager, L.-R. (1960), *Amiratus-Αμερας: l'émirat et les origines de l'admirauté (XIe–XIIIe siècles)*, Paris

Ménager, L.-R. (1969), 'La législation sud-italienne sous la domination normande', *Settimane di Studio del Centro Italiano di Studi sull'Alto Medioevo* 16: 439–96

Norwich, J. J. (1970), *The Kingdom in the Sun*, London

Pacaut, M. (1981), 'Papauté, royauté et épiscopat dans le royaume de Sicile (deuxième moitié du XIIème siècle)', in *Potere, società e popolo nell'età dei due Guglielmi* (Atti del Centro di Studi Normanno-Svevi 4), Bari, pp. 31–61

Peri, I. (1978), *Uomoni, città e campagne in Sicilia dall'XI al XIII secolo*, Bari

Reisinger, C. (1992), *Tankred von Lecce: normannischer König von Sizilien*, Cologne

Rowe, J. G. (1969), 'Hadrian IV, the Byzantine empire and the Latin Orient', in L. Sandquist and M. Powicke (eds.), *Essays in Medieval History Presented to Bertie Wilkinson*, Toronto, pp. 3–16

Schaller, H. M. (1957), 'Die Kanzlei Kaiser Friedrichs II. Ihr Personal und ihr Sprachstil, I', *Archiv für Diplomatik* 3: 209–86

Schwarz, U. (1978), *Amalfi im frühen Mittelalter*, Tübingen

Takamaya, H. (1985), 'The financial and administrative organization of the Norman kingdom of Sicily', *Viator* 16: 129–55

Takamaya, H. (1989), '*Familiares regis* and the royal inner council in twelfth-century Sicily', *EHR* 104: 357–72

Takamaya, H. (1993), *The Administration of the Norman Kingdoms of Sicily*, Leiden

Tramontana, S. (1983), 'La monarchia normanna e sveva', in A. Guillou *et al.* (eds.), *Il Mezzogiorno dai Bizantini a Federico II*, Turin, pp. 447–768

White, L. T. (1938), *Latin Monasticism in Norman Sicily*, Cambridge, MA

Wieruszowski, H. (1963), 'Roger II of Sicily, Rex-Tyrannus in twelfth-century political thought', *Speculum* 38: 46–78

16 SPAIN IN THE TWELFTH CENTURY

Alonso, M. (ed.) (1943), *Diego García: Planeta*, Madrid

Alvárez Palenzuela, V. A. (1978), *Monasterios cistercienses en Castilla (siglos XII–XIII)*, Valladolid

d'Alverny, M. T. (1982), 'Translations and translators', in R. L. Benson and G. Constable (eds.), *Renaissance and Renewal in the Twelfth Century*, Oxford, pp. 421–62

Arvizu, F. de (1988), 'Las cortes de León de 1188 y sus decretos: un ensayo de crítica institucional', in *El reino de León en la alta edad media*, I: *Cortes, concilios y fueros*, León, pp. 11–141

Avalle, S. d'A. (1960), *Peire Vidae: Poesie*, Milan and Naples

Barrios García, A. (1983–4), *Estructuras agrarias y de poder en Castilla: el ejemplo de Avila (1085–1320)*, 2 vols., Salamanca

Barton, S. (1997), *The Aristocraey in Twelfth-Century León and Castile*, Cambridge

Beltrán de Heredia (1935), 'La universidad de Palencia. – Santo Domingo de Guzmán en Palencia. – San Pedro González Telmo', in *Semana 'Pro Ecclesia et Patria': conferencias pronunciadas en los dias 3 al 6 de septiembre de 1934 en el Salón de Actos del Seminario Conciliar de Palencia*, Palencia, pp. 215–43

Beltrán de Heredia (ed.) (1970), *Cartulario de la Universidad de Salamanca (1218–1600)*, I, Salamanca

Bishko, C. J. (1975), 'The Spanish and Portuguese reconquest, 1095–1492', in K. M. Setton (gen. ed.), *A History of the Crusades*, III, Madison, pp. 396–456

Bisson, T. N. (1977), 'The organized peace in southern France and Catalonia, ca. 1140–ca. 1233', *AHR* 82: 290–311

Bisson, T. N. (1984a), 'L'essor de la Catalogne: identité, pouvoir et idéologie dans une société du XIIe siècle', in *Annales ESC* 39: 454–79

Bisson, T. N. (1986), *The Medieval Crown of Aragón: A Short History*, Oxford

Bisson, T. N. (ed.) (1984b), *Fiscal Accounts of Catalonia under the Early Count-Kings (1151–1213)*, 2 vols., Berkeley

Blöcker-Walter, M. (1966), *Alfons I. von Portugal*, Zurich

Bonnassie, P. (1980), 'Du Rhône à la Galice: genèse et modalités du régimt féodale', in *Structures féodale et féodalisme dans l'Occident méditerranéen (Xe–XIIIe siècles): bilan et perspectives de recherches*, Rome, pp. 17–55

Cabestany, J.-F. (1960), 'Alfons el Cast', in P. E. Schramm *et al.* (eds.), *Els Primers Comtes-Reis*, Barcelona, pp. 57–104

Canal Sánchez-Pagin, J. M. (1980), '¿Crónica Silense o Crónica Domnis Sanctis?', *Cuadernos de Historia de España*, 63–4: 94–103

David, P. (1947), *Etudes historiques sur la Galice et le Portugal du VIe au XIIe siècle*, Lisbon and Paris

Defourneaux, M. (1949), *Les Français en Espagne aux XIe et XIIe siècles*, Paris

Dillard, H. (1984), *Daughters of the Reconquest: Women in Castilian Town Society 1100–1300*, Cambridge

Duggan, J. J. (1989), *The 'Cantar de mio Cid': poetic creation and its economic and social contexts*, Cambridge

Erdmann, C. (1928), *Das Papssttum und Portugal im ersten Jahrhundert der portugiesischen Geschichte* (Abhandlungen der Preußischen Akademie der Wissenschaften, phil.-hist. klasse 5), Berlin

Estepa Díez, C. (1988), 'Curia y cortes en el reino de León', in *Las cortes de Castilla y León en la edad media: actas de la primera etapa del congreso cientifico sobre la historia de las cortes de Castilla y León, Burgos 1986*, I, Valladolid, pp. 23–103

Feige, P. (1978), 'Die Anfänge des portugiesischen Königstums und seiner Landeskirche', *Spanische Forschungen der Görresgesellschaft* 29: 85–436

Ferreira, J. A. (1928), *Fastos episcopaes da Igreja primacial de Braga*, I, Famalição

Fletcher, R. A. (1984), *St James's Catapult: The Life and Times of Diego Gelmírez of Santiago de Compostela*, Oxford

Fletcher, R. A. (1987), 'Reconquest and crusade in Spain c.1050–1150', *TRHS* 5th series 37: 31–47

Forey, A. J. (1973), *The Templars in the 'Corona de Aragón'*, Oxford

Forey, A. J. (1980–1), 'The will of Alfonso I of Aragon and Navarre', *Durham University Journal* 73: 56–65

Freedman, P. H. (1983), *The Diocese of Vic: Tradition and Regeneration in Medieval Catalonia*, New Brunswick

García-Arenal, M. (1984), 'Los moros de Navarra en la baja edad media', in M. García-Arenal and B. Leroy (eds.), *Moros y judíos en Navarra en la baja edad media*, Madrid, pp. 11–139

García de Cortazar, J. A. (1990), *La sociedad rural el la España medieval*, 2nd edn, Madrid

García Gallo, A. (1945), 'El imperio medieval español', *Arbor* 4: 199–228

García Gallo, A. (1975), 'Los fueros de Toledo', *Anuario de Historia del Derecho Español* 45: 341–488

García y García, A. (1985), *Iglesia, sociedad y derecho*, I, Salamanca

García Larragueta, S. A. (1957), *El Gran Priorado de Navarra de la orden de S. Juan de Jerusalén s.XII–XIII*, 2 vols., Pamplona

Gautier Dalché, J. (1979), *Historia urbana de León y Castilla en la edad media (siglos IX–XIII)*, Madrid

Gibbon, E. (1972), 'Outlines of the history of the world', in P. B. Craddock (ed.), *The English Essays of Edward Gibbon*, Oxford

Goñi Gaztambide, J. (1958), *Historia de la bula de la cruzada en España*, Vitoria

González, J. (1944), *Alfonso IX*, Madrid

González, J. (1960), *El reino de Castilla en la época de Alfonso VIII*, 3 vols., Madrid

Hehl, E. D. (1980), *Kirche und Krieg im 12. Jahrhundert: Studien zu kanonischem Recht und politischer Wirklichkeit*, Stuttgart

Herculano, A. (n.d.), *História de Portugal desde o começo da monarquia até a fim do reinado de D. Afonso III*, 8 vols., Lisbon

Hernández, F. J. (1985), 'Los mozárabes del siglo XII en la ciudad y la iglesia de Toledo', *Toletum* 16: 57–124

Hernández, F. J. (1988), 'Las cortes de Toledo de 1207', in *Las cortes de Castilla y León en la edad media: actas de la primera etapa del congreso científico sobre la historia de las cortes de Castilla y León, Burgos 1986*, I, Valladolid, pp. 221–63

Hohler, C. (1972), 'A note on *Jacobus*', *Journal of the Warburg and Courtauld Institutes* 35: 31–80

Huici Miranda, A. (1956), *Las grandes batallas de la Reconquista durante las invasiones africanas*, Madrid

Lacarra, J. M. (1952), 'El rey Lobo de Murcia y la formación del señorío de Albarracín', in *Estudios dedicados a Menéndez Pidal*, III, Madrid, pp. 515–26

Lacarra, J. M. (1971), *Vida de Alfonso el Batallador*, Saragossa

Lacarra, J. M. (1972), *História política del reino de Navarra desde sus orígenes hasta su incorporación a Castilla*, 3 vols., Pamplona

Lacarra, J. M. (1976), *Historia del reino de Navarra en la edad media*, Pamplona

Le Tourneau, R. (1969), *The Almohad Movement in North Africa in the Twelfth and Thirteenth Centuries*, Princeton

Lindley Cintra, L. F. (1957), 'Sobre a formaèção e evolução da lenda de Ourique (até à Crónica de 1419)', in *Miscelànea de estudos em honra do prof. Hernâni Cidade*, Lisbon, pp. 168–215

Linehan, P. (1971), *The Spanish Church and the Papacy in the Thirteenth Century*, Cambridge

Linehan, P. (1980), 'The Synod of Segovia (1166)', *Bulletin of Medieval Canon Law* n.s. 10: 31–44

Linehan, P. (1993), *History and the Historians of Medieval Spain*, Oxford

Livermore, H. V. (1966), *A New History of Portugal*, Cambridge

Lomax, D. W. (1978), *The Reconquest of Spain*, London

Lomax, D. W. (1988), 'La conquista de Andalucía a través de la historiografía europea de la epoca', in E. Cabrera (ed.), *Andalucía entre Oriente y Occidente (1236–1492): actas del V coloquio internacional de historia medieval de Andalucía*, Cordoba, pp. 37–49

Lomax, D. W. (1989), 'Heresy and Orthodoxy in the fall of Almohad Spain', in D. W. Lomax and D. Mackenzie (eds.), *God and Man in Medieval Spain: Essays in Honour of J. R. L. Highfield*, Warminster, pp. 37–48

Lopes, D. (1941), 'O Cid português: Geraldo Sem Pavor', *Revista Portuguesa de História* 1: 93–104

Lourie, E. (1966), 'A society organized for war: medieval Spain', *PaP* 35: 54–76

Lourie, E. (1975), 'The will of Alfonso I, "El Batallador", king of Aragón and Navarre', *Speculum* 50: 635–51

Lourie, E. (1984–5), 'The will of Alfonso I of Aragon and Navarre: a reply to Dr Forey', *Durham University Journal* 77: 165–72

McCrank, L. J. (1983), 'The Cistercians of Poblet as medieval frontiersmen: an historiographic essay and case study', in *Estudios en homenaje a D. Claudio Sánchez-Albornoz en sus 90 años*, II, Buenos Aires, pp. 313–60

Maffei, D. (1990), 'Fra Cremona, Montpellier e Palencia nel secolo XII: ricerche su Ugolino da Sesso', *Rivista Internazionale di Diritto Comune* 1: 9–30

Maravall, J. A. (1964), *El concepto de España en la edad media*, Madrid

Marongiu, A. (1968), *Medieval Parliaments: A Comparative Study*, trans. S. J. Wolff, London

Martínez Díez, G. (1988), 'Curia y cortes en el reino de Castilla', in *Las cortes de Castilla y León en la edad media: actas de la primera etapa del congreso científico sobre la historia de las cortes de Castilla y León, Burgos 1986*, I, Valladolid, pp. 105–51

Mattoso, J. (1986), *Identificação de um país: ensaio sobre as origens de Portugal 1096–1325*, 2 vols., Lisbon

Menéndez Pidal, R. (1969), *La España del Cid*, 2 vols., Madrid

Michael, I. (1991), 'Per Abbat, ¿avtor o copista? Enfoque de la cuestión', in *Homenaje a Alonso Zamora Vicente*, III: *Literaturas medievales: Literatura españda de los Siglos XV–XVII*, I, Madrid, pp. 179–205

Miret y Sans, J. (1912), 'Le roi Louis VII et le compte de Barcelone à Jaca en 1155', *MA* 16: 289–300

Moxó, S. de (1979), *Repoblación y sociedad en la España cristiana medieval*, Madrid

O'Callaghan, J. F. (1975), *A History of Medieval Spain*, Ithaca

O'Callaghan, J. F. (1989), *The Cortes of Castile-León 1188–1350*, Philadelphia

Palacios-Martín, B. (1988), 'Investidura de armas de los reyes españoles en los siglos XII y XIII', in *Gladius*, tomo especial, pp. 153–92

Pallares Méndez, M. del C. and Portela Silva, E. (1971), *El Bajo valle del Miño en los siglos XII y XIII: economia agraria y estructura social*, Santiago de Compostela

Pastor de Togneri, R. (1973), *Conflictos sociales y estancamiento económico de la España medieval*, Barcelona

Pérez-Prendes y Muños de Arraco, J. M. (1988), 'La potestad legislativa en el reino de León', in *El reino de León en la alta edad media*, I: *Cortes, concilios y fueros*, León, pp. 497–545

Portela, E. (1985), 'Del Duero al Tajo', in J. M. García de Cortázar *et al.* (eds.), *Organización social del espacio en la España medieval: la corona de Castilla en los siglos VIII a XV*, Barcelona, pp. 86–122

Post, G. (1964), *Studies in Medieval Thought*, Princeton

Powers, J. F. (1979), 'Frontier municipal baths and social interaction in thirteenth-century Spain', *Speculum* 84: 649–67

Powers, J. F. (1988), *A Society Organized for War: The Iberian Municipal Militias in the Central Middle Ages, 1000–1284*, Berkeley

Procter, E. S. (1980), *Curia and Cortes in León and Castile 1072–1295*, Cambridge

Rassow, P. (1950), *Dev Prinzgemahl: Ein Pactum Matrimoniale ars dem Jahre 1188*, Weimar

Recuero Astray, M. (1979), *Alfonso VII, emperador: el Imperio Hispánico en el siglo XII*, León

Reilly, B. F. (1982), *The Kingdom of León-Castilla under Queen Urraca 1109–1126*, Princeton

Rico, F. (1985), 'La clericía del mester', *Hispanic Review* 53: 1–23, 127–50

Sáez, E. (ed.) (1953), *Los fueros de Sepúlveda*, Segovia

Sánchez Alonso, B. (1947), *Historia de la historiografía española*, I, Madrid

Sánchez Belda, L. (1951), 'Notas de diplomática: en torno a tres diplomas de Alfonso VII', *Hispania* II: 47–61

Serrão, J. V. (1979), *História de Portugal*, I: *Estado, pátria e nação (1080–1415)*, 2 vols., n.p.

Shideler, J. (1983), *A Medieval Catalan Noble Family: The Montcadas 1000–1230*, Berkeley

Smith, C. (1983), *The Making of the 'Poema de mio Cid'*, Cambridge

Soldevila, F. (1962), *Història de Catalunya*, I, Barcelona

Torres Balbás, L. (1954), *Algunos aspectos del mudejarismo urbano medieval*, Madrid

Valdeavellano, L. G. de (1968), *Historia de España*, 2 vols., Madrid

Valdeavellano, L. G. de (1969), *Orígenes de la burguesía en la España medieval*, Madrid

Vázquez de Parga, L., Lacarra, J. M. and Uría Ríu, J. (1948–9), *Las peregrinaciones a Santiago de Compostela*, 3 vols., Madrid

Vicens Vives, J. (1967), *Manual de historia económica de España*, Barcelona

Villanueva, J. (1851), *Viage literario a las iglesias de España*, XIX Madrid

Vones, L. (1980), *Die 'História Compostellana' und die Kirchenpolitik des nordwest-spanischen Raumes 1070–1130*, Cologne and Vienna

Wright, R. (1982), *Late Latin and Early Romance in Spain and Carolingian France*, Liverpool

17(a) CROWN AND GOVERNMENT IN TWELFTH-CENTURY FRANCE

Audouin, E. (1913), *Essai sur l'armée royale au temps de Philippe Auguste*, Paris

Baldwin, J. W. (1986), *The Government of Philip Augustus: Foundations of French Royal Power in the Middle Ages*, Berkeley; French edn Paris, 1991

Bautier, R.-H. (ed.) (1982), *La France de Philippe Auguste: le temps des mutations* (Colloques Internationaux du Centre National de la Recherche Scientifique 602), Paris

Bournazel, E. (1975), *Le Gouvernement capétien au XIIe siècle (1108–1180): structures sociales et mutations institutionnelles*, Limoges

Cartellieri, A. (1899–1922), *Philipp II. August, König von Frankreich*, 4 vols., Leipzig

Duby, G. (1973), *Le Dimanche de Bouvines* (Trente Journées qui ont fait la France), Paris

Dunbabin, J. (1985), *France in the Making, 843–1180*, Oxford

Hallam, E. M. (1980), *Capetian France, 987–1328*, London

Lewis, A. W. (1981), *Royal Succession in Capetian France: Studies on Familial Order and the State*, Cambridge, MA

Lot, F. and Fawtier, R. (1957–62), *Histoire des institutions Françaises au moyen âge*, 3 vols., Paris

Luchaire, A. (1890), *Louis le Gros: annales de sa vie et de son règne (1081–1137)*, Paris

Newman, W. M. (1937), *Le Domaine royal sous les premiers capétiens (987–1180)*, Paris

Pacaut, M. (1957), *Louis VII et les élections épiscopales dans le royaume de France*, (Bibliothèque de la Société Ecclesiastique de la France), Paris

Pacaut, M. (1964), *Louis VII et son royaume* (Bibliothèque Générale de l'Ecole Pratique des Hautes Etudes, VIe Section), Paris

Powicke, M. (1961), *Loss of Normandy, 1189–1204: Studies in the History of the Angevin Empire*, 2nd edn, Manchester

Schneidmuller, B. (1987), *Nomen Patriae: die Entstehung Frankreichs in der politisch-geographischen Terminologie (10.–13. Jahrhundert)* (Nationes: Historische und Philologische Untersuchungen zur Entstehung der Europäischen Nationen im Mittelalter 7), Sigmaringen

Schramm, P. E. (1960), *Der König von Frankreich: das Wesen der Monarchie vom 9. zum 16. Jahrhundert*, rev. edn, Darmstadt

17(b) THE SEIGNEURIES IN TWELFTH-CENTURY FRANCE

Barthelémy, D. (1984), *Les Deux Ages de la seigneurie banale: Coucy (XIe–XIIIe siècles)*, Paris

Bisson, T. (1984), 'L'essor de la Catalogne: identité, pouvoir, et idéologie dans une société du XIIe siècle', *Annales ESC* 3: 454–479

Boutruche, R. (1970), *Seigneurie et féodalité*, II: *L'apogée (XIe–XIIIe siècles)*, Paris

Bur, M. (1977), *La Formation du comté de Champagne (v.950–v.1150)*, Nancy

Bur, M. (1983), 'L'image de la parenté chez les comtes de Champagne', *Annales ESC* 5: 1016–39

Bur, M. (1985), 'Remarques sur la formation des principautés en France (IXe–XIIIe siècles)', in *Centralismno y descentralization: modelos y procesos historicos en Francia y en España* (Comité Espanol de Ciencias Historicas), Madrid, pp. 215–32

Chédeville, A. and Tonnerre, N. Y. (1987), *La Bretagne féodale (XIe–XIIIe siècles)*, Rennes

Corbet, P. (1977), 'Les collégiales comtales en Champagne', *Annales de l'Est* 3: 195–241

Debord, A. (1987), *La Société laïque dans les pays de la Charente (Xe–XIIe siècles)*, Paris

Duby, G. (1973), *Hommes et structures du moyen âge: recueil d'articles*, Paris

Desportes, P. (1979), *Réims et les Rémois aux XIIIe et XIVe siècles*, Paris

Desportes, P. (1989), 'Les pairs de France et la couronne', *Revue Historique* 282: 305–40

Guyotjeannin, O. (1987), *Episcopus et comes: affirmation et déclin de la seigneurie épiscopale au nord du royaume de France, Beauvais-Noyon, Xe–début du XIIIe siècle,* Geneva and Paris

Lot, F. and Fawtier, R. (1957), *Histoire des institutions Françaises au moyen âge,* 1: *Institutions seigneuriales,* Paris

Musset, L. (1985), *Autour du pouvoir ducal normand* (Cahier des Annales de Normandie 17), Caen

Richard, J. (1954), *Les Ducs de Bourgogne et la formation du duché (XIe–XIVe siècles),* Paris

Schneider, J. (1979), 'Le problème des principautés en France et dans l'empire (Xe–XVe siècles)', in *Principautés et territoires: actes du 103e congrès national des sociétés savantes, Nancy-Metz 1978,* Paris, pp. 9–39

Verhulst, A. (1967), 'Initiative comtale et développement économique en Flandre au XIIe siècle: le rôle de Thierry et de Philippe d'Alsace', in *Miscellanea in memoriam J. F. Niermeyer,* Groningen, pp. 227–40

Werner, K. F. (1978), 'Kingdom and principalities in twelfth century France', in T. Reuter (ed.), *The Medieval Nobility,* Amsterdam, pp. 243–90

18 ENGLAND AND THE ANGEVIN DOMINIONS, 1137–1204

Alexander, J. W. (1970), 'The Becket controversy in recent historiography', *Journal of British History* 9: 1–26

Alexander, J. W. (1983), *Ranulph of Chester, a Relic of the Conquest,* Athens, GA

Alexander, J. W. (1985), 'A historiographical survey: Norman and Plantagenet kings since World War II', *Journal of British History* 24: 94–109

Altschul, M. (1965), *A Baronial Family in Medieval England: The Clares, 1217–1314,* Baltimore

Amt, E. M. (1988), 'Richard de Lucy, Henry II's Justiciar', *Medieval Prosopography* 9: 61–88

Amt, E. M. (1990), 'The Forest Regard of 1155', *Haskins Society Journal* 2: 189–95

Amt, E. M. (1991), 'The meaning of waste in the early Pipe Rolls of Henry II', *Economic History Review* 44: 239–48

Appleby, J. T. (1960), *King John of England,* London

Appleby, J. T. (1962a), *Henry II, the Vanquished King,* London

Appleby, J. T. (1962b), 'The monastic foundations of Henry II', *Catholic Historical Review* 48: 205–15

Appleby, J. T. (1965), *England without Richard,* London

Appleby, J. T. (1970), *The Troubled Reign of King Stephen,* New York

Avent, R. and Kenyon, J. (eds.) (1987), *Castles in Wales and the Marches,* Cardiff

Bachrach, B. (1978), 'The idea of the Angevin empire', *Albion* 10: 293–9

Bachrach, B. (1984), 'The Angevin tradition of family hostility', *Albion* 16: 111–30

Bachrach, B. (1985), 'Henry II and Angevin claims to the Saintonage', *Medieval Prosopography* 6: 23–45

Baldwin, J. (1986), *Philip II Augustus: Foundations of French Royal Power in the Middle Ages,* Berkeley and Los Angeles

Barber, R. (1964), *Henry Plantagenet,* London

Barlow, F. (1979), *The English Church 1066–1154*, London

Barlow, F. (1986), *Thomas Becket*, London

Barlow, F. (1988), *The Feudal Kingdom of England, 1042–1216*, 4th edn, London

Barrow, G. W. S. (1973), *The Kingdom of the Scots*, London

Barrow, G. W. S. (1980), *The Anglo-Norman Era in Scottish History*, Oxford

Barrow, G. W. S. (1981), *Kingship and Unity in Scotland, 1000–1306*, London

Barrow, G. W. S. (1985), *David of Scotland (1124–1153): The Balance of New and Old* (University of Reading, Stenton Lecture 1984), Reading

Bates, D. (1989), 'Normandy and England after 1066', *EHR* 104: 851–80

Bautier, R.-H. (1986), '"Empire Plantagenet" ou "Espace Plantagenet"?' *CCM* 29: 139–47

Beeler, J. H. (1956), 'Castles and strategy in Norman and early Angevin England', *Speculum* 31: 581–601

Beeler, J. H. (1966), *Warfare in England, 1066–1189*, Ithaca

Benjamin, R. (1986), 'The Angevin empire', *History Today* 36: 17–22

Benjamin, R. (1988), 'A forty-years war: Toulouse and the Plantagenets, 1156–1196', *Historical Research* 61: 270–85

Benton, J. F. (1967), 'The revenues of Louis VII', *Speculum* 42: 84–91

Bienvenu, J.-M. (1986), 'Aliénor d'Aquitaine et Fontevraud', *CCM* 29: 15–27

Bournazel, E. (1975), *Le Gouvernement capétien au XIIe siècle, 1108–1180*, Limoges

Boussard, J. (1938), *Le Comté d'Anjou sous Henri Plantagenet et ses fils (1151–1204)*, Paris

Boussard, J. (1945–6), 'Les mercenaires au XIIe siècle: Henri II Plantagenet et les origines de l'armée de métier', *BEC* 106: 189–224

Boussard, J. (1956), *Le Gouvernement d'Henri II Plantagenet*, Paris

Boussard, J. (1982), 'Philippe Auguste et les Plantagenets', in R.-H. Bautier (ed.), *La France de Philippe Auguste: le temps de mutation*, Paris, pp. 263–87

Brand, P. A. (1990), '"Multis vigiliis excogitatam et inventam": Henry II and the creation of the English common law', *Haskins Society Journal* 2: 197–222

Brooke, C. N. L. (1961), *From Alfred to Henry III, 871–1272*, London

Brooke, C. N. L. (1988), 'The marriage of Henry II and Eleanor of Aquitaine', *Historian* 20: 3–8

Brooke, Z. N. (1931), *The English Church and the Papacy from the Conquest to the Reign of King John*, Cambridge

Brooke, Z. N. and Brooke, C. N. L. (1946), 'Henry II, duke of Normandy and Aquitaine', *EHR* 61: 81–9

Brown, R. A. (1959), 'A list of castles, 1154–1216', *EHR* 74: 259–77

Brown, R. A. (1970), *English Castles*, revised edn, London

Brown, S. (1989), 'Military service and monetary reward in the eleventh and twelfth centuries', *History* 74: 20–38

Bradbury, J. (1990a), 'The early years of the reign of Stephen, 1135–1139', in D. Williams (ed.), *England in the Twelfth Century: Proceedings of the 1988 Harlaxton Symposium*, Woodbridge, pp. 17–30

Bradbury, J. (1990b), 'Geoffrey V of Anjou, count and knight', in C. Harper-Bill and R. Harvey (eds.), *The Ideal and Practice of Medieval Knighthood, III: Papers from the Fourth Strawberry Hill Conference 1988*, Woodbridge, pp. 21–38

Brundage, J. (1974), *Richard Lion Heart*, New York

Callahan, T. (1974a), 'The impact of anarchy on English monasticism, 1135–1154', *Albion* 6: 218–32

Callahan, T. (1974b), 'A re-evaluation of the anarchy of Stephen's reign, 1135–1154: the case of the Black Monks', *RBén* 84: 338–51

Callahan, T. (1974c), 'The renaissance of monastic bishops in England, 1135–1154', *Studia Monastica* 16: 55–67

Callahan, T. (1975), 'King Stephen and the Black Monks: abbatical elections during the anarchy', *RBén* 85: 348–57

Callahan, T. (1976a), 'The notion of anarchy in England, 1135–1154', *British Studies Monitor* 6: 23–35

Callahan, T. (1976b), 'Sinners and saintly retribution: the timely death of King Stephen's son Eustace', *Studia Monastica* 18: 109–17

Callahan, T. (1978), 'Ecclesiastical reparations and the soldiers of the anarchy', *Albion* 10: 300–11

Chaplais, P. (1973), 'Henry II's reissue of the canons of the Council of Lillebonne', *Journal of the Society of Archivists* 4: 627–32

Cheney, C. R. (1956), *From Becket to Langton*, Manchester

Cheney, C. R. (1967), *Hubert Walter*, London

Cheney, C. R. (1976), *Pope Innocent III and England*, Stuttgart

Cheney, M. G. (1981), *Roger Bishop of Worcester 1164–1179: An English Bishop in the Age of Becket*, Oxford

Chibnall, M. (1984), *The World of Orderic Vitalis*, Oxford

Chibnall, M. (1986), *Anglo-Norman England 1066–1166*, Oxford

Chibnall, M. (1988a), 'The Empress Matilda and Bec-Hellouin', *ANS* 10: 35–49

Chibnall, M. (1988b), 'The Empress Matilda and Church Reform', *TRHS* 5th series 38: 107–30

Chibnall, M. (1989), 'Orderic Vitalis on Castles', in C. Harper-Bill, C. J. Holdsworth and J. L. Nelson (eds.), *Studies in Medieval History Presented to R. Allen Brown*, Woodbridge, pp. 43–56

Chibnall, M. (1991), *The Empress Matilda: Queen Consort, Queen Mother and Lady of England*, Oxford

Christelow, S. E. (1990), 'All the king's men: prosopography and the Santa Barbara school', *Medieval Prosopography* 11: 1–15

Clanchy, M. T. (1983), *England and its Rulers, 1066–1272*, London

Corner, D. (1983), 'The "Gesta regis Henrici Secundi" and "Chronica" of Roger, Parson of Howden', *BIHR* 56: 126–44

Coulson, C. (1983), 'Fortress-policy in Capetian tradition and Angevin practice: aspects of the conquest of Normandy by Philip II Augustus', *ANS* 6: 12–38

Craig, M. A. (1977), 'A second daughter of Geoffrey of Brittany', *BIHR* 50: 112–15

Cronne, H. A. (1970), *The Reign of King Stephen: Anarchy in England*, London

Crouch, D. (1984), 'Oddities in the early history of the marcher lordship of Gower, 1107–1166', *Bulletin of the Board of Celtic Studies* 31: 133–42

Crouch, D. (1985), 'Robert, earl of Gloucester, and the daughter of Zelophehad', *JMH* 11: 227–43

Crouch, D. (1986), *The Beaumont Twins: The Roots and Branches of Power in the Twelfth Century*, Cambridge

Crouch, D. (1988a), 'Earl William of Gloucester and the end of anarchy: new evidence relating of the honor of Eudo Dapifer', *EHR* 103: 69–75

Crouch, D. (1988b), 'Strategies of lordship in Angevin England and the career of William Marshal', in C. Harper-Bill and R. Harvey (eds.), *The Ideals and Practice of Medieval Knighthood*, II: *Papers from the Third Strawberry Hill Conference*, Woodbridge, pp. 1–25

Crouch, D. (1990), *William Marshal: Court, Career and Chivalry in the Angevin Empire*, London

Dalton, P. (1990), 'William earl of York and royal authority in Yorkshire in the reign of Stephen', *Haskins Society Journal* 2: 155–65

Davies, R. R. (1987), *Conquest, Coexistence and Change in Wales, 1063–1415*, Oxford

Davis, H. W. C. (1903), 'The anarchy of King Stephen's reign', *EHR* 18: 630–41

Davis, R. H. C. (1960a), 'King Stephen and the earl of Chester revised', *EHR* 75: 654–60

Davis, R. H. C. (1960b), 'Treaty between William, earl of Gloucester, and Roger, earl of Hereford', in *A Medieval Miscellany for Doris Mary Stenton* (Pipe Roll Society, n.s. 36), London, pp. 141–2

Davis, R. H. C. (1964a), 'Geoffrey de Mandeville Reconsidered', *EHR* 79: 299–307

Davis, R. H. C. (1964b), 'What happened in Stephen's reign', *History* 49: 1–12

Davis, R. H. C. (1971), 'An unknown Coventry charter', *EHR* 86: 533–47

Davis, R. H. C. (1972), 'The College of St Martin's-Le-Grand and the anarchy, 1135–1154', *London Topographical Record*, 23: 9–26

Davis, R. H. C. (1990), *King Stephen*, 3rd edn, London

Douie, D. L. (1960), *Archbishop Geoffrey Plantagenet*, New York

Dunbabin, J. (1985), *France in the Making, 843–1180*, Oxford

Duggan, A. (1980), *Thomas Becket: A Textual History of his Letters*, Oxford

Duggan, C. (1966), 'Richard of Ilchester, royal servant and bishop', *TRHS* 5th series 16: 1–21

Duncan, A. A. M. (1975), *Scotland: The Making of the Kingdom*, Edinburgh

Eales, R. (1986), 'Local loyalties in Norman England: Kent in Stephen's reign', *ANS* 8: 88–108

Eales, R. (1990), 'Royal power and castles in Norman England', in C. Harper-Bill and R. Harvey (eds.), *The Ideals and Practice of Medieval Knighthood*, III: *Papers from the Fourth Strawberry Hill Conference*, Woodbridge, pp. 49–78

Elkins, S. K. (1988), *Holy Women of Twelfth Century England*, Chapel Hill, NC

English, B. (1979), *The Lords of Holderness, 1086–1260: A Study in Feudal Society*, Oxford

Eyton, R. W. (1878), *Court, Household and Itinerary of King Henry II*, London

Falls, J. S. (1978), 'Rannulf de Glanville's formative years, c.1120–1179: the family background and his ascent to the justiciarship', *Medieval Studies* 40: 312–27

Farmer, D. L. (1956), 'Some price fluctuations in Angevin England', *Economic History Review* 2nd series, 9: 34–43

Fawtier, R. (1960), *The Capetian Kings of France*, London

Flanagan, M. T. (1989), *Irish Society, Anglo-Norman Settlers, Angevin Kingship: Interaction in Ireland in the Late Twelfth Century*, Oxford

Foreville, R. (1943), *L'Eglise et la royauté en Angleterre sous Henri II Plantagenet (1154–1189)*, Paris

Foreville, R. (1989), 'Thomas Becket et la France capétienne', in C. Harper-Bill, C. J. Holdsworth and J. L. Nelson (eds.), *Studies in Medieval History Presented to R. Allen Brown*, Woodbridge, pp. 117–28

Frame, R. (1981), *Colonial Ireland, 1169–1369*, Dublin

Frame, R. (1989), 'England and Ireland, 1171–1399', in M. Jones and M. Vale (eds.), *England and her Neighbours, 1066–1453: Essays in Honour of Pierre Chaplais*, London, pp. 139–55

Frame, R. (1990), *The Political Development of the British Isles, 1100–1400*, Oxford

Franklin, M. (1990), 'The bishops of Winchester and the monastic revolution', *Anglo-Norman Studies* 12: 47–66

Gillingham, J. (1978), *Richard the Lionheart*, London

Gillingham, J. (1979), 'The unromantic death of Richard I', *Speculum* 54: 18–41

Gillingham, J. (1980), 'Richard I and Berengaria of Navarre', *BIHR* 53: 157–73

Gillingham, J. (1981), 'Some legends of Richard the Lionheart: their development and their influence', in *Riccardo Cuor di Leone nella storia e nella leggenda* (Accademia Nazionale dei Lincei. Problemi Attuali de Scienza e di Cultura, 253), pp. 35–50

Gillingham, J. (1984a), *The Angevin Empire*, London

Gillingham, J. (1984b), 'Richard I and the science of war in the middle ages', in J. Gillingham and J. C. Holt (eds.), *War and Government in the Middle Ages*, Woodbridge, pp. 78–91

Gillingham, J. (1985), 'The art of Kingship: Richard I, 1189–1199', *History Today* 35: 17–23

Gillingham, J. (1986), 'The fall of the Angevin empire', *History Today* 36: 30–5

Gillingham, J. (1989), 'War and chivalry in the history of William Marshal', in *Thirteenth Century England, II: Proceedings of the Newcastle-upon-Tyne Conference 1987*, Woodbridge, pp. 1–13

Gransden, A. (1974), *Historical Writing in England, c.550–c.1307*, London

Grant, L. (1988), 'The architecture of the early Savignacs and Cistercians in Normandy', *ANS* 10: 111–44

Green, J. (1981), 'The last century of Danegeld', *EHR* 96: 241–58

Green, J. (1986), *The Government of England under Henry I*, Cambridge

Green, J. (1988), 'King Henry I and the aristocracy of Normandy', in *La 'France anglaise' au moyen âge, actes du IIIe congrès national de sociétés savantes, Poitiers, 1986*, Paris, pp. 161–73

Green, J. (1989), 'Anglo-Scottish relations, 1066–1174', in M. Jones and M. Vale (eds.), *England and her Neighbours, 1066–1453: Essays in Honour of Pierre Chaplais*, London, pp. 53–72

Guilloreau, L. (1907), 'Aliénor de Bretagne: quelques details relatifs à sa captivité (1203–41)', *Revue de Bretagne* 37: 257–75, 326–36

Hallam, E. M. (1975), 'Henry II, Richard I, and Order of Grandmont', *JMH* 1: 165–86

Hallam, E. M. (1977), 'Henry II as a Founder of Monasteries', *JEH* 28: 113–32

Hallam, E. M. (1980), *Capetian France, 987–1328*, New York

Hallam, E. M. (1981), *Rural England, 1066–1348*, Glasgow

Hallam, E. M. (ed.) (1986), *The Plantagenet Chronicles*, London

Harper-Bill, C. (1989), 'The struggle for benefices in twelfth-century East Anglia', *ANS* 11: 113–32

Harper-Bill, C. and Harvey, R. (eds.) (1990), *The Ideal and Practice of Medieval Knighthood*, III: *Papers from the Fourth Strawberry Hill Conference 1988*, Woodbridge

Harvey, P. D. A. (1973), 'The English inflation of 1180–1220', *PaP* 61: 3–30

Haskins, C. H. (1918), *Norman Institutions*, Cambridge, MA

Hays, L. and Jones, E. D. (1990), 'Policy on the run: Henry II and Irish Sea diplomacy', *Journal of British Studies* 29: 293–316

Heiser, R. (1989), 'The royal *familiares* of King Richard I', *Medieval Prosopography* 10: 25–50

Heiser, R. (1990), 'The households of the justiciars of Richard I: an inquiry into the second level of medieval English government', *Haskins Society Journal* 2: 223–35

Heltzel, B. (1947), *Fair Rosamund* (Northwestern University Studies in Humanities 16), Evanston

Heslin, A. (1965), 'The coronation of the young king in 1170', *Studies in Church History* 2: 165–78

Hicks, S. (1979), 'The impact of William Clito upon the continental policies of Henry I of England', *Viator* 10: 1–21

Hill, B. (1968), *English Cistercian Monasteries and their Patrons in the Twelfth Century*, Urbana, IL.

Hill, R. (1989), 'The battle of Stockbridge, 1141?', in C. Harper-Bill, C. J. Holdsworth and J. L. Nelson (eds.), *Studies in Medieval History Presented to R. Allen Brown*, Woodbridge, pp. 173–8

Hillion, Y. (1985), 'La Bretagne et la rivalité Capetiens-Plantagenet: un exemple la duchesse Constance (1186–1202)', *Annales de Bretagne* 92: 111–44

Hollister, C. W. (1961), 'King John and the historians', *Journal of British Studies* 1: 1–19

Hollister, C. W. (1965), *The Military Organization of Norman England*, Oxford

Hollister, C. W. (1973), 'The misfortunes of the Mandevilles', *History* 58: 19–26

Hollister, C. W. (1974), 'Stephen's anarchy', *Albion* 6: 233–9

Hollister, C. W. (1975), 'The Anglo-Norman succession debate of 1126', *JMH* 1: 19–24

Hollister, C. W. (1976), 'Normandy, France and the Anglo-Norman regnum', *Speculum* 51: 202–42

Hollister, C. W. (1982), 'Recent trends in Anglo-Norman scholarship: the new political history', *Albion* 14: 254–7

Hollister, C. W. (1986), *Monarchy, Magnates and Institutions in the Anglo-Norman World*, London

Hollister, C. W. and Keefe, T. K. (1973), 'The making of the Angevin empire', *Journal of British Studies* 12: 1–25

Holt, J. C. (1961), *The Northerners: A Study in the Reign of King John*, Oxford

Holt, J. C. (1963), *King John* (Historical Association), London

Holt, J. C. (1972), 'Politics and property in early medieval England', *PaP* 57: 3–52

Holt, J. C. (1975), 'The end of the Anglo-Norman realm', *PBA* 61: 223–65

Holt, J. C. (1981), 'Richardus Rex Anglorum et Dux Normannorum', in *Riccardo Cuor di Leone nella storia e nella leggenda* (Accademia Nazionale dei Lincei. Problemi Attuali di Scienza e di Cultura, 253), pp. 17–33

Holt, J. C. (1984a), 'The loss of Normandy and royal finance', in J. Gillingham and J. C. Holt (eds.), *War and Government in the Middle Ages*, Woodbridge, pp. 92–105

Holt, J. C. (1984b), 'Patronage and politics', *TRHS* 5th series 34: 1–26

Holt, J. C. (1985), *Magna Carta and Medieval Government*, London

Holt, J. C. (1986), 'Aliénor d'Aquitaine, Jean sans Terre et la succession de 1199', *CCM* 29: 95–100

Holt, J. C. (1989), 'The acta of Henry II and Richard I of England, 1154–1199: the archive and its historical implications', in P. Ruck (ed.), *Fotografische Sammlungen mittelalterlicher Urkunden in Europa*, Sigmaringen, pp. 137–40

Holt, J. C. (1990), 'The *casus regis*: the law and politics of succession in the Plantagenet dominions, 1185–1247', in E. B. King and S. J. Ridyard (eds.), *Law in Medieval Life and Thought*, Sewannee, TN, pp. 21–42

Howell, M. (1962), *Regalian Right in Medieval England*, London

Hudson, J. (1990), 'Life-grants of land and the development of inheritance in Anglo-Norman England', *ANS* 12: 67–80

Ide, A. F. (1986), *Calendar of Death: Socio-Psychological Factors in Thomas of Canterbury's Attitude towards his Own Death*, Irving, TX

Johnston, R. C. (1976), 'The historicity of Jordan Fantosme's *Chronicle*', *JMH* 2: 135–57

Jolliffe, J. (1963), *Angevin Kingship*, 2nd edn, London

Jones, M. (1990), 'The Capetians and Brittany', *History* 63: 1–16

Jones, T. M. (1973), 'The generation gap of 1173–1174: the war between the two Henrys', *Albion* 5: 24–40

Jones, T. M. (1980), *War of the Generations: The Revolt of 1173–1174*, Ann Arbor, MI

Jordan, K. (1986), *Henry the Lion: A Biography*, trans. P. Falla, Oxford

Kealey, E. (1972), *Roger of Salisbury, Viceroy of England*, Berkeley and Los Angeles

Kealey, E. (1974), 'King Stephen: government and anarchy', *Albion* 6: 201–17

Keefe, T. K. (1974), 'Geoffrey Plantagenet's will and the Angevin succession', *Albion* 6: 266–74

Keefe, T. K. (1981), 'King Henry II and the earls: the Pipe Roll evidence', *Albion* 13: 191–222

Keefe, T. K. (1982), 'The 1165 levy for the army of Wales', *Notes and Queries* 29: 194–6

Keefe, T. K. (1983), *Feudal Assessments and the Political Community under Henry II and his Sons*, Berkeley and Los Angeles

Keefe, T. K. (1989), 'Counting those who count: a computer-assisted analysis of charter-witness lists and the itinerant court in the first year of the reign of King Richard I', *Haskins Society Journal* 1: 135–45

Keefe, T. K. (1990), 'Place–date distribution of royal charters and the historical geography of patronage strategies at the court of King Henry II Plantagenet', *Haskins Society Journal* 2: 179–88

Kelly, A. (1952), *Eleanor of Aquitaine and the Four Kings*, London

Kibler, W. W. (ed.) (1977), *Eleanor of Aquitaine: Patron and Politician*, Austin, TX

King, E. (1973), *Peterborough Abbey, 1086–1310: A Study in the Land Market*, Cambridge

King, E. (1974a), 'King Stephen and the Anglo-Norman aristocracy', *History* 59: 180–94

King, E. (1974b), 'The tenurial crisis of the early twelfth century', *PaP* 65: 110–17

King, E. (1980), 'Mountsorrel and its region in King Stephen's reign', *Huntingdon Library Quarterly* 44: 1–10

King, E. (1984), 'The anarchy of King Stephen's reign', *TRHS* 5th series 34: 133–53

King, E. (1985), 'Waleran, count of Meulan, earl of Worcester (1104–1166)', in D. E. Greenway, C. J. Holdsworth and J. E. Sayers (eds.), *Traditions and Change: Essays in Honour of Marjorie Chibnall Presented by her Friends on the Occasion of her Seventieth Birthday*, Cambridge, pp. 165–82

King, E. (1988), *Medieval England*, Oxford

King, E. (1990), 'The foundation of Pipewell Abbey, Northamptonshire', *Haskins Society Journal* 2: 167–77

Knowles, D. (1951), *The Episcopal Colleagues of Archbishop Thomas Becket*, Cambridge

Knowles, D. (1966), *The Monastic Order in England*, 2nd edn, Cambridge

Knowles, D. (1970), *Thomas Becket*, Stanford

Labande, E.-R. (1952), 'Pour une image véridique d'Aliénor d'Aquitaine', *Bulletin de la Société des Antiquaires de l'Ouest* 4.II: 173–233

Labande, E.-R. (1986), 'Les filles d'Aliénor d'Aquitaine: étude comparative', *CCM* 29: 101–12

Lalley, J. E. (1976), 'Secular patronage at the court of King Henry II', *BIHR* 49: 159–84

Latimer, P. (1986), 'Grants of *totus comitatus* in twelfth century England: their origins and meaning', *BIHR* 59: 137–45

Latimer, P. (1989), 'Henry II's campaign against the Welsh in 1165', *Welsh History Review* 14: 523–52

Leach, H. G. (1921), *Angevin Britain and Scandinavia*, Cambridge, MA

Legge, M. D. (1982), 'William Marshal and Arthur of Brittany', *BIHR* 55: 18–24

Leedom, J. W. (1974), 'William of Malmesbury and Robert of Gloucester reconsidered', *Albion* 6: 251–63

Leedom, J. W. (1980), 'The English settlement of 1153', *History* 65: 347–64

Le Maho, J. (1976), 'L'apparition de seigneuries châtelaines dans le Grand-Caux à l'époque ducal', *Archéologie Médiévale* 6: 8–148

Lemarignier, J.-F. (1965), *Le Gouvernement royal aux premiers temps capétiens*, Paris

Le Patourel, J. (1965), 'The Plantagenet dominions', *History* 50: 289–308

Le Patourel, J. (1973), 'What did not happen in King Stephen's reign', *History* 67: 1–17

Le Patourel, J. (1976), *The Norman Empire*, Oxford

Le Patourel, J. (1978), 'The Norman Conquest, 1066, 1106, 1154?', *ANS* 1: 103–20, 216–20

Le Patourel, J. (1984), 'Angevin succession and the Angevin empire', in *Feudal Empires: Norman and Plantagenet*, London, art. IX: 1–17

Lewis, A. (1981), *Royal Succession in Capetian France: Studies in Familial Order and the State*, Cambridge, MA

Leyser, K. (1975), 'Frederick Barbarossa, Henry II and the hand of St James', *EHR* 90: 489–95

Lyon, B. (1989), 'Henry II: a non-Victorian interpretation', in J. S. Hamilton *et al.* (eds.), *Documenting the Past: Essays in Medieval History Presented to George Peddy Cuttino*, Woodbridge, pp. 21–31

Lyttelton, G. (1769–73), *History of the Life of King Henry II*, 3rd edn, 6 vols., London

McGurk, J. (1973), 'Henry II and the revolts of 1173', *History Today* 23: 280–9

Mack, R. P. (1966), 'Stephen and the anarchy 1135–1154', *British Numismatic Journal* 35: 38–112

Maple, J. T. (1989), 'Anglo-Norman Conquest of Ireland and the Irish economy: stagnation or stimulation?', *Historian* 52: 61–81

Martindale, J. (1989), 'Succession and politics in the Romance-speaking world, c.1000–1140', in M. Jones and M. Vale (eds.), *England and her Neighbours, 1066–1453: Essays in Honour of Pierre Chaplais*, London, pp. 19–41

Mason, E. (1976), 'The Mauduits and their chamberlainship of the Exchequer', *BIHR* 49: 1–23

Mason, E. (1980), 'The king, the chamberlain and Southwark Priory', *BIHR* 53: 1–10

Matthew, D. J. A. (1962), *The Norman Monasteries and their English Possessions*, London

Mayr-Harting. H. (1963), 'Hilary, bishop of Chichester and Henry II', *EHR* 78: 209–24

Megaw, I. (1949), 'The ecclesiastical policy of Stephen, 1135–1139: a reinterpretation', in H. A. Cronne *et al.* (eds.), *Essays in British and Irish History in Honour of James Eadie Todd*, London, pp. 24–46

Meisel, J. (1980), *Barons of the Welsh Frontier: The Corbet, Pantulf and Fitz Warin Families, 1066–1272*, Lincoln, NB

Miller, E. (1951), *The Abbey and Bishopric of Ely*, Cambridge

Miller, E. (1971), 'The English economy in the 12th and 13th centuries: an economic contrast', *Economic History Review* 2nd series, 24: 1–14

Miller, E. and Hatcher, J. (1978), *Medieval England: Rural Society and Economic Change, 1086–1348*, London

Mitchell, S. K. (1914), *Studies in Taxation under John and Henry III*, New Haven

Mitchell, S. K. (1951), *Taxation in Medieval England*, ed. S. Painter, New Haven

Moore, O. H. (1925a), 'Bertran de Born et le jeune roi', *Romania* 51: 46–75

Moore, O. H. (1925b), *The Young King Henry Plantagenet, 1155–1183*, Columbus, OH

Morey, A. (1937), *Bartholomew of Exeter, Bishop and Canonist: A Study in the Twelfth Century*, Cambridge

Mortimer, R. (1978), 'Religious and secular motives for some English monastic foundations', *Studies in Church History* 9: 77–85

Mortimer, R. (1981a), 'The family of Rannulf de Glanville', *BIHR* 54: 1–16

Mortimer, R. (1981b), 'The beginnings of the honour of Clare', *ANS* 3: 119–41

Mortimer, R. (1986), 'Land and service: the tenants of the honour of Clare', *ANS* 8: 177–97

Mortimer, R. (1990), 'The charters of Henry II: what are the criteria for authenticity', *ANS* 12: 119–34

Musset, L. (1986), 'Y-eut-il une aristocratie d'affaires commune aux grandes villes de Normandie et d'Angleterre entre 1066 et 1204?', *Etudes Normandes* 35: 7–19

Musset, L. (1988), 'Les études d'histoire en Normandie (1951–1988). II – La Normandie du Viéme siècle à 1204', *Annales de Normandie* 38: 373–91

Musset, L. (ed.) (1985), *Autour du pouvoir ducal Normande Xe–XIIe siecles*, Caen

Nicholl, D. (1964), *Thurstan, Archbishop of York (1114–1140)*, London

Norgate, K. (1887), *England under the Angevin Kings*, 2 vols., London

Norgate, K. (1900), 'The alleged condemnation of King John by the court of France in 1202', *TRHS* 2nd series, 14: 53–67

Norgate, K. (1902), *John Lackland*, New York

Norgate, K. (1924), *Richard the Lionheart*, London

Nortier, M. (1970), 'Le comté de Mortain au début du XIIIe siècle', in *Mélanges d'histoire normande dédiées à René Jouanne* (numero spécial du *Pays bas-normand*), Flers, pp. 225–35

Nortier, M. and Baldwin, J. W. (1990), 'Contributions à l'étude des finances de Philippe Auguste', *BEC* 138: 5–33

Pacaut, M. (1964), *Louis VII and son royaume*, Paris

Pain, N. (1978), *Empress Matilda*, London

Painter, S. (1933), *William Marshal*, Baltimore

Painter, S. (1943), *Studies in the History of the English Feudal Barony*, Baltimore

Painter, S. (1949), *The Reign of King John*, Baltimore

Painter, S. (1961), *Feudalism and Liberty*, ed. F. A. Cazel, Baltimore

Painter, S. and Cazel, F. (1952), 'The marriage of Isabella of Angoulême', *EHR* 67: 233–5

Patterson, R. (1965), 'William of Malmesbury's Robert of Gloucester: a reevaluation of the *Historia novella*', *AHR* 70: 983–7

Patterson, R. (1968), 'Stephen's Shaftesbury charter: another case against William of Malmesbury', *Speculum* 43: 487–92

Patterson, R. (1972), 'An un-edited charter of Henry fitz Empress and Earl William of Gloucester's comital status', *EHR* 87: 755–7

Patterson, R. (1974), 'Anarchy in England, 1135–1154: the theory of the constitution', *Albion* 6: 190–200

Patterson, R. (1990), 'Robert Fitz Harding of Bristol: profile of an early Angevin burgess-baron patrician and his family's urban involvement', *Haskins Society Journal* 1: 109–22

Patterson, R. (1991), 'Bristol: an Angevin baronial capital under royal siege', *Haskins Society Journal* 3: 171–81

Pernoud, R. (1967), *Eleanor of Aquitaine*, London

Petit-Dutaillis, C. (1933), *La Monarchie féodale en France et en Angleterre*, Paris

Pocquet du Haut-Jusse, B.-A. (1946), 'Les Plantagenets et la Bretagne', *Annales de Bretagne* 53: 1–27

Poole, A. L. (1940), 'Livestock prices in the twelfth century', *EHR* 55: 284–95

Poole, A. L. (1955), *From Domesday Book to Magna Carta 1087–1216*, 2nd edn, Oxford

Poole, R. L. (1912), *The Exchequer in the Twelfth Century*, Oxford

Pounds, N. J. G. (1990), *The Medieval Castle in England and Wales: A Political and Social History*, Cambridge

Powicke, F. M. (1928), *Stephen Langton*, Oxford

Powicke, F. M. (1961), *The Loss of Normandy*, 2nd edn, Manchester

Prestwich, J. O. (1981), 'Richard Cœur de Lion: rex bellicosus', in *Riccardo Cuor di Leone nella storia e nella leggenda* (Accademia Nazionale dei Lincei. Problemi Attuali di Scienza e di Cultura, 253), pp. 3–15

Prestwich, J. O. (1988), 'The treason of Geoffrey de Mandeville', *EHR* 103: 283–312, 960–7 (see pp. 313–17, 967–8 for R. H. C. Davis's reply)

Ramsey, J. H. (1898), *The Foundations of England*, 2 vols., London

Ramsey, J. H. (1903), *The Angevin Empire 1154–1216*, London

Renouard, Y. (1945), 'Essai sur le rôle de l'empire Angevin dans formation de la France', *Revue Historique* 195: 289–304

Richard, A. (1903), *Histoire de comtes de Poitou, 778–1204*, 2 vols., Paris

Richardson, H. G. (1932), 'William of Ely the king's treasurer, 1195–1215', *TRHS* 4th series 15: 45–90

Richardson, H. G. (1946), 'The marriage and coronation of Isabelle of Angouleme', *EHR* 61: 289–314

Richardson, H. G. (1950), 'King John and Isabelle of Angouleme', *EHR* 65: 360–71

Richardson, H. G. (1960), *The English Jewry under the Angevin Kings*, London

Richardson, H. G. and Sayles, G. O. (1963), *The Governance of Medieval England from the Conquest to Magna Carta*, Edinburgh

Ritchie, R. L. G. (1954), *The Normans in Scotland*, Edinburgh

Roderick, A. J. (1952), 'The feudal relations between the English crown and Welsh princes', *History* 37: 201–12

Round, J. H. (1892), *Geoffrey de Mandeville: A Study of the Anarchy*, London

Round, J. H. (1895), *Feudal England*, London

Rowley, T. (1983), *The Norman Heritage, 1066–1200*, London

Russel, J. (1970), 'Rannulf de Glanville', *Speculum* 45: 69–79

Saltman, A. (1956), *Theobald, Archbishop of Canterbury*, London

Scammel, G. V. (1956), *Hugh du Puiset, Bishop of Durham*, Cambridge

Schnith, K. (1976), 'Regni et pacis inquietatrix', *JMH* 2: 135–58

Schriber, C. (1990), *Arnulf of Lisieux: The Dilemmas of a Twelfth Century Norman Bishop*, Bloomington, IN

Shaw, I. P. (1950–1), 'The ecclesiastical policy of Henry II on the continent', *Church Quarterly Review* 151: 137–55

Southern, R. W. (1966), *Saint Anselm and his Biographery*, Cambridge; new edn 1990

Southern, R. W. (1970a), *Medieval Humanism and Other Studies*, Oxford

Southern, R. W. (1970b), *Western Society and the Church in the Middle Ages*, London

Spear, D. S. (1982), 'The Norman empire and the secular clergy', *Journal of British Studies* 21: 1–10

Spear, D. S. (1983), 'Les doyens du chapitre cathédrale de Rouen durant la période ducale', *Annales de Normandie* 33: 91–119

Spear, D. S. (1984a), 'Les archidiacres de Rouen au cours de la période ducale', *Annales de Normandie* 34: 15–50

Spear, D. S. (1984b), 'Membership in the Norman cathedral chapters during the ducal period: some preliminary findings', *Medieval Prosopography* 5: 1–18

Spear, D. S. (1987), 'Les dignitaires de la cathédrale de Rouen pendant la pèriode ducale', *Annales de Normandie* 37: 129–33

Spear, D. S. (1991), 'Les chanoines de la cathédrale de Rouen pendant la pèriode ducale', *Annales de Normandie* 41: 135–76

Spufford, P. (1986), *Money and its Uses in Medieval Europe*, Cambridge

Stalley, R. A. (1971), 'A twelfth-century patron of architecture: a study of the buildings erected by Roger, bishop of Salisbury, 1102–1139', *Journal of the British Archaeological Association* (3) 34: 62–82

Stenton, D. M. (1958), 'King John and the courts of Justice', *PBA* 44: 103–28

Stenton, D. M. (1962), *English Society in the Early Middle Ages*, 3rd edn, London

Stenton, D. M. (1965), *English Justice between the Norman Conquest and the Great Charter*, London

Stenton, F. M. (1961), *The first century of English feudalism 1066–1166*, 2nd edn, Oxford

Strickland, M. (1990), 'Securing the north: invasion and the strategy of defence in twelfth-century Anglo-Scottish warfare', *ANS* 12: 175–98

Stringer, K. (1985), *Earl David of Huntingdon, 1152–1219*, Edinburgh

Thomson, R. M. (1987), *William of Malmesbury*, Woodbridge

Thorpe, L. (1978), 'Walter Map and Gerald of Wales', *Medium Aevum* 47: 6–21

Turner, R. V. (1985), *The English Judiciary in the Age of Glanville and Bracton*, Cambridge

Turner, R. V. (1986), 'Les contacts entre l'Angleterre Normanno-Angevine et la Sicile Normande', *Etudes Normandes* 35: 39–60

Turner, R. V. (1988a), 'Eleanor of Aquitaine and her children: an inquiry in medieval family attachment', *JMH* 14: 21–35

Turner, R. V. (1988b), *Men Raised from the Dust: Administrative Service and Upward Mobility in Angevin England*, Philadelphia

Turner, R. V. (1989), 'The Mandeville inheritance, 1189–1236: its legal, political and social context', *Haskins Society Journal* 1: 147–72

Turner, R. V. (1990), 'Changing perceptions of the new administrative class in Anglo-Norman and Angevin England: the *curiales* and their conservative critics', *Journal of British Studies* 29: 93–117

Ullmann, W. (1979), 'Arthur's homage to King John', *EHR* 94: 356–64

Valin, L. (1909), *Le Duc de Normandie et sa cour (912–1204): étude d'histoire juridique*, Paris

Walker, D. (1958), 'Miles of Gloucester, earl of Hereford', in *Transactions of the Bristol and Gloucester Archaeological Society* 77: 66–84

Walker, D. (1983), 'Crown and episcopacy under the Normans and the Angevins', *ANS* 5: 220–33

Ward, J. C. (1989), 'Royal service and reward: the Clare family and the crown, 1066–1154', *ANS* 11: 261–78

Wardrop, J. (1987), *Fountains Abbey and its Benefactors, 1132–1300*, Kalamazoo, MI

Warren, W. L. (1957), 'What was wrong with King John?', *History Today* 7: 806–12

Warren, W. L. (1961), *King John*, Berkeley and Los Angeles; repr. 1978

Warren, W. L. (1969), 'The interpretation of twelfth-century Irish history', *Historical Studies* 7: 1–19

Warren, W. L. (1973), *Henry II*, Berkeley and Los Angeles

Warren, W. L. (1976), 'John in Ireland in 1185', in J. A. Bossy and P. J. Jupp (eds.), *Essays Presented to Michael Roberts*, Belfast, pp. 11–23

Warren, W. L. (1981), 'King John and Ireland', in J. Lyon (ed.), *England and Ireland in the Later Middle Ages: Essays in Honour of Jocelyn Otway-Ruthven*, Dublin, pp. 26–42

Warren, W. L. (1987), *The Governance of Norman and Angevin England*, Stanford

White, G. H. (1948), 'The household of the Norman kings', *TRHS* 3rd series 30: 127–56

White, G. J. (1974), 'The restoration of order in England, 1153–1165', University of Cambridge, PhD thesis

White, G. J. (1976), 'King Stephen, Duke Henry, and Ranulf de Gernons, earl of Chester', *EHR* 91: 555–65

White, G. J. (1985), 'The devastated midlands? The remissions for "waste" in the Danegeld accounts of 1156', *Midland History* 10: 26–46

White, G. J. (1990), 'The end of Stephen's reign', *History* 75: 3–22

Wightman, W. E. (1966), *The Lacy Family in England and Normandy*, Oxford

Yoshitake, K. (1988a), 'The arrest of the bishops in 1139 and its consequences', *JMH* 14: 97–114

Yoshitake, K. (1988b), 'The Exchequer in the reign of King Stephen', *EHR* 103: 950–9

Young, A. (1979), *William Cumin: Border Politics and the Bishopric of Durham 1141–1144* (University of York, Borthwick Papers, no. 54), York

Young, C. (1968), *Hubert Walter, Lord of Canterbury and Lord of England*, Durham, NC

Young, C. (1979), *The Royal Forests of Medieval England*, Philadelphia

Yver, J. (1955–6), 'Les châteaux forts en Normandie jusqu'au milieu du XIIe siècle: contribution a l'étude du pouvoir ducal', *Bulletin de la Société des Antiquaires de Normandie* 54: 78–115

19   SCOTLAND, WALES AND IRELAND IN THE TWELFTH CENTURY

Scotland

General

Anderson, A. O. (1963), 'Anglo-Scottish relations from Constantine II to William I', *Scottish Historical Review* 42: 1–20

Barrell, A. D. M. (2000), *Medieval Scotland*, Cambridge

Barrow, G. W. S. (1973), *The Kingdom of the Scots*, London

Barrow, G. W. S. (1980), *The Anglo-Norman Era in Scottish History*, Oxford

Barrow, G. W. S. (1981), *Kingship and Unity, Scotland 1000–1306*, Edinburgh; 2nd edn 1989

Barrow, G. W. S. (1992), *Scotland and its Neighbours in the Middle Ages*, London

Barrow, G. W. S. (1994), 'The Scots and the North of England', in E. King (ed.), *The Anarchy of King Stephen's Reign*, Oxford, pp. 231–53

Broun, D. (1998), 'Defining Scotland and the Scots before the Wars of Independence', in D. Broun *et al.* (eds.), *Image and Identity: The Making and Remaking of Scotland through the Ages*, Edinburgh, pp. 4–17

Broun, D. (1999), *The Irish Identity of the Kingdom of the Scots in the Twelfth and Thirteenth Centuries*, Woodbridge

Clapperton, C. M. (ed.) (1983), *Scotland: A New Study*, Newton Abbot

Cowan, E. J. and McDonald, R. A. (eds.) (2000), *Alba: Celtic Scotland in the Middle Ages*, East Linton

Davies, R. R. (1990), *Domination and Conquest: The Experience of Ireland, Scotland and Wales 1100–1300*, Cambridge

Dodgshon, R. A. (1981), *Land and Society in Early Scotland*, Oxford

Duffy, S. (1999), 'The Anglo-Norman era in Scotland: convergence and diversity', in T. M. Devine and J. F. McMillan (eds.), *Celebrating Columba – Irish–Scottish Connections 597–1997*, Edinburgh, pp. 15–34

Duffy, S. (2000), 'Ireland and Scotland, 1014–1169: contacts and caveats', in A. P. Smyth (ed.), *Seanchas*, Dublin, pp. 348–56

Duncan, A. A. M. (1975), *The Making of the Kingdom*, Edinburgh

Frame, R. (1990), *The Political Development of the British Isles 1100–1400*, Oxford; rev. edn 1995

MacKie, E. W. (1975), *Scotland: An Archaeological Guide*, London

McNeill, P., MacQueen, H. L. and Nicholson, R. (1975), *An Historical Atlas of Scotland c. 400–1600*, St Andrews; new edn as *Atlas of Scottish History to 1707*, Edinburgh, 1996

Ritchie, R. L. G. (1954), *The Normans in Scotland*, Edinburgh

Smith, B. (ed.) (1999), *Britain and Ireland 900–1300: Insular Responses to Medieval European Change*, Cambridge

Webster, B. (1997), *Medieval Scotland: The Making of an Identity*, Basingstoke

Whittington, G. and Whyte, I. D. (eds.) (1983), *An Historical Geography of Scotland*, London

The Norse in Scotland

Batey, C. E., Jesch, J. and Morris, C. D. (eds.) (1995), *The Viking Age in Caithness, Orkney and the North Atlantic*, Edinburgh

Crawford, B. E. (1987), *Scandinavian Scotland*, Leicester

McDonald, R. A. (1997), *The Kingdom of the Isles: Scotland's Western Seaboard in the Central Middle Ages c. 1100–1336*, East Linton

Power, R. (1986), 'Magnus Barelegs' expeditions to the West', *Scottish Historical Review* 65: 107–32

The Normans in Scotland

Aird, W. (1994), 'St Cuthbert, the Scots and the Normans', *ANS* 16: 1–20

Barrow, G. W. S. (1994), 'The kings of Scotland and Durham', in D. Rollason, M. Harvey and M. Prestwich (eds.), *Anglo-Norman Durham 1093–1193*, Woodbridge, pp. 311–23

Green, J. (1990), 'Aristocratic loyalties on the northern frontier of England c. 1100–1174', in D. Williams (ed.), *England in the Twelfth Century*, Woodbridge, pp. 83–100

Kapelle, W. (1979), *The Norman Conquest of the North. The region and its transformation 1000–1135*, London

Oram, R. D. (1991), 'Fergus, Galloway and the Scots', in R. D. Oram and G. P. Stell (eds.), *Galloway, Land and Lordship*, Edinburgh, pp. 117–30

Oram, R. D. and Stell, G. (1991), *Galloway, Land and Lordship*, Edinburgh

Sellar, W. D. H. (1966), 'The origins and ancestry of Somerled', *Scottish Historical Review* 45: 123–42

Stringer, K. J. (1997), 'State-building in twelfth-century Britain: David I, king of Scots, and northern England', in J. C. Appleby and P. Dalton (eds.), *Government, Religion and Society in Northern England*, Stroud, pp. 40–62

The succession and politics

Barrow, G. W. S. (1975), 'Macbeth and other mormaers of Moray', in *The Hub of the Highlands* (Inverness Field Club centenary volume 1875–1975), Inverness, pp. 109–22

Brooke, D. (1994), *Wild Men and Holy Places: St Ninian, Whithorn and the Medieval Realm of Galloway*, Edinburgh

Broun, D. (1999), *The Irish Identity of the Kingdom of the Scots*, Woodbridge and Rochester, NY

Crawford, B. E. (1976–7), 'The earldom of Caithness and the kingdom of Scotland', *Northern Scotland* 2: 97–117

Davies, W. (1993), 'Celtic kingships in the early middle ages', in A. Duggan (ed.), *Kings and Kingship in Medieval Europe* (Kings College London Medieval Studies 10), London, pp. 101–24

Duncan, A. A. M. and Brown, A. L. (1957–7), 'Argyll and the Isles in the earlier middle ages', *Proceedings of the Society of Antiquaries in Scotland* 90: 192–220

Hudson, B. T. (1994), *Kings of Celtic Scotland*, Wesport, CT, and London

Owen, D. D. R. (1997), *William the Lion 1143–1214*, East Linton

Stringer, K. (1993), 'Periphery and core: Alan of Galloway', in A. Grant and K. Stringer (eds.), *Medieval Scotland*, Edinburgh, pp. 82–113

Wormald, P. (1986), 'Celtic and Anglo-Saxon kingship', in P. E. Szarmach and V. D. Oggins (eds.), *Sources of Anglo-Saxon Culture*, Kalamazoo, MI, pp. 151–83

Government

Anderson, M. O. (1980), *Kings and Kingship in Early Scotland*, 2nd edn, Edinburgh

Barrow, G. W. S. (1981), 'Popular courts in early medieval Scotland', *Scottish Studies* 25: 1–24

Barrow, G. W. S. (1988–9), 'Badenoch and Strathspey, 1130–1312', *Northern Scotland* 9: 1–16

Grant, A. (1993), 'Thanes and thanages from the eleventh to the fourteenth centuries', in A. Grant and K. Stringer (eds.), *Medieval Scotland*, Edinburgh, pp. 39–81

Grant, A. (2000), 'The construction of the early Scottish state', in J. Maddicott and D. Palliser (eds.), *The Medieval State: Essays Presented to James Campbell*, London, pp. 47–71

Scots and incomers; the aristocracy

Anderson, A. O. (1963), 'Anglo-Scottish relations from Constantine II to William', *Scottish Historical Review* 41: 1–20

Bannerman, J. (1990), 'The Scots language and the kin-based society', in D. S. Thomson (ed.), *Gaelic and Scots in Harmony*, Glasgow, pp. 1–19

Barrow, G. W. S. (1992), 'The Lost Gàidhealtachd', in G. W. S. Barrow, *Scotland and its neighbours*, London, pp. 105–26

Jackson, K. (1972), *The Gaelic notes in the Book of Deer*, Cambridge

Reid, N. H. (1990), *Scotland in the reign of Alexander III*, Edinburgh

Strickland, M. (1989), 'Securing the North: invasion and the strategy of defence in twelfth-century Anglo-Scottish warfare', *ANS* 12: 177–98

Stringer, K. (ed.) (1985a), *Earl David of Huntingdon*, Edinburgh

Stringer, K. (ed.) (1985b), *Essays on the Nobility of Medieval Scotland*, Edinburgh

Young, A. (1997), *Robert the Bruce's Rivals: The Comyns 1212–1314*, East Linton

Land and settlement

Baker, A. R. H. and Butlin, R. A. (eds.) (1973), *Studies in Field Systems in the British Isles*, Cambridge

Dodgshon, R. A. (1981), *Land and Society in Early Scotland*, Oxford

Oram, R. D. (1993), 'A family business? Colonisation and settlement in twelfth and
    thirteenth century Galloway', *Scottish Historical Review* 72: 111–45
Parry, M. L. and Slater, T. R. (1980), *The Making of the Scottish Countryside*, London
Whyte, I. D. (1995), *Scotland before the Industrial Revolution*, London and New York

The burghs

Dicks, B. (1983), 'The Scottish medieval town: a search for origins', in G. Gordon and
    B. Dicks (eds.), *Scottish Urban History*, Aberdeen, pp. 23–51
Lynch, M. *et al.* (eds.) (1988), *The Scottish Medieval Town*, Edinburgh
Mackenzie, W. (1949), *Scottish Burghs*, Edinburgh

The church

Barrell, A. D. M. (1995), 'The background to *Cum universi*: Scoto–papal relations
    1159–1192', *Innes Review* 46: 116–38
Cowan, I. and Easson, D. (1976), *Medieval Religious Houses, Scotland*, 2nd edn, London
Donaldson, G. (1985), *Scottish Church History*, Edinburgh
Dumville, D. N. (1997), *Councils and Synods of the Gaelic Early and Central Middle
    Ages* (Quiggin Pamphlet 3), Cambridge
Hudson, B. T. (1994), 'Kings and church in early Scotland', *Scottish Historical Review*
    73: 145–70
McDonald, R. A. (1995), 'Scoto-Norse kings and the reformed religious orders: patterns
    of monastic patronage in twelfth-century Galloway and Argyll', *Albion* 27: 187–
    219
McDonald, R. A. (1998), 'The foundation and patronage of nunneries by native elites
    in twelfth- and early thirteenth-century Scotland', in E. Ewan and M. M. Meikle
    (eds.), *Women in Scotland c.1100–c.1750*, East Linton, pp. 3–15
Macquarrie, A. (1992), 'Early Christian religious houses in Scotland: foundation
    and function', in W. J. Blair and R. Sharpe (eds.), *Pastoral Care before the Parish*,
    Leicester pp. 110–33
Morgan, M. (1947), 'The organization of the Scottish church in the twelfth century',
    TRHS 4th series 29: 135–49
Oram, R. A. (1991), 'In obedience and reverence: Whithorn and York, c.1128–c.1250',
    Innes Review 42: 83–100
Reeves, W. (1864), *The Culdees of the British Isles*, Dublin
Watt, D. E. R. (1991), *Ecclesia Scoticana* (Series Episcoporum Ecclesiae Catholicae
    Occidentalis, Series 6.1), Stuttgart

                                     Wales
General

Bowen, E. G. (1957), *Wales: A Physical, Historical and Regional Geography*, London
Davies, W. (1982), *Wales in the Early Middle Ages*, Leicester
Emery, F. V. (1969), *Wales*, London
Evans, G. (1974), *Land of My Fathers: 2000 Years of Welsh History*, Swansea

Lloyd, J. E. (1911), *A History of Wales from the Earliest Times to the Edwardian Conquest*, 2 vols., London; 3rd edn 1939

Rees, W. (1959), *An Historical Atlas of Wales from Early to Modern Times*, 2nd edn, London

Richards, M. (1969), *Welsh Administrative and Territorial Units, Medieval and Modern*, Cardiff

Thomas, D. (ed.) (1977), *Wales: A New Study*, Newton Abbot

Wade-Evans, A. W. *et al.* (1950), *The Historical Basis of Welsh Nationalism*, Cardiff

Williams, A. H. (1941–8), *An Introduction to the History of Wales*, 2 vols., Cardiff

Welsh law

Carr, A. D. and Jenkins, D. (1985), *A Look at Hywel's Law*, Whitland

Charles-Edwards, T. M. (1989), *The Welsh Laws*, Cardiff

Charles-Edwards, T. M. (1993), *Early Irish and Welsh Kinship*, Oxford

Charles-Edwards, T. M. *et al.* (eds.) (1986), *Lawyers and Laymen*, Cardiff

Ellis, T. P. (1926), *Welsh Tribal Law and Custom in the Middle Ages*, 2 vols., Oxford

Jenkins, D. (1973), *Celtic Law Papers Introductory to Welsh Medieval Law and Government*, Brussels

Jenkins, D. (1977), 'The significance of the Law of Hywel', *Transactions of the Honourable Society of Cymmrodorion*: 54–76

Pierce, T. J. (1972), *Medieval Welsh Society*, Cardiff

Seebohm, F. (1904), *The Tribal System in Wales*, 2nd edn, London

Politics

Davies, W. (1981), 'Property rights and property claims in Welsh *Vitae* of the eleventh century', in E. Patlagean and P. Riché (eds.), *Hagiographie, cultures et sociétés, IVe–XIIe siècles*, Paris, pp. 515–33

Lloyd, J. E. (1899–1900), 'Wales and the coming of the Normans (1039–1093)', *Transactions of the Honourable Society of Cymmrodorion* (1899–1900), pp. 122–79

Maund, K. L. (1985), 'Cynan ab Iago and the killing of Gruffudd ap Llywelyn', *Cambridge Medieval Celtic Studies* 10: 57–65

Maund, K. L. (1986–7), 'Trahaearn ap Caradog: legitimate usurper?', *Welsh History Review* 13: 468–76

Maund, K. L. (1991), *Ireland, Wales and England in the Eleventh Century*, Woodbridge

The Norman impact

Davies, R. R. (1979), 'Kings, lords and liberties in the March of Wales, 1066–1272', *TRHS* 5th series 29: 41–61

Davies, R. R. (1987), *Conquest, Coexistence and Change: Wales 1063–1415*, Oxford; repr. as *The Age of Conquest: Wales, 1063–1415*, Oxford, 1991

Edwards, J. G. (1956), 'The Normans and the Welsh March', *PBA* 42: 155–77

Rowlands, I. W. (1980), 'The making of the March: aspects of the Norman settlement in Dyfed', *Proceedings of the Battle Conference on Anglo-Norman Studies* 3: 142–57, 221–5

Tait, J. (1925), 'Flintshire in Domesday Book', *Flintshire Historical Society Publications* 11: 1–37

Walker, D. (1978), 'The Norman settlement in Wales', *Proceedings of the Battle Conference on Anglo-Norman Studies* 1: 131–43, 222–4

Twelfth-century accommodations

Barrow, G. W. S. (1956), *Feudal Britain: The Completion of the Medieval Kingdoms, 1066–1314*, London

Bartlett, R. (1982), *Gerald of Wales 1146–1223*, Oxford

Brooke, C. N. L. (1986), *The Church and the Welsh Border in the Central Middle Ages*, Woodbridge

Caerwyn Williams, J. E. (1978), *The Poets of the Welsh Princes*, Cardiff

Charles-Edwards, T. M. (1989), *The Welsh Laws*, Cardiff

Cowley, F. G. (1977), *The Monastic Order in South Wales, 1066–1349*, Cardiff

Davies, J. R. (1998), 'Liber Landavensis: its date and the identity of its editor', *Cambrian Medieval Celtic Studies* 35: 1–11

Davies, R. R. (1974), 'Colonial Wales', *PaP* 65: 3–23

Davies, R. R. (1990), *Domination and Conquest: The Experience of Ireland, Scotland and Wales, 1100–1300*, Cambridge

Davies, W. (1979), *The Llandaff Charters*, Aberystwyth

Huws, D. (1987–8), 'The making of Liber Landavensis', *National Library of Wales Journal* 25: 133–60

Maund, K. L. (1996), *Gruffudd ap Cynan: A Collaborative Biography*, Woodbridge

Pryce, H. (1986), 'The prologues to the Welsh lawbooks', *Bulletin of the Board of Celtic Studies* 33: 151–87

Pryce, H. (1988), 'Church and society in Wales, 1150–1250: an Irish perspective', in R. R. Davies (ed.), *The British Isles 1100–1500: Comparisons, Contrasts and Connections*, Edinburgh, pp. 27–47

Pryce, H. (1993), *Native Law and the Church in Medieval Wales*, Oxford

Richter, M. (1976), *Giraldus Cambrensis: The Growth of the Welsh Nation*, 2nd edn, Aberystwyth

Stokes, K. (1999), *The Myth of Wales: Constructions of Ethnicity 1100–1300*, Clayton

Suppe, F. C. (1994), *Military Institutions on the Welsh Marches: Shropshire, 1066–1300*, Woodbridge

Wada, Y. (1997), 'Gerald on Gerald: self-presentation by Giraldus Cambrensis', *ANS* 20: 223–46

Williams, G. (1976), *The Welsh Church from Conquest to Reformation*, 2nd edn, Cardiff

Christianity in Wales and the south-west

Brooke, C. N. L. (1986), *The Church and the Welsh Border in the Central Middle Ages*, Woodbridge

Knowles, D. and Hadcock, R. N. (1971), *Medieval Religious Houses, England and Wales*, 2nd edn, London

Lapidge, M. and Sharpe, R. (1985), *A Bibliography of Celtic Latin Literature 400–1200*, Dublin

Pryce, H. (1993), *Native Law and the Church in Medieval Wales*, Oxford

Ireland

Reference

Duffy, S. (1997), *Ireland in the Middle Ages*, Basingstoke

Flanagan, D. and Flanagan, L. (1994), *Irish Place Names*, Dublin

Hogan, E. (1910), *Onomasticon Goedelicum*, Dublin

Kenney, J. F. (1929), *Sources for the Early History of Ireland: Ecclesiastical*, rev. imp. by L. Bieler, New York, 1966

Ó Corraín, D. (1972), *Ireland before the Normans*, Dublin

Ó Corraín, D. (1976), 'A hand-list of publications in early Irish history', *Historical Studies* (Irish Conference of Historians) 10: 172–203

Ó Corraín, D. and Maguire, F. (1990), *Irish Names*, 2nd edn, Dublin

Ó Cróinín, D. (1995), *Early Medieval Ireland, 400–1200*, London

Quiggin pamphlets

Broun, D. (1995), *The Charters of Gaelic Scotland and Ireland in the Early and Central Middle Ages*, Cambridge

Carey, J. (1994), *The Irish National Origin-legend: Synthetic Pseudo-history*, Cambridge

Charles-Edwards, T. M. (1999), *The Early Medieval Gaelic Lawyer*, Cambridge

Dumville, D. N. (1997), *Councils and Synods of the Gaelic Early and Central Middle Ages*, Cambridge

Archaeology and art

Barry, T. B. (1987), *The Archaeology of Medieval Ireland*, London

Butlin, R. A. (ed.) (1977), *The Development of the Irish Town*, London

Edwards, N. (1990), *The Archaeology of Early Medieval Ireland*, London

Hamlin, A. and Lynn, C. (eds.) (1988), *Pieces of the Past: Archaeological Excavations by the Department of the Environment for Northern Ireland 1970–1986*, Belfast

Henry, F. (1965–70), *Irish Art*, 3 vols., London

Hughes, K. and Hamlin, A. (1977), *The Modern Traveller to the Early Irish Church*, London; new edn Dublin, 1997

Manning, C. (1985), *Irish Field Monuments*, Dublin

Norman, E. R. and St Joseph, J. K. S. (1969), *The Early Development of Irish Society: The Evidence of Aerial Photography*, Cambridge

Ó Ríordáin, S. P. [and R. de Valera] (1979), *Antiquities of the Irish Countryside*, 5th edn, London

Proudfoot, V. B. (1961), 'The economy of the Irish rath', *Medieval Archaeology* 5: 94–122

Proudfoot, V. B. (1977), 'Economy and settlement in rural Ireland', in L. Laing (ed.), *Studies in Celtic Survival*, Oxford, pp. 83–106

Scott, B. G. (ed.) (1974), *Perspectives in Irish Archaeology*, Dublin and Belfast
Simms, K. (1987), *From Kings to Warlords*, Woodbridge

Legal treatises and social order

Charles-Edwards, T. M. (1976), 'Boundaries in Irish law', in P. H. Sawyer (ed.),
  Medieval Settlement: Continuity and Change, London, pp. 83–7
Charles-Edwards, T. M. (1986), '*Críth Gablach* and the law of status', *Peritia* 5: 53–73
Charles-Edwards, T. M. (1993), *Early Irish and Welsh Kinship*, Oxford
Gerriets, M. (1981), 'The organization of exchange in early Christian Ireland', *Journal
  of Economic History* 41: 171–8
Gerriets, M. (1983), 'Economy and society: clientship according to the Irish laws',
  Cambridge Medieval Celtic Studies 6: 43–62
Kelly, F. (1988), *A Guide to Early Irish Law*, Dublin
Kelly, F. (1998), *Early Irish Farming*, Dublin
Ó Corráin, D. (1978), 'Women in early Irish history', in M. MacCurtain and D. Ó
  Corráin (eds.), *Women in Irish Society: The Historical Dimension*, Dublin, pp. 1–13
Ó Cróinín, D. (1995), *Early Medieval Ireland 400–1200*, London
Patterson, N. T. (1994), *Cattle-lords and Clansmen: The Social Structure of Early Ireland*,
  2nd edn, Notre Dame, IN

Kingship and political organization

MacNeill, E. J. (1911–12), 'Early Irish population groups', *Proceedings of the Royal Irish
  Academy* 29C: 59–114
Ó Corráin, D. (1971), 'Irish regnal succession: a reappraisal', *Studia Hibernica* 11: 7–39
Ó Corráin, D. (1975), 'Nationality and kingship in pre-Norman Ireland', *Historical
  Studies* (Irish Conference of Historians) 11: 1–35
Scott, B. G. (1970–3), '"Tribes" and "tribalism" in early Ireland', *Ogam* 22–5: 197–
  208
Simms, K. (1987), *From Kings to Warlords*, Woodbridge
Wailes, B. (1982), 'The Irish "royal sites" in history and archaeology', *Cambridge
  Medieval Celtic Studies* 3: 1–29
Warner, R. B. (1988), 'The archaeology of early historic Irish kingship', in S. T. Driscoll
  and M. R. Nieke (eds.), *Power and Politics in Early Medieval Britain and Ireland*,
  Edinburgh, pp. 47–68

The Irish Church

Bethell, D. (1969), 'English monks and Irish reform in the eleventh and twelfth
  centuries', *Historical Studies* (Irish Conference of Historians) 8: 111–35
Flanagan, M. T. (1989), *Irish Society, Anglo-Norman Settlers, Angevin Kingship*, Oxford
Gwynn, A. (1941), 'Papal legates in Ireland during the twelfth century', *Irish
  Ecclesiastical Record* 58: 361–70
Gwynn, A. (1945–6), 'The first Synod of Cashel', *Irish Ecclesiastical Record* 66: 81–92;
  67: 109–22

Gwynn, A. (1968), *The Twelfth-Century Reform*, Dublin
Henry, F. (1970), *Irish Art in the Romanesque Period 1020–1170*, London
Lawlor, H. J. (1922), 'A fresh authority for the Synod of Kells 1152', *Proceedings of the Royal Irish Academy* 36C: 16–22
Martin, F. X. (1975), *No Hero in the House* (O'Donnell Lecture 1975), Dublin
O'Doherty, J. F. (1933), 'Rome and the Anglo-Norman invasion of Ireland', *Irish Ecclesiastical Record* 42: 131–45
O'Doherty, J. F. (1937–8), 'Sir Laurence O'Toole and the Anglo-Norman invasion', *Irish Ecclesiastical Record* 50: 449–77, 600–25; 51: 131–46
Watt, J. A. (1970), *The Church and the Two Nations in Medieval Ireland*, Cambridge

The Anglo-French intervention in Ireland
General
Duffy, S. (1997), *Ireland in the Middle Ages*, Basingstoke
Flanagan, M. T. (1976–7), 'Hiberno-papal relations in the late twelfth century', *Archivium Hibernicum* 34: 55–70
Flanagan, M. T. (1989), *Irish Society, Anglo-Norman Settlers, Angevin Kingship*, Oxford
Gwynn, A. (1944), 'Papal legates in Ireland during the twelfth century', *Irish Ecclesiastical Record* 5th series 63: 361–70
Sheehy, M. (1975) *When the Normans came to Ireland*, Cork; 2nd edn, 1998
Warren, W. L. (1967), 'The interpretation of twelfth-century Irish history', *Historical Studies* (Irish Conference of Historians) 7: 1–19

Anglo-Norman and Angevin England
Flanagan, M. T. (1984), 'Strongbow, Henry II and Anglo-Norman intervention in Ireland', in J. Gillingham and J. C. Holt (eds.), *War and Government in the Middle Ages*, Woodbridge, pp. 62–77
Hudson, B. T. (1994–5), 'William the Conqueror and Ireland', *Irish Historical Studies* 29: 145–58
Kenney, J. F. (1929), *The Sources for the Early History of Ireland. Ecclesiastical*, New York; rev. imp. 1966
Philpott, M. (1997), 'Some interaction between the English and Irish churches', *ANS* 20: 187–204
Warren, W. L. (1973), *Henry II*, London

The Irish background
Curtis, E. (1921), 'Murchertach O'Brien, high king of Ireland, and his Norman son-in-law', *Journal of the Royal Society of Antiquaries of Ireland* 51: 116–24
Duffy, S. (1992), 'Irishmen and Islesmen in the kingdoms of Ireland and Man, 1052–1171', *Ériu* 43: 93–133
Martin, F. X. (1975), *No Hero in the House* (O'Donnell Lecture 1975), Dublin

The conquest
Duffy, S. (1997), 'Ireland's Hastings: the Anglo-Norman conquest of Dublin', *ANS* 20: 69–85

The views of the colonists
Bartlett, R. (1982), *Gerald of Wales, (1146–1223)*, Oxford
Gillingham, J. (1997), 'The travels of Roger Howden and his views of the Irish, Scots and Welsh', *ANS* 20: 151–69

The churches of Ireland after 1170
Mooney, C. (1969), *The Church in Gaelic Ireland, 13th–15th Centuries*, Dublin
Watt, J. A. (1970), *The Church and the Two Nations in Medieval Ireland*, Cambridge

The Irish after 1170
Flanagan, M. T. (1997), 'Strategies of lordship in pre-Norman and post-Norman Leinster', *ANS* 20: 107–26
Frame, R. (1981), *Colonial Ireland 1169–1369*, Dublin
Nicholls, K. W. (1972), *Gaelic and Gaelicised Ireland in the Later Middle Ages*, Dublin
O Neill, P., (1997), 'The impact of the Norman invasion on Irish literature', *ANS* 20: 171–85
Simms, K. (1987), *From Kings to Warlords*, Woodbridge

20 THE BYZANTINE EMPIRE, 1118–1204

Ahrweiler, H. and Laiou, A. E. (1998), *Studies on the Internal Diaspora of the Byzantine Empire*, Washington DC
Angold, M. (1995), *Church and Society under the Comneni, 1081–1261*, Cambridge
Angold, M. (1997), *The Byzantine Empire 1025–1204: A Political History*, 2nd edn, London
Angold, M. (1999), 'The state of research: the road to 1204: the Byzantine background to the Fourth Crusade', *JMH* 25: 257–78
Beaucamp, J. and Dagron, G. (1998), *La Transmission du patrimoine: Byzance et l'aire méditerranéenne*, Paris
Brand, C. M. (1968), *Byzantium Confronts the West, 1180–1204*, Cambridge, MA
Chalandon, F. (1912), *Les Comnène*, II: *Jean II Comnène (1118–1143) et Manuel I Comnène (1143–1180)*, 2 vols., Paris; repr. London, 1962
Cheynet, J.-C. (1990), *Pouvoir et contestations à Byzance (963–1210)*, Paris
Ciggaar, K. (1996), *Western Travellers to Constantinople: The West and Byzantium, 962–1204*, Leiden
Dagron, G. (1996), *Empereur et prêtre: étude sur le 'césaropapisme' byzantin*, Paris
Harvey, A. (1989), *Economic Expansion in the Byzantine Empire, 900–1200*, Cambridge
Hendy, M. F. (1985), *Studies in the Byzantine Monetary Economy, c.300–1450*, Cambridge
Jacoby, D. (1994), 'Italian privileges and trade in Byzantium before the Fourth Crusade: a reconsideration', *Anuario de Estudios Medievales* 24: 349–69; repr. in Jacoby (1997)
Jacoby, D. (1997), *Trade, Commodities and Shipping in the Medieval Mediterranean*, Aldershot
Kazhdan, A. P. and Epstein, A. W. (1985), *Change in Byzantine Culture in the Eleventh and Twelfth Centuries*, Berkeley, Los Angeles and London
Kazhdan, A. P. with Ronchey, S. (1997), *L'aristocrazia bizantina dal principio del XI allo fine de XII secolo*, Palermo

Laiou, A. E. and Simon, D. (eds.) (1994), *Law and Society in Byzantium, Ninth–Twelfth Centuries*, Washington DC

Lilie, R.-J. (1984), *Handel und Politik zwischen dem byzantinischen Reich und den italienischen Kommunen Venedig, Pisa, und Genoa in der Epoche der Komnenen und der Angeloi (1081–1204)*, Amsterdam

Lilie, R.-J. (1993), *Byzantium and the Crusader States, 1096–1204*, trans. J. C. Morris and E. Ridings, Oxford

Macrides, R. (2000), *Kinship and Justice in Byzantium, 11th–15th Centuries*, Aldershot

Magdalino, P. (1991), *Tradition and Transformation in Medieval Byzantium*, Aldershot

Magdalino, P. (1993), *The Empire of Manuel I Komnenos, 1143–1180*, Cambridge

Magdalino, P. (1996a), *Constantinople médiévale: études sur l'évolution des structures urbaines* (*TM* Monographies 9), Paris

Magdalino, P. (1996b), 'Eustathios and Thessalonica', in C. N. Constantinides, N. M. Panagiotakes, E. Jeffreys and A. D. Angelou (eds.), *ΦΙΛΕΛΛΗΝ: Studies in Honour of Robert Browning*, Venice, pp. 225–38

Magdalino, P. (ed.) (1994), *New Constantines: The Rhythm of Imperial Renewal in Byzantium, 4th–13th Centuries*, Aldershot

Maguire, H. (ed.) (1997), *Byzantine Court Culture, 829–1204*, Washington DC

Mango, C. and Dagron, G. (eds.) (1995), *Constantinople and its Hinterland*, Aldershot

Mullett, M. E. and Smythe, D. (1996), *Alexios I Komnenos, I: Papers* (Belfast Byzantine Texts and Translations 4.1), Belfast

Oikonomides, N. (1996), *Byzantium from the Ninth Century to the Fourth Crusade*, Aldershot

Oikonomides, N. (1996), *Fiscalité et exemption fiscale à Byzance (IXe–XIe s.)*, Athens

Ostrogorsky, G. (1968), *History of the Byzantine State*, trans. J. Hussey (Oxford)

Phillips, J. (1996), *Defenders of the Holy Land: Relations between the Latin East and the West, 1119–1187*, Oxford

Prinzing, G. and Salamon, M. (eds.) (1999), *Byzanz und Mitteleuropa 950–1453: Beiträge zu einer table-ronde des XIX International Congress of Byzantine Studies, Copenhagen 1996* (Mainzer Veröffentlichungen zur Byzantinistik 3), Wiesbaden

Shepard, J. and Franklin, S. (eds.) (1992), *Byzantine Diplomacy*, Aldershot

Stephenson, P. (1994), 'Manuel I Comnenus and Geza II: a revised context and chronology for Hungaro-Byzantine relations, 1148–1155', *BS* 55: 251–77

Stephenson, P. (1996), 'John Cinnamus, John II Comnenus and the Hungarian campaign of 1127–1129', *Byzantion* 66: 177–87

Stephenson, P. (1999), 'Political authority in Dalmatia during the reign of Manuel I Comnenus (1143–1180)', in G. Prinzing and M. Salamon (eds.), *Byzanz und Mitteleuropa 950–1453*, Wiesbaden, pp. 127–50

Tinnefeld, F. (1995), 'Byzanz und die Herrscher des Hauses Hohenstaufen (1138–1259)', *Archiv für Diplomatik* 41: 105–27

Tsiknakis, K. (ed.) (1997), *Byzantium at War (9th–12th c.)*, Athens

Whittow, M. (1995), 'Rural fortifications in western Europe and Byzantium: tenth to twelfth centuries', *BF* 21: 57–74

21 THE LATIN EAST, 1098–1204

Amouroux-Mourad, M. (1988), *Le Comté d'Edesse 1098–1150* (Bibliothèque Archéologique et Historique 128), Paris

Antweiler, W. (1991), *Das Bistum Tripolis im 12. und 13. Jahrhundert: Personengeschichtliche und strukturelle Probleme* (Studia Humaniora 20), Dusseldorf

Arnold, U. (1978), 'Jerusalem und Akkon: zur Frage von Kontinuität oder Neügrundung des Deutschen Ordens 1190', *MIÖG* 86: 416–32

Arnold, U. (1980), 'Entstehung und Frühzeit des Deutschen Ordens: zu Gründung und innerer Struktur des Deutschen Hospitals von Akkon und des Ritterordens in der ersten Hälfte des 13. Jahrhunderts', in J. Fleckenstein and M. Hellman (eds.), *Die geistlichen Ritterorden Europas* (Vorträge und Forschungen 26), Sigmaringen, pp. 81–107

Asbridge, T. (2000), *The Creation of the Principality of Antioch, 1098–1130*, Woodbridge

Balard, M., Kedar, B. Z., Riley-Smith, J. (eds.) (2001), *Dei gesta per Francos: études sur les croisades dédiées à Jean Richard*, Aldershot

Baldwin, M. W. (1936), *Raymond III of Tripolis and the Fall of Jerusalem (1140–1187)*, Princeton; repr. New York, 1978

Barasch, M. (1971), *Crusader Figural Sculpture in the Holy Land: Twelfth Century Examples from Acre, Nazareth and Belvoir Castle*, Ramat Gan

Barber, M. (1994), *The New Knighthood: A History of the Order of the Temple*, Cambridge

Beyer, G. (1936), 'Das Gebiet der Kreuzfahrerherrschaft Caesarea in Palästina siedlungs- und territorial-geschichtlich untersucht', *ZDPV* 59: 1–91

Beyer, G. (1940), 'Neapolis (Nablus) und sein Gebiet in der Kreuzfahrerzeit: eine topographische und historisch-geographische Studie', *ZDPV* 63: 155–209

Beyer, G. (1942), 'Die Kreuzfahrer gebiete von Jerusalem und S. Abraham (Hebron)', *ZDPV* 65: 165–211

Beyer, G. (1944–5), 'Die Kreuzfahrergebiete Akko und Galilaea', *ZDPV* 67: 183–260

Beyer, G. (1946–51), 'Die Kreuzfahrergebiete Südwestpalästinas', *Beiträge zur biblischen Landes- und Altertumskunde (hervorgegangen aus der ZDPV)* 68: 148–92, 249–81

Bieberstein, K. and Bloedhorn, H. (1994), *Jerusalem: Grundzuge der Baugeschichte vom Chalkolithikum bis zur Frühzeit der osmanischen Herrschaft* (Beihefte zum Tübinger Atlas des Vorderen Orients, Reihe B, Nr. 100, 1–3), 3 vols., Wiesbaden

Boas, A. J. (1999), *Crusader Archaeology: The Material Culture of the Latin East*, London

Brand, C. M. (1968), *Byzantium Confronts the West, 1180–1204*, Cambridge, MA

Brincken, A. D. von den (1973), *Die 'Nationes Christianorum orientalium' im Verständnis der lateinischen Historiographie von der Mitte des 12. bis in die zweite Hälfte des 14. Jahrhunderts* (Kölner Historische Abhandlungen 22), Cologne and Vienna

Buchthal, H. (1957), *Miniature Painting in the Latin Kingdom of Jerusalem, with Liturgical and Palaeographical Chapters by Francis Wormald*, Oxford

Bulst-Thiele, M. L. (1974), *Sacrae domus militiae Templi Hierosolymitani magistri: Untersuchungen zur Geschichte des Templerordens 1118/19–1314* (Abhandlungen der Akademie der Wissenschaften in Göttingen, phil.-hist. klasse, 3rd series, 86), Göttingen

Buschhausen, H. (1978), *Die süditalienische Bauplastik im Königreich Jerusalem von König Wilhelm II. bis Kaiser Friedrich II* (Österreichische Akademie der Wissenschaften, phil.-hist. klasse, Denkschriften 108), Vienna

Cahen, C. (1940), *La Syrie du Nord à l'époque des croisades et la principauté franque d'Antioche* (Institut Français de Damas, Bibliothèque Orientale 1), Paris

Cahen, C. (1950–1), 'Notes sur l'histoire des croisades et de l'Orient latin: 2. Le régime rural syrien au temps de la domination franque', *Bulletin de la Faculté des Lettres de l'Université de Strasbourg* 29: 286–310

Chalandon, F. (1900–12), *Les Comnène: étude sur l'empire byzantin au XIe et au XIIe siècles* (Mémoires et Documents Publiés par la Société de l'Ecole des Chartes 4), 2 vols., Paris; repr. New York, 1960

Deschamps, P. (1934–73), *Les Châteaux des croisés en Terre Sainte, I: Le Crac des Chevaliers; II: La Défense du royaume de Jérusalem; III: La Défense du Comté de Tripoli et de la principauté d'Antioche* (Bibliothèque Archéologique et Historique 19, 34, 90), 3 vols., and 3 albums of plates, Paris

Dijkstra, C. T. J. (1995), *La Chanson de croisade: étude thématique d'un genre hybride*, Amsterdam

Duparc-Quioc, S. (1955), *Le Cycle de la croisade*, Paris

Dussaud, R. (1927), *Topographie historique de la Syrie antique et médiévale* (Bibliothéque Archéologique et Historique 4), Paris

Eck, T. (2000), *Die Kreuzfahrerbistümer Beirut und Sidon im 12. und 13. Jahrhundert auf prosopographischer Grundlage* (Kieler Werkstucke, Reihe C, Band 3), Frankfurt am Main

Edbury, P. W. (1977), 'Feudal obligations in the Latin east', *Byzantion* 47: 328–56

Edbury, P. W. (1993), 'Propaganda and faction in the kingdom of Jerusalem: the background to Hattin', in M. Shatzmiller (ed.), *Crusaders and Muslims in Twelfth-Century Syria* (The Medieval Mediterranean 1), Leiden, pp. 173–89

Edbury, P. W. (1995), 'Law and custom in the Latin east: les letres dou sepulcre', in B. Arbel (ed.), *Intercultural Contacts in the Medieval Mediterranean: Studies in Honour of David Jacoby* (Mediterranean Historical Review 10), pp. 71–9

Edbury, P. W. (ed.) (1985), *Crusade and Settlement*, Cardiff

Eddé, A. M. (1999), *La Principauté ayyoubide d'Alep (579/1183–658/1260)* (Freiburger Islamstudien 21), Stuttgart

Elisséeff, N. (1967), *Nur ad-Din: un grand prince musulman de Syrie au temps des croisades (511–569 H./1118–1174)* (Institut Français de Damas), 3 vols., Damascus

Ellenblum, R. (1998), *Frankish Rural Settlement in the Latin Kingdom of Jerusalem*, Cambridge

Enlart, C. (1925–28), *Les Monuments des croisés dans le royaume de Jérusalem: architecture religieuse et civile* (Bibliothéque Archèologique et Historique 7–8), 2 vols. and 2 albums, Paris

Favreau, M. L. (1974), *Studien zur Frühgeschichte des Deutschen Ordens* (Kieler Historische Studien 21), Stuttgart

Favreau, M. L. (1977), 'Die Kreuzfahrerherrschaft "Scandalion" (Iskanderune)', *ZDPV* 93: 12–29

Favreau-Lilie, M. L. (1989), *Die Italiener im Heiligen Land vom ersten Kreuzzug bis zum Tode Heinrichs von Champagne (1098–1197)*, Amsterdam

Fleckenstein, J. and Hellmann, M. (eds.) (1980), *Die geistlichen Ritterorden Europas* (Vorträge und Forschungen 26), Sigmaringen

Folda, J. (1976), *Crusader Manuscript Illumination at Saint Jean d'Acre, 1275–1291*, Princeton

Folda, J. (1995), *The Art of the Crusaders in the Holy Land, 1098–1187*, Cambridge

Forstreuter, K. (1967), *Der Deutsche Orden am Mittelmeer* (Quellen und Studien zur Geschichte des Deutschen Ordens 2), Bonn

Gennes, J. P. de (1995), *Les Chevaliers du Saint-Sépulcre de Jérusalem: essai critique*, 1, n.p.

Grousset, R. (1934–6), *Histoire des croisades et du royaume franc de Jérusalem*, 3 vols., Paris

Hamilton, B. (1978a), 'The Elephant of Christ: Reynald of Châtillon', *Studies in Church History* 15: 97–108

Hamilton, B. (1978b), 'Women in the crusader states: the queens of Jerusalem (1100–1190)', in D. Baker (ed.), *Medieval Women: Dedicated and Presented to Rosalind M. T. Hill on the Occasion of her Seventieth Birthday* (Studies in Church History Subsidia 1), Oxford, pp. 143–74

Hamilton, B. (1980), *The Latin Church in the Crusader States: The Secular Church*, London

Hamilton, B. (1999), *Crusaders, Cathars and the Holy Places* (Collected Studies Series 656), Aldershot

Hamilton, B. (2000), *The Leper King and his Heirs: Baldwin IV and the Crusader Kingdom of Jerusalem*, Cambridge

Hartmann, A. (1975), *An-Nasir li-Din Allah (1180–1225): Politik, Religion, Kultur in der spaten 'Abbasidenzeit* (Studien zur Sprache, Geschichte und Kultur des Islamischen Orients. Beihefte zur Zeitschrift "Der Islam", Neue Folge 8), Berlin

Hatem, A. (1932), *Les Poèmes épiques des croisades: genèse, historicité, localisation: essai sur l'activité littéraire dans les colonies franques de Syrie au moyen âge*, Paris

Hellenkemper, H. (1976), *Burgen der Kreuzritterzeit in der Grafschaft Edessa und im Königreich Kleinarmenien* (Geographica Historica 1), Bonn

Heyd, W. (1879), *Geschichte des Levantehandels im Mittelalter*, 2 vols., Stuttgart; trans. F. Raynaud, *Histoire du commerce du Levant au moyen âge*, 2 vols., Leipzig (1885–6); repr. Leipzig, 1936, and Amsterdam, 1959

Hiestand, R. (1978), 'Zum Leben und zur Laufbahn Wilhelms von Tyrus', *DA* 34: 345–80

Hiestand, R. (1980), 'Die Anfänge der Johanniter', in J. Fleckenstein and M. Hellmann (eds.), *Die geistlichen Ritterorden Europas* (Vorträge und Forschungen 26), Sigmaringen, pp. 31–80

Hiestand, R. (1988a), 'Die Integration der Maroniten in die römische Kirche: zum ältesten Zeugnis der päpstlichen Kanzlei', *Orientalia Christiana Periodica* 54: 119–52

Hiestand, R. (1988b), 'Kardinal-bischof Matthaus von Albano, das Konzil von Troyes und die Entstehung des Templerordens', *Zeitschrift für Kirchengeschichte* 99: 295–325

Hiestand, R. (1997), 'Die Herren von Sidon und die Thronfolgekrise des Jahres 1163', in B. Z. Kedar, J. Riley-Smith and R. Hiestand (eds.), *Montjoie: Studies in Crusade History in Honour of Hans Eberhard Mayer*, Aldershot, pp. 77–90

Hillenbrand, C. (1990), *A Muslim Principality in Crusader Times: The Early Artuqid State* (Uitgaven van het Nederlands Historisch-Archaeologisch Instituut te Istanbul 66), Leiden

Hoch, M. (1993), *Jerusalem, Damaskus und der Zweite Kreuzzug: Konstitutionelle Krise und äußere Sicherheit des Kreuzfahrerkönigreiches Jerusalem AD 1126–1154* (Europäische Hochschulschriften, Reihe 3, Band 560), Frankfurt am Main

Hodgson, M. G. S. (1955), *The Order of the Assassins: The Struggle of the Early Nizârî Isma'ilis against the Islamic World*, The Hague; repr. New York, 1980

Hotzelt, W. (1940), *Kirchengeschichte Palästinas im Zeitalter der Kreuzzüge 1099–1291*, Cologne

Humphreys, R. S. (1977), *From Saladin to the Mongols: The Ayyubids of Damascus, 1193–1260*, Albany

Huygens, R. B. C. (1964), *Latijn in 'Outremer': een blik op de Latijnse letterkunde der Kruisvaarderstaten in het Nabije Oosten*, Leiden

Jacoby, D. (1993), 'Conrad, marquis of Montferrat and the kingdom of Jerusalem (1187–1192)', in L. Balletto, *Atti del congresso internazionale 'Dai feudi monferrini e dal Piemonte ai nuovi mondi oltre gli Oceani'*, Alessandria, pp. 187–238

Jacoby, D. (1997), 'The Venetian privileges in the Latin kingdom of Jerusalem: twelfth and thirteenth century interpretations and implementations', in B. Z. Kedar, J. Riley-Smith and R. Hiestand (eds.), *Montjoie: Studies in Crusade History in Honour of Hans Eberhard Mayer*, Aldershot, pp. 155–75

Jankrift, K. P. (1996), *Leprose als Streiter Gottes: Institutionalisierung und Organisation des Ordens vom Heiligen Lazarus zu Jerusalem von seinen Anfängen bis zum Jahre 1350* (Vita Regularis 4), Münster

Jotischky, A. (1995), *The Perfection of Solitude: Hermits and Monks in the Crusader States*, University Park, PA

Kedar, B. Z. (1974), 'The general tax of 1183 in the crusading kingdom of Jerusalem: innovation or adaptation?', *EHR* 89: 339–45

Kedar, B. Z. (1982), 'The Patriarch Eraclius', in B. Z. Kedar, H. E. Mayer and R. C. Smail (eds.), *Outremer: Studies in the History of the Crusading Kingdom of Jerusalem Presented to Joshua Prawer*, Jerusalem, pp. 177–204

Kedar, B. Z. (1983), 'Gerard of Nazareth: a neglected twelfth-century writer in the Latin east', *DOP* 37: 55–77

Kedar, B. Z. (1984), *Crusade and Mission: European Approaches toward the Muslims*, Princeton

Kedar, B. Z. (1989), '[The Samaritans in] the Frankish Period', in A. D. Crown (ed.), *The Samaritans*, Tübingen, pp. 82–94

Kedar, B. Z. (1990), 'The subjected Muslims of the Frankish Levant', in J. M. Powell (ed.), *Muslims under Latin Rule, 1100–1300*, Princeton, pp. 135–74

Kedar, B. Z., Mayer, H. E. and Smail, R. C. (eds.) (1982), *Outremer: Studies in the History of the Crusading Kingdom of Jerusalem Presented to Joshua Prawer*, Jerusalem

Kirstein, K. P. (2002), *Die lateinischen Patriarchen von Jerusalem von der Eroberung der Heiligen Stadt durch die Kreuzfahrer 1099 bis zum Ende der Kreuzfahrerstaaten 1291* (ends, however, in 1214) (Berliner Historische Studien 35 = Ordensstudien 16), Berlin

Köhler, M. (1991), *Allianzen und Verträge zwischen fränkischen und islamischen Herrschern im Vorderen Orient* (Studien zur Sprache, Geschichte und Kultur des Islamischen Orients, Neue Folge 12), Berlin

Kühnel, G. (1988), *Wall Painting in the Latin Kingdom of Jerusalem* (Frankfurter Forschungen zur Kunst 14), Berlin

La Monte, J. L. (1932), *Feudal Monarchy in the Latin Kingdom of Jerusalem, 1100 to 1291* (Mediaeval Academy of America Monographs 4), Cambridge, MA.

La Monte, J. L. (1938a), 'The rise and decline of a Frankish seigneury in Syria in the time of the crusades', *Revue Historique du Sud-Est Européen* 15:301–22

La Monte, J. L. (1938b), 'The viscounts of Naplouse in the twelfth century', *Syria* 19: 272–8

La Monte, J. L. (1942), 'The lords of Le Puiset on the crusades', *Speculum* 17: 100–18

La Monte, J. L. (1944–5), 'The lords of Sidon in the twelfth and thirteenth centuries', *Byzantion* 17: 183–211

La Monte, J. L. (1947), 'The lords of Caesarea in the period of the crusades', *Speculum* 22: 145–61

Lawrence, T. E. (1988), *Crusader Castles*, new edn by D. Pringle, Oxford

Lewis, B. (1968), *The Assassins: A Radical Sect in Islam*, New York

Lilie, R. J. (1993), *Byzantium and the Crusader States 1096–1204*, trans. J. C. Morris and J. E. Ridings, Oxford

Lyons, M. C. and Jackson, D. E. P. (1982), *Saladin: The Politics of the Holy War* (University of Cambridge Oriental Publications 30), Cambridge

Magdalino, P. (1993), *The Empire of Manuel I Komnenos 1143–1180*, Cambridge

Mayer, H. E. (1968), 'On the beginnings of the communal movement in the Holy Land: the commune of Tyre', *Traditio* 24: 443–57

Mayer, H. E. (1972a), 'Kaiserrecht und Heiliges Land', in H. Fuhrmann, H. E. Mayer and K. Wriedt (eds.), *Aus Reichsgeschichte und Nordischer Geschichte* (Kieler Historische Studien 16), Stuttgart, pp. 193–208

Mayer, H. E. (1972b), 'Studies in the history of Queen Melisende of Jerusalem', *DOP* 26: 93–182

Mayer, H. E. (1977), *Bistümer, Klöster und Stifte im Königreich Jerusalem* (*MGH* Schriften 26), Stuttgart

Mayer, H. E. (1978a), 'Latins, Muslims and Greeks in the Latin kingdom of Jerusalem', *History* 63: 175–92

Mayer, H. E. (1978b), *Das Siegelwesen in den Kreuzfahrerstaaten* (Bayerische Akademie der Wissenschaften, phil.-hist. klasse, Abhandlungen n.s. 83), Munich

Mayer, H. E. (1980a), 'Ein Deperditum König Balduins III. von Jerusalem als Zeugnis seiner Pläne zur Eroberung Ägyptens', *DA* 36: 549–66

Mayer, H. E. (1980b), 'Jérusalem et Antioche au temps de Baudouin II', *Académie des Inscriptions et Belles-Lettres: Comptes Rendus*, pp. 717–34

Mayer, H. E. (1980c), 'Die Seigneurie de Joscelin und der Deutschen Orde', in J. Fleckenstein and M. Hellmann (eds.), *Die geistlichen Ritterorden Europas* (Vorträge und Forschungen 26), Sigmaringen, pp. 171–216

Mayer, H. E. (1982a), 'Carving up crusaders: the early Ibelins and Ramla', in B. Z. Kedar, H. E. Mayer and R. C. Smail (eds.), *Outremer: Studies in the History of the Crusading Kingdom of Jerusalem Presented to Joshua Prawer*, Jerusalem, pp. 101–18

Mayer, H. E. (1982b), 'The Concordat of Nablus', *JEH* 33: 531–43

Mayer, H. E. (1984), *Mélanges sur l'histoire du royaume latin de Jérusalem* (Mémoires de l'Académie des Inscriptions et Belles-Lettres n.s. 5), Paris

Mayer, H. E. (1985a), 'Die Herrschaftsbildung in Hebron', *ZDPV* 101: 64–81

Mayer, H. E. (1985b), 'The origins of the county of Jaffa', *Israel Exploration Journal* 35: 35–45

Mayer, H. E. (1985c), 'The origins of the lordships of Ramla and Lydda in the kingdom of Jerusalem', *Speculum* 60: 537–52

Mayer, H. E. (1985d), 'The succession to Baldwin II of Jerusalem: English impact on the east', *DOP* 39: 139–47

Mayer, H. E. (1985–6), 'Guillaume de Tyr à l'école', *Mémoires de l'Académie des Sciences, Arts et Belles-Lettres de Dijon* 127: 257–65 (published 1988)

Mayer, H. E. (1988a), *The Crusades*, trans. J. Gillingham, 2nd edn., Oxford; 9th edn. of German version, with updated notes and bibliography, as *Geschichte der Kreuzzüge*, Stuttgart, 2000

Mayer, H. E. (1988b), 'Die Hofkapelle der Könige von Jerusalem', *DA* 44: 489–509

Mayer, H. E. (1988c), 'Die Legitimität Balduins IV. von Jerusalem und das Testament der Agnes von Courtenay', *Historisches Jahrbuch* 108: 63–89

Mayer, H. E. (1990a), *Die Kreuzfahrerherrschaft Montréal (Šōbak): Jordanien im 12. Jahrhundert* (Abhandlungen des Deutschen Palästina-Vereins 14), Wiesbaden

Mayer, H. E. (1990b), 'The wheel of fortune: seignorial vicissitudes under Kings Fulk and Baldwin III of Jerusalem', *Speculum* 65: 860–77

Mayer, H. E. (1991), 'Fontevrault und Bethanien: Kirchliches Leben in Anjou und Jerusalem im 12. Jahrhundert', *Zeitschrift für Kirchengeschichte* 102: 14–44

Mayer, H. E. (1992), 'The beginnings of King Amalric of Jerusalem', in B. Z. Kedar (ed.), *The Horns of Hattin*, Jerusalem and London, pp. 121–35

Mayer, H. E. (1993), *Varia Antiochena: Studien zum Kreuzfahrerkürstentum Antiochia im 12. und frühen 13. Jahrhundert (MGH Studien und Texte* 6), Hanover

Mayer, H. E. (1994), 'The crusader principality of Galilee between Saint-Omer and Bures-sur-Yvette', in R. Curiel and R. Gyselen (eds.), *Itinéraires d'Orient: hommages à Claude Cahen* (Res Orientales 6), Bures-sur-Yvette, pp. 157–67

Mayer, H. E. (1995), 'Herrschaft und Verwaltung im Kreuzfahrerkönigreich Jerusalem', *HZ* 261: 695–738

Mayer, H. E. (1996), *Die Kanzlei der lateinischen Könige von Jerusalem (MGH Schriften* 40), 2 vols., Hanover

Mayer, H. E. (2001), 'Die Register der Secrète des Königreichs Jerusalem', *DA* 57: 165–70

Melville, M. (1974), *La Vie des Templiers*, 2nd edn, Paris

Metcalf, D. M. (1995), *Coinage of the Crusades and the Latin East in the Ashmolean Museum, Oxford*, 2nd edn, London

Mouton, J. M. (1994), *Damas et sa principauté sous les Saljoukkides et les Bourides (468–549/1076–1154): Vie politique et religieuse* (Institut Français d'Archéologie Orientale. Textes Arabes et Etudes Islamiques 33), Cairo

Murray, A. V. (1998), 'Daimbert of Pisa, the Domus Godefridi and the accession of Baldwin I of Jerusalem', in A. V. Murray (ed.), *From Clermont to Jerusalem: The Crusades and Crusader Societies 1095–1500*, Turnhout, pp. 81–102

Murray, A. V. (2000), *The Crusader Kingdom of Jerusalem: A Dynastic History 1099–1125*, Oxford

Nicholson, R. L. (1940), *Tancred: A Study of His Career and Work*, Chicago; repr. New York, 1978

Nicholson, R. L. (1954), *Joscelin I, Prince of Edessa* (Illinois Studies in the Social Sciences 34–4), Urbana; repr. New York, 1983

Pahlitzsch, J. (2000), *Graeci und Suriani im Pälastina der Kreuzfahrerzeit: Beiträge und Quellen zur Geschichte des griechisch-orthodoxen Patriarchats von Jerusalem* (Berliner Historische Studien 33 = Ordensstudien 15), Berlin

Palmer, A. (1991–2), 'The history of the Syrian Orthodox in Jerusalem', *Oriens Christianus* 75: 16–43; 76: 74–94

Phillips, J. (1996), *Defenders of the Holy Land: Relations between the Latin East and the West, 1119–1187*, Oxford

Prawer, J. (1969–70), *Histoire du royaume latin de Jérusalem*, 2 vols., Paris; 2nd edn, 1975

Prawer, J. (1980), *Crusader Institutions*, Oxford

Prawer, J. (1988), *The History of the Jews in the Latin Kingdom of Jerusalem*, Oxford

Pringle, D. (1993–8), *The Churches of the Crusader Kingdom of Jerusalem: A Corpus*, 2 vols. so far, of 3, Cambridge

Pringle, D. (1997), 'The castle and lordship of Mirabel', in B. Z. Kedar, J. Riley-Smith and R. Hiestand (eds.), *Montjoie: Studies in Crusade History in Honour of Hans Eberhard Mayer*, Aldershot, pp. 91–112

Pringle, D. (2000), *Fortification and Settlement in Crusader Palestin* (Collected Studies Series 675), Aldershot

Prutz, H. (1883) *Kulturgeschichte der Kreuzzüge*, Berlin; repr. Hildesheim, 1964

Prutz, H. (1908), *Die geistlichen Ritterorden: ihre Stellung zur kirchlichen, politischen, gesellschaftlichen und wirtschaftlichen Entwicklung des Mittelalters*, Berlin

Pryor, J. H. (1988), *Geography, Technology and War: Studies in the Maritime History of the Mediterranean, 649–1571*, Cambridge

Rey, E. G. (ed.) (1869), *Les Familles d'Outre-Mer de Du Cange* (Collection de Documents Inédits sur l'Histoire de France), Paris

Rheinheimer, M. (1990), *Das Kreuzfahrerfürstentum Galiläa* (Kieler Werkstücke, Reihe C, Band 1), Frankfurt am Main

Richard, J. (1945), *Le Comté de Tripoli sous la dynastie toulousaine (1102–1187)* (Bibliothèque Archéologique et Historique 39), Paris; repr. New York, 1980

Richard, J. (1976), *Orient et Occident au moyen âge: contacts et relations (XIIe–XVe s.)* (Collected Studies Series 49), London

Richard, J. (1977), *Les Relations entre l'Orient et l'Occident au moyen âge* (Collected Studies Series 69), London

Richard, J. (1979), *The Latin Kingdom of Jerusalem*, trans. J. Shirley (Europe in the Middle Ages Selected Studies, vols. 11A and 11B), Amsterdam

Richard, J. (1983), *Croisés, missionaires et voyageurs. Les perspectives orientales du monde latin médiévale* (Collected Studies Series 182), London

Richard, J. (1989), 'Aux origines d'un grand lignage: des Palladii à Renaud de Châtillon', in *Media in Francia... recueil de mélanges offert a Karl Ferdinand Werner à l'occasion de son 65e anniversaire par ses amis et collègues français*, Maulévrier, pp. 409–18

Richard, J. (1992), *Croisades et états latins d'Orient: points de vue et documents* (Collected Studies Series 383), Aldershot

Riley-Smith, J. (1967), *The Knights of St John in Jerusalem and Cyprus c.1050–1310* (A History of the Order of the Hospital of St John of Jerusalem 1), London and New York

Riley-Smith, J. (1971a), 'The assise sur la Ligèce and the commune of Acre', *Traditio* 27:179–204

Riley-Smith, J. (1971b), 'A note on confraternities in the Latin kingdom of Jerusalem', *BIHR* 44: 301–8

Riley-Smith, J. (1972), 'Some lesser officials in Latin Syria', *EHR* 87: 1–26

Riley-Smith, J. (1973), *The Feudal Nobility and the Kingdom of Jerusalem, 1174–1277*, London

Riley-Smith, J. (1978), 'Peace never established: the case of the kingdom of Jerusalem', *TRHS* 5th series 28: 87–102

Riley-Smith, J. (1983), 'The motives of the earliest crusaders and the settlement of Latin Palestine', *EHR* 98: 721–36

Riley-Smith, J. (1985), 'Further thoughts on Baldwin II's établissement on the confiscation of fiefs', in P. W. Edbury (ed.), *Crusade and Settlement*, Cardiff, pp. 176–80

Röhricht, R. (1898), *Geschichte des Königreichs Jerusalem (1100–1291)*, Innsbruck; repr. Amsterdam, 1967

Röhricht, R. (ed.) (1893–1904), *Regesta regni Hierosolymitani, 1097–1291* and *Additamentum*, Innsbruck; repr. New York, 1960

Rowe, J. G. (1957), 'Paschal II and the relation between the spiritual and temporal powers in the kingdom of Jerusalem', *Speculum* 32: 470–501

Rowe, J. G. (1960), 'The papacy and the ecclesiastical province of Tyre (1100–1187)', *Bulletin of the John Rylands Library* 43: 160–89

Runciman, S. (1951–2), *A History of the Crusades*, I and II, Cambridge

Schaube, A. (1906), *Handelgeschichte der romanischen Volker des Mittelmeergebiets bis zum Ende der Kreuzzüge* (Handbuch der Mittelalterlichen und Neueren Geschichte, Sect. 3, 5), Munich and Berlin

Schlumberger, G., Chalandon, F. and Blanchet, A. (1943), *Sigillographie de l'Orient latin* (Bibliothèque Archéologique et Historique 37), Paris

Setton, K. M. (gen. ed.) (1955), *A History of the Crusades*, I, *The First Hundred Years*, ed. M. W. Baldwin, Philadelphia; revised edn Madison, 1969

Smail, R. C. (1956), *Crusading Warfare, 1097–1193* (Cambridge Studies in Medieval Life and Thought n.s. 3), Cambridge

Smail, R. C. (1969), 'Latin Syria and the west, 1149–1187', *TRHS* 5th series 19: 1–20

Spreckelmeyer, G. (1974), *Das Kreuzzugslied des lateinischen Mittelalters* (Munstersche Mittelalter Schriften 21), Munich

Stevenson, W. B. (1907), *The Crusaders in the East*, Cambridge

Ter-Grigorian Iskenderian, G. (1915), *Die Kreuzfahrer und ihre Beziehungen zu den armenischen Nachbarfürsten bis zum Untergange der Grafschaft Edessa* (Diss., Leipzig), Weida

Tibble, S. (1989), *Monarchy and Lordships in the Latin Kingdom of Jerusalem 1099–1291*, Oxford

Tischler, C. (2000), *Die Burgenses von Jerusalem im 12. Jahrhundert: eine Prosopographie über die nichtadligen Einwohner Jerusalems von 1120 bis 1187* (Studien und Quellen zur Geschichte der Kreuzzüge und des Papsttums 1), Frankfurt am Main

Tumler, M. (1955), *Der Deutsche Orden im Werden, Wachsen und Wirken bis 1400*, Montreal and Vienna

Vincent, L. H. and Abel, F. M. (1912–26), *Jérusalem: recherches de topographie, d'archéologie et d'histoire*, 2 vols. in 4, Paris

Vogtherr, T. (1994), 'Die Regierungsdaten der lateinischen Könige von Jerusalem', *ZDPV* 110: 51–81

Vogüé, C. J. M. de (1860), *Les Eglises de la Terre Sainte*, Paris

Wentzlaff-Eggebert, F. (1960), *Kreuzzugsdichtung des Mittelalters: Studien zu ihrer geschichtlichen und dichterischen Wirklichkeit*, Berlin

Yewdale, R. B. (1924), *Bohemond I, Prince of Antioch*, Princeton; repr. New York, 1980

22 'ABBASIDS, FATIMIDS AND SELJUQS

Al-Duri, A. A. (1969), 'The origins of Iqta' in Islam', *Al-Abhāth* 22: 3–22

Amari, M. (1937–9), *Storia dei Musulmani di Sicilia*, 2nd revised edn by C. A. Nallino, 2 vols., Catania

Ashtor, E. (1972), 'Un mouvement migratoire au haut moyen âge: migration de l'Irak vers les pays mediterranéens', *Annales ESC* 27: 185–214; repr. in E. Ashtor, *The Medieval Near East: Social and Economic History*, London, 1978

Assaad, S. (1974), *The Reign of al-Hākim bi Amr Allah (386/996–411/1021): A Political Study*, Beirut

Bianquis, T. (1978), 'Al-Hākim bi Amr Allah', in C.-A. Julien *et al.* (eds.), *Les Africains*, XI, Paris, pp. 103–33

Bianquis, T. (1980), 'Une crise frumentaire dans l'Egypte fatimide', *Journal of Economic and Social History of the Orient* 22: 67–101

Bianquis, T. (1986), *Damas et la Syrie sous la domination fatimide (359–468/969–1076)*, Damascus

Bianquis, T. (1992), 'Le fonctionnement des dīwān financiers d'après al-Musabbihi', *Annales Islamologiques* 26: 47–61

Bosworth, C. E. (1962), 'The imperial policy of the early Ghaznavids', *Islamic Studies* 1: 49–82

Bosworth, C. E. (1963), *The Ghaznavids: Their empire in Afghanistan and Eastern Iran*, Edinburgh

Bosworth, C. E. (1967), *The Islamic Dynasties*, Edinburgh

Bosworth, C. E. (1968), 'The political and dynastic history of the Iranian world (AD 1000–1217)', *Cambridge History of Iran*, IV Cambridge, pp. 1–202

Bosworth, C. E. (1975), 'The early Ghaznavids', *Cambridge History of Iran*, IV, pp. 162–97

Braudel, F. (1972), *The Mediterranean and the Mediterranean World in the Age of Philip II*, 2 vols., London

Brett, M. (1969), 'Ifriqiya as a market for Saharan trade, from the tenth to the twelfth century AD', *Journal of African History* 10: 347–64

Brett, M. (1974–5), 'The Zughba at Tripoli, 429H (1037–8)', *Society for Libyan Studies, Sixth Annual Report*, pp. 41–7

Brett, M. (1982), 'Fatimid historiography: a case study – the quarrel with the Zirids, 1048–58', in D. O. Morgan (ed.), *Medieval Historical Writing in the Christian and Islamic Worlds*, London, pp. 47–59

Brett, M. (1983), 'Islam and trade in the Bilād al-Sūdān, tenth–eleventh century AD', *Journal of African History* 24: 431–40

Brett, M. (1984), 'The way of the peasant', *BSOAS* 47: 44–56

Brett, M. (1994a), 'The Mim, the ʿAyn, and the making of Ismāʿilism', *BSOAS* 57: 27–39

Brett, M. (1994b), 'The unification of North Africa by Islam in the seventh to thirteenth centuries', *Morocco: Occasional Papers* 1: 3–12

Brett, M. (1995a), 'The origins of the Mamluk military system in the Fatimid period', in U. Vermeulen (ed.), *Egypt and Syria in the Fatimid, Ayyubid and Mamluk Eras* (Orientalia Lovaniensia 73), Leuven, pp. 39–52

Brett, M. (1995b), 'The battles of Ramla, 1099–1105', in U. Vermeulen (ed.), *Egypt and Syria in the Fatimid, Ayyubid and Mamluk Eras* (Orientalia Lovaniensia 73), Leuven, pp. 17–37

Brett, M. (2001), *The Rise of the Fatimids: The World of the Mediterranean and the Middle East in the Fourth Century AH, tenth century CE*, Leiden

Brett, M. and Fentress, L. (1995), *The Berbers*, Oxford

Bryer, D. (1975–6), 'The origin of the Druze religion', *Der Islam* 52: 47–84, 239–62; 53: 5–27

Cahen, C. (1953), 'L'évolution de l'iqtaʿ du XIe au XIIIe siècle', *Annales ESC* 8: 25–52; repr. in C. Cahen, *Les Peuples musulmans dans l'histoire médiévale*, Damascus, 1977, pp. 231–69

Cahen, C. (1971), 'Ikṭāʿ', *Encyclopaedia of Islam*, 2nd edn, III, pp. 1088–91

Cahen, C. (1974), *Turcobyzantina et Oriens Christianus*, London

The Cambridge History of Africa (1978), II, ed. J. D. Fage, Cambridge

The Cambridge History of Iran (1968), V, ed. J. A. Boyle, Cambridge

The Cambridge History of Iran (1975), IV, ed. R. N. Frye, Cambridge

Canard, M. (1951), 'Le cérémonial fatimite et le cérémonial byzantin: essai de comparaison', *Byzantion* 21: 355–420; repr. in M. Canard, *Byzance et les musulmans du Proche-Orient*, London, 1973

Canard, M. (1952), 'La procession du Nouvel An chez les Fatimides', *Annales de l'Institut des Etudes Orientales*, Algiers, 10: 364–98; repr. in M. Canard, *Miscellanea Orientalia*, London, 1973

Canard, M. (1958), 'Al-Basāsirī', in *Encyclopaedia of Islam*, 2nd edn, I, pp. 1073–5

Canard, M. (1961), 'Les sources arabes de l'histoire byzantine aux confins des Xe et XIe siècles', *Revue des Etudes Byzantines* 19: 284–314

Canard, M. (1971), 'Al-Hākim bi-amr Allah', in *Encyclopaedia of Islam*, 2nd edn, III, pp. 76–82

Chaudhuri, K. N. (1985), *Trade and Civilization in the Indian Ocean*, Cambridge

Cheddadi, A. (1986), *Ibn Khaldūn: peuples et nations du monde*, 2 vols., Paris

Coulson, N. J. (1964), *A History of Islamic Law*, Edinburgh

Crone, P. and Hinds, M. (1986), *God's Caliph: Religious Authority in the First Centuries of Islam*, Cambridge

Daftary, F. (1990), *The Ismāʿīlīs: Their History and Doctrines*, Cambridge

Encyclopaedia of Islam (1913–35), 1st edn, 4 vols. and supplement, Leiden and London; 2nd edn 10 vols. and supplement, Leiden and London, 1954–

Gibb, H. A. R. (1962), *Studies on the Civilization of Islam*, ed. S. J. Shaw and W. R. Polk, London

Goitein, S. D. (1942), 'The origin of the vizierate and its true character', *Islamic Culture* 16: 255–62, 380–92

Goitein, S. D. (1961), 'On the origin of the term vizier', *Journal of American Oriental Studies* 80: 425–6

Goitein, S. D. (1966), *Studies in Islamic History and Institutions*, Leiden

Gottheil, R. (1906), 'A distinguished family of Fatimid Cadis (Al-Nu'man) in the tenth century', *Journal of the American Oriental Society* 27: 217–96

Halm, H. (1978), *Kosmologie und Heilslehre der frühen Ismāʿīlīya*, Wiesbaden

Hamblin, W. J. (1987), 'The Fatimid army during the early crusades', PhD Michigan 1985; fascimile reprint, Ann Arbor

Hasan, Y. F. (1967), *The Arabs and the Sudan*, Edinburgh

Hazard, H. W. (1952), *The Numismatic History of Late Medieval North Africa*, New York

Hodgson, M. G. S. (1955), *The Order of Assassins*, The Hague

Hodgson, M. G. S. (1962), 'Al-Darazī and Hamza in the origin of the Druze religion', *Journal of the American Oriental Society* 82: 5–20

Hodgson, M. G. S. (1968), 'The Ismāʿīlī state', in *Cambridge History of Iran* (1968), v, pp. 422–82

Hodgson, M. G. S. (1974), *The Venture of Islam*, 3 vols., Chicago and London

Idris, H. R. (1962), *La Bérberie orientale sous les Zirides*, 2 vols., Paris

Johns, J. (1993), 'The Norman kings of Sicily and the Fatimid caliphate', *ANS* 15: 133–59

Kennedy, H. (1986), *The Prophet and the Age of the Caliphates*, Harlow

Ladak, H. A. (1971), 'The Fatimid caliphate and the Ismāʿīlī Daʿwa: from the appointment of Mustaʿlī to the suppression of the dynasty', PhD, London

Lambton, A. K. S. (1965), 'Reflections of the Iqtaʿ', in G. Makdisi (ed.), *Arabic and Islamic Studies in Honor of Hamilton A. R. Gibb*, Leiden, pp. 358–76

Lambton, A. K. S. (1981), *State and Government in Medieval Islam*, Oxford

Lane-Poole, S. (1906), *The Story of Cairo*, London

Lane-Poole, S. (1914), *A History of Egypt in the Middle Ages*, 2nd edn, London

Launois, A. (1964), 'Influence des docteurs malékites sur le monnayage ziride de type sunnite et sur celui des Almoravides', *Arabica* 11: 127–50

Lev, Y. (1981), 'The Fatimid vizier Yaʿqūb ibn Killis and the beginning of the Fatimid administration in Egypt', *Der Islam* 58: 237–49

Lewis, B. (1967), *The Assassins*, London

Lewis, B. (1974), *Islam from the Prophet Muhammed to the Capture of Constantinople*, 2 vols., New York

Lombard, M. (1975), *The Golden Age of Islam*, Amsterdam, Oxford and New York

Lyons, M. C. and Jackson, D. E. P. (1982), *Saladin: The Politics of Holy War*, Cambridge

Makarem, S. N. (1970), 'Al-Ḥākim bi-amrillah's appointment of his successors', *Al-Abhāth* 23: 319–24

Mamour, P. H. (1934), *Polemics on the Origin of the Fatimi Caliphs*, London

Maspéro, J. and Wiet, G. (1919), *Matériaux pour servir à la géographie de l'Egypte*, Cairo

Mez, A. (1937), *The Renaissance of Islam*, trans. S. K. Baksh and D. Margoliouth, Patna

Momen, M. (1985), *An Introduction to Shiʿi Islam*, New Haven and London

Mottahedeh, R. P. (1980), *Loyalty and Leadership in an Early Islamic Society*, Princeton

Poonwala, I. K. (1977), *Biobibliography of Ismaʿili Literature*, Malibu

Rabie, H. (1972), *The Financial System of Egypt*, AH 564–741 / AD 1169–1341, Oxford

Raymond, A. (1993), *Le Caïre*, Paris

Rosenthal, E. I. J. (1962), *Political Thought in Medieval Islam*, Cambridge
Runciman, S. (1951–4), *A History of the Crusades*, 3 vols., Cambridge
Sanders, P. A. (1989), 'From court ceremony to urban language: ceremonial in Fatimid Cairo and Fustāt', in C. E. Bosworth *et al.* (eds.), *The Islamic World from Classical to Modern Times: Essays in Honor of Bernard Lewis*, Princeton, pp. 311–21
Sanders, P. A. (1992), 'Claiming the past: Ghadir Khumm and the rise of Hāfizī historiography in late Fatimid Egypt', *Studia Islamica* 75: 81–104
Sanders, P. A. (1994), *Ritual, Politics and the City in Fatimid Cairo*, New York
Sato, T. (1982), 'The Iqtāʿ system of Iraq under the Buwayhids', *Orient* 18: 83–105
Shaban, M. A. (1976), *Islamic History: A New Interpretation*, II: *750–1055 (AH 132–448)*, Cambridge
Stern, S. M. (1949), 'Ismāʿīlī propaganda and Fatimid rule in Sind', *Islamic Culture* 23: 298–308
Stern, S. M. (1950), 'The epistle of the Fatimid Caliph al-Āmir (al-Hidāya al-Āmiriyya) – its date and purpose', *JRAS*: 20–31
Stern, S. M. (1951), 'The succession to the Fatimid Imam al-Āmir, the claims of the later Fatimids to the imamate, and the rise of Tayyibī Ismāʿīlism', *Oriens* 4: 193–255
Stern, S. M. (1955), 'Heterodox Ismāʿīlism at the time of al-Muʿizz', *BSOAS* 17: 10–33
Stern, S. M. (1983), *Studies in Early Ismāʿīlism*, Jerusalem and Leiden
Stern, S. M. (1984), *History and Culture of the Medieval Muslim World*, London
Turner, B. S. (1974), *Weber and Islam*, London
Vatikiotis, P. J. (1957), *The Fatimid Theory of State*, Lahore
Von Grunebaum, G. E. (1955), *Islam: Essays in the Nature and Growth of a Cultural Tradition*, London
Walker, P. E. (1993), 'The Ismaʿili Daʿwa in the reign of the Fatimid Caliph al-Hakim', *Journal of the American Research Center in Egypt* 30: 161–82
Watt, W. M. (1953), *The Faith and Practice of al-Ghazali*, London
Williams, C. (1983, 1985), 'The cult of ʿAlid saints in the Fatimid monuments of Cairo', *Muqarnas* 1: 37–52; 3: 39–60

23 ZENGIDS, AYYUBIDS AND SELJUQS

Ashtor, E. (1969), *Histoire des prix et des salaires dans l'Orient médéval*, Paris
Ashtor-Strauss, E. (1956), 'L'administration urbaine en Syrie médiévalé', *Rivista degli Studi Orientali* 31: 73–128
Ayalon, D. (1977), 'Aspects of the Mamluk phenomenon: Ayyubids, Kurds, and Mamluks', *Der Islam* 54: 1–32
Ayalon, D. (1981), 'From Ayyubids to Mamluks', *Revue des Etudes Islamiques* 49: 43–57
Barthold, W. (Bartoľd, V. V.) (1968), *Turkestan down to the Mongol Invasion*, 3rd rev. edn, London
Berchem, M. van (1922, 1927), *Matériaux pour un Corpus Inscriptionum Arabicarum: deuxième partie: Syrie du Sud, Jérusalem* (Mémoires de l'Institut Français d'Archeologie Orientale au Caire 43–4), 2 vols., Paris and Cairo
Bosworth, C. E. (1968), 'The political and dynastic history of the Iranian world (AD 1000–1217)', in J. H. Boyle (ed.), *Cambridge History of Iran*, V, Cambridge, pp. 1–202
Bosworth, C. E. (1995), 'Saldjukids', in *Encyclopaedia of Islam*, 2nd edn, VIII, pp. 936–59

Cahen, C. (1940), *La Syrie du Nord à l'époque des croisades et la principauté franque d'Antioche*, Paris

Cahen, C. (1953), 'L'évolution de l'iqta' du IXe au XIIIe siècle', *Annales ESC* 8: 25–52

Cahen, C. (1958–9), 'Mouvements populaires et autonomisme urbain dans l'Asie musulmane du moyen âge', *Arabica* 5: 225–50; 6: 25–56, 233–65

Cahen, C. (1960a), 'Atabak', in *Encyclopaedia of Islam*, 2nd edn, I, pp. 731–2

Cahen, C. (1960b), 'Ayyubids', in *Encyclopaedia of Islam*, 2nd edn, I, pp. 796–807

Cahen, C. (1977), *Makhzumiyyat: études sur l'histoire économique et financière de l'Egypte médiévale*, Leiden

Chamberlain, M. (1994), *Knowledge and Social Practice in Medieval Damascus, 1190–1350*, Cambridge

Eddé, A.-M. (1986), 'Ridwan, prince d'Alep de 1095 a 1113', *Revue des Etudes Islamiques* 54: 101–25

Eddé, A.-M. (1999), *La principauté d'Alep (579/1183-658/12)* (Freiburger Islamstudien zi), Skuttgart

Ehrenkreutz, A. S. (1955), 'The place of Saladin in the naval history of the Mediterranean Sea', *Journal of the Americal Oriental Society* 75: 100–16

Ehrenkreutz, A. S. (1972), *Saladin*, Albany, NY

Elisseeff, N. (1952–54), 'La titulature de Nur ad-Din d'après ses inscriptions', *Bulletin d'Etudes Orientales* 14: 155–96

Elisseeff, N. (1967), *Nur ad-Din: un grand prince musulman de Syrie au temps des croisades (511–569 H / 1118–1167 AD)*, 3 vols., Damascus

Gaube, H. and Worth, E. A. (1984), *Aleppo: Historische und geographische Beiträge zur baulichen Gestaltung, zur sozialen Organisation, und zur wirtschaftlichen Dynamik einer vorderasiastischen Fernhandelmetropole* (Tübinger Atlas des Vorderen Orients: Beihefte, Reihe B, no. 58), Wiesbaden

Gibb, H. A. R. (1962), 'The Armies of Saladin', in H. A. R. Gibb, *Studies on the Civilization of Islam*, ed. S. J. Shaw and W. R. Polk, London

Gibb, H. A. R. (1969a), 'Zengi and the Fall of Edessa', in K. M. Setton (gen. ed.), *A History of the Crusades*, 2nd edn, I, Madison, WI, pp. 449–62

Gibb, H. A. R. (1969b), 'The career of Nur al-Din', in K. M. Setton (gen. ed.), *A History of the Crusades*, 2nd edn, I, Madison, WI, pp. 513–27

Gibb, H. A. R. (1969c), 'The rise of Saladin', in K. M. Setton (gen. ed.), *A History of the Crusades*, 2nd edn, I, Madison, WI, pp. 563–89

Gibb, H. A. R. (1969d), 'The Aiyubids', in K. M. Setton (gen. ed.), *A History of the Crusades*, 2nd edn, vol. II, Madison, WI, pp. 693–714

Gibb, H. A. R. (1973), *Saladin*, Oxford

Gottschalk, H. L. (1958), *Al-Malik al-Kamil von Egypten und seine Zeit*, Wiesbaden

Havemann, A. (1975), *Ri'āsa und Qadā': Institutionen als Ausdruck wechselnder Kräfteverhältnisse in syrische Städten vom 10. bis zum 12. Jahrhundert*, Freiburg im Breisgau

Havemann, A. (1989), 'The vizier and the ra'is in Saljuq Syria: the struggle for urban self-representation', *International Journal of Middle East Studies* 21: 233–42

Heyd, W. (1885–6), *Geschichte des Levantehandels im Mittelalter*, 2 vols., Stuttgart (1879); trans. F. Raynaud, *Histoire du commerce du Levant au moyen âge*, 2 vols., Leipzig, 1885–6; repr. Leipzig, 1936 and Amsterdam, 1967

Hillenbrand, C. (1981), 'The career of Najm al-Din Il-Ghazi', *Der Islam* 58: 250–92

Hoch, M. (1993), *Jerusalem, Damaskus und der zweite Kreuzzug*, Frankfurt

Holt, P. M. (1986), *The Age of the Crusades: The Near East from the Eleventh Century to 1517*, London

Horst, H. (1964), *Die Staatsverwaltung der Grosselǧuqen und Ḫorazmshahs*, Wiesbaden

Humphreys, R. S. (1977a), *From Saladin to the Mongols: The Ayyubids of Damascus 1193–1260*, Albany, NY

Humphreys, R. S. (1977b), 'The emergence of the Mamluk army', *Studia Islamica* 45: 67–99; 46: 147–82

Humphreys, R. S. (1989), 'Politics and architecture patronage in Ayyubid Damascus', in C. E. Bosworth *et al.* (eds.), *The Islamic World from Classical to Modern Times: Essays in Honour of Bernard Lewis*, Princeton, pp. 151–74

Humphreys, R. S. (1994), 'Women as patrons of architecture in Ayyubid Damascus', *Muqarnas* 11: 35–54

Humphreys, R. S. (1998), 'Ayyubids, Mamluks, and the Latin east in the thirteenth century', *Mamluk Studies Review* 2: 1–18

Klausner, K. (1973), *The Seljuk Vezirate: A Study of Civil Administration, 1055–1194*, Cambridge, MA

Kohler, M. (1991), *Allianzen und Vorträge zwischen fränkischen und islamischen Herrschen im Vorderen Orient*, Berlin

Labib, S. (1965), *Handelsgeschichte Ägyptens im Spätmittelalter, 1171–1517*, Wiesbaden

Lambton, A. K. S. (1953), *Landlord and Peasant in Persia*, London

Lambton, A. K. S. (1968), 'The internal structure of the Saljuq empire', in J. A. Boyle (ed.), *The Cambridge History of Iran*, v, Cambridge, pp. 203–82

Lambton, A. K. S. (1988), *Continuity and Change in Medieval Persia: Aspects of Administrative, Economic and Social History, 11th–14th Century*, Albany, NY

Lewis, B. (1967), *The Assassins: A Radical Sect in Islam*, London

Lyons, M. C. and Jackson, D. E. P. (1982), *Saladin: The Politics of Holy War*, Cambridge

Mouton, J.-M. (1994), *Damas et sa principauté sous les Saljoukides et les Bourides, 468–549 / 1076–1154*, Cairo

Patton, D. (1991), *Badr al-Din Luʼluʼ: Atabeg of Mosul, 1211–1259*, Seattle, WA

Pouzet, L. (1988), *Damas au VIIe/XIIIe siècle: vie et structures religieuses dans une métropole islamique*, Beirut

Pryor, J. H. (1988), *Geography, Technology and War: Studies in the Maritime History of the Mediterranean, 649–1571*, Cambridge

Rabie, H. (1972), *The Financial System of Egypt*, AH 564–741 / AD 1169–1341, London

Répertoire chronologique d'épigraphie arabe, ed. E. Combe, J. Sauvaget and G. Wiet, 17 vols. so far, Cairo (1931–)

Sato Tsugitaka (1997), *State and Rural Society in Medieval Islam: Sultans, Muqtaʻs and Fallahin*, Leiden

Sauvaget, J. (1934), 'Esquisse d'une histoire de la ville de Damas', *Revue des Etudes Islamiques* 8: 421–80

Sauvaget, J. (1941), *Alep: essai sur le développement d'une grande ville syrienne des origines au milieu du XIXe siècle*, 2 vols., Paris

Schaube, A. (1906), *Handelsgeschichte der romanischen Völker des Mittelmeergebiets bis zum Ende der Kreuzzüge*, Berlin

Sivan, E. (1968), *L'Islam et la croisade: idéologie et propagande dans les réactions musulmanes aux croisades*, Paris

Sourdel, D. (1949–51), 'Les professeurs de madrasa à Alep aux XIIe–XIIIe siècles', *Bulletin d'Etudes Orientales* 13: 95–115

Al-Tabba, Y. (1982), 'The architectural patronage of Nur al-Din (1146–1174)', 2 vols., PhD, New York

Tabbaa, Y. (al-Tabba) (1997), *Constructions of Power and Piety in Medieval Aleppo*, University Park, PA

Yared-Riachi, M. (1997), *La Politique extérieure de la principauté de Damas, 468–549 H / 1076–1154*, Damascus

INDEX

Milan (*cont.*)
  and papal schism, 422
  rebuilding, 432
  status, 396
  war with Pavia, 424, 430
Miles of Gloucester, 554
Miles of Plancy, 659
Mileto monastery, 118
military orders, 347, 496–7, 498, 666
Millau, 547
Milsko, 277, 279
Milzi, 277
Minden, 44
mining, 468
Miño river, 477, 485
Mirebeau, 565, 570, 579
Mirabel, 669
Miramamolin, 506
Mirdasids, 683, 688, 690, 693, 694, 695, 699,
    702, 704
Mirebeau, 565, 570
Miroslav Nemanja, 269
Misilmeri, 109
Modena, 426, 427
Modon, 615
Moissac monastery, 150
Molesme, 149
Molise, county of, 458, 473
Molise family, 118, 451 n. 19, 473
Monaghan, 606
monasteries
  10th century, 9
  11th century
    abbots, 13, 71, 89
    Byzantium, 217, 246–7
    England, 201
    France, 124, 132, 149–52, 151, 518
    Hungary, 314, 315
    Italy, 91, 117, 118
    land gifts to, 91, 152
    León-Castile, 177
    Normandy, 195–6
    Poland, 280
    privileges, 11–12, 324
    property, 10
    Sicily, 117
    Wales, 205
  12th century
    Aragon, 493
    France, 533, 534
    generally, 324–7
    Ireland, 604
    Scotland, 593
    Sicily, 469
    Spain, 494
  see also specific orders and abbeys

Mondego river, 164
Mongols, 703, 714, 726, 738
Monomachos family, 224
Monophysite Jacobites, 646
Monopoli, 103
Monothelite Maronites, 646
Monreale, 469, 470
Montaigu Castle, 511
Montánchez, 497
Montasola, 22
Montauban, 545
Montcada, 489
Montdidier, 521
Mont-Dieu, 360
Monte Cassino Abbey
  abbots, 65, 76, 84, 118
  chronicle, 368
  and Henry III, 78
  John of Gaeta, 19
  and Lothar II, 423
  and Normans, 106, 109, 112, 117, 118
  oppression by Pandulf IV, 102
  and papacy, 87, 325
Monte Gargano, 99, 461
Monte Sant'Angelo, counts of, 111, 444
Monteagudo, 506
Montearagón, 185
Monteforte, countess of, 48
Montepeloso, 103
Montereau, 537
Monteroso, 164
Montescaglioso, count of, 110
Montferrat, 429, 570
Montfort l'Amaury family, 206
Montgomery family, 596, 597
Montlhéry Castle, 511
Montlhéry family, 6–7, 512
Montmajour monastery, 150
Montmirail, treaty of, 569
Montpellier, 361, 547
Montréal Castle, 647, 663, 670
Montreuil-Bellay, 561, 562
Montrose, 590
Monza, 396
Monzón, 185, 475
Mopsuestia, 617
Mora, 495
Morava river, 266, 270
Moravia, 279
Moray Firth, 589
Morcar, Earl, 199
Morella, 495
Morgannwg, 595
mormaers, 585
Morocco, 182, 457, 482, 697
Mortagne, 557

CPSIA information can be obtained at www.ICGtesting.com
Printed in the USA
LVOW01s0029090515

437828LV00001B/6/P

9 781107 460638